50
BEST
PLAYS
OF THE
AMERICAN
THEATRE

★★★

50
BEST
PLAYS
OF THE
AMERICAN
THEATRE

✦✦✦

Selected by
CLIVE BARNES

with Individual Play Introductions by
JOHN GASSNER

CROWN PUBLISHERS, INC., NEW YORK

NOTE: All plays contained in this volume are fully protected under the copyright laws of the United States of America, the British Empire, including the Dominion of Canada, and all other countries of the Copyright Union. Permission to reproduce, wholly or in part, by any method, must be obtained from the copyright owners or their agents. (See notices at the beginning of each play.)

SECOND PRINTING, JANUARY, 1970

© 1969 BY CROWN PUBLISHERS, INC.
LIBRARY OF CONGRESS CATALOG CARD NUMBER: 57–12830
PRINTED IN THE UNITED STATES OF AMERICA
PUBLISHED SIMULTANEOUSLY IN CANADA BY GENERAL PUBLISHING COMPANY LIMITED

Table of Contents

THE TIME OF YOUR LIFE
  William Saroyan *1*

ARSENIC AND OLD LACE
  Joseph Kesselring *47*

HARVEY
  Mary Chase *99*

THE GLASS MENAGERIE
  Tennessee Williams *137*

STATE OF THE UNION
  Howard Lindsay and Russel Crouse *175*

DREAM GIRL
  Elmer Rice *225*

BORN YESTERDAY
  Garson Kanin *271*

MEDEA
  Robinson Jeffers *319*

A STREETCAR NAMED DESIRE
  Tennessee Williams *339*

MISTER ROBERTS
  Thomas Heggen and Joshua Logan *385*

DEATH OF A SALESMAN
  Arthur Miller *425*

THE MEMBER OF THE WEDDING
  Carson McCullers *473*

50
BEST
PLAYS
OF THE
AMERICAN
THEATRE

★★★

THE TIME OF YOUR LIFE

By WILLIAM SAROYAN

THE TIME OF YOUR LIFE was first presented by the Theatre Guild in association with Eddie Dowling in New York City on October 25, 1939.

THE PEOPLE

JOE..A young loafer with money and a good heart
TOM...His admirer, disciple, errand boy, stooge and friend
KITTY DUVAL..A young woman with memories
NICK.......Owner of Nick's Pacific Street Saloon, Restaurant, and Entertainment Palace
ARAB...An Eastern philosopher and harmonica-player
KIT CARSON..An old Indian-fighter
MC CARTHY...........................An intelligent and well-read longshoreman
KRUPP.................His boyhood friend, a waterfront cop who hates his job but doesn't
                                        know what else to do instead
HARRY....................A natural-born hoofer who wants to make people laugh but can't
WESLEY..........A colored boy who plays a mean and melancholy boogie-woogie piano
DUDLEY...A young man in love
ELSIE..A nurse, the girl he loves
LORENE...An unattractive woman
MARY L...................................An unhappy woman of quality and great beauty
WILLIE..A marble-game maniac

BLICK..............................A heel   A SAILOR
MA.........................Nick's mother   A SOCIETY GENTLEMAN
A KILLER   A SOCIETY LADY
HER SIDE KICK   THE DRUNKARD
A COP   THE NEWSBOY
ANOTHER COP   ANNA.............................Nick's daughter

---

THE PLACE

Nick's Pacific Street Saloon, Restaurant, and Entertainment Palace at the foot of Embarcadero, in San Francisco. A suggestion of room 21 at The New York Hotel, upstairs, around the corner.

The Time: Afternoon and night of a day in October, 1939.

THE AUTHOR

William Saroyan, the Armenian flame from Fresno, California, already had a reputation as an original short-story writer when the Group Theatre introduced him as an equally original playwright with My Heart's in the Highlands. *This long one-acter, brilliantly staged by Robert Lewis, was produced on April 13, 1939. A portion of the press expressed utter bewilderment, but some of our most prominent critics acclaimed the piece as a remarkable work of artistry; a few of them went so far as to vote it the "best play of the season" at the Drama Critics Circle annual conclave.*

Mr. Saroyan was born in 1908 and knocked about for many years as an itinerant worker, a Western Union messenger, and a laborer in his uncle's vineyard. He forsook his native haunts "for some of the rest of the world" at the age of seventeen. Without any formal education other than the customary exposure to grammar school in his home town, the young man resolved that he had enough experience to write and that he had enough to say for anybody's money. Short Story *magazine printed his first piece* The Daring Young Man on a Flying Trapeze *in its February, 1934 issue. This was all the encouragement Saroyan needed; he began writing with lightning speed, and later in 1934 he had enough substance for a first volume. For these stories he arrived at a number of rules that were to apply not only to all his stories but to his later plays. The first rule, which he claims to have set down at the age of eleven, reads: "Do not pay attention to the rules other people make. . . . They make them for their own protection, and to hell with them." Rule number two, which he discovered somewhat later, reads: "Forget everybody who ever wrote anything." The third rule was: "Learn to typewrite, so you can turn out stories as fast as Zane Grey." He considers this last precept one of his best rules, and the haste with which he has turned out plays, as well as stories, has often been regrettably apparent. Concerning his later fiction we may confine ourselves to noting a delightful collection of fictionized memories* My Name Is Aram *(1940), a charming first novel* The Human Comedy *(1943), and a dubious war-novel* The Adventures of Wesley Jackson *(1946) drawn somewhat from the author's unhappy experiences in the Army. He spent some time in the Signal Corps' Photographic Center in Astoria, Long Island where he wrote film scripts. Subsequently he was transferred to the European theatre of operations. He was discharged some time before the end of the war and returned to California for convalescence.*

Saroyan wrote his first play Subway Circus *in 1935 but never got it to Broadway.* My Heart's in the Highlands *was written in 1938. Encouraged by the interest in this first production, Saroyan wrote his first full-length drama* The Time of Your Life *in record time and received a notable production in the fall of 1939 from Eddie Dowling and the Theatre Guild. Brooks Atkinson defined it aptly as "a prose poem in ragtime." The play provided an occasion for full agreement between the Drama Critics Circle and the Pulitzer Prize Committee, but Saroyan refused to accept the Pulitzer Prize. This chef d'oeuvre was followed in the spring of 1940 by the less successful production of* Love's Old Sweet Song. *A year later he turned producer with his elusively fanciful piece* The Beautiful People. *A good many short and long plays followed:* Sweeney in the Trees, Across the Board of Tomorrow Morning, Jim Dandy *(produced by the National Theatre Conference),* Get Away, Old Man *(produced by George Abbott in 1943),* Afton Water, *and various unproduced pieces. His superb one-acter* Hello Out There *was presented by Eddie Dowling in conjunction with a revival of Chesterton's* Magic *in September, 1942.*

THE TIME OF YOUR LIFE

ACT ONE

In the time of your life, live—so that in that good time there shall be no ugliness or death for yourself or for any life your life touches. Seek goodness everywhere, and when it is found, bring it out of its hiding-place and let it be free and unashamed. Place in matter and in flesh the least of the values, for these are the things that hold death and must pass away. Discover in all things that which shines and is beyond corruption. Encourage virtue in whatever heart it may have been driven into secrecy and sorrow by the shame and terror of the world. Ignore the obvious, for it is unworthy of the clear eye and the kindly heart. Be the inferior of no man, nor of any man be the superior. Remember that every man is a variation of yourself. No man's guilt is not yours, nor is any man's innocence a thing apart. Despise evil and ungodliness, but not men of ungodliness or evil. These, understand. Have no shame in being kindly and gentle, but if the time comes in the time of your life to kill, kill and have no regret. In the time of your life, live—so that in that wondrous time you shall not add to the misery and sorrow of the world, but shall smile to the infinite delight and mystery of it.

Nick's is an American place: a San Francisco waterfront honky-tonk. At a table, JOE: always calm, always quiet, always thinking, always eager, always bored, always superior. His expensive clothes are casually and youthfully worn and give him an almost boyish appearance. He is thinking. Behind the bar, NICK: a big red-headed young Italian-American with an enormous naked woman tattooed in red on the inside of his right arm. He is studying The Racing Form. The ARAB, at his place at the end of the bar. He is a lean old man with a rather ferocious old-country mustache, with the ends twisted up. Between the thumb and forefinger of his left hand is the Mohammedan tattoo indicating that he has been to Mecca. He is sipping a glass of beer. It is about eleven-thirty in the morning. SAM is sweeping out. We see only his back. He disappears into the kitchen. The SAILOR at the bar finishes his drink and leaves, moving thoughtfully, as though he were trying very hard to discover how to live. The NEWSBOY comes in.

NEWSBOY (*cheerfully*). Good-morning, everybody. (*No answer. To* NICK.) Paper, Mister? (NICK *shakes his head, no. The* NEWSBOY *goes to* JOE.) Paper, Mister?

(JOE *shakes his head, no. The* NEWSBOY *walks away, counting papers.*)

JOE (*noticing him*). How many you got?

NEWSBOY. Five.

(JOE *gives him a quarter, takes all the papers, glances at the headlines with irritation, throws them away.*)

(*The* NEWSBOY *watches carefully, then goes.*)

ARAB (*picks up paper, looks at headlines, shakes head as if rejecting everything else a man might say about the world*). No foundation. All the way down the line.

(*The* DRUNK *comes in. Walks to the telephone, looks for a nickel in the chute, sits down at* JOE's *table.*)

(NICK *takes the* DRUNK *out. The* DRUNK *returns.*)

DRUNK (*champion of the Bill of Rights*). This is a free country, ain't it?

(WILLIE, *the marble-game maniac, explodes through the swinging doors and*

*lifts the forefinger of his right hand com-
ically, indicating one beer. He is a very
young man, not more than twenty. He is
wearing heavy shoes, a pair of old and
dirty corduroys, a light green turtle-neck
jersey with a large letter "F" on the chest,
an oversize two-button tweed coat, and a
green hat, with the brim up.* NICK *sets out
a glass of beer for him, he drinks it,
straightens up vigorously, saying Aaah,
makes a solemn face, gives* NICK *a one-
finger salute of adieu, and begins to leave,
refreshed and restored in spirit. He walks
by the marble game, halts suddenly, turns,
studies the contraption, gestures as if to
say, Oh, no. Turns to go, stops, returns to
the machine, studies it, takes a handful of
small coins out of his pants pocket, lifts a
nickel, indicates with a gesture, One game,
no more. Puts the nickel in the slot, pushes
in the slide, making an interesting noise.)*

NICK. You can't beat that machine.

WILLIE. Oh, yeah?

*(The marbles fall, roll, and take their
place. He pushes down the lever, placing
one marble in position. Takes a very deep
breath, walks in a small circle, excited at
the beginning of great drama. Stands
straight and pious before the contest. Himself vs. the machine. Willie vs. Destiny.
His skill and daring vs. the cunning and
trickery of the novelty industry of America,
and the whole challenging world. He is
the last of the American pioneers, with
nothing more to fight but the machine,
with no other reward than lights going
on and off, and six nickels for one. Before
him is the last champion, the machine.
He is the last challenger, the young man
with nothing to do in the world.* WILLIE
*grips the knob delicately, studies the situa-
tion carefully, draws the knob back, holds
it a moment, and then releases it. The first
marble rolls out among the hazards, and
the contest is on. At the very beginning
of the play "The Missouri Waltz" is coming from the phonograph. The music ends
here.)*

*(This is the signal for the beginning of
the play.)*

*(*JOE *suddenly comes out of his reverie.
He whistles the way people do who are
calling a cab that's about a block away,*

only he does it quietly. WILLIE *turns
around, but* JOE *gestures for him to return to his work.* NICK *looks up from The
Racing Form.)*

JOE *(calling).* Tom. *(To himself.)* Where
the hell is he, every time I need him?
*(He looks around calmly: the nickel-in-
the-slot phonograph in the corner; the
open public telephone; the stage; the marble-game; the bar; and so on. He calls
again, this time very loud.)* Hey, Tom.

NICK *(with morning irritation).* What
do you want?

JOE *(without thinking).* I want the boy
to get me a watermelon, that's what *I*
want. What do *you* want? Money, or
love, or fame, or what? You won't get
them studying The Racing Form.

NICK. I like to keep abreast of the times.

*(*TOM *comes hurrying in. He is a great
big man of about thirty or so who appears
to be much younger because of the child-
like expression of his face: handsome,
dumb, innocent, troubled, and a little bewildered by everything. He is obviously
adult in years, but it seems as if by all
rights he should still be a boy. He is defensive as clumsy, self-conscious, overgrown boys are. He is wearing a flashy
cheap suit.* JOE *leans back and studies him
with casual disapproval.* TOM *slackens his
pace and becomes clumsy and embarrassed,
waiting for the bawling-out he's pretty
sure he's going to get.)*

JOE *(objectively, severely, but a little
amused).* Who saved your life?

TOM *(sincerely).* You did, Joe. Thanks.

JOE *(interested).* How'd I do it?

TOM *(confused).* What?

JOE *(even more interested).* How'd I do
it?

TOM. Joe, you know how you did it.

JOE *(softly).* I want you to answer me.
How'd I save your life? I've forgotten.

TOM *(remembering, with a big sorrowful
smile).* You made me eat all that chicken
soup three years ago when I was sick and
hungry.

JOE (*fascinated*). Chicken soup?

TOM (*eagerly*). Yeah.

JOE. Three years? Is it that long?

TOM (*delighted to have the information*). Yeah, sure. 1937. 1938. 1939. This is 1939, Joe.

JOE (*amused*). Never mind what year it is. Tell me the whole story.

TOM. You took me to the doctor. You gave me money for food and clothes, and paid my room rent. Aw, Joe, you know all the different things you did.

(JOE *nods, turning away from* TOM *after each question.*)

JOE. You in good health now?

TOM. Yeah, Joe.

JOE. You got clothes?

TOM. Yeah, Joe.

JOE. You eat three times a day. Sometimes four?

TOM. Yeah, Joe. Sometimes five.

JOE. You got a place to sleep?

TOM. Yeah, Joe.

(JOE *nods. Pauses. Studies* TOM *carefully.*)

JOE. Then, where the hell have you been?

TOM (*humbly*). Joe, I was out in the street listening to the boys. They're talking about the trouble down here on the waterfront.

JOE (*sharply*). I want you to be around when I need you.

TOM (*pleased that the bawling-out is over*). I won't do it again. Joe, one guy out there says there's got to be a revolution before anything will ever be all right.

JOE (*impatient*). I know all about it. Now, here. Take this money. Go up to the Emporium. You know where the Emporium is?

TCM. Yeah, sure, Joe.

JOE. All right. Take the elevator and go up to the fourth floor. Walk around to the

back, to the toy department. Buy me a couple of dollars' worth of toys and bring them here.

TOM (*amazed*). Toys? What *kind* of toys, Joe?

JOE. Any kind of toys. Little ones that I can put on this table.

TOM. What do you want toys for, Joe?

JOE (*mildly angry*). What?

TOM. All right, all right. You don't have to get sore at *everything*. What'll people think, a big guy like me buying toys?

JOE. *What people?*

TOM. Aw, Joe, you're always making me do crazy things for you, and *I'm* the guy that gets embarrassed. You just sit in this place and make me do all the dirty work.

JOE (*looking away*). Do what I tell you.

TOM. O.K., but I wish I knew *why*. (*He makes to go.*)

JOE. Wait a minute. Here's a nickel. Put it in the phonograph. Number seven. I want to hear that waltz again.

TOM. Boy, I'm glad *I* don't have to stay and listen to it. Joe, what do you hear in that song anyway? We listen to that song ten times a day. Why can't we hear number six, or two, or nine? There are a lot of other numbers.

JOE (*emphatically*). Put the nickel in the phonograph. (*Pause.*) Sit down and wait till the music's over. Then go get me some toys.

TOM. O.K. O.K.

JOE (*loudly*). Never mind being a martyr about it either. The cause isn't worth it.

(TOM *puts the nickel into the machine, with a ritual of impatient and efficient movement which plainly shows his lack of sympathy or enthusiasm. His manner also reveals, however, that his lack of sympathy is spurious and exaggerated. Actually, he is fascinated by the music, but is so confused by it that he pretends he dislikes it.*)

(The music begins. It is another variation of "The Missouri Waltz," played dreamily and softly, with perfect orchestral form, and with a theme of weeping in the horns repeated a number of times.)

(At first TOM *listens with something close to irritation, since he can't understand what is so attractive in the music to* JOE, *and what is so painful and confusing in it to himself. Very soon, however, he is carried away by the melancholy story of grief and nostalgia of the song.)*

(He stands, troubled by the poetry and confusion in himself.)

*(*JOE, *on the other hand, listens as if he were not listening, indifferent and unmoved. What he's interested in is* TOM. *He turns and glances at* TOM.*)*

*(*KITTY DUVAL, *who lives in a room in The New York Hotel, around the corner, comes beyond the swinging doors, quietly, and walks slowly to the bar, her reality and rhythm a perfect accompaniment to the sorrowful American music, which is her music, as it is Tom's. Which the world drove out of her, putting in its place brokenness and all manner of spiritually crippled forms. She seems to understand this, and is angry. Angry with herself, full of hate for the poor world, and full of pity and contempt for its tragic, unbelievable, confounded people. She is a small powerful girl, with that kind of delicate and rugged beauty which no circumstance of evil or ugly reality can destroy. This beauty is that element of the immortal which is in the seed of good and common people, and which is kept alive in some of the female of our kind, no matter how accidently or pointlessly they may have entered the world.* KITTY DUVAL *is somebody. There is an angry purity, and a fierce pride, in her.)*

(In her stance, and way of walking, there is grace and arrogance. JOE *recognizes her as a great person immediately. She goes to the bar.)*

KITTY. Beer.

*(*NICK *places a glass of beer before her mechanically.)*

(She swallows half the drink, and listens to the music again.)

*(*TOM *turns and sees her. He becomes dead to everything in the world but her. He stands like a lump, fascinated and undone by his almost religious adoration for her.* JOE *notices* TOM.*)*

JOE *(gently).* Tom. *(*TOM *begins to move toward the bar, where* KITTY *is standing. Loudly.)* Tom. *(*TOM *halts, then turns, and* JOE *motions to him to come over to the table.* TOM *goes over. Quietly.)* Have you got everything straight?

TOM *(out of the world).* What?

JOE. What do you mean, what? I just gave you some instructions.

TOM *(pathetically).* What do you want, Joe?

JOE. I want you to come to your senses.

(He stands up quietly and knocks Tom's hat off. TOM *picks up his hat quickly.)*

TOM. I got it, Joe. I got it. The Emporium. Fourth floor. In the back. The toy department. Two dollars' worth of toys. That you can put on a table.

KITTY *(to herself).* Who the hell is he to push a big man like that around?

JOE. I'll expect you back in a half hour. Don't get side-tracked anywhere. Just do what I tell you.

TOM *(pleading).* Joe? Can't I bet four bits on a horse race? There's a long shot—Precious Time—that's going to win by ten lengths. I got to have money.

*(*JOE *points to the street.* TOM *goes out.* NICK *is combing his hair, looking in the mirror.)*

NICK. I thought you wanted him to get you a watermelon.

JOE. I forgot. *(He watches* KITTY *a moment. To* KITTY, *clearly, slowly, with great compassion.)* What's the dream?

KITTY *(moving to* JOE, *coming to).* What?

JOE *(holding the dream for her).* What's the dream, *now?*

KITTY *(coming still closer).* What dream?

JOE. What dream! The dream you're dreaming.

NICK. Suppose ne did bring you a watermelon? What the hell would you do with it?

JOE (*irritated*). I'd put it on this table. I'd look at it. Then I'd eat it. What do you *think* I'd do with it, sell it for a profit?

NICK. How should I know what *you'd* do with *anything*? What I'd like to know is, where do you get your money from? What work do you do?

JOE (*looking at* KITTY). Bring us a bottle of champagne.

KITTY. Champagne?

JOE (*simply*). Would you rather have something else?

KITTY. What's the big idea?

JOE. I thought you might like some champagne. I myself am very fond of it.

KITTY. Yeah, but what's the big idea? You can't push *me* around.

JOE (*gently but severely*). It's not in my nature to be unkind to another human being. I have only contempe for wit. Otherwise I might say something obvious. there fore cruel, and perhaps untrue.

KITTY. You be careful what you think about me.

JOE (*slowly, not looking at her*). I have only the noblest thoughts for both your person, and your spirit.

NICK (*having listened carefully and not being able to make it out*). What are you talking about?

KITTY. You shut up. You—

ICE. He owns this place. He's an important man. All kinds of people come to nim looking for work. Comedians. Singers. Dancers.

KITTY. I don't care. He can't call me names.

NICK. All right, sister. I know how it is with a two-dollar whore in the morning.

KITTY (*furiously*). Don't you dare call me names. I used to be in burlesque.

NICK. If you were ever in burlesque, I used to be Charlie Chaplin.

KITTY (*angry and a little pathetic*). I *was* in burlesque. I played the burlesque circuit from coast to coast. I've had flowers sent to me by European royalty. I've had dinner with young men of wealth and social position.

NICK. You're dreaming.

KITTY (*to* JOE). I was in burlesque. Kitty Duval. That was my name. Life-size photographs of me in costume in front of burlesque theaters all over the country.

JOE (*gently, coaxingly*). I believe you. Have some champagne.

NICK (*going to table, with champagne bottle and glasses*). There he goes again.

JOE. Miss Duval?

KITTY (*sincerely, going over*). That's not my *real* name. That's my *stage* name.

JOE. I'll call you by your stage name.

NICK (*pouring*). All right, sister, make up your mind. Are you going to have champagne with him, or not?

JOE. Pour the lady some wine.

NICK. O.K., Professor. Why you come to this joint instead of one of the high-class dumps uptown is more than I can understand. Why don't you have champagne at the St. Francis? Why don't you drink with a lady?

KITTY (*furiously*). Don't you call me names—you dentist.

JOE. Dentist?

NICK (*amazed, loudly*). What kind of cussing is that? (*Pause. Looking at* KITTY, *then at* JOE, *bewildered.*) This guy doesn't belong here. The only reason I've got champagne is because *he* keeps ordering it all the time. (*To* KITTY.) Don't think you're the only one he drinks champagne with. He drinks with *all* of them. (*Pause.*) He's crazy. Or something.

JOE (*confidentially*). Nick, I think you're going to be all right in a couple of centuries.

NICK. I'm sorry, I don't understand your English.

(JOE *lifts his glass.*)

(KITTY *slowly lifts hers, not quite sure of what s going on.*)

JOE (*sincerely*). To the spirit, Kitty Duval.

KITTY (*beginning to understand, and very grateful, looking at him*). Thank you.

(*They drink.*)

JOE (*calling*). Nick.

NICK. Yeah?

JOE. Would you mind putting a nickel in the machine again? Number—

NICK. Seven. I know. I know. I don't mind at all, Your Highness, although, personally, I'm not a lover of music. (*Going to the machine.*) As a matter of fact I think Tchaikowsky was a dope

JOE. Tchaikowsky? Where'd you ever hear of Tchaikowsky.

NICK. He was a dope.

JOE. Yeah. Why?

NICK. They talked about him on the radio one Sunday morning. He was a sucker. He let a woman drive him crazy.

JOE. I see.

NICK. I stood behind that bar listening to the God damn stuff and cried like a baby. *None but the lonely heart!* He was a dope.

JOE. What made you cry?

NICK. What?

JOE (*sternly*). What made you cry, Nick?

NICK (*angry with himself*). I don't know.

JOE. I've been underestimating you, Nick. Play number seven.

NICK. They get everybody worked up. They give everybody stuff they shouldn't have.

(NICK *puts the nickel into the machine and the Waltz begins again. He listens to the music. Then studies* The Racing Form.)

KITTY (*to herself, dreaming*). I like champagne, and everything that goes with it. Big houses with big porches, and big rooms with big windows, and big lawns, and big trees, and flowers growing everywhere, and big shepherd dogs sleeping in the shade.

NICK. I'm going next door to Frankie's to make a bet. I'll be right back.

JOE. Make one for me.

NICK (*going to* JOE). Who do you like?

JOE (*giving him money*). Precious Time.

NICK. *Ten dollars?* Across the board?

JOE. No. On the nose.

NICK. O.K. (*He goes.*)

(DUDLEY R. BOSTWICK, *as he calls himself, breaks through the swinging doors, and practically flings himself upon the open telephone beside the phonograph.*)

(DUDLEY *is a young man of about twenty-four or twenty-five, ordinary and yet extraordinary. He is smallish, as the saying is, neatly dressed in bargain clothes, overworked and irritated by the routine and dullness and monotony of his life, apparently nobody and nothing, but in reality a great personality. The swindled young man. Educated, but without the least real understanding. A brave, dumb, salmon-spirit struggling for life in weary, stupefied flesh, dueling ferociously with a banal mind which has been only irritated by what it has been taught. He is a great personality because, against all these handicaps, what he wants is simple and basic: a woman. This urgent and violent need, common yet miraculous enough in itself, considering the unhappy environment of the animal, is the force which elevates him from nothingness to greatness. A ridiculous greatness, but in the nature of things beautiful to behold. All that he has been taught, and everything he believes, is phony, and yet he himself is real, almost super-real, because of this indestructible force in himself. His face is ridiculous. His personal rhythm is tense and jittery. His speech is shrill and violent. His gestures are wild. His ego is disjointed and epileptic. And yet deeply he possesses the same wholeness of spirit, and directness of energy, that is in all species of animals. There is little innate or cultivated spirit in him, but there is no absence of innocent animal force. He is a young man who has been taught that he has a chance, as a person, and believes it. As a matter of fact, he hasn't a chance in the world, and should have been told by somebody, or should not have had his natural and valuable ignorance spoiled by education, ruining an otherwise perfectly good and charming member of the human race.*)

(At the telephone he immediately begins to dial furiously, hesitates, changes his mind, stops dialing, hangs up furiously, and suddenly begins again.)

(Not more than half a minute after the firecracker arrival of DUDLEY R. BOSTWICK, *occurs the polka-and-waltz arrival of* HARRY.)

*(*HARRY *is another story.)*

(He comes in timidly, turning about uncertainly, awkward, out of place everywhere, embarrassed and encumbered by the contemporary costume, sick at heart, but determined to fit in somewhere. His arrival constitutes a dance.)

(His clothes don't fit. The pants are a little too large. The coat, which doesn't match, is also a little too large, and loose.)

(He is a dumb young fellow, but he has ideas. A philosophy, in fact. His philosophy is simple and beautiful. The world is sorrowful. The world needs laughter. HARRY *is funny. The world needs* HARRY. HARRY *will make the world laugh.)*

(He has probably had a year or two of high school. He has also listened to the boys at the pool room.)

(He's looking for Nick. He goes to the ARAB, *and says, Are you Nick? The* ARAB *shakes his head. He stands at the bar, waiting. He waits very busily.)*

HARRY *(as* NICK *returns).* You Nick?

NICK *(very loudly).* I am Nick.

HARRY *(acting).* Can you use a great comedian?

NICK *(behind the bar).* Who, for instance?

HARRY *(almost angry).* Me.

NICK. You? What's funny about you?

*(*DUDLEY *at the telephone, is dialing. Because of some defect in the apparatus the dialing is very loud.)*

DUDLEY. Hello. Sunset 7349? May I speak to Miss Elsie Mandelspiegel?

(Pause.)

HARRY *(with spirit and noise, dancing).* I dance and do gags and stuff.

NICK. In costume? Or are you wearing your costume?

DUDLEY. All I need is a cigar.

KITTY *(continuing the dream of grace).* I'd walk out of the house, and stand on the porch, and look at the trees, and smell the flowers, and run across the lawn, and lie down under a tree, and read a book. *(Pause.)* A book of poems, maybe.

DUDLEY *(very, very clearly).* Elsie Mandelspiegel. *(Impatiently.)* She has a room on the fourth floor. She's a nurse at the Southern Pacific Hospital. Elsie Mandelspiegel. She works at night. Elsie. Yes. *(He begins waiting again.)*

*(*WESLEY, *a colored boy, comes to the bar and stands near* HARRY, *waiting.)*

NICK. Beer?

WESLEY. No, sir. I'd like to talk to you.

NICK *(to* HARRY). All right. Get funny.

HARRY *(getting funny, an altogether different person, an actor with great energy, both in power of voice, and in force and speed of physical gesture).* Now, I'm standing on the corner of Third and Market. I'm looking around. I'm figuring it out. There it is. Right in front of me. The whole city. The whole world. People going by. They're going somewhere. I don't know where, but they're going. I ain't going *anywhere.* Where the hell can you go? I'm figuring it out. All right, I'm a citizen. A fat guy bumps his stomach into the face of an old lady. They were in a hurry. Fat and old. *They bumped.* Boom. I don't know. It may mean war. *War.* Germany. England. Russia. I don't know for sure. *(Loudly, dramatically, he salutes, about faces, presents arms, aims, and fires.)* WAAAAAR. *(He blows a call to arms.* NICK *gets sick of this, indicates with a gesture that* HARRY *should hold it, and goes to* WESLEY.)

NICK. What's on *your* mind?

WESLEY *(confused).* Well—

NICK. Come on. Speak up. Are you hungry, or what?

WESLEY. Honest to God, I ain't hungry. All I want is a job. I don't want no charity.

NICK. Well, what can you do, and how good are you?

WESLEY. I can run errands, clean up, wash dishes, anything.

DUDLEY (*on the telephone, very eagerly*). Elsie? Elsie, this is Dudley. Elsie, I'll jump in the bay if you don't marry me. Life isn't worth living without you. I can't sleep. I can't think of anything but you. All the time. Day and night and night and day. Elsie, I love you. I love you. What? (*Burning up.*) Is this Sunset 7-3-4-9? (*Pause.*) 7943? (*Calmly, while* WILLIE *begins making a small racket.*) Well, what's *your* name? *Lorene?* Lorene Smith? I thought you were Elsie Mandelspiegel. What? Dudley. Yeah. Dudley R. Bostwick. Yeah. R. It stands for Raoul, but I never spell it out. I'm pleased to meet *you*, too. What? There's a lot of noise around here. (WILLIE *stops hitting the marblegame.*) Where am I? At Nick's, on Pacific Street. I work at the S. P. I told them I was sick and they gave me the afternoon off. Wait a minute. I'll ask them. I'd like to meet *you*, too. Sure. I'll ask them. (*Turns around to* NICK.) What's this address?

NICK. Number 3 Pacific Street, you cad.

DUDLEY. Cad? You don't know how I've been suffering on acount of Elsie. I take things too ceremoniously. I've got to be more lackadaisical. (*Into telephone.*) Hello, Elenore? I mean, Lorene. It's number 3 Pacific Street. Yeah. Sure. I'll wait for you. How'll you know me? You'll *know* me. I'll recognize you. Good-bye, now. (*He hangs up.*)

HARRY (*continuing his monologue, with gestures, movements, and so on*). I'm standing there. I didn't do anything to anybody. Why should *I* be a soldier? (*Sincerely, insanely.*) BOOOOOOOOOM. *WAR!* O.K. War. *I* retreat. *I* hate war. I move to Sacramento.

NICK (*shouting*). All right, Comedian. Lay off a minute.

HARRY (*broken-hearted, going to* WILLIE). Nobody's got a sense of humor any more. The world's dying for comedy like never before, but nobody knows how to *laugh*.

NICK (*to* WESLEY). Do you belong to the union?

WESLEY. What union?

NICK. For the love of Mike, where've you been? Don't you know you can't come into a place and ask for a job and get one and go to work, just like that. You've got to belong to one of the unions.

WESLEY. I didn't know. I got to have a job. Real soon.

NICK. Well, you've got to belong to a union.

WESLEY. I don't want any favors. All I want is a chance to earn a living.

NICK. Go on into the kitchen and tell Sam to give you some lunch.

WESLEY. Honest, I ain't hungry.

DUDLEY (*shouting*). What I've gone through for Elsie.

HARRY. I've got all kinds of funny ideas in my head to help make the world happy again.

NICK (*holding* WESLEY). No, he isn't hungry.

(WESLEY *almost faints from hunger.* NICK *catches him just in time. The* ARAB *and* NICK *go off with* WESLEY *into the kitchen.*)

HARRY (*to* WILLIE). See if you think this is funny. It's my own idea. I created this dance myself. It comes after the monologue.

(HARRY *begins to dance.* WILLIE *watches a moment, and then goes back to the game. It's a goofy dance, which* HARRY *does with great sorrow, but much energy.*)

DUDLEY. Elsie. Aw, gee, Elsie. What the hell do I want to see Lorene Smith for? Some girl I don't know.

(JOE *and* KITTY *have been drinking in silence. There is no sound now except the soft shoe shuffling of* HARRY, *the Comedian.*)

JOE. What's the dream now, Kitty Duval?

KITTY (*dreaming the words and pictures*). I dream of home. Christ, I always dream of home. I've no *home*. I've no place. But I always dream of all of us together again. We had a farm in Ohio. There was nothing good about it. It was always sad. There was always trouble. But I always dream about it as if I could go back and Papa would be there and Mamma and Louie and my little brother Stephen and my sister Mary. I'm Polish. Duval! My name isn't Duval, it's Koranovsky. Katerina Koranovsky. We lost everything. The house, the farm, the trees, the horses, the cows, the chickens. Papa died. He was old. He was thirteen years older than Mamma. We moved to Chicago. We tried to work. We tried to stay together. Louie got into trouble. The fellows he was with killed him for something. I don't know what. Stephen ran away from home. Seventeen years old. I don't know where he is. Then Mamma died. *(Pause.)* What's the dream? I dream of home.

(NICK comes out of the kitchen with WESLEY.)

NICK. Here. Sit down here and rest. That'll hold you for a *while*. Why didn't you tell me you were hungry? You all right now?

WESLEY *(sitting down in the chair at the piano)*. Yes, I am. Thank you. I didn't know I was *that* hungry.

NICK. Fine. *(To HARRY who is dancing.)* Hey. What the hell do you think you're doing?

HARRY *(stopping)*. That's my own idea. I'm a natural-born dancer and comedian.

(WESLEY begins slowly, one note, one chord at a time, to play the piano.)

NICK. You're no good. Why don't you try some other kind of work? Why don't you get a job in a store, selling something? What do you want to be a comedian for?

HARRY. I've got something for the world and they haven't got sense enough to let me give it to them. Nobody knows me.

DUDLEY. Elsie. Now I'm waiting for some dame I've never seen before. Lorene Smith. Never saw her in my life. Just happened to get the wrong number. She turns on the personality, and I'm a cooked Indian. Give me a beer, please.

HARRY. Nick, you've got to see my act. It's the greatest thing of its kind in America. All I want is a chance. No salary to begin. Let me try it out tonight. If I don't wow 'em, O.K., I'll go home. If vaudeville wasn't dead, a guy like me would have a chance.

NICK. You're not funny. You're a sad young punk. What the hell do you want to try to be funny for? You'll break every-

body's heart. What's there for you to be funny about? You've been poor all your life, haven't you?

HARRY. I've been poor all right, but don't forget that some things count more than some other things.

NICK. What counts more, for instance, than what else, for instance?

HARRY. Talent, for instance, counts more than money, for instance, that's what, and I've got talent. I get new ideas night and day. Everything comes natural to me. I've got style, but it'll take me a little time to round it out. That's all.

(By now WESLEY is playing something of his own which is very good and out of the world. He plays about half a minute, after which HARRY begins to dance.)

NICK *(watching)*. I run the lousiest dive in Frisco, and a guy arrives and makes me stock up with champagne. The whores come in and holler at me that they're ladies. Talent comes in and begs me for a chance to show itself. Even society people come here once in a while. I don't know what for. Maybe it's liquor. Maybe it's the location. Maybe it's my personality. Maybe it's the crazy personality of the joint. The old honky-tonk. *(Pause.)* Maybe they can't feel at home anywhere else.

(By now WESLEY is really playing, and HARRY is going through a new routine. DUDLEY grows sadder and sadder.)

KITTY. Please dance with me.

JOE *(loudly)*. I never learned to dance.

KITTY. Anybody can dance. Just hold me in your arms.

JOE. I'm very fond of you. I'm *sorry*. I *can't* dance. I wish to God I could.

KITTY. Oh, please.

JOE. Forgive me. I'd like to very much.

(KITTY dances alone. TOM comes in with a package. He sees KITTY and goes ga-ga again. He comes out of the trance and puts the bundle on the table in front of JOE.)

JOE *(taking the package)*. What'd you get?

TOM. Two dollars' worth of toys. That's what you sent me for. The girl asked me what I wanted with toys. I didn't know what to tell her. *(He stares at* KITTY, *then back at* JOE.) Joe? I've got to have some money. After all you've done for me, I'll do anything in the world for you, but, Joe, you got to give me some money once in a while.

JOE. What do you want it for?

*(*TOM *turns and stares at* KITTY *dancing.)*

JOE *(noticing).* Sure. Here. Here's five. *(Shouting.)* Can you dance?

TOM *(proudly).* I got second prize at the Palomar in Sacramento five years ago.

JOE *(loudly, opening package).* O.K., dance with her.

TOM. You mean *her?*

JOE *(loudly).* I mean Kitty Duval, the burlesque queen. I mean the queen of the world burlesque. Dance with her. She wants to dance.

TOM *(worshipping the name Kitty Duval, helplessly).* Joe, can I tell you something?

JOE *(he brings out a toy and winds it).* You don't have to. I know. You love her. You *really* love her. I'm not blind. I know. But take care of yourself. Don't get sick that way again.

NICK *(looking at and listening to* WESLEY *with amazement).* Comes in here and wants to be a dish-washer. Faints from hunger. And then sits down and plays better than Heifetz.

JOE. Heifetz plays the violin.

NICK. All right, don't get careful. He's good, ain't he?

TOM *(to* KITTY*).* Kitty.

JOE *(he lets the toy go, loudly).* Don't *talk.* Just *dance.*

*(*TOM *and* KITTY *dance.* NICK *is at the bar, watching everything.* HARRY *is dancing.* DUDLEY *is grieving into his beer.* LORENE SMITH, *about thirty-seven, very overbearing and funny-looking, comes to the bar.)*

NICK. What'll it be, lady?

LORENE *(looking about and scaring all the young men).* I'm looking for the young man I talked to on the telephone. Dudley R. Bostwick.

DUDLEY *(jumping, running to her, stopping, shocked).* Dudley R. *(Slowly.)* Bostwick? Oh, yeah. He left here ten minutes ago. You mean Dudley Bostwick, that poor man on crutches?

LORENE. Crutches?

DUDLEY. Yeah. Dudley Bostwick. That's what he *said* his name was. He said to tell you not to wait.

LORENE. Well. *(She begins to go, turns around.)* Are you sure *you're* not Dudley Bostwick?

DUDLEY. Who—me? *(Grandly.)* My name is Roger Tenefrancia. I'm a French-Canadian. I never saw the poor fellow before.

LORENE. It seems to me your voice is like the voice I heard over the telephone.

DUDLEY. A coincidence. An accident. A quirk of fate. One of those things. Dismiss the thought. That poor cripple hobbled out of here ten minutes ago.

LORENE. He said he was going to commit suicide. I only wanted to be of help. *(She goes.)*

DUDLEY. Be of help? What kind of help could she be, of? *(*DUDLEY *runs to the telephone in the corner.)* Gee whiz, Elsie. Gee whiz. I'll never leave you again. *(He turns the pages of a little address book.)* Why do I always forget the number? I've tried to get her on the phone a hundred times this week and I still forget the number. She won't come to the phone, but I keep trying anyway. She's out. She's not in. She's working. I get the wrong number. Everything goes haywire. I can't sleep. *(Defiantly.)* She'll come to the phone one of these days. If there's anything to true love at all, she'll come to the phone. Sunset 7349.

(He dials the number, as JOE *goes on studying the toys. They are one big mechanical toy, whistles, and a music box.* JOE *blows into the whistles, quickly, by way of getting casually acquainted with them.)*

*(*TOM *and* KITTY *stop dancing.* TOM *stares at her.)*

DUDLEY. Hello. Is this Sunset 7349? May I speak to Elsie? Yes. *(Emphatically, and bitterly.)* No, this is *not* Dudley Bostwick. This is Roger Tenefrancia of Montreal,

Canada. I'm a childhood friend of Miss Mandelspiegel. We went to kindergarten together. (*Hand over phone.*) God damn it. (*Into phone.*) Yes. I'll wait, thank you.

TOM. I love you.

KITTY. You want to go to my room? (TOM *can't answer.*) Have you got two dollars?

TOM (*shaking his head with confusion*). I've got *five* dollars, but I *love* you.

KITTY (*looking at him*). You want to spend *all* that money?

(TOM *embraces her. They go.* JOE *watches. Goes back to the toy.*)

JOE. Where's that longshoreman, McCarthy?

NICK. He'll be around.

JOE. What do you think he'll have to say today?

NICK. Plenty, as usual. I'm going next door to see who won that third race at Laurel.

JOE. Precious Time won it.

NICK. That's what you think. (*He goes*).

JOE (*to himself*). A horse named McCarthy is running in the sixth race today.

DUDLEY (*on the phone*). Hello. Hello, Elsie? Elsie? (*His voice weakens; also his limbs.*) My God. She's come to the phone. Elsie, I'm at Nick's on Pacific Street. You've got to come here and talk to me. Hello. Hello, Elsie? (*Amazed.*) Did she hang up? Or was I disconnected?

(*He hangs up and goes to bar.*)

(WESLEY *is still playing the piano.* HARRY *is still dancing.* JOE *has wound up the big mechanical toy and is watching it work.*)

(NICK *returns.*)

NICK (*watching the toy*). Say. That's some gadget.

JOE. How much did I win?

NICK. How do you know you *won*?

JOE. Don't be silly. He said Precious Time was going to win by ten lengths, didn't he? He's in love, isn't he?

NICK. O.K. I don't know why, but Precious Time won. You got eighty for ten. How do you do it?

JOE (*roaring*). Faith. Faith. How'd he win?

NICK. By a nose. Look him up in The Racing Form. The slowest, the cheapest, the worst horse in the race, and the worst jockey. What's the matter with my luck?

JOE. How much did you lose?

NICK. Fifty cents.

JOE. You should never gamble.

NICK. Why not?

JOE. You always bet fifty cents. You've got no more faith than a flea, that's why.

HARRY (*shouting*). How do you like this, Nick? (*He is really busy now, all legs and arms.*)

NICK (*turning and watching*). Not bad. Hang around. You can wait table. (*To* WESLEY.) Hey. Wesley. Can you play that again tonight?

WESLEY (*turning, but still playing the piano*). I don't know for sure, Mr. Nick. I can play *something*.

NICK. Good. *You* hang around, too. (*He goes behind the bar.*)

(*The atmosphere is now one of warm, natural, American ease; every man innocent and good; each doing what he believes he should do, or what he must do. There is deep American naïveté and faith in the behavior of each person. No one is competing with anyone else. No one hates anyone else. Every man is living, and letting live. Each man is following his destiny as he feels it should be followed; or is abandoning it as he feels it must, by now, be abandoned; or is forgetting it for the moment as he feels he should forget it. Although everyone is dead serious, there is unmistakable smiling and humor in the scene; a sense of the human body and spirit emerging from the world-imposed state of stress and fretfulness, fear and awkwardness, to the more natural state of casualness and grace. Each person belongs to the environment, in his own person, as himself:* WESLEY *is playing better than ever.* HARRY *is hoofing better than ever.* NICK *is behind the bar shining glasses.* JOE *is smiling at the toy and studying it.* DUDLEY, *although still troubled, is at least calm now and full of melancholy poise.* WILLIE, *at the marble-game, is happy. The* ARAB *is deep in his memories, where he wants to be.*)

(*Into this scene and atmosphere comes* BLICK.)

(BLICK *is the sort of human being you dislike at sight. He is no different from anybody else physically. His face is an ordinary face. There is nothing obviously wrong with him, and yet you know that it is impossible, even by the most generous expansion of understanding, to accept him as a human being. He is the strong man without strength—strong only among the weak—the weakling who uses force on the weaker.*)

(BLICK *enters casually, as if he were a customer, and immediately* HARRY *begins slowing down.*)

BLICK (*oily, and with mock-friendliness*). Hello, Nick.

NICK (*stopping his work and leaning across the bar*). What do you want to come here for? You're too big a man for a little honky-tonk.

BLICK (*flattered*). Now, Nick.

NICK. Important people never come here. *Here.* Have a drink. (*Whiskey bottle.*)

BLICK. Thanks, I don't drink.

NICK (*drinking the drink himself*). Well, why don't you?

BLICK. I have responsibilities.

NICK. You're head of the lousy Vice Squad. There's no vice here.

BLICK (*sharply*). Street-walkers are working out of this place.

NICK (*angry*). What do you want?

BLICK (*loudly*). I just want you to know that it's got to stop.

(*The music stops. The mechanical toy runs down. There is absolute silence, and a strange fearfulness and disharmony in the atmosphere now.* HARRY *doesn't know what to do with his hands or feet.* WESLEY'S *arms hang at his sides.* JOE *quietly pushes the toy to one side of the table eager to study what is happening.* WILLIE *stops playing the marble-game, turns around and begins to wait.* DUDLEY *straightens up very, very vigorously, as if to say: "Nothing can scare me. I know love is the only*

thing." *The* ARAB *is the same as ever, but watchful.* NICK *is arrogantly aloof. There is a moment of this silence and tension, as though* BLICK *were waiting for everybody to acknowledge his presence. He is obviously flattered by the acknowledgment of Harry, Dudley, Wesley, and Willie, but a little irritated by Nick's aloofness and unfriendliness.*)

NICK. Don't look at me. I can't tell a street-walker from a lady. You married?

BLICK. You're not asking *me* questions. *I'm* telling *you.*

NICK (*interrupting*). You're a man of about forty-five or so. You *ought* to know better.

BLICK (*angry*). Street-walkers are working out of this place.

NICK (*beginning to shout*). Now, don't start any trouble with me. People come here to drink and loaf around. I don't care who they are.

BLICK. Well, I do.

NICK. The only way to find out if a lady is a street-walker is to walk the streets with her, go to bed, and make sure. You wouldn't want to do that. You'd *like* to, of course.

BLICK. Any more of it, and I'll have your joint closed.

NICK (*very casually, without ill-will*). Listen. I've got no use for you, or anybody like you. You're out to change the world from something bad to something worse. Something like yourself.

BLICK (*furious pause, and contempt*). I'll be back tonight. (*He begins to go.*)

NICK (*very angry but very calm*). Do yourself a big favor and don't come back tonight. Send somebody else. I don't like your personality.

BLICK (*casually, but with contempt*). Don't break any laws. I don't like yours, either.

(*He looks the place over, and goes.*)

(*There is a moment of silence. Then* WILLIE *turns and puts a new nickel in the slot and starts a new game.* WESLEY *turns to the piano and rather falteringly begins to play. His heart really isn't in it.* HARRY *walks about, unable to dance.* DUDLEY *lapses*

into his customary melancholy, at a table.
NICK *whistles a little: suddenly stops.* JOE
winds the toy.)

JOE *(comically).* Nick. You going to kill
that man?

NICK. I'm disgusted.

JOE. Yeah? Why?

NICK. Why should I get worked up over
a guy like that? Why should I hate *him?*
He's nothing. He's nobody. He's a mouse.
But every time he comes into this place
I get burned up. He doesn't want to drink.
He doesn't want to sit down. He doesn't
want to take things easy. Tell me one
thing?

JOE. Do my best.

NICK. What's a punk like *that* want to go
out and try to change the world for?

JOE *(amazed).* Does *he* want to change
the world, too?

NICK *(irritated).* You know what I mean.
What's he want to bother people for? He's
sick.

JOE *(almost to himself, reflecting on the
fact that* BLICK *too wants to change the
world).* I guess he wants to change the
world at that.

NICK. So I go to work and hate him.

JOE. It's not him, Nick. It's everything.

NICK. Yeah, *I know.* But I've still got no
use for him. He's no good. You know
what I mean? He hurts little people.
(Confused.) One of the girls tried to commit suicide on account of him. *(Furiously.)*
I'll break his head if he hurts anybody
around here. This is *my* joint. *(After-
thought.)* Or anybody's *feelings,* either.

JOE. He may not be so bad, deep down
underneath.

NICK. I know all about him. He's no good.

(During this talk WESLEY *has really begun
to play the piano, the toy is rattling again,
and little by little* HARRY *has begun to
dance.* NICK *has come around the bar, and*

*now, very much like a child—forgetting
all his anger—is watching the toy work.
He begins to smile at everything: turns
and listens to* WESLEY: *watches* HARRY:
nods at the ARAB: *shakes his head at* DUD-
LEY: *and gestures amiably about* WILLIE.
It's his joint all right.)

*(It's a good, low-down, honky-tonk Amer-
ican place that lets people alone.)*

NICK. I've got a good joint. There's nothing wrong here. Hey. Comedian. Stick to
the dancing tonight. I think you're O.K.
Wesley? Do some more of that tonight.
That's fine!

HARRY. Thanks, Nick. Gosh, I'm on my
way at last. *(On telephone.)* Hello, Ma?
Is that you, Ma? Harry. I got the job. *(He
hangs up and walks around, smiling.)*

NICK *(watching the toy all the time).* Say,
that really is something. What is that, anyway?

*(*MARY L. *comes in.)*

JOE *(holding it toward* NICK, *and* MARY L.*).*
Nick, this is a toy. A contraption devised
by the cunning of man to drive boredom,
or grief, or anger out of children. A noble
gadget. A gadget, I might say, infinitely
nobler than any other I can think of at the
moment.
(Everybody gathers around JOE'S *table to
look at the toy. The toy stops working.* JOE
*winds the music box. Lifts a whistle:
blows it, making a very strange, funny and
sorrowful sound.)*
Delightful. Tragic, but delightful.

*(*WESLEY *plays the music-box theme on the
piano.* MARY L. *takes a table.)*

NICK. Joe. That girl, Kitty. What's she
mean, calling me a dentist? I wouldn't
hurt anybody, let alone a tooth.

*(*NICK *goes to* MARY L.'s *table.* HARRY *imitates the toy. Dances. The piano music
comes up, the light dims slowly, while the
piano solo continues.)*

CURTAIN

ACT TWO

An hour later. All the people who were at Nick's when the curtain came down are still there. JOE *at his table, quietly shuffling and turning a deck of cards, and at the same time watching the face of the woman, and looking at the initials on her handbag, as though they were the symbols of the lost glory of the world. The* WOMAN, *in turn, very casually regards* JOE *occasionally. Or rather senses him; has sensed him in fact the whole hour. She is mildly tight on beer, and* JOE *himself is tight, but as always completely under control; simply sharper. The others are about, at tables, and so on.*

JOE. Is it Madge—Laubowitz?

MARY. Is what *what?*

JOE. Is the name Mabel Lepescu?

MARY. What name?

JOE. The name the initials M. L. stand for. The initials on your bag.

MARY. No.

JOE (*after a long pause, thinking deeply what the name might be, turning a card, looking into the beautiful face of the woman*). Margie Longworthy?

MARY (*all this is very natural and sincere, no comedy on the part of the people involved: they are both solemn, being drunk*). No.

JOE (*his voice higher-pitched, as though he were growing alarmed*). Midge Laurie? (MARY *shakes her head.*) My initials are J. T.

MARY (*Pause*). John?

JOE. No. (*Pause.*) Martha Lancaster?

MARY. No. (*Slight pause.*) Joseph?

JOE. Well, not exactly. That's my first name, but everybody calls me Joe. The last name is the tough one. I'll help you a little. I'm Irish. (*Pause.*) Is it just plain Mary?

MARY. Yes, it is. I'm Irish, too. At least on my father's side. English on my mother's side.

JOE. I'm Irish on both sides. Mary's one of my favorite names. I guess that's why I didn't think of it. I met a girl in Mexico City named Mary once. She was an American from Philadelphia. She got married there. In Mexico City, I mean. While I was *there*. We were in love, too. At least *I* was. You never know about anyone else. They were engaged, you see, and her mother was with her, so they went through with it. Must have been six or seven years ago. She's probably got three or four children by this time.

MARY. Are you still in love with her?

JOE. Well—no. To tell you the truth, I'm not sure. I guess I am. I didn't even knew she was engaged until a couple of days before they got married. I thought *I* was going to marry her. I kept thinking all the time about the kind of kids we would be likely to have. My favorite was the third one. The first two were fine. Handsome and fine and intelligent, but that third one was different. Dumb and goofy-looking. I liked *him* a lot. When she told me she was going to be married, I didn't feel so bad about the first two, it was that dumb one.

MARY (*after a pause of some few seconds*). What do you do?

JOE. Do? To tell you the truth, nothing.

MARY. Do you always drink a great deal?

JOE (*scientifically*). Not *always*. Only when I'm awake. I sleep seven or eight hours every night, you know.

MARY. How nice. I mean to drink when you're awake.

JOE (*thoughtfully*). It's a privilege.

MARY. Do you really *like* to drink?

JOE (*positively*). As much as I like to *breathe.*

MARY (*beautifully*). Why?

JOE (*dramatically*). Why do I like to drink? (*Pause.*) Because I don't like to be gypped. Because I don't like to be dead most of the time and just a little alive every once in a long while. (*Pause.*) If I don't drink, I become fascinated by unimportant things—like everybody else. I get busy. Do things. All kinds of little stupid things, for all kinds of little stupid reasons. Proud, selfish, *ordinary* things. I've done them. Now I don't do anything. *I live all the time.* Then I go to sleep. *(Pause.)*

MARY. Do you sleep well?

JOE *(taking it for granted).* Of course.

MARY *(quietly, almost with tenderness).* What are your plans?

JOE *(loudly, but also tenderly).* Plans? I haven't *got* any. *I just get up.*

MARY *(beginning to understand everything).* Oh, yes. Yes, of course.

(DUDLEY puts a nickel in the phonograph.)

JOE *(thoughtfully).* Why do I drink? *(Pause, while he thinks about it. The thinking appears to be profound and complex, and has the effect of giving his face a very comical and naïve expression.)* That question calls for a pretty complicated answer. *(He smiles abstractly.)*

MARY. Oh, I didn't mean—

JOE *(swiftly, gallantly).* No. No. I *insist.* I *know* why. It's just a matter of finding words. Little ones.

MARY. It really doesn't matter.

JOE *(seriously).* Oh, yes, it does. *(Clinically.)* Now, why do I drink? *(Scientifically.)* No. Why does *anybody* drink? *(Working it out.)* Every day has twenty-four hours.

MARY *(sadly, but brightly).* Yes, that's true.

JOE. Twenty-four hours. Out of the twenty-four hours at *least* twenty-three and a half are—my God, I don't know why— dull, dead, boring, empty, and murderous. Minutes on the clock, *not time of living.* It doesn't make any difference who you are or what you do, twenty-three and a half hours of the twenty-four are spent *waiting.*

MARY. Waiting?

JOE *(gesturing, loudly).* And the more you wait, the less there is to wait for.

MARY *(attentively, beautifully his student).* Oh?

JOE *(continuing).* That goes on for days and days, and weeks and months and years, and years, and the first thing you know *all* the years are dead. All the minutes are dead. You yourself are dead.

There's nothing to wait for any more. Nothing except *minutes* on the *clock.* No time of life. Nothing but minutes, and idiocy. Beautiful, bright, intelligent idiocy. *(Pause.)* Does that answer your question?

MARY *(earnestly).* I'm afraid it does. Thank you. You shouldn't have gone to all the trouble.

JOE. No trouble at all. *(Pause.)* You have children?

MARY. Yes. Two. A son and a daughter.

JOE *(delighted).* How swell. Do they look like you?

MARY. Yes.

JOE. Then why are you sad?

MARY. I was always sad. It's just that after I was married I was allowed to drink.

JOE *(eagerly).* Who are you waiting for?

MARY. No one.

JOE *(smiling).* I'm not waiting for anybody, either.

MARY. My husband, of course.

JOE. Oh, sure.

MARY. He's a lawyer.

JOE *(standing, leaning on the table).* He's a great guy. I like him. I'm very fond of him.

MARY *(listening).* You have responsibilities?

JOE *(loudly).* One, and *thousands.* As a matter of fact, I feel responsible to everybody. At least to everybody I met. I've been trying for three years to find out if it's possible to live what I think is a civilized life. I mean a life that can't hurt any other life.

MARY. You're famous?

JOE. Very. Utterly unknown, but very famous. Would you like to dance?

MARY. All right.

JOE *(loudly).* I'm *sorry.* I don't dance. I didn't think you'd like to.

MARY. To tell you the truth, I don't like to dance at all.

JOE *(proudly. Commentator).* I can hardly walk.

MARY. You mean you're tight?

JOE (*smiling*). No. I mean *all* the time.

MARY (*looking at him closely*). Were you ever in Paris?

JOE. In 1929, and again in 1934.

MARY. What month of 1934?

JOE. Most of April, all of May, and a little of June.

MARY. I was there in November and December that year.

JOE. We were there almost at the same time. You were married?

MARY. Engaged. (*They are silent a moment, looking at one another. Quietly and with great charm.*) Are you *really* in love with me?

JOE. Yes.

MARY. Is it the champagne?

JOE. Yes. Partly, at least. (*He sits down.*)

MARY. If you don't see me again will you be very unhappy?

JOE. Very.

MARY (*getting up*). I'm so pleased. (*JOE is deeply grieved that she is going. In fact, he is almost panic-stricken about it, getting up in a way that is full of furious sorrow and regret.*) I must go now. Please don't get up. (*JOE is up, staring at her with amazement.*) Good-by.

JOE (*simply*). Good-by.

(*The* WOMAN *stands looking at him a moment, then turns and goes.* JOE *stands staring after her for a long time. Just as he is slowly sitting down again, the* NEWSBOY *enters, and goes to Joe's table.*)

NEWSBOY. Paper, Mister?

JOE. How many you got this time?

NEWSBOY. Eleven.

(*JOE buys them all, looks at the lousy headlines, throws them away.*)

(*The* NEWSBOY *looks at* JOE, *amazed. He walks over to* NICK *at the bar.*)

NEWSBOY (*troubled*). Hey, Mister, do you own this place?

NICK (*casually but emphatically*). I own this place.

NEWSBOY. Can you use a great lyric tenor?

NICK (*almost to himself*). Great lyric tenor? (*Loudly.*) Who?

NEWSBOY (*loud and the least bit angry*). Me. I'm getting too big to sell papers. I don't want to holler headlines all the time. I want to *sing*. You can use a great lyric tenor, can't you?

NICK. What's lyric about you?

NEWSBOY (*voice high-pitched, confused*). My voice.

NICK. Oh. (*Slight pause, giving in.*) All right, then—sing!

(*The* NEWSBOY *breaks into swift and beautiful song: "When Irish Eyes Are Smiling."* NICK *and* JOE *listen carefully:* NICK *with wonder,* JOE *with amazement and delight.*)

NEWSBOY (*singing*).
When Irish eyes are smiling,
Sure 'tis like a morn in Spring.
In the lilt of Irish laughter,
You can hear the angels sing.
When Irish hearts are happy,
All the world seems bright and gay.
But when Irish eyes are smiling—

NICK (*loudly, swiftly*). Are you Irish?

NEWSBOY (*speaking swiftly, loudly, a little impatient with the irrelevant question*). No. I'm Greek. (*He finishes the song, singing louder than ever.*)

Sure they steal your heart away.

(*He turns to* NICK *dramatically, like a vaudeville singer begging his audience for applause.* NICK *studies the boy eagerly.* JOE *gets to his feet and leans toward the* BOY *and* NICK.)

NICK. Not bad. Let me hear you again about a year from now.

NEWSBOY (*thrilled*). Honest?

NICK. Yeah. Along about November 7th, 1940.

NEWSBOY (*happier than ever before in his life, running over to* JOE). Did you hear it too, Mister?

JOE. Yes, and it's great. What part of Greece?

NEWSBOY. Salonica. Gosh, Mister. Thanks.

JOE. Don't wait a year. Come back with some papers a little later. You're a great singer.

NEWSBOY *(thrilled and excited)*. Aw, thanks, Mister. So long. *(Running, to* NICK.*)* Thanks, Mister.

(He runs out. JOE *and* NICK *look at the swinging doors.* JOE *sits down.* NICK *laughs.)*

NICK. Joe, people are so wonderful. Look at that kid.

JOE. Of course they're wonderful. Every one of them is wonderful.

*(*MC CARTHY *and* KRUPP *come in, talking.)*

*(*MC CARTHY *is a big man in work clothes, which make him seem very young. He is wearing black jeans, and a blue workman's shirt. No tie. No hat. He has broad shoulders, a lean intelligent face, thick black hair. In his right back pocket is the longshoreman's hook. His arms are long and hairy. His sleeves are rolled up to just below his elbows. He is a casual man, easy-going in movement, sharp in perception, swift in appreciation of charm or innocence or comedy, and gentle in spirit. His speech is clear and full of warmth. His voice is powerful, but modulated. He enjoys the world, in spite of the mess it is, and he is fond of people, in spite of the mess they are.)*

*(*KRUPP *is not quite as tall or broad-shouldered as* MC CARTHY. *He is physically encumbered by his uniform, club, pistol, belt, and cap. And he is plainly not at home in the role of policeman. His movement is stiff and unintentionally pompous. He is a naïve man, essentially good. His understanding is less than McCarthy's, but he is honest and he doesn't try to bluff.)*

KRUPP. You don't understand what I mean. Hi-ya, Joe.

JOE. Hello, Krupp.

MC CARTHY. Hi-ya, Joe.

JOE. Hello, McCarthy.

KRUPP. Two beers, Nick. *(To* MC CARTHY.*)* All I do is carry out orders, carry out orders. I don't know what the idea is behind the order. Who it's for, or who it's against, or why. All I do is carry it out.

*(*NICK *gives them beer.)*

MC CARTHY. You don't read enough.

KRUPP. I do read. I read *The Examiner* every morning. *The Call-Bulletin* every night.

MC CARTHY. And carry out orders. What are the orders now?

KRUPP. To keep the peace down here on the waterfront.

MC CARTHY. Keep it for who? *(To* JOE.*)* Right?

JOE *(sorrowfully)*. Right.

KRUPP. How do I know for who? The peace. Just keep it.

MC CARTHY. It's got to be kept for somebody. Who would you suspect it's kept for?

KRUPP. For citizens!

MC CARTHY. I'm a citizen!

KRUPP. All right, I'm keeping it for you.

MC CARTHY. By hitting me over the head with a club? *(To* JOE.*)* Right?

JOE *(melancholy, with remembrance)*. I don't know.

KRUPP. Mac, you know I never hit you over the head with a club.

MC CARTHY. But you will if you're on duty at the time and happen to stand on the opposite side of myself, on duty.

KRUPP. We went to Mission High together. We were always good friends. The only time we ever fought was that time over Alma Haggerty. Did you marry Alma Haggerty? *(To* JOE.*)* Right?

JOE. Everything's right.

MC CARTHY. No. Did you? *(To* JOE.*)* Joe, are you with me or against me?

JOE. I'm with everybody. One at a time.

KRUPP. No. And that's just what I mean.

MC CARTHY. You mean neither one of us is going to marry the thing we're fighting for?

KRUPP. *I don't even know what it is.*

MC CARTHY. You don't read enough, I tell you.

KRUPP. Mac, you don't know what you're fighting for, either.

MC CARTHY. It's so simple, it's fantastic.

KRUPP. All right, what are you fighting for?

MC CARTHY. For the rights of the inferior. Right?

JOE. Something like that.

KRUPP. The who?

MC CARTHY. The inferior. The world is full of Mahoneys who haven't got what it takes to make monkeys out of everybody else, near by. The men who were created equal. Remember?

KRUPP. Mac, you're not inferior.

MC CARTHY. I'm a longshoreman. And an idealist. I'm a man with too much brawn to be an intellectual, exclusively. I married a small, sensitive, cultured woman so that my kids would be sissies instead of suckers. A strong man with any sensibility has no choice in this world but to be a heel, or a *worker*. I haven't the heart to be a heel, so I'm a worker. I've got a son in high school who's already thinking of being a writer.

KRUPP. I wanted to be a writer once.

JOE. Wonderful. (*He puts down the paper, looks at* KRUPP *and* MC CARTHY.)

MC CARTHY. They *all* wanted to be writers. Every maniac in the world that ever brought about the murder of people through war started out in an attic or a basement writing poetry. It stank. So they got even by becoming important heels. And it's still going on.

KRUPP. Is it really, Joe?

JOE. Look at today's paper.

MC CARTHY. Right now on Telegraph Hill is some punk who is trying to be Shakespeare. Ten years from now he'll be a senator. Or a communist.

KRUPP. Somebody ought to do something about it.

MC CARTHY (*mischievously, with laughter in his voice*). The thing to do is to have more magazines. Hundreds of them. *Thousands*. Print everything they write, so they'll believe ,they're immortal. That way keep them from going haywire.

KRUPP. Mac, you ought to be a writer yourself.

MC CARTHY. I hate the tribe. They're mischief-makers. Right?

JOE (*swiftly*). Everything's right. Right and wrong.

KRUPP. Then why do you read?

MC CARTHY (*laughing*). It's relaxing. It's soothing. (*Pause.*) The lousiest people born into the world are writers. Language is all right. It's the people who use language that are lousy. (*The* ARAB *has moved a little closer, and is listening carefully.*) (*To the* ARAB.) What do you think, Brother?

ARAB (*after making many faces, thinking very deeply*). No foundation. All the way down the line. What. What-not. Nothing. I go walk and look at sky. (*He goes.*)

KRUPP. What? What-not? (*To* JOE.) What's that mean?

JOE (*slowly, thinking, remembering*). What? What-not? That means this side, that side. Inhale, exhale. What: birth. What-not: death. The inevitable, the astounding, the magnificent seed of growth and decay in all things. Beginning, and end. That man, in his own way, is a prophet. He is one who, with the help of *beer,* is able to reach that state of deep understanding in which what and what-not, the reasonable and the unreasonable, are one.

MC CARTHY. Right.

KRUPP. If you can understand that kind of talk, how can you be a longshoreman?

MC CARTHY. I come from a long line of McCarthys who never married or slept with anything but the most powerful and quarrelsome flesh. (*He drinks beer.*)

KRUPP. I could listen to you two guys for hours, but I'll be damned if I know what the hell you're talking about.

MC CARTHY. The consequence is that all the McCarthys are too great and too strong to be heroes. Only the weak and unsure perform the heroic. They've *got* to. The more heroes you have, the worse the history of the world becomes. Right?

JOE. Go outside and look at it.

KRUPP. You sure can philos—philosoph— Boy. you can talk.

MC CARTHY. I wouldn't talk this way to anyone but a man in uniform, and a man who couldn't understand a word of what I was saying. The party I'm speaking of, my friend, is YOU.

(The phone rings.)

(HARRY gets up from his table suddenly and begins a new dance.)

KRUPP *(noticing him, with great authority)*. Here, here. What do you think you're doing?

HARRY *(stopping)*. I just got an idea for a new dance. I'm trying it out. Nick. Nick, the phone's ringing.

KRUPP *(to MC CARTHY)*. Has he got a right to do that?

MC CARTHY. The living have danced from the beginning of time. I might even say, the dance and the life have moved along together, until now we have— *(To HARRY.)* Go into your dance, son, and show us what we have.

HARRY. I haven't got it worked out *completely* yet, but it starts out like this. *(He dances.)*

NICK *(on phone)*. Nick's Pacific Street Restaurant, Saloon, and Entertainment Palace. Good afternoon. Nick speaking. *(Listens.)* Who? *(Turns around.)* Is there a Dudley Bostwick in the joint?

(DUDLEY jumps to his feet and goes to phone.)

DUDLEY *(on phone)*. Hello. Elsie? *(Listens.)* You're coming down? *(Elated. To the saloon.)* She's coming down. *(Pause.)* No. I won't drink. Aw, gosh, Elsie.

(He hangs up, looks about him strangely, as if he were just born, walks around touching things, putting chairs in place, and so on.)

MC CARTHY *(to HARRY.)* Splendid. Splendid.

HARRY. Then I go into this little routine. *(He demonstrates.)*

KRUPP. Is that good, Mac?

MC CARTHY. It's awful, but it's honest and ambitious, like everything else in this great country.

HARRY. Then I work along into this. *(He demonstrates.)* And *this* is where I *really* get going. *(He finishes the dance.)*

MC CARTHY. Excellent. A most satisfying demonstration of the present state of the American body and soul. Son, you're a genius.

HARRY *(delighted, shaking hands with MC CARTHY)*. I go on in front of an audience for the first time in my life tonight.

MC CARTHY. They'll be delighted. Where'd you learn to dance?

HARRY. Never took a lesson in my life. I'm a natural-born dancer. And *comedian*, too.

MC CARTHY *(astounded)*. You can make people *laugh?*

HARRY *(dumbly)*. I can be funny, but they won't laugh.

MC CARTHY. That's odd. Why not?

HARRY. I don't know. They just won't laugh.

MC CARTHY. Would you care to be funny now?

HARRY. I'd like to try out a new monologue I've been thinking about.

MC CARTHY. Please do. I promise you if it's funny I shall *roar* with laughter.

HARRY. This is it. *(Goes into the act, with much energy.)* I'm up at Sharkey's on Turk Street. It's a quarter to nine, daylight saving. Wednesday, the eleventh. What I've got is a headache and a 1918 nickel. What I *want* is a cup of coffee. If I buy a cup of coffee with the nickel, I've got to walk home. I've got an eight-ball problem. George the Greek is shooting a game of snooker with Pedro the Filipino. *I'm in rags.* They're wearing thirty-five dollar suits, made to order. I haven't got a cigarette. They're smoking Bobby Burns panatelas. I'm thinking it over, like I always do. George the Greek is in a tough spot. If I buy a cup of coffee, I'll want another cup. What happens? My *ear* aches! My ear. George the Greek takes the cue. Chalks it. Studies the table. Touches the cue-ball delicately. Tick. What happens? He makes the three-ball! What do I do. I get confused. *I go out and buy a morning paper.* What the hell do I want with a morning paper? What I *want* is a cup of coffee, and a good used car. I go out and buy a morning paper. Thursday, the twelfth. Maybe the headline's about *me*. I take a quick look. *No. The headline is not about me.* It's about Hitler. Seven thousand miles away. I'm here. Who the hell is Hitler? Who's behind the eight-ball? I turn around. *Everybody's behind the eight-ball!*

(Pause. KRUPP *moves toward* HARRY *as if to make an important arrest.* HARRY *moves to the swinging doors.* MC CARTHY *stops* KRUPP.)

MC CARTHY *(to* HARRY*).* It's the funniest thing I've ever heard. Or *seen,* for that matter.

HARRY *(coming back to* MC CARTHY*).* Then, why don't you laugh?

MC CARTHY. I don't know, *yet.*

HARRY. I'm always getting funny ideas that nobody will laugh at.

MC CARTHY *(thoughtfully).* It may be that you've stumbled headlong into a new kind of comedy.

HARRY. Well, what good is it if it doesn't make anybody laugh?

MC CARTHY. There are *kinds* of laughter, son. I must say, in all truth, that I *am* laughing, although not *out loud.*

HARRY. I want to *hear* people laugh. *Out loud.* That's why I keep thinking of funny things to say.

MC CARTHY. Well. They may catch on in time. Let's go, Krupp. So long, Joe. *(*MC CARTHY *and* KRUPP *go.)*

JOE. So long. *(After a moment's pause.)* Hey, Nick.

NICK. Yeah.

JOE. Bet McCarthy in the last race.

NICK. You're crazy. That horse is a double-crossing, no-good—

JOE. Bet everything you've got on McCarthy.

NICK. I'm not betting a nickel on him. *You* bet everything you've got on McCarthy.

JOE. I don't need money.

NICK. What makes you think McCarthy's going to win?

JOE. McCarthy's name's McCarthy, isn't it?

NICK. Yeah. So what?

JOE. The *horse* named McCarthy is going to win, *that's all.* Today.

NICK. Why?

JOE. You do what I tell you, and everything will be all right.

NICK. McCarthy likes to talk, that's all. *(Pause.)* Where's Tom?

JOE. He'll be around. He'll be miserable, but he'll be around. Five or ten minutes more.

NICK. You don't believe that Kitty, do you? About being in burlesque?

JOE *(very clearly).* I believe dreams sooner than statistics.

NICK *(remembering).* She sure is somebody. Called me a dentist.

*(*TOM, *turning about, confused, troubled, comes in, and hurries to Joe's table.)*

JOE. What's the matter?

TOM. Here's your five, Joe. I'm in trouble again.

JOE. If it's not organic, it'll cure itself. If it is organic, science will cure it. What is it, organic or non-organic?

TOM. Joe, I don't know— *(He seems to be completely broken-down.)*

JOE. What's eating you? I want you to go on an errand for me.

TOM. It's Kitty.

JOE. What about her?

TOM. She's up in her room, crying.

JOE. Crying?

TOM. Yeah, she's been crying for over an hour. I been talking to her all this time, but she won't stop.

JOE. What's she crying about?

TOM. I don't know. I couldn't understand anything. She kept crying and telling me about a big house and collie dogs all around and flowers and one of her brother's dead and the other one lost somewhere. Joe, I can't stand Kitty crying.

JOE. You want to marry the girl?

TOM (*nodding*). Yeah.

JOE (*curious and sincere*). Why?

TOM. I don't know why, exactly, Joe. (*Pause.*) Joe, I don't like to think of Kitty out in the streets. I guess I love her that's all.

JOE. She's a nice girl.

TOM. She's like an angel. She's not like those other street-walkers.

JOE (*swiftly*). Here. Take all this money and run next door to Frankie's and bet it on the nose of McCarthy.

TOM (*swiftly*). All this money, Joe? Mc-Carthy?

JOE. Yeah. Hurry.

TOM (*going*). Ah, Joe. If McCarthy wins we'll be rich.

JOE. Get going, will you?

(TOM *runs out and nearly knocks over the* ARAB *coming back in.* NICK *fills him a beer without a word.*)

ARAB. No foundation, anywhere. Whole world. No foundation. All the way down the line.

NICK (*angry*). McCarthy! Just because you got a little lucky this morning, you have to go to work and throw away eighty bucks.

JOE. He wants to marry her.

NICK. Suppose she doesn't want to marry *him*?

JOE (*amazed*). Oh, yeah. (*Thinking*). Now, why wouldn't she want to marry a nice guy like Tom?

NICK. She's been in burlesque. She's had flowers sent to her by European royalty. She's dined with young men of quality and social position. She's above Tom.

(TOM *comes running in.*)

TOM (*disgusted*). They were running when I got there. Frankie wouldn't take the bet. McCarthy didn't get a call till the stretch. I thought we were going to save all this money. Then McCarthy won by two lengths.

JOE. What'd he pay, fifteen to one?

TOM. Better, but Frankie wouldn't take the bet.

NICK (*throwing a dish towel across the room*). Well, for the love of Mike.

JOE. Give me the money.

TOM (*giving back the money*). We would have had about a thousand five hundred dollars.

JOE (*bored, casually, inventing*). Go up to Schwabacher-Frey and get me the biggest Rand-McNally map of the nations of Europe they've got. On your way back stop at one of the pawn shops on Third Street, and buy me a good revolver and some cartridges.

TOM. She's up in her room crying, Joe.

JOE. Go get me those things.

NICK. What are you going to do, study the map, and then go out and shoot somebody?

JOE. I want to read the names of some European towns and rivers and valleys and mountains.

NICK. What do you want with the revolver?

JOE. I want to study it. I'm interested in things. Here's twenty dollars, Tom. Now go get them things.

TOM. A big map of Europe. And a revolver.

JOE. Get a good one. Tell the man you don't know anything about firearms and you're trusting him not to fool you. Don't pay more than ten dollars.

TOM. Joe, you got something on your mind. Don't go fool with a revolver.

JOE. Be sure it's a good one.

TOM. Joe.

JOE (*irritated*). What, Tom?

TOM. Joe, what do you send me out for crazy things for all the time?

JOE (*angry*). They're not crazy, Tom. Now, get going.

TOM. What about Kitty, Joe?

JOE. Let her cry. It'll do her good.

TOM. If she comes in here while I'm gone, talk to her, will you, Joe? Tell her about me.

JOE. O.K. Get going. Don't load that gun. Just buy it and bring it here.

TOM (*going*). You won't catch me loading any gun.

JOE. Wait a minute. Take these toys away.

TOM. Where'll I take them?

JOE. Give them to some kid. (*Pause.*) No. Take them up to Kitty. Toys stopped me from crying once. That's the reason I had you buy them. I wanted to see if I could find out *why* they stopped me from crying. I remember they seemed awfully stupid at the time.

TOM. Shall I, Joe? Take them up to Kitty? Do you think they'd stop *her* from crying?

JOE. They might. You get curious about the way they work and you forget whatever it is you're remembering that's making you cry. That's what they're for.

TOM. Yeah. Sure. The girl at the store asked me what I wanted with toys. I'll take them up to Kitty. (*Tragically.*) She's like a little girl. (*He goes.*)

WESLEY. Mr. Nick, can I play the piano again?

NICK. Sure. Practice all you like—until I tell you to stop.

WESLEY. You going to pay me for playing the piano?

NICK. Sure. I'll give you enough to get by on.

WESLEY (*amazed and delighted*). Get money for playing the piano?

(*He goes to the piano and begins to play quietly.* HARRY *goes up on the little stage and listens to the music. After a while he begins a soft shoe dance.*)

NICK. What were you crying about?

JOE. My mother.

NICK. What about her?

JOE. She was dead. I stopped crying when they gave me the toys.

(NICK'S MOTHER, *a little old woman of sixty or so, dressed plainly in black, her face shining, comes in briskly, chattering loudly in Italian, gesturing.* NICK *is delighted to see her.*)

NICK'S MOTHER (*in Italian*). Everything all right, Nickie?

NICK (*in Italian*). Sure, Mamma.

(NICK'S MOTHER *leaves as gaily and as noisily as she came, after half a minute of loud Italian family talk.*)

JOE. Who was that?

NICK (*to* JOE, *proudly and a little sadly*). My mother. (*Still looking at the swinging doors.*)

JOE. What'd she say?

NICK. Nothing. Just wanted to see me. (*Pause.*) What do you want with that gun?

JOE. I study things, Nick.

(*An old man who looks as if he might have been Kit Carson at one time walks in importantly, moves about, and finally stands at Joe's table.*)

KIT CARSON. Murphy's the name. Just an old trapper. Mind if I sit down?

JOE. Be delighted. What'll you drink?

KIT CARSON (*sitting down*). Beer. Same as I've been drinking. And thanks.

JOE (*to* NICK). Glass of beer, Nick.

(NICK *brings the beer to the table,* KIT CARSON *swallows it in one swig, wipes his big white mustache with the back of his right hand.*)

KIT CARSON (*moving in*). I don't suppose you ever fell in love with a midget weighing thirty-nine pounds?

JOE (*studying the man*). Can't say I have, but have another beer.

KIT CARSON (*intimately*). Thanks, thanks. Down in Gallup, twenty years ago. Fellow by the name of Rufus Jenkins came to town with six white horses and two black ones. Said he wanted a man to break the horses for him because his left leg was wood and he couldn't do it. Had a meeting at Parker's Mercantile Store and finally came to blows, me and Henry Walpal. Bashed his head with a brass cuspidor and ran away to Mexico, but he didn't die.

Couldn't speak a word. Took up with a cattle-breeder named Diego, educated in California. Spoke the language better than you and me. Said, Your job, Murph, is to feed them prize bulls. I said, Fine, what'll I feed them? He said, Hay, lettuce, salt, beer, and aspirin.

Came to blows two days 'ater over an

accordion he claimed I stole. I had *borrowed* it. During the fight I busted it over his head; ruined one of the finest accordions I ever saw. Grabbed a horse and rode back across the border. Texas. Got to talking with a fellow who looked honest. Turned out to be a Ranger who was looking for me.

JOE. Yeah. You were saying, a thirty-nine-pound midget.

KIT CARSON. Will I ever forget that lady? Will I ever get over that amazon of small proportions?

JOE. Will you?

KIT CARSON. If I live to be sixty.

JOE. Sixty? You look more than sixty now.

KIT CARSON. That's trouble showing in my face. Trouble and complications. I was fifty-eight three months ago.

JOE. That accounts for it, then. Go ahead, tell me more.

KIT CARSON. Told the Texas Ranger my name was Rothstein, mining engineer from Pennsylvania, looking for something worth while. Mentioned two places in Houston. Nearly lost an eye early one morning, going down the stairs. Ran into a six-footer with an iron-claw where his right hand was supposed to be. Said, You broke up my home. Told him I was a stranger in Houston. The girls gathered at the top of the stairs to see a fight. Seven of them. Six feet and an iron claw. That's bad on the nerves. Kicked him in the mouth when he swung for my head with the claw. Would have lost an eye except for quick thinking. He rolled into the gutter and pulled a gun. Fired seven times. I was back upstairs. Left the place an hour later, dressed in silk and feathers, with a hat swung around over my face. Saw him standing on the corner, waiting. Said, Care for a wiggle? Said he didn't. I went on down the street and left town. I don't suppose you ever had to put a dress on to save your skin, did you?

JOE. No, and I never fell in love with a midget weighing thirty-nine pounds. Have another beer?

KIT CARSON. Thanks. *(Swallows glass of beer.)* Ever try to herd cattle on a bicycle?

JOE. No. I never got around to that.

KIT CARSON. Left Houston with sixty cents in my pocket, gift of a girl named Lucinda. Walked fourteen miles in fourteen hours. Big house with barb-wire all around, and big dogs. One thing I never could get around. Walked past the gate, anyway, from hunger and thirst. Dogs jumped up and came for me. Walked right into them, growing older every second. Went up to the door and knocked. Big negress opened the door, closed it quick. Said, On your way, white trash.

Knocked again. Said, On your way. Again. On your way. Again. This time the old man himself opened the door, ninety, if he was a day. Sawed-off shotgun, too.

Said, I ain't looking for trouble, Father. I'm hungry and thirsty, name's Cavanaugh.

Took me in and made mint juleps for the two of us.

Said, Living here alone, Father?

Said, Drink and ask no questions. Maybe I am and maybe I ain't. You saw the lady. Draw your own conclusions.

I'd heard of that, but didn't wink out of tact. If I told you that old Southern gentleman was my grandfather, you wouldn't believe me, would you?

JOE. I might.

KIT CARSON. Well, it so happens he wasn't. Would have been romantic if he had been, though.

JOE. Where did you herd cattle on a bicycle?

KIT CARSON. Toledo, Ohio, 1918.

JOE. Toledo, Ohio? They don't herd cattle in Toledo.

KIT CARSON. They don't anymore. They did in 1918. One fellow did, leastaways. Bookkeeper named Sam Gold. Straight from the East Side, New York. Sombrero, lariats, Bull Durham, two head of cattle and two bicycles. Called his place The Gold Bar Ranch, two acres, just outside the city limits.

That was the year of the War, you'll remember.

JOE. Yeah, I remember, but how about herding them two cows on a bicycle? How'd you do it?

KIT CARSON. Easiest thing in the world. Rode no hands. Had to, otherwise couldn't lasso the cows. Worked for Sam Gold till the cows ran away. Bicycles scared them. They went into Toledo. Never saw hide nor hair of them again. Advertised in every paper, but never got them back. Broke his heart. Sold both bikes and returned to New York.

Took four aces from a deck of red cards and walked to town. Poker. Fellow in the game named Chuck Collins, liked to gamble. Told him with a smile I didn't suppose he'd care to bet a hundred dollars I wouldn't hold four aces the next hand. Called it. My cards were red on the blank side. The other cards were blue. Plumb forgot all about it. Showed him four aces. Ace of spades, ace of clubs, ace of diamonds, ace of hearts. I'll remember them four cards if I live to be sixty. Would have been killed on the spot except for the hurricane that year.

JOE. Hurricane?

KIT CARSON. You haven't forgotten the Toledo hurricane of 1918, have you?

JOE. No. There was no hurricane in Toledo in 1918, or any other year.

KIT CARSON. For the love of God, then what do you suppose that commotion was? And how come I came to in Chicago, dream-walking down State Street?

JOE. I guess they scared you.

KIT CARSON. No, that wasn't it. You go back to the papers of November 1918, and I think you'll find there was a hurricane in Toledo. I remember sitting on the roof of a two-story house, floating northwest.

JOE (seriously). Northwest?

KIT CARSON. Now, son, don't tell me *you* don't believe me, either?

JOE (pause. Very seriously, energetically and sharply). Of course I believe you. Living is an art. It's not bookkeeping. It takes a lot of rehearsing for a man to get to be himself.

KIT CARSON (thoughtfully, smiling, and amazed). You're the first man I've ever met who believes me.

JOE (seriously). Have another beer.

(TOM comes in with the Rand-McNally book, the revolver, and the box of cartridges. KIT goes to bar.)

JOE (to TOM). Did you give her the toys?

TOM. Yeah, I gave them to her.

JOE. Did she stop crying?

TOM. No. She started crying harder than ever.

JOE. That's funny. I wonder why.

TOM. Joe, if I was a minute earlier, Frankie would have taken the bet and now we'd have about a thousand five hundred dollars. How much of it would you have given me, Joe?

JOE. If she'd marry you—*all* of it.

TOM. Would you, Joe?

JOE (opening packages, examining book first, and revolver next). Sure. In this realm there's only one subject, and you're it. It's my duty to see that my subject is happy.

TOM. Joe, do you think we'll ever have eighty dollars for a race sometime again when there's a fifteen-to-one shot that we like, weather good, track fast, they get off to a good start, our horse doesn't get a call till the stretch, we think we're going to lose all that money, and then it wins, by a nose?

JOE. I didn't quite get that.

TOM. You know what I mean.

JOE. You mean the impossible. No, Tom, we won't. We were just a little late, that's all.

TOM. We might, Joe.

JOE. It's not likely.

TOM. Then how am I ever going to make enough money to marry her?

JOE. I don't know, Tom. Maybe you aren't.

TOM. Joe, I got to marry Kitty. (Shaking his head.) You ought to see the crazy room she lives in.

JOE. What kind of a room is it?

TOM. It's little. It crowds you in. It's bad, Joe. Kitty don't belong in a place like that.

JOE. You want to take her away from there?

TOM. Yeah. I want her to live in a house where there's room enough to live. Kitty ought to have a garden, or something.

JOE. You want to take care of her?

TOM. Yeah, sure, Joe. I ought to take care of somebody good that makes me feel like *I'm* somebody.

JOE. That means you'll have to get a job. What can you do?

TOM. I finished high school, but I don't know what I can do.

JOE. Sometimes when you think about it, what do you think you'd like to do?

TOM. Just sit around like you, Joe, and have somebody run errands for me and drink champagne and take things easy and never be broke and never worry about money.

JOE. That's a noble ambition.

NICK (*to* JOE). How do you do it?

JOE. I really don't know but I think you've got to have the full co-operation of the Good Lord.

NICK. I can't understand the way you talk.

TOM. Joe, shall I go back and see if I can get her to stop crying?

JOE. Give me a hand and I'll go with you.

TOM (*amazed*). What! You're going to get up already?

JOE. She's crying, isn't she?

TOM. She's crying. Worse than ever now.

JOE. I thought the toys would stop her.

TOM. I've seen you sit in one place from four in the morning till two the next morning.

JOE. At my best, Tom, I don't travel by foot. That's all. Come on. Give me a hand. I'll find some way to stop her from crying.

TOM (*helping* JOE). Joe, I never did tell you. You're a different kind of guy.

JOE (*swiftly, a little angry*). Don't be silly. I don't understand things. I'm trying to understand them.

(JOE *is a little drunk. They go out together. The lights go down slowly, while* WESLEY *plays the piano, and come up slowly on:*)

ACT THREE

A cheap bed in Nick's to indicate room 21 of The New York Hotel, upstairs, around the corner from Nick's. The bed can be at the center of Nick's or up on the little stage. Everything in Nick's is the same, except that all the people are silent, immobile and in darkness, except WESLEY *who is playing the piano softly and sadly.* KITTY DUVAL, *in a dress she has carried around with her from the early days in Ohio, is seated on the bed, tying a ribbon in her hair. She looks at herself in a hand mirror. She is deeply grieved at the change she sees in herself. She takes off the ribbon, angry and hurt. She lifts a book from the bed and tries to read. She begins to sob again. She picks up an old picture of herself and looks at it. Sobs harder than ever, falling on the bed and burying her face. There is a knock, as if at the door.*

KITTY (*sobbing*). Who is it?

TOM'S VOICE. Kitty, it's me. Tom. Me and Joe.

(JOE, *followed by* TOM, *comes to the bed quietly.* JOE *is holding a rather large toy carousel.* JOE *studies* KITTY *a moment.*)

(He *sets the toy carousel on the floor, at the foot of Kitty's bed.*)

TOM (*standing over* KITTY *and bending down close to her*). Don't cry any more, Kitty.

KITTY (*not looking, sobbing*). I don't like this life.

(JOE *starts the carousel which makes a strange, sorrowful, tinkling music. The music begins slowly, becomes swift, gradually slows down, and ends.* JOE *himself is interested in the toy, watches and listens to it carefully.*)

TOM (*eagerly*). Kitty. Joe got up from his chair at Nick's just to get you a toy and come here. This one makes music. We rode all over town in a cab to get it. Listen.

(KITTY *sits up slowly, listening, while* TOM *watches her. Everything happens slowly and somberly.* KITTY *notices the photograph of herself when she was a little girl. Lifts it, and looks at it again.*)

TOM *(looking)*. Who's that little girl, Kitty?

KITTY. That's me. When I was seven.

(KITTY *hands the photo to* TOM.)

TOM *(looking, smiling)*. Gee, you're pretty, Kitty.

(JOE *reaches up for the photograph, which* TOM *hands to him.* TOM *returns to* KITTY *whom he finds as pretty now as she was at seven.* JOE *studies the photograph.* KITTY *looks up at* TOM. *There is no doubt that they really love one another.* JOE *looks up at them.*)

KITTY. Tom?

TOM *(eagerly)*. Yeah, Kitty.

KITTY. Tom, when you were a little boy what did you want to be?

TOM *(a little bewildered, but eager to please her)*. What, Kitty?

KITTY. Do you remember when you were a little boy?

TOM *(thoughtfully)*. Yeah, I remember sometimes, Kitty.

KITTY. What did you want to be?

TOM *(looks at* JOE. JOE *holds Tom's eyes a moment. Then* TOM *is able to speak)*. Sometimes I wanted to be a locomotive engineer. Sometimes I wanted to be a policeman.

KITTY. I wanted to be a great actress. *(She looks up into Tom's face.)* Tom, didn't you ever want to be a doctor?

TOM *(looks at* JOE. JOE *holds Tom's eyes again, encouraging Tom by his serious expression to go on talking)*. Yeah, now I remember. Sure, Kitty. I wanted to be a doctor—*once*.

KITTY *(smiling sadly)*. I'm so glad. Because I wanted to be an actress and have a young doctor come to the theater and see me and fall in love with me and send me flowers.

(JOE *pantomimes to* TOM, *demanding that he go on talking.*)

TOM. I would do that, Kitty.

KITTY. I wouldn't know who it was, and then one day I'd see him in the street and fall in love with him. I wouldn't know *he* was the one who was in love with me. I'd think about him all the time. I'd dream about him. I'd dream of being near him the rest of my life. I'd dream of having children that looked like him. I wouldn't be an actress all the time. Only until I found him and fell in love with him. After that we'd take a train and go to beautiful cities and see the wonderful people everywhere and give money to the poor and whenever people were sick he'd go to them and make them well again.

(TOM *looks at* JOE, *bewildered, confused, and full of sorrow.* KITTY *is deep in memory, almost in a trance.*)

JOE *(gently)*. Talk to her, Tom. Be the wonderful young doctor she dreamed about and never found. Go ahead. Correct the errors of the world.

TOM. Joe. *(Pathetically.)* I don't know what to say.

(*There is rowdy singing in the hall. A loud young* VOICE *sings: "Sailing, sailing, over the bounding main."*)

VOICE. Kitty. Oh. Kitty! (KITTY *stirs, shocked, coming out of the trance.*) Where the hell are you? Oh, Kitty.

(TOM *jumps up, furiously.*)

WOMAN'S VOICE *(in the hall)*. Who you looking for, Sailor Boy?

VOICE. The most beautiful lay in the world.

WOMAN'S VOICE. Don't go any further.

VOICE *(with impersonal contempt)*. You? No. Not you. Kitty. You stink.

WOMAN'S VOICE *(rasping, angry)*. Don't you dare talk to me that way. You pickpocket.

VOICE *(still impersonal, but louder)*. Oh, I see. Want to get tough, hey? Close the door. Go hide.

WOMAN'S VOICE. You pickpocket. All of you.

(The door slams.)

VOICE *(roaring with laughter which is very sad)*. Oh—Kitty.

Room 21. Where the hell is that room?

TOM *(to* JOE*)*. Joe, I'll kill him.

KITTY *(fully herself again, terribly frightened)*. Who is it?

(She looks long and steadily at TOM *and* JOE. TOM *is standing, excited and angry.* JOE *is completely at ease, his expression full of pity.* KITTY *buries her face in the bed.)*

JOE *(gently)*. Tom Just take him away.

VOICE. Here it is. Number 21. Three naturals. Heaven. My blue heaven. The west, a nest, and you. Just Molly and me. *(Tragically.)* Ah, to hell with everything.

(A young SAILOR, *a good-looking boy of no more than twenty or so, who is only drunk and lonely, comes to the bed, singing sadly.)*

SAILOR. Hi-ya, Kitty. *(Pause.)* Oh. Visitors. Sorry. A thousand apologies. *(To* KITTY.*)* I'll come back later.

TOM *(taking him by the shoulders, furiously)*. If you do, I'll kill you.

*(*JOE *holds* TOM. TOM *pushes the frightened boy away.)*

JOE *(somberly)*. Tom. You stay here with Kitty. I'm going down to Union Square to hire an automobile. I'll be back in a few minutes. We'll ride out to the ocean and watch the sun go down. Then we'll ride down the Great Highway to Half Moon Bay. We'll have supper down there, and you and Kitty can dance.

TOM *(stupefied, unable to express his amazement and gratitude)*. Joe, you mean you're going to go on an errand for me? You mean you're not going to send me?

JOE. That's right.

(He gestures toward KITTY, *indicating that* TOM *shall talk to her, protect the innocence in her which is in so much danger when* TOM *isn't near, which* TOM *loves so deeply.* JOE *leaves.* TOM *studies* KITTY, *his face becoming child-like and somber. He sets the carousel into motion, listens, watching* KITTY, *who lifts herself slowly, looking only at* TOM. TOM *lifts the turning carousel and moves it slowly toward* KITTY, *as though the toy were his heart. The piano music comes up loudly and the lights go down, while* HARRY *is heard dancing swiftly.)*

BLACKOUT

ACT FOUR

A little later.
WESLEY, *the colored boy, is at the piano.*
HARRY *is on the little stage, dancing.*
NICK *is behind the bar.*
The ARAB *is in his place.*
KIT CARSON *is asleep on his folded arms.*
The DRUNKARD *comes in. Goes to the telephone for the nickel that might be in the return-chute.* NICK *comes to take him out. He gestures for* NICK *to hold on a minute. Then produces a half dollar.* NICK *goes behind the bar to serve the* DRUNKARD *whiskey.*

THE DRUNKARD. To the old, God bless them. *(Another.)* To the new, God love them. *(Another.)* To—children and small animals, like little dogs that don't bite. *(Another. Loudly.)* To reforestation. *(Searches for money. Finds some.)* To—President Taft. *(He goes out.)*

(The telephone rings.)

KIT CARSON *(jumping up, fighting)*. Come on, *all* of you, if you're looking for trouble. I never asked for quarter and I always gave it.

NICK *(reproachfully)*. Hey, Kit Carson.

DUDLEY *(on the phone)*. Hello. Who? Nick? Yes. He's here. *(To* NICK.*)* It's for you. I think it's important.

NICK *(going to the phone)*. Important! *What's* important?

DUDLEY. He sounded like big-shot.

NICK. Big *what*? (*To* WESLEY *and* HARRY.) Hey, you. Quiet. I want to hear this important stuff.

(WESLEY *stops playing the piano.* HARRY *stops dancing.* KIT CARSON *comes close to* NICK.)

KIT CARSON. If there's anything I can do, name it. I'll do it for you. I'm fifty-eight years old; been through three wars; married four times; the father of countless children whose *names* I don't even know. I've got no money. I live from hand to mouth. But if there's anything I can do, name it. I'll do it.

NICK (*patiently*). Listen, Pop. For a moment, please sit down and go back to sleep—*for me.*

KIT CARSON. I can do that, too.

(*He sits down, folds his arms, and puts his head into them. But not for long. As* NICK *begins to talk, he listens carefully, gets to his feet, and then begins to express in pantomime the moods of each of Nick's remarks.*)

NICK (*on phone*). Yeah? (*Pause.*) Who? Oh, I see. (*Listens.*) Why don't you leave them alone? (*Listens.*) The church-people? Well, to hell with the church-people. I'm a Catholic myself. (*Listens.*) All right. I'll send them away. I'll tell them to lay low for a couple of days. Yeah, I know how it is. (*Nick's daughter* ANNA *comes in shyly, looking at her father, and stands unnoticed by the piano.*) What? (*Very angry.*) Listen. I don't like that Blick. He was here this morning, and I told him not to come back. I'll keep the girls out of here. You keep Blick out of here. (*Listens.*) I know his brother-in-law is important, but I don't want him to come down here. He looks for trouble everywhere, and he always finds it. I don't break any laws. I've got a dive in the lousiest part of town. Five years nobody's been robbed, murdered, or gypped. I leave people alone. Your swanky joints uptown make trouble for you every night. (NICK *gestures to* WESLEY—*keeps listening on the phone—puts his hand over the mouthpiece. To* WESLEY *and* HARRY.) Start playing again. My ears have got a headache. Go into your dance, son. (WESLEY *begins to play again.* HARRY *begins to dance.* NICK,

into mouthpiece.) Yeah. I'll keep them out. Just see that Blick doesn't come around and start something. (*Pause.*) O.K. (*He hangs up.*)

KIT CARSON. Trouble coming?

NICK. That lousy Vice Squad again. It's that gorilla Blick.

KIT CARSON. Anybody at all. You can count on me. What kind of a gorilla is this gorilla Blick?

NICK. Very dignified. Toenails on his fingers.

ANNA (*to* KIT CARSON, *with great warm, beautiful pride, pointing at* NICK). That's my father.

KIT CARSON (*leaping with amazement at the beautiful voice, the wondrous face, the magnificent event*). Well, bless your heart, child. Bless your lovely heart. I had a little daughter point me out in a crowd once.

NICK (*surprised*). Anna. What the hell are you doing here? Get back home where you belong and help Grandma cook me some supper.

(ANNA *smiles at her father, understanding him, knowing that his words are words of love. She turns and goes, looking at him all the way out, as much as to say that she would cook for him the rest of her life.* NICK *stares at the swinging doors.* KIT CARSON *moves toward them, two or three steps.* ANNA *pushes open one of the doors and peeks in, to look at her father again. She waves to him. Turns and runs.* NICK *is very sad. He doesn't know what to do. He gets a glass and a bottle. Pours himself a drink. Swallows some. It isn't enough, so he pours more and swallows the whole drink.*)

(*To himself.*) My beautiful, beautiful baby. Anna, she is you again. (*He brings out a handkerchief, touches his eyes, and blows his nose.* KIT CARSON *moves close to* NICK, *watching Nick's face.* NICK *looks at him. Loudly, almost making* KIT *jump.*) You're broke, aren't you?

KIT CARSON. Always. Always.

NICK. All right. Go into the kitchen and give Sam a hand. Eat some food and when you come back you can have a couple of beers.

KIT CARSON (*studying* NICK). Anything at all. I know a good man when I see one.

(*He goes.*)

(ELSIE MANDELSPIEGEL *comes into Nick's. She is a beautiful, dark girl, with a sorrowful, wise, dreaming face, almost on the verge of tears, and full of pity. There is an aura of dream about her. She moves softly and gently, as if everything around her were unreal and pathetic.* DUDLEY *doesn't notice her for a moment or two. When he does finally see her, he is so amazed, he can barely move or speak. Her presence has the effect of changing him completely. He gets up from his chair, as if in a trance, and walks toward her, smiling sadly.*)

ELSIE (*looking at him*). Hello, Dudley.

DUDLEY (*broken-hearted*). Elsie.

ELSIE. I'm sorry. (*Explaining.*) So many people are sick. Last night a little boy died. I love you, but— (*She gestures, trying to indicate how hopeless love is. They sit down.*)

DUDLEY (*staring at her, stunned and quieted*). Elsie. You'll never know how glad I am to see you. Just to *see* you. (*Pathetically.*) I was afraid I'd never see you again. It was driving me crazy. I didn't want to live. Honest. (*He shakes his head mournfully, with dumb and beautiful affection.* TWO STREETWALKERS *come in, and pause near* DUDLEY, *at the bar.*) I know. You told me before, but I can't help it, Elsie. I love you.

ELSIE (*quietly, somberly, gently, with great compassion*). I know you love me, and I love you, but don't you see love is impossible in this world?

DUDLEY. Maybe it isn't, Elsie.

ELSIE. Love is for birds. They have wings to fly away on when it's time for flying. For tigers in the jungle because they don't know their end. We know *our* end. Every night I watch over poor, dying men. I hear them breathing, crying, talking in their sleep. Crying for air and water and love, for mother and field and sunlight. *We* can never know love or greatness. We *should* know both.

DUDLEY (*deeply moved by her words*). Elsie, I love you.

ELSIE. You want to live. *I* want to live, too, but where? Where can we escape our poor world?

DUDLEY. Elsie, we'll find a place.

ELSIE (*smiling at him*). All right. We'll try again. We'll go together to a room in a cheap hotel, and dream that the world is beautiful, and that living is full of love and greatness. But in the morning, can we forget debts, and duties, and the cost of ridiculous things?

DUDLEY (*with blind faith*). Sure, we can, Elsie.

ELSIE. All right, Dudley. Of course. Come on. The time for the new pathetic war has come. Let's hurry, before they dress you, stand you in line, hand you a gun, and have you kill and be killed.

(ELSIE *looks at him gently, and takes his hand.* DUDLEY *embraces her shyly, as if he might hurt her. They go, as if they were a couple of young animals. There is a moment of silence. One of the* STREETWALKERS *bursts out laughing.*)

KILLER. Nick, what the hell kind of a joint are you running?

NICK. Well, it's not out of the world. It's on a street in a city, and people come and go. They bring whatever they've got with them and they say what they must say.

THE OTHER STREETWALKER. It's floozies like her that raise hell with our racket.

NICK (*remembering*). Oh, yeah. Finnegan telephoned.

KILLER. That mouse in elephant's body?

THE OTHER STREETWALKER. What the hell does *he* want?

NICK. Spend your time at the movies for the next couple of days.

KILLER. They're all lousy. (*Mocking.*) All about love.

NICK. Lousy or not lousy, for a couple of days the flat-foots are going to be romancing you, so stay out of here, and lay low.

KILLER. I always was a pushover for a man in uniform, with a badge, a club and a gun.

(KRUPP *comes into the place. The girls put down their drinks.*)

NICK. O.K., get going.

(*The* GIRLS *begin to leave and meet* KRUPP.)

THE OTHER STREETWALKER. We was just going.

KILLER. We was formerly models at Magnin's. (*They go.*)

KRUPP (*at the bar*). The strike isn't enough, so they've got to put us on the tails of the girls, too. I don't know. I wish to God I was back in the Sunset holding the hands of kids going home from school, where I belong. I don't like trouble. Give me a beer.
(NICK *gives him a beer. He drinks some.*) Right now, McCarthy, my best friend, is with sixty strikers who want to stop the finks who are going to try to unload the *Mary Luckenbach* tonight. Why the hell McCarthy ever became a longshoreman instead of a professor of some kind is something I'll never know.

NICK. Cowboys and Indians, cops and robbers, longshoremen and finks.

KRUPP. They're all guys who are trying to be happy; trying to make a living; support a family; bring up children; enjoy sleep. Go to a movie; take a drive on Sunday. They're all good guys, so out of nowhere, comes trouble. All they want is a chance to get out of debt and relax in front of a radio while Amos and Andy go through their act. What the hell do they always want to make trouble for? I been thinking everything over, Nick, and you know what I think?

NICK. No. What?

KRUPP. I think we're all crazy. It came to me while I was on my way to Pier 27. All of a sudden it hit me like a ton of bricks. A thing like that never happened to me before. Here we are in this wonderful world, full of all the wonderful things— here we are—all of us, and look at us. Just look at us. We're crazy. We're nuts. We've got everything, but we always feel lousy and dissatisfied just the same.

NICK. Of course we're crazy. Even so, we've got to go on living together. (*He waves at the people in his joint.*)

KRUPP. There's no hope. I don't suppose it's right for an officer of the law to feel the way I feel, but, by God, right or not right, that's how I feel. Why are we all so lousy? This is a good world. It's wonderful to get up in the morning and go out for a little walk and smell the trees and see the streets and the kids going to school and the clouds in the sky. It's wonderful just to be able to move around and whistle a song if you feel like it, or maybe try to sing one. This is a nice world. So why do they make all the trouble?

NICK. I don't know. Why?

KRUPP. We're crazy, that's why. We're no good any more. All the corruption everywhere. The poor kids selling themselves. A couple of years ago they were in grammar school. Everybody trying to get a lot of money in a hurry. Everybody betting the horses. Nobody going quietly for a little walk to the ocean. Nobody taking things easy and not wanting to make some kind of a killing. Nick, I'm going to quit being a cop. Let somebody else keep law and order. The stuff I hear about at headquarters. I'm thirty-seven years old, and I still can't get used to it. The only trouble is, the wife'll raise hell.

NICK. Ah, the wife.

KRUPP. She's a wonderful woman, Nick. We've got two of the swellest boys in the world. Twelve and seven years old. (*The* ARAB *gets up and moves closer to listen.*)

NICK. I didn't know that.

KRUPP. Sure. But what'll I do? I've wanted to quit for seven years. I wanted to quit the day they began putting me through the school. I didn't quit. What'll I do if I quit? Where's money going to be coming in from?

NICK. That's one of the reasons we're all crazy. We don't know where it's going to be coming in from, except from wherever it happens to be coming in from at the time, which we don't usually like.

KRUPP. Every once in a while I catch myself being mean, hating people just because they're down and out, broke and hungry, sick or drunk. And then when I'm with the stuffed shirts at headquarters, all of a sudden I'm nice to them, trying to make an impression. On who? People I don't like. And I feel disgusted. (*With finality.*) I'm going to quit. That's all. Quit. Out.

I'm going to give them back the uniform and the gadgets that go with it. I don't want any part of it. This is a good world. What do they want to make all the trouble for all the time?

ARAB (*quietly, gently, with great understanding*). No foundation. All the way down the line.

KRUPP. What?

ARAB. No foundation. No foundation.

KRUPP. I'll say there's no foundation.

ARAB. All the way down the line.

KRUPP (*to* NICK). Is that all he ever says?

NICK. That's all he's been saying *this* week.

KRUPP. What is he, anyway?

NICK. He's an Arab, or something like that.

KRUPP. No, I mean what's he do for a living?

NICK (*to* ARAB). What do you do for a living, brother?

ARAB. Work. Work all my life. All my life, work. From small boy to old man, work. In old country, work. In new country, work. In New York. Pittsburgh. Detroit. Chicago. Imperial Valley. San Francisco. Work. No beg. Work. For what? Nothing. Three boys in old country. Twenty years, not see. Lost. Dead. Who knows? What. What-not. No foundation. All the way down the line.

KRUPP. What'd he say last week?

NICK. Didn't say anything. Played the harmonica.

ARAB. Old country song, I play. (*He brings a harmonica from his back pocket.*)

KRUPP. Seems like a nice guy.

NICK. Nicest guy in the world.

KRUPP (*bitterly*). But crazy. Just like all the rest of us. Stark raving mad.

(WESLEY *and* HARRY *long ago stopped playing and dancing. They sat at a table together and talked for a while; then began playing casino or rummy. When the* ARAB *begins his solo on the harmonica, they stop their game to listen.*)

WESLEY. You hear that?

HARRY. That's *something*.

WESLEY. That's crying. That's crying.

HARRY. I want to make people laugh.

WESLEY. That's deep, deep crying. That's crying a long time ago. That's crying a thousand years ago. Some place five thousand miles away.

HARRY. Do you think you can play to that?

WESLEY. I want to *sing* to that, but I can't *sing*.

HARRY. You try and play to that. I'll try to dance.

(WESLEY *goes to the piano, and after closer listening, he begins to accompany the harmonica solo.* HARRY *goes to the little stage and after a few efforts begins to dance to the song. This keeps up quietly for some time.*)

(KRUPP *and* NICK *have been silent, and deeply moved.*)

KRUPP (*softly*). Well, anyhow, Nick.

NICK. Hmmmmmmm?

KRUPP. What I said. Forget it.

NICK. Sure.

KRUPP. It gets me down once in a while

NICK. No harm in talking.

KRUPP (*the* POLICEMAN *again, loudly*) Keep the girls out of here.

NICK (*loud and friendly*). Take it easy.

(*The music and dancing are now at their height.*)

CURTAIN

ACT FIVE

That evening. Fog-horns are heard throughout the scene. A man in evening clothes and a top hat, and his woman, also in evening clothes, are entering.

WILLIE is still at the marble-game. NICK is behind the bar. JOE is at his table, looking at the book of maps of the countries of Europe. The box containing the revolver and the box containing the cartridges are on the table, beside his glass. He is at peace, his hat tilted back on his head, a calm expression on his face. TOM is leaning against the bar, dreaming of love and Kitty. The ARAB is gone. WESLEY and HARRY are gone. KIT CARSON is watching the boy at the marble-game.

LADY. Oh, come on, please.

(The gentleman follows miserably.)

(The SOCIETY MAN and WIFE take a table. NICK gives them a menu.)

(Outside, in the street, the Salvation Army people are playing a song. Big drum, tambourines, cornet and singing. They are singing "The Blood of the Lamb." The music and words come into the place faintly and comically. This is followed by an old sinner testifying. It is the DRUNKARD. His words are not intelligible, but his message is unmistakable. He is saved. He wants to sin no more. And so on.)

DRUNKARD *(testifying, unmistakably drunk)*. Brothers and sisters. I was a sinner. I chewed tobacco and chased women. Oh, I sinned, brothers and sisters. And then I was saved. Saved by the Salvation Army, God forgive me.

JOE. Let's see now. Here's a city. Pribor. Czecho-slovakia. Little, lovely, lonely Czecho-slovakia. I wonder what kind of a place Pribor was? *(Calling.)* Pribor! Pribor! *(TOM leaps.)*

LADY. What's the matter with him?

MAN *(crossing his legs, as if he ought to go to the men's room)*. Drunk.

TOM. Who you calling, Joe?

JOE. Pribor.

TOM. Who's Pribor?

JOE. He's a Czech. And a Slav. A Czecho-slovakian.

LADY. How interesting.

MAN *(uncrosses legs)*. He's drunk.

JOE. Tom, Pribor's a city in Czecho-slovakia.

TOM. Oh. *(Pause.)* You sure were nice to her, Joe.

JOE. Kitty Duval? She's one of the finest people in the world.

TOM. It sure was nice of you to hire an automobile and take us for a drive along the ocean-front and down to Half Moon Bay.

JOE. Those three hours were the most delightful, the most somber, and the most beautiful I have ever known.

TOM. Why, Joe?

JOE. Why? I'm a student. *(Lifting his voice.)* Tom. *(Quietly.)* I'm a student. I study all things. All. All. And when my study reveals something of beauty in a place or in a person where by all rights only ugliness or death should be revealed, then I know how full of goodness this life is. And that's a good thing to know. That's a truth I shall always seek to verify.

LADY. Are you *sure* he's drunk?

MAN *(crossing his legs)*. He's either drunk, or just naturally crazy.

TOM. Joe?

JOE. Yeah.

TOM. You won't get sore or anything?

JOE *(impatiently)*. What is it, Tom?

TOM. Joe, where do you get all that money? You paid for the automobile. You paid for supper and the two bottles of champagne at the Half Moon Bay Restaurant. You moved Kitty out of the New York Hotel around the corner to the St. Francis Hotel on Powell Street. I saw you pay her rent. I saw you give her money for new clothes. Where do you get all that money, Joe? Three years now and I've never asked.

JOE *(looking at TOM sorrowfully, a little*

irritated, not so much with TOM *as with the world and himself, his own superiority. He speaks clearly, slowly and solemnly).* Now don't be a fool, Tom. Listen carefully. If anybody's got any money—to hoard or to throw away—you can be sure he stole it from other people. Not from rich people who can spare it, but from poor people who can't. From their lives and from their dreams. I'm no exception. I *earned* the money I throw away. I stole it like everybody else does. I hurt people to get it. Loafing around this way, I *still* earn money. The money itself earns *more*. I *still* hurt people. I don't know who they are, or where they are. If I did, I'd feel worse than I do. I've got a Christian conscience in a world that's got no conscience at all. The world's trying to get some sort of a *social* conscience, but it's having a devil of a time trying to do *that*. I've got money. I'll always have money, as long as this world stays the way it is. I don't work. I don't make anything. *(He sips.)* I drink. I worked when I was a kid. I worked *hard*. I mean hard, Tom. People are supposed to enjoy living. I got tired. *(He lifts the gun and looks at it while he talks.)* I decided to get even on the world. Well, you can't enjoy living unless you work. Unless you do something. I don't do anything. I don't *want* to do anything any more. There isn't anything I can do that won't make me feel embarrassed. Because I can't do simple, good things. I haven't the patience. And I'm too smart. Money is the guiltiest thing in the world. It stinks. Now, don't ever bother me about it again.

TOM. I didn't mean to make you feel bad, Joe.

JOE *(slowly)*. Here. Take this gun out in the street and give to to some worthy hold-up man.

LADY. What's he saying?

MAN *(uncrosses legs)*. You wanted to visit a honky-tonk. Well, *this* is a honky-tonk. *(To the world.)* Married twenty-eight years and she's still looking for adventure.

TOM. How should I know who's a hold-up man?

JOE. Take it away. Give it to somebody.

TOM *(bewildered)*. Do I *have* to give it to somebody?

JOE. Of course.

TOM. Can't I take it back and get some of our money?

JOE. Don't talk like a business man. Look around and find somebody who appears to be in need of a gun and give it to him. It's a good gun, isn't it?

TOM. The man said it was, but how can I tell who needs a gun?

JOE. Tom, you've seen good people who needed guns, haven't you?

TOM. I don't remember. Joe, I might give it to the wrong kind of guy. He might do something crazy.

JOE. All right. I'll find somebody myself. *(TOM rises.)* Here's some money. Go get me this week's *Life, Liberty, Time,* and six or seven packages of chewing gum.

TOM *(swiftly, in order to remember each item)*. *Life, Liberty, Time,* and six or seven packages of chewing gum?

JOE. That's right.

TOM. All that chewing gum? What kind?

JOE. Any kind. Mix 'em up. All kinds.

TOM. Licorice, too?

JOE. Licorice, by all means.

TOM. Juicy Fruit?

JOE. Juicy Fruit.

TOM. Tutti-frutti?

JOE. Is there such a gum?

TOM. I think so.

JOE. All right. Tutti-frutti, too. Get *all* the kinds. Get as many kinds as they're selling.

TOM. *Life, Liberty, Time,* and all the different kinds of gum. *(He begins to go.)*

JOE *(calling after him loudly)*. Get some jelly beans too. All the different colors.

TOM. All right, Joe.

JOE. And the longest panatela cigar you can find. Six of them.

TOM. Panatela. I got it.

JOE. Give a news-kid a dollar.

TOM. O.K., Joe.

JOE. Give some old man a dollar.

TOM. O.K., Joe.

JOE. Give them Salvation Army people in the street a couple of dollars and ask them to sing that song that goes— *(He sings loudly.)* Let the lower lights be burning, send a gleam across the wave.

TOM *(swiftly).* Let the lower lights be burning, send a gleam across the wave.

JOE. That's it. *(He goes on with the song, very loudly and religiously.)* Some poor, dying, struggling seaman, you may rescue, you may save. *(Halts.)*

TOM. O.K., Joe. I got it. *Life, Liberty, Time,* all the kinds of gum they're selling, jelly beans, six panatela cigars, a dollar for a news-kid, a dollar for an old man, two dollars for the Salvation Army. *(Going.)* Let the lower lights be burning, send a gleam across the wave.

JOE. That's it.

LADY. He's absolutely insane.

MAN *(wearily crossing legs).* You asked me to take you to a honky-tonk, instead of to the Mark Hopkins. You're *here* in a honky-tonk. I can't help it if he's crazy. Do you want to go back to where people *aren't* crazy?

LADY. No, not just yet.

MAN. Well, all right then. Don't be telling me every minute that he's crazy.

LADY. You needn't be huffy about it.

(MAN refuses to answer, uncrosses legs.)

(When JOE began to sing, KIT CARSON turned away from the marble-game and listened. While the man and woman are arguing he comes over to Joe's table.)

KIT CARSON. Presbyterian?

JOE. I attended a Presbyterian Sunday School.

KIT CARSON. Fond of singing?

JOE. On occasion. Have a drink?

KIT CARSON. Thanks.

JOE. Get a glass and sit down.

(KIT CARSON gets a glass from NICK, returns to the table, sits down, JOE pours him a drink, they touch glasses just as the Salvation Army people begin to fulfill the request. They sip some champagne, and at the proper moment begin to sing the song together, sipping champagne, raising hell with the tune, swinging it, and so on. The SOCIETY LADY *joins them, and is stopped by her* HUSBAND.)*

Always was fond of that song. Used to sing it at the top of my voice. Never saved a seaman in my life.

KIT CARSON *(flirting with the* SOCIETY LADY *who loves it).* I saved a seaman once. Well, he wasn't exactly a seaman. He was a darky named Wellington. Heavy-set sort of a fellow. Nice personality, but no friends to speak of. Not until I came along, at any rate. In New Orleans. In the summer of the year 1899. No. Ninety-eight. I was a lot younger of course, and had no mustache, but was regarded by many people as a man of means.

JOE. Know anything about guns?

KIT CARSON *(flirting).* All there is to know. Didn't fight the Ojibways for nothing. Up there in the Lake Takalooca Country, in Michigan. *(Remembering.)* Along about in 1881 or two. Fought 'em right up to the shore of the Lake. Made 'em swim for Canada. One fellow in particular, an Indian named Harry Daisy.

JOE *(opening the box containing the revolver).* What sort of a gun would you say this is? Any good?

KIT CARSON *(at sight of gun, leaping).* Yep. That looks like a pretty nice hunk of shooting iron. That's a six-shooter. Shot a man with a six-shooter once. Got him through the palm of his right hand. Lifted his arm to wave to a friend. Thought it was a bird. Fellow named, I believe, Carroway. Larrimore Carroway.

JOE. Know how to work one of these things? *(He offers* KIT CARSON *the revolver, which is old and enormous.)*

KIT CARSON *(laughing at the absurd question).* Know how to work it? Hand me that little gun, son, and I'll show you all about it. *(JOE hands KIT the revolver.)* *(Importantly.)* Let's see now. This is probably a new kind of six-shooter. After my time. Haven't nicked an Indian in years. I believe this here place is supposed to move out. (*He fools around and get the barrel out for loading.*) That's it. There it is.

JOE. Look all right?

KIT CARSON. It's a good gun. You've got a good gun there, son. I'll explain it to you. You see these holes? Well, that's where you put the cartridges.

JOE (*taking some cartridges out of the box*). Here. Show me how it's done.

KIT CARSON (*a little impatiently*). Well, son, you take 'em one by one and put 'em in the holes, like this. There's one. Two. Three. Four. Five. Six. Then you get the barrel back in place. Then cock it. Then all you got to do is aim and fire.

(*He points the gun at the* LADY *and* GENTLEMAN *who scream and stand up, scaring* KIT CARSON *into paralysis.*)

(*The gun is loaded, but uncocked.*)

JOE. It's all set?

KIT CARSON. Ready to kill.

JOE. Let me hold it.

(KIT *hands* JOE *the gun. The* LADY *and* GENTLEMAN *watch, in terror.*)

KIT CARSON. Careful, now, son. Don't cock it. Many a man's lost an eye fooling with a loaded gun. Fellow I used to know named Danny Donovan lost a nose. Ruined his whole life. Hold it firm. Squeeze the trigger. Don't snap it. Spoils your aim.

JOE. Thanks. Let's see if I can unload it.

(*He begins to unload it.*)

KIT CARSON. Of course you can.

(JOE *unloads the revolver, looks at it very closely, puts the cartridges back into the box.*)

JOE (*looking at gun*). I'm mighty grateful to you. Always wanted to see one of those things close up. Is it really a good one?

KIT CARSON. It's a beaut, son.

JOE (*aims the empty gun at a bottle on the bar*). Bang!

WILLIE (*at the marble-game, as the machine groans*). Oh, Boy! (*Loudly, triumphantly.*) There you are, Nick. Thought I couldn't do it, hey? *Now*, watch. (*The machine begins to make a special kind of*

noise. *Lights go on and off. Some red, some green. A bell rings loudly six times.*) One. Two. Three. Four. Five. Six. (*An American flag jumps up.* WILLIE *comes to attention. Salutes.*) Oh, boy, what a beautiful country. (*A loud music-box version of the song* "America." JOE, KIT, *and the* LADY *get to their feet.*) (*Singing.*) My country, 'tis of thee, sweet land of liberty, of thee I sing. (*Everything quiets down. The flag goes back into the machine.* WILLIE *is thrilled, amazed, delighted.* EVERYBODY *has watched the performance of the defeated machine from wherever he happened to be when the performance began.* WILLIE, *looking around at everybody, as if they had all been on the side of the machine.*) O.K. How's that? I knew I could do it. (*To* NICK.) Six nickels.

(NICK *hands him six nickels.* WILLIE *goes over to* JOE *and* KIT.) Took me a little while, but I finally did it. It's scientific, really. With a little skill a man can make a modest living beating the marble-games. Not that that's what I want to do. I just don't like the idea of anything getting the best of me. A machine or anything else. Myself, I'm the kind of a guy who makes up his mind to do something, and then goes to work and does it. There's no other way a man can be a success at anything.

(*Indicating the letter* "F" *on his sweater.*)

See that letter? That don't stand for some little-bitty high school somewhere. That stands for *me*. Faroughli. Willie Faroughli. I'm an Assyrian. We've got a civilization six or seven centuries old, I think. Somewhere along in there. Ever hear of Osman? Harold Osman? He's an Assyrian, too. He's got an orchestra down in Fresno.

(*He goes to the* LADY *and* GENTLEMAN.)

I've never seen you before in my life, but I can tell from the clothes you wear and the company you keep (*Graciously indicating the* LADY.) that you're a man who looks every problem straight in the eye, and then goes to work and *solves* it. I'm that way myself. Well. (*He smiles beautifully, takes* GENTLEMAN's *hand furiously.*) It's been wonderful talking to a nicer type of people for a change. Well. I'll be seeing you. So long. (*He turns, takes two steps, returns to the table. Very politely and seriously.*) Good-bye, lady. You've got a good man there. Take good care of him.

(WILLIE *goes, saluting* JOE *and the world.*)

KIT CARSON (*to* JOE). By God, for a while there I didn't think that young Assyrian was going to do it. That fellow's got something.

(TOM *comes back with the magazines and other stuff.*)

JOE. Get it all?

TOM. Yeah. I had a little trouble finding the jelly beans.

JOE. Let's take a look at them.

TOM. These are the jelly beans.

(JOE *puts his hand into the cellophane bag and takes out a handful of the jelly beans, looks at them, smiles, and tosses a couple into his mouth.*)

JOE. Same as ever. Have some. (*He offers the bag to* KIT.)

KIT CARSON (*flirting*). Thanks! I remember the first time I ever ate jelly beans. I was six, or at the most seven. Must have been in (*Slowly.*) eighteen—seventy-seven. Seven or eight. Baltimore.

JOE. Have some, Tom. (TOM *takes some.*)

TOM. Thanks, Joe.

JOE. Let's have some of that chewing gum.

(*He dumps all the packages of gum out of the bag onto the table.*)

KIT CARSON (*flirting*). Me and a boy named Clark. Quinton Clark. Became a Senator.

JOE. Yeah. Tutti-frutti, all right. (*He opens a package and folds all five pieces into his mouth.*) Always wanted to see how many I could chew at one time. Tell you what, Tom. I'll bet I can chew more at one time than you can.

TOM (*delighted*). All right. (*They both begin to fold gum into their mouths.*)

KIT CARSON. I'll referee. Now, one at a time. How many you got?

JOE. Six.

KIT CARSON. All right. Let Tom catch up with you.

JOE (*while* TOM'S *catching up*). Did you give a dollar to a news-kid?

TOM. Yeah, sure.

JOE. What'd he say?

TOM. Thanks.

JOE. What sort of a kid was he?

TOM. Little, dark kid. I guess he's Italian.

JOE. Did he seem pleased?

TOM. Yeah.

JOE. That's good. Did you give a dollar to an old man?

TOM. Yeah.

JOE. Was he pleased?

TOM. Yeah.

JOE. Good. How many you got in your mouth?

TOM. Six.

JOE. All right. I got six, too. (*Folds one more in his mouth.* TOM *folds one too.*)

KIT CARSON. Seven. Seven each. (*They each fold one more into their mouths, very solemnly, chewing them into the main hunk of gum.*) Eight. Nine. Ten.

JOE (*delighted*). Always wanted to do this. (*He picks up one of the magazines.*) Let's see what's going on in the world. (*He turns the pages and keeps folding gum into his mouth and chewing.*)

KIT CARSON. Eleven. Twelve. (KIT *continues to count while* JOE *and* TOM *continue the contest. In spite of what they are doing, each is very serious.*)

TOM. Joe, what'd you want to move Kitty into the St. Francis Hotel for?

JOE. She's a better woman than any of them tramp society dames that hang around that lobby.

TOM. Yeah, but do you think she'll feel at home up there?

JOE. Maybe not at first, but after a couple of days she'll be all right. A nice big room. A bed for sleeping in. Good clothes. Good food. She'll be all right, Tom.

TOM. I hope so. Don't you think she'll get lonely up there with nobody to talk to?

JOE (*looking at* TOM *sharply, almost with admiration, pleased but severe*). There's nobody *anywhere* for *her* to talk to—except *you.*

TOM (*amazed and delighted*). Me, Joe?

JOE (*while* TOM *and* KIT CARSON *listen carefully,* KIT *with great appreciation*). Yes, you. By the grace of God, you're the other half of that girl. Not the angry woman that swaggers into this waterfront dive and shouts because the world has kicked her around. *Anybody* can have *her*. You belong to the little kid in Ohio who once dreamed of living. Not with her carcass, for *money,* so she can have food and clothes, and pay rent. With *all* of her. I put her in that hotel, so she can have a chance to gather herself together again. She can't do that in the New York Hotel. You saw what happens there. There's nobody anywhere for her to talk to, except you. They all make her talk like a whore. After a while, she'll *believe* them. Then she won't be able to remember. She'll get lonely. Sure. People can get lonely for *misery,* even. I want her to go on being lonely for *you,* so she can come together again the way she was meant to be from the beginning. Loneliness is good for people. Right now it's the only thing for Kitty. Any more licorice?

TOM (*dazed*). What? Licorice? (*Looking around busily.*) I guess we've chewed all the licorice in. We still got Clove, Peppermint, Doublemint, Beechnut, Teaberry, and Juicy Fruit.

JOE. Licorice used to be my favorite. Don't worry about her, Tom, she'll be all right. You really want to marry her, don't you?

TOM (*nodding*). Honest to God, Joe. (*Pathetically.*) Only, I haven't got any money.

JOE. Couldn't you be a prize-fighter or something like that?

TOM. Naaaah. I couldn't hit a man if I wasn't sore at him. He'd have to do something that made me hate him.

JOE. You've got to figure out something to do that you won't mind doing very much.

TOM. I wish I could, Joe.

JOE (*thinking deeply, suddenly*). Tom, would you be embarrassed driving a truck?

TOM (*hit by a thunderbolt*). Joe, I never thought of that. I'd like that. Travel. Highways. Little towns. Coffee and hot cakes. Beautiful valleys and mountains and streams and trees and daybreak and sunset.

JOE. There *is* poetry in it, at that.

TOM. Joe, that's just the kind of work I *should* do. Just sit there and travel, and look, and smile, and bust out laughing. Could Kitty go with me, sometimes?

JOE. I don't know. Get me the phone book. Can you drive a truck?

TOM. Joe, you know I can drive a truck, or any kind of thing with a motor and wheels. (TOM *takes* JOE *the phone book.* JOE *turns the pages.*)

JOE (*looking*). Here! Here it is. Tuxedo 7900. Here's a nickel. Get me that number. (TOM *goes to telephone, dials the number.*)

TOM. Hello.

JOE. Ask for Mr. Keith.

TOM (*mouth and language full of gum*). I'd like to talk to Mr. Keith. (*Pause.*) Mr. Keith.

JOE. Take that gum out of your mouth for a minute. (TOM *removes the gum.*)

TOM. Mr. Keith. Yeah. That's right. Hello, Mr. Keith?

JOE. Tell him to hold the line.

TOM. Hold the line, please.

JOE. Give me a hand, Tom. (TOM *helps* JOE *to the telephone. At phone, wad of gum in fingers delicately.*) Keith? Joe. Yeah. Fine. Forget it. (*Pause.*) Have you got a place for a good driver? (*Pause.*) I don't think so. (*To* TOM.) You haven't got a driver's license, have you?

TOM (*worried*). No. But I can get one, Joe.

JOE (*at phone*). No, but he can get one easy enough. To hell with the union. He'll join later. All right, call him a Vice-President and say he drives for relaxation. Sure. What do you mean? Tonight? I don't know why not. San Diego? All right, let him start driving without a license. What the hell's the difference? Yeah. Sure. Look him over. Yeah. I'll send him right over. Right. (*He hangs up.*) Thanks. (*To telephone.*)

TOM. Am I going to get the job?

JOE. He wants to take a look at you.

TOM. Do I look all right, Joe?

JOE (*looking at him carefully*). Hold up your head. Stick out your chest. How do you feel? (TOM *does these things.*)

TOM. Fine.

JOE. You *look* fine, too.

(JOE *takes his wad of gum out of his mouth and wraps* Liberty *magazine around it.*)

JOE. You win, Tom. Now, look. (*He bites off the tip of a very long panatela cigar, lights it, and hands one to* TOM, *and another to* KIT.) Have yourselves a pleasant smoke. Here. (*He hands two more to* TOM.) Give those slummers each one. (*He indicates the* SOCIETY LADY *and* GENTLEMAN.)

(TOM *goes over and without a word gives a cigar each to the* MAN *and the* LADY.)

(*The* MAN *is offended; he smells and tosses aside his cigar. The* WOMAN *looks at her cigar a moment, then puts the cigar in her mouth.*)

MAN. What do you think you're doing?

LADY. Really, dear. I'd like to.

MAN. Oh, this is too much.

LADY. I'd *really*, really like to, dear. (*She laughs, puts the cigar in her mouth. Turns to* KIT. *He spits out tip. She does the same.*)

MAN (*loudly*). The mother of five grown men, and she's still looking for *romance*. (*Shouts as* KIT *lights her cigar.*) No. I forbid it.

JOE (*shouting*). What's the matter with you? Why don't you leave her alone? What are you always pushing your women around for? (*Almost without a pause.*) Now, look, Tom. (*The* LADY *puts the lighted cigar in her mouth, and begins to smoke, feeling wonderful.*) Here's ten bucks.

TOM. Ten bucks?

JOE. He may want you to get into a truck and begin driving to San Diego tonight.

TOM. Joe, I got to tell Kitty.

JOE. I'll tell her.

TOM. Joe, take care of her.

JOE. She'll be all right. Stop worrying about her. She's at the St. Francis Hotel. Now, look. Take a cab to Townsend and Fourth. You'll see the big sign. Keith Motor Transport Company. He'll be waiting for you.

TOM. O.K., Joe. (*Trying hard.*) Thanks, Joe.

JOE. Don't be silly. Get going.

(TOM *goes.*)

(LADY *starts puffing on cigar.*)

(*As* TOM *goes,* WESLEY *and* HARRY *come in together.*)

NICK. Where the hell have you been? We've got to have some entertainment around here. Can't you see them fine people from uptown? (*He points at the* SOCIETY LADY *and* GENTLEMAN.)

WESLEY. You said to come back at ten for the second show.

NICK. Did I say that?

WESLEY. Yes, sir, Mr. Nick, that's exactly what you said.

HARRY. Was the first show all right?

NICK. That wasn't a show. There was no one here to see it. How can it be a show when no one sees it? People are afraid to come down to the waterfront.

HARRY. Yeah. We were just down to Pier 27. One of the longshoremen and a cop had a fight and the cop hit him over the head with a blackjack. We saw it happen, didn't we?

WESLEY. Yes, sir, we was standing there looking when it happened.

NICK (*a little worried*). Anything else happen?

WESLEY. They was all talking.

HARRY. A man in a big car came up and said there was going to be a meeting right away and they hoped to satisfy everybody and stop the strike.

WESLEY. Right away. *Tonight.*

NICK. Well, it's about time. Them poor cops are liable to get nervous and—shoot somebody. (*To* HARRY, *suddenly.*) Come back here. I want you to tend bar for a while. I'm going to take a walk over to the pier.

HARRY. Yes, sir.

NICK (to the SOCIETY LADY and GENTLEMAN). You society people made up your minds yet?

LADY. Have you champagne?

NICK (indicating JOE). What do you think he's pouring out of that bottle, water or something?

LADY. Have you a chilled bottle?

NICK. I've got a dozen of them chilled. He's been drinking champagne here all day and all night for a month now.

LADY. May we have a bottle?

NICK. It's six dollars.

LADY. I think we can manage.

MAN. I don't know. I *know* I don't know.

(NICK *takes off his coat and helps* HARRY *into it.* HARRY *takes a bottle of champagne and two glasses to the* LADY *and the* GENTLEMAN, *dancing, collects six dollars, and goes back behind the bar, dancing.* NICK *gets his coat and hat.*)

NICK (to WESLEY). Rattle the keys, a little, son. Rattle the keys.

WESLEY. Yes, sir, Mr. Nick. (NICK *is on his way out. The* ARAB *enters.*)

NICK. Hi-ya, *Mahmed.*

ARAB. No foundation.

NICK. All the way down the line. (*He goes.*)

(WESLEY *is at the piano, playing quietly. The* ARAB *swallows a glass of beer, takes out his harmonica, and begins to play.* WESLEY *fits his playing to the Arab's.*)

(KITTY DUVAL, *strangely beautiful, in new clothes, comes in. She walks shyly, as if she were embarrassed by the fine clothes, as if she had no right to wear them. The* LADY *and* GENTLEMAN *are very impressed.* HARRY *looks at her with amazement.* JOE *is reading* Time *magazine.* KITTY *goes to his table.* JOE *looks up from the magazine, without the least amazement.*)

JOE. Hello, Kitty.

KITTY. Hello, Joe.

JOE. It's nice seeing you again.

KITTY. I came in a cab.

JOE. You been crying again? (KITTY *can't answer. To* HARRY.) Bring a glass. (HARRY *comes over with a glass.* JOE *pours* KITTY *a drink.*)

KITTY. I've got to talk to you.

JOE. Have a drink.

KITTY. I've never been in burlesque. We were just poor.

JOE. Sit down, Kitty.

KITTY (*sits down*). I tried other things.

JOE. Here's to you, Katerina Koranovsky. Here's to you. And Tom.

KITTY (*sorrowfully*). Where *is* Tom?

JOE. He's getting a job tonight driving a truck. He'll be back in a couple of days.

KITTY (*sadly*). I told him I'd marry him.

JOE. He wanted to see you and say good-by.

KITTY. He's too good for me. He's like a little boy. (*Wearily.*) I'm— Too many things have happened to me.

JOE. Kitty Duval, you're one of the few truly innocent people I have ever known. He'll be back in a couple of days. Go back to the hotel and wait for him.

KITTY. That's what I mean. I can't stand being alone. I'm no good. I tried very hard. I don't know what it is. I miss— (*She gestures.*)

JOE (*gently*). Do you really want to come back here, Kitty?

KITTY. I don't know. I'm not sure. Everything *smells* different. I don't know how to feel, or what to think. (*Gesturing pathetically.*) I know I don't belong there. It's what I've wanted all my life, but it's too *late.* I try to be happy about it, but all I can do is remember everything and cry.

JOE. I don't know what to tell you, Kitty. I didn't mean to hurt you.

KITTY. You haven't hurt me. You're the only person who's ever been good to me. I've never known anybody like you. I'm not sure about love any more, but I know I love you, and I know I love Tom.

JOE. I love you too, Kitty Duval.

KITTY. He'll want babies. I know he will. I know *I* will, too. Of course I will. I can't— (*She shakes her head.*)

JOE. Tom's a baby himself. You'll be very happy together. He wants you to ride with him in the truck. Tom's good for you. You're good for Tom.

KITTY (*like a child*). Do you want me to go back and wait for him?

JOE. I can't *tell* you what to do. I think it would be a good idea, though.

KITTY. I wish I could tell you how it makes me feel to be alone. It's almost worse.

JOE. It might take a whole week, Kitty. (*He looks at her sharply, at the arrival of an idea.*) Didn't you speak of reading a book? A book of poems?

KITTY. I didn't know what I was saying.

JOE (*trying to get up*). Of course you knew. I think you'll like poetry. Wait here a minute, Kitty. I'll go see if I can find some books.

KITTY. All right, Joe. (*He walks out of the place, trying very hard not to wobble.*)

(*Fog-horn. Music. The* NEWSBOY *comes in. Looks for* JOE. *Is broken-hearted because* JOE *is gone.*)

NEWSBOY (*to* SOCIETY GENTLEMAN). Paper?

MAN (*angry*). No.

(*The* NEWSBOY *goes to the* ARAB.)

NEWSBOY. Paper, Mister?

ARAB (*irritated*). No foundation.

NEWSBOY. What?

ARAB (*very angry*). No foundation. (*The* NEWSBOY *starts out, turns, looks at the* ARAB, *shakes head.*)

NEWSBOY. No foundation? How do you figure?

(BLICK *and* TWO COPS *enter.*)

NEWSBOY (*to* BLICK). Paper, mister?

(BLICK *pushes him aside. The* NEWSBOY *goes.*)

BLICK (*walking authoritatively about the place, to* HARRY). Where's Nick?

HARRY. He went for a walk.

BLICK. Who are you?

HARRY. Harry.

BLICK (*to the* ARAB *and* WESLEY). Hey, you. Shut up. (*The* ARAB *stops playing the harmonica,* WESLEY *the piano.*)

BLICK (*studies* KITTY). What's your name, sister?

KITTY (*looking at him*). Kitty Duval. What's it to you?

(KITTY'S *voice is now like it was at the beginning of the play: tough, independent, bitter and hard.*)

BLICK (*angry*). Don't give me any of your gutter lip. Just answer my questions.

KITTY. You go to hell, you.

BLICK (*coming over, enraged*). Where do you live?

KITTY. The New York Hotel. Room 21.

BLICK. Where do you work?

KITTY. I'm not working just now. I'm look-for work.

BLICK. What kind of work? (KITTY *can't answer.*) What kind of work? (KITTY *can't answer.*) (*Furiously.*) WHAT KIND OF WORK? (KIT CARSON *comes over.*)

KIT CARSON. You can't talk to a lady that way in *my* presence. (BLICK *turns and stares at* KIT. *The* COPS *begin to move from the bar.*)

BLICK (*to the* COPS). It's all right, boys. I'll take care of this. (*To* KIT.) *What'd you say?*

KIT CARSON. You got no right to hurt people. Who are *you?*

(BLICK, *without a word, takes* KIT *to the street. Sounds of a blow and a groan.* BLICK *returns, breathing hard.*)

BLICK (*to the* COPS). O.K., boys. You can go now. Take care of him. Put him on his feet and tell him to behave himself from now on. (*To* KITTY *again.*) Now answer my question. What kind of work?

KITTY (*quietly*). I'm a whore, you son of a bitch. You know what kind of work I do. And I know what kind you do.

MAN (*shocked and really hurt*). Excuse me, officer, but it seems to me that your attitude—

BLICK. Shut up.

MAN (*quietly*). —is making the poor child say things that are not true.

BLICK. Shut up, I said.

LADY. Well. (*To the* MAN.) Are you going to stand for such insolence?

BLICK (*to* MAN, *who is standing*). Are you?

MAN (*taking the* WOMAN's *arm*). I'll get a divorce. I'll start life all over again. (*Pushing the* WOMAN). Come on. Get the hell out of here!

(*The* MAN *hurries his* WOMAN *out of the place,* BLICK *watching them go.*)

BLICK (*to* KITTY). Now. Let's begin again, and see that you tell the truth. What's your name?

KITTY. Kitty Duval.

BLICK. Where do you live?

KITTY. Until this evening I lived at the New York Hotel. Room 21. This evening I moved to the St. Francis Hotel.

BLICK. Oh. To the St. Francis Hotel. Nice place. Where do you work?

KITTY. I'm looking for work.

BLICK. What kind of work do you do?

KITTY. I'm an actress.

BLICK. I see. What movies have I seen you in?

KITTY. I've worked in burlesque.

BLICK. You're a liar.

(WESLEY *stands, worried and full of dumb resentment.*)

KITTY (*pathetically, as at the beginning of the play*). It's the truth.

BLICK. What are you doing here?

KITTY. I came to see if I could get a job here.

BLICK. Doing what?

KITTY. Singing—and—dancing.

BLICK. You can't sing or dance. What are you lying for?

KITTY. I can. I sang and danced in burlesque all over the country.

BLICK. You're a liar.

KITTY. I said lines, too.

BLICK. So you danced in burlesque?

KITTY. Yes.

BLICK. All right. Let's see what you did.

KITTY. I can't. There's no music, and I haven't got the right clothes.

BLICK. There's music. (*To* WESLEY). Put a nickel in that phonograph. (WESLEY *can't move.*) Come on. Put a nickel in that phonograph. (WESLEY *does so. To* KITTY). All right. Get up on that stage and do a hot little burlesque number. (KITTY *stands. Walks slowly to the stage, but is unable to move.* JOE *comes in, holding three books.*) Get going, now. Let's see you dance the way you did in burlesque, all over the country. (KITTY *tries to do a burlesque dance. It is beautiful in a tragic way.*)

BLICK. All right, start taking them off!

(KITTY *removes her hat and starts to remove her jacket.* JOE *moves closer to the stage, amazed.*)

JOE (*hurrying to* KITTY). Get down from there. (*He takes* KITTY *into his arms. She is crying. To* BLICK.) What the hell do you think you're doing!

WESLEY (*like a little boy, very angry*). It's that man, Blick. *He* made her take off her clothes. He beat up the old man, too.

(BLICK *pushes* WESLEY *off, as* TOM *enters.* BLICK *begins beating up* WESLEY.)

TOM. What's the matter, Joe? What's happened?

JOE. Is the truck out there?

TOM. Yeah, but what's happened? Kitty's crying again!

JOE. You driving to San Diego?

TOM. Yeah, Joe. But what's he doing to that poor colored boy?

JOE. Get going. Here's some money. Everything's O.K. (*To* KITTY.) Dress in the truck. Take these books.

WESLEY'S VOICE. You can't hurt me. You'll get yours. You wait and see.

TOM. Joe, he's hurting that boy. I'll kill him!

JOE (*pushing* TOM). Get out of here! Get married in San Diego. I'll see you when you get back. (TOM *and* KITTY *go.* NICK *enters and stands at the lower end of the bar.* JOE *takes the revolver out of his pocket. Looks at it.*) I've always wanted to kill somebody, but I never knew who it should be. (*He cocks the revolver, stands real straight, holds it in front of him firmly and walks to the door. He stands a moment watching* BLICK, *aims very carefully, and pulls trigger. There is no shot.*)

(NICK *runs over and grabs the gun, and takes* JOE *aside.*)

NICK. What the hell do you think you're doing?

JOE (*casually, but angry*). That dumb Tom. Buys a six-shooter that won't even shoot once.

(JOE *sits down, dead to the world.*)

(BLICK *comes out, panting for breath.*)

(NICK *looks at him. He speaks slowly.*)

NICK. Blick! I told you to stay out of here! Now get out of here. (*He takes* BLICK *by the collar, tightening his grip as he speaks, and pushing him out.*) If you come back again, I'm going to take you in that room where you've been beating up that colored boy, and I'm going to murder you— slowly—with my hands. Beat it! (*He pushes* BLICK *out. To* HARRY.) Go take care of the colored boy. (HARRY *runs out.*) (WILLIE *returns and doesn't sense that anything is changed.* WILLIE *puts another nickel into the machine, but he does so very violently. The consequence of this violence is that the flag comes up again.* WILLIE, *amazed, stands at attention and salutes. The flag goes down. He shakes his head.*)

WILLIE (*thoughtfully*). As far as I'm concerned, this is the *only* country in the world. If you ask me, *nuts* to Europe! (*He is about to push the slide in again when the flag comes up again. Furiously, to* NICK, *while he salutes and stands at attention, pleadingly.*) Hey, Nick. This machine is out of order.

NICK (*somberly*). Give it a whack on the side.

(WILLIE *does so. A hell of a whack. The result is the flag comes up and down, and* WILLIE *keeps saluting.*)

WILLIE (*saluting*). Hey, Nick. Something's wrong.

(*The machine quiets down abruptly.* WILLIE *very stealthily slides a new nickel in, and starts a new game.*)

(*From a distance two pistol shots are heard, each carefully timed.*)

(NICK *runs out.*)

(*The* NEWSBOY *enters, crosses to Joe's table, senses something is wrong.*)

NEWSBOY (*softly*). Paper, Mister?

(JOE *can't hear him.*)

(*The* NEWSBOY *backs away, studies* JOE, *wishes he could cheer* JOE *up. Notices the phonograph, goes to it, and puts a coin in it, hoping music will make* JOE *happier.*)

(*The* NEWSBOY *sits down. Watches* JOE. *The music begins. "The Missouri Waltz."*)

(*The* DRUNKARD *comes in and walks around. Then sits down.* NICK *comes back.*)

NICK (*delighted*). Joe, Blick's dead! Somebody just shot him, and none of the cops are trying to find out who. (JOE *doesn't hear.* NICK *steps back, studying* JOE.)

NICK (*shouting*). Joe.

JOE (*looking up*). What?

NICK. Blick's dead.

JOE. Blick? Dead? Good! That God damn gun wouldn't go off. I *told* Tom to get a good one.

NICK (*picking up gun and looking at it*). Joe, you wanted to kill that guy! (HARRY *returns.* JOE *puts the gun in his coat pocket.*) I'm going to buy you a bottle of champagne.

(NICK *goes to bar.* JOE *rises, takes hat from rack, puts coat on. The* NEWSBOY *jumps up, helps* JOE *with coat.*)

NICK. What's the matter, Joe?

JOE. Nothing. Nothing.

NICK. How about the champagne?

JOE. Thanks. (*Going.*)

NICK. It's not eleven yet. Where you going, Joe?

JOE. I don't know. Nowhere.

NICK. Will I see you tomorrow?

JOE. I don't know. I don't think so.

(KIT CARSON *enters, walks to* JOE. JOE *and* KIT *look at one another knowingly.*)

JOE. Somebody just shot a man. How are you feeling?

KIT. Never felt better in my life. (*Loudly, bragging, but somber.*) I shot a man once. In San Francisco. Shot him two times. In 1939, I think it was. In October. Fellow named Blick or Glick or something like that. Couldn't stand the way he talked to ladies. Went up to my room and got my old pearl-handled revolver and waited for him on Pacific Street. Saw him walking, and let him have it, two times. Had to throw the beautiful revolver into the Bay.

(HARRY, NICK, *the* ARAB *and the* DRUNKARD *close in around him.*)

(JOE *searches his pockets, brings out the revolver, puts it in Kit's hand, looks at him with great admiration and affection.* JOE *walks slowly to the stairs leading to the street, turns and waves.* KIT, *and then one by one everybody else, waves, and the marble-game goes into its beautiful American routine again: flag, lights, and music. The play ends.*)

CURTAIN

ARSENIC AND OLD LACE

By JOSEPH KESSELRING

ARSENIC AND OLD LACE was presented by Howard Lindsay and Russel Crouse at the Fulton Theatre in New York, on January 10, 1941, with the following cast:

ABBY BREWSTER............Josephine Hull

THE REV. DR. HARPER
Wyrley Birch

TEDDY BREWSTER....John Alexander

OFFICER BROPHY............John Quigg

OFFICER KLEIN............Bruce Gordon

MARTHA BREWSTER........Jean Adair

ELAINE HARPER............Helen Brooks

MORTIMER BREWSTER....Allyn Joslyn

MR. GIBBS......................Henry Herbert

JONATHAN BREWSTER
Boris Karloff

DR. EINSTEIN................Edgar Stehli

OFFICER O'HARA............Anthony Ross

LIEUTENANT ROONEY
Victor Sutherland

MR. WITHERSPOON.....William Parks

SCENES

The entire action of the play takes place in the living room of the Brewster home in Brooklyn. Time: the present.

ACT I: An afternoon in September.

ACT II: The same night.

ACT III: Scene 1. Later that night.

Scene 2. Early the next morning.

THE AUTHOR

It was Joseph Otto Kesselring's great good fortune in 1940 to meet up with Howard Lindsay and Russel Crouse. The not quite young playwright (he was born in New York in 1902) had lately written a melodrama about sweet old ladies and their penchant for relieving people of the burdens of this world. The script fell into the lap of Dorothy Stickney, Mrs. Lindsay, who was then playing Mother to Howard Lindsay's irascible Father in Life With Father. *Mrs. Lindsay found the idea both impossible and amusing, and so informed her husband, who in turn informed Mr. Crouse, who was then busily engaged in Hollywood on the screenplay of* The Great Victor Herbert. *The friends acquired the script, guided the author in the delicate matter of revisions, helped him to evolve the Boris Karloff character, and persuaded Mr. Karloff to impersonate himself. They also rounded up a host of twenty-one backers who will remain eternally grateful to them.*

The benign melodrama, Arsenic and Old Lace, *opened in New York on January 10, 1941. Mr. Lindsay told his co-producer before the rise of the curtain: "We either have a hit or we'll be run out of town." They were not run out of town, which would have been the town's loss in any event. To their "angels" they wrote, enclosing the first checks for quickly accrued profits: "If there is anything in this about which you wish to complain we shall be glad to hear from you. Just address us in care of the Dead Letter Office, Washington, D. C."*

Mr. Kesselring tried his playwriting hand again after Arsenic and Old Lace *with a piece called* Maggie McGilligan *which got no further than the Woodstock Playhouse in 1942. Prior to his lurid tour de force he had tried acting, and had written* There's Wisdom in Women, *which D. A. Doran produced in 1935 with a cast that included Walter Pidgeon. The production ran for forty-six performances. Another of Mr. Kesselring's plays,* Cross-Town, *produced on Broadway in 1937, had met with scantier favor.*

ARSENIC AND OLD LACE

ACT ONE

TIME: *Late afternoon. September. Present.*

PLACE: *The living-room of the old Brewster home in Brooklyn, N. Y. It is just as Victorian as the two sisters* ABBY *and* MARTHA BREWSTER, *who occupy the house with their nephew,* TEDDY.

Down stage right is the front door of the house, a large door with frosted glass panels in the upper half, beyond which, when it is open, can be seen the front porch and the lawn and shrubbery of the front garden of the Brewster house. On either side of the door are narrow windows of small panes of glass, curtained. The remainder of the right wall is taken up by the first flight of stairs leading to the upper floors. In the up-stage corner is a landing where the stairs turn to continue along the back wall of the room. At the top of the stairs, along the back wall, is another landing, from which a door leads into the second-floor bedrooms, and an arch at the left end of this landing suggests the stairs leading to the third floor.

On stage level under this landing is a door which leads to the cellar. To the left of this door is a recess which contains a sideboard, on the top of which at either end are two small cabinets, where the sisters keep, among other things, bottles of elderberry wine. To the left of the recess is the door leading to the kitchen.

In the left wall of the room, there is a large window looking out over the cemetery of the neighboring Episcopal Church. This window has the usual lace curtains and thick drapes, which open and close by the use of a heavy curtain cord. Below the window is a large window seat. When this lid is raised, the hinges creak audibly.

At the left of the foot of the stairs is a small desk, on which stands a dial telephone, and by this desk is a stool. Along the back wall, to the right of the cellar door, is an old-fashioned sofa. Left center in the room is a round table. There is a small chair right of this table and behind it, to the left of the table, a larger, comfortable armchair. On the walls are the usual pictures, including several portraits of the rather eccentric Brewster ancestors.

As the curtain rises, ABBY BREWSTER, *a plump little darling in her late sixties, is presiding at tea. She is sitting behind the table in front of a high silver tea service. At her left, in the comfortable armchair, is the* REVEREND DR. HARPER, *the elderly rector of the near-by church. Standing, stage center, thoughtfully sipping a cup of tea, is her nephew,* TEDDY, *in a frock coat, and wearing pince-nez attached to a black ribbon.* TEDDY *is in his forties and has a large mustache.*

ABBY. Yes indeed, my sister Martha and I have been talking all week about your sermon last Sunday. It's really wonderful, Dr. Harper—in only two short years you've taken on the spirit of Brooklyn.

HARPER. That's very gratifying, Miss Brewster.

ABBY. You see, living here next to the church all our lives, we've seen so many ministers come and go. The spirit of Brooklyn we always say is friendliness— and your sermons are not so much sermons as friendly talks.

TEDDY. Personally, I've always enjoyed my talks with Cardinal Gibbons—or have I met him yet?

ABBY. No, dear, not yet. *(Changing the subject.)* Are the biscuits good?

TEDDY *(he sits on sofa).* Bully!

ABBY. Won't you have another biscuit, Dr. Harper?

HARPER. Oh, no, I'm afraid I'll have no appetite for dinner now. I always eat too many of your biscuits just to taste that lovely jam.

ABBY. But you haven't tried the quince. We always put a little apple in with it to take the tartness out.

HARPER. No, thank you.

ABBY. We'll send you over a jar.

HARPER. No, no. You keep it here so I can be sure of having your biscuits with it.

ABBY. I do hope they don't make us use that imitation flour again. I mean with

49

this war trouble. It may not be very chari-
table of me, but I've almost come to the
conclusion that this Mr. Hitler isn't a
Christian.

HARPER (*with a sigh*). If only Europe
were on another planet!

TEDDY (*sharply*). Europe, sir?

HARPER. Yes, Teddy.

TEDDY. Point your gun the other way!

HARPER. Gun?

ABBY (*trying to calm him*). Teddy.

TEDDY. To the West! There's your danger!
There's your enemy! Japan!

HARPER. Why, yes—yes, of course.

ABBY. Teddy!

TEDDY. No, Aunt Abby! Not so much talk
about Europe and more about the canal!

ABBY. Well, let's not talk about war. Will
you have another cup of tea, dear?

TEDDY. No, thank you, Aunt Abby.

ABBY. Dr. Harper?

HARPER. No, thank you. I must admit, Miss
Abby, that war and violence seem far
removed from these surroundings.

ABBY. It is peaceful here, isn't it?

HARPER. Yes—peaceful. The virtues of
another day—they're all here in this house.
The gentle virtues that went out with
candlelight and good manners and low
taxes.

ABBY (*glancing about her contentedly*).
It's one of the oldest houses in Brooklyn.
It's just as it was when Grandfather Brewster built and furnished it—except for the
electricity—and we use it as little as possible. It was Mortimer who persuaded us
to put it in.

HARPER (*beginning to freeze*). Yes, I can
understand that. Your nephew Mortimer
seems to live only by electric light.

ABBY. The poor boy has to work so late.
I understand he's taking Elaine with him
to the theatre again tonight. Teddy, your
brother Mortimer will be here a little later.

TEDDY (*baring his teeth in a broad grin*).
Dee-lighted!

ABBY (*to* HARPER). We're so happy it's
Elaine Mortimer takes to the theatre with
him.

HARPER. Well, it's a new experience for
me to wait up until three o'clock in the
morning for my daughter to be brought
home.

ABBY. Oh, Dr. Harper, I hope you don't
disapprove of Mortimer.

HARPER. Well—

ABBY. We'd feel so guilty if you did—sister
Martha and I. I mean since it was here in
our home that your daughter met Mortimer.

HARPER. Of course, Miss Abby. And so I'll
say immediately that I believe Mortimer
himself to be quite a worthy gentleman.
But I must also admit that I have watched
the growing intimacy between him and
my daughter with some trepidation. For
one reason, Miss Abby.

ABBY. You mean his stomach, Dr. Harper?

HARPER. Stomach?

ABBY. His dyspepsia—he's bothered with
it so, poor boy.

HARPER. No, Miss Abby, I'll be frank with
you. I'm speaking of your nephew's unfortunate connection with the theatre.

ABBY. The theatre! Oh, no, Dr. Harper!
Mortimer writes for a New York newspaper.

HARPER. I know, Miss Abby, I know. But
a dramatic critic is constantly exposed to
the theatre, and I don't doubt but what
some of them do develop an interest in it.

ABBY. Well, not Mortimer. You need have
no fear of that. Why, Mortimer hates the
theatre.

HARPER. Really?

ABBY. Oh, yes! He writes awful things
about the theatre. But you can't blame
him, poor boy. He was so happy writing
about real estate, which he really knew
something about, and then they just made
him take this terrible night position.

HARPER. My! My!

ABBY. But, as he says, the theatre can't last
much longer anyway and in the meantime
it's a living. (*Complacently.*) Yes, I think
if we give the theatre another year or two,

perhaps . . . (*A knock on* R. *door.*) Well, now, who do you suppose that is? (*They all rise as* ABBY *goes to door* R. TEDDY *starts for door at same time, but* ABBY *stops him.*) No, thank you, Teddy. I'll go. (*She opens door to admit two cops,* OFFICERS BROPHY *and* KLEIN.) Come in, Mr. Brophy.

BROPHY. Hello, Miss Brewster.

ABBY. How are you, Mr. Klein?

KLEIN. Very well, Miss Brewster.

(*The* COPS *cross to* TEDDY *who is standing near desk, and salute him.* TEDDY *returns salute.*)

TEDDY. What news have you brought me?

BROPHY. Colonel, we have nothing to report.

TEDDY. Splendid! Thank you, gentlemen! At ease!

(COPS *relax and drop* D. S. ABBY *has closed door, and turns to* COPS.)

ABBY. You know Dr. Harper.

KLEIN. Sure! Hello, Dr. Harper.

BROPHY (*turns to* ABBY, *doffing cap*). We've come for the toys for the Christmas Fund.

ABBY. Oh, yes.

HARPER (*standing below table.*) That's a splendid work you men do—fixing up discarded toys to give poor children a happier Christmas.

KLEIN. It gives us something to do when we have to sit around the station. You get tired playing cards and then you start cleaning your gun, and the first thing you know you've shot yourself in the foot. (KLEIN *drifts* U. L. *around to window-seat.*)

ABBY (*crossing to* TEDDY). Teddy, go upstairs and get that big box from your Aunt Martha's room. (TEDDY *crosses upstage toward stairs.* ABBY *speaks to* BROPHY.) How is Mrs. Brophy today? Mrs. Brophy has been quite ill, Dr. Harper.

BROPHY (*to* HARPER). Pneumonia!

HARPER. I'm sorry to hear that.

(TEDDY *has reached first landing on stairs where he stops and draws an imaginary sword.*)

TEDDY (*shouting*). CHARGE! (*He charges up stairs and exits off balcony. The others pay no attention to this.*)

BROPHY. Oh, she's better now. A little weak still—

ABBY (*starting toward kitchen*). I'm going to get you some beef broth to take to her.

BROPHY. Don't bother, Miss Abby! You've done so much for her already.

ABBY (*at kitchen door*). We made it this morning. Sister Martha is taking some to poor Mr. Benitzky right now. I won't be a minute. Sit down and be comfortable, all of you. (*She exits into kitchen.*)

(HARPER *sits again.* BROPHY *crosses to table and addresses the other two.*)

BROPHY. She shouldn't go to all that trouble.

KLEIN. Listen, try to stop her or her sister from doing something nice—and for nothing! They don't even care how you vote. (*He sits on window-seat.*)

HARPER. When I received my call to Brooklyn and moved next door my wife wasn't well. When she died and for months before—well, if I know what pure kindness and absolute generosity are, it's because I've known the Brewster sisters.

(*At this moment* TEDDY *steps out on balcony and blows a bugle call. They all look.*)

BROPHY (*stepping* U. S. . . . *Remonstrating*). Colonel, you promised not to do that.

TEDDY. But I have to call a Cabinet meeting to get the release of those supplies. (TEDDY *wheels and exits.*)

BROPHY. He used to do that in the middle of the night. The neighbors raised cain with us. They're a little afraid of him, anyway.

HARPER. Oh, he's quite harmless.

KLEIN. Suppose he does think he's Teddy Roosevelt. There's a lot worse people he could think he was.

BROPHY. Damn shame—a nice family like this hatching a cuckoo.

KLEIN. Well, his father—the old girls' brother, was some sort of a genius, wasn't he? And their father—Teddy's grandfather—seems to me I've heard he was a little crazy too.

BROPHY. Yeah—he was crazy like a fox. He made a million dollars.

HARPER. Really? Here in Brooklyn?

BROPHY. Yeah. Patent medicine. He was a kind of a quack of some sort. Old Sergeant Edwards remembers him. He used the house here as a sort of a clinic—tried 'em out on people.

KLEIN. Yeah, I hear he used to make mistakes occasionally, too.

BROPHY. The department never bothered him much because he was pretty useful on autopsies sometimes. Especially poison cases.

KLEIN. Well, whatever he did he left his daughters fixed for life. Thank God for that ——

BROPHY. Not that they ever spend any of it on themselves.

HARPER. Yes, I'm well acquainted with their charities.

KLEIN. You don't know a tenth of it. When I was with the Missing Persons Bureau I was trying to trace an old man that we never did find *(Rises.)* —do you know there's a renting agency that's got this house down on its list for furnished rooms? They don't rent rooms—but you can bet that anybody who comes here lookin' for a room goes away with a good meal and probably a few dollars in their kick.

BROPHY. It's just their way of digging up people to do some good to.

(R. door opens and MARTHA BREWSTER *enters.* MARTHA *is also a sweet elderly woman with Victorian charm. She is dressed in the old-fashioned manner of* ABBY, *but with a high lace collar that covers her neck.* MEN *all on feet.)*

MARTHA *(at door)*. Well, now, isn't this nice? *(Closes door.)*

BROPHY *(crosses to* MARTHA*)*. Good afternoon, Miss Brewster.

MARTHA. How do you do, Mr. Brophy? Dr. Harper. Mr. Klein.

KLEIN. How are you, Miss Brewster? We dropped in to get the Christmas toys.

MARTHA. Oh, yes, Teddy's Army and Navy. They wear out. They're all packed. *(She turns to stairs.* BROPHY *stops her.)*

BROPHY. The Colonel's upstairs after them —it seems the Cabinet has to O.K. it.

MARTHA. Yes, of course. I hope Mrs. Brophy's better?

BROPHY. She's doin' fine, ma'am. Your sister's getting some soup for me to take to her.

MARTHA *(crossing below* BROPHY *to* C.*)*. Oh, yes, we made it this morning. I just took some to a poor man who broke ever so many bones.

(ABBY enters from kitchen carrying a covered pail.)

ABBY. Oh, you're back, Martha. How was Mr. Benitzky?

MARTHA. Well, dear, it's pretty serious, I'm afraid. The doctor was there. He's going to amputate in the morning.

ABBY *(hopefully)*. Can we be present?

MARTHA *(disappointment)*. No. I asked him but he says it's against the rules of the hosiptal. *(MARTHA crosses to sideboard, puts pail down. Then puts cape and hat on small table* U. L.*)*

(TEDDY enters on balcony with large cardboard box and comes downstairs to desk, putting box on stool. KLEIN *crosses to toy box.* HARPER *speaks through this.)*

HARPER. You couldn't be of any service— and you must spare yourselves something.

ABBY *(to* BROPHY*)*. Here's the broth, Mr. Brophy. Be sure it's good and hot.

BROPHY. Yes, ma'am. *(Drops* U. S.*)*

KLEIN. This is fine—it'll make a lot of kids happy. *(Lifts out toy soldier.)* That O'Malley boy is nuts about soldiers.

TEDDY. That's General Miles. I've retired him. *(KLEIN removes ship.)* What's this! The Oregon!

MARTHA *(crosses to* U. L.*)*. Teddy, dear, put it back.

TEDDY. But the Oregon goes to Australia.

ABBY. Now, Teddy—

TEDDY. No, I've given my word to Fighting Bob Evans.

MARTHA. But, Teddy—

KLEIN. What's the difference what kid gets it—Bobby Evans, Izzy Cohen? (*Crosses to R. door with box, opens door.* BROPHY *follows.*) We'll run along, ma'am, and thank you very much.

ABBY. Not at all. (*The* COPS *stop in doorway, salute* TEDDY *and exit.* ABBY *crosses and shuts door as she speaks.* TEDDY *starts upstairs.*) Good-bye.

HARPER (*crosses to sofa, gets hat*). I must be getting home.

ABBY. Before you go, Dr. Harper—

(TEDDY *has reached stair landing.*)

TEDDY. CHARGE! (*He dashes upstairs. At top he stops and with a sweeping gesture over the balcony rail, invites all to follow him as he speaks.*) Charge the blockhouse! (*He dashes through door, closing it after him.*)

(HARPER *looks after him.* MARTHA, *to L. of* HARPER, *is fooling with a pin on her dress.* ABBY R. *of* HARPER.)

HARPER. The blockhouse?

MARTHA. The stairs are always San Juan Hill.

HARPER. Have you ever tried to persuade him that he wasn't Teddy Roosevelt?

ABBY. Oh, no!

MARTHA. He's so happy being Teddy Roosevelt.

ABBY. Once, a long time ago— (*She crosses below to* MARTHA.) remember, Martha? We thought if he would be George Washington it might be a change for him—

MARTHA. But he stayed under his bed for days and just wouldn't be anybody.

ABBY. And we'd so much rather he'd be Mr. Roosevelt than nobody.

HARPER. Well, if he's happy—and what's more important you're happy— (*He takes blue-backed legal paper from inside pocket.*) You'll see that he signs these.

MARTHA. What are they?

ABBY. Dr. Harper has made all arrangements for Teddy to go to Happy Dale Sanitarium after we pass on.

MARTHA. But why should Teddy sign any papers now?

HARPER. It's better to have it all settled. If the Lord should take you away suddenly perhaps we couldn't persuade Teddy to commit himself and that would mean an unpleasant legal procedure. Mr. Witherspoon understands they're to be filed away until the times comes to use them.

MARTHA. Mr. Witherspoon? Who's he?

HARPER. He's the Superintendent of Happy Dale.

ABBY (*to* MARTHA). Dr. Harper has arranged for him to drop in tomorrow or the next day to meet Teddy.

HARPER (*crossing to R. door and opening it*). I'd better be running along or Elaine will be over here looking for me.

(ABBY *crosses to door and calls out after him.*)

ABBY. Give our love to Elaine—and Dr. Harper, please don't think harshly of Mortimer because he's a dramatic critic. Somebody has to do those things. (ABBY *closes door, comes back into room.*)

(MARTHA *crosses to sideboard, puts legal papers on it . . . notices tea things on table.*)

MARTHA. Did you just have tea? Isn't it rather late?

ABBY (*as one who has a secret*). Yes—and dinner's going to be late too.

(TEDDY *enters on balcony, starts downstairs to first landing.* MARTHA *steps to* ABBY.)

MARTHA. So? Why?

ABBY. Teddy! (TEDDY *stops on landing.*) Good news for you. You're going to Panama and dig another lock for the canal.

TEDDY. Dee-lighted! That's bully! Just bully! I shall prepare at once for the journey. (*He turns to go upstairs, stops as if puzzled, hurries back to landing, cries CHARGE!, and rushes up and off.*)

MARTHA (*elated*). Abby! While I was out?

ABBY (*taking* MARTHA's *hand*). Yes, dear! I just couldn't wait for you. I didn't know when you'd be back and Dr. Harper was coming.

MARTHA. But all by yourself?

ABBY. Oh, I got along fine!

MARTHA. I'll run right downstairs and see.

(She starts happily for cellar door.)

ABBY. Oh, no, there wasn't time, and I was all alone.

(MARTHA looks around room toward kitchen.)

MARTHA. Well—

ABBY (coyly). Martha—just look in the window-seat. (MARTHA almost skips to window-seat, and just as she gets there a knock is heard on R. door. She stops. They both look toward door. ABBY hurries to door and opens it. ELAINE HARPER enters. ELAINE is an attractive girl in her twenties; she looks surprisingly smart for a minister's daughter.) Oh, it's Elaine. (Opens door.) Come in, dear.

(ELAINE crosses to C. ABBY closes door, crosses to C.)

ELAINE. Good afternoon, Miss Abby. Good afternoon, Miss Martha. I thought Father was here.

MARTHA (stepping to L. of table). He just this minute left. Didn't you meet him?

ELAINE (pointing to window in L. wall). No, I took the short cut through the cemetery. Mortimer hasn't come yet?

ABBY. No, dear.

ELAINE. Oh? He asked me to meet him here. Do you mind if I wait?

MARTHA. Not at all.

ABBY. Why don't you sit down, dear?

MARTHA. But we really must speak to Mortimer about doing this to you.

ELAINE (sits chair R. of table). Doing what?

MARTHA. Well, he was brought up to know better. When a gentleman is taking a young lady out he should call for her at her house.

ELAINE (to both). Oh, there's something about calling for a girl at a parsonage that discourages any man who doesn't embroider.

ABBY. He's done this too often—we're going to speak to him.

ELAINE. Oh, please don't. After young men whose idea of night life was to take me to prayer meeting, it's wonderful to go to the theatre almost every night of my life.

MARTHA. It's comforting for us, too, because if Mortimer has to see some of those plays he has to see—at least he's sitting next to a minister's daughter. (MARTHA steps to back of table.)

(ABBY crosses to back of table, starts putting tea things on tray. ELAINE and MARTHA help.)

ABBY. My goodness, Elaine, what must you think of us—not having tea cleared away by this time. (She picks up tray and exits to kitchen.)

(MARTHA blows out one candle and takes it to sideboard. ELAINE blows out other, takes to sideboard.)

MARTHA (as ABBY exits). Now don't bother with anything in the kitchen until Mortimer comes, and then I'll help you. (To ELAINE.) Mortimer will be here any minute now.

ELAINE. Yes. Father must have been surprised not to find me at home. I'd better run over and say good night to him. (She crosses to R. door.)

MARTHA. It's a shame you missed him, dear.

ELAINE (opening door). If Mortimer comes you tell him I'll be right back. (She has opened door, but sees MORTIMER just outside.) Hello, Mort!

(MORTIMER BREWSTER walks in. He is a dramatic critic.)

MORTIMER. Hello, Elaine. (As he passes her going toward MARTHA, thus placing himself between ELAINE and MARTHA, he reaches back and pats ELAINE on the fanny . . . then embraces MARTHA.) Hello, Aunt Martha.

(MARTHA exits to kitchen, calling as she goes.)

MARTHA. Abby, Mortimer's here!

(ELAINE slowly closes door.)

MORTIMER (*turning* R.). Were you going somewhere?

ELAINE. I was just going over to tell Father not to wait up for me.

MORTIMER. I didn't know that was still being done, even in Brooklyn. (*He throws his hat on sofa.*)

(ABBY *enters from kitchen.* MARTHA *follows, stays in doorway* R.)

ABBY (*crosses to* MORTIMER *at* C.) Hello, Mortimer.

MORTIMER (*embraces and kisses her*). Hello, Aunt Abby.

ABBY. How are you, dear?

MORTIMER. All right. And you look well. You haven't changed much since yesterday.

ABBY. Oh, my goodness, it was yesterday, wasn't it? We're seeing a great deal of you lately. (*She crosses and starts to sit in chair above table.*) Well, come, sit down. Sit down.

(MARTHA *stops her from sitting.*)

MARTHA. Abby—haven't we something to do in the kitchen?

ABBY. Huh?

MARTHA. You know—the tea things.

ABBY (*suddenly seeing* MORTIMER *and* ELAINE, *and catching on*). Oh, yes! Yes! The tea things— (*She backs toward kitchen.*) Well—you two just make yourselves at home. Just—

MARTHA. —make yourselves at home.

(*They exit kitchen door,* ABBY *closing door.*)

ELAINE (*stepping to* MORTIMER, *ready to be kissed*). Well, can't you take a hint?

MORTIMER (*complaining*). No . . . that was pretty obvious. A lack of inventiveness, I should say.

ELAINE (*only slightly annoyed as she crosses to table, and puts handbag on it*). Yes—that's exactly what you'd say.

MORTIMER (*he is at desk, fishing various pieces of notepaper from his pockets, and separating dollar bills that are mixed in with papers*). Where do you want to go for dinner?

ELAINE (*opening bag, looking in hand mirror*). I don't care. I'm not very hungry.

MORTIMER. Well, I just had breakfast. Suppose we wait until after the show?

ELAINE. But that'll make it pretty late, won't it?

MORTIMER. Not with the little stinker we're seeing tonight. From what I've heard about it we'll be at Blake's by ten o'clock.

ELAINE (*crosses to* U. S. C.). You ought to be fair to these plays.

MORTIMER. Are these plays fair to me?

ELAINE. *I've* never seen you walk out on a musical.

MORTIMER. That musical isn't opening tonight.

ELAINE (*disappointed*). No?

MORTIMER. Darling, you'll have to learn the rules. With a musical there are always four changes of title and three postponements. They liked it in New Haven but it needs a lot of work.

ELAINE. Oh, I was hoping it was a musical.

MORTIMER. You have such a light mind.

ELAINE. Not a bit. Musicals somehow have a humanizing effect on you. (*He gives her a look.*) After a serious play we join the proletariat in the subway and I listen to a lecture on the drama. After a musical you bring me home in a taxi, (*Turning away.*) and you make a few passes.

MORTIMER (*crossing* D. C.). Now wait a minute, darling, that's a very inaccurate piece of reporting.

ELAINE (*leaning against* D. S. *end of table*). Oh, I will admit that after the Behrman play you told me I had authentic beauty— and that's a hell of a thing to say to a girl. It wasn't until after our first musical you told me I had nice legs. And I have too.

(MORTIMER *stares at her legs a moment, then walks over and kisses her.*)

MORTIMER. For a minister's daughter you know a lot about life. Where'd you learn it?

ELAINE (*casually*). In the choir loft.

MORTIMER. I'll explain that to you some time, darling—the close connection between eroticism and religion.

ELAINE. Religion never gets as high as the choir loft. *(Crosses below table, gathers up bag.)* Which reminds me, I'd better tell Father please not to wait up for me tonight.

MORTIMER *(almost to himself)*. I've never been able to rationalize it.

ELAINE. What?

MORTIMER. My falling in love with a girl who lives in Brooklyn.

ELAINE. Falling in love? You're not stooping to the articulate, are you?

MORTIMER *(ignoring this)*. The only way I can regain my self-respect is to keep you in New York.

ELAINE *(few steps toward him.)* Did you say keep?

MORTIMER. No, no. I've come to the conclusion that you're holding out for the legalities.

ELAINE *(crossing to him as he backs away)*. I can afford to be a good girl for quite a few years yet.

MORTIMER *(stops and embraces her)*. And I can't wait that long. Where could we be married in a hurry—say tonight?

ELAINE. I'm afraid Father will insist on officiating.

MORTIMER *(turning away R. from her)*. Oh, God; I'll bet your father could make even the marriage service sound pedestrian.

ELAINE. Are you by any chance writing a review of it?

MORTIMER. Forgive me, darling. It's an occupational disease. *(She smiles at him lovingly and walks toward him. He meets her halfway and they forget themselves for a moment in a sentimental embrace and kiss. When they come out of it, he turns away from her quickly . . . breaking U. s. near desk.)* I may give that play tonight a good notice.

ELAINE. Now, darling, don't pretend you love me that much.

MORTIMER *(looks at her with polite lechery. then starts toward her)*. Be sure to tell your father not to wait up tonight.

ELAINE *(aware that she can't trust either of them, and backing U. s.)*. I think tonight I'd better tell him to wait up.

MORTIMER *(following her)*. I'll telephone Winchell to publish the banns.

ELAINE *(backing D. s.)* Nevertheless—

MORTIMER. All right, everything formal and legal. But not later than next month.

ELAINE *(runs into his arms)*. Darling! I'll talk it over with Father and set the date.

MORTIMER. No—we'll have to see what's in rehearsal. There'll be a lot of other first nights in October.

(TEDDY enters from balcony and comes downstairs dressed in tropical clothes and a solar topee. At foot of stairs he sees MORTIMER, crosses to him and shakes hands.)

TEDDY. Hello, Mortimer!

MORTIMER *(gravely)*. How are you, Mr. President?

TEDDY. Bully, thank you. Just bully! What news have you brought me?

MORTIMER. Just this, Mr. President—the country is squarely behind you.

TEDDY *(beaming)*. Yes, I know. Isn't it wonderful? *(He shakes MORTIMER's hand again.)* Well, good-bye. *(He crosses to ELAINE and shakes hands with her.)* Good-bye. *(He goes to cellar door.)*

ELAINE. Where are you off to, Teddy?

TEDDY. Panama. *(He exits through cellar door, shutting it. ELAINE looks at MORTIMER inquiringly.)*

MORTIMER. Panama's the cellar. He digs locks for the canal down there.

(ELAINE takes his arm and they stroll D. L. to R. of table.)

ELAINE You're so sweet with him—and he's very fond of you.

MORTIMER. Well, Teddy was always my favorite brother.

ELAINE *(stopping and turning to him)*. Favorite? Were there more of you?

MORTIMER. There's another brother—Jonathan.

ELAINE. I never heard of him. Your aunts never mention him.

MORTIMER. No, we don't like to talk about Jonathan. He left Brooklyn very early—

by request. Jonathan was the kind of boy who liked to cut worms in two—with his teeth.

ELAINE. What became of him?

MORTIMER. I don't know. He wanted to become a surgeon like Grandfather but he wouldn't go to medical school first and his practice got him into trouble.

(ABBY *enters from kitchen, crossing* D. L. *of table.*)

ABBY. Aren't you two going to be late for the theatre?

(MORTIMER'S L. *arm around* ELAINE'S *neck, he looks at his wristwatch.*)

MORTIMER. We're skipping dinner. We won't have to start for half an hour.

ABBY (*backing* U. L.). Well, then I'll leave you two alone together again.

ELAINE. Don't bother, darling. (*Breaking* R. *in front of* MORTIMER.) I'm going to run over to speak to Father. (*To* MORTIMER.) Before I go out with you he likes to pray over me a little. (*She runs to* R. *door and opens it, keeping her* L. *hand on outside doorknob.*) I'll be right back—I'll cut through the cemetery.

MORTIMER (*crossing to her, puts his hand on hers*). If the prayer isn't too long, I'd have time to lead you beside distilled waters.

(ELAINE *laughs and exits.* MORTIMER *shuts door.*)

ABBY (*happily, as she crosses to* C.). Mortimer, that's the first time I've ever heard you quote the Bible. We knew Elaine would be a good influence for you.

MORTIMER (*laughs, crosses* L., *then turns to* ABBY). Oh, by the way—I'm going to marry her.

ABBY. What? Oh, darling! (*She runs and embraces him. Then she dashes toward kitchen door as* MORTIMER *crosses to window* L. *and looks out.*) Martha! Martha! (MARTHA *enters from kitchen.*) Come right in here. I've got the most wonderful news for you—Mortimer and Elaine are going to be married.

MARTHA. Married? Oh, Mortimer! (*She runs over to* R. *of* MORTIMER, *who is looking out window* L., *embraces and kisses*

him. ABBY *comes down to his* L. *He has his arms around both of them.*)

ABBY. We hoped it would happen just like this.

MARTHA. Well, Elaine must be the happiest girl in the world.

MORTIMER (*pulls curtain back, looks out window*). Happy! Just look at her leaping over those gravestones. (*As he looks out window* MORTIMER'S *attention is suddenly drawn to something.*) Say! What's that?

MARTHA (*looking out on his* R. ABBY *is on his* L.). What's what, dear?

MORTIMER. See that statute there. That's a horundinida carnina.

MARTHA. Oh, no, dear—that's Emma B. Stout ascending to heaven.

MORTIMER. No, no,—standing on Mrs. Stout's left ear. That bird—that's a red-crested swallow. I've only seen one of those before in my life.

ABBY (*crosses around above table and pushes chair* R. *into table*). I don't know how you can be thinking about a bird now—what with Elaine and the engagement and everything.

MORTIMER. It's a vanishing species. (*He turns away from window.*) Thoreau was very fond of them. (*As he crosses to desk to look through various drawers and papers.*) By the way, I left a large envelope around here last week. It was one of the chapters of my book on Thoreau. Have you seen it?

MARTHA (*pushing armchair into table*). Well, if you left it here it must be here somewhere.

ABBY (*crossing to* D. L. *of* MORTIMER). When are you going to be married? What are your plans? There must be something more you can tell us about Elaine.

MORTIMER. Elaine? Oh, yes, Elaine thought it was brilliant. (*He crosses to sideboard, looks through cupboards and drawers.*)

MARTHA. What was, dear?

MORTIMER. My chapter on Thoreau. (*He finds a bundle of papers (script) in* R. *drawer and takes them to table and looks through them.*)

ABBY *(at c.)*. Well, when Elaine comes back I think we ought to have a little celebration. We must drink to your happiness. Martha, isn't there some of that Lady Baltimore cake left?

(During last few speeches MARTHA *has picked up pail from sideboard and her cape, hat and gloves from table in* U. L. *corner.)*

MARTHA *(crossing* D. L.*)*. Oh, yes!

ABBY. And I'll open a bottle of wine.

MARTHA *(as she exits to kitchen)*. Oh, and to think it happened in this room!

MORTIMER *(has finished looking through papers, is gazing around room)*. Now where could I have put that?

ABBY. Well, with your fiancée sitting beside you tonight, I do hope the play will be something you can enjoy for once. It may be something romantic. What's the name of it?

MORTIMER. "Murder Will Out."

ABBY. Oh dear! *(She disappears into kitchen as* MORTIMER *goes on talking.)*

MORTIMER. When the curtain goes up the first thing you'll see will be a dead body.

(He lifts window-seat and sees one. Not believing it, he drops window-seat again and starts downstage. He suddenly stops with a "take," then goes back, throws window-seat open and stares in. He goes slightly mad for a moment. He backs away, then hears ABBY *humming on her way into the room. He drops window-seat again and holds it down, staring around the room.* ABBY *enters carrying a silencer and table cloth which she puts on armchair, then picks up bundle of papers and returns them to drawer in sideboard.*

MORTIMER *(speaks in a somewhat strained voice)*. Aunt Abby!

ABBY *(at sideboard)*. Yes, dear?

MORTIMER. You were going to make plans for Teddy to go to that . . . sanitarium —Happy Dale—

ABBY *(bringing legal papers from sideboard to* MORTIMER*)*. Yes, dear, it's all arranged. Dr. Harper was here today and brought the papers for Teddy to sign. Here they are.

(He takes them from her.)

MORTIMER. He's got to sign them right away.

ABBY *(arranging silencer on table.* MARTHA *enters from kitchen door with table silver and plates on a tray. She sets tray on sideboard. Goes to table* R.*)*. That's what Dr. Harper thinks. Then there won't be any legal difficulties after we pass on.

MORTIMER. He's got to sign them this minute! He's down in the cellar—get him up here right away.

MARTHA *(unfolding tablecloth. She's above table on* R.*)*. There's no such hurry as that.

ABBY. No. When Teddy starts working on the canal you can't get his mind on anything else.

MORTIMER. Teddy's got to go to Happy Dale now—tonight.

MARTHA. Oh, no, dear, that's not until after we're gone.

MORTIMER. Right away, I tell you!—right away!

ABBY *(turning to* MORTIMER*)*. Why, Mortimer, how can you say such a thing? Why, as long as we live we'll never be separated from Teddy.

MORTIMER *(trying to be calm)*. Listen, darlings, I'm frightfully sorry, but I've got some shocking news for you. *(The* AUNTS *stop work and look at him with some interest.)* Now we've all got to try and keep our heads. You know we've sort of humored Teddy because we thought he was harmless.

MARTHA. Why he *is* harmless!

MORTIMER. He *was* harmless. That's why he has to go to Happy Dale. Why he has to be confined.

ABBY *(stepping to* MORTIMER*)*. Mortimer, why have you suddenly turned against Teddy?—your own brother?

MORTIMER. You've got to know sometime. It might as well be now, Teddy's—killed a man!

MARTHA. Nonsense, dear.

*(*MORTIMER *rises and points to window-seat.)*

MORTIMER. There's a body in the window-seat!

ABBY. Yes, dear, we know.

(MORTIMER "takes" as ABBY and MARTHA busy themselves again at table.)

MORTIMER. You *know?*

MARTHA. Of course, dear, but it has nothing to do with Teddy. (Gets tray from sideboard—arranges silver and plates on table: three places, U. L. and R.)

ABBY. Now, Mortimer, just forget about it —forget you ever saw the gentleman.

MORTIMER. *Forget?*

ABBY. We never dreamed you'd peek.

MORTIMER. But who is he?

ABBY. His name's Hoskins—Adam Hoskins. That's really all I know about him —except that he's a Methodist.

MORTIMER. That's all you know about him? Well, what's he doing here? What happened to him?

MARTHA. He died.

MORTIMER. Aunt Martha, men don't just get into window-seats and die.

ABBY (silly boy). No, he died first.

MORTIMER. Well, how?

ABBY. Oh, Mortimer, don't be so inquisitive. The gentleman died because he drank some wine with poison in it.

MORTIMER. How did the poison get in the wine?

MARTHA. Well, we put it in wine because it's less noticeable—when it's in tea it has a distinct odor.

MORTIMER. *You* put it in the wine?

ABBY. Yes. And I put Mr. Hoskins in the window-seat because Dr. Harper was coming.

MORTIMER. So you knew what you'd done! You didn't want Dr. Harper to see the body!

ABBY. Well, not at tea—that wouldn't have have been very nice. Now, Mortimer, you know the whole thing, just forget about it. I do think Martha and I have the right to our own little secrets. (She crosses to sideboard to get two goblets from L. cup-board as MARTHA comes to table from sideboard with salt dish and pepper shaker.)

MARTHA. And don't you tell Elaine! (She gets third goblet from sideboard, then turns to ABBY who takes tray from sideboard.) Oh, Abby, while I was out I dropped in on Mrs. Schultz. She's much better but she would like us to take Junior to the movies again.

ABBY. Well, we must do that tomorrow or next day.

MARTHA. Yes, but this time we'll go where we want to go. (She starts for kitchen door. ABBY follows.) Junior's not going to drag me into another one of those scary pictures. (They exit into kitchen as MORTIMER wheels around and looks after them. ABBY shuts door.)

MORTIMER (dazed, looks around the room. His eyes come to rest on phone on desk; he crosses to it and dials a number. Into phone.) City desk! (There is a pause.) Hello, Al. Do you know who this is? (Pause.) That's right. Say, Al, when I left the office, I told you where I was going, remember?—Well, where did I say? (Pause.) Uh-huh. Well, it would take me about half an hour to get to Brooklyn. What time have you got? (He looks at his watch.) That's right. I must be here. (He hangs up, sits for a moment, then suddenly leaps off stool toward kitchen.) Aunt Abby! Aunt Martha! Come in here! (He backs to C. stage as the two AUNTS bustle in. MARTHA has tray with plates, cups, saucers and soup cups.) What are we going to do? What are we going to do?

MARTHA (R. of table). What are we going to do about what, dear?

MORTIMER (pointing to window-seat). There's a body in there.

ABBY (U. L. of MORTIMER). Yes—Mr. Hoskins.

MORTIMER. Well, good heavens, I can't turn you over to the police! But what am I going to do?

MARTHA. Well, for one thing, dear, stop being so excited.

ABBY. And for pity's sake stop worrying. We told you to forget the whole thing.

MORTIMER. Forget! My dear Aunt Abby, can't I make you realize that something has to be done?

ABBY (*a little sharply*). Now, Mortimer, you behave yourself. You're too old to be flying off the handle like this.

MORTIMER. But Mr. Hotchkiss—

(ABBY, *on her way to sideboard, stops and turns to* MORTIMER.)

ABBY. Hoskins, dear. (*She continues on her way to sideboard and gets napkins and rings from* L. *drawer.* MARTHA *puts her tray, with cups, plates, etc., on table.* MORTIMER *continues speaking through this.*)

MORTIMER. Well, whatever his name is, you can't leave him there.

MARTHA. We don't intend to, dear.

ABBY (*crossing to table* L. *with napkins and rings*). No, Teddy's down in the cellar now digging the lock.

MORTIMER. You mean you're going to bury Mr. Hotchkiss in the cellar?

MARTHA (*stepping to him*). Oh, yes, dear, —that's what we did with the others.

MORTIMER (*walking away to* R.). No! You can't bury Mr.— (*Double take. Turns back to them.*) —others?

ABBY. The other gentlemen.

MORTIMER. When you say others—do you mean—others? More than one others?

MARTHA. Oh, yes, dear. Let me see, this is eleven. (*To* ABBY U. L. *of table.*) Isn't it, Abby?

ABBY. No, dear, this makes twelve.

(MORTIMER *backs away from them, stunned, toward phone stool at desk.*)

MARTHA. Oh, I think you're wrong, Abby. This is only eleven.

ABBY. No, dear, because I remember when Mr. Hoskins first came in, it occurred to me that he would make just an even dozen.

MARTHA. Well, you really shouldn't count the first one.

ABBY. Oh, *I* was counting the first one. So that makes it twelve.

(*Phone rings.* MORTIMER, *in a daze, turns*

toward it and without picking up receiver, speaks.)

MORTIMER. Hello! (*He comes to, picks up receiver.*) Hello. Oh, hello, Al. My, it's good to hear your voice.

(ABBY, *at table is still holding out for a "twelve" count.*)

ABBY. Well, anyway, they're all down in the cellar—

MORTIMER (*to* AUNTS). Ssshhh— (*Into phone, as* AUNTS *cross to sideboard and put candelabras from top to bottom shelf.*) Oh, no, Al, I'm sober as a lark. I just called you because I was feeling a little Pirandello—Piran—you wouldn't know, Al. Look, I'm glad you called. Get hold of George right away. He's got to review the play tonight. I can't make it. No, Al, you're wrong. I'll tell you all about it tomorrow. Well, George has got to cover the play tonight! This is my department and I'm running it! You get ahold of George! (*He hangs up and sits a moment trying to collect himself.*) Now let's see, where were we? (*He suddenly leaps from stool.*) TWELVE!

MARTHA. Yes, Abby thinks we ought to count the first one and that makes twelve. (*She goes back to sideboard.*)

(MORTIMER *takes chair* R. *of table and faces it toward* R. *stage, then takes* MARTHA *by the hand, leads her to chair and sets her in it.*)

MORTIMER. All right—now—who was the first one?

ABBY (*crossing from above table to* MORTIMER). Mr. Midgely. He was a Baptist.

MARTHA. Of course, I still think we can't claim full credit for him because he just died.

ABBY. Martha means without any help from us. You see, Mr. Midgely came here looking for a room—

MARTHA. It was right after you moved to New York.

ABBY. —And it didn't seem right for that lovely room to be going to waste when there were so many people who needed it—

MARTHA. —He was such a lonely old man. . . .

ABBY. All his kith and kin were dead and it left him so forlorn and unhappy—

MARTHA. —We felt so sorry for him.

ABBY. And then when his heart attack came—and he sat dead in that chair *(Pointing to armchair.)* looking so peaceful—remember, Martha—we made up our minds then and there that if we could help other lonely old men to that same peace —we would!

MORTIMER *(all ears)*. He dropped dead right in that chair! How awful for you!

MARTHA. Oh, no, dear. Why, it was rather like old times. Your grandfather always used to have a cadaver or two around the house. You see, Teddy had been digging in Panama and he thought Mr. Midgely was a Yellow Fever victim.

ABBY. That meant he had to be buried immediately.

MARTHA. So we all took him down to Panama and put him in the lock. *(She rises, puts her arm around ABBY.)* Now that's why we told you not to worry about it because we know exactly what's to be done.

MORTIMER. And that's how all this started —that man walking in here and dropping dead.

ABBY. Of course, we realized we couldn't depend on that happening again. So—

MARTHA *(crosses to MORTIMER)*. You remember those jars of poison that have been up on the shelves in Grandfather's laboratory all these years—?

ABBY. You know your Aunt Martha's knack for mixing things. You've eaten enough of her piccalilli.

MARTHA. Well, dear, for a gallon of elderberry wine I take one teaspoonful of arsenic, then add a half teaspoonful of strychnine and then just a pinch of cyanide.

MORTIMER *(appraisingly)*. Should have quite a kick.

ABBY. Yes! As a matter of fact one of our gentlemen found time to say "How delicious!"

MARTHA *(stepping U. S.)*. Well, I'll have to get things started in the kitchen.

ABBY *(to MORTIMER)*. I wish you could stay for dinner.

MARTHA. I'm trying out a new recipe.

MORTIMER. I couldn't eat a thing.

(MARTHA goes out to kitchen.)

ABBY *(calling after MARTHA)*. I'll come and help you, dear. *(She pushes chair R. into table.)* Well, I feel so much better now. Oh, you have to wait for Elaine, don't you? *(She smiles.)* How happy you must be. *(She goes to kitchen doorway.)* Well, dear, I'll leave you alone with your thoughts. *(She exits, shutting door.)*

(The shutting of the door wakes MORTIMER from his trance. He crosses to windowseat, kneels down, raises cover, looks in. Not believing, he lowers cover, rubs his eyes, raises cover again. This time he really sees Mr. Hoskins. Closes window-seat hastily, rises, steps back. Runs over and closes drapes over window. Backs up to above table. Sees water glass on table, picks it up, raises it to lips, suddenly remembers that poisoned wine comes in glasses, puts it down quickly. Crosses to cellar door, opens it. ELAINE enters R., he closes cellar door with a bang. As ELAINE puts her bag on top of desk he looks at her, and it dawns on him that he knows her. He speaks with faint surprise.)

MORTIMER. Oh, it's you. *(He drops D. S. ELAINE crosses to him, takes his hand.)*

ELAINE. Don't be cross, darling! Father could see that I was excited—so I told him about us and that made it hard for me to get away. But listen, darling—he's not going to wait up for me tonight.

MORTIMER *(looking at window-seat)*. You run along home, Elaine, and I'll call you up tomorrow.

ELAINE. Tomorrow!

MORTIMER *(irritated)*. You know I always call you up every day or two.

ELAINE. But we're going to the theatre tonight.

MORTIMER. No—no we're not!

ELAINE. Well, why not?

MORTIMER *(turning to her)*. Elaine, something's come up.

ELAINE. What, darling? Mortimer—you've lost your job!

MORTIMER. No—no—I haven't lost my job. I'm just not covering that play tonight. *(Pushing her R.)* Now you run along home, Elaine.

ELAINE. But I've got to know what's happened. Certainly you can tell me.

MORTIMER. No, dear, I can't.

ELAINE. But if we're going to be married—

MORTIMER. Married?

ELAINE. Have you forgotten that not fifteen minutes ago you proposed to me?

MORTIMER *(vaguely)*. I did? Oh—yes! Well, as far as I know that's still on. *(Urging her R. again.)* Now you run along home, Elaine. I've got to do something.

ELAINE. Listen, you can't propose to me one minute and throw me out of the house the next.

MORTIMER *(pleading)*. I'm not throwing you out of the house, darling. Will you get out of here?

ELAINE. No. I won't get out of here. *(MORTIMER crosses toward kitchen. ELAINE crosses below to window-seat.)* Not until I've had some kind of explanation. *(ELAINE is about to sit on window-seat. MORTIMER grabs her by the hand. Phone rings.)*

MORTIMER. Elaine! *(He goes to phone, dragging ELAINE with him.)* Hello! Oh, hello, Al. Hold on a minute, will you?— All right, it's important! But it can wait a minute, can't it? Hold on! *(He puts receiver on desk. Takes ELAINE's bag from top of desk and hands it to her. Then takes her by hand and leads her to door R. and opens it.)* Look, Elaine, you're a sweet girl and I love you. But I have something on my mind now and I want you to go home and wait until I call you.

ELAINE *(in doorway)*. Don't try to be masterful.

MORTIMER *(annoyed to the point of being literate)*. When we're married and I have problems to face I hope you're less tedious and uninspired!

ELAINE. And when we're married *if* we're married—I hope I find you adequate! *(She exits. MORTIMER does take, then runs out on porch after her, calling—)*

MORTIMER. Elaine! Elaine! *(He runs back in, shutting door, crosses and kneels on window-seat to open window. Suddenly remembers contents of window-seat and leaps off it. Dashes into kitchen but remembers Al is on phone, re-enters immediately and crosses to phone.)* Hello, Al? Hello . . . hello. . . . *(He pushes hook down and starts to dial when doorbell rings. He thinks it's the phone. ABBY enters from kitchen.)* Hello. Hello, Al?

ABBY *(crossing to R. door and opening it)*. That's the doorbell, dear, not the telephone. *(MORTIMER pushes hook down . . . dials. MR. GIBBS steps in doorway R.)* How do you do? Come in.

GIBBS. I understand you have a room to rent.

(MARTHA enters from kitchen. Puts "Lazy Susan" on sideboard, then gets to R. of table.)

ABBY. Yes. Won't you step in?

GIBBS *(stepping into room)*. Are you the lady of the house?

ABBY. Yes, I'm Miss Brewster. And this is my sister, another Miss Brewster.

GIBBS. My name is Gibbs.

ABBY *(easing him to chair R. of table)*. Oh, won't you sit down? I'm sorry we were just setting the table for dinner.

MORTIMER *(into phone)*. Hello—let me talk to Al again. City desk. *(Loud.)* AL!! CITY DESK! WHAT? I'm sorry, wrong number. *(He hangs up and starts dialling again as GIBBS looks at him. GIBBS turns to ABBY.)*

GIBBS. May I see the room?

MARTHA *(D. L. of table)*. Why don't you sit down a minute and let's get acquainted.

GIBBS. That won't do much good if I don't like the room.

ABBY. Is Brooklyn your home?

GIBBS. Haven't got a home. Live in a hotel. Don't like it.

MORTIMER *(into phone)*. Hello. City desk.

MARTHA. Are your family Brooklyn people?

GIBBS. Haven't got any family.

ABBY (another victim). All alone in the world?

GIBBS. Yep.

ABBY. Well, Martha— (MARTHA goes happily to sideboard, gets bottle of wine from U. L. cupboard, and a wine glass, and sets them on table, U. S. end. ABBY eases GIBBS into chair R. of table and continues speaking to him, then to above table.) Well, you've come to just the right house. Do sit down.

MORTIMER (into phone). Hello, Al? Mort. We got cut off. Al, I can't cover the play tonight—that's all there is to it, I can't!

MARTHA (L. of table). What church do you go to? There's an Episcopal church practically next door. (Her gesture toward window brings her to window-seat and she sits.)

GIBBS. I'm Presbyterian. Used to be.

MORTIMER (into phone). What's George doing in Bermuda? (Rises and gets loud.) Certainly I told him he could go to Bermuda—it's my department, isn't it? Well, you've got to get somebody. Who else is there around the office? (He sits on second chair.)

GIBBS (annoyed. Rises and crosses below table to L. of it). Is there always this much noise?

MARTHA. Oh, he doesn't live with us.

(ABBY sits above table.)

MORTIMER (into phone). There must be somebody around the place. Look, Al, how about the office boy? You know the bright one—the one we don't like? Well, you look around the office, I'll hold on.

GIBBS. I'd really like to see the room.

ABBY (after seating GIBBS R. of table she has sat in chair above table). It's upstairs. Won't you try a glass of our wine before we start up?

GIBBS. Never touch it.

MARTHA. We make this ourselves. It's elderberry wine.

GIBBS (to MARTHA). Elderberry wine. Hmmph. Haven't tasted elderberry wine since I was a boy. Thank you. (He pulls armchair around and sits as ABBY uncorks bottle and starts to pour wine.)

MORTIMER (into phone). Well, there must be some printers around. Look, Al, the fellow who sets my copy. He ought to know about what I'd write. His name is Joe. He's the third machine from the left. But, Al, he might turn out to be another Burns Mantle!

GIBBS (to MARTHA). Do you have your own elderberry bushes?

MARTHA. No, but the cemetery is full of them.

MORTIMER (rising). No, I'm not drinking, but I'm going to start now.

GIBBS. Do you serve meals?

ABBY. We might, but first just see whether you like our wine.

(MORTIMER hangs up, puts phone on top of desk and crosses L. He sees wine on table. Goes to sideboard, gets glass, brings it to table and pours drink. GIBBS has his glass in hand and is getting ready to drink.)

MARTHA (sees MORTIMER pouring wine). Mortimer! Eh eh eh eh! (GIBBS stops and looks at MARTHA. MORTIMER pays no attention.) Eh eh eh eh!

(As MORTIMER raises glass to lips with L. hand, ABBY reaches up and pulls his arm down.)

ABBY. Mortimer. Not that. (MORTIMER, still dumb, puts his glass down on table. Then he suddenly sees GIBBS who has just got glass to his lips and is about to drink. He points across table at GIBBS and gives a wild cry. GIBBS looks at him, putting his glass down. MORTIMER, still pointing at GIBBS, goes around above table toward him. GIBBS, seeing a madman, rises slowly and backs toward c., then turns and runs for exit R., MORTIMER following him. GIBBS opens R. door and MORTIMER pushes him out, closing door after him. Then he turns and leans on door in exhausted relief. Meantime, MARTHA has risen and crossed to below armchair, while ABBY has risen and crossed to D. C. [To cover GIBBS' cross and exit, MORTIMER has the following lines . . . "Get out of here! Do you want to be poisoned? Do you want to be killed? Do you want to be murdered?"])

ABBY (great disappointment). Now you've spoiled everything. (She goes to sofa and sits.)

(MARTHA *sits in armchair.* MORTIMER *crosses to* C. *and looks from one to the other . . . then speaks to* ABBY.)

MORTIMER. You can't do things like that. I don't know how to explain this to you, but it's not only against the law. It's wrong! (*To* MARTHA.) It's not a nice thing to do. (MARTHA *turns away from him as* ABBY *has done in his lines to her.*) People wouldn't understand. (*Points to door after* GIBBS.) He wouldn't understand.

MARTHA. Abby, we shouldn't have told Mortimer!

MORTIMER. What I mean is—well, this has developed into a very bad habit.

ABBY (*rises*). Mortimer, we don't try to stop you from doing things you like to do. I don't see why you should interfere with us.

(*Phone rings.* MORTIMER *answers.* MARTHA *rises to below table.*)

MORTIMER. Hello? (*It's Al again.*) All right, I'll see the first act and I'll pan the hell out of it. But look, Al, you've got to do something for me. Get hold of O'Brien —our lawyer, the head of our legal department. Have him meet me at the theatre. Now, don't let me down. O.K. I'm starting now. (*He hangs up and turns to* AUNTS.) Look, I've got to go to the theatre. I can't get out of it. But before I go will you promise me something?

MARTHA (*crossing to* ABBY *at* C.). We'd have to know what it was first.

MORTIMER. I love you very much and I know you love me. You know I'd do anything in the world for you and I want you to do just this little thing for me.

ABBY. What do you want us to do?

MORTIMER. Don't *do* anything. I mean don't do *anything.* Don't let anyone in this house—and leave Mr. Hoskins right where he is.

MARTHA. Why?

MORTIMER. I want time to think—and I've got quite a little to think about. You know I wouldn't want anything to happen to you.

ABBY. Well, what on earth could happen to us?

MORTIMER (*beside himself*). Anyway— you'll do this for me, won't you?

MARTHA. Well—we were planning on holding services before dinner.

MORTIMER. Services!

MARTHA (*a little indignant*). Certainly. You don't think we'd bury Mr. Hoskins without a full Methodist service, do you? Why he was a Methodist.

MORTIMER. But can't that wait until I get back?

ABBY. Oh, then you could join us.

MORTIMER (*going crazy himself*). Yes! Yes!

ABBY. Oh, Mortimer, you'll enjoy the services—especially the hymns. (*To* MARTHA.) Remember how beautifully Mortimer used to sing in the choir before his voice changed?

MORTIMER. And remember, you're not going to let anyone in this house while I'm gone—it's a promise!

MARTHA. Well—

ABBY. Oh, Martha, we can do that now that Mortimer's cooperating with us. (*To* MORTIMER.) Well, all right, Mortimer.

(MORTIMER *heaves a sigh of relief. Crosses to sofa and gets his hat. Then on his way to opening* R. *door, he speaks.*)

MORTIMER. Have you got some paper? I'll get back just as soon as I can. (*Taking legal papers from coat pocket as he crosses.*) There's a man I've got to see.

(ABBY *has gone to desk for stationery. She hands it to* MORTIMER.)

ABBY. Here's some stationery. Will this do?

MORTIMER (*taking stationery*). That'll be fine. I can save time if I write my review on the way to the theatre. (*He exits* R.)

(*The* AUNTS *stare after him.* MARTHA *crosses and closes door.* ABBY *goes to sideboard and brings two candelabras to table. Then gets matches from sideboard—lights candles during lines.*)

MARTHA. Mortimer didn't seem quite himself today.

ABBY (*lighting candles*). Well, that's only natural—I think I know why.

MARTHA (*lighting floor lamp*). Why?

ABBY. He's just become engaged to be married. I suppose that always makes a man nervous.

MARTHA *(during this speech she goes to first landing and closes drapes over window, then comes downstairs and turns off remote switch).* Well, I'm so happy for Elaine—and their honeymoon ought to give Mortimer a real vacation. I don't think he got much rest this summer.

ABBY. Well, at least he didn't go kiting off to China or Spain.

MARTHA. I could never understand why he wanted to go to those places.

ABBY. Well, I think to Mortimer the theatre has always seemed pretty small potatoes. He needs something big to criticize—something like the human race. *(She sets one candelabra* D. L., *the other* U. R. *on table.)*

MARTHA *(at* C.*).* Oh, Abby, if Mortimer's coming back for the services for Mr. Hoskins, we'll need another hymnal. There's one in my room. *(She starts upstairs to first landing.)*

ABBY. You know, dear, it's really my turn to read the services, but since you weren't here when Mr. Hoskins came I want you to do it.

MARTHA *(pleased).* That's very nice of you, dear—but, are you sure you want me to?

ABBY. It's only fair.

MARTHA. Well, I think I'll wear my black bombazine and Mother's old brooch. *(She starts up again when doorbell rings.)*

ABBY *(crossing as far as desk).* I'll go, dear.

MARTHA *(hushed).* We promised Mortimer we wouldn't let anyone in.

ABBY *(trying to peer through curtained window in door).* Who do you suppose it is?

MARTHA. Wait a minute, I'll look. *(She turns to landing window and peeks out the curtains.)* It's two men—and I've never seen them before.

ABBY. Are you sure?

MARTHA. There's a car at the curb—they must have come in that.

ABBY. Let me look! *(She hurries up stairs. There is a knock on door.* ABBY *peeks out the curtains.)*

MARTHA. Do you recognize them?

ABBY. They're strangers to me.

MARTHA. We'll just have to pretend we're not at home. *(The two of them huddle back in corner of landing.)*

(Another knock at the door R., *the knob is turned, and door swings slowly open. A tall* MAN *walks to* C., *looking about the room. He walks in with assurance and ease as though the room were familiar to him—in every direction but that of the stairs. There is something sinister about the man—something that brings a slight chill in his presence. It is in his walk, his bearing, and his strange resemblance to Boris Karloff. From stair-landing* ABBY *and* MARTHA *watch him, almost afraid to speak. Having completed his survey of the room, the* MAN *turns and addresses someone outside the front door.)*

JONATHAN. Come in, Doctor. *(*DR. EINSTEIN *enters* R. *He is somewhat ratty in appearance. His face wears the benevolent smirk of a man who lives in a pleasant haze of alcohol. There is something about him that suggests the unfrocked priest. He stands just inside the door, timid but expectant.)* This is the home of my youth. As a boy I couldn't wait to escape from this place—now I'm glad to escape back into it.

EINSTEIN *(shutting door. His back to* AUNTS.*)* Yah, Chonny, it's a fine hideout.

JONATHAN. The family must still live here. There's something so unmistakably Brewster about the Brewsters. I hope there's a fatted calf awaiting the return of the prodigal.

EINSTEIN. Yah, I'm hungry. *(He suddenly sees the fatted calf in the form of the two glasses of wine on table.)* Look, Chonny, drinks! *(He runs over below to table.* JONATHAN *crosses to above side.)*

JONATHAN. As though we were expected. A good omen.

(They raise glasses to their lips as ABBY *steps down a couple of stairs and speaks.)*

ABBY. Who are you? What are you doing here?

(They both put glasses down. EINSTEIN *picks up his hat from armchair, ready to run for it.* JONATHAN *turns to* ABBY.*)*

JONATHAN. Why, Aunt Abby! Aunt Martha! It's Jonathan.

MARTHA (*frightened*). You get out of here.

JONATHAN (*crossing to* AUNTS). I'm Jonathan—your nephew, Jonathan.

ABBY. Oh, no, you're not. You're nothing like Jonathan, so don't pretend you are! You just get out of here!

JONATHAN (*crossing closer*). But I am Jonathan. And this (*Indicating* EINSTEIN.) is Dr. Einstein.

ABBY. And he's not Dr. Einstein either.

JONATHAN. Not Dr. Albert Einstein—Dr. Herman Einstein.

ABBY (*down another step*). Who are you? You're not our nephew, Jonathan.

JONATHAN (*peering at* ABBY's *outstretched hand*). I see you're still wearing the lovely garnet ring that Grandma Brewster bought in England. (ABBY *gasps, looks at ring.*) And you, Aunt Martha, still the high collar—to hide the scar where Grandfather's acid burned you.

(MARTHA's *hand goes to her throat. The* AUNTS *look at* JONATHAN. MARTHA *comes down a few steps to behind* ABBY. EINSTEIN *gets to* C.)

MARTHA. His voice is like Jonathan's.

ABBY (*stepping down to stage floor*). Have you been in an accident?

JONATHAN (*his hand goes to side of his face*). No— (*He clouds.*) —my face—Dr. Einstein is responsible for that. He's a plastic surgeon. He changes people's faces.

MARTHA (*comes down to* ABBY). But I've seen that face before. (*To* ABBY.) Abby, remember when we took the little Schultz boy to the movies and I was so frightened? It was that face!

(JONATHAN *grows tense and looks toward* EINSTEIN. EINSTEIN *crosses to* C. *and addresses* AUNTS.)

EINSTEIN. Easy, Chonny—easy! (*To* AUNTS.) Don't worry, ladies. The last five years I give Chonny three new faces. I give him another one right away. This last face —well, I saw that picture too—just before I operate. And I was intoxicated.

JONATHAN (*with a growing and dangerous intensity as he walks toward* EINSTEIN, *who backs* D. S.). You see, Doctor—you see what you've done to me. Even my own family—

EINSTEIN (*to calm him, as he is forced around* R. *stage*). Chonny—you're home —in this lovely house— (*To* AUNTS.) How often he tells me about Brooklyn—about this house—about his aunts that he lofes so much. (*To* JONATHAN.) They know you, Chonny. (*To* ABBY *as he leads her toward* JONATHAN.) You know it's Jonathan. Speak to him. Tell him so. (*He drifts above table to* D. L. *of it.*)

ABBY. Well—Jonathan—it's been a long time—what have you been doing all these years?

MARTHA (*has come to far* D. R.). Yes, Jonathan, where have you been?

JONATHAN (*recovering his composure*). Oh, England, South Africa, Australia,— the last five years Chicago. Dr. Einstein and I were in business there together

ABBY. Oh, we were in Chicago for the World's Fair.

MARTHA (*for want of something to say*). Yes—we found Chicago awfully warm.

EINSTEIN (*he has wandered above* U. L. *and down to below table*). Yah—it got hot for us too.

JONATHAN (*turning on the charm as he crosses above* ABBY, *placing himself between the* AUNTS.) Well, it's wonderful to be in Brooklyn again. And you—Abby—Martha you don't look a day older. Just as I remembered you—sweet—charming—hospitable. (*The* AUNTS *don't react too well to this charm.*) And dear Teddy— (*He indicates with his hand a lad of eight or ten.*) —did he get into politics? (*He turns to* EINSTEIN.) My little brother, Doctor, was determined to become President.

ABBY. Oh, Teddy's fine! Just fine! And Mortimer's well too.

JONATHAN (*a bit of a sneer*). I know about Mortimer. I've seen his picture at the head of his column. He's evidently fulfilled all the promise of his early nasty nature.

ABBY (*defensively*). We're very fond of Mortimer.

(There is a slight pause. Then MARTHA

speaks uneasily as she gestures toward R. *door.)*

MARTHA. Well, Jonathan, it's very nice to have seen you again.

JONATHAN (*expanding*). Bless you, Aunt Martha. (*Crosses and sits chair* R. *of table.*) It's good to be home again.

(*The* AUNTS *look at each other with dismay.*)

ABBY. Well, Martha, we mustn't let what's on the stove boil over. (*She starts to kitchen, then sees* MARTHA *isn't following. She crosses back and tugs at* MARTHA, *then crosses toward kitchen again.* MARTHA *follows to* C., *then speaks to* JONATHAN.*)

MARTHA. Yes. If you'll excuse us for a minute, Jonathan. Unless you're in a hurry to go somewhere.

(JONATHAN *looks at her balefully.* MARTHA *crosses around above table, takes bottle of wine and puts it back in sideboard, then exits with* ABBY. ABBY, *who has been waiting in kitchen doorway for* MARTHA, *closes door after them.* EINSTEIN *crosses* U. L. *around to behind* JONATHAN.*)

EINSTEIN. Well, Chonny, where do we go from here? We got to think fast. The police. The police have got pictures of that face. I got to operate on you right away. We got to find some place for that—and we got to find a place for Mr. Spenalzo too.

JONATHAN. Don't waste any worry on that rat.

EINSTEIN. But, Chonny, we got a hot stiff on our hands.

JONATHAN (*flinging hat onto sofa*). Forget Mr. Spenalzo.

EINSTEIN. But you can't leave a dead body in the rumble seat. You shouldn't have killed him, Chonny. He's a nice fellow— he gives us a lift—and what happens?

JONATHAN (*remembering bitterly*). He said I looked like Boris Karloff! (*He starts for* EINSTEIN.*) That's your work, Doctor. You did that to me!

EINSTEIN (*he's backed away to* D. L. *of table*). Now, Chonny—we find a place somewhere—I fix you up quick!

JONATHAN. Tonight!

EINSTEIN. Chonny—I got to eat first. I'm hungry—I'm weak.

(*The* AUNTS *enter from kitchen.* ABBY *comes to* JONATHAN *at* C. MARTHA *remains in kitchen doorway.*)

ABBY. Jonathan—we're glad that you remembered us and took the trouble to come in and say "Hello." But you were never happy in this house and we were never happy while you were in it—so, we've just come in to say good-bye.

JONATHAN (*takes a menacing step toward* ABBY. *Then decides to try the "charm" again*). Aunt Abby, I can't say that your feelings toward me come as a surprise. I've spent a great many hours regretting the many heartaches I must have given you as a boy.

ABBY. You were quite a trial to us, Jonathan.

JONATHAN. But my great disappointment is for Dr. Einstein. (EINSTEIN *is a little surprised.*) I promised him that no matter how rushed we were in passing through Brooklyn, I'd take the time to bring him here for one of Aunt Martha's home-cooked dinners.

(MARTHA *rises to this a bit, stepping* D. S.*)

MARTHA. Oh . . .

ABBY (*backing* U. L.*). I'm sorry. I'm afraid there wouldn't be enough.

MARTHA. Abby, it's a pretty good-sized pot roast.

JONATHAN (*how wonderful*). Pot roast!

MARTHA. I think the least we can do is to—

JONATHAN. Thank you, Aunt Martha! We'll stay to dinner.

ABBY (*backing to kitchen door and not at all pleased*). Well, we'll hurry it along.

MARTHA. Yes! (*She exits into kitchen.*)

ABBY (*stopping in doorway*). Oh, Jonathan, if you want to freshen up—why don't you use the washroom in Grandfather's old laboratory?

JONATHAN (*crossing to her*). It that still there?

ABBY. Oh, yes. Just as he left it. Well, I'll help Martha get things started—since we're all in a hurry. (*She exits into kitchen.*)

EINSTEIN (*stepping* U. S.). Well, we get a meal anyway.

JONATHAN (*above table*). Grandfather's laboratory! (*Looks upstairs*). And just as it was. Doctor, a perfect operating room.

EINSTEIN. Too bad we can't use it.

JONATHAN. After you've finished with me—Why, we could make a fortune here. The laboratory—that large ward in the attic—ten beds, Doctor—and Brooklyn is crying for your talents.

EINSTEIN. Vy vork yourself up, Chonny? Anyway, for Brooklyn I think we're a year too late.

JONATHAN. You don't know this town, Doctor. Practically everybody in Brooklyn needs a new face.

EINSTEIN. But so many of the old faces are locked up.

JONATHAN. A very small percentage—and the boys in Brooklyn are famous for paying generously to stay out of jail.

EINSTEIN. Take it easy, Chonny. Your aunts—they don't want us here.

JONATHAN. We're here for dinner, aren't we?

EINSTEIN. Yah—but after dinner?

JONATHAN (*crossing up to sofa*). Leave it to me, Doctor. I'll handle it. Why, this house'll be our headquarters for years.

EINSTEIN (*a pretty picture*). Oh, that would be beautiful, Chonny! This nice

quiet house. Those aunts of yours—what sweet ladies. I love them already. I get the bags, yah?

JONATHAN (*stopping him*). Doctor! We must wait until we're invited.

EINSTEIN. But you chust said that—

JONATHAN. We'll be invited.

EINSTEIN. And if they say no—?

JONATHAN. Doctor—two helpless old women—? (*He sits on sofa.*)

EINSTEIN (*takes bottle flask from hip pocket and unscrews cork as he crosses to window-seat*). It's like comes true a beautiful dream— Only I hope you're not dreaming. (*He stretches out on window-seat, taking a swig from bottle.*) It's so peaceful.

JONATHAN (*stretched out on sofa*). That's what makes this house so perfect for us—it's so peaceful.

(TEDDY *enters from cellar, blows a terrific blast on his bugle, as* JONATHAN *backs* R. TEDDY *marches to stairs and on up to first landing, as the two* MEN *look at his tropical garb with some astonishment.*)

TEDDY. CHARGE! (*He rushes up the stairs and off.*)

(JONATHAN *watches him from foot of stairs.* EINSTEIN, *sitting on window-seat, takes a hasty swig from his flask as the curtain comes down on the word CHARGE!*)

ACT TWO

SCENE: *The same. Later that night.*

JONATHAN, *with an after-dinner cigar, is occupying armchair* L. *of table, completely at his ease.* ABBY *and* MARTHA, *seated on window-seat, are giving him a nervous attention in the attitude of people who wish their guests would go home.* EINSTEIN *is relaxed and happy in chair* R. *of table. Dinner dishes have been cleared. There is a red cloth on table, with a saucer to serve as ash-tray for* JONATHAN. *The room is in order. All doors are closed, as are drapes over windows.*

JONATHAN. Yes, Aunties, those five years in Chicago were amongst the busiest and happiest of my life.

EINSTEIN. And from Chicago we go to South Bend, Indiana. (*He shakes his head as though he wishes they hadn't.*)

(JONATHAN *gives him a look.*)

JONATHAN. They wouldn't be interested in our experience in Indiana.

ABBY. Well, Jonathan, you've led a very interesting life, I'm sure—but we really shouldn't have allowed you to talk so late.

(She starts to rise. JONATHAN *seats her just by the tone of his voice.)*

JONATHAN. My meeting Dr. Einstein in London, I might say, changed the whole course of my life. You remember I had been in South Africa, in the diamond business—then Amsterdam, the diamond market. I wanted to go back to South Africa—and Dr. Einstein made it possible for me.

EINSTEIN. A good job, Chonny. *(To* AUNTS.*)* When we take off the bandages—his face look so different, the nurse had to introduce me.

JONATHAN. I loved that face. I still carry the picture with me. *(He produces snapshot-size picture from inside coat pocket, looks at it a moment, then hands it to* MARTHA. *She looks at it and hands it to* ABBY.*)*

ABBY. This looks more the way you used to look, but still I wouldn't know you.

JONATHAN. I think we'll go back to that face, Doctor.

EINSTEIN. Yah, it's safe now.

ABBY *(rising).* Well, I know you both want to get to—where you're going.

JONATHAN *(relaxing even more.)* My dear aunts—I'm so full of that delicious dinner I'm unable to move a muscle.

EINSTEIN *(relaxing too).* Yah, it's nice here.

MARTHA *(rises).* After all—it's very late and—

*(*TEDDY *enters on balcony wearing his solar topee, carrying a book, open, and another topee.)*

TEDDY *(descending stairs).* I found it! I found it!

JONATHAN. What did you find, Teddy?

TEDDY. The story of my life—my biography. *(He crosses above to* L. *of* EINSTEIN.*)* Here's the picture I was telling you about, General. *(He lays open book on table showing picture to* EINSTEIN.*)* Here we are, both of us. "President Roosevelt and General Goethals at Culebra Cut." That's me, General, and that's you.

*(*EINSTEIN *looks at picture.)*

EINSTEIN. My, how I've changed.

*(*TEDDY *looks at* EINSTEIN, *a little puzzled but makes adjustment.)*

TEDDY. Well, you see that picture hasn't been taken yet. We haven't even started work on Culebra Cut. We're still digging locks. And now, General, we will both go to Panama and inspect the new lock.

ABBY. No, Teddy—not to Panama.

EINSTEIN. We go some other time. Panama's a long way off.

TEDDY. Nonsense, it's just down in the cellar.

JONATHAN. The cellar?

MARTHA. We let him dig the Panama Canal in the cellar.

TEDDY *(severely).* General Goethals, as President of the United States, Commander-in-Chief of the Army and Navy and the man who gave you this job, I demand that you accompany me on the inspection of this new lock.

JONATHAN. Teddy! I think it's time you went to bed.

TEDDY. I beg your pardon! *(He crosses above to* L. *of* JONATHAN, *putting on his pinc-nez as he crosses.)* Who are you?

JONATHAN. I'm Woodrow Wilson. Go to bed.

TEDDY. No—you're not Wilson. But your face is familiar. Let me see— You're not anyone I know now. Perhaps later— On my hunting trip to Africa—yes, you look like someone I might meet in the jungle.

*(*JONATHAN *stiffens.* ABBY *crosses in front of* TEDDY, *getting between him and* JONATHAN.*)*

ABBY. It's your brother, Jonathan, dear.

MARTHA *(rising).* He's had his face changed.

TEDDY. So that's it—a nature faker!

ABBY. And perhaps you had better go to bed, Teddy—Jonathan and his friend have to go back to their hotel.

JONATHAN *(rising).* General Goethals, *(To* EINSTEIN.*)* inspect the canal. *(He crosses to* U. C.*)*

EINSTEIN (*rising*). All right, Mr. President. We go to Panama.

TEDDY. Bully! Bully! (*He crosses to cellar door, opens it.*) Follow me, General. (EINSTEIN *goes up to* L. *of* TEDDY. TEDDY *taps solar topee in* EINSTEIN's *hand, then taps his own head.*) It's down south you know. (*He exits downstairs.*)

(EINSTEIN *puts on topee, which is too large for him. Then turns in cellar doorway and speaks.*)

EINSTEIN. Well—bon voyage. (*He exits, closing door.*)

JONATHAN. Aunt Abby, I must correct your misapprehension. You spoke of our hotel. We have no hotel. We came directly here—

MARTHA. Well, there's a very nice little hotel just three blocks down the—

JONATHAN (*cutting her off*). Aunt Martha, this is my home.

ABBY. But, Jonathan, you can't stay here. We need our rooms.

JONATHAN. You need them?

ABBY. Yes, for our lodgers.

JONATHAN (*alarmed*). Are there lodgers in this house?

MARTHA. Well, not just now, but we plan to have some.

JONATHAN (*cutting her off again*). Then my old room is still free.

ABBY. But, Jonathan, there's no place for Dr. Einstein.

JONATHAN (*crosses below table, drops cigar ashes into saucer*). He'll share the room with me.

ABBY. No, Jonathan, I'm afraid you can't stay here.

(JONATHAN *is below table. He grinds cigar out in saucer, then starts toward* AUNTS. *They back around above table to* C., MARTHA *first.* JONATHAN *turns back and crosses below table to* ABBY *at* C.)

JONATHAN. Dr. Einstein and I need a place to sleep. You remembered, this afternoon, that as a boy I could be disagreeable. It wouldn't be very pleasant for any of us if—

MARTHA (R. C., *and frightened*). Perhaps we'd better let them stay here tonight—

ABBY. Well, just overnight, Jonathan.

JONATHAN. That's settled. Now, if you'll get my room ready—

MARTHA (*starting upstairs,* ABBY *following*). It only needs airing out.

ABBY. We keep it ready to show our lodgers. I think you and Dr. Einstein will find it comfortable.

(JONATHAN *follows them to first landing and leans on newel-post.* AUNTS *are on balcony.*)

JONATHAN. You have a most distinguished guest in Dr. Einstein. I'm afraid you don't appreciate his skill. But you will. In a few weeks you'll see me looking like a very different Jonathan.

MARTHA. He can't operate on you here.

JONATHAN (*ignoring*). When Dr. Einstein and I get organized—when we resume practice— Oh, I forgot to tell you. We're turning Grandfather's laboratory into an operating room. We expect to be quite busy.

ABBY. Jonathan, we will not let you turn this house into a hospital.

JONATHAN (*laughing*). A hospital—heavens no! It will be a beauty parlor.

(EINSTEIN *enters excitedly from cellar.*)

EINSTEIN. Hey, Chonny, down in the cellar— (*He sees* AUNTS *and stops.*)

JONATHAN. Dr. Einstein—my dear aunts have invited us to live with them.

EINSTEIN. Oh, you fixed it?

ABBY. Well, you're sleeping here tonight.

JONATHAN. Please get our room ready immediately.

MARTHA. Well—

ABBY. For tonight.

(*They exit through arch.* JONATHAN *comes to foot of stairs.*)

EINSTEIN. Chonny, when I go down in the cellar, what do you think I find?

JONATHAN. What?

EINSTEIN. The Panama Canal.

JONATHAN (*disgusted, crossing to* C.). The Panama Canal.

EINSTEIN. It just fits Mr. Spenalzo. It's a hole Teddy dug. Six feet long and four feet wide.

JONATHAN (*gets the idea. Opens cellar door and looks down*). Down there!

EINSTEIN. You'd think they knew we were bringing Mr. Spenalzo along. That's hospitality.

JONATHAN (*closing cellar door*). Rather a good joke on my aunts—their living in a house with a body buried in the cellar.

EINSTEIN. How do we get him in?

JONATHAN (*drops* D. S.). Yes. We can't just walk him through the door. (*He sees window in* L. *wall.*) We'll drive the car up between the house and the cemetery— then when they've gone to *bed,* we'll bring Mr. Spenalzo in through the window.

EINSTEIN (*taking out bottle flask*). Bed! Just think, we've got a bed tonight! (*He starts swigging.*)

JONATHAN (*grabbing his arm*). Easy, Doctor. Remember you're operating tomorrow. And this time you'd better be sober.

EINSTEIN. I fix you up beautiful.

JONATHAN. And if you don't— (*Gives* EINSTEIN *shove to door.*)

ABBY (*she and* MARTHA *enter on balcony*). Jonathan! Your room is ready.

JONATHAN. Then you can go to bed. We're moving the car up behind the house.

MARTHA. It's all right where it is—until morning.

JONATHAN (EINSTEIN *has opened door*). I don't want to leave it in the street— that might be against the law. (*He exits.*)

(EINSTEIN *follows him out, closing door.* ABBY *and* MARTHA *start downstairs and reach below table.*)

MARTHA. Abby, what are we going to do?

ABBY. Well, we're not going to let them stay more than one night in this house for one thing. What would the neighbors think? People coming in here with one face and going out with another.

(*She has reached table* D. S. MARTHA *is at her* R.*)*

MARTHA. What are we going to do about Mr. Hoskins?

ABBY (*crosses to window-seat.* MARTHA *follows*). Oh, Mr. Hoskins. It can't be very comfortable for him in there. And he's been so patient, the poor dear. Well, I think Teddy had better get Mr. Hoskins downstairs right away.

MARTHA (*adamant*). Abby—I will not invite Jonathan to the funeral services.

ABBY. Oh, no. We'll wait until they've gone to bed and then come down and hold the services.

(TEDDY *enters from cellar, gets book from table and starts* R. ABBY *stops him at* C.*)*

TEDDY. General Goethals was very pleased. He says the Canal is just the right size.

ABBY (*crosses to* C.) Teddy! Teddy, there's been another Yellow Fever victim.

TEDDY (*takes off pince-nez*). Dear me—this will be a shock to the General.

MARTHA (*stepping* R.). Then we mustn't tell him about it.

TEDDY (*crosses below* ABBY *to* MARTHA). But it's his department.

ABBY. No, we mustn't tell him, Teddy. It would just spoil his visit.

TEDDY. I'm sorry, Aunt Abby. It's out of my hands—he'll have to be told. Army regulations, you know.

ABBY. No, Teddy, we *must* keep it a secret.

MARTHA. Yes!

TEDDY (*he loves them*). A state secret?

ABBY. Yes, a state secret.

MARTHA. Promise?

TEDDY (*what a silly request*). You have the word of the President of the United States. Cross my heart and hope to die. (*He spits.*) Now let's see— (*Puts pince-nez on, then puts arms around both* AUNTS.) how are we going to keep it a secret?

ABBY. Well, Teddy, you go back down in the cellar and when I turn out the lights —when it's all dark—you come up and take the poor man down to the Canal. (*Urging him to cellar door, which he opens.*) Now go along, Teddy.

MARTHA (*following* U. S.). And we'll come down later and hold services.

TEDDY (*in doorway*). You may announce the President will say a few words. (*He starts, then turns back.*) Where is the poor devil?

MARTHA. He's in the window-seat.

TEDDY. It seems to be spreading. We've never had Yellow Fever there before. (*He exits, closing door.*)

ABBY. Martha, when Jonathan and Dr. Einstein come back, let's see if we can get them to go to bed right away.

MARTHA. Yes. Then by the time they're asleep, we'll be dressed for the funeral. (*Sudden thought.*) Abby, I've never even seen Mr. Hoskins.

ABBY. Oh, my goodness, that's right—you were out. Well, you just come right over and see him now. (*They go to window-seat,* ABBY *first.*) He's really very nice looking—considering he's a Methodist. (*As they go to lift window-seat,* JONATHAN *throws window open from outside with a bang.* AUNTS *scream and draw back.* JONATHAN *puts his head in through drapes.*)

JONATHAN. We're bringing—the luggage through here.

ABBY (*now at* C.). Jonathan, your room's waiting for you. You can go right up.

(*Two dusty bags and a large instrument case are passed through window by* EINSTEIN. JONATHAN *puts them on floor.*)

JONATHAN. I'm afraid we don't keep Brooklyn hours—but you two run along to bed.

ABBY. Now, you must be very tired, both of you—and we don't go to bed this early.

JONATHAN. Well, you should. It's time I came home to take care of you.

MARTHA. We weren't planning to go until—

JONATHAN (*the master*). Aunt Martha, did you hear me say go to bed! (AUNT MARTHA *starts upstairs as* EINSTEIN *comes in through window and picks up two bags.* JONATHAN *takes instrument case and puts it* U. S. *of window-seat.*) The instruments can go to the laboratory in the morning.

(EINSTEIN *starts upstairs.* JONATHAN *closes window.* MARTHA *is partway upstairs as* EINSTEIN *passes her.* ABBY *is at* R. C.) Now, then, we're all going to bed. (*He crosses to* C. *as* ABBY *breaks* D. R. *to light-switch.*)

ABBY. I'll wait till you're up, then turn out the lights.

(JONATHAN, *going upstairs, sees* EINSTEIN *pausing at balcony door.* MARTHA *is almost up to balcony.*)

JONATHAN. Another flight, Doctor. (*To* MARTHA.) Run along, Aunt Martha. (MARTHA *hurries into doorway.* EINSTEIN *goes through arch to third floor.* JONATHAN *continues on to* L. *end of balcony.* ABBY *is at light-switch.*) All right, Aunt Abby.

ABBY (*stalling. Looks toward cellar door*). I'll be right up.

JONATHAN. Now, Aunt Abby. (*Definite.*) Turn out the lights!

(ABBY *turns switch, plunging stage into darkness except for spot shining down stairway from arch.* ABBY *goes up stairs to her door where* MARTHA *is waiting. She takes a last frightened look at* JONATHAN *and exits.* MARTHA *closes door.* JONATHAN *goes off through arch, closing that door, blotting out the spot. A street light shines through main door* R. *on stage floor.* TEDDY *opens cellar door, then turns on cellar light, outlining him in the doorway. He crosses to window-seat and opens it—the window-seat cover giving out its usual rusty squeak. He reaches in and pulls Mr. Hoskins over his shoulder and, leaving window-seat open, crosses to cellar door and goes down into cellar with Mr. Hoskins. Closes door.* JONATHAN *and* EINSTEIN *come through arch. It is dark. They light matches and listen at the* AUNTS' *door for a moment.* EINSTEIN *speaks.*)

EINSTEIN. All right, Chonny.

(*The matches go out.* JONATHAN *lights another and they come down to foot of stairs.*)

JONATHAN. I'll get the window open. You go around and hand him through.

EINSTEIN. No, he's too heavy for me. You go outside and push—I stay here and pull. Then together we get him down to Panama.

JONATHAN. All right. *(He blows out match, crosses and opens door.* EINSTEIN *to his* L.*)* I'll take a look around outside the house. When I tap on the glass, you open the window.

EINSTEIN. All right. *(*JONATHAN *exits, closing door.* EINSTEIN *lights match and crosses* L. *He bumps into table and match goes out. He feels his way* L. *from there. We hear ejaculations and noise.* EINSTEIN *has fallen into window-seat. In window-seat he lights another match and slowly rises up to a sitting position and looks around. He blows out match and hauls himself out of window-seat, speaking.)* Who left dis open? Dummkopf! *(We hear the creak of the cover as he closes it. In the darkness we hear a tap on* L. *window.* EINSTEIN *opens it. Then in a hushed voice.)* Chonny? O.K. Allez Oop. Wait—wait a minute. You lost a leg somewhere.—Ach —now I got him— Come on—ugh— *(He falls on floor and there is a crash of a body and the sound of a "Sshhhh" from outside.)* That was me, Chonny. I schlipped.

JONATHAN *(voice)*. Be more careful.

(Pause.)

EINSTEIN. Well, his shoe came off. *(Pause.)* All right, Chonny. I got him! *(There is a knock at* R. *door.)* Chonny! Somebody at the door! Go quick. NO. I manage here —go quick!

(A second knock at door. A moment's silence and we hear the creak of window-seat as EINSTEIN *puts Mr. Spenalzo in Mr. Hoskins' place. A third knock, as* EINSTEIN *struggles with body. A fourth knock and then the creak of the window-seat as* EINSTEIN *closes it. He scurries around to beside desk, keeping low to avoid being seen through door.* ELAINE *enters* R.*, calling softly.)*

ELAINE. Miss Abby! Miss Martha! *(In the dim path of light she comes toward* C.*, calling toward balcony.)* Miss Abby! Miss Martha! *(Suddenly* JONATHAN *steps through door and closes it. The noise swings* ELAINE *around and she gasps.)* Uhhh! Who is it? Is that you, Teddy? *(*JONATHAN *comes toward her as she backs into chair* R. *of table.)* Who are you?

JONATHAN. Who are *you?*

ELAINE. I'm Elaine Harper—I live next door!

JONATHAN. Then what are you doing here?

ELAINE. I came over to see Miss Abby and Miss Martha.

JONATHAN *(to* EINSTEIN, *without turning.* EINSTEIN *has crept to light-switch after* JONATHAN'S *cross)*. Turn on the lights, Doctor. *(The lights go on.* ELAINE *gasps as she sees* JONATHAN *and sits in chair.* JONATHAN *looks at her for a moment.)* You chose rather an untimely moment for a social call. *(He crosses toward window-seat, looking for Spenalzo, but doesn't see him. He looks up, behind table. Looks out window, then comes back into the room.)*

ELAINE *(trying to summon courage)*. I think you'd better explain what *you're* doing here.

JONATHAN *(*D. L. *of table)*. We happen to live here.

ELAINE. You *don't* live here. I'm in this house every day and I've never seen you before. *(Frightened.)* Where are Miss Abby and Miss Martha? What have you done to them?

JONATHAN *(a step to below table)*. Perhaps we'd better introduce ourselves. This— *(Indicating.)* —is Dr. Einstein.

ELAINE *(looks at* EINSTEIN*)*. Dr. Einstein? *(She turns back to* JONATHAN. EINSTEIN, *behind her back, is gesturing to* JONATHAN *the whereabouts of Spenalzo.)*

JONATHAN. A surgeon of great distinction— *(He looks under table for Spenalzo, and not finding him—)* —and something of a magician.

ELAINE. And I suppose you're going to tell me you're Boris Kar—

JONATHAN. I'm Jonathan Brewster.

ELAINE *(drawing back almost with fright)*. Oh—you're Jonathan!

JONATHAN. I see you've heard of me.

*(*EINSTEIN *drifts to front of sofa.)*

ELAINE. Yes—just this afternoon for the first time.

JONATHAN (*stepping toward her*). And what did they say about me?

ELAINE. Only that there was another brother named Jonathan—that's all that was said. (*Calming.*) Well, that explains everything. Now that I know who you are— (*Running to* R. *door.*) I'll be running along back home. (*The door is locked. She turns to* JONATHAN.) If you'll kindly unlock the door.

(JONATHAN *crosses to her, then, before reaching her, he turns* D. S. *to* R. *door and unlocks it.* EINSTEIN *drifts down to chair* R. *of table. As* JONATHAN *opens door partway,* ELAINE *starts toward it. He turns and stops her with a gesture.*)

JONATHAN. "That explains everything"? Just what did you mean by that? Why did you come here at this time of night?

ELAINE. I thought I saw someone prowling around the house. I suppose it was you.

(JONATHAN *closes door and locks it, leaving key in lock.*)

JONATHAN. You thought you saw someone prowling around the house?

ELAINE. Yes—weren't you outside? Isn't that your car?

JONATHAN. You saw someone at the car?

ELAINE. Yes.

JONATHAN (*coming toward her as she backs* U. L.). What else did you see?

ELAINE. Just someone walking around the house to the car.

JONATHAN. What else did you see?

ELAINE. Just that—that's all. That's why I came over here. I wanted to tell Miss Abby to call the police. But if it was you, and that's your car, I don't need to bother Miss Abby. I'll be running along. (*She takes a step toward door above* JONATHAN. *He steps in her path.*)

JONATHAN. What was the man doing at the car?

ELAINE (*excited*). I don't know. You see I was on my way over here.

JONATHAN (*forcing her as she backs* L.). I think you're lying.

EINSTEIN (*crosses to* U. R. C.). I think she tells the truth, Chonny. We let her go now, huh?

JONATHAN (*still forcing her* L.). I think she's lying. Breaking into a house this time of night. I think she's dangerous. She shouldn't be allowed around loose.

(*He seizes* ELAINE's *arm. She screams.*)

ELAINE. Take your hands off me—

JONATHAN. Doctor—

(*As* EINSTEIN *starts* L., TEDDY *enters from cellar, shutting door. He looks at* JONATHAN L., *then speaks to* EINSTEIN R.)

TEDDY (*simply*). It's going to be a private funeral. (*He goes up stairs to first landing.* ELAINE *crosses to desk, dragging* JONATHAN *with her.*)

ELAINE. Teddy! Teddy! Tell these men who I am.

(TEDDY *turns and looks at her.*)

TEDDY. That's my daughter—Alice. (*He cries "CHARGE!" Dashes up stairs and exits.*)

ELAINE (*struggling to get away from* JONATHAN *and dragging him to* R. C.). No! No! Teddy!

(JONATHAN *has* ELAINE's *arm twisted in back of her, his other hand is over her mouth.*)

JONATHAN. Doctor! Your handkerchief! (*As* EINSTEIN *hands him a handkerchief,* JONATHAN *releases his hand from* ELAINE's *mouth to take it. She screams. He puts his hand over her mouth again. Spies the cellar door and speaks to* EINSTEIN.) The cellar!

(EINSTEIN *runs and opens cellar door. Then he runs back and turns off light-switch, putting stage in darkness.* JONATHAN *pushes* ELAINE *through cellar doorway.* EINSTEIN *runs back and down cellar stairs with* ELAINE. JONATHAN *shuts door, remaining on stage as the* AUNTS *enter on balcony above in their mourning clothes. Everything is in complete darkness except for street lamp.*)

ABBY. What's the matter?

MARTHA. What's happening down there?

(MARTHA *shuts her door and* ABBY *puts on*

lights from switch on balcony. They look down at the room a moment, then come downstairs, speaking as they come.)

ABBY. What's the matter? *(Reaching foot of stairs as she sees* JONATHAN.*)* What are you doing?

JONATHAN. We caught a burglar—a sneak thief. Go back to your room.

ABBY. We'll call the police.

JONATHAN. We've called the police. We'll handle this. Go back to your room. Do you hear me?

(The doorbell rings, followed by several knocks. ABBY *runs and opens* R. *door.* MORTIMER *enters with suitcase. At the same time,* ELAINE *runs out of cellar and into* MORTIMER's *arms.* JONATHAN *makes a grab for* ELAINE *but misses. This leaves him* D. S. C. EINSTEIN *sneaks* D. S. *behind* JONATHAN.*)*

ELAINE. Mortimer! *(He drops suitcase.)* Where have you been?

MORTIMER. To the Nora Bayes Theatre and I should have known better. *(He sees* JONATHAN.*)* My God!—I'm still there.

*(*ABBY *is at* R. *of* MORTIMER.*)*

ABBY. This is your brother Jonathan—and this is Dr. Einstein.

*(*MORTIMER *surveys his* AUNTS *all dressed in black.)*

MORTIMER. I know this isn't a nightmare, but what is it?

JONATHAN. I've come back home, Mortimer.

MORTIMER *(looking at him, and then to* ABBY*).* Who did you say this was?

ABBY. It's your brother Jonathan. He's had his face changed. Dr. Einstein performed the operation.

MORTIMER *(taking a closer look at* JONATHAN*).* Jonathan! Jonathan, you always were a horror, but do you have to look like one?

*(*JONATHAN *takes a step toward him.* EINSTEIN *pulls on his sleeve.* ELAINE *and* MARTHA *draw back to desk.)*

EINSTEIN. Easy, Chonny! Easy.

JONATHAN. Mortimer, have you forgotten the things I used to do to you when we were boys? Remember the time you were tied to the bedpost—the needles under your fingernails—?

MORTIMER. By God, it is Jonathan.—Yes, I remember. I remember you as the most detestable, vicious, venomous form of animal life I ever knew.

*(*JONATHAN *grows tense.* ABBY *steps between them.)*

ABBY. Now don't you two boys start quarrelling again the minute you've seen each other.

MORTIMER *(crosses to door, opens it).* There won't be any fight, Aunt Abby. Jonathan, you're not wanted here—get out!

JONATHAN. Dr. Einstein and I have been invited to stay.

MORTIMER. Not in this house.

ABBY. Just for tonight.

MORTIMER. I don't want him anywhere near me.

ABBY. But we did invite them for tonight, and it wouldn't be very nice to go back on our word.

MORTIMER *(unwillingly).* All right, tonight. But the first thing in the morning —out! *(He picks up his suitcase.)* Where are they sleeping?

ABBY. We put them in Jonathan's old room.

MORTIMER. That's my old room. *(Starts upstairs.)* I'm sleeping in that room. I'm here to stay.

MARTHA. Oh, Mortimer, I'm so glad.

EINSTEIN. Chonny, we sleep down here.

MORTIMER. You bet your life you sleep down here.

EINSTEIN *(to* JONATHAN*).* You sleep on the sofa and I sleep on the window-seat.

(At the mention of window-seat, MORTIMER *has reached the landing; after hanging his hat on hall tree, he turns and comes slowly downstairs, speaking as he reaches the floor and crossing over to window-seat. He drops back at* U. S. *end of window-seat.)*

MORTIMER. The window-seat! Oh, well, let's not argue about it. That window-seat's good enough for me for tonight. I'll sleep on the window-seat. (*As* MORTIMER *crosses above table,* EINSTEIN *makes a gesture as though to stop him from going to window-seat, but he's too late. He turns to* JONATHAN *as* MORTIMER *sits on window-seat.*)

EINSTEIN. You know, Chonny—all this argument--it makes me think of Mr. Spenalzo.

JONATHAN. Spenalzo! (*He steps* U. S. *looking around for Spenalzo again. Realizing it would be best for them to remain downstairs, he speaks to* MORTIMER.) Well, now, Mortimer— It really isn't necessary to inconvenience you like this—we'll sleep down here.

MORTIMER (*rising*). Jonathan, your sudden consideration for me is very unconvincing.

EINSTEIN (*goes upstairs to landing*). Come along, Chonny. We get our things out of the room, eh?

MORTIMER. Don't bother, Doctor!

JONATHAN. By the way, Doctor, I've completely lost track of Mr. Spenalzo.

MORTIMER. Who's this Mr. Spenalzo?

EINSTEIN (*from landing*). Just a friend of ours Chonny's been looking for.

MORTIMER. Well, don't bring anyone else in here!

EINSTEIN. It's all right, Chonny. While we pack I tell you all about it. (*He goes up and through arch.* JONATHAN *starts upstairs.*)

ABBY (*dropping* D. S.). Mortimer, you don't have to sleep down here. I can go in with Martha and you can take my room.

JONATHAN (*he has reached the balcony*). No trouble at all, Aunt Abby. We'll be packed in a few minutes. And then you can have the room, Mortimer. (*He exits through arch.*)

(MORTIMER *crosses up to sofa.* MARTHA *crosses to above armchair at* L. *of table and as* MORTIMER *speaks she picks up sport shoe belonging to Spenalzo, that* EINSTEIN *put there in blackout scene, unnoticed by anyone. She pretends to dust hem of her dress.*)

MORTIMER. You're just wasting your time —I told you I'm sleeping down here.

(ELAINE *leaps up from stool into* MORTIMER'S *arms.*)

ELAINE. Mortimer!

MORTIMER. What's the matter with you. dear?

ELAINE (*semi-hysterical*). I've almost been killed.

MORTIMER. You've almost been— (*He looks quickly at the* AUNTS.) Abby! Martha!

MARTHA. No! It was Jonathan.

ABBY. He mistook her for a sneak-thief.

ELAINE. No, it was more than that. He's some kind of maniac. Mortimer, I'm afraid of him.

MORTIMER. Why, darling, you're trembling. (*Seats her on sofa. To* AUNTS.) Have you got any smelling salts?

MARTHA. No, but do you think some hot tea, or coffee—?

MORTIMER. Coffee. Make some for me, too —and some sandwiches. I haven't had any dinner.

MARTHA. We'll make something for both of you.

(MORTIMER *starts to question* ELAINE *as* ABBY *takes off her hat and gloves and puts them on sideboard. Talking to* MARTHA *at the same time.*)

ABBY. Martha, we can leave our hats downstairs here, now.

MORTIMER. You weren't going out somewhere, were you? Do you know what time it is? It's after twelve. (*The word twelve rings a bell.*) TWELVE! (*He turns to* ELAINE.) Elaine, you've got to go home!

ELAINE. Whaa-t?

ABBY. Why, you wanted some sandwiches for you both. It won't take a minute. (*She exits into kitchen.*)

(MORTIMER *is looking at* ELAINE *with his back to* MARTHA. MARTHA *crosses to him with shoe in hand by her* U. S. *side.*)

MARTHA. Why, don't you remember—we wanted to celebrate your engagement? (*She punctuates the word "engagement" by pointing the shoe at* MORTIMER'S *back. She looks at the shoe in wonderment.*

Wondering how that shoe ever got in her hand. She stares at it a moment [the other two do not see it, of course], then puts it on top of the table. Finally dismissing it she turns to MORTIMER *again.)* That's what we'll do, dear. We'll make a nice supper for both of you. *(She starts out kitchen door, then turns back.)* And we'll open a bottle of wine! *(She exits kitchen door.)*

MORTIMER *(vaguely).* All right. *(Suddenly changes his mind and runs to kitchen door.)* No WINE! *(He closes the door and comes back to* C. *as* ELAINE *rises from the sofa to him. She is still very upset.)*

ELAINE. Mortimer! What's going on in this house?

MORTIMER *(suspicious).* What do you mean—what's going on in this house?

ELAINE. You were supposed to take me to dinner and the theatre tonight—you called it off. You asked me to marry you—I said I would—and five minutes later you threw me out of the house. Tonight, just after your brother tries to strangle me, you want to chase me home. Now, listen, Mr. Brewster—before I go home, I want to know where I stand. Do you love me?

MORTIMER *(taking her hands).* I love you very much, Elaine. In fact I love you so much I can't marry you.

ELAINE. Have you suddenly gone crazy?

MORTIMER. I don't think so but it's just a matter of time. *(They both sit on sofa as* MORTIMER *begins to explain.)* You see, insanity runs in my family. *(He looks upstairs and toward kitchen.)* It practically gallops. That's why I can't marry you, dear.

ELAINE. Now wait a minute, you've got to do better than that.

MORTIMER. No, dear—there's a strange taint in the Brewster blood. If you really knew my family it's—well—it's what you'd expect if Strindberg had written *Hellzapoppin.*

ELAINE. Now just because Teddy is a little—

MORTIMER. No, it goes way back. The first Brewster—the one who come over on the Mayflower. You know in those days the Indians used to scalp the settlers—he used to scalp the Indians.

ELAINE. Mortimer, that's ancient history—

MORTIMER. No, the whole family . . . *(He rises and points to a picture of Grandfather over the sideboard.)* Take my grandfather—he tried his patent medicines out on dead people to be sure he wouldn't kill them.

ELAINE. He wasn't so crazy. He made a million dollars.

MORTIMER. And then there's Jonathan. You just said he was a maniac—he tried to kill you.

ELAINE *(rises, crosses to him).* But he's your brother, not you. I'm in love with you.

MORTIMER. And there's Teddy, too. You *know* Teddy. He thinks he's Roosevelt. No, dear, no Brewster should marry. I realize now that if I'd met my father in time I'd have stopped him.

ELAINE. Now, darling, all this doesn't prove *you're* crazy. Look at your aunts—they're Brewsters, aren't they?—and the sanest, sweetest people I've ever known.

*(*MORTIMER *crosses above table to window-seat, speaking as he goes.)*

MORTIMER. Well, even they have their peculiarities.

ELAINE *(turning and drifting* R.*).* Yes, but what lovely peculiarities!—Kindness, generosity—human sympathy—

*(*MORTIMER *sees* ELAINE'S *back is to him. He lifts window-seat to take a peek, and sees Mr. Spenalzo instead of Mr. Hoskins. He puts window-seat down again and staggers to table, and leans on it.)*

MORTIMER *(to himself).* There's another one!

ELAINE *(turning to* MORTIMER*).* Oh, Mortimer, there are plenty of others. You can't tell me anything about your aunts.

MORTIMER. I'm not going to. *(Crossing to her.)* Look, Elaine, you've got to go home. Something very important has just come up.

ELAINE. Up, from where? We're here alone together.

MORTIMER. I know I'm acting irrationally, but just put it down to the fact that I'm a mad Brewster.

ELAINE. If you think you're going to get out of this by pretending you're insane—you're crazy. Maybe you're not going to marry me, but I'm going to marry you. I love you, you dope.

MORTIMER (urging her to R. door). Well, if you love me you will get the hell out of here!

ELAINE. Well, at least take me home, won't you, I'm afraid.

MORTIMER. Afraid! A little walk through the cemetery?

(ELAINE crosses to door, then changing tactics, turns to MORTIMER.)

ELAINE. Mortimer, will you kiss me good night?

MORTIMER (holding out arms). Of course, dear. (What MORTIMER plans to be a desultory peck, ELAINE turns into a production number. He comes out of it with no less of poise.) Good night, dear. I'll call you up in a day or two.

ELAINE (walks to R. door in a cold fury, opens it and turns to MORTIMER). You—you critic! (She slams door after her.)

(MORTIMER looks at the door helplessly then turns and stalks to the kitchen door.)

MORTIMER (in doorway). Aunt Abby! Aunt Martha! Come in here!

ABBY (offstage). We'll be in in a minute, dear.

MORTIMER. Come in here now! (He stands down by U. S. end of window-seat.)

(ABBY enters from kitchen.)

ABBY. Yes, dear, what is it? Where's Elaine?

MORTIMER. I thought you promised me not to let anyone in this house while I was gone!

(The following speeches overlap.)

ABBY. Well, Jonathan just walked in—

MORTIMER. I don't mean Jonathan—

ABBY. And Dr. Einstein was with him—

MORTIMER. I don't mean Dr. Einstein. Who's that in the window-seat?

ABBY. We told you—Mr. Hoskins.

(MORTIMER throws open the window-seat and steps back U. L.)

MORTIMER. It is not Mr. Hoskins.

(ABBY, a little puzzled, walks to window-seat and looks in at D. S. end then speaks very simply.)

ABBY. Who can that be?

MORTIMER (R. of ABBY). Are you trying to tell me you've never seen this man before?

ABBY. I certainly am. Why, this is a fine how do you do! It's getting so anybody thinks he can walk into this house.

MORTIMER. Now Aunt Abby, don't you try to get out of this. That's another one of your gentlemen!

ABBY. Mortimer, how can you say such a thing! That man's an impostor! And if he came here to be buried in our cellar he's mistaken.

MORTIMER. Oh, Aunt Abby, you admitted to me that you put Mr. Hoskins in the window-seat.

ABBY. Yes, I did.

MORTIMER. Well, this man couldn't have just got the idea from Mr. Hoskins. By the way—where is Mr. Hoskins? (He looks toward cellar door.)

(ABBY crosses above table to U. C.)

ABBY. He must have gone to Panama.

MORTIMER. Oh, you buried him?

ABBY. No, not yet. He's just down there waiting for the services, poor dear. We haven't had a minute what with Jonathan in the house. (At the mention of JONATHAN's name, MORTIMER closes the window-seat.) Oh, dear. We've always wanted to hold a double funeral, (Crossing to kitchen door.) but I will not read services over a total stranger.

MORTIMER (going up to her). A stranger! Aunt Abby, how can I believe you? There are twelve men in the cellar and you admit you poisoned them.

ABBY. Yes, I did. But you don't think I'd stoop to telling a fib. Martha! (She exits into kitchen.)

(At the same time JONATHAN enters through the arch onto balcony and comes down quickly to foot of stairs. MORTIMER *crosses to* D. R. C. JONATHAN *sees him and crosses to him.*)

JONATHAN. Oh, Mortimer—I'd like to have a word with you.

MORTIMER (*standing up to him*). A word's about all you'll have time for, Jonathan, because I've decided you and your Doctor friend are going to have to get out of this house just as quickly as possible.

JONATHAN (*smoothly*). I'm glad you recognize the fact that you and I can't live under the same roof—but you've arrived at the wrong solution. Take your suitcase and get out! (*He starts to cross above* MORTIMER, *anxious to get to the window-seat, but* MORTIMER *makes big sweep around above table and comes back to him at* D. S. C.)

MORTIMER. Jonathan!—You're beginning to bore me. You've played your one night stand in Brooklyn—move on!

JONATHAN. My dear Mortimer, just because you've graduated from the back fence to the typewriter, don't think you've grown up. . . . (*He takes a sudden step* U. S. *around* MORTIMER *and gets to the window-seat and sits.*) I'm staying, and you're leaving—and I mean now!

MORTIMER (*crossing to him*). If you think I can be frightened—if you think there's anything I fear—

JONATHAN (*he rises, they stand facing each other*). I've lived a strange life, Mortimer. But it's taught me one thing—to be afraid of nothing! (*They glare at each other with equal courage when* ABBY *marches in from the kitchen, followed by* MARTHA.)

ABBY. Martha, just look and see what's in that window-seat.

(*Both* MEN *throw themselves on the window-seat simultaneously.* JONATHAN D. S. *end.*)

MORTIMER *and* JONATHAN. Now, Aunt Abby!

(MORTIMER *turns his head slowly to* JONATHAN, *light dawning on his face. He rises with smiling assurance.*)

MORTIMER. Jonathan, let Aunt Martha see what's in the window-seat (JONATHAN *freezes dangerously.* MORTIMER *crosses below table up to* ABBY.) Aunt Abby, I owe

you an apology. (*He kisses her on forehead.*) I have very good news for you. Jonathan is leaving. He's taking Dr. Einstein and their cold companion with him. (JONATHAN *rises but holds his ground.*) Jonathan, you're my brother. You're a Brewster. I'm going to give you a chance to get away and take the evidence with you—you can't ask for more than that. (JONATHAN *doesn't move.*) Very well,—in that case I'll have to call the police. (MORTIMER *crosses to phone and picks it up.*)

JONATHAN. Don't reach for that telephone. (*He crosses to* L. *of* MORTIMER.) Are you still giving me orders after seeing what's happened to Mr. Spenalzo?

MARTHA (*she's above table*). Spenalzo?

ABBY (U. C.). I knew he was a foreigner.

JONATHAN. Remember what happened to Mr. Spenalzo can happen to you too.

(*There is a knock on* R. *door.* ABBY *crosses and opens it and* OFFICER O'HARA *sticks his head in.*)

O'HARA. Hello, Miss Abby.

ABBY. Oh, Officer O'Hara. Is there something we can do for you?

(MORTIMER *puts phone down and drifts down close to* O'HARA. JONATHAN *turns* L.)

O'HARA. I saw your lights on and thought there might be sickness in the house. (*He sees* MORTIMER.) Oh, you got company—I'm sorry I disturbed you.

MORTIMER (*taking* O'HARA *by the arm*). No, no, come in.

ABBY. Yes, come in.

MARTHA (*crossing to door*). Come right in, Officer O'Hara. (MORTIMER *leads* O'HARA *in a couple of steps and shuts door.* ABBY *crosses back to* U. S. C. MARTHA *is near desk.* JONATHAN *is in front of sofa* R. *of* ABBY. MARTHA, *to* O'HARA.) This is our nephew, Mortimer.

O'HARA. Pleased to meet you.

(JONATHAN *starts toward kitchen.*)

ABBY (*stopping* JONATHAN). And this is another nephew, Jonathan.

O'HARA (*crosses below* MORTIMER *and gestures to* JONATHAN *with his night stick*)

Pleased to make your acquaintance. (JONA-THAN *ignores him.* O'HARA *speaks to* AUNTS.) Well, it must be nice havin' your nephews visitin' you. Are they going to stay with you for a bit?

MORTIMER. I'm staying. My brother Jona-aathan is just leaving.

(JONATHAN *starts for stairs.* O'HARA *stops him.*)

O'HARA. I've met you here before, haven't I?

ABBY. I'm afraid not. Jonathan hasn't been home for years.

O'HARA. Your face looks familiar to me. Maybe I seen a picture of you somewheres.

JONATHAN. I don't think so. (*He hurries up stairs.*)

MORTIMER. Yes, Jonathan, I'd hurry if I were you. Your things are all packed any-way, aren't they?

O'HARA. Well, you'll be wanting to say your good-byes. I'll be running along.

MORTIMER. What's the rush? I'd like to have you stick around until my brother goes.

(JONATHAN *exits through arch.*)

O'HARA. I just dropped in to make sure everything was all right.

MORTIMER. We're going to have some cof-fee in a minute. Won't you join us?

ABBY. Oh, I forgot the coffee. (*She goes out to kitchen.*)

MARTHA (*crossing to kitchen door*). Well, I'd better make some more sandwiches. I ought to know your appetite by this time, Officer O'Hara. (*She goes out to kitchen as* O'HARA *follows as far as* C.)

O'HARA. Don't bother. I'm due to ring in in a few minutes.

MORTIMER. You can have a cup of coffee with us. My brother will be gone soon. (*He leads* O'HARA *below table to armchair.*) Sit down.

O'HARA. Say—ain't I seen a photograph of your brother around here some place?

MORTIMER. I don't think so. (*He sits* R. *of table.*)

O'HARA. He certainly reminds me of some-body.

MORTIMER. He looks like somebody you've probably seen in the movies.

O'HARA. I never go to the movies. I hate 'em! My mother says the movies is a bas-tard art.

MORTIMER. Yes, it's full of them.—Your, er, mother said that?

O'HARA. Yeah. My mother was an actress—a stage actress. Perhaps you heard of her—Peaches Latour.

MORTIMER. It sounds like a name I've seen on a program. What did she play?

O'HARA. Well, her big hit was "Mutt and Jeff." Played it for three years. I was born on tour—the third season.

MORTIMER. You were?

O'HARA. Yep. Sioux City, Iowa. I was born in the dressing room at the end of the second act, and Mother made the finale.

MORTIMER. What a trouper! There must be a good story in your mother—you know, I write about the theatre.

O'HARA. You do? Say!—you're not Mor-timer Brewster, the dramatic critic!

MORTIMER. Yes.

O'HARA. Well, I certainly am glad to meet you. (*He moves his hat and stick prepara-tory to shaking hands with* MORTIMER. *He also picks up the sport shoe which* MARTHA *has left on the table. He looks at it just for a split second and puts it on the* D. S. *end of table.* MORTIMER *sees it and stares at it.*) Say, Mr. Brewster—we're in the same line of business.

MORTIMER (*still intent on shoe*). We are?

O'HARA. Yeah. I'm a playwright. Oh, this being on the police force is just temporary.

MORTIMER. How long have you been on the force?

O'HARA. Twelve years. I'm collecting mate-rial for a play.

MORTIMER. I'll bet it's a honey.

O'HARA. Well, it ought to be. With all the drama I see being a cop. Mr. Brewster—you got no idea what goes on in Brooklyn.

MORTIMER. I think I have. (*He puts the*

shoe under his chair, then looks at his watch, then looks toward balcony.)

O'HARA. Say, what time you got?

MORTIMER. Ten after one.

O'HARA. Gee, I gotta ring in. (He starts for R. door but MORTIMER stops him at C.)

MORTIMER. Wait a minute, O'Hara. On that play of yours—I may be able to help you. (Sits him in chair R.)

O'HARA (ecstasy). You would! (Rises.) Say, it was fate my walking in here tonight. Look—I'll tell you the plot!

(At this point JONATHAN enters on the balcony followed by DR. EINSTEIN. They each have a bag. At the same moment ABBY enters from the kitchen. Helpful as the cop has been, MORTIMER does not want to listen to his plot. As he backs away from him he speaks to JONATHAN as they come down stairs.)

MORTIMER. Oh, you're on your way, eh? Good! You haven't got much time, you know.

ABBY (U. L.). Well, everything's just about ready. (Sees JONATHAN and EINSTEIN at foot of stairs.) Oh, you leaving now, Jonathan? Good-bye. Good-bye, Dr. Einstein. (She sees instrument case above window-seat.) Oh, doesn't this case belong to you?

(This reminds MORTIMER of Mr. Spenalzo, also.)

MORTIMER. Yes, Jonathan—you can't go without all your things. (Now to get rid of O'HARA. He turns to him.) Well, O'Hara, it was nice meeting you. I'll see you again and we'll talk about your play.

O'HARA (refusing to leave). Oh, I'm not leaving now, Mr. Brewster.

MORTIMER. Why not?

O'HARA. Well, you just offered to help me with my play, didn't you? You and me are going to write my play together.

MORTIMER. I can't do that, O'Hara—I'm not a creative writer.

O'HARA. I'll do the creating. You just put the words to it.

MORTIMER. But, O'Hara—

O'HARA. No, sir, Mr. Brewster. I ain't leaving this house till I tell you the plot.

(He crosses and sits on window-seat.)

JONATHAN (starting for R. door). In that case, Mortimer . . . we'll be running along.

MORTIMER. Don't try that. You can't go yet. You've got to take everything with you, you know. (He turns and sees O'HARA on window-seat and runs to him.) Look, O'Hara, you run along now, eh? My brother's just going—

O'HARA. I can wait. I've been waiting twelve years.

(MARTHA enters from kitchen with a tray of coffee and sandwiches.)

MARTHA. I'm sorry I was so long.

MORTIMER. Don't bring that in here. O'Hara, would you join us for a bite in the kitchen?

MARTHA. The kitchen?

ABBY (to MARTHA). Jonathan's leaving.

MARTHA. Oh. Well, that's nice. Come along, Officer O'Hara. (She exits to kitchen.)

(O'HARA gets to kitchen doorway as ABBY speaks.)

ABBY. Sure you don't mind eating in the kitchen, Mr. O'Hara?

O'HARA. And where else would you eat?

ABBY. Good-bye, Jonathan, nice to have seen you again.

(O'HARA exits to kitchen, followed by ABBY. MORTIMER crosses to kitchen doorway and shuts door, then turns to JONATHAN.)

MORTIMER. I'm glad you came back to Brooklyn, Jonathan, because it gives me a chance to throw you out—and the first one out is your boy friend, Mr. Spenalzo. (He lifts up window-seat. As he does so, O'HARA, sandwich in hand, enters from kitchen. MORTIMER drops window-seat.)

O'HARA. Look, Mr. Brewster, we can talk in here.

MORTIMER (pushing him into kitchen). Coming right out.

JONATHAN. I might have known you'd grow up to write a play with a policeman.

MORTIMER (from kitchen doorway). Get going now—all three of you. (He exits, shutting door.)

(JONATHAN puts bag down and crosses to window-seat.)

JONATHAN. Doctor, this affair between my brother and me has got to be settled.

EINSTEIN *(crossing to window-seat for instrument case and bringing it back to foot of stairs).* Now, Chonny, we got trouble enough. Your brother gives us a chance to get away—what more could you ask?

JONATHAN. You don't understand. *(He lifts window-seat.)* This goes back a good many years.

EINSTEIN *(foot of stairs).* Now, Chonny, let's get going.

JONATHAN *(harshly).* We're not going. We're going to sleep right here tonight.

EINSTEIN. With a cop in the kitchen and Mr. Spenalzo in the window-seat.

JONATHAN. That's all he's got on us. *(Puts window-seat down.)* We'll take Mr. Spenalzo down and dump him in the bay, and come right back here.—Then if he tries to interfere— *(He crosses to C. EINSTEIN crosses to L. of him and faces him.)*

EINSTEIN. Now, Chonny.

JONATHAN. Doctor, you know when I make up my mind—

EINSTEIN. Yeah—when you make up your mind, you lose your head. Brooklyn ain't a good place for you.

JONATHAN *(peremptorily).* Doctor!

EINSTEIN. O.K. We got to stick together. *(He crosses to bags.)* Some day we get stuck together. If we're coming back here do we got to take these with us?

JONATHAN. No. Leave them here. Hide them in the cellar. Move fast! *(He moves to bags to L. end of sofa as EINSTEIN goes down cellar with instrument case.)* Spenalzo can go out the same way he came in! *(He kneels on window-seat and looks out. Then as he starts to lift window-seat, EINSTEIN comes in from the cellar with some excitement.)*

EINSTEIN. Hey, Chonny, come quick!

JONATHAN *(crossing to him).* What's the matter?

EINSTEIN. You know that hole in the cellar?

JONATHAN. Yes.

EINSTEIN. We got an *ace* in the hole. Come on I show you. *(They both exit into cellar.* JONATHAN *shuts door.)*

(MORTIMER enters from kitchen, sees their bags still there. He opens window-seat and sees Spenalzo. Then he puts his head out window and yells.)

MORTIMER. Jonathan! Jonathan! *(JONA-THAN comes through cellar door unnoticed by MORTIMER and crosses to back of him.* EINSTEIN *comes down into C. of room.)* Jonathan!

JONATHAN *(quietly).* Yes, Mortimer.

MORTIMER *(leaping backwards to below table).* Where have you two been? I thought I told you to get—

JONATHAN. We're not going.

MORTIMER. Oh, you're not? You think I'm not serious about this, eh? Do you want O'Hara to know what's in that window-seat?

JONATHAN. We're staying here.

MORTIMER *(crossing around above table to kitchen door).* All right! You asked for it. This gets me rid of you and Officer O'Hara at the same time. *(Opens kitchen door, yells out.)* Officer O'Hara, come in here!

JONATHAN. If you tell O'Hara what's in the window-seat, I'll tell him what's down in the cellar.

(MORTIMER closes kitchen door quickly.)

MORTIMER. The cellar?

JONATHAN. There's an elderly gentleman down there who seems to be very dead

MORTIMER. What were you doing down in the cellar?

EINSTEIN. What's *he* doing down in the cellar?

(O'HARA's voice is heard offstage.)

O'HARA. No, thanks, ma'am. They were fine. I've had plenty.

JONATHAN. Now what are you going to say to O'Hara?

(O'HARA walks in kitchen door.)

O'HARA. Say, Mr. Brewster, your aunts want to hear it too. Shall I get them in here?

MORTIMER (*pulling him* R.). No, O'Hara, you can't do that now. You've got to ring in.

(O'HARA *stops at* C. *as* MORTIMER *opens the door.*)

O'HARA. The hell with ringing in. I'll get your aunts in here and tell you the plot.

(*He starts for kitchen door.*)

MORTIMER (*grabbing him*). No, O'Hara, not in front of all these people. We'll get together alone, some place later.

O'HARA. How about the back room at Kelly's?

MORTIMER (*passing* O'HARA R. *in front of him*). Fine! You go ring in, and I'll meet you at Kelly's.

JONATHAN (*at window-seat*). Why don't you two go down in the cellar?

O'HARA. That's all right with me. (*Starts for cellar door.*) Is this the cellar?

MORTIMER (*grabbing him again, pushing toward door*). Nooo! We'll go to Kelly's. But you're going to ring in on the way.

O'HARA (*as he exits* R.). All right, that'll only take a couple of minutes. (*He's gone.*) (MORTIMER *takes his hat from hall tree and crosses to open* R. *door.*)

MORTIMER. I'll ditch this guy and be back in five minutes. I'll expect to find you gone. (*Changes his mind.*) Wait for me.

(*He exits* R.)

(EINSTEIN *sits* R. *of table.*)

JONATHAN. We'll wait for him, Doctor. I've waited a great many years for a chance like this.

EINSTEIN. We got him right where we want him. Did he look guilty!

JONATHAN (*rising*). Take the bags back up to our room, Doctor.

(EINSTEIN *gets bags and reaches foot of stairs with them.* ABBY *and* MARTHA *enter from kitchen.* ABBY *speaks as she enters.*)

ABBY. Have they gone? (*Sees* JONATHAN *and* EINSTEIN.) Oh—we thought we heard somebody leave.

JONATHAN (*crossing to* R. C.). Just Mortimer, and he'll be back in a few minutes. Is there any food left in the kitchen? I think Dr. Einstein and I would enjoy a bite.

MARTHA (L. *of table*). But you won't have time.

ABBY (*at* C.). No, if you're still here when Mortimer gets back he won't like it.

EINSTEIN (*dropping* D. S. R.). He'll like it. He's gotta like it.

JONATHAN. Get something for us to eat while we bury Mr. Spenalzo in the cellar.

MARTHA (*crossing to below table*). Oh no!

ABBY. He can't stay in our cellar. No, Jonathan, you've got to take him with you.

JONATHAN. There's a friend of Mortimer's downstairs waiting for him.

ABBY. A friend of Mortimer's?

JONATHAN. He and Mr. Spenalzo will get along fine together. They're both dead.

MARTHA. They must mean Mr. Hoskins.

EINSTEIN. Mr. Hoskins?

JONATHAN. You know about what's downstairs?

ABBY. Of course we do, and he's no friend of Mortimer's. He's one of our gentlemen.

EINSTEIN. Your chentlemen?

MARTHA. And we won't have any strangers buried in our cellar.

JONATHAN (*noncomprehending*). But Mr. Hoskins—

MARTHA. Mr. Hoskins isn't a stranger.

ABBY. Besides, there's no room for Mr. Spenalzo. The cellar's crowded already.

JONATHAN. Crowded? With what?

ABBY. There are twelve graves down there now.

(*The two* MEN *draw back in amazement.*)

JONATHAN. Twelve graves!

ABBY. That leaves very little room and we're going to need it.

JONATHAN. You mean you and Aunt Martha have murdered—?

ABBY. Murdered! Certainly not. It's one of our charities.

MARTHA (*indignantly*). Why, what we've been doing is a mercy.

ABBY (*gesturing outside*). So you just take your Mr. Spenalzo out of here.

JONATHAN (*still unable to believe*). You've done that—here in this house— (*Points to floor.*) and you've buried them down there!

EINSTEIN. Chonny—we've been chased all over the world—they stay right here in Brooklyn and do just as good as you do.

JONATHAN (*facing him*). What?

EINSTEIN. You've got twelve and they've got twelve.

JONATHAN (*slowly*). I've got thirteen.

EINSTEIN. No, Chonny, twelve.

JONATHAN. Thirteen! (*Counting on fingers.*) There's Mr. Spenalzo. Then the first one in London—two in Johannesburg —one in Sydney—one in Melbourne—two in San Francisco—one in Phoenix, Arizona—

EINSTEIN. Phoenix?

JONATHAN. The filling station. The three

in Chicago and the one in South Bend. That makes thirteen!

EINSTEIN. But you can't count the one in South Bend. He died of pneumonia.

JONATHAN. He wouldn't have got pneumonia if I hadn't shot him.

EINSTEIN (*adamant*). No, Chonny, he died of pneumonia. He don't count.

JONATHAN. He counts with me. I say thirteen.

EINSTEIN. No, Chonny. You got twelve and they got twelve. (*Crossing to* AUNTS.) The old ladies are just as good as you are. (*The two* AUNTS *smile at each other happily.* JONATHAN *turns, facing the three of them and speaks menacingly.*)

JONATHAN. Oh, they are, are they? Well, that's easily taken care of. All I need is one more, that's all—just one more.

(MORTIMER *enters hastily* R., *closing door behind him, and turns to them with a nervous smile.*)

MORTIMER. Well, here I am!

(JONATHAN *turns and looks at him with the widening eyes of someone who has just solved a problem, as the curtain falls.*)

ACT THREE

SCENE I

The scene is the same. Still later that night. The curtain rises on an empty stage. The window-seat is open and we see that it's empty. The armchair has been shifted to R. *of table. The drapes over the windows are closed. All doors except cellar are closed.* ABBY's *hymnal and black gloves are on sideboard.* MARTHA's *hymnal and gloves are on table. Otherwise the room is the same. As the curtain rises we hear a row from the cellar, through the open door. The speeches overlap in excitement and anger until the* AUNTS *appear on the stage, from cellar door.*

MARTHA. You stop doing that!

ABBY. This is our house and this is our cellar and you can't do that.

EINSTEIN. Ladies! Please!—Go back upstairs where you belong.

JONATHAN. Abby! Martha! Go upstairs!

MARTHA. There's no use your doing what you're doing because it will just have to be undone.

ABBY. I tell you we won't have it and you'd better stop it right now.

MARTHA (*entering from cellar*). All right! You'll find out. You'll find out whose house this is. (*She crosses to door* D. R., *opens it and looks out. Then closes it.*)

ABBY (*entering*). I'm warning you! You'd better stop it! (D. S. C. *To* MARTHA.) Hasn't Mortimer come back yet?

MARTHA. No.

ABBY. It's a terrible thing to do—to bury a good Methodist with a foreigner. (*She crosses to window-seat.*)

MARTHA *(crossing to cellar door).* I will not have our cellar desecrated!

ABBY *(drops window-seat).* And we promised Mr. Hoskins a full Christian funeral. Where do you suppose Mortimer went?

MARTHA *(drops D. S.).* I don't know, but he must be doing something—because he said to Jonathan, "You just wait, I'll settle this."

ABBY *(crossing up to sideboard).* Well, he can't very well settle it while he's out of the house. That's all we want settled— what's going on down there.

(MORTIMER enters R., closes door.)

MORTIMER *(as one who has everything settled).* All right. Now, where's Teddy?

(The AUNTS are very much annoyed with MORTIMER.)

ABBY. Mortimer, where have you been?

MORTIMER. I've been over to Dr. Gilchrist's. I've got his signature on Teddy's commitment papers.

MARTHA. Mortimer, what is the matter with you?

ABBY *(to below table).* Running around getting papers signed at a time like this!

MARTHA. Do you know what Jonathan's doing?

ABBY. He's putting Mr. Hoskins and Mr. Spenalzo in together.

MORTIMER *(to cellar door).* Oh, he is, is he? Well, let him. *(He shuts cellar door.)* Is Teddy in his room?

MARTHA. Teddy won't be any help.

MORTIMER. When he signs these commitment papers I can tackle Jonathan.

ABBY. What have they got to do with it?

MORTIMER. You had to go and tell Jonathan about those twelve graves. If I can make Teddy responsible for those I can protect you, don't you see?

ABBY. No, I don't see. And we pay taxes to have the police protect us.

MORTIMER *(going upstairs).* I'll be back down in a minute.

ABBY *(takes gloves and hymnal from table).* Come, Martha. We're going for the police.

(MARTHA gets her gloves and hymnal from sideboard. They both start R. to door.)

MORTIMER *(on landing).* All right. *(He turns and rushes downstairs to R. door before they can reach it.)* The police. You can't go for the police.

MARTHA *(D. R., but L. of ABBY).* Why can't we?

MORTIMER *(near R. door).* Because if you tell the police about Mr. Spenalzo they'd find Mr. Hoskins too, *(Crosses to MARTHA.)* and that might make them curious, and they'd find out about the other twelve gentlemen.

ABBY. Mortimer, we know the police better than you do. I don't think they'd pry into our private affairs if we asked them not to.

MORTIMER. But if they found your twelve gentlemen they'd have to report to headquarters.

MARTHA *(pulling on her gloves).* I'm not so sure they'd bother. They'd have to make out a very long report—and if there's one thing a policeman hates to do, it's to write.

MORTIMER. You can't depend on that. It might leak out!—and you couldn't expect a judge and jury to understand.

MARTHA. Oh, Judge Cullman would.

ABBY *(drawing on her gloves).* We know him very well.

MARTHA. He always comes to church to pray—just before election.

ABBY. And he's coming here to tea some day. He promised.

MARTHA. Oh, Abby, we must speak to him again about that. *(To MORTIMER.)* His wife died a few years ago and it's left him very lonely.

ABBY. Well, come along, Martha. *(She starts toward door R. MORTIMER gets there first.)*

MORTIMER. No! You can't do this. I won't let you. You can't leave this house, and you can't have Judge Cullman to tea.

ABBY. Well, if you're not going to do something about Mr. Spenalzo, we are.

MORTIMER. I am going to do something. We may have to call the police in later, but if we do, I want to be ready for them.

MARTHA. You've got to get Jonathan out of this house!

ABBY. And Mr. Spenalzo, too!

MORTIMER. Will you please let me do this my own way? (*He starts upstairs.*) I've got to see Teddy.

ABBY (*facing* MORTIMER *on stairs*). If they're not out of here by morning, Mortimer, we're going to call the police.

MORTIMER (*on balcony*). They'll be out, I promise you that! Go to bed, will you? And for God's sake get out of those clothes —you look like Judith Anderson. (*He exits into hall, closing door.*)

(*The* AUNTS *watch him off.* MARTHA *turns to* ABBY.)

MARTHA. Well, Abby, that's a relief, isn't it?

ABBY. Yes—if Mortimer's going to do something at last, it just means Jonathan's going to a lot of unnecessary trouble. We'd better tell him. (ABBY *starts to cellar door as* JONATHAN *comes in. They meet* U. S. C. *front of sofa. His clothes are dirty.*) Oh, Jonathan—you might as well stop what you're doing.

JONATHAN. *It's all done.* Did I hear Mortimer?

ABBY. Well, it will just have to be undone. You're all going to be out of this house by morning. Mortimer's promised.

JONATHAN. Oh, are we? In that case, you and Aunt Martha can go to bed and have a pleasant night's sleep.

MARTHA (*always a little frightened by* JONATHAN, *starts upstairs*). Yes. Come, Abby.

(ABBY *follows* MARTHA *upstairs.*)

JONATHAN. Good night, Aunties.

ABBY. Not good night, Jonathan. Good-bye. By the time we get up you'll be out of this house. Mortimer's promised.

MARTHA (*on balcony*). And he has a way of doing it too!

JONATHAN. Then Mortimer is back?

ABBY. Oh, yes, he's up here talking to Teddy.

MARTHA. Good-bye, Jonathan.

ABBY. Good-bye, Jonathan.

JONATHAN. Perhaps you'd better say good-bye to Mortimer.

ABBY. Oh, you'll see Mortimer.

JONATHAN (*sitting on stool*). Yes—I'll see Mortimer.

(ABBY *and* MARTHA *exit.* JONATHAN *sits without moving. There is murder in his thought.* EINSTEIN *enters from cellar. He dusts off his trouser cuffs, lifting his leg, and we see he is wearing Spenalzo's sport shoes.*)

EINSTEIN. Whew! That's all fixed up. Smooth like a lake. Nobody'd ever know they were down there. (JONATHAN *still sits without moving.*) That bed feels good already. Forty-eight hours we didn't sleep. (*Crossing to second chair.*) Come on, Chonny, let's go up, yes?

JONATHAN. You're forgetting, Doctor.

EINSTEIN. Vat?

JONATHAN. My brother Mortimer.

EINSTEIN. Chonny—tonight? We do that tomorrow or the next day.

JONATHAN (*just able to control himself*). No, tonight! Now!

EINSTEIN (*down to floor*). Chonny, please —I'm tired—and tomorrow I got to operate.

JONATHAN. Yes, you're operating tomorrow, Doctor. But tonight we take care of Mortimer.

EINSTEIN (*kneeling in front of* JONATHAN, *trying to passify him*). But, Chonny, not tonight—we go to bed, eh?

JONATHAN (*rising.* EINSTEIN *straightens up too*). Doctor, look at me. You can see it's going to be done, can't you?

EINSTEIN (*retreating*). Ach, Chonny—I can see. I know dat look!

JONATHAN. It's a little too late for us to dissolve our partnership.

EINSTEIN. O.K., we do it. But the quick way. The quick twist like in London. (*He gives that London neck another twist with his hands and makes a noise suggesting strangulation.)*

JONATHAN. No, Doctor, I think this calls for something special. *(He walks toward* EINSTEIN, *who breaks* U. S. JONATHAN *has the look of beginning to anticipate a rare pleasure.)* I think perhaps the Melbourne method.

EINSTEIN. Chonny—no—not that. Two hours! And when it was all over, what? The fellow in London was just as dead as the fellow in Melbourne.

JONATHAN. We had to work too fast in London. There was no esthetic satisfaction in it—but Melbourne, ah, there was something to remember.

EINSTEIN *(dropping* D. S. *as* JONATHAN *crosses him).* Remember! *(He shivers.)* I vish I didn't. No, Chonny—not Melbourne—not me!

JONATHAN. Yes, Doctor. Where are the instruments?

EINSTEIN. I won't do it, Chonny.—I won't do it.

JONATHAN *(advancing on him as* EINSTEIN *backs* D. S.*).* Get your instruments!

EINSTEIN. No, Chonny!

JONATHAN. Where are they? Oh, yes—you hid them in the cellar. Where?

EINSTEIN. I won't tell you.

JONATHAN *(going to cellar door).* I'll find them, Doctor. *(He exits to cellar, closing door.)*

*(*TEDDY *enters on balcony and lifts his bugle to blow.* MORTIMER *dashes out and grabs his arm.* EINSTEIN *has rushed to cellar door. He stands there as* MORTIMER *and* TEDDY *speak.)*

MORTIMER. Don't do that, Mr. President.

TEDDY. I cannot sign any proclamation without consulting my cabinet.

MORTIMER. But this must be a secret.

TEDDY. A secret proclamation? How unusual.

MORTIMER. Japan mustn't know until it's signed.

TEDDY. Japan! Those yellow devils. I'll sign it right away. *(Taking legal paper from* MORTIMER.*)* You have my word for it. I can let the cabinet know later.

MORTIMER. Yes, let's go and sign it.

TEDDY. You wait here. A secret proclamation has to be signed in secret.

MORTIMER. But at once, Mr. President.

TEDDY. I'll have to put on my signing clothes. *(*TEDDY *exits.)*

*(*MORTIMER *comes downstairs.* EINSTEIN *crosses and takes* MORTIMER's *hat off of hall tree and hands it to him.)*

EINSTEIN *(anxious to get* MORTIMER *out of the house).* Ah, you go now, eh?

MORTIMER *(takes hat and puts it on desk).* No, Doctor, I'm waiting for something. Something important.

EINSTEIN *(*L. *of* MORTIMER*).* Please—you go now!

MORTIMER. Dr. Einstein, I have nothing against you personally. You seem to be a nice fellow. Take my advice and get out of this house and get just as far away as possible.

EINSTEIN. Trouble, yah! You get out.

MORTIMER *(crossing to* C.*).* All right, don't say I didn't warn you.

EINSTEIN. I'm warning you—get away quick.

MORTIMER. Things are going to start popping around here any minute.

EINSTEIN *(*D. R.*).* Listen—Chonny's in a bad mood. When he's like dis, he's a madman—things happen—terrible things.

MORTIMER. Jonathan doesn't worry me now.

EINSTEIN. Ach, himmel—don't those plays you see teach you anything?

MORTIMER. About what?

EINSTEIN. Vell, at least people in plays act like they got sense—that's more than you do.

MORTIMER *(interested in this observation).* Oh, you think so, do you? You think people in plays act intelligently. I wish you had to sit through some of the ones I have to sit through. Take the little opus I saw tonight for instance. In this play, there's

a man—he's supposed to be bright . . .
(JONATHAN *enters from cellar with instrument case, stands in doorway and listens to* MORTIMER.) —he knows he's in a house with murderers—he ought to know he's in danger—he's even been warned to get out of the house—but does he go? No, he stays there. Now I ask you, Doctor, is that what an intelligent person would do?

EINSTEIN. You're asking me?

MORTIMER. He didn't even have sense enough to be frightened, to be on guard. For instance, the murderer invites him to sit down.

EINSTEIN (*he moves so as to keep* MORTIMER *from seeing* JONATHAN). You mean —"Won't you sit down?"

MORTIMER (*reaches out and pulls armchair to him* R. *of table without turning his head from* EINSTEIN). Believe it or not, that one was in there too.

EINSTEIN. And what did he do?

MORTIMER (*sitting in armchair*). He sat down. Now mind you, this fellow's supposed to be bright. There he sits—just waiting to be trussed up. And what do you think they used to tie him with.

EINSTEIN. Vat?

MORTIMER. The curtain cord.

(JONATHAN *spies curtain cords on either side of window in* L. *wall. He crosses, stands on window-seat and cuts cords with penknife.*)

EINSTEIN. Vell, why not? A good idea. Very convenient.

MORTIMER. A little too convenient. When are playwrights going to use some imagination! The curtain cord!

(JONATHAN *has got the curtain cord and is moving in slowly behind* MORTIMER.)

EINSTEIN. He didn't see him get it?

MORTIMER. See him? He sat there with his back to him. That's the kind of stuff we have to suffer through night after night. And they say the critics are killing the theatre—it's the playwrights who are killing the theatre. So there he sits—the big dope—this fellow who's supposed to be bright—just waiting to be trussed up and gagged.

(JONATHAN *drops loop of curtain cord over* MORTIMER's *shoulder and draws it taut. At the same time he throws other loop of cord on floor beside* EINSTEIN. *Simultaneously,* EINSTEIN *leaps to* MORTIMER *and gags him with handkerchief, then takes his curtain cord and ties* MORTIMER's *legs to chair.*)

EINSTEIN (*finishing up the tying*). You're right about dat fella—he vasn't very bright.

JONATHAN. Now, Mortimer, if you don't mind—we'll finish the story. (*He goes to sideboard and brings two candelabras to table and speaks as he lights them.* EINSTEIN *remains kneeling beside* MORTIMER.) Mortimer, I've been away for twenty years, but never once in all that time—my dear brother—were you out of my mind. In Melbourne one night, I dreamed of you—when I landed in San Francisco I felt a strange satisfaction—once more I was in the same country with you. (JONATHAN *has finished lighting candles. He crosses* D. R. *and flips light-switch, darkening stage. As he crosses,* EINSTEIN *gets up and crosses to window-seat.* JONATHAN *picks up instrument case at cellar doorway and sets it on table between candelabras and opens it, revealing various surgical instruments both in the bottom of case and on the inside of cover.*) Now, Doctor, we go to work! (*He removes an instrument from the case and fingers it lovingly, as* EINSTEIN *crosses and kneels on chair* L. *of table. He is not too happy about all this.*)

EINSTEIN. Please, Chonny, for me, the quick way!

JONATHAN. Doctor! This must really be an artistic achievement. After all, we're performing before a very distinguished critic.

EINSTEIN. Chonny!

JONATHAN (*flaring*). Doctor!

EINSTEIN (*beaten*). All right. Let's get it over. (*He closes drapes tightly and sits on window-seat.* JONATHAN *takes three or four more instruments out of the case and fingers them. At last, having the necessary equipment laid out on the towel he begins to put on a pair of rubber gloves.*)

JONATHAN. All ready for you, Doctor!

EINSTEIN. I gotta have a drink. I can't do this without a drink.

(He takes bottle from pocket. Drinks. Finds it empty. Rises.)

JONATHAN. Pull yourself together, Doctor.

EINSTEIN. I gotta have a drink. Ven ve valked in here this afternoon there was wine here—remember? Vere did she put that? *(He looks at sideboard and remembers. He goes to it, opens L. cupboard and brings bottle and two wine glasses to D. S. end of table top.)* Look, Chonny, we got a drink. *(He pours wine into the two glasses, emptying the bottle.* MORTIMER *watches him.)* Dat's all dere is. I split it with you. We both need a drink. *(He hands one glass to* JONATHAN, *then raises his own glass to his lips.* JONATHAN *stops him.)*

JONATHAN. One moment, Doctor—please. Where are your manners? *(He drops D. S. to R. of* MORTIMER *and looks at him.)* Yes, Mortimer, I realize now it was you who brought me back to Brooklyn. . . . *(He looks at wine, then draws it back and forth under his nose smelling it. He decides that it's all right apparently for he raises his glass—)* Doctor—to my dear dead brother—

(As they get the glasses to their lips, TEDDY *steps out on the balcony and blows a terrific call on his bugle.* EINSTEIN *and* JONATHAN *drop their glasses, spilling the wine.* TEDDY *turns and exits.)*

EINSTEIN. Ach Gott!

JONATHAN. Damn that idiot! *(He starts for stairs.* EINSTEIN *rushes over and intercepts him.)* He goes next! That's all—he goes next!

EINSTEIN. No, Chonny, not Teddy—that's where I shtop—not Teddy!

JONATHAN. We get to Teddy later!

EINSTEIN. We don't get to him at all.

JONATHAN. Now we've got to work fast! *(He crosses above to L. of* MORTIMER. EINSTEIN *in front of* MORTIMER.)*

EINSTEIN. Yah, the quick way—eh, Chonny?

JONATHAN. Yes, Doctor, the quick way! *(He pulls a large silk handkerchief from his inside pocket and drops it around* MORTIMER'S *neck.)*

(At this point the door bursts open and OFFICER O'HARA *comes in to* C., *very excited.)*

O'HARA. Hey! The Colonel's gotta quit blowing that horn!

JONATHAN *(he and* EINSTEIN *are standing in front of* MORTIMER, *hiding him from* O'HARA*).* It's all right, Officer. We're taking the bugle away from him.

O'HARA. There's going to be hell to pay in the morning. We promised the neighbors he wouldn't do that any more.

JONATHAN. It won't happen again, Officer. Good night.

O'HARA. I'd better speak to him myself. Where are the lights? *(*O'HARA *puts on lights and goes upstairs to landing, when he sees* MORTIMER*.)* Hey! You stood me up. I waited an hour at Kelly's for you. *(He comes downstairs and over to* MORTIMER *and looks at him then speaks to* JONATHAN *and* EINSTEIN*.)* What happened to him?

EINSTEIN *(thinking fast).* He was explaining the play he saw tonight—that's what happened to the fella in the play.

O'HARA. Did they have that in the play you saw tonight? *(*MORTIMER *nods his head— yes.)* Gee, they practically stole that from the second act of my play—*(He starts to explain.)* Why, in my second act, just before the— *(He turns back to* MORTIMER.*)* I'd better begin at the beginning. It opens in my mother's dressing room where I was born—only I ain't born yet— *(*MORTIMER *rubs his shoes together to attract* O'HARA'S *attention.)* Huh? Oh, yeah. *(*O'HARA *starts to remove the gag from* MORTIMER'S *mouth and then decides not to.)* No! You've got to hear the plot. *(He gets stool and brings it to R. of* MORTIMER *and sits, continuing on with his "plot" as the curtain falls.)* Well, she's sitting there making up, see— when all of a sudden through the door— a man with a black mustache walks in— turns to my mother and says—"Miss La-tour, will you marry me?" He doesn't know she's pregnant.

CURTAIN

SCENE II

Scene is the same. Early the next morning. When the curtain rises again, daylight is streaming through the windows. All doors closed. All drapes open. Mor-TIMER is still tied in his chair and seems to be in a semi-conscious state. JONATHAN is asleep on sofa. EINSTEIN, pleasantly intoxicated, is seated L. of table, his head resting on table top. O'HARA, with his coat off and his collar loosened, is standing over the stool which is between him and MORTIMER. He has progressed to the most exciting scene of his play. There is a bottle of whiskey and a water tumbler on the table along with a plate full of cigarette butts.

O'HARA. —there she is lying unconscious across the table in her lingerie—the Chink is standing over her with a hatchet— *(He takes the pose.)* —I'm tied up in a chair just like you are—the place is an inferno of flames—it's on fire—when all of a sudden—through the window—in comes Mayor LaGuardia. (EINSTEIN *raises his head and looks out the window. Not seeing anyone he reaches for the bottle and pours himself another drink.* O'HARA *crosses above to him and takes the bottle.)* Hey, remember who paid for that—go easy on it.

EINSTEIN. Vell, I'm listening, ain't I? *(He crosses to JONATHAN on the sofa.)*

O'HARA. How do you like it so far?

EINSTEIN. Vell, it put Chonny to sleep.

(O'HARA has just finished a swig from the bottle.)

O'HARA. Let him alone. If he ain't got no more interest than that—he don't get a drink. (EINSTEIN *takes his glass and sits on bottom stair. At the same time* O'HARA *crosses, puts stool under desk and whiskey bottle on top of desk, then comes back to center and goes on with his play—)* All right. It's three days later—I been transferred and I'm under charges—that's because somebody stole my badge. (He pantomimes through following lines.) All right. I'm walking my beat on Staten Island—forty-sixth precinct—when a guy I'm following, it turns out—is really following me. (There is a knock on door. EINSTEIN goes up and looks out landing window. Leaves glass behind D. S. drape.) Don't let anybody in.—So I figure I'll outsmart him. There's a vacant house on the corner. I goes in.

EINSTEIN. It's cops!

O'HARA. I stands there in the dark and I see the door handle turn.

EINSTEIN *(rushing downstairs, shakes JONATHAN by the shoulder.)* Chonny! It's cops! Cops! (JONATHAN *doesn't move.* EINSTEIN *rushes upstairs and off through the arch.)*

(O'HARA is going on with his story without a stop.)

O'HARA. I pulls my guns—braces myself against the wall—and I says—"Come in." (OFFICERS BROPHY *and* KLEIN *walk in* R., *see* O'HARA *with gun pointed at them and raise their hands. Then, recognizing their fellow officer, lower them.)* Hello, boys.

BROPHY. What the hell is going on here?

O'HARA *(goes to BROPHY).* Hey, Pat, whaddya know? This is Mortimer Brewster! He's going to write my play with me. I'm just tellin' him the story.

KLEIN *(crossing to MORTIMER and untying him).* Did you have to tie him up to make him listen?

BROPHY. Joe, you better report in at the station. The whole force is out looking for ya.

O'HARA. Did they send you here for me?

KLEIN. We didn't know you was here.

BROPHY. We came to warn the old ladies that there's hell to pay. The Colonel blew that bugle again in the middle of the night.

KLEIN. From the way the neighbors have been calling in about it you'd think the Germans had dropped a bomb on Flatbush Avenue.

(He has finished untying MORTIMER. *Puts cords on sideboard.)*

BROPHY. The Lieutenant's on the warpath. He says the Colonel's got to be put away some place.

MORTIMER *(staggers to feet).* Yes! Yes!

O'HARA *(going to* MORTIMER*).* Gee, Mr. Brewster, I got to get away, so I'll just run through the third act quick.

MORTIMER *(staggering* R.*).* Get away from me.

*(*BROPHY *gives* KLEIN *a look, goes to phone and dials.)*

KLEIN. Say, do you know what time it is? It's after eight o'clock in the morning.

O'HARA. It is? *(He follows* MORTIMER *to stairs.)* Gee, Mr. Brewster, them first two acts run a little long, but I don't see anything we can leave out.

MORTIMER *(almost to landing).* You can leave it *all* out.

*(*BROPHY *sees* JONATHAN *on sofa.)*

BROPHY. Who the hell is this guy?

MORTIMER *(hanging on railing, almost to balcony).* That's my brother.

BROPHY. Oh, the one that ran away? So he came back.

MORTIMER. Yes, he came back!

*(*JONATHAN *stirs as if to get up.)*

BROPHY *(into phone).* This is Brophy. Get me Mac. *(To* O'HARA, *sitting on bottom stair.)* I'd better let them know we found you, Joe. *(Into phone.)* Mac? Tell the Lieutenant he can call off the big manhunt —we got him. In the Brewster house. *(*JONATHAN *hears this and suddenly becomes very much awake, looking up to see* KLEIN *to* L. *of him and* BROPHY *to his* R.*)* Do you want us to bring him in? Oh —all right, we'll hold him right here. *(He hangs up.)* The Lieutenant's on his way over.

JONATHAN *(rising).* So I've been turned in, eh? *(*BROPHY *and* KLEIN *look at him with some interest.)* All right, you've got me! *(Turning to* MORTIMER, *who is on balcony looking down.)* And I suppose you and

that stool-pigeon brother of mine will split the reward?

KLEIN. Reward?

(Instinctively KLEIN *and* BROPHY *both grab* JONATHAN *by an arm.)*

JONATHAN *(dragging* COPS D. S. C.*).* Now I'll do some turning in! You think my aunts are sweet charming old ladies, don't you? Well, there are thirteen bodies buried in their cellar.

MORTIMER *(as he rushes off to see* TEDDY*).* Teddy! Teddy! Teddy!

KLEIN. What the hell are you talking about?

BROPHY. You'd better be careful what you're saying about your aunts—they happen to be friends of ours.

JONATHAN *(raving as he drags them toward the cellar door).* I'll show you! I'll prove it to you! You come to the cellar with me!

KLEIN. Wait a minute! Wait a minute!

JONATHAN. Thirteen bodies! I'll show you where they're buried.

KLEIN *(refusing to be kidded).* Oh, yeah?

JONATHAN. You don't want to see what's down in the cellar?

BROPY *(releases* JONATHAN's *arm, then to* KLEIN*).* Go on down in the cellar with him, Abe.

KLEIN *(drops* JONATHAN's *arm, backs* D. S. *a step and looks at him).* I'm not so sure I want to be down in the cellar with him. Look at that puss. He looks like Boris Karloff. *(*JONATHAN, *at mention of Karloff, grabs* KLEIN *by the throat, starts choking him.)* Hey—what the hell— Hey, Pat! Get him off me.

*(*BROPHY *takes out rubber blackjack.)*

BROPHY. Here, what do you think you're doing! *(He socks* JONATHAN *on head.* JONATHAN *falls unconscious, face down.)* *(*KLEIN, *throwing* JONATHAN's *weight to floor, backs away, rubbing his throat.)*

KLEIN. Well what do you know about that?

(There is a knock on door R.*)*

O'HARA. Come in.

(LIEUTENANT ROONEY *bursts in* R., *slamming door after him. He is a very tough, driving, dominating officer.*)

ROONEY. What the hell are you men doing here? I told you *I* was going to handle this.

KLEIN. Well, sir, we was just about to— (KLEIN's *eyes go to* JONATHAN *and* ROONEY *sees him.*)

ROONEY. What happened? Did he put up a fight?

BROPHY. This ain't the guy that blows the bugle. This is his brother. He tried to kill Klein.

KLEIN (*feeling his throat*). All I said was he looked like Boris Karloff.

ROONEY (*his face lights up*). Turn him over.

(*The two* COPS *turn* JONATHAN *over on his back.* KLEIN *steps back.* ROONEY *crosses front of* BROPHY *to take a look at* JONATHAN. BROPHY *drifts to* R. *of* ROONEY. O'HARA *is still at foot of stairs.*)

BROPHY. We kinda think he's wanted somewhere.

ROONEY. Oh, you kinda *think* he's wanted somewhere? If you guys don't look at the circulars we hang up in the station, at least you could read *True Detective.* Certainly he's wanted. In Indiana! Escaped from the prison for the Criminal Insane! He's a lifer. For God's sake that's how he was described—he *looked* like Karloff!

KLEIN. Was there a reward mentioned?

ROONEY. Yeah—and *I'm* claiming it.

BROPHY. He was trying to get us down in the cellar.

KLEIN. He said there was thirteen bodies buried down there.

ROONEY (*suspicious*). Thirteen bodies buried in the cellar? (*Deciding it's ridiculous.*) And that didn't tip you off he came out of a nut-house!

O'HARA. I thought all along he talked kinda crazy.

(ROONEY *sees* O'HARA *for the first time. Turns to him.*)

ROONEY. Oh, it's Shakespeare! (*Crossing to him.*) Where have you been all night? And you needn't bother to tell me.

O'HARA. I've been right here, sir. Writing a play with Mortimer Brewster.

ROONEY (*tough*). Yeah? Well, you're gonna have plenty of time to write that play. You're suspended! Now get back and report in!

(O'HARA *takes his coat, night stick, and cap from top of desk. Goes to* R. *door and opens it. Then turns to* ROONEY.)

O'HARA. Can I come over sometime and use the station typewriter?

ROONEY. No!—Get out of here. (O'HARA *runs out.* ROONEY *closes door and turns to the* COPS. TEDDY *enters on balcony and comes downstairs unnoticed and stands at* ROONEY's *back to the* R. *of him.* ROONEY, *to* COPS.) Take that guy somewhere else and bring him to. (*The* COPS *bend down to pick up* JONATHAN.) See what you can find out about his accomplice. (*The* COPS *stand up again in a questioning attitude.* ROONEY *explains.*) The guy that helped him escape. He's wanted too. No wonder Brooklyn's in the shape it's in, with the police force full of flatheads like you—falling for that kind of a story—thirteen bodies in the cellar!

TEDDY. But there are thirteen bodies in the cellar.

ROONEY (*turning on him*). Who are you?

TEDDY. I'm President Roosevelt.

(ROONEY *does a walk* U. S. *on this, then comes down again.*)

ROONEY. What the hell is this?

BROPHY. He's the fellow that blows the bugle.

KLEIN. Good morning, Colonel.

(*They salute* TEDDY, *who returns it.* ROONEY *finds himself saluting* TEDDY *also. He pulls his hand down in disgust.*)

ROONEY. Well, Colonel, you've blown your last bugle.

TEDDY (*seeing* JONATHAN *on floor*). Dear me—another Yellow Fever victim?

ROONEY. What-at?

TEDDY. All the bodies in the cellar are Yellow Fever victims.

(ROONEY *crosses exasperatedly to* R. *door on this.*)

BROPHY. No, Colonel, this is a spy we caught in the White House.

ROONEY (*pointing to* JONATHAN). Will you get that guy out of here!

(COPS *pick up* JONATHAN *and drag him to kitchen.* TEDDY *follows them.* MORTIMER *enters, comes down stairs.*)

TEDDY (*turning back to* ROONEY). If there's any questioning of spies, that's my department!

ROONEY. You keep out of this!

TEDDY. You're forgetting! As President, I am also head of the Secret Service.

(BROPHY *and* KLEIN *exit with* JONATHAN *into kitchen.* TEDDY *follows them briskly.* MORTIMER *has come to* C.)

MORTIMER. Captain—I'm Mortimer Brewster.

ROONEY. Are you sure?

MORTIMER. I'd like to talk to you about my brother Teddy—the one who blew the bugle.

ROONEY. Mr. Brewster, we ain't going to talk about that—he's got to be put away!

MORTIMER. I quite agree with you. In fact, it's all arranged for. I had these commitment papers signed by Dr. Gilchrist, our family physician. Teddy has signed them himself, you see—and I've signed them as next of kin.

ROONEY. Where's he going?

MORTIMER. Happy Dale.

ROONEY. All right, I don't care where he goes as long as he goes!

MORTIMER. Oh, he's going all right. But I want you to know that everything that's happened around here Teddy's responsible for. Now, those thirteen bodies in the cellar—

ROONEY (*he's had enough of those thirteen*). Yeah—yeah—those thirteen bodies in the cellar! It ain't enough that the neighbors are all afraid of him, and his

disturbing the peace with that bugle—but can you imagine what would happen if that cock-eyed story about thirteen bodies in the cellar got around? And now he's starting a Yellow Fever scare. Cute, ain't it?

MORTIMER (*greatly relieved, with an embarrassed laugh*). Thirteen bodies. Do you think anybody would believe that story?

ROONEY. Well, you can't tell. Some people are just dumb enough. You don't know what to believe sometimes. About a year ago a crazy guy starts a murder rumor over in Greenpoint, and I had to dig up a half acre lot, just to prove that—

(*There is a knock on* R. *door.*)

MORTIMER. Will you excuse me? (*He goes to door and admits* ELAINE *and* MR. WITHERSPOON, *an elderly, tight-lipped disciplinarian. He is carrying a brief case.*)

ELAINE (*briskly*). Good morning, Mortimer.

MORTIMER (*not knowing what to expect*). Good morning, dear.

ELAINE. This is Mr. Witherspoon. He's come to meet Teddy.

MORTIMER. To meet Teddy?

ELAINE. Mr. Witherspoon's the superintendent of Happy Dale.

MORTIMER (*eagerly*). Oh, come right in. (*They shake hands.* MORTIMER *indicates* ROONEY.) This is Captain—

ROONEY. *Lieutenant* Rooney. I'm glad you're here, Super, because you're taking him back with you today!

WITHERSPOON. Today? I didn't know that—

ELAINE (*cutting in*). Not today!

MORTIMER. Look, Elaine, I've got a lot of business to attend to, so you run along home and I'll call you up.

ELAINE. Nuts! (*She crosses to window-seat and sits.*)

WITHERSPOON. I had no idea it was this immediate.

ROONEY. The papers are all signed, he goes today!

(TEDDY *backs into room from kitchen, speaking sharply in the direction whence he's come.*)

TEDDY. Complete insubordination! You men will find out I'm no mollycoddle. (*He slams door and comes down to below table.*) When the President of the United States is treated like that—what's this country coming to?

ROONEY. There's your man, Super.

MORTIMER. Just a minute! (*He crosses to* TEDDY *and speaks to him as to a child.*) Mr. President, I have very good news for you. Your term of office is over.

TEDDY. Is this March the Fourth?

MORTIMER. Practically.

TEDDY (*thinking*). Let's see—OH!—Now I go on my hunting trip to Africa! Well, I must get started immediately. (*He starts across the room and almost bumps into* WITHERSPOON *at* C. *He looks at him then steps back to* MORTIMER.) Is he trying to move into the White House before I've moved out?

MORTIMER. Who, Teddy?

TEDDY (*indicating* WITHERSPOON). Taft!

MORTIMER. This isn't Mr. Taft, Teddy. This is Mr. Witherspoon—he's to be your guide in Africa.

TEDDY (*shakes hands with* WITHERSPOON *enthusiastically*). Bully! Bully! I'll bring down my equipment. (*He crosses to stairs.* MARTHA *and* ABBY *have entered on balcony during last speech and are coming downstairs.*) When the safari comes, tell them to wait. (*As he passes the* AUNTS *on his way to landing, he shakes hands with each, without stopping his walk.*) Good-bye, Aunt Abby. Good-bye, Aunt Martha. I'm on my way to Africa—isn't it wonderful? (*He has reached the landing.*) CHARGE!

(*He charges up the stairs and off.*)

(*The* AUNTS *are at foot of stairs.*)

MORTIMER (*crossing to aunts*). Good morning, darlings.

MARTHA. Oh, we have visitors.

MORTIMER (*he indicates* ROONEY *at* C.). This is Lieutenant Rooney.

ABBY (*crossing, shakes hands with him*).

How do you do, Lieutenant? My, **you** don't look like the fussbudget the policemen say you are.

MORTIMER. Why the Lieutenant is here— You know, Teddy blew his bugle again last night.

MARTHA. Yes, we're going to speak to Teddy about that.

ROONEY. It's a little more serious than that, Miss Brewster.

MORTIMER (*easing* AUNTS *to* WITHERSPOON *who is above table where he has opened his brief case and extracted some papers*). And you haven't met Mr. Witherspoon. He's the Superintendent of Happy Dale.

ABBY. Oh, Mr. Witherspoon—how do you do?

MARTHA. You've come to meet Teddy.

ROONEY (*somewhat harshly*). He's come to *take* him.

(*The* AUNTS *turn to* ROONEY *questioningly.*)

MORTIMER (*making it as easy as possible*). Aunties—the police want Teddy to go there, today.

ABBY (*crossing to* R. *of chair*). Oh—no!

MARTHA (*behind* ABBY). Not while we're alive!

ROONEY. I'm sorry, Miss Brewster, but it has to be done. The papers are all signed and he's going along with the Superintendent.

ABBY. We won't permit it. We'll promise to take the bugle away from him.

MARTHA. We won't be separated from Teddy.

ROONEY. I'm sorry, ladies, but the law's the law! He's committed himself and he's going!

ABBY. Well, if he goes, we're going too.

MARTHA. Yes, you'll have to take us with him.

MORTIMER (*has an idea. Crosses to* WITHERSPOON). Well, why not?

WITHERSPOON (*to* MORTIMER). Well, that's sweet of them to want to, but it's impossible. You see, we can't take *sane* people at Happy Dale.

MARTHA (*turning to* WITHERSPOON). Mr. Witherspoon, if you'll let us live there with Teddy, we'll see that Happy Dale is in our will—and for a very generous amount.

WITHERSPOON. Well, the Lord knows we could use the money, but—I'm afraid—

ROONEY. Now let's be sensible about this, ladies. For instance, here I am wasting my morning when I've got serious work to do. You know there are still *murders* to be solved in Brooklyn.

MORTIMER. Yes! (*Covering.*) Oh, are there?

ROONEY. It ain't only his bugle blowing and the neighbors all afraid of him, but things would just get worse. Sooner or later we'd be put to the trouble of digging up your cellar.

ABBY. Our cellar?

ROONEY. Yeah.—Your nephew's been telling around that there are thirteen bodies in your cellar.

ABBY. But there are thirteen bodies in our cellar.

(ROONEY *looks disgusted.* MORTIMER *drifts quietly to front of cellar door.*)

MARTHA. If that's why you think Teddy has to go away—you come down to the cellar with us and we'll prove it to you. (*Goes* U. S.)

ABBY. There's one—Mr. Spenalzo—who doesn't belong here and who will have to leave—but the other twelve are our gentlemen. (*She starts* U. S.)

MORTIMER. I don't think the Lieutenant wants to go down in the cellar. He was telling me that only last year he had to dig up a half-acre lot—weren't you, Lieutenant?

ROONEY. That's right.

ABBY (*to* ROONEY). Oh, you wouldn't have to dig here. The graves are all marked. We put flowers on them every Sunday.

ROONEY. Flowers? (*He steps up toward* ABBY, *then turns to* WITHERSPOON, *indicating the* AUNTS *as he speaks.*) Superintendent—don't you think you can find room for these ladies?

WITHERSPOON. Well, I—

ABBY (*to* ROONEY). You come along with us, and we'll show you the graves.

ROONEY. I'll take your word for it, lady—I'm a busy man. How about it, Super?

WITHERSPOON. Well, they'd have to be committed.

MORTIMER. Teddy committed himself. Can't they commit themselves? Can't they sign the papers?

WITHERSPOON. Why, certainly.

MARTHA (*sits in chair* L. *of table as* WITHERSPOON *draws it out for her*). Oh, if we can go with Teddy, we'll sign the papers. Where are they?

ABBY (*sitting* R. *of table.* MORTIMER *helps her with chair*). Yes, where are they?

(WITHERSPOON *opens brief case for more papers.* KLEIN *enters from kitchen.*)

KLEIN. He's coming around, Lieutenant.

ABBY. Good morning, Mr. Klein.

MARTHA. Good morning, Mr. Klein. Are you here too?

KLEIN. Yeah. Brophy and me have got your other nephew out in the kitchen.

ROONEY. Well, sign 'em up, Superintendent. I want to get this all cleaned up. (*He crosses to kitchen door, shaking his head as he exits and saying:*) Thirteen bodies.

(KLEIN *follows him out.* MORTIMER *is to the* L. *of* ABBY, *fountain pen in hand.* WITHERSPOON *to* R. *of* MARTHA, *also with pen.*)

WITHERSPOON (*handing* MARTHA *pen*). If you'll sign right here.

(MARTHA *signs.*)

MORTIMER. And you here, Aunt Abby.

(ABBY *signs.*)

ABBY (*signing*). I'm really looking forward to going—the neighborhood here has changed so.

MARTHA. Just think, a front lawn again.

(EINSTEIN *enters through arch and comes down stairs to door* D. R. *carrying suitcase. He picks hat from hall tree on way down.*)

WITHERSPOON. Oh, we're overlooking something.

MARTHA. What?

WITHERSPOON. Well, we're going to need the signature of a doctor.

MORTIMER. Oh! *(He sees* EINSTEIN *about to disappear through the door.)* Dr. Einstein! Will you come over here—we'd like you to sign some papers.

EINSTEIN. Please, I must—

MORTIMER *(crosses to him)*. Just come right over, Doctor. At one time last night, I thought the Doctor was going to operate on me. *(*EINSTEIN *puts down suitcase and his hat just inside the door.)* Just come right over, Doctor. *(*EINSTEIN *crosses to table, L. of* ABBY.*)* Just sign right here, Doctor.

(The DOCTOR *signs* ABBY's *paper and* MARTHA's *paper.* ROONEY *and* KLEIN *enter from kitchen.* ROONEY *crosses to desk and dials phone.* KLEIN *stands near kitchen door.)*

ABBY. Were you leaving, Doctor?

EINSTEIN *(signing papers)*. I think I must go.

MARTHA. Aren't you going to wait for Jonathan?

EINSTEIN. I don't think we're going to the same place.

*(*MORTIMER *sees* ELAINE *on window-seat and crosses to her.)*

MORTIMER. Hello, Elaine. I'm glad to see you. Stick around, huh?

ELAINE. Don't worry, I'm going to.

*(*MORTIMER *stands back of* MARTHA's *chair.* ROONEY *speaks into phone.)*

ROONEY. Hello, Mac. Rooney. We've picked up that guy that's wanted in Indiana. Now there's a description of his accomplice—it's right on the desk there—read it to me. *(*EINSTEIN *sees* ROONEY *at phone. He starts toward kitchen and sees* KLEIN *standing there. He comes back to* R. *of table and stands there dejectedly waiting for the pinch.* ROONEY *repeats the description given him over phone, looking blankly at* EINSTEIN *the while.)* Yeah—about fifty-four—five foot six—hundred and forty pounds—blue eyes—talks with a German accent. Poses as a doctor. Thanks, Mac. *(He hangs up as* WITHERSPOON *crosses to him with papers in hand.)*

WITHERSPOON. It's all right, Lieutenant. The Doctor here has just completed the signatures.

*(*ROONEY *goes to* EINSTEIN *and shakes his hand.)*

ROONEY. Thanks, Doc. You're really doing Brooklyn a service.

*(*ROONEY *and* KLEIN *exit to kitchen.)*

*(*EINSTEIN *stands amazed for a moment then grabs up his hat and suitcase and disappears through* R. *door. The* AUNTS *rise and cross over, looking out after him.* ABBY *shuts the door and they stand there* D. R.*)*

WITHERSPOON *(above table)*. Mr. Brewster, you sign now as next of kin.

(The AUNTS *whisper to each other as* MORTIMER *signs.)*

MORTIMER. Yes, of course. Right here?

WITHERSPOON. That's fine.

MORTIMER. That makes everything complete—everything legal?

WITHERSPOON. Oh, yes.

MORTIMER *(with relief)*. Well, Aunties, now you're safe.

WITHERSPOON *(to* AUNTS*)*. When do you think you'll be ready to start?

ABBY *(stepping* L.*)*. Well, Mr. Witherspoon, why don't you go upstairs and tell Teddy just what he can take along?

WITHERSPOON. Upstairs?

MORTIMER. I'll show you.

ABBY *(stopping him)*. No, Mortimer, you stay here. We want to talk to you. *(To* WITHERSPOON.*)* Yes, Mr. Witherspoon, just upstairs and turn to the left.

*(*WITHERSPOON *puts his brief case on sofa and goes upstairs, the* AUNTS *keeping an eye on him while talking to* MORTIMER.*)*

MARTHA. Well, Mortimer, now that we're moving, this house really is yours.

ABBY. Yes, dear, we want you to live here now.

MORTIMER *(below table)*. No, Aunt Abby, this house is too full of memories.

MARTHA. But you'll need a home when you and Elaine are married.

MORTIMER. Darlings, that's very indefinite.

ELAINE *(rises and crosses to* L. *of* MORTIMER*)*. It's nothing of the kind—we're going to be married right away.

*(*WITHERSPOON *has exited off balcony.)*

ABBY. Mortimer—Mortimer, we're really very worried about something.

MORTIMER. Now, darlings, you're going to love it at Happy Dale.

MARTHA. Oh, yes, we're very happy about the whole thing. That's just it—we don't want anything to go wrong.

ABBY. Will they investigate those signatures?

MORTIMER. Don't worry, they're not going to look up Dr. Einstein.

MARTHA. It's not his signature, dear, it's yours.

ABBY. You see, you signed as next of kin.

MORTIMER. Of course. Why not?

MARTHA. Well, dear, it's something we never wanted to tell you. But now you're a man—and it's something Elaine should know too. You see, dear—you're not really a Brewster.

*(*MORTIMER *stares as does* ELAINE*.)*

ABBY. Your mother came to us as a cook —and you were born about three months afterward. But she was such a sweet woman—and such a good cook we didn't want to lose her—so brother married her.

MORTIMER. I'm—not—really—a—Brewster?

MARTHA. Now, don't feel badly about it, dear.

ABBY. And Elaine, it won't make any difference to you?

MORTIMER *(turning slowly to face* ELAINE. *His voice rising).* Elaine! Did you hear? Do you understand? I'm a bastard!

*(*ELAINE *leaps into his arms. The two* AUNTS *watch them, then* MARTHA *starts* U. L. *a few steps.)*

MARTHA. Well, now I really must see about breakfast.

ELAINE *(leading* MORTIMER *to* R. *door; opening door).* Mortimer's coming over to my house. Father's gone to Philadelphia, and Mortimer and I are going to have breakfast together.

MORTIMER. Yes, I need some coffee—I've had quite a night.

ABBY. In that case I should think you'd want to get to bed.

MORTIMER *(with a sidelong glance at* ELAINE*).* I do. *(They exit* R.*, closing door.)*

*(*WITHERSPOON *enters on balcony, carrying two canteens. He starts downstairs when* TEDDY *enters carrying large canoe paddle. He is dressed in Panama outfit with pack on his back.)*

TEDDY. One moment, Witherspoon. Take this with you! *(He exits off balcony again as* WITHERSPOON *comes on downstairs to sofa. He puts canteens on sofa and leans paddle against wall.)*

(At the same time ROONEY *and the two cops with* JONATHAN *between them enter. The* COPS *have twisters around* JONATHAN'S *wrists.* ROONEY *enters first and crosses to* R. C. *The other three stop* D. L. *of table. The* AUNTS *are* R. *of the table.)*

ROONEY. We won't need the wagon. My car's out front.

MARTHA. Oh, you leaving now, Jonathan?

ROONEY. Yeah—he's going back to Indiana. There's some people there want to take care of him for the rest of his life. Come on.

*(*ROONEY *opens door as the two* COPS *and* JONATHAN *cross to* R. C. ABBY *steps* D. S. *after they pass.)*

ABBY. Well, Jonathan, it's nice to know you have some place to go.

MARTHA. We're leaving too.

ABBY. Yes, we're going to Happy Dale.

JONATHAN. Then this house is seeing the last of the Brewsters.

MARTHA. Unless Mortimer wants to live here.

JONATHAN. I have a suggestion to make. Why don't you turn this property over to the church?

ABBY. Well, we never thought of that.

JONATHAN. After all, it *should* be part of the cemetery.

ROONEY. All right, get going, I'm a busy man.

JONATHAN (*holding his ground for his one last word*). Good-bye, Aunties. Well, I can't better my record now but neither can you—at least I have that satisfaction. The score stands even, *twelve* to *twelve*.

(JONATHAN *and the* COPS *exit* R., *as the* AUNTS *look out after them.*)

(WITHERSPOON *crosses above to window-seat and stands quietly looking out the window. His back is to the* AUNTS.)

MARTHA (*starting toward* R. *door to close it*). Jonathan always was a mean boy. Never could stand to see anyone get ahead of him. (*She closes door.*)

ABBY (*turning slowly around* L. *as she speaks*). I wish we could show him he isn't so smart! (*Her eyes fall on* WITHERSPOON. *She studies him.* MARTHA *turns from door and sees* ABBY's *contemplation.* ABBY *speaks sweetly.*) Mr. Witherspoon? (WITHERSPOON *turns around facing them.*) Does your family live with you at Happy Dale?

WITHERSPOON. I have no family.

ABBY. Oh—

MARTHA (*stepping into room*). Well, I suppose you consider everyone at Happy Dale your family?

WITHERSPOON. I'm afraid you don't quite understand. As head of the institution, I have to keep quite aloof.

ABBY. That must make it very lonely for you.

WITHERSPOON. It does. But my duty is my duty.

ABBY (*turning to* MARTHA). Well, Martha— (MARTHA *takes her cue and goes to sideboard for bottle of wine. Bottle in* L. *cupboard is empty. She puts it back and takes out full bottle from* R. *cupboard. She brings bottle and wine-glass to table.* ABBY *continues talking.*) If Mr. Witherspoon won't join us for breakfast, I think at least we should offer him a glass of elderberry wine.

WITHERSPOON (*severely*). Elderberry wine?

MARTHA. We make it ourselves.

WITHERSPOON (*melting slightly*). Why, yes . . . (*Severely again.*) Of course, at Happy Dale our relationship will be more formal—but here— (*He sits in chair* L. *of table as* MARTHA *pours wine.* ABBY *is beside* MARTHA.) You don't see much elderberry wine nowadays—I thought I'd had my last glass of it.

ABBY. Oh, no—

MARTHA (*handing him glass of wine*). No, here it is.

(WITHERSPOON *toasts the ladies and lifts glass to his lips, but the curtain falls before he does. . . .*)

CURTAIN

HARVEY
Mary Chase

Harvey was produced by Brock Pemberton at the Forty-Eighth Street Theatre, New York City, on November 1, 1944. It was directed by Antoinette Perry, with settings by John Root. The cast was as follows:

MYRTLE MAE SIMMONS.. Jane Van Duser
VETA LOUISE SIMMONS... Josephine Hull
ELWOOD P. DOWD .... Frank Fay
MISS JOHNSON.......... Eloise Sheldon
MRS. ETHEL CHAUVENET Frederica Going
RUTH KELLY, R.N. .... Janet Tyler
DUANE WILSON .... Jesse White

LYMAN SANDERSON, M.D. ... Tom Seidel
WILLIAM R. CHUMLEY, M.D.
              Fred Irving Lewis
BETTY CHUMLEY .... Dora Clement
JUDGE OMAR GAFFNEY.......John Kirk
E. J. LOFGREN .... Robert Gist

The action of the play takes place in a city in the Far West in the library of the old Dowd family mansion and the reception room of Chumley's Rest. Time is the present.

ACT ONE. *Scene One:* The library, late afternoon. *Scene Two:* Chumley's Rest, an hour later.

ACT TWO. *Scene One:* The library, an hour later. *Scene Two:* Chumley's Rest, four hours later.

ACT THREE: Chumley's Rest, a few minutes later.

INTRODUCTION

The author of *Harvey*, Mary Coyle Chase, has followed a busy career, and although an assiduous writer, has led a full rich life. Perhaps the well appreciated humor she has lavished on *Mrs. McThing* and *Bernardine* as well as *Harvey* is something she developed as wife and mother in her native Denver, high above the oppressive valleys and considerably removed from the frantic show-place of Broadway.

Born on February 25, 1907 in Denver, Colorado, Mary Coyle was educated in that city's public schools and for three years (1921-23) at the University of Denver, after which she spent a year at the University of Colorado, at Boulder. She married the Denver journalist Robert Lamont Chase in 1928 and became the mother of three sons. In 1924, she became a newspaper reporter, and worked regularly for the *Rocky Mountain News* in Denver from 1928 to 1931. Following this stint, she worked as a free-lance correspondent for the International News Service and the United Press from 1932 to 1936. Subsequently she became a publicity director and served the local Teamsters' Union in that capacity from 1942 to 1944.

She wrote her first play, *Now You've Done It*, in 1937, and had another play called *Sorority House* produced as a motion picture in 1938. In 1938 she also wrote another work for the stage, *Too Much Business*. But she attained success as a playwright late, in 1944, with the Brock Pemberton production of *Harvey*, following which she succeeded on Broadway twice again, in 1952, with the fantasy *Mrs. McThing*, in which Helen Hayes delighted the public with a bizarre characterization, and in the same year with *Bernardine*, which commended itself to playgoers with a fresh treatment of adolescence, about which it is to be presumed the mother of three children would know a thing or two.

Mrs. Chase is reported to have worked for two years on her *chef d'oeuvre*; she wrote eighteen versions of *Harvey* before getting this delicately poised play, which blends comedy of character with fantasy, ready for the stage. Even then, she and her producer, Brock Pemberton, faced a problem—what to do with an eight-foot rubber rabbit made specially for the production. The problem was solved when *The Pooka*, as the play was then called, had its tryout in Boston. One look at the rabbit crossing the stage during the dress rehearsal, and both the author and the producer decided to do away with the pixilated Elwood P. Dowd's synthetic companion! Another problem, whom to cast as the lovable lush, was fortunately solved earlier when Pemberton chose the former vaudevillian Frank Fay. The success of the play was assured by the presence of Frank Fay and the absence of his furry companion— and, let us not forget, the assistance of the delightful Josephine Hull in the chief supporting role. No small portion of credit goes, of course, to Mrs. Chase herself. Plays have come and plays have gone since 1945, but New York playgoers have yet to see a more endearing comic fantasy.

ACT ONE

Scene One

TIME: *Mid-afternoon of a spring day. The present.*

SCENE: *The library of the old Dowd family mansion—a room lined with books and set with heavy, old-fashioned furniture of a faded grandeur. The most conspicuous item in the room is an oil painting over a black marble Victorian mantelpiece at the lower part of the wall at stage L. This is the portrait of a lantern-jawed older woman. There are double doors at R. These doors, now pulled apart, lead to the hallway and across to the parlor, which is not seen. Telephone is on small table L. This afternoon there is a festive look to the room— silver bowls with spring flowers set about. From the parlor R. comes the sound of a bad female voice singing, "I'm Called Little Buttercup."*

AT RISE: *MYRTLE MAE is discovered coming through door R. and as telephone rings, she goes to it.*

———

MYRTLE. Mrs. Simmons? Mrs. Simmons is my mother, but she has guests this afternoon. Who wants her? (*Respectful change in tone after she hears who it is.*) Oh—wait just a minute. Hang on just a minute. (*Goes to doorway R. and calls.*) Psst—Mother! (*Cranes her neck more.*) Psst —Mother! (*Crooks her finger insistently several times. Singing continues.*)

VETA (*enters R., humming "Buttercup"*). Yes, dear?

MYRTLE. Telephone.

VETA (*turning to go out again*). Oh, no, dear. Not with all of them in there. Say I'm busy.

MYRTLE. But, Mother. It's the Society Editor of the Evening News Bee—

VETA (*turning*). Oh—the Society Editor. She's very important. (*She fixes her hair and goes to phone. Her voice is very sweet. She throws out chest and assumes dignified pose.*) Good afternoon, Miss Ellerbe. This is Veta Simmons. Yes—a tea and reception for the members of the Wednesday Forum. You might say—program tea. My mother, you know—(*Waves hand toward portrait.*) the late Marcella Pinney Dowd, pioneer cultural leader—she came here by ox-team as a child and she founded the Wednesday Forum. (MYR-

TLE *is watching out door.*) Myrtle—how many would you say?

MYRTLE. Seventy-five, at least. Say a hundred.

VETA (*on phone*). Seventy-five. Miss Tewksbury is the soloist, accompanied by Wilda McCurdy, accompanist.

MYRTLE. Come on! Miss Tewksbury is almost finished with her number.

VETA. She'll do an encore.

MYRTLE. What if they don't give her a lot of applause?

VETA. I've known her for years. She'll do an encore. (MYRTLE *again starts to leave.*) You might say that I am entertaining, assisted by my daughter, Miss Myrtle Mae Simmons. (*To Myrtle—indicates her dress.* MYRTLE MAE *crosses to* C.) What color would you call that?

MYRTLE. Rancho Rose, they told me.

VETA (*into phone*). Miss Myrtle Mae Simmons looked charming in a modish Rancho Rose toned crepe, picked up at the girdle with a touch of magenta on emerald. I wish you could see her, Miss Ellerbe.

MYRTLE (*crossing up* R. *Looks through door*). Mother—please—she's almost finished and where's the cateress?

VETA (*to Myrtle*). Everything's ready. The minute she's finished singing we open the dining-room doors and we begin pouring. (*Into phone.*) The parlors and halls are festooned with smilax. Yes, festooned. (*Makes motion in air with finger.*) That's right. Yes, Miss Ellerbe, this is the first party we've had in years. There's a reason but I don't want it in the papers. We all have our troubles, Miss Ellerbe. The guest list? Oh, yes—

MYRTLE. Mother—come.

VETA. If you'll excuse me now, Miss Ellerbe. I'll call you later. (*Hangs up.*)

MYRTLE. Mother—Mrs. Chauvenet just came in!

VETA (*arranging flowers on phone table*). Mrs. Eugene Chauvenet Senior! Her father was a scout with Buffalo Bill.

MYRTLE. So that's where she got that hat!

VETA (*as she and* MYRTLE *start to exit*). Myrtle, you must be nice to Mrs. Chauvenet. She has a grandson about your age.

MYRTLE. But what difference will it make, with Uncle Elwood?—Mac!

VETA. Myrtle—remember! We agreed not to talk about that this afternoon. The point of this whole party· is to get you started. We work through those older women to the younger group.

MYRTLE. We can't have anyone here in the evenings, and that's when men come to see you—in the evenings. The only reason we can even have a party this afternoon is because Uncle Elwood is playing pinochle at the Fourth Avenue Firehouse. Thank God for the firehouse!

VETA. I know—but they'll just have to invite you out and it won't hurt them one bit. Oh, Myrtle—you've got so much to offer. I don't care what anyone says, there's something sweet about every girl. And a man takes that sweetness, and look what he does with it! (*Crosses to mantel with flowers.*) But you've got to meet somebody, Myrtle. That's all there is to it.

MYRTLE. If I do they say, That's Myrtle Mae Simmons! Her uncle is Elwood P. Dowd—the biggest screwball in town. Elwood P. Dowd and his pal—

VETA (*puts hand on her mouth*). You promised.

MYRTLE (*crossing above table, sighs*). All right—let's get them into the dining-room.

VETA. Now when the members come in here and you make your little welcome speech on behalf of your grandmother—be sure to do this. (*Gestures toward portrait on mantel.*)

MYRTLE (*in fine disgust*). And then after that, I mention my Uncle Elwood and say a few words about his pal Harvey. Damn Harvey! (*In front of table, as she squats.*)

VETA (*the effect on her is electric. She runs over and closes doors. Crosses behind table to* C). Myrtle Mae—that's right! Let everybody in the Wednesday Forum hear you. You said that name. You promised you wouldn't say that name and you said it.

MYRTLE (*rising, starting to cross* L.). I'm sorry, Mother. But how do you know Uncle Elwood won't come in and introduce Harvey to everybody? (*To mantel. Places flowers on it.*)

VETA. This is unkind of you, Myrtle Mae. Elwood is the biggest heartache I have. Even if people do call him peculiar he's still my brother, and he won't be home this afternoon.

MYRTLE. Are you sure?

VETA. Of course I'm sure.

MYRTLE. But Mother, why can't we live like other people?

VETA. Must I remind you again? Elwood is not living with us—we are living with him.

MYRTLE. Living with him and Harvey! Did Grandmother know about Harvey?

VETA. I've wondered and wondered about that. She never wrote me if she did.

MYRTLE. Why did she have to leave all her property to Uncle Elwood?

VETA. Well, I suppose it was because she died in his arms. People are sentimental about things like that.

MYRTLE. You always say that and it doesn't make sense. She couldn't make out her will after she died, could she?

VETA. Don't be didactic, Myrtle Mae. It's not becoming in a young girl, and men loathe it. Now don't forget to wave your hand.

MYRTLE. I'll do my best. (*Opens door.*)

VETA. Oh, dear—Miss Tewksbury's voice is certainly fading!

MYRTLE. But not fast enough. (*She exits.*)

VETA (*exits through door, clapping hands, pulling down girdle*). Lovely, Miss Tewksbury—perfectly lovely. I loved it.

(*Through door* U.L. *enters* ELWOOD P. DOWD. *He is a man about 47 years old with a dignified bearing, and yet a dreamy expression in his eyes. His expression is benign, yet serious to the point of gravity. He wears an overcoat and a battered old hat. This hat, reminiscent of the Joe College era, sits on the top of his head. Over his arm he carries another hat and coat. As he enters, although he is alone, he seems to be ushering and bowing someone else in with him. He bows the invisible person over to a chair. His step is light, his movements quiet and his voice low-pitched*).

ELWOOD (*to invisible person*). Excuse me a moment. I have to answer the phone. Make yourself comfortable, Harvey. (*Phone rings.*) Hello. Oh, you've got the wrong number. But how are you, anyway? This is Elwood P. Dowd speaking. I'll do? Well, thank you. And what is your name, my dear? Miss Elsie Greenawalt? (*To chair.*) Harvey, it's a Miss Elsie Greenawalt. How are you today, Miss Greenawalt? That's fine. Yes, my dear. I would be happy to join your club. I belong to several clubs now—the University Club, the Country Club and the Pinochle Club at the

Fourth Avenue Firehouse. I spend a good deal of my time there, or at Charlie's Place, or over at Eddie's Bar. And what is your club, Miss Greenawalt? (*He listens—then turns to empty chair.*) Harvey, I get the Ladies Home Journal, Good Housekeeping and the Open Road for Boys for two years for six twenty-five. (*Back to phone.*) It sounds fine to me. I'll join it. (*To chair.*) How does it sound to you, Harvey? (*Back to phone.*) Harvey says it sounds fine to him also, Miss Greenawalt. He says he will join, too. Yes— two subscriptions. Mail everything to this address. . . . I hope I will have the pleasure of meeting you some time, my dear. Harvey, she says she would like to meet me. When? When would you like to meet me, Miss Greenawalt? Why not right now? My sister seems to be having a few friends in and we would consider it an honor if you would come and join us. My sister will be delighted. 343 Temple Drive—I hope to see you in a very few minutes. Good-by, my dear. (*Hangs up.*) She's coming right over. (*Moves C. to* HARVEY.) Harvey, don't you think we'd better freshen up? Yes, so do I. (*He takes up hats and coats and exits* L.)

VERA (*enters, followed by* MAID). I can't seem to remember where I put that guest list. I must read it to Miss Ellerbe. . . . Have you seen it, Miss Johnson?

MAID. No, I haven't, Mrs. Simmons.

VETA. Look on my dresser. (MAID *exits* L.)

MYRTLE (*enters* R.). Mother—Mrs. Chauvenet—she's asking for you. (*Turning—speaking in oh-so-sweet tone to someone in hall.*) Here's Mother, Mrs. Chauvenet. Here she is. (*Enter* MRS. CHAUVENET. *She is a woman of about 65—heavy, dressed with the casual sumptuousness of a wealthy Western society woman—in silvery gold and plush, and mink scarf even though it is a spring day. She rushes over to* VETA.)

MRS. CHAUVENET. Veta Louise Simmons! I thought you were dead. (*Gets to her and takes hold of her.*)

VETA (*rushing to her, they kiss*). Aunt Ethel! (*Motioning to* MYRTLE *to come forward and meet the great lady.*) Oh, no— I'm very much alive—thank you—

MRS. CHAUVENET (*turning to* MYRTLE).— and this full-grown girl is your daughter I've known you since you were a baby.

MYRTLE. I know.

MRS. CHAUVENET. What's your name,

dear?

VETA (*proudly*). This is Myrtle—Aunt Ethel. Myrtle Mae—for the two sisters of her father. He's dead. That's what confused you.

MRS. CHAUVENET. Where's Elwood?

VETA (*with a nervous glance at* MYRTLE MAE). He couldn't be here, Aunt Ethel — now let me get you some tea. (*Cross to* R. *of table* R.)

MRS. CHAUVENET. Elwood isn't here?

VETA. No—

MRS. CHAUVENET. Oh, shame on him. That was the main reason I came. (*Takes off scarf—puts it on chair* L. *of table.*) I want to see Elwood.

VETA. Come—there are loads of people anxious to speak to you.

MRS. CHAUVENET. Do you realize, Veta, it's been years since I've seen Elwood?

VETA. No—where does the time go?

MRS. CHAUVENET. But I don't understand it. I was saying to Mr. Chauvenet only the other night—what on earth do you suppose has happened to Elwood Dowd? He never comes to the club dances any more. I haven't seen him at a horse show in years. Does Elwood see anybody these days?

VETA (*and* MYRTLE *glance at each other*). Oh, yes—Aunt Ethel. Elwood sees somebody.

MYRTLE. Oh, yes.

MRS. CHAUVENET (*to* MYRTLE). Your Uncle Elwood, child, is one of my favorite people. (VETA *rises and crosses around chair* R. *of table.*) Always has been.

VETA. Yes, I remember.

MRS. CHAUVENET. Is Elwood happy, Veta?

VETA. Elwood's very happy, Aunt Ethel. You don't need to worry about Elwood——(*Looks through* R. *doorway. She is anxious to get the subject on something else.*) Why, there's Mrs. Frank Cummings— just came in. Don't you want to speak to her?

MRS. CHAUVENET (*crosses above chair to peer out* R). My—but she looks ghastly! Hasn't she failed though?

VETA. If you think she looks badly you should see him!

MRS. CHAUVENET. Is that so? I must have them over. (*Looks again.*) She looks frightful. I thought she was dead.

VETA. Oh, no.

MRS. CHAUVENET. Now—what about tea, Veta?

VETA. Certainly—(*Starts forward to lead the way.*) If you will forgive me, I will precede you——(ELWOOD *enters.* MRS. CHAUVENET *turns back to pick up her scarf from chair, and sees him.*)

MRS. CHAUVENET (*rushing forward*). Elwood! Elwood Dowd! Bless your heart.

ELWOOD (*coming forward and bowing as he takes her hand*). Aunt Ethel! What a pleasure to come in and find a beautiful woman waiting for me!

MRS. CHAUVENET (*looking at him fondly*). Elwood—you haven't changed.

VETA (*moves forward quickly, takes hold of her*). Come along, Aunt Ethel—you mustn't miss the party.

MYRTLE. There's punch if you don't like tea.

MRS. CHAUVENET. But I do like tea. Stop pulling at me, you two. Elwood, what night next week can you come to dinner?

ELWOOD. Any night. Any night at all, Aunt Ethel—I would be delighted.

VETA. Elwood, there's some mail for you today. I took it up to your room.

ELWOOD. Did you, Veta? That was nice of you. Aunt Ethel—I want you to meet Harvey. As you can see he's a Pooka. (*Turns toward air beside him.*) Harvey, you've heard me speak of Mrs. Chauvenet? We always called her Aunt Ethel. She is one of my oldest and dearest friends. (*Inclines head toward space and goes "Hmm!" and then listens as though not hearing first time. Nods as though having heard someone next to him speak.*) Yes—yes—that's right. She's the one. This is the one. (*To* MRS. CHAUVENET.) He says he would have known you anywhere. (*Then as a confused, bewildered look comes over* MRS. CHAUVENET's *face and as she looks to* L. *and* R. *of* ELWOOD *and cranes her neck to see behind him—*ELWOOD, *not seeing her expression, crosses her toward* VETA *and* MYRTLE MAE.) You both look lovely. (*Turns to the air next to him.*) Come in with me, Harvey—We must say hello to all of our friends——(*Bows to* MRS. CHAUVENET.) I beg your pardon, Aunt Ethel. If you'll excuse me for one moment—(*Puts his hand gently on her arm, trying to turn her.*)

MRS. CHAUVENET. What?

ELWOOD. You are standing in his way — (SHE *gives a little—her eyes wide on him.*) Come along, Harvey. (HE *watches the invisible Harvey cross to door, then stops him.*) Uh-uh! (ELWOOD *goes over to door. He turns and pantomimes as he arranges the tie and brushes off the head of the invisible Harvey. Then he does the same thing to his own tie. They are* ALL *watching him,* MRS. CHAUVENET *in horrified fascination. The heads of* VETA *and* MYRTLE, *bowed in agony.*) Go right on in, Harvey. I'll join you in a minute. (*He pantomimes as though slapping him on the back, and ushers him out. Then turns and comes back to* MRS. CHAUVENET.) Aunt Ethel, I can see you are disturbed about Harvey. Please don't be. He stares like that at everybody. It's his way. But he liked you. I could tell. He liked you very much. (*Pats her arm reassuringly, smiles at her, then calmly and confidently goes on out at* R. *After his exit,* MRS. CHAUVENET, MYRTLE *and* VETA *are silent. Finally* VETA—*with a resigned tone—clears her throat.*)

VETA (*looking at* MRS. CHAUVENET). Some tea—perhaps—

MRS. CHAUVENET. Why, I—not right now—I—well—I think I'll be running along. (*Crosses back of table.*)

MYRTLE. But—

VETA (*putting a hand over hers to quiet her*). I'm so sorry—

MRS. CHAUVENET. I'll—I'll be talking to you soon. Good-by—good-by—(*She exits quickly out* L. VETA *stands stiffly—her anger paralyzing her.* MYRTLE *finally tiptoes over and closes one side of door—peeking over, but keeping herself out of sight.*)

MYRTLE. Oh, God—(*Starts to run for doorway.*) Oh, my God!

VETA. Myrtle—where are you going?

MYRTLE. Up to my room. He's introducing Harvey to everybody. I can't face those people now. I wish I were dead.

VETA. Come back here. Stay with me. We'll get him out of there and upstairs to his room.

MYRTLE. I won't do it. I can't. I can't.

VETA. Myrtle Mae! (MYRTLE *stops.* VETA *goes over to her and pulls her down* C., *where they are directly in line with doorway.*) Now—pretend I'm fixing your corsage.

MYRTLE (*covering her face with her hands in shame*). Oh, Mother!

VETA. We've got to. Pretend we're having a gay little chat. Keep looking. When you catch his eye, tell me. He always comes when I call him. Now, then—do you see him yet?

MYRTLE. No—not yet. How do you do, Mrs. Cummings.

VETA. Smile, can't you? Have you no pride? I'm smiling— (*Waves off* R. *and laughs.*) and he's my own brother!

MYRTLE. Oh, Mother—people get run over by trucks every day. Why can't something like that happen to Uncle Elwood?

VETA. Myrtle Mae Simmons, I'm ashamed of you. This thing is not your uncle's fault. (*Phone rings.*)

MYRTLE. Ouch! You're sticking me with that pin!

VETA. That's Miss Ellerbe. Keep looking. Keep smiling. (*She goes to phone.*)

MYRTLE. Mrs. Cummings is leaving. Uncle Elwood must have told her what Harvey is. Oh, God!

VETA (*on phone*). Hello—this is Mrs. Simmons. Should you come in the clothes you have on—What have you on? Who is this? But I don't know any Miss Greenawalt. Should you what?—May I ask who invited you? Mr. Dowd! Thank you just the same, but I believe there has been a mistake.—Well, I never!

MYRTLE. Never what?

VETA. One of your Uncle Elwood's friends. She asked me if she should bring a quart of gin to the Wednesday Forum!

MYRTLE. There he is—he's talking to Mrs. Halsey.

VETA. Is Harvey with him?

MYRTLE. What a thing to ask! How can I tell? How can anybody tell but Uncle Elwood?

VETA (*calls*). Oh, Elwood, could I see you a moment, dear? (*To Myrtle.*) I promise you your Uncle Elwood has disgraced us for the last time in this house. I'm going to do something I've never done before.

MYRTLE. What did you mean just now when you said this was not Uncle Elwood's fault? If it's not his fault, whose fault is it?

VETA. Never you mind. I know whose fault it is. Now lift up your head and smile and go back in as though nothing had happened.

MYRTLE. You're no match for Uncle Elwood.

VETA. You'll see. (ELWOOD *is coming.*)

MYRTLE (*as* THEY *pass at door*). Mother's waiting for you. (*She exits.*)

VETA. Elwood! Could I see you for a moment, dear?

ELWOOD. Yes, sister. Excuse me, Harvey. (VETA *steps quickly over and pulls double doors together.*)

VETA. Elwood, would you mind sitting down in here and waiting for me until the party is over? I want to talk to you. It's very important.

ELWOOD (*crossing* C). Of course, sister. I happen to have a little free time right now and you're welcome to all of it, Veta. Do you want Harvey to wait too?

VETA (*To* R. *of* ELWOOD. *Quite seriously —not in a pampering, humoring tone at all*). Yes, Elwood. I certainly do. (*She steals out—watching him as she crosses through* R. *door. After she has gone out we see doors being pulled together from the outside and hear the click of a lock.* ELWOOD *goes calmly over to bookcase, peruses it carefully, and then when he has found the book he wants, takes it out and from behind it pulls a half-filled pint bottle of liquor.*)

ELWOOD (*looking at book he holds in one hand*). Ah—Jane Austen. (*He gets one chair, pulls it down, facing front. Gets chair* L. *and pulls it right alongside. Sits down, sets bottle on floor between chairs.*) Sit down, Harvey. Veta wants to talk to us. She said it was important. I think she wants to congratulate us on the impression we made at her party. (*Reads. Turns to Harvey. Inclines head and listens, then looks at back of book and answers as though Harvey had asked what edition it is, who published it and what are those names on the fly leaf; turning head toward empty chair each time and twice saying "Hmm?"*) Jane Austen—De Luxe Edition—Limited—Grosset and Dunlap— The usual acknowledgements. Chapter One—

AND THE CURTAIN FALLS

ACT ONE

SCENE TWO

SCENE: *The office in the main building of Chumley's Rest—a sanitarium for mental patients. The wall at back is half plaster and half glass. There is a door* U.C. *Through this we can see the corridor of the sanitarium itself. In the wall lower* R. *is a door which is lettered "Dr. Chumley." Above on* R. *wall is a bookcase, a small filing-case on top of it. Across the room at upper* L. *is another door lettered "Dr. Sanderson." Down* L. *is the door leading from the outside. There is a big desk* L.C. *at right angles with footlights, with chair either side of desk. At* R. *is a table with chairs on either side. One small chair upstage* C.

TIME: *An hour after the curtain of Scene One.*

AT RISE: MISS RUTH KELLY, *head nurse at Chumley's Rest, is seated* L. *of desk, taking notes as she talks to* VETA SIMMONS, *who stands* C. MISS KELLY *is a very pretty young woman of about twenty-four. She is wearing a starched white uniform and cap. As she talks to Veta she writes on a slip of paper with a pencil.*

———

KELLY (*writing*). Mrs. O. R. Simmons, 343 Temple Drive, is that right?

VETA (*nodding, taking handkerchief from handbag*). We were born and raised there. It's old but we love it. It's our home. (*Crosses to table* R., *puts down handbag.*)

KELLY. And you wish to enter your brother here at the sanitarium for treatment. Your brother's name?

VERA (*coming back to desk—raising handkerchief to eyes and dabbing*). It's—oh—

KELLY. Mrs. Simmons, what is your brother's name?

VETA. I'm sorry. Life is not easy for any of us. I'll have to hold my head up and go on just the same. That's what I keep telling Myrtle and that's what Myrtle Mae keeps telling me. She's heart-broken about her Uncle Elwood—Elwood P. Dowd. That's it. (*Sits chair* R. *of desk.*)

KELLY (*writing*). Elwood P. Dowd. His age?

VETA. Forty-seven the 24th of last April. He's Taurus—Taurus—the bull. I'm Leo, and Myrtle is on a cusp.

KELLY. Forty-seven. Is he married?

VETA. No, Elwood has never married. He stayed with Mother. He was always a great home boy. He loved his home.

KELLY. You have him with you now?

VETA. He's in a taxicab down in the driveway. (KELLY *rings buzzer.*) I gave the driver a dollar to watch him, but I didn't tell the man why. You can't tell these things to perfect strangers. (*Enter* WILSON, C. *He is the sanitarium strongarm. He is a big burly attendant, black-browed, about 28.* KELLY *crosses in front of desk toward bookcase.*)

KELLY. Mr. Wilson, would you step down to a taxi in the driveway and ask a Mr. Dowd if he would be good enough to step up to Room number 24—South Wing G?

WILSON (*glaring at* L. *upper corner of desk*). Ask him?

KELLY (*above table* R., *with a warning glance toward Veta*). This is his sister, Mrs. Simmons. (KELLY *crosses to cabinet* R. *for card.*)

WILSON (*with a feeble grin*). How do— why, certainly—be glad to *escort* him. (*Exits down* L.)

VETA. Thank you.

KELLY (*coming* C. *to* R. *of Veta—handing her printed slip*). The rates here, Mrs. Simmons— you'll find them printed on this card.

VETA (*waving it away*). That will all be taken care of by my mother's estate. The late Marcella Pinney Dowd. Judge Gaffney is our attorney.

KELLY. Now I'll see if Dr. Sanderson can see you. (*Starts toward office* L.)

VETA. Dr. Sanderson? I want to see Dr. Chumley himself.

KELLY (*backs down* C). Oh, Mrs. Simmons, Dr. Sanderson is the one who sees everybody. Dr. Chumley sees no one.

VETA. He's still head of this institution, isn't he? He's still a psychiatrist, isn't he?

KELLY (*shocked at such heresy*). Still a psychiatrist! Dr. Chumley is more than that. He is a psychiatrist with a national reputation. Whenever people have mental breakdowns they at once think of Dr. Chumley.

VETA (*pointing*). That's his office, isn't it? Well, you march right in and tell him I want to see him. If he knows who's in here he'll come out here.

KELLY. I wouldn't dare disturb him, Mrs. Simmons. I would be discharged if I did.

VETA. Well, I don't like to be pushed off onto any second fiddle.

KELLY. Dr. Sanderson is nobody's second fiddle. (*Crosses to back of desk, her eyes aglow.*) He's young, of course, and he hasn't been out of medical school very long, but Dr. Chumley tried out twelve and kept Dr. Sanderson. He's really wonderful—(*Catches herself.*) to the patients.

VETA. Very well. Tell him I'm here.

KELLY (*straightens her cap. As she exits into door* L., *primps*). Right away. (VETA *rises, takes off coat—puts it on back of chair* R. *of desk, sighs.*) Oh dear—oh dear (*and crosses to table* R. WILSON *and* ELWOOD *appear in corridor.* ELWOOD *pulls over a little from* WILSON *and sees* VETA.)

ELWOOD. Veta—isn't this wonderful! (WILSON *takes him forcefully off upstairs.* VETA *is still jumpy and nervous from the surprise, and her back is to door* U.L. *as* DR.

SANDERSON *enters.* LYMAN SANDERSON *is a good-looking man of 27 or 28. He is wearing a starched white coat over dark trousers. His eyes follow* MISS KELLY, *who has walked out before him and gone out* C., *closing* C. *doors. Then he sees* VETA, *pulls down his jacket, and gets a professional bearing.* VETA *has not heard him come in. She is busy with her compact.*)

SANDERSON (*looking at slip in his hand. Crosses to* C). Mrs. Simmons?

VETA (*startled—she jumps*). Oh—oh dear—I didn't hear you come in. You startled me. You're Dr. Sanderson?

SANDERSON (*he nods*). Yes. Will you be seated, please?

VETA (*sits chair* L. *of table* R). Thank you. I hope you don't think I'm jumpy like that all the time, but I—

SANDERSON (*crossing in front of table to chair* R). Of course not. Miss Kelly tells me you are concerned about your brother. Dowd, is it? Elwood P. Dowd?

VETA. Yes, Doctor—he's—this isn't easy for me, Doctor.

SANDERSON (*kindly*). Naturally these things aren't easy for the families of patients. I understand.

VETA (*twisting her handkerchief nervously*). It's what Elwood's doing to himself, Doctor—that's the thing. Myrtle Mae has a right to nice friends. She's young and her whole life is before her. That's my daughter.

SANDERSON (*sits* R. *of table*). Your daughter. How long has it been since you began to notice any peculiarity in your brother's actions?

VETA. I noticed it right away when Mother died, and Myrtle Mae and I came back home from Des Moines to live with Elwood. I could see that he—that he— (*Twists handkerchief—looks pleadingly at Sanderson.*)

SANDERSON. That he—what? Take your time, Mrs. Simmons. Don't strain. Let it come. I'll wait for it.

VETA. Doctor—everything I say to you is confidential? Isn't it?

SANDERSON. That's understood.

VETA. Because it's a slap in the face to everything we've stood for in this community the way Elwood is acting now.

SANDERSON. I am not a gossip, Mrs. Simmons. I am a psychiatrist.

VETA. Well—for one thing—he drinks.

SANDERSON. To excess?

VETA. To excess? Well—don't you call it excess when a man never lets a day go by without stepping into one of those cheap taverns, sitting around with riff-raff and people you never heard of? Inviting them to the house—playing cards with them—giving them food and money. And here I am trying to get Myrtle Mae started with a nice group of young people. If that isn't excess I'm sure I don't know what excess is.

SANDERSON. I didn't doubt your statement, Mrs. Simmons. I merely asked if your brother drinks.

VETA. Well, yes, I say definitely Elwood drinks and I want him committed out here permanently, because I cannot stand another day of that Harvey. Myrtle and I have to set a place at the table for Harvey. We have to move over on the sofa and make room for Harvey. We have to answer the telephone when Elwood calls and asks to speak to Harvey. Then at the party this afternoon with Mrs. Chauvenet there—We didn't even know anything about Harvey until we came back here. Doctor, don't you think it would have been a little bit kinder of Mother to have written and told me about Harvey? Be honest, now—don't you?

SANDERSON. I really couldn't answer that question, because I——

VETA. I can. Yes—it certainly would have.

SANDERSON. This person you call Harvey—who is he?

VETA. He's a rabbit.

SANDERSON. Perhaps—but just who is he? Some companion—someone your brother has picked up in these bars, of whom you disapprove?

VETA (*patiently*). Doctor—I've been telling you. Harvey is a rabbit—a big white rabbit—six feet high—or is it six feet and a half? Heaven knows I ought to know. He's been around the house long enough.

SANDERSON (*regarding her narrowly*). Now, Mrs. Simmons, let me understand this—you say—

VETA (*impatient*). Doctor—do I have to keep repeating myself? My brother insists that his closest friend is this big white rabbit. This rabbit is named Harvey. Harvey lives at our house. Don't you understand? He and Elwood go every place together. Elwood buys railroad tickets, theater tickets, for both of them. As I told Myrtle Mae—if your uncle was so lonesome he had to bring something home   why couldn't he bring home something human? He has me, doesn't he? He has Myrtle Mae, doesn't he? (*She leans forward.*) Doctor—(*She rises to him.* HE *inclines toward her.*) I'm going to tell you something I've never told anybody in the world before. (*Puts her hand on his shoulder.*) Every once in a while I see that big white rabbit myself. Now isn't that terrible? I've never even told that to Myrtle Mae.

SANDERSON (*now convinced. Starts to rise*). Mrs. Simmons—

VETA (*straightening*). And what's more — he's every bit as big as Elwood says he is. Now don't ever tell that to anybody, Doctor. I'm ashamed of it. (*Crosses to* C., *to chair* R. *of desk.*)

SANDERSON (*crosses to* VETA). I can see that you have been under a great nervous strain recently.

VETA. Well—I certainly have.

SANDERSON. Grief over your mother's death depressed you considerably?

VETA (*sits chair* R. *of desk*). Nobody knows how much.

SANDERSON. Been losing sleep?

VETA. How could anybody sleep with that going on?

SANDERSON (*crosses to back of desk*). Short-tempered over trifles?

VETA. You just try living with those two and see how your temper holds up.

SANDERSON (*presses buzzer*). Loss of appetite?

VETA. No one could eat at a table with my brother and a big white rabbit. Well, I'm finished with it. I'll sell the house— be appointed conservator of Elwood's estate, and Myrtle Mae and I will be able to entertain our friends in peace. It's too much, Doctor. I just can't stand it.

SANDERSON (*has been repeatedly pressing a buzzer on his desk. He looks with annoyance toward hall door. His answer now to* VETA *is gentle*). Of course, Mrs. Simmons. Of course it is. You're tired.

VETA (*she nods*). Oh, yes I am.

SANDERSON. You've been worrying a great deal.

VETA (*nods*). Yes, I have. I can't help it.

SANDERSON. And now I'm going to help you.

VETA. Oh, Doctor . . .

SANDERSON (*goes cautiously to door— watching her*). Just sit there quietly, Mrs. Simmons. I'll be right back. (*He exits* C.)

VETA (*sighing with relief, rises and calls out as she takes coat*). I'll just go down to the cab and get Elwood's things. (*She exits out down* L. SANDERSON, KELLY, *and* WILSON *come from* C.)

SANDERSON. Why didn't someone answer the buzzer?

KELLY. I didn't hear you, Doctor—

SANDERSON. I rang and rang. (*Looks into his office. It is empty.*) Mrs. Simmons— (*Looks out door* L., *shuts it, comes back.*) Sound the gong, Wilson. That poor woman must not leave the grounds.

WILSON. She's made with a getaway, huh, Doc? (WILSON *presses a button on the wall and we hear a loud gong sounding.*)

SANDERSON. Her condition is serious. Go after her. (WILSON *exits* C.)

KELLY. I can't believe it. (*Above chair* R. *of desk.* SANDERSON *sits* L. *of desk and picks up phone.*)

SANDERSON. Main gate. Henry, Dr. Sanderson. Allow no one out of the main gate. We're looking for a patient. (*Hangs up.*) I shouldn't have left her alone, but no one answered the buzzer.

KELLY. Wilson was in South, Doctor.

SANDERSON (*making out papers*). What have we available, Miss Kelly?

KELLY. Number 13, upper West R., is ready, Doctor.

SANDERSON. Have her taken there immediately, and I will prescribe preliminary treatment. I must contact her brother. Dowd is the name. Elwood P. Dowd. Get him on the telephone for me, will you please, Miss Kelly?

KELLY. But Doctor—I didn't know it was the woman who needed the treatment. She said it was for her brother.

SANDERSON. Of course she did. It's the oldest dodge in the world—always used by a cunning type of psychopath. She apparently knew her brother was about to commit her, so she came out to discredit him. Get him on the telephone, please.

KELLY. But, Doctor—I thought the woman was all right, so I had Wilson take the brother up to No. 24 South Wing G. He's there now.

SANDERSON (*staring at her with horror*). You had Wilson take the brother in? No gags, please, Kelly. You're not serious, are you?

KELLY. Oh, I did, Doctor. I did. Oh, Doctor, I'm terribly sorry.

SANDERSON. Oh, well then, if you're sorry, that fixes everything. (*He starts to pick up house phone and finishes the curse under his breath.*) Oh—no! (*Buries his head in his hands.*)

KELLY. I'll do it, Doctor. I'll do it. (*She takes phone.*) Miss Dunphy—will you please unlock the door to Number 24—and give Mr. Dowd his clothes and——? (*Looks at Sanderson for direction.*)

SANDERSON. Ask him to step down to the office right away.

KELLY (*into phone*). Ask him to step down to the office right away. There's been a terrible mistake and Dr. Sanderson wants to explain—

SANDERSON (*crosses below table to* C). Explain? Apologize!

KELLY (*hanging up*). Thank heaven they hadn't put him in a hydro tub yet. She'll let him out.

SANDERSON (*staring at her*). Beautiful—and dumb, too. It's almost too good to be true.

KELLY (*crosses to* L. *of Sanderson*). Doctor—I feel terrible. I didn't know. Judge Gaffney called and said Mrs. Simmons and her brother would be out here, and when she came in here—you don't have to be sarcastic.

SANDERSON. Oh, don't I? Stop worrying. We'll squirm out of it some way. (*Thinking—starts toward* R.)

KELLY. Where are you going?

SANDERSON. I've got to tell the chief about it, Kelly. He may want to handle this himself.

KELLY. He'll be furious. I know he will. He'll die. And then he'll terminate me.

SANDERSON (*below table, catches her shoulders*). The responsibility is all mine, Kelly.

KELLY. Oh, no—tell him it was all my fault, Doctor.

SANDERSON. I never mention your name. (*Crossing to door* R.) Except in my sleep.

KELLY. But this man Dowd——(*Kneels on chair* R.)

SANDERSON. Don't let him get away. I'll be right back.

KELLY (*crosses to* L. *of chair* R. *of table*). But what shall I say to him? What shall I do? He'll be furious.

SANDERSON. Look, Kelly—he'll probably be fit to be tied—but he's a man, isn't he?

KELLY. I guess so—his name is Mister. (*Off chair.*)

SANDERSON (*across chair from her*). Go into your old routine—you know—the eyes—the swish—the works. I'm immune—but I've seen it work with some people—some of the patients out here. Keep him here, Kelly—if you have to do a strip tease. (*He exits* R.)

KELLY (*very angry. Speaks to closed door*). Well, of all the—oh—you're wonderful, Dr. Sanderson! You're just about the most wonderful person I ever met in my life. (*Kicks chair.*)

WILSON (*has entered from* C. *in time to hear last sentence*). Yeah—but how about giving me a lift here just the same?

KELLY. What?

WILSON. That Simmons dame.

KELLY (*crosses to Wilson*). Did you catch her?

WILSON. Slick as a whistle. She was comin' along the path hummin' a little tune. I jumped out at her from behind a tree. I says "Sister—there's a man wants to see you." Shoulda heard her yell! She's whacky, all right.

KELLY. Take her to No. 13 upper West R. (*Crosses* WILSON *to back of desk.*)

WILSON. She's there now. Brought her in through the diet kitchen. She's screamin' and kickin' like hell. I'll hold her if you'll come and undress her.

KELLY. Just a second, Wilson. Dr. Sanderson told me to stay here till her brother comes down—(*Round back of desk.*)

WILSON. Make it snappy—(*Goes out* C. ELWOOD *enters* C. KELLY *rises*).

KELLY. You're Mr. Dowd?

ELWOOD (*carrying another hat and coat over his arm. He bows*). Elwood P.

KELLY. I'm Miss Kelly.

ELWOOD. Let me give you one of my cards. (*Fishes in vest pocket—pulls out card.*) If you should want to call me—call me at this number. Don't call me at that one.

KELLY. Thank you.

ELWOOD. Perfectly all right, and if you lose it—don't worry, my dear. I have plenty more.

KELLY. Won't you have a chair, please, Mr. Dowd?

ELWOOD. Thank you. I'll have two. Allow me. (*He brings another chair down from* U.C. *to* L. *of table. Puts extra hat and coat on table* C. *Motions Harvey to sit in chair* L. *of table. He stands waiting.*)

KELLY. Dr. Sanderson is very anxious

to talk to you. He'll be here in a minute. Please be seated.

ELWOOD (*waving her toward chair* R. *of desk*). After you, my dear.

KELLY. Oh, I really can't, thank you. I'm in and out all the time. But you mustn't mind me. Please sit down.

ELWOOD (*bowing*). After you.

KELLY (*she sits chair* R. *of desk. He sits on chair he has just put in place*). Could I get you a magazine to look at?

ELWOOD. I would much rather look at you, Miss Kelly, if you don't mind. You really are very lovely.

KELLY. Oh—well. Thank you. Some people don't seem to think so.

ELWOOD. Some people are blind. That is often brought to my attention. And now, Miss Kelly—I would like to have you meet—(*Enter* SANDERSON *from* R. MISS KELLY *rises and backs up to below desk.* ELWOOD *rises when she does, and he makes a motion to the invisible Harvey to rise, too.*)

SANDERSON (*going to him, extending hand*). Mr. Dowd?

ELWOOD. Elwood P. Let me give you one of my cards. If you should want—

SANDERSON (*crossing to* C). Mr. Dowd— I am Dr. Lyman Sanderson, Dr. Chumley's assistant out here.

ELWOOD. Well, good for you! I'm happy to know you. How are you, Doctor?

SANDERSON. That's going to depend on you, I'm afraid. Please sit down. You've met Miss Kelly, Mr. Dowd?

ELWOOD. I have had that pleasure, and I want both of you to meet a very dear friend of mine—

SANDERSON. Later on—be glad to. Won't you be seated, because first I want to say—

ELWOOD. After Miss Kelly—

SANDERSON. Sit down, Kelly—(SHE *sits* L. *of desk, as does* ELWOOD—*who indicates to Harvey to sit also.*) Is that chair quite comfortable, Mr. Dowd?

ELWOOD. Yes, thank you. Would you care to try it? (*He takes out a cigarette.*)

SANDERSON. No, thank you. How about an ash tray there? Could we give Mr. Dowd an ash tray? (KELLY *gets up— gets it from wall* L. ELWOOD *and Harvey rise also.* ELWOOD *beams as he turns and watches her.* KELLY *puts ash tray by* DOWD, *who moves it to share with Harvey.*) Is it too warm in here for you, Mr. Dowd? Would you like me to open a window? (ELWOOD

hasn't heard. He is watching Miss Kelly.)

KELLY (*turning, smiling at him*). Mr. Dowd—Dr. Sanderson wants to know if he should open a window?

ELWOOD. That's entirely up to him. I wouldn't presume to live his life for him. (*During this dialogue* SANDERSON *is near window.* KELLY *has her eyes on his face.* ELWOOD *smiles at Harvey fondly.* KELLY *sits at* L. *of desk.*)

SANDERSON. Now then, Mr. Dowd, I can see that you're not the type of person to be taken in by any high-flown phrases or beating about the bush. (*Sits on lower* R. *corner of desk.*)

ELWOOD (*politely*). Is that so, Doctor?

SANDERSON. You have us at a disadvantage here. You know it. We know it. Let's lay the cards on the table.

ELWOOD. That certainly appeals to me, Doctor.

SANDERSON. Best way in the long run. People are people, no matter where you go.

ELWOOD. That is very often the case.

SANDERSON. And being human are therefore liable to mistakes. Miss Kelly and I have made a mistake here this afternoon, Mr. Dowd, and we'd like to explain it to you.

KELLY. It wasn't Doctor Sanderson's fault, Mr. Dowd. It was mine.

SANDERSON. A human failing—as I said.

ELWOOD. I find it very interesting, nevertheless. You and Miss Kelly here? (THEY *nod.*) This afternoon—you say? (THEY *nod.* ELWOOD *gives Harvey a knowing look.*)

KELLY. We do hope you'll understand, Mr. Dowd.

ELWOOD. Oh, yes. Yes. These things are often the basis of a long and warm friendship.

SANDERSON. And the responsibility is, of course, not hers—but mine.

ELWOOD. Your attitude may be old-fashioned, Doctor—but I like it.

SANDERSON. Now, if I had seen your sister first—that would have been an entirely different story.

ELWOOD. Now there you surprise me. I think the world and all of Veta—but I had supposed she had seen her day. (KELLY *sits chair* R. *of desk.*)

SANDERSON. You must not attach any blame to her. She is a very sick woman. Came in here insisting you were in need of treatment. That's perfectly ridiculous.

ELWOOD. Veta shouldn't be upset about me. I get along fine.

SANDERSON. Exactly—but your sister had already talked to Miss Kelly, and there had been a call from your family lawyer, Judge Gaffney

ELWOOD. Oh, yes, I know him. Know his wife, too. Nice people. (*He turns to Harvey takes cigarette; he needs a match.*)

SANDERSON. Is there something I can get for you, Mr. Dowd?

ELWOOD. What did you have in mind?

SANDERSON. A light—here—let me give you a light. (*Crosses to* DOWD, *lights his cigarette.* ELWOOD *brushes smoke away from the rabbit*). Your sister was extremely nervous and plunged right away into a heated tirade on your drinking. (*Crosses back to sit on chair* R. *of desk.*)

ELWOOD. That was Veta.

SANDERSON. She became hysterical.

ELWOOD. I tell Veta not to worry about that. I'll take care of that.

SANDERSON. Exactly. Oh, I suppose you take a drink now and then—the same as the rest of us?

ELWOOD. Yes, I do. As a matter of fact, I would like one right now.

SANDERSON. Matter of fact, so would I, but your sister's reaction to the whole matter of drinking was entirely too intense. Does your sister drink, Mr. Dowd?

ELWOOD. Oh, no, Doctor. No. I don't believe Veta has ever taken a drink.

SANDERSON. Well, I'm going to surprise you. I think she has and does—constantly.

ELWOOD. I am certainly surprised.

SANDERSON. But it's not her alcoholism that's going to be the basis for my diagnosis of her case. It's much more serious than that. It was when she began talking so emotionally about this big white rabbit—Harvey—yes, I believe she called him Harvey—

ELWOOD (*nodding*). Harvey is his name.

SANDERSON. She claimed you were persecuting her with this Harvey.

ELWOOD. I haven't been persecuting her with Harvey. Veta shouldn't feel that way. And now, Doctor, before we go any further I must insist you let me introduce—(*He starts to rise.*)

SANDERSON. Let me make my point first, Mr. Dowd. This trouble of your sister's didn't spring up overnight. Her condition stems from trauma.

ELWOOD (*sits down again*). From what?

SANDERSON. From trauma spelled T-R-A-U-M-A. It means shock. Nothing unusual about it. There is the birth trauma. The shock to the act of being born.

ELWOOD (*nodding*). That's the one we never get over—

SANDERSON. You have a nice sense of humor, Dowd—hasn't he, Miss Kelly?

KELLY. Oh, yes, Doctor.

ELWOOD. May I say the same about both of you?

SANDERSON. To sum it all up—your sister's condition is serious, but I can help her. She must however remain out here temporarily.

ELWOOD. I've always wanted Veta to have everything she needs.

SANDERSON. Exactly.

ELWOOD. But I wouldn't want Veta to stay out here unless she liked it out here and wanted to stay here.

SANDERSON. Of course. (*To Kelly.*) Did Wilson get what he went after? (KELLY *nods.*)

KELLY. Yes, Doctor. (*She rises.*)

SANDERSON. What was Mrs. Simmons' attitude, Miss Kelly?

KELLY (*crosses above desk to file cabinet* R). Not unusual, Doctor.

SANDERSON (*rising*). Mr. Dowd, if this were an ordinary delusion—something reflected on the memory picture—in other words, if she were seeing something she had seen once—that would be one thing. But this is more serious. It stands to reason nobody has ever seen a white rabbit six feet high.

ELWOOD (*smiles at Harvey*). Not very often, Doctor.

SANDERSON. I like you, Dowd.

ELWOOD. I like you, too, Doctor. And Miss Kelly here. (*Looks for* MISS KELLY, *who is just crossing in front of window seat.* ELWOOD *springs to his feet.* KELLY *sits quickly.* ELWOOD *motions Harvey down and sits, himself.*) I like her, too.

SANDERSON. So she must be committed here temporarily. Under these circumstances I would commit my own grandmother. (*Goes to* L. *of desk.*)

ELWOOD. Does your grandmother drink, too?

SANDERSON. It's just an expression. (*Leans over desk.*) Now will you sign these temporary commitment papers as next-of-kin—just a formality?

ELWOOD (*rises, crosses to* R. *of desk*). You'd better have Veta do that, Doctor. She always does all the signing and managing for the family. She's good at it. (*Pushes chair* R. *of desk under desk.*)

SANDERSON. We can't disturb her now. (*Sits* L. *of desk.*)

ELWOOD. Perhaps I'd better talk it over with Judge Gaffney?

SANDERSON. You can explain it all to him later. Tell him I advised it. And it isn't as if you couldn't drop in here any time and make inquiries. Glad to have you. I'll make out a full visitor's pass for you. When would you like to come back? Wednesday, say? Friday, say?

ELWOOD. You and Miss Kelly have been so pleasant I can come back right after dinner. About an hour.

SANDERSON (*taken aback*). Well—we're pretty busy around here, but I guess that's all right.

ELWOOD. I don't really have to go now. I'm not very hungry.

SANDERSON. Delighted to have you stay—but Miss Kelly and I have to get on upstairs now. Plenty of work to do. But I tell you what you might like to do.

ELWOOD. What might I like to do?

SANDERSON. We don't usually do this— but just to make sure in your mind that your sister is in good hands why don't you look around here? If you go through that door—(*Rises—points beyond stairway.*) and turn right just beyond the stairway you'll find the occupational therapy room down the hall, and beyond that the conservatory, the library, and the diet kitchen.

ELWOOD. For Veta's sake I believe I'd better do that, Doctor.

SANDERSON. Very well, then. (*He is now anxious to terminate the interview. Rises, shakes hands.*) It's been a great pleasure to have this little talk with you, Mr. Dowd. (*Gives him pass.*)

ELWOOD (*walking toward her*). I've enjoyed it too, Doctor—meeting you and Miss Kelly.

SANDERSON. And I will say that for a layman you show an unusually acute perception into psychiatric problems.

ELWOOD. Is that a fact? I never thought I knew anything about it. Nobody does, do you think?

SANDERSON. Well—the good psychiatrist is not found under every bush.

ELWOOD. You have to pick the right bush. Since we all seem to have enjoyed this so much, let us keep right on. I would like to invite you to come with me now down to Charlie's Place and have a drink. When I enjoy people I like to stay right with them.

SANDERSON. Sorry—we're on duty now. Give us a rain check. Some other time be glad to.

ELWOOD. When?

SANDERSON. Oh—can't say right now. Miss Kelly and I don't go off duty till ten o'clock at night.

ELWOOD. Let us go to Charlie's at ten o'clock tonight.

SANDERSON. Well—

ELWOOD. And you, Miss Kelly?

KELLY. I—(*Looks at Sanderson.*)

SANDERSON. Dr. Chumley doesn't approve of members of the staff fraternizing, but since you've been so understanding perhaps we could manage it.

ELWOOD. I'll pick you up out here in a cab at ten o'clock tonight and the four of us will spend a happy evening. I want you both to become friends with a very dear friend of mine. You said later on— so later on it will be. Good-by, now. (*Motions good-by to Harvey. Tips hat, exits* C.)

KELLY (*places chair and ash tray against back wall*). Whew—now I can breathe again!

SANDERSON. Boy, that was a close shave all right, but he seemed to be a pretty reasonable sort of fellow. That man is proud—what he has to be proud of I don't know. I played up to that pride. You can get to almost anybody if you want to. Now I must look in on that Simmons woman. (*Crosses below desk toward* C.)

KELLY (*at* R. C.). Dr. Sanderson—! (SANDERSON *turns.*) You say you can get to anybody if you want to. How can you do that?

SANDERSON. Takes study, Kelly. Years of specialized training. There's only one thing I don't like about this Dowd business.

KELLY. What's that?

SANDERSON. Having to make that date with him. Of course the man has left here as a good friend and booster of this sanitarium—so I guess I'll have to go with him tonight—but you don't have to go.

KELLY. Oh! (*Back of chair* L. *of table.*)

SANDERSON. No point in it. I'll have a drink with him, pat him on the back and leave. I've got a date tonight, anyway.

KELLY (*freezing*). Oh, yes—by all means. I didn't intend to go, anyway. The idea bored me stiff. I wouldn't go if I never went anywhere again. I wouldn't go if my life depended on it.

SANDERSON (*stepping back to her*). What's the matter with you, Kelly? What are you getting so emotional about?

KELLY. He may be a peculiar man with funny clothes, but he knows how to act. His manners were perfect.

SANDERSON. I saw you giving him the doll-puss stare. I didn't miss that.

KELLY. He wouldn't sit down till I sat down. He told me I was lovely and he called me dear. I'd go to have a drink with him if you weren't going.

SANDERSON. Sure you would. And look at him! All he does is hang around bars. He doesn't work. All that corny bowing and getting up out of his chair every time a woman makes a move. Why, he's as outdated as a cast-iron deer. But you'd sit with him in a bar and let him flatter you—You're a wonderful girl, Kelly.

KELLY. Now let me tell you something—you—(*Enter from down* R. *the great* DR. WILLIAM CHUMLEY. DR. CHUMLEY *is a large, handsome man of about 57. He has gray hair and wears rimless glasses, which he removes now and then to tap on his hand for emphasis. He is smartly dressed. His manner is confident, pompous, and lordly. He is good and he knows it*).

CHUMLEY (*enters with book*). Dr. Sanderson! Miss Kelly! (THEY *break apart and jump to attention like two buck privates before a C.O.*)

KELLY AND SANDERSON. Yes, Doctor?

CHUMLEY. Tell the gardener to prune more carefully around my prize dahlias along the fence by the main road. They'll be ready for cutting next week. (*At upper corner of bookcase.*) The difficulty of the woman who has the big white rabbit— has it been smoothed over?

SANDERSON. Yes, Doctor. I spoke to her brother and he was quite reasonable.

CHUMLEY. While I have had many patients out here who saw animals, I have never before had a patient with an animal that large. (*Puts book in bookcase.*)

SANDERSON. Yes, Doctor. She called him Harvey.

CHUMLEY. Harvey. Unusual name for an animal of any kind. Harvey is a man's name. I have known several men in my day named Harvey, but I have never heard of any type of animal whatsoever with that name. The case has an interesting phase, Doctor. (*Finishes straightening books.*)

SANDERSON. Yes, Doctor.

CHUMLEY. I will now go upstairs with you and look in on this woman. It may be that we can use my formula 977 on her. I will give you my advice in prescribing the treatment, Doctor. (*Crosses to below table.*)

SANDERSON. Thank you, Doctor.

CHUMLEY. (*Starts to move across stage toward* C. *and stops, draws himself up sternly.*) And now—may I ask—what is that hat and coat doing on that table? Whose is it?

SANDERSON. I don't know. Do you know, Miss Kelly? Was it Dowd's?

KELLY (*above table, picking up hat and coat*). He had his hat on, Doctor. Perhaps it belongs to a relative of one of the patients.

CHUMLEY (*crosses to* C.). Hand me the hat. (KELLY *hands it. Looking inside:*) There may be some kind of identification— Here—what's this   what's this? (*Pushes two fingers up through the holes.*) Two holes cut in the crown of this hat. See!

KELLY. That's strange!

CHUMLEY. Some new fad—put them away. Hang them up—get them out of here. (KELLY *takes them into upper* L. *office.* CHUMLEY *starts crossing to table.* KELLY *has come out of* L. WILSON *comes in through* C.)

WILSON (*very impressed with Dr. Chumley and very fond of him.*) Hello, Dr. Chumley.

CHUMLEY. Oh, there you are.

WILSON. How is every little old thing? (DR. CHUMLEY *picks up pad of notes from* R. *of desk;* R. *of table, looking at notes.* KELLY *re-enters from upper left.*)

CHUMLEY. Fair, thank you, Wilson, fair.

WILSON (*top of desk*). Look—somebody's gonna have to give me a hand with this Simmons dame—order a restraining jacket or something. She's terrible. (*To Kelly.*) Forgot me, didn't you? Well, I got her corset off all by myself.

CHUMLEY. We're going up to see this patient right now, Wilson.

WILSON. She's in a hydro tub now— my God—I left the water running on her! (*Runs off* C. *upstairs, followed by*

KELLY.) (BETTY CHUMLEY, *the Doctor's wife, enters down* L. *She is a good-natured, gay, bustling woman of about 55.*)

BETTY. Willie—remember your promise—Hello, Dr. Sanderson. Willie, you haven't forgotten Dr. McClure's cocktail party? We promised them faithfully. (*Sits* L. *of table* R.)

CHUMLEY. That's right. I have to go upstairs now and look in on a patient. Be down shortly—(*Exits* C. *upstairs.*)

BETTY (*calling after him; as she crosses down to chair* L. *of table, she sits, fixes her shoe*). Give a little quick diagnosis, Willie—we don't want to be late to the party. I'm dying to see the inside of that house. (*Enter* ELWOOD *from* C. *He doesn't see Betty at first. He looks around the room carefully.*) Good evening.

ELWOOD (*removing his hat and bowing*). Good evening. (*Puts hat on desk. Walks over to her.*)

BETTY. I am Mrs. Chumley. Doctor Chumley's wife.

ELWOOD. I'm happy to know that. Dowd is my name. Elwood P. Let me give you one of my cards. (*Gives her one.*) If you should want to call me—call me at this one. Don't call me at that one, because that's—(*Points at card.*) the old one. (*Starts one step. Looking.*)

BETTY. Thank you. Is there something I can do for you?

ELWOOD (*turns to her*). What did you have in mind?

BETTY. You seem to be looking for someone.

ELWOOD (*walking*). Yes, I am. I'm looking for Harvey. I went off without him.

BETTY. Harvey? Is he a patient here?

ELWOOD (*turns*). Oh, no. Nothing like that. (*Cross to door down* L.)

BETTY. Does he work here?

ELWOOD (*looking out down* L. *door*). Oh, no. He is what you might call my best friend. He is also a pooka. He came out here with me and Veta this afternoon.

BETTY. Where was he when you last saw him?

ELWOOD (*behind chair* L. *of desk*). In that chair there—with his hat and coat on the table.

BETTY. There doesn't seem to be any hat and coat around here now. Perhaps he left?

ELWOOD. Apparently. I don't see him anywhere. (*Looks in* SANDERSON'S *office.*)

BETTY. What was that word you just said—pooka?

ELWOOD (*crosses* C. *He is looking in hallway* C.) Yes—that's it.

BETTY. Is that something new? (*Looks in hallway.*)

ELWOOD (*coming down*). Oh, no. As I understand it, that's something very old.

BETTY. Oh, really? I had never happened to hear it before.

ELWOOD. I'm not too surprised at that. I hadn't myself, until I met him. I do hope you get an opportunity to meet him. I'm sure he would be quite taken with you. (*Down* C. *on a line with Betty.*)

BETTY. Oh, really? Well, that's very nice of you to say so, I'm sure.

ELWOOD. Not at all. If Harvey happens to take a liking to people he expresses himself quite definitely. If he's not particularly interested, he sits there like an empty chair or an empty space on the floor. Harvey takes his time making his mind up about people. Choosey, you see. (*Crosses above table to door* R.)

BETTY. That's not such a bad way to be in this day and age.

ELWOOD. Harvey is fond of my sister, Veta. That's because he is fond of me, and Veta and I come from the same family. Now you'd think that feeling would be mutual, wouldn't you? (*Looks in office* R. *Crosses to chair* R. *of table.*) But Veta doesn't seem to care for Harvey. Don't you think that's rather too bad, Mrs. Chumley?

BETTY. Oh, I don't know, Mr. Dowd. I gave up a long time ago expecting my family to like my friends. It's useless.

ELWOOD. But we must keep on trying. (*Sits chair* R. *of table.*)

BETTY. Well, there's no harm in trying, I suppose.

ELWOOD. Because if Harvey has said to me once he has said a million times—"Mr. Dowd, I would do anything for you." Mrs. Chumley—

BETTY. Yes—

ELWOOD. Did you know that Mrs. McElhinney's Aunt Rose is going to drop in on her unexpectedly tonight from Cleveland?

BETTY. Why, no I didn't—

ELWOOD. Neither does she. That puts you both in the same boat, doesn't it?

BETTY. Well, I don't know anybody named—Mrs.—

ELWOOD. Mrs. McElhinney? Lives next door to us. She is a wonderful woman. Harvey told me about her Aunt Rose. That's an interesting little news item, and you are perfectly free to pass it around.

BETTY. Well, I——

ELWOOD. Would you care to come downtown with me now, my dear? I would be glad to buy you a drink.

BETTY. Thank you very much, but I am waiting for Dr. Chumley and if he came down and found me gone he would be liable to raise—he would be irritated!

ELWOOD. We wouldn't want that, would we? Some other time, maybe? (*He rises.*)

BETTY. I'll tell you what I'll do, however.

ELWOOD. What will you do, however? I'm interested.

BETTY. If your friend comes in while I'm here I'd be glad to give him a message for you.

ELWOOD (*gratefully*). Would you do that? I'd certainly appreciate that. (*Goes up* C. *to top of desk for his hat.*)

BETTY. No trouble at all. I'll write it down on the back of this. (*Holds up card. Takes pencil from purse.*) What would you like me to tell him if he comes in while I'm still here?

ELWOOD. Ask him to meet me downtown—if he has no other plans.

BETTY (*writing*). Meet Mr. Dowd downtown. Any particular place downtown?

ELWOOD. He knows where. Harvey knows this town like a book.

BETTY (*writing*). Harvey—you know where. Harvey what?

ELWOOD. Just Harvey.

BETTY (*rises—crosses to desk*). I'll tell you what.

ELWOOD. What?

BETTY (*swings chair* R. *of desk in position*). Doctor and I are going right downtown—to 12th and Montview. Dr. McClure is having a cocktail party.

ELWOOD (*at* L. *of desk; he writes that down on pad on desk*). A cocktail party at 12th and Montview.

BETTY. We're driving there in a few minutes. We could give your friend a lift into town.

ELWOOD. I hate to impose on you— but I would certainly appreciate that.

BETTY. No trouble at all. Dr. McClure is having this party for his sister from Wichita.

ELWOOD. I didn't know Dr. McClure had a sister in Wichita.

BETTY. Oh—you *know* Dr. McClure?

ELWOOD. No.

BETTY (*puts Elwood's card down on desk*). But——(*Sits chair* R. *of desk.*)

ELWOOD. You're quite sure you haven't time to come into town with me and have a drink?

BETTY. I really couldn't—but thank you just the same.

ELWOOD. Some other time, perhaps?

BETTY. Thank you.

ELWOOD. It's been very pleasant to meet you, and I hope to see you again.

BETTY. Yes, so do I.

ELWOOD. Good-night, my dear. (*Tips hat—bows—goes to door, turns.*) You can't miss Harvey. He's very tall—(*Shows with hands.*) Like that—(*Exits down* L. *From back* C. *now comes* CHUMLEY, *followed by* SANDERSON *and* KELLY. CHUMLEY *goes to chair* R. *of desk.* KELLY *crosses above table to* R. C. *office for Chumley's hat and coat.* SANDERSON *goes to top of desk.*)

CHUMLEY (*working with pen on desk-pad*). That Simmons woman is unco-operative, Doctor. She refused to admit to me that she has this big rabbit. Insists it's her brother. Give her two of these at nine—another at ten—if she continues to be so restless. Another trip to the hydro-room at eight, and one in the morning at seven. Then we'll see if she won't co-operate tomorrow, won't we, Doctor?

SANDERSON. Yes, Doctor.

CHUMLEY (*putting pen away*). You know where to call me if you need me. Ready, pet?

BETTY. Yes, Willie—and oh, Willie—

CHUMLEY. Yes—

BETTY. There was a man in here—a man named—let me see—(*picks up card from desk.*) Oh, here is his card—Dowd—Elwood P. Dowd. KELLY *enters from* R. *to below table—she has Dr. Chumley's hat.*)

SANDERSON. That's Mrs. Simmons' brother, Doctor. I told him he could look around, and I gave him full visiting privileges.

CHUMLEY. She mustn't see anyone to-night. Not anyone at all. Tell him that.

SANDERSON. Yes, Doctor.

BETTY. He didn't ask to see her. He was looking for someone—some friend of his.

CHUMLEY. Who could that be, Dr. Sanderson?

SANDERSON. I don't know, Doctor.

BETTY. He said it was someone he came out here with this afternoon.

SANDERSON. Was there anyone with Dowd when you saw him, Miss Kelly?

KELLY (R. C. *giving hat to* SANDERSON). No, Doctor—not when I saw him.

BETTY. Well, he said there was. He said he last saw his friend sitting right in that chair there with his hat and coat. He seemed quite disappointed.

KELLY (*at top of table—a funny look is crossing her face*). Dr. Sanderson—

BETTY. I told him if we located his friend we'd give him a lift into town. He could ride in the back seat. Was that all right, Willie?

CHUMLEY. Of course—of course—

BETTY. Oh here it is. I wrote it down on the back of this card. His friend's name was Harvey.

KELLY. Harvey!

BETTY. He didn't give me his last name. He mentioned something else about him—pooka—but I didn't quite get what that was.

SANDERSON AND CHUMLEY. Harvey!

BETTY (*rises*). He said his friend was very tall—Well, why are you looking like that, Willie? This man was a very nice, polite man, and he merely asked that we give his friend a lift into town, and if we can't do a favor for someone, why are we living? (*Back to down* R.)

SANDERSON (*gasping*). Where—where did he go, Mrs. Chumley? How long ago was he in here?

CHUMLEY (*thundering*). Get me that hat! By George, we'll find out about this! (KELLY *goes out upper* L. *to get it.* BETTY *crosses* R. *to chair* R. *of table.* CHUMLEY *and* SANDERSON *sit at* R. *of desk.*)

BETTY. I don't know where he went. Just a second ago. (SANDERSON, *his face drawn, sits at* L. *of desk and picks up house phone.* CHUMLEY, *with a terrible look on his face, has started to thumb through phone book.*)

SANDERSON (*on house phone*). Main gate —Henry—Dr. Sanderson—

CHUMLEY (*thumbing through book*). Gaffney—Judge Gaffney——

SANDERSON. Henry—did a man in a brown suit go out through the gate a minute ago? He did? He's gone? (*Hangs up and looks stricken.* KELLY *enters from* L. *with hat, comes* C.)

CHUMLEY (*has been dialing*). Judge Gaffney—this is Dr. William Chumley —the psychiatrist. I'm making a routine checkup on the spelling of a name before entering it into our records. Judge—you telephoned out here this afternoon about having a client of yours committed? How is that name spelled? With a W, not a U—Mr. Elwood P. Dowd. Thank you, Judge—(*Hangs up—rises—pushes chair in to desk—takes hat from* KELLY. *Stands silently for a moment, contemplating* SANDERSON.) Dr. Sanderson—I believe your name is Sanderson?

SANDERSON. Yes, Doctor.

CHUMLEY. You know that much, do you? You went to medical school—you specialized in the study of psychiatry? You graduated—you went forth. (*Holds up hat and runs two fingers up through holes in it.*) Perhaps they neglected to tell you that a rabbit has large pointed ears! That a hat for a rabbit would have to be perforated to make room for those ears?

SANDERSON. Dowd seemed reasonable enough this afternoon, Doctor.

CHUMLEY. Doctor—the function of a psychiatrist is to tell the difference between those who are reasonable, and those who merely talk and act reasonably. (*Presses buzzer. Flings hat on desk.*) Do you realize what you have done to me? You don't answer. I'll tell you. You have permitted a psycopathic case to walk off these grounds and roam around with an overgrown white rabbit. You have subjected me—a psychiatrist—to the humiliation of having to call—of all things—a lawyer to find out who came out here to be committed—and who came out here to commit! (WILSON *enters.*)

SANDERSON. Dr. Chumley—I—

CHUMLEY. Just a minute, Wilson—I want you. (*Back to* SANDERSON.) I will now have to do something I haven't done in fifteen years. I will have to go out after this patient, Elwood P. Dowd, and I will have to bring him back, and when I do bring him back, your connection with this institution is ended—as of that moment! (*Turns to* WILSON—OTHERS *are standing frightened.*) Wilson, get the car. (*To* BETTY.) Pet, call the McClures and say we can't make it. Miss Kelly—come upstairs with me and we'll get that woman out of the tub—(*Starts upstairs on the run.*)

KELLY (*follows him upstairs*). Yes—Doctor—

(SANDERSON *turns on his heel, goes into his office.* WILSON *is getting into a coat in hall.*)

BETTY (*at bookcase* R.) I'll have to tell the cook we'll be home for dinner. She'll be furious. (*She turns.*) Wilson—

WILSON. Yes, ma'am.

BETTY. What is a pooka?

WILSON. A what?

BETTY. A pooka.

WILSON. You can search me, Mrs. Chumley.

BETTY. I wonder if it would be in the Encyclopedia here? (*Goes to bookcase and takes out book.*) They have everything here. I wonder if it is a lodge, or what it is! (*Starts to look in it, then puts it on table open.*) Oh, I don't dare to stop to do this now. Dr. Chumley won't want to find me still here when he comes down. (*Starts to cross to lower* L. *door very fast.*) He'll raise —I mean—oh, dear! (*She exits down* L.)

WILSON (*goes above tables, picks up book, looks in it. Runs forefinger under words.*) P-o-o-k-a. "Pooka. From old Celtic mythology. A fairy spirit in animal form. Always very large. The pooka appears here and there, now and then, to this one and that one at his own caprice. A wise but mischievous creature. Very fond of rum-pots, crackpots," and how are you, Mr. Wilson. (*Looks at book startled—looks at* C. *doorway fearfully— then back to book.*) How are you, Mr. Wilson? (*Shakes book, looks at it in surprise.*) Who in the encyclopedia wants to know? (*Looks at book again, drops it on table.*) Oh— to hell with it! (*He exits quickly out down* L.)

CURTAIN

ACT TWO

SCENE ONE

SCENE: *The Dowd library again.*

TIME: *About an hour after the curtain of Act One.*

AT RISE: *Doorbell is ringing and* MYRTLE *enters from door up* L. *She calls behind her.*

MYRTLE (*calling*). That's right. The stairs at the end of the hall. It goes to the third floor. Go right up. I'll be with you in a minute. (*Crosses to chair* L. *of table.* JUDGE OMAR GAFFNEY *enters* R., *an elderly white-haired man. He looks displeased.*)

JUDGE (*entering and looking around*). Well, where is she? (*Back of table.*)

MYRTLE. Where is who? Whom do you mean, Judge Gaffney? Sit down, won't you?

JUDGE. I mean your mother. Where's Veta Louise? (*Crosses in front of chair.*)

MYRTLE. Why Judge Gaffney! You know where she is. She took Uncle Elwood out to the sanitarium.

JUDGE. I know that. But why was I called at the club with a lot of hysteria? Couldn't even get what she was talking about. Carrying on something fierce. (*Sits chair* R. *of table* R.)

MYRTLE. Mother carrying on! What about? (*Crosses down to chair* L. *of table* R.)

JUDGE. I don't know. She was hysterical.

MYRTLE. That's strange! She took Uncle Elwood out to the sanitarium. All she had to do was put him in. (*Goes back* R., *opens door and looks through, calling.*) Did you find it? I'll be right up. (*Waits. Turns to him.*) They found it.

JUDGE. Who? Found what? What are you talking about?

MYRTLE. When Mother left the house with Uncle Elwood I went over to the real estate office to put the house on the market. And what do you think I found there? (*She sits.*)

JUDGE. I'm not a quiz kid.

MYRTLE. Well, I found a man there who was looking for an old house just like this to cut up into buffet apartments. He's going through it now.

JUDGE. Now see here, Myrtle Mae. This house doesn't belong to you. It belongs to your Uncle Elwood.

MYRTLE. But now that Elwood is locked up, mother controls the property, doesn't she?

JUDGE. Where is your mother? Where is Veta Louise?

MYRTLE. Judge, she went out to Chumley's Rest to tell them about Harvey and put Uncle Elwood in.

JUDGE. Why did she call me at the club when I was in the middle of a game, and scream at me to meet her here about something important?

MYRTLE. I don't know. I simply don't know. Have you got the deed to this house?

JUDGE. Certainly, it's in my safe. Myrtle, I feel pretty bad about this thing of locking Elwood up.

MYRTLE. Mother and I will be able to take a long trip now—out to Pasadena.

JUDGE. I always liked that boy. He could have done anything—been anything—made a place for himself in this community.

MYRTLE. And all he did was get a big rabbit.

JUDGE. He had everything. Brains, personality, friends. Men liked him. Women liked him. I liked him.

MYRTLE. Are you telling me that once Uncle Elwood was like other men—that women actually liked him—I mean in that way?

JUDGE. Oh, not since he started running around with this big rabbit. But they did once. Once that mailbox of your grandmother's was full of those little blue-scented envelopes for Elwood.

MYRTLE. I can't believe it.

JUDGE. Of course there was always something different about Elwood.

MYRTLE. I don't doubt that.

JUDGE. Yes—he was always so calm about any sudden change in plans. I used to admire it. I should have been suspicious. Take your average man looking up and seeing a big white rabbit. He'd do something about it. But not Elwood. He took that calmly, too. And look where it got him!

MYRTLE. You don't dream how far overboard he's gone on this rabbit.

JUDGE. Oh, yes I do. He's had that rabbit in my office many's the time. I'm old but I don't miss much. (*Noise from upstairs.*) What's that noise?

MYRTLE. The prospective buyer on the third floor. (*Looks up.* VETA *is standing in doorway, looking like something the cat dragged in. Shakes her head sadly; looks into the room and sighs; her hat is crooked.* MYRTLE *jumps up.*) Mother! Look, Judge—

JUDGE (*rising*). Veta Louise—what's wrong, girl?

VETA (*shaking her head*). I never thought I'd see either of you again. (MYRTLE *and* JUDGE *take* VETA *to chair* L. *of table* R.)

MYRTLE. Take hold of her, Judge. She looks like she's going to faint. (JUDGE *gets hold of her on one side and* MYRTLE *on the other. They start to bring her into the room.*) Now, Mother—you're all right. You're going to be perfectly all right.

JUDGE. Steady—steady, girl, steady.

VETA. Please—not so fast.

JUDGE. Don't rush her, Myrtle—Ease her in.

VETA. Let me sit down. Only get me some place where I can sit down.

JUDGE (*guiding her to a big chair*). Here you are, girl. Easy, Myrtle—easy. (VETA *is about to lower herself into chair. She sighs. But before she can complete the lowering,* MYRTLE MAE *lets out a yelp and* VETA *straightens up quickly.*)

MYRTLE. Oh—(*She picks up envelope off chair. Holds it up.*) The gas bill.

VETA (*hand at head*). Oh—oh, my—(*Sits.*)

JUDGE. Get her some tea, Myrtle. Do you want some tea, Veta?

MYRTLE. I'll get you some tea, Mother. Get her coat off, Judge.

JUDGE. Let Myrtle get your coat off, Veta. Get her coat off, Myrtle.

VETA. Leave me alone. Let me sit here. Let me get my breath.

MYRTLE. Let her get her breath, Judge.

VETA. Let me sit here a minute and then let me get upstairs to my own bed where I can let go.

MYRTLE. What happened to you, Mother?

VETA. Omar, I want you to sue them. They put me in and let Elwood out.

JUDGE. What's this?

MYRTLE. Mother!

VETA (*taking off hat*). Just look at my hair.

MYRTLE. But why? What did you say? What did you do? (*Kneels at* VETA's *feet.*) You must have done something.

VETA. I didn't do one thing. I simply told them about Elwood and Harvey.

JUDGE. Then how could it happen to you? I don't understand it. (*Sits chair* R.)

VETA. I told them about Elwood, and then I went down to the cab to get his things. As I was walking along the path—this awful man stepped out. He was a white slaver. I know he was. He had on one of those white suits. That's how they advertise.

MYRTLE. A man—what did he do, Mother?

VETA. What did he do? He took hold of me and took me in there and then he—(*Bows her head.* MYRTLE *and* JUDGE *exchange a look.*)

JUDGE (*softly*). Go on, Veta Louise. Go on, girl.

MYRTLE (*goes over, takes her hand*). Poor Mother—Was he a young man?

JUDGE. Myrtle Mae—perhaps you'd better leave the room.

MYRTLE. Now? I should say not! Go on, Mother.

JUDGE (*edging closer*). What did he do, Veta?

VETA. He took me upstairs and tore my clothes off.

MYRTLE (*shrieking*). Oh—did you hear that, Judge! Go on, Mother. (*She is all ears.*)

JUDGE. By God—I'll sue them for this!

VETA. And then he sat me down in a tub of water.

MYRTLE (*disappointed*). Oh! For heaven's sake! (*Rises.*)

VETA. I always thought that what you were, showed on your face. Don't you believe it, Judge! Don't you believe it, Myrtle. This man took hold of me like I was a woman of the streets—but I fought. I always said if a man jumped at me—I'd fight. Haven't I always said that, Myrtle?

MYRTLE. She's always said that, Judge. That's what Mother always told me to do.

VETA. And then he hustled me into that sanitarium and set me down in that tub of water and began treating me like I was a—

MYRTLE. A what—?

VETA. A crazy woman—but he did that just for spite.

JUDGE. Well, I'll be damned!

VETA. And those doctors came upstairs and asked me a lot of questions—all about sex-urges—and all that filthy stuff. That place ought to be cleaned up, Omar. You better get the authorities to clean it up. Myrtle, don't you ever go out there. You hear me?

JUDGE. This stinks to high heaven, Veta. By God, it stinks!

VETA. You've got to do something about it, Judge. You've got to sue them.

JUDGE. I will, girl. By God, I will! If Chumley thinks he can run an unsavory place like this on the outskirts of town he'll be publicly chastised. By God, I'll run him out of the state!

VETA. Tell me, Judge. Is that all those doctors do at places like that—think

about sex?

JUDGE. I don't know.

VETA. Because if it is they ought to be ashamed—of themselves. It's all in their head anyway. Why don't they get out and go for long walks in the fresh air? (*To* MYRTLE.) Judge Gaffney walked everywhere for years—didn't you, Judge?

JUDGE. Now let me take some notes on this. (MYRTLE *goes to back of table.*) You said—these doctors came up to talk to you—Dr. Chumley and—What was the other doctor's name?

VETA. Sanderson—(*Sits up straight, glances covertly at them, and becomes very alert.*) But, Judge, don't you pay any attention to anything he tells you. He's a liar. Close-set eyes. They're always liars. Besides—I told him something in strictest confidence and he blabbed it.

MYRTLE. What did you tell him, Mother? (*She is back of table.*)

VETA. Oh, what difference does it make? Let's forget. I don't even want to talk about it. (*Rises—crosses to back of chair.*) You can't trust anybody.

JUDGE. Anything you told this Dr. Sanderson you can tell us, Veta Louise. This is your daughter and I am your lawyer.

VETA. I know which is which. I don't want to talk about it. I want to sue them and I want to get in my own bed. (JUDGE *rises.*)

MYRTLE. But, Mother—this is the important thing, anyway. Where is Uncle Elwood?

VETA (*to herself*). I should have known better than to try to do anything about him. Something protects him—that awful Pooka—

MYRTLE. Where is Uncle Elwood? Answer me.

VETA (*trying to be casual*). How should I know? They let him go. (*Crosses to door* R.) They're not interested in men at places like that. Don't act so naïve, Myrtle Mae. (*Noise from upstairs.*) What's that noise?

MYRTLE. I've found a buyer for the house.

VETA. What?

MYRTLE. Listen, Mother, we've got to find Uncle Elwood—no matter who jumped at you, we've still got to lock up Uncle Elwood.

VETA. I don't know where he is. The next time *you* take him, Judge. Wait until Elwood hears what they did to me. He

won't stand for it. Don't forget to sue
them, Judge—Myrtle Mae, all I hope is
that never, never as long as you live a
man pulls the clothes off you and dumps
you down into a tub of water. (*She exits* R.)

MYRTLE (*turning to* JUDGE. *Behind chair* L).
Now, see—Mother muffed everything.
No matter what happened out there—
Uncle Elwood's still wandering around
with Harvey.

JUDGE (*pondering*). The thing for me
to do is take some more notes.

MYRTLE. It's all Uncle Elwood's fault.
He found out what she was up to—and
he had her put in. Then he ran.

JUDGE. Oh, no—don't talk like that.
(*Crosses up to back of chair.*) Your uncle
thinks the world and all of your mother.
Ever since he was a little boy he always
wanted to share everything he had with
her.

MYRTLE. I'm not giving up. We'll get
detectives. We'll find him. And, besides
—you'd better save some of that sympathy for me and Mother—you don't
realize what we have to put up with.
Wait till I show you something he brought
home about six months ago, and we hid
it out in the garage. You just wait—

JUDGE. I'm going up to talk to Veta.
There's more in this than she's telling.
I sense that.

MYRTLE (*as she exits* L). Wait till I show
you, Judge.

JUDGE. All right. I'll wait. (WILSON
enters from R.)

WILSON (*crosses to table* R). Okay—is he
here?

JUDGE (*crosses to chair* R. *of table* R).
What? What's this?

WILSON. That crackpot with the rabbit.
Is he here?

JUDGE. No—and who, may I ask, are
you?

WILSON (*stepping into hallway, calling*).
Not here, Doctor—okay—(*To* JUDGE.)
Doctor Chumley's comin' in, anyway.
What's your name?

JUDGE. Chumley—well, well, well—
I've got something to say to him! (*Sits.*)

WILSON. What's your name? Let's
have it.

JUDGE. I am Judge Gaffney—where is
Chumley?

WILSON. The reason I asked your name
is the Doctor always likes to know who
he's talkin' to. (*Enter* CHUMLEY.) This guy
says his name is Judge Gaffney, Doctor.

JUDGE. Well, well, Chumley—

CHUMLEY. Good evening, Judge. Let's
not waste time. Has he been here? (*Crosses to* L. *of table.*)

JUDGE. Who? Elwood—no—but see
here, Doctor—

WILSON. Sure he ain't been here? He's
wise now. He's hidin'. It'll be an awful
job to smoke him out.

CHUMLEY. It will be more difficult, but
I'll do it. They're sly. They're cunning.
But I get them. I always get them. Have
you got the list of the places we've been,
Wilson? (*Crosses to* WILSON.)

WILSON (*pulling paper out of his pocket*).
Right here, Doctor.

CHUMLEY (*sits*). Read it.

WILSON (*crosses to* CHUMLEY). We've
been to seventeen bars, Eddie's Place,
Charlie's Place, Bessie's Barn-dance, the
Fourth Avenue Firehouse, the Tenth
and Twelfth and Ninth Avenue fire-
houses, just to make sure. The Union
Station, the grain elevator—say, why
does this guy go down to a grain elevator?

JUDGE. The foreman is a friend of his.
He has many friends—many places.

CHUMLEY. I have stopped by here to
ask Mrs. Simmons if she has any other
suggestions as to where we might look for
him.

JUDGE. Doctor Chumley, I have to inform you that Mrs. Simmons has re-
tained me to file suit against you—

DR. CHUMLEY. What?

JUDGE. —for what happened to her
at the sanitarium this afternoon . . .

CHUMLEY. A suit!

JUDGE. And while we're on that subject—

WILSON (*crosses to back of table*). That's
pretty, ain't it, Doctor? After us draggin'
your tail all over town trying to find that
guy.

CHUMLEY. What happened this afternoon was an unfortunate mistake. I've
discharged my assistant who made it.
And I am prepared to take charge of this
man's case personally. It interests me.
And my interest in a case is something
no amount of money can buy. You can
ask any of them.

JUDGE. But this business this afternoon,
Doctor—

CHUMLEY. Water under the dam. This
is how I see this thing. I see it this way—
(MYRTLE *has come into the room. She is carrying a big flat parcel, wrapped in brown paper.*

Stands it up against wall and listens, by chair L.) The important item now is to get this man and take him out to the sanitarium where he belongs.

MYRTLE (*coming forward*). That's right, Judge—that's just what I think—

JUDGE. Let me introduce Miss Myrtle Mae Simmons, Mr. Dowd's niece, Mrs. Simmon's daughter. (CHUMLEY *rises*.)

MYRTLE. How do you do, Dr. Chumley.

CHUMLEY (*giving her the careful scrutiny he gives all women*). How do you do, Miss Simmons.

WILSON. Hello, Myrtle—

MYRTLE (*now seeing him and looking at him with a mixture of horror and intense curiosity*). What? Oh—

CHUMLEY. Now, then let me talk to Mrs. Simmons.

MYRTLE. Mother won't come down, Doctor. I know she won't. (*To Judge.*) You try to get Mother to talk to him, Judge. (*Puts package down.*)

JUDGE. But, see here—your mother was manhandled. She was—God knows what she was—the man's approach to her was not professional, it was personal. (*Looks at Wilson.*)

CHUMLEY. Wilson—this is a serious charge.

WILSON. Dr. Chumley, I've been with you for ten years. Are you gonna believe—what's your name again?

JUDGE. Gaffney. Judge Omar Gaffney.

WILSON. Thanks. You take the word of this old blister Gaffney—

CHUMLEY. Wilson!

WILSON. Me! Me and a dame who sees a rabbit!

JUDGE. It's not Mrs. Simmons who sees a rabbit. It's her brother.

MYRTLE. Yes, it's Uncle Elwood.

JUDGE. If you'll come with me, Doctor—

CHUMLEY. Very well, Judge. Wilson, I have a situation here. Wait for me. (HE *and* JUDGE *exit* R.)

WILSON. OK, Doctor. (MYRTLE MAE *is fascinated by* WILSON. *She lingers and looks at him.* HE *comes over to her, grinning.*)

WILSON. So your name's Myrtle Mae?

MYRTLE. What? Oh—yes—(*She backs up.* HE *follows.*)

WILSON. If we grab your uncle you're liable to be comin' out to the sanitarium on visiting days?

MYRTLE. Oh, I don't really know—I—

WILSON. Well, if you do, I'll be there.

MYRTLE. You will? Oh—

WILSON. And if you don't see me right away—don't give up. Stick around. I'll show up.

MYRTLE. You will—? Oh—

WILSON. Sure. (*He is still following her.*) You heard Dr. Chumley tell me to wait?

MYRTLE. Yeah—

WILSON. Tell you what—while I'm waiting I sure could use a sandwich and a cup of coffee.

MYRTLE. Certainly. If you'll forgive me I'll precede you into the kitchen. (*She tries to go.* HE *traps her.*)

WILSON. Yessir—you're all right, Myrtle.

MYRTLE. What?

WILSON. Doctor Chumley noticed it right away. He don't miss a trick. (*Crowds closer; raises finger and pokes her arm for emphasis.*) Tell you somethin' else, Myrtle—

MYRTLE. What?

WILSON. You not only got a nice build—but, kid, you got something else, too.

MYRTLE. What?

WILSON. You got the screwiest uncle that ever stuck his puss inside our nut-house. (MYRTLE *starts to exit in a huff, and* WILSON *raises hand to give her a spank, but she turns and so he puts up raised hand to his hair. They exit. The stage is empty for a half-second, and then through* R. *comes* ELWOOD. HE *comes in, goes to phone, dials a number.*)

ELWOOD. Hello, Chumley's Rest? Is Doctor Chumley there? Oh—it's Mrs. Chumley! This is Elwood P. Dowd speaking. How are you tonight? Tell me, Mrs. Chumley, were you able to locate Harvey?—Don't worry about it. I'll find him. I'm sorry I missed you at the McClure cocktail party. The people were all charming and I was able to leave quite a few of my cards. I waited until you phoned and said you couldn't come because a patient had escaped. Where am I? I'm here. But I'm leaving right away. I must find Harvey. Well, good-by, Mrs. Chumley. My regards to you and anybody else you happen to run into. Good-by. (*Hangs up, then he sees the big flat parcel against wall. He gets an "Ah, there it is!" expression on his face, goes over, and takes off paper. We see revealed a very strange thing. It is an oil painting of Elwood seated on a chair while behind him stands a large white rabbit, in a blue polka-dot collar and red necktie.* ELWOOD *holds it away from him and surveys it proudly. Then looks around for a place to put it. Takes it over and sets it on mantel. It obscures the picture of Marcella Pinney Dowd completely. He gathers up wrapping paper, admires the rabbit again, tips his hat to it, and exits R. Phone rings and* VETA *enters* L., *followed by* DR. CHUMLEY.)

VETA. Doctor, you might as well go home and wait. I'm suing you for fifty thousand dollars and that's final. (*Crosses to phone—her back is to mantel, she hasn't looked up.*)

CHUMLEY (*follows her to chair* L). Mrs. Simmons—

VETA (*into phone*). Yes—Well, all right.

CHUMLEY. This picture over your mantel.

VETA. That portrait happens to be the pride of this house.

CHUMLEY (*looking at her*). Who painted it?

VETA. Oh, some man. I forget his name. He was around here for the sittings, and then we paid him and he went away. Hello—yes—No. This is Dexter 1567. (*Hangs up.*)

CHUMLEY. I suppose if you have the money to pay people, you can persuade them to do anything.

VETA. Well, Dr. Chumley—(*Walks over and faces him.*) When you helped me out of that tub at your place, what did I say to you?

CHUMLEY. You expressed yourself. I don't remember the words.

VETA. I said, "Dr. Chumley, this is a belated civility." Isn't that what I said?

CHUMLEY. You said something of the sort—

VETA. You brought this up; you may as well learn something quick. I took a course in art this last winter. The difference between a fine oil painting and a mechanical thing like a photograph is simply this: a photograph shows only the reality; a painting shows not only the reality but the dream behind it—It's our dreams that keep us going. That separate us from the beasts. I wouldn't even want to live if I thought it was all just eating and sleeping and taking off my clothes. Well—putting them on again—(*Turns— sees picture—screams—totters—falls back.*) Oh—Doctor—oh—hold me—oh—

CHUMLEY (*taking hold of her*). Steady now—steady—don't get excited. Everything's all right. (*Seats her in chair* L.) Now —what's the matter?

VETA (*pointing*). Doctor—that is *not* my mother!

CHUMLEY. I'm glad to hear that.

VETA. Oh, Doctor. Elwood's been here. He's been here.

CHUMLEY. Better be quiet. (*Phone rings.*) I'll take it. (*He answers it.*) Hello. Yes, yes—who's calling? (*Drops his hands over mouthpiece quickly.*) Here he is. Mrs. Simmons, it's your brother!

VETA (*getting up. Weak no longer*). Oh— let me talk to him!

CHUMLEY. Don't tell him I'm here. Be casual.

VETA. Hello, Elwood—(*Laughs.*) Where are you? What? Oh—just a minute. (*Covers phone.*) He won't say where he is. He wants to know if Harvey is here.

CHUMLEY. Tell him Harvey *is* here.

VETA. But he isn't.

CHUMLEY. Tell him. That will bring him here, perhaps. Humor him. We have to humor them.

VETA. Yes—Elwood. Yes, dear. Harvey is here. Why don't you come home? Oh, oh, oh—well—all right. (*Looks around uncomfortably. Covers phone again.*) It won't work. He says for me to call Harvey to the telephone.

CHUMLEY. Say Harvey is here, but can't come to the telephone. Say—he— say—he's in the bathtub.

VETA. Bathtub?

CHUMLEY. Say he's in the bathtub, and you'll send him over there. That way we'll find out where he is.

VETA. Oh, Doctor!

CHUMLEY. Now, you've got to do it, Mrs. Simmons.

VETA. Hello, Elwood. Yes, dear. Harvey is here but he can't come to the telephone, he's in the bathtub. I'll send him over as soon as he's dry. Where are you? Elwood? (*Bangs phone.*)

CHUMLEY. Did he hang up?

VETA. Harvey just walked in the door! He told me to look in the bathtub—it must be a stranger. But I know where he is. He's at Charlie's Place. That's a bar over at 12th and Main.

CHUMLEY (*picking up his hat from table* R). 12th and Main. That's two blocks down and one over, isn't it?

VETA. Doctor—where are you going?

CHUMLEY. I'm going over there to get your brother and take him out to the sanitarium, where he belongs.

VETA. Oh, Dr. Chumley—don't do that. Send one of your attendants. I'm warning you.

CHUMLEY. But, Mrs. Simmons, if I am to help your brother—

VETA. He can't be helped. (*Looks at picture.*) There is no help for him. He must be picked up and locked up and left.

CHUMLEY. You consider your brother a dangerous man?

VETA. Dangerous!

CHUMLEY. Why?

VETA. I won't tell you why, but if I didn't, why would I be asking for a permanent commitment for him?

CHUMLEY. Then I must observe this man. I must watch the expression on his face as he talks to this rabbit. He does talk to the rabbit, you say?

VETA. They tell each other everything.

CHUMLEY. What's that?

VETA. I said, of course he talks to him. But don't go after him, Doctor. You'll regret it if you do.

CHUMLEY. Nonsense—(*He is going toward* R.) You underestimate me, Mrs. Simmons.

VETA. Oh, no, Doctor. You underestimate my brother.

CHUMLEY. Not at all. Don't worry now. I can handle him! (*He exits* R.)

VETA (*after he has gone*). You can handle him? That's what you think! (*Calls up* L.) Myrtle Mae! See who's in the bathtub. OH!

CURTAIN

ACT TWO

SCENE TWO

SCENE: *The main office at* CHUMLEY'S REST *again.*

TIME: *Four hours after the curtain of Scene One, Act Two.*

AT RISE: KELLY *is on the phone.* WILSON *is helping* SANDERSON *carry boxes of books out of his office up* L. *and onto table* C.

KELLY. Thank you. I may call later. (*Hangs up.*)

WILSON (L. *of table* R). How about the stuff in your room, Doctor—upstairs?

SANDERSON (*to table, puts box on it*). All packed—thanks Wilson.

WILSON. Tough your gettin' bounced.

I had you pegged for the one who'd make the grade.

SANDERSON. Those are the breaks.

WILSON. When you takin' off?

SANDERSON. As soon as Dr. Chumley gets back.

WILSON (*to* KELLY). Did you get a report back yet from the desk sergeant in the police accident bureau?

KELLY. Not yet. I just talked to the downtown dispensary. They haven't seen him.

WILSON. It's beginning to smell awful funny to me. Four hours he's been gone and not a word from him. (*Goes to* SANDERSON—*extends hand.*) I may not see you again, Doctor, so I want to say I wish you a lot of luck and I'm mighty sorry you got a kick in the atpray.

SANDERSON. Thanks, Wilson—good luck to you, too—

WILSON (*starts to exit, but stops at door back* C., *turns toward* KELLY.) Look, Kelly, let me know when you hear from the desk sergeant again. If there's no sign of the doctor, I'm goin' into town and look for him. He should know better'n to go after a psycho without me. (*Starts up* C.)

SANDERSON. I'd like to help look for the doctor, too, Wilson.

WILSON. That's swell of you, Doctor, right after he give you the brush.

SANDERSON. I've no resentment against Dr. Chumley. He was right. I was wrong. (*He rises.*) Chumley is the biggest man in his field. It's my loss not to be able to work with him. (*Crosses up to bookcase.*)

WILSON. You're not so small yourself, Doctor—

SANDERSON. Thanks, Wilson.

WILSON. Don't mention it. (*Exits* U.C.)

KELLY (*taking deep breath and standing above desk*). Dr. Sanderson—

SANDERSON (*without looking up*). Yes—

KELLY (*plunging in*). Well, Doctor— (*Takes another deep breath.*) I'd like to say that *I* wish you a lot of luck, too, and I'm sorry to see you leave.

SANDERSON (*going on with his work*). Are you sure you can spare these good wishes, Miss Kelly?

KELLY (*she flushes*). On second thought —I guess I can't. Forget it. (*Starts for below desk.*)

SANDERSON (*now looking up*). Miss Kelly —(*To back of table.*) This is for nothing— just a little advice. I'd be a little careful if I were you about the kind of company I kept.

KELLY. I beg you pardon, Doctor?

SANDERSON (*crosses* C). You don't have to. I told you it was free. I saw you Saturday night—dancing with that drip in the Rose Room down at the Frontier Hotel.

KELLY (*putting books on desk*). Oh, did you? I didn't notice you.

SANDERSON. I'd be a little careful of him, Kelly. He looked to me like a schizophrenic all the way across the floor.

KELLY. You really shouldn't have given him a thought, Doctor. He was my date—not yours. (*Hands book to* SANDERSON.)

SANDERSON. That was his mentality. The rest of him—well—(*Puts book in box front of table.*)

KELLY. But she was beautiful, though—

SANDERSON. Who?

KELLY. That girl you were with—

SANDERSON. I thought you didn't notice?

KELLY. You bumped into us twice. How could I help it?

SANDERSON. Not that it makes any difference to you, but that girl is a charming little lady. *She* has a sweet kind disposition and *she* knows how to conduct herself.

KELLY. Funny she couldn't rate a better date on a Saturday night!

SANDERSON. And she has an excellent mind.

KELLY. Why doesn't she use it?

SANDERSON (*crossing toward* KELLY). Oh, I don't suppose you're to be censured for the flippant hard shell you have. You're probably compensating for something.

KELLY. I am not, and don't you use any of your psychiatry on me.

SANDERSON. Oh—if I could try something else on you—just once! Just to see if you'd melt under any circumstances. I doubt it.

KELLY. You'll never know, Doctor.

SANDERSON. Because you interest me as a case history—that's all. I'd like to know where you get that inflated ego—(*Goes back of desk.*)

KELLY (*now close to tears*). If you aren't the meanest person—inflated ego—case history! (*Turns and starts out* C.)

SANDERSON. Don't run away. Let's finish it. (PHONE *rings.*)

KELLY. Oh, leave me alone. (*Goes to answer it.*)

SANDERSON. Gladly. (*Exits.*)

KELLY (*in angry, loud voice*). Chumley's Rest. Yes—Sergeant. No accident report on him either in town or the suburbs. Look, Sergeant—maybe we better— (*Looks up as door down* L. *opens and* ELWOOD *enters. He is carrying a bouquet of dahlias.*) Oh, never mind, Sergeant. They're here now. (*Hangs up. Goes toward* ELWOOD.) Mr. Dowd!

ELWOOD (*crosses to* C. *Handing her flowers*). Good evening, my dear. These are for you.

KELLY (*crosses to* C). For me—oh, thank you!

ELWOOD. They're quite fresh, too. I just picked them outside.

KELLY. I hope Dr. Chumley didn't see you. They're his prize dahlias. Did he go upstairs? (*Backing up.*)

ELWOOD. Not knowing, I cannot state. Those colors are lovely against your hair.

KELLY. I've never worn burnt orange. It's such a trying color.

ELWOOD. You would improve any color, my dear.

KELLY. Thank you. Did Dr. Chumley go over to his house?

ELWOOD. I don't know. Where is Dr. Sanderson?

KELLY. In his office there—I think. (*Crosses back to desk.*)

ELWOOD (*going over to door and knocking*). Thank you.

SANDERSON (*enters*). Dowd! There you are!

ELWOOD. I have a cab outside, if it's possible for you and Miss Kelly to get away now.

SANDERSON. Where is Dr. Chumley?

ELWOOD. Is he coming with us? That's nice.

KELLY (*answering question on* SANDERSON's *face*). I don't know, Doctor.

ELWOOD. I must apologize for being a few seconds late. I thought Miss Kelly should have some flowers. (*Crosses to table.*) After what happened out here this afternoon, the flowers really should be from you, Doctor. As you grow older and pretty women pass you by, you will think with deep gratitude of these generous girls of your youth. Shall we go now? (KELLY *exits.*)

SANDERSON (*pressing buzzer*). Just a moment, Dowd—(*Starts* R.) The situation has changed since we met this afternoon. But I urge you to have no resentments.

Dr. Chumley is your friend. He only wants to help you.

ELWOOD. That's very nice of him. I would like to help him, too. (*At table.*)

SANDERSON. If you'll begin by taking a co-operative attitude—that's half the battle. We all have to face reality, Dowd—sooner or later.

ELWOOD. Doctor, I wrestled with reality for forty years, and I am happy to state that I finally won out over it. (KELLY *enters.*) Won't you and Miss Kelly join me—down at Charlie's? (*Enter* WILSON *from* C.)

WILSON. Here you are! (*Goes over to* ELWOOD.) Upstairs, buddy—we're going upstairs. Is the doctor O.K.? (*He asks* SANDERSON *this.*)

ELWOOD. There must be some mistake. Miss Kelly and Dr. Sanderson and I are going downtown for a drink. I'd be glad to have you come with us, Mr.———

WILSON. Wilson.

ELWOOD. —Wilson. They have a wonderful floor show.

WILSON. Yeah? Well—wait'll you see the floor show we've got—Upstairs, buddy!

SANDERSON. Just a minute, Wilson. Where did you say Dr. Chumley went, Dowd?

ELWOOD. As I said, he did not confide his plans in me.

WILSON. You mean the doctor ain't showed up yet? (*Crosses to desk.*)

KELLY. Not yet.

WILSON. Where is he?

SANDERSON. That's what we're trying to find out.

KELLY. Mr. Dowd walked in here by himself.

WILSON. Oh, he did, eh? Listen, you—talk fast or I'm workin' you over!

ELWOOD. I'd rather you didn't do that, and I'd rather you didn't even mention such a thing in the presence of a lovely young lady like Miss Kelly —

SANDERSON. Mr. Dowd, Dr. Chumley went into town to pick you up. That was four hours ago.

ELWOOD. Where has the evening gone to?

WILSON. Listen to that! Smart, eh?

SANDERSON. Just a minute, Wilson. Did you see Dr. Chumley tonight, Dowd?

ELWOOD. Yes, I did. He came into Charlie's Place at dinnertime. It is a cozy spot. Let's all go there and talk it over with a tall one.

WILSON. We're going no place—(*Crosses between* ELWOOD *and* SANDERSON.) Now I'm askin' you a question, and if you don't button up your lip and give me some straight answers I'm gonna beat it out of you!

ELWOOD. What you suggest is impossible.

WILSON. What's that?

ELWOOD. You suggest that I button up my lip and give you some straight answers. It can't be done. (*Sits chair* L. *of table.*)

SANDERSON. Let me handle this, Wilson. (*Puts* WILSON *to* L.)

WILSON. Well, handle it, then. But find out where the doctor is. (*Back of desk.*)

SANDERSON. Dr. Chumley *did* come into Charlie's Place, you say?

ELWOOD. He did, and I was very glad to see him.

WILSON. Go on—

ELWOOD. He had asked for me, and naturally the proprietor brought him over and left him. We exchanged the conventional greetings. I said, "How do you do, Dr. Chumley," and he said, "How do you do, Mr. Dowd." I believe we said that at least once.

WILSON. Okay—okay—

ELWOOD. I am trying to be factual. I then introduced him to Harvey.

WILSON. To who?

KELLY. A white rabbit. Six feet tall.

WILSON. Six feet!

ELWOOD. Six feet one and a half!

WILSON. Okay—fool around with him, and the doctor is probably some place bleedin' to death in a ditch.

ELWOOD. If those were his plans for the evening he did not tell me.

SANDERSON. Go on, Dowd.

ELWOOD. Dr. Chumley sat down in the booth with us. I was sitting on the outside like this. (*Shows.*) Harvey was on the inside near the wall, and Dr. Chumley was seated directly across from Harvey where he could look at him.

WILSON (*crosses a step* R). That's right. Spend all night on the seatin' arrangements!

ELWOOD. Harvey then suggested that I buy him a drink. Knowing that he does not like to drink alone, I suggested to Dr. Chumley that we join him.

WILSON. And so?

ELWOOD. We joined him.

WILSON. Go on—go on.

ELWOOD. We joined him again.

WILSON. Then what?

ELWOOD. We kept right on joining him.

WILSON. Oh, skip all the joining!

ELWOOD. You are asking me to skip a large portion of the evening—

WILSON. Tell us what happened—come on— please—

ELWOOD. Dr. Chumley and Harvey got into a conversation—quietly at first. Later it became rather heated and Dr. Chumley raised his voice.

WILSON. Yeah—why?

ELWOOD. Harvey seemed to feel that Dr. Chumley should assume part of the financial responsibility of the joining, but Dr. Chumley didn't seem to want to do that.

KELLY (*it breaks out from her*). I can believe *that* part of it!

WILSON. Let him talk. See how far he'll go. This guy's got guts.

ELWOOD. I agreed to take the whole thing because I did not want any trouble. We go down to Charlie's quite often —Harvey and I—and the proprietor is a fine man with an interesting approach to life. Then the other matter came up.

WILSON. Cut the damned double-talk and get on with it!

ELWOOD. Mr. Wilson, you are a sincere type of person, but I must ask you not to use that language in the presence of Miss Kelly. (*He makes a short bow to her.*)

SANDERSON. You're right, Dowd, and we're sorry. You say—the other matter came up?

ELWOOD. There was a beautiful blonde woman—a Mrs. Smethills—and her escort seated in the booth across from us. Dr. Chumley went over to sit next to her, explaining to her that they had once met. In Chicago. Her escort escorted Dr. Chumley back to me and Harvey and tried to point out that it would be better for Dr. Chumley to mind his own affairs. Does he have any?

WILSON. Does he have any what?

ELWOOD. Does he have any affairs?

WILSON. How would I know?

KELLY. Please hurry, Mr. Dowd—we're all so worried.

ELWOOD. Dr. Chumley then urged Harvey to go with him over to Blondie's Chicken Inn. Harvey wanted to go to Eddie's instead. While they were arguing about it I went to the bar to order another drink, and when I came back they were gone.

WILSON. Where did they go? I mean where did the doctor go?

ELWOOD. I don't know—I had a date out here with Dr. Sanderson and Miss Kelly, and I came out to pick them up— hoping that later on we might run into Harvey and the doctor and make a party of it.

WILSON. So you satisfied? You got his story—(*Goes over to* ELWOOD, *fists clenched.*) O.K. You're lyin' and we know it!

ELWOOD. I never lie, Mr. Wilson.

WILSON. You've done somethin' with the doctor and I'm findin' out what it is—

SANDERSON (*moving after him*). Don't touch him, Wilson—

KELLY. Maybe he isn't lying, Wilson—

WILSON (*turning on them. Furiously*). That's all this guy is, a bunch of lies! You two don't believe this story he tells about the doctor sittin' there talkin' to a big white rabbit, do you?

KELLY. Maybe Dr. Chumley *did* go to Charlie's Place.

WILSON. And saw a big rabbit, I suppose.

ELWOOD. And why not? Harvey was there. At first the doctor seemed a little frightened of Harvey, but that gave way to admiration as the evening wore on— The evening wore on! That's a nice expression. With your permission I'll say it again. The evening wore on.

WILSON (*lunging at him*). With your permission I'm gonna knock your teeth down your throat!

ELWOOD (*not moving an inch*). Mr. Wilson—haven't you some old friends you can go play with? (SANDERSON *has grabbed* WILSON *and is struggling with him.*)

WILSON (*he is being held. Glares fiercely at* ELWOOD. KELLY *dials phone*). The nerve of this guy! He couldn't come out here with an ordinary case of D.T.'s. No. He has to come out with a six-foot rabbit.

ELWOOD (*rises—goes toward desk* L). Stimulating as all this is, I really must be getting downtown.

KELLY (*on phone*). Charlie's Place? Is Dr. Chumley anywhere around there?

He was there with Mr. Dowd earlier in the evening. What? Well, don't bite my head off! (*Hangs up.*) My, that man was mad. He said Mr. Dowd was welcome any time, but his friend was not.

ELWOOD. That's Mr. McNulty the bartender. He thinks a lot of me. Now let's all go down and have a drink.

WILSON. Wait a minute—

KELLY. Mr. Dowd—(*Goes over to him.*)

ELWOOD. Yes, my dear—may I hold your hand?

KELLY. Yes—if you want to. (ELWOOD *does.*) Poor Mrs. Chumley is so worried. Something must have happened to the doctor. Won't you please try and remember something—something else that might help her? Please—

ELWOOD. For you I would do anything. I would almost be willing to live my life over again. Almost. But I've told it all.

KELLY. You're sure?

ELWOOD. Quite sure—but ask me again, anyway, won't you? I liked that warm tone you had in your voice just then.

SANDERSON (*without realizing he is saying it*). So did I. (*Looks at* KELLY.)

WILSON. Oh, nuts!

ELWOOD. What?

WILSON. Nuts!

ELWOOD. Oh! I must be going. I have things to do.

KELLY. Mr. Dowd, what is it you do?

ELWOOD (*sits, as* KELLY *sits* R. *of desk*). Harvey and I sit in the bars and we have a drink or two and play the jukebox. Soon the faces of the other people turn toward mine and smile. They are saying: "We don't know your name, Mister, but you're a lovely fellow." Harvey and I warm ourselves in all these golden moments. We have entered as strangers —soon we have friends. They come over. They sit with us. They drink with us. They talk to us. They tell about the big terrible things they have done. The big wonderful things they *will* do. Their hopes, their regrets, their loves, their hates. All very large because nobody ever brings anything small into a bar. Then I introduce them to Harvey. And he is bigger and grander than anything they offer me. When they leave, they leave impressed. The same people seldom come back—but that's envy, my dear. There's a little bit of envy in the best of us—too bad, isn't it?

SANDERSON (*leaning forward*). How did you happen to call him Harvey?

ELWOOD. Harvey is his name.

SANDERSON. How do you know that?

ELWOOD. That was rather an interesting coincidence, Doctor. One night several years ago I was walking early in the evening along Fairfax Street— between 18th and 19th. You know that block?

SANDERSON. Yes, yes.

ELWOOD. I had just helped Ed Hickey into a taxi. Ed had been mixing his rye with his gin, and I felt he needed conveying. I started to walk down the street when I heard a voice saying: "Good evening, Mr. Dowd." I turned, and there was this great white rabbit leaning against a lamp-post. Well, I thought nothing of that, because when you have lived in a town as long as I have lived in this one, you get used to the fact that everybody knows your name. Naturally, I went over to chat with him. He said to me: "Ed Hickey is a little spiffed this evening, or could I be mistaken?" Well, of course he was not mistaken. I think the world and all of Ed, but he was spiffed. Well, anyway, we stood there and talked, and finally I said—"You have the advantage of me. You know my name and I don't know yours." Right back at me he said: "What name do you like?" Well, I didn't even have to think a minute: Harvey has always been my favorite name. So I said, "Harvey," and this is the interesting part of the whole thing. He said— "What a coincidence! My name happens to be Harvey."

SANDERSON (*crossing above desk*). What was your father's name, Dowd?

ELWOOD. John. John Frederick.

SANDERSON. Dowd, when you were a child you had a playmate, didn't you? Someone you were very fond of—with whom you spent many happy, carefree hours?

ELWOOD. Oh, yes, Doctor. Didn't you?

SANDERSON. What was his name?

ELWOOD. Verne. Verne McElhinney. Did you ever know the McElhinneys, Doctor?

SANDERSON. No.

ELWOOD. Too bad. There were a lot of them, and they circulated. Wonderful people.

SANDERSON. Think carefully, Dowd. Wasn't there someone, somewhere, sometime, whom you knew by the name of Harvey? Didn't you ever know anybody by that name?

ELWOOD. No, Doctor. No one. Maybe that's why I always had such hopes for it.

SANDERSON. Come on, Wilson, we'll take Mr. Dowd upstairs now.

WILSON. I'm taking him nowhere. You've made this your show—now run it. Lettin' him sit here—forgettin' all about Dr. Chumley! O.K. It's your show—you run it.

SANDERSON. Come on, Dowd— (*Pause. Putting out his hand.*) Come on, Elwood—

ELWOOD (*rises*). Very well, Lyman. (SANDERSON *and* KELLY *take him to door.*) But I'm afraid I won't be able to visit with you for long. I have promised Harvey I will take him to the floor-show. (THEY *exit* U.C. WILSON *is alone. Sits at desk, looks at his watch.*)

WILSON. Oh, boy! (*Puts head in arms on desk.* DR. CHUMLEY *enters* L. WILSON *does not see him until he gets almost* C. *stage.*)

WILSON (*jumping up, going to him*). Dr. Chumley—Are you all right?

CHUMLEY. All right? Of course I'm all right. I'm being followed. Lock that door.

WILSON (*goes to door* L., *locks it.*) Who's following you?

CHUMLEY. None of your business. (*Exits into office* R., *locks door behind him.*) (WILSON *stands a moment perplexed, then shrugs shoulders, turns off lights and exits* U.C. *The stage is dimly lit. Then from door* L. *comes the rattle of the doorknob. Door opens and shuts, and we hear locks opening and closing, and see light from hall on stage. The invisible Harvey has come in. There is a count of eight while he crosses the stage, then door of* CHUMLEY'S *office opens and closes, with sound of locks clicking. Harvey has gone in—and then—*

CURTAIN

ACT THREE

SCENE: *The sanitarium office at Chumley's Rest.*

TIME: *A few minutes after the curtain of Act Two.*

AT RISE: *Lights are still dim as at preceding curtain. There is a loud knocking at* L. *and the sound of* CHUMLEY'S *voice calling,* "Wilson! Wilson!"

WILSON (*enters from* C., *opens door* L. CHUMLEY *enters, whitefaced*). How didja get out here, Doctor? I just saw you go in there.

CHUMLEY. I went out through my window. Wilson—don't leave me!

WILSON. No, Doctor.

CHUMLEY. Get that man Dowd out of here.

WILSON. Yes, Doctor. (*Starts to exit* C.)

CHUMLEY. No—don't leave me!

WILSON (*turning back—confused*). But you said—

CHUMLEY. Dumphy—on the telephone.

WILSON. Yes, Doctor. (*Crosses to phone.*) Dumphy—give that guy Dowd his clothes and get him down here right away. (*A knock on the door.*)

CHUMLEY. Don't leave me!

WILSON. Just a minute, Doctor. (*Crosses up and turns on lights. Crosses down and opens door* L.) Judge Gaffney.

JUDGE. I want to see Dr. Chumley. (*Enter* JUDGE *and* MYRTLE MAE.)

WILSON. Hiya, Myrtle.

MYRTLE. Hello.

JUDGE. Chumley, we've got to talk to you. This thing is serious.

MYRTLE. It certainly is.

GAFFNEY. More serious than you suspect. Where can we go to talk? (*Moves toward Chumley's office.*)

CHUMLEY (*blocking door*). Not in there.

WILSON. The doctor doesn't want you in his office.

CHUMLEY. No, sir.

JUDGE. Then sit down, Dr. Chumley. Sit down, Myrtle Mae.

CHUMLEY (*dazed*). Sit down, Dr. Chumley. Sit down, Myrtle Mae. Don't go, Wilson. Don't leave me.

JUDGE. Now, Chumley, here are my notes—the facts. Can anybody hear me?

WILSON. Yeah, we can all hear you. Is that good?

JUDGE (*gives Wilson a look of reproof*). Now, Chumley, has it ever occurred to you that possibly there might *be* something like this rabbit Harvey?

MYRTLE. Of course there isn't. And

anybody who thinks so is crazy. (CHUM-LEY *stares at her.*) Well, don't look at me like that. There's nothing funny about me. I'm like my father's family they're all dead.

JUDGE. Now, then, my client, the plaintiff, Mrs. Veta Louise Simmons, under oath, swears that on the morning of November second while standing in the kitchen of her home, hearing her name called, she turned and saw this great white rabbit, Harvey. He was staring at her. Resenting the intrusion, the plaintiff made certain remarks and drove the creature from the room. He went.

CHUMLEY. What did she say to him?

JUDGE. She was emphatic. The remarks are not important.

CHUMLEY. I want to know how she got this creature out of her sanitarium— I mean—her home.

MYRTLE. I hate to have you tell him, Judge. It isn't a bit like Mother.

WILSON. Quit stalling. Let's have it.

GAFFNEY. She looked him right in the eye and exclaimed in the heat of anger — "To hell with you!"

CHUMLEY (*looking at door*). "To hell with you!" He left?

JUDGE. Yes, he left. But that's beside the point. The point is—is it perjury or is it something we can cope with? I ask for your opinion. (KELLY *enters from stairs* U.C. SANDERSON *comes from* U.C. *diet kitchen.*)

SANDERSON. Ruthie! I've been looking all over for you.

CHUMLEY. Dr. Sanderson, disregard what I said this afternoon. I want you on my staff. You are a very astute young man.

KELLY. Oh, Lyman! Did you hear?

SANDERSON. Oh, baby!

KELLY. See you later. (*Exits* U.C., *blowing him a kiss.* SANDERSON *exits into his office.*)

MYRTLE. You've just got to keep Uncle Elwood out here, Doctor. (JUDGE *crosses to desk.*)

CHUMLEY. No. I want this sanitarium the way it was before that man came out here this afternoon.

MYRTLE. I know what you mean.

CHUMLEY. You do?

MYRTLE. Well, it certainly gets on anyone's nerves the way Uncle Elwood knows what's going to happen before it

happens. This morning, for instance, he told us that Harvey told him Mrs. McElhinney's Aunt Rose would drop in on her unexpectedly tonight from Cleveland.

CHUMLEY. And did she?

MYRTLE. Did she what?

CHUMLEY. Aunt Rose—did she come just as Harvey said she would?

MYRTLE. Oh, yes. Those things always turn out the way Uncle Elwood says they will—but what of it? What do we care about the McElhinneys?

CHUMLEY. You say this sort of thing happens often?

MYRTLE. Yes, and isn't it silly? Uncle Elwood says Harvey tells him everything. Harvey knows everything. How could he when there is no such thing as Harvey?

CHUMLEY (*goes over, tries lock at door* R). Fly-specks. I've been spending my life among fly-specks while miracles have been leaning on lamp-posts on 18th and Fairfax.

VETA (*enters down* L. *Looks around cautiously. Sighs with relief*). Good. Nobody here but people.

MYRTLE. Oh, Mother! You promised you wouldn't come out here.

VETA. Well, good evening. Now, Myrtle Mae, I brought Elwood's bathrobe. Well, why are you all just sitting here? I thought you'd be committing him.

JUDGE. Sit down there, girl. (*Motioning to chair near Wilson.*)

VETA. I will not sit down there. (*Sits chair* R. *of desk.*)

WILSON. How about you and me stepping out Saturday night, Myrtle Mae?

VETA. Certainly not. Myrtle Mae, come here.

MYRTLE. I'm sorry. (*Goes down to* VETA.)

VETA. Is everything settled?

CHUMLEY. It will be.

SANDERSON (*enters from his office*). Doctor, may I give an opinion?

CHUMLEY. Yes, do. By all means.

VETA (*sniffing*). His opinion! Omar— he's the doctor I told you about. The eyes!

SANDERSON. It's my opinion that Elwood P. Dowd is suffering from a third-degree hallucination and the—(*Pointing at Veta's back.*) other party concerned is the victim of autosuggestion. I recommend shock formula number 977 for him and bed-rest at home for—(*Points again.*)

CHUMLEY. You do?

SANDERSON. That's my diagnosis, Doctor. (*To Veta.*) Mr. Dowd will not see this rabbit any more after this injection. We've used it in hundreds of psychopathic cases.

VETA. Don't you call my brother a psychopathic case! There's never been anything like that in our family.

MYRTLE. If you didn't think Uncle Elwood was psychopathic, why did you bring him out here?

VETA. Where else could I take him? I couldn't take him to jail, could I? Besides, this is not your uncle's fault. Why did Harvey have to speak to him in the first place? With the town full of people, why did he have to bother Elwood?

JUDGE. Stop putting your oar in. Keep your oar out. If this shock formula brings people back to reality, give it to him. That's where we want Elwood.

CHUMLEY. I'm not sure that it would work in a case of this kind, Doctor.

SANDERSON. It always has.

VETA. Harvey always follows Elwood home.

CHUMLEY. He does?

VETA. Yes. But if you give him the formula and Elwood doesn't see Harvey, he won't let him in. Then when he comes to the door, I'll deal with him.

MYRTLE. Mother, won't you stop talking about Harvey as if there was such a thing?

VETA. Myrtle Mae, you've got a lot to learn and I hope you never learn it. (*She starts up toward* Wilson.)

(ELWOOD *is heard offstage, humming.*)

JUDGE. Sh! Here he is.

ELWOOD (*enters* C). Good evening, everybody.

(ALL *nod.*)

VETA. Good evening, Elwood. I've brought you your bathrobe.

ELWOOD. Thank you, Veta.

JUDGE. Well, Chumley, what do we do? We've got to do something.

VETA. Oh, yes, we must.

MYRTLE. I should say so.

CHUMLEY (*looking at door*). Yes, it's imperative.

ELWOOD. Well, while you're making up your minds, why don't we all go down to Charlie's and have a drink?

VETA. You're not going anywhere, Elwood. You're staying here.

MYRTLE. Yes, Uncle Elwood.

JUDGE. Stay here, son.

ELWOOD. I plan to leave. You want me to stay. An element of conflict in any discussion is a good thing. It means everybody is taking part and nobody is left out. I like that. Oh— how did you get along with Harvey, Doctor?

CHUMLEY. Sh-h!

JUDGE. We're waiting for your answer, Doctor.

CHUMLEY. What?

JUDGE. What is your decision?

CHUMLEY. I must be alone with this man. Will you all step into the other room? (MYRTLE *exits* U.L.) I'll have my diagnosis in a moment.

VETA. Do hurry, Doctor.

CHUMLEY. I will.

VETA. You stay here, Elwood. (*She and* JUDGE GAFFNEY *exit* U.L.)

CHUMLEY. Here, Mr. Dowd. Let me give you this chair. (*Indicates chair* L. *of table* R.) Let me give you a cigar. (*Does so.*) Is there anything else I can get you?

ELWOOD (*seated in chair*). What did you have in mind?

CHUMLEY. Mr. Dowd (*Lowers voice, looks toward office.*) What kind of a man are you? Where do you come from?

ELWOOD (*getting out card*). Didn't I give you one of my cards?

CHUMLEY. And where on the face of this tired old earth did you find a thing like him?

ELWOOD. Harvey the Pooka?

CHUMLEY (*sits chair* R. *of table*). Is it true that he has a function—that he—

ELWOOD. Gets advance notice? I'm happy to say it is. Harvey is versatile. Harvey can stop clocks.

DR. CHUMLEY. What?

ELWOOD. You've heard that expression, "His face would stop a clock"?

CHUMLEY. Yes. But why? To what purpose?

ELWOOD. Harvey says that he can look at your clock and stop it and you can go away as long as you like with whomever you like and go as far as you like. And when you come back not one minute will have ticked by.

CHUMLEY. You mean that he actually — (*Looks toward office.*)

ELWOOD. Einstein has overcome time

and space. Harvey has overcome not only time and space—but any objections.

CHUMLEY. And does he do this for you?

ELWOOD. He is willing to at any time, but so far I've never been able to think of any place I'd rather be. I always have a wonderful time just where I am, whomever I'm with. I'm having a fine time right now with you, Doctor. (*Holds up cigar.*) Corona-Corona.

CHUMLEY. I know where I'd go.

ELWOOD. Where?

CHUMLEY. I'd go to Akron.

ELWOOD. Akron?

CHUMLEY. There's a cottage camp outside Akron in a grove of maple trees, cool, green, beautiful.

ELWOOD. My favorite tree.

CHUMLEY. I would go there with a pretty young woman, a strange woman, a quiet woman.

ELWOOD. Under a tree?

CHUMLEY. I wouldn't even want to know her name. I would be—just Mr. Brown.

ELWOOD. Why wouldn't you want to know her name? You might be acquainted with the same people.

CHUMLEY. I would send out for cold beer. I would talk to her. I would tell her things I have never told anyone— things that are locked in here. (*Beats his breast.* ELWOOD *looks over at his chest with interest.*) And then I would send out for more cold beer.

ELWOOD. No whiskey?

CHUMLEY. Beer is better.

ELWOOD. Maybe under a tree. But she might like a highball.

CHUMLEY. I wouldn't let her talk to me, but as I talked I would want her to reach out a soft white hand and stroke my head and say, "Poor thing! Oh, you poor, poor thing!"

ELWOOD. How long would you like that to go on?

CHUMLEY. Two weeks.

ELWOOD. Wouldn't that get monotonous? Just Akron, beer, and "poor, poor thing" for two weeks?

CHUMLEY. No. No, it would not. It would be wonderful.

ELWOOD. I can't help but feel you're making a mistake in not allowing that woman to talk. If she gets around at all, she may have picked up some very interesting little news items. And I'm sure you're making a mistake with all that beer and no whiskey. But it's your two weeks.

CHUMLEY (*dreamily*). Cold beer at Akron and one last fling! God, man!

ELWOOD. Do you think you'd like to lie down for awhile?

CHUMLEY. No. No. Tell me Mr. Dowd, could he—would he do this for me?

ELWOOD. He could and he might. I have never heard Harvey say a word against Akron. By the way, Doctor, where is Harvey?

CHUMLEY (*rising. Very cautiously*). Why, don't you know?

ELWOOD. The last time I saw him he was with you.

CHUMLEY. Ah!

ELWOOD. Oh! He's probably waiting for me down at Charlie's

CHUMLEY (*with a look of cunning toward his office*). That's it! He's down at Charlie's.

ELWOOD. Excuse me, Doctor. (*Rises, starts upstage.*)

CHUMLEY (*going* U.L. *of table*). No, no, Mr. Dowd. Not in there.

ELWOOD. I couldn't leave without saying good-night to my friend, Dr. Sanderson.

CHUMLEY. Mr. Dowd, Dr. Sanderson is not your friend. None of those people are your friends. *I* am your friend.

ELWOOD. Thank you, Doctor. And I'm yours.

CHUMLEY. And this sister of yours— she is at the bottom of this conspiracy against you. She's trying to persuade me to lock you up. Today she had commitment papers drawn up. She's got your power of attorney and the key to your safety box. She brought you out here

ELWOOD. My sister did all that in one afternoon? Veta is certainly a whirlwind.

CHUMLEY (*moving down below desk*). God, man, haven't you any righteous indignation?

ELWOOD. Dr. Chumley, my mother used to say to me, "In this world, Elwood"—she always called me Elwood —she'd say, "In this world, Elwood, you must be oh, so smart or oh, so pleasant." For years I was smart. I recommend pleasant. You may quote me.

CHUMLEY. Just the same, I will protect you if I have to commit her. Would you like me to do that?

ELWOOD. No, Doctor, not unless Veta wanted it that way. Oh, not that you don't have a nice place out here, but I think Veta would be happier at home with me and Harvey and Myrtle Mae. (KELLY *enters from* C. *with flower in hair, goes to put magazines on table* R. ELWOOD *turns to her.*) Miss Kelly! "Diviner grace has never brightened this enchanting face!" (*To Chumley.*) Ovid's Fifth Elegy. (*To Miss Kelly.*) My dear, you will never look lovelier!

KELLY. I'll never feel happier, Mr. Dowd. I know it. (*Kisses him.*)

CHUMLEY. Well!

KELLY. Yes, Doctor. (*Exits up stairs* C.) (WILSON *enters hall in time to see the kiss.*)

ELWOOD. I wonder if I would be able to remember any more of that poem?

WILSON. Say, maybe this rabbit gag is a good one. Kelly never kissed me.

ELWOOD (*looking at Wilson*). Ovid has always been my favorite poet.

WILSON. O.K., pal — You're discharged. This way out—(*Takes him by arm downstage.*)

CHUMLEY. Wilson! Take your hands off that man!

WILSON. (R. *of desk*). What?

CHUMLEY. Apologize to Mr. Dowd.

WILSON. Apologize to him—this guy with the rabbit? (*He is below desk.*)

CHUMLEY (*looking toward his office*). Apologize! Apologize—

WILSON. I apologize. This is the door.

ELWOOD. If I leave, I'll remember. (WILSON *exits* D.L.)

CHUMLEY. Wait a minute, Dowd. Do women often come up to you and kiss you like Miss Kelly did just now?

ELWOOD. Every once in a while.

CHUMLEY. Yes?

ELWOOD. I encourage it, too.

CHUMLEY (*to himself*). To hell with decency! I've got to have that rabbit! Go ahead and knock. (ELWOOD *starts for Sanderson's door just as* SANDERSON *comes out.*)

ELWOOD. Dr. Sanderson, I couldn't leave without—

SANDERSON. Just a minute, Dowd— (*To Chumley.*) Doctor, do you agree with my diagnosis?

CHUMLEY. Yes, yes! Call them all in.

SANDERSON. Thank you, Doctor. Mrs. Simmons—Judge Gaffney—will you step in here for a minute, please?

VETA (*enters*). Is it settled? (MYRTLE *and* JUDGE *enter.*)

CHUMLEY. I find I concur with Dr. Sanderson!

SANDERSON. Thank you, Doctor.

MYRTLE. Oh, that's wonderful! What a relief!

JUDGE. Good boy!

ELWOOD. Well, let's celebrate—(*Takes little book out of his pocket.*) I've got some new bars listed in the back of this book.

CHUMLEY (*speaking to others in low tone*). This injection carries a violent reaction. We can't give it to him without his consent. Will he give it?

VETA. Of course he will, if I ask him.

CHUMLEY. To give up this rabbit—I doubt it.

MYRTLE. Don't ask him. Just give it to him.

ELWOOD. "Bessie's Barn Dance. Blondie's Chicken Inn. Better Late Than Never—Bennie's Drive In"—

VETA. Elwood!

ELWOOD. We'll go to Bennie's Drive In—We should telephone for a table. How many of us will there be, Veta?

VETA (*starting to count, then catching herself*). Oh—Elwood!

CHUMLEY. Mr. Dowd, I have a formula—977—that will be good for you. Will you take it?

JUDGE. Elwood, you won't see this rabbit any more.

SANDERSON. But you will see your responsibilities, your duties—

ELWOOD. I'm sure if you thought of it, Doctor, it must be a very fine thing. And if I happen to run into anyone who needs it, I'll be glad to recommend it. For myself, I wouldn't care for it.

VETA. Hear that, Judge! Hear that, Doctor! That's what we have to put up with.

ELWOOD (*turning to look at her*). Veta, do you want me to take this?

VETA. Elwood, I'm only thinking of you. You're my brother and I've known you for years. I'd do anything for you. That Harvey wouldn't do anything for you. He's making a fool out of you, Elwood. Don't be a fool.

ELWOOD. Oh, I won't.

VETA. Why, you could amount to something. You could be sitting on the Western Slope Water Board right now if you'd only go over and ask them.

ELWOOD. All right, Veta. If that's what you want, Harvey and I will go over and ask them tomorrow.

VETA. Tomorrow! I never want to see another tomorrow. Not if Myrtle Mae and I have to live in the house with that rabbit. Our friends never come to see us—we have no social life; we have no life at all. We're both miserable. I wish I were dead—but maybe you don't care!

ELWOOD (*slowly*). I've always felt that Veta should have everything she wants. Veta, are you sure? (VETA *nods*.) I'll take it. Where do I go, Doctor?

CHUMLEY. In Dr. Sanderson's office, Dowd.

ELWOOD. Say good-by to the old fellow for me, won't you? (*Exits* U.L. CHUMLEY *exits* C.)

JUDGE. How long will this take, Doctor?

SANDERSON. Only a few minutes. Why don't you wait? (*Exits.*)

JUDGE. We'll wait. (*Sits* L. *of desk.*)

VETA (*sighs*). Dr. Sanderson said it wouldn't take long.

MYRTLE. Now, Mother, don't fidget.

VETA. Oh, how can I help it?

MYRTLE (*picks up edge of draperies*). How stunning! Mother, could you see me in a housecoat of this material.

VETA (*to Myrtle—first looking at draperies. Sighs again*). Yes, dear, but let me get a good night's sleep first. (*Loud knocking at door.*)

JUDGE. Come in. (*Enter* CAB DRIVER.)

JUDGE. What do you want?

CAB DRIVER. I'm lookin' for a little, short—(*Seeing Veta.*) Oh, there you are! Lady, you jumped outta the cab without payin' me.

VETA. Oh, yes. I forgot. How much is it?

CAB DRIVER. All the way out here from town? $2.75.

VETA (*looking in purse*). $2.75! I could have sworn I brought my coin purse—where is it? (*Gets up, goes to table, turns pocketbook upside down, in full view of audience. Nothing comes out of it but a compact and a handkerchief.*) Myrtle, do you have any money?

MYRTLE. I spent that money Uncle Elwood gave me for my new hair-do for the party.

VETA. Judge, do you have $2.75 I could give this man?

JUDGE. Sorry. Nothing but a check.

CAB DRIVER. We don't take checks.

JUDGE. I know.

VETA. Dr. Chumley, do you happen to have $2.75 I could borrow to pay this cab driver?

CHUMLEY (*He has just entered* C., *now wearing white starched jacket*). Haven't got my wallet. No time to get it now. Have to get on with this injection. Sorry. (*Exits* L.)

VETA. Well, I'll get it for you from my brother, but I can't get it right now. He's in there to get an injection. It won't be long. You'll have to wait.

CAB DRIVER. You're gonna get my money from your brother and he's in there to get some of that stuff they shoot out here?

VETA. Yes, it won't be but a few minutes.

CAB DRIVER. Lady, I want my money now.

VETA. But I told you it would only be a few minutes. I want you to drive us back to town, anyway.

CAB DRIVER. And I told you I want my money now or I'm nosin' the cab back to town, and you can wait for the bus—at six in the morning.

VETA. Well, of all the pig-headed, stubborn things!

MYRTLE. I should say so.

JUDGE. What's the matter with you?

CAB DRIVER. Nothin' that $2.75 won't fix. You heard me. Take it or leave it.

VETA (*getting up, going* L). I never heard of anything so unreasonable in my life. (*Knocks.*) Dr. Chumley, will you let Elwood step out here a minute. This cab driver won't wait.

CHUMLEY (*off* L). Don't be too long. (*Enter* ELWOOD. CHUMLEY *follows.*)

VETA. Elwood, I came off without my coin purse. Will you give this man $2.75? But don't give him any more. He's been very rude.

ELWOOD (*extending his hand*). How do you do? Dowd is my name. Elwood P.

CAB DRIVER. Lofgren's mine. E. J.

ELWOOD. I'm glad to meet you, Mr. Lofgren. This is my sister, Mrs. Simmons. My charming little niece, Myrtle Mae Simmons. Judge Gaffney and Dr. Chumley. (ALL *bow coldly.*)

CAB DRIVER. Hi—

ELWOOD. Have you lived around here long, Mr. Lofgren?

CAB DRIVER. Yeah, I've lived around here all my life.

ELWOOD. Do you enjoy your work?

CAB DRIVER. It's O.K. I been with the Apex Cabs fifteen years and my brother Joe's been drivin' for Brown Cabs pretty near twelve.

ELWOOD. You drive for Apex and your brother Joe for Brown's? That's interesting, isn't it, Veta? (VETA *reacts with a sniff.*) Mr. Lofgren—let me give you one of my cards. (*Gives him one.*)

CHUMLEY. Better get on with this, Mr. Dowd.

ELWOOD. Certainly. One minute. My sister and my charming little niece live here with me at this address. Won't you and your brother come and have dinner with us some time?

CABBY. Sure—be glad to.

ELWOOD. When—when would you be glad to?

CABBY. I couldn't come any night but Tuesday. I'm on duty all the rest of the week.

ELWOOD. You must come on Tuesday, then. We'll expect you and be delighted to see you, won't we, Veta?

VETA. Oh, Elwood, I'm sure this man has friends of his own.

ELWOOD. Veta, one can't have too many friends.

VETA. Elwood, don't keep Dr. Chumley waiting—that's rude.

ELWOOD. Of course. (*Gives him bill.*) Here you are—keep the change. I'm glad to have met you and I'll expect you Tuesday with your brother. Will you excuse me now?

LOFGREN. Sure. (ELWOOD *exits* U.L. CHUMLEY *follows.*)

CAB DRIVER. A sweet guy.

VETA. Certainly. You could just as well have waited.

CAB DRIVER. Oh, no. Listen, lady. I've been drivin' this route fifteen years. I've brought 'em out here to get that stuff and drove 'em back after they had it. It changes 'em. (*Crosses to desk.*)

VETA. Well, I certainly hope so.

CAB DRIVER. And you ain't kiddin'. On the way out here they sit back and enjoy the ride. They talk to me. Sometimes we stop and watch the sunsets and look at the birds flyin'. Sometimes we stop and watch the birds when there ain't no birds and look at the sunsets when it's rainin'. We have a swell time

and I always get a big tip. But afterward—oh—oh—(*Starts to exit again.*)

VETA. Afterwards—oh—oh! What do you mean afterwards—oh—oh?

CAB DRIVER. They crab, crab, crab. They yell at me to watch the lights, watch the brakes, watch the intersections. They scream at me to hurry. They got no faith—in me or my buggy—yet it's the same cab—the same driver—and we're goin' back over the very same road. It's no fun—and no tips—(*Turns to door.*)

VETA. But my brother would have tipped you, anyway. He's very generous. Always has been.

CAB DRIVER. Not after this he won't be. Lady, after this, he'll be a perfectly normal human being and you know what bastards they are! Glad I met you. I'll wait. (*Exits* L.)

VETA (*starts to run for door* U.L.). Oh, Judge Gaffney—Myrtle Mae! Stop it —stop it—don't give it to him! Elwood, come out of there.

JUDGE. You can't do that. Dr. Chumley is giving the injection.

MYRTLE. Mother—stop this—

VETA (*pounding on door*). I don't want Elwood to have it! I don't want Elwood that way. I don't like people like that.

MYRTLE. Do something with her, Judge   Mother, stop it—

VETA (*turning on her*). You shut up! I've lived longer than you have. I remember my father. I remember your father. I remember—

CHUMLEY (*opens door*). What's this? What's all this commotion?

WILSON (*enters* U.C.). What's the trouble, Doctor? She soundin' off again?

JUDGE. She wants to stop the injection.

VETA. You haven't—you haven't already given it to him, have you?

CHUMLEY. No, but we're ready. Take Mrs. Simmons away, Wilson.

VETA. Leave me alone. Take your hands off me, you whiteslaver!

JUDGE. You don't know what you want. You didn't want that rabbit, either.

VETA. And what's wrong with Harvey? If Elwood and Myrtle Mae and I want to live with Harvey it's nothing to you! You don't even have to come around. It's our business. Elwood—

Elwood! (ELWOOD *enters from* U.L. SHE *throws herself weepingly into his arms.* HE *pats her shoulder.*)

ELWOOD. There, there, Veta. (*To others.*) Veta is all tired out. She's done a lot today.

JUDGE. Have it your own way. I'm not giving up my game at the club again, no matter how big the animal is. (*He exits down* L.)

VETA (*crossing Elwood to desk*). Come on, Elwood—let's get out of here. I hate this place. I wish I'd never seen it!

CHUMLEY. But—see—here—

ELWOOD. It's whatever Veta says, Doctor.

VETA. Why, look at this! That's funny. (*It's her coin purse.*) It must have been there all the time. I could have paid that cab driver myself. Harvey!

VETA. Come on, Myrtle Mae. Come on, Elwood. Hurry up. (*She exits down left.* MYRTLE *follows.*)

ELWOOD. Good night, Doctor Chumley. Good night, Mr. Wilson.

VETA (*offstage*). Come along, Elwood.

ELWOOD. Doctor, for years I've known what my family thinks of Harvey. But I've often wondered what Harvey's family thinks of me. (*He looks beyond* CHUMLEY *to the door of his office* R.) Oh—there you are! Doctor—do you mind? (*Gestures for him to step back.*) You're standing in his way. (*There is the sound of a lock clicking open and the door of* CHUMLEY's *office opens wide. The invisible Harvey crosses to him and as they exit together:*) Where've you been? I've been looking all over for you—

CURTAIN

THE GLASS MENAGERIE
By TENNESSEE WILLIAMS

———

THE GLASS MENAGERIE was first produced by Eddie Dowling and Louis J. Singer at the Playhouse Theatre, New York City, on March 31, 1945. The play was staged by Eddie Dowling and Margo Jones; setting by Jo Mielziner; original music by Paul Bowles. The cast was as follows:

THE MOTHER..............Laurette Taylor
HER SON.........................Eddie Dowling
HER DAUGHTER.............Julie Haydon
THE GENTLEMAN CALLER
                                        Anthony Ross

———

The scene is an Alley in St. Louis.

PART I. Preparation for a Gentleman Caller.

PART II. The Gentleman calls.

Time: Now and the Past.

———

THE AUTHOR

As a descendant of Indian-fighting Tennessee pioneers Tennessee Williams, who was born in Columbus, Mississippi (in 1914), comes naturally by his restiveness. He has traveled extensively in America and Mexico. In fact, it is always a problem for his agents and producers where to locate him. Broadway is his beat only when he has business to transact or when he cannot roam elsewhere.

After graduation from the University of Iowa, he began serving an indirect apprenticeship to literature and the theatre as a bell hop in New Orleans, a handyman in a shoe-warehouse (like the hero of The Glass Menagerie), *a teletypist with a corps of engineers in Jacksonville, Florida, and a waiter and reciter of verse in a Greenwich Village night club. Throughout all these efforts to hold body and soul together he was writing furiously, mostly for the stage.*

His talents were recognized several years before he received a professional production. The Group Theatre awarded him a cash prize for four one-act pieces appropriately entitled American Blues, *since the young author was one well acquainted with the pre-war depression and memorialized it. Theresa Helburn and John Gassner gave him a scholarship to their advanced playwrights' seminar at the New School for Social Research. It was in this class that he wrote his second full-length play* The Battle of Angels. *It was the first to get a professional production after the instructors, who were both Theatre Guild associates, presented the script officially to the Guild. Lawrence Langner, the other member of the Guild trio that concerned itself with playwrights, took charge of the lyrical play, Margaret Webster was assigned to direct it, and Miriam Hopkins was engaged for the leading role. Unfortunately,* The Battle of Angels *was abandoned in Boston where it caused a minor scandal, and plans to revamp the play for New York failed to materialize. According to report, Mr. Williams considers it his best effort to date, and he is perhaps not far from right. If it is ever given some intelligent revision and a sound production, it is certain to enhance its author's reputation. Mr. Williams also received a Rockefeller Foundation Fellowship in 1940 and was awarded a thousand dollar grant for work in drama by the American Academy and National Institute of Arts and Letters.*

The Glass Menagerie *frightened Broadway producers. Eddie Dowling and Louis Singer tested it in Chicago before bringing it to New York in March, 1945. Mr. Williams was fortunate in having Eddie Dowling as the director of his play, and the production was the occasion for the triumphant return of Laurette Taylor to the New York stage. The mother in* The Glass Menagerie *was also to be Miss Taylor's last role on the stage of this world, and her seasoned performance was the high-water mark of her notable career.*

Mr. Williams' earlier written collaboration, You Touched Me, *a dramatization of a D. H. Lawrence story, was produced in the fall of 1945. Although it fell short of the success of* The Glass Menagerie, *it again revealed an aptitude for sensitive characterization and dialogue.*

THE GLASS MENAGERIE

SCENE I

The Wingfield apartment is in the rear of the building, one of those vast hive-like conglomerations of cellular living-units that flower as warty growths in overcrowded urban centers of lower middle-class population and are symptomatic of the impulse of this largest and fundamentally enslaved section of American society to avoid fluidity and differentiation and to exist and function as one interfused mass of automatism.

The apartment faces an alley and is entered by a fire-escape, a structure whose name is a touch of accidental poetic truth, for all of these huge buildings are always burning with the slow and implacable fires of human desperation. The fire-escape is included in the set—that is, the landing of it and steps descending from it.

The scene is memory and is therefore nonrealistic. Memory takes a lot of poetic license. It omits some details; others are exaggerated, according to the emotional value of the articles it touches, for memory is seated predominantly in the heart. The interior is therefore rather dim and poetic.

At the rise of the curtain, the audience is faced with the dark, grim rear wall of the Wingfield tenement. This building, which runs parallel to the footlights, is flanked on both sides by dark, narrow alleys which run into murky canyons of tangled clotheslines, garbage cans and the sinister lattice-work of neighboring fire-escapes. It is up and down these side alleys that exterior entrances and exits are made, during the play. At the end of Tom's *opening commentary, the dark tenement wall slowly reveals (by means of a transparency) the interior of the ground floor Wingfield apartment.*

Downstage is the living room, which also serves as a sleeping room for Laura, *the sofa unfolding to make her bed. Upstage, center, and divided by a wide arch or second proscenium with transparent faded portieres (or second curtain), is the dining room. In an old-fashioned what-not in the living room are seen scores of transparent glass animals. A blown-up photograph of the father hangs on the wall of the living room, facing the audience, to the left of the archway. It is the face of a very handsome young man in a doughboy's First World War cap. He is gallantly smiling, ineluctably smiling, as if to say, "I will be smiling forever."*

The audience hears and sees the opening scene in the dining room through both the transparent fourth wall of the building and the transparent gauze portieres of the dining-room arch. It is during this revealing scene that the fourth wall slowly ascends, out of sight. This transparent exterior wall is not brought down again until the very end of the play, during Tom's *final speech.*

The narrator is an undisguised convention of the play. He takes whatever license with dramatic convention as is convenient to his purposes:

Tom *enters dressed as a merchant sailor from alley, stage left, and strolls across the front of the stage to the fire-escape. There he stops and lights a cigarette. He addresses the audience.*

TOM. Yes, I have tricks in my pocket, I have things up my sleeve. But I am the opposite of a stage magician. He gives you illusion that has the appearance of truth. I give you truth in the pleasant disguise of illusion.

To begin with, I turn back time. I reverse it to that quaint period, the thirties, when the huge middle class of America was matriculating in a school for the blind. Their eyes had failed them, or they had failed their eyes, and so they were having their fingers pressed forcibly down on the fiery Braille alphabet of a dissolving economy.

In Spain there was revolution. Here there was only shouting and confusion.

In Spain there was Guernica. Here there were disturbances of labor, sometimes pretty violent, in otherwise peaceful cities such as Chicago, Cleveland, Saint Louis . . .

This is the social background of the play.

(MUSIC.)

The play is memory.

Being a memory play, it is dimly lighted, it is sentimental, it is not realistic.

In memory everything seems to happen to music. That explains the fiddle in the wings.

I am the narrator of the play, and also a character in it.

The other characters are my mother, Amanda, my sister, Laura, and a gentleman caller who appears in the final scenes. He is the most realistic character in the play, being an emissary from a world of reality that we were somehow set apart from.

But since I have a poet's weakness for symbols, I am using this character also as a symbol; he is the long delayed but always expected something that we live for.

There is a fifth character in the play who doesn't appear except in this larger-than-life-size photograph over the mantel.

This is our father who left us a long time ago.

He was a telephone man who fell in love with long distances; he gave up his job with the telephone company and skipped the light fantastic out of town . . .

The last we heard of him was a picture post-card from Mazatlan, on the Pacific coast of Mexico, containing a message of two words—

"Hello— Good-bye!" and no address.

I think the rest of the play will explain itself. . . .

(AMANDA's *voice becomes audible through the portieres.*)

(LEGEND ON SCREEN: "OU SONT LES NEIGES.") (*He divides the portieres and enters the upstage area.*)

(AMANDA *and* LAURA *are seated at a drop-leaf table. Eating is indicated by gestures without food or utensils.* AMANDA *faces the audience.* TOM *and* LAURA *are seated in profile.*)

(*The interior has lit up softly and through the scrim we see* AMANDA *and* LAURA *seated at the table in the upstage area.*)

AMANDA (*calling*). Tom?

TOM. Yes, Mother.

AMANDA. We can't say grace until you come to the table!

TOM. Coming, Mother. (*He bows slightly and withdraws, reappearing a few moments later in his place at the table.*)

AMANDA (*to her son*). Honey, don't *push* with your *fingers.* If you have to push with something, the thing to push with is a crust of bread. And chew—chew! Animals have sections in their stomachs which enable them to digest food without mastication, but human beings are supposed to chew their food before they swallow it down. Eat food leisurely, son, and really enjoy it. A well-cooked meal has lots of delicate flavors that have to be held in the mouth for appreciation. So chew your food and give your salivary glands a chance to function!

(TOM *deliberately lays his imaginary fork down and pushes his chair back from the table.*)

TOM. I haven't enjoyed one bite of this dinner because of your constant directions on how to eat it. It's you that makes me rush through meals with your hawk-like attention to every bite I take. Sickening—spoils my appetite—all this discussion of —animals' secretion—salivary glands—mastication!

AMANDA (*lightly*). Temperament like a Metropolitan star! (*He rises and crosses downstage.*) You're not excused from the table.

TOM. I'm getting a cigarette.

AMANDA. You smoke too much.

(LAURA *rises.*)

LAURA. I'll bring in the blanc mange.

(*He remains standing with his cigarette by the portieres during the following.*)

AMANDA (*rising*). No, sister, no, sister—you be the lady this time and I'll be the darky.

LAURA. I'm already up.

AMANDA. Resume your seat, little sister— I want you to stay fresh and pretty—for gentlemen callers!

LAURA. I'm not expecting any gentlemen callers.

AMANDA (crossing out to kitchenette. Airily). Sometimes they come when they are least expected! Why, I remember one Sunday afternoon in Blue Mountain—

(Enters kitchenette.)

TOM. I know what's coming!

LAURA. Yes. But let her tell it.

TOM. Again?

LAURA. She loves to tell it.

(AMANDA returns with bowl of dessert.)

AMANDA. One Sunday afternoon in Blue Mountain—your mother received—seventeen!—gentlemen callers! Why, sometimes there weren't chairs enough to accommodate them all. We had to send the nigger over to bring in folding chairs from the parish house.

TOM (remaining at portieres). How did you entertain those gentlemen callers?

AMANDA. I understood the art of conversation!

TOM. I bet you could talk.

AMANDA. Girls in those days knew how to talk, I can tell you.

TOM. Yes?

(IMAGE: AMANDA AS A GIRL ON A PORCH, GREETING CALLERS.)

AMANDA. They knew how to entertain their gentlemen callers. It wasn't enough for a girl to be possessed of a pretty face and a graceful figure—although I wasn't slighted in either respect. She also needed to have a nimble wit and a tongue to meet all occasions.

TOM. What did you talk about?

AMANDA. Things of importance going on in the world! Never anything coarse or common or vulgar. (She addresses TOM as though he were seated in the vacant chair at the table though he remains by portieres. He plays this scene as though he held the book.) My callers were gentlemen—all! Among my callers were some of the most prominent young planters of the Mississippi Delta—planters and sons of planters!

(TOM motions for music and a spot of light on AMANDA.)

(Her eyes lift, her face glows, her voice becomes rich and elegiac.)

(SCREEN LEGEND: "OU SONT LES NEIGES.")

There was young Champ Laughlin who later became vice-president of the Delta Planters Bank.

Hadley Stevenson who was drowned in Moon Lake and left his widow one hundred and fifty thousand in Government bonds.

There were the Cutrere brothers, Wesley and Bates. Bates was one of my bright particular beaux! He got in a quarrel with that wild Wainwright boy. They shot it out on the floor of Moon Lake Casino. Bates was shot through the stomach. Died in the ambulance on his way to Memphis. His widow was also well-provided for, came into eight or ten thousand acres, that's all. She married him on the rebound —never loved her—carried my picture on him the night he died!

And there was that boy that every girl in the Delta had set her cap for! That beautiful, brilliant young Fitzhugh boy from Greene County!

TOM. What did he leave his widow?

AMANDA. He never married! Gracious, you talk as though all of my old admirers had turned up their toes to the daisies!

TOM. Isn't this the first you've mentioned that still survives?

AMANDA. That Fitzhugh boy went North and made a fortune—came to be known as the Wolf of Wall Street! He had the Midas touch, whatever he touched turned to gold!

And I could have been Mrs. Duncan J. Fitzhugh, mind you! But—I picked your father!

LAURA (rising). Mother, let me clear the table.

AMANDA. No, dear, you go in front and study your typewriter chart. Or practice your shorthand a little. Stay fresh and pretty!—It's almost time for our gentlemen callers to start arriving. (She flounces girlishly toward the kitchenette.) How many do you suppose we're going to entertain this afternoon?

(TOM throws down the paper and jumps up with a groan.)

LAURA (*alone in the dining room*). I don't believe we're going to receive any, Mother.

AMANDA (*reappearing, airily*). What? No one—not one? You must be joking! (LAURA *nervously echoes her laugh. She slips in a fugitive manner through the half-open portieres and draws them gently behind her. A shaft of very clear light is thrown on her face against the faded tapestry of the curtains.* MUSIC: "THE GLASS MENAGERIE" UNDER FAINTLY. *Lightly.*) Not one gentleman caller? It can't be true! There must be a flood, there must have been a tornado!

LAURA. It isn't a flood, it's not a tornado, Mother. I'm just not popular like you were in Blue Mountain. . . . (TOM *utters another groan.* LAURA *glances at him with a faint, apologetic smile, her voice catching a little.*) Mother's afraid I'm going to be an old maid.

THE SCENE DIMS OUT WITH "GLASS MENAGERIE" MUSIC

SCENE II

"Laura, Haven't You Ever Liked Some Boy?"
On the dark stage the screen is lighted with the image of blue roses.
Gradually LAURA's *figure becomes apparent and the screen goes out.*
The music subsides.
LAURA *is seated in the delicate ivory chair at the small claw-foot table.*
She wears a dress of soft violet material for a kimono—her hair tied back from her forehead with a ribbon.
She is washing and polishing her collection of glass.
AMANDA *appears on the fire-escape steps. At the sound of her ascent,* LAURA *catches her breath, thrusts the bowl of ornaments away and seats herself stiffly before the diagram of the typewriter keyboard as though it held her spellbound.*
Something has happened to AMANDA. *It is written in her face as she climbs to the landing: a look that is grim and hopeless and a little absurd.*
She has on one of those cheap or imitation velvety-looking cloth coats with imitation fur collar. Her hat is five or six years old, one of those dreadful cloche hats that were worn in the late twenties and she is clasping an enormous black patent-leather pocketbook with nickel clasps and initials. This is her full-dress outfit, the one she usually wears to the D.A.R.
Before entering she looks through the door.
She purses her lips, opens her eyes very wide, rolls them upward and shakes her head.
Then she slowly lets herself in the door. Seeing her mother's expression LAURA *touches her lips with a nervous gesture.*

LAURA. Hello, Mother, I was— (*She makes a nervous gesture toward the chart on the wall.* AMANDA *leans against the shut door and stares at* LAURA *with a martyred look.*)

AMANDA. Deception? Deception? (*She slowly removes her hat and gloves, continuing the sweet suffering stare. She lets the hat and gloves fall on the floor—a bit of acting.*)

LAURA (*shakily*). How was the D.A.R. meeting? (AMANDA *slowly opens her purse and removes a dainty white handkerchief which she shakes out delicately and delicately touches to her lips and nostrils.*) Didn't you go to the D.A.R. meeting, Mother?

AMANDA (*faintly, almost inaudibly*). —No. —No. (*Then more forcibly.*) I did not have the strength—to go to the D.A.R. In fact, I did not have the courage! I wanted to find a hole in the ground and hide myself in it forever! (*She crosses slowly to the wall and removes the diagram of the typewriter keyboard. She holds it in front of her for a second, staring at it sweetly and sorrowfully—then bites her lips and tears it in two pieces.*)

LAURA (*faintly*). Why did you do that, Mother? (AMANDA *repeats the same procedure with the chart of the Gregg Alphabet.*) Why are you—

AMANDA. Why? Why? How old are you Laura?

LAURA. Mother, you know my age.

AMANDA. I thought that you were an adult; it seems that I was mistaken. (*She crosses slowly to the sofa and sinks down and stares at* LAURA.)

LAURA. Please don't stare at me, Mother.

(AMANDA *closes her eyes and lowers her head. Count ten.*)

AMANDA. What are we going to do, what is going to become of us, what is the future? (*Count ten.*)

LAURA. Has something happened, Mother? (AMANDA *draws a long breath and takes out the handkerchief again. Dabbing process.*) Mother, has—something happened?

AMANDA. I'll be all right in a minute, I'm just bewildered— (*Count five.*) —by life. . . .

LAURA. Mother, I wish that you would tell me what's happened!

AMANDA. As you know, I was supposed to be inducted into my office at the D.A.R. this afternoon. (IMAGE: A SWARM OF TYPEWRITERS.) But I stopped off at Rubicam's business college to speak to your teachers about your having a cold and ask them what progress they thought you were making down there.

LAURA. Oh. . . .

AMANDA. I went to the typing instructor and introduced myself as your mother. She didn't know who you were. Wingfield, she said. We don't have any such student enrolled at the school!

I assured her she did, that you had been going to classes since early in January.

"I wonder," she said, "if you could be talking about that terribly shy little girl who dropped out of school after only a few days' attendance?"

"No," I said, "Laura, my daughter, has been going to school every day for the past six weeks!"

"Excuse me," she said. She took the attendance book out and there was your name, unmistakably printed, and all the dates you were absent until they decided that you had dropped out of school.

I still said, "No, there must have been some mistake! There must have been some mix-up in the records!"

And she said, "No—I remember her perfectly now. Her hands shook so that she couldn't hit the right keys! The first time we gave a speed-test, she broke down completely—was sick at the stomach and almost had to be carried into the wash-room! After that morning she never showed up any more. We phoned the house but never got any answer—while I was working at Famous and Barr, I suppose, demonstrating those— Oh!"

I felt so weak I could barely keep on my feet!

I had to sit down while they got me a glass of water!

Fifty dollars' tuition, all of our plans—my hopes and ambitions for you—just gone up the spout, just gone up the spout like that.

(LAURA *draws a long breath and gets awkwardly to her feet. She crosses to the victrola and winds it up.*)

What are you doing?

LAURA. Oh! (*She releases the handle and returns to her seat.*)

AMANDA. Laura, where have you been going when you've gone out pretending that you were going to business college?

LAURA. I've just been going out walking.

AMANDA. That's not true.

LAURA. It is. I just went walking.

AMANDA. Walking? Walking? In winter? Deliberately courting pneumonia in that light coat? Where did you walk to, Laura?

LAURA. All sorts of places—mostly in the park.

AMANDA. Even after you'd started catching that cold?

LAURA. It was the lesser of two evils, Mother. (IMAGE: WINTER SCENE IN PARK.) I couldn't go back up. I—threw up—on the floor!

AMANDA. From half past seven till after five every day you mean to tell me you walked around in the park, because you wanted to make me think that you were still going to Rubicam's Business College?

LAURA. It wasn't as bad as it sounds. I went inside places to get warmed up.

AMANDA. Inside where?

LAURA. I went in the art museum and the bird-houses at the Zoo. I visited the penguins every day! Sometimes I did without lunch and went to the movies. Lately I've been spending most of my afternoons in the Jewel-box, that big glass house where they raise the tropical flowers.

AMANDA. You did all this to deceive me, just for deception? (LAURA *looks down.*) Why?

LAURA. Mother, when you're disappointed, you get that awful suffering look on your face, like the picture of Jesus' mother in the museum!

AMANDA. Hush!

LAURA. I couldn't face it.

(*Pause. A whisper of strings.*)

(LEGEND: "THE CRUST OF HUMILITY.")

AMANDA (*hopelessly fingering the huge pocketbook*). So what are we going to do the rest of our lives? Stay home and watch the parades go by? Amuse ourselves with the glass menagerie, darling? Eternally play those worn-out phonograph records your father left as a painful reminder of him?

We won't have a business career—we've given that up because it gave us nervous indigestion! (*Laughs wearily.*) What is there left but dependency all our lives? I know so well what becomes of unmarried women who aren't prepared to occupy a position. I've seen such pitiful cases in the South—barely tolerated spinsters living upon the grudging patronage of sister's husband or brother's wife!—stuck away in some little mouse-trap of a room—encouraged by one in-law to visit another— little birdlike women without any nest— eating the crust of humility all their life! Is that the future that we've mapped out for ourselves?

I swear it's the only alternative I can think of!

It isn't a very pleasant alternative, is it?

Of course—some girls *do marry.*

(LAURA *twists her hands nervously.*)

Haven't you ever liked some boy?

LAURA. Yes. I liked one once. (*Rises.*) I came across his picture a while ago.

AMANDA (*with some interest*). He gave you his picture?

LAURA. No, it's in the year-book.

AMANDA (*disappointed*). Oh—a high-school boy.

(SCREEN IMAGE: JIM AS HIGH-SCHOOL HERO BEARING A SILVER CUP.)

LAURA. Yes. His name was Jim. (LAURA *lifts the heavy annual from the claw-foot table.*) Here he is in *The Pirates of Penzance.*

AMANDA (*absently*). The what?

LAURA. The operetta the senior class put on. He had a wonderful voice and we sat across the aisle from each other Mondays, Wednesdays and Fridays in the Aud. Here he is with the silver cup for debating! See his grin?

AMANDA (*absently*). He must have had a jolly disposition.

LAURA. He used to call me—Blue Roses.

(IMAGE: BLUE ROSES.)

AMANDA. Why did he call you such a name as that?

LAURA. When I had that attack of pleurosis —he asked me what was the matter when I came back. I said pleurosis—he thought that I said Blue Roses! So that's what he always called me after that. Whenever he saw me, he'd holler, "Hello, Blue Roses!" I didn't care for the girl that he went out with. Emily Meisenbach. Emily was the best-dressed girl at Soldan. She never struck me, though, as being sincere . . . It says in the Personal Section—they're engaged. That's—six years ago! They must be married by now.

AMANDA. Girls that aren't cut out for business careers usually wind up married to some nice man. (*Gets up with a spark of revival.*) Sister, that's what you'll do!

(LAURA *utters a startled, doubtful laugh. She reaches quickly for a piece of glass.*)

LAURA. But, Mother—

AMANDA. Yes? (*Crossing to photograph.*)

LAURA (*in a tone of frightened apology*). I'm—crippled!

(IMAGE: SCREEN.)

AMANDA. Nonsense! Laura, I've told you never, never to use that word. Why, you're not crippled, you just have a little defect—hardly noticeable, even! When people have some slight disadvantage like that, they cultivate other things to make up for it—develop charm—and vivacity—and—*charm!* That's all you have to do! (*She turns again to the photograph.*) One thing your father had *plenty of*—was *charm!*

(TOM *motions to the fiddle in the wings.*)

THE SCENE FADES OUT WITH MUSIC

SCENE III

LEGEND ON SCREEN: "AFTER THE FIASCO—"
TOM *speaks from the fire-escape landing.*

TOM. After the fiasco at Rubicam's Business College, the idea of getting a gentleman caller for Laura began to play a more and more important part in Mother's calculations.

It became an obsession. Like some archetype of the universal unconscious, the image of the gentleman caller haunted our small apartment. . . .

(IMAGE: YOUNG MAN AT DOOR WITH FLOWERS.)

An evening at home rarely passed without some allusion to this image, this sceptre, this hope. . . .

Even when he wasn't mentioned, his presence hung in Mother's preoccupied look and in my sister's frightened, apologetic manner—hung like a sentence passed upon the Wingfields!

Mother was a woman of action as well as words.

She began to take logical steps in the planned direction.

Late that winter and in the early spring—realizing that extra money would be needed to properly feather the nest and plume the bird—she conducted a vigorous campaign on the telephone, roping in subscribers to one of those magazines for matrons called *The Home-maker's Companion,* the type of journal that features the serialized sublimations of ladies of letters who think in terms of delicate cup-like breasts, slim, tapering waists, rich, creamy thighs, eyes like wood-smoke in autumn, fingers that soothe and caress like strains of music, bodies as powerful as Etruscan sculpture.

(SCREEN IMAGE: GLAMOR MAGAZINE COVER.)

(AMANDA *enters with phone on long extension cord. She is spotted in the dim stage.*)

AMANDA. Ida Scott? This is Amanda Wingfield!

We *missed* you at the D.A.R. last Monday! I said to myself: She's probably suffering with that sinus condition! How is that sinus condition?

Horrors! Heaven have mercy!—You're a Christian martyr, yes, that's what you are, a Christian martyr!

Well, I just now happened to notice that your subscription to the *Companion's* about to expire! Yes, it expires with the next issue, honey!—just when that wonderful new serial by Bessie Mae Hopper is getting off to such an exciting start. Oh, honey, it's something that you can't miss! You remember how *Gone With the Wind* took everybody by storm? You simply couldn't go out if you hadn't read it. All everybody *talked* was Scarlett O'Hara. Well, this is a book that critics already compare to *Gone With the Wind.* It's the *Gone With the Wind* of the post-World War generation!—What?—Burning?—Oh, honey, don't let them burn, go take a look in the oven and I'll hold the wire! Heavens—I think she's hung up!

DIM OUT

(LEGEND ON SCREEN: "YOU THINK I'M IN LOVE WITH CONTINENTAL SHOEMAKERS?")

(*Before the stage is lighted, the violent voices of* TOM *and* AMANDA *are heard.*)

(*They are quarrelling behind the portieres. In front of them stands* LAURA *with clenched hands and panicky expression*)

(A clear pool of light on her figure throughout this scene.)

TOM. What in Christ's name am I—

AMANDA *(shrilly)*. Don't you use that—

TOM. Supposed to do!

AMANDA. Expression! Not in my—

TOM. Ohhh!

AMANDA. Presence! Have you gone out of your senses?

TOM. I have, that's true, *driven* out!

AMANDA. What is the matter with you, you —big—big—IDIOT!

TOM. Look!—I've got *no thing,* no single thing—

AMANDA. Lower your voice!

TOM. In my life here that I can call my OWN! Everything is—

AMANDA. Stop that shouting!

TOM. Yesterday you confiscated my books! You had the nerve to—

AMANDA. I took that horrible novel back to the library—yes! That hideous book by that insane Mr. Lawrence. *(TOM laughs wildly.)* I cannot control the output of diseased minds or people who cater to them— *(TOM laughs still more wildly.)* BUT I WON'T ALLOW SUCH FILTH BROUGHT INTO MY HOUSE! No, no, no, no, no!

TOM. House, house! Who pays rent on it, who makes a slave of himself to—

AMANDA *(fairly screeching)*. Don't you DARE to—

TOM. No, no, *I* mustn't say things! *I've* got to just—

AMANDA. Let me tell you—

TOM. I don't want to hear any more! *(He tears the portieres open. The upstage area is lit with a turgid smoky red glow.)*

(AMANDA's hair is in metal curlers and she wears a very old bathrobe, much too large for her slight figure, a relic of the faithless Mr. Wingfield.)

(An upright typewriter and a wild disarray of manuscripts is on the drop-leaf table. The quarrel was probably precipitated by AMANDA's interruption of his creative labor.

A chair is lying overthrown on the floor.)

(Their gesticulating shadows are cast on the ceiling by the fiery glow.)

AMANDA. You *will* hear more, you—

TOM. No, I won't hear more, I'm going out!

AMANDA. You come right back in—

TOM. Out, out, out! Because I'm—

AMANDA. Come back here, Tom Wingfield! I'm not through talking to you!

TOM. Oh, go—

LAURA *(desperately)*. —Tom!

AMANDA. You're going to listen, and no more insolence from you! I'm at the end of my patience!

(He comes back toward her.)

TOM. What do you think I'm at? Aren't I supposed to have any patience to reach the end of, Mother? I know, I know. It seems unimportant to you, what I'm *doing*— what I *want* to do—having a little *difference* between them! You don't think that—

AMANDA. I think you've been doing things that you're ashamed of. That's why you act like this. I don't believe that you go every night to the movies. Nobody goes to the movies night after night. Nobody in their right minds goes to the movies as often as you pretend to. People don't go to the movies at nearly midnight, and movies don't let out at two A.M. Come in stumbling. Muttering to yourself like a maniac! You get three hours' sleep and then go to work. Oh, I can picture the way you're doing down there. Moping, doping, because you're in no condition.

TOM *(wildly)*. No, I'm in no condition!

AMANDA. What right have you got to jeopardize your job? Jeopardize the security of us all? How do you think we'd manage if you were—

TOM. Listen! You think I'm crazy *about* the *warehouse?* *(He bends fiercely toward her slight figure.)* You think I'm in love with the Continental Shoemakers? You think I want to spend fifty-five *years* down there in that—*celotex interior!* with— *fluorescent—tubes!* Look! I'd rather somebody picked up a crowbar and battered out my brains—than go back mornings! I *go!*

Every time you come in yelling that God damn *"Rise and Shine!" "Rise and Shine!"* I say to myself, "How *lucky dead* people are!" But I get up. I *go!* For sixty-five dollars a month I give up all that I dream of doing and being *ever!* And you say self—*self's* all I ever think of. Why, listen, if self is what I thought of, Mother, I'd be where he is—GONE! *(Pointing to father's picture.)* As far as the system of transportation reaches! *(He starts past her. She grabs his arm.)* Don't grab at me, Mother!

AMANDA. Where are you going?

TOM. I'm going to the *movies!*

AMANDA. I don't believe that lie!

TOM *(crouching toward her, overtowering her tiny figure. She backs away, gasping).* I'm going to opium dens! Yes, opium dens, dens of vice and criminals' hang-outs, Mother. I've joined the Hogan gang, I'm a hired assassin, I carry a tommy-gun in a violin case! I run a string of cat-houses in the Valley! They call me Killer, Killer Wingfield, I'm leading a double-life, a simple, honest warehouse worker by day, by night a dynamic *czar* of the *underworld, Mother.* I go to gambling casinos, I spin away fortunes on the roulette table! I wear a patch over one eye and a false mustache, sometimes I put on green whiskers. On those occasions they call me—*El Diablo!* Oh, I could tell you things to make you sleepless! My enemies plan to dynamite this place. They're going to blow us all sky-high some night! I'll be glad, very happy, and so will you! You'll go up,

up on a broomstick, over Blue Mountain with seventeen gentlemen callers! You ugly—babbling old—*witch.* . . . *(He goes through a series of violent, clumsy movements, seizing his overcoat, lunging to the door, pulling it fiercely open. The women watch him, aghast. His arm catches in the sleeve of the coat as he struggles to pull it on. For a moment he is pinioned by the bulky garment. With an outraged groan he tears the coat off again, splitting the shoulder of it, and hurls it across the room. It strikes against the shelf of* LAURA's *glass collection, there is a tinkle of shattering glass.* LAURA *cries out as if wounded.)*

*(*MUSIC. LEGEND: "THE GLASS MENAGERIE."*)*

LAURA *(shrilly).* My glass!—menagerie. . . . *(She covers her face and turns away.)*

(But AMANDA *is still stunned and stupefied by the "ugly witch" so that she barely notices this occurrence. Now she recovers her speech.)*

AMANDA *(in an awful voice).* I won't speak to you—until you apologize! *(She crosses through portieres and draws them together behind her.* TOM *is left with* LAURA. LAURA *clings weakly to the mantel with her face averted.* TOM *stares at her stupidly for a moment. Then he crosses to shelf. Drops awkwardly on his knees to collect the fallen glass, glancing at* LAURA *as if he would speak but couldn't.)*

("The Glass Menagerie" steals in as)

THE SCENE DIMS OUT

SCENE IV

The interior is dark. Faint light in the alley.
A deep-voiced bell in a church is tolling the hour of five as the scene commences.
TOM appears at the top of the alley. After each solemn boom of the bell in the tower, he shakes a little noise-maker or rattle as if to express the tiny spasm of man in contrast to the sustained power and dignity of the Almighty. This and the unsteadiness of his advance makes it evident that he has been drinking.
As he climbs the few steps to the fire-escape landing light steals up inside. LAURA *appears in night-dress, observing* TOM's *empty bed in the front room.*
TOM fishes in his pockets for door-key, removing a motley assortment of articles in the search, including a perfect shower of movie-ticket stubs and an empty bottle. At last he finds the key, but just as he is about to insert it, it slips from his fingers. He strikes a match and crouches below the door.

TOM *(bitterly).* One crack—and it falls through!

*(*LAURA *opens the door.)*

LAURA. Tom! Tom, what are you doing?

TOM. Looking for a door-key.

LAURA. Where have you been all this time?

TOM. I have been to the movies.

LAURA. All this time at the movies?

TOM. There was a very long program. There was a Garbo picture and a Mickey Mouse and a travelogue and a newsreel and a preview of coming attractions. And there was an organ solo and a collection for the milk-fund—simultaneously—which ended up in a terrible fight between a fat lady and an usher!

LAURA (innocently). Did you have to stay through everything?

TOM. Of course! And, oh, I forgot! There was a big stage show! The headliner on this stage show was Malvolio the Magician. He performed wonderful tricks, many of them, such as pouring water back and forth between pitchers. First it turned to wine and then it turned to beer and then it turned to whiskey. I know it was whiskey it finally turned into because he needed somebody to come up out of the audience to help him, and I came up— both shows! It was Kentucky Straight Bourbon. A very generous fellow, he gave souvenirs. (He pulls from his back pocket a shimmering rainbow-colored scarf.) He gave me this. This is his magic scarf. You can have it, Laura. You wave it over a canary cage and you get a bowl of gold-fish. You wave it over the gold-fish bowl and they fly away canaries. . . . But the wonderfullest trick of all was the coffin trick. We nailed him into a coffin and he got out of the coffin without removing one nail. (He has come inside.) There is a trick that would come in handy for me—get me out of this 2 by 4 situation! (Flops onto bed and starts removing shoes.)

LAURA. Tom—Shhh!

TOM. What're you shushing me for?

LAURA. You'll wake up Mother.

TOM. Goody, goody! Pay 'er back for all those "Rise an' Shines." (Lies down, groaning.) You know it don't take much intelligence to get yourself into a nailed-up coffin, Laura. But who in hell ever got himself out of one without removing one nail?

(As if in answer, the father's grinning photograph lights up.)

SCENE DIMS OUT

(Immediately following: The church bell is heard striking six. At the sixth stroke the alarm clock goes off in AMANDA's room, and after a few moments we hear her calling: "Rise and Shine! Rise and Shine! Laura, go tell your brother to rise and shine!")

TOM (sitting up slowly). I'll rise—but I won't shine.

(The light increases.)

AMANDA. Laura, tell your brother his coffee is ready.

(LAURA slips into front room.)

LAURA. Tom!—It's nearly seven. Don't make Mother nervous. (He stares at her stupidly. Beseechingly.) Tom, speak to Mother this morning. Make up with her, apologize, speak to her!

TOM. She won't to me. It's her that started not speaking.

LAURA. If you just say you're sorry she'll start speaking.

TOM. Her not speaking—is that such a tragedy?

LAURA. Please—please!

AMANDA (calling from kitchenette). Laura, are you going to do what I asked you to do, or do I have to get dressed and go out myself?

LAURA. Going, going—soon as I get on my coat! (She pulls on a shapeless felt hat with nervous, jerky movement, pleadingly glancing at TOM. Rushes awkwardly for coat. The coat is one of AMANDA's, inaccurately made-over, the sleeves too short for LAURA.) Butter and what else?

AMANDA (entering upstage). Just butter. Tell them to charge it.

LAURA. Mother, they make such faces when I do that.

AMANDA. Sticks and stones can break our bones, but the expression on Mr. Garfinkel's face won't harm us! Tell your brother his coffee is getting cold.

LAURA (at door). Do what I asked you, will you, will you, Tom?

(He looks sullenly away.)

AMANDA. Laura, go now or just don't go at all!!

LAURA (*rushing out*). Going—going! (*A second later she cries out.* TOM *springs up and crosses to door.* AMANDA *rushes anxiously in.* TOM *opens the door.*)

TOM. Laura?

LAURA. I'm all right. I slipped, but I'm all right.

AMANDA (*peering anxiously after her*). If anyone breaks a leg on those fire-escape steps, the landlord ought to be sued for every cent he possesses! (*She shuts door. Remembers she isn't speaking and returns to other room.*)

(*As* TOM *enters listlessly for his coffee, she turns her back to him and stands rigidly facing the window on the gloomy gray vault of the areaway. Its light on her face with its aged but childish features is cruelly sharp, satirical as a Daumier print.*)

(MUSIC UNDER: "AVE MARIA.")

(TOM *glances sheepishly but sullenly at her averted figure and slumps at the table. The coffee is scalding hot; he sips it and gasps and spits it back in the cup. At his gasp,* AMANDA *catches her breath and half turns. Then catches herself and turns back to window.*)

(TOM *blows on his coffee, glancing sidewise at his mother. She clears her throat.* TOM *clears his. He starts to rise. Sinks back down again, scratches his head, clears his throat again.* AMANDA *coughs.* TOM *raises his cup in both hands to blow on it, his eyes staring over the rim of it at his mother for several moments. Then he slowly sets the cup down and awkwardly and hesitantly rises from the chair.*)

TOM (*hoarsely*). Mother. I—I apologize, Mother. (AMANDA *draws a quick, shuddering breath. Her face works grotesquely. She breaks into childlike tears.*) I'm sorry for what I said, for everything that I said, I didn't mean it.

AMANDA (*sobbingly*). My devotion has made me a witch and so I make myself hateful to my children!

TOM. *No,* you *don't.*

AMANDA. I worry so much, don't sleep, it makes me nervous!

TOM (*gently*). I understand that.

AMANDA. I've had to put up a solitary battle all these years. But you're my right-hand bower! Don't fall down, don't fail!

TOM (*gently*). I try, Mother.

AMANDA (*with great enthusiasm*). Try and you will SUCCEED! (*The notion makes her breathless.*) Why, you—you're just *full* of natural endowments! Both of my children —they're *unusual* children! Don't you think I know it? I'm so—*proud!* Happy and—feel I've—so much to be thankful for but— Promise me one thing, Son!

TOM. What, Mother?

AMANDA. Promise, Son, you'll never be a drunkard!

TOM (*turns to her grinning*). I will never be a drunkard, Mother.

AMANDA. That's what frightened me so, that you'd be drinking! Eat a bowl of Purina!

TOM. Just coffee, Mother.

AMANDA. Shredded wheat biscuit?

TOM. No. No, Mother, just coffee.

AMANDA. You can't put in a day's work on an empty stomach. You've got ten minutes—don't gulp! Drinking too-hot liquids makes cancer of the stomach. . . . Put cream in.

TOM. No, thank you.

AMANDA. To cool it.

TOM. No! No, thank you, I want it black.

AMANDA. I know, but it's not good for you. We have to do all that we can to build ourselves up. In these trying times we live in, all that we have to cling to is—each other . . . . That's why it's so important to— Tom, I— I sent out your sister so I could discuss something with you. If you hadn't spoken I would have spoken to you. (*Sits down.*)

TOM (*gently*). What is it, Mother, that you want to discuss?

AMANDA. *Laura!*

(TOM *puts his cup down slowly.*)

(LEGEND ON SCREEN: "LAURA.")

(MUSIC: "THE GLASS MENAGERIE.")

TOM. —Oh.—Laura . . .

AMANDA (*touching his sleeve*). You know how Laura is. So quiet but—still water runs deep! She notices things and I think she—broods about them. (TOM *looks up.*) A few days ago I came in and she was crying.

TOM. What about?

AMANDA. You.

TOM. Me?

AMANDA. She has an idea that you're not happy here.

TOM. What gave her that idea?

AMANDA. What gives her any idea? However, you do act strangely. I—I'm not criticizing, understand *that!* I know your ambitions do not lie in the warehouse, that like everybody in the whole wide world—you've had to—make sacrifices, but—Tom—Tom—life's not easy, it calls for Spartan endurance! There's so many things in my heart that I cannot describe to you! I've never told you but I—*loved* your father. . . .

TOM (*gently*). I know that, Mother.

AMANDA. And you—when I see you taking after his ways! Staying out late—and—well, you *had* been drinking the night you were in that—terrifying condition! Laura says that you hate the apartment and that you go out nights to get away from it! Is that true, Tom?

TOM. No. You say there's so much in your heart that you can't describe to me. That's true of me, too. There's so much in my heart that I can't describe to *you!* So let's respect each other's—

AMANDA. But, why—*why,* Tom—are you always so *restless?* Where do you *go* to, nights?

TOM. I—go to the movies.

AMANDA. Why do you go to the movies so much, Tom?

TOM. I go to the movies because—I like adventure. Adventure is something I don't have much of at work, so I go to the movies.

AMANDA. But, Tom, you go to the movies *entirely* too *much!*

TOM. I like a lot of adventure.

(AMANDA *looks baffled, then hurt. As the familiar inquisition resumes he becomes hard and impatient again.* AMANDA *slips back into her querulous attitude toward him.*)

(IMAGE ON SCREEN: SAILING VESSEL WITH JOLLY ROGER.)

AMANDA. Most young men find adventure in their careers.

TOM. Then most young men are not employed in a warehouse.

AMANDA. The world is full of young men employed in warehouses and offices and factories.

TOM. Do all of them find adventure in their careers?

AMANDA. They do or they do without it! Not everybody has a craze for adventure.

TOM. Man is by instinct a lover, a hunter, a fighter, and none of those instincts are given much play at the warehouse!

AMANDA. Man is by instinct! Don't quote instinct to me! Instinct is something that people have got away from! It belongs to animals! Christian adults don't want it!

TOM. What do Christian adults want, then, Mother?

AMANDA. Superior things! Things of the mind and the spirit! Only animals have to satisfy instincts! Surely your aims are somewhat higher than theirs! Than monkeys—pigs—

TOM. I reckon they're not.

AMANDA. You're joking. However, that isn't what I wanted to discuss.

TOM (*rising*). I haven't much time.

AMANDA (*pushing his shoulders*). Sit down.

TOM. You want me to punch in red at the warehouse, Mother?

AMANDA. You have five minutes. I want to talk about Laura.

(LEGEND: "PLANS AND PROVISIONS.")

TOM. All right! What about Laura?

AMANDA. We have to be making some plans and provisions for her. She's older than you, two years, and nothing has happened. She just drifts along doing nothing. It frightens me terribly how she just drifts along.

TOM. I guess she's the type that people call home girls.

AMANDA. There's no such type, and if there is, it's a pity! That is unless the home is hers, with a husband!

TOM. What?

AMANDA. Oh, I can see the handwriting on the wall as plain as I see the nose in front of my face! It's terrifying!

More and more you remind me of your father! He was out all hours without explanation!—Then *left! Good-bye!*

And me with the bag to hold. I saw that letter you got from the Merchant Marine. I know what you're dreaming of. I'm not standing here blindfolded.

Very well, then. Then *do* it!

But not till there's somebody to take your place.

TOM. What do you mean?

AMANDA. I mean that as soon as Laura has got somebody to take care of her, married, a home of her own, independent—why, then you'll be free to go wherever you please, on land, on sea, whichever way the wind blows you!

But until that time you've got to look out for your sister. I don't say me because I'm old and don't matter! I say for your sister because she's young and dependent.

I put her in business college—a dismal failure! Frightened her so it made her sick at the stomach.

I took her over to the Young People's League at the church. Another fiasco. She spoke to nobody, nobody spoke to her. Now all she does is fool with those pieces of glass and play those worn-out records. What kind of a life is that for a girl to lead?

TOM. What can I do about it?

AMANDA. Overcome selfishness! Self, self, self is all that you ever think of!

(TOM *springs up and crosses to get his coat. It is ugly and bulky. He pulls on a cap with earmuffs.*)

Where is your muffler? Put your wool muffler on!

(*He snatches it angrily from the closet and tosses it around his neck and pulls both ends tight.*)

Tom! I haven't said what I had in mind to ask you.

TOM. I'm too late to—

AMANDA (*catching his arm—very importunately. Then shyly*). Down at the warehouse, aren't there some—nice young men?

TOM. No!

AMANDA. There *must* be—*some* . . . .

TOM. Mother—

(*Gesture.*)

AMANDA. Find out one that's clean-living—doesn't drink and—ask him out for sister!

TOM. What?

AMANDA. For *sister! To meet! Get acquainted!*

TOM (*stamping to door*). Oh, my go-osh!

AMANDA. Will you? (*He opens door. Imploringly.*) Will you? (*He starts down.*) Will you? *Will* you, dear?

TOM (*calling back*). YES!

(AMANDA *closes the door hesitantly and with a troubled but faintly hopeful expression.*)

(SCREEN IMAGE: GLAMOR MAGAZINE COVER.)

(*Spot* AMANDA *at phone.*)

AMANDA. Ella Cartwright? This is Amanda Wingfield!

How are you, honey?

How is that kidney condition?

(*Count five.*)

Horrors!

(*Count five.*)

You're a Christian martyr, yes, honey, that's what you are, a Christian martyr! Well, I just now happened to notice in my little red book that your subscription to the *Companion* has just run out! I knew that you wouldn't want to miss out on the wonderful serial starting in this new issue. It's by Bessie Mae Hopper, the first thing she's written since *Honeymoon for Three.*

Wasn't that a strange and interesting story? Well, this one is even lovelier, I believe. It has a sophisticated, society background. It's all about the horsey set on Long Island!

FADE OUT

SCENE V

LEGEND ON SCREEN: "ANNUNCIATION." *Fade with music.*

It is early dusk of a spring evening. Supper has just been finished in the Wingfield apartment. AMANDA *and* LAURA *in light-colored dresses are removing dishes from the table, in the upstage area, which is shadowy, their movements formalized almost as a dance or ritual, their moving forms as pale and silent as moths.*

TOM, *in white shirt and trousers, rises from the table and crosses toward the fire-escape.*

AMANDA *(as he passes her).* Son, will you do me a favor?

TOM. What?

AMANDA. Comb your hair! You look so pretty when your hair is combed! *(TOM slouches on sofa with evening paper. Enormous caption "Franco Triumphs.")* There is only one respect in which I would like you to emulate your father.

TOM. What respect is that?

AMANDA. The care he always took of his appearance. He never allowed himself to look untidy. *(He throws down the paper and crosses to fire-escape.)* Where are you going?

TOM. I'm going out to smoke.

AMANDA. You smoke too much. A pack a day at fifteen cents a pack. How much would that amount to in a month? Thirty times fifteen is how much, Tom? Figure it out and you will be astounded at what you could save. Enough to give you a night-school course in accounting at Washington U! Just think what a wonderful thing that would be for you, Son!

(TOM is unmoved by the thought.)

TOM. I'd rather smoke. *(He steps out on landing, letting the screen door slam.)*

AMANDA *(sharply).* I know! That's the tragedy of it. . . . *(Alone, she turns to look at her husband's picture.)*

(DANCE MUSIC: "ALL THE WORLD IS WAITING FOR THE SUNSHINE!")

TOM *(to the audience).* Across the alley from us was the Paradise Dance Hall. On evenings in spring the windows and doors were open and the music came outdoors. Sometimes the lights were turned out except for a large glass sphere that hung from the ceiling. It would turn slowly about and filter the dusk with delicate rainbow colors. Then the orchestra played a waltz or a tango, something that had a slow and sensuous rhythm. Couples would come outside, to the relative privacy of the alley. You could see them kissing behind ash-pits and telephone poles.

This was the compensation for lives that passed like mine, without any change or adventure.

Adventure and change were imminent in this year. They were waiting around the corner for all these kids.

Suspended in the mist over Berchtesgaden, caught in the folds of Chamberlain's umbrella—

In Spain there was Guernica!

But here there was only hot swing music and liquor, dance halls, bars, and movies, and sex that hung in the gloom like a chandelier and flooded the world with brief, deceptive rainbows. . . .

All the world was waiting for bombardments!

(AMANDA turns from the picture and comes outside.)

AMANDA *(sighing).* A fire-escape landing's a poor excuse for a porch. *(She spreads a newspaper on a step and sits down, gracefully and demurely as if she were settling into a swing on a Mississippi veranda.)* What are you looking at?

TOM. The moon.

AMANDA. Is there a moon this evening?

TOM. It's rising over Garfinkel's Delicatessen.

AMANDA. So it is! A little silver slipper of a moon. Have you made a wish on it yet?

TOM. Um-hum.

AMANDA. What did you wish for?

TOM. That's a secret.

AMANDA. A secret, huh? Well, I won't tell mine either. I will be just as mysterious as you.

TOM. I bet I can guess what yours is.

AMANDA. Is my head so transparent?

TOM. You're not a sphinx.

AMANDA. No, I don't have secrets. I'll tell you what I wished for on the moon. Success and happiness for my precious children! I wish for that whenever there's a moon, and when there isn't a moon, I wish it, too.

TOM. I thought perhaps you wished for a gentleman caller.

AMANDA. Why do you say that?

TOM. Don't you remember asking me to fetch one?

AMANDA. I remember suggesting that it would be nice for your sister if you brought home some nice young man from the warehouse. I think that I've made that suggestion more than once.

TOM. Yes, you have made it repeatedly.

AMANDA. Well?

TOM. We are going to have one.

AMANDA. *What?*

TOM. A gentleman caller!

(THE ANNUNCIATION IS CELEBRATED WITH MUSIC.)

(AMANDA *rises.*)

(IMAGE ON SCREEN: CALLER WITH BOUQUET.)

AMANDA. You mean you have asked some nice young man to come over?

TOM. Yep. I've asked him to dinner.

AMANDA. You really did?

TOM. I did!

AMANDA. You did, and did he—*accept?*

TOM. He did!

AMANDA. Well, well—well, well! That's —lovely!

TOM. I thought that you would be pleased.

AMANDA. It's definite, then?

TOM. Very definite.

AMANDA. Soon?

TOM. Very soon.

AMANDA. For heaven's sake, stop putting on and tell me some things, will you?

TOM. What things do you want me to tell you?

AMANDA. *Naturally* I would like to know when he's *coming!*

TOM. He's coming tomorrow.

AMANDA. *Tomorrow?*

TOM. Yep. Tomorrow.

AMANDA. But, Tom!

TOM. Yes, Mother?

AMANDA. Tomorrow gives me no time!

TOM. Time for what?

AMANDA. Preparations! Why didn't you phone me at once, as soon as you asked him, the minute that he accepted? Then, don't you see, I could have been getting ready!

TOM. You don't have to make any fuss.

AMANDA. Oh, Tom, Tom, Tom, of course I have to make a fuss! I want things nice, not sloppy! Not thrown together. I'll certainly have to do some fast thinking, won't I?

TOM. I don't see why you have to think at all.

AMANDA. You just don't know. We can't have a gentleman caller in a pig-sty! All my wedding silver has to be polished, the monogrammed table linen ought to be laundered! The windows have to be washed and fresh curtains put up. And how about clothes? We have to *wear* something, don't we?

TOM. Mother, this boy is no one to make a fuss over!

AMANDA. Do you realize he's the first young man we've introduced to your sister? It's terrible, dreadful, disgraceful that poor little sister has never received a single gentleman caller! Tom, come inside! (*She opens the screen door.*)

TOM. What for?

AMANDA. I want to ask you some things.

TOM. If you're going to make such a fuss, I'll call it off, I'll tell him not to come!

AMANDA. You certainly won't do anything of the kind. Nothing offends people worse than broken engagements. It simply means I'll have to work like a Turk! We won't be brilliant, but we will pass inspection. Come on inside. (TOM *follows, groaning.*) Sit down.

TOM. Any particular place you would like me to sit?

AMANDA. Thank heavens I've got that new sofa! I'm also making payments on a floor lamp I'll have sent out! And put the chintz covers on, they'll brighten things up! Of course I'd hoped to have these walls repapered. . . . What is the young man's name?

TOM. His name is O'Connor.

AMANDA. That, of course, means fish—tomorrow is Friday! I'll have that salmon loaf—with Durkee's dressing! What does he do? He works at the warehouse?

TOM. Of course! How else would I—

AMANDA. Tom, he—doesn't drink?

TOM. Why do you ask me that?

AMANDA. Your father *did*!

TOM. Don't get started on that!

AMANDA. He *does* drink, then?

TOM. Not that I know of!

AMANDA. Make sure, be certain! The last thing I want for my daughter's a boy who drinks!

TOM. Aren't you being a little bit premature? Mr. O'Connor has not yet appeared or the scene!

AMANDA. But will tomorrow. To meet your sister, and what do I know about his character? Nothing! Old maids are better off than wives of drunkards!

TOM. Oh, my God!

AMANDA. Be still!

TOM (*leaning forward to whisper*). Lots of fellows meet girls whom they don't marry!

AMANDA. Oh, talk sensibly, Tom—and don't be sarcastic! (*She has gotten a hairbrush.*)

TOM. What are you doing?

AMANDA. I'm brushing that cow-lick down! What is this young man's position at the warehouse?

TOM (*submitting grimly to the brush and the interrogation*). This young man's position is that of a shipping clerk, Mother.

AMANDA. Sounds to me like a fairly responsible job, the sort of a job *you* would be in if you just had more *get-up*. What is his salary? Have you any idea?

TOM. I would judge it to be approximately eighty-five dollars a month.

AMANDA. Well—not princely, but—

TOM. Twenty more than I make.

AMANDA. Yes, how well I know! But for a family man, eighty-five dollars a month is not much more than you can just get by on. . . .

TOM. Yes, but Mr. O'Connor is not a family man.

AMANDA. He might be, mightn't he? Some time in the future?

TOM. I see. Plans and provisions.

AMANDA. You are the only young man that I know of who ignores the fact that the future becomes the present, the present the past and the past turns into everlasting regret if you don't plan for it!

TOM. I will think that over and see what I can make of it.

AMANDA. Don't be supercilious with your Mother! Tell me some more about this—what do you call him?

TOM. James D. O'Connor. The D. is for Delaney.

AMANDA. Irish on *both* sides! *Gracious!* And doesn't drink?

TOM. Shall I call him up and ask him right this minute?

AMANDA. The only way to find out about those things is to make discreet inquiries at the proper moment. When I was a girl in Blue Mountain and it was suspected that a young man drank, the girl whose attentions he had been receiving, if any girl *was,* would sometimes speak to the minister of his church, or rather her father would if her father was living, and sort of feel out on the young man's character. That is the way such things are discreetly handled to keep a young woman from making a tragic mistake!

TOM. Then how did you happen to make a tragic mistake?

AMANDA. That innocent look of your father's had everyone fooled!

He *smiled*—the world was *enchanted!*

No girl can do worse than put herself at the mercy of a handsome appearance!

I hope that Mr. O'Connor is not too good-looking.

TOM. No, he's not too good-looking. He's covered with freckles and hasn't too much of a nose.

AMANDA. He's not right-down homely, though?

TOM. Not right-down homely. Just medium homely, I'd say.

AMANDA. Character's what to look for in a man.

TOM. That's what I've always said, Mother.

AMANDA. You never said anything of the kind and I suspect you would never give it a thought.

TOM. Don't be so suspicious of me.

AMANDA. At least I hope he's the type that's up and coming.

TOM. I think he really goes in for self-improvement.

AMANDA. What reason have you to think so?

TOM. He goes to night school.

AMANDA *(beaming).* Splendid! What does he do, I mean study?

TOM. Radio engineering and public speaking!

AMANDA. Then he has visions of being advanced in the world!

Any young man who studies public speaking is aiming to have an executive job some day!

And radio engineering? A thing for the future!

Both of these facts are very illuminating. Those are the sort of things that a mother should know concerning any young man who comes to call on her daughter. Seriously or—not.

TOM. One little warning. He doesn't know about Laura. I didn't let on that we had dark ulterior motives. I just said, why don't you come and have dinner with us? He said okay and that was the whole conversation.

AMANDA. I bet it was! You're eloquent as an oyster.

However, he'll know about Laura when he gets here. When he sees how lovely and sweet and pretty she is, he'll thank his lucky stars he was asked to dinner.

TOM. Mother, you mustn't expect too much of Laura.

AMANDA. What do you mean?

TOM. Laura seems all those things to you and me because she's ours and we love her. We don't even notice she's crippled any more.

AMANDA. Don't say crippled! You know that I never allow that word to be used!

TOM. But face facts, Mother. She is and—that's not all—

AMANDA. What do you mean "not all"?

TOM. Laura is very different from other girls.

AMANDA. I think the difference is all to her advantage.

TOM. Not quite all—in the eyes of others—strangers—she's terribly shy and lives in a world of her own and those things make her seem a little peculiar to people outside the house.

AMANDA. Don't say peculiar.

TOM. Face the facts. She is.

(THE DANCE-HALL MUSIC CHANGES TO A TANGO THAT HAS A MINOR AND SOMEWHAT OMINOUS TONE.)

AMANDA. In what way is she peculiar—may I ask?

TOM (*gently*). She lives in a world of her own—a world of—little glass ornaments, Mother. . . . (*Gets up.* AMANDA *remains holding brush, looking at him, troubled.*) She plays old phonograph records and—that's about all— (*He glances at himself in the mirror and crosses to door.*)

AMANDA (*sharply*). Where are you going?

TOM. I'm going to the movies. (*Out screen door.*)

AMANDA. Not to the movies, every night to the movies! (*Follows quickly to screen door.*) I don't believe you always go to the movies! (*He is gone.* AMANDA *looks worriedly after him for a moment. Then vitality and optimism return and she turns from the door. Crossing to portieres.*) Laura! Laura! (*LAURA answers from kitchenette.*)

LAURA. Yes, Mother.

AMANDA. Let those dishes go and come in front! (*LAURA appears with dish towel. Gaily.*) Laura, come here and make a wish on the moon!

(SCREEN IMAGE: MOON.)

LAURA (*entering*). Moon—moon?

AMANDA. A little silver slipper of a moon. Look over your left shoulder, Laura, and make a wish!

(*LAURA looks faintly puzzled as if called out of sleep.* AMANDA *seizes her shoulders and turns her at an angle by the door.*)

Now!

Now, darling, *wish!*

LAURA. What shall I wish for, Mother?

AMANDA (*her voice trembling and her eyes suddenly filling with tears*). Happiness! Good fortune!

(*The violin rises and the stage dims out.*)

CURTAIN

SCENE VI

IMAGE: HIGH SCHOOL HERO.

TOM. And so the following evening I brought Jim home to dinner. I had known Jim slightly in high school. In high school Jim was a hero. He had tremendous Irish good nature and vitality with the scrubbed and polished look of white chinaware. He seemed to move in a continual spotlight. He was a star in basketball, captain of the debating club, president of the senior class and the glee club and he sang the male lead in the annual light operas. He was always running or bounding, never just walking. He seemed always at the point of defeating the law of gravity. He was shooting with such velocity through his adolescence that you would logically expect him to arrive at nothing short of the White House by the time he was thirty. But Jim apparently ran into more interference after his graduation from Soldan. His speed had definitely slowed. Six years after he left high school he was holding a job that wasn't much better than mine.

(IMAGE: CLERK.)

He was the only one at the warehouse with whom I was on friendly terms. I was valuable to him as someone who could remember his former glory, who had seen him win basketball games and the silver cup in debating. He knew of my secret practice of retiring to a cabinet of the wash-room to work on poems when business was slack in the warehouse. He called me Shakespeare. And while the other boys in the warehouse regarded me with suspicious hostility, Jim took a humorous attitude toward me. Gradually his attitude affected the others, their hostility wore off and they also began to smile at me as people smile at an oddly fashioned dog who trots across their path at some distance.

I knew that Jim and Laura had known each other at Soldan, and I had heard Laura speak admiringly of his voice. I didn't know if Jim remembered her or not. In high school Laura had been as unobtrusive as Jim had been astonishing. If he did remember Laura, it was not as my sister, for when I asked him to dinner, he grinned and said, "You know, Shakespeare, I never thought of you as having folks!"

He was about to discover that I did. . . .

(LIGHT *up* STAGE.)

(LEGEND ON SCREEN: "THE ACCENT OF A COMING FOOT.")

(*Friday evening. It is about five o'clock of a late spring evening which comes "scattering poems in the sky.")

(*A delicate lemony light is in the Wingfield apartment.*)

(AMANDA *has worked like a Turk in preparation for the gentleman caller. The results are astonishing. The new floor lamp with its rose-silk shade is in place, a colored paper lantern conceals the broken light fixture in the ceiling, new billowing white curtains are at the windows, chintz covers are on chairs and sofa, a pair of new sofa pillows make their initial appearance.*)

(*Open boxes and tissue paper are scattered on the floor.*)

(LAURA *stands in the middle with lifted arms while* AMANDA *crouches before her, adjusting the hem of the new dress, devout and ritualistic. The dress is colored and designed by memory. The arrangement of* LAURA'S *hair is changed; it is softer and more becoming. A fragile, unearthly prettiness has come out in* LAURA: *she is like a piece of translucent glass touched by light, given a momentary radiance, not actual, not lasting.*)

AMANDA (*impatiently*). Why are you trembling?

LAURA. Mother, you've made me so nervous!

AMANDA. How have I made you nervous?

LAURA. By all this fuss! You make it seem so important!

AMANDA. I don't understand you, Laura. You couldn't be satisfied with just sitting home, and yet whenever I try to arrange something for you, you seem to resist it. (*She gets up.*)

Now take a look at yourself.

No, wait! Wait just a moment—I have an idea!

LAURA. What is it now?

(AMANDA *produces two powder puffs which she wraps in handkerchiefs and stuffs in* LAURA'S *bosom.*)

LAURA. Mother, what are you doing?

AMANDA. They call them "Gay Deceivers"!

LAURA. I won't wear them!

AMANDA. You will!

LAURA. Why should I?

AMANDA. Because, to be painfully honest, your chest is flat.

LAURA. You make it seem like we were setting a trap.

AMANDA. All pretty girls are a trap, a pretty trap, and men expect them to be.

(LEGEND: "A PRETTY TRAP.")

Now look at yourself, young lady. This is the prettiest you will ever be!

I've got to fix myself now! You're going to be surprised by your mother's appearance! (*She crosses through portieres, humming gaily.*)

(LAURA *moves slowly to the long mirror and stares solemnly at herself.*)

(*A wind blows the white curtains inward in a slow, graceful motion and with a faint, sorrowful sighing.*)

AMANDA (*off stage*). It isn't dark enough yet. (*She turns slowly before the mirror with a troubled look.*)

(LEGEND ON SCREEN: "THIS IS MY SISTER: CELEBRATE HER WITH STRINGS!" MUSIC.)

AMANDA (*laughing, off*). I'm going to show you something. I'm going to make a spectacular appearance!

LAURA. What is it, Mother?

AMANDA. Possess your soul in patience—you will see!

Something I've resurrected from that old trunk! Styles haven't changed so terribly much after all. . . .

(*She parts the portieres.*)

Now just look at your mother!

(*She wears a girlish frock of yellowed voile with a blue silk sash. She carries a bunch of jonquils—the legend of her youth is nearly revived. Feverishly.)*

This is the dress in which I led the cotillion. Won the cakewalk twice at Sunset Hill, wore one spring to the Governor's ball in Jackson!

See how I sashayed around the ballroom, Laura?

(She raises her skirt and does a mincing step around the room.)

I wore it on Sundays for my gentlemen callers! I had it on the day I met your father—

I had malaria fever all that spring. The change of climate from East Tennessee to the Delta—weakened resistance—I had a little temperature all the time—not enough to be serious—just enough to make me restless and giddy!—Invitations poured in —parties all over the Delta!—"Stay in bed," said Mother, "you have fever!"—but I just wouldn't.—I took quinine but kept on going, going!—Evenings, dances!— Afternoons, long, long rides! Picnics— lovely!—So lovely, that country in May.— All lacy with dogwood, literally flooded with jonquils!—That was the spring I had the craze for jonquils. Jonquils became an absolute obsession. Mother said, "Honey, there's no more room for jonquils." And still I kept on bringing in more jonquils. Whenever, wherever I saw them, I'd say, "Stop! Stop! I see jonquils!" I made the young men help me gather the jonquils! It was a joke, Amanda and her jonquils! Finally there were no more vases to hold them, every available space was filled with jonquils. No vases to hold them? All right, I'll hold them myself! And then I— *(She stops in front of the picture. MUSIC.)* met your father!

Malaria fever and jonquils and then—this —boy. . . .

(She switches on the rose-colored lamp.)

I hope they get here before it starts to rain.

(She crosses upstage and places the jonquils in bowl on table.)

I gave your brother a little extra change so he and Mr. O'Connor could take the service car home.

LAURA *(with altered look).* What did you say his name was?

AMANDA. O'Connor.

LAURA. What is his first name?

AMANDA. I don't remember. Oh, yes, I do. It was—Jim!

(LAURA sways slightly and catches hold of a chair.)

(LEGEND ON SCREEN: "NOT JIM!")

LAURA *(faintly).* Not—Jim!

AMANDA. Yes, that was it, it was Jim! I've never known a Jim that wasn't nice!

(MUSIC: OMINOUS.)

LAURA. Are you sure his name is Jim O'Connor?

AMANDA. Yes. Why?

LAURA. Is he the one that Tom used to know in high school?

AMANDA. He didn't say so. I think he just got to know him at the warehouse.

LAURA. There was a Jim O'Connor we both knew in high school— *(Then, with effort.)* If that is the one that Tom is bringing to dinner—you'll have to excuse me, I won't come to the table.

AMANDA. What sort of nonsense is this?

LAURA. You asked me once if I'd ever liked a boy. Don't you remember I showed you this boy's picture?

AMANDA. You mean the boy you showed me in the year book?

LAURA. Yes, that boy.

AMANDA. Laura, Laura, were you in love with that boy?

LAURA. I don't know, Mother. All I know is I couldn't sit at the table if it was him!

AMANDA. It won't be him! It isn't the least bit likely. But whether it is or not, you will come to the table. You will not be excused.

LAURA. I'll have to be, Mother.

AMANDA. I don't intend to humor your silliness, Laura. I've had too much from you and your brother, both!

So just sit down and compose yourself till they come. Tom has forgotten his key so you'll have to let them in, when they arrive.

LAURA *(panicky)*. Oh, Mother, *you* answer the door!

AMANDA *(lightly)*. I'll be in the kitchen—busy!

LAURA. Oh, Mother, please answer the door, don't make me do it!

AMANDA *(crossing into kitchenette)*. I've got to fix the dressing for the salmon. Fuss, fuss—silliness!—over a gentleman caller!

(Door swings shut. LAURA is left alone.)

(LEGEND: "TERROR!")

(She utters a low moan and turns off the lamp—sits stiffly on the edge of the sofa, knotting her fingers together.)

(LEGEND ON SCREEN: "THE OPENING OF A DOOR!")

(TOM and JIM appear on the fire-escape steps and climb to landing. Hearing their approach, LAURA rises with a panicky gesture. She retreats to the portieres.)

(The doorbell. LAURA catches her breath and touches her throat. Low drums.)

AMANDA *(calling)*. Laura, sweetheart! The door!

(LAURA stares at it without moving.)

JIM. I think we just beat the rain.

TOM. Uh-huh. *(He rings again, nervously. JIM whistles and fishes for a cigarette.)*

AMANDA *(very, very gaily)*. Laura, that is your brother and Mr. O'Connor! Will you let them in, darling?

(LAURA crosses toward kitchenette door.)

LAURA *(breathlessly)*. Mother—you go to the door!

(AMANDA steps out of kitchenette and stares furiously at LAURA. She points imperiously at the door.)

LAURA. Please, please!

AMANDA *(in a fierce whisper)*. What is the matter with you, you silly thing?

LAURA *(desperately)*. Please, you answer it, *please!*

AMANDA. I told you I wasn't going to humor you, Laura. Why have you chosen this moment to lose your mind?

LAURA. Please, please, please, you go!

AMANDA. You'll have to go to the door because I can't!

LAURA *(despairingly)*. I can't either!

AMANDA. *Why?*

LAURA. I'm *sick!*

AMANDA. I'm sick, too—of your nonsense! Why can't you and your brother be normal people? Fantastic whims and behavior!

(TOM gives a long ring.)

Preposterous goings on! Can you give me one reason— *(Calls out lyrically.)* COMING! JUST ONE SECOND!—why you should be afraid to open a door? Now you answer it, Laura!

LAURA. Oh, oh, oh . . . *(She returns through the portieres. Darts to the victrola and winds it frantically and turns it on.)*

AMANDA. Laura Wingfield, you march right to that door!

LAURA. Yes—yes, Mother!

(A faraway, scratchy rendition of "Dardanella" softens the air and gives her strength to move through it. She slips to the door and draws it cautiously open.)

(TOM enters with the caller, JIM O'CONNOR.)

TOM. Laura, this is Jim. Jim, this is my sister, Laura.

JIM *(stepping inside)*. I didn't know that Shakespeare had a sister!

LAURA *(retreating stiff and trembling from the door)*. How—how do you do?

JIM *(heartily extending his hand)*. Okay!

(LAURA touches it hesitantly with hers.)

JIM. Your hand's *cold*, Laura!

LAURA. Yes, well—I've been playing the victrola. . . .

TOM *(disinterest)*. Yeah? *(Lights cigarette and crosses back to fire-escape door.)*

JIM. Where are *you* going?

TOM. I'm going out on the terrace.

JIM *(goes after him)*. You know, Shakespeare—I'm going to sell you a bill of goods!

TOM. What goods?

JIM. A course I'm taking.

TOM. Huh?

JIM. In public speaking! You and me, we're not the warehouse type.

TOM. Thanks—that's good news.
But what has public speaking got to do with it?

JIM. It fits you for—executive positions!

TOM. Awww.

JIM. I tell you it's done a helluva lot for me.

(IMAGE: EXECUTIVE AT DESK.)

TOM. In what respect?

JIM. In every! Ask yourself what is the difference between you an' me and men in the office down front? Brains?—No!—Ability?—No! Then what? Just one little thing—

TOM. What is that one little thing?

JIM. Primarily it amounts to—social poise! Being able to square up to people and hold your own on any social level!

AMANDA (off stage). Tom?

TOM. Yes, Mother?

AMANDA. Is that you and Mr. O'Connor?

TOM. Yes, Mother.

AMANDA. Well, you just make yourselves comfortable in there.

TOM. Yes, Mother.

AMANDA. Ask Mr. O'Connor if he would like to wash his hands.

JIM. Aw, no—no—thank you—I took care of that at the warehouse. Tom—

TOM. Yes?

JIM. Mr. Mendoza was speaking to me about you.

TOM. Favorably?

JIM. What do you think?

TOM. Well—

JIM. You're going to be out of a job if you don't wake up.

TOM. I am waking up—

JIM. You show no signs.

TOM The signs are interior.

(IMAGE ON SCREEN: THE SAILING VESSEL WITH JOLLY ROGER AGAIN.)

TOM. I'm planning to change. (He leans over the rail speaking with quiet exhilaration. The incandescent marquees and signs of the first-run movie houses light his face from across the alley. He looks like a voyager.) I'm right at the point of committing myself to a future that doesn't include the warehouse and Mr. Mendoza or even a night-school course in public speaking.

JIM. What are you gassing about?

TOM. I'm tired of the movies.

JIM. Movies!

TOM. Yes, movies! Look at them— (A wave toward the marvels of Grand Avenue.) All of those glamorous people—having adventures—hogging it all, gobbling the whole thing up! You know what happens? People go to the movies instead of moving! Hollywood characters are supposed to have all the adventures for everybody in America, while everybody in America sits in a dark room and watches them have them! Yes, until there's a war. That's when adventure becomes available to the masses! Everyone's dish, not only Gable's! Then the people in the dark room come out of the dark room to have some adventures themselves—Goody, goody!—It's our turn now, to go to the South Sea Island—to make a safari—to be exotic, far-off!—But I'm not patient. I don't want to wait till then. I'm tired of the movies and I am about to move!

JIM (incredulously). Move?

TOM. Yes.

JIM. When?

TOM. Soon!

JIM. Where? Where?

(THEME THREE MUSIC SEEMS TO ANSWER THE QUESTION, WHILE TOM THINKS IT OVER. HE SEARCHES AMONG HIS POCKETS.)

TOM. I'm starting to boil inside. I know I seem dreamy, but inside—well, I'm boiling!—Whenever I pick up a shoe, I shudder a little thinking how short life is and what I am doing!—Whatever that means, I know it doesn't mean shoes—except as something to wear on a traveler's feet! (Finds paper.) Look—

JIM. What?

TOM. I'm a member.

JIM *(reading)*. The Union of Merchant Seamen.

TOM. I paid my dues this month, instead of the light bill.

JIM. You will regret it when they turn the lights off.

TOM. I won't be here.

JIM. How about your mother?

TOM. I'm like my father. The bastard son of a bastard! See how he grins? And he's been absent going on sixteen years!

JIM. You're just talking, you drip. How does your mother feel about it?

TOM. Shhh!—Here comes Mother! Mother is not acquainted with my plans!

AMANDA *(enters portieres)*. Where are you all?

TOM. On the terrace, Mother.

(They start inside. She advances to them. TOM is distinctly shocked at her appearance. Even JIM blinks a little. He is making his first contact with girlish Southern vivacity and in spite of the night-school course in public speaking is somewhat thrown off the beam by the unexpected outlay of social charm.)

(Certain responses are attempted by JIM but are swept aside by AMANDA's gay laughter and chatter. TOM is embarrassed but after the first shock JIM reacts very warmly. Grins and chuckles, is altogether won over.)

(IMAGE: AMANDA AS A GIRL.)

AMANDA *(coyly smiling, shaking her girlish ringlets)*. Well, well, well, so this is Mr. O'Connor. Introductions entirely unnecessary. I've heard so much about you from my boy. I finally said to him, Tom—good gracious!—why don't you bring this paragon to supper? I'd like to meet this nice young man at the warehouse!—Instead of just hearing him sing your praises so much!

I don't know why my son is so stand-offish —that's not Southern behavior!

Let's sit down and—I think we could stand a little more air in here! Tom, leave the door open. I felt a nice fresh breeze a moment ago. Where has it gone to?

Mmm, so warm already! And not quite summer, even. We're going to burn up when summer really gets started.

However, we're having—we're having a very light supper. I think light things are better fo' this time of year. The same as light clothes are. Light clothes an' light food are what warm weather calls fo.' You know our blood gets so thick during th' winter—it takes a while fo' us to *adjust* ou'selves!—when the season changes . . .

It's come so quick this year. I wasn't prepared. All of a sudden—heavens! Already summer!—I ran to the trunk an' pulled out this light dress— Terribly old! Historical almost! But feels so good--so good an' co-ol, y' know. . . .

TOM. Mother—

AMANDA. Yes, honey?

TOM. How about—supper?

AMANDA. Honey, you go ask Sister if supper is ready! You know that Sister is in full charge of supper!

Tell her you hungry boys are waiting for it.

(To JIM.)

Have you met Laura?

JIM. She—

AMANDA. Let you in? Oh, good, you've met already! It's rare for a girl as sweet an' pretty as Laura to be domestic! But Laura is, thank heavens, not only pretty but also very domestic. I'm not at all. I never was a bit. I never could make a thing but angel-food cake. Well, in the South we had so many servants. Gone, gone, gone. All vestige of gracious living! Gone completely! I wasn't prepared for what the future brought me. All of my gentlemen callers were sons of planters and so of course I assumed that I would be married to one and raise my family on a large piece of land with plenty of servants. But man proposes—and woman accepts the proposal!—To vary that old, old saying a little bit—I married no planter! I married a man who worked for the telephone company!—That gallantly smiling gentleman over there! (*Points to the picture.*) A telephone man who—fell in love with long-distance!—Now he travels and I don't even know where!—But what am I going on for about my—tribulations?

Tell me yours—I hope you don't have any! Tom?

TOM (*returning*). Yes, Mother?

AMANDA. Is supper nearly ready?

TOM. It looks to me like supper is on the table.

AMANDA. Let me look— (*She rises prettily and looks through portieres.*) Oh, lovely! —But where is Sister?

TOM. Laura is not feeling well and she says that she thinks she'd better not come to the table.

AMANDA. What?—Nonsense!—Laura? Oh, Laura!

LAURA (*off stage, faintly*). Yes, Mother.

AMANDA. You really must come to the table. We won't be seated until you come to the table!

Come in, Mr. O'Connor. You sit over there, and I'll—

Laura? Laura Wingfield!

You're keeping us waiting, honey! We can't say grace until you come to the table!

(*The back door is pushed weakly open and* LAURA *comes in. She is obviously quite faint, her lips trembling, her eyes wide and staring. She moves unsteadily toward the table.*)

(LEGEND: "TERROR!")

(*Outside a summer storm is coming abruptly. The white curtains billow inward at the windows and there is a sorrowful murmur and deep blue dusk.*)

(LAURA *suddenly stumbles—she catches at a chair with a faint moan.*)

TOM. Laura!

AMANDA. Laura!

(*There is a clap of thunder.*)

(LEGEND: "AH!")

(*Despairingly.*)

Why, Laura, you *are* sick, darling! Tom, help your sister into the living room, dear! Sit in the living room, Laura—rest on the sofa.

Well!

(*To the gentleman caller.*)

Standing over the hot stove made her ill! —I told her that it was just too warm this evening, but—

(TOM *comes back in.* LAURA *is on the sofa.*)

Is Laura all right now?

TOM. Yes.

AMANDA. What *is* that? Rain? A nice cool rain has come up!

(*She gives the gentleman caller a frightened look.*)

I think we may—have grace—now . . .

(TOM *looks at her stupidly.*)

Tom, honey—you say grace!

TOM. Oh . . .

"For these and all thy mercies—"

(*They bow their heads,* AMANDA *stealing a nervous glance at* JIM. *In the living room* LAURA, *stretched on the sofa, clenches her hand to her lips, to hold back a shuddering sob.*)

God's Holy Name be praised—

THE SCENE DIMS OUT

SCENE VII

A Souvenir.

Half an hour later. Dinner is just being finished in the upstage area which is concealed by the drawn portieres.

As the curtain rises LAURA *is still huddled upon the sofa, her feet drawn under her, her head resting on a pale blue pillow, her eyes wide and mysteriously watchful. The new floor lamp with its shade of rose-colored silk gives a soft, becoming light to her face, bringing out the fragile, unearthly prettiness which usually escapes attention. There is a steady murmur of rain, but it is slackening and stops soon after the scene begins; the air outside becomes pale and luminous as the moon breaks out.*

A moment after the curtain rises, the lights in both rooms flicker and go out.

JIM. Hey, there, Mr. Light Bulb!

(AMANDA *laughs nervously.*)

(LEGEND: "SUSPENSION OF A PUBLIC SERV-ICE.")

AMANDA. Where was Moses when the lights went out? Ha-ha. Do you know the answer to that one, Mr. O'Connor?

JIM. No, Ma'am, what's the answer?

AMANDA. In the dark!

(JIM *laughs appreciatively.*)

Everybody sit still. I'll light the candles. Isn't it lucky we have them on the table? Where's a match? Which of you gentlemen can provide a match?

JIM. Here.

AMANDA. Thank you, sir.

JIM. Not at all, Ma'am!

AMANDA. I guess the fuse has burnt out. Mr. O'Connor, can you tell a burnt-out fuse? I know I can't and Tom is a total loss when it comes to mechanics.

(SOUND: GETTING UP: VOICES RECEDE A LIT-TLE TO KITCHENETTE.)

Oh, be careful you don't bump into something. We don't want our gentleman caller to break his neck. Now wouldn't that be a fine howdy-do?

JIM. Ha-ha!

Where is the fuse-box?

AMANDA. Right here next to the stove. Can you see anything?

JIM. Just a minute.

AMANDA. Isn't electricity a mysterious thing?

Wasn't it Benjamin Franklin who tied a key to a kite?

We live in such a mysterious universe, don't we? Some people say that science clears up all the mysteries for us. In my opinion it only creates more!

Have you found it yet?·

JIM. No, Ma'am. All these fuses look okay to me.

AMANDA. Tom!

TOM. Yes, Mother?

AMANDA. That light bill I gave you several days ago. The one I told you we got the notices about?

(LEGEND: "HA!")

TOM. Oh.—Yeah.

AMANDA. You didn't neglect to pay it by any chance?

TOM. Why, I—

AMANDA. Didn't! I might have known it!

JIM. Shakespeare probably wrote a poem on that light bill, Mrs. Wingfield.

AMANDA. I might have known better than to trust him with it! There's such a high price for negligence in this world!

JIM. Maybe the poem will win a ten-dollar prize.

AMANDA. We'll just have to spend the remainder of the evening in the nineteenth century, before Mr. Edison made the Mazda lamp!

JIM. Candlelight is my favorite kind of light.

AMANDA. That shows you're romantic! But that's no excuse for Tom.

Well, we got through dinner. Very considerate of them to let us get through dinner before they plunged us into everlasting darkness, wasn't it, Mr. O'Connor?

JIM. Ha-ha!

AMANDA. Tom, as a penalty for your carelessness you can help me with the dishes.

JIM. Let me give you a hand.

AMANDA. Indeed you will not!

JIM. I ought to be good for something.

AMANDA. Good for something? (*Her tone is rhapsodic.*)

You? Why, Mr. O'Connor, nobody, *nobody's* given me this much entertainment in years—as you have!

JIM. Aw, now, Mrs. Wingfield!

AMANDA. I'm not exaggerating, not one bit! But Sister is all by her lonesome. You go keep her company in the parlor!

I'll give you this lovely old candelabrum that used to be on the altar at the church of the Heavenly Rest. It was melted a little out of shape when the church burnt.down. Lightning struck it one spring. Gypsy

Jones was holding a revival at the time and he intimated that the church was destroyed because the Episcopalians gave card parties.

JIM. Ha-ha.

AMANDA. And how about you coaxing Sister to drink a little wine? I think it would be good for her! Can you carry both at once?

JIM. Sure. I'm Superman!

AMANDA. Now, Thomas, get into this apron!

(*The door of kitchenette swings closed on* AMANDA's *gay laughter; the flickering light approaches the portieres.*)

(LAURA *sits up nervously as he enters. Her speech at first is low and breathless from the almost intolerable strain of being alone with a stranger.*)

(THE LEGEND: "I DON'T SUPPOSE YOU REMEMBER ME AT ALL!")

(*In her first speeches in this scene, before* JIM's *warmth overcomes her paralyzing shyness,* LAURA's *voice is thin and breathless as though she has just run up a steep flight of stairs.*)

(JIM's *attitude is gently humorous. In playing this scene it should be stressed that while the incident is apparently unimportant, it is to* LAURA *the climax of her secret life.*)

JIM. Hello, there, Laura.

LAURA (*faintly*). Hello. (*She clears her throat.*)

JIM. How are you feeling now? Better?

LAURA. Yes. Yes, thank you.

JIM. This is for you. A little dandelion wine. (*He extends it toward her with extravagant gallantry.*)

LAURA. Thank you.

JIM. Drink it—but don't get drunk!

(*He laughs heartily.* LAURA *takes the glass uncertainly; laughs shyly.*)

Where shall I set the candles?

LAURA. Oh—oh, anywhere . . .

JIM. How about here on the floor? Any objections?

LAURA. No.

JIM. I'll spread a newspaper under to catch the drippings. I like to sit on the floor. Mind if I do?

LAURA. Oh, no.

JIM. Give me a pillow?

LAURA. What?

JIM. A pillow!

LAURA. Oh . . . (*Hands him one quickly.*)

JIM. How about you? Don't you like to sit on the floor?

LAURA. Oh—yes.

JIM. Why don't you, then?

LAURA. I—will.

JIM. Take a pillow! (LAURA *does. Sits on the other side of the candelabrum.* JIM *crosses his legs and smiles engagingly at her.*) I can't hardly see you sitting way over there.

LAURA. I can—see you.

JIM. I know, but that's not fair, I'm in the limelight. (LAURA *moves her pillow closer.*) Good! Now I can see you! Comfortable?

LAURA. Yes.

JIM. So am I. Comfortable as a cow! Will you have some gum?

LAURA. No, thank you.

JIM. I think that I will indulge, with your permission. (*Musingly unwraps it and holds it up.*) Think of the fortune made by the guy that invented the first piece of chewing gum. Amazing, huh? The Wrigley Building is one of the sights of Chicago.—I saw it summer before last when I went up to the Century of Progress. Did you take in the Century of Progress?

LAURA. No, I didn't.

JIM. Well, it was quite a wonderful exposition. What impressed me most was the Hall of Science. Gives you an idea of what the future will be in America, even more wonderful than the present time is! (*Pause. Smiling at her.*) Your brother tells me you're shy. Is that right, Laura?

LAURA. I—don't know.

JIM. I judge you to be an old-fashioned

type of girl. Well, I think that's a pretty good type to be. Hope you don't think I'm being too personal—do you?

LAURA (*hastily, out of embarrassment*). I believe I *will* take a piece of gum, if you —don't mind. (*Clearing her throat.*) Mr. O'Connor, have you—kept up with your singing?

JIM. Singing? Me?

LAURA. Yes. I remember what a beautiful voice you had.

JIM. When did you hear me sing?

(VOICE OFF STAGE IN THE PAUSE.)

VOICE (*off stage*).

O blow, ye winds, heigh-ho,
A-roving I will go!
I'm off to my love
With a boxing glove—
Ten thousand miles away!

JIM. You say you've heard me sing?

LAURA. Oh, yes! Yes, very often . . . I—don't suppose—you remember me—at all?

JIM (*smiling doubtfully*). You know I have an idea I've seen you before. I had that idea soon as you opened the door. It seemed almost like I was about to remember your name. But the name that I started to call you—wasn't a name! And so I stopped myself before I said it.

LAURA. Wasn't it—Blue Roses?

JIM (*springs up. Grinning*). Blue Roses! —My gosh, yes—Blue Roses!

That's what I had on my tongue when you opened the door!

Isn't it funny what tricks your memory plays? I didn't connect you with high school somehow or other.

But that's where it was; it was high school. I didn't even know you were Shakespeare's sister!

Gosh, I'm sorry.

LAURA. I didn't expect you to. You—barely knew me!

JIM. But we did have a speaking acquaintance, huh?

LAURA. Yes, we—spoke to each other.

JIM. When did you recognize me?

LAURA. Oh, right away!

JIM. Soon as I came in the door?

LAURA. When I heard your name I thought it was probably you. I knew that Tom used to know you a little in high school. So when you came in the door—

Well, then I was—sure.

JIM. Why didn't you *say* something, then?

LAURA (*breathlessly*). I didn't know what to say, I was—too surprised!

JIM. For goodness' sakes! You know, this sure is funny!

LAURA. Yes! Yes, isn't it, though . . .

JIM. Didn't we have a class in something together?

LAURA. Yes, we did.

JIM. What class was that?

LAURA. It was—singing—Chorus!

JIM. Aw!

LAURA. I sat across the aisle from you in the Aud.

JIM. Aw.

LAURA. Mondays, Wednesdays and Fridays.

JIM. Now I remember—you always came in late.

LAURA. Yes, it was so hard for me, getting upstairs. I had that brace on my leg—it clumped so loud!

JIM. I never heard any clumping.

LAURA (*wincing at the recollection*). To me it sounded like—thunder!

JIM. Well, well, well, I never even noticed.

LAURA. And everybody was seated before I came in. I had to walk in front of all those people. My seat was in the back row. I had to go clumping all the way up the aisle with everyone watching!

JIM. You shouldn't have been self-conscious.

LAURA. I know, but I was. It was always such a relief when the singing started.

JIM. Aw, yes, I've placed you now! I used to call you Blue Roses. How was it that I got started calling you that?

LAURA. I was out of school a little while with pleurosis. When I came back you asked me what was the matter. I said I had pleurosis—you thought I said Blue Roses. That's what you always called me after that!

JIM. I hope you didn't mind.

LAURA. Oh, no—I liked it. You see, I wasn't acquainted with many—people. . . .

JIM. As I remember you sort of stuck by yourself.

LAURA. I—I—never have had much luck at—making friends.

JIM. I don't see why you wouldn't.

LAURA. Well, I—started out badly.

JIM. You mean being—

LAURA. Yes, it sort of—stood between me—

JIM. You shouldn't have let it!

LAURA. I know, but it did, and—

JIM. You were shy with people!

LAURA. I tried not to be but never could—

JIM. Overcome it?

LAURA. No, I—I never could!

JIM. I guess being shy is something you have to work out of kind of gradually.

LAURA (sorrowfully). Yes—I guess it—

JIM. Takes time!

LAURA. Yes—

JIM. People are not so dreadful when you know them. That's what you have to remember! And everybody has problems, not just you, but practically everybody has got some problems.

You think of yourself as having the only problems, as being the only one who is disappointed. But just look around you and you will see lots of people as disappointed as you are. For instance, I hoped when I was going to high school that I would be further along at this time, six years later, than I am now— You remember that wonderful write-up I had in *The Torch?*

LAURA. Yes! (*She rises and crosses to table.*)

JIM. It said I was bound to succeed in anything I went into! (LAURA *returns with the annual.*) Holy Jeez! *The Torch!* (*He accepts it reverently. They smile across it with mutual wonder.* LAURA *crouches beside him and they begin to turn through it.* LAURA's *shyness is dissolving in his warmth.*)

LAURA. Here you are in *The Pirates of Penzance!*

JIM (*wistfully*). I sang the baritone lead in that operetta.

LAURA (*raptly*). So—*beautifully!*

JIM (*protesting*). Aw—

LAURA. Yes, yes—beautifully—beautifully!

JIM. You heard me?

LAURA. All three times!

JIM. No!

LAURA. Yes!

JIM. All three performances?

LAURA (*looking down*). Yes.

JIM. Why?

LAURA. I—wanted to ask you to—autograph my program.

JIM. Why didn't you ask me to?

LAURA. You were always surrounded by your own friends so much that I never had a chance to.

JIM. You should have just—

LAURA. Well, I—thought you might think I was—

JIM. Thought I might think you was—what?

LAURA. Oh—

JIM (*with reflective relish*). I was beleaguered by females in those days.

LAURA. You were terribly popular!

JIM. Yeah—

LAURA. You had such a—friendly way—

JIM. I was spoiled in high school.

LAURA. Everybody—liked you!

JIM. Including you?

LAURA. I—yes, I—I did, too— (*She gently closes the book in her lap.*)

JIM. Well, well, well!—Give me that program, Laura. (*She hands it to him. He signs it with a flourish.*) There you are—better late than never!

LAURA. Oh, I—what a—surprise!

JIM. My signature isn't worth very much right now.

But some day—maybe—it will increase in value!

Being disappointed is one thing and being discouraged is something else. I am disappointed but I am not discouraged.

I'm twenty-three years old.

How old are you?

LAURA. I'll be twenty-four in June.

JIM. That's not old age!

LAURA. No, but—

JIM. You finished high school?

LAURA *(with difficulty)*. I didn't go back.

JIM. You mean you dropped out?

LAURA. I made bad grades in my final examinations. *(She rises and replaces the book and the program. Her voice strained.)* How is—Emily Meisenbach getting along?

JIM. Oh, that kraut-head!

LAURA. Why do you call her that?

JIM. That's what she was.

LAURA. You're not still—going with her?

JIM. I never see her.

LAURA. It said in the Personal Section that you were—engaged!

JIM. I know, but I wasn't impressed by that—propaganda!

LAURA. It wasn't—the truth?

JIM. Only in Emily's optimistic opinion!

LAURA. Oh—

(LEGEND: "WHAT HAVE YOU DONE SINCE HIGH SCHOOL?")

(JIM lights a cigarette and leans indolently back on his elbows smiling at LAURA with a warmth and charm which lights her inwardly with altar candles. She remains by the table and turns in her hands a piece of glass to cover her tumult.)

JIM *(after several reflective puffs on a cigarette)*. What have you done since high school? *(She seems not to hear him.)* Huh? *(LAURA looks up.)* I said what have you done since high school, Laura?

LAURA. Nothing much.

JIM. You must have been doing something these six long years.

LAURA. Yes.

JIM. Well, then, such as what?

LAURA. I took a business course at business college—

JIM. How did that work out?

LAURA. Well, not very—well—I had to drop out, it gave me—indigestion—

(JIM laughs gently.)

JIM. What are you doing now?

LAURA. I don't do anything—much. Oh, please don't think I sit around doing nothing! My glass collection takes up a good deal of time. Glass is something you have to take good care of.

JIM. What did you say—about glass?

LAURA. Collection I said—I have one— *(She clears her throat and turns away again, acutely shy.)*

JIM *(abruptly)*. You know what I judge to be the trouble with you?

Inferiority complex! Know what that is? That's what they call it when someone low-rates himself!

I understand it because I had it, too. Although my case was not so aggravated as yours seems to be. I had it until I took up public speaking, developed my voice, and learned that I had an aptitude for science. Before that time I never thought of myself as being outstanding in any way whatsoever!

Now I've never made a regular study of it, but I have a friend who says I can analyze people better than doctors that make a profession of it. I don't claim that to be necessarily true, but I can sure guess a person's psychology, Laura! *(Takes out his gum.)* Excuse me, Laura. I always take it out when the flavor is gone. I'll use this scrap of paper to wrap it in. I know how it is to get it stuck on a shoe.

Yep—that's what I judge to be your principal trouble. A lack of confidence in yourself as a person. You don't have the proper amount of faith in yourself. I'm basing that fact on a number of your remarks and also on certain observations I've made. For instance that clumping you thought was so awful in high school. You say that you even dreaded to walk into class. You see what you did? You dropped out of school, you gave up an education because of a clump, which as far as I know was practically non-existent! A little physical defect is what you have. Hardly noticeable even! Magnified thousands of times by imagination!

You know what my strong advice to you is? Think of yourself as *superior* in some way!

LAURA. In what way would I think?

JIM. Why, man alive, Laura! Just look about you a little. What do you see? A world full of common people! All of 'em born and all of 'em going to die!

Which of them has one-tenth of your good points! Or mine! Or anyone else's, as far as that goes—Gosh!

Everybody excels in some one thing. Some in many!

(Unconsciously glances at himself in the mirror.)

All you've got to do is discover in *what!* Take me, for instance.

(He adjusts his tie at the mirror.)

My interest happens to lie in electro-dynamics. I'm taking a course in radio engineering at night school, Laura, on top of a fairly responsible job at the warehouse. I'm taking that course and studying public speaking.

LAURA. Ohhhh.

JIM. Because I believe in the future of television!

(Turning back to her.)

I wish to be ready to go up right along with it. Therefore I'm planning to get in on the ground floor. In fact I've already made the right connections and all that remains is for the industry itself to get under way! Full steam—

(His eyes are starry.)

Knowledge—Zzzzzp! Money—Zzzzzzp! —Power!

That's the cycle democracy is built on!

(His attitude is convincingly dynamic. LAURA stares at him, even her shyness eclipsed in her absolute wonder. He suddenly grins.)

I guess you think I think a lot of myself!

LAURA. No—o-o-o, I—

JIM. Now how about you? Isn't there something you take more interest in than anything else?

LAURA. Well, I do—as I said—have my—glass collection—

(A peal of girlish laughter from the kitchen.)

JIM. I'm not right sure I know what you're talking about.

What kind of glass is it?

LAURA. Little articles of it, they're ornaments mostly!

Most of them are little animals made out of glass, the tiniest little animals in the world. Mother calls them a glass menagerie!

Here's an example of one, if you'd like to see it!

This one is one of the oldest. It's nearly thirteen.

(MUSIC: "THE GLASS MENAGERIE.")

(He stretches out his hand.)

Oh, be careful—if you breathe, it breaks!

JIM. I'd better not take it. I'm pretty clumsy with things.

LAURA. Go on, I trust you with him!

(Places it in his palm.)

There now—you're holding him gently! Hold him over the light, he loves the light! You see how the light shines through him?

JIM. It sure does shine!

LAURA. I shouldn't be partial, but he is my favorite one.

JIM. What kind of a thing is this one supposed to be?

LAURA. Haven't you noticed the single horn on his forehead?

JIM. A unicorn, huh?

LAURA. Mmm-hmmm!

JIM. Unicorns, aren't they extinct in the modern world?

LAURA. I know!

JIM. Poor little fellow, he must feel sort of lonesome.

LAURA *(smiling)*. Well, if he does he doesn't complain about it. He stays on a shelf with some horses that don't have horns and all of them seem to get along nicely together.

JIM. How do you know?

LAURA *(lightly)*. I haven't heard any arguments among them!

JIM *(grinning)*. No arguments, huh? Well, that's a pretty good sign! Where shall I set him?

LAURA. Put him on the table. They all like a change of scenery once in a while!

JIM *(stretching)*. Well, well, well, well— Look how big my shadow is when I stretch!

LAURA. Oh, oh, yes—it stretches across the ceiling!

JIM *(crossing to door)*. I think it's stopped raining. *(Opens fire-escape door.)* Where does the music come from?

LAURA. From the Paradise Dance Hall across the alley.

JIM. How about cutting the rug a little, Miss Wingfield?

LAURA. Oh, I—

JIM. Or is your program filled up? Let me have a look at it. *(Grasps imaginary card.)* Why, every dance is taken! I'll just have to scratch some out. (WALTZ MUSIC: "LA GOLONDRINA.") Ahhh, a waltz! *(He executes some sweeping turns by himself then holds his arms toward LAURA.)*

LAURA *(breathlessly)*. I—can't dance!

JIM. There you go, that inferiority stuff!

LAURA. I've never danced in my life!

JIM. Come on, try!

LAURA. Oh, but I'd step on you!

JIM. I'm not made out of glass.

LAURA. How—how—how do we start?

JIM. Just leave it to me. You hold your arms out a little.

LAURA. Like this?

JIM. A little bit higher. Right. Now don't tighten up, that's the main thing about it —relax.

LAURA *(laughing breathlessly)*. It's hard not to.

JIM. Okay.

LAURA. I'm afraid you can't budge me.

JIM. What do you bet I can't? *(He swings her into motion.)*

LAURA. Goodness, yes, you can!

JIM. Let yourself go, now, Laura, just let yourself go.

LAURA. I'm—

JIM. Come on!

LAURA. Trying!

JIM. Not so stiff— Easy does it!

LAURA. I know but I'm—

JIM. Loosen th' backbone! There now, that's a lot better.

LAURA. Am I?

JIM. Lots, lots better! *(He moves her about the room in a clumsy waltz.)*

LAURA. Oh, my!

JIM. Ha-ha!

LAURA. Oh, my goodness!

JIM. Ha-ha-ha! *(They suddenly bump into the table.* JIM *stops.)* What did we hit on?

LAURA. Table.

JIM. Did something fall off it? I think—

LAURA. Yes.

JIM. I hope it wasn't the little glass horse with the horn!

LAURA. Yes.

JIM. Aw, aw, aw. Is it broken?

LAURA. Now it is just like all the other horses.

JIM. It's lost its—

LAURA. Horn! It doesn't matter. Maybe it's a blessing in disguise.

JIM. You'll never forgive me. I bet that that was your favorite piece of glass.

LAURA. I don't have favorites much. It's no tragedy, Freckles. Glass breaks so easily.

No matter how careful you are. The traffic jars the shelves and things fall off them.

JIM. Still I'm awfully sorry that I was the cause.

LAURA (*smiling*). I'll just imagine he had an operation.

The horn was removed to make him feel less—freakish!

(*They both laugh.*)

Now he will feel more at home with the other horses, the ones that don't have horns. . . .

JIM. Ha-ha, that's very funny!

(*Suddenly serious.*)

I'm glad to see that you have a sense of humor.

You know—you're—well—very different! Surprisingly different from anyone else I know!

(*His voice becomes soft and hesitant with a genuine feeling.*)

Do you mind me telling you that?

(LAURA *is abashed beyond speech.*)

I mean it in a nice way . . .

(LAURA *nods shyly, looking away.*)

You make me feel sort of—I don't know how to put it!

I'm usually pretty good at expressing things, but—

This is something that I don't know how to say!

(LAURA *touches her throat and clears it— turns the broken unicorn in her hands.*) (*Even softer.*)

Has anyone ever told you that you were pretty?

(PAUSE: MUSIC.)

(LAURA *looks up slowly, with wonder, and shakes her head.*)

Well, you are! In a different way from anyone else.

And all the nicer because of the difference, too.

(*His voice becomes low and husky.* LAURA *turns away, nearly faint with the novelty of her emotions.*)

I wish that you were my sister. I'd teach you to have some confidence in yourself. The different people are not like other people, but being different is nothing to be ashamed of. Because other people are not such wonderful people. They're one hundred times one thousand. You're one times one! They walk all over the earth. You just stay here. They're common as—weeds, but—you—well, you're—*Blue Roses!*

(IMAGE ON SCREEN: BLUE ROSES.)

(MUSIC CHANGES.)

LAURA. But blue is wrong for—roses . . .

JIM. It's right for you!—You're—pretty!

LAURA. In what respect am I pretty?

JIM. In all respects—believe me! Your eyes —your hair—are pretty! Your hands are pretty!

(*He catches hold of her hand.*)

You think I'm making this up because I'm invited to dinner and have to be nice. Oh, I could do that! I could put on an act for you, Laura, and say lots of things without being very sincere. But this time I am. I'm talking to you sincerely. I happened to notice you had this inferiority complex that keeps you from feeling comfortable with people. Somebody needs to build your confidence up and make you proud instead of shy and turning away and—blushing—

Somebody—ought to—

Ought to—*kiss* you, Laura!

(*His hand slips slowly up her arm to her shoulder.*)

(MUSIC SWELLS TUMULTUOUSLY.)

(*He suddenly turns her about and kisses her on the lips.*)

(*When he releases her,* LAURA *sinks on the sofa with a bright, dazed look.*)

(JIM *backs away and fishes in his pocket for a cigarette.*)

(LEGEND ON SCREEN: "SOUVENIR.")

Stumble-john!

(*He lights the cigarette, avoiding her look.*)

(*There is a peal of girlish laughter from* AMANDA *in the kitchen.*)

(LAURA *slowly raises and opens her hand*

It still contains the little broken glass animal. She looks at it with a tender, bewildered expression.)

Stumble-john!

I shouldn't have done that— That was way off the beam.

You don't smoke, do you?

(She looks up, smiling, not hearing the question.)

(He sits beside her a little gingerly. She looks at him speechlessly—waiting.)

(He coughs decorously and moves a little farther aside as he considers the situation and senses her feelings, dimly, with perturbation.)

(Gently.) Would you—care for a—mint?

(She doesn't seem to hear him but her look grows brighter even.)

Peppermint—Life-Saver?

My pocket's a regular drug store—wherever I go . . .

(He pops a mint in his mouth. Then gulps and decides to make a clean breast of it. He speaks slowly and gingerly.)

Laura, you know, if I had a sister like you, I'd do the same thing as Tom. I'd bring out fellows and—introduce her to them. The right type of boys of a type to—appreciate her.

Only—well—he made a mistake about me. Maybe I've got no call to be saying this. That may not have been the idea in having me over. But what if it was?

There's nothing wrong about that. The only trouble is that in my case—I'm not in a situation to—do the right thing.

I can't take down your number and say I'll phone.

I can't call up next week and—ask for a date.

I thought I had better explain the situation in case you—misunderstood it and—hurt your feelings. . . .

(Pause.)

(Slowly, very slowly, LAURA's *look changes, her eyes returning slowly from his to the ornament in her palm.)*

*(*AMANDA *utters another gay laugh in the kitchen.)*

LAURA *(faintly).* You—won't call again?

JIM. No, Laura, I can't.

(He rises from the sofa.)

As I was just explaining, I've—got strings on me.

Laura, I've—been going steady!

I go out all of the time with a girl named Betty. She's a home-girl like you, and Catholic, and Irish, and in a great many ways we—get along fine.

I met her last summer on a moonlight boat trip up the river to Alton, on the *Majestic.* Well—right away from the start it was— love!

(LEGEND: LOVE!)

*(*LAURA *sways slightly forward and grips the arm of the sofa. He fails to notice, now enrapt in his own comfortable being.)*

Being in love has made a new man of me!

(Leaning stiffly forward, clutching the arm of the sofa, LAURA *struggles visibly with her storm. But* JIM *is oblivious, she is a long way off.)*

The power of love is really pretty tremendous!

Love is something that—changes the whole world, Laura!

(The storm abates a little and LAURA *leans back. He notices her again.)*

It happened that Betty's aunt took sick, she got a wire and had to go to Centralia. So Tom—when he asked me to dinner—I naturally just accepted the invitation, not knowing that you—that he—that I—

(He stops awkwardly.)

Huh—I'm a stumble-john!

(He flops back on the sofa.)

(The holy candles in the altar of LAURA's *face have been snuffed out. There is a look of almost infinite desolation.)*

*(*JIM *glances at her uneasily.)*

I wish that you would—say something.

(She bites her lip which was trembling and then bravely smiles. She opens her hand again on the broken glass ornament. Then she gently takes his hand and raises

it level with her own. She carefully places the unicorn in the palm of his hand, then pushes his fingers closed upon it.) What are you—doing that for? You want me to have him?—Laura? *(She nods.)* What for?

LAURA. A—souvenir . . . *(She rises unsteadily and crouches beside the victrola to wind it up.)*

(LEGEND ON SCREEN: "THINGS HAVE A WAY OF TURNING OUT SO BADLY!")

(OR IMAGE: "GENTLEMAN CALLER WAVING GOOD-BYE!—GAILY.")

(At this moment AMANDA rushes brightly back in the front room. She bears a pitcher of fruit punch in an old-fashioned cut-glass pitcher and a plate of macaroons. The plate has a gold border and poppies painted on it.)

AMANDA. Well, well, well! Isn't the air delightful after the shower? I've made you children a little liquid refreshment. *(Turns gaily to the gentleman caller.)*

Jim, do you know that song about lemonade?

"Lemonade, lemonade
Made in the shade and stirred with a spade—
Good enough for any old maid!"

JIM *(uneasily)*. Ha-ha! No—I never heard it.

AMANDA. Why, Laura! You look so serious!

JIM. We were having a serious conversation.

AMANDA. Good! Now you're better acquainted!

JIM *(uncertainly)*. Ha-ha! Yes.

AMANDA. You modern young people are much more serious-minded than my generation. I was so gay as a girl!

JIM. You haven't changed, Mrs. Wingfield.

AMANDA. Tonight I'm rejuvenated! The gaiety of the occasion, Mr. O'Connor! *(She tosses her head with a peal of laughter. Spills lemonade.)*

Oooo! I'm baptizing myself!

JIM. Here—let me—

AMANDA *(setting the pitcher down)*. There

now. I discovered we had some maraschino cherries. I dumped them in, juice and all!

JIM. You shouldn't have gone to that trouble, Mrs. Wingfield.

AMANDA. Trouble, trouble? Why, it was loads of fun!

Didn't you hear me cutting up in the kitchen? I bet your ears were burning! I told Tom how outdone with him I was for keeping you to himself so long a time! He should have brought you over much, much sooner! Well, now that you've found your way, I want you to be a frequent caller! Not just occasional but all the time. Oh, we're going to have a lot of gay times together! I see them coming!

Mmm, just breathe that air! So fresh, and the moon's so pretty!

I'll skip back out—I know where my place is when young folks are having a—serious conversation!

JIM. Oh, don't go out, Mrs. Wingfield. The fact of the matter is I've got to be going.

AMANDA. Going, now? You're joking! Why, it's only the shank of the evening, Mr. O'Connor!

JIM. Well, you know how it is.

AMANDA. You mean you're a young workingman and have to keep workingmen's hours. We'll let you off early tonight. But only on the condition that next time you stay later.

What's the best night for you? Isn't Saturday night the best night for you workingmen?

JIM. I have a couple of time-clocks to punch, Mrs. Wingfield. One at morning, another one at night!

AMANDA. My, but you *are* ambitious! You work at night, too?

JIM. No, Ma'am, not work but—Betty!

(He crosses deliberately to pick up his hat. The band at the Paradise Dance Hall goes into a tender waltz.)

AMANDA. Betty? Betty? Who's—Betty!

(There is an ominous cracking sound in the sky.)

JIM. Oh, just a girl. The girl I go steady with! (*He smiles charmingly. The sky falls.*)

(LEGEND: "THE SKY FALLS.")

AMANDA (*a long-drawn exhalation*). Ohhhh . . . Is it a serious romance, Mr. O'Connor?

JIM. We're going to be married the second Sunday in June.

AMANDA. Ohhhh—how nice!

Tom didn't mention that you were engaged to be married.

JIM. The cat's not out of the bag at the warehouse yet.

You know how they are. They call you Romeo and stuff like that. (*He stops at the oval mirror to put on his hat. He carefully shapes the brim and the crown to give a discreetly dashing effect.*)

It's been a wonderful evening, Mrs. Wingfield. I guess this is what they mean by Southern hospitality.

AMANDA. It really wasn't anything at all.

JIM. I hope it don't seem like I'm rushing off. But I promised Betty I'd pick her up at the Wabash depot, an' by the time I get my jalopy down there her train'll be in. Some women are pretty upset if you keep 'em waiting.

AMANDA. Yes, I know— The tyranny of women!

(*Extends her hand.*)

Good-bye, Mr. O'Connor.

I wish you luck—and happiness—and success! All three of them, and so does Laura! —Don't you, Laura?

LAURA. Yes!

JIM (*taking her hand*). Good-bye, Laura. I'm certainly going to treasure that souvenir. And don't you forget the good advice I gave you.

(*Raises his voice to a cheery shout.*)

So long, Shakespeare!

Thanks again, ladies— Good night!

(*He grins and ducks jauntily out.*)

(*Still bravely grimacing,* AMANDA *closes the door on the gentleman caller. Then she* turns back to the room with a puzzled expression. She and LAURA don't dare to face each other. LAURA crouches beside the victrola to wind it.)

AMANDA (*faintly*). Things have a way of turning out so badly.

I don't believe that I would play the victrola.

Well, well—well—

Our gentleman caller was engaged to be married!

Tom!

TOM (*from back*). Yes, Mother?

AMANDA. Come in here a minute. I want to tell you something awfully funny.

TOM (*enters with macaroon and a glass of the lemonade*). Has the gentleman caller gotten away already?

AMANDA. The gentleman caller has made an early departure.

What a wonderful joke you played on us!

TOM. How do you mean?

AMANDA. You didn't mention that he was engaged to be married.

TOM. Jim? Engaged?

AMANDA. That's what he just informed us.

TOM. I'll be jiggered! I didn't know about that.

AMANDA. That seems very peculiar.

TOM. What's peculiar about it?

AMANDA. Didn't you call him your best friend down at the warehouse?

TOM. He is, but how did I know?

AMANDA. It seems extremely peculiar that you wouldn't know your best friend was going to be married!

TOM. The warehouse is where I work, not where I know things about people!

AMANDA. You don't know things anywhere! You live in a dream; you manufacture illusions!

(*He crosses to door.*)

Where are you going?

TOM. I'm going to the movies.

AMANDA. That's right, now that you've had

us make such fools of ourselves. The effort, the preparations, all the expense! The new floor lamp, the rug, the clothes for Laura! All for what? To entertain some other girl's fiancé!

Go to the movies, go! Don't think about us, a mother deserted, an unmarried sister who's crippled and has no job! Don't let anything interfere with your selfish pleasure!

Just go, go, go—to the movies!

TOM. All right, I will! The more you shout about my selfishness to me the quicker I'll go, and I won't go to the movies!

AMANDA. Go, then! Then go to the moon— you selfish dreamer!

(TOM *smashes his glass on the floor. He plunges out on the fire-escape, slamming the door.* LAURA *screams—cut by door.*)

(*Dance-hall music up.* TOM *goes to the rail and grips it desperately, lifting his face in the chill white moonlight penetrating the narrow abyss of the alley.*)

(LEGEND ON SCREEN: "AND SO GOOD-BYE . . .")

(TOM's *closing speech is timed with the interior pantomime. The interior scene is played as though viewed through sound-proof glass.* AMANDA *appears to be making a comforting speech to* LAURA *who is huddled upon the sofa. Now that we cannot hear the mother's speech, her silliness is gone and she has dignity and tragic beauty.* LAURA's *dark hair hides her face until at the end of the speech she lifts it to smile at her mother.* AMANDA's *gestures are slow and graceful, almost dance-like, as she comforts the daughter. At the end of her speech she glances a moment at the father's picture—then withdraws through the portieres. At close of* TOM's *speech,* LAURA *blows out the candles, ending the play.*)

TOM. I didn't go to the moon, I went much

further—for time is the longest distance between two places—

Not long after that I was fired for writing a poem on the lid of a shoe-box.

I left Saint Louis. I descended the steps of this fire-escape for a last time and followed, from then on, in my father's footsteps, attempting to find in motion what was lost in space—

I traveled around a great deal. The cities swept about me like dead leaves, leaves that were brightly colored but torn away from the branches.

I would have stopped, but I was pursued by something.

It always came upon me unawares, taking me altogether by surprise. Perhaps it was a familiar bit of music. Perhaps it was only a piece of transparent glass—

Perhaps I am walking along a street at night, in some strange city, before I have found companions. I pass the lighted window of a shop where perfume is sold. The window is filled with pieces of colored glass, tiny transparent bottles in delicate colors, like bits of a shattered rainbow.

Then all at once my sister touches my shoulder. I turn around and look into her eyes . . .

Oh, Laura, Laura, I tried to leave you behind me, but I am more faithful than I intended to be!

I reach for a cigarette, I cross the street, I run into the movies or a bar, I buy a drink, I speak to the nearest stranger— anything that can blow your candles out!

(LAURA *bends over the candles.*)

—for nowadays the world is lit by lightning! Blow out your candles, Laura—and so good-bye. . . .

(*She blows the candles out.*)

THE SCENE DISSOLVES

State of the Union

BY HOWARD LINDSAY and RUSSEL CROUSE

First presented by Leland Hayward at the Hudson Theatre in New York on November 14, 1945, with the following cast:

JAMES CONOVER	Minor Watson	SAM PARRISH	Herbert Heyes
SPIKE MacMANUS	Myron McCormick	SWENSON	Fred Ayres Cotton
KAY THORNDYKE	Kay Johnson	JUDGE JEFFERSON DAVIS ALEXANDER	
GRANT MATTHEWS	Ralph Bellamy		G. Albert Smith
NORAH	Helen Ray	MRS. ALEXANDER	Maidel Turner
MARY MATTHEWS	Ruth Hussey	JENNY	Madeline King
STEVENS	John Rowe	MRS. DRAPER	Aline McDermott
BELLBOY	Howard Graham	WILLIAM HARDY	Victor Sutherland
WAITER	Robert Toms	SENATOR LAUTERBACK	George Lessey

ACT ONE

Scene One: The study in James Conover's home in Washington, D. C.
Scene Two: A bedroom in the Conover home. The following evening.

ACT TWO

The living room of a suite in the Book-Cadillac Hotel, Detroit. Several weeks later.

ACT THREE

Scene One: The living room of the Matthews' apartment in New York. Two weeks later.

Scene Two: The same, an hour later.

WITH *State of the Union,* which received the Pulitzer Prize in 1946, Lindsay and Crouse reached the peak of a joint artistic career already exalted by their *Life with Father.* The authors applied their well-tested talent for comedy to an immediate political issue—that of making fair and liberal politics prevail in the land of the free and the home of the brave. The liberal spirit was at its zenith then, the American eagle having acquitted itself triumphantly against the vultures of Nazism and Fascism. Now was the time for all good men to get together and expel native monstrosities of race hatred from the land and to clean up politics in general by denouncing whatever tendencies to play one ethnic group against another might exist or might arise in the political game. Some such idea buzzed in the busy factory of the two expert fun-makers, who are among the most reputable as well as successful of Broadway's showmen.

The story of their separate careers and partnership is by now authentic Broadway history, and there is no reason to revise the report written in the previous volume of our *Best Plays* series.

Mr. Lindsay, who was born in Waterford, New York, in 1889, became an elocutionist at the tender age of ten in Atlantic City, and his unprofessional success led him to cast an eye on the stage until the close of his freshman year at Harvard. Although he then entertained notions of preparing himself for the ministry (he would have filled a pulpit quite impressively), he soon found himself examining a catalogue of the American Academy of Dramatic Arts. He abandoned Harvard for the Academy and, after a year's preparation, started his stage career in 1909 by appearing in *Polly of the Circus.* He spent four years in road companies, worked as an extra in Hollywood, played in vaudeville, and joined Margaret Anglin's repertory as an actor and assistant stage manager. He regards his five years with Miss Anglin as his university education. The first World War found him in the infantry sporting a corporal's stripes. When he reappeared on Broadway, it was to play in Kaufman and Connelly's celebrated farce-comedy *Dulcy.* He also began to write plays, in collaboration with Bertrand Robinson: *Tommy, Your Uncle Dudley* (1929), and *Oh Promise Me* (1930). After another term in Hollywood, he directed *Gay Divorce,* starring Fred Astaire on Broadway, and both wrote and directed the successful college play *She Loves Me Not* (1933), which started the acting career of Burgess Meredith. The year 1935 saw a collaboration with Damon Runyon, *A Slight Case of Murder.* Lindsay and Crouse were introduced to each other in the summer of 1934 by Vinton Freedley, who was then trying to launch the musical comedy *Anything Goes,* for which he needed a new story. Mr. Lindsay was then recuperating from the "flu" and needed support from Mr. Crouse, who is a generous dispenser of sunshine, humor, and wit.

Mr. Crouse hailed from Findlay, Ohio, where he had been born in 1893 to an editor and owner of various Midwestern newspapers. Mathematics was the vulnerable part of Mr. Crouse's education, and it lost him an appointment to Annapolis. Journalism and the theatre gained thereby. Mr. Crouse did a two years' stint as reporter on the Cincinnati *Commercial-Tribune,* moved to the Kansas City *Star,* and after seeing service with the Navy during the first World War, worked on New York newspapers and graduated into the ranks of columnists on the *Post.* He published books (one of them was on Currier and Ives) and wrote two musical comedies; one of these was the successful Joe Cook show *Hold Your Horses.*

The first Lindsay-Crouse collaboration, *Anything Goes,* with music by Cole Porter, was a striking success. The next, somewhat less successful, collaborative effort was the musical *Red, Hot and Blue* (1936), which introduced Bob Hope to the public. Then the friends served Ed Wynn with the clever musical satire on "merchants of death" and international espionage, *Hooray for What.* This was in 1937, and in that year they began speculating on a dramatization of Clarence Day's books of reminiscence which eventuated in the memorable *Life with Father* in 1939. Next, Lindsay and Crouse branched out as the producers of *Arsenic and Old Lace* and *The Hasty Heart,* and put a portion of their fabulous earnings into the purchase of the Hudson Theatre. They did not lay down their pens, however. They tried to contribute to war-time morale with *Strip for*

Action, which fell short of success, and they retrieved their laurels with *State of the Union* in the season of 1945-46.

State of the Union, we must add, did not represent a commitment to political writing, as one could infer from the substantial presence of domestic comedy in the play. In the season of 1948-49, they produced their overdue sequel to *Life with Father*, the quite enchanting if rather tenuous comedy *Life with Mother*. They then made an even more strenuous return to unadulterated show-business by producing the musical *Call Me Madam*, and astutely cast Ethel Merman in the role of our first lady ambassador. And at this writing they are completely upsetting the public's equanimity with the farce-melodrama *Remains to Be Seen*, a fabrication of theirs to which they have added non-verbal percussion with an ampler set of drum-traps than any seen on the stage rather than under it. It is, however, conceivable that when the genial partners appear before the judgment seat, *State of the Union* will speak more loudly or at least more persuasively for them.

ACT ONE

Scene One

The study in the home of James Conover in Washington, D. C. It is a wood-paneled library. There is a recessed window upstage, with the curtains drawn. The wall brackets and lamps are lighted. There is a large desk at the right of the room and several easy chairs. At the left of the room there is a table on which stands a tray containing bottles of liquor, soda, glasses and a container filled with ice cubes.

Four persons are seated in the room: James Conover, a quiet-spoken man of about 60, not quite the type the audience would expect as a politician. Mrs. Katherine Thorndyke, known hereafter as Kay, a handsome woman in her late thirties, the kind you would find talking to men more often than women. Spike MacManus, who has been for years a Washington political reporter, pudgy and genial and with a rough charm. Grant Matthews, a distinguished-looking man in his middle forties, a successful business man, but also much more than that.

James Conover is seated to the right of his desk engaged in a telephone conversation. His share of the conversation consists almost entirely of listening, with an occasional murmur of assent. The other three are obviously waiting for him to finish. Their attention wanders away from Conover to themselves. Kay consults her handbag mirror and passes her hand over her hair. Grant takes a fresh cigarette and lights it from the one he is about to discard. Spike takes a paper out of his pocket, glances at some notes on it and puts it back. Kay looks toward Grant and, when their eyes meet, she smiles and nods an indication that everything is going all right.

In reply Grant shrugs noncommittally. They both look at Spike, who makes a reassuring gesture with his hands, palms down.

Conover interrupts the flow of conversation coming from the other end of the telephone, speaking with quiet authority.

———

CONOVER *(into telephone)*. Dave, I'm sorry, but I have to give the Senator a free hand in this. *(Pause)* Has this occurred to you? The reason you and the Senator are fighting over this one appointment is because we lost the last election and the one before that and the one before that! We have to win the next one! The Senator feels that an appointment will strengthen the party in his district. So there's no argument. *(Short pause)* Certainly, any time. Good night, Dave. *(He hangs up and turns to the others)*

SPIKE. You're being pretty tough on Tisdale, Jim. If he can't swing that appointment, how's he going to stay out of jail?

CONOVER. Spike, you know too much.

SPIKE *(grinning)*. I've been blackmailing Tisdale for years. He's one of my best sources.

CONOVER. Spike's just trying to show off in front of his boss, Mrs. Thorndyke.

KAY. He doesn't have to. I'm not the only publisher who thinks Spike's the best newspaper man in Washington.

CONOVER. Well, I think Walter Lippmann writes a little better.

KAY. Oh, we wouldn't let Spike write a paragraph.

SPIKE. They even took away my typewriter—but they gave me six telephones.

KAY. Spike knows more about what's going on in Washington than you and Bob Hannegan put together. That's why I'm willing to lend him to you for the campaign—but I want him back!

CONOVER *(half kidding)*. Too bad you weren't running Dewey's campaign, Spike.

SPIKE. Well, if Dewey had listened to me when I saw him in Pawling he'd have had a much better chance. *(The others look at Spike with smiling disbelief)* I didn't say he'd have had a *chance*. I said he'd have had a much better chance.

KAY *(to Conover)*. Jim, do you think you're going to have trouble stopping Dewey?

CONOVER *(quietly)*. He's built up a strong organization. But I think it can be done. That's why we have to start early.

SPIKE. Republicans never have nominated a defeated candidate. That's on the record. The boys feel that way about Dewey, don't they, Jim?

CONOVER. I can't speak for the Republican Party . . .

SPIKE. Hell, who can these days? But, Jim, you're certainly strong enough to stop anyone on the horizon now. So why can't you name your own man?

CONOVER. If we get a strong candidate in '48 we've got better than a fighting chance. Jim, my newspapers are city papers, but small cities, with a rural circulation too. They make a pretty good sounding board. Here's what comes back to me. The party's best chance in '48 is to put up a candidate who's never been identified with politics.

SPIKE. Look what happened in '40. If the election had been held a month after Philadelphia, Willkie would have won.

KAY. Yes, and why? Because people had the idea Willkie was someone you politicians didn't want.

SPIKE *(to Conover)*. You wouldn't mind if that impression got around about the candidate in '48, would you?

CONOVER. Not if the candidate was someone I *did* want.

SPIKE. That's what I mean.

CONOVER. It seems to me at this point we ought to hear from Mr. Matthews. *(They all look at Grant.)*

GRANT. Let me make this clear—I don't want to be President of the United States. *(They smile at his vehemence.)*

CONOVER. That decision may not be in your hands.

GRANT. Mr. Conover, I can understand Mrs. Thorndyke telling me I should be President. But you—you must be talking about somebody else.

CONOVER. You're a national figure—and you have been ever since the war started.

SPIKE. Is Henry Kaiser a national figure? For every ship he's built you've built a hundred planes.

KAY. Grant, everybody in the country knows you and everybody respects you.

GRANT. Oh, they know I make good airplanes and I've made a hell of a lot of them.

SPIKE. They know more than that. *(He rises and goes to Grant)* When you fought the aluminum combine! When you slugged it out with the War Production Board until they broke those bottlenecks! The time you talked back to that Senate Investigating Committee! Three times you crowded the war off the front page!

CONOVER. Mrs. Thorndyke and I aren't the only Republicans who've been thinking about you. Those speeches you've been making—especially that last one in Cleveland.

GRANT *(putting his glass down on the table)*. When I made that speech in Cleveland I was trying to put both parties on the spot. I wasn't speaking as a Republican. I was speaking as a citizen. *(He rises and moves toward Conover, as he warms to his subject)* I'm worried about what's happening in this country. We're splitting apart. Business, labor, farmers, cattlemen, lumbermen—they're all trying to get the biggest bite of the apple. We talk about the war being over—well, we've got a war on here at home now—a civil war—an economic war. That's what I said in Cleveland. That's why I was surprised you asked me down here.

CONOVER. Why were you surprised?

GRANT. Because you politicians are trying to make capital out of this situation—you appeal to each one of these pressure groups just to get their votes. But let me tell you something. I don't think that's good politics. A lot of people wrote me after that speech in Cleveland. *(With a grin)* Of course I will admit that the business men liked best what I said about labor, and the unions said I was absolutely right about big business, and the farmers were pretty pleased with what I said about everybody but the farmers. *(He becomes serious again)* But they all knew what I was talking about. They know we've all got to work in harness, if we're going to take our place in this world. And if we don't there won't be any world. We may be kidding ourselves that our party is going to win in '48—that the people here will want a change the way they did in England—but if our party does win, whoever is President has to have guts enough to pull us together and keep us together. I'm for that man, Mr. Conover—I don't care who he is.

KAY. That man is you, Grant.

GRANT. You're prejudiced, Kay. *(To Conover)* The boys who are back from fighting the war deserve something better . . .

(There is a knock on the door.)

CONOVER. Go ahead, finish.

GRANT. No, that may be important.

CONOVER. Come in.

(Norah, a middle-aged maid, wearing glasses, enters. She has a slip of paper in her hand.)

NORAH. I'm sorry to interrupt you. It's a telephone call. *(She hands Conover the slip of paper. He looks at it)*

CONOVER. Thank you. You go to bed, Norah. I'll take the rest of the calls myself.

NORAH *(starting out)*. Thank you, Mr. Conover. *(Turns back at the door)* It's turned cool. I've put an extra blanket in your room, Mrs. Thorndyke. Yours, too, Mr. Matthews.

GRANT. Thank you, Norah. Good night.

KAY. Good night, Norah.

(Norah exits.)

CONOVER. Do you mind? I'll try to make this short. *(He picks up telephone and speaks into it)* Hello, there! How are you? *(Pause)* Oh—can you call me on that in the morning? *(Pause)* Well, hold on. I'll have to take this in another room. Spike MacManus is here.

(Conover rises, holding the telephone. Spike crosses to the desk, reaching for the telephone.)

SPIKE. I'll hang up as soon as you're on.

CONOVER *(giving him a look, then extending the telephone to Kay)*. Mrs. Thorndyke, do you mind? Spike has a little Drew Pearson blood. *(Conover exits)*

SPIKE *(to Kay)*. If he doesn't want me to hear that, it's something we ought to hear.

(There is a long pause, Kay holding the receiver to her ear.)

KAY *(watching Spike, but speaking into the telephone)*. Are you on? All right, I'll hang up. *(To amuse Spike she listens for a moment before putting the receiver down. Grant has been pacing the room nervously. Spike sits in Conover's chair and picks up a volume of Who's Who that is on Conover's desk and opens it)*

GRANT. I've never felt so uncomfortable in my life. When he comes back, I'm going to tell him to drop the whole subject.

KAY *(going to Grant)*. I didn't come all the way to Washington to tell Jim Conover not to talk about something we came down here to talk about.

GRANT *(taking Kay's hands in his)*. Now, Kay, we've had a lot of fun between ourselves dreaming about all this—but damn it, to ask a man like Conover to take it seriously . . .

KAY *(pushing Grant into his chair)*. Now behave yourself. Mr. Conover and I are going to talk about you and you're going to sit right down and listen.

(Grant looks up and grins.)

GRANT. All right, I'll listen. But if Conover is serious about considering me, the Republican Party must be pretty desperate.

SPIKE *(looking up from the book)*. You're damn right they're desperate!

GRANT. But Conover—he's always played along with the reactionaries. Why should he be interested in me?

SPIKE. If Conover isn't the guy who picks the Republican candidate for '48, he might as well turn Democrat.

KAY. You know, Grant, the last thing he has to boast about is Warren Harding. *(Spike is studying the book in his lap.)*

SPIKE. And don't think he isn't serious about you! There was a bookmark in this *Who's Who* at your page. You know this even impresses me. *(He runs his finger down a page)* Twelve boards of directors! Say, there's a lot of swell angles about you! For instance, Honorary President of the Society for the Preservation of Wild Life. *(He puts the book back on the desk)* How can we use that in the campaign?

KAY. Spike, I don't think the wild-life vote is very important.

SPIKE. No, I mean from a publicity angle. Say, for instance, a picture in *Life.* *(He points to Grant)* You and a grateful duck.

(Conover enters.)

CONOVER. After that call I need a drink.

SPIKE *(pointing to the telephone)*. Oh, Senator Taft!

CONOVER *(laughs, then turns to mix a drink)*. Anyone else?

SPIKE. I'll tend bar. *(Spike mixes drinks and serves them during the following)*

CONOVER. Oh, thank you.

KAY *(to Conover)*. Jim, do you think Taft's serious about being a candidate himself?

CONOVER. You can always figure that Senator Taft is serious. *(He returns to his chair and sits)* He'll go into the convention with Ohio and some Southern delegations.

GRANT. Don't kid yourselves. Truman isn't going to be easy to beat. He's made some strong appointments.

KAY. He's also made some weak ones.

CONOVER. Those are the ones that interest me—the weak ones. Between now and the campaign the Administration can run into some ugly trouble.

SPIKE. Well, all we can do is hope. *(He places drinks in front of Kay and Conover)*

KAY. Jim, Labor's already asking Truman for more than he can give them. I think we've got a chance for the labor vote if we have the right candidate.

SPIKE. That rules out Sewell Avery!

KAY. But it doesn't rule out Grant. *(She rises)* No employer in the country's got a better labor record. And business is bound to go along with him. Jim, don't you see the strength we have in Mr. Matthews? Phil Murray and Sewell Avery would both vote for him.

GRANT. I'm not so sure—because I wouldn't promise either one of them anything.

SPIKE. You'd have to promise them something. *(He hands Grant a drink and pauses for thought)* Still, Dewey outpromised Roosevelt and it didn't get him anywhere.

GRANT. That's one of our most serious problems. There's not enough difference between the two parties.

SPIKE. Well, not to change the subject, I would like to pause at this moment and take a one-man Gallup poll. What do you think of Mr. Matthews' chances, Jim?

CONOVER. That's not an easy question to answer. I haven't got much to go on. After Mr. Matthews makes his speech here Monday night I'd know a little more about what the feeling is here in Washington. Is Mrs. Matthews coming down to hear you speak?

GRANT *(amiably)*. No, she takes bringing up the children more seriously than she does my speeches. And I think she's right. This has all been very flattering—but as I said to Mrs. Thorndyke while you were out of the room—let's drop the whole idea.

KAY *(quickly. To Conover)*. Jim, Tuesday Grant's starting a tour of his plants. Everywhere he's going he's been invited to speak.

SPIKE. Minneapolis, Seattle, San Francisco, Los Angeles, Denver, Wichita, Detroit—

KAY. If Grant made those speeches, at the end of the tour could you tell him whether he had a chance, or whether we should give up the whole idea?

CONOVER *(with a little thought)*. That covers a lot of territory. Yes, I think if Mr. Matthews made those speeches I could be pretty definite.

KAY *(going to Grant)*. Grant, you've got to go along with us that far! You've got to make those speeches!

GRANT *(looking up at Kay)*. Kay, I'm going to be pretty busy on this trip. I've got problems in every one of those plants. I've got to do my damnedest to keep those men working. Besides, I wish I knew how much you had to do with those invitations for me to speak.

KAY *(decisively)*. Spike, you're going to make the trip with him. You've been telling everyone for years how to run a political campaign. Now we'll find out whether you can run one. The bureau can get along without you for a couple of weeks. It will be a vacation for you.

CONOVER. It will be a vacation for everyone in Washington. *(Briskly)* Now that we've reached that decision, there's a lot for all of us to talk about. On this tour, Mr. Matthews . . . *(Telephone rings)* Damn! Pardon me! *(Conover answers the telephone)* Hello. *(With some interest)* Oh, yes, I've been waiting to hear from you. *(Looks around room unhappily)* Hold on. Wait a minute. *(He rises)* Spike, why don't you go home? *(He hands the telephone to Kay)* Do you mind, Mrs. Thorndyke?

KAY *(rises and takes the telephone)*. I'm glad you trust publishers.

CONOVER *(going to the door)*. Just Republican publishers.

SPIKE. I thought it was agreed we were all to trust each other.

CONOVER. Only when we're in the same room. *(He exits)*

SPIKE *(gleefully rubbing his hands)*. Mr. Conover has just leaped gracefully onto the front seat of the bandwagon.

GRANT. Take it easy, Spike. Conover hasn't brought up the payoff yet.

SPIKE. Well, there's one promise I want.

GRANT. What?

SPIKE. That I'm not to be the next Postmaster General.

GRANT. I'll settle for that, Spike—you're not the next Postmaster General. And that's the only commitment I'm going to make.

SPIKE. You settled awfully quick. I just threw that in for a laugh. *(He turns to*

Kay) Mrs. Thorndyke—tell Sir Galahad here . . .

KAY *(into the telephone).* Are you on? All right, I'll hang up. *(Again to amuse Spike, she keeps her ear to the receiver. Suddenly her expression changes sharply. She presses down the disconnector with her free hand, then releases it immediately and continues to listen in, giving the men a warning gesture. Grant rises indignantly and starts toward her)*

GRANT. Kay!

(Spike stops him with a gesture. Grant obviously disapproves and walks unhappily away, as if he will have none of it. Spike beams in admiration of Kay at first, but as she listens in and flashes a look toward Grant, Spike realizes it is a serious matter and his smile vanishes. Even Grant's attention is arrested. The two men stand watching Kay. She hangs up and goes immediately to Grant, speaking quickly and with deep concern.)

KAY. It's a report from New York. He's had someone looking you up. They've picked up some gossip about you and me.

SPIKE. Oh—oh!

KAY. And there's been talk about Mary, too—Mary and some Major.

SPIKE. Who's Mary?

KAY. Mrs. Matthews.

SPIKE. Oh—ho!

GRANT. What Major? What's his name?

KAY. I couldn't get his name.

GRANT. What'd the name sound like?

(Kay gestures him to be quiet.)

KAY. Sh-h. He'll be back in a minute. *(She raises her voice, making a pretense of normal conversation)* Of course, Spike, that's one way of looking at it, but you never can be sure.

GRANT *(sitting down).* A Major!

SPIKE *(to Grant as Conover enters).* On the other hand, if what you say is true, Mr. Matthews, that makes the migratory flamingo a very interesting bird.

CONOVER. What makes the flamingo an interesting bird, Spike?

SPIKE *(caught short, but not very).* Tell him what you just told us, Mr. Matthews.

GRANT *(at no loss whatever).* I don't think Mr. Conover's interested in the wild life of America.

CONOVER. Staying up this late is a little more wild life than I'm used to. I think we'd better call it a night.

(They are caught flatfooted by his tone of dismissal.)

SPIKE *(tentatively).* Nothing else you want to bring up, Jim?

CONOVER. Not now. *(Grant rises)* Spike, you may have a little trouble getting a taxi. Good night. *(Conover shakes hands with Spike)*

SPIKE. Good night, Jim. Good night, Boss. *(He turns to Grant)* Grant, if the lights are still on in the White House, I'll drop in and tell the Trumans to start packing.

KAY. Spike, you'd better get off some wires accepting those speaking dates for Grant.

CONOVER. I'd like to give some of those cities a little more thought. *(Spike gets his hat and crosses to the door)* Tomorrow's time enough for that, isn't it?

GRANT. Yes—I guess so. *(He goes to Conover)* Well, Mr. Conover, if I never get any closer to the White House than this, it's been a very pleasant evening. I'll say good night, too.

CONOVER. You and I might take time to finish our drinks.

KAY. I haven't finished mine— *(No one asks her to stay)* I'll finish it in my room. *(She starts to rise, picking up her bag and drink)*

CONOVER. I thought Mr. Matthews and I might chat for a few minutes longer.

KAY. I'll run along then. I can't tell you how grateful we are for your having us here. Good night. Good night, Grant.

GRANT. Good night, Kay.

KAY *(she starts to door, stops and turns back to Conover; Spike is holding door open for her).* Jim, I want you to know how completely we trust you. *(She goes directly to Grant)* Good night, darling. *(She puts her arms around him and they kiss. She starts out again)*

CONOVER. Mrs. Thorndyke! *(Kay stops and turns)* You might as well finish your drink here. That's what I was going to talk about. *(Kay raises her eyebrows, comes back and sits down. Spike closes the door, and drops his hat on a chair)* Naturally, Mr. Matthews, when your name first came up as a possible candidate, I made some inquiries. It seems there's been some talk about you and Mrs. Thorndyke.

GRANT. What kind of talk?

CONOVER *(easily).* I think you know what I mean when I say talk.

KAY. We wouldn't pretend to deny there's basis for it, but it can't be very widespread.

GRANT. Kay, let Mr. Conover tell us what he's heard.

CONOVER. That's about all. There's been some gossip. That's nothing unusual, and as long as it's about a man who makes airplanes, even though you're very well known, I don't think it would spread a great deal, but the minute you become a public figure . . .

KAY. You think it might be used against Mr. Matthews?

CONOVER. Not openly. What it would come down to would be a whispering campaign.

GRANT *(firmly)*. Frankly, Mr. Conover, I don't give a damn for the kind of opinion that sort of thing would influence.

CONOVER. I haven't any respect for it, either; but I have to reckon with it. You see, Mr. Matthews, while Mrs. Thorndyke happens to be divorced, you're a married man.

GRANT. Well, if you think that's a major— *(His mind sticks momentarily on the word)* —a vital factor . . . Kay, that seems to settle it.

KAY. Wait a minute, Grant! Jim, there must be some way around this.

CONOVER. Yes, there's a very obvious one.

GRANT. So? What is it?

CONOVER. I'd like to see your wife with you when you speak here Monday night, and I'd like to see her make this trip with you.

GRANT *(laughing)*. That's not the solution. If Mary knew that I even thought of myself as President of the United States . . .

KAY. Jim, we've got to think of something else. It's a little difficult for me to talk about Mrs. Matthews in this situation but—you've seen the kind of wife—the more important her husband becomes the more determined she is to make him feel unimportant.

GRANT. Now, wait a minute, Kay! Be fair to Mary. *(To Conover)* I don't want you to get the wrong impression of my wife, Mr. Conover. She's no shrew. She's a damn bright woman.

KAY. Grant, you know Mary's always cutting you down.

GRANT. I can't deny that. Still, I suppose her criticism of me has been valuable sometimes. *(To Conover)* But a man doe'n reach a saturation point.

CONOVER. If you become a candidate you'll have to take a lot of criticism.

SPIKE. Yes, your wife might be good training for you. Toughen you up.

KAY. I think it's more important that Grant should have his self-confidence.

CONOVER *(sitting on the edge of his desk)*. The most important thing of all is to kill this gossip. We haven't got a chance unless we do. The American people like to think of a married candidate as happily married. They want to see him and his wife together. They like to see them make the campaign together. It's an American tradition. You'd have to face that sooner or later. I think the sooner you face it the better.

GRANT. Yes, Mary may solve the whole situation for us. I'm not so sure she would campaign with me even if I asked her to.

CONOVER. Why don't you call her and find out?

(Kay and Grant exchange a look of mutual inquiry.)

GRANT *(to Conover)*. Why not? *(Conover picks up the telephone and dials)*

SPIKE. There's been that gossip about every candidate except Herbert Hoover. They didn't pull it on Hoover because nobody would have believed it

CONOVER *(into telephone)*. This is Dupont 4108. I want a New York call. I want to speak to Mrs. Grant Matthews at . . . *(He looks inquiringly at Grant)*

GRANT. Plaza 5-8249.

CONOVER *(into phone)*. Plaza 5-8249. *(He rises and hands the telephone to Grant)* Invite her to stay here, of course.

GRANT *(taking the telephone)*. There's no way of a man being elected President before his wife hears about it, is there? *(He sits beside the desk)* Hello. Well, put it through as soon as you can and call me. *(He hangs up and there is an uneasy pause. They are not looking at each other. Finally Spike speaks up brightly)*

SPIKE. Shall we dance?

(Jim Conover gives him a look that's an answer, but not to his question.)

GRANT. Mr. Conover, I'm glad there's a delay in that call because before it comes through there's something I'd like to ask you.

CONOVER. Yes?

GRANT. If it works out that we can go

ahead, you and I, what are you going to expect of me?

CONOVER. I'd expect you to be elected.

GRANT. Mr. Conover, I'm inexperienced in politics, but I am not—shall I say—completely naive. Let's put it this way—if I were elected, naturally I'd be very grateful to you. Is there any particular way in which you'd expect me to show my gratitude?

KAY. Grant, aren't you being a little premature? *(To Conover)* It's probably pre-natal influence. Grant was a premature baby.

SPIKE. You were? Say, drop that into an interview some time. There may be some votes in that. There are a lot of bastards who think they were seven-month babies.

CONOVER. In answer to your question, Mr. Matthews, if you mean have I a list of Federal appointments in my pocket?—No.

GRANT. I'd be very glad to see any list of names you wanted to show me. I just want it to be clear I'm not making any commitments.

CONOVER. I can't ask for more than an open mind. Mrs. Thorndyke said you two came down here for my advice. Well, politics is my business. If we do get into a campaign together I hope you'll be open-minded about any advice I might give you then.

GRANT. I'd welcome it—only I can't promise I'd always follow it.

KAY. Now, Grant, don't turn down advice before you get it.

GRANT *(to Conover, with a disarming laugh)*. All right. Give me some!

CONOVER *(amused, but still serious)*. Well, in that list of speaking dates, you mentioned Minneapolis. I wouldn't speak there. You might just stir up trouble. That's Stassen territory. The local boys would resent it and you might start a backfire.

GRANT. That's damn good advice. I'll take it. How do you feel about Stassen?

CONOVER. There's a good deal of opposition to him in the party. Oh, that prompts me to venture some more advice, if you don't mind?

GRANT. No—shoot!

CONOVER. If you make this preliminary tour, keep whatever you have to say pretty general. Don't be too specific.

GRANT. There I'm afraid I can't go all the way with you. The only reason I have for speaking at all is because there are some things I feel deeply about.

KAY. Grant, it's only that at this early stage . . .

GRANT. No, Kay! I'm not going to pull any punches! I want that understood!

KAY. Grant, if you keep on being belligerent about your honesty, we'll begin to suspect you.

CONOVER *(serenely)*. Mr. Matthews, most candidates have to spend a lot of time explaining things they wish they hadn't said. You're not carrying that weight because you haven't said very much yet. Your danger at this point might be in raising minor issues that would come back to plague you later.

KAY. Grant, this isn't the airplane business. You're used to dealing with tangible things. I know what Jim's talking about because I have to go out after circulation. You'll have to go out after votes.

GRANT. Oh, I know you have to appeal for votes. But I think what I believe in . . .

(The telephone rings. Spike picks it up.)

SPIKE *(into telephone)*. Hello. New York? Just a minute. *(He hands the telephone to Grant. Kay goes to a chair on the farther side of the room and sits)*

GRANT *(into telephone)*. Hello, Hello. What's that? *(With a little impatience)* Well, get them back. No, I'll hang on.

CONOVER. Have you your speech for Monday night prepared?

GRANT. Yes. Want to look at it tomorrow? I'll listen to anything you have to say.

KAY. And on the tour you listen to Spike. He can be very valuable.

GRANT *(grinning)*. If I know Spike, he's going to give me plenty of advice.

SPIKE. No, Mr. Matthews, my big job is to humanize you.

GRANT *(in amused surprise)*. Oh, is it?

SPIKE. I've got a lot of things dreamed up. Do you know what first sold Willkie to the country as a human being? His going on Information Please. He came over as a regular guy and he held his own, too.

GRANT. Just a minute! I'm no Wendell Willkie—I'm willing to take on Harry Truman, but not John Kieran.

SPIKE. We've got to do something to counteract those speeches.

GRANT. Counteract them! Well then, why am I making them?

SPIKE. Oh, no, you've got to make them. But sometimes your speeches get a little fancy. We don't want people to think you're stuffy.

GRANT. Do you know, Spike, you sound just like my wife. (*At this moment he hears his wife's voice on the telephone and speaks to her with some surprise*) Hello, Mary. (*Pause*) I'm in Washington. How's Joyce? (*Pause*) Doctor been there today? (*Pause*) That's fine . . . If she's that well, Sonny won't catch it now. (*Pause*) Mary, I'm making another speech down here Monday night. (*Pause—then somewhat indignantly*) No, they *asked* me to! I'd like to have you come down and listen to it, if it wouldn't bore you too much (*Pause*) As a matter of fact, I won't *be* home for a few weeks. I'm making a tour of the plants. How'd you like to make the trip with me?—I wish you would. We haven't made the circuit together in a long time. (*Pause*) But how about coming down here, anyway? We'll be house guests at Jim Conover's. (*Pause*) Conover—a friend of mine, but in spite of that you'll like him. (*Pause*) Get here tomorrow night—It doesn't matter how late. I'll send the plane back for you— Swell! (*Pause*) Bring enough clothes for the trip, anyway. We can talk it over when you get here. Mary, you'll need a dinner dress here Monday night. It's a banquet. (*Gaily*) You'll get my speech for dessert. (*Pause*) What? (*Not so gaily*) All right— Of course you'll look a little funny sitting there with earmuffs on. Good night. (*He hangs up*) I'm not sure the Presidency's worth it.

CONOVER. She's coming?

GRANT. Yes, Heaven help me.

KAY. Grant, you know what that means. If Mary's coming here I've got to go home tomorrow.

CONOVER. I confess that would ease the housing situation. The National Committee seems to think I run a hotel.

KAY (*starting for the door*). Well, for the next few weeks I'll be sitting alone in New York, while you tour the country with your wife.

SPIKE (*thoughtfully*). Politics makes strange bedfellows.

(*Kay looks at him sharply. Spike catches the look, picks up his hat and starts out of the room.*)

CURTAIN

SCENE TWO

The next night.

A bedroom in Jim Conover's house. There is a double bed with bed tables on each side of bed. There are two over-stuffed chairs with a small table between them. The entrance to the bedroom is up-stage to the left. There is a window down-stage left. On the right there is a door leading to a dressing room and bathroom offstage. Below the door is a desk with a chair.

Grant, wearing horn-rimmed glasses, is discovered alone, seated at the desk, editing the loose pages of his typewritten speech. There is a knock at the door.

———

GRANT (*taking off his glasses*). Come in!

(*Conover enters.*)

CONOVER. How's the speech coming along?

GRANT. All right, I guess. What Spike said last night had me worried. I'm trying to unfancy it a little bit.

CONOVER. Don't let Spike worry you. I think it's very good. When you finish, drop back downstairs. I think it would be a good idea to have the boys see as much of you as possible. You made a very good impression at dinner.

GRANT. I was thrown a little by the way Senator Fosdick kept yessing me. He's an America Firster, isn't he?

CONOVER. He was—until he was defeated. (*He starts to leave*) I'll see you later then. (*Turns back*) Oh! I came up to tell you I've sent the car down to the airport.

GRANT (*looking at his watch*). He might have quite a wait. I don't think Mary will be in much before midnight. (*A little disturbed*) If she could have told me when she was getting in I could have met her myself.

(*Spike enters.*)

SPIKE. Jim, Governor Dunn just arrived.

CONOVER (*to Grant*). Oh, that's fine!)

want you to meet him. He can be very valuable to you in the Northwest. I'm glad he dropped in.

SPIKE. Like hell you are! He brought his bags with him.

CONOVER. Oh, damn! Where am I going to put him? Well, I guess I'll have to take him into my room, and I was hoping for a good night's sleep. Spike, you're an expert in these matters. Why do all Governors snore?

SPIKE. It's an occupational disease.

GRANT. Where are you putting Mary? (*Conover is taken a little by surprise.*)

CONOVER. In here with you. If we're going to create the impression about you two that we want to, this would be a good start.

GRANT (*troubled*). I don't think she'd welcome the idea. We rushed into this decision and it's been on my conscience ever since. Look, Jim, when Mary finds out what's up, she can still say no. But moving her in here with me tonight . . .

CONOVER (*thinking*). Well, Senator Fosdick's room is about the only one. He's in there alone. But where can I put the Senator? There's nothing left but the billiard table.

SPIKE. Why not? The son-of-a-bitch didn't even carry his own state.

CONOVER. I'll put him on a cot somewhere. Come on down with me. I want you to meet the Governor.

SPIKE. He's got to finish that speech. I want to take it with me tonight.

GRANT. I'm almost through.

CONOVER (*turning at the door*). Shall I send up a drink?

SPIKE. Send up a couple.

(*Conover exits.*)

GRANT. Why are you in such a hurry? There's plenty of time to get this copied before tomorrow night.

SPIKE. All the wire services will want it by noon, and even if they don't want it they're going to get it. If they don't have it in advance you may only get a couple of paragraphs. Are you out on a limb anywhere in here? (*He picks up first few pages of the manuscript and starts glancing through it*) Because we could play it the other way. Not give out any copies— then you could always claim you've been misquoted.

GRANT. I wish I was as sure as you seem to be that I'll be quoted at all.

SPIKE. This isn't as bad as I thought it was going to be.

GRANT. Those changes were all made for your benefit.

SPIKE (*placing one sheet in front of Grant*). This spot in here sounds a little like a speech. (*He points*)

GRANT. Damn it!—It *is* a speech!

SPIKE. That's what I meant.

(*There is a knock on the door.*)

GRANT. Come in!

(*Norah enters, loaded down with two bags and a hatbox.*)

NORAH (*from doorway*). These are Mrs. Matthews' bags.

GRANT (*rising*). Oh, is my wife here?

NORAH. She just came. I'll put these in the dressing room.

(*Grant stops her.*)

GRANT. No, they don't go there. Mrs. Matthews is in another room.

NORAH (*bewildered*). What other room? (*Conover enters.*)

CONOVER. Grant, Mrs. Matthews is here! (*Mary follows Conover in. Mary is an attractive woman in her thirties, brisk and self-assured. She is dressed in a smart traveling suit and hat.*)

GRANT. Hello, dear.

MARY. Hello, Grant. (*She goes to Grant and they kiss*)

GRANT. I didn't expect you to get here this early.

MARY. I think we broke the record— and both my ear drums.

GRANT. Spike, I want you to meet Mrs. Matthews. (*To Mary*) This is Mr. Mac-Manus.

MARY. How do you do, Mr. MacManus?

SPIKE (*standing near window*). Hello, Mrs. Matthews.

GRANT. You seem to have met Mr. Conover.

MARY. Oh, yes, downstairs. (*She smiles at Conover*) It's so nice of you to have us here. I'm really quite excited. I hope you'll notice, Grant, I've packed for the whole trip. (*She points to the bags, which Norah is still holding, then speaks to Norah*) Just put those down anywhere.

NORAH. I was told you were going to be in another room. (*Norah looks toward Conover*)

CONOVER. Leave the bags here for a minute, Norah. You're moving Senator Fosdick.

NORAH. Again?

CONOVER. Put him in the south bedroom with Mr. Godfrey.

NORAH. The Commissioner's in there with Mr. Godfrey.

CONOVER. We have another cot, haven't we?

NORAH. That army cot.

MARY. That's nonsense. Don't move Senator Fosdick. Grant and I can stay here. *(She looks around at the group)* We're really married. *(Conover hesitates)* Unless the rest of the Senate is in here with Grant.

GRANT. Mr. Conover just thought you'd be more comfortable with a room to yourself.

MARY *(to Norah)*. I'll stay here. *(Norah crosses to the dressing room with the bags. Grant holds the door open for her. Mary goes to the bed and throws hat and bag on it. She starts removing her gloves)* After all, Senator Fosdick's an isolationist. I think he ought to be isolated.

SPIKE *(grinning)*. I'm going to like you.

(Mary answers him with a smile.)

NORAH *(at dressing-room door)*. Shall I unpack for you, Ma'am?

MARY. Just the small bag. And you can take the shoes out of my hat box. *(Norah starts out)* Oh, there's a print dress in the suitcase I'd like to wear tomorrow. Could it be pressed for me?

NORAH. Surely. *(She exits into the dressing room with the bags)*

MARY *(pressing her ears)*. Those plane trips always leave me deaf.

GRANT. If that lasts through tomorrow you'll be spared hearing my speech.

MARY *(smiling at him)*. That's a little more than I could hope for.

(The others are politely amused. There is a knock on the door. Stevens, the butler, enters with two drinks on a tray. He's a little bewildered to find four people.)

STEVENS. Scotch and soda?

MARY. I'm not as deaf as I thought I was. What a perfect host! *(She takes one of the highballs)*

CONOVER. I'll take the other one, Stevens. *(To Grant)* You and Spike get your drinks downstairs. I want you to meet the Governor.

(Stevens exits.)

GRANT. Want to meet a Governor, Mary?

MARY. I'd like to get a little better acquainted with this highball.

CONOVER. That was my idea. You and I, let's finish our drinks quietly up here. *(To Grant)* We'll join you later.

SPIKE. How about the rest of this Gettysburg Address? Finished with it?

GRANT. Yes, I think the end's all right. Take it along. *(He hands Spike his speech)*

CONOVER. Spike, see that Grant and Governor Dunn get together.

SPIKE *(exiting)*. All right.

CONOVER. Grant, I'm sure the Governor will be very interested in meeting you.

GRANT *(with a touch of self-importance)*. I'll be glad to talk to him. *(Grant exits. Mary smiles at Conover and goes to one of the easy chairs and sits down)*

MARY. This is very pleasant.

CONOVER. It is for me.

MARY. Now I can boast that I've really been behind the scenes in Washington.

CONOVER. You certainly can! The Republican Party's been behind the scenes for fourteen years. However, that's about over. I think we're going to win next time.

MARY. If I needed an excuse to drink, that would be it. *(She lifts her glass to Conover. They drink)* But you'll have to offer the Democrats a good reason for voting Republican.

CONOVER. Your husband's been lecturing me along those lines.

MARY. Then I'd better change the subject. Grant can be very outspoken—but not by anybody I know.

CONOVER. Everything he said about politicians we had coming to us. I have a great admiration for your husband.

MARY. I'm many years ahead of you on that.

CONOVER. Of course, everyone admires him as a business man. What impresses me is that he doesn't limit his thinking to his own field. *(Conover sits in the other easy chair)* He has a very clear vision about the whole country—what it needs— what the world needs. Any man who sees our problems as clearly as he does—it imposes on him a certain responsibility.

MARY. Oh, I think you're sure of a big check from him.

(Conover smiles, then becomes serious.)

CONOVER. No, I mean a responsibility to the country. I've been trying to persuade your husband to take an active part in the Government.

MARY. Mr. Conover, Grant's talking politics is one thing—but he has a big enough job ahead of him—that is, if you know anything about his plans for post-war aviation.

CONOVER. I don't think his usefulness should be limited to that. I think the country will feel that way, too, after hearing what he says here tomorrow night, and the speeches he's going to make on this trip.

MARY. Is he going to make speeches on the trip?

CONOVER. Yes, in several places.

MARY (dismayed). Oh, dear. (Catching herself) Oh, I didn't mean that the way it sounded. Grant really can make a very good speech. But public appearances for me—I'm not good at that—I'm so uncomfortable. Would it be bad form if I just stayed quietly at the hotel and listened to him over the radio?

CONOVER. Yes, I'm afraid it would. It would defeat the whole purpose.

MARY. Purpose? What purpose?

CONOVER (avoiding a direct answer). Mrs. Matthews, you must know how concerned your husband is about this country's splitting apart—how deeply he feels that it must be held together.

MARY. Oh, yes. We've been talking about it for months. Grant's been trying to figure out what could be done.

CONOVER. I think you can help him do something about it.

MARY. Oh, not me. I just get angry! I can't read the newspapers any more! While the war was on we were a united country—we were fighting Germany and Japan. Now we're just fighting each other. No, I just get angry.

CONOVER. I'm glad you feel that strongly about it because it's important that wherever Grant goes now—wherever he makes these speeches—you're right there alongside of him.

(Mary senses for the first time that there is more than meets the ear in Conover's conversation.)

MARY. Why should that be important?

CONOVER (smoothly). Well, for a man who's going to be in the public-eye—people like to know his wife—like to see what she looks like—like to see the two of them together.

MARY (thoughtfully, putting her drink on the table). I was a little puzzled by Grant's invitation to make this trip with him.

CONOVER. Oh, Grant wants you to go along. These public appearances—they're my idea. It's just an old politician's habit of cashing in on an opportunity.

MARY (rising and walking away). It all fits in a little too neatly, Mr. Conover. I don't know whether you know—(She stops and looks at him sharply)—or perhaps you do—that Grant and I haven't been very close for the last year or so.

CONOVER. Wouldn't you prefer to create a contrary impression?

MARY. Oh, then you do know! Let's be open about this. These public appearances that Grant and I are to make together—are they designed to kill off any talk about my husband and Mrs. Thorndyke?

CONOVER. There's that kind of talk about every important man. But if there are any rumors about your husband, this would be a good chance to kill them. (Conover is watching Mary carefully) You see, Mrs. Matthews . . .

(Norah enters from the dressing room, carrying a print dress.)

NORAH. Is this the dress, Ma'am? (Mary stares at the dress and then comes to the surface.)

MARY. Oh, yes. But don't bother to press it.

NORAH. It's no trouble at all, Ma'am. It won't take me long. I'll have it back tonight.

MARY. No! Please! (But Norah has gone. Mary to Conover) May I use your telephone?

CONOVER. Certainly.

MARY. I want to get back to New York tonight if I can. (She goes to the telephone, picks up the receiver and starts to dial)

CONOVER (rising). Mrs. Matthews, I think any man who has a chance to become President of the United States deserves that chance.

(Mary slowly puts down the telephone, turns and stares at Conover in astonishment.)

MARY. President of the United States?

CONOVER. Yes. (There is a short pause) Don't you think he'd make a good President?

MARY (after consideration). Yes, I do.

CONOVER. Then you understand this goes beyond personal considerations. Let's not think of this in terms of you—and Grant—

MARY. —and Mrs. Thorndyke.

CONOVER. And Mrs. Thorndyke. I'm sure you will go along with us. You're a good citizen.

MARY. Right now, Mr. Conover, I'm not feeling like a good citizen! I'm feeling like a woman!

CONOVER. All right, as a woman!

MARY. As a woman, no, I won't go along with you. I resent being used!

CONOVER. Mrs. Matthews, let's think of it in terms of the country. That's what I've had to do. I am prepared to make some sacrifices.

MARY *(turning to him)*. What sacrifices?

CONOVER. Frankly, your husband isn't the kind of man a politician would prefer to deal with.

MARY. I've been wondering why any political party should choose Grant, knowing the things he stands for.

CONOVER. I want the people to make the choice.

MARY. That's damn white of you!

CONOVER. That's the purpose of this trip. I want the American people to get better acquainted with your husband. We don't know yet what's coming out of it, but I've told him that when this trip is over I can let him know whether to go ahead with the idea or forget the whole thing.

MARY. Oh, I don't think Grant could ever forget it. I'll bet he's running a pretty high fever right now. When he left the room I thought he walked as though he was trying to be two inches taller.

CONOVER. Mrs. Matthews, you see your husband at pretty close range. Take my word for it, he's a big man.

MARY. There's no argument about that, Mr. Conover. I know he's a big man and you know he's a big man. My bad days are when *he* knows he's a big man! *(She thinks for a moment)* You don't suppose there's any way of Grant being elected President and keeping it a secret from him, do you? *(Conover laughs. Mary sits on the side of the bed)* Is Grant speaking in Seattle?

CONOVER. Yes, why?

MARY. We were married in Seattle.

When I think of Grant speaking there as a candidate for President—

CONOVER *(going to her quickly)*. He's not speaking now as a candidate. That's a deep, dark secret. The whole idea of this trip is to create the demand.

MARY. That clears up something you just said—he's your choice first and then the people's choice.

CONOVER. I'm a citizen. I have a right to a choice. I think I've made a good one. And I want to help Grant all I can. He's new at this and needs advice.

MARY. What advice are you giving him?

CONOVER. Oh, so far it's chiefly along the lines of what not to say. Your husband is so afraid of not being completely honest.

MARY. You want him to be honest, don't you?

CONOVER. Oh, yes! *(There is a knock on the door)* Yes? Come in!

(Stevens enters.)

STEVENS. There's a long-distance call for you, sir. It's Wilkes-Barre.

CONOVER. Thank you, Stevens. *(He hesitates for a moment)* I'll take it here. *(He goes to the telephone. Stevens exits)*

MARY. Am I in the way?

CONOVER. Not at all. I won't be a minute. *(He picks up the receiver)* Hello. Put him on. *(Pause)* Yes, how are you? *(Pause)* Uh-huh. Yes, Joe, I want the campaign in your district strictly along those lines. If what happens down there is what I think will happen, it'll be a large part of the campaign in '48. How many Italians down there? *(Pause)* What's the size of your Polish vote? *(Pause)* That many? Well, tell them their hope lies in our party. Russia can't be trusted and we'll be tough with her—force her to correct those injustices. *(Mary turns and looks at Conover)* You don't have to tell 'em *how.* *(Mary rises, still watching Conover)* Go after it, hammer and tongs. You swing that district and we'll get you that veterans' hospital. *(Pause)* Not at all. Good luck. And thanks for calling. *(He hangs up)* Sorry for the interruption.

MARY. I'm glad it happened. It gave me a chance to change my mind. I'll go with Grant.

CONOVER *(heartily)*. That's fine. That pleases me very much. *(He goes to the table and picks up his glass)* That's our first big campaign contribution. To you, my dear, the most attractive plank in your husband's platform.

MARY. That's a hell of a thing to call a woman.

CONOVER (laughing). Suppose we go downstairs? I'd like to have you meet the rest of my guests.

MARY. Would it be rude if I postponed that until tomorrow? I have to get a little used to this idea—and I have to get a little used to Grant.

CONOVER. Well, this trip—working along with Grant—by the time you come back you two may be much closer together.

MARY. Even if that could happen, I don't think you'd want it to. It might cost you the support of Mrs. Thorndyke's newspapers.

CONOVER (laughing). Don't worry about that. They're Republican newspapers in Republican territory. They couldn't afford to risk their circulation. A chain of newspapers is a very valuable property.

MARY. Mrs. Thorndyke must have thought so. In the divorce settlement Dick Thorndyke got the children and she got the newspapers. And if that sounds bitchy, I hoped it would. You may succeed in killing the rumors, but unfortunately you won't kill Mrs. Thorndyke.

CONOVER (knowingly). We may kill more than one rumor.

MARY. Oh, dear! Is there someone I don't know about?

CONOVER (with a smile). There have been some rumors about you.

MARY (enormously pleased, she walks over to Conover). There have?

CONOVER. Yes. About you and a certain Major.

MARY. That's wonderful! That's the best news I've had in weeks. Does Grant know about the Major?

CONOVER. Not so far as I know.

MARY. Well, you're going to tell him, aren't you? I deserve something out of this! I was hoping he'd told you.

CONOVER. No, Mrs. Matthews, I have a little intelligence service of my own.

MARY. Well, it can't be too intelligent. They're considerably behind the times. The Major's been in China for six months. But when you tell Grant about him, don't let him know the Major's out of the country.

CONOVER. As far as I'm concerned, the whole thing's a military secret.

MARY (gaily). You know, I think I'll go downstairs with you at that! I feel a lot better than I did! Can you wait until I put on a new face? (She picks up her bag. The door opens and Grant enters. To Grant) We were just starting down.

GRANT. You're a little late. The party's breaking up.

CONOVER. We forgot all about you. We've been having a very interesting talk.

GRANT. That puts you one up on me. I've been listening to Governor Dunn. He's just about talked himself to sleep.

CONOVER. I'd better get down there! He doesn't even know where his room is! I'm the night clerk around here. I'll make your excuses, Mrs. Matthews.

MARY. Thanks. Thanks for everything!

CONOVER. Good night. Good night, Grant. (He starts for the door)

GRANT. See you in the morning.

CONOVER (at the door). Grant, I couldn't wait. I told Mrs. Matthews all about it. (He gives Grant a reassuring smile and exits quickly. Grant turns and looks at Mary. He seems a little uncertain. There is a pause)

MARY. Grant, I'm very proud of you.

GRANT. Well, Mary, don't think I'm taking this too seriously.

MARY. I'm taking it seriously. (Grant gives her a quick look) I think it would be a wonderful thing for the country.

GRANT. That's about as nice a thing as you could say, Mary. It's a damn big job. I'm not so sure I've got what it takes.

MARY. Well, I am. It isn't only that you have the brains for it—the important thing to me is—you've always tried to be honest.

GRANT. Tried to be?

MARY. Oh, you've cut some corners in business to get where you wanted to. That's what frightens me a little. But I will say this—you always had the decency to be unhappy about it.

GRANT (wryly). With some help from you.

MARY. But when you weren't thinking of yourself—when it came to what was best for the airplane industry as a whole, I've seen you take some pretty big losses.

GRANT. Right now I'm thinking about the country as a whole. I'm scared, Mary. (He sits down on the side of the bed)

MARY. About being President?

GRANT. No, about what's happening to the country. It's breaking up again . . .

MARY. What do you think you can do about it?

GRANT. I think somebody can appeal to what's best in people instead of what's worst.

MARY. And still be in politics?

GRANT. That's my whole case, Mary. If I can make the people see the choice they've got to make—the choice between their own interests and the interests of the country as a whole—damn it, I think the American people are sound. I think they can be unselfish.

MARY. All of them?

GRANT. Hell, we both know there are plenty of bastards in this world who'll always be out for themselves. But that's where I differ from Conover. I think they're in the minority.

MARY. I do, too. *(Mary sits on the other side of the bed, facing him)* How much do you and Conover differ?

GRANT. He's a politician. Politicians think you have to bribe people to vote for you—one way or another.

MARY. You mean groups like the Poles and the Italians?

GRANT. Yes—and labor and the farmers and the rest of them. But I'm not going to play politics.

MARY. That will take a lot of courage.

GRANT. No, it won't. I have faith in the American people.

MARY. So have I. *(There is a pause)* The Presidency's a great temptation!

GRANT. I don't even want the job. Whether I become President or not is completely unimportant.

(They look at each other for a moment. Then Mary turns away.)

MARY. Grant, when I first learned the purpose of this trip, I wasn't very happy about making it with you.

GRANT. I can understand that.

MARY *(looking back at Grant)*. But I am now.

GRANT. Mary, there are some things I should say—*(There is a pause, and then he turns away)*—but I can't.

(The moment is almost too intense. Mary stares at Grant's back for a moment or two, then rises, taking up her hat, gloves and bag from bed.)

MARY. I think I'll get out of these clothes. *(She exits into the dressing room, leaving the door open. Grant rises and turns to watch the door for a moment. Then Mary's voice comes from the dressing room)* Grant!

GRANT. Yes?

MARY *(offstage)*. I wish you'd call up Joyce tomorrow.

GRANT *(sitting in one of the easy chairs)*. She'll be in school, won't she?

MARY *(offstage)*. No, the doctor thinks she shouldn't go back until Wednesday. Oh, she's better. She had no temperature at all today.

GRANT. I'll call around dinner time. Then I can talk to Sonny, too.

MARY *(offstage)*. They were both pretty disappointed they couldn't go along.

GRANT *(dreamily)*. We ought to be thinking about a good boarding school for those kids.

MARY *(offstage)*. For heaven's sake, why?

GRANT. Well, I'm not so sure the White House is a good place to raise children.

MARY *(offstage)*. Grant!

GRANT. Yes?

MARY *(offstage)*. When are you going to break the news?

GRANT. You mean that I'm a candidate?

MARY *(offstage)*. Oh, you're way beyond the nomination—you've elected yourself.

GRANT *(grinning)*. I walked into that one—*(Then, defensively)*—but I didn't mean it quite the way it sounded.

MARY *(offstage)*. Which one of the plants are we going to first?

GRANT. Minneapolis.

MARY *(offstage)*. What are you speaking about there?

GRANT. I'm not making a speech there. That's Stassen territory. Conover thought I might just stir up trouble.

MARY *(offstage)*. Uh-huh. I suppose that's good politics. Tell me some more about your differences with Conover.

GRANT *(irritated)*. Now wait a minute, Mary! *(He goes to dressing-room door)* That was my decision! I'm making all the decisions! I've told Conover where I stand and he knows I'm going to tell the American people where I stand. *(Starts walking around the room)* The American people are facing problems today that will affect the future of the entire world. There's only one way to face them—with complete honesty—with utter frankness—

MARY (offstage). Grant!

GRANT. What?

MARY (offstage). Take it easy. I'm going to vote for you.

GRANT. No, I want to straighten you out on this too! If I have anything to offer, it's to change the whole complexion of political campaigns. I'm not going before the American people telling them what I can do for them. (Mary enters in nightgown, negligee and mules) But what I can do for them is to show them that the strength of this country, within our own borders . . .

MARY. Grant! I'm through with the dressing room.

GRANT. I'm in no hurry. (Resuming his "broadcast") The power of this country, outside our own borders . . .

MARY. Wouldn't you feel more comfortable if you took off that stuffed shirt? (Grant throws himself down in the chair, sulkily.)

GRANT. Aw, hell—I don't want to be President.

MARY (going to him). Darling, when we were talking a little while ago, you said the same things and they sounded so right—I wish you could just talk to the people that way.

GRANT (not entirely mollified). That's the way I plan to talk to them.

MARY. That's all I meant. Got a cigarette? (Grant offers her one from his case and lights it for her) Bill and Amy know we're coming to Seattle? (She crosses to the bench at foot of bed and sits)

GRANT. Bill knows—he expects me at the plant. But they don't know you're coming.

MARY. I'll wire Amy. (She shakes her head) Amy—with eight children?

GRANT. Yep, Bill's got the best production record of anyone in the industry.

MARY. I hope Amy's done something about the way she dresses. She always looks as though somebody bet her she couldn't.

GRANT (laughing). Do you remember the way she looked as your bridesmaid?

MARY. No, I was in a complete daze until we got to Victoria.

GRANT. And even in Victoria! When we went into the dining room you shook hands with the headwaiter! (They both laugh. There is an embarrassed pause.

Grant straightens up in his chair, steals a look at Mary who is stealing a look at him at the same time. Grant rises) Well, I've got a tough day tomorrow. (He exits into the dressing room, unbuttoning his coat as he goes and leaving the door open. Mary goes back into her memories for a moment, then throws them off and starts for her drink on the table. There is a knock on the door and Mary goes to door and opens it. Norah enters with Mary's dress, pressed)

NORAH. I was afraid you might have gone to bed. I'll hang it up for you. (Norah starts for the dressing room)

MARY (running in front of Norah to dressing-room door). My husband's in there!

NORAH. Oh.

GRANT (offstage). Did you say something, darling?

MARY. No, dear. It's just the maid with my dress. (She closes the dressing-room door. Norah drapes the dress carefully over the back of a chair) What's your name?

NORAH. Norah, Ma'am. (She takes a blanket from the bed and puts it over the back of chair)

MARY. Thank you for pressing it, Norah. I'll hang it up later. (Norah starts preparing the bed, removing spread and turning back the covers.)

NORAH. I'm sorry I was so late with it. Just as the iron got hot we got another guest.

MARY. Gracious, where did you put him?

NORAH. He's on a cot in Mr. Conover's room.

MARY. Oh, dear, that makes me feel very guilty.

NORAH. Don't you worry, Mrs. Matthews. A cot's good enough for most of them. They just come down here to get something out of Mr. Conover. Not the people we put in this room. This room is for special guests. We even had a Democrat in this bed one night.

MARY. Oh, I wish you hadn't told me that.

NORAH. He wasn't a Roosevelt Democrat. (Norah has finished with the bed and turns on the bed light on table near the bed, then turns to the service-bell cord) When you wake up in the morning just press this button and I'll have breakfast right up for you.

MARY. Thank you, Norah. Good night.

NORAH. Good night, Ma'am. *(She starts out, then stops and turns)* Oh, I was going to ask your husband but maybe you can tell me. Do you know Mrs. Thorndyke's address?

MARY. Mrs. Thorndyke?

NORAH. She forgot her glasses when she left this morning. And I know what it is to be without glasses. I want to mail them back to her.

MARY. Are you sure they're Mrs. Thorndyke's?

NORAH *(getting the glasses from pocket and showing them)*. Yes, they're them Chinese kind. What women won't do! Won't they?

MARY. Yes—won't they? *(Mary places her drink on the desk with considerable emphasis, goes to dressing-room door and opens it, calling in to Grant)* Grant, can you step out for a minute? Norah wants some information.

GRANT *(offstage)*. Be right with you. *(Mary goes to the window and looks out, standing immovable. Grant appears, tying his dressing gown)* Hello, Norah, What can I do for you?

NORAH. Mrs. Thorndyke left her glasses. I wanted to know where to mail them back to her.

GRANT. Oh!— *(He glances toward Mary)* —1276 Park Avenue. Shall I write it down for you?

NORAH. No, I can remember it. 1276. 76 —that's the year of the revolution, and twelve for the Twelve Commandments.

(Norah exits. Grant glances toward Mary, who raises the window sharply, her back to him. Grant retreats into the dressing room, closing the door. Mary turns, looks after him, studies the bed for a moment and then her eyes go to the overstuffed chairs. She goes into action. She removes three cushions from the overstuffed chairs, placing them in a line on the floor. She then goes to the bed and removes the sheets and blankets. Folding one sheet and one blanket, she makes a bed for one person on one side of the double bed. Then with the other sheet and blanket, she makes a bed on the three cushions on the floor. As she is finishing this, Grant enters from the dressing room in pajamas and dressing gown. He takes in the situation.

GRANT. Mary, what do you think you're doing? Now stop that nonsense and make up that bed again. *(Mary finishes fixing the bed on the floor)* Damn it, I'm not going to let you do this! *(Grant goes to her. Mary, ignoring him, takes off her dressing gown, switches off the lights, leaving only the bed lamp burning)* You wouldn't get any sleep down there on the floor and I wouldn't get any sleep lying there worrying about you. *(He points to the double bed. Mary crosses quickly to the double bed)*

MARY. Good night, Mr. President! *(She pops into the double bed, turning off the bed lamp. Grant looks at the bed on the floor with dismay as the curtain falls)*

ACT TWO

The living room of a suite at the Book-Cadillac Hotel in Detroit. It is furnished the way a living room in the Book-Cadillac Hotel would be furnished—in fact the Book-Cadillac has furnished it for us—a desk, a telephone, a sofa, several easy chairs, and a highboy. The pictures on the wall are surprisingly enough not French prints but modern paintings.

The entrance from the hall is upstage, center. Down right and down left are the two doors leading into the bedroom of the suite.

At rise the stage is dark; then the door to the hall opens and a bellboy enters, puts down three bags he is carrying and switches on the lights.

Mary and Grant follow him, arm-in-arm. Grant is carrying a handful of telegrams, some of them already opened.

———

BELLBOY. Well, we made it.

GRANT. Thanks! That was slick. We'd have never got through that crowd in the lobby.

BELLBOY. Remember that if you get trapped again. The service elevators are right back of the passenger elevators.

MARY. It was exciting, wasn't it? At the station, too. What a mob!

GRANT. I thought Spike would meet us. I guess he didn't get my telegram.

MARY. Just the same I'm glad he came on ahead. This is more like it.

BELLBOY. Where shall I put the bags?

GRANT. Mary, pick a room for yourself,

will you? (*Grant throws his coat and hat on a chair, goes to the desk, puts down the telegrams, and picks up the telephone. Mary opens the door of the bedroom to the left and looks in*) Hello, what room is Mr. MacManus in?

MARY. That's a nice room. (*She crosses to the right bedroom*)

GRANT (*into the telephone*). What? (*Pause*) E. J. MacManus. (*Pause*) Ring it, will you?

MARY (*looking into the right bedroom*). One room's as good as another. (*She turns to the bellboy*) Where are Mr. Matthews' bags?

BELLBOY. I'll bring them right up.

MARY. Well, you can put those in here. (*She exits into the right bedroom followed by Bellboy with her bags*)

GRANT (*into the telephone*). Hello, Spike. (*Pause*) Just this minute. We were grounded in Springfield. Come on up. We're in 2519. (*Pause*) Jim? The hell he is! Telephone the desk and tell them when he gets here to send him right up to the suite. (*Pause*) We're having a drink. What will you have, an old-fashioned? (*Pause*) Right. I'll order a drink for Jim too. Come on up. (*He clicks the receiver, staying on the phone*) Room service. (*Pause*) Room service? This is 2519. Will you send up two martinis— (*Mary enters from the right bedroom*) —one old-fashioned, and a Scotch and soda right away? Thanks.

MARY. Who are all the drinks for?

GRANT. Spike and Jim.

MARY. Is Conover here?

GRANT. He's on his way up from the station. That's a good sign, Mary. It looks as though Jim's afraid somebody might get his front seat on the bandwagon. (*Grant has started opening the telegrams*) Here! Let's get to work on these telegrams. (*He hands Mary some of the wires, then goes left to sofa and sits*)

MARY. I'm not so sure that's the reason Jim came out here.

GRANT (*absorbed in the telegrams*). Yeah?

MARY (*going to him*). Grant, don't talk to Jim about what you're going to say tonight.

GRANT (*excitedly*). These wires are all about the Wichita speech. They're terrific. I've never had anything like this before.

MARY. That's what I mean. Spike tried to talk you out of making that speech. So remember what I just said.

GRANT (*looking up*). What'd you just say?

MARY. Don't talk to Jim about your speech tonight.

GRANT. O.K. Mary, listen to this one. . . . (*The Bellboy enters from the right bedroom.*)

BELLBOY. I turned on the radiator and opened the windows. You've got plenty of towels. Is there anything else I can do?

MARY. Yes, you can get the other bags.

BELLBOY. Oh, yes. Coming right up. (*He exits*)

MARY (*glancing through the telegrams*). Grant—these are simply wonderful! You see, you didn't have to be afraid of shooting the works. That's the way they want to hear you talk.

GRANT. Just look at these, Mary—it shows how hungry the American people are for leadership.

MARY. This one's nice, Grant. It mentions your modesty and humility.

GRANT. Well, here's one who didn't like it.

MARY. Who's that?

GRANT. I don't know. Executive Secretary, Local 801. . . . (*He crumples the telegram and throws it away*)

MARY. Look, darling—they want you to speak in Omaha next Monday.

GRANT. That's nothing. They want me in New Orleans on Thursday and Atlanta on Friday.

MARY. Let's go— (*She sits on the sofa beside him*) —let's go to all three of them!

GRANT. Mary, Omaha is way back there— (*He gestures*) —New Orleans and Atlanta are way down there— (*He gestures*) —New York is over there— (*Another gesture*) —and the work on my desk is up to here. (*He indicates his chin*)

MARY. I don't know why you bother with business when this is so much fun. (*They grin at each other.*)

GRANT. Do you know, this trip has done you a lot of good? You have no right to look that young at your age! On the field at Denver, just before we took off, I had the damnedest sensation. You were standing there in the moonlight with the wind from the propeller blowing your hair and your dress—I knew we were in Denver, but you were the girl standing on the deck of the boat on our way to Victoria.

MARY (*after a reminiscent pause*). Now I'll tell you something. Remember in Victoria when we stood on the balcony of the hotel and you were telling me what the world should be like? That same boy was standing on the platform last night in Wichita.

GRANT. I'm glad you said that, Mary. It was a wonderful satisfaction, that speech —just saying what I really believed.

MARY (*she holds up the telegrams*). You see what that speech did! (*She looks down at the top telegram*) Grant, who's Herbert Bayard Swope?

(*There is a knock on the door.*)

GRANT. Come in! (*Spike enters, carrying the Detroit newspapers. Mary and Grant rise and greet him*) Hello, Spike.

SPIKE. Hi-ya.

MARY. Hello, Spike, we finally got here.

SPIKE. You had me worried. You jammed up a lot of appointments when your plane was grounded.

MARY. Don't tell Grant I said so—but there's nothing like a train.

GRANT. Those the evening papers? (*He takes the papers from Spike and starts reading them*) Hmm! Front-page spread!

SPIKE. Did the newspaper boys get you at the station?

GRANT (*sitting in chair left*). Yeah—a flock of them. (*He is still reading paper*) Mary! (*In the play Grant reads a headline that would be in a Detroit newspaper the night of the performance. This headline is changed every night*) Jim's coming out here makes things look pretty hot.

MARY. Is he staying here?

SPIKE. Yes, damn it—and I have to split my bed with him. You know what kind of split a politician takes.

MARY. That's silly. We have two bedrooms here and we don't need both of them. Grant, you're moving in with me. We're putting Jim in the other bedroom. (*Grant is absorbed in the paper*) Grant! Yoo-hoo! Mr. Candidate! Mr. President!

GRANT (*looking up*). Huh?

MARY. That got him! (*To Grant*) I'm playing a little politics for you. I'm saving Jim from sleeping with Spike. We're putting him in our extra bedroom.

GRANT. Fine! Be with you in a minute, Spike. Let me finish this editorial.

(*There is a knock on the door.*)

SPIKE. I've got some people coming to see you but they're not due this early.

(*Spike goes to the door and opens it. Conover enters*) Hello, Jim!

CONOVER. Hello, Spike. (*He greets Mary*) Mary!

MARY. So nice seeing you, Jim. We didn't expect you. (*She offers him her cheek, which he kisses. Grant rises*)

CONOVER (*going to Grant and shaking hands*). Hello, Grant! Politics agrees with you—you're looking fine.

GRANT. I feel great. Look, headlines and a damn good editorial! It's about the Wichita speech—the responsibility of the labor unions. Says it's about time somebody brought it out into the open.

MARY. Jim, it was the best speech Grant ever made. It was the first time I felt sure he could be elected. You never heard such applause.

CONOVER. Mary, if applause elected Presidents, William Jennings Bryan would have had three terms.

GRANT. It's good to see you.

MARY. We're putting you in our other bedroom.

CONOVER. Fine! My bags are down in the lobby.

GRANT. What news have you brought us? I'm certainly glad you're here.

MARY. Yes, it will give you a chance to see Grant in front of an audience.

CONOVER. Oh, I'm not making any public appearances. I'm not supposed to be in Detroit. Don't let anyone know I'm in town. I thought I should come out and bring you up to date on things and go over the situation. What are you talking about here tonight?

GRANT. Well, it's the last speech of the tour, Jim. It's got a little bit of everything.

CONOVER. Anything controversial?

MARY. Not for anybody that agrees with him. I want you to see these telegrams. (*Mary goes to the desk*)

SPIKE. They got here three hours late. (*To Grant*) I was pretty sure you'd make the broadcast. You don't go on until after the banquet.

MARY. Is this another banquet?

SPIKE. Yeah.

MARY. Then we'd better have dinner before we go. (*Mary picks up the telephone and speaks into it*) Room service, please. What do you want to eat, Grant?

(*Spike takes the telegrams from Mary and hands them to Conover who glances at them casually.*)

GRANT. Anything that's ready—hamburger if they've got it.

SPIKE. I won't have time to eat with you. Better make it snappy. You're going to be busy.

MARY. Jim, what shall I order for you?

CONOVER. I'll have some chicken—and some coffee.

MARY. You can't have chicken and eat with us. I never want to see another chicken.

GRANT. Every time we sit down in a chair, somebody puts chicken in front of us. (He pulls up a trouser-leg and points to his calf) Look—pin-feathers!

CONOVER. All right. I'll have hamburger too—hamburger and onions.

MARY (into the telephone). Room service? (Pause) This is room— (She looks inquiringly toward the men)

SPIKE. 2519.

MARY. 2519. Have you any hamburger? (Pause) That's fine. Three hamburger steaks, one with onions—two without, damn it, and whatever goes with it—except spinach. (To the men) Anybody want dessert? Ice cream's always safe.

GRANT. Fine!

CONOVER. None for me.

MARY (into the telephone). One chocolate ice cream. And three coffees. Will you hurry it, please? (She hangs up. There is a knock on the door) Come in! (The Bellboy enters with Grant's bags. He is followed by Waiter with a tray of drinks. To the Bellboy) Put all the bags in there. (She indicates the right bedroom. She takes a cocktail from the tray) We ordered a highball for you, Jim.

CONOVER. Thanks.

(The waiter serves the others their drinks.)

SPIKE. Are you the floor waiter?

WAITER. Yes, sir.

SPIKE. There's a dinner order in. Hurry it up for us, will you? (To Grant) I've got a lot of people lined up for you to see.

GRANT. Can't I see them after the banquet?

SPIKE. You were supposed to see them this afternoon, but you didn't get in, so I bunched them all between seven and seven-thirty.

CONOVER. Well, I can't have dinner here if a lot of people are coming in.

SPIKE. No, it's O.K. I can keep this room clear. I'll juggle the visiting firemen between the two bedrooms. Grant can duck in and say hello, and come back and eat. We'll clear them all up in a hurry.

(The Bellboy enters from the right bedroom.)

BELLBOY. I've turned off the radiator and closed the windows. Anything else I can do?

GRANT. No, thanks. (Grant tips the Bellboy, who exits. The Waiter goes to Grant who takes the check and writes on it)

CONOVER. Are you touching on labor again tonight?

GRANT. No!

MARY (cutting in quickly). Grant, we won't have time to dress after dinner. We ought to be changing now.

GRANT. Yes, we can be changed by the time dinner gets here.

(The Waiter starts out and Mary stops him.)

MARY. Waiter! Another drink, Jim?

CONOVER. No, thanks.

MARY. Spike?

SPIKE. Not now.

MARY. How about you, Grant? Another cocktail while you're dressing?

GRANT. I don't dare. I've got to make a speech.

MARY (to the Waiter). Bring another martini to the bedroom.

WAITER. Right away, Ma'am. (He exits)

MARY (moving toward the right bedroom). That's the difference between Grant and me—I'd rather be tight than be President. (She exits)

GRANT. Spike, we haven't opened all those telegrams. Look through them, will you? (He starts to exit)

CONOVER. Grant, while you're dressing, have you got a copy of your speech tonight that I could be glancing at?

GRANT (at the bedroom door). It's not a set speech, Jim. I'm talking from notes.

CONOVER. Could I be looking over the notes?

GRANT. They're just some memos I scribbled down—I'm sorry, Jim, they wouldn't mean a thing to you. (Spike has picked up the telegrams) I'll tell you what you can read. Spike, show him some more of my fan mail. (Grant exits into the right bedroom. Spike turns to look at Conover)

CONOVER (angrily). You're a hell of a campaign manager!

SPIKE (on the defensive). That's why I

wired for you, Jim. He's gotten away from me.

CONOVER. It's a damn shame! The boys in the Northwest and all along the Coast —they were swinging right in behind him. Then he had to stick out his chin in Wichita.

SPIKE. How much damage has he done?

CONOVER. We may have lost labor. I must have had thirty calls after that speech. How did you let it happen?

SPIKE. I talked him out of that labor stuff in Denver—that is, I gave him something to use instead—local stuff—Rocky Mountain stuff.

CONOVER. Didn't you get a look at the speech for Wichita?

SPIKE. No, and I'll tell you why. She— (*He points to the right bedroom*) —knew he was planning to talk about labor in Denver and when he didn't she spent the rest of the night tossing harpoons into him. But the next day on the plane to Wichita they were clubby as hell—and I couldn't get any advance copy of the speech. You just sent the wrong dame with him!

CONOVER. I even talked him into taking her along.

SPIKE. When we get back to New York, Kay can straighten him out. She put this Presidential bee in his bonnet. She never tears Grant down. She always builds him up. If you ask me, that's why he fell for her. But that doesn't help us tonight.

CONOVER. What are you afraid of tonight?

SPIKE. I don't know— (*The telephone rings*) —but she's too damn happy. (*Spike answers the telephone*) Hello. (*Pause*) Oh —give me the desk. (*To Conover*) That's why I sent for you. We can't take a chance on his making another mistake here tonight. (*Into the telephone*) Hello. This is MacManus. There are some people down there to see Mr. Matthews. And there are a lot more coming. Send them all up to the twenty-fifth floor, Parlor B, and tell them to wait for me there. (*He hangs up. Then speaks to Conover*) You've got to find out what he's talking about here. (*Spike picks up telegrams and joins Conover on the sofa*)

CONOVER. That's what I was trying to do —and you saw how far I got. (*Conover glances through some of the telegrams, then tosses them aside*)

SPIKE. Well, keep after him.

CONOVER. If you've got people coming to see him, what chance have I?

SPIKE. I wasn't sure you were going to get here. I figured I had to put some kind of pressure on him. I've got everybody— dairy farmers, automobile people, even the labor boys, mad as they are.

CONOVER. Maybe they ought to be talking to Mrs. Matthews.

SPIKE. Look, Jim, this guy's vulnerable. He's got the bug.

CONOVER. That's what I was counting on. How bad has he got it?

SPIKE. He wants to be President, all right. So what I keep throwing at him is votes—get those votes—don't lose those votes. (*Conover rises. Spike looks up from the telegrams he has been reading*) Say, maybe that Wichita speech didn't do as much harm as we thought it did.

CONOVER. Oh, those are just from people.

SPIKE. They don't count, eh?

CONOVER. You don't see any signed "State Chairman," do you?

SPIKE. Don't kid yourself, this guy does something to people. I've been on a lot of campaigns. They don't shake hands with Grant just to say they've shaken hands with him. They're up there with a light in their eyes—they practically mob him. If he gets away from us, you may be heading a "Stop Matthews" movement.

CONOVER. Stopping him wouldn't be any trouble. He hasn't any organization. I don't want to stop him. I think we can elect him, if we can keep him in line. (*Spike is studying another telegram.*)

SPIKE. Say, Jim, did you arrange this?

CONOVER. What?

SPIKE. He's speaking in New York—the 23rd—Foreign Policy Association.

CONOVER. The hell he is! Why doesn't he consult us?

SPIKE. He didn't even mention it to me. Just because I don't trust him doesn't mean he shouldn't trust me.

CONOVER. That forces us right out into the open. What's that date?

SPIKE. The twenty-third.

CONOVER. He can't speak there and pretend he's not a candidate. Besides that, he's got to go along with us on foreign policy. Our big chance to win is with the foreign vote. Well, I guess we've got to fence him in. Damn!

SPIKE. He wants that nomination. He wants to be President.

CONOVER. Then I'd better face him with some people who can deliver delegates— people he knows he has to have to win— I'd like to throw them at him all at once.

SPIKE. Better line up a big shot from labor.

CONOVER. Yes—Bill Hardy would do that for me. I could get Senator Lauterback to scare hell out of him on the farm vote.

SPIKE. You'd better have Kay there. I know damn well he listens to her.

CONOVER. Who would talk for business? Look around at the banquet tonight, Spike, and see if there's anybody who could be useful.

(There is a knock at the door.)

SPIKE. Damn it. I told them to send everybody to Parlor B. *(He goes to door and opens it. It is the Waiter)*

WAITER. I have the dinner—and the extra cocktail.

SPIKE. Wheel it in!

(The Waiter wheels in a table with service for three and Mary's second cocktail. Spike goes to the bedroom door and knocks.)

GRANT *(offstage)*. Yes?

SPIKE. Dinner's here.

GRANT *(offstage)*. We'll be right out.

SPIKE. Does Mary want her other cocktail in there?

MARY *(offstage)*. Cocktails don't have to come to me. I come to them. *(Mary enters in a dinner dress. The Waiter serves Mary the cocktail)*

WAITER. I have the dinner right outside. *(He exits and returns immediately with portable oven. During the following scene, he sets the table and puts three chairs in their proper places)*

SPIKE *(going to the bedroom door)*. Grant, is your room free?

GRANT *(offstage)*. All set. I'm just tying my tie.

SPIKE. When you're through, will you unlock the hall door to your room?

GRANT *(offstage)*. Okay.

MARY *(to the Waiter)*. Serve it as soon as you're ready.

SPIKE *(hurriedly going to the other bedroom)*. I'd better unlock the hall door to this one, too. *(Spike exits into left bedroom)*

CONOVER *(to Mary)*. My dear, that's a little unfair.

MARY. What?

CONOVER. I'm afraid that instead of listening to Grant they'll be just looking at you tonight.

MARY. Thank you, Jim. I'm so willing to believe that, I'm going to pretend you're not a politician.

(Spike returns from the left bedroom.)

SPIKE. All right. Here we go. I'll bring in the first batch of patriots. *(To Mary)* Remind Grant they've got votes.

MARY. Spike does take the nobility out of a crusade.

SPIKE *(at the hall doorway)*. Am I expected to be noble? On my salary! *(He exits into the hall)*

CONOVER. Why don't you just spend the evening here with me? You've probably read Grant's speech anyway, haven't you?

MARY. I'm sorry you won't be there.

CONOVER. I'll listen to it on the radio— if I can get a radio—and if I can't—what's he speaking about?

MARY. Oh, I think we can get you a radio. *(She goes to the telephone. Grant enters from the right bedroom)*

GRANT. I damn near left these notes in my other suit. *(He starts looking through some notes he has in his hand)*

MARY *(into the telephone)*. Could you have a radio sent up to 2519 right away? *(Pause)* It's very important. *(Pause)* Thank you! *(She hangs up)* It looks as though you'll have to listen, Jim. They think you can have one.

CONOVER *(to Grant)*. If you want to rehearse any of that, Grant, I'll be glad to have you try it out on me.

GRANT. I'll give you the start— *(He speaks as though he were addressing a large auditorium)* Ladies—and members of the Automotive Council of Detroit. I know that I am among friends here tonight—and it would be unfriendly of me not to talk to you with utter frankness and naked honesty. In the economic anarchy we are facing today—

(The Waiter has taken two plates of food out of the portable oven.)

WAITER. Who's with onions?

CONOVER *(sourly)*. I'm with onions.

(Mary goes to the center place at the table and sits. The two men go to either side and sit. The Waiter serves them.)

WAITER. Watch the plates—they're very hot.

GRANT. Looks good—I can hardly wait.

Waiter, you've got a starving man on your hands.

WAITER. Watch the plate. I'll bring the dessert in fifteen minutes. (*He exits, with the portable oven*)

GRANT. Ah—meat! And can I use it? (*He has his knife and fork poised when Spike enters from the right bedroom*)

SPIKE. Grant, your public is waiting.

GRANT. My hamburger's waiting.

SPIKE. Hamburgers don't vote. These are dairy farmers. (*He goes to Grant and hands him a slip of paper, pointing to a name at the top*) The fellow with the mustache is the one to play for.

GRANT. Just the Number Five handshake, Spike?

SPIKE. No, a little talk. You know— cows, butter, milk, cheese—since the war American cheese has become big industry.

GRANT. What do I know about American cheese?

SPIKE. Walk this way and meet three perfect specimens. (*Grant rises and starts out*) Remember— (*Grant turns*) They mean votes! (*Grant exits into the right bedroom*) Well—now I'll set 'em up in the other alley. (*He exits into the hall*)

MARY (*eagerly*). How do you think Grant's doing? What are your reports?

CONOVER. First let me tell you about my reports on you. You've done a great job, and I want to congratulate you.

MARY. Well, I'd like to admit something if I could be sure it wouldn't be used against me. I've enjoyed it—every minute of it.

CONOVER. Even the speeches?

MARY. That's been the best part of it. I don't mean just listening to Grant. I mean listening to the people—feeling the way they respond. Of course they laugh and yell when he talks about the troubles he's had getting things through in Washington . . .

CONOVER (*busily eating*). Yes, I've heard those laughs. He does it very cleverly. That's what they like to hear.

MARY. Jim, over the radio you only hear the audience when it's making noise. What you don't hear is the silence—when Grant has them so that they're not thinking of themselves—when he has them thinking of the country—that's when it takes your breath away.

CONOVER. I'm glad to hear Grant can do

that. I know how effective it can be in a speaker.

MARY. Jim, I'm not talking about Grant. When they rush up after the speeches—I wish you could see their faces. You know, I'd forgotten how good it was to be with people—I used to see a lot of them when Grant first started and had small plants— when we moved to New York I got too far away from them— They're so eager to do whatever is the best thing to do—and they're so quick—they're so intelligent. (*She laughs*) They've thrown a couple of questions at Grant that had him stopped cold. He just had to admit he didn't know enough to answer them. And they liked him for it.

CONOVER. That's smart. Shows he uses his head.

MARY (*sitting back in her chair and regarding Conover quizzically*). Jim, you fascinate me. You have such a complete lack of faith in sincerity—and you're so sincere about it. (*Conover gives her an understanding smile*) What puzzles me is that I dislike so thoroughly the way your mind works—and yet I'm so very fond of you.

CONOVER. It is puzzling, isn't it, because I feel the same way toward you.

(*Mary pats his hand with fond reproof.*)

MARY. You're so cynical.

(*Conover pats her hand in same manner.*)

CONOVER. You're so unrealistic.

(*They grin at each other. Grant enters from the right bedroom.*)

MARY (*to Grant*). Well, how's the farmer's choice?

GRANT (*going to the table*). After the beautiful things I have just said about cows, I shouldn't touch this hamburger. It's like eating an old friend. But I'm going to. (*He sits down and gets ready to eat the hamburger. Spike enters from the left bedroom*)

SPIKE. Ah, back from the pastures. Wipe off your feet and come in and meet the A. F. of L.

GRANT. Look, Spike, give me a chance to eat . . .

SPIKE. Nope. This is a crisis. I have to know you're holding the A. F. of L. in there while I sneak the C.I.O. into the other bedroom.

GRANT. Put them both in the same room. I'll talk to them both at the same time.

SPIKE. Little Boy Blue, haven't you

heard? They ain't keeping steady company any more. Besides these aren't big shots—just small fry—officers in the locals.

GRANT. They're both labor groups. They both want the same thing. That's what I've been talking about all this time—getting people to work together—now let's put it into action.

SPIKE. Now, boss . . .

GRANT. I'm serious about this, Spike. Tell those men in there you're bringing in the C.I.O., and then I'll come in and talk to them!

(Spike shrugs and exits into the left bedroom. Mary preens herself, looking proudly from Grant to Conover.)

CONOVER. Grant, aren't you just asking for trouble?

GRANT. Jim, I've got both organizations working in my plants. I can walk into a recreation room where C.I.O. and A. F. of L. men are there together and talk to them—talk labor to them. Bill Green and Phil Murray will both sit down with each other. The big boys in labor are all right, except for Lewis. *(He points to the left bedroom)* This is the type of men we've got to get together.

CONOVER. I don't mind your having your head in the clouds—but I wish you'd keep your feet in the voting booth.

GRANT. Jim, if I can ever make people like these in the next room see something bigger than their job as head of their own locals and the little power they get from that . . .

MARY *(to Conover)*. There may be some votes in that, too.

CONOVER. One of the things I came down to talk to you about—I got a very bad reaction to your speech in Wichita.

GRANT. Did you read those telegrams?

CONOVER. You may have picked up a few votes there in the auditorium, but you've chilled off most of the labor leaders in the country. I know! I've talked to them!

GRANT. I said that business had to give labor a voice in management. That didn't chill them off, did it?

CONOVER. No, no, that was all right—for labor.

GRANT. I said that labor had to have a fairer share of the profits. Did they object to that?

CONOVER. No, damn it—it was the stand you took on strikes.

GRANT *(earnestly)*. No, Jim, not on strikes. I mentioned only one kind of strike. I asked labor to give the people of this country the answer to this question: "Is there any moral justification for the jurisdictional strike?" Can you answer that question? Can the labor leaders you talked to answer that question?

CONOVER. Of course they can't. That's what makes them so sore. Too bad you didn't talk about the other kind of strikes.

GRANT. All right, it's true—some unions are abusing their right to strike at this time. They're sacrificing the country for their own special interest. What do you propose to do? Take their right to strike away from them? Freedom of the press is being abused. Do you want to take that right away from publishers?

CONOVER *(grudgingly)*. Well—labor's pretty sore about what you said about opening their books, too.

GRANT. Not all of them are. Some of the biggest and best unions in the country have opened their books.

MARY. Jim, the audience was full of union men—I don't mean union leaders, I mean union members—and they cheered Grant. I had a feeling they'd like to get a look at those books themselves.

CONOVER. Some of that money goes into campaign contributions.

(Spike enters from the left bedroom.)

GRANT. Well?

SPIKE. No dice. They're even mad they're in the same hotel together.

GRANT. That makes me pretty mad, too.

SPIKE. Boss, you've got to speak to them.

GRANT *(he throws down napkin and rises)*. Of course I'll speak to them. How am I going to do what I want to do if I don't speak to them?

SPIKE. Here are the names. *(He hands Grant a slip of paper)* Watch out for the little guy they call Mac. *(Grant angrily grabs the paper, and exits into the left bedroom)* Now for some counter-espionage. *(Spike exits into the hall.)*

MARY *(earnestly)*. Jim, Grant's got something. Don't take it away from him! When he's just cockeyed drunk with sincerity people can't resist him!

CONOVER. That statement sounds as though it includes you, too.

MARY. Let me straighten you out about Grant and me. Our personal relations are strictly political.

CONOVER. I thought I saw Grant throw

a look or two at you tonight that wasn't entirely impersonal.

MARY. Jim, you're a bachelor, aren't you?

CONOVER. Theoretically. Why?

MARY. It's just that if you'd been married, you'd understand?

CONOVER. Understand what?

MARY. When a man and woman have been married for a long time even their closest friends can't always tell whether they're still in love with each other. They themselves wonder about it sometimes.

CONOVER. Well, then the trip's accomplished something—if you're at the point of wondering.

MARY. No, there are things that happen that make you sure—little things that don't really mean anything except that you know how much they do mean. For instance, Grant found out once the girls at school used to call me Maizie. He knew I hated it. So sometimes he used to call me Maizie—just to tease me—but you don't tease people that way unless you love each other. Well, Maizie doesn't live here any more. And another thing—Grant always hated to hear me swear—whenever I let go with something—he used to smack me on the behind—hard. I've done a lot of swearing on this trip—

CONOVER. And no smacks?

MARY *(wistfully)*. It's a small request— but I'd give anything for a good smack on the behind.

CONOVER. I wish there were something I could do about that.

(Spike enters from the right bedroom.)

SPIKE. Still in with them?

MARY. Yes, and all's quiet on the Western front.

SPIKE. Well, the Eastern front is ready. *(Grant enters from the left bedroom, closing the door behind him.)*

GRANT *(to Spike)*. Are the C.I.O. boys in there?

SPIKE. Yes—and in what I would call an ugly mood.

GRANT. Keep your back turned, Jim. *(Grant opens the left bedroom door)* This way, gentlemen. *(Three stony-faced labor leaders march in front the left bedroom, and Grant leads them toward the right bedroom. Mary springs up to greet them. As each one is introduced, they shake hands with Mary, then continue into the*

right bedroom) This is Mrs. Matthews! Mr. Vincent.

MARY. How do you do?

GRANT. Mr. Solly.

MARY. How do you do?

GRANT. Mr. Mack.

MARY. How do you do?

GRANT. Right in here, gentlemen. *(He opens the right bedroom door and they file in. Grant turns and gives a broad wink to Mary and Conover and follows in after them, closing the door. Spike puts his fingers in his ears and stands shuddering as though he expects an explosion behind him, then relaxes with a grin)*

SPIKE. You know, Grant might be able to unite the United Nations. *(He starts out, sees Grant's food, walks to Grant's place, sits and picks up the knife and fork)*

MARY. Spike, don't you dare touch that! *(Spike rises.)*

SPIKE. All right, I can starve. But that's the way you make Communists. *(He exits into the hall)*

MARY. Poor Grant. He's not getting a thing to eat. *(She goes to the desk and gets a cigarette from her evening bag and lights it)*

CONOVER. I was hoping we three could have a quiet dinner together and talk.

MARY. We'll see you after we get back here.

CONOVER. I'd like to go over with Grant what he's speaking about tonight. Tell me something about it.

MARY. Well, it's his last speech of the trip. It's sort of a summary.

CONOVER. Detroit's a dangerous city politically—almost anything you say here is controversial.

MARY. Isn't a Presidential campaign supposed to be controversial?

CONOVER. Yes, but they've had a lot of trouble here—strikes—race riots—and for some reason or other it seems to be the headquarters of the lunatic fringe.

MARY. You mean the subversive groups . . .

CONOVER. Mary, subversive is a very dangerous word— *(Apprehensively)* Grant's not using that word in his speech tonight, is he?

MARY. I think Grant's saving anything like that—and the international situation —for his speech in New York.

CONOVER. Oh, is he speaking in New York?

MARY. Yes! *(Grant enters from the right bedroom)* Still alive?

GRANT. Yes, and so are they. *(He goes to the table)* As a matter of fact, the Congress of Industrial Organization has just extended an invitation to the American Federation of Labor to have a glass of beer.

CONOVER *(with a bit of a grin)*. Under whose jurisdiction?

GRANT. The Arcade Bar and Grill! *(He starts to eat)*

CONOVER. Mary tells me you're making a speech in New York.

GRANT *(gratified)*. Yes. The twenty-third. Foreign Policy Association! That's moving into the big time!

CONOVER. You couldn't postpone that, could you? I don't see how you can open up on the international situation and still pretend you're not a candidate.

GRANT. I didn't think I could turn it down.

CONOVER. Well, it's too late, I guess. *(Disturbed)* I couldn't very well advise you about something I didn't know anything about.

(Spike enters from the left bedroom.)

SPIKE. Okay, Grant, if you're ready!

GRANT *(starting to eat again)*. Spike, they can't be more important than this hamburger.

SPIKE. Well, they're all your friends. It's the Detroit tycoon set.

GRANT *(rising with alacrity)*. Oh, somebody I really want to see? You're slipping, Spike. *(He exits into the left bedroom)*

SPIKE. I've got one more set. They're gate crashers. Even I don't know who they are. *(He exits into the hall)*

MARY *(putting out her cigarette)*. I wonder whether I have time to sneak a look in a mirror? *(She starts for the right bedroom, then stops. Conover rises)* Oh, I forgot to thank you for telling Grant the gossip about me.

CONOVER. I didn't tell him.

MARY. Well, somebody must have told him.

CONOVER. Has he said anything?

MARY. No, but he's very rude to all army Majors. *(Conover chuckles)* And it's so unfair to those poor Majors. My Major's been a Colonel for months.

CONOVER. I hadn't heard about that.

MARY. Jim, your secret service works backwards. They keep secrets from you! *(Grant enters from the left bedroom.)*

GRANT. Mary, Sam Parrish is in here. He'd like to say hello to you.

MARY. Good! I haven't seen Sam for ages.

CONOVER. Wait, Mary! Grant, I'd like to have a few words with Parrish myself. Could you have him step in here?

GRANT. Sure, I'll tell him.

CONOVER. Oh, Grant—don't let the others know I'm here.

(Grant exits into the left bedroom. Conover moves up out of range of door, pulling his chair with him.)

MARY. We've known Sam for years. We're very fond of him.

CONOVER. So am I. He's raised a lot of money for the party.

(Sam Parrish enters from the left bedroom. He is the successful American business man and looks it. He sees Mary and goes to her.)

SAM. Hello, Mary! You're a sight for sore eyes! *(He kisses her)*

MARY. Hello, Sam!

SAM. Mary, I'll be in New York for our annual dinner on the seventeenth. This time it's on me!

MARY. No, Sam, you're having dinner with us.

SAM. My, you're just as pretty as you ever were! I could eat you with a spoon. . . . *(He swings Mary around exuberantly and catches sight of Conover)* Why, Jim Conover, you old son-of-a-gun!

CONOVER. Hi-ya, Sam!

SAM. What are you doing here?

CONOVER. Take it easy, Sam. You're the only one in Detroit who knows I am here —and keep it to yourself!

SAM. What the hell's going on? Say— *(He looks from Conover to Mary and then the dawn breaks)* Damn it, I might have known! Jim, do you know you're psychic? I'm due in Washington on the eighteenth —I had it all planned to come and see you with the idea of selling you Grant Matthews for President, and damn it you beat me to it. Frankly, I was going to bribe you—with the biggest campaign contribution you ever saw.

CONOVER *(grabbing Sam's hand and shaking it)*. That's a date, Sam! Lunch in Washington on the eighteenth and bring cash!

SAM (*gleefully*). Mary, you go right home and start packing. You're moving into the White House. Give me another kiss! (*He kisses her again*) I've never been so happy about anything in my life. Wait until I tell Hilda!

CONOVER. Sam, you're not telling anybody, including Hilda.

MARY. How is Hilda? Is she coming to the banquet?

SAM. No, damn it, she's in bed with the flu. She's so mad she's going to miss Grant's speech she's not fit to live with. Look—why don't you call her up? Niagara 2956.

MARY. I'd better call her now because I'm not sure you and Hilda will be speaking to us after Grant's speech tonight. (*She goes to the telephone and picks up the receiver*)

CONOVER (*to Mary, sharply*). Why do you say that?

SAM (*to Conover*). The last time I was in New York, Grant and I had a hell of a knockdown drag-out fight about reconversion and full employment.

CONOVER (*to Mary*). Mary, is that what Grant's talking about tonight?

MARY (*into the telephone*). Just a minute. (*To Sam*) What's that number again, Sam?

SAM. Niagara 2956.

MARY (*into the telephone*). Niagara 2956.

SAM (*to Conover*). You know Grant—likes to talk like a radical, but, hell, anybody that's made as much money as Grant has is a sound American.

(*Grant enters from the left bedroom.*)

GRANT. The other boys thought they ought to hurry over there, Sam. Why don't you stick around a while and go over with us?

SAM. No, I've got to go with them. I'm chairman of the committe.

GRANT. You can catch them at the elevator. I'll let you out this way. (*He takes Sam to the hall door*)

SAM. I'll come back after the banquet. Got something to talk to you about, eh, Jim? (*He gives Conover a wink, then to Grant*) That was a hell of a good speech you made in Wichita. I could go along with two-thirds of it—especially that stuff about strikes. The other third—I suppose you've got to say those things—but look out people don't get the idea you're too far to the left. Talk to you about it later.

MARY (*into the telephone*). Keep trying and call me when you get them. (*She hangs up*)

SAM. See you later, Mary.

MARY. Good-bye, Sam.

SAM (*shaking hands with Grant*). Damn it, Grant! I'll be telling people I knew you when.

GRANT. Don't tell them yet!

SAM (*outside the door*). Hey, wait! Going down! (*Grant closes the door after him*)

CONOVER (*accusingly*). You're talking about reconversion and full employment tonight.

GRANT. Touching on them, among other things. (*He lights a cigarette*)

CONOVER. What angle are you taking?

GRANT. We talked about it in Washington. You know how I stand.

CONOVER. In Washington you were pretty specific. You're not being that specific here tonight?

GRANT. You're damn right I am!

CONOVER. What are you going to say?

GRANT. I'm going to tell them they did a great job in war production—and they did! But I'm going to remind them there wasn't any risk in that— The Government paid them for it. They had their engineering brains, and plenty of manpower to do the work.

CONOVER. All right. Why don't you let it go at that?

GRANT. Oh, no! I've got to tell them that now they're up against the test. Now they're on their own. They talk about how they want to save the private-enterprise system. All right, now they've got a chance to do it!

CONOVER (*agreeably*). Yes?

GRANT. They're not going to save it by lowering production so they can raise prices. And they're not going to save it by closing down plants to cut down competition. They're not going to save it if they don't work with unions instead of against them. And those babies who are stirring up war veterans to fight labor— I'm going to take their hide off!

CONOVER. Grant, you can't do that!

GRANT. Jim, you know reconversion goes deeper than re-tooling our plants. We need a moral reconversion. Take full employment—I don't mean the Bill—I mean the principle of it. What's behind most of the opposition to full employment—behind opposing the whole idea of the Government supplying work. To give private enterprise the chance to supply the employment? Nuts! It's to keep prices up on everything but labor. Let labor starve for a while! Jim, there isn't going to be a free-enterprise system if it means that men are free to starve!

CONOVER. Grant, you can't say those things now, and you can't say them here! This town is one of my best sources for silent money!

GRANT. You'll have to take your chances on the silent money, Jim!

MARY. What is silent money?

CONOVER (ignoring her). I warn you, Grant, you can't get out on this limb before the nomination.

MARY. People ought to know where he stands before they nominate him.

CONOVER (angrily). The people have damn little to say about the nomination. You two have lived in this country all your lives. Haven't you got that through your heads yet? You're not nominated by the people—you're nominated by the politicians! Why? Because the voters are too damned lazy to vote in the primaries! Well, politicians are not lazy! Remember what happened to Willkie in Wisconsin!

GRANT. They've got to know what I think, Jim! I told you that from the start. I've got to be on record.

CONOVER. All right—but not here—not tonight! Later. When you're out in Nebraska or Oklahoma.

(Spike enters from the right bedroom.)

SPIKE. O.K., Grant. This is the last group. And are they fruity?

CONOVER. Stall them, Spike. We're discussing something.

GRANT. No, Jim, I'm seeing them. (Grant turns to Spike) Who are they?

SPIKE. I don't know. They call themselves the Americans Incorruptible.

GRANT. I never heard of them.

SPIKE. They're dressed for the McKinley campaign. I didn't take their names. The Head Incorruptible is the fat dame with the big cowcatcher.

GRANT. What's their angle? What are they for?

MARY. With a name like that they're not for anything. They're against something.

SPIKE. Yes. (He takes Grant's cigarette away from him) Let's take no chances! But remember—they've got votes!

(Grant opens the door to the right bedroom, looks in and then turns back to Spike.)

GRANT. They shouldn't have! (He exits into the right bedroom. Mary crosses to the sofa and picks up a newspaper and starts reading the editorial on Grant)

SPIKE. I think I'd better go and air out Parlor B. (He starts out. The telephone rings)

MARY. That's probably Hilda Parrish for me.

SPIKE (into the telephone). Hello . . . This is MacManus. (He shakes head negatively at Mary) It's for you, Jim. (Spike exits. Conover goes to the desk and picks up the receiver)

CONOVER (into the telephone, casually as though talking to an old political friend). Hello. Oh, hello. How are you? (Pause) Who told you I was here—Sam? (Pause) Where are you? (Pause) All right. I'll come up to your room. (He hangs up and turns to Mary) Mary, will you tell Grant— (The telephone rings again)

MARY (drops the paper and starts for the telephone). That must be Hilda.

CONOVER. Tell Grant I'll be right back. (He exits into the hall)

(The waiter enters with ice cream and coffee; he pours the coffee.)

MARY (into the telephone). Hello . . . Oh, hello, Hilda. (Pause) This is Mary . . . Mary Matthews! (Pause) Yes. I'm here with Grant. I'm so sorry you're sick. (Pause) Well, if it isn't too much for you we'd love to run out for a few minutes after the banquet. (Pause) Good. Oh, Grant's busy in the next room with some women. (She laughs) No, he's safe. There's a whole committee of them. (Pause) All right . . . see you later. Good-bye, dear. (Mary hangs up and turns to the Waiter) Have you the check?

WAITER. Yes, Ma'am. (Waiter hands Mary a pencil and offers the check. She starts writing on the check)

MARY. I'll write your tip on the check.

WAITER. Is your husband Grant Matthews?

MARY. Yes.

WAITER. He certainly don't pull any punches, does he?

MARY (smiling). You said that just in time. (She writes the tip on the check and *hands it to the Waiter. He looks at it and smiles broadly)*

WAITER. Oh, thank you! *(He hurries out)*

GRANT *(entering from the right bedroom, carrying his hat and coat, which he places on a table near the door)*. Well, we've lost the Americans Incorruptible.

MARY *(taking a cup of coffee)*. Who were they? What did they want?

GRANT *(sitting down to his ice cream and coffee)*. They don't want America to be too harsh on poor little Germany and Japan. We shouldn't have gotten into it in the first place!

MARY. Oh, that crowd! Against war— but we may have to fight the Russians!

GRANT. Exactly! I wound up making a campaign speech for Stalin. *(He looks around)* Where's Jim?

MARY. He'll be back in a minute. He had a telephone call. Grant, what is silent money?

GRANT. Oh, it's a way they get around the Hatch Act.

MARY. What's the Hatch Act?

GRANT. It's a law they passed a few years ago about campaign funds. Only individuals can give money and nobody more than $5,000, and you have to account for how it's spent. It's a very pretty law—and we feel very moral that it's on the books —but it just doesn't work.

MARY. There must have been some reason for passing it.

GRANT. Yes, there was! It had gotten to be a bad situation. But you know how we do things in this country sometimes. When human nature gets to behaving like human nature, they pass a law repealing human nature. But the Hatch Act is too tough. So men who can afford it, walk in and put silent money down on the barrel-head—cash that can't be traced. It's been done by both parties before the law was passed and since. I've told you before, Mary, there's damn little difference between Democrats and Republicans.

MARY. But if silent money's illegal, I don't think you should take it!

GRANT. Oh, I wouldn't take it. That would be Jim's business.

MARY. But, Grant— *(She puts her coffee cup on the table)*

GRANT *(stopping her)*. Now, Mary, we both drank during Prohibition, didn't we? Put it down to political education, the

way the PAC does. *(Seeing she is still troubled)* I can't be too righteous about taking silent money. I've given it.

MARY. If you take money, you have to pay it back some way.

GRANT *(indignantly)*. Mary! You know damn well I'm not for sale!

MARY *(sharply)*. You've arranged that very neatly in your mind, Grant. All they have to do is buy Conover! I warned you the Presidency was a great temptation!

GRANT *(after a tight-lipped pause)*. You certainly have a gift for making it tough for me.

MARY *(distressed with herself)*. I know. I hear myself saying those things. I suppose it's a gift I picked up in exchange for some illusions.

GRANT *(with sober reasoning)*. Mary. people change. We've both changed. Life does that to you. We would have been happier if we could have stayed the two kids who went on a honeymoon to Victoria. I'm just as unhappy as you are that we didn't.

(There is a pause. Mary moves about the room restlessly, then turns the conversation to a less personal subject.)

MARY. I'm sorry Jim got a line on what you're going to say here.

GRANT. Yes, damn it! I was all keyed up for tonight's speech.

MARY *(disturbed)*. Are you going to change it?

GRANT. Oh, no! Don't worry. I'm going to speak my mind about reconversion.

MARY. Grant, you have to! You told labor they had to take the responsibility that goes with their power! You certainly have to be just as frank with business!

GRANT. I'm going to! Jim's argument was just not to say it here in Detroit.

MARY. In Wichita you said what you really believed. *(She goes to Grant)* Remember the satisfaction it gave you? I hope you feel that way tonight.

GRANT. I'd like to feel that way all the time. But you know yourself, you get into spots where you just can't afford it. *(He turns away. Mary realizes Grant is torn between ambition and integrity. She speaks to him quietly and sincerely)*

MARY. Grant—you know you don't have to be President.

GRANT *(the big liar)*. Oh—I don't even expect to be! *(Then with deep sincerity)*

But I know this much—I could do a lot of good.

MARY (*smoothing his hair*). Well, Grant, you may have to make up your mind whether you want that inner satisfaction or . . .

(*Conover enters from the outer hall.*)

GRANT (*rising and putting on his coat*). Hello, where's Spike? It's getting late. We ought to be going.

CONOVER. He may be getting the car around. Grant, before you go, I'd like to pick up where we left off about your speech tonight.

GRANT. Jim, we haven't got time for it. Let's talk about my speech after I've made it.

(*Spike enters from the left bedroom.*)

SPIKE. I hate to pull this on you, Grant, but there's one more delegation.

GRANT. To hell with them! Tell them I've left.

SPIKE (*handing a slip of paper to Grant*). You can't do that. They might see you on your way out.

GRANT (*taking the slip and glancing at it*). Okay. (*He starts for the left bedroom*)

MARY. Grant, we're the guests of honor. We can't be late.

GRANT. I'll make this short. Get your things, Mary. (*Grant exits into the left bedroom*)

SPIKE. Mary, you've got at least five minutes. I'll go down and check up on the police escort. (*He exits into the outer hall*)

MARY. It's a wonderful country! You take the police along with you so they can help you break the speed laws. (*She exits into the right bedroom, leaving the door open. Conover wanders down to the open door*)

CONOVER. Take your time, Mary. The way you look tonight I want everybody there before you make your entrance.

MARY (*offstage*). Don't be so flattering, Jim, or I'll think you want something from me!

CONOVER (*laughing*). As a matter of fact, I do. I was just going to ask you a favor.

MARY (*entering from the right bedroom wearing her evening wrap*). Fine! What can I do for you?

CONOVER. You're having Sam Parrish to dinner on the seventeenth. Do you mind inviting me, too?

MARY. Why, no. I'd love to have you.

CONOVER. Can I impose on you by inviting some other guests—say four or five?

MARY (*hesitating*). I hadn't planned that kind of a party on the seventeenth but . . .

CONOVER. If Grant's speaking on the twenty-third on International Policy, it may be important for him to see these people first.

(*Mary hesitates again, then comes to a decision.*)

MARY. All right, Jim. I think we can handle it! Do I know any of these people?

CONOVER. Well, you know Sam— And there's one other I'd like to talk to you about. You remember the reason I wanted you to make this trip in the first place?

MARY (*tightening*). Yes, I remember well enough.

CONOVER. Mary, I've been looking into how that talk got started. Mrs. Thorndyke used to be a frequent guest at your house. Then about a year ago she was crossed off your list, but Grant went on seeing her.

MARY. Yes.

CONOVER. Let's kill off those rumors once and for all. I want Mrs. Thorndyke there on the seventeenth.

MARY (*in cold anger*). No, Jim! Not in my house! And of all nights not on the seventeenth! It happens to be our wedding anniversary.

CONOVER (*with some heat*). Mary, I'm doing my damnedest to go along with Grant, even though he doesn't always go along with me. I need Mrs. Thorndyke there for more reasons than one. Let me win this one, will you?

MARY. Sorry, Jim, that's more than I can take. (*There is a knock on the door*) Come in! (*The Bellboy enters with a radio*)

BELLBOY. Here's your radio. I had to steal it from another room.

MARY. That's fine. Can you connect it for us?

CONOVER. Let's talk about this some more after the banquet.

(*The Bellboy puts the radio on the desk and plugs it in. Grant enters from the left bedroom.*)

MARY. Ready!

(*Grant takes a swig of coffee and Mary gets his hat. The Bellboy switches on the radio.*)

BELLBOY. Everybody wanted a radio tonight.

GRANT (*pleased*). So?

BELLBOY. Special broadcast from Holly-wood—Bob Hope and Jack Benny.

GRANT. Yes, I've got a break tonight, Jim—I'm following Hope and Benny.

MARY *(handing Grant his hat)*. After all that nonsense they'll be glad to hear Grant make some sense.

(The door opens and Spike sticks his head in.)

SPIKE. All set? I've got the elevator waiting for you.

MARY. Grant, fix your tie. Listen in, Jim. You'll find out what Grant's talking about!

GRANT. Good-bye, Jim. *(Grant and Mary exit into the hall)*

CONOVER. Good luck.

(We hear some music over the radio; then the Bellboy turns it off. Mary rushes back in excitement, looking desperately around the room.)

MARY. Where's my bag, my bag, my bag?

CONOVER. What's that in your hand? *(She looks down and sees her bag in her hand)*

MARY. That's my bag! *(She wheels and runs out)*

BELLBOY *(at the radio)*. Works all right. Do you want it on?

CONOVER. No. I can turn a radio on—and off. *(He tips the Bellboy, who thanks him and exits. Conover takes a chair from the table and places it at the right of the desk. Then he crosses to the left bedroom, opens the door, and speaks through it)* We may as well sit in here and be comfortable! *(Conover turns back into the room. Kay Thorndyke enters. She strolls across the room to the chair by the desk, places her furs and hat on the desk and sits down. Conover draws up a chair)* I have a radio. Do I dare listen?

KAY. I think so. Of course, I had less than five minutes with him.

CONOVER. Yes. And Mary's had five weeks! *(He lights a cigar)*

KAY *(confidently)*. I think he was glad to see me. I told you in Washington I could handle him.

CONOVER. Well, we'll find out. *(He sits down)*

KAY. I made it pretty strong. I said the Democrats would never take a chance like that. But that brought up a question that's on his mind, Jim, and you'd better have an answer ready for him.

CONOVER. An answer to what?

KAY. Is there any real difference between the Democratic Party and the Republican Party?

CONOVER. All the difference in the world. *(He turns on the radio)* They're in—and we're out!

CURTAIN

ACT THREE

SCENE ONE

The living room of the Matthews' apartment in New York. It is a fairly large room, the entrance from the hall being from an arch upstage, left of center; the door from the elevator is somewhere off-stage left. In this left arch we see stairs leading to an upper floor. Right of center there is a corresponding arch. Recessed behind this arch is an alcove bar with bottles of liquor and glasses, and it is through this arch that the guests proceed to the dining room, which is off right. Down-stage left there is a single door leading to a powder room and a place for the ladies' wraps.

There is a fireplace in the right wall. There is a small table and an ottoman below the fireplace. On a line with the fire-place and facing the audience is an up-holstered couch. On stage left there are two large comfortable upholstered chairs with a small table between them. Upstage between the two arches, there is a cabinet with single chairs at either end. On the cabinet is a vase of flowers, and above it on the wall hangs a painting of Mary and the two children.

Spike is sitting on the sofa, his hat be-side him. On the floor at his feet are an ashtray and a package which obviously contains a bottle of liquor. He has a piece of paper in his hand and a pencil.

Swenson, the butler, is standing facing Spike, with a piece of note-paper in his hand and a pencil.

———

SPIKE *(consulting the slip of paper he holds)*. Judge Alexander—bourbon—bour-bon and plain water—he may take a cock-tail, but I doubt it—he'll probably stick to straight bourbon.

SWENSON. Yes, sir. *(He makes a note)*

SPIKE. Now his wife—do you know how to mix a Sazarac?

SWENSON. No, sir, but I can look it up.

SPIKE. Well, I'll tell you. Take an old-fashioned glass and put a lump of sugar in it, soaked in Pernod.

SWENSON. I don't think we have any Pernod, sir.

SPIKE. I brought some. It's in there. *(He points to the package)* Then a jigger of bourbon, a twist of lemon peel on the top and give it a good stir. Don't sample that one, Swenson, it'll light up your vest buttons. *(Swenson makes a note)* That's all Mrs. Alexander drinks, but she drinks a lot of them. It's all right for her to get tight, if she wants to—but take it easy on the rest of them. We want to keep them sober. The Senator likes martinis before dinner, then he goes on a steady diet of Scotch and sodas.

SWENSON. Yes, sir.

SPIKE. Now, Mr. Parrish . . .

SWENSON. Manhattans for Mr. Parrish, and then rye.

SPIKE. And Mrs. Thorndyke—?

SWENSON. Mrs. Thorndyke likes a martini before dinner—very dry.

SPIKE. All right, give her one. Same for Mrs. Draper. Just have plenty of martinis and Manhattans—and Scotch and soda for Mr. Conover. And remember, Swenson, except for Mrs. Alexander nobody gets too much to drink—and that goes for Mr. and Mrs. Matthews too.

(Grant has entered through the left arch during the last sentence of Spike's speech. He is wearing a hat and a topcoat, and carries a small wrapped box. He drops the hat and the box on a chair.)

GRANT. What goes for Mr. and Mrs. Matthews?

SPIKE. I'm straightening Swenson out on the drinks—and nobody's to get too many. If there's one thing I don't want around here tonight, it's too much frankness—especially from you. I'm thinking of that time you got tight in San Francisco. We'd been in a hell of a fix if the newspaper men hadn't gotten drunker. Swenson wanted to know where to put the place cards. I've got a diagram here. *(He takes a piece of cardboard out of his pocket)*

GRANT. Wait till I get Mary. *(He hurries up the stairs)*

SWENSON. There's a Mr. Hardy on the list, sir.

SPIKE. Those labor boys are smart cookies. He doesn't drink anything.

(Swenson picks up the package at Spike's feet and goes through the right arch to the bar. He leaves the package behind the bar and exits right. We hear Grant before we see him.)

GRANT. Well, make it as soon as you can. I'm late. I should be changing. *(He comes downstairs, taking off his topcoat and holding it over his arm)* She'll be here in a minute. *(He goes to the fireplace)*

SPIKE. Nervous about tonight?

GRANT. Yes, a little. I feel as though I'm being quietly surrounded.

SPIKE. Take it easy. Let them do the talking.

GRANT. Oh, I'm not making any commitments here tonight. You and Jim and I are meeting over at Kay's after they've gone.

SPIKE. Look, they're going to throw the book at you tonight. That goes for Conover too. They don't expect you to take it all—it's just as Kay said last night—they'll be willing to compromise.

GRANT. Before I got into this, it all seemed so clear and simple. I suppose it does to almost everybody who doesn't have to make the decisions.

SPIKE. Yeah, Mary, for instance.

GRANT. I know now it isn't just black and white—but damn it, where do you draw the line? *(He thinks a moment)* I know damn well once I got to be President—*(A pause)* Well!

SPIKE. I'll drop back about midnight and pick you up and we can talk it out at Kay's.

GRANT. Spike, keep that to yourself—we're supposed to be meeting . . .

(Mary enters down the stairs. She is in evening dress. There is a lack of warmth between her and Grant.)

MARY *(crossing to arm of sofa and sitting)*. Hello, Spike. I'm sorry to get you up here, but I told Grant you had to help seat these people.

SPIKE. I've got a diagram here. *(He shows Mary the diagram)* You're here—and Grant's at the other end.

GRANT *(sitting on the sofa beside Spike)*. Well, if we're going to observe any protocol, Senator Lauterback ranks. I think he ought to be on Mary's right.

SPIKE. Okay, and I'll put Mrs. Draper on your right. We're short of women, some of the men will have to sit together.

MARY. Why don't you put Sam Parrish on Grant's left?

GRANT. Don't you want Sam up near you? It'll give you someone to talk to.

MARY. Well, I thought that after what you *didn't* say about reconversion in Detroit, you and Sam might want to hold hands under the table.

GRANT. Mary, we've been over that often enough. I *did* talk about reconversion in Detroit.

MARY. I wouldn't say about it, Grant. I'd say around it. You did come right out and mention the word once.

GRANT *(rising, and speaking with angry finality)*. Mary, I've heard all I want to hear about Detroit.

SPIKE *(to the rescue)*. Here's a good couple to pair off. Hardy and Mrs. Alexander. He never opens his mouth and she never closes hers. *(He writes their names down)* How about Mrs. Thorndyke up here? *(He points to one end of the diagram)*

MARY. How about Mrs. Thorndyke down there? *(She points to the other end of the diagram)*

SPIKE. Okay. Then the Judge here, and Jim here. *(He writes and then holds up the diagram)* That looks all right. *(He hands it to Mary)*

GRANT *(looking at his watch)*. Hell, I've got to get dressed. *(He starts for the stairs)*

MARY. Grant, you're looking in on Sonny and Joyce?

GRANT. I certainly am. *(He goes back to Mary)* Mary, I know this dinner isn't going to be much fun for you. It's damn nice of you to do it for me. I appreciate it.

MARY. Nonsense, Grant. I hope it's everything you want it to be. I'll do my best. Just to show you how serious I am about it, I'm not even going to have a cocktail.

GRANT. I'm going light myself. *(He starts off, then notices his hat and the box on the chair. He picks them up)* Oh, Mary, I almost forgot. This is for tonight. *(He hands her the box and hurries upstairs. Mary rises and watches Grant as he leaves)*

MARY. I didn't think he even remembered it.

SPIKE. Remembered what?

MARY. Today's our wedding anniversary. Excuse me, Spike! *(She takes off the wrapping eagerly, revealing a box of cigars)* My error! *(Jenny, a maid, enters from the right arch)* Jenny!

JENNY. Yes, Madam?

MARY. Here's the table diagram. Will you take care of the place cards? And these cigars?

JENNY *(taking both diagram and cigars)*. Very good, Madam. *(She exits left into the hall)*

SPIKE *(with forced gaiety)*. Those cigars are Llaranaguas, the only brand Conover smokes. Don't tell me Grant doesn't know how to play politics.

MARY. Oh, I know he plays politics! I've found that out! *(In unhappy puzzlement)* I *wish* I knew *why* he changed his speech in Detroit!

SPIKE *(casually)*. Jim talked to him, didn't he? Warned him not to say anything that would cost us any campaign contributions?

MARY. No, Spike, it wasn't for money. So if you do know, you won't tell me. You're not on my team. And I've often wondered why. You know, Spike, you've got a very wide streak of decency.

SPIKE. Yes, and if I don't watch it, it gets in my way. *(Seriously)* Mary, I'll pull every trick I know to get Grant in the White House, but once he's there and I'm back on the newspaper, I'll be on the same team with you; and if Grant isn't in there pitching for the people, I'll burn his pants off!

MARY. I'll light the matches for you.

SPIKE *(rising)*. But don't start any bonfires here tonight. *(Jenny crosses the hall, on her way to the outer door)* These educated apes that are coming here—Grant can't be nominated without their support, and in the election they can deliver a lot of votes.

MARY *(scornfully)*. How can you deliver the votes of a free people?

SPIKE. Mary, lazy people and ignorant people and prejudiced people are not free. *(We hear the voice of Judge Alexander offstage.)*

ALEXANDER *(offstage)*. Is Mrs. Matthews in?

JENNY *(offstage)*. This way, sir.

SPIKE *(picking up the ashtray and putting it on the table)*. Somebody's here.

I'd better run. I'll be back in time to help you sweep them out.

MARY. Wait until whoever this is comes in, will you, Spike? I don't know them all.

(*Judge Jefferson Davis Alexander and Mrs. Lulubelle Alexander enter. She is still wearing her wrap, which she hands to Jenny who exits with it to room down left. The Alexanders are from the deep South. He is tall and lean. She is short and plump.*)

SPIKE (*holding out his hand*). Hello, Judge. I'm Spike MacManus. Remember me?

ALEXANDER (*expansively, crossing to shake hands with Spike*). Indeed I do! It's a great pleasure to see you again, sir! This is Mrs. Alexander.

SPIKE. How do you do? Mrs. Matthews, this is Judge Alexander and Mrs. Alexander.

MARY (*holding out her hand*). How do you do, Judge Alexander?

ALEXANDER (*shaking hands*). It's an honor to be here, Mrs. Matthews.

MARY (*to Lulubelle*). I'm especially glad you could come, Mrs. Alexander. We women are going to be outnumbered here tonight.

LULUBELLE. That's nothing new to me, Mrs. Matthews. When I go to dinner with the Judge's Republican friends I'm always outnumbered. I make it a point to tell my hostess right off that while Jeff's a Republican, I'm a Democrat. But you can speak freely. You Republicans can't say anything about the Administration mean enough for us Democrats down South. (*She laughs; she is incurably good-natured*)

SPIKE (*amused*). I'll leave you my proxy, Mrs. Alexander. I've got to run along. Good night. Good night, Mary. Good night, Judge. (*He exits left.*)

ALEXANDER (*calling after him heartily*). It's been very pleasant seeing you again, sir! Good night! (*He turns to Mary*) Who is he?

MARY. A newspaperman. He's been helping my husband. Won't you sit down? (*Lulubelle goes to one of the easy chairs and sits. Jenny enters from the room down left and exits through the arch toward the outer door.*)

MARY. Mr. Matthews will be down in a minute.

ALEXANDER. Mrs. Alexander and I are certainly looking forward to meeting him. (*Swenson enters from the left arch and stands awaiting Mary's orders.*)

MARY. You must be looking forward to a cocktail, too.

LULUBELLE. Frankly, I'm looking forward to both.

SWENSON (*to Alexander*). Bourbon, sir?

ALEXANDER. You read my mind.

LULUBELLE. He can't read my mind.

SWENSON (*turning to Lulubelle*). A Sazarac, I believe?

ALEXANDER. Lulubelle, your reputation's getting too far north.

MARY. Swenson, can you make a Sazarac?

SWENSON. I think so, Ma'am.

LULUBELLE. If he just thinks so, Jeff, you'd better mix that Sazarac.

ALEXANDER. Yes, honey.

MARY (*indicating*). The bar's right over there.

SWENSON. This way, sir. (*He leads Alexander to the alcove bar, where the Judge goes to work mixing a Sazarac*)

MARY. Do you get up North often?

LULUBELLE. Being a Republican down South, the Judge only gets important every four years, around Convention time. Jim Conover getting him way up here this early must mean they're pretty serious about running your husband for President, which I hope they don't.

MARY. Really?

LULUBELLE. Yes, you seem like such a nice woman. Politics is too good an excuse for a man to neglect his wife.

MARY. Well, if you're neglected tonight —you and I will be neglected together. (*She hears voices in the hall and moves up to greet the new guests*)

(*Jenny ushers in Mrs. Grace Draper and Jim Conover. They are followed by Bill Hardy, and later Senator Lauterback. Mrs. Draper is a positive woman whose mind has been closed ever since Roosevelt's first term. Conover is dressed in a conservative business suit. Bill Hardy, the labor leader, obviously hasn't just come from the factory. He is dressed in dinner clothes and wishes he weren't. Senator Lauterback represents the farm bloc, but has been doing his farming in the Senate for a great many years. Jenny takes Mrs. Draper's wrap and exits with it into the room downstage left.*)

CONOVER. Hello, Mary. This is Mrs. Draper, Mrs. Matthews. Hello, Lulubelle. Where's the Judge?

LULUBELLE. Mixing me a drink.

CONOVER. Well, this is where I went out. *(He waves to the Judge)* Hello, Judge!

ALEXANDER *(from the bar)*. Hello, Jim!

MRS. DRAPER *(to Lulubelle)*. You're Judge Alexander's wife. I met you in Chicago.

LULUBELLE. Oh, yes, at the Convention. I was so glad to get back down South away from that heat. *(Mrs. Draper crosses to the sofa and sits down. Swenson has entered from the bar with a tray of drinks.)*

MRS. DRAPER *(crossing to Mary and shaking hands)*. I've been so eager to meet you and your husband.

MARY. It's so nice that you could come. Do you know Mrs. Alexander? *(Mrs. Draper goes to Lulubelle.)*

CONOVER. Mrs. Matthews, this is Bill Hardy. *(Hardy shakes hands with Mary.)*

MARY. Hello, Mr. Hardy.

HARDY *(aggrieved)*. Nobody told me not to dress.

CONOVER. My fault, Bill. I slipped up on that.

MARY. I'm glad you did dress. Men are getting all too lazy about dressing.

CONOVER. Isn't that what you're after, Bill? Put labor in evening clothes and let the rest of us go without? Have a drink! *(He points to the bar)* Oh, Mary, this is Senator Lauterback.

SENATOR *(shaking hands with Mary)*. Wanted to meet you ever since you made that trip with your husband. You were just as big a hit as he was. He talks well, but you're prettier.

CONOVER. Mr. Matthews will be down in a minute, Senator, and the bar's over there.

(The Senator goes to the bar.)

MARY *(as Swenson comes up with the tray)*. You want a highball, don't you, Jim?

CONOVER. Well, we've just come from a little caucus in my room at the hotel. We did some drinking there. Oh, all right. *(He takes a highball. Swenson turns to offer a drink to Mary)*

MARY. No, thank you, Swenson. I'm not having anything to drink tonight. *(Swenson serves a drink to Mrs. Draper. Kay Thorndyke enters and stands in the left arch. Mary turns and sees her. There is a moment of tension)* Hello, Kay.

KAY. Hello, Mary. *(Kay walks forward with outstretched hand)* You're looking very pretty tonight.

MARY *(taking a martini from Swenson's tray and putting it in Kay's outstretched hand)*. You're just in time for a cocktail. Do you know everyone here?

KAY. I know Mrs. Draper. *(The Judge has entered from the bar with Lulubelle's Sazarac, which he takes to her. The Senator and Bill Hardy remain at the bar.)*

MARY. Mrs. Alexander, this is Mrs. Thorndyke—and Judge Alexander.

KAY. How do you do?

LULUBELLE. Hello, Mrs. Thorndyke. *(She starts her drinking)*

ALEXANDER. Mrs. Thorndyke, I'm very pleased to meet you. I was raised in the old traditions of the South, where it was looked down on for a woman to go into anything like newspaper business. But no gentleman of the South could deny as attractive a woman as you your outstanding success. Which reminds me of a story! A number of years ago when I was a small boy . . .

LULUBELLE. Jeff, this is the best Sazarac I ever had in my life. Mix me another one right away!

ALEXANDER. Yes, honey.

MRS. DRAPER. Kay, after you left, Jim and I went into the situation in Chicago. Jim, tell her what you said.

KAY. Oh, Grace, let's take time out of politics for a little drinking. You're in for a bad evening, Mary.

(The Judge, having lost his audience, goes to the bar.)

MARY. Oh no! Politics is new to me, but I'm very interested.

CONOVER *(amiably, but sardonically)*.

You've got the "very" in the wrong place, Mary. Interested, but very new.

MARY (to the others, smiling). Mr. Conover means I haven't lost my amateur standing.

CONOVER. You're learning—I hope!

MARY. That's a dangerous hope, Jim. You politicians have stayed professionals because the voters have remained amateurs.

(Sam Parrish appears in the left arch.)

SAM. Hello, everybody! Late as usual! Had a hell of a day! (He goes to Mary) How's my sweetheart?

MARY. Hello, Sam.

(Sam kisses her.)

SAM. That's for Hilda! (He kisses her again) That's for me! (Hearing Sam, Hardy and the Senator drift into the room) Jim, I won't get down to Washington until afternoon. How about dinner instead of lunch?

CONOVER. That suits me even better.

SENATOR. Hello, Sam.

SAM. Senator! You'll be glad to hear I'm starting a back-to-the-farm movement. Just closed down two plants. (Hardy steps into view from behind the Senator) Oh, hello, Bill! Shouldn't have said that in front of you! Mary, do I have to sit down with Labor again tonight? Where's Grant?

MARY. He'll be down any minute.

MRS. DRAPER. Hello, Sam!

SAM. Hello, Grace!

MARY. Do you know Mrs. Alexander? Mr. Parrish.

SAM. How are you, Mrs. Alexander?

MARY. And have you met Mrs. Thorndyke?

KAY. Oh, yes, we know each other. Nice seeing you, Mr. Parrish.

SAM (to Kay). Where did you get to that night? I looked all over the banquet hall for you.

KAY (after a second's pause). I didn't go to the banquet.

CONOVER (to change the subject). Say, how's Hilda?

SAM. She's fine now. Mrs. Thorndyke, I thought that was why you were in Detroit—to hear Grant's speech.

MARY. Were you in Detroit when we were there, Kay?

SAM. Yes, you must have seen her, Mary. She was on her way to your suite. I'd just left you, remember?

MARY. I didn't see Mrs. Thorndyke in Detroit. (Fitting the pieces together) Oh, you must have dropped in to talk to Grant about reconversion.

SAM. What Grant said about reconversion in his speech that night was all right. You couldn't argue with it.

MARY. Well, I think you can thank Mrs. Thorndyke for that.

CONOVER (interrupting and going center to Sam). Sam, did you get that finance report I sent you?

SAM. Yes, and it's a damn bad job. I've made you a whole new list. (He searches through his pockets)

KAY (to Mrs. Draper). Grace, I'm having another cocktail.

MRS. DRAPER. I'll have one, too. (They both go to the bar.)

MARY (turning to Conover). Well, Jim, you hoped I'd learn. I'm learning.

(The Judge enters from the bar with two Sazaracs and goes to Lulubelle.)

SAM. Left it in my overcoat. I'll get it. (He starts out and sees the Judge) Hello, Judge! You drinking with both hands now?

ALEXANDER. Hello, Sam! These aren't for me. (Sam exits into the hall. The Judge places the drinks on the table beside Lulubelle) Honey, I want to talk to some of these people, so I brought you two of them.

LULUBELLE. Thank you, Jeff. (She takes a fresh drink)

MARY. Judge, I'll have one of those. (The Judge hands her a drink.)

CONOVER (concerned). Mary, those are pretty powerful. I thought you weren't drinking anything tonight.

MARY (incisively). I've just been reconverted! (She takes a healthy swallow)

LULUBELLE. Jeff, make another one for me right away.

ALEXANDER. Yes, honey. (He starts for the bar)

MARY. Hm-m, I like these. Judge, would you make another one for me too? (Mary sits in the comfortable chair next to Lulubelle. The Judge starts toward the bar. Grant Matthews comes down the stairs into the arch as Sam enters from the left with a sheaf of papers in his hand.)

GRANT. Hello, Sam!

SAM. Grant! All I've got to decide tonight is whether we're going to run you for a third term.

(They shake hands and come into the room together.)

CONOVER. How're you, Grant? You certainly took time to pretty yourself up.

GRANT. Was it successful? Sorry I'm late.

(The Judge has crossed down in front of sofa.)

ALEXANDER. Mr. Matthews, I'm Judge Alexander.

GRANT *(with a gesture)*. Not guilty!

(He crosses to the Judge and they shake hands. Sam takes Conover aside into conference)

ALEXANDER. Sir, I reject your plea. I'm sentencing you to four years in the White House!

GRANT *(laughing)*. You're taking Jim Conover more seriously than I am.

(Mary and Lulubelle are drinking steadily.)

ALEXANDER. Mr. Conover's a man to be taken seriously. Due to his efforts I almost had the honor of being the last man appointed to public office by Herbert Hoover. But the Federal Judge we expected to die held on a few days and the first thing we knew Mr. Roosevelt was in office. So I'm still on the State bench. However, my term expires in 1948. So ...

LULUBELLE. Jeff!

ALEXANDER. Yes, honey?

LULUBELLE. I'm going to be needing my other drink.

ALEXANDER. Yes, honey.

MARY. Grant, this is Mrs. Alexander.

(Grant turns to Lulubelle. Again without an audience, the Judge returns to the bar.)

GRANT. How do you do, Mrs. Alexander?

LULUBELLE *(to Mary)*. Handsome, isn't he? *He's* the first good reason I've ever seen for voting Republican. *(To Grant)* I warned your wife I was a Democrat.

GRANT. Some of my best friends are Democrats.

LULUBELLE. Well, you know us Southerners. We vote Democratic at home, but we've got an awfully good Republican record in Congress.

(Kay, Mrs. Draper, Hardy and the Senator come in from the bar. Swenson arrives at this moment at Grant's side with a tray of drinks. Grant takes a martini and turns to Mary.)

GRANT. Cocktail, Mary? Oh, you're not drinking anything, are you?

MARY *(holding glass aloft)*. Yes! Sazaracs!

GRANT *(surprised)*. Oh?

KAY. Hello, Grant!

(Grant turns and goes to her.)

GRANT. Oh, hello, Kay! Nice seeing you again.

(They shake hands.)

KAY. Do you know Bill Hardy?

GRANT. Glad you're here, Mr. Hardy.

HARDY. Nobody told me not to dress.

(He shakes hands with Grant, then turns to the fireplace to nurse his sense of social injustice)

KAY. And this is Grace Draper.

GRANT. I've been looking forward to meeting you, Mrs. Draper. You're on the National Committee, I believe.

KAY. And they're going to run Mrs. Draper for Congress.

GRANT. Fine! I always say a woman's place is in the House.

SENATOR *(coming down to Grant)*. Just so they stay out of the Senate. How are you, Mr. Matthews? I'm Senator Lauterback.

(They shake hands.)

GRANT. Oh, of course.

(Conover comes down and joins the group.)

SENATOR. We met before, in a manner of speaking. Remember? You testified before my Committee. You made a very strong impression on us.

GRANT *(amused)*. Well, I would never have guessed it from the Committee's report.

CONOVER. The Senator was just telling me about that, Grant. He can give you the inside on it. I think you'll find it very interesting.

(Swenson approaches the group around Grant with a tray of drinks.)

GRANT. Senator, we'll have to go into that later. I'd like to hear about it. Another cocktail, Mrs. Draper?

MRS. DRAPER. Thank you. They're very good. *(She takes one)*

GRANT. How about you, Kay?

LULUBELLE *(to Mary)*. You see, that's what happens when your husband gets into politics. You just sit off in a corner.

MARY. We have each other for company tonight and it gives us time to attend to our drink-

KAY. No, two's my limit.

GRANT. How about you, Senator? Or would you rather have a highball?

SENATOR. No, I'll stick to these. (He takes a cocktail) And very good too!

GRANT (to Hardy). Want that refreshed, Mr. Hardy?

HARDY. No, you can drink just so much Coca-Cola.

ing. (She finishes her Sazarac just as the Judge arrives with two more. Both women take fresh drinks)

LULUBELLE. Just in time, Jeff. Fix us some more right away.

ALEXANDER, Honey, there are a lot of things I want to talk to Mr. Matthews about.

LULUBELLE. Mix the drinks before you start talkin', Jeff; you know how I hate to interrupt you.

ALEXANDER. Yes, honey.

(Judge hurries back to bar, muttering.)

(Swenson returns to bar and then disappears into dining room.)

KAY. Grant, Mrs. Draper is very interested in what you plan to say at the Foreign Policy Association Thursday night.

GRANT (to Mrs. Draper). Yes, Thursday's the night I settle world affairs.

KAY. Grace is the Party's expert on the foreign vote.

MRS. DRAPER. I think the election in '46 is going to turn on it, and in '48 too.

KAY. Take the Italians, for instance. Everybody knows we've made a mess of things in Italy.

MRS. DRAPER. The Italians over here are all unhappy about it, and they're going to be even unhappier when the final peace terms are drawn up.

KAY. Truman has to take responsibility for the peace terms. So it's not going to be hard to appeal to the Italian vote.

GRANT. I think we have to wait and find out what the peace terms are.

KAY. We don't have to wait. We just have to demand justice for Italy.

MARY (who has been listening to this, speaks up, with Sazarac-inspired articulateness). If you favor Italy, won't that lose you the Abyssinian vote?

MRS. DRAPER (turning to Mary). Mrs. Matthews, there isn't any Abyssinian vote.

MARY. Good! We don't have to worry

about justice for the Abyssinians. (She goes back to her drinking)

KAY (to Grant). Grace thinks that in this election the Polish vote is the most important.

MRS. DRAPER. Indeed I do! Now in your speech Thursday night you should come out for the reopening of the whole Polish question—boundaries, government, reparations—

KAY. Any strong stand, Grant, would clinch the Polish vote.

MARY. I thought the Poles voted in Poland.

KAY (to Mary, kindly). We're talking about Polish-Americans.

MARY. Oh, can you be both?

SAM (looking up from his papers). Mary, you're a sweet girl and I love you, but this is practical politics, and you're way out over your head.

MARY. If they're Americans I should think you'd ask them to vote as Americans, not as Poles!

GRANT (too heartily). Mary, I think we could all use some more hors d'œuvres.

(Mary rises and goes to bell in the left wall, which she presses.)

KAY. Take Pennsylvania for instance...

MARY. Is this what's called power politics?

SENATOR (strolling toward Mary). Mrs. Matthews, power politics is what they play in Europe.

MARY (crossing back to her chair). It seems to me we're beginning to play it right here. Let's disunite the United Nations and keep Pennsylvania safe for the Republicans. (She sits. Judge Alexander comes out of the bar with a tray holding four Sazaracs. He crosses to Lulubelle)

ALEXANDER. Doggone it, I miss everything. Who says we're not going to carry Pennsylvania? (He places the tray on the table and addresses Lulubelle) Honey, I made four this time. I'm missing out on everything. I'm starved for some good Republican talk.

(Jenny enters from left arch in answer to bell. Mary and Lulubelle each take a fresh Sazarac.)

LULUBELLE (raising her glass to Mary). More power to you!

MARY. Thanks! They're full of it, aren't they? (She starts on her third Sazarac.)

GRANT (to Jenny). Jenny, some hors d'œuvres, please.

(Jenny takes a tray of hors d'œuvres from a table at the foot of the stairs and passes them.)

ALEXANDER. Mr. Matthews, if I may say so, I think you're the hope of the new South.

SENATOR. Here we go again! The Judge is going to promise that we'll break the solid South.

ALEXANDER. Senator, you don't understand the conditions down there!

SENATOR. All I have to say is that when a state votes the same way for one hundred years, it a reflection on the intelligence of the electorate. *(Turns to Mary)* Don't you agree with me, Mrs. Matthews?

MARY. I'm from Vermont. *(She drinks)*

SENATOR. That's not the same thing. Vermont's always been a good sound Republican state *(To Grant)* Mr. Matthews, in your speech Thursday I know you have to tie up world peace with tariff reductions and we realize industry has to make some sacrifice along that line . . .

SAM. Oh, industry has to make the sacrifices!

SENATOR. But I think you'll have to reassure the American farmer that he won't be forced to compete with Russian wheat and Danish butter and Argentine beef.

GRANT. Senator, there's a direct connection between world trade and world peace.

KAY. Grant, the farmer has a special case.

SENATOR. And twenty million votes!

GRANT. Senator, I want you to talk to me very, very frankly and very fully, and give me all the information you can—but please don't expect me to make any decisions here tonight.

MARY. That's the way Grant works. He likes to listen to people before he makes any decish—*(Mary stops short, looks down at the drink, puts the drink on the table, then continues somewhat defiantly)* —before he decides anything.

SAM. I thought we were going to taik turkey tonight. If I'm going to raise this money, I've got to take word back to Detroit how Grant stands on certain issues.

CONOVER *(following Sam down to center)*. After you've gone, Grant and I are going to hold a caucus. We'll have word for all of you tomorrow.

SENATOR *(to Sam)*. Sam, Mr. Matthews' strength is with big business. Why should they be worried about him?

SAM. You know what we're worried about. Are we going to be in for a lot of government competition, or is this country going to be put back in the hands of private enterprise?

(Swenson enters from arch left and tries to catch Mary's eye.)

MARY *(rising)*. Oh, Grant believes in private enterprise. *(She stares across at Kay)* Doesn't he, Kay?

SWENSON. Dinner is served, Ma'am. *(Swenson exits.)*

GRANT. Dinner. Good! Take your cocktails with you if you haven't finished. *(He crosses to center)* Mary!

MARY *(leading the guests out)*. Just find your own place cards. I hope some of you men don't mind sitting together. There aren't enough women to go around.

(Mary exits through the right arch, followed by Mrs. Draper and Lulubelle, then Hardy, Alexander, Sam, Senator and Conover. Kay delays following the others so that when all are gone but Grant she can seize the opportunity to speak to him.)

KAY *(with cold anger)*. Grant, Mary's tight. Is there any way you can talk to her—do something with her?

GRANT *(worried)*. What happened?

KAY. It was Sam. The minute he walked into the room he . . .

(Mary enters from dining room, speaking back over her shoulder.)

MARY. Find your place cards, everyone. I forgot my—*(She turns and sees Grant and Kay)*—cocktail.

(Kay brushes past her to dining room. Mary stares after her.)

GRANT. Mary, I'm depending on you to help me tonight.

MARY *(crossing to the table)*. I'm afraid I interrupted you and Kay before she had a chance to tell you what you think. *(She picks up drink from table)*

GRANT. Leave that drink here, and get some food into you as soon as you can!

MARY *(challengingly)*. Well! Seems to me you're getting a little belligerel.

GRANT. Mary, I'm on a spot here tonight. We both are. We have to be ready to do some quick thinking.

MARY *(starting for the dining room)*. Don't worry about me. *(She stops and looks back at Grant)* I'm a very thick quinker.

(Mary continues toward the dining room,

*walking with careful deliberation. Grant
starts to follow.)*

CURTAIN

SCENE TWO

The same, some time after dinner.
*Mary and Lulubelle are seated in the
comfortable chairs. Mary is drinking coffee with a certain desperation.*

*On the table between them is Lulu-
belle's demitasse, untouched. Lulubelle is
at work on a bourbon and soda. Mary
finishes her coffee, puts it down on the
table and notices Lulubelle's full cup. She
eyes it for a second and then speaks to
Lulubelle.*

———

MARY. You haven't touched your coffee.

LULUBELLE. Never use it. Keeps me
awake nights.

MARY *(picking up the cup).* Do you
mind?

LULUBELLE. Help yourself, honey.
*(Mary starts on Lulubelle's coffee. Lulu-
belle is sipping her highball as though her
immediate memories gave her some
amusement. Swenson appears with a coffee pot on a tray. He approaches the
empty cup which Mary has put down.)*

SWENSON *(to Lulubelle).* More coffee,
Ma'am?

MARY *(promptly).* Yes, Swenson.
*(He fills the empty cup, then turns to
Mary.)*

SWENSON. Coffee, Ma'am?

MARY. Yes, please. *(She quickly finishes
coffee in her cup, then holds it out for
Swenson to refill)* Be sure everyone in the
dining room is taken care of. And did
you remember Mr. Conover's cigars?

SWENSON. Yes, Ma'am.
*(Swenson starts back to the dining room.
Mrs. Draper enters. He allows her to pass
and then exits. Mrs. Draper heads for the
powder room, but stops center and points
toward it.)*

MRS. DRAPER. Am I right?
*(Mary nods, giving her the best smile she
can muster. Mrs. Draper hurries into the
powder room.)*

LULUBELLE *(to Mary, reassuringly).* I
thought she spoke to you real friendly.

MARY. Shouldn't she have? What did I
say to *her?*

LULUBELLE. I can't quite remember,
honey, but it was followed by one of the
loudest silences I've ever heard.
(Mary suffers and gulps some coffee.)

MARY. I can't remember anything that
happened before the salad.

LULUBELLE. You missed the best part.
You certainly were whamming away at
them. You picked them off one by one—
like settin' birds. I haven't enjoyed myself
so much since Huey Long died.

MARY *(after taking another gulp of coffee).* Can you remember any of the things
I said?

LULUBELLE *(thinking).* Now let me see
—what was it you said to the Senator? I
kept wishing I had a pencil so I could
write 'em down. It may come back to me
later. That was the time Sam Parrish had
the choking spell. You remember that,
don't you?

MARY *(disconsolately).* No.

LULUBELLE. Oh, he had to leave the
table. Then when he came back you
started on *him.*

MARY. Oh, dear! *(She puts her empty
cup down and takes up Lulubelle's full
one and starts drinking from it)*

LULUBELLE. It was something personal
that I couldn't rightly follow. Your husband got it. That's when he knocked over
his wine. My!—And that looked like an
expensive dress Mrs. Thorndyke is wearing. *(Mary comes out of coffee cup with a
broad smile and turns to Lulubelle)* I
don't think she likes you, honey. She was
the only one that tried to get back at you.
But you took care of her!

MARY. What were they talking about?

LULUBELLE. It was kinda hard to keep
track of it, because every time you said
something they changed the subject.
(Mary suffers) After we've gone, you'd
better make up to your husband. I don't
think he thought that talk about the thermometer was very funny.

MARY *(bewildered).* Thermometer? What
thermometer?

LULUBELLE. Oh, you just kept bedevil-
ing him to take his temperature.

MARY. Why?

LULUBELLE. Well, you said he was getting another one of his attacks of gallopin'
self-importance. *(Mary winces)* I remember that one! I'm saving that up to use on
Jeff! *(She finishes her drink)*

MARY. I certainly picked a good day for

this. *(Turns to Lulubelle)* It's our wedding anniversary.

LULUBELLE *(thoughtfully)*. Well, honey, this is one anniversary you'll both always remember. *(Jenny crosses back of arch toward the outer door. Swenson enters from the dining room with a tray holding a silver coffee pot and a bourbon and soda. Lulubelle helps herself to the highball)* Thank you!

SWENSON *(pouring coffee for Mary)*. Shall I leave this here?

MARY. Yes, please. Thanks, Swenson. *(He puts the tray with the coffee pot on the table. Spike enters through the arch)*

SPIKE *(blithely)*. Hello, there! How's everything going?

MARY. Just daisy.

(Swenson picks up Lulubelle's empty glass and starts to exit.)

SPIKE *(to Swenson)*. Will you tell Mr. Matthews I'm here?

(Swenson bows and exits.)

MARY. They're still in the dining room, talking politics.

SPIKE. Did it get too much for you?

MARY. I got too much for them.

SPIKE *(concerned)*. Oh-oh!

MARY. And don't ask for a copy of my speech. No matter what they tell you, I've been misquoted.

(Grant appears in the right arch.)

GRANT. Hello, Spike, come on in! You know everybody.

SPIKE. How's it going?

GRANT. I don't know.

SPIKE. If it's a smoke-filled room, I can tell you—you're nominated.

(Spike exits into dining room. Grant looks at his watch. He speaks in Mary's general direction.)

GRANT. I didn't know it was that late. Spike came to get Jim and me. We're going over to Jim's hotel afterwards for a post-mortem. Swenson taking care of you, Mrs. Alexander?

LULUBELLE. Yes, thank you. We're having a good time in here.

GRANT. We're having a good time in there—now. *(He exits into the dining room. Mary hastily drinks more coffee.)*

LULUBELLE. You blame it all on me, honey. You tell him I started you drinking those Sazaracs.

MARY *(painfully)*. What's in those buzz bombs?

(Mrs. Draper enters from the powder room.)

LULUBELLE. Mrs. Draper, you've given me an idea. *(She rises and exits into the powder room)*

MARY *(to Mrs. Draper)*. Won't you sit down and have a drink with us?

MRS. DRAPER. I have to catch a train. I'm just going back to say my good nights. *(Conover enters from the dining room.)*

CONOVER. Oh, Grace, I was afraid you'd gone. The talk has swung around to your territory. They need some information.

MRS. DRAPER. I can only stay a couple of minutes. *(She exits. Conover looks at Mary thoughtfully)*

CONOVER. Can I get you a drink?

MARY. Not until about 1952.

CONOVER. Oh, I forgot to tell you. There's been a shake-up in my secret service. I'll prove it to you. The Colonel, who used to be a Major, is now a General.

MARY *(disinterestedly)*. Really?

CONOVER. He must be quite a guy.

MARY. He is.

CONOVER. Better keep in touch with him. Send him congratulations.

MARY. No, Jim. When he was a Major —I admit he was a major interest. But now, although he's a General, he's just a general interest.

(Conover studies Mary for a minute.)

CONOVER. Mary, you once spoke of a spanking as an indication of deep affection. There were some moments tonight when I could have turned you over my knee, but there wouldn't have been any affection in it.

MARY. All right, Jim. I'll agree I've behaved badly as a hostess. I'm not proud of my bad manners. But I'll bet you I'd be proud of what I said—if I could remember what I said.

CONOVER *(amused in spite of himself)*. You did let go some beauts.

MARY. Well, I think they're all stupid, selfish people.

CONOVER. I'd like to tell you how stupid I think you are. *(He goes to her)* Mary, I think it's time you were a little selfish, *and* a little intelligent. There's such a thing as enlightened self-interest you know. Why should you be stupid, just because Kay's being stupid?

MARY. Jim, that's one thing even I can't say about Kay—she's not stupid.

CONOVER. Isn't she? She's in there now

doing her damnedest to get Grant into the White House. And the White House is the one place where she can't be with him. She can't follow him there, Mary. Have you ever thought of that?

MARY *(given pause)*. No, I hadn't.

CONOVER. Well, isn't it a little unintelligent of you to do anything to stop Grant from getting there? If he doesn't become President, I'm not so sure what's going to happen between you and him. But if he is elected—then you'll be the First Lady—in more ways than one.

MARY *(painfully)*. That doesn't necessarily follow.

CONOVER. I think it does—and I'll tell you why. I know how you feel toward Grant. You've never bothered to conceal it from me.

MARY. Okay. So I love him.

CONOVER. Mary, when I saw you and Grant in Detroit—before he spoke that night—there were two people in love. Maybe Grant hadn't said so—maybe Grant hadn't shown it in those little ways you were looking for—but if you had had another month alone together, you know what would have happened.

MARY *(not daring to believe it)*. I think you're wrong, Jim.

CONOVER. No, my dear, what he feels toward you goes pretty deep—and I'll tell you how he gives himself away. It's in his respect for your opinion—for what you think.

MARY. Don't kid me, Jim. We both know what happened to Grant's speech on reconversion.

CONOVER *(sitting on the arm of her chair)*. Well, here's something you don't know—how unhappy Grant is about that. He's good and sore at himself and I know in my bones that some day what he thinks about reconversion—and Big Business—and what you think—is going to pop right out in the middle of a speech. I'm only praying that it doesn't happen before the nomination, and you'd better add a prayer, too.

MARY. But I want him to say it.

CONOVER. No, Mary! Not before the nomination! That's playing Kay's game. *(Spike enters.)*

SPIKE. Jim, can you come back in here? They're just breaking up.

CONOVER. I'll be there in a minute. *(Spike exits)* Mary, use your head. You can keep Grant from being President, but if you do, you're going to lose him. *(He rises)* Will you do something for me before I go tonight?

MARY. What?

CONOVER. I'd like to hear you say something to Grant that would let him know that if he does come our way just a little, you won't make life miserable for him. *(Mary is silent)* You're not the only one to be considered, Mary. Think of your children. That's a pretty good heritage— to be able to say, "My father was President of the United States."

MARY. Thanks, Jim. You're better than black coffee. You'd better get back in there.

CONOVER *(strolling toward the dining room)*. Oh, I'll hear it all later.

MARY. Oh, yes, Grant and Spike are going over to your hotel with you. *(Conover stops in the arch and looks back at Mary.)*

CONOVER. No, Mary, we're going over to Mrs. Thorndyke's. *(Conover stands for a minute watching Mary who slowly turns and stares at him; then he exits. Mary sits thinking for a moment; then rises with determination and starts for the dining room but hears voices offstage and stops.)*

MRS. DRAPER *(offstage)*. Good night, everybody! *(She enters with Grant and Hardy)* I'm sorry I have to run. I'm afraid I broke up the party.

GRANT. I'm sure you'll have time to get your train.

MRS. DRAPER. I have to stop at the hotel first. I'll get my wrap.

MARY. Can I help you?

MRS. DRAPER. No. I know right where it is. *(She exits into the powder room. The Senator and Conover enter but stay in the bar alcove talking together confidentially)*

HARDY *(to Mary)*. I'll say good night, Mrs. Matthews.

MARY. Good night. It was very nice having you here.

HARDY *(to Grant)*. I hope to hear from you on that.

GRANT. You'll be in touch with Jim.

HARDY. Just keep in mind what I said. Our funds are our secret weapon. If an employer knows how much we've got in the bank, he knows just how long we can stay out on strike. We can't afford to open our books.

GRANT (*smiling*). As an employer I can understand that. Of course, I have to show my books.

HARDY. Well, good night. Good night, Mrs. Matthews. See you in Washington, Senator. (*He exits*)

SENATOR (*going to Mary*). What you said about Sam Parrish—I can't wait to get back to Washington to tell it on him— (*Turns to Grant*) Good night, Mr. Matthews— (*He draws him downstage*) Look, will you promise me this? Before you speak in the Middle West again, will you have another talk with me—and I'd like to have Ed O'Neal and Earl Smith there. We can handle the farm problems in Congress, but we'd like to be sure we won't run into any vetoes.

GRANT (*laughing*). Vetoes! Senator, you're moving a little too fast for me. I haven't even started to work on my inaugural address.

MARY (*trying to take part*). Inaugural address! My, that makes me nervous—and excited!

CONOVER. I'll be there holding your hand, Mary.

SENATOR. Jim, I know everything's safe in your hands. (*We hear a laugh from dining room*) Good night, Mr. Matthews. (*He shakes hands with Grant*) Good night, Mrs. Matthews. (*Kay and Alexander enter*) Good night, everybody! (*He exits*)

KAY. I'll remember that, Judge, the next time I'm in New Orleans.

ALEXANDER. Where's Lulubelle?

MRS. DRAPER (*who has just entered with wrap*). She's in the bedroom getting her things.

KAY (*crossing Mrs. Draper downstage to door at left*). I'd better get mine. (*She exits*)

ALEXANDER. My coat is out there, isn't it? (*He indicates hall and exits into it*)

MRS. DRAPER (*going to Mary*). It was so nice meeting you, Mrs. Matthews.

MARY. Thank you. I hope we see each other soon.

MRS. DRAPER. You don't mind my falling in love with your husband, do you?

MARY. I don't see how you could help it.

MRS. DRAPER (*to Grant*). I hope you and Jim get together on everything.

GRANT. Whoever the candidate is, you're going to be very valuable to him. I realize that.

(*Kay enters from the powder room with her wrap.*)

MRS. DRAPER. Well, if there's one group I do know how to swing, it's the foreigners. I don't pretend to be an intellectual, but since our so-called great minds have gotten us into the United Nations, we can't overlook the political advantage it gives us. Remember, there are lots of voters who are afraid of Russia!—And you'd be surprised how many people hate the British!

GRANT. I don't think we can capitalize on that, Mrs. Draper. We can't build world peace on hate. We have a certain leadership in the United Nations. We have to be very jealous of it.

KAY. Yes, but, Grant, if the Party's to win, remember each nationality in America will be thinking of their home country. We can use that. Am I right, Jim?

CONOVER. In Jersey City, Mayor Hague promised the Italians we'd rebuild Italy.

KAY. Exactly!

MRS. DRAPER. We've got to promise them that, and more, too!

CONOVER. It's bound to be part of the campaign. I don't see how we can very well avoid it. (*He has been eyeing Mary*) Do you, Mary?

MARY (*taking time to swallow*). Well, some of the Democrats are being pretty open about it.

MRS. DRAPER. I do have to run. Goodbye, Mr. Matthews. You'll find I'm right about all this! (*She shakes hands with Grant. To Mary*) Good night, Mrs. Matthews. It was a wonderful dinner—and such good talk! (*She crosses to the left arch and pauses to speak again to Mary who has followed her*) Of course my friends accuse me of thinking God is a Republican. But I'm fair-minded. I thank Him every night for Senator Bilbo.

(*Mrs. Draper and Mary exit together. Kay crosses to sofa and sits. Lulubelle enters from the powder room, wearing her wrap. Judge Alexander enters from the left arch, with his topcoat on, carrying his hat.*)

ALEXANDER (*crossing to Grant*). Mr. Matthews, I just happened to find in my overcoat pocket here a little pamphlet. It's a reprint of some of my most important decisions. I thought you might like to look it over. (*He hands pamphlet to Grant*)

GRANT. I'll be very glad to study it.

ALEXANDER. And I think I can safely

promise you the votes of five Southern States.

GRANT (*unbelieving*). In the election?

ALEXANDER. Hell, no!—In the convention! (*He crosses to the left arch*)

LULUBELLE. Mr. Matthews, I can't tell you how crazy I am about that wife of yours. And that reminds me— (*She offers her hand to shake*) Congratulations!

GRANT. Congratulations? I don't think the Democrats have conceded yet.

LULUBELLE. No, I mean on your anniversary—your weddin' anniversary!

(*Grant looks a bit blank, then it comes to him.*)

GRANT (*shaking her hand vigorously*). Oh, yes, of course! Well, thank you!

(*Sam and Spike enter from the dining room.*)

SAM. Spike, I hate to bother you with it . . .

ALEXANDER (*to Grant*). Remember, when you speak in New Orleans, you're going to be our house guest.

LULUBELLE. Good night, Mr. Matthews. But if you campaign through the South, you'd better change your name from Grant to Lee!

(*Lulubelle and Alexander exit through left arch.*)

SPIKE (*to Conover*). Jim, I'm going to try to switch Sam to your train tomorrow. You're on the Congressional, aren't you?

CONOVER. Yes.

SPIKE (*to Sam*). Better give me your space.

(*Sam hands Spike a railroad envelope. Spike sits down and makes notes on the envelope.*)

CONOVER. Yes, that's fine, Sam. I think on the way down we can have a pretty definite talk.

SPIKE. I'll get to work on it in the morning.

(*Mary enters from the left arch.*)

SAM. Well, I've got to catch up on my beauty sleep. Can I drop you, Mrs. Thorndyke?

GRANT. I'm going over to Jim's hotel with him. We can drop Mrs. Thorndyke. It's on the way.

SAM. Grant, the evening turned out fine. It was a great idea getting all these people together. Must have been something of an education for you. You see, Grant, you have to run your politics the same way you run your business. It's a question of taking practical measures.

(*Mary has come down to left of Sam. Conover is watching Mary.*)

GRANT. Sam, you'd better go home. You know you rule me. Pretty soon we'll be in an argument. (*He gives Sam a affectionate push*)

SAM. You're in a spot now where you can't indulge in any more of that radical talk. My God, look at the effect it's had on Mary!

GRANT. Sam, if you have nightmares, I'll bet they're all about Henry Wallace!

SAM (*remembering something*). Oh, say! —Hilda'd never forgive me if I forgot to show you this. (*He takes a leather picture case from his pocket*) Look! It's Bobby, taken in Japan. Made a hell of a record— sixteen Jap planes.

GRANT. You must be very proud of Bobby.

SAM. He'll be out soon. He wants to go right into the business when he gets back. No more college. And I'm going to let him. Want to train him. I haven't got too many more years left. I want to leave him the soundest business in these whole United States. (*To Mary with almost pathetic justification*) That isn't anything to be ashamed of, is it, Mary?

MARY (*distressed*). Give him my love when you write—and next time bring Hilda.

SAM. Good night, Mary. (*He kisses Mary and shakes hands with Grant*)

SPIKE. I'll leave your ticket at the hotel in the morning.

(*Jenny enters from the right arch with a tray.*)

SAM. See you on the train, Jim.

CONOVER. Good night, Sam.

(*Sam exits.*)

GRANT (*to Jenny*). Jenny, will you ask Swenson to bring down my coat? I left it upstairs.

(*Jenny exits and goes upstairs. Grant goes to the ottoman and sits.*)

KAY. Spike, why don't you get Jim's coat?

(*Spike rises and starts for the left arch. Swenson is seen going upstairs.*)

CONOVER. Well, Grant, you're still alive. I know you didn't look forward to this evening—but it wasn't so tough, was it?

GRANT. They certainly don't mind asking for heaven and earth, do they?

CONOVER. They don't expect to get heaven.

SPIKE. No, they'll settle for the earth. *(He exits into hall left. Mary sits on the arm of one of the chairs)*

KAY. I was pretty frank with them. I told them there were some things they just couldn't ask Mr. Matthews to do. They were pretty reasonable—on the whole. Of course, there's no question about it—we'll have to meet them half way. *(She sees Grant looking at her and smiles at him)* Part way, at least.

CONOVER. I'll get all these people alone. They know they can't get too tough with me. Of course there are some points we'll have to concede. We can't get through life without conceding some things, can we, Mary? *(He goes to Mary and puts his arm around her shoulder as if in reminder, but doesn't wait for an answer. Spike enters with Conover's coat)* I think all the Senator wanted to know was that Grant wouldn't fight the farm bloc. Hell, we all know we can't fight the farm bloc. They're too powerful.

(Spike helps Jim into his coat.)

GRANT. I'm afraid, Jim, that when it comes to concessions, the Senator and his crowd will have to make some. *(Swenson enters with Grant's coat and hat)* They want a floor under farm prices but no ceiling. They can't have it both ways.

CONOVER. Oh, there's always a margin of give and take. We won't have any trouble there.

GRANT *(getting into his coat)*. Don't wait up, Swenson. I'm going to be late. *(He hands Swenson the Judge's pamphlet)* And throw this away, will you? *(To the others)* Well, we'd better get going.

SPIKE. I don't think the Senator is going to be half as tough as Mrs. Draper. I started kidding her. I said it was too bad we couldn't dig up Hitler. There might be some votes in it. *(He chuckles)*. She didn't know whether I was on the level or not. And from her answer, I don't know whether she was on the level or not.

GRANT *(buttoning up his coat)*. If you ask me, I don't think she was kidding. I can't go whole hog with her, Jim.

CONOVER. Of course she goes a little overboard—but you can't dismiss the fact those issues are coming up, and we've got to find some way of making a play for the foreign vote.

KAY. We know that every nation is going to feel the peace terms have done them an injustice. We can make a perfectly honest appeal for justice, and if that gets us some votes—I don't think we should quibble.

GRANT. Which are you thinking of first, the votes or the justice?

CONOVER. Grant, we can't help ourselves! The Democrats are going to play that side of the street—they're doing it already! Mary agrees with us on that. *(He has been watching Mary. She, instead of making any comment, rises and starts for the stairway)* We can find some way to take a stand for justice and still appeal to the foreign vote—and with a clear conscience. Don't you think so, Mary?

MARY *(turns)*. No! I don't! I tried to get out of the room before I got sick, but you wouldn't let me! I've sat here listening to you making plans for Grant to trade away the peace of the world to get a few votes! Now that we're in the United Nations let's use it—use it to get Italian votes and Polish votes—let's use it to get the votes of those who hate the Russians and those who hate the British! How long is it going to be before you ask us to forgive Germany to get the German vote?

CONOVER *(warningly)*. Mary!

MARY. You heard Mrs. Draper and how much did it mean to you? "She's a little overboard"—"You can't quite go whole hog with her." And you heard Kay, too, cheering her on! None of you had the guts to tell them they are starting another war and to slap them down for it!

KAY. Now, Grant. Really!

CONOVER. Mary, do you know what you're doing?

MARY. Yes, Jim, I know what I'm doing! Look at Sam—he wants to leave a fortune to Bobby. What kind of a world is he going to leave to Bobby? The kind he wants isn't good enough for my children. Don't you know what's happened in the world? Are you willing to trust the people you brought here tonight with atomic power?

CONOVER *(harshly)*. We may not be as bright as you are, Mary, but the people here tonight were pretty representative.

MARY. Representative of what? Nobody represented the American people! They don't even represent the Republican Party. You represent what's dead in the Republican Party . . . and what's dead in the Democratic Party!

KAY. For Heaven's sake, Mary, have a little faith in Grant!

MARY. What have you got faith in? The people? You're afraid to let them know what Grant really thinks. Don't you believe in democracy?

KAY (sharply). Why do you suppose we were here tonight? What do you think we were doing? All we were planning was the next election.

MARY. Yes, I know. Everybody here tonight was thinking of the next election. Well, it's time somebody began thinking of the next generation! (She covers her face with her hands, sobbing, as she runs upstairs. There is a pause)

KAY. Well! . . . (She turns to look at Grant. Jim is also watching him. Grant is standing in thought, without moving. There is another pause) I think we could all use a drink. Let's go over to my house and go to work on some highballs. (There is another pause as they wait for Grant to break away from his thoughts)

CONOVER. Grace Draper will do what I tell her to do. But we have some things to settle. I want to be able to kid these people along.

GRANT. I'm not going to kid anybody along. I never have.

KAY (pleadingly). Grant, everybody here tonight was thinking of the future—which is how to get you elected. It's stupid right now to think in any other terms.

(Grant unbuttons his coat and takes it off. Kay turns to Conover in alarm.)

CONOVER (going to Grant). Grant, I've got to talk to these people, and that means you've got to talk to me!

GRANT. I'm talking to a lot of people in my speech Thursday night. You'll be one of them. I promised myself when I went into this that I'd appeal to the best in the American people. The only advice I've ever had from any of you was to appeal to their worst. And that's what both parties are starting to do today. Let's end rationing! Who cares if Europe starves? Let's lift price ceilings—suppose it does bring inflation. Let's lower taxes and all get rich!

CONOVER. I see. You're the only honest man in politics.

GRANT. No, Jim! We have some damn good men! There are some wonderful men in the Senate and in the House, too—

Democrats and Republicans. But damn it, Jim, there aren't enough of them to shape party policies. So, to get votes, both parties are out to buy the American public. I can't do that, Jim. So I'm afraid I can't be of any use to you.

(There is a slight pause.)

KAY. Well, Grant, I won't accept that decision. Oh, Grant, we've always talked these things out together. All right, we won't discuss it any more tonight. You're upset. I'll be in touch with you tomorrow. Come on, Jim. (She starts to exit and turns back) Be sure to tell Mary it was a charming evening. (She exits)

CONOVER. I think Kay's right, Grant. You'd better sleep on it. I can stay over for another day.

GRANT. No, Jim. I've made up my mind.

CONOVER. Grant, you're wrong! In this country we play politics—and to play politics you have to play ball! (He starts out)

GRANT. I'm sorry, Jim. I've become very fond of you.

CONOVER. Oh, don't send any flowers. It's not my funeral. (He exits)

SPIKE (after a pause). Mr. Matthews, will you marry me?

GRANT (laughing). Be careful, Spike. I'm in the mood for it! I've never felt so relieved in my life. Thank God, that's settled. I hope they're all listening in Thursday night! I'm going to burn their ears off. Any candidate for any office who threatens world peace for the sake of a few votes—there's the international criminal for you, Spike! I'll take care of them Thursday night—and from now on!

SPIKE. You know, Jim may have to take you on your own terms.

GRANT. No, Spike, it's all over but the shouting—but, oh, boy, am I going to shout!

(Grant starts to take off his coat and roll up his shirt sleeves. Mary enters downstairs, is surprised to find Grant and Spike there. Grant pays no attention to her; he is busy with his thoughts.)

MARY. I thought you were gone. Where's Jim?

SPIKE. I think he's cabling General MacArthur.

GRANT (pacing). We've got to run business on a different basis . . .

MARY. What's happened?

SPIKE. Quiet, please, we're on the air.

GRANT. Sam and his type are dead! They

want to go back to something they've had before. We've got to move on to something we've never had before. And I'm going to tell off the Senator, too. . . . (*Goes to Mary*) It's time somebody spoke up for the farmers. The American farmer is not the unpatriotic, selfish, grasping bastard the farm bloc makes him out to be! Thank God, I can speak my mind now— (*He looks back at Spike*) I don't have to worry about being a candidate!

SPIKE. Now you're on the beam. Talk as though you're not a candidate and I think they'll have to make you one.

GRANT. Forget it, Spike. (*He goes to Spike and shakes his hand*) It's been great working with you. But it's all over. I'll be seeing you. This isn't good-bye.

SPIKE. You're damn right it isn't good-bye. I'll be around first thing Friday morning. (*He starts out*) See you later, Mary.

GRANT. No, Spike, it's cold. But I'm in a great spot for my speech Thursday night. I haven't any commitments.

SPIKE. You've got one.

GRANT. What?

SPIKE. You promised not to make me Postmaster General. But I'll tell you what I'm doing, Grant—I'm releasing you from that. I'll be Postmaster General. (*He exits*)

MARY. But, Grant, what happened?

GRANT. Mary, I'm not running for President. But that doesn't mean I'm out of politics. Nobody can afford to be out of politics. I'm going to be yelling from the sidelines; you've got to be yelling; everybody's got to be yelling! I'm going to be in there asking questions, and I'm going to see that the people get the answers!

MARY. There are a lot of questions to ask, Grant. You're going to be a busy man.

GRANT. You're damned right I'll be busy. Say, I didn't do a real job in any one of my plants. Let's make the trip all over again.

MARY. But, Grant, you need a rest first. We both do.

GRANT. All right. What do you say we go back to Victoria?

MARY. Victoria?

GRANT. Say—do you know something? (*He crosses to Mary, shaking finger at her*) You forgot this is our wedding anniversary!

MARY (*pretending surprise*). I did? Oh, damn it all to hell!

(*Grant gives Mary a resounding smack on the behind.*)

GRANT. Cut that out, Maizie! (*The realization comes to Mary that he has smacked her and called her "Maizie." Her face slowly lights up. Grant continues pacing and talking to Mary and the world*) I've got to get back to work! We've all got to get back to work! There is a big job ahead for all of us! (*He stops and looks at Mary and then goes to her*) Darling, you're right about the future. We've got something great to work for! (*He reaches Mary and takes her in his arms*)

CURTAIN

DREAM GIRL

By ELMER RICE

DREAM GIRL was originally presented by The Playwrights' Company at the Coronet Theatre, New York City, on December 14, 1945. The play was staged by the author; settings by Jo Mielziner. The cast was as follows:

GEORGINA ALLERTON......Betty Field	GEORGE HAND................Edmon Ryan
LUCY ALLERTON.........Evelyn Varden	BERT.....................................Don Stevens
A RADIO ANNOUNCER	A MEXICAN.....................Wendell Corey
Keene Crockett	TWO OTHER MEXICANS:
DR. J. GILMORE PERCIVAL	David Pressman
William A. Lee	James Gregory
GEORGE ALLERTON	A WAITER...........................Stuart Nedd
William A. Lee	ARABELLA....................Sonya Stokowski
MIRIAM ALLERTON LUCAS	LUIGI...............................David Pressman
Sonya Stokowski	AN USHER...... ....Gaynelle Nixon
THE OBSTETRICIAN	
William A. Lee	MISS DELEHANTY........Helen Bennett
THE NURSE..................Evelyn Varden	ANTONIO...........................Don Stevens
JIM LUCAS.......................Kevin O'Shea	SALARINO.....................Robert Fletcher
CLAIRE BLAKELEY.........Helen Marcy	A THEATRE MANAGER
A STOUT WOMAN.....Philippa Bevans	William A. Lee
A DOCTOR...........................Don Stevens	A HEADWAITER..........Keene Crockett
CLARK REDFIELD.......Wendell Corey	A WAITER.....................Robert Fletcher
A POLICEMAN.................James Gregory	JUSTICE OF THE PEACE
THE JUDGE..................William A. Lee	BILLINGS..................William A. Lee
THE DISTRICT ATTORNEY	A CHAUFFEUR..................Stuart Nedd
Keene Crockett	

THE AUTHOR

Elmer Rice has been one of the standard-bearers of the progressively minded theatre for over three decades. Mr. Rice, who was born in New York in 1892, endured a bout with business and law for some six years before turning playwright with On Trial *in 1914. The play was produced by the firm of George M. Cohan and Sam Harris and became a sensation owing to a fairly exciting story and an original use of the flashback technique. Since the first World War atmosphere was not congenial to the author's brand of thinking, and Mr. Rice was out of sympathy with what he regarded as an imperialistic imbroglio, his next plays* The Iron Cross *and* The Home of the Free *failed to attract the public. He wooed Broadway after the war with* For the Defense *(1919),* Wake Up Jonathan *(1921), a collaboration with Hatcher Hughes in which Mrs. Fiske did the honors, and* It Is the Law *(1922). These post-war contributions, however, added nothing to his stature and to the modern theatre until he wrote his satire on the industrial age* The Adding Machine, *to which the* Theatre Guild *gave an estimable production in 1923. Its stylization was derived from post-war European expressionism, but Mr. Rice employed it with verve and the play remains his most original piece of writing.*

Mr. Rice made theatre history again with Street Scene *after unsuccessful collaborations with Dorothy Parker,* Close Harmony *(1924), and Philip Barry,* Cock Robin *(1928).* Street Scene, *which was produced in 1929 by William Brady, proved a powerful realistic panorama, as well as an extraordinarily successful enterprise, and earned the Pulitzer Prize for its author. Two years later, after some indifferent efforts, Mr. Rice opened two successful plays* The Left Bank *and* Counsellor-at-Law *within one month of each other. The former took a realistic view of expatriation, which had been a popular pastime of the pre-depression intelligentsia, and* Counsellor-at-Law, *which provided Paul Muni with one of his best stage roles, was well anchored in character comedy.*

The depression evoked Mr. Rice's protest in the hard-driving multi-scened We the People *(1933), Hitler's rise provoked* Judgment Day *(1934), and the conflict between American and Russian ideologies inspired the conversation piece* Between Two Worlds *(1934). Mr. Rice also produced and directed these plays, and their failure on Broadway aroused the embattled author against the New York critics. He retired from the theatre after writing an ingenious satire on the theatre* Not for Children *(1935), which had no Broadway production (it was produced by the London Stage Society and the Pasadena Theatre), and wrote a novel.*

Mr. Rice returned to the theatre to organize The Playwrights Producing Company with Robert Sherwood, S. N. Behrman, Maxwell Anderson, and Sidney Howard, to write plays for the company, and to direct his own and his colleagues' pieces. American Landscape *(1938) fared poorly in spite of its timeliness and its ingenious construction.* Two on an Island *presented an appealing tale of young adventure in Manhattan.* Flight to the West *(1940) stayed for some time on Broadway and won the interest of alert playgoers, but had a hard struggle at the box-office.* A New Life *lacked luster.* Dream Girl, *in which Betty Field scored a personal triumph, became an instant success for Mr. Rice both as playwright and director.*

Perhaps it should be added that no truly liberal cause ever failed to win Mr. Rice's intelligent support, and that the Authors' League found in him one of its most sagacious leaders. Strenuous citizenship and generally strenuous playwriting have been this playwright's twin interests. They have made him a highly regarded man of the American theatre. He is reaping another harvest at this writing with a distinguished Kurt Weill musical version of Street Scene.

DREAM GIRL

ACT ONE

As the curtain rises on a dark stage, a deep-toned, distant bell is striking the hour of eight. On the eighth stroke, an alarm clock begins its incessant clamor and, as the lights go up, slowly and dimly at center, a bed glides into view. Beside it is a night table on which are the alarm clock and a small radio. In the bed, a girl, struggling against the rude awakening, turns and twists, then sits bolt upright. She is GEORGINA ALLERTON, young, slender, and pretty. She shakes her head and rubs her closed eyes with her fists. The alarm clock is still ringing.

GEORGINA *(yawning heavily).* Ohhhh! *(Then, angrily, to the alarm clock.)* For heaven's sake, will you please shut up? *(She shuts off the alarm clock; then leans over and pulls up an imaginary window shade. The bed is flooded with morning sunlight.* GEORGINA *moans, shakes her head, and stretches her arms.)* Oh, dear! Another day! How awful! Who was it that said: "Must we have another day?" Dorothy Parker, I suppose. I wonder if she really says all those things. *(With a sigh.)* Well, time to get up, I guess. *(She plumps herself down again and snuggles her head in the pillow.)*

MRS. ALLERTON *(off right).* Georgina! It's time to get up!

GEORGINA *(calling).* Yes, I know. I've been up for hours! *(Indignantly.)* Goodness, you'd think sleep was some sort of a crime. *(Gloomily, as she looks toward the window.)* Yes, another day. And what a day! Beautiful sunshine. Not a cloud in the sky. How wonderful it must be to be able to enjoy it. *(She sighs, then says firmly.)* Well, come on, Georgina, snap out of it, and get yourself up out of bed! *(She switches on the radio and an orchestra is heard softly playing "Paris in the Spring.")* I wonder how long a person can go on like this without developing a psychosis or something. For all I know, I may have a psychosis already. Good grief, what a thought! I wish I could remember that awful nightmare I had last night. Still, they say it's awfully hard to make anything out of your own dreams. That damned little psychic censor gets in your way. And besides, I really don't know very much about dream symbols. Just the obvious ones, like Maypoles and church steeples—and I never seem to dream about them. Oh, well, to hell with it! *(She throws back the covers, swings her legs out of bed, and gets into her slippers and negligee. The music stops, and the voice of a radio announcer is heard.)*

ANNOUNCER'S VOICE. And so we bring to a close our half hour of recorded music. And friends, don't forget your date tonight at eight-thirty, with your counselor on human relations, Dr. J. Gilmore Percival, brought to you through the courtesy of Kellogg's Kidney Capsules. If you are maladjusted, if you are worried about some emotional problem, come and tell your troubles to Dr. Percival, whose wise and kindly counsel has helped hundreds to solve—

GEORGINA *(switching off the radio indignantly).* How ridiculous! As though that little quack could really solve people's emotional problems for them! Still, I suppose the poor deluded people who go to him get a kind of relief just from spilling their troubles to somebody. After all, that's what psychiatry is—only on a scientific basis, of course. *(She sits musing on the bed, her chin in her palm.)* Maybe I should try psychiatry. Only what's the use when I know so well what's the matter with me? Except that the right psychiatrist might help me to forget Jim. But do I want to forget Jim? And suppose it isn't just Jim that's the matter with me! What if it all goes back to something that's lurking deep in my unconscious, quietly festering away? *(Sharply.)* How absurd! In the first place, it costs a fortune. And besides, what do I need a psychiatrist for? I'm a perfectly healthy, normal person. All that's the matter with me is that I'm in love with the wrong man. But that's plenty! Anyhow, how do I know I'm really normal? Is anybody? *(Angrily.)* Honestly, it's disgraceful that they allow charlatans like that Dr. Percival on the air! Imagine standing up in front of a microphone and revealing the things that— (*As she sits musing, the radio lights up again and the voice of the* ANNOUNCER *is heard.*)

ANNOUNCER'S VOICE. And remember, folks, it's the kidneys that are the key to your health. And now here is Dr. Percival.

PERCIVAL'S VOICE. Good evening, friends. Tonight we begin with the problem of Miss G. A. Now, Miss, just step right up to the microphone and tell me what is troubling you.

(GEORGINA *picks up the bedside lamp and speaks into it, as though it were a microphone.*)

GEORGINA (*low*). Well, I—

PERCIVAL'S VOICE. A little louder, please, so that we can all hear you. There's nothing to be nervous about.

GEORGINA. I'm not nervous. It's just—well, it's just that it's a little hard to discuss your personal problems with several million people listening in.

PERCIVAL'S VOICE. I can't help you, unless you—

GEORGINA. I know. Well, you see, I'm in love with a man named Jim—

PERCIVAL'S VOICE. No names, please! No one's identity is ever revealed on this program.

GEORGINA. Oh, I'm sorry! I—

PERCIVAL'S VOICE. Go on, please. You are in love with a man named J. And he does not reciprocate your feeling for him, is that it?

GEORGINA. Oh, that's not the point! It's that he—he—

PERCIVAL'S VOICE. Well, what?

GEORGINA. Well, he happens to be my brother-in-law.

PERCIVAL'S VOICE. One moment, please! Do I understand you to say that you are in love with your brother-in-law?

GEORGINA. Yes. Yes, I am. I have been, for years and years.

PERCIVAL'S VOICE. This is really quite an extraordinary case. And, if I understand you correctly, he is not in love with you.

GEORGINA. Well, I used to think he was. And then suddenly he married Miriam and—

PERCIVAL'S VOICE. No names, please!

GEORGINA. Sorry! He married my sister, two years ago, and that was just about the end of everything for me.

PERCIVAL'S VOICE. And is he aware of your feeling for him?

GEORGINA (*indignantly*). Certainly not! What kind of a girl do you think I am? Why, I'd die rather than let him know. Nobody knows or even suspects. (*Weepily.*) But I just can't keep it bottled up any longer. That's why I thought I'd—

PERCIVAL'S VOICE. Yes. You have a feeling of guilt about it, haven't you?

GEORGINA. In a way, I suppose. Being in love with your own brother-in-law—well, it seems just a little—a little incestuous.

PERCIVAL'S VOICE (*hastily*). One moment, Miss A. That is not a word that is acceptable on the air.

GEORGINA. I'm terribly sorry, I—

PERCIVAL'S VOICE. Well, young woman, if you want my advice, you'll put this brother-in-law completely out of your mind and—

GEORGINA. Yes, that's easy to say. I've tried and tried. In fact, there's a man I'm having lunch with, a Mr.—

PERCIVAL'S VOICE. Careful!

GEORGINA. Well. I've been careful, up to now. Oh, you mean about his name. Well, he's a Mr. H.

PERCIVAL'S VOICE. And this Mr. H. is interested in you?

GEORGINA. Well, when a man keeps asking a girl out all the time—especially a married man—

PERCIVAL'S VOICE. Your involvements seem to be exclusively with married men.

GEORGINA. I know.

PERCIVAL'S VOICE. Miss A., I think your situation is a very serious one, indeed. It is hard for me—

MRS. ALLERTON (*off right*). Georgina! Are you daydreaming again in there? It's almost nine!

GEORGINA *(leaping up)*. All right, Mother. I'm practically dressed. *(The lights fade on the scene and come up, at left, on* GEORGINA's *bathroom, which she enters, talking all the while.)* Maybe your mother is right, Georgina. Maybe it's time you cut out the daydreaming—time you stopped mooning around and imagining yourself to be this extraordinary creature with a strange and fascinating psychological life. *(She has removed her negligee and donned a bathing cap; and she now goes around behind the bathroom, invisible but still audible. The sound of a shower is heard.)* Oh, damn it! Cold as ice. There, that's better! *(She sings "Night and Day" lustily. Then the shower is turned off and she reappears wrapped in a large bath towel and stands, her back to the audience, rubbing herself vigorously.)* Still, to be honest, I must admit that, compared to the average girl you meet, I'm really quite complex. Intelligent and well informed too; and a good conversationalist. *(Indignantly, as over her shoulder, she sees someone looking in at her.)* Well, for heaven's sake! Honestly, some people! *(She pulls down an imaginary window shade and the scene is blacked out, her voice coming out of the darkness.)* And my looks are nothing to be ashamed of, either. I have a neat little figure and my legs are really very nice. Of course, my nose is sort of funny, but my face definitely has character—not just one of those magazine-cover deadpans. *(With a yawn.)* Oh, I never seem to get enough sleep! *(The lights come up, as she raises the imaginary shade. She is dressed now in her shoes, stockings, and slip. She seats herself at her dressing table, facing the audience, and brushes her hair.)* If I could only stop lying awake for hours, dreaming up all the exciting things that could happen but never do. Well, maybe this is the day when things really will begin to happen to me. Maybe Wentworth and Jones will accept my novel. They've had it over a month now, and all the other publishers turned it down in less than two weeks. It certainly looks promising. And especially with Jim's recommendation. Wouldn't that be wonderful! With a published novel, I'd really be somebody. Reviews in all the book sections; royalty checks coming in; women nudging each other at Schrafft's and whispering: "Don't look now, but that girl over there—the one with the smart hat —that's Georgina Allerton, the novelist." *(Going to the washbasin.)* Gee, that would be thrilling! To feel that I'd accomplished something. To feel that I had a purpose in life. To feel that— *(She busies herself with a toothbrush, becoming momentarily unintelligible.)* Ubble-ba-glug-ab-lub-mum. Only it wouldn't make up for Jim. *(Going back to the dressing table.)* Fifty novels wouldn't make up for Jim. If Miriam only appreciated him. But she doesn't. She doesn't understand him. All his fine sensitive qualities—they're completely lost on her. It's really ironic. *(Baring her teeth.)* Gosh, my teeth could certainly stand a good cleaning. It's awful the way I put off going to the dentist. Maybe that's psychopathic too. What to do? What to do? Here I am twenty-three years old—no, let's face it, twenty-four next month! And that's practically thirty. Thirty years old—and nothing to show for it. Suppose nothing ever does happen to me. That's a frightening thought! Just to go on and on like this, on through middle age, on to senility, never experiencing anything—what a prospect! *(Putting on her make-up.)* Of course I suppose that up to a certain point there's nothing abnormal about virginity. But the question is, how can you ever be sure you haven't passed that point? Heavens, is that a gray hair? No, thank goodness. What a scare! Still, there must be a lot of women who go right on being virgins until the very day they die. It can be done, I guess. Doesn't sound like much fun though. *(She rises and gets into her dress.)* Well, that brings me right smack back to George Hand. Maybe I shouldn't have accepted his invitation for today. He really is rushing me. Of course, he may not have any intentions at all. No, he's too busy a man to keep on dating up a girl, without having something on his mind. So that puts it squarely up to me. Well, anyhow, if I'm going to play with fire, I may as well look my best. So here goes.

MRS. ALLERTON *(off right)*. Georgina, I'm getting tired of keeping the coffee hot.

GEORGINA. Coming! Coming! *(As she quickly crosses the stage, the light fades out on the bathroom and comes up at right on a breakfast table, at which her parents are seated.* MRS. ALLERTON *is a stoutish, good-looking woman in a negligee;* MR. ALLERTON, *a pleasant round-faced man in a business suit. He is busy with the morning's mail.*)

GEORGINA (*briskly, as she takes her place at the table*). Morning, Mother. Morning, Dad.

ALLERTON (*looking up from the letter he is reading*). Oh, good morning, Georgie.

MRS. ALLERTON. Don't tell me you're wearing that new dress to work.

GEORGINA. I have a lunch date.

MRS. ALLERTON (*with lively interest*). Oh?

GEORGINA. No, Mother, he is *not* a matrimonial prospect. We just happen to be going to a swanky place so—

MRS. ALLERTON. I didn't say—I didn't say— (*Suppressing a sneeze.*) a single—solitary —word. (*The sneeze bursts forth.*) Excuse me!

GEORGINA. Goodness, Mother, have you got a cold?

MRS. ALLERTON. Well, what does it sound like—appendicitis?

GEORGINA. I told you not to put your fur coat in storage yet.

MRS. ALLERTON (*sharply*). That has nothing —nothing whatever—nothing whatever to do with it. (*Another sneeze.*) Oh, damn it! I hate colds.

GEORGINA. Some aspirin might do it good.

MRS. ALLERTON. Nothing does a cold any good. And if you want to know how I got it, I got it from sleeping next to an open window. Your father, after consulting the calendar, decided that spring is here, so of course up went the window all the way.

ALLERTON (*mildly*). I offered to change beds with you, Lucy.

MRS. ALLERTON. That would have only meant your getting a cold and I'd have not only had to nurse you, but would have caught it myself. It was much simpler to catch my own cold in the first place.

GEORGINA (*pouring herself some coffee*). But why didn't you close the window?

MRS. ALLERTON. Well, we discussed the pros and cons of that at some length,

but, in the middle of your father's second rebuttal, I fell asleep, with the result that— (*A sneeze.*)

ALLERTON. Some butter, Georgie?

GEORGINA. Dad, aren't you ever going to learn that I don't take butter?

MRS. ALLERTON. How can you swallow that dry toast?

GEORGINA. You get used to it.

MRS. ALLERTON. I would never get used to it. Has it ever occurred to you that if nature had intended our skeletons to be visible it would have put them—on the outside—on the outside of our bodies? (*A sneeze.*)

ALLERTON. Oh, there's a letter for you, Georgie. (*He hands it to her.*)

GEORGINA. From Wentworth and Jones! (*She tears it open, eagerly, then registers deep disappointment.*) Oh, damn! They've turned down my novel.

ALLERTON. Too bad! But you mustn't be discouraged.

GEORGINA. Well, I am! I was sure they were going to accept it. Especially after Jim recommended it for publication.

MRS. ALLERTON. Sounds to me like an excellent reason for turning it down.

GEORGINA. I don't see why you're always picking on poor Jim.

MRS. ALLERTON. Well, I'm fed up with poor Jim. I think a fellow his age shouldn't just be sitting around reading manuscripts at thirty-five dollars a week.

ALLERTON. Oh, give the boy a chance, my dear. He hasn't found himself yet.

GEORGINA. That's exactly it!

MRS. ALLERTON. Well, I'm sick and tired of financing the search. First, I had to see him through law school. Then—

GEORGINA. Don't go all over that again, Mother. Just because he's too sensitive to bring himself—

ALLERTON. Yes. Law, as it's practiced today, is hardly the profession for an idealist.

MRS. ALLERTON. Well, *you* should know! What *is* this case you're going to Washington on?

ALLERTON. It's the Sons of Solomon case.

GEORGINA. Who are they, Dad?

ALLERTON. A religious sect in Montana that's being prosecuted for advocating polygamy. We've lost all along the line, but I'm very hopeful of winning in the Supreme Court.

MRS. ALLERTON. And that will mean a whopping fee, I'm sure.

ALLERTON (rising). No fee at all, win or lose. I'm handling the case as a matter of principle. Free speech, freedom of religion.

GEORGINA. But, Dad, do you believe in polygamy?

ALLERTON. Personally speaking, no.

MRS. ALLERTON. And a lot of good it would do him if he did!

ALLERTON. But I can say with Voltaire: I disapprove of what you say, but I will defend to the death your right to say it.

GEORGINA. Oh, did Voltaire say that?

MRS. ALLERTON (interrupting). George, doesn't anybody ever walk into your office who's been run over by a millionaire's limousine or who's robbed a bank and is willing to give you—to give you half—to get him—get him out of it? (A sneeze.)

GEORGINA. Why, Mother, aren't there enough ambulance-chasers and police-court shysters without Dad becoming one?

ALLERTON. Thank you, Georgie. (He kisses her.) Good-by, dear. (About to kiss MRS. ALLERTON.) Good-by, Lucy.

MRS. ALLERTON (drawing back). Don't kiss me, or you'll have the entire Supreme Court sneezing their heads off.

ALLERTON (solicitously). I'm worried about you. Maybe a little aspirin—

MRS. ALLERTON. If aspirin is mentioned again—I'll—I'll—I'll— (A sneeze.) Sometimes I think that even monogamy is going too far.

ALLERTON. I'll be back late tonight. Don't be downcast about the novel, Georgie. These things take time.

GEORGINA. Yes, it certainly looks that way.

(ALLERTON exits.)

MRS. ALLERTON. Do you have to encourage him?

GEORGINA. Well, I admire him for sticking unselfishly to his principles, instead of just practicing law on a sordid, commercial basis.

MRS. ALLERTON. Yes, there is certainly no taint of commercialism upon this family, including the connections by marriage. And it's a fortunate coincidence that I am able to foot the bills on the income from Grandpa's sordid commercial estate.

GEORGINA. Well, I have every intention of contributing my share, just as soon as—

(MRS. ALLERTON sneezes.)

MRS. ALLERTON. Excuse me. How much did the bookshop lose last month.

GEORGINA. Only a hundred and eighteen dollars. Claire says it's the best month we've had yet.

MRS. ALLERTON (rising). Why, you're right on the highroad to success. (She sneezes.) Well, I'm going to go and suffer in solitude.

GEORGINA. Good-by, Mother. I do hope—

(MRS. ALLERTON has gone off right. GEORGINA sighs as MIRIAM LUCAS, a young attractive woman, enters at left.)

MIRIAM. 'Lo, Sis.

GEORGINA. Why, Miriam!

MIRIAM. Why, look at you, all dressed up to kill.

GEORGINA. Well, I'm lunching at the Canard Rouge, so I thought I'd—

MIRIAM. Oh-oh!

GEORGINA. Nothing like that. Just somebody who's in the book trade. Since when do you get up at daybreak?

MIRIAM. I had a date with a doctor. Where are Mother and Dad?

GEORGINA. Dad's gone to Washington, and Mother's got an awful cold.

MIRIAM. That's good. I mean I'd rather not spring this on the whole family at once. I hate collective reactions.

GEORGINA. Is anything wrong?

MIRIAM. That's a matter of opinion. It seems that the old medico went into a huddle with some mouse or rabbit that he keeps around and they've decided that you're about to become an aunt.

GEORGINA. But Miriam, how exciting! When's it going to be?

MIRIAM. Oh, not for a hell of a while— a good five or six months. All those engineers, with their blueprints, knocking hours off the transcontinental flying time, but not one day do they save us mothers. Well, I guess I'll go break the news to Mother.

GEORGINA. I'll bet Jim is happy about it.

MIRIAM. He doesn't know it yet. I saw no point in getting him into an interesting condition until I was really sure myself. (*Vehemently.*) And to come right out with it, I don't care a hoot whether he's happy about it or not.

GEORGINA (*greatly embarrassed*). Well, I know it's going to make all the difference in the world for you both. Gee, I certainly envy you.

MIRIAM. And may I say that I certainly envy you. Here am I, a seething mass of unpleasant symptoms, and there are you, fit as a fiddle, and positively suffused with the soft glow of vicarious maternity.

GEORGINA. I just wish I could change places with you, that's all.

MIRIAM. It's a deal. I'll send my agent around after lunch. And I hope you have a boy.

GEORGINA. Maybe it'll be twins.

MIRIAM. Don't say things like that! You never know who's listening. (*She exits at right.*)

(GEORGINA *sits looking dreamily after* MIRIAM. *Then, as the light fades on the scene, a chorus of female voices sings "Sleep, Baby, Sleep." The stage is in darkness for a few moments, then the singing dies out and merges into a chorus of wailing infants. The lights come up slowly at the center, revealing a hospital bed, completely surrounded by flowers, in which* GEORGINA *sits propped up. She wears a silk bed jacket and holds a large doll*

in each arm, one wrapped in a blue blanket, the other in pink. At one side of the bed stands an OBSTETRICIAN, *who looks like* ALLERTON; *at the other side, a* NURSE *who looks like* MRS. ALLERTON.)

THE OBSTETRICIAN. Well, my dear, you've come through wonderfully.

GEORGINA. All thanks to you, Doctor. You've been like a father to me.

THE OBSTETRICIAN. In all my years, I've never known a harder confinement or a braver patient. Yes, you're a plucky little woman.

GEORGINA. A lucky one, you mean! (*Smiling down at the babies.*) Just look at my little darlings!

THE OBSTETRICIAN. I've never seen two finer ones.

THE NURSE. You're the envy of every mother in the hospital.

GEORGINA (*beaming*). Well, what's a little suffering compared to that? Besides, pain is a part of life, and to live fully, we must taste every form of human experience.

THE NURSE. Oh, that's beautifully expressed!

GEORGINA. And, Doctor, I definitely *don't* want them to go on the bottle. It's such a joy!

THE OBSTETRICIAN (*patting her head*). Good girl! (*As the* OBSTETRICIAN *exits,* JIM LUCAS *enters. He is an attractive young man, with a face and manner that are almost too sensitive.*)

JIM. Georgina, darling!

GEORGINA. Oh, Jim!

THE NURSE. Not too long, Mr. Lucas. We mustn't tire her.

JIM. No, no. I understand. (*As the* NURSE *exits, he goes to* GEORGINA.)

GEORGINA. Oh, Jim, isn't it wonderful?

JIM. Yes, wonderful! Birth, the most universal experience, and yet the greatest of all miracles. Are you happy, darling?

GEORGINA. Just look at me! I've waited so long for this, afraid it was never going to happen. I'm a new woman, Jim.

JIM. And I'm a new man—with someone to understand me, someone to have faith in me.

GEORGINA. And a new world to build for ourselves—and for them: Gerald and Geraldine.

MIRIAM (*entering at right, smoking a cigarette*). Hand them over quick, Georgina. I'm parked in front of a fire plug.

GEORGINA (*clinging to the babies*). No, you shan't have them! They're mine.

MIRIAM (*coming to the bed*). Yours? Look, darling, it wasn't my idea to have a baby! But having produced a couple of brats, in the customary, antiquated manner, I don't think I'm unreasonable in contending that they're mine.

JIM. Only in the crudest physiological sense.

MIRIAM. Oh, forgive me! Is there some other sense?

GEORGINA. There is indeed!

JIM. You wouldn't have to be told that, Miriam, if you had any feeling for the deeper values of life. There's no real marriage between you and me—no love, no understanding, no spiritual communion. The children of my body may be yours, but the children of my spirit will always be Georgina's.

MIRIAM. All right. I'll settle for that. (*Calling.*) Nurse!

THE NURSE. Coming!

MIRIAM (*snatching one baby and pointing to the other*). Here, you take that one. And hurry up before I get a ticket. (*The* NURSE *takes the other baby from* GEORGINA *and follows* MIRIAM *off, sneezing into the baby's face.*)

MIRIAM (*as she exits*). And watch that sneezing!

JIM (*taking a step after her*). Miriam, I—

GEORGINA (*as the scene fades out*). Jim! Jim! Don't leave me! Don't leave me!

JIM (*stretching his arms toward the disappearing* GEORGINA). I'm sorry, Georgina! I know it isn't right! I know it shouldn't be this way! Georgina! Georgina! Georgina! (*He exits.*)

MRS. ALLERTON (*off right*). Georgina! Georgina, are you still there? (*The lights come up right on* GEORGINA *as she sits at the breakfast table, as before.*)

GEORGINA (*startled*). What? Yes. Yes, I am. (*She hastily wipes her eyes, as* MRS. ALLERTON *enters.*)

MRS. ALLERTON. You'll be late again at the shop. What on earth are you moping about now?

GEORGINA. Just happy about Miriam. And a little wistful at the prospect of being a maiden aunt. Don't you feel sort of—

MRS. ALLERTON. I'm much too furious to feel sort of anything.

GEORGINA. Why? What's the matter?

MRS. ALLERTON. Didn't Miriam tell you about Jim?

GEORGINA (*anxiously*). No, what about him?

MRS. ALLERTON. He's out of a job again.

GEORGINA. He's left Wentworth and Jones?

MRS. ALLERTON. Well, that's one way of putting it. In less diplomatic language, they fired him.

GEORGINA. So that's why she was so upset. Poor Jim!

MRS. ALLERTON. What do you mean, poor Jim! What about poor Miriam?

GEORGINA. It's much worse for him. He's just had nothing but hard luck.

MRS. ALLERTON. Why, the way you stand up for him, anybody would think you were madly in love with him.

GEORGINA (*angrily*). Don't talk such nonsense! Just because I happen to feel some sympathy for a boy who—

MRS. ALLERTON. All right, you can feel all the sympathy you like for him. But, in my opinion, the sooner Miriam gets herself unattached from that balmy dreamer, the better off she'll be.

GEORGINA. Well, I hope you don't tell her anything like that.

MRS. ALLERTON. I just this minute—just this minute—finished telling her! (*A sneeze.*)

GEORGINA. How *could* you, just when she's going to have a baby?

MRS. ALLERTON. That's just exactly it. She'd be a fool to hang on to him, now that he's accomplished what will probably be the only affirmative act of his life.

GEORGINA. But it's just the time when a woman needs her husband most!

MRS. ALLERTON. You read too many serious books. What on earth does she need him for now?

GEORGINA. I don't see how you can be so cynical about your daughter's happiness.

MRS. ALLERTON. I'm not the least bit cynical. If she gets rid of that piece of excess baggage, she has a chance to make a fresh start. Otherwise, she's just stuck with him. Everybody else seems to fire him. Why shouldn't she?

GEORGINA. Well, I trust and pray that Miriam won't pay any attention to you. In fact, I'm going to call her up and tell her so.

MRS. ALLERTON. You keep out of this. If Miriam had wanted your advice, she'd have asked for it. And if that unemployed Galahad comes crying to you, I wish you'd tell him for me that—that—that— *(She sneezes.)* For goodness' sake, will you run along to work now, before I use language unbecoming a grandmother?

GEORGINA. All right, good-by, then. And for heaven's sake, take care of yourself.

MRS. ALLERTON *(as GEORGINA exits).* If you—if I—if anybody—

(The lights fade on the scene and come up, at left, on a corner of a small bookshop. The telephone is ringing. On the third ring, CLAIRE BLAKELY, a brisk young woman about GEORGINA's age, enters and answers it.)

CLAIRE. Mermaid Bookshop. No, madam, I'm terribly sorry. This is not the Bide-a-wee Home. You must have the wrong number. *(A STOUT WOMAN enters and CLAIRE turns to her.)* Good morning. Can I help you?

THE WOMAN. I was just wondering if you happen to have a copy of *Always Opal?*

CLAIRE. No. I'm afraid not at the moment.

THE WOMAN. Oh, dear. This is about the fifth shop I've been to.

CLAIRE. We have a dozen copies but they're all out. And a waiting list of at least fifty. But here's something you might like. Mary Myrtle Miven's latest, *My Heart Is Like a Trumpet.* It's a sort of idyllic love story about two horses. Very tender and poetic.

THE WOMAN. No, I really don't think—

CLAIRE. Well, how about *The Dnieper Goes Rolling Along?* It's that new Soviet novel about the electrification of collective farms. Very stark and powerful.

THE WOMAN. No, what I really want is *Always Opal.* You see, all my friends are reading it, and I feel so out of it. I understand it's very—very—

CLAIRE. Well, it certainly doesn't leave much to the imagination in the way of—

THE WOMAN. Yes, so I understand. *(As she starts to go.)* Oh, I wonder if you happen to have a three-cent stamp.

CLAIRE. Yes, I think so. *(She opens a tin cashbox on the desk.)*

THE WOMAN *(fumbling in her handbag).* Oh, dear, I'm afraid the smallest I have is a five-dollar bill. Could you possibly—?

CLAIRE. I guess I can make it. One, and four is five.

THE WOMAN. Oh, thank you so much.

CLAIRE. Not a bit. Stop in again.

THE WOMAN. Indeed I will! *(She goes out at the right, as GEORGINA enters).*

GEORGINA. Hello, Claire. Sorry I'm late again. Have you had a busy morning?

CLAIRE. You betcha. I directed two people to Oppenheim Collins, one gal wanted to look at the phone book, another had to go to the john, and I just made a cash sale of a three-cent stamp.

GEORGINA. It's discouraging.

CLAIRE. Oh, I knew there was something else. Frank McClellan called up to say that that asthma of his has got completely out of hand and the doctor has ordered him to Arizona, pronto.

GEORGINA. Oh, the poor guy! But what about his bookshop?

CLAIRE. Well, he thought we might like to take it over.

GEORGINA *(excitedly)*. But Claire, how wonderful! Why, compared to this dinky little—

CLAIRE. You can spare me the comparison. He says he clears five or six hundred a month.

GEORGINA. Why, we lost nearly that much one month.

CLAIRE. Yes, dear.

GEORGINA. Well, let's tell him yes, before he changes his mind.

CLAIRE. He wants ten thousand dollars for the business.

GEORGINA. Ten thousand dollars! For heaven's sake!

CLAIRE. Did you think he wanted to make us a present of it? You don't happen to know where we could dig up ten thousand, do you?

GEORGINA. Who, me?

CLAIRE. No, I guess not. Well, it's too bad. *(With firmness.)* Georgie, I don't think you and I are cut out for business. I think the best thing for us to do is board up this hole in the wall and call it a day.

GEORGINA. What, give up the business, when we've put so much into it?

CLAIRE. We could have had sables on what we've put into it.

GEORGINA. But we're not interested in sables.

CLAIRE. We're not?

GEORGINA. Well, what I mean is, we're not the frivolous type, that's willing just to gad around and fritter our time away.

CLAIRE. But what type are we? and what are we good for? What can we do?

GEORGINA. Well, we could go to secretarial school.

CLAIRE. Back to school at twenty-four? Listen, darling, beginning with play school at three, I went to school—let me see, now—sixteen, seventeen, eighteen, nineteen . . . ! My God, nineteen consecutive years! Nineteen years, thousands of dollars, and the efforts of hundreds of

specially trained people have been spent in making us not want to do all the useful things we don't know how to do.

GEORGINA. And I'm getting terribly discouraged about my novel, too. Wentworth and Jones have just turned it down. And after Jim Lucas recommended it. I'm beginning to think that maybe I'm not a novelist.

CLAIRE. Oh, don't take that attitude. William DeMorgan had his first novel published at sixty-six.

GEORGINA. But he must have had something to keep him occupied in the meantime. I still have one teeny hope. Jim Lucas said he'd give the manuscript to Clark Redfield. You know—the book reviewer.

CLAIRE. Oh, yes.

GEORGINA. If he turns thumbs down, I'll just—! Oh, well, no use brooding over it. By the way, speaking of Jim Lucas, Miriam is going to have a baby.

CLAIRE. Congratulations! Well, that's something that even we would be capable of, I suppose.

GEORGINA. They say it takes two.

CLAIRE. Yes, that's the hell of it. We're choosy too. Well, let's not be defeatist about things. Can't you think of some way we could raise that ten thousand? How about your grandfather's estate? It's a perfectly safe investment—

GEORGINA. Not a chance of that. It's all tied up in a trust fund with some bank, as long as my mother lives.

CLAIRE. And I suppose she's good for another twenty-five years.

GEORGINA. Why, what a thing to say!

CLAIRE. Oh, I didn't mean it that way. It's just that—oh, you know—always some dead hand, holding us back. Oh, well, I've got to get out this month's bills. *(She starts to go.)* Don't take any more reservations for *Always Opal.* Our lease will be up by the time we fill all we have now. *(She exits behind the book shelves.* GEORGINA *sighs, lights a cigarette, gets up and walks about the shop, lost in thought. Suddenly the telephone rings.)*

GEORGINA *(without going near the telephone).* Hello? Yes, this is she. What? Oh, no, I can't believe it! Yes! Yes! I'll be right there. *(As she hurries center, the lights come up, revealing a* MAN *in a surgeon's uniform with a stethoscope about his neck.)* Oh, Doctor, Doctor, it can't be true about my mother!

THE DOCTOR. Yes, my dear, I'm afraid it is.

GEORGINA. What was it—her heart?

THE DOCTOR. That—and other things. It happens that way, sometimes. We tried to save her, but it was hopeless.

GEORGINA. Did you try sodium pentathol?

THE DOCTOR. Yes, my dear. Everything was done that medical science can do. But there are still some things we haven't mastered. And now, I shall leave you with your father. He needs you, my dear. *(He recedes into the darkness as* ALLERTON *comes forward.)*

GEORGINA *(in his arms).* Dad!

ALLERTON. I'm all alone now, Georgie—except for you!

GEORGINA. You have Miriam, too, Dad.

ALLERTON *(shaking his head).* She has Jim to look out for. And a baby coming soon. So there's only you.

GEORGINA. You can depend on me, Dad. I'll never leave you. You're all I have in the world, too.

ALLERTON. You're a rich girl now, Georgie. Anything that your heart desires—

GEORGINA. Oh, I don't care about the money, Dad. If I do use any of it, it will only be so that Claire and I—

*(*CLARK REDFIELD, *a young man of twenty-eight, enters at left. He staggers under the load of a double armful of books. He goes to the desk, plumps down the books, looks toward the center, and coughs tentatively. As* GEORGINA *turns and sees him, the lights fade quickly on* ALLERTON.)*

CLARK. Good morning, Miss Allerton.

GEORGINA *(approaching* REDFIELD). Oh! Good morning, Mr. Redfield.

CLARK. You seemed preoccupied. I hope I haven't derailed some train of cosmic thought.

GEORGINA *(somewhat flustered).* Of course not. I was just— *(Seeing the books.)* Goodness! More review copies?

CLARK. You betcha! I've got—

GEORGINA *(preoccupied).* Do you mind waiting a minute while I call my mother? She wasn't feeling well this morning and—

CLARK. Nothing serious, I hope!

GEORGINA. Well, I think it's only a cold, but you know how these respiratory disorders flare up sometimes. *(She dials a number. A telephone rings at the right and the lights go up on* MRS. ALLERTON. *She is seated on a chaise longue, dressed as before, and reading a book. The telephone is beside her and she answers it.)*

MRS. ALLERTON. Hello!

GEORGINA. This is me, Mother. How are you feeling?

MRS. ALLERTON. What do you mean, how am I feeling? I'm feeling—feeling fine. *(She sneezes.)*

GEORGINA. You sound awful.

MRS. ALLERTON. I've got a cold in the head and every now and then—I—I—I—have to sneeze. What are you calling up for?

GEORGINA. To find out how you are, of course. I've been worried about you.

MRS. ALLERTON. You mean to say you called up just to ask about my sneezes? You certainly must have very little on your mind.

GEORGINA. Well, you might at least appreciate my—

MRS. ALLERTON. I was appreciating Opal's hot affair with Monseigneur de Montrouget and you interrupted me just as they were about to—to— *(She sneezes and hangs up.)*

GEORGINA *(as the lights fade on* MRS. ALLERTON). All right. I'm just glad you— *(She hangs up.)*

CLARK. Is she all right?

GEORGINA. She seems all right. Just sneezing and very cranky.

CLARK. The typical American mother. *(Rubbing his hands.)* Well, are you ready to do business now?

GEORGINA. What have you there?

CLARK. A fine mixed bag. Three whodunits, a couple of epics of the soil, a survey of the natural resources of Bolivia, and a volume called *Fun with a Chafing Dish.* And here is the prize of the lot: Professor Oglethorpe's two-volume *Life of Napoleon,* with the pages still uncut.

GEORGINA. You mean you haven't read it.

CLARK. Do I look like a boy who, six years out of college, would wade through eleven hundred pages on Napoleon?

GEORGINA. But I read your review of it in the *Globe.*

CLARK. I didn't say I didn't review it. I said I didn't read it.

GEORGINA. How could you review it without reading it?

CLARK. Easy. First I quoted liberally from the introduction and quarreled with the author's approach. Next, I leafed quickly through and called attention to three typographical errors. Then I praised the illustrations, grumbled about the footnotes, and intimated that the book added little to what had already been written. Result, a scholarly column and all done in exactly fifty-seven minutes.

GEORGINA. Is that your idea of literary criticism?

CLARK. Look! I'm a working newspaperman and a member of the Newspaper Guild, whose contract guarantees me a minimum wage for a maximum working week. There's nothing in it that requires me to ruin my eyesight and addle my brain in the interests of a Corsican upstart.

GEORGINA. Well, I've often heard that newspapermen are cynical, but I wouldn't have believed that a man who is entrusted with reviewing books could have so little sense of responsibility.

CLARK. You make me feel like a great big brute.

GEORGINA. I don't see anything funny about it. I think it's disgraceful.

CLARK. Don't twist the sword, Miss Allerton. Just give me the price of my shame and let me go in peace. Well, what do you say? How much am I bid for the lot?

GEORGINA *(examining the books).* Most of these aren't much use to us. How about five dollars?

CLARK. Like all idealists, you drive a hard bargain. But I'm not going to lug these damned things any further, so they're yours.

GEORGINA. Well, I don't want you to feel I'm taking advantage of you. I'll make it six dollars.

CLARK *(holding up his hand).* No, no! Even a cynical newspaperman has his pride. Give!

GEORGINA *(handing him a bill).* You don't have to be so sarcastic about it. We really don't need your secondhand books. Maybe, hereafter, you'd better take them somewhere else.

CLARK. Unfortunately, I'm a creature of habit, Miss Allerton. Let me but tuck a review copy under my arm and immediately there is set in motion a whole series of muscular reflexes that takes me straight to your door.

GEORGINA. If reviewing books is so distasteful to you, why do you do it?

CLARK. Well, you see, I have a periodic rendezvous with my stomach. And I find that reviewing books requires less leg work than covering the police courts. And, not to withhold anything from you, I'm sitting in a very pretty spot for the first opening on the sports page.

GEORGINA *(in amazement).* You mean you'd rather be a sports writer than a literary critic?

CLARK. I'm afraid you don't grasp the practical realities of journalism. What you euphemistically call a literary critic is only a miserable penny-a-liner, whereas a sports writer nestles snugly in the upper brackets.

GEORGINA. I wasn't thinking about the money—

CLARK. Pardon the indelicacy. So you think that writing about books is on a higher level than writing about sports?

GEORGINA. I just think there's no comparison.

CLARK. You're right; there isn't. Any young squirt, fresh out of college, can write book reviews. Just as any beginner in the theater can play Polonius. In fact, the technique is much the same. You put on false whiskers and spout platitudes in a high, squeaky voice. But to go in there and play Hamlet and follow all the sinuous twists and turnings of that tortured soul; or, on the other hand, to analyze the strategy of an intricate football formation or judge a fast ten-round bout on points—that's something else again. To do that, you really have to know your stuff.

GEORGINA. Oh, yes, you're very clever and paradoxical, aren't you?

CLARK. Thank you for the compliment, tinged though it is with a certain asperity. But you see, getting on the sports page is only what might be called a primary objective. For to a really good sports writer, every door is open: literature, movies, radio, politics, anything. Look at Ring Lardner. Look at Heywood Broun. Look at John Kieran. Look—if you can bear it—at Westbrook Pegler. In my daydreams, I write a story about the deciding game of the World Series that stampedes the Democratic Convention, and lands me in the White House. And on my tentative cabinet slate, you're down for Secretary of Labor. Ta-ta, Madam Allerton, I'll see you in Washington.

GEORGINA (as he is about to go). Oh, just a minute. Did Jim Lucas ever give you—

CLARK. Did I hear you aright? Did you mention the name of Jim Lucas?

GEORGINA. Have you got something sarcastic to say about him, too?

CLARK. Not sarcastic, my dear young woman. Sarcasm would be a wholly inadequate instrument for a commentary on that epic character. But perhaps you haven't heard the news about Jim?

GEORGINA. I've heard that he's parted company with Wentworth and Jones, if that's what you mean.

CLARK. Parted company, did you say? Really, Miss Allerton, you have a gift for hyperbolic understatement. The impact of Jim's violent expulsion has rocked Publishers' Row to its foundations. Would you mind telling an inquiring reporter, Miss Allerton, how it feels to be the sister-in-law of the man who sent back the manuscript of *Always Opal,* without even turning in a report on it?

GEORGINA. Is that really true? Did Jim do that?

CLARK. Oh, so you haven't heard. An enterprising book peddler like you should get around more. This Lucas is a celebrity, the greatest bonehead player since Fred Merkle forgot to touch second base.

GEORGINA. Well, that book deserved to be turned down. It's nothing but a lot of dressed-up smut, atrociously written, and all in very bad taste, if you ask me.

CLARK. Wait a minute, Carrie Nation. The verdict of history is already in. Don't try to alibi Jim, or folks will get the impression that you take more than a sisterly-in-law interest in him.

GEORGINA (flaring up). That's an uncalled-for and highly impertinent remark.

CLARK. Or is it just a case of one hand washing the other?

GEORGINA. And what is that supposed to mean?

CLARK. Well, I got the impression that Jim thinks rather highly of that novel of yours that he asked me to read.

GEORGINA (eager for his verdict). Oh, then he did give it to you?

CLARK. Yes, he did.

GEORGINA. And I suppose, following your usual practice, you haven't read it.

CLARK. No, you're wrong. I have read it. All of it—well, almost all.

GEORGINA (after a pause). Well?

CLARK. You mean you want my opinion of it?

GEORGINA. Well, why do you suppose I let Jim give it to you?

CLARK. I wasn't sure. Well, to put the thing as delicately as possible, I think it stinks.

GEORGINA (enraged). Oh, you do, do you?

CLARK. Yes, I do. (Contemplatively.) Yes, that really is a malodorous morsel! In the first place—

GEORGINA (*almost in tears*). Never mind! I'm not interested in what you have to say.

CLARK. Oh, then you really *didn't* want my opinion. That's what I thought.

GEORGINA. I don't call that an opinion. Just a nasty, insulting—

CLARK. I see! You only wanted a favorable opinion.

GEORGINA. Nobody wants criticism that's just destructive. I say if a critic can't be constructive—

CLARK. You mean you want the critic to do the creative job that you failed to do? If that's his function, we might as well dispense with the writer in the first place. Now, if you'll let me give a piece of friendly advice—

GEORGINA. I don't want your advice. I'd never have let Jim give you the manuscript if I had known that you're just a hockey fan.

CLARK. There's a good hockey match at the Garden Saturday night. Want to go?

GEORGINA. No, I don't! And if you'll excuse me now, I have a lot of work to do.

CLARK. You haven't a damn thing to do. You just sit around this shop all day to give yourself the illusion that you're doing something.

GEORGINA. Will you please get out of here?

CLARK. Sore as a boil, aren't you?

GEORGINA. Not in the least. It just happens that I find you very unpleasant. I think you're not only lazy and dishonest, but sadistic and vulgar.

CLARK. Well, I'm glad you're not sore. And I think that novel of yours is just about the most terrific thing I've read since *War and Peace.*

GEORGINA. And another thing, I wish you would not ever come here again.

CLARK. I'll try to remember that. By, now. And thanks for the five bucks. (CLARK *exits right.*)

GEORGINA (*with tears of anger*). You great big ape! (*She stands looking after him for a moment, trembling with rage and humiliation. Then she begins threshing* about, *in uncontrollable fury. She strides to the desk and violently pushes* CLARK's *books to the floor. Then she stands with clenched fists glaring in the direction that* CLARK *has gone and with sudden resolution strides center into the darkness. There is a flash of lightning and a peal of thunder. The lights fade on the bookshop and come up at the right, as the pitiful meowing of a cat is heard.* CLARK, *in his shirt sleeves and wearing a green eyeshade, is seated before a typewriter at an untidy table, piled high with books. Beside him on the floor is a stuffed cat whose tail he is twisting. The meowing is heard again.* CLARK *laughs fiendishly, pours himself a stiff drink of whisky, gulps it down, and begins pecking at the typewriter. Again lightning and thunder, followed by a sharp knocking.*)

CLARK. Who the hell is that? (*He leans over and twists the cat's tail again. There is a wail of pain, as* GEORGINA *enters, wearing a hooded cloak.*)

CLARK (*sneeringly*). Oh, it's you, is it?

GEORGINA. Yes, it's me. I mean it's I.

CLARK. I'm just having a little fun with kitty.

GEORGINA (*grimly*). And I'm going to have a little fun with you! (*She takes a revolver from beneath her cloak and levels it at him.*)

CLARK (*cowering in terror.*) No! No! Not that!

(GEORGINA *fires two shots.* CLARK *shrieks and slumps to the floor. A* POLICEMAN *rushes on at the right and seizes* GEORGINA *roughly.*)

THE POLICEMAN. Come along, you!

GEORGINA (*with quiet dignity*). All right. You needn't be rough about it. I did it and I'm willing to take the consequences.

(*As the* POLICEMAN *takes her off, the lights fade. A tumult of voices and the thumping of a gavel is heard. The lights come up at center. A* JUDGE, *who resembles* ALLERTON, *is seated at the bench, beside which, in the witness chair,* GEORGINA *sits. The* DISTRICT ATTORNEY *and* JIM LUCAS *are seated at the counsel table.*)

THE JUDGE (*banging his gavel*). Order! Order! If there are any more demonstrations, I'll have the courtroom cleared. (*As quiet is restored.*) Proceed with your examination, Mr. District Attorney.

THE DISTRICT ATTORNEY (*pointing an accusing finger*). Then you admit that you went there with the deliberate intention of killing Clark Redfield?

GEORGINA. Yes, I admit it. But I had every justification. He was a savage brute, a man without—

THE DISTRICT ATTORNEY. I object!

THE JUDGE (*banging his gavel*). Objection sustained!

JIM (*jumping up*). Your Honor, I protest. This young woman is on trial for her life. Is she to be railroaded to the chair without even an opportunity to speak in her own defense?

THE JUDGE. The point is well taken. Proceed, Miss Allerton.

GEORGINA. Well, let me just ask you this. If he had attacked me, wouldn't you all agree that I had a right—?

THE JUDGE. One moment! Are we to understand that Clark Redfield attempted to—?

GEORGINA. No, he didn't. But compared to what he did to me, it would have been easy to submit to—to— Well, not easy, but almost preferable. He struck at my dignity, humiliated me, trampled my pride in the dust. And if you men think that an injury to a woman's body is a greater provocation to murder than an injury to her spirit, then you know nothing about feminine nature. That's all! That's my case! (*She glares about defiantly.*)

THE DISTRICT ATTORNEY. Your Honor, the people of the State of New York demand the death penalty!

THE JUDGE. Counsel for the defense will now address the jury. Proceed, Mr. Lucas.

JIM (*rising and addressing the unseen jury*). Ladies and gentlemen of the jury. I speak to you not merely as counsel for Georgina Allerton, but as her brother. And by that I do not refer to my accidental marital relationship to her sister, but to the deep, spiritual, fraternal bond that has long existed between the defendant and myself. I can say, in all honesty, that no one understands her as I do: no

other living being has plumbed so profoundly the depths of that tender, sensitive soul. And, in the light of my knowledge and understanding, I say to you that when she struck down Clark Redfield it was no act of murder, but a simple, human gesture of self-defense. (*A murmur from the unseen* JURORS.) Yes, ladies and gentlemen, self-defense! For what was this novel of hers, that Clark Redfield sought to annihilate with the cruel strokes of his sharp-edged tongue and stabbing wit? It was her baby, ladies and gentlemen, the child of her spirit, as real to her and as dear to her as though it had been, indeed, the flesh-and-blood creation of her body. For it was conceived in the beautiful ecstasy of spiritual passion, nurtured for long months in the dark, secret recesses of her soul, brought forth in an agony of travail. And as it lay nestling in her bosom, so to speak, Clark Redfield struck at it, with his lethal weapons! And with the noble, unerring instinct of outraged maternity, she struck back, struck back at the would-be assassin of her baby. Could any mother, could any woman do less? I leave the answer to you. (*He sits down amid cheers and applause.*)

THE JUDGE (*pounding for order*). What is your verdict, ladies and gentlemen of the jury?

CHORUS OF UNSEEN JURORS. Not guilty!

(*The* DISTRICT ATTORNEY *leaves in a huff.*)

THE JUDGE. The defendant is dismissed.

GEORGINA (*shaking hands with him*). Thank you, Your Honor.

THE JUDGE (*as he leaves the bench*). Not at all. But just a word of fatherly advice, Miss Allerton. In the future, try to avoid the use of firearms.

GEORGINA (*earnestly*). I will, Your Honor. (*Turning to Jim, as the judge exits.*) Oh, Jim, darling, I knew I could depend on you! (*She walks toward* JIM, *but as the telephone rings in the bookshop, she ignores his outstretched arms and hurries to answer it. The lights fade on the courtroom and come up, at left, on the bookshop.*)

GEORGINA. Mermaid Bookshop. No, madam, I'm sorry; we're all out of *Always Opal*. You're welcome.

CLAIRE (*who has entered*). Why, what's the matter with you? You look as though you were ready to commit murder.

GEORGINA. Oh, it's nothing. I'm just mad at myself for losing my temper.

CLAIRE. Who did what to you?

GEORGINA. It's too trivial to talk about. It's just that that Clark Redfield was in and began shooting off his face about a lot of— Honestly, of all the brash, egotistical fools I ever met—!

CLAIRE. Well, I've only met him once or twice, but I had an idea he was kind of nice. How did he like your novel?

GEORGINA. Oh, I really don't know. I didn't even bother to ask him.

CLAIRE. Sorry. Excuse it, please. (*She exits. As* GEORGINA *picks up the scattered books,* JIM LUCAS *enters at right.*)

JIM. Hello, Georgina.

GEORGINA. Oh, hello, Jim.

JIM. Are you busy?

GEORGINA. Well, I have a lunch date at one-thirty and—

JIM. Oh, you've got lots of time.

GEORGINA. I was going to stop at Collette's first, to pick up a new hat she's making for me. But it doesn't matter. Sit down.

JIM (*complying*). I have something to tell you. But maybe you heard it already from Miriam.

GEORGINA. You mean about your leaving Wentworth and Jones?

JIM. Oh, that, yes! Trust Miriam to waste no time in spreading it around.

GEORGINA. It wasn't from Miriam I heard it. Clark Redfield was just in—

JIM. Good old Clark! Always the reporter. I suppose he told you why they fired me.

GEORGINA. Well, he did mention something about *Always Opal*—

JIM. You don't have to be tactful. I'm not in the least bit sensitive about it. If I had it to do over again, I'd still turn that book down. It's just a piece of trash.

GEORGINA. Well, that's exactly what I said to Redfield

JIM. Good for you! But what I came in to tell you is that Miriam and I are splitting up.

GEORGINA. Oh, no, Jim. You mustn't do that! Just because you've had some silly quarrel about losing your job—

JIM. It goes much deeper than that. We never were right for each other. She's much too down to earth for me, and I'm much too undependable for her.

GEORGINA. It just doesn't seem right to me. And when you get to thinking it over—

JIM. There's nothing more to think over. It's all settled, and Miriam is just as relieved about it as I am. I haven't felt so free and so hopeful in years. Well, you'd better run along to your lunch date. I just wanted to give you my version of the situation, before you heard about it from the other side of the family.

GEORGINA. Well, I'm glad you did.

JIM (*going to her*). So am I! It's wonderful to be able to talk to somebody who has some idea of what you're getting at. One of the things I want most, Georgina, is for you and me to get back on our old footing again. I've felt a kind of restraint in you these past two years and I—

GEORGINA (*greatly troubled*). Well, I—

JIM. Yes, it was natural enough, I suppose. But it doesn't have to be that way any more. Now we can be friends as we used to be. (*Taking her hand.*) Good-by, Georgina. I'll see you soon.

GEORGINA. Yes, Jim.

(JIM *exits quickly.* GEORGINA, *on the verge of tears, stands looking after him.*)

CLAIRE (*entering*). Didn't you say something about a lunch date?

GEORGINA (*startled*). What? Oh, yes! (*Looking at her watch.*) Heavens, I'm going to keep him waiting again!

CLAIRE. Somebody interesting?

GEORGINA (*with attempted nonchalance*). Just George Hand.

CLAIRE. George Hand is taking you to lunch again?

GEORGINA. Well, what's wrong about that? He's a book jobber and we run a bookshop—

CLAIRE. Where do you get that "we"? Am I in on this lunch date?

GEORGINA. What a mind you have! Just because Mr. Hand and I happen to discover that we have a few things in common—

CLAIRE. Which he hopes will eventually include a bed.

GEORGINA. Claire, will you please stop! You'll make me so self-conscious that I won't know what to say to him.

CLAIRE. Well, if you can't think of anything else, you can always say no.

GEORGINA. Maybe I should phone the Canard Rouge and tell him I'm not coming. I'm terribly upset and in no mood for one of those fencing matches.

CLAIRE. Goodness, does a little tiff with Clark Redfield make you—

GEORGINA. Certainly not! I've even forgotten Clark Redfield's existence. Jim Lucas was just in to tell me that he and Miriam are divorcing. Isn't that dreadful?

CLAIRE. People do it every day, with the greatest of ease. And from where I sit, Miriam is well rid of that Jim.

GEORGINA. That seems to be a general opinion with which I disagree. Oh, well, I may as well have lunch with George Hand and get it over with. I'll be back as soon as I can.

CLAIRE (as GEORGINA exits at right). Don't hurry! And don't say no, until after the liqueurs. (The telephone rings.) Mermaid Bookshop. No, madam, I'm sorry, we're all out of Always Opal. Well, we're expecting— (Her voice and scene fade out. The lights come up at right on a semicircular upholstered booth in a corner of the Canard Rouge, a chi-chi midtown restaurant. GEORGINA and GEORGE HAND are seated over their coffee and brandy. HAND is a brisk, good-looking man, getting on to forty. GEORGINA is wearing a gay, plumed hat.)

HAND. Think you could manage another brandy?

GEORGINA. I definitely could not manage one other thing. Except maybe a cigarette.

HAND (giving her one and lighting it for her). Oh, sure! What made you go on the wagon?

GEORGINA. Two cocktails and two brandies for lunch! Is that your idea of being on the wagon?

HAND. I used to know a girl who took three Cuba libres with breakfast.

GEORGINA. What interesting people you know! Did she work?

HAND. Well, not in the daytime, I guess. She was a night telephone operator. Is that bookshop keeping you busy?

GEORGINA. Afraid not. In fact, we've about decided to close it.

HAND. That's a good idea. What astrologer advised you to pick that grim location?

GEORGINA. I guess we didn't use very good judgment, did we?

HAND. I don't think you're cut out for a business career.

GEORGINA. That's what my partner says. But what career am I cut out for?

HAND. Have you tried love?

GEORGINA. You won't take me seriously, will you?

HAND. Sure, if I can't have you any other way.

GEORGINA. No, I mean it!

HAND. Well, what would be the point of both of us taking you seriously? No sense in overdoing the thing.

GEORGINA. You think I take myself too seriously?

HAND. Well, let's say seriously enough.

GEORGINA. I suppose I do. And that's bad, isn't it?

HAND. Terrible.

GEORGINA. Why?

HAND. Think of all the fun you miss.

GEORGINA. Yes, maybe I do. I've often wished that I could be just—well, just completely reckless and irresponsible, like —like—oh, I don't know who

HAND. Like Opal?

GEORGINA. Well, yes, now that you mention it! Is that why everybody is so mad to read that silly book?

HAND. What are you being so snooty about? Why, that book is positively a boon to womankind! For two-fifty flat or three cents a day any *Hausfrau* in the land can identify herself with the most luscious yes-woman in all literature.

GEORGINA. Is that really what every woman wants?

HAND. All I can go by is the sales figures.

GEORGINA. So you think we're all harlots at heart?

HAND. Well, I wouldn't want to run for Congress on that platform.

GEORGINA. Still, even if you're right, there seem to be an awful lot of women who manage not to—

HAND. I know. That's what makes life so difficult for a man.

GEORGINA. Oh, poor Mr. Hand! Do we make things difficult for you?

HAND. Very. But I don't complain. No victory without labor, my Sunday-school teacher used to say. And, by the way, my name is George.

GEORGINA. Yes, George.

HAND. That's better. George and Georgina. We sound like a team of adagio dancers. I consider that very auspicious.

GEORGINA. I was named after my father. He's George, too.

HAND. Now, don't tell me you're attracted to me because I remind you of your father.

GEORGINA. You don't remind me in the least of my father. And who told you that I'm attracted to you?

HAND. You know, I am really beginning to go for you in a big way. *(Shaking his head.)* I can't figure this out.

GEORGINA. You mean there's really something you can't figure out?

HAND. Uh-huh. Just one thing. You!

GEORGINA. Oh, so I'm an enigma! What fun!

HAND. No fooling, how does a girl who has all that you have happen to be so unattached?

GEORGINA. Maybe my virtues—no, that isn't the word! Maybe my charms aren't as apparent to everyone as they are to you.

HAND. I don't believe that! Or are you one of those girls who think they're only interested in marriage?

GEORGINA. I'm not in the least interested in marriage.

HAND. You're not? Why?

GEORGINA. Because from what I've seen of it, I think the odds are all against you.

HAND. You're so right! Well, that makes everything much simpler.

GEORGINA. For whom?

HAND. For you, of course. It doesn't cramp your style, doesn't limit the range of your experiences.

GEORGINA. Why, that's true, isn't it? You have a wonderful gift for clarifying things.

HAND. Don't be coy, Georgina. You'll never get me to believe that a sophisticated girl like you has never had any experiences.

GEORGINA. Well, it would be hard to believe that a sophisticated girl could get to be twenty-two without having had *some* experiences.

HAND. Then what the hell? Or does your aversion to marriage extend to men who are already married?

GEORGINA. I often wonder how I'd feel if I were the man's wife. Or is that very unsophisticated?

HAND. Not a bit. Does credit to your upbringing. Only Mollie isn't a bit like that. We get along fine together except when she has a drink too many and then we really go to town. Otherwise, I don't interfere with her and she doesn't interfere with me.

GEORGINA. That's what I mean about marriage.

HAND. I agreed with you, didn't I? But you'll admit I'm not one of the lads who comes crying for sympathy because he's so misunderstood.

GEORGINA. No, that's true. I knew there was *something* about you that was different.

HAND. No flattery, please! Tell me, have you ever been to Mexico?

GEORGINA. Thanks for changing the subject. No, I haven't been to Mexico. But I've always wanted to go.

HAND. Wonderful! But I haven't changed the subject. I have to go down next month and I've been thinking what fun it would be if you and I could sort of meet up there.

GEORGINA. Oh, have you?

HAND. It's a great country. I've been there before and I know my way around. We'd take in jai-alai matches and bullfights—

GEORGINA. I should say not!

HAND. All right, we'll stay away from bullfights. Anyhow, we'd find some village fiestas, look at the Rivera frescoes, and drift along on the flower boats at Xochimilco. And talk about food! Have you ever eaten mole?

GEORGINA. No, I don't think I have.

HAND. It's turkey with a sauce made of chocolate and about fifteen different kinds of pepper. Sounds revolting, doesn't it?

GEORGINA. It certainly does!

HAND. I'm telling you it's tops. Especially when washed down with a bottle of tequila. You've heard of Taxco, haven't you?

GEORGINA. Yes, of course.

HAND. Well, a friend of mine has a house there that he hardly ever uses. Up on a terraced hill, looking down onto the little village plaza. We'd have dinner in the patio and the local folks would come up and serenade us. Why, I can just see you, done up in a rebozo and—

GEORGINA. You *are* a salesman, aren't you?

(Before HAND can reply, a MAN enters at the left and goes right.)

THE MAN *(as he passes the table)*. Hi, George! How are you doing? *(He waves and goes out at right.)*

HAND. Why, hello, Bert! *(Excitedly to GEORGINA.)* This is really from the gods!

You know who that is? Bert Glover, the fellow who owns the house in Taxco. *(Jumping up.)* Excuse me! I'll be right back!

GEORGINA. No, wait, please!

HAND. I won't be a minute! *(He exits quickly at right. GEORGINA looks after him for a moment, considerably agitated, then sits back, dreamily, lost in her imaginings. As the lights fade slowly on the scene, the sound of singing is heard, center. The lights come up on a corner of an exotic patio bathed in moonlight. A trio of musical-comedy Mexicans is strumming guitars and singing a sentimental Spanish love song. The leader of the trio, a tall, good-looking young man, has the face of CLARK REDFIELD. After a moment, GEORGINA and HAND stroll on at the right, GEORGINA wearing a mantilla and bright shawl and carrying a fan. He has his arm about her. They stand listening to the music. The song ends and the SERENADERS cover their hearts with their sombreros and bow low.)*

GEORGINA *(clapping her hands)*. Oh, lovely, lovely! Buena! Buena! Muchas gracias!

HAND. That was great! *(Reaching into his pocket.)* Here's something for you, boys. *(The LEADER comes forward, holding out his sombrero. HAND drops a fistful of coins into it.)*

THE SINGER. Gracias, señor! Muchas gracias! Buenas noches, señor! Buenas noches, señorita! *(He bends over GEORGINA's hand and kisses it.)*

GEORGINA. Buenas noches! Hasta la vista, caballero!

THE SINGER. Hasta la vista, señorita! Viva los Americanos! *(Bowing and smiling, the SERENADERS exit.)*

GEORGINA. Viva Mé-hi-co! Oh, this is really heavenly. That wonderful moon, this clear cool air, filled with the scent of flowers, and that charming song—

HAND. What about that charming singer? Good thing I'm broad-minded. That young man seemed to take quite a fancy to you.

GEORGINA. It's strange. There's something so familiar about him. And yet I can't think of whom he reminds me. *(She fans herself throughout.)*

HAND. Well, don't bother. You're supposed to be concentrating on me, you know. By the way, where did you pick up all that Spanish? Why, you talk it like a native.

GEORGINA *(modestly).* Oh, don't be silly. But I was always good at languages, and Señor Gonzales at Berlitz did tell me I have a good accent.

HAND. Next time you see him, you can tell him I said you're an all-around good girl.

GEORGINA. Well, I'm glad you think so. Oh, that exquisite food! Who would have believed that turkey with chocolate sauce could taste like that!

HAND. I was right about it, wasn't I?

GEORGINA. Indeed you were! You were right about lots of things. Only—well, I can't help thinking that tomorrow all this will end.

HAND. Georgina, there's something I want to say to you. I knew darned well that when you finally agreed to this, it was only because you thought maybe I could help you forget somebody it made you unhappy to think about. It's true, isn't it?

GEORGINA. Yes, it's true. I was trying to escape, desperately running away from a situation I didn't know how to cope with.

HAND. Then tell me something else. Have I helped you forget?

GEORGINA. Yes, George, you have. That's why it's so hard— No, I won't say it!

HAND. You've said all you need to say, all I wanted to know. Georgina, I thought I had nothing more to learn about women, but I was wrong. I don't want this to be the end, but just the beginning.

GEORGINA. Why do you say such things, when you know it's impossible?

HAND. No, it's not impossible. In fact it's all arranged. While you were at the market this afternoon, I called up my wife. I told her I want a divorce and—

GEORGINA. No, I won't hear of it! I'm not one of those girls that breaks up marriages.

That's one reason I've said no to every married man who—

HAND. Wait a minute! You're not breaking up any marriage. My wife jumped at the suggestion. It seems she's interested in some band leader and she had just about made up her mind to ask me for a divorce.

GEORGINA. Are you telling me the truth?

HAND. I couldn't lie to you. I respect you too much, and anyhow I know you're too smart for me to get away with it. Georgina, this is really from the gods! You *can't* say no!

GEORGINA. I—I don't know, George. You've got to give me time to think— *(As they move right and the lights fade on the scene.)* I must have time to think!

(The lights come up slowly at the right. GEORGINA is seated at the table, as before, lost in her dreams and fanning herself with the luncheon check. She does not see HAND as he hurries on at the right.)

HAND *(coming up to the table).* Well, we're in great luck. Everything is—

GEORGINA *(almost jumping out of her seat).* Oh! Goodness, you nearly frightened me out of my wits!

HAND. Sorry! You look as though you'd been a million miles away. *(Sitting beside her.)* Listen, Georgina, I've fixed it all up with Bert.

GEORGINA. Bert?

HAND. Yes, about the house in Taxco. He just was down there and won't be going again for months. It's just sitting there waiting for us. Well, what do you say?

GEORGINA. Well, goodness, I can't give you an answer just like that!

HAND. Yes, you can! Never fight your impulses. Take it from me, the things we really regret in life are not those we do, but those we don't do.

GEORGINA. I've got to have time to make up my mind.

HAND. All right. How much time do you want—two days, a week?

GEORGINA. Do you have to pin me down like that?

HAND. Sure I do! Because when a gay time is lost, it's lost forever.

GEORGINA. Well, I'll—I'll think it over. *(Looking at her watch.)* Goodness, it's nearly three o'clock. I've got to get back to the shop. *(She rises.)*

HAND *(signing the check).* And I've got a deskful of work. Can I drop you?

GEORGINA. No, you run along. I want to powder my nose. *(Extending her hand.)* Thanks for a marvelous lunch.

HAND *(holding her hand).* Remember what the voice of experience is saying to you: Don't resist your impulses. Goodby! I won't leave you in peace for long!

GEORGINA *(as he goes off).* Well—! *(She stands looking after him, greatly flustered. A* WAITER *enters, picks up the check, and starts to clear the table.)* Oh, do you think I could have another brandy?

THE WAITER. Certainly, madam. The imported?

GEORGINA. What? Oh, yes, the imported, by all means.

THE WAITER. Yes, madam. *(He goes.* GEORGINA *sits at the table.)*

GEORGINA *(gloomily).* So now you're taking to drink, are you? Just like all the other misfits who can't face their problems and try to make alcohol a substitute for character. Oh, Georgina, Georgina, my girl, you're really in a bad way! *(She shakes her head dolefully, as the lights fade and the curtain falls.)*

CURTAIN

ACT TWO

As the curtain rises, the lights come up on the bookshop, at stage left, as in Act 1. CLAIRE *is straightening books on the shelves. A moment later,* GEORGINA *enters, considerably exhilarated.*

GEORGINA. I'm back.

CLAIRE. I was just about to call the Juvenile Delinquents' Court. *(Seeing Georgina's new hat.)* Well, for heaven's sake! *(She examines it at close range.)* Colette has really outdone herself.

GEORGINA. Like it?

CLAIRE. I'm green with envy. How did Mr. Hand react to it?

GEORGINA. He was very polite about it.

CLAIRE. Now, don't hold out on me. Come on, tell Auntie Claire everything that happened.

GEORGINA. Well, we ate and ate, and drank and drank, and talked and talked.

CLAIRE. What did you talk about?

GEORGINA. Oh, all sorts of things. You were right about his intentions. He wants me to go to Mexico with him.

CLAIRE. Just like that? Well, he's obviously not a man who lets the grass grow under his feet.

GEORGINA. No, he isn't. He's been to Mexico and knows all the places to go. Besides that, a friend of his has a house in Taxco and we could have the use of it.

CLAIRE. But how romantic!

GEORGINA. It is sort of. And I've always wanted to go to Mexico.

CLAIRE. Yes, they say that travel broadens the mind. And *he* certainly sounds like a broad-minded boy.

GEORGINA. Well, I must say he was nice and frank about the whole thing. He didn't try to give me any line or pretend a lot of things. He just frankly put it up to me.

CLAIRE. Uh-huh! The direct frontal attack or appeal to the intelligence. After all, we're living in the twentieth century. Let's be modern about this thing. Very flattering.

GEORGINA *(removing her hat).* I suppose so. But I prefer it to the usual line of flattery. If I'm going into something like this, I'd rather go in with my eyes open.

CLAIRE. And are you going into it?

GEORGINA. I promised him I'd think it over.

CLAIRE. Why, Georgina Allerton!

GEORGINA. Does that shock you?

CLAIRE. Well, it just doesn't sound like you. Tell me, are you in love with him?

GEORGINA. Well, he's a clever, successful, good-looking man. And I am attracted to him. He's not making any demand of me, or pretending he's in love with me. If it's all right for him, why isn't it for me?

CLAIRE. You're desperately logical about it.

GEORGINA. Why do men have to have a monopoly on logic?

CLAIRE. I don't know. But somehow, when a woman falls back on logic—

GEORGINA. That's just a hangover from the days when women led sheltered lives. It's time we stopped being a lot of fluttery, scatterbrained little ninnies, who have to rely on something called intuition. Why can't we work out our own problems, just as men do, by using our intelligence?

CLAIRE. It really looks as though Mr. Hand *has* been using the right technique!

GEORGINA. He's not fooling me with any technique. I'm thinking very clearly about the whole thing, and entirely from my own point of view. After all, what would be the harm in it? It's not so unusual these days for a girl to—

CLAIRE. Oh, I don't think it's likely that you'd be put in the stocks and branded with a large, scarlet capital A.

GEORGINA. You mean I might be hurt emotionally? All right, suppose I did get hurt a little! It might be the best thing in the world for me—just what I need, maybe. If I don't begin to have some experiences soon, when will I begin?

CLAIRE. And yet I never met a girl who seemed less eager to go off on a toot with George Hand.

GEORGINA. He thinks I'm puritanical, and I'm afraid he may be right.

CLAIRE. Afraid?

GEORGINA. Well, after all, what is a puritan? Just somebody with such strong desires that she doesn't dare let herself cut loose.

CLAIRE. Oh, so that's what you're afraid of! You think if you say yes to him it will just be your first step on the road to hell?

GEORGINA. That *would* be pretty awful, wouldn't it?

CLAIRE. It would indeed! Well, darling, I think I'll pop out and do some shopping. Think you can look after the trade by yourself?

GEORGINA. Oh, damn it! I wish you'd be a little helpful.

CLAIRE. No, my pet! This is between you and your guardian angel—and I can't wait to see who wins!

GEORGINA (*as* CLAIRE *exits*). Neither can I! (*She sits lost in thought as the lights fade slowly on the scene. To the music of "Poor Butterfly," the lights come up at center on a red fire-alarm lamppost. In the background is an illuminated sign bearing the legend "Joyland."* GEORGINA *enters and swaggers to the lamppost. She wears a cheap red coat with a ratty fur collar and a gaudy hat perched on a tousled blonde wig.* GEORGE HAND, *accompanied by a girl who resembles* MIRIAM, *emerges from the darkness, at the right.*)

HAND (*as they cross*). Well, Arabella, if you've never eaten at Antoine's in New Orleans, you really don't know what food is.

ARABELLA. Yes, so I've heard.

HAND (*glancing at* GEORGINA *as he passes her*). We'd start with oysters Rockefeller, which Ford Madox Ford, who was a great epicure, describes as swimming in a kind of green scum. (*Stopping at left.*) Excuse me a moment! (*He turns and goes back to* GEORGINA, *who starts to go, as she sees him approaching.*)

HAND (*detaining her*). Just a minute, please!

GEORGINA (*in a rough voice*). Hands off, you!

HAND (*turning her about*). Why, I was right! It's Georgina Allerton.

GEORGINA. Well, what's it *to* you?

HAND. What are you doing here, hanging around a street corner?

GEORGINA. Looking after my trade, that's what!

HAND. But—a girl like you! What's brought you to this?

GEORGINA. It would give you a kick, wouldn't it, to hear all about it? You're all like that!

HAND. But in Mexico, you were such a gay, proud girl, full of the joy of living; and dreaming of all the things you were going to do.

GEORGINA (harshly). I didn't know how easy it would be to say yes, the next time someone asked me. And the next time after that, it was easier still. Then they stopped asking me—and I began asking them. Now you know all about it. So, go ahead and scram.

HAND. Georgina, if there's anything I can—

GEORGINA. To hell with that! I don't want your pity.

HAND. Well, let me, at least— (He takes a bill from his pocket and offers it to her. GEORGINA snatches it and tears it up.)

GEORGINA. Go on, now! Beat it! Your girl friend is waiting for you!

(HAND sighs, shakes his head, and goes left.)

ARABELLA (as he rejoins her). For heaven's sake, what was that all about?

HAND (as they exit). It's tragic. I used to know that girl, years ago. And, believe it or not, she was a sweet, modest little—

(His voice trails off. The tune changes to "Broadway Rose." GEORGINA buries her face in her hands and sobs, then as she hears a MAN whistling off right, she straightens up and resumes her place at the lamppost. CLARK REDFIELD strides on, whistling merrily. He glances quickly at GEORGINA as he passes her.)

GEORGINA. Got a date for tonight, dearie?

CLARK. Sorry, baby, but I've got a little wife waiting for me. (He is about to exit, then stops and turns.) Say, haven't I seen you somewhere before?

GEORGINA (brazenly). Have you?

CLARK. Why, sure enough! You're that girl who used to run that crummy little bookshop on East—! Well, I'll be damned!

GEORGINA (savagely). What the hell's so funny about it?

CLARK. Why, who'd have thought it? Little Miss—whatever your name is! The budding literary genius, the highly cultivated young college grad, who lectured me about my manners and thought sports writing was vulgar. Well, it looks like you're doing a little in the sporting line yourself.

GEORGINA. Shut up, you great big ape! (She slaps his face.)

CLARK (in a rage). Oh, that's how you feel about it, is it? Well, I'll show you! There's a place for tramps like you. (He goes left.) Officer! Officer! (He disappears in the darkness. GEORGINA looks about, in terror, then opens her handbag, takes out a small bottle, and drains it. The tune changes to "Hearts and Flowers.")

JIM (off right). Georgina! Stop! For God's sake, stop! (He rushes on.)

GEORGINA (with a wan smile, as she throws the bottle away). You're too late, Jim. Nothing can save me, now.

JIM. Why have you done this, Georgina? Why? Why didn't you come to me? I would have—

GEORGINA. No, Jim, I couldn't do that. You have Miriam and those three lovely children. Once I brought you two together again, there was no place for me in your life. There's no place for me anywhere. (She totters.) Hold me, Jim, hold me! I'm— (She collapses into his arms.)

JIM. Georgina, I—

GEORGINA (faintly). Don't say anything, Jim. Just hold me. I wanted to live in your arms, but it wasn't meant to be. So let me die in them. It's the only happiness I'll ever know now. Good-by, Jim. Kiss Mother and Dad for me. And ask them to forgive me. And try not to forget me, Jim. There was never anybody for me but you—

JIM. I'll never forget you—never!

GEORGINA. Thank you, Jim. Good-by, darling. (Standing erect, for a moment.) It is a far, far better thing that I do than I have ever done. It is a far, far better rest I go to than I have ever known.

(She clasps her abdomen in agony, pivots on her heels, and falls inert.)

JIM *(kneeling beside her).* Georgina! Georgina, my darling! *(*CLARK *reappears at left, accompanied by a* POLICEMAN.*)*

THE POLICEMAN. Is that her?

CLARK. Yes, she accosted me! She's nothing but a common—! My God, what's happened to her?

JIM *(looking up).* She's gone where no one can harm her, now.

CLARK *(removing his hat).* You mean she's—?

JIM. Yes, Clark Redfield, she is.

CLARK *(with an agonized cry).* Oh, no! Oh, why did I do it? If only I'd been a little human to her—! *(Turning to the policeman.)* Officer, arrest me! Take me away!

THE POLICEMAN. What for?

CLARK. I'm a murderer. I killed that girl as surely as though I had stabbed her to the heart.

THE POLICEMAN. Then, come along! *(He snaps handcuffs onto* CLARK *as the light fades on the scene and the clanging of a patrol-wagon bell is heard. The sound merges into that of a ringing telephone. The lights come up left on the bookshop.* GEORGINA, *seated moodily, is startled by the ringing of the telephone. She hurries to it and answers it.)*

GEORGINA *(greatly flustered).* Hello! Mermaid Bookshop! *(As she speaks, the lights come up, stage right, on a telephone booth in which* CLARK REDFIELD *is standing.)*

CLARK. Is Miss Allerton there?

GEORGINA. This is she.

CLARK. Oh, I didn't recognize your voice. You sound scared to death.

GEORGINA *(sharply).* Who is this, please?

CLARK. Clark Redfield.

GEORGINA *(who knew it all along).* Oh, it's you, is it? Well, what is it?

CLARK. I want to ask you to—

GEORGINA. I don't care to hear any apologies. The whole thing is of no consequence whatever. I was foolish to let my temper get the better of me. And, as far as I'm concerned, the whole incident is closed.

CLARK. Yes, you have got a temper, haven't you? But are you under the impression that I called up to apologize for something?

GEORGINA. Well, I guess that's foolish too—to expect you to have that much graciousness. Look, I'm quite busy and if you don't mind—

CLARK. I'll bet you haven't done a thing all afternoon.

GEORGINA. If you'll excuse me, Mr. Redfield—

CLARK. Whoa! Wait a minute! Don't hang up on me! I'm calling to ask you—

GEORGINA. Well, what? Please get to the point, will you?

CLARK. I've got a pair of tickets for a show tonight and I thought you might like to—

GEORGINA. Well, of all the unmitigated—! You really *have* got the hide of an elephant. What makes you think I'd consider—

CLARK. Well, it's the opening of *The Merchant of Venice,* with James Zerney as Shylock. And I thought that might appeal to a lover of the classics.

GEORGINA. Well, under ordinary circumstances, it certainly would. Especially with Hilda Vincent playing Portia; but I'm afraid—

CLARK. Is she a favorite of yours?

GEORGINA. It just happens that we went to college together and—

CLARK. Good! Then it's a date!

GEORGINA *(indignantly).* It certainly is *not* a date! But thank you all the same, though I can't imagine why you—

CLARK. I can't, either. It was just an impulse and I—

GEORGINA. You don't strike me as the impulsive type. I should rather think of you as decidedly calculating.

CLARK. All right. What do you say we settle for a calculated impulse? *(As the operator cuts in.)* All right, just a minute!

GEORGINA. What's that?

CLARK (*fishing in his pockets*). The operator wants another nickel.

GEORGINA. Well, there's no necessity for prolonging—

CLARK. No, wait a minute, Georgina! No, I'm not talking to you, operator. Listen, I haven't got a nickel, operator. (*Flourishing a bill.*) Can you change five dollars for me? Well, where's all that service you people do so much advertising about? Just a second! Look, Georgina, call me back, will you?

GEORGINA. I have nothing further to—

CLARK. No, call me back! The number is Circle 5-7933. Hello! Hello! Oh, damn it! (*He bangs down the receiver, leans back in the booth, and lights a cigarette.*)

GEORGINA. I tell you I—hello! (*She hangs up, and slowly jots down the number on a pad. Then she sits staring at the telephone. She raises her forefinger as though to dial, then lowers it again. The phone rings and she jumps. Picking up the phone.*) I thought you didn't have another—

(*The lights come up quickly at center on* GEORGE HAND *seated at his desk, and talking into the telephone. Throughout,* CLARK *keeps looking at his telephone, waiting for it to ring.*)

HAND. Hello? Is that you, Georgina?

GEORGINA. Yes. Who is this? (*Knowing full well.*)

HAND. This is George. Anything wrong? You sound jumpy.

GEORGINA. It must be all those brandies. I'm not used to—

HAND. Why, I'll have to put you back in training. Look, honey, a business dinner date just blew up on me, so I thought maybe you'd take pity on a poor guy with an evening on his hands and—

GEORGINA (*nervously*). Oh, I really don't think I can tonight, George— (CLARK *is beginning to get impatient.*)

HAND. We can take our time over a nice dinner somewhere and then go dancing —or to a show, if you'd rather.

GEORGINA. I only wish I could. If you'd

only called up a half hour sooner! I just promised somebody I'd go to the theater.

HAND. Tough luck! But I called the minute I knew I'd be free. Why don't you get out of it?

GEORGINA. I don't see how, after just saying yes, ten minutes ago.

HAND. Well, then, how about cocktails and dinner? Or a drink after the show?

GEORGINA. I'm afraid that's all included.

HAND. Say, who is this monopolist? I'll sick the Attorney General on him!

GEORGINA. It's nothing like that. Just one of those things that you get into and can't get out of.

HAND. Well, try to get out of at least some part of it. I do want to see you.

GEORGINA. All right, I'll try my best.

HAND. Shall I call you back?

GEORGINA. No, I'm just leaving. If I can fix it, I'll call you.

(CLARK *leaves the booth, and starts to exit, then changes his mind and comes back.*)

HAND. Well, I'll keep my fingers crossed. Because I've got you very much on my mind. And if I do lose tonight, I'll owe you lunch tomorrow—yes?

GEORGINA. All right! Good-by, George. And thanks.

HAND. Good-by, dear.

(*He hangs up and the lights fade out quickly on him.* GEORGINA *hangs up and leans back with a deep sigh. Then she stares at the telephone number, hesitates a moment, then starts slowly to dial.*)

CLARK (*with sudden anger*). Oh, to hell with it! (*He leaves the booth and strides off, right. The phone in the booth rings, then again and once again.* GEORGINA, *very much annoyed, is about to hang up, but* CLARK *comes tearing back and picks up the phone in the booth just in time.*) Hello! Is that you?

GEORGINA. Well, you certainly took your time about answering.

CLARK. I fell asleep waiting for you to call. What's the matter, have you got telephone operator's cramp or something?

GEORGINA. I happened to have another call. You seem to forget I'm running a business.

CLARK. Running conveys an idea of activity.

GEORGINA. The only reason I called back is that I don't want you to have the false impression that I'm sufficiently interested in anything you may have said, this morning or at any other time, to make me feel the slightest bit of resentment.

CLARK *(whistling)*. Phew! I was afraid you were never going to get to the end of that one! Now, to get back to *The Merchant of Venice*—

GEORGINA. Yes, exactly. In the first place, I have no interest whatever in being taken to the theater by you. But I *would* like to see Hilda Vincent play Portia, so—

CLARK. Right! So you'll go.

GEORGINA. Will you please let me finish?

CLARK. If you think you can by eight-forty.

GEORGINA. What I started to say is that I'll consider it only on a strictly business basis.

CLARK. I have a feeling that neither of us knows what you're talking about.

GEORGINA. What I mean is that if you have an extra ticket on your hands, I'll be glad to buy it from you.

CLARK. Can't be done. These are press seats.

GEORGINA *(interestedly)*. Oh, are you going to review the play?

CLARK. I am not. I got them from our movie critic. His mother is getting married tonight and he has to give her away.

GEORGINA. Do the movie critics get tickets for plays, too?

CLARK. Look, Georgina, this is one of those phones where you have to stand up. How about meeting me at—

GEORGINA. Are you dressing?

CLARK. Certainly not! Nobody dresses for Shakespeare, unless Bea Lillie happens to be in it.

GEORGINA. Then I'll meet you in the lobby at eight-thirty. Unless you want to leave the ticket with the ticket-taker.

CLARK. No, I don't! How about dinner?

GEORGINA. I'll have dinner somewhere.

CLARK. You're a resourceful girl. I think I'll do likewise. Maybe we could have it at the same place—purely by coincidence, of course.

GEORGINA. Thank you, but I don't care to—

CLARK. Look, one of the things I don't like to do is eat alone. It makes me feel so unwanted. You don't have to say a word. I'll do all the talking. And you can read a book or sulk in your beer or whatever you like.

GEORGINA. Well—only if it's clearly understood that we go Dutch.

CLARK. I was thinking of going Italian. Do you know Emilio's?

GEORGINA. No, I don't.

CLARK. Well, it's just a spaghetti and red ink joint, but what would be called, in France, a serious house. They have—

GEORGINA. There's no reason why you should take me to dinner and I—

CLARK. There are two reasons—both valid from my point of view. The first is that that five bucks I got from you is burning a hole in my pocket. And the second is that I have something to celebrate.

GEORGINA. Well, I'm afraid I haven't.

CLARK. All right, then, you can watch *me* celebrate. Listen, I'm getting acute claustrophobia. Emilio's at seven.

GEORGINA. I don't know why I'm doing this.

CLARK. Good! That will give you something to brood over at dinner while I talk. I'm hanging up now.

GEORGINA. Just a minute! Where is this Emilio's?

CLARK. Oh, yes, you may as well know *that*. Forty-seventh, just west of Eighth. Good-by!

GEORGINA. Oh, just one other thing— *(Then, hastily, as* JIM *enters.)* All right,

Emilio's at seven. (*She hangs up. The light fades quickly on* CLARK.)

GEORGINA (*flustered*). Oh, hello, Jim!

JIM. Yes, here I am, back again. But only to ask you if you can have dinner with me.

GEORGINA. Oh, I'm sorry, Jim! I just this minute made a date. Maybe I can break it—only I'm not sure that I know where to—

JIM. That's too bad. I was hoping we could—

GEORGINA. How about lunch tomorrow? I have a sort of tentative date, but I guess I can get out of it.

JIM. I won't be here tomorrow. I'm leaving for Reno tonight.

GEORGINA. You're going to Reno? But I thought you said Miriam—

JIM. Yes, I've had another session with Miriam. She made a great to-do about being separated from her obstetrician, so I said I'd go. Georgina, I've got something very important to say to you, and since I have only these few minutes, you'll forgive me if I seem blunt about it.

GEORGINA. Well, what is it?

JIM. Well, I came here this morning, without knowing why; it was just sheer impulse. But now I do know why. It was because it's you I've always wanted, because unconsciously I've always been reaching out for you.

GEORGINA (*greatly agitated*). You're just imagining all that. It's the way people always behave when they're going through an emotional crisis.

JIM. Yes, I knew you'd say that. You think I'm just turning to you on the bounce. But it isn't so, and I know now that you're the answer to everything I want and need. Does that make you unhappy?

GEORGINA. Oh, no, Jim. Not unhappy. It's just that this is the last thing in the world I was expecting.

JIM. Well, if it disturbs you so, it must mean that you have some deep feeling for me, too. Does it, Georgina? Please be honest with me.

GEORGINA. All right! I will be honest! Yes, I do care for you. I always have, ever since I've known you.

JIM. Then why are you so troubled about it?

GEORGINA. Because I'm afraid you may feel quite differently about it, sitting out there in Reno for six weeks with plenty of time to think it over. Why don't we wait and see if you still feel the same way when you come back to New York?

JIM. I'm not coming back to New York. I've had enough of cities and the treadmill life you have to lead in them. I want to be able to breathe for once. I'm going to find myself a place where I can see the stars and smell the earth.

GEORGINA. Yes, I've often dreamed of that. Just running off somewhere, anywhere—and with you, too!

JIM. Then why don't you get on that plane with me tonight?

GEORGINA. It's not as simple as all that, Jim. People daydream about all sorts of things. But when you're faced with actuality, you have to stop and think. If a man and woman are going to spend their lives together, they must have some plan, some way of living.

JIM. Of course they do. But why can't it be a simple one? Why can't we get ourselves a little farm, or a ranch? We'll work the land together, and work at other things too. I've always wanted to paint, and you have your writing—

GEORGINA. No, I don't think I want to go on with that. Clark Redfield says my novel is a piece of tripe.

JIM. Why do you pay any attention to him? I'll back my judgment of that book to the limit. It expresses all the things that you and I believe in, and beautifully too. Georgina, if you feel that you'd rather not go with me now, promise me at least that you'll come out and join me when I've got my decree.

GEORGINA. It all means too much to me, Jim, to be able to say yes, just like that. First, I want to be absolutely sure that this is right for both of us.

JIM. Well, I'm completely confident about your decision, because I know that this is meant to be. Well, I've got to run along now and pick up my ticket. I wish I could see you again, before I leave, if only for a moment.

GEORGINA. So do I. But I'm afraid I won't be free until after the theater.

JIM. Well, my plane doesn't leave until one. Why don't you meet me at the air terminal about twelve and ride out to the airport with me?

(The telephone rings.)

GEORGINA *(going to the telephone)*. Excuse me, Jim. Mermaid Bookshop.

(As she answers the telephone, the lights go up at right on MRS. ALLERTON, *seated at the telephone in her negligee, as in Act I. A book is beside her.)*

MRS. ALLERTON. I have some news for you, Georgina.

GEORGINA. Oh, just a minute, please. *(Covering the transmitter.)* All right, Jim. I'll be at the air terminal at twelve.

JIM. Thank you, Georgina. *(He presses her free hand, and exits.)*

GEORGINA. I'm sorry, Mother. I had to get rid of a customer.

MRS. ALLERTON. That's right. Don't encourage them. Tell me, have you heard from Miriam?

GEORGINA. No, I haven't.

MRS. ALLERTON. Jim, either?

GEORGINA. No, why? Is anything wrong?

MRS. ALLERTON. On the contrary. They're divorcing. Jim is leaving for Reno tonight. Miriam didn't want to go and since Jim is at leisure again, we decided to ship him out. Of course, I'm footing the bills; but this is one expenditure poor old Grandpa would certainly have approved of.

GEORGINA. Well, I don't approve. I think it's awful.

MRS. ALLERTON. I expected you would. That's why I'm calling you—to warn you not to try to upset things, in case Jim comes crying to you.

GEORGINA. What makes you think he has any intention of doing that?

MRS. ALLERTON. Just a hunch. I suspect that it's you he's always been in love with. *(She sneezes.)*

GEORGINA. Why, Mother, how can you say things like that!

MRS. ALLERTON. Well, maybe it's just this irritation of my mucous membrane that makes me think so. But, if he does turn up, be careful not to say anything that will keep him off that plane. I only hope and pray that he's subject to airsickness. *(A sneeze.)* Well, now that everything is settled I can get back to Opal. I certainly do envy that girl.

GEORGINA. Really, Mother!

MRS. ALLERTON. I just don't understand how she can spend so much time without any clothes on and not catch her death of cold. Well, good-by.

GEORGINA. Oh, I won't be home till late. I'm having dinner out and going to the opening of *The Merchant of Venice*—and somewhere else afterwards.

MRS. ALLERTON. Oh, I hope there's a promising male involved.

GEORGINA. No, there isn't. It's just a boorish, conceited newspaperman in whom nobody could have the slightest interest.

MRS. ALLERTON. Sounds like a charming evening.

GEORGINA. Well, I haven't been to a first night in years. Besides, Hilda Vincent is playing Portia and I want to see her.

MRS. ALLERTON. What is there in it for the young man?

GEORGINA. I don't know. I haven't any idea why he asked me, except that he's sadistic and is planning to spend the evening making me feel uncomfortable.

MRS. ALLERTON. Well, it certainly looks as though Mr. Right had come along at last. Well, have fun. *(As she hangs up, the lights fade on her.* GEORGINA *hangs up. She sits for a moment, steeped in gloom, then rises, and picks up her hat.)*

GEORGINA *(looking at the hat)*. No, not for that uncouth person. *(She replaces the hat on the desk and exits. The lights fade on the scene and come up center, on* CLARK, *seated at a table in Emilio's, a modest*

Italian restaurant. He is munching a bread stick and listening to a Caruso record.)

GEORGINA *(entering as the record comes to an end).* Sorry to be late.

CLARK *(half rising).* O.K. I was just listening to Caruso and wondering if you'd decided to stand me up.

GEORGINA *(sitting at the table).* That doesn't happen to be my way of doing things.

CLARK. All right. Let's not start fighting right away. We have the whole evening ahead of us. *(Calling.)* Oh, Luigi!

LUIGI *(entering).* Yes, Meester Redfield.

CLARK. I think we'll order now. *(To GEORGINA.)* How about a drink first?

GEORGINA. I'd like a Martini.

CLARK. Not with good Italian food. Look, do you mind if I do the ordering?

GEORGINA. Of course not! You know what I want much better than I do.

CLARK. Now you're talking sense! All right, Luigi, we'll have a mixed Vermouth to start with—two parts dry and one part sweet, frappéed and with a slice of lemon peel.

LUIGI. O.K., Meester Redfield. And some antipasto?

CLARK. No, not all that miscellaneous stuff. Just those little bitter olives and some prosciutto.

LUIGI. Then a little minestrone?

GEORGINA. Not for me, thanks. I'm on a diet and I had a huge lunch.

CLARK *(to LUIGI).* Yes, let's have minestrone. Then some spaghetti.

LUIGI. Marinara?

CLARK. No, Bolognese. And then how about a nice scallopini à la Parmigiana?

LUIGI. Ees very good!

CLARK. No, wait a minute! Let's have the scallopini à la Marsala. And eggplant Parmigiana with it.

LUIGI. O.K.

GEORGINA. I hope you're not ordering all this for me, because I really—

CLARK *(ignoring her).* And a mixed green salad. Any zuppe Inglese tonight?

LUIGI. I think so.

CLARK. Well, save a couple portions for us.

GEORGINA *(tartly.)* You already ordered soup!

CLARK. Soup? Oh, you mean zuppe Inglese. Yes, literally English soup, but actually a kind of rum cake. What they call trifle in England. Depend on the English to make any kind of food sound unappetizing.

LUIGI. And about the wine. Some Chianti? Or maybe Lacrime Cristi?

CLARK. Have you got any of that Falerno left?

LUIGI. I guess we got a few bottles.

CLARK. Let's have that. All right, I think that's all for the present.

LUIGI. O.K., Meester Redfield. *(He exits.)*

GEORGINA. What are we going to do with all that when it comes?

CLARK. Eat it. I'm not sure that the Falerno is better than the Lacrime Cristi, but it gives me a kick to drink a wine that is a lineal descendant of the Falernian of ancient Rome. Attica nectareum turbatis mella Falernum. Honey of Attica make thick the nectar-like Falernian. I forget who said it. Do you know?

GEORGINA. No, I don't. I went in for modern languages. Spanish and—

CLARK. I tried that once, thickening the wine with honey. But maybe I had the wrong formula. Or maybe the Romans had different tastes. So you're a friend of Hilda Vincent's?

GEORGINA. Well, not a friend, exactly. We just happened to be at college together. So, naturally, I've always been interested in her work.

CLARK. I know, the old school tie.

GEORGINA. Besides, I once played Portia.

CLARK. You what?

GEORGINA. It was our high school graduation play. Of course, it was only an amateur production, but I don't think I did too badly. I still know the whole thing by heart. At that time, I wanted very much to become an actress.

CLARK. Well, why didn't you?

GEORGINA. Oh, I don't know. My father wanted me to be a lawyer, so I just went along with that, for a while. I even tried one semester at law school. (*Sighing.*) And now, of course, it's too late to do anything about acting.

CLARK. So you turned to literature?

GEORGINA. Let's keep off that subject, if you don't mind.

CLARK. Which reminds me that I've brought back your novel. (*He produces a large envelope from under the table.*)

GEORGINA (*tartly*). That's very thoughtful of you, I'm sure. But it might have been a little more practical to have brought it back tomorrow, instead of lugging it all through dinner and theater.

CLARK. Aren't you forgetting that you told me never to enter your shop again?

GEORGINA (*tight-lipped*). You could have mailed it.

CLARK (*weighing the envelope in his hand*). A heck of a lot of postage. And suppose some little postal inspector had peeped into it? Those poor devils have a hard enough life as it is.

GEORGINA. You said you were celebrating something tonight. Did some friend of yours die?

CLARK. Well, it's almost as good as that. Oliver Quinn is leaving the paper.

GEORGINA. I suppose I *should* know who Oliver Quinn is.

CLARK. Yes, you certainly should. He writes one of the three best sports columns in the country.

GEORGINA. Excuse my ignorance. But I never read the sports page—

CLARK. Yes, so you told me. But several million other people do. Of course, most of them are not important people, but still, as you'll hear Portia say, later in the evening, God made them, so therefore let them pass for men. Well, anyhow, Oliver is leaving the paper to take the chair of Icelandic literature at the University of Michigan. That means promotions all

along the line and an opening at the bottom, which the chief says is for me. (*As* LUIGI *enters.*) And here, opportunely, is Luigi, so we'll drink to my good luck. (*He picks up the glass which Luigi has set before him.* LUIGI *exits.*)

GEORGINA (*picking up her glass.*) Well, if you consider it good luck—

CLARK. I do indeed, and thanks for the toast.

GEORGINA (*savoring the drink*). This is quite good.

CLARK. Careful! Don't commit yourself. These olives go well with it.

GEORGINA (*taking one*). Thank you.

CLARK. And try a little of this raw ham. (*He helps her to some.*)

GEORGINA. I hope it doesn't give us trichinosis.

CLARK. What in hell is that?

GEORGINA. It's a horrible intestinal disorder you get from eating undercooked pork.

CLARK. Really? Well, if we do get it, it will probably be the only thing we'll ever have in common, so let's go to it. (*He takes a large mouthful.*)

GEORGINA. I didn't believe that you were serious, this morning, about wanting to be a sports writer.

CLARK. If I have a fault, Georgina, it's that I incline to the serious side.

GEORGINA. I can't understand it. People getting all excited about which team scores the most runs or who knocks out who.

CLARK. Nothing hard about that. Every time the champ comes up with a haymaker, forty thousand customers are taking a swing at the boss or the traffic cop. And when the King of Swat whams it into the bleachers, a million flat-chested runts are right in there, whizzing around the bases.

GEORGINA. That's nothing but escapism.

CLARK. That's right. Like the girls out of college who slam the door with Nora, take a nose dive into the brook with Ophelia, or tumble into a lot of Louis Quartorze beds with Opal.

GEORGINA. We'll just pass over the personal implications and confine ourselves to the abstract question whether an interest in sports and an interest in literature—

CLARK. There is no such thing as an abstract discussion between a man and a woman.

GEORGINA. Well, *that* certainly reveals a narrow and conventional mind.

CLARK. Who's getting personal now? You see, every road we take leads right back to that novel of yours.

GEORGINA. Will you stop harping on that? What's my novel got to do—! I was certainly an idiot ever to show it to you.

CLARK. But you did! And the reason you did was that you thought you'd produced something creative and wanted to show it off.

GEORGINA. Nothing of the kind! I mistook you for a literary critic and I wanted—

CLARK. Baloney! You were just a fond mamma, showing off her baby and blindly oblivious to the fact that it was just an old rag doll with the straw stuffing coming through. Talk about escapism! Why, there isn't a genuine moment in it—just a rehash of all the lady writers from Jane Austen to Virginia Woolf.

GEORGINA. All right, I've heard enough about that!

CLARK. That's what you think! My God, can't a girl who's been around for twenty-three or -four years find—

GEORGINA. Twenty-two, if you don't mind.

CLARK. I don't mind a bit. If you want to write, can't you produce something better than a lot of moony daydreaming about an idiotic young couple who can't bear escalators and modern plumbing and who go off to the great open spaces to live in simple, unwashed happiness among the mosquitoes and shad flies? There's a tasty dish for you—*Love among the Heifers:* a pastoral in nine cantos, with costumes by Abercrombie and Fitch.

GEORGINA. Anything can be made to sound silly, if you're stupid and literal about it. I happened to be writing a fantasy, about two sensitive people who find themselves hemmed in by the steel and stone of the city and who can find freedom only in—

CLARK. Skip it! Can you imagine any girl in her right mind behaving the way that heroine of yours does?

GEORGINA. Yes, I can. If she cared enough about the man, why wouldn't she be willing to give up a lot of meaningless things for him?

CLARK. What! And go tooting off to some nebulous never-never land with that balmy Jim Lucas of a character.

GEORGINA. What's Jim Lucas got to do with it?

CLARK. That just slipped out. But it's not so far off, at that. No wonder he thinks the story is a world-beater. Why, I'm beginning to think that maybe he sat for that portrait.

GEORGINA. I hope I'm not so literal-minded that I have to write about—

CLARK. I know! I know! Why bother to step outside and look at life, when it's so cozy indoors and there's always a shelfful of books handy? For God's sake, hasn't anything ever happened to you? Have you never been drunk? Or socked a guy for making a pass at you? Or lost your panties on Fifth Avenue?

GEORGINA. You think you're going to make me lose my temper, don't you? Well, I'm sorry to disappoint you, but you're not. However, I do find you even more offensive than I had expected, so, if you'll excuse me, I think I'll just leave you to your splendid repast, while I— (*She starts to rise.*)

CLARK (*pushing her back into her seat*). You'll certainly do nothing of the kind! I told you I don't like eating alone. And what's more, I'm going to protect these friends of mine here. They're artists: the preparation and serving of food is a serious business to them. (*As* LUIGI *enters.*) Here's Luigi now, with the minestrone and a dusty bottle of Falerno. Do you think I'm going to have his feelings lacerated by having you walk out on the soup course? No! It's time you learned some manners.

GEORGINA (*aghast*). I beg your pardon! And to think that I turned down two other invitations to—!

CLARK. Well, that was your mistake. Just as it was my mistake to pass up the Wilinski-O'Connell fight at the Garden. But since we are here, you'll just have to see it through. You can say or do whatever you like to me, but I will not allow Emilio's minestrone to be slighted.

LUIGI (*smiling, as he starts to serve the soup*). Ees nice and hot.

GEORGINA (*with great self-restraint*). Very well, I shall eat the minestrone.

LUIGI. A leetle cheese, mees?

GEORGINA. No, thank you.

LUIGI (*distressed*). Oh, ees no good weed-out cheese.

GEORGINA. Well, just a little then. (*As he serves her.*) Thank you, that's very nice.

CLARK. A lot for me, Luigi.

LUIGI (*beaming*). Sure ting, Meester Redfield! (*He serves* CLARK *and goes for the wine.*)

CLARK. They really do a beautiful minestrone here, don't they? (GEORGINA *eats her soup without replying.*) You'd think I owned the joint, wouldn't you, the way I go on? You ought to eat here three or four times a week and build yourself up. You're too damned skinny. (*She throws him a look but does not reply.*) Personally, I find the natural curves of the female body quite appealing. (*As* LUIGI *approaches with the wine bottle.*) Ah, here we are! Luigi, did you know that the ancient Romans drank this wine?

LUIGI. No, I didn' know. I come from Napoli. (*He fills the glasses and goes.*)

CLARK (*sniffing the wine*). I want you to taste this. But finish your soup first. I'm glad to see you concentrating on your dinner. I can't stand girls who are so busy gabbing that they just pick at their food.

(GEORGINA *throws him a withering look. Apparently oblivious of it, he tears off a morsel of bread and pops it into his mouth. As they go on eating their soup, the lights fade slowly on the scene. To the sound of a string quartet playing Elizabethan music, the lights come up dimly at the left on a section of a theater, consisting of eight or ten seats arranged in three rows. The seats face right and the stage of the theater is presumably off right, beyond the proscenium arch. The aisle of the theater runs right and left, downstage of the seats. All the seats are occupied, except the aisle pair in the first and third rows. After a moment, an* USHER *enters at left, followed by* CLARK *and* GEORGINA. CLARK *has* GEORGINA's *script tucked under his arm.*)

THE USHER (*stopping at the third row*). First two on the aisle. (*She hands* CLARK *the stubs and programs and exits left.* GEORGINA *takes the second seat and* CLARK *the one on the aisle.*)

GEORGINA. Well, I'm glad we're not late. I hate to come in after the curtain is up.

CLARK. I knew a girl who was dropped from the social register for admitting that she had seen the first act of a play. She finally put an end to herself, by taking an overdose of caviar.

GEORGINA. Why do you come to the theater at all?

CLARK. It fills that awkward gap between liqueurs and highballs.

GEORGINA. Please don't mention food or drink again!

CLARK. Good dinner, wasn't it?

GEORGINA. Oh, yes, the dinner was fine.

CLARK. There's some reservation there.

GEORGINA (*looking at her program*). That's lovely music. I wonder what it is.

CLARK. Sounds iike Purcell.

GEORGINA (*finding it in the program*). Why, it *is* Purcell!

CLARK. Sorry! I always seem to be saying the wrong thing.

GEORGINA. It's certainly a mystery to me— (*She breaks off.*)

CLARK. Oh, come on! Say it!

GEORGINA. Well, it's just that I don't understand why a person who knows as much as you do has so little knowledge of human nature.

CLARK. You mean I have no knowledge of your nature?

GEORGINA. I mean anybody's nature! Either that or what's even worse, you take pleasure in making people feel uncomfortable.

CLARK. What are you uncomfortable about?

GEORGINA. How would you like it if I had spent the whole evening harping on your shortcomings?

CLARK. I might have found it very instructive.

GEORGINA. There you go again—implying that I am afraid to hear about my deficiencies. That's not what I meant at all.

CLARK. Then what did you mean?

GEORGINA. I mean that there are ways of saying things. No sensible person objects to having things pointed out in a—

CLARK. I see! We're back again on destructive versus constructive criticism.

GEORGINA. Yes, we are. It's one thing to be told, in a friendly spirit, how you might improve yourself in certain respects—

CLARK. In other words, you like to hear about your faults in a way that high-lights your virtues.

GEORGINA. If I listened to you, I'd soon believe that I didn't have any virtues. I don't know anything. I can't do anything. I'm just a total loss. Luckily, I don't attach any importance to your opinion of me.

CLARK. Is that why you keep bringing it up?

GEORGINA (indignantly). Well, what do you think I am, some kind of a jellyfish that's just going to sit and let you—

CLARK. If you'd ever tangled with a jellyfish you'd know they're anything but submissive creatures.

(She buries her nose in the program. The USHER comes down the aisle, followed by GEORGE HAND and a YOUNG WOMAN in a spectacular evening gown. The USHER stops beside the unoccupied row.)

USHER. These two.

HAND (as the USHER exits). Thank you! (Seeing GEORGINA and going up to her.) Why, hello, Georgina! Fancy meeting you here!

GEORGINA. Why, hello, George! (CLARK rises.)

HAND. This is Miss Delehanty. Tessie, Miss Allerton.

MISS DELEHANTY. Hi!

GEORGINA. How do you do? And this is Mr. Redfield. Miss Delehanty, Mr. Hand.

MISS DELEHANTY (to CLARK). Hi!

HAND (shaking hands with CLARK). Are you the Redfield who writes those book reviews?

CLARK (eying MISS DELEHANTY). Afraid so.

GEORGINA. But he doesn't read the books.

HAND (laughing). Well, thank God for that! Think of what he'd say if he did read them. Well, I guess we'd better settle down, Tessie.

MISS DELEHANTY. Yeah! (She and HAND sit in the first row.)

CLARK (sotto voce). What's his name— Hand?

GEORGINA. George Hand. He's one of the biggest book jobbers in—

CLARK. Oh, yes! I thought it rang a bell somewhere.

GEORGINA. Something wrong about it?

CLARK. No. Not a thing. If books must be sold, there must be people to sell them. I'll bet he catches hell from Tessie, when she finds out this isn't a musical. Well, I guess that accounts for one of the dinner dates you turned down.

GEORGINA. Yes, it does. And I almost wish I hadn't.

CLARK. Why did you?

GEORGINA. Because I already had accepted your invitation.

CLARK. You could have called me off.

GEORGINA. Well, that is certainly a gracious remark! As a matter of fact, I would have, if I'd known where to reach you.

CLARK. Always call the paper. If I'm not there, somebody's likely to know where I am.

GEORGINA. I'll remember that—but I doubt that I'll ever have any need for the information.

CLARK. They say this Hand is quite a chaser.

GEORGINA. Do they? Well, I wouldn't know about that.

CLARK. I thought you might.

GEORGINA. What made you think that?

CLARK. I don't know. I get hunches like that sometimes. I have Indian blood in me.

GEORGINA. Well, in the future I wish you would please—

(The music comes to an end, amid scattered applause.)

CLARK *(applauding)*. Sh! Curtain going up!

(The lights dim, except that GEORGINA's and CLARK's faces remain brightly lighted. They look off right, where a glow is now visible, as the curtain presumably rises. There is scattered applause followed by a flourish of trumpets, and then the voices of the unseen actors of "The Merchant of Venice" are heard off right.)

ANTONIO.
In sooth, I know not why I am so sad:
It wearies me; you say it wearies you;
But how I caught it, found it, or came by it,
What stuff 'tis made of, whereof it is born,
I am to learn;
And such a want-wit sadness makes of me,
That I have much ado to know myself.

SALARINO.
Your mind is tossing on the ocean;
There, where your argosies with portly sail,
Like signiors and rich burghers on the flood,
Or, as it were, the pageants of the sea,
Do overpeer the petty traffickers
That curtsy to them, do them reverence,
As they fly by them with their woven wings.

(During the latter part of SALARINO's speech, his words grow fainter, as GEORGINA's attention wanders from the stage. She sits staring into space, and only a distant murmur of voices is now heard. After a moment, the THEATER MANAGER, wearing a dinner jacket and looking for all the world like MR. ALLERTON, hurries on at left, downstage of the seats. He makes straight for GEORGINA and leans across CLARK to speak to her.)

THE MANAGER *(tensely)*. Excuse me, are you Miss Georgina Allerton?

GEORGINA *(in surprise)*. Why, yes, I am.

THE MANAGER. I'm the manager of the theater. Miss Hilda Vincent, who was to play Portia tonight, has just collapsed in her dressing room and—

GEORGINA. Oh, how perfectly awful! Is she seriously—?

THE MANAGER. Well, I hope not. But she won't be able to go on. And we have no understudy.

GEORGINA. But what will you do?

THE MANAGER. That's what I've come to see you about.

GEORGINA. Me?

THE MANAGER. Yes, Miss Vincent is under the impression that you are familiar with the role of Portia—

GEORGINA. Well, I did play it once. But that was in high school, years ago.

THE MANAGER. Are you up in the part?

GEORGINA. Oh, I remember every word of it. But I couldn't possibly go on and—

THE MANAGER. Well, won't you please help us out and try it?

GEORGINA *(hesitantly)*. Well, I don't know. *(Turning to CLARK.)* Do you think I should, Clark?

CLARK *(laughing)*. Are you being funny? You couldn't get up there and act that part for a first-night audience.

GEORGINA *(to the MANAGER)*. I guess he's right. I couldn't do it.

THE MANAGER. Please try! It's that or refunding thousands of dollars and sending away all these people disappointed. Miss Vincent told me to beg you in the name of your alma mater to—

GEORGINA. All right! I will! I'll try it!

CLARK *(trying to detain her)*. You'll make a fool of yourself!

GEORGINA *(pushing past him)*. I'd rather be a fool than a coward.

THE MANAGER. That's the spirit, Miss Allerton! I know you'll come through. This way, please. *(Her head high, she follows him across the stage into the darkness at the right. The light fades out at the left, then there is scattered applause, followed by the voice of the* MANAGER, *off right.)* Ladies and gentlemen, I regret to inform you that Miss Hilda Vincent, who was to be seen as Portia tonight, will be unable to appear. *(Murmurs and exclamations from the unseen audience.)* However, there happens to be in the audience a young lady, Miss Georgina Allerton, who, though not a professional actress, is familiar with the role, and has graciously consented to replace Miss Vincent.

(Scattered applause and murmurs.)

CLARK *(loudly).* Boo!

THE MANAGER. I am sure you will show Miss Allerton every indulgence, in view of the fact that she is going on at a moment's notice, and without even a rehearsal. I thank you.

(Applause, followed by a flourish of music. Then the lights come up at right, on a small section of an elevated stage. GEORGINA, *in the dress of a Venetian doctor of laws, stands on the stage, facing the spectators at left, among whom only* CLARK *can be seen, as a spotlight focuses on his face. He grins sardonically, as* GEORGINA *begins to speak.)*

GEORGINA.
The quality of mercy is not strain'd,
It droppeth as the gentle rain from heaven
Upon the place beneath: it is twice blest;
It blesseth him that gives and him that takes:
'Tis mightiest in the mightiest: it becomes
The throned monarch better than his crown;
His sceptre shows the force of temporal power,
The attribute to awe and majesty,
Wherein doth sit the dread and fear of kings;
But mercy is above this sceptred sway;
It is enthroned in the hearts of kings,
It is an attribute to God himself;
And earthly power doth then show likest God's
When mercy seasons justice. Therefore, Jew,
Though justice be thy plea, consider this,
That, in the course of justice, none of us
Should see salvation: we do pray for mercy;
And that same prayer doth teach us all to render
The deeds of mercy.

(As the speech goes on, CLARK's *expression begins to soften until at the end he is moved almost to tears. When the speech is finished, there is an outburst of applause, cheers, and cries of "Bravo!"* CLARK *sniffles, then takes out a handkerchief and blows his nose.* GEORGINA *bows, smiles, and blows kisses to the unseen audience. Two ushers cross quickly from left to right, carrying huge bouquets which they hand up to* GEORGINA. *Her arms filled with flowers, she bows again. Then she disappears. There is another upsurge of applause, as the lights fade out at right. Then* CLARK *springs to his feet as he sees* GEORGINA *approaching from the right and meets her stage center.)*

CLARK. Georgina! You were magnificent!

GEORGINA *(as they go toward their seats).* Don't try to flatter me. I know you don't mean it.

CLARK. But I do! I swear to you I do! You were superb: sincere, moving, eloquent, forceful, charming.

GEORGINA. That's a lot, isn't it, for a girl who doesn't know anything, a girl who can't do anything?

CLARK. I take it all back, Georgina—every word of it. I've done you an injustice, completely misunderstood you—

GEORGINA. Next time, maybe you'll be a little more careful. Only I'm afraid there'll be no next time for you, as far as I'm concerned.

(They are seated by now.)

CLARK. Georgina, you mean you want to be rid of me?

GEORGINA. Yes, and a good riddance too.

PORTIA *(off right).*
A gentle riddance. Draw the curtains, go.
Let all of his complexion choose me so.

(There is applause as the unseen curtain falls. As the lights come up again at left, GEORGINA, *startled, begins to applaud. The Elizabethan music is resumed and continues throughout.)*

CLARK *(to* GEORGINA*).* Well, I'm glad you're back with us.

(The other SPECTATORS *begin to rise and file out.)*

GEORGINA. It's good, isn't it?

CLARK. Why, I don't believe you heard a word of it.

GEORGINA *(indignantly)*. Why, I heard every syllable. What do you mean—?

CLARK. Go on! You were off in some Cloud-Cuckoo-Land.

GEORGINA. I was nothing of the kind!

CLARK *(looking toward* HAND *and* MISS DELEHANTY*)*. Sh! We mustn't give them the impression that we're not en rapport. Besides, I'm dying to know how Tessie interprets the casket plot.

HAND *(as he and* MISS DELEHANTY *join* CLARK *and* GEORGINA*)*. Say, that Vincent girl is a good Portia, isn't she? Why, to meet her at a cocktail party, you'd never think she had it in her.

CLARK. The world is full of girls like that. You have to live with them to know them. Miss Delehanty, how about a cigarette?

MISS DELEHANTY. Yeah, why not?

CLARK *(as they go left)*. Well, there might be a number of reasons. Let's look at it, first, from the purely esthetic angle— *(He and* MISS DELEHANTY *exit.)*

HAND. So you turned me down for a book reviewer!

GEORGINA. I had already said yes to him when you—

HAND. Never mind, I can take it. But remember, we're playing a return engagement tomorrow at the Canard Rouge. I've dug up a lot more dope about Mexico. It seems that—

GEORGINA. Save it until tomorrow. We really should join the others.

HAND *(as they go left)*. Yes, I guess so. Kind of brash, this Redfield, isn't he?

GEORGINA. Oh, yes—very!

(As they exit, the lights fade on the scene and the music changes to a jazz rhythm. The lights come up, center, on a table in a night club. A HEADWAITER *appears, at left, followed by* GEORGINA *and* CLARK, *who still carries the script.)*

THE HEADWAITER. How about this?

CLARK. Yes, this'll do. *(He and* GEORGINA *seat themselves at the table.)*

THE HEADWAITER. Can I take your order?

GEORGINA. Nothing for me. I've only got about a half hour—

CLARK. That's time enough for a drink. Scotch and soda?

GEORGINA. Now, don't spoil things by beginning to ask me what *I* want.

CLARK *(to the* HEADWAITER*)*. Two Scotches and soda. And two smoked whitefish sandwiches on rye toast.

GEORGINA. Do you really think you can eat two sandwiches?

CLARK *(to the* HEADWAITER*)*. Well, just bring one to start with.

THE HEADWAITER. Yes, sir. *(He exits. The band selection comes to an end.)*

CLARK. Now we can really relax and talk things over.

GEORGINA. I couldn't relax even if we had anything to talk over. I don't know why I let you drag me here, when I have to—

CLARK. I know! I got my eye glued on the time. Where is that you have to be at midnight, Cinderella?

GEORGINA. My, but you ask a lot of questions, don't you?

CLARK. Newspaperman. Get the story or get another job.

GEORGINA. Well, if you must know, I'm going to the airport to see somebody off.

CLARK. Good! I'll go with you!

GEORGINA. You'll do nothing of the sort.

CLARK. Well, that's settled! *(He suddenly laughs aloud.)*

GEORGINA *(vexed)*. Am I missing something again?

CLARK. I'm thinking of George Hand.

GEORGINA. What's so funny about that?

CLARK. On the way out of the theater, he asked me where we were bound for, and I said we were going to the Blue Grotto and why didn't he join us there. I can just see him turning that gloomy joint upside down in search of us, while Miss

Delehanty sits wrapped in her thoughts —the naked creature!

GEORGINA. Well, of all the adolescent—! *(She laughs in spite of herself.)* I'm only laughing at the picture of Miss Delehanty—

CLARK. It's all right. Don't apologize. Is this George Hand trying to seduce you?

GEORGINA. Heavens, who's talking book language now?

CLARK. Well, I've learned that I mustn't always use the first word that springs to my lips. Of course, if you'd rather I asked you if he's trying to—

GEORGINA *(hastily)*. No, I wouldn't! He's asked me to go to Mexico with him. You can put your own interpretation on that.

CLARK. I have. It doesn't worry me.

GEORGINA. Why should it worry *you?*

CLARK. I've just told you it doesn't. I mean it's not what's worrying you, either.

GEORGINA. Who said anything was worrying me?

CLARK *(preoccupied)*. Nobody. Tell me something, Georgina. Are you a virgin?

GEORGINA. Didn't you say that the Newspaper Guild limits your working hours?

CLARK *(thoughtfully)*. It really doesn't matter much. Well, I'm glad we went to that play. Because suddenly everything clicked. Do you remember my telling you that you were off in a trance?

GEORGINA. I was off in some Cloud-Cuckoo-Land, you said.

CLARK. Yes. I happened to look at you and I saw that you were no longer Georgina Allerton, that college grad who plays at running a bookshop. You were suddenly being somebody up there on the stage, who was pretending to be Portia of Belmont who was pretending to be a doctor of laws in an imaginary Venetian court of justice.

GEORGINA. Well, that's what art is supposed to do for us, isn't it? Make us identify ourselves with—

CLARK. No! Art should reveal reality to us. It shouldn't be something that we use to screen ourselves from reality.

GEORGINA. Is that what you're trying to tell me—that I hide from reality?

CLARK. Yes. Sitting there beside you in the theater and looking at you—

GEORGINA. Weren't you interested in the play?

CLARK. What's that got to do with it?

GEORGINA. I was wondering what made you look at *me.*

CLARK. Let's stick to the point, please.

GEORGINA. I'm sorry!

CLARK. The point is that you're a daydreamer. You live in a world of fantasy, instead of the world of reality.

GEORGINA. What is this reality you keep talking about?

CLARK. I was hoping you wouldn't ask me that because I'm not sure that I know the answer. But I'm pretty sure it means living your life out and not dreaming it away.

GEORGINA. If a dream is real to you, why isn't it as real as something you do?

CLARK. Because dreaming is easy and life is hard. Because when you dream, you make your own rules, but when you try to *do* something, the rules are made for you by the limitations of your own nature and the shape of the world you live in. Because no matter how much you win in your dreams, your gains are illusory, and you always come away empty-handed. But in life, whether you win or lose, you've always got something to show for it—even if it's only a scar or a painful memory.

GEORGINA. Scars are ugly and pain hurts.

CLARK. Without ugliness, there would be no beauty. And if you're afraid to know pain, you'll never know the value of pleasure.

GEORGINA. You're a tough guy, aren't you?

CLARK. Well, I've had to fight my own way through life, ever since I can remember. You either get tough, or else you go under.

GEORGINA. It's not the way I was brought up. I always had people to protect me.

CLARK. If you bandage a muscle long enough, it withers. And that goes for your emotions, too. If you keep smothering them with dreams, they'll die after a while.

GEORGINA. Don't say it. It's what I'm afraid of.

CLARK. Then it's time somebody said it.

GEORGINA. I know. Push her off the dock and she'll learn to swim. But suppose I'm not the one that gets tough. Suppose I'm the one that goes under.

CLARK. All right then. If that's the way you feel about it, go on sitting on the end of the dock for the rest of your life and let the moonbeams turn your blood to water.

GEORGINA. No, I mustn't do that, must I? Keep on telling me. I mustn't do that. Only what do you do, if the thing you always dreamed suddenly faces you? Suppose—well, suppose you cared very much for someone. Couldn't get him out of your thoughts, day or night. And all the while you knew it was hopeless, knew you could never have him. But still you went on, weeping and longing and dreaming. And then, just like that, what you thought could never be, suddenly became possible. What you had prayed for was yours for the asking. Only it was all different—not a bit the way you dreamed it. And he was different, too. But it was reality; it was no longer a dream. And that's your recipe—reality. So that's what I go for, according to you.

CLARK. Not according to me, at all.

GEORGINA. But you said—

CLARK. I said live your life. Lots of people have a beautiful time, yearning unhappily for the pot of gold at the end of the rainbow. But when the rainbow fades, and the pot turns out to be full of ashes, they don't have to hug it to their bosoms. They can leave it be, and say: "Well, looks like I staked out the wrong claim." That is, if they have any guts and any sense of humor they can. If you can make a dream come to life, grab hold of it. But if it dies on you, roll up your sleeves and give it a decent burial, instead of trying to haul the corpse around with you.

(The band begins to play another dance tune.)

GEORGINA *(rising)*. Thank you, teacher.

CLARK *(also rising)*. Do you have to go already?

GEORGINA. Well, the bus to the airport won't wait.

CLARK. Why is it so important that you go?

GEORGINA. I told you I'd promised somebody I'd see them off.

CLARK. What would happen if you didn't?

GEORGINA. Nothing would happen, I guess. Except that they might be disappointed.

CLARK *(as the waiter appears with the drinks and sandwich)*. Well, if you do go, I'll have to eat and drink alone, and I've told you I don't like that.

GEORGINA *(hesitantly)*. Well, if I don't go, I should at least phone the air terminal and say I'm not coming.

(The waiter exits.)

CLARK. Why? If you don't show up, they'll figure out that you're not there.

GEORGINA. Yes, I suppose that's true.

CLARK. Of course, if you enjoy unnecessary telephone conversations—

GEORGINA. No, I really don't.

CLARK *(resuming his seat)*. Then let's sit down.

GEORGINA *(complying)*. I wonder why I listen to you.

CLARK. I have a magnetic personality. *(Raising his glass.)* God, I've talked my throat dry. Here's to you.

GEORGINA *(raising her glass)*. And here's to you. I'm sorry your throat is dry, but I'm glad you talked to me. Do you mind telling me why?

CLARK *(with a shrug)*. I don't know. I guess I hate to see anybody with such pretty legs walking around in a trance. *(Taking a bite of the sandwich.)* Say, this is damned good!

GEORGINA. Could I have a bite?

CLARK *(pushing the plate over)*. Why, sure! Maybe I'd better order another one.

GEORGINA. No, let's finish this one, first.

(Taking a bite.) It *is* good. You're always right, aren't you?

CLARK. About ninety per cent of the time. Well—say ninety-five. I hope I'm right about that Wilinski-O'Connell fight. I'm backing Wilinski on the short end of a two-to-one bet.

GEORGINA *(her mouth full)*. It's too bad you didn't go.

CLARK. Oh, that's all right. This is fun, for a change.

GEORGINA. Gee, thanks.

CLARK. You should eat more. You're too skinny.

GEORGINA. You told me that before.

CLARK *(looking at her)*. Jim Lucas?

GEORGINA *(startled)*. What?

CLARK. You heard me. I said Jim Lucas.

GEORGINA. How did you guess?

CLARK. I have a knack for putting one and one together.

GEORGINA. He's going to Reno to get a divorce.

CLARK. Well, what the hell else would anybody go to Reno for?

GEORGINA. He wants me to join him there.

CLARK. And are you going to?

GEORGINA. Maybe.

CLARK. Say, I'd like to have a piece of the agency that handles your travel arrangements. And if you do get there, what then?

GEORGINA. We'd get married and get ourselves a ranch.

CLARK. A ranch. *(Suddenly.)* My God, it's right straight out of that novel of yours.

GEORGINA. Just pushing the girl off the dock isn't enough for you. You have to kick her off. *(Rising.)* Get up!

CLARK. Why?

GEORGINA. I feel like dancing.

CLARK. With me?

GEORGINA. Well, I'm a shy girl. I'd feel funny about accosting some stranger. Don't you like to dance?

CLARK *(rising)*. It depends upon with whom.

GEORGINA. You have a charming way of saying things. Years of experience, I suppose.

(They dance back and forth, across the stage, a spotlight following them.)

CLARK. Well, working on a newspaper, you get around.

GEORGINA. That's what I mean.

CLARK. Your eyes aren't too bad, either.

GEORGINA. Now, don't feel that you have to overdo it.

CLARK. That's a sound criticism. Overstatement is one of my worst faults.

GEORGINA. I'm sure you have plenty of bad ones.

CLARK. Well—enough.

GEORGINA. Is that why no girl has ever married you?

CLARK. I've never asked one to.

GEORGINA. Never met anyone worthy, I suppose.

CLARK. That's partly it. But it's also because I think I'd make a lousy husband.

GEORGINA. Would you? Why?

CLARK. Well, in the first place— *(Breaking off.)* Do you really want to know?

GEORGINA. Well, it gives us something to talk about.

CLARK. We wouldn't have to talk.

GEORGINA. That's true. Only you don't seem very happy when you're not talking.

CLARK. Well, that's the first thing. I'm gabby.

GEORGINA. Maybe that's because you really have a lot of things to say.

CLARK. That doesn't follow. The world is full of windbags. Then again I'm blunt and caustic. I come right out with things.

GEORGINA. That might be honesty.

CLARK. As for egotism—that's my middle name.

GEORGINA. It's a quality that a lot of creative people seem to have.

CLARK. I'm a hard guy to know.

GEORGINA. Complex people usually are.

CLARK. I'm lacking in reverence.

GEORGINA. It could be that you're too penetrating to be taken in by sham.

CLARK. It bores me to listen to other people's troubles.

GEORGINA. Perhaps you think they should stand on their own feet and solve their own problems.

CLARK. The idea of supporting a wife irks me.

GEORGINA. A man who is independent himself might not respect an able-bodied woman who was willing to be a dependent.

CLARK. I'm an unpredictable bastard. If I have a strong impulse, I'm as likely as not to follow it.

GEORGINA. That could denote imagination and courage.

(*The music comes to an end. They stop dancing and applaud, mechanically, both transfused with new-found emotion.*)

CLARK. You dance all right.

GEORGINA. Thank you. So do you.

CLARK (*as they go back to the table*). Why don't we order another drink?

GEORGINA (*seating herself*). That's a wonderful idea.

CLARK. You order it. I want to make some phone calls. (*Fishing in his pockets.*) Have you got any nickels? You know how I always get stuck in phone booths without nickels.

GEORGINA (*opening her handbag*). I think I have. How many do you want?

CLARK. Oh, three or four. (*She hands him some nickels.*) Thanks. And don't forget to order the drinks.

GEORGINA. I won't.

CLARK. Oh, better order another sandwich, too.

GEORGINA. All right, I will.

CLARK (*picking up the remains of his sandwich.*) I may as well finish this, while I'm phoning.

(*He takes a bite, as he exits. As* GEORGINA *sits gazing after him, the lights fade out on the scene. A persistent knocking is heard off stage right. The lights come up center on the empty stage. A* MAN *in slippers and an old-fashioned flannel nightshirt comes on at left, carrying a lighted kerosene lamp. He looks like* MR. ALLERTON.)

THE MAN (*peering off right, as the knocking continues*). Consarn it all, who's there?

CLARK (*off*). Is Justice of the Peace Billings in?

BILLINGS. Where in tarnation do you think I'd be this time of night?

CLARK (*off*). Well, open up and let us in.

BILLING. What in thunder for?

CLARK (*off*). We want to get married.

BILLINGS. Well, jiminy crickets, can't you wait till mornin'?

CLARK (*off*). No, we can't. It's an emergency.

BILLINGS (*as he goes off right*). Some folks ain't got the sense they was born with. (*A sound of bolts opening and a door creaking. Then* BILLINGS *reappears, followed by* CLARK *and* GEORGINA.)

CLARK (*producing a paper*). Here's the license, Judge. Now give us the works.

(BILLINGS *peers at the license, as a cuckoo clock sounds two.*)

BILLINGS. Well, I'll be danged! Two o'clock. Time you young folks was in bed, 'stead of gallivantin' around.

CLARK. We know it. But we thought we ought to get married first.

BILLINGS (*reading the license*). Do you, Georgina Allerton, aim to take this bachelor, Clark Redfield, to be your lawful wedded husband?

GEORGINA. I do.

BILLINGS. And do you, Clark Redfield, hanker to take this spinster, Georgina Allerton, to be your lawful wedded wife?

CLARK. That's what I'm here for.

BILLINGS. To love and to cherish. To honor and to obey.

CLARK. No!

GEORGINA (*simultaneously*). No!

BILLINGS. What's that?

CLARK. Cut out that "obey."

BILLINGS (*grumpily*). It's part o' the ceremony. Folks ain't expected to take it serious.

GEORGINA. We're very serious people—very serious and very honest.

BILLINGS. When I do the marryin', I don't want no back talk. In sickness and in health. In joy and in sorrow. Until death do you part.

CLARK. I do.

GEORGINA. I— (*She stops, as a clatter of horse's hoofs is heard off left.*)

JIM (*off*). Whoa! (*The hoofbeats stop and* JIM *rushes on, dressed as a cowboy.*)

JIM. No! No! Stop!

GEORGINA. Jim!

CLARK. Oh, so you're here, are you?

JIM. Yes, I am! And just in the nick of time, it seems.

CLARK. What do you want?

JIM (*ignoring him*). Georgina, do you realize what you're doing?

GEORGINA. Well, not altogether, Jim. But it gives me such a wonderful feeling, as though I were really alive for the first time.

JIM. You're just yielding to a romantic impulse, just throwing yourself away.

CLARK (*to* JIM). You keep out of this, Lucas. You're all washed up, as far as this girl is concerned; and I'm taking over now.

JIM. Answer him, Georgina!

GEORGINA. I don't know what to say. I never met anyone like him before. He's a tough guy—he really is. He scares the daylights out of me.

JIM. All right. I'll answer him then. (*To* CLARK.) She's mine—mine! Do you understand?

CLARK. How do you figure that?

JIM. Because she loves me—she's always loved me. For years she's built her whole secret life around me—yearning, dreaming, hoping against hope. And now I'm free and I want her and I'm going to make her mine.

GEORGINA (*to* CLARK). It's true what he's saying. He wants me, and I've always loved him and—

CLARK. Scuttlebutt! He doesn't know what he wants and never will. And you don't love him and never did. You've just been in love with some Romeo of your imagination, that never was on land or sea.

GEORGINA. Do you think so? Do you think that's the way it is?

JIM. Don't listen to him, Georgina.

GEORGINA. I have to listen to him, Jim. He may be right. He is—ninety-five per cent of the time.

BILLINGS (*impatiently*). Well, young lady, I'm goin' back to bed. The law don't require me to stay up all night, waitin' for folks to make up their minds.

GEORGINA. No, wait! It's true. I've got to make up my mind. If I don't now, I never will. All right, Judge, proceed with the ceremony.

BILLINGS. Well, that's better. Do you, Georgina Allerton—

JIM. No, Georgina. You mustn't do this.

BILLINGS. You keep out of this, young feller, unless you want to spend the night in the lockup.

CLARK. Go on, cowboy. Beat it.

(JIM *looks appealingly at Georgina, but she averts her head and he exits, dolefully.*)

GEORGINA. All right. I'm ready. In sickness and in health. In joy and in sorrow. Until death— (*She breaks off as the jazz music from the night club blares forth.*) No, no! Stop it, Georgina! You mustn't go on like this! You mustn't! (CLARK *and* BILLINGS *have gone and as the night-club scene appears again, she goes back to her place at the table.*) I'm at it again—drugging myself with dreams. And when I come to, all I'll get from him is a slap in the face. He doesn't care a damn for me. He's just having fun with me—just giving me the run-around, that's all. He's calling up to find out if he won his bet on Wilinski—that means more to him than I do. *(Springing to her feet.)* No, I can't take it! I'll never see him again. I'll go before he gets back. I'll—I'll—oh, I don't know. Anything—anything not to hear the bitter truth from him. *(She starts to exit.)*

CLARK *(entering)*. I won! Wilinski knocked him out in the— *(Looking at her.)* You look as though you think you're going somewhere.

GEORGINA. Yes, I am. Good-by and congratulate Wilinski for me.

CLARK. We'll send him a joint wire. Where are you going?

GEORGINA. I'm going to take a taxi to the airport and get on that plane with Jim.

CLARK. Why?

GEORGINA. Because you've convinced me that doing something is better than doing nothing. And if I don't go away with Jim, I haven't anything.

CLARK. Well, of course, if that's what you want to do! Only I wish you'd told me just a few minutes sooner.

GEORGINA. What do you mean by that?

CLARK. Well, you know those impulses I get. I suddenly decided to round off the evening by blowing in that dough I won on Wilinski. So I ordered one of those rented limousines to come around and pick us up. The guy wears a peaked cap and gauntlets. It's pretty damned impressive.

GEORGINA. Where were you planning to go?

CLARK. Oh, I thought we could decide that as we went along. We could whirl around Central Park a couple of times, and then maybe work our way up to Bronx Park—or even beyond. It's a nice night for a ride, and sitting back in a car, you get a chance to talk. I haven't been able to get in a word edgewise, all evening. *(He pays the check.)* Oh, didn't you order that sandwich?

GEORGINA. Oh, I'm sorry! I forgot all about it.

CLARK. Daydreaming again?

GEORGINA. Afraid so. About you and me.

CLARK. Why, you're improving. I think this one may really pay off.

(A liveried chauffeur enters.)

THE CHAUFFEUR. Excuse me, are you Mr. Redfield?

CLARK. Yes. Keep your motor racing. We'll be right with you.

THE CHAUFFEUR. Yes, sir. *(He exits.)*

CLARK *(looking after him)*. What did I tell you? Well, are you ready?

GEORGINA. Clark—Clark, I'm a serious girl. I wouldn't know how to take any more jokes.

CLARK. Well, I have my serious moments, too. Look, if you don't want to ride around with me, I'll drop you at the airport and take a spin by myself. Only let's get going. You have to pay these birds whether they're moving or standing still.

(He takes her arm, and, as they exit at right, the lights fade quickly on the scene. A telephone rings at left and the lights come up, revealing MRS. ALLERTON in bed, as she turns on the lamp on the night table beside her. In a twin bed, on the other side of the night table, MR. ALLERTON groans and turns over.)

MRS. ALLERTON *(picking up the telephone, sleepily)*. Hello!

(She sneezes and gropes under her pillow for cleansing tissue as the lights come up quickly at right, on a double bed. GEORGINA, telephone in hand, is seated on the bed with CLARK close beside her.)

GEORGINA. Hello, Mother! Goodness, you sound worse.

MRS. ALLERTON *(irritably)*. What's that? What number are you calling?

(MR. ALLERTON groans again.)

GEORGINA. It's Georgina, Mother.

MRS. ALLERTON. Well, for goodness' sakes! What time is it?

GEORGINA. About three-thirty, I guess. Listen Mother, I'm—

MRS. ALLERTON. What are you calling up at this hour for? Are you in jail?

GEORGINA. No, I'm in Greenwich.

MRS. ALLERTON. What are you doing there?

GEORGINA. I just got married.

MRS. ALLERTON (sneezing). You just got what? Talk a little louder. This damned cold seems to have gone to my ears.

GEORGINA. I said I just got married.

MRS. ALLERTON. Well, for God's sake! George, did you hear that? She's married.

(ALLERTON mumbles unintelligibly.)

GEORGINA. I thought you'd—

MRS. ALLERTON (angrily). Wait a minute, will you? I can't talk to two people at once. (Poking MR. ALLERTON.) George, will you please wake up? She's married.

GEORGINA (to CLARK). She's furious at me for waking her up.

CLARK. I don't blame her.

ALLERTON (raising himself to a sitting position). Who's married?

MRS. ALLERTON. Georgina, of course. Who do you suppose?

ALLERTON. To whom is she married?

MRS. ALLERTON. How the devil should I know?

ALLERTON. Well, ask her.

MRS. ALLERTON (at the telephone). Georgina, your father wants to know to whom you're married.

GEORGINA. Oh, to a man I know.

MRS. ALLERTON. Well, I should hope so. (To ALLERTON.) I can't get a thing out of her.

ALLERTON. Let me talk to her. (Taking the telephone.) Hello, Georgie.

GEORGINA. Hello, Dad! I'm married!

ALLERTON. Can you tell us who your husband is?

GEORGINA. His name is Clark Redfield. He took me to dinner and the theater and then—

MRS. ALLERTON (to ALLERTON). Well, who is it?

ALLERTON (to MRS. ALLERTON). I didn't get the name. Someone who took her to dinner and the theater and—

MRS. ALLERTON. Good grief! (Snatching the telephone.) Don't tell me it's that boorish, conceited newspaperman!

GEORGINA (happily). Yes, that's the one. Wait, I'll let you talk to him. (Handing CLARK the telephone.)

CLARK. Hello, Mrs. Allerton. This is your new son-in-law, Clark Redfield.

MRS. ALLERTON. Clark who? Talk a little louder, can't you? (She sneezes.)

CLARK. Redfield. Red as in Russia, field as in football. Have you got a cold?

MRS. ALLERTON. Only a newspaperman could ask such a foolish question. (She sneezes.)

CLARK. Have you ever tried a little—

MRS. ALLERTON. Look, young man, don't give me any of your advice. You're going to need all you've got for that girl you've married. (To ALLERTON.) I think she's going to have her hands full with him.

CLARK. What's that?

ALLERTON. Let me talk to him. (Taking the telephone.) Hello. This is Georgina's father.

CLARK. Oh, yes. This is her husband.

ALLERTON. Yes, so I understand. I just wondered whether you have any plans.

CLARK. Do you mean future plans or immediate plans?

GEORGINA. Let me talk to him. (Taking the telephone.) Good night, Dad. Tell Mother—

ALLERTON. You'd better tell her. (He hands the telephone to MRS. ALLERTON.)

GEORGINA. I just wanted to say good night, Mother.

MRS. ALLERTON. Have you got everything you need?

GEORGINA. Yes, we bought toothbrushes and popcorn in Mamaroneck!

MRS. ALLERTON. Well, if it's chilly up there, don't let him talk you into leaving the window open. (She sneezes.)

GEORGINA. I won't. Good night. (She hangs up.)

MRS. ALLERTON *(hanging up)*. I hope I didn't sound too damned mushy.

*(*ALLERTON *sneezes loudly, as the lights fade quickly.)*

CLARK *(looking at his watch)*. It's three-thirty. I'm not used to being up so late. *(He puts out the lamp beside the bed, leaving the scene in semidarkness.)*

GEORGINA. Wait! There's just one thing I'd like to know. Do I have to give up dreaming altogether? Couldn't I just sort of taper off?

CLARK. Well, I'll be reasonable about it, as long as you run your dreams, instead of letting them run you.

GEORGINA. I know! If you can dream and not make dreams your master—! Do you think Kipling will live?

CLARK *(as he pulls down an imaginary shade)*. Look, I didn't come all the way up here to discuss literature!

(The stage is plunged into darkness. The curtain falls.)

CURTAIN

BORN YESTERDAY

By GARSON KANIN

BORN YESTERDAY was presented by Max Gordon at the Lyceum Theatre, New York City, on February 4, 1946. It was staged by the author. Donald Oenslager designed the setting. The cast was as follows:

BILLIE DAWN	Judy Holliday	THE ASSISTANT MANAGER	
HARRY BROCK	Paul Douglas		Carroll Ashburn
PAUL VERRALL	Gary Merrill	HELEN, A MAID	Ellen Hall
ED DEVERY	Otto Hulett	A BELLHOP	William Harmon
SENATOR NORVAL HEDGES		ANOTHER BELLHOP	Rex King
	Larry Oliver	A BARBER	Ted Mayer
MRS. HEDGES	Mona Bruns	A MANICURIST	Mary Laslo
EDDIE BROCK	Frank Otto	A BOOTBLACK	Parris Morgan
		A WAITER	C. L. Burke

The scene is Washington, D. C.

ACT I: September, 1945.

ACT II: Two months later.

ACT III: Late that night.

THE AUTHOR

After a slow start as Western Union messenger, Macy's clerk, vaudevillian, saxophonist, and bit player, following some study at the American Academy of Dramatic Arts, Garson Kanin developed meteoric qualities. He did not achieve any singularity as an actor, but he came to the attention of George Abbott as a willing young man with a flair for staging. Mr. Kanin could not have had a better mentor in the field of directing than Mr. Abbott, with whom he was associated in the profitable ventures of Three Men on a Horse, Boy Meets Girl, Room Service, *and* Brother Rat. *An alert acolyte could learn a good deal from the famous Abbott aptitude for fast and telling timing. Mr. Kanin, in turn, gave good value for the instruction by helping to discover Betty Field, Sam Levene, Allyn Joslyn and other capable players for the productions.*

Sam Goldwyn, who has a keen eye for talent and backs his judgment with conspicuous action, brought the young man to Hollywood in 1937 when Kanin was only twenty-five and gave him an opportunity to familiarize himself with motion picture technique. R.K.O. allowed him to direct A Man to Remember, *and Kanin became "the boy wonder" of the Barbary Coast. Subsequently, he directed the Ginger Rogers picture* Bachelor Mother, My Favorite Wife, They Knew What They Wanted, *and* Tom, Dick and Harry. *When the war came he enlisted as a private and emerged a captain. The army was astute enough to keep him to his last, and in consequence Kanin was able to direct numerous and valuable documentary films. He climaxed this phase of his career with* The True Glory.

Released from military service, Captain Kanin turned to the challenging task of directing Robert Sherwood's The Rugged Path *and took his first public fling at writing a play. The result was the extraordinarily successful* Born Yesterday, *which he also directed. The play opened in New York on February 4, 1946. He had hardly settled down to enjoying his literary success than the distaff side of his household represented by Ruth Gordon called upon his services. He staged Miss Gordon's autobiographical reminiscence* Years Ago *out of town and then restaged it in the fall of 1946 with conspicuous success. Whether Mr. Kanin will enliven the stage by writing more plays of the calibre of* Born Yesterday *remains to be seen. Broadway will be in his debt if he does. His is the freshest new talent for Broadway comedy to appear on the stage in many years.*

BORN YESTERDAY

ACT ONE

SCENE: This happens in the sitting room of Suite 67D, a large part of the best hotel in Washington, D. C. 67D is so called because it is a duplex apartment on the sixth and seventh floors of the hotel. It is a masterpiece of offensive good taste, colorful and lush and rich. There are mops and brooms in the doorway when the curtain rises and in the room a chambermaid's cleaning unit. The main door is open and the telephone bell is ringing. A maid comes down the staircase which leads from the bedrooms, carrying a large vase of yellow roses. She sets them down, and goes off to the service wing, paying the phone no mind. It rings some more. In a moment, the maid returns and tends to a few more chores in the room. The phone stops. A man walks by the open door. He looks in, but passes. A moment later he returns and stands in the doorway. This is PAUL VERRALL, of the New Republic's Washington staff. VERRALL is in his middle thirties, handsome, alert, and energetic. There is nothing wrong with him at all, in fact, with the possible exception of a tendency to take things, and himself, too seriously. He knows this. He is carrying several books, magazines, and newspapers. He wears eyeglasses. He lights a cigarette and leans in the doorway.

PAUL. Who's coming in here, Helen, do you know?

HELEN. Hello, Mr. Verrall. No, I don't.

PAUL. A Harry Brock, by any chance?

HELEN. I'm not the room clerk, please.

PAUL. I'm supposed to meet this guy, that's all. I wondered if maybe he was coming in here.

(HELEN *looks at the card stuck in among the roses.*)

HELEN. Brock. (*She goes about her work.*)

PAUL (*looking around*). I figured. (*He steps into the room.*)

HELEN. Who's Brock?

PAUL. *Harry* Brock.

HELEN. Never heard of him.

PAUL. You will, Helen. Big man. Ran a little junk yard into fifty million bucks, with no help from anyone or anything— except maybe World War II.

HELEN. Anybody checks into 67D I got no desire to meet. Believe me.

PAUL. Why not?

HELEN. Listen, you know what they charge for this layout? (*She is about to continue, impressively, when* PAUL *interrupts.*)

PAUL. Two hundred and thirty-five a day.

HELEN. Who told you?

PAUL. Frank.

HELEN. Oh.

PAUL. What about it?

HELEN. Listen, anybody's got two hundred and thirty-five dollars a day to spend on a hotel room there ought to be a law.

PAUL. Too many laws already.

HELEN. While I'm getting eighteen a week I don't see why anybody should spend two hundred and thirty-five a day.

PAUL. For a hotel room.

HELEN. That's what I say.

PAUL (*smiling*). I know some people who'd call you a communist.

HELEN (*darkly*). Tell them I'm thinking about it. Seriously.

(PAUL *is at the window, looking out over the city.*)

HELEN. Changed much, do you think?

PAUL. What?

HELEN. Washington?

PAUL. Not enough. I could stand a little more change. The idea of the war wasn't to leave everything the same, you know.

HELEN. The trouble with you, Mr. Verrall, you think too much. Most fellows your age get more—

(*She breaks off as a bellhop enters, carrying a large leather box and several brief cases. He is followed by* EDDIE BROCK, *who is* HARRY BROCK'S *cousin—and servant.*)

EDDIE. This stays down. The rest goes up.

THE BELLHOP. Yes, sir.

(HELEN *picks up her paraphernalia and goes.* PAUL *is on his way out. So is the* BELLHOP. *As they reach the door, however, they step aside.* HARRY BROCK *stamps in, followed by the* ASSISTANT MANAGER. *Then* BILLIE DAWN *appears wearing a mink coat and carrying another.* BROCK *is a huge man in his late thirties. Gross is the word for him.* BILLIE *is breathtakingly beautiful and breathtakingly stupid. The* BELLHOP *leaves.*)

THE ASSISTANT MANAGER (*a Rotarian*). Here we are.

(BROCK *and* BILLIE *are looking around.* BROCK *is impressed by the room, but tries not to show it. As he looks around he sees* PAUL, *but doesn't particularly notice him.*)

BROCK (*without enthusiasm*). It's all right.

THE ASSISTANT MANAGER (*pointing*). Service wing. Terrace. (*Going toward the staircase.*) And the bedchambers are right this way.

(*He goes up.* BILLIE *follows.* EDDIE *is unpacking bottles of liquor from the leather box and putting them on a side table.* BROCK *sits on a large modern sofa, the principal piece of furniture in the room, and removes his shoes.* PAUL *comes down to him.*)

PAUL (*extending his hand*). Hello, Mr. Brock.

BROCK (*brusquely, ignoring* PAUL's *hand*). How are you? (*He turns away.* PAUL *thinks a moment, then leaves.*)

BROCK. Who the hell was that?

EDDIE. Search me.

BROCK. What kind of a joint is this—people in and out of your place all the time?

(*The* ASSISTANT MANAGER *returns.*)

THE ASSISTANT MANAGER. Mrs. Brock seems delighted with the bedchambers.

BROCK. It's not Mrs. Brock.

THE ASSISTANT MANAGER (*gulping*). I see.

BROCK. All right. Just don't get nosey.

THE ASSISTANT MANAGER. Not at all.

BROCK. There ain't no Mrs. Brock, except my mother. And she's dead.

THE ASSISTANT MANAGER. I see.

BROCK (*snapping his fingers*). Eddie! Take care of him. (EDDIE *comes over, reaches into his pocket, and takes out a roll of bills. He looks at* BROCK. *They reach a swift, silent, understanding as to how much.* EDDIE *hands the* ASSISTANT MANAGER *two ten-dollar bills.*)

THE ASSISTANT MANAGER (*to Eddie*). Thank you. (*Then, to* BROCK.) That is, thank *you.* So much.

BROCK. All right, all right. Just listen. Anybody works in this room just tell 'em to do it good and do it quick and nobody'll get hurt. I'm a big tipper, tell 'em, and I don't like a lot of people around all the time and I don't like to wait for nothin'. I ain't used to it.

THE ASSISTANT MANAGER. I'm sure everything will be just that, Mr. Brock.

BROCK (*with a wave*). Okay. Knock off.

THE ASSISTANT MANAGER. Thank you *very* much, Mr. Brock. (*He leaves.*)

BROCK (*rising and shouting*). Billie!!

BILLIE (*appearing on the balcony*). What?

BROCK (*indicating the room*). Not bad, huh?

BILLIE (*without enthusiasm*). It's all right.

(*The door buzzer sounds.* EDDIE *goes to answer it.*)

BROCK (*sore*). All right, she says. You know what this place costs a day?

BILLIE. Two hundred and thirty-five. You told me.

(*She leaves, with a bored wave of her hips.* EDDIE *opens the door.* ED DEVERY *comes in, slightly drunk.*)

DEVERY. Hello, Eddie.

EDDIE. Hello.

(*About* ED DEVERY. *Thirty years ago, when he was secretary to a great Supreme Court Justice, he was known as a young man destined for greatness. The white star shone clearly on his forehead. Fifteen years later, he was still so known—except to himself. He knew then that he had lost his way. Now everyone knows. They speak of his past brilliance in law and charitably forget that he now has but one client,* HARRY BROCK, *who might have difficulty in finding a reputable lawyer to serve him. But* ED DEVERY *is past caring.* BROCK *represents over $100,000 a year, which buys plenty of the best available Scotch.)*

DEVERY. Welcome to our city.

BROCK. Yeah.

EDDIE. Say I got this ticket to be fixed.

(He reaches into his pocket, searching for it.)

DEVERY *(annoyed)*. What's it about?

EDDIE. Ah, some louse just as we blew into town. Here. *(He hands over a pink traffic summons.)*

DEVERY *(loud and mean)*. I should like to impress one thing on your nonexistent intellect . . . the fact that I am a lawyer does not mean that I own the law.

EDDIE. What'd *I* do? What'd I *do?*

DEVERY. All right. I'll see what I can manage. *(He takes a deep, weary breath.)*

BROCK. You plastered again?

DEVERY. Still.

BROCK. I told you I got a couple things can't wait.

DEVERY. Don't worry about me, massa, I can see a loophole at twenty paces.

BROCK. How'd we make out?

DEVERY. It's going to be all right. May cost slightly more than we estimated, but there is no cause for alarm.

BROCK. How much more?

DEVERY. It's negligible.

BROCK. Why more?

DEVERY. Supply and demand, Harry. A crook is becoming a rare item in these parts. Therefore, he comes high. Don't worry.

BROCK. What do you mean, "don't worry"? This kind of stuff ain't deductible, you know.

DEVERY. I'm not sure. Perhaps we should make a trial issue of it. *(Dictating.)* To the Collector of Internal Revenue. Herewith additional deduction for Tax Return now on file, one bribe, $80,000.

BROCK *(outraged)*. Eighty?

(The phone rings.)

DEVERY. What's the matter?

BROCK. You said—uh—negligible.

DEVERY. We figured fifty, didn't we?

EDDIE *(answering phone)*. Yeah?

BROCK *(to* DEVERY*)*. You're very handy with *my* dough, you know it?

EDDIE *(on the phone)*. . . . Yes, he is. Who wants him? Wait a second. *(To* DEVERY*)*. Some guy for *you*. Verrall.

DEVERY *(going to phone)*. Thanks. *(Into phone.)* How are you, Paul? . . . Good. . . . How's the crusade business? . . . Sure, any time now. Sooner the better. Fine. . . . See you. . . . *(He hangs up)*.

BROCK. What's all that?

DEVERY. Paul Verrall. I told you about him.

BROCK. I don't remember no Verrall.

DEVERY. He's a writer. *New Republic*. Wants an interview. Smart boy. He's just back from a long time in the service with lots of ideas and lots of energy.

BROCK. I don't want to talk to no writers. I got to get shaved.

DEVERY. I think you'd better talk to this one.

BROCK. What's so important?

DEVERY. Just do it.

BROCK. Why?

DEVERY. This is one of the few fellows in Washington to look out for. Thing to do is take him in. Then he doesn't go poking.

BROCK *(loudly)*. Eddie!

DEVERY. How's Billie?

BROCK. She's all right. Upstairs. *(*EDDIE *comes in.)* Get me a shave up here.

EDDIE. Right.

DEVERY. Harry—

BROCK. What?

EDDIE (on the phone). Barber shop.

DEVERY. Tell Billie to wear something nice and plain for the Senator. He may be bringing his wife.

BROCK. Tell her yourself. You ain't pregnant.

EDDIE (on the phone). This is Harry Brock's apartment. Send up a barber and a manicure. Right away. . . . Harry Brock. . . . That's right. . . . Okay, make it snappy.

BROCK (yelling). And a shine!

EDDIE (echoing him). And a shine! (He hangs up.) Be right up.

DEVERY. Eddie, how would you like to save my life?

EDDIE. Soda or plain water?

DEVERY. Neat.

EDDIE. Right! (He goes to work with the liquor.)

BROCK (removing his jacket and tie). Don't worry about Billie. One thing, she knows how to dress. You know what it costs me for clothes for her?

DEVERY. That's not all I'm worried about, Harry.

BROCK. What?

DEVERY. Well, did you have to bring Billie?

BROCK. I may be here God knows how long.

DEVERY. Trouble is, this is a city of few secrets and much chat.

BROCK. Anybody chats me I'll bust 'em in half.

DEVERY. Fine. That'll get you right where you want to go. Up with the dress-for-dinner bunch.

BROCK. What do I care?

DEVERY. I don't know. What do you care? (EDDIE hands him a drink.) Thanks. (Sitting down beside BROCK.) Listen, Harry, you've got a chance to be one of the men who runs this country. Better than that. You can run the men who run

it. It takes power. You've got some. It takes money. You've got plenty. Above all, it takes judgment and intelligence. (A pause.) That's why you pay me a hundred thousand a year.

BROCK. What's all the excitement?

DEVERY. Nothing. I'm just trying to make it clear where I fit in.

BROCK. You don't have to holler.

DEVERY. All right.

BROCK. Honest to God, I thought I done somethin' wrong. (He rises and moves away.)

DEVERY. When Verrall gets here, be friendly. Treat him nicely. Don't bull him. Just be yourself. Treat him like a woman you're trying to make.

BROCK. Wait a minute!

(The buzzer sounds.)

DEVERY. I'll leave you alone with him. Better that way. I want to see Billie, anyway. (DEVERY opens the door and admits VERRALL.) Hello, Paul.

PAUL. Ed. (They shake hands.)

DEVERY. Harry Brock, Paul Verrall.

PAUL. How do you do, sir? (He bows, slightly and sharply. A habit.)

BROCK. How are you? (He looks at Paul, quizzically.) Ain't I seen you some place before? (PAUL just smiles at him.) Excuse me for my coat off. I have to get shaved and so forth. I hope you don't mind.

PAUL (to DEVERY). What have you been telling this guy about me?

DEVERY. If you gentlemen will excuse me—

(He goes upstairs.)

BROCK. Sit down. What'll you drink?

(PAUL sits.)

PAUL. Scotch, please—if you've got it.

BROCK (with a short laugh). If I've got it. (He calls out, loudly.) Eddie!! (To PAUL.) I got everything. Where do you think you are? (EDDIE appears.) Stick around, willya, for Christ's sake, and give the man a Scotch and— (To PAUL.) soda?

PAUL. Plain water.

BROCK (*to* EDDIE). Plain water.

EDDIE. Right. Rye ginger ale for you?

BROCK. Right. (*To* PAUL, *happily.*) He always knows what I feel to drink. Yeah. He's worked for me I don't know how many years. Also, he's my cousin. He knows me insides out. (*To* EDDIE.) Right?

EDDIE. That's right.

PAUL. Maybe I should be interviewing Eddie. (*A great howl of laughter from* BROCK.)

BROCK. Hey, you maybe got somethin' there. That's pretty good. What's it gonna be, pal? A plug or a pan?

PAUL. Why—

BROCK. I like to know these things. Then I know how to talk, if I know your angle.

PAUL. No angle. Just, well—just the facts.

BROCK. Oh, a pan! (*He laughs, confident of his boorish charm.* EDDIE *brings their drinks.*)

PAUL. Not exactly. (*Taking the drink.*) Thanks.

(EDDIE *pads around the room, placing cigarettes, matches, and cigars in the right places.*)

BROCK. It's okay! Don't worry. Write what you want. See, the way I look at it is like this. You can't hurt me and you can't help me. Nobody can. (*They drink.*) I'm only talkin' with you because Ed Devery asked me. What the hell, I pay a guy a hundred grand a year for advice so I'm a sucker if I don't take it. Right?

EDDIE (*from a remote part of the room, answers automatically*). That's right.

BROCK (*screaming at him*). Butt out, willya? (EDDIE *looks up, confused and hurt, then goes on with his activity.*) Devery likes it when I get wrote about.

(*He goes to a newly placed humidor.*)

PAUL. Well, of course, in Washington, Mr. Brock, there's a certain amount of value in the right kind of—

BROCK (*getting out a magnificently boxed cigar and bringing it to* PAUL). Cut it out, willya? You're breakin' my heart. Washington! I licked every town I ever decided, so what's different? Have a cigar!

PAUL (*taking it*). Thanks. (*He looks at it carefully.*) I'll give it to a Congressman.

BROCK. Five bucks apiece they cost me. From Cuba someplace.

PAUL. Well, in that case, I'll give it to a Senator. (*He puts it in his pocket.*)

BROCK (*thoughtfully*). Senators are pretty big stuff around here, huh?

PAUL (*hardly knowing how to answer this*). Yes.

BROCK (*in disgust*). Christ!

PAUL. Why? Shouldn't they be?

BROCK. Listen, you know what a Senator is to me? A guy who makes a hundred and fifty bucks a week.

(PAUL *smiles, then takes a few sheets of folded note paper from his breast pocket, a pencil from another pocket, and makes a note.*)

BROCK. What are you puttin' in?

PAUL (*writing*). Your little joke.

BROCK (*delighted*). You like it, huh?

PAUL. First class.

BROCK. Maybe I oughta be on the radio.

PAUL. Maybe.

BROCK. How much you wanna bet I make more money than Amos and Andy?

PAUL. No bet.

(EDDIE *carries a bottle of Poland Water upstairs.* BROCK *lights a cigarette and stretches out on the sofa, happily. He feels he is doing well. He puts his feet up.*)

BROCK (*expansively*). Well, fella, what do you wanna know?

PAUL (*suddenly*). How much money have you got?

BROCK (*startled*). What?

PAUL. How much money have you got?

BROCK. How should I know? What am I, an accountant?

PAUL (*moving to him*). You don't know?

BROCK. Not exactly.

PAUL. Fifty million?

BROCK. I'll tell you the truth. I don't know.

PAUL. Ten million?

BROCK. Maybe.

PAUL. One million?

BROCK. More.

PAUL (pressing). How much?

BROCK. Plenty.

(PAUL gives up, turns away, and crosses back to his chair.)

PAUL. Okay.

BROCK. And listen. I made every nickel. Nobody ever give me nothin'.

PAUL. Nice work. (He sits.)

BROCK (putting out his cigarette and rising). I can tell already. You're gonna give me the business.

PAUL (trying to charm him). Wait a minute—

BROCK. Go ahead! I like it.

PAUL. —you've got me wrong.

BROCK. Go ahead. Work for me. I got more people workin' for me than knows it. (He moves away.)

PAUL (after a pause). What do you think about—?

BROCK (turning violently). Go ahead! Pan me. Tell how I'm a mugg and a roughneck. You'll do me good.

PAUL. Listen, Mr. Brock—

BROCK. Lemme tell you about Cleveland. In 1937 there's a big dump there, see? And the city wants to get rid of it. High class scrap. So I go out there to look it over myself. There's a lot of other guys there, too. From Bethlehem even and like that. I didn't have a chance and I knew it. I figure I'm out of my class on the deal and I'm ready to pull out when all of a sudden the God-damnedest thing comes out there in one of the papers. About me. A big write-up. It says my name and about how come the city is gonna do business with hoodlums. Mind you, I was out of my class. I didn't have the kind of buttons a guy needs for a deal like that. So the next day—again. This time they got a picture of me. Next thing you know, a guy calls me up. A guy from the Municipal Commission. He comes up

to see me and he says they don't want no trouble. So I naturally string him along and I get busy on the phone and I raise some dough with a couple of boys from *Detroit*. Then comes the big pan. On the front page. Next day I close the deal and in a week, I'm cartin'.

(EDDIE comes downstairs.)

PAUL (after a pause). What's your point?

BROCK. My point is you can't do me no harm if you make me out to be a mugg. Maybe you'll help me. Everybody gets scared, and for me that's good. Everybody scares easy.

PAUL. Well, not everybody.

BROCK. Well, enough. You can't hurt me. All you can do is build me up or shut up. Have a drink. (He snaps his fingers at EDDIE.)

(EDDIE picks up PAUL's glass.)

PAUL (to EDDIE). No, thanks. Really.

(EDDIE puts the glass down and starts to turn away.)

BROCK (to EDDIE). Do what I'm tellin' you! Who the hell pays you around here? (EDDIE picks up the glass again, quickly, and does as he is told.) When I'm home, he shaves me in the mornin'. I've got my own barber chair. (To EDDIE.) Right?

EDDIE. That's right.

BROCK (moving back to the sofa). Well, go ahead, pal. I thought you wanted to interview me.

(There is a pause.)

PAUL. Where were you born?

BROCK (settling back again). Jersey. Plainfield, New Jersey. 1907. I went to work when I was twelve years old and I been workin' ever since. I'll tell you my first job. A paper route. I bought a kid out with a swift kick in the keester.

PAUL (writing). And you've been working ever since.

BROCK (missing the point). Right. I'll tell you how I'm the top man in my racket. I been in it over twenty-five years. In the same racket.

PAUL. Steel.

BROCK. Junk. Not steel. *Junk.*

PAUL. Oh.

BROCK. Look, don't butter me up. I'm a junk man. I ain't ashamed to say it.

PAUL. All right.

BROCK. Lemme give you some advice, sonny boy. Never crap a crapper. I can sling it with the best of 'em.

(EDDIE *goes upstairs.*)

PAUL. Twenty-five years, you say?

BROCK. I'll tell you. I'm a kid with a paper route. I've got this little wagon. So on my way home nights, I come through the alleys pickin' up stuff. I'm not the only one. All the kids are doin' it. The only difference is, they keep it. Not me. I sell it. First thing you know, I'm makin' seven, eight bucks a week from that. Three bucks from papers. So I figure out right off which is the right racket. I'm just a kid, mind you, but I could see that. Pretty soon, the guy I'm sellin' to is handin' me anywheres from fifteen to twenty a week. So he offers me a job for ten. Dumb jerk. I'd be sellin' this guy his own stuff back half the time and he never knew.

PAUL. How do you mean?

BROCK (*relishing the memory*). Well, in the night, see, I'm under the fence and I drag it out and load up. In the mornin', I bring it in the front way and collect.

PAUL. Twelve years old, you were?

BROCK. Somethin' like that.

PAUL. So pretty soon you owned the whole yard.

BROCK. Damn right! This guy, the jerk? He works for me now. And you know who else works for me? The kid whose paper route I swiped. I figure I owe him. That's how I am.

PAUL. Pretty good years for the—junk business, these last few.

BROCK (*with a mysterious grin*). I ain't kickin'.

PAUL. Do you anticipate a decline now?

BROCK (*frowning suddenly*). Talk plain, pal.

(*The buzzer sounds.*)

PAUL. Is it still going to be good, do you think?

BROCK (*darkly*). We'll make it good.

PAUL (*quickly*). Who's we?

(*A pause.* BROCK *senses he is being cornered.*)

BROCK. We is me, that's who.

PAUL. I see.

BROCK. Fancy talk don't go with me.

(EDDIE *opens the door for the barber, the manicurist, and the bootblack.*)

THE BARBER. Good evening. In here, sir?

BROCK. Yeah. (*He removes his shirt and hands it to* EDDIE.)

PAUL (*rising*). Well, I'll get out of your—

BROCK. Don't go. Sit down. Sit down.

(*The* BARBER *and* MANICURIST *go about their work.* PAUL *sits down.* BROCK *looks at him and smiles.*)

BROCK. Sit down—I like you. You play your cards right, I'll put you on the payroll. You know what I mean?

PAUL. Sure.

BROCK (*to the barber*). Once over easy and no talkin'. (*To the* MANICURIST.) Just brush 'em up. I get a manicure every day.

THE MANICURIST. Yes, sir.

(*The* BOOTBLACK *gets into position, then notices that* BROCK *is not wearing shoes. He looks up, confused.*)

BROCK. Over there someplace.

(*The* BOOTBLACK *moves his equipment, finds the shoes, and works on them.*)

BROCK (*to* PAUL). Keep goin'. It's okay.

PAUL. I've been wondering what you're doing in Washington.

BROCK (*genially*). None of your God damn business.

PAUL. Sure it is.

BROCK. How come?

PAUL. You're a big man, Mr. Brock.

(*The* BARBER *is putting a towel around* BROCK's *neck.*)

BROCK (*for no reason*). Not so tight!

THE BARBER. Sorry, sir.

BROCK (*to Paul*). Sightseein'. That's what I'm in Washington for. Sightseein'.

PAUL. All right.

BROCK. Put that in the write-up, then nobody'll be scared.

PAUL. How long do you think you'll be around?

BROCK. Depends on how many sights I got to see.

PAUL. There's some talk you may be around for a long, long time.

BROCK. Where'd you get that?

PAUL. Around.

BROCK. Bull. What the hell do I care about politics? I got trouble enough in my own racket. I don't know nothin' about the politics racket.

PAUL. I hear you've come to find out.

BROCK. Listen, pal, so far I been nice to you. Don't pump me.

PAUL. My life's work.

BROCK. Well, don't work on me. I like to be friends with you.

(DEVERY *appears on the balcony and starts downstairs.*)

DEVERY (*to PAUL*). How are you getting on with the monarch of all he surveys?

PAUL. Great. I found out he was born in Plainfield, New Jersey. He sure is a tough man to dig.

(*A grunt from* BROCK, *as the* BARBER *works on his face. A* BELLHOP *knocks and enters, carrying a freshly pressed suit. He gives it to* EDDIE, *who takes it upstairs.*)

DEVERY. I can't believe that. He loves to talk.

PAUL. Not to me.

BROCK. Why, I told you the story of my life, practically.

(BILLIE *comes down.*)

PAUL (*to* DEVERY). He wouldn't even tell me how much money he's got.

BROCK. I don't know, I'm tellin' you.

(BILLIE *goes to the liquor table and selects a bottle.*)

PAUL (*to* DEVERY). And he wouldn't tell me what he was doing in Washington.

BROCK. Because it's none of your business.

DEVERY. No secret. Just a little tax stuff. I told you.

PAUL. Yes, I know, but I didn't believe you.

(BILLIE *starts back upstairs carrying the bottle.*)

DEVERY. Oh, Billie, this is my friend Paul Verrall. (*To* PAUL.) Billie Dawn.

PAUL (*making his bow*). How do you do?

(BILLIE *nods and continues to move.*)

BROCK. Wait a minute.

BILLIE (*slightly scared*). What's the matter?

BROCK. Where do you think you're goin' with that?

BILLIE. Upstairs.

BROCK. Put it back.

BILLIE. I just wanted—

BROCK. I know what you wanted. Put it back.

BILLIE. Why can't I—?

BROCK (*mean*). Because I say you can't, that's why. We got somebody comin'. Somebody important. I don't want you stinkin'.

BILLIE. Well, can't I just have—?

BROCK. No! Now put it back and go upstairs and change your clothes and don't give me no trouble.

(BILLIE *stands motionless, humiliated.*)

BROCK (*too loud*). Do what I'm tellin' you!!

(BILLIE *obeys.* PAUL *and* DEVERY *have half turned away in embarrassment.* BROCK *settles back in his chair to let the* BARBER *continue.* BILLIE *goes back upstairs. There is silence in the room. Nobody watches her go. About halfway up, she turns and regards* PAUL *with strange interest, but continues her move. If you were close enough, you might even recognize the faint beginnings of a smile. She goes into her room.* EDDIE *returns.*)

DEVERY. Barber, what'll you take to cut his throat?

(BROCK *sits up so suddenly that the barber almost does so.*)

BROCK *(in a fury).* There's some kind of jokes I don't like, Ed.

DEVERY. Don't get excited.

BROCK. Don't tell me what to do!

(*He strides over to* DEVERY *and pushes his face, hard.* DEVERY *is thrown off balance, but* PAUL *keeps him from falling.*)

DEVERY *(weakly).* Jesus, Harry. It was just a joke.

BROCK *(to the barber).* That's all.

BARBER. Not quite finished, sir.

BROCK. That's all, I told you. Beat it.

BARBER. Very good, sir.

BROCK *(to the* MANICURIST*).* You too. (*To* EDDIE, *indicating the help.*) Eddie, take care of 'em.

(*The* BARBER, *the* MANICURIST, *and the* BOOTBLACK *prepare to leave.*)

PAUL. I guess I'd better be—

(EDDIE *is attending to the tips.*)

BROCK. Don't go.

PAUL. I really should. I've got some work.

BROCK. Stick around, can't you? Looks like you're about the only friend I got left around here.

PAUL. Well, I'm not far. If anyone starts beating you, just scream and I'll come running.

(BROCK *laughs. The* BARBER, *the* MANICURIST, *and the* BOOTBLACK *leave.* EDDIE *picks up the shoes and takes them upstairs.*)

BROCK. You live in the hotel here?

PAUL. Right down the hall.

BROCK. Fine.

(*They shake hands.*)

PAUL. Other side of the tracks, of course.

BROCK. Say, don't kid me. I hear you do fine.

PAUL *(to* DEVERY*).* Good night, Ed.

DEVERY *(quietly).* Night.

(*He walks to the liquor table and pours himself a stiff drink.*)

BROCK *(to* PAUL*).* See you soon.

PAUL *(as he leaves).* Good night. Thanks for everything.

BROCK. Don't mention it.

DEVERY *(getting his brief case).* I need Billie's signature on a few things. Eddie, too.

BROCK. Sure. (*Yells.*) Billie!

BILLIE'S VOICE. What?

BROCK. Come on down here. Right away. (*To* DEVERY.) What are you sore about?

DEVERY. Not sore, Harry.

BROCK. You look funny.

DEVERY. I know.

BROCK. Don't you feel good? You want an aspirin?

DEVERY. No, no. I'm fine. In fact, considering that I have been dead for sixteen years, I am in remarkable health.

(BILLIE *comes down, wearing her most dignified dress.*)

BROCK *(to* DEVERY*).* Swear to God, sometimes I don't understand you at all.

DEVERY *(smiling).* Sometimes?

BILLIE. What do you want?

BROCK. Ed.

DEVERY. A few things I want you to sign, honey.

BILLIE. That's all I do around here is sign.

BROCK. Too bad about you. (*To* DEVERY.) When is he comin'? This Senator guy?

DEVERY. Any time now.

BROCK. I better get fixed up, huh?

(*Still in his undershirt, and shoeless, he picks up his jacket and tie and starts up. He glances at* BILLIE, *stops, and moves to examine every detail of her get-up.*)

BROCK. She look all right to you?

BILLIE. Look who's talkin'!

DEVERY. Perfect.

BROCK. You *sure* now?

BILLIE (*in a prideful whine*). What's the matter with me?

(BROCK *pays no attention to her.*)

BROCK. Tell me if somethin's wrong. I don't want to start off on no left foot.

DEVERY. Don't worry.

(BROCK *leaves.* DEVERY *brings out a sheaf of legal papers and spreads them out for* BILLIE *to sign. He hands her his fountain pen.*)

BILLIE. What's got into *him*?

DEVERY. Nothing. He just wants to make a good impression.

BILLIE. So let him.

DEVERY (*pointing out a line*). Two places on this one, please.

(EDDIE *enters and goes upstairs.*)

BILLIE (*signing, her head quite close to the paper*). What happened to all that stuff I signed last week?

DEVERY (*smiling*). All used up.

BILLIE. I bet I've signed about a million of these.

DEVERY. What you get for being a multiple corporate officer.

BILLIE. I *am*? (DEVERY *nods.*) What do you know?

DEVERY. You've come a long way from the chorus all right.

BILLIE. I wasn't only in the chorus. In *Anything Goes* I spoke lines.

DEVERY. Really?

BILLIE. Of course.

DEVERY. How many?

BILLIE. How many what?

DEVERY (*blotting*). Lines did you speak?

BILLIE. Five.

DEVERY. I never knew that.

BILLIE. Ask anybody.

DEVERY. I believe you.

BILLIE (*signing*). I could of been a star probably. If I'd of stuck to it.

DEVERY. Why didn't you?

BILLIE (*signing*). Harry didn't want me being in the show. He likes to get to bed early.

DEVERY. I see.

BILLIE. He's changed, Harry. Don't you think so?

DEVERY. How?

BILLIE. I don't know. He used to be like more satisfied. Now he's always runnin' around. Like this. What did he have to come to Washington, D. C., for?

DEVERY (*blotting*). Long story.

BILLIE. Well, don't tell it to me, I don't care where he goes. I just wish he'd settle down.

DEVERY. Ambitious.

BILLIE (*signing*). I know. He *talks* all the time now. He never used to. Now he's got me up half the night tellin' me what a big man he is. And how he's gonna be bigger. Run everything.

DEVERY. He may, at that.

BILLIE. Personally, I don't care one way or the other.

DEVERY. Very few people do, that's why he may get to do it. The curse of civilization. Don't-care-ism. Satan's key to success.

BILLIE. What kind of talk is that? You drunk or sump'n?

DEVERY (*blotting*). I'm drunk *and* "sump'n."

BILLIE. All right. I give up. (*She goes to the liquor table.*)

DEVERY (*without looking at her*). Take it easy.

BILLIE. Look now, don't *you* start.

DEVERY. Better if you drink later, Billie, after they've gone.

BILLIE. What's the deal, anyway?

DEVERY. No deal. Just important people, that's all.

BILLIE. Who? This Senator guy?

DEVERY. And *Mrs.* Hedges.

BILLIE. Harry told me this fellow works for him.

DEVERY. In a way.

BILLIE. So what's he puttin' it on for?

DEVERY. I suppose he wants him to *keep* working for him.

BILLIE. Too deep for me.

(The buzzer sounds. EDDIE *comes downstairs and goes to the door.)*

DEVERY *(dropping his voice).* All you have to do is be nice and no rough language.

BILLIE. I won't open my mush.

DEVERY. I didn't mean that.

BILLIE. I don't have to be down here, at all, you know. I *could* go upstairs. *(She starts out.)* In fact, I think I will.

*(*DEVERY *moves to her.)*

DEVERY. I'm telling you, Billie. Harry wouldn't like it.

BILLIE *(making a violent about-face).* All right all right all right! *(She moves to the sofa and sits.)*

*(*EDDIE *opens the door to admit* SENATOR NORVAL HEDGES *and* MRS. HEDGES. DEVERY *moves to greet them.)*

DEVERY. How are you, Norval?

HEDGES. Can't complain.

DEVERY *(to* MRS. HEDGES*).* Haven't seen you for a long time, Anna.

MRS. HEDGES. No, you haven't.

DEVERY. Come on in.

*(*SENATOR HEDGES *is a worried man of sixty—thin, pale, and worn.* MRS. HEDGES *bears out Fanny Dixwell Holmes's comment that Washington is a city filled with great men and the women they married when they were very young. Except that the Senator is not a great man. He just looks like a great man.)*

HEDGES *(to* BILLIE*).* Good evening.

BILLIE. Good evening.

DEVERY. Senator, you ought to remember this little lady. A great first-nighter like you. She used to be Billie Dawn?

HEDGES *(vaguely).* Oh yes . . . Yes, indeed.

DEVERY. Billie, this is Senator Norval Hedges I've told you so much about.

*(*HEDGE *offers his hand.* BILLIE *takes it.)*

HEDGES. How do you do?

BILLIE. How do you do?

DEVERY. And this is Mrs. Hedges, Billie.

MRS. HEDGES. Glad to meet you.

BILLIE. Glad to meet you.

*(*MRS. HEDGES *seats herself beside* BILLIE. *There is an awkward pause.* MRS. HEDGES *suddenly extends her hand.* BILLIE *takes it.)*

DEVERY. What do you say to a drink?

MRS. HEDGES. Love one.

HEDGES. Sounds all right to me.

DEVERY. Whiskey?

HEDGES. Be fine.

DEVERY *(to* EDDIE*).* Whiskey all around, Eddie.

EDDIE. Right. *(He goes to work on the drinks.)*

HEDGES. That's going to hit the spot just fine. *(He sits down.)*

MRS. HEDGES *(to* BILLIE*).* He's awfully tired.

DEVERY *(to* HEDGES*).* What have you been doing? Standing over a hot resolution all day?

HEDGES. Just about.

MRS. HEDGES. How do you like Washington, Mrs. Brock?

(There is a tiny pause. BILLIE, *turned slightly away, does not realize for an instant that she is being addressed.* DEVERY, *having taken such pains to avoid identifying her too exactly during the course of the introductions, is afraid* BILLIE *may now correct* MRS. HEDGES *and ruin his careful diplomacy.* BILLIE *catches his eye.)*

BILLIE. I haven't seen it yet.

MRS. HEDGES. You mean to say this is the very first time you've been here?

BILLIE. That's what I mean. I never went on the road.

HEDGES. Well, we must show you around. Beautiful city.

MRS. HEDGES. Too bad the Supreme Court isn't in session. You'd love that.

(*A pause.*)

BILLIE. What is it?

(MRS. HEDGES *doesn't know what to make of this. She looks over at the* SENATOR *to see if he has any ideas.* DEVERY *saves the moment by bursting into laughter.*)

DEVERY. Lots of people would like to know the answer to that one, Billie.

(*The* SENATOR *and* MRS. HEDGES *now settle for* BILLIE's *remark as a brand of metropolitan humor which they have never been able to get, quite. They join in the laughter.* EDDIE *serves the drinks.*)

DEVERY. What's this jam Wallace has gotten himself into?

HEDGES. Give him enough rope. I've said so from the start.

DEVERY. I know.

HEDGES. Trouble with these professional do-gooders is they never seem to— (*He stops as* BROCK *enters from above, carefully brushed and dressed.*)

BROCK. Hello, everybody!

DEVERY. Here we are.

(*The* SENATOR *rises. For some reason,* MRS. HEDGES *rises, too.*)

DEVERY. Senator Hedges, Harry Brock.

BROCK (*very hearty*). Say, it's about time us two got together, Senator. (*He shakes hands with* HEDGES *using both hands.*)

HEDGES. About time.

BROCK (*moving across the room*). And I suppose this is Mrs. Hedges.

MRS. HEDGES. That's right.

(*They shake hands, and* BROCK *nearly knocks her down with cordiality.*)

BROCK. I certainly am happy to make your acquaintance. Sit down. (*To* HEDGES.) Senator, sit down.

(SENATOR *and* MRS. HEDGES *sit.*)

HEDGES. Have a good trip down?

BROCK. Oh, sure. I come down in my own car. I came. Had to stop in Baltimore on the way down. I got a yard there, you know. A junk yard.

HEDGES. Is that so?

BROCK. Yeah. Just a *little* racket. Tell you the truth, it ain't worth the trouble it takes to run it, but I like it. It was the second yard I picked up. Before that I only had one yard.

MRS. HEDGES. How many do you have now?

BROCK. Hell, I don't know.

(*He stops abruptly, then addresses a blushing apology to* MRS. HEDGES.)

BROCK. *Excuse me.*

MRS. HEDGES (*being big about it*). Oh, that's all right.

BROCK (*to* HEDGES). I don't know why I like that little Baltimore outfit. I just always get kind of a feelin' from it. You know what I mean?

HEDGES. Sentimental.

BROCK. That's it! I'm sentimental. Like you say.

MRS. HEDGES. I think we're *all* a bit sentimental.

(*There is a pause. It seems* BILLIE's *turn to speak.*)

BILLIE. Well— (*They all look at her.*) It's a free country.

BROCK (*covering quickly*). How's things with you, Senator?

HEDGES. Same old grind.

BROCK. Lemme tell you something, Senator. You got one job I don't never wanna be. Everybody pesterin' you all the time, probably.

HEDGES. Part of the job.

MRS. HEDGES. Do you play bridge, Mrs. Brock?

BILLIE. No. Only gin.

MRS. HEDGES. I beg your pardon?

BILLIE. Gin rummy.

MRS. HEDGES. Oh, yes, of course. I was going to ask you to join us. A few of the girls? We meet now and then.

BILLIE. Yuh. Well, I don't play bridge.

BROCK *(to* BILLIE*).* You could learn to if you wanted.

BILLIE. I don't think so.

BROCK. Sure you could. *(To* MRS. HEDGES*.)* She couldn't play gin till I learned her. Now she beats my brains out.

DEVERY. How are you fixed for time tomorrow, Norval?

HEDGES. Pretty tight, I'm afraid.

DEVERY. Oh. I wanted to bring Harry over on a few things.

HEDGES. Ten o'clock all right?

DEVERY. How's that for you, Harry?

BROCK. In the mornin'?

HEDGES. Yes.

BROCK. Pretty early for me.

BILLIE. I'll say.

*(*BROCK *throws her a look.)*

HEDGES. Eleven?

BROCK. Okay.

DEVERY. Where'll you be?

HEDGES *(awkwardly).* Well, I can drop by here if that's all right.

DEVERY. Sure.

HEDGES *(lamely).* It's right on my way.

(There is a pause. BILLIE *rises and speaks to* MRS. HEDGES*.)*

BILLIE. You wanna wash your hands or anything, honey?

MRS. HEDGES *(so shocked that her reply is inaudible).* No, thank you.

*(*BILLIE *moves upstairs, through an atmosphere of tense embarrassment.)*

DEVERY *(to* HEDGES*).* I hope you're free on Friday night.

HEDGES. I think so. Are we, dear?

MRS. HEDGES. Well, we *can* be.

BROCK. Atta girl! *(He moves to sit beside her and puts his arm on the back of the sofa just behind her.)*

DEVERY. Fine. I'm doing a little dinner. Few people I want Harry to meet.

HEDGES. And who want to meet *him,* I'm sure.

BROCK *(coyly).* Say, listen, Senator. I'm just a junk man.

HEDGES. That's no disgrace in America.

DEVERY *(almost sardonic).* No—not if you're a *big* junk man.

(A pause. SENATOR HEDGES *rises and moves to* BROCK*.)*

HEDGES *(softly).* I want to thank you, Mr. Brock. For everything.

BROCK. Call me Harry, Senator, willya?

HEDGES. I haven't written you about it. Harry. Not considered good form. But I want you to know that I'm grateful for all you've done. For your support.

BROCK. Don't mention it. Just tit for tat. *(He stops, confused, then turns to* MRS. HEDGES*.)* Excuse *me!*

MRS. HEDGES *(at sea).* Quite all right.

BROCK. You see, Senator, what I think is —there's a certain kind of people ought to stick together.

HEDGES. My feeling.

BROCK. You know what I'm interested in. Scrap iron. I wanna buy it—I wanna move it—and I wanna sell it. And I don't want a lot of buttin' in with rules and regulations at no stage of the game.

HEDGES. Obviously.

BROCK *(rising).* I ain't talkin' about peanuts, mind you. All this junk I been sellin' for the last fifteen years—well, it's junk again. And I can sell it again once I lay my hands on it. Do you know how much scrap iron is layin' around all over Europe? Where the war's been?

HEDGES. No, I don't.

BROCK. Well, I don't either. Nobody knows. Nobody ever *will* know. It's more than you can think of. Well, I want to pick it up and bring it back where it belongs. Where it came from. Where I can use it. Who does it belong to anyway?

MRS. HEDGES. Why—isn't that interesting?

HEDGES. I have a copy for you of the preliminary survey made by—

BROCK (*sitting opposite* HEDGES). Boil it down and give it to me fast. I didn't come down here to have to do a lot of paper work. See, the way I work is like this. It's every man for himself—like dog eat dog. Like you gotta get the other guy before he gets you.

HEDGES. Exactly.

BROCK. What I got in mind is an operatin' combo—all over the world. There's enough in it for everybody—if they're *in,* that is. Up to now, I'm doin' fine. Everybody's lined up, everybody understands everybody. I want to get movin', see?—that's all. Only thing is, Ed here comes up with some new trouble every day. *This* law, *that* law, tariffs, taxes, State Department, *this* department, *that* department—

DEVERY. I'm sure you understand, Norval, that in an operation of this kind—

BROCK. Listen, all that stuff is just a lot of hot air to me. There's a way to do anything. That's all I know. It's up to you guys to find out how.

DEVERY. Norval's been working along those lines.

HEDGES. Yes. The Hedges-Keller Amendment, for example, guarantees no interference with free enterprise—foreign or domestic. We're doing everything we can to get it through quickly.

BROCK. Well, see that you do, 'cause that's why I'm here, to see that I get what I paid for.

DEVERY (*picking up the* SENATOR's *glass*). One more?

HEDGES. I think not.

BROCK. One for the road.

HEDGES. All right.

(DEVERY *hands the glass to* EDDIE.)

BROCK. How do things look to you, Senator?

HEDGES. Generally?

BROCK. Yeah, generally.

HEDGES. Well, not too bad. Just a question of staying on the alert. Too many crackpots around with their foot in the White House door.

BROCK. Tellin' me.

HEDGES (*confidentially*). He listens to everything, you know.

BROCK. Sure.

HEDGES. I said to Sam only last week, "This country will soon have to decide if the people are going to run the government or the government is going to run the people."

BROCK. You said it. (EDDIE *distributes fresh drinks.*) You know where I'd be if I had to start my business today? Up the creek. (*He looks at* MRS. HEDGES.) Excuse me.

(*This time she simply nods.*)

DEVERY. That's good sound thinking, Norval.

HEDGES. Thank you.

DEVERY. Worthy of Holmes.

HEDGES. Great man, Holmes.

DEVERY. My personal god.

BROCK. Who?

DEVERY. Oliver Wendell Holmes, Junior.

HEDGES. A wonderful man.

BROCK. Is he comin' Friday night?

(*An awkward pause.*)

DEVERY (*quietly*). I don't think so.

BROCK. Oh.

HEDGES. Well, we mustn't keep you.

MRS. HEDGES. No, we mustn't.

(*They rise and prepare to leave.*)

BROCK. Don't go. We stay up all the time.

HEDGES. Well, don't think of this as a proper visit. We just wanted to say hello. We'll be seeing a lot of each other, I'm sure.

BROCK. Right. Wait a second! (*He moves quickly to the cigar box and takes out a handful.*) Brought these down special.

(*He hands them to* HEDGES.)

HEDGES (*taking them.*) Very kind of you.

BROCK. Don't mention it.

HEDGES. Good night, Harry.

(They shake hands. BILLIE *returns.)*

BROCK. Senator, it's a pleasure.

MRS. HEDGES. Good night, Mrs. Brock.

BILLIE. Good night.

MRS. HEDGES *(to* BROCK*).* Good night and thank you so much.

BROCK. For what? Wait till I get settled down here. I'll show you somethin' to thank me for.

MRS. HEDGES. Good night. Good night, Ed.

DEVERY. See you tomorrow, Norval.

HEDGES. That's right. Good night.

BILLIE. Good night, all.

(The HEDGES *leave.* EDDIE *picks up the empty glasses.)*

BROCK. Okay, Eddie. Knock off.

EDDIE. Right.

*(*EDDIE *starts out.)*

DEVERY. Wait a minute.

*(*EDDIE *stops.* DEVERY *goes to his brief case and gets out some papers which* EDDIE *signs during the following.)*

BILLIE. Drips.

BROCK. What?

BILLIE. I said they're drips.

BROCK. Who the hell are you to say?

BILLIE *(stretching out on the sofa).* I'm myself, that's who.

BROCK. Well, shut up. Nobody asked you.

(He sits down and removes his shoes.)

BILLIE. Pardon me for living.

BROCK. Get upstairs.

BILLIE. Not yet.

BROCK *(rising).* Get upstairs, I told you.

*(*BILLIE *goes, quietly, attempting to retain her little dignity by giving him a look of contempt.)*

EDDIE *(signing).* Here too?

DEVERY. Yes.

EDDIE. Since when I'm only Vice-President?

DEVERY. You're slipping.

BROCK *(worried).* She's gonna be in the way, that dame.

DEVERY. What are you going to do about it?

BROCK *(sitting).* I don't know. Right now I feel like to give her the brush.

DEVERY. Pretty complicated.

BROCK. I know.

DEVERY. At the moment, she owns more of you than *you* do. On paper.

BROCK. Your idea.

DEVERY. Yes, and a damned good one, too. Keeps you in the clear and you know what it saves you?

BROCK. I know, I know. You told me a million times.

DEVERY. Sorry.

BROCK. You better think somethin' up. She's gonna louse me up all the way down the line. God-damn dumb broad.

DEVERY. Send her home.

BROCK. No.

DEVERY. Why not?

BROCK *(softly).* I'm nuts about her.

*(*DEVERY *looks at him quickly, in surprise.)*

DEVERY *(turning away).* Can't have your cake and eat it.

BROCK. What?

DEVERY. Just a saying?

BROCK. It don't make sense.

DEVERY. All right.

(There is a long, long pause.)

BROCK. What's cakes got to do with it?

DEVERY. Nothing, Harry.

*(*EDDIE *finishes signing.)*

EDDIE. Okay?

*(*DEVERY *picks up the papers and looks them over.)*

DEVERY. Okay.

*(*EDDIE *leaves.)*

BROCK. Must be a way to smarten her up a little. Ain't there?

DEVERY. I suppose so.

BROCK. Some kinda school we could send her to, maybe?

DEVERY. I doubt that.

BROCK. Then what?

DEVERY. Well, we might be able to find someone who could smooth the rough edges off.

BROCK. How?

DEVERY. Let me think about it. And while I'm thinking about that, Harry, there's something you might be turning over in *your* mind.

BROCK. Yeah, what?

DEVERY. Well, if you've got to have her around you--the possibility of getting married.

BROCK. Not me.

DEVERY. Why not?

BROCK. I *been* married. I don't like it.

DEVERY. How long have you—you know --been with Billie?

BROCK. I don't know. Eight, nine years. Why?

DEVERY. Well, what the hell?

BROCK. It gets different when you get mar-ried.

DEVERY. Why should it?

BROCK. How do I know why should it? It just does, that's all.

DEVERY. All right.

BROCK. This way, I give her somethin', I'm a hell of a fella. We get married, she's got it comin', she thinks.

DEVERY. Billie's not like that.

BROCK. A broad's a broad.

DEVERY. Time may come you'll be sorry.

BROCK *(rising)*. Listen, don't shove me.

DEVERY. All right. *(He gives BROCK a patronizing look, and pours a drink.)*

BROCK *(irritated)*. Don't make out like I'm some kind of a dope. I know what I'm doin'.

DEVERY. Sure you do.

BROCK. All right. So don't make them Harvard College expressions on your face. So far you still work for me.

DEVERY. That's right, Harry.

BROCK. Okay. Just tell me what you think. If I feel like it, I'll do it. If not, no. And don't give me them looks down your nose.

(DEVERY nods, quietly. BROCK slumps into a chair and sulks for a moment.)

BROCK. What's so important I should get married all of a sudden?

DEVERY. You're moving up, Harry. Bigger places. Bigger people. No matter what goes on underneath, these people make sure of their respectable fronts.

BROCK. The hell with 'em.

DEVERY. That's just talk. You're in the Big League now, and there are certain rules.

BROCK. Like what? Like you got to be married?

DEVERY. No. Like you can't expect to just pass off a setup like this. There's such a thing as being *too* colorful.

BROCK. All right. I'll let you know. But if I do or if I don't we got to do somethin' with her. She just don't fit in. Do you think so?

DEVERY. You're right.

BROCK. Every time she opened her kisser tonight, somethin' wrong come out.

DEVERY. The hell of it is she doesn't realize.

BROCK *(desperately)*. Ed, couldn't you have a talk with her?

DEVERY. Take more than a talk, I'm afraid.

BROCK. Then what?

DEVERY. It's a big job, Harry. It's not easy to make a person over. Maybe impossible. She has to have a great many things ex-plained to her. I won't be around enough, and even if I were, I couldn't do it. No patience, too old, and I don't know enough myself. Not the kind of things she—

(BROCK has been thinking hard. Now he cuts in, suddenly.)

BROCK. Wait a minute!

DEVERY. What?

(BROCK *doesn't get ideas often. When he does, he thrills to the sensation.*)

BROCK (*very quietly*). The guy from down the hall?

DEVERY. Who?

BROCK. The interview guy. There's a smart little cookie.

DEVERY. Well—

BROCK (*selling it*). Knows the town. Knows the angles. Very classy, with that bowing. (*He illustrates, in an imitation of Paul's mannerism.*)

DEVERY. He could do it, probably, but he won't.

BROCK. Why not?

DEVERY. Well, he's not—

BROCK. I'll pay him whatever he **wants**.

DEVERY. I don't think so.

BROCK. Make you a bet. (*He goes to the phone.*) What's his name again?

DEVERY. Wait a minute, Harry.

BROCK. What?

DEVERY. Verrall. Paul Verrall. Harry, I'm not sure—

BROCK. I like it. (*Into the phone.*) Give me Verrall. . . . Yeah . . . Mr. Verrall.

DEVERY (*losing his temper*). I wish you wouldn't sail into things.

BROCK. Shut up. (*Into phone.*) Hello, pal. . . . Harry Brock. . . . You got a minute? I wanna have a little talk. . . . Got a proposition to make you. . . . What? No, no. Nothin' like that. This is all right. . . . Absolutely legitimate. . . . Do that, will you? . . . Fine. . . . I'll be right here. (*He hangs up.*) I like that guy.

DEVERY. Well enough to have him around with Billie all the time?

BROCK. Are you kiddin'? With them glasses? Listen, this is all right. I can feel it. I might even tap him for a little dope myself once in a while.

DEVERY. What about Billie? She may not care for the idea.

BROCK. She'll do what I tell her.

DEVERY. That's not the point, Harry. People don't learn anything unless they want to.

BROCK. She knows what's good for her, she'll want to.

DEVERY. You know best.

BROCK. Damn right. Listen, what do you think I ought to give him?

DEVERY. Seems to me you ought to try just putting it on a friendly basis.

BROCK. I don't believe in nothin' on no friendly basis.

(*The buzzer sounds.*)

DEVERY. I know this fellow.

BROCK. I know lots of fellas. Money talks. I don't want nobody doing me no favors.

DEVERY. Why not talk it over with him and see what—?

(BROCK *goes to the door and opens it.* PAUL *comes in.*)

BROCK (*heartily*). Come on in, pal. Come on in.

PAUL. Thanks.

BROCK. Have a drink.

PAUL. No, thanks. I'm just in the middle of something.

BROCK. Sit down, I want to ask you somethin'.

(PAUL *sits.*)

PAUL. Sure.

BROCK. How much do you make a week?

PAUL. How should I know? What am I, an acountant?

(BROCK *is delighted to hear himself quoted. He laughs.*)

BROCK (*to* DEVERY). I love this guy. (*To* PAUL, *as he sits down beside him.*) What's your name again?

PAUL. Verrall.

BROCK. No, I mean your regular name.

PAUL. Paul.

BROCK. Listen, Paul. Here's the layout. got a friend. Nice kid. I think you prob ably seen her in here before. Billie?

PAUL. Oh, yes.

BROCK. Well, she's a good kid, see? Only to tell you the truth, a little on the stupid side. Not her fault, you understand. I got her out of the chorus. For the chorus she was smart enough, but I'm scared she's gonna be unhappy in this town. She's never been around with such kind of people, you know what I mean?

PAUL. No.

BROCK. Well, I figure a guy like you could help her out. And me, too.

PAUL. How?

BROCK. Show her the ropes, sort of. Explain her what goes on and all like that. In your spare time. What do you say?

PAUL. No, I don't think I could handle it, Mr. Brock.

BROCK. Means a lot to me. I'll give you two hundred bucks a week.

PAUL. All right, I'll do it.

(BROCK *looks at* DEVERY *and laughs again.*)

BROCK. I'm tellin' you. I love this guy.

PAUL. When do I start?

BROCK. Right now. Why not right now?

PAUL. Fine.

BROCK. Let me introduce you like and you take it from there.

PAUL. Good.

BROCK (*getting up and calling loudly*). Billie!

BILLIE'S VOICE. What?

BROCK. Come on down here a minute. (*To* PAUL.) She's a hell of a good kid. You'll like her.

(BILLIE *comes out onto the landing, brushing her hair. She is wearing a negligee that does all the proper things.* PAUL *rises.*)

BILLIE (*as she sees* PAUL). I'm not dressed.

BROCK. It's all right. It's all right. He's a friend of the family. (BILLIE *hesitates*). Come on, I'm tellin' you! (BILLIE *comes down into the room.*) Honey, this is Paul Verrall!

BILLIE. Yes, I know.

BROCK. He wants to talk to you.

BILLIE. What about?

BROCK. You'll find out. Sit down. (BILLIE *sits.*) Come on up a minute, willya, Ed?

DEVERY. Sure.

BROCK. Bring the stuff.

(DEVERY *picks up his brief case and follows* BROCK *out of the room. There is a pause when they have gone. Finally, Paul smiles at* BILLIE. *No response. He stops smiling.*)

PAUL. Your—friend, Mr. Brock, has an idea he'd like us to spend a little time together. You and me, that is.

BILLIE. You don't say.

PAUL. Yes.

BILLIE. What are you? Some kind of gigolo?

PAUL. Not exactly.

BILLIE. What's the idea?

PAUL. Nothing special. (*He sits on the sofa, some distance from* BILLIE.) He just wants me to put you wise to a few things. Show you the ropes. Answer any questions.

BILLIE. I got no questions.

PAUL. I'll give you some.

BILLIE. Thanks.

PAUL. Might be fun for you, in a way. There's a lot to see down here. I'd be glad to show you around.

BILLIE. You know this Supreme Court?

PAUL. Yes.

BILLIE. I'd like to take that in.

PAUL. Sure. We're on, then?

BILLIE. How do you mean?

PAUL. The arrangement.

BILLIE. I don't mind. I got nothin' much to do.

PAUL. Good.

BILLIE. What's he payin' you?

PAUL. Two hundred.

BILLIE. You're a sucker. You could of got more. He's got plenty.

PAUL. I'd have done it for nothing. (BILLIE *looks at him with rare disbelief and gives a mirthless little laugh.*) I would.

BILLIE. Why?

PAUL. This isn't work. I like it.

(BILLIE *smiles.*)

BILLIE. He thinks I'm too stupid, huh?

PAUL. Why, no—

BILLIE. He's right. I'm stupid and I like it.

PAUL. You do?

BILLIE. Sure. I'm happy. I got everything I want. Two mink coats. Everything. If there's somethin' I want, I ask. And if he don't come across—I don't come across. (*This candor has* PAUL *off balance.*) If you know what I mean.

PAUL (*with a gulp*). Yes, I do.

BILLIE. So as long as I know how to get what I want, that's all I want to know.

PAUL. As long as you know what you want.

BILLIE. Sure. What?

PAUL. As long as you know what you want.

BILLIE. You tryin' to mix me up?

PAUL. No.

(*A pause.*)

BILLIE. I'll tell you what I *would* like.

PAUL. Yes?

BILLIE. I'd like to learn how to talk good.

PAUL. All right.

BILLIE. Is it hard to learn?

PAUL. I don't think so.

BILLIE. What do I have to do?

PAUL. Well, I might give you a few books to start with. Then, if you don't mind, I'll correct you now and then.

BILLIE. Go ahead.

PAUL. When *I* know, that is. I don't—talk so good myself.

BILLIE. You'll do.

PAUL. Fine.

BILLIE. I never say "ain't." Did you notice that? Never.

PAUL. I do.

BILLIE. Well, I'll correct *you* then.

PAUL. Do that.

BILLIE. Since I was very small, I never say it. We had this teacher. She used to slug you if you did it.

PAUL. Did what?

BILLIE. Said ain't.

PAUL. Oh.

BILLIE. So I got out of the habit.

PAUL. I wonder if it was worth the slugging.

BILLIE. Well, not hard.

PAUL. It's the principle of the thing. There's too much slugging. I don't believe in it.

BILLIE. All right, I don't believe in it either.

PAUL. Good.

BILLIE. I learn pretty fast, don't I?

PAUL (*smiling*). You're great, Miss Dawn.

BILLIE. Billie.

PAUL. Billie. (*A tiny pause.*) Sort of an odd name, isn't it?

BILLIE. What are you talkin'? Half the kids I know are named it. Anyway, it's not my real name.

PAUL. What is?

(*She has to think a moment before she can answer.*)

BILLIE. My God! Emma.

PAUL. What's the matter?

BILLIE. Do I look to you like an Emma?

PAUL. No. You don't look like a Billie, either.

BILLIE. So what do I look like?

PAUL. To me?

BILLIE. Yuh, to you.

PAUL. You look like a little angel.

(*A pause.*)

BILLIE. Lemme ask you. Are you one these talkers, or would you be interes in a little action?

PAUL (*stunned*). Huh?

BILLIE. I got a yen for you right off.

PAUL. Do you get many?

BILLIE. Now and then.

PAUL. What do you do about them?

BILLIE. Stick around. You'll find out.

PAUL. All right, I will.

BILLIE. And if you want a tip, I'll tell you. Sweet-talk me. I like it. Like that angel line. (PAUL *looks upstairs with a frown.*) Don't worry about him. He don't see a thing. He's too dizzy from being a big man.

PAUL (*rising and moving away*). This is going to be a little different than I thought.

BILLIE. You mind?

PAUL. No.

BILLIE. It's only fair. We'll educate each other.

PAUL (*in a weak attempt to get on safer ground*). Now, about those books.

BILLIE. Yes?

PAUL. I'll get them for you tomorrow. I'll look around my place, too. If there's anything interesting, I'll drop it by later.

BILLIE. All right.

PAUL. We can figure out time every day the day before.

(BILLIE *beckons.* PAUL *comes to her. She reaches up, takes his lapel, and brings his ear close.*)

BILLIE. Or the night.

PAUL (*straightening*). Sure.

(BROCK *and* DEVERY *come down.* BROCK *now wears a silk lounging jacket.*)

BROCK. Well! You two gonna get together?

PAUL. I think we're all set.

BROCK. Great, great!

(DEVERY *picks up his hat.*)

PAUL. Well, if you'll excuse me—

BROCK. Have a drink.

PAUL. No, thanks.

DEVERY. See you tomorrow, Harry.

BROCK. Right.

DEVERY. Good night, Billie.

BILLIE. So long.

(DEVERY *leaves.*)

PAUL (*to* BILLIE). Good night.

BILLIE. Good night.

BROCK (*taking* PAUL *to the door*). So long, kid. Appreciate it.

PAUL (*with a look at* BILLIE). So do I.

(*He leaves.* BROCK, *beaming satisfaction, comes back into the room. He stops, looks at* BILLIE, *and takes a deck of cards out of his pocket. He moves over to the table and starts to shuffle the cards.* BILLIE *falls automatically into this nightly routine. She brings a box of cigarettes to the table. They cut the cards. He wins. He sits down and begins to deal.* BILLIE *mixes two drinks and brings them to the table. She sits down, takes up her hand, and arranges her cards with flourish. The game begins. They play swiftly, professionally, with no sense of enjoyment. She takes three of his discards in quick succession. He grows tenser and tenser.*)

BILLIE (*laying down her hand*). Gin.

BROCK. Forty-one.

(BILLIE *shoves the cards to him and picks up the score pad.*)

BILLIE. Forty-one?

BROCK. Forty-one.

(*She marks the score, after computing it by drumming her fingers on her temple. He shuffles, cuts, and hands her the pack. She deals. They pick up their cards and play again.*)

BROCK. If you pay attention, that Verrall guy can do you some good.

BILLIE. All right.

BROCK. You're in the Big League now. I want you to watch your step.

BILLIE. All right.

BROCK. You got to learn to fit in. If not, I can't have you around, and that's no bull. (*A pause, as they play.*) You got to be careful what you do. (*He draws a card, looks at it, discards it.*) And—what you say. (*She picks it up and lays down her hand.*)

BILLIE. Three!

BROCK. Twenty-eight.

BILLIE. Twenty-eight?

BROCK. Twenty-eight.

(She scores. He shuffles, cuts. She deals. They play again.)

BILLIE. You could use a little education yourself, if you ask me.

BROCK. Who asked you?

BILLIE. Nobody.

BROCK. So shut up.

BILLIE. Can't I talk?

BROCK. Play your cards.

(A pause.)

BILLIE *(mumbling).* It's a free country.

BROCK. That's what *you* think. *(They play.* BILLIE *starts to hum "Anything Goes."* BROCK's *nerves are further shaken.)* Do you mind?!!

BILLIE *(laying down her hand).* Gin.

BROCK. Thirty-four.

BILLIE. Thirty-four?

BROCK. Thirty-four.

(He shuffles the cards as she scores.)

BILLIE. Schneider.

BROCK. Where do you get the schneid?

*(*BILLIE *hands him the score.)*

BILLIE. Fifty-five dollars. And sixty cents.

BROCK. All right, that's all!

*(*BROCK *throws down the cards and rises. He crosses and pours a drink.)*

BILLIE. Pay me now.

BROCK *(yelling).* What the hell's the matter? Don't you trust me?

BILLIE. What are you hollerin' for? You always make *me* pay.

BROCK. Christ's sake!

BILLIE *(taunting him).* Sore loser.

BROCK. Shut up!

BILLIE. Fifty-five dollars. And sixty cents.

(He brings a large roll of bills from his pocket, peels off a few, and puts them on the table. BILLIE *looks at him, hard, until he provides the sixty cents.)*

BILLIE. Thanks.

*(*BROCK *starts for the staircase.)*

BROCK. Come on up.

BILLIE. In a minute.

BROCK. Now.

BILLIE. In a minute, I told you.

(This is the one moment of the day of which BILLIE *is boss.* BROCK *goes up quietly and shuts the door.* BILLIE *lays out a hand of solitaire. As she plays, she sings, softly, and interpolates little orchestral figures.)*

"In olden days a glimpse of stocking
Was looked on as something shocking,
But now Lord knows (tyah dah)
Anything goes. (tata tata—tata tata—tzing!)

Good authors, too, who once—"

(The door buzzer. She stops singing, throws a look up the stairs, makes a few personal adjustments, and goes to the door. PAUL *enters, carrying a few books and two newspapers.)*

PAUL. Hello.

BILLIE. Hello.

PAUL. Morning papers.

*(*BILLIE *takes them.)*

BILLIE. You could of saved yourself the trouble. I don't read papers.

PAUL. Never?

BILLIE. Once in a while the back part.

PAUL. I think you should. The front part.

BILLIE. Why?

PAUL. It's interesting.

BILLIE. Not to me.

PAUL. How do you know if you never read it?

BILLIE. Look, if you're gonna turn out to be a pest, we could call the whole thing off right now.

PAUL. Sorry.

BILLIE. I look at the papers sometimes. I just never understand it. So what's the sense?

PAUL. Tell you what you do. You look through these. Anything you don't understand, make a mark. (*He hands her a red editing pencil.*) Then tomorrow, I'll explain whatever I can. All right?

BILLIE. All right.

PAUL (*handing her the books*). And I thought you might like these.

BILLIE. I'll try. (*She puts the books and papers on a near-by table.*)

PAUL. No, don't do that. Just start reading. If you don't like it, stop. Start something else.

BILLIE. There's only one thing. My eyesight isn't so hot.

PAUL. Well, why don't you wear glasses?

BILLIE. Glasses!

PAUL. Why not?

BILLIE. Because it's terrible.

(*They look at each other for a time. She notices his glasses, but can't think of anything to say that will soften her remark. She moves in closer to him. Then closer still. It looks as though they are about to dance. She leans toward him. Now they are touching.* PAUL *responds. He puts his arms about her and kisses her. A long, expert kiss. They come out of it.*)

BILLIE. Of course, they're not so bad **on** men.

PAUL (*softly*). Good night, Billie.

BILLIE. Good night.

(PAUL *leaves.* BILLIE *looks around for the light switch, finds it, and turns out the lights in the sitting room. The balcony, however, is still illuminated. She starts up the stairs, slowly, and begins singing again.*)

BILLIE. "Good authors, too, who once knew better words
Now only use four-letter words
Writing prose (tyah dah)—"

(*She stops, turns, and looks back at the books and papers, her new key to something or other. She moves back into the room, picks them up, and, clutching them tightly, starts up again, continuing the song.*)

"Writing prose (tyah dah)—"

(*She turns out the balcony light, sings the "tyah dah" at the door to* BROCK'S *room as two notes of derision, then goes into her room and slams the door as we hear her last triumphant.*)

"Anything goes—!"

                                        CURTAIN

ACT TWO

SCENE: *Two months or so have passed. The room looks lived in. A new piece of furniture has been added—a desk, which stands to one side. It is loaded with books, papers, magazines, and clippings. On the walls are some lovely framed reproductions of French and American moderns, and one or two small originals. In another part of the room stands a large globe-map. There is also a library dictionary on a stand near the desk. At the other side of the room, a Capehart. On the floor beside the instrument are stacks of record albums. In every part of the room, more books, magazines, pictures, and books. It is early evening and* BILLIE, *wearing lounging pajamas and eyeglasses, is sitting on the sofa, her legs stretched out before her, reading a newspaper. She makes a mark on the paper, then lifts it high to continue her reading. The front page of the paper is covered with red marks. It looks like a newspaper with the measles. She puts the paper down with a sign of fatigue and moves to the Capehart, stretching. She selects a few records, puts them on the machine, starts it, and goes back to the sofa. The room is soon filled with the soothing sounds of the Sibelius "Concerto in D Minor for Violin and Orchestra, op. 47." The door buzzer sounds.* EDDIE *comes through, still wearing his hat, and opens the door to admit* PAUL. BILLIE *looks around and smiles. She takes off her glasses, quickly.*

PAUL. How are you, Eddie?

EDDIE. Great.

BILLIE. Hello.

(EDDIE *goes.*)

PAUL. Hello, smarty-pants. *(He moves to her.)* How you coming?

BILLIE. Not so bad?

PAUL. Hm?

BILLIE. *-ly,* bad*ly.* Would you like some tea?

PAUL *(sitting down).* No, thanks. *(He indicates the music.)* Nice, that.

BILLIE. Sibelius, opp forty-seven. *(They listen for a moment.)* Guess who I just had for tea? To tea?

PAUL. Who?

BILLIE. Mrs. Hedges.

PAUL. Really? How was it?

BILLIE. Don't ask! You know, she's pretty stupid, too, but in a refined sort of way. Of course, we didn't have very much to talk about—so then she happened to notice my book laying there—

PAUL. Lying.

BILLIE. —my book lying there, and she said, "Oh, I've been meaning to read that again for years!"

PAUL. What was it?

BILLIE. *David Copperfield.*

PAUL. Oh, yes.

BILLIE. So then we got to talking about it and you want to know something?

PAUL. What?

BILLIE. She's never read it at all.

PAUL. How do you know?

BILLIE. I could tell from the way we were talking.

PAUL. Does that surprise you?

BILLIE. What, that she'd never read it?

PAUL. Yes.

BILLIE. No.

PAUL. Then what?

BILLIE. Well, why should she make out like she did? It's no crime if she didn't.

PAUL. Everybody does that, more or less.

BILLIE. Do you?

PAUL. Sometimes.

BILLIE. I don't.

PAUL. I know, Billie. You have the supreme virtue of honesty.

BILLIE. Thanks.

(A WAITER *comes in from the service wing, crosses to the coffee table, and picks up the tray. A letter lies under it.)*

BILLIE. I'm glad I got something after two months of this.

(The WAITER *starts out.)*

PAUL. You didn't get that from me, I'm afraid.

BILLIE. I'm not so sure.

PAUL *(prompting).* Thank you.

BILLIE. You're welcome.

PAUL *(indicating the waiter).* No.

BILLIE. Oh . . . *(She calls out to the* WAITER.*)* Thank you! *(The* WAITER *nods and leaves. She picks up the letter.)* I got this letter today. From my father.

PAUL. New York?

BILLIE. Yes. I can't get over it.

PAUL. Why?

BILLIE. Well, it's the first time he ever wrote me in about eight years. We had a fight, sort of. He didn't want me to go with Harry.

PAUL. What does he do?

BILLIE. My father?

PAUL. Yes.

BILLIE. Gas Company. He used to read meters, but in this letter he says how he can't get around so good any more so they gave him a different job. Elevator man. *(A pause, as she remembers back. The music is still playing.)* Goofy old guy. He used to take a little frying pan to work every morning, and a can of Sterno, and cook his own lunch. He said everybody should have a hot lunch. *(Another pause.)* I swear I don't know how he did it. There were four of us. Me and my three brothers, and he had to do everything. My mother died. I never knew her. He used to feed us and give us a bath and buy our clothes. Everything. That's why all my life I used to think how some day I'd like to pay him back. Funny how it worked out. One night, I brought home a hundred dollars and I gave it to him. You know what he did? He threw it in the toilet and pulled the chain. I thought he was going to hit me, sure, but he didn't. In his whole life, he never hit me once.

PAUL (*carefully*). How'd he happen to write you? I mean, after all this time.

BILLIE. Because I wrote *him*.

PAUL (*smiling*). Oh.

BILLIE. He says he's thought about me every day. God. I haven't thought about him, I bet, once even, in five years. That's nothing against him. I haven't thought of anything.

PAUL. Be nice to see him, maybe.

BILLIE. I guess so—but he said I should write him again and I should have a hot lunch every day and I should let him know how I am but that he didn't want to see me if I was still living the life of a concubine. I looked it up. . . . He always used to say: "Don't ever do nothin' you wouldn't want printed on the front page of the *New York Times*." (*A pause.*) Hey— I just realized. I've practically told you the whole story of my life by now, practically.

PAUL. I've enjoyed it very much.

BILLIE. How about the story of *your* life?

PAUL. Oh, no. It's too long—and mostly untrue. (BILLIE *takes the letter over to the desk and puts it in a drawer.*) What'd you do·this morning?

BILLIE (*brightening*). Oh, I went to the newsreel and then over to the National Gallery like you said.

PAUL. How was it?

BILLIE. Wonderful. Quiet and peaceful and so interesting and did you ever notice? It smells nice. (PAUL *smiles.*) It does.

PAUL. How long did you stay?

BILLIE. Oh—a couple hours. I'm going again.

PAUL. Good.

BILLIE. Only the next time I wish you could come along.

PAUL. All right.

BILLIE. Boy, there's sure some things *there* that could use some explaining. (*She moves toward* PAUL.) Oh, and you know what else I did today? I went down to Brentano's and I just walked around, like you said I should, and looked at all the different kinds of books, and then the ones I thought maybe I'd like to read I took.

PAUL. That's right.

BILLIE. Well, pretty soon I had a whole big pile, too big to carry even. So I stopped. And I thought, my God, it'll take me about a year to read this many. Then I looked around, and compared to all the books there, my little pile was like nothing. So then I realized that even if I read my eyes out till the day I die I couldn't even make a little dent in that one store. Next thing you know I bust out crying.

(*She sits down, dejected.*)

PAUL. Nobody reads everything.

BILLIE. They don't?

PAUL. Of course not.

BILLIE. I've sure been trying to.

PAUL (*rising and going to the desk*). I don't suppose you got a chance to read *my* piece? (*He holds up a copy of the* New Republic.)

BILLIE. What are you talking? Of course I read it. Twice. (*A pause.*)

PAUL. What'd you think?

BILLIE (*slowly*). Well, I think it's the best thing I ever read. I didn't understand one word.

PAUL. What didn't you understand?

BILLIE. None of it.

PAUL. Here. Show me what.

(BILLIE *puts on her eyeglasses and moves to join him at the desk.* PAUL *laughs.*)

BILLIE. What's so funny? That I'm blind, practically?

PAUL. Practically blind.

BILLIE. —practically blind?

PAUL. You're wonderful.

BILLIE. I'm sorry I look funny to you.

PAUL. You don't. They make you look lovelier than ever.

BILLIE. You sound like one of those ads for eyeglasses. (*She sits down at the desk and puts her attention on the article.* PAUL *points to it.*)

PAUL. What?

BILLIE. Well, like the name of it. "The Yellowing Democratic Manifesto."

PAUL. Simple.

BILLIE. To who? Whom.—Whom? Well, anyway, not to me.

PAUL. Well, look. You know what "yellowing" means?

BILLIE. Not this time.

PAUL. When a piece of paper gets old, what happens to it?

(BILLIE *thinks.*)

BILLIE. You throw it away.

PAUL. No, it turns yellow.

BILLIE. It does?

PAUL. Of course.

BILLIE. What do you know?

PAUL. Now, "democratic." You know what that means, don't you?

BILLIE (*nodding*). Not Republican.

PAUL. Well, not exactly. It just means pertaining to our form of government, which is a democracy.

(*There is a pause.*)

BILLIE (*understanding*). Oh. (*A sudden frown.*) What's "pertaining"?

PAUL (*with a gesture*). Has to do with.

BILLIE (*musing*). Pertaining. Nice word.

(*She makes a note of it.*)

PAUL. All right, now—"manifesto."

BILLIE. I don't know.

PAUL. Why didn't you look it up?

BILLIE. I did look it up. I still don't know.

PAUL. Well, look—when I say "manifesto," I mean the set of rules and ideals and— principles and hopes on which the United States is based.

BILLIE. And you think it's turning yellow.

PAUL. Well, yes. I think the original inspiration has been neglected, and forgotten.

BILLIE. And that's bad.

PAUL. And that's bad.

(*She thinks it over for a moment, hard. We seem to see it soaking in. She picks up the magazine.*)

BILLIE (*reading*). "Even a— (*She looks at* PAUL.) —cursory? (*He nods.*) —examination of contemporary society in terms of the Greek philosophy which defines the whole as a representation of its parts, sends one immediately to a consideration of the individual as a citizen and the citizen as an individual."

PAUL. Well—

BILLIE. I looked up every word!

PAUL. Well, listen—thousands of years ago, a Greek philosopher— (*He pauses to make sure she is following.*) —once said that the world could only be as good as the people who lived in it.

(*There is a pause as* BILLIE *thinks this over.*)

BILLIE. Makes sense.

PAUL. All right. So I said, you take one look at America today and right away you figure you better take a look at the people in it. One by one, sort of.

BILLIE. Yuh.

PAUL. That's all.

BILLIE (*pointing to the article*). That's this?

PAUL. Sure.

BILLIE. Well, why didn't you say so?

PAUL. Too fancy, huh? (*He moves to the other side of the room.*) You know, I think I'm going to do that piece again Plainer.

BILLIE. Oh, and you know that little thing you gave me about Napoleon?

PAUL. No, what?

BILLIE. By Robert G. Ingersoll?

PAUL. Oh, yes.

BILLIE. Well, I'm not sure if I get that either.

PAUL. No deep meaning there.

BILLIE. There must be. He says about how he goes and looks in Napoleon's tomb.

PAUL. Yuh.

BILLIE. And he thinks of Napoleon's whole sad life.

PAUL. Yuh.

BILLIE. And then in the end he says he himself would have rather been a happy farmer.

PAUL (quoting). "—and I said I would rather have been a French peasant and worn wooden shoes. I would rather have lived in a hut with a vine growing over the door, and the grapes growing purple in the kisses of the autumn sun. I would rather have been that poor peasant, with my loving wife by my side, knitting as the day died out of the sky—with my children upon my knees and their arms about me—I would rather have been that man and gone down to the tongueless silence of the dreamless dust, than to have been that imperial impersonation of force and murder, known as 'Napoleon the Great.'"

BILLIE (impressed). How can you remember all that stuff?

(The music, which has by now become part of the background, suddenly changes. A Debussy record comes to a close and a wild Benny Goodman side replaces it. PAUL is startled, so is BILLIE. Then BILLIE rushes over and turns it off.)

BILLIE. Once in a while. Just for a change.

(PAUL laughs.)

PAUL. Don't try so hard, Billie. Please. You miss the whole point.

BILLIE. Well, I like to like what's better to like.

PAUL. There's room for all sorts of things in you. The idea of learning is to be bigger, not smaller.

BILLIE. You think I'm getting bigger?

PAUL. Yes.

BILLIE. Glad to hear it. (She sits at the desk again.) So he would rather be a happy peasant than be Napoleon. So who wouldn't?

PAUL. So Harry wouldn't, for one.

BILLIE. What makes you think not?

PAUL. Ask him.

BILLIE. He probably never heard of Napoleon.

PAUL. What's worse, he probably never heard of a peasant.

BILLIE. Do you hate him like poison?

PAUL. Who, Harry?

BILLIE. Yuh.

PAUL. No.

BILLIE. But you don't like him.

PAUL (moving away). No.

BILLIE. On account of me and him?

PAUL. One reason. There are lots more.

BILLIE. What?

PAUL. Well, if you think about it, you'll see that Harry is a menace.

BILLIE. He's not so bad. I've seen worse.

PAUL. Has he ever done anything for anyone, except himself?

BILLIE. Me.

PAUL. What?

BILLIE. Well, I got two mink coats.

PAUL. That was a trade. You gave him something, too.

(There is an awkward pause before BILLIE replies, very quietly.)

BILLIE. Don't get dirty. You're supposed to be so wonderful, so don't get dirty.

PAUL. Has he ever thought about anybody but himself?

BILLIE. Who does?

PAUL (with increasing fervor and volume). Millions of people, Billie. The whole damned history of the world is the story of a struggle between the selfish and the unselfish!

BILLIE. I can hear you.

PAUL *(patiently)*. All the bad things in the world are bred by selfishness. Sometimes selfishness even gets to be a cause, an organized force, even a government. Then it's called Fascism. Can you understand that?

BILLIE. Sort of.

PAUL *(loudly)*. Well, think about it, Billie.

BILLIE *(softly)*. You're crazy about me, aren't you.

PAUL. Yes.

BILLIE. That's why you get so mad at Harry.

PAUL. Billie, listen, I hate his life, what he does, what he stands for. Not him. He just doesn't know any better.

BILLIE. I go for you, too.

PAUL. I'm glad, Billie.

BILLIE. That's why I started doing all this. I guess you know.

PAUL. No, I didn't.

BILLIE. A lot of good it did me. I never had this kind of trouble before, I can tell you.

PAUL. Trouble?

BILLIE. After that first night when I met you—I figured it was all going to work dandy. Then, when you wouldn't step across the line—I figured maybe the way to *you* was through your head.

PAUL *(very slowly)*. Well—no.

BILLIE. Anyway, it doesn't matter now—but I like you anyway. Too late for the rest.

PAUL. Why?

BILLIE. Why? Look, Paul, there's a certain time between a fellow and a girl when it either comes off or not and if it doesn't then, then it never does.

PAUL. Maybe we haven't got to our time yet.

BILLIE. I think we did. And you dropped the ball.

PAUL. Don't be so sure.

BILLIE. I know. I've had lots of fellas and I *haven't* had lots of fellas. If you know what I mean.

PAUL. Yes.

BILLIE *(moving away)*. But I sure never thought I'd go through a thing like this for anybody.

PAUL. Like what?

BILLIE. Like getting all mixed up in my head. Wondering and worrying and *thinking*—and stuff like that. And, I don't know if it's good to find out so much so quick. *(She sits on the sofa.)*

PAUL. What the hell, Billie. Nobody's *born* smart. You know what's the stupidest thing on earth? An infant.

BILLIE. What've you got against babies all of a sudden?

PAUL. Nothing. I've got nothing against a brain three weeks old and empty. But when it hangs around for thirty years without absorbing anything, I begin to think something's the matter with it.

BILLIE *(rising in fury)*. What makes you think I'm thirty?

PAUL. I didn't mean you, especially.

BILLIE. Yes, you did.

PAUL. I swear.

BILLIE. You certainly know how to get me sore.

PAUL. I'm sorry.

BILLIE. Thirty! Do I look thirty to you?

PAUL. No.

BILLIE. Then what'd you say it for?

PAUL. I don't know. *(A short pause.)* How old *are* you?

BILLIE. Twenty-nine.

(They look at each other. PAUL smiles. She responds. He comes over and kisses her, softly.)

PAUL. Don't stop. *(She kisses him.)* I meant don't stop studying.

BILLIE. Oh.

PAUL. Will you?

BILLIE. I don't know why it's so important to you.

PAUL. It's sort of a cause. I want everybody to be smart. As smart as they can be. A world full of ignorant people is too dangerous to live in.

BILLIE (*sitting again*). I know. That's why I wish I was doing better.

PAUL. You're doing wonderfully.

BILLIE. Yeah, but it's just no use. I bet most people would laugh at me if they knew what I was trying to do.

PAUL. I'm not laughing.

BILLIE. I am. I'm sort of laughing at myself. Who do I think I am anyway?

PAUL. What's the matter?

BILLIE. All them books!

PAUL (*coming to her*). It isn't only books, Billie. I've told you a hundred times.

BILLIE. It's mostly.

PAUL (*sitting beside her*). Not at all. Listen, who said this? "The proper study of Mankind is Man."

BILLIE. I don't know.

PAUL. You should.

BILLIE. Why?

PAUL. I've told you.

BILLIE. I forgot.

PAUL. Pope.

BILLIE. The Pope?

PAUL. No, not the Pope. Alexander Pope.

BILLIE. "The proper study of—

PAUL. —Mankind is Man."

BILLIE. —Mankind is Man." Of course, that means women, too.

PAUL. Yes.

BILLIE. Yes, I know.

PAUL. Don't worry about books so much.

BILLIE. I *been* studying different mankind lately. The ones you told me. Jane Addams last week, and this week Tom Paine. And then all by myself I got to thinking about Harry. He works so hard to get what he

wants, for instance, but he doesn't know what he wants.

PAUL. More of what he's got, probably.

BILLIE. Money.

PAUL. Money, more people to push around, money.

BILLIE. He's not so bad as you think he is.

PAUL. I know. He's got a brain of gold.

(*There is the sound of a key in the door. Brock comes in.*)

BROCK. Hello.

PAUL. Hello, Harry. We were just talking about you.

BROCK (*removing his hat and coat and putting them on a chair*). Yeah? Well, that ain't what I pay you for. She knows enough about me. Too much, in fact. Ed here?

BILLIE. No.

BROCK. God damn it! He's supposed to meet me. (*He sits down and removes his shoes.*)

PAUL (*to* BILLIE). What did you find out about Tom Paine?

BILLIE. Well, he was quite a fella.

PAUL. Where was he born? Do you remember?

BILLIE. London. Or England. Some place like that.

BROCK. What do you mean London or England? It's the same thing.

BILLIE. It is?

BROCK. London is *in* England. It's a city, London. England is a whole country.

BILLIE. I forgot.

BROCK (*to* PAUL). Honest to God, boy. You got some patience.

PAUL. Take it easy.

BROCK. How can anybody get so dumb?

PAUL. We can't all know everything, Harry.

BILLIE (*to* BROCK). Who's Tom Paine, for instance?

BROCK. What?

BILLIE. You heard me. Tom Paine.

BROCK. What the hell do I care who he is?

BILLIE. *I* know.

BROCK. So what? If I wanted to know who he is I'd know who he is. I just don't care. *(To* PAUL.*)* Go ahead. Don't let me butt in.

PAUL *(to* BILLIE*)*. Which of his books did you like best?

BILLIE. Well, I didn't read *by* him yet—only about him.

PAUL. Oh.

BILLIE. But I made a list of—

BROCK *(suddenly)*. Who's Rabbit Maranville?

BILLIE. Who?

BROCK. Rabbit Maranville.

BILLIE. I don't know any rabbits.

BROCK. Think you're so smart.

PAUL. Used to play shortstop for the Braves, didn't he?

BROCK *(to* PAUL*)*. What are you? Some kind of genius?

PAUL. No.

BROCK. I hire and fire geniuses every day.

PAUL. I'm sure you do. *(He turns to* BILLIE.*)* Where's that list?

BILLIE *(handing it over)*. Here.

PAUL *(studying it)*. Well, suppose you start with *The Age of Reason.*

BILLIE *(writing it down)*. The—Age—of—Reason.

PAUL. Then, next, you might—

BROCK. Who's Willie Hop?

PAUL *(turning slightly)*. National billiard champion. And I think it's pronounced —Hoppe.

BROCK. That's what I said. Anyway, I didn't ask you, I asked her.

PAUL. Sorry. *(He turns back to* BILLIE.*)* Where were we?

BILLIE. *Age of Reason.*

PAUL. All right, then try *The Rights of Man.*

BILLIE *(writing)*. The—Rights—of—Man.

PAUL. I think that'll give you a rough idea of what—

BROCK *(coming over to them)*. What's a peninsula?

BILLIE. Sshhh!!

BROCK. Don't give me that shush—! You think you know so much—what's a peninsula?

PAUL. It's a—

BROCK. Not you.

BILLIE *(with condescending superiority)*. It's that new medicine!

BROCK. It is not.

BILLIE. What then?

BROCK. It's a body of land surrounded on three sides by water.

BILLIE. So what's that to know?

BROCK. So what's this Sam Paine to know?

BILLIE. Some difference! Tom Paine—not Sam Paine—*Tom* Paine practically started this whole country.

BROCK. You mean he's dead?

BILLIE. Of course.

BROCK *(to* PAUL*)*. What the hell are you learnin' her about dead people? I just want her to know how to act with live people.

PAUL. Education is a difficult thing to control or to channel, Harry. One thing leads to another. It's a matter of awakening curiosity—stimulating imagination—developing a sense of independence.

BROCK *(cutting in)*. Work on her, not me.

PAUL. No extra charge.

BROCK. I don't need nothin' you can tell me.

PAUL. Oh, I'm sure we could tell each other lots of interesting things, Harry.

BROCK *(a warning tone)*. What the hell does that mean?

PAUL. Just trying to be friendly.

BROCK. Who asked you? You know, every time I see you I don't like you as much. For a chump who's got no place, you're pretty fresh. You better watch out—I got an eye on you.

PAUL. All right. Let's both watch out.

BROCK. You know, I could knock your block off, if I wanted.

PAUL. Yes, I know.

BROCK. All right, then—just go ahead and do what you're supposed to—and that's all.

PAUL. It's all right—we'll stop for now.

BROCK. No, go ahead. I want to see how you do it.

PAUL. Not just now, if you don't mind— I've got to go lie down. You don't realize how hard I work.

BILLIE. Ha ha. Some joke.

BROCK (*petulant*). Two hundred bucks a week and I can't even watch!

PAUL (*to* BILLIE). See you later.

BILLIE. Goodbye, Paul. Thanks.

PAUL. Not a bit.

(*He leaves.*)

BROCK. London or England. Honest to God.

(*He opens an envelope on the desk and studies its contents throughout the following, without once looking at* BILLIE.)

BILLIE. Harry.

BROCK. Yeah?

BILLIE. What's this business we're in down here? Could you tell me?

BROCK. What do you mean—*we?*

BILLIE. Well, I figure I'm sort of a partner, in a way.

BROCK. A silent partner.

BILLIE. So?

BROCK. So shut up.

BILLIE. I got a right to know.

BROCK. You got a right to get the hell out of my hair. Just put your nose in your book and keep it.

BILLIE. I don't want to do anything if it's against the law. That's one sure thing.

BROCK. You'll do what I tell you.

BILLIE. I think I know what it is—only I'm not sure.

BROCK. You should worry. You're doin' all right. Somethin' you want you ain't got maybe?

BILLIE. Yuh.

BROCK. What?

BILLIE. I want to be like the happy peasant.

BROCK. I'll buy it for you.

(HELEN *enters from the service wing, carrying a book.*)

BROCK. *Now* will you stop crabbing?

(Helen *puts the book on one of the shelves.*)

HELEN. Well, I finished finally. Thanks loads for the loan of it.

BILLIE. How'd you like it?

HELEN. Pretty punk.

BILLIE. Really, Helen? I enjoyed it.

HELEN. Not me. I don't go for these stories where it shows how miserable it is to be rich.

BILLIE. Well, it can be.

BROCK. All—right—can the coffee klotch. (*To* HELEN.) Knock off.

HELEN. Sorry, Mr. Brock. (*She leaves, quickly, with a little see-you-later wave to* BILLIE.)

BROCK. Don't get so pally with everybody.

BILLIE. Paul says it's all right.

BROCK. Never mind Paul says. I don't like it.

BILLIE. You know what you are?

BROCK. What?

BILLIE. Uh—

(*She can't think of it, so she goes to the large dictionary and starts looking for the word. The door buzzer sounds.* EDDIE *comes in to open the front door.* BILLIE *finds what she has been looking for. She looks up from the dictionary.*)

BILLIE. Antisocial!

BROCK. You're God damn right I am!

(EDDIE *opens the door to admit* DEVERY *and* SENATOR HEDGES.)

DEVERY. Good evening.

BROCK. Where the hell have you guys been? You know what time it is?

DEVERY. Sorry.

BROCK. You're always sorry.

HEDGES. My fault. *(To* BILLIE*).* Good evening.

BILLIE. Good evening. Won't you sit down?

HEDGES. Thank you.

DEVERY. How are you, Billie?

BILLIE. Superb. New word.

BROCK. All right—all right. What happened?

(An awkward pause. DEVERY *and* HEDGES *exchange a look and silently gird their loins.)*

HEDGES *(softly).* It's just this, Harry. I'm afraid it's going to take a little more time and— *(He pauses.)*

DEVERY *(picking it up).* —and a little more money.

BROCK *(angry).* Why?

DEVERY. Well, for one thing, the whole amendment has to be re-drafted.

BROCK. I don't want no re-drafted and I don't want to wait.

HEDGES. I'm afraid you'll have to.

BROCK. Don't tell me what I have to!

HEDGES. If you'd let me—

BROCK. Listen, I don't like you. You're makin' me feel like some sucker.

DEVERY. I'm sure Norval's doing his best.

BROCK. Well, his best ain't good enough.

DEVERY. Don't be unreasonable, Harry. There are ninety-six votes up there. Norval's just one guy.

BROCK. He's the wrong guy. What the hell? We've handled it before.

HEDGES. Things aren't the same.

BROCK. We'll make 'em the same. That's your job, ain't it?

DEVERY. Pretty tough assignment.

BROCK. What do I care? *(To* HEDGES.*)* And you. You better get movin' or I'll butcher you—you'll wind up a God damn YMCA secretary again before you know it.

DEVERY. Harry—

BROCK. I'm gonna get it fixed so I can do business where I want and how I want and as big as I want. If you ain't with me, you're against me.

HEDGES. I'm with you.

BROCK *(starting up the stairs).* All right, then, you'll have to pull your weight in the God damn boat or I'll get somebody who can. You understand me?

(He slams out. There is an awkward pause.)

HEDGES. He has quite a temper, hasn't he?

DEVERY. Don't mind him, he's always lived at the top of his voice. *(Pouring a drink.)* Anybody with me? Norval?

HEDGES. No, thank you.

BILLIE *(to* HEDGES*).* I don't think Harry should talk to you like that. After all, you're a Senator.

HEDGES. Oh, well.

BILLIE. I don't think anybody should talk to a Senator like that or be able to. A Senator is a wonderful thing.

HEDGES. Thank you.

BILLIE. The way it looks to me—if he pushes you around, it's like he's pushing a few million people around.

HEDGES. How do you mean?

BILLIE. The people who picked you.

HEDGES. Well, not quite that many.

BILLIE. How many then?

HEDGES. Eight hundred and six thousand, four hundred and thirty-four.

BILLIE. Well, *that's* quite a few to push around.

HEDGES. *You're* not one of my constituents by any chance, are you?

BILLIE *(after thinking a moment).* I don't think I know that one.

DEVERY. The Senator means are you one of the people who voted for him?

BILLIE. I never voted for anybody.

HEDGES *(smiling).* Why not?

BILLIE. I don't know. I guess I wouldn't know how.

DEVERY. Very simple. You just press a button.

BILLIE. Yuh, but which one? Like suppose it's between different people?

DEVERY (smiling). Well, you listen to the speeches—you read the papers—you make up your own mind. You take a look and see who's for who—that's *very* important. Once you take a stand on something— take a look and see who's on the other side and who's on your side.

HEDGES (lightly). That's all there is to it.

BILLIE (to HEDGES). Well, why do you take it from Harry? That's what I want to know. You're more important than him. You're a Senator.

HEDGES. Yes, and as such, you see—I have a great many duties and responsibilities—

BILLIE. Yuh?

HEDGES (stalling). The operation of government is very complex.

BILLIE. Why should it be? I understand it pretty good in the books and when Paul tells me—but then when I see a thing like this—it's like different.

HEDGES. How?

BILLIE. Well, when it comes down to what should be the laws and what shouldn't— is Harry more important than anybody else?

HEDGES (meaning yes). No.

BILLIE. Then how come he's got so much to say? After all, nobody ever voted for *him.*

HEDGES (rising and starting out). Well, we'll have a nice long talk about it some-time.

BILLIE. All right.

HEDGES. Goodbye.

BILLIE. Goodbye.

(DEVERY takes HEDGES up to the door.)

HEDGES. Quite a little girl.

DEVERY. Oh, yes.

HEDGES. Goodbye.

DEVERY. Goodbye.

(HEDGES leaves. DEVERY goes quietly to his brief case and takes out a sheaf of papers.)

DEVERY (to BILLIE). Few things here for you.

(He spreads the papers out for signing. BILLIE comes over. She picks up her glasses. He hands her his fountain pen, then goes over and pours another drink. BILLIE puts on her glasses and stands looking at the papers. She starts to read the top one. A moment later, DEVERY turns back into the room. He looks at BILLIE in amazement, then takes a step or two into the room.)

BILLIE. What is this?

DEVERY. Same old stuff.

BILLIE. What?

DEVERY. Take too long to explain.

BILLIE. No it wouldn't. I like having things explained to me. I found that out.

DEVERY. Some other time.

BILLIE. Now.

DEVERY. You want me to tell Harry?

BILLIE. Tell him what?

DEVERY. That you won't sign this stuff?

BILLIE. Who said anything about that? I just want to know what it is.

DEVERY. A merger.

BILLIE. What's that?

DEVERY. Several companies being formed into one.

BILLIE. All Harry's?

DEVERY. No.

BILLIE. Whose then?

DEVERY. A few of Harry's and some others. French, Italian, and so on.

BILLIE (with the shock of recognition). A cartel!

DEVERY. What are you talking about?

BILLIE. About cartels. If that's what this is, then I'm against it. Paul explained me the whole thing.

(DEVERY is dumbfounded.)

DEVERY. It's perfectly all right. Don't worry.

BILLIE. You sure?

DEVERY. Ask Harry.

BILLIE. All right.

DEVERY. He won't like it.

BILLIE. Why not?

DEVERY. He just won't, that's all. He doesn't like people butting in.

BILLIE. I'm not people.

DEVERY. Listen to me, Billie. Be smart.

BILLIE. How can I be smart if nobody ever tells me anything?

DEVERY. I'm telling you something.

BILLIE. What?

DEVERY. Sign the stuff and don't start up with him.

BILLIE. Tomorrow.

DEVERY. Why tomorrow?

BILLIE. I want to look them over, so I'll know what I'm doing.

DEVERY *(losing his temper)*. It's all right!

BILLIE. Must be something fishy. If not, you'd tell me.

DEVERY. Take my word for it.

BILLIE. No.

(DEVERY tries hard to think of another approach.)

BILLIE. I know what you feel bad about. You don't like to be doing all his dirty work—because you know you're better than him.

DEVERY *(white)*. That's enough.

BILLIE. But I'm not so sure—maybe you're worse!

(DEVERY looks at her for a moment, then rushes up the stairs in angry determination. BILLIE picks up the papers, also a small dictionary, brings them to the sofa, and sits down to read. Now BROCK appears on the balcony. He comes down into the room, slowly. Too slowly. BILLIE looks up, once, and continues what she is doing. BROCK crosses the room. She senses his silent fury as he passes behind her. He goes to where the liquor is, directly behind BILLIE, and takes a drink. Then he moves into the room and sits down, facing her. He watches her, quietly. BILLIE looks up at him for a moment, but says nothing. She is frightened. BROCK gives no sign of anger or violence. He just looks at her. Finally, he breaks the silence.)

BROCK. Interesting?

BILLIE *(without looking up)*. Not very.

BROCK. I suppose you're used to reading more high-toned stuff.

BILLIE. Yes, I am.

(There is another long pause.)

BROCK. What's the matter, kid?

BILLIE. Nothing.

BROCK. All of a sudden.

BILLIE. I don't like that Ed.

BROCK. Why, what'd he do to you?

BILLIE. He didn't do nothing, *anything*, to me. It's what he's done to himself.

BROCK. Done what?

BILLIE. He used to be Assistant Attorney General of the United States.

BROCK. Who?

BILLIE. Ed.

BROCK. So what's wrong with that?

BILLIE. Nothing's wrong. Just look at him now.

(BROCK frowns, trying hard to follow.)

BILLIE. Did you know he once wrote a book? *The Roots of Freedom.* That was the name of it. I read it. It was wonderful.

BROCK. Where'd you get all this?

BILLIE. I looked it up.

BROCK. Why?

BILLIE. No reason. I was just in the library. And look at him now. He hangs around and helps you promote and lets you walk all over him just because you pay for it.

BROCK. Oh, so we finally got around to me.

BILLIE. Yuh. I'm not so sure I like you either. You're selfish, that's your trouble.

BROCK. Since when is all this?

BILLIE. Since now.

BROCK. You don't say.

BILLIE. I used to think you were a big man, Harry. Now I'm beginning to see you're not. All through history there's been bigger men than you and better. Now, too.

BROCK. Who, for instance?

BILLIE. Thousands.

BROCK. Name one.

BILLIE. My father.

BROCK (*contemptuously*). Twenty-five a week.

BILLIE. "—a brain of gold."

BROCK (*confused*). What?

BILLIE. Never mind.

(BROCK *rises, moves across the room, and sits beside her.*)

BROCK. Listen, cutie, don't get nervous just because you read a book. You're as dumb as you ever were.

BILLIE. You think so?

BROCK. Sure, but I don't mind. You know why? (*He makes a rude pass.*) Because you've got the best little—

BILLIE (*rising and moving away swiftly*). Leave me alone, Harry.

BROCK. Come here.

BILLIE. No.

BROCK. I never seen you like this.

BILLIE. I never been like this. I feel like I want to go away someplace.

BROCK. Where?

BILLIE. I don't know.

BROCK. I may wind up here in a few weeks. We'll go to Florida maybe.

BILLIE. I mean alone.

BROCK. You know what I think? I think you've gone nuts.

BILLIE. Maybe.

BROCK. Calm down.

BILLIE. I can't.

BROCK. Why not?

BILLIE. I don't know. I just know I hate my life. There's a better kind, I know it. If you read some of these books, you'd know it, too. Maybe it's right what you say, I'm still dumb, but I know one thing I never knew before. There's a better kind of life than the one I got. Or you.

BROCK (*as he gets up and moves to her*). I suppose you figure you'da been better off with that lousy saxophone player.

BILLIE. At least he was honest.

BROCK. He was a dime-a-dozen chump.

BILLIE. He worked for a living, that's one thing—

BROCK. I work. I been workin' since I was twelve years old—nobody ever give me nothin'.

BILLIE. If a man goes and robs a house—that's work, too.

BROCK. In my whole life—

(HELEN, *carrying towels, enters from the service wing and goes upstairs.* BROCK *holds it until she is out of sight.*)

BROCK. —in my whole life I never robbed a house. What the hell are you talkin' about?

BILLIE. You can hardly understand anything, can you?

BROCK. Get off that high horse—you dumb little pot!

BILLIE. You— (*She tries hard to think of something worse.*) —menace!

BROCK. I picked you up out of the gutter and I can throw you back there, too. Why, you never had a decent meal before you met me.

BILLIE. Yeah, but I had to have 'em with you. You eat terrible. You got no manners. Takin' your shoes off all the time—that's another thing . . . and pickin' your teeth. You're just not couth!

(HELEN *comes down the stairs and goes out through the service entrance.*)

BROCK (*shouting*). I'm as couth as you are!

BILLIE (*with considerable disgust*). And that cheap perfume you put on yourself.

BROCK. Cheap? I don't own nothin' cheap. Except you.

BILLIE (*very quietly*). You don't own me. Nobody can own anybody. There's a law says.

BROCK. Don't tell me about the law. If I was scared of the law, I wouldn't be where I am.

BILLIE. Where are you?

BROCK. All right, you've talked enough. If you don't like it here, beat it. You'll be back.

(BILLIE *starts out of the room.*)

BROCK. Wait a minute. (*He gets the documents from the coffee table.*) First this.

BILLIE. Not now.

BROCK. Right now.

BILLIE. No. (*She starts up the stairs.*)

BROCK (*loudly*). Come here!

BILLIE. I'm not going to sign anything any more till I know what I'm signing. From now on.

BROCK. Do what I'm telling you!

(BILLIE *stands rigid and frightened.* BROCK *is suddenly in front of her. He raises his arm to strike her.*)

BILLIE (*cringing*). Harry, please! Don't!

(*Her last word is cut in two by a stinging slap. Then another. The seed of her rebellion is suddenly uprooted. She sags and sobs, defeated.* BROCK *propels her to the desk in a series of rough shoves. Still sobbing, she follows his directions and signs the documents, one by one. When she has finished,* BROCK *takes them up, folds them, and puts them into his pocket.* BILLIE's *head goes to her folded arms on the desk.* BROCK *crosses to the liquor and gets a drink.*)

BROCK. All right, now get the hell out of here.

BILLIE. What?

BROCK. Don't be bawlin' around here, that's what. I don't like it. I been treatin' you too good, that's the trouble. You don't appreciate it. Nothin'. I ain't gonna have nobody around here who don't know their place. So get the hell out of here. Go sit on a park bench someplace till you're ready to behave yourself. (BILLIE *is rigid with fright.*) Go on! (*She starts for the stairs.* BROCK *points to the front door.*) This way out.

BILLIE (*in a small voice*). I've got to put something on.

BROCK. Well, hurry up—I don't want you around here like this. You bother me.

(BILLIE *starts up the stairs. Halfway up, she stops and turns to* BROCK.)

BILLIE. Big Fascist!

BROCK. What?

(*She goes into her room quickly.* BROCK *turns and sees a pile of books before him. Instantly, he identifies them as the reason for his present despair. He pushes them to the floor, violently—he kicks them out of his way—he finds a strange release in this, so he picks up one of the books, and begins tearing out the pages. There is mingled fury, excitement, and satisfaction in his heart as he completes the destruction of the book. He starts on a second as* DEVERY *comes down.* BROCK *stops, as though discovered in an indecent act.*)

DEVERY. All set?

BROCK. Certainly all set. What'd you think —I'm gonna let a broad talk back?

DEVERY. Where is she?

BROCK. I told her to take a walk. If there's one thing I can't stand it's a crier.

DEVERY. What's she crying about?

BROCK. What do I know?

DEVERY. She's becoming a strange girl.

BROCK. She's all right. All this book stuff's got her nervous, that's all.

DEVERY (*softly*). "A little learning is a dangerous thing."

BROCK. What?

DEVERY (*sitting*). Nothing, Harry. Looks like your passion for educating her was a mistake.

BROCK. I didn't know it would turn out like this, did I?—Remind me to fire that four-eyed Verrall skunk.

DEVERY. Why blame him?

BROCK. He must have told her *too* much. (*A pause.*) You know what she called me before? A Fach-ist.

DEVERY (*almost smiling*). She did?

BROCK. What the hell's that? Some kinda European, ain't it? It don't make sense. I was born in Plainfield, New Jersey. She knows that.

(*He stares at the door of* BILLIE's *room moodily.*)

DEVERY. What's the matter, Harry?

BROCK. I love that broad. (*There is a pause.* BROCK *appears to be thinking. He looks up, in despair.*) Ed. You think we could maybe find somebody to make her dumb again?

(BILLIE *comes down, dressed for the street, and moves toward the front door.*)

BROCK (*without turning*). And don't be late if you don't want a bloody nose.

(BILLIE *stops and moves a step into the room.*)

BILLIE (*very, very gently*). Would you do me a favor, Harry?

BROCK (*mean*). What?

BILLIE. Drop dead?

(*She leaves quickly, before* BROCK *recovers.*)

CURTAIN

ACT THREE

SCENE: *Later that evening.* DEVERY, *coatless, is on the sofa working over a pile of documents. He is somewhat drunker than before.* BROCK, *in pajamas and dressing gown, is pacing the floor.*

BROCK. What time is it already?

DEVERY. One-thirty.

BROCK. I'll slug her senseless when she comes back.

DEVERY. *If.*

BROCK. Listen, I've had this with her before. She always winds up where I want her.

DEVERY. I hope so.

(*There is a pause.*)

BROCK. What time is it?

DEVERY. One-thirty.

BROCK. You said that before.

DEVERY. One-thirty-one.

BROCK. What time she go out?

DEVERY. I don't know. Five, six o'clock.

BROCK. Eight hours.

DEVERY. What?

BROCK. She's been gone eight hours.

DEVERY. Maybe she's seeing a double feature.

BROCK. Yeah. . . . *That* don't take eight hours! (*A pause.*) She coulda got into an accident.

DEVERY. You'd hear.

BROCK. She coulda got raped! (DEVERY *looks at him.*) It happens all the time.

DEVERY. Not to Billie. Maybe the other way around, but not to Billie.

BROCK. You'd think Eddie'd call up at least.

(*A pause.*)

DEVERY. Be damned inconvenient if he doesn't find her. I've got some more for her to sign. It can't wait.

(EDDIE *comes in.*)

EDDIE. She here?

BROCK. What do you mean, "she here"? *No!*

EDDIE. The guy downstairs said he seen her go out and then he seen her come in.

BROCK. He's blind. Go out and look some more.

EDDIE. I been all over town.

BROCK. Well, go over it again. (*There is the slightest possible hesitation from* EDDIE.) Do what I'm tellin' you!

EDDIE. Sure. (*He starts for his room.*) Just change my shoes. (*He goes out.*)

DEVERY. If I thought I could make those stairs I'd go lie down.

(*There is a tiny pause.*)

BROCK. I sure never thought she was gonna turn out like this.

DEVERY. Have you thought any more about that matter we discussed in connection with her?

BROCK. What connection?

DEVERY. Marrying her.

BROCK. Still harpin', huh?

DEVERY. Seems to have gone beyond the reasons of appearance, Harry. If she's going to be truculent, I'm thinking of your legal safety. On paper, she owns—

BROCK. I know what she owns.

DEVERY. You've got to do it, Harry.

(A long pause.)

BROCK *(softly).* They always hook you in the end, them broads. *(He pours a drink.)* It's crazy, you know it?

DEVERY. How?

BROCK. A whole trouble because a dame reads a book.

DEVERY. Just goes to show you.

BROCK. Yuh.

DEVERY. It's the new world, Harry—force and reason change places. Knowledge is power. You can lead a horse to water.

BROCK. What?

DEVERY. Honesty is the best policy. A stitch in time saves nine. *(He starts up the stairs and trips.)*

BROCK. I don't like the way things are going around here. You stewed all the time—the broad outa line—and that's some fine Senator you bought me.

DEVERY. I think he's cute.

BROCK. I could get me a better Senator out of Lindy's.

DEVERY. Best I could do.

BROCK. I'd like to trade him in, no kiddin'.

DEVERY. They're not all for sale, Harry. That's the trouble with this town—too many honest men in it.

(DEVERY goes off into BROCK's room. BROCK paces, lights a cigarette—then stops and stares at the books. He selects a particu- larly slender one and moves to the sofa. He reads. EDDIE comes through.)*

EDDIE. I'll take a look downstairs and see if she's—

(He stops abruptly at the unbelievable sight before his eyes. BROCK turns to see him gaping.)

BROCK. What's the matter?

EDDIE. Nuthin'.

BROCK. Didn't you ever see a person readin' a book, for Christ's sake?

EDDIE. Sure.

BROCK. All right then. Get the hell out of here!

EDDIE. Sure.

(He goes quietly. BROCK reads. Behind him the door opens noiselessly and BILLIE looks in. She closes the door. BROCK reads a bit longer, then gives up. He tears the book in two and throws it away. He goes upstairs and into his room, turning off the main light on his way. A moment later BILLIE comes in and looks around.

She goes up the stairs, stops at BROCK's door, and listens. Then she comes down to the door again and whispers to someone just outside.

PAUL joins her and closes the door. BILLIE moves to the desk and starts looking through the papers on it. She holds one out to PAUL. He examines it carefully, and nods. Quietly, systematically, they go through the desk. PAUL makes a pile of documents, letters, checkbooks, and papers. BILLIE crosses and picks up the material left by DEVERY. PAUL follows her and adds this to his.)

BILLIE *(in a whisper).* Okay?

PAUL. This ought to do it fine.

BILLIE. I probably won't see you again, Paul—

PAUL. What!

BILLIE. Ssshh!

PAUL *(whispering).* What?!

BILLIE. So I want to say goodbye and thank you for everything.

PAUL. Where are you going?

BILLIE. Just away from here, that's all I know.

PAUL. Where? You can tell *me*.

BILLIE. I don't know. I thought I might go see my father for a while.

PAUL. And have a hot lunch every day?

BILLIE. Yeah.

PAUL. I've got a better idea.

BILLIE. What?

PAUL. Let's get married.

BILLIE. You must be daffy.

PAUL. I love you, Billie.

BILLIE. You don't love me. You just love my brain.

PAUL. That, too.

BILLIE. What would the boss of the *New Republic* say?

PAUL. I don't know. Probably—congratulations.

BILLIE. I'll think it over, but I can tell you now the answer is no. And I wish you'd hurry up out of here. (PAUL *kisses her.*) What are you doing?

PAUL. Well, if you don't know, I must be doing it wrong. (*He kisses her again.*)

BILLIE (*sitting on the sofa*). What's more important right now—crabbing Harry's act—or romancing?

PAUL (*sitting next to her*). They're one and the same thing to me.

BILLIE. Honest, Paul—I wish you'd—

(*The door opens and* EDDIE *comes in. He switches on the lights. He stops on the landing, surprised.* PAUL *and* BILLIE *rise.*)

EDDIE. What's this? Night school? (*To* BILLIE.) Where were you anyway? I looked all over town.

BILLIE. I walked over to the White House and back.

EDDIE. How's everybody over there? (*To* PAUL.) You better knock off, brother.

PAUL. Why?

EDDIE. I'm supposed to tell him she's back. I don't think he'll like you horsin' around

with his girl in the middle of the night. He's funny that way.

PAUL. I'll take a chance.

BILLIE. You better go.

EDDIE. She's right. Take my advice.

PAUL. What's it to you?

EDDIE. Listen—noise I can stand, but blood makes me nervous. (*He goes upstairs and into* BROCK's *room.*)

BILLIE. Please, Paul.

PAUL. Sure you'll be all right?

BILLIE. Don't worry.

PAUL. Goodbye, Billie.

BILLIE. Goodbye.

(PAUL *goes.* BILLIE *picks up the phone.*)

BILLIE. Porter, please. (*She sorts out a few things on the desk.*) Hello, porter? This is 67D. Could you send somebody up for my bags? . . . No, right now . . . thank you.

(EDDIE *appears on the balcony, rubbing his stomach, and gasping softly.*)

BILLIE. What's the matter?

EDDIE. Right in the stomach he hit me.

BILLIE. Why didn't you hit him back?

EDDIE. What?

BILLIE. Why didn't you hit him back?

EDDIE. He's been sayin' you've gone nuts. I could believe it, you know it?

BILLIE. Would you do me a favor?

EDDIE. What?

BILLIE. Pack my things up there?

EDDIE. You scrammin' again?

BILLIE. For good.

EDDIE. I'll tell you the truth, I'm sorry. I think he's gonna be sorry, too.

BILLIE. He's going to be worse than sorry.

EDDIE. Where you goin'?

BILLIE. Never mind.

EDDIE. You sore at me, too?

BILLIE. In a way.

EDDIE. What'd *I* do? What'd I *do?*

BILLIE. It's a new thing with me, Eddie. I'm going to be sore at anybody who just takes it. From now on.

EDDIE. Listen, don't get me thinkin'. I got enough trouble now.

(He goes into BILLIE's *room.* BILLIE *begins to sort out her belongings, as* BROCK *appears.)*

BROCK. Fine time.

BILLIE *(gay)*. Hello, Harry.

BROCK *(coming down)*. Where you been?

BILLIE. I took a walk like you told me.

BROCK. That took you till now?

BILLIE. What's the matter, Harry? You miss me?

BROCK. I decided somethin' to tell you. Somethin' good. I don't like to wait when I get an idea.

BILLIE. Yuh, I know.

BROCK. Now I see you, I don't know if I should tell you it.

BILLIE. Why not?

BROCK. Runnin' out, talkin' fresh, slammin' doors. I knew you'd be back, though.

BILLIE. You did, huh?

BROCK. I told Ed, even. He was worried. Not me.

BILLIE. Not yet.

BROCK. What took you so long?

BILLIE. I had a lot to think.

BROCK. For instance?

BILLIE. Just where I stand around here.

BROCK. That's what I'm tryin' to tell you.

BILLIE. What?

BROCK. Where you stand.

BILLIE. Yuh.

BROCK. Well—first thing, that Verrall stuff is through. It gets in my way—and I don't like you upset so much. It's bad for you. And the next thing—we're gonna get married.

BILLIE. No.

BROCK. Only you got to behave yourself . . . No?! What do you mean, no?

BILLIE. I don't want to, that's what I mean. No. In fact, I've never been so insulted.

BROCK *(in a whisper)*. Well, that's the God damndest thing I ever heard.

BILLIE. Why?

BROCK. Who the hell are you to say no, if I tell you?

BILLIE. Don't knock yourself out, you've got a lot of surprises coming.

BROCK. Just tell me first.

BILLIE. What?

BROCK. How can *you* not want to marry *me?*

BILLIE. Well, you're too dumb—for one thing. I've got a different kind of life in mind, Harry. Entirely. I'm sorry, but you just wouldn't fit in.

BROCK. Listen, Billie, I don't understand what the hell's happenin'!

BILLIE. I do.

BROCK. What'd I do? What did I? All right, I talked rough to you once in a while. Maybe I hit you a couple of times. Easy. Is that a reason to treat me like this? I done good for you, too. Couldn't we straighten it out?

BILLIE. No.

BROCK. Why not?

BILLIE *(very simply)*. Well, all this stuff I've been reading—all that Paul's been telling me—it just mixed me up. But when you hit me before, it was like everything knocked itself together in my head—and made sense. All of a sudden I realized what it means. How some people are always giving it and some taking. And it's not fair. So I'm not going to let you any more. *Or anybody else.*

(She goes back to the desk.)

BROCK. Listen, kid. I got an idea. Come on upstairs and I'll calm you down. *(*BILLIE *continues her work.)* We used to have a pretty good time, remember? *(*BILLIE *slams a drawer.)* You want to come to Florida? I think you ought to marry me, don't you? *(He is suddenly off the handle.)* Listen, Billie. I want you to marry me. I don't want to argue about it. I've heard enough. Now you do what I'm tellin' you or you'll be damn good and sorry.

BILLIE. I'm not scared of you any more, Harry, that's another thing.

BROCK. You're not, huh?

(*He starts moving toward her, ominously, but stops as the door buzzer sounds. The door opens and two bellhops appear.*)

BILLIE. Come on in! Right up there.

BROCK. What the hell's this?

BILLIE. Oh, didn't I tell you? I'm leaving.

BROCK. What?

BILLIE. Yuh, for good.

BROCK (*to the bellhops*). Wait a second. (*They stop.*) Beat it. (*The bellhops hesitate.*) Hurry up! (*They hurry down and out.*)

BELLHOP (*at the door*). Thank you, sir.

BROCK (*to* BILLIE). Let's get organized around here! You can't just walk out, cutie. You're in too deep with me. I'm right in the middle of the biggest thing I ever done. Maybe I made a mistake hookin' you in with it—but you're in.

BILLIE. Well, I'm not going to be. I decided.

BROCK. All right, fine. You want to wash it up, we'll wash it up. I'm too important to monkey around with what you think. (*He shouts up.*) Ed! (*He looks through the papers on the desk.*) I'll fix it so you can be out of here in no time. You're spoiled. I spoiled you. You're no good to me no more. I was ready to make you a real partner. So you don't want it? So fine. See how you'll do without me. You don't look like you looked nine years ago. In fact, you look lousy, if you want the truth. I'm glad to get rid of you.

BILLIE. And as far as I'm concerned . . .

BROCK. Yeah?

BILLIE. *Visa versa!*

(DEVERY *comes down.*)

DEVERY (*to* BILLIE). You're back. (*To* BROCK.) All set?

BROCK. Shut up!

DEVERY. What's the matter?

BROCK (*rummaging through the desk*). She's off her nut. We're gonna settle everything up and get her the hell outa here.

DEVERY (*to* BILLIE). You sure you know what you're doing?

BILLIE. First time in my life I *do* know.

BROCK. What'd you do with that stuff you wanted her to . . . ?

DEVERY (*pointing to the sofa*). Right there.

BROCK. Where right there?

(DEVERY *moves to the desk. They begin looking, feverishly.*)

BILLIE (*nonchalantly*). With blue covers?

DEVERY. Yeah.

(*A pause.*)

BILLIE. Three copies?

BROCK. That's right.

(*Another pause.*)

BILLIE. I gave 'em to Paul.

(BROCK *and* DEVERY *freeze at the desk in odd positions.*)

BROCK. When?

BILLIE. Just now.

DEVERY. What for?

BILLIE. What do you think for? To put in the paper. I guess.

BROCK. There's some kinda jokes I don't like.

BILLIE. It's no joke. Paul says it's the worst swindle since—uh—the teapot. Something like that.

(DEVERY *and* BROCK *exchange a horrified look.*)

BILLIE. What are you getting so white about? You told me yourself it was perfectly all right.

BROCK. You double-crossing little—

BILLIE. I don't see it like that. If there's a fire and I call the engines—so who am I double-crossing—the fire?

DEVERY. I'd better get Norval.

BROCK. I know who to get. Eddie!!

DEVERY *(on the phone)*. Decatur 9124.

(EDDIE appears.)

BROCK. You know where Verrall's room is?

EDDIE. Sure.

BROCK. Tell him to get in here right away.

EDDIE. Right. *(He starts out.)*

BROCK. Wait a minute—tell him Billie wants him.

(EDDIE goes.)

DEVERY *(on the phone.)* Hello, Norval? Ed. Wake you? . . . Oh, good. I'm over here at Harry's. Can you drop by? Important. . . . No, it can't. . . . All right.

(He hangs up.)

BILLIE. Paul's got nothing to do with this. It was my own idea.

BROCK. I'll show you ideas.

BILLIE. If you think you can strong-arm him—you're wasting your time. For a fellow with eyeglasses, he's very stubborn.

DEVERY *(pouring a drink)*. Oh, dear.

BROCK *(to DEVERY)*. If you don't stop belly-achin', get the hell out of here!

DEVERY. We're in trouble, Harry.

BROCK. Is that gonna help?

DEVERY. No. *(He downs his drink.)*

BROCK. I'll trim this guy. Watch me.

DEVERY. All right.

BROCK. You get in a spot, you fold up. Remind me to have a heart-to-heart talk with you.

DEVERY. Be that as it may—if this stuff breaks—nobody'll play with us.

BROCK. So what's to do?

DEVERY. Might be best—under the circumstances—to forget the whole deal. Let him publish. If nothing happens, he looks silly.

BROCK. What do you mean if nothin' happens? I've spent two months down here and I don't know how much dough. I'm supposed to let all that ride?

DEVERY. If you want to play it safe.

BROCK. Well, I don't. I want what I'm after.

DEVERY. Going to be tough to get.

BROCK. Why? Because some little weasel with eyeglasses wants to get noisy? I'll cut his tongue out!

DEVERY. Listen, Harry!

BROCK. You're chicken!

DEVERY. You think so?

BROCK. I think so.

DEVERY. You're off the handle because it looks like I've been right and you've been wrong.

BROCK. Talk.

DEVERY. I've told you again and again. Get too big and you become a target. It's easier to steal diamonds than elephants.

BROCK. Shut up! I'll handle this.

DEVERY. All right.

BROCK. You brought this guy around in the first place. Remember that. *(DEVERY sighs.)* You're about as much help to me as a boil on the—

(EDDIE comes back with PAUL, who immediately senses the trap. BROCK crosses to him and speaks with quiet menace.)

BROCK. I think you got somethin' by mistake that belongs to me.

PAUL. That so?

BROCK. How about it?

(There is no answer. BROCK signals EDDIE, who grabs PAUL's arms. BROCK frisks him.)

BROCK. Sit down.

(PAUL sits beside BILLIE.)

PAUL. Hello.

BILLIE. How've you been?

PAUL. Fine, and you?

BILLIE. Fine.

BROCK *(to DEVERY)*. Get the stuff out of his room.

(DEVERY starts out.)

PAUL. Not there, Ed.

(DEVERY stops.)

BROCK. Where, then? (PAUL *looks at him and smiles.*) All right, if you want to play it rough. I know how to do that, too.

(BROCK *walks to the service wing and bolts the door. Then* EDDIE *moves to the front door and does the same.* BROCK's *determination and purpose strike a kind of terror in the room. He moves back to the sofa.*)

BROCK. Now you listen, you two heels. I mean business. I got too much at stake down here. You got somethin' that belongs to me. And if you wanna get out of here alive—you're gonna give it back. I'm no blowhard. (*To* BILLIE.) Tell him.

BILLIE. He's no blowhard. He's had people killed before. Like once, about six years ago, there was a strike at one of his—

BROCK. Shut up! You ain't gonna be tellin' nobody nothin' pretty soon.

BILLIE (*derisively*). Double negative. (*To* PAUL.) Right?

PAUL. Right.

BROCK. You don't seem to be gettin' the idea. You never been in trouble like you're gonna be if you don't do what I'm tellin' you.

DEVERY. Wait a minute, Harry. There's another way to handle this. (*To* PAUL.) I really think you've pulled a boner, Paul. My advice to you is to lay off.

PAUL. And my advice to you is to stop sticking your noses into my business.

BILLIE. Yuh!

BROCK. Look who's talkin' about stickin' noses. You're the God-damndest buttinski I ever run into!

PAUL. I think I told you once before, Harry, that's my job.

BROCK. What? Gettin' in my way?

PAUL. Not exactly.

BROCK. What then? I'd like to know. No kiddin'.

PAUL. To find out what goes on and get it to the people.

BROCK. What people?

PAUL. The people.

BROCK. Never heard of them.

BILLIE. You will, Harry, some day. They're getting to be more well-known all the time. (EDDIE *brings* BROCK *a drink.*)

DEVERY. What if I told you this whole operation is strictly according to law?

PAUL. Then I'd say the law needs revision.

BROCK. Who are you? The government?

PAUL. Of course.

BROCK. Since when?

BILLIE. Since—uh—1779! (*To* PAUL.) Right?

BROCK. What?

PAUL. Of course I'm the government. What do you think the government is, Harry? A man, a monster, a machine? It's you and me and a few million more. We've got to learn to look after each other.

BROCK. Thanks, I can look after myself.

BILLIE (*to* PAUL). He doesn't get it. I think it's because you still talk too fancy. (*To* BROCK.) Look, Harry, the idea is that you can only get away with your kind of shenanigans if nobody cares about it.

BROCK. I know what I'm doin'. I got my rights the same as anybody else.

BILLIE. More! You keep buying more and more rights for yourself.

BROCK. You got nothin' to say to me.

(*The door buzzer.* EDDIE *goes to the door, unlocks and opens it, and* SENATOR HEDGES *comes in. Then he locks it again.*)

HEDGES. Good evening, Eddie! (*Gay.*) Well, this is a late little party, isn't it?

BROCK. Shut up!.

HEDGES. What?

BROCK. Don't be so happy!

HEDGES. What's the trouble?

DEVERY. Well, Verrall here has—uh—stumbled on a whole pocketful of information. I don't know what he thinks it means.

PAUL. I'll tell you. Just that the connection between Harry's combine and the Senator's amendment is more than coincidence.

HEDGES. Now, just a moment, son. I've got nothing against you young radicals—used to be one myself—but you simply won't be practical. Now, what we're doing is common practice. Done every day. I don't know why you single us out to make a fuss about.

BROCK. Yeah, why?

PAUL. It's done every day, sir, right. I have no doubt that an undiscovered murder is committed every day. What does that prove? All this under-cover pressure—this bribery—and corruption—this government between friends—sure it goes on all the time and it's tough to crack. Ask me. I've tried for years. You need more than the knowing about it. You've got to have the facts and the figures and, most important —the names.

BILLIE. And he's got 'em.

HEDGES *(angry)*. You be careful, young man, when you use the word bribery in my presence.

BILLIE. Eighty thousand dollars you got. What word would you like him to use?

(HEDGES pales and looks helplessly over to BROCK.)

HEDGES. Harry, I honestly feel—

BROCK. What the hell do I care what you feel? I feel, too.

HEDGES. I can't take any smearing now. It's a bad time.

BROCK. Knock off. *(To PAUL.)* All right, now we've all had our little beat around the bush, let's get down to it. What can we work out?

PAUL. You just heard your lawyer say it was all according to law.

BROCK. Yeah.

PAUL. If that's the case, what's bothering you?

BROCK. I don't like a lot of noise, that's all.

PAUL. I'll be very quiet.

DEVERY. It just starts a lot of snooping, you know that. Gets to be uncomfortable.

BILLIE. Maybe if it gets to be uncomfortable enough, you'll cut it out.

(HEDGES sits down, miserable.)

BROCK. What'll you take, Paul?

PAUL. I'll take a drink, please, if I may.

BROCK. Don't be fancy with me. I never met a guy yet who didn't have his price.

PAUL *(pouring drink)*. I have.

BROCK *(to PAUL)*. I'm talkin' about big numbers.

BILLIE. You and your big numbers. If you don't watch out you'll be wearing one across your chest.

BROCK. I'll get to you later. *(To PAUL.)* Make up your mind. There's just two ways we can do business. One—you play ball— make it worth your while. Two—you better start watchin' your step: There'll be no place you can walk—no place you can live, if you monkey-wrench me! What do you say?

PAUL. I'd like to think it over!

BROCK. All right. You got two minutes.

(PAUL sits down and thinks. He looks at BILLIE. He smiles. She smiles. He looks at DEVERY. She looks at HEDGES. They both look at BROCK. Suddenly, PAUL rises.)

PAUL. Come on, Billie.

(BILLIE rises. PAUL is moving to the door. EDDIE seems about to intercept him. BROCK is moving toward him.)

DEVERY. Wait a minute, Harry!

HEDGES. Now, let's not lose our tempers.

(BROCK, in a sudden inhuman burst, swings PAUL around, grabs him by the throat, and begins to choke him. PAUL goes to his knees. BROCK hangs on.)

DEVERY *(in a panic)*. Stop it!

BILLIE. Harry!

HEDGES. Oh, my God!

(HEDGES, DEVERY, and EDDIE are desperately attempting to prevent murder. BILLIE rushes to the phone and screams.)

BILLIE. Operator! *Operator!!!*

(A signal from DEVERY, and EDDIE goes to BILLIE, removes the phone from her hands, and seats her. The combined forces of DEVERY and HEDGES now tear BROCK loose. They throw him on the sofa, where he sits, spent, and subdued. BILLIE is helping PAUL, who sits on the stairs, groggy.)

DEVERY *(to BROCK)*. You God-damned fool! Where the hell do you think you are?

Can't you see all this muscle stuff is a thing of the past? You cut it out, or you'll be a thing of the past, too.

BROCK. I got mad.

PAUL (*coming down to* BROCK). Who are *you* to get mad? You big baboon! You ought to be grateful you're allowed to walk around free.

BROCK (*in a warning tone*). You don't know me good enough for that kind of talk.

PAUL. I know you. I've seen your kind down here for years—with red hair and white hair and no hair—but you're always the same—you're usually right here in this room. What the hell do you guys want, anyway? You've *got* damn near all the oil and the lumber and the steel and coal and aluminum—what do you want now —all the people? All the laws?

BROCK (*rising*). Don't blow your top. I'm still ready to do business. How's a hundred grand?

PAUL. A hundred grand is beautiful—but I can't do it.

BROCK. Why not?

(*A pause.*)

PAUL. My wife wouldn't like it.

BILLIE (*softly*). She certainly wouldn't.

BROCK. All right, then, what's your idea?

PAUL. To try and stop you from buying and selling legislation as though it were junk.

BILLIE. "This country with its institutions belongs to the people who inhibit it."

PAUL. "Inhabit."

BILLIE. "Inhabit."

BROCK. What the hell are you two battin' about? I don't see what I'm doin' so wrong. This is America, ain't it? Where's all this free enterprise they're always talkin' about?

DEVERY (*toasting*). To free enterprise.

BROCK. You're just sore because I made good and you ain't. Everybody had the same chance as me—all them kids I used to know—so where are they now?

BILLIE. No place. Because you beat them out, like you said. You always want to hold everybody down so you can get it all for yourself. That's why there's people like my father—and like me. He couldn't give me what he wanted—so I wind up with an empty head and with you.

BROCK. I always did what I want and I'm always gonna.

BILLIE. Try it.

BROCK. Who's gonna stop me?

BILLIE. Us two.

BROCK. Youse two? Don't make me split a gut. Be some fine country where a hundred-and-a-quarter-a-week hick and a broad that ain't been off her end for ten years can stop *me*. (*He turns and crosses to* DEVERY, *in a fury*.) What the hell are you standin' around like a deaf-and-dumby? What do I pay you for? Go on, say somethin'!

DEVERY. All right. I'll say something.

BROCK. Well?

DEVERY. They're right.

BROCK. You think they can stop me? Stop a Senator? What the hell kind of a world is it if your money's no good? How can they lick me? *I* got all the money.

DEVERY. The Republicans had all the money, too. Remember?

(EDDIE *puts another drink into* BROCK'S *hand*.)

BROCK (*to* EDDIE). What the hell do *you* want?

EDDIE. Rye ginger ale.

BROCK. Who asked you? Knock off!

(EDDIE *retreats*.)

PAUL. Maybe another time, Harry, not now. And if you're going to try again—do it fast. It gets harder all the time—people get wiser—they hear more—they read more—they talk more. When enough of them know enough—that'll be the end of you.

BROCK. Don't worry about me.

PAUL. I do, though. I worry like hell. I stay up nights. When you live in Washington, it's enough to break your heart. You see a perfect piece of machinery—the demo-cratic structure—and somebody's always tampering with it and trying to make it hit the jackpot.

DEVERY *(toasting)*. To the jackpot.

BROCK. I'm no gambler. I'm a business man.

PAUL. You certainly are, but you're in the wrong business now.

BILLIE. When you steal from the govern-ment, you're stealing from yourself, you dumb ox.

PAUL. Sure, you nearsighted empire-build-ers have managed to *buy* little pieces of it once in a while—but you can't have it all —if you do, it won't be this country any more.

BROCK *(to DEVERY, softly)*. Of all the guys in this town—why the hell did you have to pick *him* out? *(To PAUL)*. Do what you want. I'm goin' ahead.

BILLIE. Wait a minute! I'll tell you where you're going.

BROCK. You?!

BILLIE. Sure. In this whole thing—I guess you forgot about me—about how I'm a partner? Ed once told me—a hundred and twenty-six different yards I own.

DEVERY. Control.

BILLIE *(to DEVERY)*. Same thing. *(To BROCK.)* So here's how it's going to be. I don't want them. I don't want anything of yours—or to do with you. So I'm going to sign them all back.

BROCK. All right!

BILLIE. Only not all at once—just one at a time—*one a year!* (BROCK *is stunned.)* Only you've got to behave yourself—be-cause if you don't, I'm going to let go on everything. For what you've done—even since I've known you only—I bet you could be put in jail for about nine hundred years. You'd be a pretty old man when you got out.

BROCK *(to DEVERY)*. What's goin' on around here?

DEVERY. A revolution.

BROCK. You got me into this—*get me out!*

DEVERY. Somehow, I don't feel as clever as I used to.

BILLIE. Come on, Paul. *(To BROCK.)* I'll send for my things.

BROCK. You little crumb—you'll be sorry for this day—wait and see. Go on—go with him—you ain't got a chance. If I ever seen anybody outsmart themself, it's you.

BILLIE *(starts to go)*. Goodbye, all.

BROCK *(to PAUL)*. And you!

PAUL. Me?

BROCK. Yeah—you're fired!

PAUL. I'm sorry, Harry. I've enjoyed work-ing for you very much indeed.

(BILLIE *is at the door*).

BILLIE *(to EDDIE)*. Open up!

EDDIE. All right, Harry?

BILLIE *(to EDDIE, in imitation of BROCK)*. Do what I'm tellin' you!

(EDDIE *opens the door quickly.* BILLIE *and* PAUL *go out, smiling.* DEVERY *pours himself a drink.)*

BROCK *(trying hard to laugh off his dis-aster)*. How do you like that? He coulda had a hundred grand—and she coulda had me. So they both wind up with nothin'. *(A pause.)* Dumb chump.

HEDGES. Yes.

BROCK. Crazy broad.

HEDGES. Quite right.

DEVERY *(toasting, his glass held high)*. To all the dumb chumps and all the crazy broads, past, present, and future—who thirst for knowledge—and search for truth—who fight for justice—and civilize each other—and make it so tough for sons-of-bitches like you— *(To HEDGES.)* —and you— *(To BROCK.)* —and me. *(He drinks.)*

CURTAIN

Medea

Freely Adapted from the "Medea" of Euripides

BY ROBINSON JEFFERS

First presented by Robert Whitehead and Oliver Rea at the National Theatre in New York on October 20, 1947, with the following cast:

THE NURSE.....................................Florence Reed
THE TUTOR...................................Don McHenry
THE CHILDREN.................Gene Lee, Peter Moss
FIRST WOMAN OF CORINTH.........Grace Mills
SECOND WOMAN OF CORINTH..Kathryn Grill
THIRD WOMAN OF CORINTH....Leone Wilson
MEDEA ....Judith Anderson
CREON ....Albert Hecht

JASON ....John Gielgud
AEGEUS ....Hugh Franklin
JASON'S SLAVE............................Richard Hylton
ATTENDANTS TO MEDEA
  Martha Downes, Marian Seldes
SOLDIERS ....Ben Morse, Jon Dawson,
  Richard Boone, Dennis McCarthy

The entire action of the play occurs before Medea's house in Corinth.

OUR THEATRE is indebted to Judith Anderson not only for memorable performances, among which the one she gave in *Medea* is the most unforgettable, but for a large share in introducing Robinson Jeffers as a playwright. It was her West Coast performance as Clytemnestra in John Gassner's adaptation of *The Tower Beyond Tragedy* that first called Broadway's attention to the power of Jeffers' dramatic verse, although that power had been recognized in literary circles some fifteen years earlier. The John Gassner version had been made for the Theatre Guild in 1938 but had been shelved by the Guild's directorate in favor of a less distinguished but more topical play, Stefan Zweig's *Jeremiah* as adapted by Worthington Miner and John Gassner. The Guild's Lawrence Langner, however, made an attempt to put the play into production a year or so later and invited Miss Anderson to assume the leading role. Although Miss Anderson responded to the call, it was found difficult to cast the other parts of this exacting poetic drama, and the project was dropped. From then on, interest in the play cropped up in one quarter or another, but it finally yielded precedence to *Medea*, which Miss Anderson urged Mr. Jeffers to adapt for her from Euripides' play. *The Tower Beyond Tragedy*, in the meantime produced in various adaptations by community theatres, did finally reach New York in a stage version prepared by Jeffers himself, and was given an ANTA (American National Theatre and Academy) production in 1950. An attempt was also made to present his dramatic poem *Dear Judas* as a play. But it was *Medea*, produced on Broadway by Oliver Rea and Robert Whitehead, that made Jeffers known to a large body of playgoers who would not have otherwise made the acquaintance of this harrowing Euripidean drama and of Mr. Jeffers' dramatic poetry. *Medea* properly bears the following dedication: "To Judith Anderson for whom this was written."

Robinson Jeffers was born in Pittsburgh in 1887, but was taken to Europe by his parents on two occasions and educated there from the ages of thirteen to fifteen. At fifteen, he enrolled at Occidental College in Los Angeles and was graduated three years later. Subsequently he studied at the University of Southern California, the University of Zurich, and a medical school in Los Angeles. In 1914, however, he abandoned every intention to pursue a profession when a legacy of $10,000 enabled him to devote himself to the writing of poetry. He built himself a home in Carmel, California, and isolating himself from modern civilization, whose commercialism and tameness repelled him, he composed numerous poems expressive of his nihilistic philosophy and admiration for primitive nature. Especially notable were his long narratives dealing with the lusts, passions, and pride of men and women who despise a commonplace life or an easy felicity, succumb to dark inner promptings and violate taboos. For his violent subject matter, moreover, he developed a granitic style of poetry in the form of long, clause- and phrase-studded lines.

Jeffers had always been a dramatic, as well as epic, poet, but in *Medea* he wrote a completely dramatic work directly intended for the stage. It follows the outlines of Euripides' celebrated tragedy, but Jeffers' style and grim view of life are his own. The play departs considerably not only from Euripides' lyricism, but from the old master's liberal feminism and sympathy with victims of discrimination and oppression. If Jeffers' *Medea* is a dream of love frustrated and turned vengeful, this is not merely because the Greek Argonaut legend used by Euripides contains this often retold story, but because it accords with Jeffers' formidable, Nay-saying disposition and his fascination with destructive passion. This disposition and interest appeared early in the powerful poetry of *Tamar* (1924), *Roan Stallion* (1925), *Cawdor* (1928), and other volumes. *Medea* is the one distinguished high tragedy written by an American poet. Underlying this poetic drama is the same view, too extreme to be Greek or classic, that Jeffers expressed so plainly in the lines of his poem *Meditation on Saviors*, written in 1928:

> "But while he lives let each man make his health in his mind,
>   to love the coast opposite humanity
> And so be freed of love, laying it like bread on the waters; it is worst
>   turned inward, it is best shot farthest.
> Love, the mad wine of good and evil, the saint's and murderer's,
>   the mote in the eye that makes its object
> Shine the sun black . . ."

ACT ONE

The NURSE *comes from the door Left toward the front of the stage)*

THE NURSE.

I wish the long ship Argo had never passed that peri-
lous channel between the Symplegades,
I wish the pines that made her mast and her oars still
waved in the wind on Mount Pelion, and the gray
fishhawk
Still nested in them, the great adventurers had never
voyaged
Into the Asian sunrise to the shores of morning for
the Golden Fleece
                    For then my mistress Medea
Would never have seen Jason, nor loved and saved him,
nor cut herself off from home to come with him
Into this country of the smiling chattering Greeks and
the roofs of Corinth: over which I see evil
Hang like a cloud. For she is not meek but fierce, and
the daughter of a king.
                    Yet at first all went well.
The folk of Corinth were kind to her, they were proud
of her beauty, and Jason loved her. Happy is the
house
Where the man and the woman love and are faithful.
    Now all is changed; all is black hatred. For Jason
has turned from her; he calls the old bond a barbarian mating, not a Greek marriage; he has cast
her off
And wedded the yellow-haired child of Creon, the
ruler here. He wants worldly advantage, fine
friends,
And a high place in Corinth. For these he is willing to
cast Medea like a harlot, and betray the children
That she has borne him. He is not wise, I think
                    But Medea
Lies in the house, broken with pain and rage; she will
neither eat nor drink, except her own tears,
She turns her face toward the earth, remembering her
father's house and her native land, which she
abandoned
For the love of this man: who now despises her.
And if I try to speak comfort to her she only stares at
me, great eyes like stones. She is like a stone on
the shore
Or a wave of the sea, and I think she hates
Even her children.
She is learning what it is to be a foreigner,
    cast out, alone and despised.
She will never learn to be humble, she will never learn
    to drink insult
Like harmless water. O I'm in terror of her: whether
she'll thread a knife through her own heart,
Or whether she'll hunt the bridegroom and his new
bride, or what more dreadful evil stalks in the
forest
Of her dark mind. I know that Jason would have been
wiser to tempt a lioness, or naked-handed
Steal the whelps of a tiger.

(From up Right she sees MEDEA'S BOYS *coming
with their* TUTOR, ELDER BOY *first with seashell,* YOUNGER BOY *on* TUTOR'S *back.)*
                    Here comes the happy
children. Little they know
Of their mother's grief.
(During this speech TUTOR *lets* BOY *off his back.* BOYS
go up and sit up Right corner of house. TUTOR
crosses down Center to Left of NURSE.)

THE TUTOR.

                    Old servant of my lady, why do
you stand out here, keeping watch in solitude
With those grim eyes? Is it some trouble of your own
that you are lamenting? I should think Medea
Would need your care.

THE NURSE.

It is all one to Medea, whether I am there or here. Yes,
it is mine,
My trouble. My lady's grief is my grief. And it has
hurt me .

So that I had to come out and speak it to the earth and
sky.

THE TUTOR.

Is she still in that deep despair?

THE NURSE.

                    You are lucky,
Old watchdog of Jason's boys. I envy you,
You do not see her. This evil is not declining, it is just
at dawn. I dread the lion-eyed
Glare of its noon.

THE TUTOR.

                    Is she so wrought? Yet neither you
nor Medea
Knows the latest and worst.

THE NURSE. *(Rises from rock)*
                    What? What?

THE TUTOR. *(Crosses to Center)*
                            I shouldn't
have spoken.

THE NURSE.

                    Tell me the truth, old man. You and
I are two slaves, we can trust each other,
We can keep secrets.

THE TUTOR

                    I heard them saying—when we
walked beside the holy fountain Peirene,
Where the old men sit in the sun on the stone benches
    —they were saying that Creon, the lord of this
    land,
Intends to drive out Medea and the children with her,
    these innocent boys, out of this house
And out of Corinth, and they must wander through the
    wild world
Homeless and helpless.

THE NURSE.

                    I don't believe it. Ah, no! Jason
may hate the mother, but he would hardly
Let his sons be cast out.

THE TUTOR.

                    Well—he has made a new
alliance.
He is not a friend of this house.

THE NURSE. *(She crosses below* TUTOR *to Left)*
If this were true!—

MEDEA. *(Within house. She is Asiatic and laments
loudly)* Death.

THE NURSE.

Listen! I hear her voice

MEDEA. *(Within)*

Death. Death is my wish. For myself, my enemies, my
children. Destruction.

THE NURSE.

Take the children away, keep them away from her.
Take them to the other door. Quickly.

(During "Deaths" YOUNGER BOY *rises from
rock.* TUTOR *crosses, picks him up and exits
Left, followed by* ELDER BOY. *They go out,
toward rear door of the house.* THE NURSE
looks after them, wringing her hands.)

MEDEA.

That's the word. Grind, crush, burn. Destruction. Ai—
Ai—

THE NURSE. *(Wringing her hands)*
                    This is my terror:
To hear her always harking back to the children, like
    a fierce hound at fault. O unhappy one,
They're not to blame.
                    (Sits step Right of pillar down Left.)

MEDEA. *(Within)*

                    If any god hears me: let me die.
Ah, rotten, rotten, rotten: death is the only
Water to wash this dirt.

(FIRST and SECOND WOMAN are coming in

up Right, but the NURSE *does not yet notice them. She is intent on* MEDEA'S *cries and her own thoughts.)*

THE NURSE.

Oh, it's a bad thing

To be born of high race, and brought up wilful and
    powerful in a great house, unruled.
And ruling many: for then if misfortune comes it is
    unendurable, it drives you mad. I say that poor
    people
Are happier: the little commoners and humble people,
    the poor in spirit: they can lie low
Under the wind and live:
        (Enter THIRD WOMAN; *joins* FIRST *and*
        SECOND *up Right Center.)*
                    while the tall oaks and cloud-
raking mountain pines go mad in the storm,
Writhe, groan and crash.
MEDEA.
Ai!
THE NURSE.
This is the wild and terrible justice of God: it brings
    on great persons
The great disasters.
MEDEA.
Ai!!!
THE NURSE. *(Becomes aware of the* WOMEN *who
have come in, and is startled from her reverie.* FIRST
WOMAN *crosses down Center)*
    What do you want?
FIRST WOMAN.
                    I hear her crying again: it
    is dreadful.
SECOND WOMAN. *(Crosses down to Right of* FIRST
WOMAN)
                Her lamentation.
She is beautiful and deep in grief: we couldn't help
    coming.
THIRD WOMAN. *(Crosses down to Right of* SECOND
WOMAN)
We are friends of this house and its trouble hurts us.
THE NURSE.
You are right, friends; it is not a home. It is broken.
A house of grief and of weeping.
MEDEA. *(Within)*
                    Hear me, God, let me
    die. What I need: all dead, all dead, all dead
        *(*THIRD WOMAN *crosses down Right of rock.)*
Under the great cold stones. For a year and a thousand
    years and another thousand: cold as the stones,
    cold,
But noble again, proud, straight and silent, crimson-
    cloaked
In the blood of our wounds.

        *(*FIRST WOMAN *crosses to 3rd step, Center.)*

FIRST WOMAN.
                    O shining sky, divine earth,
Harken not to the song that this woman sings.
It is not her music; her mind is not here.
She does not know what she prays for.
Pain and wrath are the singers.
SECOND WOMAN. *(Crosses to second step, facing
door)*
                    Unhappy one,

Never pray for death, never pray for death,
He is here all too soon.
He strikes from the clear sky like a hawk,
He hides behind green leaves, or he waits
Around the corner of the wall.
O never pray for death, never pray for death—
Because that prayer will be answered.
MEDEA. *(The rise and fall of her voice indicate that
she is prowling back and forth beyond the main door-
way, like a caged animal)*

I know poisons. I know the bright teeth of steel. I
    know fire. But I will not be mocked by my enemies,
        *(*THIRD WOMAN *crosses up Right of rock to
        Right Center.)*
And I will not endure pity. Pity and contempt are
    sister and brother, twin-born. I will not die tamely.
I will not allow blubber-eyed pity, nor contempt either,
    to snivel over the stones of my tomb.
I am not a Greek woman.
    THIRD WOMAN. *(Crosses to step Center)*
                    No, a barbarian woman from
    savage Colchis, at the bitter end
Of the Black Sea. Does she boast of that?
SECOND WOMAN.
                        She doesn't
    know what she is saying.
MEDEA. *(Within)*
Poisons. Death-magic. The sharp sword. The hemp
    rope. Death-magic.
Death—
    SECOND WOMAN. *(Crosses down Right of rock.*
THIRD WOMAN *joins her)*
                I hate Jason, who made this sorrow.
FIRST WOMAN. *(Crosses to* NURSE *in front of doors)*
Old and honored servant of a great house, do you think
    it is wise
To leave your lady alone in there, except perhaps a
    few slaves, building that terrible acropolis
Of deadly thoughts? We Greeks believe that solitude
    is very dangerous, great passions grow into
    monsters
In the dark of the mind; but if you share them with
    loving friends they remain human, they can be
    endured.
MEDEA. *(Within)*
Ai!
FIRST WOMAN.
I think you ought to persuade Medea to come from the
    dark dwelling, and speak with us, before her heart
    breaks,
Or she does harm to herself. She has lived among us,
    we've learned to love her, we'd gladly tell her so.
It might comfort her spirit.
    THE NURSE.
                    Do you think so? She
    wouldn't listen
        (Door BOLT is heard. NURSE *rises.* FIRST WOMAN
        crosses down Right, joining other two WOMEN,
        and sits on rock)
                —Oh, oh, she is coming!
Speak carefully to her: make your words a soft music.

        *(*MEDEA *comes through the doorway, prop-
        ping herself against one of the pillars, and
        stands staring.)*

THE NURSE.
Oh, my dear, my poor child.
        *(*NURSE *sits.)*
SECOND WOMAN. *(Whispering)*
They say she is dangerous. Look at her eyes.
FIRST WOMAN.
She is a witch, but not evil. She can make old men
    young again: she did it for Jason's father.
THIRD WOMAN.
All the people of her country are witches. They know
    about drugs and magic. They are savages, but they
    have a wild wisdom.
SECOND WOMAN.
Poor soul, it hasn't helped this one much.
MEDEA. *(She does not see the gaping and whispering*
WOMEN)
I will look at the light of the sun, this last time. I wish
    from that blue sky the white wolf of lightning
Would leap, and burst my skull and my brain, and like
    a burning babe cling to these breasts— Ai!—Ai!
        (She checks and looks fiercely at the WOMEN
        below)
Someone is here?
        (Her hostile eyes range back and forth; she

sees the WOMEN *clearly now, and assumes full self-control. Her voice is cautious and insincere)*
I did not know I had visitors.—Women of Corinth:
If anything has been spoken too loudly here, consider
That I believed I was alone; and I have some provocation. You've come—let me suppose
With love and sympathy—to peer at my sorrow. I understand well enough
That nothing is ever private in a Greek city; whoever withholds anything

Is thought sullen or proud—
(With irony),
undemocratic
I think you call it. This is not always just, but we know that justice, at least on earth,
Is a name, not a fact; and as for me, I wish to avoid any appearance
Of being—proud. Of what? Of affliction? I will show you my naked heart.
(The THREE WOMEN *rise; cross to Center.)*
You know that my lord Jason
Has left me and made a second marriage, with the bright-haired child
Of wealth and power. I too was a child of power, but not in this country; and I spent my power
For love of Jason. I poured it out before him like water, I made him drink it like wine. I gave him
Success and fame; I saved him his precious life; not once, many times. You may have heard what I did for him:
I betrayed my father for him, I killed my brother to save him; I made my own land to hate me forever;
And I fled west with Jason in the Greek ship, under the thunder of the sail, weeping and laughing,
That huge journey through the Black Sea and the Bosphorus, where the rocks clang together, through the Sea of Marmora,
And through Hellespont,

watched by the spearmen of wealthy Troy, and home to Greek water: his home, my exile,
My endless exile.
(Crosses to pillar Left of house)
And here I have loved him and borne him sons; and this—man—
Has left me and taken Creon's daughter, to enjoy her fortune, and put aside her soft yellow hair
And kiss her young mouth.
(MEDEA stands rigid, struggling for self-control.)

FIRST WOMAN.
She is terrible. Stone with stone eyes.
SECOND WOMAN.
Look: the foam-flake on her lip, that flickers with her breathing.
THIRD WOMAN.
She is pitiable: she is under great injuries.
MEDEA. *(Low-voiced)*
I do not know what other woman—I do not know how much a Greek woman
Will endure. The people of my race are somewhat rash and intemperate. As for me, I want simply to die.
(She sits at pillar Left)
But Jason is not to smile at his bride over my grave, nor that great man Creon
Hang wreaths and make a feast-day in Corinth. Or let the wreaths be bright blinding fire, and the songs a high wailing,
And the wine, blood.
FIRST WOMAN. *(Crosses to Center)*
Daughter of sorrow, beware.

It is dangerous to dream of wine; it is worse
To speak of wailing or blood:
For the images that the mind makes
Find a way out, they work into life.

MEDEA.
Let them work into life!
FIRST WOMAN.
There are evils that cannot be cured by evil.
Patience remains, and the gods watch all.
MEDEA. *(Dully, without hope)*
Let them watch my enemies go down in blood.

(First TRUMPET off up Right is heard. The THREE WOMEN *cross up Right.)*

SECOND WOMAN.
Medea, beware!
Some great person is coming.—
(Second TRUMPET is heard)
It is Creon himself.
(Third TRUMPET)
THIRD WOMAN.
Creon is coming.

(The THREE WOMEN *cross down stage of rock Right.)*

THE NURSE.
He is dark with anger. O my lady—my child—bend in this wind,
And not be broken!

(MEDEA rises. CREON comes in up Right with MEN *attending him. The* WOMEN *move to one side. He speaks to* MEDEA, *with an angry gesture toward* WOMEN.)*

CREON. *(At Center)*
You have admirers, I see. Abate your pride: these people will not be with you where you are going.
(A pause. MEDEA *does not answer.* CREON *brings his wrath under control and crosses up to second step to Right of* MEDEA)
Medea, woman of the stone forehead and hate-filled eyes: I have made my decision. I have decided
That you must leave this land at once and go into banishment
THREE WOMEN.
Oohh!
CREON.
with your children.
THREE WOMEN.
Oohh.
CREON.
I intend to remove
A root of disturbance out of the soil of Corinth. I am here to see to it. I will not return home
Until it is done.

(The THREE WOMEN *sit.)*

MEDEA.
You mean—banishment?
CREON.
Exile: banishment: go where you may, Medea, but here
You abide no more.
MEDEA.
—I with my children?
CREON.
I will not take them away from you.
MEDEA.
The children, my lord—
(Her lips move angrily, but the voice is not heard.)
CREON.
What are you muttering?
MEDEA.
Nothing—I am praying to my gods for wisdom,
And you for mercy. My sons are still very young, tender and helpless. You know, my lord,
What exile means—to wander with fear and famine for guide and driver, through all the wild winter storms

And the rage of the sun; and beg a bread-crust and be
    derided; pelted with stones in the villages,
Held a little lower than the scavenger dogs, kicked,
    scorned and slaved—the children, my lord,
Are Jason's children. Your chosen friend, I believe,
    and now
Even closer bound. And as for me, your servant, O
    master of Corinth, what have I done? Why
Must I be cast?

CREON.

                I will tell you frankly: because you
nourish rancorous ill will toward persons
Whom I intend to protect: I send you out before you've
    time to do harm here. And you are notorious
For occult knowledge: sorcery, poisons, magic. Men
    say you can even sing down the moon from heaven,
And make the holy stars to falter and run backward,
    against the purpose
And current of nature. Ha? As to that I know not: I
    know you are dangerous. You threaten my daugh-
    ter: you have to go.

MEDEA.

But I wish her well, my lord! I wish her all happiness.
    I hope that Jason may be as kind to her
As—to me.

CREON.

        That is your wish?

MEDEA.

                I misspoke. I thought of
old days—
    (She seems to weep.)

CREON.

        I acknowledge, Medea,
That you have some cause for grief. I all the more
    must guard against your dark wisdom and bitter
    heart.

MEDEA.

You misjudge me cruelly. It is true that I have some
    knowledge of drugs and medicines: I can some-
    times cure sickness.
Is that a crime? These dark rumors, my lord,
Are only the noise of popular gratitude.
    (Crosses down to one step above him)
You must have observed
    it often: if any person
Knows a little more than the common man, the people
    suspect him. If he brings a new talent,
How promptly the hateful whispers begin. But you
    are not a common man, lord of Corinth; you
Will not fear knowledge.

CREON.

            No. Nor change my decision.
    I am here to see you leave this house and the city:
And not much time. Move quickly, gather your things
    and go. I pity you, Medea,
But you must go.
    (He crosses off steps, with back to her down
    Right Center.)

MEDEA.

        You pity me? You—pity me?
    (She comes close to him, wild with rage)
I will endure a dog's pity or a wart-grown toad's. May
God who hears me— We shall see in the end
Who's to be pitied.

    (NURSE rises, crosses in to steps. MEDEA
    crosses down Left, then up Right between
    pillar and edge of house, then back to NURSE in
    her arms.)

CREON.

            Yes, and I'll keep her safe of your
    female hatred: therefore I send you
Out of this land.

    (NURSE resumes her sitting position down
    Left.)

MEDEA.

        It is not true, I am not jealous. I
never hated her.

Jealous for the sake of Jason? I am far past wanting
    Jason, my lord. You took him and gave him to her,
And I will say you did well, perhaps wisely. Your
    daughter is loved by all: she is beautiful: if I were
    near her
I would soon love her.

CREON.

            You can speak sweetly enough,
    you can make honey in your mouth like a brown
    bee
When it serves your turn.

MEDEA.

            Not honey: the truth.

CREON.

                Trust
    you or not, you are going out of this country,
    Medea.
What I decide is fixed;
    (MEDEA crosses away from him to Center.)
        it is like the firm rocks of Acro-
    corinth, which neither earthquake can move
Nor a flood of tears melt. Make ready quickly: I have
    a guest in my house. I should return to him.

THE NURSE. (Comes to Left of MEDEA and speaks
    to her)
What guest? O my lady, ask him
Who is the guest? If powerful and friendly
He might be a refuge for us—

MEDEA. (Pays no attention to her. Crosses; kneels;
    to CREON)
I know that your will is granite. But even on the harsh
    face of a granite mountain some flowers of mercy
May grow in season. Have mercy on my little sons,
    Creon,
Though there is none for me.

    (She reaches to embrace his knees. He steps
    backward from her.)

CREON.

            How long, woman? This
    is decided; done; finished.

    (NURSE crosses back Left and sits down.)

MEDEA. (Rising from her knees, turns half away
    from him)
            I am not a beggar.
I will not trouble you. I shall not live long.
    (Crosses two steps to Left; turns to him
    again)
Sire: grant me a few hours yet, one day to prepare in,
    one little day
Before I go out of Corinth forever.

CREON.

            What? No! I told
    you. The day is today. Medea, this day.
And the hour is now.

MEDEA.

            There are no flowers on this
    mountain: not one violet, not one anemone.
Your face, my lord, is like flint.—If I could find the
    right words, if some god would lend me a touch of
    eloquence,
I'd show you my heart.

    (Crosses to CREON)
            I'd lift it out of my breast and
    turn it over in my hands; you'd see how pure it is
Of any harm or malice toward you or your household.
    (She holds out her hands to him)
Look at it: not a speck: look, my lord. They call mercy
The jewel of kings. I am praying
To you as to one of the gods: destroy us not utterly.
    To go out with no refuge, nothing prepared,
Is plain death: I would rather kill myself quickly and
    here. If I had time but to ask the slaves
And strolling beggars where to go, how to live: and I
    must gather some means: one or two jewels
And small gold things I have,

(Crosses away from CREON *to Left)*
               to trade them for bread
and goat's milk.
   (Crosses up steps to Center of doorway)
          Wretched, wretched, wretched I am,
I and my boys.

   (She kneels again)
          I beseech you, Creon,
By the soft yellow hair and cool smooth forehead and
   the white knees
Of that young girl who is now Jason's bride: lend me
   this inch of time: one day—half a day.
For this one is now half gone—and I will go my sad
   course and vanish in the morning quietly as dew
That drops on the stones at dawn and is dry at sunrise.
You will never again be troubled by any word
Or act of mine. And this I pray you for your dear
   child's sake. Oh Creon, what is half a day
In all the rich years of Corinth?
   CREON.
              I will think of it. I am
no tyrant.
I have been merciful to my own hurt, many times.
   Even to myself I seem to be foolish
If I grant you this thing— No, Medea,
I will not grant it.
   *(*THREE WOMEN *rise, cross down Right of*
   CREON, *imploringly)*
       Well— We shall watch you: as a
hawk does a viper. What harm could she do
In the tail of one day? A ruler ought to be ruthless,
   but I am not. I am a fool
In my own eyes, whatever the world may think. I
   can be gruff with warriors; a woman weeping
   *(*MEDEA *weeps.)*
Floods me off course.—Take it, then. Make your
   preparations.
But if tomorrow's sun shines on you here—Medea,
   you die—
   *(*MEDEA *and* WOMEN *make a gesture of*
   thanks.)
       Enough words. Thank me not. I want
my hands
Washed of this business.
   (He departs quickly up Right, followed by
   his MEN. MEDEA *rises from her knees.)*

   MEDEA.
            I will thank you.
And the whole world will hear of it.
   *(*MEDEA *crosses around to Right of house*
   on top step; makes a violent gesture after
   him, then sits at pillar Right.)
   FIRST WOMAN. *(Crosses up Center watching him*
   out then turns to other WOMEN*)*
I have seen this man's arrogance, I watched and heard
   him.
I am of Corinth, and I say that Corinth
Is not well ruled.
   SECOND WOMAN. *(Crosses up Center.* THREE
   WOMEN *join hands at Center on end of this speech)*
The city where even a woman, even a foreigner,
Suffers unjustly the rods of power
Is not well ruled.

   *(*THREE WOMEN *take a step to* MEDEA.*)*

   FIRST WOMAN.
Unhappy Medea, what haven, what sanctuary, where
   will you wander?
Which of the gods, Medea,
Drives you through waves of woe, the mooring broken,
   the hawsers and the anchor-head,
Hopeless from harbor?·
   MEDEA.
          —This man—this barking dog
—this gulled fool—
   *(*MEDEA *rises)*
          gods of my father's country,
You saw me low on my knees before the great dog of

Corinth; humble, holding my heart in my hands
For a dog to bite—break this dog's teeth!

   *(*WOMEN *cross down stage of rock Right.)*
              Women: it is
a bitter thing to be a woman.
A woman is weak for warfare, she must use cunning.

   Men boast their battles: I tell you this, and we
   know it:
   (Starts down steps Center)
It is easier to stand in battle three times, in the front
   line, in the stabbing fury, than to bear one child.
And a woman, they say, can do no good but in child-
   birth. It may be so. She can do evil;
   *(*WOMEN *make pleading gesture to her)*
              she can do evil.
   (She snarls at them and they turn away)
I wept before that tall dog, I wept my tears before
   him, I degraded my knees to him, I gulled and
   flattered him.
O triple fool, he has given me
   (She crosses up Right Center. FIRST WOMAN
   sits on rock Right)
          all that I needed: a little time, a
space of time.
   (Crosses back to Left Center)
          Death is dearer to me
Than what I am now; and if today by sunset the world
   has not turned, and turned sharp too—let your
   dog Creon
Send two or three slaves to kill me and a cord to
   strangle me: I will stretch out
My throat to it. But I have a bitter hope, women. I
   begin to see light
Through the dark wood, between the monstrous trunks
   of the trees, at the end of the tangled forest an
   eyehole,
A pin-point of light:

            I shall not die perhaps
As a pigeon dies. Nor like an innocent lamb, that feels
   a hand on its head and looks up from the knife
To the man's face and dies.—No, like some yellow-
   eyed beast that has killed its hunters let me lie
   down
On the hounds' bodies and the broken spears.—Then
   how to strike them? What means to use? There
   are so many
Doors through which painful death may glide in and
   catch— Which one, which one?
   (She stands meditating down Left. The NURSE
   comes from behind her and speaks to the FIRST
   WOMAN.)*
   THE NURSE.
               Tell me: do you
know what guest
Is in Creon's house?
   FIRST WOMAN.
          What?—Oh. An Athenian ship
came from the north last night: it is Ægeus.
The lord of Athens.
   THE NURSE.
          Ægeus! My lady knows him: I
believe he will help us. Some god has brought him
   here,
Some savior god.
   FIRST WOMAN.
         He is leaving, I think, today.
   THE NURSE. *(Hobbling back toward* MEDEA*)*
                  My lady!
Lord Ægeus
Is here in Corinth, Creon's guest: Ægeus of Athens.
   *(*MEDEA *looks at her silently, without atten-*
   tion.)
If you will see him and speak him fairly,
We have a refuge.
   MEDEA.
         I have things in my hand to do. Be
   quiet.

THE NURSE.
Oh, listen to me!
You are driven out of Corinth; you must find shelter.
Ægeus of Athens is here.

(MEDEA turns from her. The NURSE catches at her clothing, servile but eager, slave and mother at the same time.)

MEDEA. *(Angrily turning on her)*
What's that to me?
THE NURSE. *(Kneels at her feet)*
I lifted you in my arms when you were—this long. I gave you milk from these breasts, that are now dead leaves.
I saw the little beautiful body straighten and grow tall: Oh—child—almost my child—how can I
Not try to save you? Life is better than death—
MEDEA.
                                        Not now.
THE NURSE.
Time's running out!
MEDEA.
                        I have time. Oh, I have time.
It would be good to stand here a thousand years and think of nothing
But the deaths of three persons.
THE NURSE.
                                Ai! There's no hope then.
Ai, child, if you could do this red thing you dream of, all Corinth
Would pour against you.
MEDEA.
                        After my enemies are punished
and I have heard the last broken moan—Corinth?
What's that? I'll sleep. I'll sleep well. I am alone against all: and so weary
That it is pitiful.

(MEDEA sits. NURSE rises, wringing her hands. On trumpet call the THREE WOMEN cross up Right.)

FIRST WOMAN.
                Look: who is coming? I see the sunlight glitter on lanceheads.

SECOND WOMAN.
Oh, it is Jason!
THIRD WOMAN.
Jason's Medea's worst enemy, who should have been Her dearest protector.

(MEDEA leans wearily against one of the pillars of the doorway, her back to the stage, unconscious of what they are saying. JASON enters in haste up Right, followed by armed ATTENDANTS, and speaks angrily.)

JASON. *(Crossing to Center on 2nd step)*
                        What business have you here,
you women
Clustered like buzzing bees at the hive-door?
Where is Medea?

(They do not answer for a moment, but look involuntarily toward MEDEA, and JASON sees her. She jerks and stiffens at the sound of his voice, but does not turn.)

FIRST WOMAN. *(Pointing)*
                        There: mourning for what you have done.

(NURSE takes a step above MEDEA, disclosing her to JASON.)

JASON.
        Ha? What she has done.

Not I. Not by my will she and my sons are exiled.
MEDEA. *(Slowly turns and faces him, her head high, rigid with inner violence)*
Is there another dog here?

(THREE WOMEN sit on steps up Right Center.)

JASON.
                        So, Medea,
You have once more affronted and insulted the head of Corinth. This is not the first time
I've seen what a fool anger is. You might have lived here happily, secure and honored—I hoped you would—
By being just a little decently respectful toward those in power. Instead you had to go mad with anger
And talk yourself into exile. To me it matters little what you say about me, but rulers are sensitive.
Time and again I've smoothed down Creon's indignation, then you like a madwoman, like a possessed imbecile,
Wag your head and let the words flow again; you never cease
From speaking evil against him and his family. So now— Call yourself lucky, Medea,
Not to get worse than exile.
                (Crosses a few steps to MEDEA on 2nd step)
                        In spite of all this, I have your interest at heart and am here to help you.
Exile's a bitter business. I want to make some provision for you. I wish you no harm,
Although you hate me.
                (He waits for her to speak, but she is silent. He continues)
                        And in particular the children, my sons; our sons.—You might have been decent enough
To have thought of our sons.
MEDEA. *(Slowly)*
                                Did you consider them
When you betrayed this house?
JASON.
                        Certainly I considered them. It was my hope that they would grow up here,
And I, having married power, could protect and favor them. And if perhaps, after many years, I become
Dynast of Corinth—for that is Creon's desire, to make me his heir—our sons
Would have been a king's sons— I hope to help them wherever they go: but now of course must look forward
To younger children.
                (Steps down off steps and turns from her.)
MEDEA. *(Trembling)*
                        Ah—it's enough. Something might happen. It is—likely that—something might happen
To the bride and the marriage.
JASON.
                        I'll guard against it. But evidently Creon is right to be rid of you.

(He crosses as if to go off Right. She stops him when he is up Right Center. He gives helmet to SLAVE; crosses down Right.)

MEDEA. *(Rises and crosses to Center)*
Have you finished now? I thought I would let you speak on and spread out your shamelessness
Before these women: the way a Tyrian trader unrolls his rare fabrics: "Do you like it, ladies?"
                                        It is the
Dog's daughter's husband. It is a brave person: it has finally got up its courage—with a guard of spears—
To come and look me in the face.
                (JASON turns away from her. MEDEA makes gestures as if to take him in her arms, then stops)

O Jason: how have you
pulled me down
To this hell of vile thoughts? I did not use to talk like
a common woman. I loved you once:
And I am ashamed of it:
(JASON *sits rock Right. She crosses two steps
Left*)
    but there are some things
That ought to be remembered by you and me. That
blue day when we drove through the Hellespont
Into Greek sea, and the great-shouldered heroes were
singing at the oars, and those birds flying
Through the blown foam: that day was too fine I sup-
pose
For Creon's daughter's man to remember
(JASON *rises as if to leave.*)
    —but you might remember
Whether I cheated my father for you and tamed the
fire-breathing
Brazen-hoofed bulls; and whether I saved your life in
the field of the teeth; and you might remember
Whether I poisoned the great serpent and got you the
Golden Fleece; and fled with you, and killed my
brother
When he pursued us, making myself abominable
In my own home; and then in yours I got your enemy
Pelias hacked to death
By his own daughter's hands—whatever these fine
Corinthian friends of yours
May say against my rapid and tricky wisdom: you it
has served,
You it has served well:
(JASON *starts to speak.*)
    here are five times, if I counted
right—and all's not counted—
That your adventure would have been dusty death
If I'd not saved you—but now you think that your
adventures are over; you are safe and high placed
in Corinth,
And will need me no more.
    It is a bit of a dog, isn't it,
women? It is well qualified
To sleep with the dog's daughter.
(JASON *makes a gesture of wrath.*)
    But for me, Jason, me
driven by the hairy snouts from the quadruped
marriage-bed,

What refuge does your prudent kindness advise? Shall
I fly home to Colchis—
To put my neck in the coil of a knotted rope, for the
crimes
I served you with? Or shall I go and kneel to the
daughter of Pelias? They would indeed be happy
To lay their hands on my head: holding the very knives
and the cleavers
That carved their sire. The world is a little closed to me,
eh?
By the things I have done for you

(*Crosses away from him to down Center.*)
THE NURSE.
    I'll go to the palace
And seek Ægeus. There is no other hope.
(*She hurries out door Left.*)
JASON. (*Slowly crossing to Center to Right of
MEDEA*)
    I see, Medea,
You have been a very careful merchant of benefits.
You forget none, you keep a strict reckoning.
But—
Some little things that I on my side have done for you
Ought to be in the books too: as, for example, that I
carried you
Out of the dirt and superstition of Asiatic Colchis into
the rational
Sunlight of Greece, and the marble music of the Greek
temples: is that no benefit? And I have brought
you
To meet the first minds of our time, and to speak as

an equal with the great heroes and the rulers of
cities:
Is that no benefit? And now—this grievous thing that
you hate me for:
That I have married Creon's young daughter, little
Creusa:
(MEDEA *sits 2nd step.*)
    do you think I did it like a boy or a woman.

Out of blind passion? I did it to achieve power here;
and I'd have used that power to protect
You and our sons, but your jealous madness has
muddled everything. And finally:
(NURSE *appears behind house and exits up
Right.* JASON *crosses above* MEDEA *to top
step*)
As to those acts of service you so loudly boast—whom
do I thank for them? I thank divine Venus, the
goddess
Who makes girls fall in love. You did them because
you had to do them; Venus compelled you; I
Enjoyed her favor.
(*Crosses down two steps to her Left*)
    A man dares things, you know; he
makes his adventure
In the cold eye of death; and if the gods care for him
They appoint an instrument to save him; if not, he dies.
You were that instrument.
MEDEA.
    Here it is: the lowest.
The obscene dregs; the slime and the loathing; the
muddy bottom of a mouthed cup: when a scoun-
drel begins
To invoke the gods
JASON.
Ha!
MEDEA.
You had better go, Jason. Vulgarity
Is a contagious disease; and in a moment what could I
do but spit at you like a peasant, or curse you
Like a drunken slave? You had better take yourself
back to
"Little Creusa."
JASON.
    I came to help you and save you if
possible.
(*Reaches down and touches her arm.*)
MEDEA.
    Your help
Is not wanted. Go. Go.
JASON. (*Crosses below her to Right Center, then
stops*)
    If I could see my boys—

MEDEA.
    Go
quickly.
JASON.
    Yours the regret then.

(*Exits up Right. Watching him go,* MEDEA
*strokes her wrist and hand to the tips of the
spread fingers, as if she were scraping off
slime.*)
MEDEA.
This is it. I did not surely know it: loathing is all. This
flesh
He has touched and fouled. These hands that wrought
for him, these knees
That ran his errands. This body that took his—what
they call love, and made children of it. If I could
peel off
The flesh, the children, the memory—
(*Again she scarifies one hand with the other.
She looks at her hand*)
    Poor misused
hand; poor defiled arm; your bones
Are not unshapely. If I could tear off the flesh and be
bones; naked bones;
Salt-scoured bones on the shore
At home in Colchis.

FIRST WOMAN. *(Rises and crosses down Right)*
God keep me from fire and the hunger of the sword,
Save me from the hateful sea and the jagged lightning,
And the violence of love.
SECOND WOMAN. *(Joins* FIRST WOMAN*)*
A little love is a joy in the house,
A little fire is a jewel against frost and darkness.

(During these two speeches THIRD WOMAN
goes up Right Center, then returns to
WOMEN *down Right.)*

FIRST WOMAN.
A great love is a fire
That burns the beams of the roof.
The doorposts are flaming and the house falls.
*(*THIRD WOMAN *kneels.)*
A great love is a lion in the cattle-pen,
The herd goes mad, the heifers run bawling
And the claws are in their flanks.
Too much love is an armed robber in the treasury.
He has killed the guards and he walks in blood.
SECOND WOMAN.
And now I see the black end,
The end of great love, and God save me from it:
The unburied horror, the unbridled hatred,
The vultures tearing a corpse!
God keep me clean of those evil beaks.
THIRD WOMAN.
What is she doing, that woman,
Staring like stone, staring?
*(*MEDEA *looks up.)*
Oh, she has moved now.
MEDEA.
Annihilation. The word is pure music: annihilation. To
annihilate the past—
Is not possible: but its fruit in the present—
Can be nipped off. Am I to look in my sons' eyes
And see Jason's forever? How could I endure the end-
less defilement, those lives
That mix Jason and me? Better to be clean
Bones on the shore. Bones have no eyes at all, how
could they weep? White bones
On the Black Sea shore—
Oh, but that's far. Not yet.
Corinth must howl first.
FIRST WOMAN.
The holy fountains flow up from the earth,
The smoke of sacrifice flows up from the earth.

The eagle and the wild swan fly up from the earth,
Righteousness also
Has flown up from the earth to the feet of God.
It is not here, but up there; peace and pity are de-
parted;
Hatred is here; hatred is heavy, it clings to the earth.
Love blows away, hatred remains.
SECOND WOMAN.
Women hate war, but men will wage it again.
Women may hate their husbands, and sons their
fathers,
But women will never hate their own children.
FIRST WOMAN.
But as for me, I will do good to my husband,
I will love my sons and daughters, and adore the gods.
MEDEA.
If I should go into the house with a sharp knife
To the man and his bride—
*(*MEDEA *rises.* THIRD WOMAN *rises.)*
Or if I could fire the room they sleep in, and hear them
Wake in the white of the fire, and cry to each other,
and howl like dogs.
THREE WOMEN.
Oh!!!
(Cringe together.)
MEDEA.
And howl and die—
But I might fail; I might be cut down first;
The knife might turn in my hand, or the fire not burn,
and my enemies could laugh at me.

No: I have subtler means, and more deadly cruel; I
have my dark art
That fools call witchcraft. Not for nothing I have
worshipped the wild gray goddess that walks in
the dark, the wise one,
The terrible one, the sweet huntress, flower of night,
Hecate,
In my house at my hearth.
(She crosses up to pillar Right and sits.)
THE NURSE. *(Hurries in toward* MEDEA, *to her Right)*
My lady: he was leaving Creon's
door: he is coming.
*(*MEDEA *pays no attention.)*
Ægeus is coming?
The power of Athens.
MEDEA. *(Prays)*
Ancient Goddess to whom I and my people
Make the sacrifice of black lambs and black female
hounds,
Holy one, haunter of cross-roads, queen of night,
Hecate,
Help me now: to remember in my mind the use of the
venomous fire, the magic song
And the sharp gems.
(She sits in deep thought. ÆGEUS *comes in up
Right.)*
THE NURSE.
He is here, my lady,
Athens is here.

*(*MEDEA *pays no attention.* THREE WOMEN
*curtsy, then resume their original positions at
rock.* FIRST WOMAN *sits.)*

ÆGEUS. *(Crosses down Left and up steps to top
step, Left of* MEDEA*)*
Medea, rejoice! There is no fairer
greeting from friend to friend.
(She ignores him. He speaks more loudly)
Hail and rejoice! Medea.
MEDEA. *(Lifts her head and stares at him)*
"Rejoice?" It may be so. It
may be I shall—rejoice
Before the sun sets.
ÆGEUS.
What has happened to you?
Your
eyes are cavernous!
And your mouth twitches.
MEDEA.
Nothing: I am quite well:
fools trouble me.—Where are you travelling from,
Ægeus?
ÆGEUS.
From Delphi, where I went to consult
The ancient oracle of Apollo.
MEDEA. *(Abstractedly)*
Oh— Delphi—
Did you get a good answer?
ÆGEUS.
An obscure one.
Some god or other has made me unable to beget a child:
that is my sorrow: but the oracle
Never gives plain responses.
(Crosses two steps nearer her)
I tell you these things
because you are skilled in mysteries, and you might
help me
To the god's meaning.
MEDEA. *(Wearily)*
You want a child? What did
Apollo
Say to you?
ÆGEUS.
That I must not unloose the hanging foot
of the wine-skin until I return
To the hearth of my fathers.
MEDEA. *(Without interest, but understanding the
anatomical reference)*

You have never had a child?

ÆGEUS.

No.

And it is bitterness.

(Turns away from her and takes one step down.)

MEDEA.

But when misfortune comes it is bitter to have children, and watch their starlike Faces grow dim to endure it.

ÆGEUS.

When death comes, Medea, It is, for a childless man, utter despair, darkness, extinction. One's children Are the life after death.

MEDEA. *(Excited)*

Do you feel it so? Do you feel it so? Then—if you had a dog-eyed enemy and needed absolute vengeance—you'd kill The man's children first. Unchild him, ha? And then unlife him.

ÆGEUS.

I do not care to think of such horrors. I have no enemy.

(MEDEA rises, making violent movement; sits again. He stares, and slightly recoils from her. Crosses back up to her)

What is it? What is the matter, Medea? You are trembling; wild fever Flames in your eyes.

MEDEA.

I am well enough— Fools trouble me, and dogs; but not that— Oh—

ÆGEUS.

What has happened to you?

THE NURSE. *(Crouches by her, trying to comfort her)*

My dear—my love—

MEDEA. *(Pushes her gently aside; looks up at ÆGEUS)*

I would not hurt my children. Their father hurts them.

ÆGEUS.

What do you mean—Jason? What has Jason done?

MEDEA.

He has betrayed and denied Both me and them.

ÆGEUS.

Jason has done that? Why? Why?

MEDEA.

He has cast me off and married Creon's young daughter. And Creon, this very day, is driving us Into black exile.

ÆGEUS.

Jason consents to that?

MEDEA.

He is glad of it.

ÆGEUS. *(Crossing down steps to WOMEN down Right)*

Why—it's atrocious, it's past belief.

THE NURSE. *(Says in MEDEA's ear)*

Ask him for refuge! Ask him to receive you in Athens!

MEDEA. *(Straight and rigid)*

Do you not think such men ought to be punished, Ægeus?

ÆGEUS.

I think it is villainous. They told me nothing of this—

MEDEA.

Do you not think such men ought to be punished, Ægeus?

(Crossing down steps to 2d step Center.)

ÆGEUS.

Where will you go?

MEDEA. *(Solemnly)*

If there is any rightness on earth or in heaven, they will be punished.

ÆGEUS.

Where will you go to, Medea?

MEDEA. *(Crossing Left, still on 2nd step)*

What? To death, of course.

THE NURSE. *(Crosses to ÆGEUS)*

Oh— She is all bewildered, sir, In the deep storm and ocean of grief, or she would ask of you Refuge in Athens.

MEDEA. *(In bitter mockery, seeing ÆGEUS hesitate)*

Ah? So I should. That startled the man.—Ægeus: Will *you* shelter me in *Athens?*

ÆGEUS.

Why—yes. Yes—I will not take you now from Corinth; it would not be right. I want no quarrel with Creon, I am his guest here.

(Crossing below NURSE to Center)

If you by your own means come to Athens I will take care of you.

(THE NURSE sits on 1st step to Right of ÆGEUS.)

MEDEA.

I could repay you for it. I know the remedies—that would make a dry stick flame into fire and fruit.

ÆGEUS. *(Eagerly)*

You'd cure my sterility?

MEDEA.

I could do so.

ÆGEUS.

You are famous for profound knowledge Of drugs and charms.

(Eagerly)

You'll come to Athens?

MEDEA.

If I choose. If the gods decide it so. But, Ægeus, Would you protect me if I came? I have certain enemies. If powerful enemies came, baying for my blood, Would you protect me?

ÆGEUS.

Why—yes. What enemies?— Yes. Athens protects.

MEDEA.

I should need peace and a free mind While I prepared the medicines to make you well.

ÆGEUS.

You'll have them, you'll have them, Medea. You've seen the huge stones In the old sacred war-belt of Athens. Come the four ends of the world, they will not break in: you're safe there: I am your pledge.

(Extends arm, which she later takes.)

MEDEA.

Will you swear it, Ægeus?

ÆGEUS.

Ah? Why? I promised.

MEDEA. *(She takes his arm)*

I trust you: the oath is formal: your cure Depends on it.

(She crosses below him to down Right and then turns to him, raising her hand)

You swear by the fruitful earth and high shining heaven that you will protect me in Athens

Against all men. Swear it.
ÆGEUS. *(Raises his hand)*
                    I swear by the fruitful earth
and high shining heaven to protect you in Athens
Against all men.

                    (BOTH lower their arms.)
MEDEA.
                    And if you should break this oath?
ÆGEUS.
I will not break it.
MEDEA.
                    If you should break it, the earth
Will give you no bread but death, and the sky no light
But darkness.
ÆGEUS. *(Visibly perturbed)*
                    I will not break it.
MEDEA.
                    You must repeat the
words, Ægeus.
ÆGEUS.
If I break it, the earth
Will give me no bread but death, and the sky no light
But darkness.
MEDEA.
                    You have sworn: the gods have heard
you.
                    (Crosses below ÆGEUS to Center. Pause.)
ÆGEUS. *(Uneasily)*
When will you come to Athens?
                    (Turning to her.)
MEDEA.
                                    To Athens?
Oh,
To Athens. Why:—if I come, if I live—it will be soon.
The yoke's
On the necks of the horses.
                    (Crosses up to top step at door of house)
                    —I have some things to do
That men will talk of afterwards with hushed voices:
while I and my children
Safe in Athens laugh. Is that it? Farewell, Ægeus.
                    *(She turns abruptly from him; goes slowly,
                    deep in thought, into the house. The doors
                    close.)*
ÆGEUS. *(Staring after her)*
May the gods comfort you, Medea.—to you also
farewell,
Women of Corinth.

                    (THREE WOMEN rise.)

FIRST WOMAN.
                    Fair be the gale behind you, sir,
and the way ahead.
                    (Exit ÆGEUS up Right. She turns to NURSE)
What is she plotting in her deep mind?
She is juggling with death and life, as a juggler
With a black ball and a white ball.

                    *(NURSE slowly goes up to 2nd step, looking at
                    door of house.)*

SECOND WOMAN. *(Crosses to Left of the FIRST
WOMAN)*
No: she is like some distracted city
Sharpening its weapons. Embassies visit her:
The heads of state come to her door:
She receives them darkly.
THE NURSE.
                    I beseech you, women,
Not to speak words against my lady whom I love. You
know that wicked injustice she has to suffer.
                    (She prays)
O God, protector of exiles, lord of the holy sky, lead us
To the high rock that Athens loves, and the olive
Garland of Athens.
                    *(THE NURSE crosses down Left and sits on
                    steps.)*

FIRST WOMAN.
                    Athens is beautiful
As a lamp on a rock.
The temples are marble-shafted; light shines and
                    lingers there.
Honey-color among the carved stones
And silver-color on the leaves of the olives.
The maidens are crowned with violets: Athens and
                    Corinth
Are the two crowns of time.
                    SECOND WOMAN. *(Crosses to FIRST WOMAN and
they join hands)*
Mycenae for spears and armor; Sparta
For the stern men and the tall blonde women; and
                    Thebes I remember,
Old Thebes and the seven gates in the gray walls—
But rather I praise Athena, the ivory, the golden,
The gray-eyed Virgin, her city.
And also I praise Corinth of the beautiful fountains,
On the fair plain between the two gulfs.
                    FIRST WOMAN.
God-favored cities of the Greek world.
Fortunate those that dwell in them, happy that behold
                    them.
SECOND WOMAN.
How can one wish to die? How can that woman
Be drowned in sorrow and bewildered with hatred?

                    *(The BOLT on door is heard opening.
                    MEDEA enters and stands in doorway.)*
For only to be alive and to see the light
Is beautiful. Only to see the light;
To see a blade of young grass,
Or the gray face of a stone.
                    FIRST WOMAN. *(Pointing toward MEDEA)*
Hush.
                    MEDEA. *(Proudly and falsely)*
                    As you say. What a marvelous privilege it is
Merely to be alive. And how foolish it would be
To spend the one day of life that remains to me—at
                    least in Corinth—this tag end of one day
On tears and hatred! Rather I should rejoice, and
                    sing, and offer gifts; and as to my enemies—
I will be reconciled with them.
                    FIRST WOMAN. *(Amazed)*
                                    Reconciled with them!

                    (THREE WOMEN cross a few steps to MEDEA.)
MEDEA.
                    As you say. Reconciled. Why should they hate me?
Surely I can appease those people.
They say that gold will buy anything; even friendship,
                    even love: at least in Greece,
Among you civilized people, you reasonable and civil-
                    ized Hellenes.—In fact,
We've seen it happen. They bought Jason; Jason's
                    love. Well—
I shall buy theirs.
I still have two or three of the treasures that I brought
                    from home, things of pure precious gold, which
                    a god
Gave to the kings of my ancestors.
                    *(The LIGHT darkens, a cloud passing over
                    the sun. HARP effect offstage. The THREE
                    WOMEN huddle together.)*
                                    Is it late? It seems
to me
That the light darkens.
                    (To THE NURSE)
                                    Is it evening?
                    THE NURSE. *(Trembling)*
                                    No— No— A cloud.
MEDEA.
                    I hope for thunder: let the sky rage: my gifts
                    *(Enter TWO SLAVES from door with gift.
                    Kneel on top step.)*
Will shine the brighter.—Listen, old woman! I want
                    you
                    (THE NURSE rises.)
To go to Jason and tell him—tell him— Tell him that

I am sick of hating and weary of evil!
I wish for peace.
> (MEDEA *crosses and stands between* TWO
> SLAVES)

I wish to send precious gifts to that pale girl with the
yellow hair
Whom he has married: tell him to come and take them
—and to kiss his boys
Before we go into exile. Tell him to come speedily. Now
run, run, find him.
> (MEDEA *turns her head away.*)

THE NURSE. (*Crossing to* WOMEN *stage Center*)
Oh, I'll go. I'll run.
> (*Tremulously, to* WOMEN)
> Let me pass, please.
> (WOMEN *make way for* THE NURSE. MEDEA
> *stands looking after her.* THE NURSE *turns
> back at the limit of the scene, Right, and says,
> wringing her hands*)

But I am terrified. I do not know— I am terrified.

Pray to the gods, women, to keep
Evil birds from our hearts!
> (*She hurries away up Right.*)

MEDEA. (*Crossing down two steps*)
Run! Run! Find him!!!!
> (MEDEA *goes into the house.*)

CURTAIN

ACT TWO

MEDEA *is sitting on the upper doorstep. A cloak of
woven gold lies across her knee and down the stone
steps. Beside her are two open cases of dark
leather. From one she takes a coronet of gold vine
leaves, looks at it and replaces it.*
Two SERVING WOMEN *stand in the doorway behind her. On the Right, at some distance, the*
THREE WOMEN *are huddled, like sheep in a storm.
The Scene is darker than it was, and the gold
cloth shines.*

MEDEA.
These are the gifts I am sending to the young bride;
this golden wreath
And this woven-gold veil. They are not without value;
there is nothing like them in the whole world, or
at least
The Western world; the God of the Sun gave them to
my father's father, and I have kept them
In the deep chest for some high occasion; which has
now come.
I have great joy in giving these jewels to Creon's
daughter, for the glory of life consists of being
generous
To one's friends, and—merciless to one's enemies—you
know what a friend she has been to me. All Corinth
knows.
The slaves talk of it. The old stones in the walls
Have watched and laughed.

(MEDEA *looks at the gold cloth, and strokes it cautiously with her hand. It seems to scorch her
fingers.* THIRD WOMAN *has come nearer to look;
now starts backward.*)

MEDEA.
See, it is almost alive. Gold is a living thing: such
pure gold.
> (NURSE *enters from up Right; crosses to foot of
> steps*)
But when her body has warmed it, how it will shine!
> (*To the* NURSE)
Why doesn't he come? What keeps him?
NURSE. (*Evidently terrified*)

Oh, my lady: presently.
I have but now returned from him. He was beyond
the gate, watching the races—where a monstrous
thing
Had happened: a young mare broke from the chariot
And tore with her teeth a stallion.
MEDEA. (*Stands up, shakes out the golden cloak,
which again smoulders. She folds it cautiously, lays it
in the leather case. The LIGHT has darkened again.
She looks anxiously at the clouded sun*)
> He takes his time, eh? It
is intolerable
To sit and wait.
> (*To the* SERVING WOMEN)
> Take these into the house. Keep them at hand
For when I call.
> (*They take them in.* MEDEA *moves restlessly, un-
> der extreme nervous tension; speaks to the* NURSE.

NURSE *crosses below steps to stage Left, then up
two steps*)
> You say that a mare attacked a stallion?
THE NURSE.
> She tore
him cruelly.
I saw him being led away: a black racer: his blood
ran down
From the throat to the fetlocks.
MEDEA.
> You're sure he's coming. You're
sure?
THE NURSE.
> He said he would.
MEDEA.
> Let him make haste, then!
SECOND WOMAN. (*She crosses to Left below* NURSE)
Frightening irrational things
Have happened lately; the face of nature is flawed
with omens.
FIRST WOMAN. (*Crosses to Left, joining* SECOND
WOMAN)
> Yesterday evening a slave
Came up to the harbor-gate, carrying a basket
Of new-caught fish: one of the fish took fire
And burned in the wet basket with a high flame: the
thing was witnessed
By many persons.
THIRD WOMAN. (*Crosses Left of other* TWO WOMEN,
joining them)
> And a black leopard was seen
Gliding through the market-place—
MEDEA. (*Abruptly, approaching the* WOMEN)
> You haven't told
me yet: do you not think that Creon's daughter
Will be glad of those gifts?
FIRST WOMAN.
> O Medea, too much wealth
Is sometimes dreadful.
MEDEA.
> She'll be glad, however. She'll
take them and put them on, she'll wear them, she'll
strut in them,
She'll peacock in them.—I see him coming now.—the
> (THREE WOMEN *retire to up Left corner.* NURSE
> *sits below Left pillar*)
whole palace will admire her.—Stand away from
me, women,
While I make my sick peace.

(MEDEA *crosses way down Right as* JASON *enters up
Right to stage Center.* NURSE *points at* MEDEA.
who goes across the scene to meet JASON, *but more
and more slowly, and stops. Her attitude indicates
her aversion.*)

JASON.
> Well, I have come. I tell you plainly,
Not for your sake: the children's. Your woman says
that you have your wits again, and are willing
To look beyond your own woes.

(MEDEA *is silent.* JASON *observes her and says*)
                                   It appears doubtful.
(She turns from him)
—Where are the children? I have made inquiry: I can
find fosterage for them
In Epidaurus; or any other of several cities
That are Creon's friends. I'll visit them from time to
time, and watch
That they're well kept.
MEDEA. *(With suppressed violence)*
                        You mean—take them from me!
Be careful, Jason, I am not patient yet.
(More quietly)
                        I am the one who labored in
pain to bear them, I cannot
Smile while I lose them. But I am learning: I am
learning.—
No, Jason: I will not give up my little ones
To the cold care of strangers.
Hard faces, harsh hands. It will be far better for
them to share
My wandering ocean of beggary and bleak exile:
I love them, Jason. Only if you would keep them and
care for them here in Corinth,
I might consent.
JASON.
        Gladly—but they are exiled.
MEDEA.
                        —In your own
house.
JASON.
        Gladly I'd do it—but you understand
They are exiled, as you are. I asked Creon and he re-
fused it.
MEDEA.
You asked Creon to take my children from me?
(She reaches her hands toward him)
Forgive me, Jason,
As I do you.
        (Crosses up steps to his Right)
                We have had too much wrath, and our acts
Are closing on us. On me, I mean. Retribution is from
the gods, and it breaks our hearts: but you
Feel no guilt, you fear nothing, nothing can touch you.
It is wonderful to stand serene above fate
While earthlings wince. If it lasts. It does not always
last.
—Do you love the children, Jason?
JASON.
                Ha? Certainly. The children? Certainly!
I am their father.
MEDEA.
        Oh, but that's not enough. If I am to give
them up to you—be patient with me,
I must question you first. And very deeply; to the
quick. If anything happens to them,
Would you be grieved?

JASON.
                Nothing will happen to them,
Medea, if in my care. Rest your mind on it.
MEDEA. *(She crosses up to top step in back of*
JASON)
You must pardon me: it is not possible to be certain
of that.
If they were—killed and their blood
Ran on the floor of the house or down the deep earth—
Would you be grieved?
JASON.
                You have a sick mind. What
a weak thing a woman is, always dreaming of evil.
MEDEA.
Answer me!
JASON.
        Yes, after I'd cut their killer into red col-
lops—I'd grieve.
MEDEA.
                That is true: vengeance
Makes grief bearable.—But—Creon's daughter, your
wife—no doubt will breed

Many other boys.—But, if something should happen
to—Creon's daughter—
JASON.
        Enough, Medea. Too much. Be silent!
MEDEA.
I am to conclude that you love—Creon's daughter—
More than your sons They'll have to take the sad
journey with me.
        (To the NURSE)
Tell the boys to come out
And bid their father farewell.
        (The NURSE goes into the house.)
JASON. *(Coming to her and taking her arm)*
                        I could take them from you
By force, Medea.
MEDEA. *(Violently)*
        Try it, you!

(Controlling herself)
                No, Creon decided otherwise; he said
        (JASON crosses down Right as if to go)
        they will share my exile.—Come, Jason,
Let's be friends at last!
        *(The BOYS come out with their TUTOR, followed
        by the NURSE. JASON makes to clasp her arm. She
        pulls away to Center)*
I am quite patient now; I have learned.—Come, boys:
come,
        (BOYS run straight to MEDEA.)
Speak to your father.
        *(NURSE and TUTOR remain on top step at
        either side of door. They shrink back)*
                No, no, we're friends again. We're not
angry any more.
JASON. *(Has gone eagerly to meet them on the steps.
He drops to one knee to be more nearly level with them,
but they are shy and reluctant)*
        Big boys. Tall fellows, ha?
You've grown up since I saw you.
MEDEA.
                        Smile for him, children.
Give him
        *(She turns, and stands rigidly turned away,
        her face sharp with pain)*
        your hands.
THE NURSE. *(To JASON)*
                I think he's afraid of you, sir.
JASON. *(To the YOUNGER BOY)*
                                        What?
What? You'll learn, my man,
        *(During this speech ELDER BOY crosses to
        him. He picks him up)*
Not to fear me. You'll make your enemies run away
from you
When you grow up.
        (To the ELDER BOY)
                        And you, Captain,
How would you like a horn-tipped bow to hunt rabbits
with?
Wolves, I mean.
        *(Takes ELDER BOY by the hand and crosses
        with him to rock Right. He sits YOUNGER BOY
        on his lap. ELDER BOY sits on floor. He plays
        with the BOYS. They are less shy of him now.)*
FIRST WOMAN. *(Coming close to MEDEA)*
                Don't give them to him,
Medea. If you do it will ache forever.
SECOND WOMAN.
                        You have refuge;
        take them there.
Athens is beautiful—
MEDEA. *(Fiercely)*
                Be silent!
Look at him: he loves them—ah? Therefore his dear
children
Are not going to that city but a darker city, where no
games are played, no music is heard.—Do you
think
I am a cow lowing after the calf? Or a bitch with
pups, licking

The hand that struck her? Watch and see. Watch this man, women: he is going to weep. I think
He is going to weep blood, and quite soon, and much more
Than I have wept. Watch and keep silence.
(She goes toward the GROUP on the steps)
Jason,
Are the boys dear to you? I think I am satisfied that you love them,
These two young heroes.
(JASON stands up and turns to her, one of the Boys clinging to each of his hands. He has made friends with them.)
MEDEA. *(She weeps)*
Oh—Oh—Oh!
JASON.
—God's hand, Medea, what is it?
What is the matter?
MEDEA. *(Makes with both hands a gesture of pushing down something, flings her head back proudly)*
Nothing. It is hard to let them go.
—This I have thought of:
You shall take them to—Creon's daughter, your wife—and make them kneel to her, and ask her
To ask her father to let them stay here in Corinth. He'll grant it, he is growing old, he denies her nothing.
Even that hard king loves his only child.
What she asks is done.—You will go with the boys, Jason, and speak for them,—they are not skillful yet
In supplication—and I'll send gifts. I'll put gifts in their hands. People say that gifts
Will persuade even the gods.—Is it well thought of?
Will she listen to us?
JASON.
Why, if I ask it! She'd hardly refuse me anything. And I believe that you're right,
She can rule Creon.
MEDEA. *(To the TUTOR)*
Bring me those gold things.
(TUTOR exits main door.)
(She extends hands to BOYS. Sits on step. They cross to her)
Dear ones, brave little falcons—little pawns of my agony—
Go, ask that proud breastless girl of her bitter charity
Whether she will let you nest here until your wings fledge, while far your mother
Flies the dark storm—
(She weeps again.)
JASON.
I'm sorry for you. Parting is hard.
(He crosses down Right off steps.)
MEDEA.
I can
bear it.
And worse too.
(The TUTOR and SERVING WOMEN bring the gifts)
Oh, here: here are the things: take them, darlings,
Into your little hands.
(Giving them to the BOYS. Crown goes to YOUNGER BOY. Cloak to ELDER BOY. Each show them to TUTOR and NURSE, then sit on the 3rd step. SERVING WOMEN exit as soon as gifts are taken from them)
Hold carefully by the cases: don't touch the gold,
Or it might—tarnish.
JASON.
Why! These are king's treasures. You shouldn't, Medea: it's too much. Creon's house
Has gold enough of its own.
MEDEA.
Oh—if she'll wear them. What should I want with woven gold vanities —Black is my wear. The woman ought to be very happy

(Throws wedding ring in box with cloak)
With such jewels—and such a husband—ah? Her sun is rising,
(MEDEA crosses Left)
mine going down—I hope
To a red sunset.—The little gold wreath is pretty, isn't it?

(YOUNGER BOY holds it up to JASON.)

JASON. *(Doubtfully)*
It looks like fire—
MEDEA.
Vine leaves: the flashing
Arrow-sharp leaves. They have weight, though.
(BOYS put down boxes)
Gold is too heavy a burden
for little hands. Carry them, you,
Until you come to the palace.
(NURSE takes gold wreath; exits up Right, followed by TUTOR with cloak. JASON follows with BOYS by the hand)
—Farewell, sweet boys: brave
little trudging pilgrims from the black wave
To the white desert: take the stuff in, be sure you lay

it in her own hands.
Come back and tell me what happens.
(Crosses up to front of pillar Right and waves goodbye to them as they leave. She turns abruptly away from them)
Tell me what happens.
(The BOYS go out reluctantly, JASON holding their hands.)
Rejoice, women,
The gifts are given; the bait is laid.
The gods roll their great eyes over Creon's house and quietly smile:
That robe of bright-flowing gold, that bride-veil, that fish-net
To catch a young slender salmon—not mute, she'll sing: her delicate body writhes in the meshes,
The golden wreath binds her bright head with light: she'll dance, she'll sing loudly:
Would I were there to hear it, that proud one howling.
(She crosses to Center between pillars)
—Look, the sun's out again, the clouds are gone,
All's gay and clear. Ai! I wish the deep earth would open and swallow us—
Before I do what comes next.
I wish all life would perish,
(Crosses down to 3rd step and sits)
and the holy gods in high heaven die,
before my little ones
Come home to my hands.
FIRST WOMAN. *(Going to MEDEA)*
It would be better for you, Medea, if the earth
Opened her jaws and took you down into darkness.

But one thing you will not do, for you cannot,
You will not hurt your own children, though wrath like plague-boils
Aches, your mind in a fire-haze
Bites the purple apples of pain—no blood-lapping
Beast of the field, she-bear nor lioness,
Nor the lean wolf-bitch,
Hurts her own tender whelps, nor the yellow-eyed,
Scythe-beaked and storm-shouldered
Eagle that tears the lambs has ever made prey
Of the fruit of her own tree—
MEDEA.
How could that girl's death slake me?
THIRD WOMAN. *(Coming forward from the OTHERS)*
I am sick with terror.
I'll run to the palace, I'll warn them.
MEDEA.
Will you?—Go. Go if you will.
God and my vengeful goddess are doing these things: you cannot prevent them, but you could easily fall
In the same fire.

THIRD WOMAN. *(Retreating)*
            I am afraid to go.
MEDEA.
                    You are wise. Anyone
Running between me and my justice will reap
What no man wants.
FIRST WOMAN.
                  Not justice; vengeance.
You have suffered evil, you wish to inflict evil.
MEDEA.
I do according to nature what I have to do.
FIRST WOMAN.
I have heard evil
Answering evil as thunder answers the lightning.
A great waste voice in the hollow sky,
And all that they say is death. I have heard vengeance
Like an echo under a hill answering vengeance,
Great hollow voices: all that they say is death.
SECOND WOMAN.
                  The sword speaks
And the spear answers: the city is desolate.
The nations remember old wrongs and destroy each
    other.
And no man binds up their wounds.
FIRST WOMAN.
               But justice
Builds a firm house.
MEDEA.
           The doors of her house are vengeance.
SECOND WOMAN.
               I dreamed that someone
Gave good for evil, and the world was amazed.
MEDEA. *(Rises. Crosses up between pillar and column Right)*
Only a coward or a madman gives good for evil.—Did
    you hear a thin music
Like a girl screaming? Or did I perhaps imagine it?
    Hark, it is music.

THIRD WOMAN. *(Crossing towards Center below steps)*
Let me go, Medea!
I'll be mute, I'll speak to no one. I cannot bear—
Let me go to my house!
MEDEA.
             You will stay here,
And watch the end.
    (The WOMEN *are beginning to mill like scared cattle, huddled and circular)*
           You will be quiet, you women. You
came to see

How the barbarian woman endures betrayal: watch
    and you'll know.
SECOND WOMAN. *(Kneels)*
My heart is a shaken cup
Of terror: the thin black wine
Spills over all my flesh down to my feet.

FIRST WOMAN.
She fled from her father's house in a storm of blood,
In a blood-storm she flew up from Thessaly,
Now here and dark over Corinth she widens
Wings to ride up the twisted whirlwind
And talons to hold with—
Let me flee this dark place and the pillared doorway.
SECOND WOMAN.
I hear the man-wolf on the snow hill
Howl to the soaring moon—
THIRD WOMAN.
The demon comes in through the locked door
And strangles the child—
SECOND WOMAN.
Blood is the seed of blood, hundredfold the harvest,
The gleaners that follow it, their feet are crimson—
FIRST WOMAN.
I see the whirlwind hanging from the black sky.
Like a twisted rope,
Like an erect serpent, its tail tears the earth,
It is braided of dust and lightning,

Who will fly in it? Let me hide myself
From these night-shoring pillars and the dark door.

MEDEA.
                  Have patience,
    women. Be quiet.
I am quite sure something has happened; presently
    someone
Will bring us news.
THIRD WOMAN.
             Look! The children are coming.
SECOND WOMAN. *(Rises)*
They have bright things in their hands: their faces are
    clear and joyous; was all that fear
A dream, a dream?

    *(*MEDEA *crosses to pillar Left. The* TUTOR *enters up Right with the* BOYS. *The* ELDER BOY *carries a decorated bow and arrows; the* YOUNGER BOY *has a doll, a brightly painted wooden warrior.* MEDEA, *gazing at the* BOYS, *retreats slowly backward from them.)*

THE TUTOR. *(Crossing up to* MEDEA *on top step;* BOYS *stand behind him on 2nd and 3rd steps)*
          Rejoice, Medea, I bring good news. The
    princess graciously
Received your presents and smiled: it is peace between
    you. She has welcomed the little boys, they are
    safe from exile.
They'll be kept here. Their father is joyful.
MEDEA. *(Coldly, her hands clenched in the effort of self control)*
                    Yes?
THE TUTOR.
All Creon's house is well pleased. When we first went in
The serving-women came and fondled the children;
    it was rumored through all the household that
    you and Jason
Were at peace again: like word of a victory
Running through a wide city, when people gather in
    the streets to be glad together: and we brought
    the boys
Into the hall; we put those costly gifts in their hands;
    then Jason
Led them before the Princess. At first she looked
    angrily at them and turned away, but Jason said,
"Don't be angry at your friends. You ought to love
Those whom I love. Look what they've brought you,
    dear," and she looked and saw
In the dark boxes the brilliant gold: she smiled then,
And marveled at it.
    (He turns to them and YOUNGER BOY *crosses up to him)*
          Afterwards she caressed the children;
    she even said that this little one's
Hair was like fine-spun gold. Then Jason gave them
    these toys and we came away.
MEDEA.
               Yes.—If this
Were all. If this were all, old man—
I'd have your bony loins beaten to a blood-froth
For the good news you bring.
TUTOR.
               My lady—!
MEDEA.
              There's more, however
It will come soon.

    (The BOYS *shyly approach her and show their toys. She, with violent self-constraint, looks at them; but folds her hands in her cloak, not to touch them.)*

ELDER BOY. *(Crosses to her. Drawing the little bow)*
Look, Mother.
MEDEA. *(Suddenly weeping)*
              Take them away from me!
I cannot bear. I cannot bear.

THE TUTOR.

Children, come quickly.
(He shepherds them up the steps, and disappears in the house.)

FIRST WOMAN.

If there is any mercy or forbearance in heaven
Let it reach down and touch that dark mind
To save it from what it dreams—

THE SLAVE. *(A young SLAVE dashes in up Right, panting and distraught. He has run from CREON'S house)*

Where is Medea?
(SLAVE crosses to base of steps Right, throwing himself across them.)

SECOND WOMAN.

What has happened? What horror drives you?
Are spears hunting behind you?

THE SLAVE. *(He sees MEDEA on the steps)*

Flee for your life, Medea! I am
Jason's man, but you were good to me
While I was here in the house. Can you hear me?
Escape, Medea!

MEDEA.

I hear you.

Draw breath; say quietly
What you have seen. It must have been something notable, the way your eyes
Bulge in the whites.

THE SLAVE.

If you have horses, Medea, drive! Or a boat on the shore,
Sail!
(Rises and crosses down stage Right.)

MEDEA.

But first you must tell me about the beautiful girl who was lately married:

SLAVE.

Ooh!

MEDEA.

your great man's daughter:

SLAVE.

Ooh!

MEDEA.

Are they all quite well?

SLAVE.

My ears ring with the crying, my eyes are scalded. She put on the gold garments—
Did you do it, Medea?

MEDEA.

I did it.

SLAVE.

Ooooh!!!

MEDEA.

Speak quietly.

THE SLAVE.

You are avenged.

You are horribly avenged. It is too much.
The gods will hate you.
(Collapses on podium.)

MEDEA. *(Avid, but still sitting)*

That is my care. Did anyone die with her?

THE SLAVE.

Creon!

THREE WOMEN.

Oooh!!!!

MEDEA. *(Solemnly)*

Where is pride now?
Tell me all that you saw. Speak slowly.

THE SLAVE.

He tried to save her—

he died! Corinth is masterless.
All's in amazed confusion, and some are looting, but they'll avenge him—
(He hears someone coming behind him)
I'm going on!

Someone is going to die.

(He runs Left to the far side of the scene, and exits while MEDEA speaks. Meanwhile the light has been changing, and soon the sun will set.)

MEDEA.

Here comes a more stable witness.
(The NURSE enters from up Right)
Old friend:
Catch your breath; take your time. I want the whole tale, every gesture and cry. I have labored for this.

THE NURSE.

Death is turned loose! I've hobbled and run, and fallen—
(Crosses to 4th step and sits.)

MEDEA.

Please

Nurse: I am very happy: go slowly.
(MEDEA sits and puts her head in NURSE's lap)
Tell me these things in order from the beginning.
As when you used to dress me, when I was little, in my father's house: you used to say
"One thing at a time; one thing and then the next."
(The LIGHT has changed to a flare of sunset)

(THREE WOMEN have assembled themselves after NURSE's entrance in following fashion: FIRST sitting first step Center, SECOND standing to her Left, THIRD standing to Left of SECOND.)

THE NURSE.

My eyes are blistered,
My throat's like a dry straw— There was a long mirror on the wall, and when her eyes saw it—
After the children had gone with Jason—she put her hands in the case and took those gold things—and I
Watched, for I feared something might happen to her, but I never thought
So horribly—she placed on her little head the bright golden wreath, she gathered the flowing gold robe
Around her white shoulders,
And slender flanks,—
(MEDEA rises; crosses to below rock down Right)
And gazed at the girl in the metal mirror, going back and forth
On tiptoe almost;
But suddenly horror began. I— Oh, oh—

MEDEA. *(Crosses up to Right of NURSE, shaking her by the shoulders)*

You are not suffering.
You saw it, you did not feel it. Speak plainly.

THE NURSE.

Her face went white;
She staggered a few steps, bending over, and fell

Into the great throne-chair; then a serving woman
Began to call for water thinking she had fainted, but saw the foam
Start on her lips, and the eyes rolling, and screamed instead. Then some of them
Ran after Jason, others ran to fetch Creon: and that doomed girl
Frightfully crying started up from the chair; she ran, she was like a torch, and the gold crown
(MEDEA races up to door of house writhing)
Like a comet streamed fire; she tore at it but it clung to her head; the golden cloak
Was white-hot, flaying the flesh from the living bones: blood mixed with fire ran down, she fell, she burned
On the floor, writhing. Then Creon came and flung himself on her, hoping to choke
That rage of flame, but it ran through him, his own agony
Made him forget his daughter's. The fire stuck to the flesh, it glued him to her; he tried to stand up,
He tore her body and his own. The burnt flesh broke

In lumps from the bones.
(She covers her eyes with her hands)
I have finished. They lie there.
Eyeless, disfaced, untouchable; middens of smoking flesh—
(Nearly a scream)
No!
I have no more.
MEDEA. *(Crossing down to NURSE; takes her arms)*
I want all.
Had they died when you came away?
THE NURSE.
I am not able—have mercy—
No, the breath
Still whistled in the black mouths. No one could touch them.
Jason stood in their smoke, and his hands tore
His unhelmeted hair.
MEDEA.
You have told good news well: I'll reward you.
As for those people, they will soon die. Their woes are over too soon.
(MEDEA crosses down, then paces up Right and back down Right; sees WOMEN at end of speech and crosses to them)
Mine are not.
Jason's are not.
(She turns abruptly from them, toward the BOYS, who have been standing by the doorway, fascinated, not comprehending but watching)
My little falcons!—Listen to me! Laugh and be glad: we have accomplished it.
Our enemies were great and powerful, they were full of cold pride, they ruled all this country—they are down in the ashes.
(Sitting on steps with BOYS)
Crying like dogs, cowering in the ashes, in their own ashes. They went down with the sun, and the sun will rise
And not see them again. He will think "Perhaps they are sleeping, they feasted late.
At noon they will walk in the garden." Oh, no, oh, no!
They will not walk in the garden. No one has ever injured me but suffered more
Than I had suffered.
(She turns from the BOYS)
Therefore this final sacrifice I intended glares in my eyes
Like a lion on a ridge.
(Turning back to the BOYS)
We still hate, you know;—a person fiearer than these, more vile, more contemptible,
Whom I—I cannot. If he were my own hands I would cut him off, or my eyes, I would gouge him out—
But not you: that was madness.
(She turns from them)
So Jason will be able to say, "I have lost much,
But not all: I have children: My sons are well."
(She stands staring, agonized, one hand picking at the other)
No! I want him crushed, boneless, crawling—
I have no choice.
(Resolutely, to the THREE WOMEN. She rises and crosses down Left to WOMEN)
You there! You thought me soft and submissive like a common woman—who takes a blow
And cries a little, and she wipes her face
And runs about the housework, loving her master? I am not such a woman.
FIRST WOMAN.
Awake, Medea!
Awake from the evil dream. Catch up your children and flee,
Farther than Athens, farther than Thrace or Spain, flee to the world's end.
Fire and death have done your bidding,
Are you not fed full with evil?

Is it not enough?
MEDEA.
No, Loathing is endless.
Hate is a bottomless cup, I will pour and pour.
(She turns fiercely to the BOYS)
Children—
(Suddenly melting)
—O my little ones!
What was I dreaming?—My babes, my own!
(She kneels to them, taking their hands)
Never, never, never, never
Shall my own babes be hurt. Not if every war-hound and spear-slave in headless Corinth
Were on the track.
(Still kneeling; to WOMEN)
Look, their sweet lips are trembling: look, women, the little mouths: I frightened them
With those wild words: they stood and faced me, they never flinched.
Look at their proud young eyes! My eaglets, my golden ones!
(She kisses them, then holds them off and gazes at them)
O sweet small faces—like the pale wild-roses
That blossom where the cliff breaks toward the brilliant sea: the delicate form and color, the dear, dear fragrance
Of your sweet breath—
(She continues gazing at them; her face changes)

THE NURSE. *(Sits up)*
My lady, make haste, haste!
Take them and flee. Flee away from here! Someone will come soon.
(MEDEA still gazes at the BOYS)
Oh—listen to me.
Spears will come, death will come. All Corinth is in confusion and headless anarchy, unkinged and amazed
Around that horror you made: therefore they linger: yet in a moment
Its avengers come!
(MEDEA looks up from staring at the BOYS. Her face has changed; the love has gone out of it. She speaks in a colorless, tired voice)
MEDEA.
I have a sword in the house.
I can defend you.
(She stands up stiffly and takes the BOYS by their shoulders; holds the ELDER in front of her, toward WOMEN: speaks with cold intensity)
Would you say that this child
Has Jason's eyes?
(The WOMEN are silent, in terror gazing at her)
—They are his cubs. They have his blood.
As long as they live I shall be mixed with him.
(Crosses to pillar up Right. She looks down at the BOYS; speaks tenderly but hopelessly.)
Children:
It is evening. See, evening has come. Come, little ones.
Into the house.
(BOYS cross to her; arms about her waist)
Evening brings all things home. It brings the bird to the bough and the lamb to the fold—
And the child to the mother.
(She pushes BOYS gently into house)
We must not think too much: people go mad
If they think too much.
(In the doorway, behind BOYS, she flings up her hands as if to tear her hair out by the roots; then quietly goes in. The great door closes; the iron noise of the BOLT is driven home.)
THE NURSE.

No!

(She rushes toward the door, helpless, her hand reaching up and beating feebly against the foot of the door.)

FIRST WOMAN.

What is going to happen?

SECOND WOMAN.

That crown of horrors—

(They speak like somnambulists, and stand frozen. There is a moment of silence.)

CHILD'S VOICE. *(In the house, shrill, broken off)*

Mother Ai—!

(The WOMEN press toward the door, crying more or less simultaneously)

THE WOMEN.

Medea, no!

Prevent her! Save them!

Open the door—

(They listen for an answer.)

THIRD WOMAN.

A god is here, Medea, he calls to you, he forbids you—

(NURSE has risen, and beats feebly on the door, stooping and bent over. FIRST WOMAN stands beside her, very erect, with her back against the door, covering her ears with her hands. They are silent.)

ELDER BOY'S VOICE. *(Clear, but as if hypnotized)*
Mother— Mother—ai!

MEDEA. Aaahh!!!!

(Lamentation — keening — is heard in the house. It rises and falls, and continues to the end, but often nearly inaudible. It is now twilight.)

THE NURSE. *(Limps down the steps and says)*

There is no hope in heaven or earth. It is done.

It was destined when she was born, now it is done.

(Wailing.)

Oh, oh, oh.

THIRD WOMAN. *(With terror, looking into the shadows)*

Who is coming?

Someone is running at us!

FIRST WOMAN. *(Quietly)*

The accursed man.

Jason.

SECOND WOMAN.

He has a sword.

FIRST WOMAN.

I am more afraid of the clinging contagion of his misfortunes.

A man the gods are destroying.

JASON. *(Enters rapidly up Right, disheveled and shaking, a drawn sword in his hand. Crosses in to Right at foot of steps)*

Where is that murderess? Here in the house?

Or has she fled? She'll have to hide in the heavy metal darkness and caves of the earth—and there

I'll crawl and find her.

(No answer. The THREE WOMEN draw away from him as he moves toward the door. He stops and turns on them, drawing his left hand across his face, as if his eyes were bewildered.)

JASON.

Are you struck dumb? Are you shielding her?

Where is Medea?

FIRST WOMAN.

You caused these things. She was faithful to you and you broke faith.

Horror is here.

JASON.

Uncaused. There was no reason— Tell me at once—

Whether she took my boys with her? Creon's people

would kill them for what she has done: I'd rather save them

Than punish her. Help me in this.

THE NURSE. *(Wailing, sinks to ground down Left)*

Oh, oh, oh—

JASON. *(Looking sharply at NURSE)*

So she has killed herself.

Good. She never lacked courage— I'll take my sons away to the far end of the earth, and never

Speak of these things again.

THE NURSE. *(Wailing)*

Oh, oh, oh—

(Lamentation from the house answers.)

JASON. *(With a queer slyness, for he is trying to cheat himself out of believing what he dreads. He glances at the door, furtively, over his shoulder)*

Is she lying in there?

Honorable at least in her death.—I might have known it.

(They remain silent)

Well, answer!

FIRST WOMAN. *(Pointing toward CREON'S house)*

Death is there; death is here.

But you are both blind and deaf: how can I tell you?

JASON. *(Is silent, then says slowly)*

But—the—

children are well?

FIRST WOMAN.

I do not know

Whether Medea lives or is dead.

JASON. *(Flings down the sword and sets his shoulder against the door; pushes in vain)*

Open! Open! Open!

(Returns halfway down the steps, and says pitiably)

Women, I am alone.

Help me.

Help me to break the bolt.

Go and find help—

(JASON runs down Right as door opens. This stops him and he turns. It is now fairly dark; the interior of the house is lighted. WOMEN draw back in fear; JASON stands on the steps, bewildered. MEDEA comes into the doorway; her hand and clothing are blood-marked. The door closes.)

MEDEA.

What feeble night-bird overcome by misfortune beats at my door?

(JASON takes two steps up to her)

Can this be that great adventurer,

The famous lord of the seas and delight of women, the heir of rich Corinth—this crying drunkard

On the dark doorstep?—Yet you've not had enough.

You have come to drink the last bitter drops.

I'll pour them for you.

(She displays her hand which is covered with blood.)

JASON.

What's that stain on your hands?

MEDEA.

The wine

I was pouring for you spilled on my hand—

Dear were the little grapes that were crushed to make it; dear were the vineyards.

JASON.

I came to kill you, Medea,

Like a caught beast, like a crawling viper. Give me my sons, that I may save them from Creon's men,

I'll go quietly away.

MEDEA.

Hush, they are sleeping. Perhaps

I will let you look at them: you cannot have them.

But the hour is late, you ought to go home to that highborn bride: the night has fallen, surely she longs for you.

Surely her flesh is not crusted black, nor her forehead
burned bald, nor her mouth a horror.
> (JASON *kneels on the steps, painfully groping
> for his sword)*

　　　　　　　　　　　　　　　　　　She
is very young. But surely she loves and desires
you—
Surely she will be fruitful.—Your sword you want?
There it is. Not that step, the next lower. No, the next
higher.
JASON. *(Stands erect. Goes up two steps to her)*
I'll kill you first and then find my sons.

MEDEA.
　　　　　　　　　　　　You must be careful, Jason.
Do you see the two fire-snakes
That guard this door?
> *(Indicating the two snakes)*
　　　　　　　Here and here: one on each side: two
serpents.
　　　Their throats are swollen with poison,
Their eyes are burning coals and their tongues are fire.
　　　They are coiled ready to strike: if you come near
　　　them,
They'll make you what Creon is. But stand there very
　　　quietly.
　　　I'll let you
Look at your sons.
> (MEDEA *crosses to pillar Left)*

Open the doors that he may see them.
> *(The doors open revealing the* TWO BOYS
> *soaked in blood.)*
JASON. *(Flinging his hands to his temples and cross-
ing up to pillar Right)*
　　　I knew it already.
I knew it before I saw it. No wild beast could have
　　　done it.
MEDEA.
　　　　　　　　　　　　　　　　I have
done it: because I loathed you more
Than I loved them.
JASON.
　　　Did you feel nothing, no pity, are you pure evil? I
　　　should have killed you
The day I saw you.
MEDEA.
　　　I tore my own heart and laughed: I was tearing
　　　yours.
JASON. Will you laugh while I strangle you?
MEDEA.
I would still laugh.

> (JASON *lunges at her but is sent back by
> snakes)*
　　　　　—Beware my door holders, Jason! these
eager serpents.—I'd still be joyful
To know that every bone of your life is broken: you
are left helpless, friendless, mateless, childless,
Avoided by gods and men, unclean with awful excess
of grief—childless

JASON.
　　　It is no matter now
Who lives, or who dies.
> *(As next speech is said* JASON *starts slowly
> down steps to Right.)*
MEDEA.
　　　You had love and betrayed it: now of all men
You are utterly the most miserable. As I of women.
　　　But I, as woman, despised, a foreigner, alone
Against you and the might of Corinth,
Have met you, throat for throat, evil for evil, vengeance
for vengeance.
JASON. *(Turning to her on bottom step)*
　　　　　What does it matter now?
Only give me my boys: the little pitiful violated bodies:
that I may bury them
In some kind place.
MEDEA.

To you?—You would betray even the little bodies:
coin them for silver.
Sell them for power. No!
JASON. *(Crawling up two more steps at her feet)*
　　　Let me touch their dear flesh, let me touch
their hair!
MEDEA.
　　　　　　　No. They are mine.
> *(HARP EFFECT off Right)*
They are going with me: the chariot is at the gate.

> *(During this speech* JASON *rises and goes
> slowly down Right)*

　　　Go down to your ship Argo and weep beside
it, that rotting hulk on the harbor-beach
Drawn dry astrand, never to be launched again—even
the weeds and barnacles on the warped keel
Are dead and stink:—that's your last companion—
And only hope: for some time one of the rotting tim-
bers
Will fall on your head and kill you—meanwhile sit
there and mourn, remembering the infinite evil,
and the good
That you made evil.
　　　Now I go forth
Under the cold eyes of heaven—those weakness-despis-
ing stars:—not me they scorn.

> (MEDEA *goes into the house*—JASON *starts after her
> but the door is bolted in his face. He collapses to
> the ground in front of doors.* MEDEA *is seen com-
> ing out Left door bearing the* TWO BOYS. *Then as
> final fanfare of MUSIC comes slow*

　　　　　　CURTAIN

A Streetcar Named Desire

BY TENNESSEE WILLIAMS

First presented by Irene Selznick at the Barrymore Theatre in New York on December 3, 1947, with the following cast:

NEGRO WOMAN	Gee Gee James	MEXICAN WOMAN	Edna Thomas
EUNICE HUBBELL	Peg Hillias	BLANCHE DUBOIS	Jessica Tandy
STANLEY KOWALSKI	Marlon Brando	PABLO GONZALES	Nick Dennis
STELLA KOWALSKI	Kim Hunter	A YOUNG COLLECTOR	Vito Christi
STEVE HUBBELL	Rudy Bond	NURSE	Ann Dere
HAROLD MITCHELL (MITCH)	Karl Malden	DOCTOR	Richard Garrick

The action of the play takes place in the spring, summer, and early fall in New Orleans. It was performed with intermissions after Scene Four and Scene Six.

WHEN Tennessee Williams' *A Streetcar Named Desire* appeared on the Broadway scene, its critics could barely restrain their admiration for its raw emotional power. Only George Jean Nathan refused to be impressed—perversely, it seemed. John Mason Brown spoke for the strong majority opinion when he called the play "the most probing script to have been written by an American since Clifford Odets wrote *Awake and Sing!*" Brooks Atkinson acclaimed "Mr. Williams' baleful insight into character, his ruthless-ness as an observer and his steel-like accuracy as a writer." Other virtues found in the author's artistry were "lyricism" and ability "to evoke mood and transcend realism." John Mason Brown referred to him as a "good Chekhovian." In rebuttal, it could be noted that a considerable portion of the drama was produced by external and not alto-gether inevitable circumstances. It could also be noted that the play, so tragical in tone and mood, fell short of tragic elevation; that Blanche's story was a singular clinical case rather than a fundamentally representative, "universal" drama. Nevertheless, the play continued to exert a spell over audiences for a long time, and it was appreciated on grounds other than mere sensationalism even when it could not be endorsed as high tragedy.

Atkinson defined *A Streetcar Named Desire* as a play about "an unequal contest between the decadence of a self-conscious civilization and the vitality of animal aimless-ness"; and somewhat more accurately, as the drama of a gentlewoman's "panicky flight from the catastrophe of a genteel way of life that can no longer sustain her in an animal-ized world." This much is certain: There was a substantial, if not absolutely formulable, residuum of meaning in the experience that harrowed the playgoer. The play communi-cated a sense of crass fatality; of life destroyed by frustration in love, against which pre-tensions and illusions are a pathetic and futile defense. The epigraph Williams chose from Hart Crane's *The Broken Tower* (Williams belongs to the avant-garde school that favors epigraphs as well as symbols) may speak for his own intentions. It expresses much the same realization of the fragility of love and the same hunger of the soul in a far from clement world that Blanche experiences:

> And so it was I entered the broken world
> To trace the visionary company of love, its voice
> An instant in the wind (I know not whither hurled)
> But not for long to hold each desperate choice.

Not invulnerable to criticism, *A Streetcar Named Desire* nonetheless towered over most of the plays written for the American theatre during the decade of the forties.

Williams was only thirty-three years old when he presented this work after the notable production of *The Glass Menagerie*. Born in 1914 in Columbus, Mississippi, Thomas Lanier ("Tennessee") Williams grew up in the South, for the most part in St. Louis, in a household that introduced him to the struggles of unsheltered gentility. His maternal grandfather, an Episcopalian clergyman, helped to shape his mind and gave him a taste for literature; he also took the impressionable lad on consolatory visits to members of his flock, among whom Williams saw prototypes of the pathetic women of his plays. His sister, to whom he was devoted, had the sort of delicate, vulnerable soul that he was later to represent in these plays, and, like them, suffered mental shipwreck. His father was a none too prosperous shoe salesman who wanted the sensitive lad to earn a living as soon as possible. He went on to the University of Washington, St. Louis, in 1931, but left college after his sophomore year. He worked for two years in the shoe factory that employed his father but after a nervous collapse caused by feverish attempts to write late at night, he returned to college in 1936 and acquired a degree from the University of Iowa. Then came lean years of roving through the South, working at odd jobs, and ushering at a motion picture theatre in New York and performing as a singing waiter in Greenwich Village.

Continuing to write poetry, stories, and plays, Williams, however, found a loyal and energetic play agent, Audrey Wood of the Liebling-Wood office. With Miss Wood's help he won a small cash prize in 1939 from the Group Theatre with four one-act plays on Depression period themes entitled *American Blues*, and in 1940 a scholarship from Theresa Helburn and John Gassner to their seminar for promising playwrights. At the end of the spring semester he submitted his full-length drama of small-town life, *Battle of Angels,* to them. They bought it for the Theatre Guild, and the play went into rehearsal under the direction of Margaret Webster and the supervision of Lawrence Langner, the Guild's co-director.

The "out-of-town" tryout in Boston was disastrous, but fortunately Williams was sustained by American Academy of Arts and Rockefeller Foundation awards and fellowships until the Eddie Dowling production of *The Glass Menagerie* in 1945 gave him material as well as critical success. His collaboration on the dramatization of a D. H. Lawrence short story, *You Touched Me,* was produced less successfully in 1946, but a year later *A Streetcar Named Desire* secured his place in the American theatre. Although his next play, *Summer and Smoke* (see page 665), failed on Broadway, he had another successful production with *The Rose Tattoo* in the season of 1949-50. Williams also published a collection of his one-act plays entitled *27 Wagons Full of Cotton and Other Plays* in 1945, and several of these have been considered well worth staging. The range of his talent was further established by a collection of short stories and a novel. To date, however, it is his plays that ensure him a position in American letters.

SCENE ONE

The exterior of a two-story corner building on a street in New Orleans which is named Elysian Fields and runs between the L & N tracks and the river. The section is poor but, unlike corresponding sections in other American cities, it has a raffish charm. The houses are mostly white frame, weathered gray, with rickety outside stairs and galleries and quaintly ornamented gables. This building contains two flats, upstairs and down. Faded white stairs ascend to the entrances of both.

It is first dark of an evening early in May. The sky that shows around the dim white building is a peculiarly tender blue, almost a turquoise, which invests the scene with a kind of lyricism and gracefully attenuates the atmosphere of decay. You can almost feel the warm breath of the brown river beyond the river warehouses with their faint redolences of bananas and coffee. A corresponding air is evoked by the music of Negro entertainers at a barroom around the corner. In this part of New Orleans you are practically always just around the corner, or a few doors down the street, from a tinny piano being played with the infatuated fluency of brown fingers. This "blue piano" expresses the spirit of the life which goes on here.

Two women, one white and one colored, are taking the air on the steps of the building. The white woman is Eunice, who occupies the upstairs flat; the colored woman a neighbor, for New Orleans is a cosmopolitan city where there is a relatively warm and easy intermingling of races in the old part of town.

Above the music of the "blue piano" the voices of people on the street can be heard overlapping.

(Two men come around the corner, Stanley Kowalski and Mitch. They are about twenty-eight or thirty years old, roughly dressed in blue denim work clothes. Stanley carries his bowling jacket and a red-stained package from a butcher's. They stop at the foot of the steps.)

STANLEY *(bellowing)*. Hey, there! Stella, baby!

(Stella comes out on the first floor landing, a gentle young woman, about twenty-five, and of a background obviously quite different from her husband's.)

STELLA *(mildly)*. Don't holler at me like that. Hi, Mitch.

STANLEY. Catch!

STELLA. What?

STANLEY. Meat!

(He heaves the package at her. She cries out in protest but manages to catch it: then she laughs breathlessly. Her husband and his companion have already started back around the corner.)

STELLA *(calling after him)*. Stanley! Where are you going?

STANLEY. Bowling!

STELLA. Can I come watch?

STANLEY. Come on. *(He goes out)*

STELLA. Be over soon. *(To the white woman)* Hello, Eunice. How are you?

EUNICE. I'm all right. Tell Steve to get him a poor boy's sandwich 'cause nothing's left here.

(They all laugh; the colored woman does not stop. Stella goes out.)

NEGRO WOMAN. What was that package he th'ew at 'er? *(She rises from steps, laughing louder)*

EUNICE. You hush, now!

NEGRO WOMAN. Catch *what!*

(She continues to laugh. Blanche comes around the corner, carrying a valise. She looks at a slip of paper, then at the building, then again at the slip and again at the building. Her expression is one of shocked disbelief. Her appearance is incongruous in this setting. She is daintily dressed in a white suit with a fluffy bodice, necklace and earrings of pearl, white gloves and hat, looking as if she were arriving at a summer tea or cocktail party in the garden district. She is about five years older than Stella. Her delicate beauty must avoid a strong light. There is something about her uncertain manner, as well as her white clothes, that suggests a moth.)

EUNICE *(finally)*. What's the matter, honey? Are you lost?

BLANCHE *(with faintly hysterical humor)*. They told me to take a streetcar named Desire, and then transfer to one called Cemeteries and ride six blocks and get off at—Elysian Fields!

EUNICE. That's where you are now.

BLANCHE. At Elysian Fields?

EUNICE. This here is Elysian Fields.

BLANCHE. They mustn't have—understood—what number I wanted . . .

EUNICE. What number you lookin' for?

(Blanche wearily refers to the slip of paper.)

BLANCHE. Six thirty-two.

EUNICE. You don't have to look no further.

BLANCHE *(uncomprehendingly)*. I'm looking for my sister, Stella DuBois. I mean—Mrs. Stanley Kowalski.

EUNICE. That's the party.—You just did miss her, though.

BLANCHE. This—can this be—her home?

EUNICE. She's got the downstairs here and I got the up.

BLANCHE. Oh. She's—out?

EUNICE. You noticed that bowling alley around the corner?

BLANCHE. I'm—not sure I did.

EUNICE. Well, that's where she's at, watchin' her husband bowl. *(There is a pause)* You want to leave your suitcase here an' go find her?

BLANCHE. No.

NEGRO WOMAN. I'll go tell her you come.

BLANCHE. Thanks.

NEGRO WOMAN. You welcome. *(She goes out)*

EUNICE. She wasn't expecting you?

BLANCHE. No. No, not tonight.

EUNICE. Well, why don't you just go in and make yourself at home till they get back.

BLANCHE. How could I—do that?

EUNICE. We own this place so I can let you in.

(She gets up and opens the downstairs door. A light goes on behind the blind, turning it light blue. Blanche slowly follows her into the downstairs flat. The surrounding areas dim out as the interior is lighted.)

(Two rooms can be seen, not too clearly defined. The one first entered is primarily a kitchen but contains a folding bed to be used by Blanche. The room beyond this is a bedroom. Off this room is a narrow door to a bathroom.)

EUNICE *(defensively, noticing Blanche's look)*. It's sort of messed up right now but when it's clean it's real sweet.

BLANCHE. Is it?

EUNICE. Uh-huh, I think so. So you're Stella's sister?

BLANCHE. Yes. *(Wanting to get rid of her)* Thanks for letting me in.

EUNICE. *Por nada,* as the Mexicans say, *por nada!* Stella spoke of you.

BLANCHE. Yes?

EUNICE. I think she said you taught school.

BLANCHE. Yes.

EUNICE. And you're from Mississippi, huh?

BLANCHE. Yes.

EUNICE. She showed me a picture of your home-place, the plantation.

BLANCHE. Belle Reve?

EUNICE. A great big place with white columns.

BLANCHE. Yes...

EUNICE. A place like that must be awful hard to keep up.

BLANCHE. If you will excuse me, I'm just about to drop.

EUNICE. Sure, honey. Why don't you set down?

BLANCHE. What I meant was I'd like to be left alone.

EUNICE *(offended)*. Aw. I'll make myself scarce, in that case.

BLANCHE. I didn't mean to be rude, but—

EUNICE. I'll drop by the bowling alley an' hustle her up. *(She goes out the door)*

(Blanche sits in a chair very stiffly with her shoulders slightly hunched and her legs pressed close together and her hands tightly clutching her purse as if she were quite cold. After a while the blind look goes out of her eyes and she begins to look slowly around. A cat screeches. She catches her breath with a startled gesture. Suddenly she notices something in a half opened closet. She springs up and crosses to it, and removes a whiskey bottle. She pours a half tumbler of whiskey and tosses it down. She carefully replaces the bottle and washes out the tumbler at the sink. Then she resumes her seat in front of the table.)

BLANCHE *(faintly to herself)*. I've got to keep hold of myself!

(Stella comes quickly around the corner of the building and runs to the door of the downstairs flat.)

STELLA *(calling out joyfully)*. Blanche!

(For a moment they stare at each other. Then Blanche springs up and runs to her with a wild cry.)

BLANCHE. Stella, oh, Stella, Stella! Stella for Star!

(She begins to speak with feverish vivacity as if she feared for either of them to stop and think. They catch each other in a spasmodic embrace.)

BLANCHE. Now, then, let me look at you. But don't you look at me, Stella, no, no, no, not till later, not till I've bathed and rested! And turn that over-light off! Turn that off! I won't be looked at in this merciless glare! *(Stella laughs and complies)* Come back here now! Oh, my baby! Stella! Stella for Star! *(She embraces her again)* I thought you would never come back to this horrible place! What am I saying? I didn't mean to say that. I meant to be nice about it and say—Oh, what a convenient location and such—Ha-a-ha! Precious lamb! You haven't said a *word* to me.

STELLA. You haven't given me a chance to, honey! *(She laughs, but her glance at Blanche is a little anxious)*

BLANCHE. Well, now you talk. Open your pretty mouth and talk while I look around for some liquor! I know you must have some liquor on the place! Where could it be, I wonder? Oh, I spy, I spy! *(She rushes to the closet and removes the bottle; she is shaking all over and panting for breath as she tries to laugh. The bottle nearly slips from her grasp.)*

STELLA *(noticing)*. Blanche, you sit down and let me pour the drinks. I don't know what we've got to mix with. Maybe a coke's in the icebox. Look'n see, honey, while I'm —

BLANCHE. No coke, honey, not with my nerves tonight— Where—where— where is—?

STELLA. Stanley? Bowling! He loves it. They're having a—found some soda!— tournament . . .

BLANCHE. Just water, baby, to chase it! Now don't get worried, your sister hasn't turned into a drunkard, she's just all shaken up and hot and tired and dirty! You sit down, now, and explain this place to me! What are you doing in a place like this?

STELLA. Now, Blanche—

BLANCHE. Oh, I'm not going to be hypocritical, I'm going to be honestly critical about it! Never, never, never in my worst dreams could I picture— Only Poe! Only Mr. Edgar Allan Poe!—could do it justice! Out there I suppose is the ghoul-haunted woodland of Weir! *(She laughs)*

STELLA. No, honey, those are the L & N tracks.

BLANCHE. No, now seriously, putting joking aside. Why didn't you tell me, why didn't you write me, honey, why didn't you let me know?

STELLA *(carefully, pouring herself a drink)*. Tell you what, Blanche?

BLANCHE. Why, that you had to live in these conditions!

STELLA. Aren't you being a little intense about it? It's not that bad at all! New Orleans isn't like other cities.

BLANCHE. This has got nothing to do with New Orleans. You might as well say —forgive me, blessed baby! *(She suddenly stops short)* The subject is closed!

STELLA *(a little drily)*. Thanks. *(During the pause, Blanche stares at her. She smiles at Blanche.)*

BLANCHE *(looking down at her glass, which shakes in her hand)*. You're all I've got in the world, and you're not glad to see me!

STELLA *(sincerely)*. Why, Blanche, you know that's not true.

BLANCHE. No?—I'd forgotten how quiet you were.

STELLA. You never did give me a chance to say much, Blanche. So I just got in the habit of being quiet around you.

BLANCHE *(vaguely)*. A good habit to get into . . . *(Then, abruptly)* You haven't asked me how I happened to get away from the school before the spring term ended.

STELLA. Well, I thought you'd volunteer that information—if you wanted to tell me.

BLANCHE. You thought I'd been fired?

STELLA. No, I—thought you might have —resigned . . .

BLANCHE. I was so exhausted by all I'd been through my—nerves broke. *(Nervously tamping cigarette)* I was on the verge of—lunacy, almost! So Mr. Graves— Mr. Graves is the high school superintendent—he suggested I take a leave of absence. I couldn't put all of those details into the wire . . . *(She drinks quickly)* Oh, this buzzes right through me and feels so *good!*

STELLA. Won't you have another?

BLANCHE. No, one's my limit.

STELLA. Sure?

BLANCHE. You haven't said a word about my appearance.

STELLA. You look just fine.

BLANCHE. God love you for a liar! Daylight never exposed so total a ruin! But you—you've put on some weight, yes, you're just as plump as a little partridge! And it's so becoming to you!

STELLA. Now, Blanche—

BLANCHE. Yes, it is, it is or I wouldn't say it! You just have to watch around the hips a little. Stand up.

STELLA. Not now.

BLANCHE. You hear me? I said stand up! (*Stella complies reluctantly*) You messy child, you, you've spilt something on that pretty white lace collar! About your hair— you ought to have it cut in a feather bob with your dainty features. Stella, you have a maid, don't you?

STELLA. No. With only two rooms it's—

BLANCHE. What? *Two* rooms, did you say?

STELLA. This one and—(*She is embarrassed*)

BLANCHE. The other one? (*She laughs sharply. There is an embarrassed silence*) I am going to take just one little tiny nip more, sort of to put the stopper on, so to speak. . . . Then put the bottle away so I won't be tempted. (*She rises*) I want you to look at *my* figure! (*She turns around*) You know I haven't put on one ounce in ten years, Stella? I weigh what I weighed the summer you left Belle Reve. The summer Dad died and you left us . . .

STELLA (*a little wearily*). It's just incredible, Blanche, how well you're looking.

BLANCHE (*they both laugh uncomfortably*). But, Stella, there's only two rooms, I don't see where you're going to put me!

STELLA. We're going to put you in here.

BLANCHE. What kind of bed's this—one of those collapsible things? (*She sits on it*)

STELLA. Does it feel all right?

BLANCHE (*dubiously*). Wonderful, honey. I don't like a bed that gives much. But there's no door between the two rooms, and Stanley—will it be decent?

STELLA. Stanley is Polish, you know.

BLANCHE. Oh, yes. They're something like Irish, aren't they?

STELLA. Well—

BLANCHE. Only not so—highbrow? (*They both laugh again in the same way*) I brought some nice clothes to meet all your lovely friends in.

STELLA. I'm afraid you won't think they are lovely.

BLANCHE. What are they like?

STELLA. They're Stanley's friends.

BLANCHE. Polacks?

STELLA. They're a mixed lot, Blanche.

BLANCHE. Heterogeneous—types?

STELLA. Oh, yes. Yes, types is right!

BLANCHE. Well—anyhow—I brought nice clothes and I'll wear them. I guess you're hoping I'll say I'll put up at a hotel, but I'm not going to put up at a hotel. I want to be *near* you, got to be *with* somebody, I *can't* be *alone!* Because—as you must have noticed—I'm—*not* very *well* . . . (*Her voice drops and her look is frightened*)

STELLA. You seem a little bit nervous or overwrought or something.

BLANCHE. Will Stanley like me, or will I be just a visiting in-law, Stella? I couldn't stand that.

STELLA. You'll get along fine together, if you'll just try not to—well—compare him with men that we went out with at home.

BLANCHE. Is he so—different?

STELLA. Yes. A different species.

BLANCHE. In what way; what's he like?

STELLA. Oh, you can't describe someone you're in love with! Here's a picture of him! (*She hands a photograph to Blanche*)

BLANCHE. An officer?

STELLA. A Master Sergeant in the Engineers' Corps. Those are decorations!

BLANCHE. He had those on when you met him?

STELLA. I assure you I wasn't just blinded by all the brass.

BLANCHE. That's not what I—

STELLA. But of course there were things to adjust myself to later on.

BLANCHE. Such as his civilian background! (*Stella laughs uncertainly*) How did he take it when you said I was coming?

STELLA. Oh, Stanley doesn't know yet.

BLANCHE (*frightened*). You—haven't told him?

STELLA. He's on the road a good deal.

BLANCHE. Oh. Travels?

STELLA. Yes.

BLANCHE. Good. I mean—isn't it?

STELLA (*half to herself*). I can hardly stand it when he is away for a night . . .

BLANCHE. Why, Stella!

STELLA. When he's away for a week I nearly go wild!

BLANCHE. Gracious!

STELLA. And when he comes back I cry on his lap like a baby . . . (*She smiles to herself*)

BLANCHE. I guess that is what is meant by being in love . . . *(Stella looks up with a radiant smile)* Stella—

STELLA. What?

BLANCHE *(in an uneasy rush)*. I haven't asked you the things you probably thought I was going to ask. And so I'll expect you to be understanding about what *I* have to tell *you*.

STELLA. What, Blanche? *(Her face turns anxious)*

BLANCHE. Well, Stella—you're going to reproach me, I know that you're bound to reproach me—but before you do—take into consideration—you left! I stayed and struggled! You came to New Orleans and looked out for yourself! I stayed at Belle Reve and tried to hold it together! I'm not meaning this in any reproachful way, but *all* the burden descended on *my* shoulders.

STELLA. The best I could do was make my own living, Blanche.

(Blanche begins to shake again with intensity.)

BLANCHE. I know, I know. But you are the one that abandoned Belle Reve, not I! I stayed and fought for it, bled for it, almost died for it!

STELLA. Stop this hysterical outburst and tell me what's happened? What do you mean fought and bled? What kind of—

BLANCHE. I knew you would, Stella. I knew you would take this attitude about it!

STELLA. About—what?—please!

BLANCHE *(slowly)*. The loss—the loss . . .

STELLA. Belle Reve? Lost, is it? No!

BLANCHE. Yes, Stella.

(They stare at each other across the yellow-checked linoleum of the table. Blanche slowly nods her head and Stella looks slowly down at her hands folded on the table. The music of the "blue piano" grows louder. Blanche touches her handkerchief to her forehead.)

STELLA. But how did it go? What happened?

BLANCHE *(springing up)*. You're a fine one to ask me how it went!

STELLA. Blanche!

BLANCHE. You're a fine one to sit there *accusing me* of it!

STELLA. *Blanche!*

BLANCHE. I, I, *I* took the blows in my face and my body! All of those deaths! The long parade to the graveyard! Father, mother! Margaret, that dreadful way! So big with it, it couldn't be put in a coffin! But had to be burned like rubbish! You just came home in time for the funerals, Stella. And funerals are pretty compared to deaths. Funerals are quiet, but deaths—not always. Sometimes their breathing is hoarse, and sometimes it rattles, and sometimes they even cry out to you, "Don't let me go!" Even the old, sometimes, say, "Don't let me go." As if you were able to stop them! But funerals are quiet, with pretty flowers. And, oh, what gorgeous boxes they pack them away in! Unless you were there at the bed when they cried out, "Hold me!" you'd never suspect there was the struggle for breath and bleeding. You didn't dream, but I saw! *Saw! Saw!* And now you sit there telling me with your eyes that I let the place go! How in hell do you think all that sickness and dying was paid for? Death is expensive, Miss Stella! And old Cousin Jessie's right after Margaret's, hers! Why, the Grim Reaper had put up his tent on our doorstep! . . . Stella. Belle Reve was his headquarters! Honey—that's how it slipped through my fingers! Which of them left us a fortune? Which of them left a cent of insurance even? Only poor Jessie—one hundred to pay for her coffin. That was all, Stella! And I with my pitiful salary at the school. Yes, accuse me! Sit there and stare at me, thinking I let the place go! *I* let the place go? Where were *you!* In bed with your—Polack!

STELLA *(springing)*. Blanche! You be still! That's enough! *(She starts out)*

BLANCHE. Where are you going?

STELLA. I'm going into the bathroom to wash my face.

BLANCHE. Oh, Stella, Stella, you're crying!

STELLA. Does that surprise you?

BLANCHE. Forgive me—I didn't mean to—

(The sound of men's voices is heard. Stella goes into the bathroom, closing the door behind her. When the men appear, and Blanche realizes it must be Stanley returning, she moves uncertainly from the bathroom door to the dressing table, looking apprehensively towards the front door. Stanley enters, followed by Steve and Mitch. Stanley pauses near his door, Steve by the foot of the spiral stair, and Mitch is slightly above and to the right of them,

about to go out. As the men enter, we hear some of the following dialogue.)

STANLEY. Is that how he got it?

STEVE. Sure that's how he got it. He hit the old weather-bird for 300 bucks on a six-number-ticket.

MITCH. Don't tell him those things; he'll believe it.

(Mitch starts out.)

STANLEY (restraining Mitch). Hey, Mitch—come back here.

(Blanche, at the sound of voices, retires in the bedroom. She picks up Stanley's photo from dressing table, looks at it, puts it down. When Stanley enters the apartment, she darts and hides behind the screen at the head of bed.)

STEVE (to Stanley and Mitch). Hey, are we playin' poker tomorrow?

STANLEY. Sure—at Mitch's.

MITCH (hearing this, returns quickly to the stair rail). No—not at my place. My mother's still sick!

STANLEY. Okay, at my place . . . (Mitch starts out again) But you bring the beer! (Mitch pretends not to hear—calls out "Goodnight all," and goes out, singing. Eunice's voice is heard, above.)

EUNICE. Break it up down there! I made the spaghetti dish and ate it myself.

STEVE (going upstairs). I told you and phoned you we was playing. (To the men) Jax beer!

EUNICE. You never phoned me once.

STEVE. I told you at breakfast—and phoned you at lunch . . .

EUNICE. Well, never mind about that. You just get yourself home here once in a while.

STEVE. You want it in the papers?

(More laughter and shouts of parting come from the men. Stanley throws the screen door of the kitchen open and comes in. He is of medium height, about five feet eight or nine, and strongly, compactly built. Animal joy in his being is implicit in all his movements and attitudes. Since earliest manhood the center of his life has been pleasure with women, the giving and taking of it, not with weak indulgence, dependently, but with the power and pride of a richly feathered male bird among hens. Branching out from this complete and satisfying center are all the auxiliary channels of his life, such as his heartiness with men, his appreciation of rough humor, his love of good drink and food and

games, his car, his radio, everything that is his, that bears his emblem of the gaudy seed-bearer. He sizes women up at a glance, with sexual classification, crude images flashing into his mind and determining the way he smiles at them.)

BLANCHE (drawing involuntarily back from his stare). You must be Stanley. I'm Blanche.

STANLEY. Stella's sister?

BLANCHE. Yes.

STANLEY. H'lo. Where's the little woman?

BLANCHE. In the bathroom.

STANLEY. Oh. Didn't know you were coming in town.

BLANCHE. I—uh—

STANLEY. Where you from, Blanche?

BLANCHE. Why, I—live in Laurel.

(He has crossed to the closet and removed the whiskey bottle.)

STANLEY. In Laurel, huh? Oh, yeah. Yeah, in Laurel, that's right. Not in my territory. Liquor goes fast in hot weather. (He holds the bottle to the light to observe its depletion) Have a shot?

BLANCHE. No, I—rarely touch it.

STANLEY. Some people rarely touch it, but it touches them often.

BLANCHE (faintly). Ha-ha.

STANLEY. My clothes're stickin' to me. Do you mind if I make myself comfortable? (He starts to remove his shirt)

BLANCHE. Please, please do.

STANLEY. Be comfortable is my motto.

BLANCHE. It's mine, too. It's hard to stay looking fresh. I haven't washed or even powdered my face and—here you are!

STANLEY. You know you can catch cold sitting around in damp things, especially when you been exercising hard like bowling is. You're a teacher, aren't you?

BLANCHE. Yes.

STANLEY. What do you teach, Blanche?

BLANCHE. English.

STANLEY. I never was a very good English student. How long you here for, Blanche?

BLANCHE. I—don't know yet.

STANLEY. You going to shack up here?

BLANCHE. I thought I would if it's not inconvenient for you all.

STANLEY. Good.

BLANCHE. Traveling wears me out.

STANLEY. Well, take it easy.

(A cat screeches near the window. Blanche springs up.)

BLANCHE. What's that?

STANLEY. Cats . . . Hey, Stella!

STELLA (*faintly, from the bathroom*). Yes, Stanley.

STANLEY. Haven't fallen in, have you? (*He grins at Blanche. She tries unsuccessfully to smile back. There is a silence*) I'm afraid I'll strike you as being the unrefined type. Stella's spoke of you a good deal. You were married once, weren't you? (*The music of the polka rises up, faint in the distance.*)

BLANCHE. Yes. When I was quite young.

STANLEY. What happened?

BLANCHE. The boy—the boy died. (*She sinks back down*) I'm afraid I'm—going to be sick!

(*Her head falls on her arms.*)

SCENE TWO

It is six o'clock the following evening. Blanche is bathing. Stella is completing her toilette. Blanche's dress, a flowered print, is laid out on Stella's bed.

Stanley enters the kitchen from outside, leaving the door open on the perpetual "blue piano" around the corner.

———

STANLEY. What's all this monkey doings?

STELLA. Oh, Stan! (*She jumps up and kisses him which he accepts with lordly composure*) I'm taking Blanche to Galatoire's for supper and then to a show, because it's your poker night.

STANLEY. How about my supper, huh? I'm not going to no Galatoire's for supper!

STELLA. I put you a cold plate on ice.

STANLEY. Well, isn't that just dandy!

STELLA. I'm going to try to keep Blanche out till the party breaks up because I don't know how she would take it. So we'll go to one of the little places in the Quarter afterwards and you'd better give me some money.

STANLEY. Where is she?

STELLA. She's soaking in a hot tub to quiet her nerves. She's terribly upset.

STANLEY. Over what?

STELLA. She's been through such an ordeal.

STANLEY. Yeah?

STELLA. Stan, we've—lost Belle Reve!

STANLEY. The place in the country?

STELLA. Yes.

STANLEY. How?

STELLA (*vaguely*). Oh, it had to be— sacrificed or something. (*There is a pause while Stanley considers. Stella is changing into her dress*) When she comes in be sure to say something nice about her appearance. And, oh! Don't mention the baby. I haven't said anything yet, I'm waiting until she gets in a quieter condition.

STANLEY (*ominously*). So?

STELLA. And try to understand her and be nice to her, Stan.

BLANCHE (*singing in the bathroom*). "From the land of the sky blue water, They brought a captive maid!"

STELLA. She wasn't expecting to find us in such a small place. You see I'd tried to gloss things over a little in my letters.

STANLEY. So?

STELLA. And admire her dress and tell her she's looking wonderful. That's important with Blanche. Her little weakness!

STANLEY. Yeah. I get the idea. Now let's skip back a little to where you said the country place was disposed of.

STELLA. Oh!—yes . . .

STANLEY. How about that? Let's have a few more details on that subjeck.

STELLA. It's best not to talk much about it until she's calmed down.

STANLEY. So that's the deal, huh? Sister Blanche cannot be annoyed with business details right now!

STELLA. You saw how she was last night.

STANLEY. Uh-hum, I saw how she was. Now let's have a gander at the bill of sale.

STELLA. I haven't seen any.

STANLEY. She didn't show you no papers, no deed of sale or nothing like that, huh?

STELLA. It seems like it wasn't sold.

STANLEY. Well, what in hell was it then, give away? To charity?

STELLA. Shhh! She'll hear you.

STANLEY. I don't care if she hears me. Let's see the papers!

STELLA. There weren't any papers, she didn't show any papers, I don't care about papers.

STANLEY. Have you ever heard of the Napoleonic code?

STELLA. No, Stanley, I haven't heard of the Napoleonic code and if I have, I don't see what it—

STANLEY. Let me enlighten you on a point or two, baby.

STELLA. Yes?

STANLEY. In the state of Louisiana we have the Napoleonic code according to which what belongs to the wife belongs to the husband and vice versa. For instance if I had a piece of property, or you had a piece of property—

STELLA. My head is swimming!

STANLEY. All right. I'll wait till she gets through soaking in a hot tub and then I'll inquire if *she* is acquainted with the Napoleonic code. It looks to me like you have been swindled, baby, and when you're swindled under the Napoleonic code I'm swindled *too*. And I don't like to be *swindled*.

STELLA. There's plenty of time to ask her questions later but if you do now she'll go to pieces again. I don't understand what happened to Belle Reve but you don't know how ridiculous you are being when you suggest that my sister or I or anyone of our family could have perpetrated a swindle on anyone else.

STANLEY. Then where's the money if the place was sold?

STELLA. Not sold—*lost, lost!* (*He stalks into bedroom, and she follows him*) Stanley!
(*He pulls open the wardrobe trunk standing in middle of room and jerks out an armful of dresses.*)

STANLEY. Open your eyes to this stuff! You think she got them out of a teacher's pay?

STELLA. Hush!

STANLEY. Look at these feathers and furs that she come here to preen herself in! What's this here? A solid-gold dress, I believe! And this one! What is these here? Fox-pieces! (*He blows on them*) Genuine fox fur-pieces, a half a mile long! Where are your fox-pieces, Stella? Bushy snow-white ones, no less! Where are your white fox-pieces?

STELLA. Those are inexpensive summer furs that Blanche has had a long time.

STANLEY. I got an acquaintance who deals in this sort of merchandise. I'll have him in here to appraise it. I'm willing to bet you there's thousands of dollars invested in this stuff here!

STELLA. Don't be such an idiot, Stanley! (*He hurls the furs to the daybed. Then he jerks open small drawer in the trunk and pulls up a fist-full of costume jewelry.*)

STANLEY. And what have we here? The treasure chest of a pirate!

STELLA. Oh, Stanley!

STANLEY. Pearls! Ropes of them! What is this sister of yours, a deep-sea diver? Bracelets of solid gold, too! Where are your pearls and gold bracelets?

STELLA. Shhh! Be still, Stanley!

STANLEY. And diamonds! A crown for an empress!

STELLA. A rhinestone tiara she wore to a costume ball.

STANLEY. What's rhinestone?

STELLA. Next door to glass.

STANLEY. Are you kidding? I have an acquaintance that works in a jewelry store. I'll have him in here to make an appraisal of this. Here's your plantation, or what was left of it, here!

STELLA. You have no idea how stupid and horrid you're being! Now close that trunk before she comes out of the bathroom!
(*He kicks the trunk partly closed and sits on the kitchen table.*)

STANLEY. The Kowalskis and the Du-Bois have different notions.

STELLA (*angrily*). Indeed they have, thank heavens—*I'm* going outside. (*She snatches up her white hat and gloves and crosses to the outside door*) You come out with me while Blanche is getting dressed.

STANLEY. Since when do you give me orders?

STELLA. Are you going to stay here and insult her?

STANLEY. You're damn tootin' I'm going to stay here.
(*Stella goes out to the porch. Blanche comes out of the bathroom in a red satin robe.*)

BLANCHE (*airily*). Hello, Stanley! Here I am, all freshly bathed and scented, and feeling like a brand new human being!
(*He lights a cigarette.*)

STANLEY. That's good.

BLANCHE (*drawing the curtains at the window*). Excuse me while I slip on my pretty new dress!

STANLEY. Go right ahead, Blanche.
(*She closes the drapes between the rooms.*)

BLANCHE. I understand there's to be a little card party to which we ladies are cordially *not* invited!

STANLEY (*ominously*). Yeah?
(*Blanche throws off her robe and slips into a flowered print dress.*)

BLANCHE. Where's Stella?

STANLEY. Out on the porch.

BLANCHE. I'm going to ask a favor of you in a moment.

STANLEY. What could that be, I wonder?

BLANCHE. Some buttons in back! You may enter! (*He crosses through drapes with a smoldering look*) How do I look?

STANLEY. You look all right.

BLANCHE. Many thanks! Now the buttons!

STANLEY. I can't do nothing with them.

BLANCHE. You men with your big clumsy fingers. May I have a drag on your cig?

STANLEY. Have one for yourself.

BLANCHE. Why, thanks! . . . It looks like my trunk has exploded.

STANLEY. Me an' Stella were helping you unpack.

BLANCHE. Well, you certainly did a fast and thorough job of it!

STANLEY. It looks like you raided some stylish shops in Paris.

BLANCHE. Ha-ha! Yes—clothes are my passion!

STANLEY. What does it cost for a string of fur-pieces like that?

BLANCHE. Why, those were a tribute from an admirer of mine!

STANLEY. He must have had a lot of—admiration!

BLANCHE. Oh, in my youth I excited some admiration. But look at me now! (*She smiles at him radiantly*) Would you think it possible that I was once considered to be—attractive?

STANLEY. Your looks are okay.

BLANCHE. I was fishing for a compliment, Stanley.

STANLEY. I don't go in for that stuff.

BLANCHE. What—stuff?

STANLEY. Compliments to women about their looks. I never met a woman that didn't know if she was good-looking or not without being told, and some of them give themselves credit for more than they've got. I once went out with a doll who said to me, "I am the glamorous type, I am the glamorous type!" I said, "So what?"

BLANCHE. And what did she say then?

STANLEY. She didn't say nothing. That shut her up like a clam.

BLANCHE. Did it end the romance?

STANLEY. It ended the conversation—that was all. Some men are took in by this Hollywood glamor stuff and some men are not.

BLANCHE. I'm sure you belong in the second category.

STANLEY. That's right.

BLANCHE. I cannot imagine any witch of a woman casting a spell over you.

STANLEY. That's—right.

BLANCHE. You're simple, straightforward and honest, a little bit on the primitive side I should think. To interest you a woman would have to—(*She pauses with an indefinite gesture*)

STANLEY (*slowly*). Lay . . . her cards on the table.

BLANCHE (*smiling*). Well, I never cared for wishy-washy people. That was why, when you walked in here last night, I said to myself—"My sister has married a man!"—Of course that was all that I could tell about you.

STANLEY (*booming*). Now let's cut the re-bop!

BLANCHE (*pressing hands to her ears*) Ouuuuu!

STELLA (*calling from the steps*). Stanley! You come out here and let Blanche finish dressing!

BLANCHE. I'm through dressing, honey.

STELLA. Well, you come out, then.

STANLEY. Your sister and I are having a little talk.

BLANCHE (*lightly*). Honey, do me a favor. Run to the drugstore and get me a lemon-coke with plenty of chipped ice in it!—Will you do that for me, Sweetie?

STELLA (*uncertainly*). Yes. (*She goes around the corner of the building*)

BLANCHE. The poor little thing was out there listening to us, and I have an idea she doesn't understand you as well as I do. . . . All right; now, Mr. Kowalski, let us proceed without any more double-talk. I'm ready to answer all questions. I've nothing to hide. What is it?

STANLEY. There is such a thing in this state of Louisiana as the Napoleonic code, according to which whatever belongs to my wife is also mine—and vice versa.

BLANCHE. My, but you have an impressive judicial air!

(*She sprays herself with her atomizer; then playfully sprays him with it. He seizes the atomizer and slams it down on the dresser. She throws back her head and laughs.*)

STANLEY. If I didn't know that you was my wife's sister I'd get ideas about you!

BLANCHE. Such as what!

STANLEY. Don't play so dumb. You know!

BLANCHE *(she puts the atomizer on the table)*. All right. Cards on the table. That suits me. *(She turns to Stanley)* I know I fib a good deal. After all, a woman's charm is fifty per cent illusion, but when a thing is important I tell the truth, and this is the truth: I haven't cheated my sister or you or anyone else as long as I have lived.

STANLEY. Where's the papers? In the trunk?

BLANCHE. Everything that I own is in that trunk.

(Stanley crosses to the trunk, shoves it roughly open and begins to open compartments.)

BLANCHE. What in the name of heaven are you thinking of! What's in the back of that little boy's mind of yours? That I am absconding with something, attempting some kind of treachery on my sister? —Let me do that! It will be faster and simpler . . . *(She crosses to the trunk and takes out a box)* I keep my papers mostly in this tin box. *(She opens it)*

STANLEY. What's them underneath? *(He indicates another sheaf of paper)*

BLANCHE. These are love-letters, yellowing with antiquity, all from one boy. *(He snatches them up. She speaks fiercely)* Give those back to me!

STANLEY. I'll have a look at them first!

BLANCHE. The touch of your hands insults them!

STANLEY. Don't pull that stuff!

(He rips off the ribbon and starts to examine them. Blanche snatches them from him, and they cascade to the floor.)

BLANCHE. Now that you've touched them I'll burn them!

STANLEY *(staring, baffled)*. What in hell are they?

BLANCHE *(on the floor, gathering them up)*. Poems a dead boy wrote. I hurt him the way that you would like to hurt me, but you can't! I'm not young and vulnerable any more. But my young husband was and I—never mind about that! Just give them back to me!

STANLEY. What do you mean by saying you'll have to burn them?

BLANCHE. I'm sorry, I must have lost my head for a moment. Everyone has something he won't let others touch because of their—intimate nature . . . *(She now seems faint with exhaustion and she sits down with the strong box and puts on a pair of glasses and goes methodically through a large stack of papers)* Ambler & Ambler. Hmmmmm. . . . Crabtree. . . . More Ambler & Ambler.

STANLEY. What is Ambler & Ambler?

BLANCHE. A firm that made loans on the place.

STANLEY. Then it *was* lost on a mortgage?

BLANCHE *(touching her forehead)*. That must've been what happened.

STANLEY. I don't want no ifs, ands or buts! What's all the rest of them papers? *(She hands him the entire box. He carries it to the table and starts to examine the papers.)*

BLANCHE *(picking up a large envelope containing more papers)*. There are thousands of papers, stretching back over hundreds of years, affecting Belle Reve as, piece by piece, our improvident grandfathers and father and uncles and brothers exchanged the land for their epic fornications—to put it plainly! *(She removes her glasses with an exhausted laugh)* The four-letter word deprived us of our plantation, till finally all that was left—and Stella can verify that!—was the house itself and about twenty acres of ground, including a graveyard, to which now all but Stella and I have retreated. *(She pours the contents of the envelope on the table)* Here all of them are, all papers! I hereby endow you with them! Take them, peruse them— commit them to memory, even! I think it's wonderfully fitting that Belle Reve should finally be this bunch of old papers in your big, capable hands! . . . I wonder if Stella's come back with my lemon-coke . . . *(She leans back and closes her eyes)*

STANLEY. I have a lawyer acquaintance who will study these out.

BLANCHE. Present them to him with a box of aspirin tablets.

STANLEY *(becoming somewhat sheepish)*. You see, under the Napoleonic code—a man has to take an interest in his wife's affairs—especially now that she's going to have a baby.

(Blanche opens her eyes. The "blue piano" sounds louder.)

BLANCHE. Stella? Stella going to have a

baby? *(Dreamily)* I didn't know she was
going to have a baby!
*(She gets up and crosses to the outside
door. Stella appears around the corner
with a carton from the drugstore.)*
*(Stanley goes into the bedroom with the
envelope and the box.)*
*(The inner rooms fade to darkness and
the outside wall of the house is visible.
Blanche meets Stella at the foot of the
steps to the sidewalk.)*
    BLANCHE. Stella, Stella for star! How
lovely to have a baby! It's all right. Everything's all right.
    STELLA. I'm sorry he did that to you.
    BLANCHE. Oh, I guess he's just not the
type that goes for jasmine perfume, but
maybe he's what we need to mix with our
blood now that we've lost Belle Reve. We
thrashed it out. I feel a bit shaky, but I
think I handled it nicely, I laughed and
treated it all as a joke. *(Steve and Pablo
appear, carrying a case of beer)* I called
him a little boy and laughed and flirted.
Yes, I was flirting with your husband! *(As
the men approach)* The guests are gathering for the poker party. *(The two men
pass between them, and enter the house)*
Which way do we go now, Stella—this
way?
    STELLA. No, this way. *(She leads Blanche
away)*
    BLANCHE *(laughing)*. The blind are
leading the blind!
(A tamale vendor is heard calling.)
    VENDOR'S VOICE. Red-hot!

SCENE THREE

THE POKER NIGHT
    *There is a picture of Van Gogh's of a
billiard-parlor at night. The kitchen now
suggests that sort of lurid nocturnal brilliance, the raw colors of childhood's spec-
trum. Over the yellow linoleum of the
kitchen table hangs an electric bulb with
a vivid green glass shade. The poker players—Stanley, Steve, Mitch and Pablo—
wear colored shirts, solid blues, a purple, a
red-and-white check, a light green, and
they are men at the peak of their physical
manhood, as coarse and direct and powerful as the primary colors. There are vivid
slices of watermelon on the table, whiskey
bottles and glasses. The bedroom is relatively dim with only the light that spills*

*between the portieres and through the
wide window on the street.*
    *For a moment, there is absorbed silence
as a hand is dealt.*

———

    STEVE. Anything wild this deal?
    PABLO. One-eyed jacks are wild.
    STEVE. Give me two cards.
    PABLO. You, Mitch?
    MITCH. I'm out.
    PABLO. One.
    MITCH. Anyone want a shot?
    STANLEY. Yeah, me.
    PABLO. Why don't somebody go to the
Chinaman's and bring back a load of chop
suey?
    STANLEY. When I'm losing you want to
eat! Ante up! Openers? Openers! Get y'r
ass off the table, Mitch. Nothing belongs
on a poker table but cards, chips and
whiskey. *(He lurches up and tosses some
watermelon rinds to the floor)*
    MITCH. Kind of on your high horse, ain't
you?
    STANLEY. How many?
    STEVE. Give me three.
    STANLEY. One.
    MITCH. I'm out again. I oughta go home
pretty soon.
    STANLEY. Shut up.
    MITCH. I gotta sick mother. She don't go
to sleep until I come in at night.
    STANLEY. Then why don't you stay home
with her?
    MITCH. She says to go out, so I go, but
I don't enjoy it. All the while I keep wondering how she is.
    STANLEY. Aw, for the sake of Jesus, go
home, then!
    PABLO. What've you got?
    STEVE. Spade flush.
    MITCH. You all are married. But I'll be
alone when she goes.—I'm going to the
bathroom.
    STANLEY. Hurry back and we'll fix you a
sugar-tit.
    MITCH. Aw, go rut. *(He crosses through
the bedroom into the bathroom)*
    STEVE *(dealing a hand)*. Seven card stud.
(Telling his joke as he deals) This ole
farmer is out in back of his house sittin'
down th'owing corn to the chickens when
all at once he hears a loud cackle and this
young hen comes lickety split around the
side of the house with the rooster right behind her and gaining on her fast.

STANLEY (*impatient with the story*). Deal!

STEVE. But when the rooster catches sight of the farmer th'owing the corn he puts on the brakes and lets the hen get away and starts pecking corn. And the old farmer says, "Lord God, I hopes I never gits *that* hongry!"

(*Steve and Pablo laugh. The sisters appear around the corner of the building.*)

STELLA. The game is still going on.

BLANCHE. How do I look?

STELLA. Lovely, Blanche.

BLANCHE. I feel so hot and frazzled. Wait till I powder before you open the door. Do I look done in?

STELLA. Why no. You are as fresh as a daisy.

BLANCHE. One that's been picked a few days.

(*Stella opens the door and they enter.*)

STELLA. Well, well, well. I see you boys are still at it!

STANLEY. Where you been?

STELLA. Blanche and I took in a show. Blanche, this is Mr. Gonzales and Mr. Hubbell.

BLANCHE. Please don't get up.

STANLEY. Nobody's going to get up, so don't be worried.

STELLA. How much longer is this game going to continue?

STANLEY. Till we get ready to quit.

BLANCHE. Poker is so fascinating. Could I kibitz?

STANLEY. You could not. Why don't you women go up and sit with Eunice?

STELLA. Because it is nearly two-thirty. (*Blanche crosses into the bedroom and partially closes the portieres*) Couldn't you call it quits after one more hand?

(*A chair scrapes. Stanley gives a loud whack of his hand on her thigh.*)

STELLA (*sharply*). That's not fun, Stanley.

(*The men laugh. Stella goes into the bedroom.*)

STELLA. It makes me so mad when he does that in front of people.

BLANCHE. I think I will bathe.

STELLA. Again?

BLANCHE. My nerves are in knots. Is the bathroom occupied?

STELLA. I don't know.

(*Blanche knocks. Mitch opens the door and comes out, still wiping his hands on a towel.*)

BLANCHE. Oh!—good evening.

MITCH. Hello. (*He stares at her*)

STELLA. Blanche, this is Harold Mitchell. My sister, Blanche DuBois.

MITCH (*with awkward courtesy*). How do you do, Miss DuBois.

STELLA. How is your mother now, Mitch?

MITCH. About the same, thanks. She appreciated your sending over that custard. —Excuse me, please.

(*He crosses slowly back into the kitchen, glancing back at Blanche and coughing a little shyly. He realizes he still has the towel in his hands and with an embarrassed laugh hands it to Stella. Blanche looks after him with a certain interest.*)

BLANCHE. That one seems—superior to the others.

STELLA. Yes, he is.

BLANCHE. I thought he had a sort of sensitive look.

STELLA. His mother is sick.

BLANCHE. Is he married?

STELLA. No.

BLANCHE. Is he a wolf?

STELLA. Why, Blanche! (*Blanche laughs*) I don't think he would be.

BLANCHE. What does—what does he do? (*She is unbuttoning her blouse*)

STELLA. He's on the precision bench in the spare parts department. At the plant Stanley travels for.

BLANCHE. Is that something much?

STELLA. No. Stanley's the only one of his crowd that's likely to get anywhere.

BLANCHE. What makes you think Stanley will?

STELLA. Look at him.

BLANCHE. I've looked at him.

STELLA. Then you should know.

BLANCHE. I'm sorry, but I haven't noticed the stamp of genius even on Stanley's forehead.

(*She takes off the blouse and stands in her pink silk brassiere and white skirt in the light through the portieres. The game has continued in undertones.*)

STELLA. It isn't on his forehead and it isn't genius.

BLANCHE. Oh. Well, what is it, and where? I would like to know.

STELLA. It's a drive that he has. You're standing in the light, Blanche!

BLANCHE. Oh, am I!

(*She moves out of the yellow streak of*

light. Stella has removed her dress and put on a light blue satin kimono.)

STELLA *(with girlish laughter)*. You ought to see their wives.

BLANCHE *(laughingly)*. I can imagine. Big, beefy things, I suppose.

STELLA. You know that one upstairs? *(More laughter)* One time *(laughing)* the plaster—*(laughing)* cracked—

STANLEY. You hens cut out that conversation in there!

STELLA. You can't hear us.

STANLEY. Well, you can hear me and I said to hush up!

STELLA. This is my house and I'll talk as much as I want to!

BLANCHE. Stella, don't start a row.

STELLA. He's half drunk!—I'll be out in a minute.

(She goes into the bathroom. Blanche rises and crosses leisurely to a small white radio and turns it on.)

STANLEY. Awright, Mitch, you in?

MITCH. What? Oh!—No, I'm out!

(Blanche moves back into the streak of light. She raises her arms and stretches, as she moves indolently back to the chair.

(Rhumba music comes over the radio. Mitch rises at the table.)

STANLEY. Who turned that on in there?

BLANCHE. I did. Do you mind?

STANLEY. Turn it off!

STEVE. Aw, let the girls have their music.

PABLO. Sure, that's good, leave it on!

STEVE. Sounds like Xavier Cugat!

(Stanley jumps up and, crossing to the radio, turns it off. He stops short at the sight of Blanche in the chair. She returns his look without flinching. Then he sits again at the poker table.

(Two of the men have started arguing hotly.)

STEVE. I didn't hear you name it.

PABLO. Didn't I name it, Mitch?

MITCH. I wasn't listenin'.

PABLO. What were you doing, then?

STANLEY. He was looking through them drapes. *(He jumps up and jerks roughly at curtains to close them)* Now deal the hand over again and let's play cards or quit. Some people get ants when they win. *(Mitch rises as Stanley returns to his seat.)*

STANLEY *(yelling)*. Sit down!

MITCH. I'm going to the "head. Deal me out.

PABLO. Sure he's got ants now. Seven five-dollar bills in his pants pocket folded up tight as spitballs.

STEVE. Tomorrow you'll see him at the cashier's window getting them changed into quarters.

STANLEY. And when he goes home he'll deposit them one by one in a piggy bank his mother give him for Christmas. *(Dealing)* This game is Spit in the Ocean.

(Mitch laughs uncomfortably and continues through the portieres. He stops just inside.)

BLANCHE *(softly)*. Hello! The Little Boys' Room is busy right now.

MITCH. We've—been drinking beer.

BLANCHE. I hate beer.

MITCH. It's—a hot weather drink.

BLANCHE. Oh, I don't think so; it always makes me warmer. Have you got any cigs? *(She has slipped on the dark red satin wrapper)*

MITCH. Sure.

BLANCHE. What kind are they?

MITCH. Luckies.

BLANCHE. Oh, good. What a pretty case. Silver?

MITCH. Yes. Yes; read the inscription.

BLANCHE. Oh, is there an inscription? I can't make it out. *(He strikes a match and moves closer)* Oh! *(Reading with feigned difficulty)*
"And if God choose,
I shall but love thee better—after—death!"
Why, that's from my favorite sonnet by Mrs. Browning!

MITCH. You know it?

BLANCHE. Certainly I do!

MITCH. There's a story connected with that inscription.

BLANCHE. It sounds like a romance.

MITCH. A pretty sad one.

BLANCHE. Oh?

MITCH. The girl's dead now.

BLANCHE *(in a tone of deep sympathy)*. Oh!

MITCH. She knew she was dying when she give me this. A very strange girl, very sweet—very!

BLANCHE. She must have been fond of you. Sick people have such deep, sincere attachments.

MITCH. That's right, they certainly do.

BLANCHE. Sorrow makes for sincerity, I think.

MITCH. It sure brings it out in people.

BLANCHE. The little there is belongs to people who have experienced some sorrow.

MITCH. I believe you are right about that.

BLANCHE. I'm positive that I am. Show me a person who hasn't known any sorrow and I'll show you a shuperficial— Listen to me! My tongue is a little—thick! You boys are responsible for it. The show let out at eleven and we couldn't come home on account of the poker game so we had to go somewhere and drink. I'm not accustomed to having more than one drink. Two is the limit—and *three! (She laughs)* Tonight I had three.

STANLEY. Mitch!

MITCH. Deal me out. I'm talking to Miss—

BLANCHE. DuBois.

MITCH. Miss DuBois?

BLANCHE. It's a French name. It means woods and Blanche means white, so the two together mean white woods. Like an orchard in spring! You can remember it by that.

MITCH. You're French?

BLANCHE. We are French by extraction. Our first American ancestors were French Huguenots.

MITCH. You are Stella's sister, are you not?

BLANCHE. Yes, Stella is my precious little sister. I call her little in spite of the fact she's somewhat older than I. Just slightly. Less than a year. Will you do something for me?

MITCH. Sure. What?

BLANCHE. I bought this adorable little colored paper lantern at a Chinese shop on Bourbon. Put it over the light bulb! Will you, please?

MITCH. Be glad to.

BLANCHE. I can't stand a naked light bulb, any more than I can a rude remark or a vulgar action.

MITCH *(adjusting the lantern)*. I guess we strike you as being a pretty rough bunch.

BLANCHE. I'm very adaptable—to circumstances.

MITCH. Well, that's a good thing to be. You are visiting Stanley and Stella?

BLANCHE. Stella hasn't been so well lately, and I came down to help her for a while. She's very rundown.

MITCH. You're not—?

BLANCHE. Married? No, no. I'm an old maid schoolteacher!

MITCH. You may teach school but you're certainly not an old maid.

BLANCHE. Thank you, sir! I appreciate your gallantry!

MITCH. So you are in the teaching profession?

BLANCHE. Yes. Ah, yes . . .

MITCH. Grade school or high school or—

STANLEY *(bellowing). Mitch!*

MITCH. *Coming!*

BLANCHE. Gracious, what lung-power! . . . I teach high school. In Laurel.

MITCH. What do you teach? What subject?

BLANCHE. Guess!

MITCH. I bet you teach art or music? *(Blanche laughs delicately)* Of course I could be wrong. You might teach arithmetic.

BLANCHE. Never arithmetic, sir; never arithmetic! *(With a laugh)* I don't even know my multiplication tables! No, I have the misfortune of being an English instructor. I attempt to instill a bunch of bobby-soxers and drugstore Romeos with reverence for Hawthorne and Whitman and Poe!

MITCH. I guess that some of them are more interested in other things.

BLANCHE. How very right you are! Their literary heritage is not what most of them treasure above all else! But they're sweet things! And in the spring, it's touching to notice them making their first discovery of love! As if nobody had ever known it before! *(The bathroom door opens and Stella comes out. Blanche continues talking to Mitch)* Oh! Have you finished? Wait—I'll turn on the radio.

(She turns the knobs on the radio and it begins to play "Wien, Wien, nur du allein." Blanche waltzes to the music with romantic gestures. Mitch is delighted and moves in awkward imitation like a dancing bear.

(Stanley stalks fiercely through the portieres into the bedroom. He crosses to the small white radio and snatches it off the table. With a shouted oath, he tosses the instrument out the window.)

STELLA. *Drunk—drunk—animal thing, you! (She rushes through to the poker table)* All of you—please go home! If any of you have one spark of decency in you—

BLANCHE *(wildly).* Stella, watch out, he's—

(Stanley charges after Stella.)

MEN *(feebly).* Take it easy, Stanley. **Easy,** fellow.—Let's all—

STELLA. You lay your hands on me and I'll—

(*She backs out of sight. He advances and disappears. There is the sound of a blow. Stella cries out. Blanche screams and runs into the kitchen. The men rush forward and there is grappling and cursing. Something is overturned with a crash.*)

BLANCHE (*shrilly*). My sister is going to have a baby!

MITCH. This is terrible.

BLANCHE. Lunacy, absolute lunacy!

MITCH. Get him in here, men.

(*Stanley is forced, pinioned by the two men, into the bedroom. He nearly throws them off. Then all at once he subsides and is limp in their grasp.*

They speak quietly and lovingly to him and he leans his face on one of their shoulders.)

STELLA (*in a high, unnatural voice, out of sight*). I want to go away, I want to go away!

MITCH. Poker shouldn't be played in a house with women.

(*Blanche rushes into the bedroom.*)

BLANCHE. I want my sister's clothes! We'll go to that woman's upstairs!

MITCH. Where is the clothes?

BLANCHE (*opening the closet*). I've got them! (*She rushes through to Stella*) Stella, Stella, precious! Dear, dear little sister, don't be afraid!

(*With her arms around Stella, Blanche guides her to the outside door and upstairs.*)

STANLEY (*dully*). What's the matter; what's happened?

MITCH. You just blew your top, Stan.

PABLO. He's okay, now.

STEVE. Sure, my boy's okay!

MITCH. Put him on the bed and get a wet towel.

PABLO. I think coffee would do him a world of good, now.

STANLEY (*thickly*). I want water.

MITCH. Put him under the shower!

(*The men talk quietly as they lead him to the bathroom.*)

STANLEY. Let the rut go of me, you sons of bitches!

(*Sounds of blows are heard. The water goes on full tilt.*)

STEVE. Let's get quick out of here!

(*They rush to the poker table and sweep up their winnings on their way out.*)

MITCH (*sadly but firmly*). Poker should not be played in a house with women.

(*The door closes on them and the place is still. The Negro entertainers in the bar around the corner play "Paper Doll" slow and blue. After a moment Stanley comes out of the bathroom dripping water and still in his clinging wet polka dot drawers.*)

STANLEY. Stella! (*There is a pause*) My baby doll's left me! (*He breaks into sobs. Then he goes to the phone and dials, still shuddering with sobs*) Eunice? I want my baby! (*He waits a moment; then he hangs up and dials again*) Eunice! I'll keep on ringin' until I talk with my baby!

(*An indistinguishable shrill voice is heard. He hurls phone to floor. Dissonant brass and piano sounds as the rooms dim out to darkness and the outer walls appear in the night light. The "blue piano" plays for a brief interval.*

Finally, Stanley stumbles half-dressed out to the porch and down the wooden steps to the pavement before the building. There he throws back his head like a baying hound and bellows his wife's name: "Stella! Stella, sweetheart! Stella!")

STANLEY. Stell-*lahhhhh!*

EUNICE (*calling down from the door of her upper apartment*). Quit that howling out there an' go back to bed!

STANLEY. I want my baby down here. Stella, Stella!

EUNICE. She ain't comin' down so you quit! Or you'll git th' law on you!

STANLEY. Stella!

EUNICE. You can't beat on a woman an' then call 'er back! She won't come! And her goin' t' have a baby! . . . You stinker! You whelp of a Polack, you! I hope they do haul you in and turn the fire hose on you, same as the last time!

STANLEY (*humbly*). Eunice, I want my girl to come down with me!

EUNICE. Hah! (*She slams her door*)

STANLEY (*with heaven-splitting violence*). STELL-LAHHHHH!

(*The low-tone clarinet moans. The door upstairs opens again. Stella slips down the rickety stairs in her robe. Her eyes are glistening with tears and her hair loose about her throat and shoulders. They stare at each other. Then they come together with low animal moans. He falls to his knees on the steps and presses his face to her belly, curving a little with maternity. Her eyes go blind with tenderness as she catches his head and raises him level with her. He snatches the screen door open and lifts her off her feet and bears her into the dark flat.*

(Blanche comes out on the upper landing in her robe and slips fearfully down the steps.)

BLANCHE. Where is my little sister? Stella? Stella?

(She stops before the dark entrance of her sister's flat. Then catches her breath as if struck. She rushes down to the walk before the house. She looks right and left as if for a sanctuary.

(The music fades away. Mitch appears from around the corner.)

MITCH. Miss DuBois?

BLANCHE. Oh!

MITCH. All quiet on the Potomac now?

BLANCHE. She ran downstairs and went back in there with him.

MITCH. Sure she did.

BLANCHE. I'm terrified!

MITCH. Ho-ho! There's nothing to be scared of. They're crazy about each other.

BLANCHE. I'm not used to such—

MITCH. Naw, it's a shame this had to happen when you just got here. But don't take it serious.

BLANCHE. Violence! Is so—

MITCH. Set down on the steps and have a cigarette with me.

BLANCHE. I'm not properly dressed.

MITCH. That don't make no difference in the Quarter.

BLANCHE. Such a pretty silver case.

MITCH. I showed you the inscription, didn't I?

BLANCHE. Yes. *(During the pause she looks up at the sky)* There's so much—so much confusion in the world . . . *(He coughs diffidently)* Thank you for being so kind! I need kindness now.

SCENE FOUR

It is early the following morning. There is a confusion of street cries like a choral chant.

Stella is lying down in the bedroom. Her face is serene in the early morning sunlight. One hand rests on her belly, rounding slightly with new maternity. From the other dangles a book of colored comics. Her eyes and lips have that almost narcotized tranquility that is in the faces of Eastern idols.

The table is sloppy with remains of breakfast and the debris of the preceding night, and Stanley's gaudy pyjamas lie across the threshold of the bathroom. The outside door is slightly ajar on a sky of summer brilliance.

Blanche appears at this door. She has spent a sleepless night and her appearance entirely contrasts with Stella's. She presses her knuckles nervously to her lips as she looks through the door, before entering.

———

BLANCHE. Stella?

STELLA *(stirring lazily)*. Hmmh?

(Blanche utters a moaning cry and runs into the bedroom, throwing herself down beside Stella in a rush of hysterical tenderness.)

BLANCHE. Baby, my baby sister!

STELLA *(drawing away from her)*. Blanche, what is the matter with you?

(Blanche straightens up slowly and stands beside the bed looking down at her sister with knuckles pressed to her lips.)

BLANCHE. He's left?

STELLA. Stan? Yes.

BLANCHE. Will he be back?

STELLA. He's gone to get the car greased. Why?

BLANCHE. Why! I've been half crazy, Stella! When I found out you'd been insane enough to come back in here after what happened—I started to rush in after you!

STELLA. I'm glad you didn't.

BLANCHE. What were you thinking of? *(Stella makes an indefinite gesture)* Answer me! What? What?

STELLA. Please, Blanche! Sit down and stop yelling.

BLANCHE. All right, Stella. I will repeat the question quietly now. How could you come back in this place last night? Why, you must have slept with him!

(Stella gets up in a calm and leisurely way.)

STELLA. Blanche, I'd forgotten how excitable you are. You're making much too much fuss about this.

BLANCHE. Am I?

STELLA. Yes, you are, Blanche. I know how it must have seemed to you and I'm awful sorry it had to happen, but it wasn't anything as serious as you seem to take it. In the first place, when men are drinking and playing poker anything can happen. It's always a powder-keg. He didn't know what he was doing. . . . He was as good as a lamb when I came back and he's really very, very ashamed of himself.

BLANCHE. And that—that makes it all right?

STELLA. No, it isn't all right for anybody to make such a terrible row, but—people do sometimes. Stanley's always smashed things. Why, on our wedding night—soon as we came in here—he snatched off one of my slippers and rushed about the place smashing the light-bulbs with it.

BLANCHE. He did—*what?*

STELLA. He smashed all the light-bulbs with the heel of my slipper! (*She laughs*)

BLANCHE. And you—you *let* him? Didn't *run*, didn't *scream?*

STELLA. I was—sort of—thrilled by it. (*She waits for a moment*) Eunice and you had breakfast?

BLANCHE. Do you suppose I wanted any breakfast?

STELLA. There's some coffee left on the stove.

BLANCHE. You're so—matter of fact about it, Stella.

STELLA. What other can I be? He's taken the radio to get it fixed. It didn't land on the pavement so only one tube was smashed.

BLANCHE. And you are standing there smiling!

STELLA. What do you want me to do?

BLANCHE. Pull yourself together and face the facts.

STELLA. What are they, in your opinion?

BLANCHE. In my opinion? You're married to a madman!

STELLA. No!

BLANCHE. Yes, you are, your fix is worse than mine is! Only you're not being sensible about it. I'm going to *do* something. Get hold of myself and make myself a new life!

STELLA. Yes?

BLANCHE. But you've given in. And that isn't right, you're not old! You can get out.

STELLA (*slowly and emphatically*). I'm not in anything I want to get out of.

BLANCHE (*incredulously*). What—Stella?

STELLA. I said I am not in anything that I have a desire to get out of. Look at the mess in this room! And those empty bottles! They went through two cases last night! He promised this morning that he

was going to quit having these poker parties, but you know how long such a promise is going to keep. Oh, well, it's his pleasure, like mine is movies and bridge. People have got to tolerate each other's habits, I guess.

BLANCHE. I don't understand you. (*Stella turns toward her*) I don't understand your indifference. Is this a Chinese philosophy you've—cultivated?

STELLA. Is what—what?

BLANCHE. This shuffling about and mumbling—"One tube smashed—beer-bottles—mess in the kitchen!"—as if nothing out of the ordinary has happened! (*Stella laughs uncertainly, and picking up the broom, twirls it in her hands*)

BLANCHE. Are you deliberately shaking that thing in my face?

STELLA. No.

BLANCHE. Stop it. Let go of that broom. I won't have you cleaning up for him!

STELLA. Then who's going to do it? Are you?

BLANCHE. I? I!

STELLA. No, I didn't think so.

BLANCHE. Oh, let me think, if only my mind would function! We've got to get hold of some money, that's the way out!

STELLA. I guess that money is always nice to get hold of.

BLANCHE. Listen to me. I have an idea of some kind. (*Shakily she twists a cigarette into her holder*) Do you remember Shep Huntleigh? (*Stella shakes her head*) Of course you remember Shep Huntleigh. I went out with him at college and wore his pin for a while. Well—

STELLA. Well?

BLANCHE. I ran into him last winter. You know I went to Miami during the Christmas holidays?

STELLA. No.

BLANCHE. Well, I did. I took the trip as an investment, thinking I'd meet someone with a million dollars.

STELLA. Did you?

BLANCHE. Yes. I ran into Shep Huntleigh—I ran into him on Biscayne Boulevard, on Christmas Eve, about dusk . . . getting into his car—Cadillac convertible; must have been a block long!

STELLA. I should think it would have been—inconvenient in traffic!

BLANCHE. You've heard of oil-wells?

STELLA. Yes—remotely.

BLANCHE. He has them, all over Texas.

Texas is literally spouting gold in his pockets.

STELLA. My, my.

BLANCHE. Y'know how indifferent I am to money. I think of money in terms of what it does for you. But he could do it, he could certainly do it!

STELLA. Do what, Blanche?

BLANCHE. Why—set us up in a—shop!

STELLA. What kind of a shop?

BLANCHE. Oh, a—shop of some kind! He could do it with half what his wife throws away at the races.

STELLA. He's married?

BLANCHE. Honey, would I be here if the man weren't married? (*Stella laughs a little. Blanche suddenly springs up and crosses to phone. She speaks shrilly*) How do I get Western Union?—Operator! Western Union!

STELLA. That's a dial phone, honey.

BLANCHE. I can't dial, I'm too—

STELLA. Just dial O.

BLANCHE. O?

STELLA. Yes, "O" for Operator! (*Blanche considers a moment; then she puts the phone down*)

BLANCHE. Give me a pencil. Where is a slip of paper? I've got to write it down first—the message, I mean . . . (*She goes to the dressing table, and grabs up a sheet of Kleenex and an eyebrow pencil for writing equipment*) Let me see now . . . (*She bites the pencil*) "Darling Shep. Sister and I are in desperate situation."

STELLA. I beg your pardon!

BLANCHE. "Sister and I in desperate situation. Will explain details later. Would you be interested in—?" (*She bites the pencil again*) "Would you be—interested—in . . ." (*She smashes the pencil on the table and springs up*) You never get anywhere with direct appeals!

STELLA (*with a laugh*). Don't be so ridiculous, darling!

BLANCHE. But I'll think of something, I've *got* to think of—*something*! Don't, don't laugh at me, Stella! Please, please don't—I—I want you to look at the contents of my purse! Here's what's in it! (*She snatches her purse open*) Sixty-five measly cents in coin of the realm!

STELLA (*crossing to bureau*). Stanley doesn't give me a regular allowance, he likes to pay bills himself, but—this morning he gave me ten dollars to smooth things over. You take five of it, Blanche, and I'll keep the rest.

BLANCHE. Oh, no. No, Stella.

STELLA (*insisting*). I know how it helps your morale just having a little pocket-money on you.

BLANCHE. No, thank you—I'll take to the streets!

STELLA. Talk sense! How did you happen to get so low on funds?

BLANCHE. Money just goes—it goes places. (*She rubs her forehead*) Sometime today I've got to get hold of a bromo!

STELLA. I'll fix you one now.

BLANCHE. Not yet—I've got to keep thinking!

STELLA. I wish you'd just let things go, at least for a—while . . .

BLANCHE. Stella, I can't live with him! You can, he's your husband. But how could I stay here with him, after last night, with just those curtains between us?

STELLA. Blanche, you saw him at his worst last night.

BLANCHE. On the contrary, I saw him at his best! What such a man has to offer is animal force and he gave a wonderful exhibition of that! But the only way to live with such a man is to—go to bed with him! And that's your job—not mine!

STELLA. After you've rested a little, you'll see it's going to work out. You don't have to worry about anything while you're here. I mean—expenses . . .

BLANCHE. I have to plan for us both, to get us both—out!

STELLA. You take it for granted that I am in something that I want to get out of.

BLANCHE. I take it for granted that you still have sufficient memory of Belle Reve to find this place and these poker players impossible to live with.

STELLA. Well, you're taking entirely too much for granted.

BLANCHE. I can't believe you're in earnest.

STELLA. No?

BLANCHE. I understand how it happened —a little. You saw him in uniform, an officer, not here but—

STELLA. I'm not sure it would have made any difference where I saw him.

BLANCHE. Now don't say it was one of those mysterious electric things between people! If you do I'll laugh in your face.

STELLA. I am not going to say anything more at all about it

BLANCHE. All right, then, don't!

STELLA. But there are things that happen between a man and a woman in the dark —that sort of make everything else seem —unimportant. *(Pause)*

BLANCHE. What you are talking about is brutal desire—just—Desire!—the name of that rattle-trap streetcar that bangs through the Quarter, up one old narrow street and down another . . .

STELLA. Haven't you ever ridden on that streetcar?

BLANCHE. It brought me here.—Where I'm not wanted and where I'm ashamed to be . . .

STELLA. Then don't you think your superior attitude is a bit out of place?

BLANCHE. I am not being or feeling at all superior, Stella. Believe me I'm not! It's just this. This is how I look at it. A man like that is someone to go out with—once —twice—three times when the devil is in you. But live with? Have a child by?

STELLA. I have told you I love him.

BLANCHE. Then I tremble for you! I just —*tremble* for you. . . .

STELLA. I can't help your trembling if you insist on trembling!

(There is a pause.)

BLANCHE. May I—speak—*plainly?*

STELLA. Yes, do. Go ahead. As plainly as you want to.

(Outside, a train approaches. They are silent till the noise subsides. They are both in the bedroom.

(Under cover of the train's noise Stanley enters from outside. He stands unseen by the women, holding some packages in his arms, and overhears their following conversation. He wears an undershirt and grease-stained seersucker pants.)

BLANCHE. Well—if you'll forgive me— he's *common!*

STELLA. Why, yes, I suppose he is.

BLANCHE. Suppose! You can't have forgotten that much of our bringing up, Stella, that you just *suppose* that any part of a gentleman's in his nature! *Not one particle, no!* Oh, if he was just—*ordinary!* Just *plain*—but good and wholesome, but —no. There's something downright—*bestial*—about him! You're hating me saying this, aren't you?

STELLA *(coldly)*. Go on and say it all, Blanche.

BLANCHE. He acts like an animal, has an animal's habits! Eats like one, moves like one, talks like one! There's even something —sub-human—something not quite to the stage of humanity yet! Yes, something— ape-like about him, like one of those pictures I've seen in—anthropological studies! Thousands and thousands of years have passed him right by, and there he is— Stanley Kowalski—survivor of the stone age! Bearing the raw meat home from the kill in the jungle! And you—*you* here— *waiting* for him! Maybe he'll strike you or maybe grunt and kiss you! That is, if kisses have been discovered yet! Night falls and the other apes gather! There in the front of the cave, all grunting like him, and swilling and gnawing and hulking! His poker night!—you call it—this party of apes! Somebody growls—some creature snatches at something—the fight is on! *God!* Maybe we are a long way from being made in God's image, but Stella—my sister—there has been *some* progress since then! Such things as art—as poetry and music—such kinds of new light have come into the world since then! In some kinds of people some tenderer feelings have had some little beginning! That we have got to make *grow!* And *cling* to, and hold as our flag! In this dark march toward whatever it is we're approaching. . . . *Don't—don't hang back with the brutes!*

(Another train passes outside. Stanley hesitates, licking his lips. Then suddenly he turns stealthily about and withdraws through front door. The women are still unaware of his presence. When the train has passed he calls through the closed front door.)

STANLEY. Hey! Hey, Stella!

STELLA *(who has listened gravely to Blanche)*. Stanley!

BLANCHE. Stell, I—

(But Stella has gone to the front door. Stanley enters casually with his packages.)

STANLEY. Hiyuh, Stella. Blanche back?

STELLA. Yes, she's back.

STANLEY. Hiyuh, Blanche. *(He grins at her)*

STELLA. You must've got under the car.

STANLEY. Them darn mechanics at Fritz's don't know their ass fr'm— *Hey!* *(Stella has embraced him with both arms, fiercely, and full in the view of Blanche. He laughs and clasps her head to him. Over her head he grins through the curtains at Blanche.*

(As the lights fade away, with a lingering

brightness on their embrace, the music of the "blue piano" and trumpet and drums is heard.)

SCENE FIVE

Blanche is seated in the bedroom fanning herself with a palm leaf as she reads over a just completed letter. Suddenly she bursts into a peal of laughter. Stella is dressing in the bedroom.

STELLA. What are you laughing at, honey?

BLANCHE. Myself, myself, for being such a liar! I'm writing a letter to Shep. *(She picks up the letter)* "Darling Shep. I am spending the summer on the wing, making flying visits here and there. And who knows, perhaps I shall take a sudden notion to *swoop* down on *Dallas!* How would you feel about that? Ha-ha!" *(She laughs nervously and brightly, touching her throat as if actually talking to Shep)* "Forewarned is forearmed, as they say!"— How does that sound?

STELLA. Uh-huh . . .

BLANCHE *(going on nervously)*. "Most of my sister's friends go north in the summer but some have homes on the Gulf and there has been a continued round of entertainments, teas, cocktails, and luncheons—"

(A disturbance is heard upstairs at the Hubbells' apartment.)

STELLA. Eunice seems to be having some trouble with Steve.

(Eunice's voice shouts in terrible wrath.)

EUNICE. I heard about you and that blonde!

STEVE. That's a damn lie!

EUNICE. You ain't pulling the wool over my eyes! I wouldn't mind if you'd stay down at the Four Deuces, but you always going up.

STEVE. Who ever seen me up?

EUNICE. I seen you chasing her 'round the balcony—I'm gonna call the vice squad!

STEVE. Don't you throw that at me!

EUNICE *(shrieking)*. You hit me! I'm gonna call the police!

(A clatter of aluminum striking a wall is heard, followed by a man's angry roar, shouts and overturned furniture. There is a crash; then a relative hush.)

BLANCHE *(brightly)*. Did he *kill* her? *(Eunice appears on the steps in daemonic disorder.)*

STELLA. No! She's coming downstairs.

EUNICE. Call the police, I'm going to call the police! *(She rushes around the corner)* *(They laugh lightly. Stanley comes around the corner in his green and scarlet silk bowling shirt. He trots up the steps and bangs into the kitchen. Blanche registers his entrance with nervous gestures.)*

STANLEY. What's a matter with Eun-uss?

STELLA. She and Steve had a row. Has she got the police?

STANLEY. Naw. She's gettin' a drink.

STELLA. That's much more practical! *(Steve comes down nursing a bruise on his forehead and looks in the door.)*

STEVE. She here?

STANLEY. Naw, naw. At the Four Deuces.

STEVE. That rutting hunk! *(He looks around the corner a bit timidly, then turns with affected boldness and runs after her)*

BLANCHE. I must jot that down in my notebook. Ha-ha! I'm compiling a notebook of quaint little words and phrases I've picked up here.

STANLEY. You won't pick up nothing here you ain't heard before.

BLANCHE. Can I count on that?

STANLEY. You can count on it up to five hundred.

BLANCHE. That's a mighty high number. *(He jerks open the bureau drawer, slams it shut and throws shoes in a corner. At each noise Blanche winces slightly. Finally she speaks)* What sign were you born under?

STANLEY *(while he is dressing)*. Sign?

BLANCHE. Astrological sign. I bet you were born under Aries. Aries people are forceful and dynamic. They dote on noise! They love to bang things around! You must have had lots of banging around in the army and now that you're out, you make up for it by treating inanimate objects with such a fury!

(Stella has been going in and out of closet during this scene. Now she pops her head out of the closet.)

STELLA. Stanley was born just five minutes after Christmas.

BLANCHE. Capricorn—the Goat!

STANLEY. What sign were *you* born under?

BLANCHE. Oh, my birthday's next month,

the fifteenth of September; that's under Virgo.

STANLEY. What's Virgo?

BLANCHE. Virgo is the Virgin.

STANLEY (*contemptuously*). Hah! (*He advances a little as he knots his tie*) Say, do you happen to know somebody named Shaw?

(*Her face expresses a faint shock. She reaches for the cologne bottle and dampens her handkerchief as she answers carefully.*)

BLANCHE. Why, everybody knows somebody named Shaw!

STANLEY. Well, this somebody named Shaw is under the impression he met you in Laurel, but I figure he must have got you mixed up with some other party because this other party is someone he met at a hotel called the Flamingo.

(*Blanche laughs breathlessly as she touches the cologne-dampened handkerchief to her temples.*)

BLANCHE. I'm afraid he does have me mixed up with this "other party." The Hotel Flamingo is not the sort of establishment I would dare to be seen in!

STANLEY. You know of it?

BLANCHE. Yes, I've seen it and smelled it.

STANLEY. You must've got pretty close if you could smell it.

BLANCHE. The odor of cheap perfume is penetrating.

STANLEY. That stuff you use is expensive?

BLANCHE. Twenty-five dollars an ounce! I'm nearly out. That's just a hint if you want to remember my birthday! (*She speaks lightly but her voice has a note of fear*)

STANLEY. Shaw must've got you mixed up. He goes in and out of Laurel all the time so he can check on it and clear up any mistake.

(*He turns away and crosses to the portieres. Blanche closes her eyes as if to faint. Her hand trembles as she lifts the handkerchief again to her forehead.*)

(*Steve and Eunice come around the corner. Steve's arm is around Eunice's shoulder and she is sobbing luxuriously and he is cooing love-words. There is a murmur of thunder as they go slowly upstairs in a tight embrace.*)

STANLEY (*to Stella*). I'll wait for you at the Four Deuces!

STELLA. Hey! Don't I rate one kiss?

STANLEY. Not in front of your sister.

(*He goes out. Blanche rises from her chair. She seems faint; looks about her with an expression of almost panic.*)

BLANCHE. Stella! What have you heard about me?

STELLA. Huh?

BLANCHE. What have people been telling you about me?

STELLA. Telling?

BLANCHE. You haven't heard any—unkind—gossip about me?

STELLA. Why, no, Blanche, of course not!

BLANCHE. Honey, there was—a good deal of talk in Laurel.

STELLA. About *you*, Blanche?

BLANCHE. I wasn't so good the last two years or so, after Belle Reve had started to slip through my fingers.

STELLA. All of us do things we—

BLANCHE. I never was hard or self-sufficient enough. When people are soft—soft people have got to shimmer and glow—they've got to put on soft colors, the colors of butterfly wings, and put a—paper lantern over the light. . . . It isn't enough to be soft. You've got to be soft *and attractive*. And I—I'm fading now! I don't know how much longer I can turn the trick.

(*The afternoon has faded to dusk. Stella goes into the bedroom and turns on the light under the paper lantern. She holds a bottled soft drink in her hand.*)

BLANCHE. Have you been listening to me?

STELLA. I don't listen to you when you are being morbid! (*She advances with the bottled coke*)

BLANCHE (*with abrupt change to gaiety*). Is that coke for me?

STELLA. Not for anyone else!

BLANCHE. Why, you precious thing, you! Is it just coke?

STELLA (*turning*). You mean you want a shot in it!

BLANCHE. Well, honey, a shot never does a coke any harm! Let me! You mustn't wait on me!

STELLA. I like to wait on you, Blanche. It makes it seem more like home. (*She goes into the kitchen, finds a glass and pours a shot of whiskey into it*)

BLANCHE. I have to admit I love to be waited on . . . (*She rushes into the bedroom. Stella goes to her with the glass. Blanche suddenly clutches Stella's free hand with a moaning sound and presses the hand to her lips. Stella is embarrassed by her show of emotion. Blanche speaks in a choked voice)* You're—you're so *good* to me! And I—

STELLA. Blanche.

BLANCHE. I know, I won't! You hate me to talk sentimental! But honey, *believe* I feel things more than I *tell* you! I *won't* stay long! I won't, I *promise* I—

STELLA. Blanche!

BLANCHE *(hysterically)*. I won't, I promise, *I'll* go! Go *soon!* I will *really!* I *won't* hang around until he—throws me out . . .

STELLA. Now will you stop talking foolish?

BLANCHE. Yes, honey. Watch how you pour—that fizzy stuff foams over!

(Blanche laughs shrilly and grabs the glass, but her hand shakes so it almost slips from her grasp. Stella pours the coke into the glass. It foams over and spills. Blanche gives a piercing cry.)

STELLA *(shocked by the cry)*. Heavens!

BLANCHE. Right on my pretty white skirt!

STELLA. Oh . . . Use my hanky. Blot gently.

BLANCHE *(slowly recovering)*. I know—gently—gently . . .

STELLA. Did it stain?

BLANCHE. Not a bit. Ha-ha! Isn't that lucky? *(She sits down shakily, taking a grateful drink. She holds the glass in both hands and continues to laugh a little)*

STELLA. Why did you scream like that?

BLANCHE. I don't know why I screamed! *(Continuing nervously)* Mitch—Mitch is coming at seven. I guess I am just feeling nervous about our relations. *(She begins to talk rapidly and breathlessly)* He hasn't gotten a thing but a goodnight kiss, that's all I have given him, Stella. I want his respect. And men don't want anything they get too easy. But on the other hand men lose interest quickly. Especially when the girl is over—thirty. They think a girl over thirty ought to—the vulgar term is—"put out." . . . And I—I'm not "putting out." Of course he—he doesn't know—I mean I haven't informed him—of my real age!

STELLA. Why are you sensitive about your age?

BLANCHE. Because of hard knocks my vanity's been given. What I mean is—he thinks I'm sort of—prim and proper, you know! *(She laughs out sharply)* I want to *deceive* him enough to make him—want me . . .

STELLA. Blanche, do you want *him?*

BLANCHE. I want to *rest!* I want to breathe quietly again! Yes—I *want* Mitch . . . *very badly!* Just think! If it happens! I can leave here and not be anyone's problem . . .

(Stanley comes around the corner with a drink under his belt.)

STANLEY *(bawling)*. Hey, Steve! Hey, Eunice! Hey, Stella!

(There are joyous calls from above. Trumpet and drums are heard from around the corner.)

STELLA *(kissing Blanche impulsively)*. It *will* happen!

BLANCHE *(doubtfully)*. It will?

STELLA. It *will!* *(She goes across into the kitchen, looking back at Blanche)* It will, honey, it *will.* . . . But don't take another drink! *(Her voice catches as she goes out the door to meet her husband)*

(Blanche sinks faintly back in her chair with her drink. Eunice shrieks with laughter and runs down the steps. Steve bounds after her with goat-like screeches and chases her around corner. Stanley and Stella twine arms as they follow, laughing. (Dusk settles deeper. The music from the Four Deuces is slow and blue.)

BLANCHE. Ah, me, ah, me, ah, me . . .

(Her eyes fall shut and the palm leaf fan drops from her fingers. She slaps her hand on the chair arm a couple of times. There is a little glimmer of lightning about the building.

(A Young Man comes along the street and rings the bell.)

BLANCHE. Come in.

(The Young Man appears through the portieres. She regards him with interest.)

BLANCHE. Well, well! What can I do for *you?*

YOUNG MAN. I'm collecting for *The Evening Star.*

BLANCHE. I didn't know that stars took up collections.

YOUNG MAN. It's the paper.

BLANCHE. I know, I was joking—feebly! Will you—have a drink?

YOUNG MAN. No, ma'am. No, thank you, I can't drink on the job.

BLANCHE. Oh, well, now, let's see. . . . No, I don't have a dime! I'm not the lady of the house. I'm her sister from Mississippi. I'm one of those poor relations you've heard about.

YOUNG MAN. That's all right. I'll drop by later. (*He starts to go out. She approaches a little*)

BLANCHE. Hey! (*He turns back shyly. She puts a cigarette in a long holder*) Could you give me a light? (*She crosses toward him. They meet at the door between the two rooms*)

YOUNG MAN. Sure. (*He takes out a lighter*) This doesn't always work.

BLANCHE. It's temperamental? (*It flares*) Ah!—thank you. (*He starts away again*) Hey! (*He turns again, still more uncertainly. She goes close to him*) Uh—what time is it?

YOUNG MAN. Fifteen of seven, ma'am.

BLANCHE. So late? Don't you just love these long rainy afternoons in New Orleans when an hour isn't just an hour—but a little piece of eternity dropped into your hands—and who knows what to do with it? (*She touches his shoulders*) You—uh—didn't get wet in the rain?

YOUNG MAN. No, ma'am. I stepped inside.

BLANCHE. In a drugstore? And had a soda?

YOUNG MAN. Uh-huh.

BLANCHE. Chocolate?

YOUNG MAN. No, ma'am. Cherry.

BLANCHE (*laughing*). Cherry!

YOUNG MAN. A cherry soda.

BLANCHE. You make my mouth water. (*She touches his cheek lightly, and smiles. Then she goes to the trunk*)

YOUNG MAN. Well, I'd better be going—

BLANCHE. (*stopping him*). Young man! (*He turns. She takes a large, gossamer scarf from the trunk and drapes it about her shoulders.*

(*In the ensuing pause, the "blue piano" is heard. It continues through the rest of this scene and the opening of the next. The young man clears his throat and looks yearningly at the door.*)

Young man! Young, young, young man! Has anyone ever told you that you look like a young Prince out of the Arabian Nights?

(*The Young Man laughs uncomfortably and stands like a bashful kid. Blanche speaks softly to him.*)

Well, you do, honey lamb! Come here. I want to kiss you, just once, softly and sweetly on your mouth!

(*Without waiting for him to accept, she crosses quickly to him and presses her lips to his.*)

Now run along, now, quickly! It would be nice to keep you, but I've got to be good—and keep my hands off children.

(*He stares at her a moment. She opens the door for him and blows a kiss at him as he goes down the steps with a dazed look. She stands there a little dreamily after he has disappeared. Then Mitch appears around the corner with a bunch of roses.*)

BLANCHE (*gaily*). Look who's coming! My Rosenkavalier! Bow to me first . . . now present them! Ahhhh—Merciiii!

(*She looks at him over them, coquettishly pressing them to her lips. He beams at her self-consciously.*)

SCENE SIX

It is about two A.M. *on the same evening. The outer wall of the building is visible. Blanche and Mitch come in. The utter exhaustion which only a neurasthenic personality can know is evident in Blanche's voice and manner. Mitch is stolid but depressed. They have probably been out to the amusement park on Lake Pontchartrain, for Mitch is bearing, upside down, a plaster statuette of Mae West, the sort of prize won at shooting-galleries and carnival games of chance.*

BLANCHE (*stopping lifelessly at the steps*). Well—(*Mitch laughs uneasily*) Well . . .

MITCH. I guess it must be pretty late—and you're tired.

BLANCHE. Even the hot tamale man has deserted the street, and he hangs on till the end. (*Mitch laughs uneasily again*) How will you get home?

MITCH. I'll walk over to Bourbon and catch an owl-car.

BLANCHE (*laughing grimly*). Is that streetcar named Desire still grinding along the tracks at this hour?

MITCH (*heavily*). I'm afraid you haven't gotten much fun out of this evening, Blanche.

BLANCHE. I spoiled it for *you*.

MITCH. No, you didn't, but I felt all the time that I wasn't giving you much—entertainment.

BLANCHE. I simply couldn't rise to the occasion. That was all. I don't think I've ever tried so hard to be gay and made such a dismal mess of it. I get ten points for trying!—I *did* try.

MITCH. Why did you try if you didn't feel like it, Blanche?

BLANCHE. I was just obeying the law of nature.

MITCH. Which law is that?

BLANCHE. The one that says the lady must entertain the gentleman—or no dice! See if you can locate my door-key in this purse. When I'm so tired my fingers are all thumbs!

MITCH *(rooting in her purse)*. This it?

BLANCHE. No, honey, that's the key to my trunk which I must soon be packing.

MITCH. You mean you are leaving here soon?

BLANCHE. I've outstayed my welcome.

MITCH. This it?

(The music fades away.)

BLANCHE. Eureka! Honey, you open the door while I take a last look at the sky. *(She leans on the porch rail. He opens the door and stands awkwardly behind her)* I'm looking for the Pleiades, the Seven Sisters, but these girls are not out tonight. Oh, yes they are, there they are! God bless them! All in a bunch going home from their little bridge party. . . . Y' get the door open? Good boy! I guess you—want to go now . . .

(He shuffles and coughs a little.)

MITCH. Can I—uh—kiss you—good-night?

BLANCHE. Why do you always ask me if you may?

MITCH. I don't know whether you want me to or not.

BLANCHE. Why should you be so doubtful?

MITCH. That night when we parked by the lake and I kissed you, you—

BLANCHE. Honey, it wasn't the kiss I objected to. I liked the kiss very much. It was the other little—familiarity—that I—felt obliged to—discourage. . . . I didn't resent it! Not a bit in the world! In fact, I was somewhat flattered that you—desired me! But, honey, you know as well as I do that a single girl, a girl alone in the world, has got to keep a firm hold on her emotions or she'll be lost!

MITCH *(solemnly)*. Lost?

BLANCHE. I guess you are used to girls that like to be lost. The kind that get lost immediately, on the first date!

MITCH. I like you to be exactly the way that you are, because in all my—experience—I have never known anyone like you.

(Blanche looks at him gravely; then she bursts into laughter and then claps a hand to her mouth.)

MITCH. Are you laughing at me?

BLANCHE. No, honey. The lord and lady of the house have not yet returned, so come in. We'll have a night-cap. Let's leave the lights off. Shall we?

MITCH. You just—do what you want to.

(Blanche precedes him into the kitchen. The outer wall of the building disappears and the interiors of the two rooms can be dimly seen.)

BLANCHE *(remaining in the first room)*. The other room's more comfortable—go on in. This crashing around in the dark is my search for some liquor.

MITCH. You want a drink?

BLANCHE. I want *you* to have a drink! You have been so anxious and solemn all evening, and so have I; we have both been anxious and solemn and now for these few last remaining moments of our lives together—I want to create—*joie de vivre!* I'm lighting a candle.

MITCH. That's good.

BLANCHE. We are going to be very Bohemian. We are going to pretend that we are sitting in a little artists' cafe on the Left Bank in Paris! *(She lights a candle stub and puts it in a bottle)* Je suis la Dame aux Camellias! Vous êtes—Armand! Understand French?

MITCH *(heavily)*. Naw. Naw, I—

BLANCHE. *Voulez-vous couchez avec moi ce soir? Vous ne comprenez pas? Ah, quelle dommage!*—I mean it's a damned good thing. . . . I've found some liquor! Just enough for two shots without any dividends, honey . . .

MITCH *(heavily)*. That's—good.

(She enters the bedroom with the drinks and the candle.)

BLANCHE. Sit down! Why don't you take off your coat and loosen your collar?

MITCH. I better leave it on.

BLANCHE. No. I want you to be comfortable.

MITCH. I am ashamed of the way I perspire. My shirt is sticking to me.

BLANCHE. Perspiration is healthy. If people didn't perspire they would die in five minutes. (*She takes his coat from him*) This is a nice coat. What kind of material is it?

MITCH. They call that stuff alpaca.

BLANCHE. Oh. Alpaca.

MITCH. It's very lightweight alpaca.

BLANCHE. Oh. Lightweight alpaca.

MITCH. I don't like to wear a wash-coat even in summer because I sweat through it.

BLANCHE. Oh.

MITCH. And it don't look neat on me. A man with a heavy build has got to be careful of what he puts on him so he don't look too clumsy.

BLANCHE. You are not too heavy.

MITCH. You don't think I am?

BLANCHE. You are not the delicate type. You have a massive bone-structure and a very imposing physique.

MITCH. Thank you. Last Christmas I was given a membership to the New Orleans Athletic Club.

BLANCHE. Oh, good.

MITCH. It was the finest present I ever was given. I work out there with the weights and I swim and I keep myself fit. When I started there, I was getting soft in the belly but now my belly is hard. It is so hard now that a man can punch me in the belly and it don't hurt me. Punch me! Go on! See? (*She pokes lightly at him*)

BLANCHE. Gracious. (*Her hand touches her chest*)

MITCH. Guess how much I weigh, Blanche?

BLANCHE. Oh, I'd say in the vicinity of— one hundred and eighty?

MITCH. Guess again.

BLANCHE. Not that much?

MITCH. No. More.

BLANCHE. Well, you're a tall man and you can carry a good deal of weight without looking awkward.

MITCH. I weigh two hundred and seven pounds and I'm six feet one and one half inches tall in my bare feet—without shoes on. And that is what I weigh stripped.

BLANCHE. Oh, my goodness, me! It's awe-inspiring.

MITCH (*embarrassed*). My weight is not a very interesting subject to talk about. (*He hesitates for a moment*) What's yours?

BLANCHE. My weight?

MITCH. Yes.

BLANCHE. Guess!

MITCH. Let me lift you.

BLANCHE. Samson! Go on, lift me. (*He comes behind her and puts his hands on her waist and raises her lightly off the ground*) Well?

MITCH. You are light as a feather.

BLANCHE. Ha-ha! (*He lowers her but keeps his hands on her waist. Blanche speaks with an affectation of demureness*) You may release me now.

MITCH. Huh?

BLANCHE (*gaily*). I said unhand me, sir. (*He fumblingly embraces her. Her voice sounds gently reproving*) Now, Mitch. Just because Stanley and Stella aren't at home is no reason why you shouldn't behave like a gentleman.

MITCH. Just give me a slap whenever I step out of bounds.

BLANCHE. That won't be necessary. You're a natural gentleman, one of the very few that are left in the world. I don't want you to think that I am severe and old maid schoolteacherish or anything like that. It's just—well—

MITCH. Huh?

BLANCHE. I guess it is just that I have— old-fashioned ideals! (*She rolls her eyes, knowing he cannot see her face. Mitch goes to the front door. There is a considerable silence between them. Blanche sighs and Mitch coughs self-consciously*)

MITCH (*finally*). Where's Stanley and Stella tonight?

BLANCHE. They have gone out. With Mr. and Mrs. Hubbell upstairs.

MITCH. Where did they go?

BLANCHE. I think they were planning to go to a midnight prevue at Loew's State.

MITCH. We should all go out together some night.

BLANCHE. No. That wouldn't be a good plan.

MITCH. Why not?

BLANCHE. You are an old friend of Stanley's?

MITCH. We was together in the Two-forty-first.

BLANCHE. I guess he talks to you frankly?

MITCH. Sure.

BLANCHE. Has he talked to you about me?

MITCH. Oh—not very much.

BLANCHE. The way you say that, I suspect that he has.

MITCH. No, he hasn't said much.

BLANCHE. But what he *has* said. What would you say his attitude toward me was?

MITCH. Why do you want to ask that?

BLANCHE. Well—

MITCH. Don't you get along with him?

BLANCHE. What do you think?

MITCH. I don't think he understands you.

BLANCHE. That is putting it mildly. If it weren't for Stella about to have a baby, I wouldn't be able to endure things here.

MITCH. He isn't—nice to you?

BLANCHE. He is insufferably rude. Goes out of his way to offend me.

MITCH. In what way, Blanche?

BLANCHE. Why, in every conceivable way.

MITCH. I'm surprised to hear that.

BLANCHE. Are you?

MITCH. Well, I—don't see how anybody could be rude to you.

BLANCHE. It's really a pretty frightful situation. You see, there's no privacy here. There's just these portieres between the two rooms at night. He stalks through the rooms in his underwear at night. And I have to ask him to close the bathroom door. That sort of commonness isn't necessary. You probably wonder why I don't move out. Well, I'll tell you frankly. A teacher's salary is barely sufficient for her living-expenses. I didn't save a penny last year and so I had to come here for the summer. That's why I have to put up with my sister's husband. And he has to put up with me, apparently so much against his wishes. . . . Surely he must have told you how much he hates me!

MITCH. I don't think he hates you.

BLANCHE. He hates me. Or why would he insult me? The first time I laid eyes on him I thought to myself, that man is my executioner! That man will destroy me, unless—

MITCH. Blanche—

BLANCHE. Yes, honey?

MITCH. Can I ask you a question?

BLANCHE. Yes. What?

MITCH. How old are you?

(She makes a nervous gesture.)

BLANCHE. Why do you want to know?

MITCH. I talked to my mother about you and she said, "How old is Blanche?" And I wasn't able to tell her. *(There is another pause)*

BLANCHE. You talked to your mother about me?

MITCH. Yes.

BLANCHE. Why?

MITCH. I told my mother how nice you were, and I liked you.

BLANCHE. Were you sincere about that?

MITCH. You know I was.

BLANCHE. Why did your mother want to know my age?

MITCH. Mother is sick.

BLANCHE. I'm sorry to hear it. Badly?

MITCH. She won't live long. Maybe just a few months.

BLANCHE. Oh.

MITCH. She worries because I'm not settled.

BLANCHE. Oh.

MITCH. She wants me to be settled down before she—*(His voice is hoarse and he clears his throat twice, shuffling nervously around with his hands in and out of his pockets)*

BLANCHE. You love her very much, don't you?

MITCH. Yes.

BLANCHE. I think you have a great capacity for devotion. You will be lonely when she passes on, won't you? *(Mitch clears his throat and nods)* I understand what that is.

MITCH. To be lonely?

BLANCHE. I loved someone, too, and the person I loved I lost.

MITCH. Dead? *(She crosses to the window and sits on the sill, looking out. She pours herself another drink)* A man?

BLANCHE. He was a boy, just a boy, when I was a very young girl. When I was sixteen, I made the discovery—love. All at once and much, much too completely. It was like you suddenly turned a blinding light on something that had always been half in shadow, that's how it struck the world for me. But I was unlucky. Deluded. There was something different about the boy, a nervousness, a softness and tenderness which wasn't like a man's, although he wasn't the least bit effeminate looking—still—that thing was there. . . . He came to me for help. I didn't know that. I didn't find out anything till after our marriage when we'd run away and come back and all I knew was I'd failed him in some mysterious way and wasn't able to give the help he needed but couldn't speak of! He was in the quicksands and clutching at me—but I wasn't holding him out, I was slipping in with him! I didn't know that. I didn't know anything except I loved him unendurably but without being able to help him or help myself. Then I found out. In the worst of all possible ways. By coming suddenly into a room that I thought was empty—which wasn't empty, but had two people in it . . . the boy I had married and an older man who had been his friend for years . . .

(A locomotive is heard approaching outside. She claps her hands to her ears and crouches over. The headlight of the locomotive glares into the room as it thunders past. As the noise recedes she straightens slowly and continues speaking.)

Afterwards we pretended that nothing had been discovered. Yes, the three of us drove out to Moon Lake Casino, very drunk and laughing all the way.

(Polka music sounds, in a minor key faint with distance.)

We danced the Varsouviana! Suddenly in the middle of the dance the boy I had married broke away from me and ran out of the casino. A few moments later—a shot!

(The Polka stops abruptly.)

(Blanche rises stiffly. Then, the Polka resumes in a major key.)

I ran out—all did!—all ran and gathered about the terrible thing at the edge of the lake! I couldn't get near for the crowding. Then somebody caught my arm. "Don't go any closer! Come back! You don't want to see!" See? See what! Then I heard voices say—Allan! Allan! The Grey boy! He'd stuck the revolver into his mouth, and fired—so that the back of his head had been—blown away!

(She sways and covers her face.)

It was because—on the dance-floor—unable to stop myself—I'd suddenly said—"I saw! I know! You disgust me . . ." And then the searchlight which had been turned on the world was turned off again and never for one moment since has there been any light that's stronger than this—kitchen—candle . . .

(Mitch gets up awkwardly and moves toward her a little. The Polka music increases. Mitch stands beside her.)

MITCH *(drawing her slowly into his arms)*. You need somebody. And I need somebody, too. Could it be—you and me, Blanche?

(She stares at him vacantly for a moment. Then with a soft cry huddles in his embrace. She makes a sobbing effort to speak but the words won't come. He kisses her forehead and her eyes and finally her lips. The Polka tune fades out. Her breath is drawn and released in long, grateful sobs.)

BLANCHE. Sometimes—there's God—so quickly!

SCENE SEVEN

It is late afternoon in mid-September.

The portieres are open and a table is set for a birthday supper, with cake and flowers.

Stella is completing the decorations as Stanley comes in.

STANLEY. What's all this stuff for?
STELLA. Honey, it's Blanche's birthday.
STANLEY. She here?
STELLA. In the bathroom.
STANLEY *(mimicking)*. "Washing out some things"?
STELLA. I reckon so.
STANLEY. How long she been in there?
STELLA. All afternoon.
STANLEY *(mimicking)*. "Soaking in a hot tub"?
STELLA. Yes.
STANLEY. Temperature 100 on the nose, and she soaks herself in a hot tub.
STELLA. She says it cools her off for the evening.
STANLEY. And you run out an' get her cokes, I suppose? And serve 'em to Her Majesty in the tub? *(Stella shrugs)* Set down here a minute.
STELLA. Stanley, I've got things to do.
STANLEY. Set down! I've got th' dope on your big sister, Stella.
STELLA. Stanley, stop picking on Blanche.
STANLEY. That girl calls *me* common!
STELLA. Lately you been doing all you can think of to rub her the wrong way, Stanley, and Blanche is sensitive and you've got to realize that Blanche and I grew up under very different circumstances than you did.
STANLEY. So I been told. And told and

told and told! You know she's been feeding us a pack of lies here?

STELLA. No, I don't, and—

STANLEY. Well, she has, however. But now the cat's out of the bag! I found out some things!

STELLA. What—things?

STANLEY. Things I already suspected. But now I got proof from the most reliable sources—which I have checked on! *(Blanche is singing in the bathroom a saccharine popular ballad which is used contrapuntally with Stanley's speech.)*

STELLA *(to Stanley)*. Lower your voice!

STANLEY. Some canary-bird, huh!

STELLA. Now please tell me quietly what you think you've found out about my sister.

STANLEY. Lie Number One: All this squeamishness she puts on! You should just know the line she's been feeding to Mitch. He thought she had never been more than kissed by a fellow! But Sister Blanche is no lily! Ha-ha! Some lily she is!

STELLA. What have you heard and who from?

STANLEY. Our supply-man down at the plant has been going through Laurel for years and he knows all about her and everybody else in the town of Laurel knows all about her. She is as famous in Laurel as if she was the President of the United States, only she is not respected by any party! This supply-man stops at a hotel called the Flamingo.

BLANCHE *(singing blithely)*. "Say, it's only a paper moon, Sailing over a cardboard sea—But it wouldn't be make-believe If you believed in me!"

STELLA. What about the—Flamingo?

STANLEY. She stayed there, too.

STELLA. My sister lived at Belle Reve.

STANLEY. This is after the home-place had slipped through her lily-white fingers! She moved to the Flamingo! A second-class hotel which has the advantage of not interfering in the private social life of the personalities there! The Flamingo is used to all kinds of goings-on. But even the management of the Flamingo was impressed by Dame Blanche! In fact they was so impressed by Dame Blanche that they requested her to turn in her room-key—for permanently! This happened a couple of weeks before she showed here.

BLANCHE *(singing)*. "It's a Barnum and

Bailey world, Just as phony as it can be—
But it wouldn't be make-believe If you believed in me!"

STELLA. What—contemptible—lies!

STANLEY. Sure, I can see how you would be upset by this. She pulled the wool over your eyes as much as Mitch's!

STELLA. It's pure invention! There's not a word of truth in it and if I were a man and this creature had dared to invent such things in my presence—

BLANCHE *(singing)*. "Without your love, It's a honky-tonk parade! Without your love, It's a melody played In a penny arcade . . ."

STANLEY. Honey, I told you I thoroughly checked on these stories! Now wait till I'm finished. The trouble with Dame Blanche was that she couldn't put on her act any more in Laurel! They got wised up after two or three dates with her and then they quit, and she goes on to another, the same old line, same old act, same old hooey! But the town was too small for this to go on forever! And as time went by she became a town character. Regarded as not just different but downright loco—nuts. *(Stella draws back)* And for the last year or two she has been washed up like poison. That's why she's here this summer, visiting royalty, putting on all this act—because she's practically told by the mayor to get out of town! Yes, did you know there was an army camp near Laurel and your sister's was one of the places called "Out-of-Bounds"?

BLANCHE. "It's only a paper moon, Just as phony as it can be—
But it wouldn't be make-believe If you believed in me!"

STANLEY. Well, so much for her being such a refined and particular type of girl. Which brings us to Lie Number Two.

STELLA. I don't want to hear any more!

STANLEY. She's not going back to teach school! In fact I am willing to bet you that she never had no idea of returning to Laurel! She didn't resign temporarily from the high school because of her nerves! No, siree, Bob! She didn't. They kicked her out of that high school before the spring term ended—and I hate to tell you the reason that step was taken! A seventeen-year-old boy—she'd gotten mixed up with!

BLANCHE. "It's a Barnum and Bailey

world, Just as phony as it can be—"
*(In the bathroom the water goes on loud;
little breathless cries and peals of laughter
are heard as if a child were frolicking in
the tub.)*

STELLA. This is making me—sick!

STANLEY. The boy's dad learned about it
and got in touch with the high school
superintendent. Boy, oh, boy, I'd like to
have been in that office when Dame
Blanche was called on the carpet! I'd like
to have seen her trying to squirm out of
that one! But they had her on the hook
good and proper that time and she knew
that the jig was all up! They told her she
better move on to some fresh territory.
Yep, it was practickly a town ordinance
passed against her!

*(The bathroom door is opened and
Blanche thrusts her head out, holding a
towel about her hair.)*

BLANCHE. Stella!

STELLA *(faintly)*. Yes, Blanche?

BLANCHE. Give me another bath-towel
to dry my hair with. I've just washed it.

STELLA. Yes, Blanche. *(She crosses in a
dazed way from the kitchen to the bathroom door with a towel)*

BLANCHE. What's the matter, honey?

STELLA. Matter? Why?

BLANCHE. You have such a strange expression on your face!

STELLA. Oh—*(She tries to laugh)* I guess
I'm a little tired!

BLANCHE. Why don't you bathe, too,
soon as I get out?

STANLEY *(calling from the kitchen)*.
How soon is that going to be?

BLANCHE. Not so terribly long! Possess
your soul in patience!

STANLEY. It's not my soul, it's my kidneys I'm worried about!

*(Blanche slams the door. Stanley laughs
harshly. Stella comes slowly back into the
kitchen.)*

STANLEY. Well, what do you think of it?

STELLA. I don't believe all of those stories
and I think your supply-man was mean
and rotten to tell them. It's possible that
some of the things he said are partly true.
There are things about my sister I don't
approve of—things that caused sorrow at
home. She was always—flighty!

STANLEY. Flighty!

STELLA. But when she was young, very
young, she married a boy who wrote poetry. . . . He was extremely good-looking.
I think Blanche didn't just love him but
worshipped the ground he walked on!
Adored him and thought him almost too
fine to be human! But then she found
out—

STANLEY. What?

STELLA. This beautiful and talented
young man was a degenerate. Didn't your
supply-man give you that information?

STANLEY. All we discussed was recent
history. That must have been a pretty long
time ago.

STELLA. Yes, it was—a pretty long time
ago . . .

*(Stanley comes up and takes her by the
shoulders rather gently. She gently withdraws from him. Automatically she starts
sticking little pink candles in the birthday
cake.)*

STANLEY. How many candles you putting in that cake?

STELLA. I'll stop at twenty-five.

STANLEY. Is company expected?

STELLA. We asked Mitch to come over
for cake and ice-cream.

*(Stanley looks a little uncomfortable. He
lights a cigarette from the one he has just
finished.)*

STANLEY. I wouldn't be expecting Mitch
over tonight.

*(Stella pauses in her occupation with
candles and looks slowly around at Stanley.)*

STELLA. *Why?*

STANLEY. Mitch is a buddy of mine. We
were in the same outfit together—Two-
forty-first Engineers. We work in the same
plant and now on the same bowling team.
You think I could face him if—

STELLA. Stanley Kowalski, did you—did
you repeat what that—?

STANLEY. You're goddam right I told
him! I'd have that on my conscience the
rest of my life if I knew all that stuff and
let my best friend get caught!

STELLA. Is Mitch through with her?

STANLEY. Wouldn't you be if—?

STELLA. I said, *Is Mitch through with
her?*

*(Blanche's voice is lifted again, serenely as
a bell. She sings "But it wouldn't be make
believe if you believed in me.")*

STANLEY. No, I don't think he's necessarily through with her—just wised up!

STELLA. Stanley, she thought Mitch was
—going to—going to marry her. I was
hoping so, too.

STANLEY. Well, he's not going to marry her. Maybe he *was,* but he's not going to jump in a tank with a school of sharks— now! *(He rises)* Blanche! Oh, Blanche! Can I please get in my bathroom? *(There is a pause)*

BLANCHE. Yes, indeed, sir! Can you wait one second while I dry?

STANLEY. Having waited one hour I guess one second ought to pass in a hurry.

STELLA. And she hasn't got her job? Well, what will she do!

STANLEY. She's not stayin' here after Tuesday. You know that, don't you? Just to make sure I bought her ticket myself. A bus-ticket!

STELLA. In the first place, Blanche wouldn't go on a bus.

STANLEY. She'll go on a bus and like it.

STELLA. No, she won't, no, she won't, Stanley!

STANLEY. *She'll go!* Period. P.S. She'll go *Tuesday!*

STELLA *(slowly).* What'll — she — do! What on earth will she—*do!*

STANLEY. Her future is mapped out for her.

STELLA. What do you mean?
(Blanche sings.)

STANLEY. Hey, canary bird! Toots! Get *OUT* of the *BATHROOM!*
(The bathroom door flies open and Blanche emerges with a gay peal of laughter, but as Stanley crosses past her, a frightened look appears in her face, almost a look of panic. He doesn't look at her but slams the bathroom door shut as he goes in.)

BLANCHE *(snatching up a hair-brush).* Oh, I feel so good after my long, hot bath, I feel so good and cool and—rested!

STELLA *(sadly and doubtfully from the kitchen).* Do you, Blanche?

BLANCHE *(brushing her hair vigorously).* Yes, I do, so refreshed! *(She tinkles her highball glass)* A hot bath and a long, cold drink always give me a brand new outlook on life! *(She looks through the portieres at Stella, standing between them, and slowly stops brushing)* Something has happened!—What is it?

STELLA *(turning away quickly).* Why, nothing has happened, Blanche.

BLANCHE. You're lying! Something has!
(She stares fearfully at Stella, who pretends to be busy at the table. The distant piano goes into a hectic breakdown.)

SCENE EIGHT

Three-quarters of an hour later.

The view through the big windows is fading gradually into a still-golden dusk. A torch of sunlight blazes on the side of a big water-tank or oil-drum across the empty lot toward the business district which is now pierced by pinpoints of lighted windows or windows reflecting the sunset.

The three people are completing a dismal birthday supper. Stanley looks sullen. Stella is embarrassed and sad.

Blanche has a tight, artificial smile on her drawn face. There is a fourth place at the table which is left vacant.

———

BLANCHE *(suddenly).* Stanley, tell us a joke, tell us a funny story to make us all laugh. I don't know what's the matter, we're all so solemn. Is it because I've been stood up by my beau? *(Stella laughs feebly)* It's the first time in my entire experience with men, and I've had a good deal of all sorts, that I've actually been stood up by anybody! Ha-ha! I don't know how to take it. . . . Tell us a funny little story, Stanley! Something to help us out.

STANLEY. I didn't think you liked my stories, Blanche.

BLANCHE. I like them when they're amusing but not indecent.

STANLEY. I don't know any refined enough for your taste.

BLANCHE. Then let me tell one.

STELLA. Yes, you tell one, Blanche. You used to know lots of good stories.
(The music fades.)

BLANCHE. Let me see, now. . . . I must run through my repertoire! Oh, yes—I love parrot stories! Do you all like parrot stories? Well, this one's about the old maid and the parrot. This old maid, she had a parrot that cursed a blue streak and knew more vulgar expressions than Mr. Kowalski!

STANLEY. Huh.

BLANCHE. And the only way to hush the parrot up was to put the cover back on its cage so it would think it was night and go back to sleep. Well, one morning the old maid had just uncovered the parrot for the day—when who should she see coming up the front walk but the preacher! Well, she rushed back to the parrot and slipped the cover back on the cage and then she let in the preacher. And the parrot was perfectly still, just as quiet as a mouse, but just as she was asking the preacher how much sugar he wanted in his coffee—the parrot broke the silence with a loud—(*She whistles*)—and said—"God *damn,* but that was a short day!" (*She throws back her head and laughs. Stella also makes an ineffectual effort to seem amused. Stanley pays no attention to the story but reaches way over the table to spear his fork into the remaining chop which he eats with his fingers.*)

BLANCHE. Apparently Mr. Kowalski was not amused.

STELLA. Mr. Kowalski is too busy making a pig of himself to think of anything else!

STANLEY. That's right, baby.

STELLA. Your face and your fingers are disgustingly greasy. Go and wash up and then help me clear the table.

(*He hurls a plate to the floor.*)

STANLEY. That's how I'll clear the table! (*He seizes her arm*) Don't ever talk that way to me! "Pig—Polack—disgusting—vulgar—greasy!"—them kind of words have been on your tongue and your sister's too much around here! What do you two think you are? A pair of queens? Remember what Huey Long said—"Every Man Is a King!" And I am the king around here, so don't forget it! (*He hurls a cup and saucer to the floor*) My place is cleared! You want me to clear your places? (*Stella begins to cry weakly. Stanley stalks out on the porch and lights a cigarette.* (*The Negro entertainers around the corner are heard.*)

BLANCHE. What happened while I was bathing? What did he tell you, Stella?

STELLA. Nothing, nothing, nothing!

BLANCHE. I think he told you something about Mitch and me! You know why Mitch didn't come but you won't tell me! (*Stella shakes her head helplessly*) I'm going to call him!

STELLA. I wouldn't call him, Blanche.

BLANCHE. I am, I'm going to call him on the phone.

STELLA (*miserably*). I wish you wouldn't.

BLANCHE. I intend to be given some explanation from someone!

(*She rushes to the phone in the bedroom. Stella goes out on the porch and stares reproachfully at her husband. He grunts and turns away from her.*)

STELLA. I hope you're pleased with your doings. I never had so much trouble swallowing food in my life, looking at that girl's face and the empty chair! (*She cries quietly*)

BLANCHE (*at the phone*). Hello. Mr. Mitchell, please. . . . Oh. . . . I would like to leave a number if I may. Magnolia 9047. And say it's important to call. . . . Yes, very important. . . . Thank you. (*She remains by the phone with a lost, frightened look*)

(*Stanley turns slowly back toward his wife and takes her clumsily in his arms.*)

STANLEY. Stell, it's gonna be all right after she goes and after you've had the baby. It's gonna be all right again between you and me the way that it was. You remember that way that it was? Them nights we had together? God, honey, it's gonna be sweet when we can make noise in the night the way that we used to and get the colored lights going with nobody's sister behind the curtains to hear us! (*Their upstairs neighbors are heard in bellowing laughter at something. Stanley chuckles*) Steve an' Eunice. . . .

STELLA. Come on back in. (*She returns to the kitchen and starts lighting the candles on the white cake*) Blanche?

BLANCHE. Yes. (*She returns from the bedroom to the table in the kitchen*) Oh, those pretty, pretty little candles! Oh, don't burn them, Stella.

STELLA. I certainly will.

(*Stanley comes back in.*)

BLANCHE. You ought to save them for baby's birthdays. Oh, I hope candles are going to glow in his life and I hope that his eyes are going to be like candles, like two blue candles lighted in a white cake!

STANLEY (*sitting down*). What poetry!

BLANCHE (*she pauses reflectively for a moment*). I shouldn't have called him.

STELLA. There's lots of things could have happened.

BLANCHE. There's no excuse for it, Stella. I don't have to put up with insults. I won't be taken for granted.

STANLEY. Goddamn, it's hot in here with the steam from the bathroom.

BLANCHE. I've said I was sorry three times. (*The piano fades out*) I take hot baths for my nerves. Hydro-therapy, they call it. You healthy Polack, without a nerve in your body, of course you don't know what anxiety feels like!

STANLEY. I am not a Polack. People from Poland are Poles, not Polacks. But what I am is a one hundred percent American, born and raised in the greatest country on earth and proud as hell of it, so don't ever call me a Polack.

(The phone rings. Blanche rises expectantly.)

BLANCHE. Oh, that's for me, I'm sure.

STANLEY. *I'm* not sure. Keep your seat. *(He crosses leisurely to phone)* H'lo. Aw, yeh, hello, Mac.

(He leans against wall, staring insultingly in at Blanche. She sinks back in her chair with a frightened look. Stella leans over and touches her shoulder.)

BLANCHE. Oh, keep your hands off me, Stella. What is the matter with you? Why do you look at me with that pitying look?

STANLEY *(bawling)*. Q U I E T I N THERE!—We've got a noisy woman on the place.—Go on, Mac. At Riley's? No, I don't wanta bowl at Riley's. I had a little trouble with Riley last week. I'm the team-captain, ain't I? All right, then, we're not gonna bowl at Riley's, we're gonna bowl at the West Side or the Gala! All right, Mac. See you! *(He hangs up and returns to the table. Blanche fiercely controls herself, drinking quickly from her tumbler of water. He doesn't look at her but reaches in a pocket. Then he speaks slowly and with false amiability)* Sister Blanche, I've got a little birthday remembrance for you.

BLANCHE. Oh, have you, Stanley? I wasn't expecting any, I—I don't know why Stella wants to observe my birthday! I'd much rather forget it—when you—reach twenty-seven! Well—age is a subject that you'd prefer to—ignore!

STANLEY. Twenty-seven?

BLANCHE *(quickly)*. What is it? Is it for me?

(He is holding a little envelope toward her.)

STANLEY. Yes, I hope you like it!

BLANCHE. Why, why—Why, it's a—

STANLEY. Ticket! Back to Laurel! On the Greyhound! Tuesday! *(The Varsouviana music steals in softly and continues playing. Stella rises abruptly and turns her back. Blanches tries to smile. Then she tries to laugh. Then she gives both up and springs from the table and runs into the next room. She clutches her throat and then runs into the bathroom. Coughing, gagging sounds are heard)* Well!

STELLA. You didn't need to do that.

STANLEY. Don't forget all that I took off her.

STELLA. You needn't have been so cruel to someone alone as she is.

STANLEY. Delicate piece she is.

STELLA. She is. She was. You didn't know Blanche as a girl. Nobody, nobody, was tender and trusting as she was. But people like you abused her, and forced her to change. *(He crosses into the bedroom, ripping off his shirt, and changes into a brilliant silk bowling shirt. She follows him)* Do you think you're going bowling now?

STANLEY. Sure.

STELLA. You're not going bowling. *(She catches hold of his shirt)* Why did you do this to her?

STANLEY. I done nothing to no one. Let go of my shirt. You've torn it.

STELLA. I want to know why. Tell me why.

STANLEY. When we first met, me and you, you thought I was common. How right you was, baby. I was common as dirt. You showed me the snapshot of the place with the columns. I pulled you down off them columns and how you loved it, having them colored lights going! And wasn't we happy together, wasn't it all okay till she showed here? *(Stella makes a slight movement. Her look goes suddenly inward as if some interior voice had called her name. She begins a slow, shuffling progress from the bedroom to the kitchen, leaning and resting on the back of the chair and then on the edge of a table with a blind look and listening expression. Stanley, finishing with his shirt, is unaware of her reaction)* And wasn't we happy together? Wasn't it all okay? Till she showed here. Hoity-toity, describing me as an ape. *(He suddenly notices the change in Stella)* Hey, what is it, Stel? *(He crosses to her)*

STELLA *(quietly)*. Take me to the hospital.

(He is with her now, supporting her with his arm, murmuring indistinguishably as they go outside.)

SCENE NINE

A while later that evening. Blanche is

seated in a tense hunched position in a bedroom chair that she has re-covered with diagonal green and white stripes. She has on her scarlet satin robe. On the table beside chair is a bottle of liquor and a glass. The rapid, feverish polka tune, the "Varsouviana," is heard. The music is in her mind; she is drinking to escape it and the sense of disaster closing in on her, and she seems to whisper the words of the song. An electric fan is turning back and forth across her.

Mitch comes around the corner in work clothes: blue denim shirt and pants. He is unshaven. He climbs the steps to the door and rings. Blanche is startled.

———

BLANCHE. Who is it, please?

MITCH *(hoarsely)*. Me. Mitch.

(The polka tune stops.)

BLANCHE. Mitch!—Just a minute. *(She rushes about frantically, hiding the bottle in a closet, crouching at the mirror and dabbing her face with cologne and powder. She is so excited that her breath is audible as she dashes about. At last she rushes to the door in the kitchen and lets him in)* Mitch!—Y'know, I really shouldn't let you in after the treatment I have received from you this evening! So utterly uncavalier! But hello, beautiful! *(She offers him her lips. He ignores it and pushes past her into the flat. She looks fearfully after him as he stalks into the bedroom)* My, my, what a cold shoulder! And such uncouth apparel! Why, you haven't even shaved! The unforgivable insult to a lady! But I forgive you. I forgive you because it's such a relief to see you. You've stopped that polka tune that I had caught in my head. Have you ever had anything caught in your head? No, of course you haven't, you dumb angel-puss, you'd never get anything awful caught in your head!

(He stares at her while she follows him while she talks. It is obvious that he has had a few drinks on the way over.)

MITCH. Do we have to have that fan on?

BLANCHE. No!

MITCH. I don't like fans.

BLANCHE. Then let's turn it off, honey. I'm not partial to them! *(She presses the switch and the fan nods slowly off. She clears her throat uneasily as Mitch plumps himself down on the bed in the bedroom, and lights a cigarette)* I don't know what

there is to drink. I—haven't investigated.

MITCH. I don't want Stan's liquor.

BLANCHE. It isn't Stan's. Everything here isn't Stan's. Some things on the premises are actually mine! How is your mother? Isn't your mother well?

MITCH. Why?

BLANCHE. Something's the matter tonight, but never mind. I won't cross-examine the witness. I'll just— *(She touches her forehead vaguely. The polka tune starts up again)*—pretend I don't notice anything different about you! That—music again . . .

MITCH. What music?

BLANCHE. The "Varsouviana"! The polka tune they were playing when Allan— Wait! *(A distant revolver shot is heard. Blanche seems relieved)* There now, the shot! It always stops after that. *(The polka music dies out again)* Yes, now it's stopped.

MITCH. Are you boxed out of your mind?

BLANCHE. I'll go and see what I can find in the way of— *(She crosses into the closet, pretending to search for the bottle)* Oh, by the way, excuse me for not being dressed. But I'd practically given you up! Had you forgotten your invitation to supper?

MITCH. I wasn't going to see you any more.

BLANCHE. Wait a minute. I can't hear what you're saying and you talk so little that when you do say something, I don't want to miss a single syllable of it. . . . What am I looking around here for? Oh, yes—liquor! We've had so much excitement around here this evening that I *am* boxed out of my mind! *(She pretends suddenly to find the bottle. He draws his foot up on the bed and stares at her contemptuously)* Here's something. Southern Comfort! What is that, I wonder?

MITCH. If you don't know, it must belong to Stan.

BLANCHE. Take your foot off the bed. It has a light cover on it. Of course you boys don't notice things like that. I've done so much with this place since I've been here.

MITCH. I bet you have.

BLANCHE. You saw it before I came. Well, look at it now! This room is almost —dainty! I want to keep it that way. I wonder if this stuff ought to be mixed with something? Ummm, it's sweet, so sweet! It's terribly, terribly sweet! Why, it's a *liqueur,* I believe! Yes, that's what it *is,* a liqueur! *(Mitch grunts)* I'm afraid you won't like it, but try it, and maybe you will.

MITCH. I told you already I don't want none of his liquor and I mean it. You ought to lay off his liquor. He says you been lapping it up all summer like a wild-cat!

BLANCHE. What a fantastic statement! Fantastic of him to say it, fantastic of you to repeat it! I won't descend to the level of such cheap accusations to answer them, even!

MITCH. Huh.

BLANCHE. What's in your mind? I see something in your eyes!

MITCH *(getting up).* It's dark in here.

BLANCHE. I like it dark. The dark is comforting to me.

MITCH. I don't think I ever seen you in the light. *(Blanche laughs breathlessly)* That's a fact!

BLANCHE. Is it?

MITCH. I've never seen you in the afternoon.

BLANCHE. Whose fault is that?

MITCH. You never want to go out in the afternoon.

BLANCHE. Why, Mitch, you're at the plant in the afternoon!

MITCH. Not Sunday afternoon. I've asked you to go out with me sometimes on Sundays but you always make an excuse. You never want to go out till after six and then it's always some place that's not lighted much.

BLANCHE. There is some obscure meaning in this but I fail to catch it.

MITCH. What it means is I've never had a real good look at you, Blanche. Let's turn the light on here.

BLANCHE *(fearfully).* Light? Which light? What for?

MITCH. This one with the paper thing on it. *(He tears the paper lantern off the light bulb. She utters a frightened gasp)*

BLANCHE. What did you do that for?

MITCH. So I can take a look at you good and plain!

BLANCHE. Of course you don't really mean to be insulting!

MITCH. No, just realistic.

BLANCHE. I don't want realism. I want magic! *(Mitch laughs)* Yes, yes, magic! I try to give that to people. I misrepresent things to them. I don't tell truth, I tell what *ought* to be truth. And if that is sinful, then let me be damned for it!—*Don't turn the light on!*

(Mitch crosses to the switch. He turns the light on and stares at her. She cries out and covers her face. He turns the light off again.)

MITCH *(slowly and bitterly).* I don't mind you being older than what I thought. But all the rest of it—Christ! That pitch about your ideals being so old-fashioned and all the malarkey that you've dished out all summer. Oh, I knew you weren't sixteen any more. But I was a fool enough to believe you was straight.

BLANCHE. Who told you I wasn't—"straight"? My loving brother-in-law. And you believed him.

MITCH. I called him a liar at first. And then I checked on the story. First I asked our supply-man who travels through Laurel. And then I talked directly over long-distance to this merchant.

BLANCHE. Who is this merchant?

MITCH. Kiefaber.

BLANCHE. The merchant Kiefaber of Laurel! I know the man. He whistled at me. I put him in his place. So now for revenge he makes up stories about me.

MITCH. Three people, Kiefaber, Stanley and Shaw, swore to them!

BLANCHE. Rub-a-dub-dub, three men in a tub! And such a filthy tub!

MITCH. Didn't you stay at a hotel called The Flamingo?

BLANCHE. Flamingo? No! Tarantula was the name of it! I stayed at a hotel called The Tarantula Arms!

MITCH *(stupidly).* Tarantula?

BLANCHE. Yes, a big spider! That's where I brought my victims. *(She pours herself another drink)* Yes, I had many intimacies with strangers. After the death of Allan—intimacies with strangers was all I seemed able to fill my empty heart with. . . . I think it was panic, just panic, that drove me from one to another, hunting for some protection—here and there, in the most—unlikely places—even, at last, in a seventeen-year-old boy but—somebody wrote the superintendent about it—"This woman is morally unfit for her position!" *(She throws back her head with convulsive, sobbing laughter. Then she repeats the statement, gasps, and drinks)* True? Yes, I suppose—unfit somehow—anyway. . . . So I came here. There was nowhere else I could go. I was played out. You know what played out is? My youth was suddenly gone up the water-spout, and—I met you. You said you needed somebody. Well, I needed somebody, too. I thanked God for you, because you seemed to be gentle— a cleft in the rock of the world that I could hide in! But I guess I was asking, hoping—too much! Kiefaber, Stanley and Shaw have tied an old tin can to the tail of the kite.

(There is a pause. Mitch stares at her dumbly.)

MITCH. You lied to me, Blanche.

BLANCHE. Don't say I lied to you.

MITCH. Lies, lies, inside and out, all lies.

BLANCHE. Never inside, I didn't lie in my heart . . .

(A vendor comes around the corner. She is a blind Mexican woman in a dark shawl, carrying bunches of those gaudy tin flowers that lower class Mexicans display at funerals and other festive occasions. She is calling barely audibly. Her figure is only faintly visible outside the building.)

MEXICAN WOMAN. Flores. Flores. Flores para los muertos. Flores. Flores.

BLANCHE. What? Oh! Somebody outside . . . *(She goes to the door, opens it and stares at the Mexican Woman)*

MEXICAN WOMAN *(she is at the door and offers Blanche some of her flowers)*. Flores? Flores para los muertos?

BLANCHE *(frightened)*. No, no! Not now! Not now! *(She darts back into the apartment, slamming the door)*

MEXICAN WOMAN *(she turns away and starts to move down the street)*. Flores para los muertos.

(The polka tune fades in.)

BLANCHE *(as if to herself)*. Crumble and fade and—regrets—recriminations . . . "If you'd done this, it wouldn't've cost me that!"

MEXICAN WOMAN. Corones para los muertos. Corones . . .

BLANCHE. Legacies! Huh . . . And other things such as bloodstained pillow-slips— "Her linen needs changing"—"Yes, Mother. But couldn't we get a colored girl to do it?" No, we couldn't of course. Everything gone but the—

MEXICAN WOMAN. Flores.

BLANCHE. Death—I used to sit here and she used to sit over there and death was as close as you are. . . . We didn't dare even admit we had ever heard of it!

MEXICAN WOMAN. Flores para los muertos, flores—flores . . .

BLANCHE. The opposite is desire. So do you wonder? How could you possibly wonder! Not far from Belle Reve, before we had lost Belle Reve, was a camp where they trained young soldiers. On Saturday nights they would go in town to get drunk—

MEXICAN WOMAN *(softly)*. Corones . . .

BLANCHE. —and on the way back they would stagger onto my lawn and call— "Blanche! Blanche!"—The deaf old lady remaining suspected nothing. But sometimes I slipped outside to answer their calls. . . . Later the paddy-wagon would gather them up like daisies . . . the long way home . . .

(The Mexican Woman turns slowly and drifts back off with her soft mournful cries. Blanche goes to the dresser and leans forward on it. After a moment, Mitch rises and follows her purposefully. The polka music fades away. He places his hands on her waist and tries to turn her about.)

BLANCHE. What do you want?

MITCH *(fumbling to embrace her)*. What I been missing all summer.

BLANCHE. Then marry me, Mitch!

MITCH. I don't think I want to marry you any more.

BLANCHE. No?

MITCH *(dropping his hands from her waist)*. You're not clean enough to bring in the house with my mother.

BLANCHE. Go away, then. *(He stares at her)* Get out of here quick before I start screaming fire! *(Her throat is tightening with hysteria)* Get out of here quick before I start screaming fire. *(He still remains staring. She suddenly rushes to the big window with its pale blue square of the soft summer light and cries wildly)* Fire! Fire! Fire!

(With a startled gasp, Mitch turns and goes out the outer door, clatters awkwardly down the steps and around the corner of the building. Blanche staggers back from the window and falls to her knees. The distant piano is slow and blue.)

SCENE TEN

It is a few hours later that night.
Blanche has been drinking fairly steadily since Mitch left. She has dragged her

wardrobe trunk into the center of the bedroom. It hangs open with flowery dresses thrown across it. As the drinking and packing went on, a mood of hysterical exhilaration came into her and she has decked herself out in a somewhat soiled and crumpled white satin evening gown and a pair of scuffed silver slippers with brilliants set in their heels.

Now she is placing the rhinestone tiara on her head before the mirror of the dressing-table and murmuring excitedly as if to a group of spectral admirers.

———

BLANCHE. How about taking a swim, a moonlight swim at the old rock-quarry? If anyone's sober enough to drive a car! Ha-ha! Best way in the world to stop your head buzzing! Only you've got to be careful to dive where the deep pool is—if you hit a rock you don't come up till tomorrow . . .

(Tremblingly she lifts the hand mirror for a closer inspection. She catches her breath and slams the mirror face down with such violence that the glass cracks. She moans a little and attempts to rise.)

(Stanley appears around the corner of the building. He still has on the vivid green silk bowling shirt. As he rounds the corner the honky-tonk music is heard. It continues softly throughout the scene.)

(He enters the kitchen, slamming the door. As he peers in at Blanche, he gives a low whistle. He has had a few drinks on the way and has brought some quart beer bottles home with him.)

BLANCHE. How is my sister?

STANLEY. She is doing okay.

BLANCHE. And how is the baby?

STANLEY *(grinning amiably)*. The baby won't come before morning so they told me to go home and get a little shut-eye.

BLANCHE. Does that mean we are to be alone in here?

STANLEY. Yep. Just me and you, Blanche. Unless you got somebody hid under the bed. What've you got on those fine feathers for?

BLANCHE. Oh, that's right. You left before my wire came.

STANLEY. You got a wire?

BLANCHE. I received a telegram from an old admirer of mine.

STANLEY. Anything good?

BLANCHE. I think so. An invitation.

STANLEY. What to? A fireman's ball?

BLANCHE *(throwing back her head)*. A cruise of the Caribbean on a yacht!

STANLEY. Well, well. What do you know?

BLANCHE. I have never been so surprised in my life.

STANLEY. I guess not.

BLANCHE. It came like a bolt from the blue!

STANLEY. Who did you say it was from?

BLANCHE. An old beau of mine.

STANLEY. The one that give you the white fox-pieces?

BLANCHE. Mr. Shep Huntleigh. I wore his ATO pin my last year at college. I hadn't seen him again until last Christmas. I ran in to him on Biscayne Boulevard. Then—just now—this wire—inviting me on a cruise of the Caribbean! The problem is clothes. I tore into my trunk to see what I have that's suitable for the tropics!

STANLEY. And come up with that—gorgeous—diamond—tiara?

BLANCHE. This old relic? Ha-ha! It's only rhinestones.

STANLEY. Gosh. I thought it was Tiffany diamonds. *(He unbuttons his shirt)*

BLANCHE. Well, anyhow, I shall be entertained in style.

STANLEY. Uh-huh. It goes to show, you never know what is coming.

BLANCHE. Just when I thought my luck had begun to fail me—

STANLEY. Into the picture pops this Miami millionaire.

BLANCHE. This man is not from Miami. This man is from Dallas.

STANLEY. This man is from Dallas?

BLANCHE. Yes, this man is from Dallas where gold spouts out of the ground!

STANLEY. Well, just so he's from somewhere! *(He starts removing his shirt)*

BLANCHE. Close the curtains before you undress any further.

STANLEY *(amiably)*. This is all I'm going to undress right now. *(He rips the sack off a quart beer-bottle)* Seen a bottle-opener? *(She moves slowly toward the dresser, where she stands with her hands knotted together)* I used to have a cousin who could open a beer-bottle with his teeth. *(Pounding the bottle cap on the corner of table)* That was his only accomplishment, all he could do—he was just a human bottle-opener. And then one time, at a wedding party, he broke his front teeth off! After that he was so ashamed of himself he used t' sneak out of the house when company came . . . *(The bottle cap pops off and a geyser of foam shoots up. Stanley laughs happily, holding up the bottle over his head)* Ha-ha! Rain from heaven! *(He extends the bottle toward her)* Shall we bury the hatchet and make it a loving-cup? Huh?

BLANCHE. No, thank you.

STANLEY. Well, it's a red letter night for us both. You having an oil-millionaire and me having a baby.

(He goes to the bureau in the bedroom and crouches to remove something from the bottom drawer.)

BLANCHE *(drawing back)*. What are you doing in here?

STANLEY. Here's something I always break out on special occasions like this. The silk pyjamas I wore on my wedding night!

BLANCHE. Oh.

STANLEY. When the telephone rings and they say, "You've got a son!" I'll tear this off and wave it like a flag! *(He shakes out a brilliant pyjama coat)* I guess we are both entitled to put on the dog. *(He goes back to the kitchen with the coat over his arm)*

BLANCHE. When I think of how divine it is going to be to have such a thing as privacy once more—I could weep with joy!

STANLEY. This millionaire from Dallas is not going to interfere with your privacy any?

BLANCHE. It won't be the sort of thing you have in mind. This man is a gentleman and he respects me. *(Improvising feverishly)* What he wants is my companionship. Having great wealth sometimes makes people lonely! A cultivated woman, a woman of intelligence and breeding, can enrich a man's life—immeasurably! I have those things to offer, and this doesn't take them away. Physical beauty is passing. A transitory possession. But beauty of the mind and richness of the spirit and tenderness of the heart—and I have all of those things—aren't taken away, but grow! Increase with the years! How strange that I should be called a destitute woman! When I have all of these treasures locked in my heart. *(A choked sob comes from her)* I think of myself as a very, very rich woman! But I have been foolish—casting my pearls before swine!

STANLEY. Swine, huh?

BLANCHE. Yes, swine! Swine! And I'm thinking not only of you but of your friend, Mr. Mitchell. He came to see me tonight. He dared to come here in his work-clothes! And to repeat slander to me, vicious stories that he had gotten from you! I gave him his walking papers . . .

STANLEY. You did, huh?

BLANCHE. But then he came back. He returned with a box of roses to beg my forgiveness! He implored my forgiveness. But some things are not forgivable. Deliberate cruelty is not forgivable. It is the one unforgivable thing in my opinion and it is the one thing of which I have never, never been guilty. And so I told him, I said to him, "Thank you," but it was foolish of me to think that we could ever adapt ourselves to each other. Our ways of life are too different. Our attitudes and our backgrounds are incompatible. We have to be realistic about such things. So farewell, my friend! And let there be no hard feelings . . .

STANLEY. Was this before or after the telegram came from the Texas oil millionaire?

BLANCHE. What telegram? No! No, after! As a matter of fact, the wire came just as—

STANLEY. As a matter of fact there wasn't no wire at all!

BLANCHE. Oh, oh!

STANLEY. There isn't no millionaire! And Mitch didn't come back with roses 'cause I know where he is—

BLANCHE. Oh!

STANLEY. There isn't a goddam thing but imagination!

BLANCHE. Oh!

STANLEY. And lies and conceit and tricks!

BLANCHE. Oh!

STANLEY. And look at yourself! Take a look at yourself in that worn-out Mardi Gras outfit, rented for fifty cents from some rag-picker! And with the crazy crown on! What queen do you think you are?

BLANCHE. Oh—God . . .

STANLEY. I've been on to you from the start! Not once did you pull any wool over this boy's eyes! You come in here and sprinkle the place with powder and spray perfume and cover the light-bulb with a paper lantern, and lo and behold the place has turned into Egypt and you are the

Queen of the Nile! Sitting on your throne and swilling down my liquor! I say—Ha! —Ha! Do you hear me? Ha—ha—ha! *(He walks into the bedroom)*

BLANCHE. Don't come in here! *(Lurid reflections appear on the walls around Blanche. The shadows are of a grotesque and menacing form. She catches her breath, crosses to the phone and jiggles the hook. Stanley goes into the bathroom and closes the door)* Operator, operator! Give me long-distance, please. . . . I want to get in touch with Mr. Shep Huntleigh of Dallas. He's so well-known he doesn't require any address. Just ask anybody who—Wait! —No, I couldn't find it right now. . . . Please understand. I—No! No, wait! . . . One moment! Someone is—Nothing! Hold on, please!

(She sets the phone down and crosses warily into the kitchen. The night is filled with inhuman voices like cries in a jungle. (The shadows and lurid reflections move sinuously as flames along the wall spaces. (Through the back wall of the rooms, which have become transparent, can be seen the sidewalk. A prostitute has rolled a drunkard. He pursues her along the walk, overtakes her and there is a struggle. A policeman's whistle breaks it up. The figures disappear.

(Some moments later the Negro Woman appears around the corner with a sequined bag which the prostitute had dropped on the walk. She is rooting excitedly through it.

(Blanche presses her knuckles to her lips and returns slowly to the phone. She speaks in a hoarse whisper.)

BLANCHE. Operator! Operator! Never mind long-distance. Get Western Union. There isn't time to be—Western—Western Union! *(She waits anxiously)* Western Union? Yes! I—want to— Take down this message! "In desperate, desperate circumstances! Help me! Caught in a trap. Caught in—" *Oh!*

(The bathroom door is thrown open and Stanley comes out in the brilliant silk pyjamas. He grins at her as he knots the tasseled sash about his waist. She gasps and backs away from the phone. He stares at her for a count of ten. Then a clicking becomes audible from the telephone, steady and rasping.)

STANLEY. You left th' phone off th' hook. *(He crosses to it deliberately and sets it*

back on the hook. After he has replaced it, he stares at her again, his mouth slowly curving into a grin, as he weaves between Blanche and the outer door.

(The barely audible "blue piano" begins to drum up louder. The sound of it turns into the roar of an approaching locomotive. Blanche crouches, pressing her fists to her ears until it has gone by.)

BLANCHE *(finally straightening)*. Let me —let me get by you!

STANLEY. Get by me? Sure. Go ahead. *(He moves back a pace in the doorway)*

BLANCHE. You—you stand over there! *(She indicates a further position)*

STANLEY *(grinning)*. You got plenty of room to walk by me now.

BLANCHE. Not with you there! But I've got to get out somehow!

STANLEY. You think I'll interfere with you? Ha-ha!

(The "blue piano" goes softly. She turns confusedly and makes a faint gesture. The inhuman jungle voices rise up. He takes a step toward her, biting his tongue which protrudes between his lips.)

STANLEY *(softly)*. Come to think of it— maybe you wouldn't be bad to—interfere with . . .

(Blanche moves backward through the door into the bedroom.)

BLANCHE. Stay back! Don't you come toward me another step or I'll—

STANLEY. What?

BLANCHE. Some awful thing will happen! It will!

STANLEY. What are you putting on now? *(They are now both inside the bedroom.)*

BLANCHE. I warn you, don't, I'm in danger!

(He takes another step. She smashes a bottle on the table and faces him, clutching the broken top.)

STANLEY. What did you do that for?

BLANCHE. So I could twist the broken end in your face!

STANLEY. I bet you would do that!

BLANCHE. I would! I will if you—

STANLEY. Oh! So you want some roughhouse! All right, let's have some roughhouse! *(He springs toward her, overturning the table. She cries out and strikes at him with the bottle top but he catches her wrist)* Tiger—tiger! Drop the bottle-top! Drop it! We've had this date with each other from the beginning!

(She moans. The bottle-top falls. She sinks

to her knees. He picks up her inert figure and carries her to the bed. The hot trumpet and drums from the Four Deuces sound loudly.)

SCENE ELEVEN

It is some weeks later. Stella is packing Blanche's things. Sound of water can be heard running in the bathroom.

The portieres are partly open on the poker players—Stanley, Steve, Mitch and Pablo—who sit around the table in the kitchen. The atmosphere of the kitchen is now the same raw, lurid one of the disastrous poker night.

The building is framed by the sky of turquoise. Stella has been crying as she arranges the flowery dresses in the open trunk.

Eunice comes down the steps from her flat above and enters the kitchen. There is an outburst from the poker table.

STANLEY. Drew to an inside straight and made it, by God.

PABLO. *Maldita sea tu suerto!*

STANLEY. Put it in English, greaseball.

PABLO. I am cursing your rutting luck.

STANLEY *(prodigiously elated)*. You know what luck is? Luck is believing you're lucky. Take at Salerno. I believed I was lucky. I figured that four out of five would not come through but I would . . . and I did. I put that down as a rule. To hold front position in this rat-race you've got to believe you are lucky.

MITCH. You . . . you . . . you. . . . Brag . . . brag . . . bull . . . bull.

(Stella goes into the bedroom and starts folding a dress.)

STANLEY. What's the matter with him?

EUNICE *(walking past the table)*. I always did say that men are callous things with no feelings, but this does beat anything. Making pigs of yourselves. *(She comes through the portieres into the bedroom)*

STANLEY. What's the matter with her?

STELLA. How is my baby?

EUNICE. Sleeping like a little angel. Brought you some grapes. *(She puts them on a stool and lowers her voice)* Blanche?

STELLA. Bathing.

EUNICE. How is she?

STELLA. She wouldn't eat anything but asked for a drink.

EUNICE. What did you tell her?

STELLA. I—just told her that—we'd made arrangements for her to rest in the country. She's got it mixed in her mind with Shep Huntleigh.

(Blanche opens the bathroom door slightly.)

BLANCHE. Stella.

STELLA. Yes, Blanche?

BLANCHE. If anyone calls while I'm bathing take the number and tell them I'll call right back.

STELLA. Yes.

BLANCHE. That cool yellow silk—the bouclé. See if it's crushed. If it's not too crushed I'll wear it and on the lapel that silver and turquoise pin in the shape of a seahorse. You will find them in the heart-shaped box I keep my accessories in. And Stella . . . Try and locate a bunch of artificial violets in that box, too, to pin with the seahorse on the lapel of the jacket.

(She closes the door. Stella turns to Eunice.)

STELLA. I don't know if I did the right thing.

EUNICE. What else could you do?

STELLA. I couldn't believe her story and go on living with Stanley.

EUNICE. Don't ever believe it. Life has got to go on. No matter what happens, you've got to keep on going.

(The bathroom door opens a little.)

BLANCHE *(looking out)*. Is the coast clear?

STELLA. Yes, Blanche. *(To Eunice)* Tell her how well she's looking.

BLANCHE. Please close the curtains before I come out.

STELLA. They're closed.

STANLEY. —How many for you?

PABLO. —Two.

STEVE. —Three.

(Blanche appears in the amber light of the door. She has a tragic radiance in her red satin robe following the sculptural lines of her body. The "Varsouviana" rises audibly as Blanche enters the bedroom.)

BLANCHE *(with faintly hysterical vivacity)*. I have just washed my hair.

STELLA. Did you?

BLANCHE. I'm not sure I got the soap out.

EUNICE. Such fine hair!

BLANCHE *(accepting the compliment)*. It's a problem. Didn't I get a call?

STELLA. Who from, Blanche?

BLANCHE. Shep Huntleigh . . .

STELLA. Why, not yet, honey!

BLANCHE. How strange! I—

(*At the sound of Blanche's voice, Mitch's arm supporting his cards has sagged and his gaze is dissolved into space. Stanley slaps him on the shoulder.*)

STANLEY. Hey, Mitch, come to!

(*The sound of this new voice shocks Blanche. She makes a shocked gesture, forming his name with her lips. Stella nods and looks quickly away. Blanche stands quite still for some moments—the silverbacked mirror in her hand and a look of sorrowful perplexity as though all human experience shows on her face. Blanche finally speaks but with sudden hysteria.*)

BLANCHE. What's going on here?

(*She turns from Stella to Eunice and back to Stella. Her rising voice penetrates the concentration of the game. Mitch ducks his head lower but Stanley shoves back his chair as if about to rise. Steve places a restraining hand on his arm.*)

BLANCHE (*continuing*). What's happened here? I want an explanation of what's happened here.

STELLA (*agonizingly*). Hush! Hush!

EUNICE. Hush! Hush! Honey.

STELLA. Please, Blanche.

BLANCHE. Why are you looking at me like that? Is something wrong with me?

EUNICE. You look wonderful, Blanche. Don't she look wonderful?

STELLA. Yes.

EUNICE. I understand you are going on a trip.

STELLA. Yes, Blanche *is*. She's going on a vacation.

EUNICE. I'm green with envy.

BLANCHE. Help me, help me get dressed!

STELLA (*handing her dress*). Is this what you—

BLANCHE. Yes, it will do! I'm anxious to get out of here—this place is a trap!

EUNICE. What a pretty blue jacket.

STELLA. It's lilac colored.

BLANCHE. You're both mistaken. It's Della Robbia blue. The blue of the robe in the old Madonna pictures. Are these grapes washed?

(*She fingers the bunch of grapes which Eunice had brought in.*)

EUNICE. Huh?

BLANCHE. Washed, I said. Are they washed?

EUNICE. They're from the French Market.

BLANCHE. That doesn't mean they've been washed. (*The cathedral bells chime*) Those cathedral bells—they're the only clean thing in the Quarter. Well, I'm going now. I'm ready to go.

EUNICE (*whispering*). She's going to walk out before they get here.

STELLA. Wait, Blanche.

BLANCHE. I don't want to pass in front of those men.

EUNICE. Then wait'll the game breaks up.

STELLA. Sit down and . . .

(*Blanche turns weakly, hesitantly about. She lets them push her into a chair.*)

BLANCHE. I can smell the sea air. The rest of my time I'm going to spend on the sea. And when I die, I'm going to die on the sea. You know what I shall die of? (*She plucks a grape*) I shall die of eating an unwashed grape one day out on the ocean. I will die—with my hand in the hand of some nice-looking ship's doctor, a very young one with a small blond mustache and a big silver watch. "Poor lady," they'll say, "the quinine did her no good. That unwashed grape has transported her soul to heaven." (*The cathedral chimes are heard*) And I'll be buried at sea sewn up in a clean white sack and dropped overboard—at noon—in the blaze of summer —and into an ocean as blue as (*Chimes again*) my first lover's eyes!

(*A Doctor and a Matron have appeared around the corner of the building and climbed the steps to the porch. The gravity of their profession is exaggerated—the unmistakable aura of the state institution with its cynical detachment. The Doctor rings the doorbell. The murmur of the game is interrupted.*)

EUNICE (*whispering to Stella*). That must be them.

(*Stella presses her fists to her lips.*)

BLANCHE (*rising slowly*). What is it?

EUNICE (*affectedly casual*). Excuse me while I see who's at the door.

STELLA. Yes.

(*Eunice goes into the kitchen.*)

BLANCHE (*tensely*). I wonder if it's for me.

(*A whispered colloquy takes place at the door.*)

EUNICE (*returning, brightly*). Someone is calling for Blanche.

BLANCHE. It *is* for me, then! (*She looks fearfully from one to the other and then to the portieres. The "Varsouviana" faintly plays*) Is it the gentleman I was expecting from Dallas?

EUNICE. I think it is, Blanche.

BLANCHE. I'm not quite ready.

STELLA. Ask him to wait outside.

BLANCHE. I . . .

(*Eunice goes back to the portieres. Drums sound very softly.*)

STELLA. Everything packed?

BLANCHE. My silver toilet articles are still out.

STELLA. Ah!

EUNICE (*returning*). They're waiting in front of the house.

BLANCHE. They! Who's "they"?

EUNICE. There's a lady with him.

BLANCHE. I cannot imagine who this "lady" could be! How is she dressed?

EUNICE. Just—just a sort of a—plain-tailored outfit.

BLANCHE. Possibly she's—(*Her voice dies out nervously*)

STELLA. Shall we go, Blanche?

BLANCHE. Must we go through that room?

STELLA. I will go with you.

BLANCHE. How do I look?

STELLA. Lovely.

EUNICE (*echoing*). Lovely.

(*Blanche moves fearfully to the portieres. Eunice draws them open for her. Blanche goes into the kitchen.*)

BLANCHE (*to the men*). Please don't get up. I'm only passing through.

(*She crosses quickly to outside door. Stella and Eunice follow. The poker players stand awkwardly at the table—all except Mitch, who remains seated, looking down at the table. Blanche steps out on a small porch at the side of the door. She stops short and catches her breath.*)

DOCTOR. How do you do?

BLANCHE. You are not the gentleman I was expecting. (*She suddenly gasps and starts back up the steps. She stops by Stella, who stands just outside the door, and speaks in a frightening whisper*) That man isn't Shep Huntleigh.

(*The "Varsouviana" is playing distantly.*)

(*Stella stares back at Blanche. Eunice is holding Stella's arm. There is a moment of silence—no sound but that of Stanley steadily shuffling the cards.*)

(*Blanche catches her breath again and slips back into the flat. She enters the flat with a peculiar smile, her eyes wide and brilliant. As soon as her sister goes past her, Stella closes her eyes and clenches her hands. Eunice throws her arms comfortingly about her. Then she starts up to her flat. Blanche stops just inside the door. Mitch keeps staring down at his hands on the table, but the other men look at her curiously. At last she starts around the table toward the bedroom. As she does, Stanley suddenly pushes back his chair and rises as if to block her way. The Matron follows her into the flat.*)

STANLEY. Did you forget something?

BLANCHE (*shrilly*). Yes! Yes, I forgot something!

(*She rushes past him into the bedroom. Lurid reflections appear on the walls in odd, sinuous shapes. The "Varsouviana" is filtered into a weird distortion, accompanied by the cries and noises of the jungle. Blanche seizes the back of a chair as if to defend herself.*)

STANLEY (*sotto voce*). Doc, you better go in.

DOCTOR (*sotto voce, motioning to the Matron*). Nurse, bring her out.

(*The Matron advances on one side, Stanley on the other. Divested of all the softer properties of womanhood, the Matron is a peculiarly sinister figure in her severe dress. Her voice is bold and toneless as a firebell.*)

MATRON. Hello, Blanche.

(*The greeting is echoed and re-echoed by other mysterious voices behind the walls, as if reverberated through a canyon of rock.*)

STANLEY. She says that she forgot something.

(*The echo sounds in threatening whispers.*)

MATRON. That's all right.

STANLEY. What did you forget, Blanche?

BLANCHE. I—I—

MATRON. It don't matter. We can pick it up later.

STANLEY. Sure. We can send it along with the trunk.

BLANCHE (*retreating in panic*). I don't know you—I don't know you. I want to be—left alone—please!

MATRON. Now, Blanche!

ECHOES (*rising and falling*). Now, Blanche—now, Blanche—now, Blanche!

STANLEY. You left nothing here but spilt

talcum and old empty perfume bottles—unless it's the paper lantern you want to take with you. You want the lantern?
(He crosses to dressing table and seizes the paper lantern, tearing it off the light bulb, and extends it toward her. She cries out as if the lantern was herself. The Matron steps boldly toward her. She screams and tries to break past the Matron. All the men spring to their feet. Stella runs out to the porch, with Eunice following to comfort her, simultaneously with the confused voices of the men in the kitchen. Stella rushes into Eunice's embrace on the porch.)

STELLA. Oh, my God, Eunice, help me! Don't let them do that to her, don't let them hurt her! Oh, God, oh, please God, don't hurt her. What are they doing to her? What are they doing? *(She tries to break from Eunice's arms)*

EUNICE. No, honey, no, no, honey. Stay here. Don't go back in there. Stay with me and don't look.

STELLA. What have I done to my sister? Oh, God, what have I done to my sister?

EUNICE. You done the right thing, the only thing you could do. She couldn't stay here; there wasn't no other place for her to go.
(While Stella and Eunice are speaking on the porch the voices of the men in the kitchen overlap them. Mitch has started toward the bedroom. Stanley crosses to block him. Stanley pushes him aside. Mitch lunges and strikes at Stanley. Stanley pushes Mitch back. Mitch collapses at the table, sobbing.)
(During the preceding scenes, the Matron catches hold of Blanche's arm and prevents her flight. Blanche turns wildly and scratches at the Matron. The heavy woman pinions her arms. Blanche cries out hoarsely and slips to her knees.)

MATRON. These fingernails have to be trimmed. *(The Doctor comes into the room and she looks at him)* Jacket, Doctor?

DOCTOR. Not unless necessary.
(He takes off his hat and now he becomes personalized. The inhuman quality goes. His voice is gentle and reassuring as he crosses to Blanche and crouches in front of her. As he speaks her name, her terror subsides a little. The lurid reflections fade from the walls, the inhuman cries and noises die out and her own hoarse crying is calmed.)

DOCTOR. Miss DuBois. *(She turns her face to him and stares at him with desperate pleading. He smiles; then he speaks to the Matron)* It won't be necessary.

BLANCHE *(faintly)*. Ask her to let go of me.

DOCTOR *(to the Matron)*. Let go.
(The Matron releases her. Blanche extends her hands toward the Doctor. He draws her up gently and supports her with his arm and leads her through the portieres.)

BLANCHE *(holding tight to his arm)*. Whoever you are—I have always depended on the kindness of strangers.
(The poker players stand back as Blanche and the Doctor cross the kitchen to the front door. She allows him to lead her as if she were blind. As they go out on the porch, Stella cries out her sister's name from where she is crouched a few steps up on the stairs.)

STELLA. Blanche! Blanche, Blanche!
(Blanche walks on without turning, followed by the Doctor and the Matron. They go around the corner of the building.)
(Eunice descends to Stella and places the child in her arms. It is wrapped in a pale blue blanket. Stella accepts the child, sobbingly. Eunice continues downstairs and enters the kitchen where the men, except for Stanley, are returning silently to their places about the table. Stanley has gone out on the porch and stands at the foot of the steps looking at Stella.)

STANLEY *(a bit uncertainly)*. Stella?
(She sobs with inhuman abandon. There is something luxurious in her complete surrender to crying now that her sister is gone.)

STANLEY *(voluptuously, soothingly)*. Now, honey. Now, love. Now, now, love. *(He kneels beside her and his fingers find the opening of her blouse)* Now, now, love. Now, love. . . .
(The luxurious sobbing, the sensual murmur fade away under the swelling music of the "blue piano" and the muted trumpet.)

STEVE. This game is seven-card stud.

CURTAIN

Mister Roberts

BY THOMAS HEGGEN and JOSHUA LOGAN

First presented by Leland Hayward at the Alvin Theatre in New York on February 18, 1948, with the following cast:

CHIEF JOHNSON................................Rusty Lane	DOLAN ....Casey Walters
LIEUTENANT (JG) ROBERTS.......Henry Fonda	GERHART ....Fred Barton
DOC ....Robert Keith	PAYNE ....James Sherwood
DOWDY ....Joe Marr	LIEUTENANT ANN GIRARD.....Jocelyn Brando
THE CAPTAIN.........................William Harrigan	SHORE PATROLMAN.......................John Jordan
INSIGNA ....Harvey Lembeck	MILITARY POLICEMAN...........Marshall Jamison
MANNION ....Ralph Meeker	SHORE PATROL OFFICER.....Murray Hamilton
LINDSTROM ....Karl Lukas	SEAMEN, FIREMEN AND OTHERS:
STEFANOWSKI ....Steven Hill	Tiger Andrews, Joe Bernard, Ellis Eringer,
WILEY ....Robert Baines	Mikel Kane, Bob Keith, Jr., Walter Mullen,
SCHLEMMER ....Lee Krieger	John (Red) Kullers, Jack Pierce, Len Smith,
REBER ....John Campbell	Jr., Sanders (Sandy) Turner

ENSIGN PULVER..............................David Wayne

Scene: Aboard the U.S. Navy Cargo Ship, *AK* 601, operating in the back areas of the Pacific.

Time: A few weeks before V-E Day until a few weeks before V-J Day.

Mister Roberts was the most successful war play of the American theatre since *What Price Glory?* It was originally a novel written by Thomas O. (Orlo) Heggen out of his experience in the Navy, from which he was discharged in the fall of 1945. Mr. Heggen, who is of Norwegian descent and therefore qualifies for seafaring, was born on December 23, 1919, in Fort Dodge, Iowa. He attended the University of Minnesota, where he successfully discharged an apprenticeship in journalism by contributing a popular comic column to the college paper, the Minnesota *Daily,* and received his bachelor's degree in 1941. Joining the American Navy, he attained the rank of lieutenant, spent three years in the service, and saw action at Guam, Iwo Jima, and Okinawa. By the time he was ready for discharge, he had as much right as any man of letters to report on naval life. He found a position on the editorial staff of *Reader's Digest.* His *Mister Roberts* was published in 1946.

Its success attracted the Texas-born and Princeton-educated Joshua Logan, until then known only as a director and as an extremely talented one who had studied with Stanislavsky in Moscow on a fellowship and had subsequently staged, since 1938, such noteworthy productions as *On Borrowed Time, I Married an Angel, Knickerbocker Holiday,* and *Charley's Aunt*—the Broadway production that introduced another Princetonian, José Ferrer, as an actor to be reckoned with. Mr. Logan, whose own overseas experience had led to a captaincy in the Air Forces Combat Intelligence, found the play agent Leland Hayward favorably disposed toward turning producer and sponsoring a production of *Mister Roberts* if it were turned into a play. Mr. Logan collaborated on the dramatization with Mr. Heggen. For the leading part he recruited Henry Fonda, who had been a member of the University Players company Logan had founded on Cape Cod after leaving Princeton. A better choice could not have been made, and the results were gratifying to everyone involved in the extremely successful enterprise. The play, like the novel, was, in the words of John Mason Brown, "tough-fibered, muscular, and exuberant in its animalism," and "wonderfully unromantic and unorthodox" in its realization "that boredom is one of the chief conditions and horrors of war." At the same time, it was appealingly romantic as a tribute to the young officer-hero who was eager to see active service instead of navigating constantly on a supply ship "from Apathy to Tedium and back again." It would have been a miracle if the American public had been able to resist the Broadway production. Encouraged by the success of the play he had written as well as staged, Mr. Logan continued to try his hand at playwriting. He collaborated on the libretto of *South Pacific* with Oscar Hammerstein the Second, and he based *The Wisteria Trees* on *The Cherry Orchard* by Anton Chekhov the first and, alas, last.

ACT ONE

Scene One

The curtain rises on the main set, which is the amidships section of a navy cargo ship. The section of the ship shown is the house, and the deck immediately forward of the house. Dominating center stage is a covered hatch. The house extends on an angle to the audience from downstage left to upstage right. At each side is a passageway leading to the after part of the ship. Over the passageways on each side are twenty-millimeter gun tubs; ladders lead up to each tub. In each passageway and hardly visible to the audience is a steep ladder leading up to a bridge. Downstage right is a double bitt. At the left end of the hatch cover is an opening. This is the entrance to the companionway which leads to the crew's compartment below. The lower parts of two kingposts are shown against the house. A life raft is also visible. A solid metal rail runs from stage right and disappears behind the house. Upstage center is the door to the Captain's cabin. The pilothouse with its many portholes is indicated on the bridge above. On the flying bridge are the usual nautical furnishings: a searchlight and two ventilators. Over the door is a loudspeaker. There is a porthole to the left of the door and two portholes to the right. These last two look into the Captain's cabin.

The only object which differentiates this ship from any other navy cargo ship is a small scrawny palm tree, potted in a five-gallon can, standing to the right of the Captain's cabin door. On the container, painted in large white letters, is the legend: "PROP.T OF CAPTAIN, KEEP AWAY."

At rise, the lighting indicates that it is shortly after dawn. The stage is empty and there is no indication of life other than the sound of snoring from below.

Chief Johnson, a bulging man about forty, enters through passageway upstage left. He wears dungaree shirt and pants and a chief petty officer's cap. He is obviously chewing tobacco, and he starts down the hatchway, notices the palm tree, crosses to the Captain's door cautiously, peering into the porthole to see that he is not being watched, then deliberately spits into the palm tree container. He wipes his mouth smugly and shuffles over to the hatch. There he stops, takes out his watch and looks at it, then disappears down the hatchway. A shrill whistle is heard.

———

JOHNSON (*offstage—in a loud singsong voice which is obviously just carrying out a ritual*). Reveille . . . Hit the deck . . . Greet the new day . . . (*The whistle is heard again*) Reveille . . .

INSIGNA (*offstage*). Okay, Chief, you done your duty—now get your big fat can out of here!

(*Johnson reappears at the head of hatchway calling back.*)

JOHNSON. Just thought you'd like to know about reveille. And you're going to miss chow again.

STEFANOWSKI (*offstage*). Thanks, Chief. Now go back to bed and stop bothering us.

(*His duty done, Johnson, still chewing, shuffles across the stage and disappears. There is a brief moment of silence, then the snoring is resumed below.*)

(*After a moment, Roberts enters from the passageway at right. He wears khaki shirt and trousers and an officer's cap. On each side of his collar he wears the silver bar indicating the rank of Lieutenant [junior grade]. He carries a rumpled piece of writing paper in his left hand, on which there is a great deal of writing and large black marks indicating that much has been scratched out. He walks slowly to the bitt, concentrating, then stands a moment looking out right. He suddenly gets an idea and goes to hatch cover, sitting and writing on the paper. Doc enters from the left passageway. Doc is between thirty-five and forty and he wears khakis and an officer's fore-and-aft cap; he wears medical insignia and the bars of Lieutenant [senior grade] on his collar. A stethoscope sticks out of his hip pocket. He is wiping the sweat off his neck with his handkerchief as he crosses above hatch cover. He stops as he sees Roberts.*)

DOC. That you, Doug?

ROBERTS (*wearily, looking up*). Hello, Doc. What are you doing up?

DOC. I heard you were working cargo today so I thought I'd get ready. On days when there's any work to be done I can always count on a big turnout at sick call.

ROBERTS *(smiles)*. Oh, yeah.

DOC. I attract some very rare diseases on cargo days. That day they knew you were going to load five ships I was greeted by six more cases of beriberi—double beriberi this time. So help me, I'm going down to the ship's library and throw that old copy of *Moby Dick* overboard!
(He sits on hatch cover.)

ROBERTS. What are you giving them these days for double beriberi?

DOC. Aspirin—what else? *(He looks at Roberts)* Is there something wrong, Doug?

ROBERTS *(preoccupied)*. No.

DOC *(lying back on the hatch)*. We missed you when you went on watch last night. I gave young Ensign Pulver another drink of alcohol and orange juice and it inspired him to relate further sexual feats of his. Some of them bordered on the supernatural!

ROBERTS. I don't doubt it. Did he tell you how he conquered a forty-five-year-old virgin by the simple tactic of being the first man in her life to ask her a direct question?

DOC. No. Last night he was more concerned with quantity. It seems that on a certain cold and wintry night in November, 1939—a night when most of us mortal men would have settled for a cup of cocoa—he rendered pregnant three girls in Washington, D. C., caught the 11:45 train, and an hour later performed the same service for a young lady in Baltimore.

ROBERTS *(laughing)*. Oh, my God!

DOC. I'm not sure what to do with young Pulver. I'm thinking of reporting his record to the American Medical Association.

ROBERTS. Why don't you just get him a job as a fountain in Radio City?

DOC. Don't be too hard on him, Doug. He thinks you are approximately God. . . . Say, there *is* something wrong, isn't there?

ROBERTS. I've been up all night, Doc.

DOC. What is it? What's the matter?

ROBERTS. I saw something last night when I was on watch that just about knocked me out.

DOC *(alarmed)*. What happened?

ROBERTS *(with emotion)*. I was up on the bridge. I was just standing there looking out to sea. I couldn't bear to look at that island any more. All of a sudden I

noticed something. Little black specks crawling over the horizon. I looked through the glasses and it was a formation of our ships that stretched for miles! Carriers and battleships and cans—a whole task force, Doc!

DOC. Why didn't you break me out? I've never seen a battleship!

ROBERTS. They came on and they passed within half a mile of that reef! Carriers so big they blacked out half the sky! And battlewagons sliding along—dead quiet! I could see the men on the bridges. And this is what knocked me out, Doc. Somehow—I thought I was on those bridges— I thought I was riding west across the Pacific. I watched them until they were out of sight, Doc—and I was right there on those bridges all the time.

DOC. I know how that must have hurt, Doug.

ROBERTS. And then I looked down from our bridge and saw our Captain's palm tree! *(Points at palm tree, then bitterly)* Our trophy for superior achievement! The Admiral John J. Finchley award for delivering more toothpaste and toilet paper than any other Navy cargo ship in the safe area of the Pacific. *(Taking letter from pocket and handing it to Doc)* Read this, Doc—see how it sounds.

DOC. What is it?

ROBERTS. My application for transfer. I've been rewriting it ever since I got off watch last night.

DOC. O God, not another one!

ROBERTS. This one's different—I'm trying something new, Doc—a stronger wording. Read it carefully.
(Doc looks for a moment skeptically, then noticing the intensity in his face decides to read the letter.)

DOC *(reading)*.
"From: Lieutenant (jg) Douglas Roberts
To: Bureau of Naval Personnel
16 April 1945
Subject: Change of Duty, Request for . . ."
(He looks up.)
Boy, this is sheer poetry.

ROBERTS *(rises nervously)*. Go on, Doc.

DOC *(reads on)*.
"For two years and four months I have served aboard this vessel as Cargo Officer. I feel that my continued service aboard can only reduce my own usefulness to the Navy and increase disharmony aboard this ship."

(He looks at Roberts and rises. Roberts looks back defiantly.)

ROBERTS. How about *that!*

DOC *(whistles softly, then continues).* "It is therefore urgently requested that I be ordered to combat duty, preferably aboard a destroyer."

ROBERTS *(tensely, going to Doc).* What do you say, Doc? I've got a chance, haven't I?

DOC. Listen, Doug, you've been sending in a letter every week for God knows how long . . .

ROBERTS. Not like this . . .

DOC. . . . and every week the Captain has screamed like a stuck pig, *dis*approved your letters and forwarded them that way. . . .

ROBERTS. That's just my point, Doc. He *does* forward them. They go through the chain of command all the way up to the Bureau . . . Just because the Captain doesn't . . .

DOC. Doug, the Captain of a Navy ship is the most absolute monarch left in this world!

ROBERTS. I know that.

DOC. If he endorsed your letter "approved" you'd get your orders in a minute . . .

ROBERTS. Naturally, but I . . . *(Turns away from Doc)*

DOC. . . . but "disapproved," you haven't got a prayer. You're stuck on this old bucket, Doug. Face it!

ROBERTS *(turns quickly back).* Well, grant me this much, Doc. That one day I'll find the perfect wording and one human guy way up on top will read those words and say, "Here's a poor son-of-a-bitch screaming for help. Let's put him on a fighting ship!"

DOC *(quietly).* Sure . . .

ROBERTS *(after a moment).* I'm not kidding myself, am I, Doc? I've got a chance, haven't I?

DOC. Yes, Doug, you've got a chance. It's about the same chance as putting your letter in a bottle and dropping it in the ocean . . .

ROBERTS *(snatching letter from Doc).* But it's still a chance, goddammit! It's still a chance!

(Roberts stands looking out to sea. Doc watches him for a moment then speaks gently.)

DOC. I wish you hadn't seen that task force, Doug. *(Pauses)* Well, I've got to go down to my hypochondriacs.

(He goes off slowly through passageway.)

(Roberts is still staring out as Dowdy enters from the hatchway. He is a hard-bitten man between thirty-five and forty and is wearing dungarees and no hat. He stands by hatchway with a cup of coffee in his hand.)

DOWDY. Morning, Mister Roberts.

ROBERTS. Good morning, Dowdy.

DOWDY. Jeez, it's even hotter up here than down in that messhall! *(He looks off)* Look at that cruddy island . . . smell it! It's so hot it *already* smells like a hog pen. Think we'll go out of here today, sir?

(Roberts takes Dowdy's cup as he speaks and drinks from it, then hands it back.)

ROBERTS. I don't know, Dowdy. There's one LCT coming alongside for supplies . . . *(Goes to hatchway, looks down)* Are they getting up yet?

DOWDY *(also looking down hatch).* Yeah, they're starting to stumble around down there—the poor punch-drunk bastards. Mister Roberts, when are you going to the Captain again and ask him to give this crew a liberty? These guys ain't been off the ship for over a year except on duty.

ROBERTS. Dowdy, the last time I asked him was last night.

DOWDY. What'd he say?

ROBERTS. He said "No."

DOWDY. We gotta get these guys ashore! They're going Asiatic! *(Pause)* Will you see him anyhow, Mister Roberts—just once more?

ROBERTS. You know I will, Dowdy. *(Hands Dowdy the letter)* In the meantime, have Dolan type that up for me. *(He starts off right)*

DOWDY *(descending hatchway).* Oh, your letter. Yes, sir!

ROBERTS *(calling over his shoulder).* Then will you bring a couple of men back aft? *(He exits through passageway)*

DOWDY. Okay, Mister Roberts. *(He disappears down hatchway. He is heard below)* All right, you guys in there. Finish your coffee and get up on deck. Stefanowski, Insigna, off your tails . . .

(After a moment the center door opens and the Captain appears wearing pajamas and bathrobe and his officer's cap. He is carrying water in an engine-room oil can.

He waters the palm tree carefully, looks at it for a moment tenderly and goes back into his cabin. After a moment, Dowdy's voice is heard from the companionway and he appears followed by members of the crew.)

DOWDY. All right, let's go! Bring me those glasses, Schlemmer. *(Schlemmer exits by ladder to the bridge. Other men appear from the hatchway. They are Insigna, Stefanowski, Mannion, Wiley, Reber and Lindstrom—all yawning, buttoning pants, tucking in shirts and, in general, being comatose. The men do not appear to like one another very much at this hour—least of all Insigna and Mannion)* All right, I got a little recreation for you guys. Stefanowski, you take these guys and get this little rust patch here. *(He hands Stefanowski an armful of scrapers and wire brushes, indicating a spot on the deck. Stefanowski looks at instruments dully, then distributes them to the men standing near him. Schlemmer returns from the bridge, carrying four pairs of binoculars and a spy glass. He drops them next to Insigna who is sitting on the hatch)* Insigna, I got a real special job for you. You stay right here and clean these glasses.

INSIGNA. Ah, let me work up forward, Dowdy. I don't want to be around this crud, Mannion.

MANNION. Yeah, Dowdy. Take Insigna with you!

DOWDY. Shut up, I'm tired of you two bellyaching! *(Nodding to others to follow him)* All right, let's go, Reber . . . Schlemmer.

(Dowdy, Reber and Schlemmer leave through passageway right. The others sit in sodden silence. Lindstrom wanders slowly over to Insigna. He picks up spy glass and examines it. He holds the large end toward him and looks into it.)

LINDSTROM. Hey, look! I can see myself!

STEFANOWSKI. Terrifying, ain't it? *(Insigna takes the spy glass from him and starts polishing it. Lindstrom removes his shoe and feels inside it, then puts it back on.)*

MANNION *(after a pause)*. Hey, what time is it in San Francisco?

INSIGNA *(scornfully)*. When?

MANNION. Anybody ask you? *(Turns to Wiley)* What time would it be there?

WILEY. I don't know. I guess about midnight last night.

STEFANOWSKI *(studying scraper in his hand)*. I wonder if you could get sent back to the States if you cut off a finger. *(Nobody answers.)*

INSIGNA *(looking offstage)*. Hey, they got a new building on that island. Fancy—two stories . . . *(Nobody shows any curiosity.)*

MANNION. You know, I had a girl in San Francisco wore flowers in her hair—instead of hats. Never wore a hat . . . *(Another sodden pause.)*

INSIGNA *(holding spy glass)*. Hey Stefanowski! Which end of this you look through?

STEFANOWSKI. It's optional, Sam. Depends on what size eyeball you've got. *(Insigna idly looks through spy glass at something out right. Another pause.)*

INSIGNA. Hey, the Japs must've took over this island—there's a red and white flag on that new building.

MANNION. Japs! We never been within five thousand miles of a Jap! Japs! You hear that, Wiley?

WILEY. Yeah, smart, ain't he?

MANNION. Japs! That's a hospital flag!

INSIGNA. Anybody ask you guys? *(Nudging Lindstrom and pointing to the other group)* The goldbrick twins! *(Looks through spy glass)* Hey, they got a fancy hospital . . . big windows and . . . *(Suddenly rises, gasping at what he sees)*

STEFANOWSKI. What's the matter, Sam?

INSIGNA. Oh, my God! She's bare-assed!

STEFANOWSKI. *She!*

INSIGNA. Taking a shower . . . in that bathroom . . . that nurse . . . upstairs window! *(Instantly the others rush to hatch cover, grab binoculars and stand looking out right.)*

WILEY. She's a blonde—see!

LINDSTROM. I never seen such a beautiful girl!

MANNION. She's sure taking a long time in that shower!

WILEY. Yeah, honey, come on over here by the window!

INSIGNA. Don't you do it, honey! You take your time!

STEFANOWSKI. There's another one over by the washbasin—taking a shampoo.

INSIGNA *(indignantly)*. Yeah. But why the hell don't she take her bathrobe off!

That's a stupid goddamn way to take a shampoo!

(For a moment the men watch in silent vigilance.)

STEFANOWSKI. Ah-hah!

WILEY. She's coming out of the shower!

MANNION. She's coming over to the window! *(A pause)* Kee-ri-mi-ny!

(For a moment the men stand transfixed, their faces radiant. They emit rapturous sighs. That is all.)

LINDSTROM. Aw, she's turning around the other way!

MANNION. What's that red mark she's got . . . there?

INSIGNA *(authoritatively)*. That's a birthmark!

MANNION *(scornfully)*. Birthmark!

INSIGNA. What do you think it is, wise guy?

MANNION. Why, that's paint! She's sat in some red paint!

INSIGNA. Sat in some red paint! I'm tellin' you, that's a birthmark!

MANNION. Did you ever see a birthmark down there?

INSIGNA *(lowers his spy glass, turns to Mannion)*. Why, you stupid jerk! I had an uncle once had a birthmark right down . . .

WILEY. Aww!

(Insigna and Mannion return quickly to their glasses.)

STEFANOWSKI *(groaning)*. She's put her bathrobe on!

MANNION. Hey, she's got the same color bathrobe as that stupid bag taking the shampoo!

(The four men notice something and exclaim in unison.)

INSIGNA. Bag, hell! Look at her now with her head out of the water . . .

LINDSTROM. She's just as beautiful as the other one . . .

STEFANOWSKI. They look exactly alike with those bathrobes on. Maybe they're twins.

MANNION. That's my gal on the right—the one with the red birthmark.

INSIGNA. You stupid crud, the one with the birthmark's on the left!

MANNION. The hell she is . . .

(Mannion and Insigna again lower their glasses.)

INSIGNA. The hell she ain't . . .

WILEY. Awwww!

(Mannion and Insigna quickly drop their argument and look.)

STEFANOWSKI. They've both leaving the bathroom together. . . .

(The men are dejected again.)

LINDSTROM. Hey, there ain't no one in there now!

STEFANOWSKI *(lowering his glasses)*. Did you figure that out all by yourself? *(He looks through his glasses again)*

MANNION *(after a pause)*. Come on, girls, let's go!

WILEY. Yeah. Who's next to take a nice zippy shower?

INSIGNA *(after a pause)*. They must think we got nothing better to do than stand here!

LINDSTROM. These glasses are getting heavy!

STEFANOWSKI. Yeah. We're wasting manpower. Let's take turns, okay? *(The others agree)* All right, Mannion, you take it first.

(Mannion nods, crosses and sits on bitt, keeping watch with his binoculars. The others pick up their scrapers and wire brushes.)

INSIGNA *(watching Mannion)*. I don't trust that crud.

LINDSTROM. Gee, I wish we was allowed to get over to that island. We could get a closer look.

STEFANOWSKI. No, Lindstrom. They'd see us and pull the shades down.

LINDSTROM. No, they wouldn't. We could cover ourselves with leaves and make out like we was bushes—and sneak up on them—like them Japs we seen in that movie . . .

(He starts to sneak around front of hatch, holding his wire brush before his face. Stefanowski hears a noise from the Captain's cabin and quickly warns the others.)

STEFANOWSKI. Flash Red! *(The men immediately begin working in earnest as the Captain, now in khaki, enters. He stands for a moment, looking at them, and then wanders over to the group scraping the rust patch to inspect their work. Then, satisfied that they are actually working, he starts toward passageway. He sees Mannion, sitting on the bitt, looking through his glasses and smiling. The Captain goes over and stands beside him, looking off in the same direction. Stefanowski tries frantically to signal a warning to Mannion by beating out code with his* scraper. *Mannion suddenly sees the Captain and quickly lowers his glasses and pretends to clean them, alternately wiping the lenses and holding them up to his eyes to see that they are clean. The Captain watches him suspiciously for a moment, then he exits by the ladder to the bridge. Stefanowski rises and looks up ladder to make certain the Captain has gone)* Flash White! *(He turns and looks at Mannion)* Hey, Mannion. Anyone in there yet?

MANNION *(watching something happily through glasses)*. No, not yet!

INSIGNA *(picks up spy glass and looks, and rises quickly)*. Why, you dirty, miserable cheat!

(Instantly all the men are at the glasses.)

LINDSTROM. There's one in there again!

STEFANOWSKI. The hell with her—she's already got her clothes on!

INSIGNA. And there she goes! *(Slowly lowers his glass, turning to Mannion threateningly)* Why, you lousy, cheating crud!

MANNION *(idly swinging his glasses)*. That ain't all. I seen three!

STEFANOWSKI. You lowdown Peeping Tom!

LINDSTROM *(hurt)*. Mannion, that's a real dirty trick.

INSIGNA. What's the big idea?

MANNION. Who wants to know?

INSIGNA. *I* want to know! And you're damn well going to tell me!

MANNION. You loud-mouthed little bastard! Why don't you make me?

INSIGNA. You're damn right I will. Right now! *(He swings on Mannion as Lindstrom steps clumsily between them)*

LINDSTROM. Hey, fellows! Fellows!

INSIGNA. No wonder you ain't got a friend on this ship . . . except this crud, Wiley. *(He jerks his head in direction of Wiley who stands behind him on hatch cover. Wiley takes him by shoulder and whirls him around)*

WILEY. What'd you say?

STEFANOWSKI *(shoving Wiley)*. You heard him!

(Mannion jumps on hatch cover to protect Wiley from Stefanowski. Insigna rushes at Mannion and for a moment they are all in a clinch. Lindstrom plows up on the hatch and breaks them apart. The men have suddenly formed into two camps—Mannion and Wiley on one side, Insigna and Stefanowski facing them, Lindstrom is just an accessory, but stands prepared to intervene if necessary.)

MANNION *(to Wiley)*. Look at them two! Everybody on the ship hates their guts! The two moochingest, no-good loudmouths on the ship!

(Stefanowski starts for Mannion but Insigna pulls him back and steps menacingly toward Mannion.)

INSIGNA. Why, you slimy, lying son-of-a-bitch!

(Suddenly Mannion hits Insigna, knocking him down. He jumps on Insigna who catches Mannion in the chest with his feet and hurls him back. Wiley and Stefanowski start fighting with Lindstrom, attempting to break them apart. Mannion rushes back at Insigna. Insigna sidesteps Mannion's lunge and knocks him to the deck. Insigna falls on him. They wrestle to their feet and stand slugging. At this point Roberts and Dowdy run on from passageway. Roberts flings Insigna and Mannion apart. Dowdy separates the others.)

ROBERTS. Break it up! Break it up, I tell you!

(Insigna and Mannion rush at each other. Roberts and Dowdy stop them.)

DOWDY. Goddamn you guys, break it up!

ROBERTS. All right! What's going on?

INSIGNA *(pointing at Mannion)*. This son-of-a-bitch here . . .

ROBERTS. Did you hear me?

MANNION *(to Insigna)*. Shut your mouth!

DOWDY. Shut up, both of you!

INSIGNA. Slimy son-of-a-bitch! *(Picks up scraper and lunges at Mannion again. Roberts throws him back)*

ROBERTS. I said to cut it out! Did you hear me? *(Wheels on Mannion)* That goes for you too! *(Includes entire group)* I'm going to give it to the first one who opens his mouth! *(The men stand subdued, breathing hard from the fight)* Now get to work! All of you! *(They begin to move sullenly off right)* Mannion, you and the rest get to work beside number two! And, Insigna, take those glasses way up to the bow and work on them! Stefanowski, keep those two apart.

STEFANOWSKI. Yes, sir.

(The men exit. Roberts and Dowdy look after them.)

DOWDY (*tightly*). You seen that, Mister Roberts. Well, last night down in the compartment I stopped three of them fights—worse than that. They've got to have a liberty, Mister Roberts.

ROBERTS. They sure do. Dowdy, call a boat for me, will you? I'm going ashore.

DOWDY. What are you going to do?

ROBERTS. I just got a new angle.

DOWDY. Are you going over the Captain's head?

ROBERTS. No, I'm going around his end —I hope. Get the lead out, Dowdy.

(*He exits left as Dowdy goes off right and the lights fade out.*)

During the darkness, voices can be heard over the squawk-box saying:

Now hear this . . . now hear this. Sweepers, man your brooms. Clean sweep-down fore and aft. Sweep-down all ladders and all passageways. Do *not* throw trash over the fantail.

Now, all men on report will see the master-at-arms for assignment to extra duty.

Now hear this . . . now hear this. Because in violation of the Captain's orders, a man has appeared on deck without a shirt on, there will be no movies again tonight—by order of the Captain.

SCENE TWO

The lights dim up revealing the state-room of Pulver and Roberts. Two lockers are shown, one marked "Ensign F. T. Pulver," the other marked "Lt. (jg) D. A. Roberts." There is a double bunk along the bulkhead right. A desk with its end against the bulkhead left has a chair at either side. There is a porthole in the bulkhead above it. Up center, right of Pulver's locker is a washbasin over which is a shelf and a medicine chest. The door is up center.

An officer is discovered with his head inside Roberts' locker, throwing skivvy shirts over his shoulder as he searches for something. Dolan, a young, garrulous, brash yeoman, second class, enters. He is carrying a file folder.

DOLAN. Here's your letter, Mister Roberts. (*He goes to the desk, taking fountain pen from his pocket*) I typed it up.

Just sign your old John Henry here and I'll take it in to the Captain . . . then hold your ears. (*No answer*) Mister Roberts! (*Pulver's head appears from the locker*) Oh, it's only you, Mister Pulver. What are you doing in Mister Roberts' locker?

PULVER (*hoarsely*). Dolan, look in here, will you? I know there's a shoe box in there, but I can't find it.

(*Dolan looks in the locker.*)

DOLAN. There ain't no shoe box in there, Mister Pulver.

PULVER. They've stolen it! There's nothing they'll stop at now. They've broken right into the sanctity of a man's own locker. (*He sits in chair at desk*)

DOLAN (*disinterested*). Ain't Mister Roberts back from the island yet?

PULVER. No.

DOLAN. Well, as soon as he gets back, will you ask him to sign this baby?

PULVER. What is it?

DOLAN. What is it! It's the best damn letter Mister Roberts writ yet. It's going to blow the Old Man right through the overhead. And them big shots at the Bureau are going to drop their drawers too. This letter is liable to get him transferred.

PULVER. Yeah, lemme see it.

DOLAN (*handing letter to Pulver*). Get a load of that last paragraph. Right here.

PULVER (*reading with apprehension*). ". . . increase disharmony aboard this ship . . ."

DOLAN (*interrupting gleefully*). Won't that frost the Old Man's knockers? I can't wait to jab this baby in the Old Man's face. Mister Pulver, you know how he gets sick to his stomach when he gets extra mad at Mister Roberts—well, when I deliver this letter I'm going to take along a wastebasket! Let me know when Mister Roberts gets back.

(*Dolan exits. Pulver continues reading the letter with great dismay. He hears Roberts and Doc talking in the passageway, offstage, and quickly goes to his bunk and hides the letter under a blanket. He goes to the locker and is replacing skivvy shirts as Roberts and Doc enter.*)

ROBERTS. . . . so after the fight I figured I had to do something and do it quick!

DOC. What did you do over on the island, Doug?

ROBERTS (*sitting in chair and searching through desk drawer*). Hey, Frank, has Dolan been in here yet with my letter?

PULVER (innocently). I don't know, Doug boy. I just came in here myself.

DOC. You don't know anybody on the island, do you, Doug?

ROBERTS. Yes. The Port Director—the guy who decides where to send this ship next. He confided to me that he used to drink a quart of whiskey every day of his life. So this morning when I broke up that fight it came to me that he might just possibly sell his soul for a quart of Scotch.

PULVER (rises). Doug, you didn't give that shoe box to the Post Director!

ROBERTS. I did. "Compliments of the Captain."

DOC. You've had a quart of Scotch in a shoe box?

ROBERTS. Johnny Walker! I was going to break it out the day I got off this ship —Resurrection Day!

PULVER. Oh, my God! It's really gone! (He sinks to the bunk)

DOC. Well, did the Port Director say he'd send us to a Liberty Port?

ROBERTS. Hell, no. He took the Scotch and said, "Don't bother me, Roberts. I'm busy." The rummy!

PULVER. How could you do it!

DOC. Well, where there's a rummy, there's hope. Maybe when he gets working on that Scotch he'll mellow a little.

PULVER. You gave that bottle to a god-damn man!

ROBERTS. Man! Will you name me another sex within a thousand miles . . . (Pulver, dejected, goes up to porthole) What the hell's eating you anyhow, Frank?

(Doc crosses to bunk. He sees two fancy pillows on bottom bunk, picks up one and tosses it to Roberts. He picks up the other.)

DOC. Well, look here. Somebody seems to be expecting company!

ROBERTS. Good Lord!

DOC (reads lettering on pillowcase). "Toujours l'amour . . . Souvenir of San Diego . . . Oh, you kid!"

ROBERTS (reading from his pillowcase). "Tonight or never . . . Compliments of Allis-Chalmers, Farm Equipment . . . We plow deep while others sleep." (He looks at Doc, then rises) Doc—that new hospital over there hasn't got nurses, has it?

DOC. Nurses! It didn't have yesterday!

PULVER (turning from porthole). It has today!

DOC. But how did you find out they were there?

PULVER (trying to recall). Now let me think . . . it just came to me all of a sudden. This morning it was so hot I was just lying on my bunk—thinking . . . There wasn't a breath of air. And then, all of a sudden, a funny thing happened. A little breeze came up and I took a big deep breath and said to myself, "Pulver boy, there's women on that island."

ROBERTS. Doc, a thing like this could make a bird dog self-conscious as hell.

PULVER (warming up). They just flew in last night. There's eighteen of them— all brunettes except for two beautiful blondes—twin sisters! I'm working on one of those. I asked her out to the ship for lunch and she said she was kind of tired. So then I got kind of desperate and turned on the old personality—and I said, "Ain't there anything in the world that'll make you come out to the ship with me?" And she said, "Yes, there is, one thing and one thing only—" (Crosses to Roberts, looks at him accusingly) "A good stiff drink of Scotch!" (He sinks into the chair)

ROBERTS (after a pause). I'm sorry, Frank. I'm really sorry. Your first assignment in a year. (He pats Pulver on the shoulder)

PULVER. I figured I'd bring her in here . . . I fixed it up real cozy . . . (Fondling pillow on desk) . . . and then I was going to throw a couple of fast slugs of Scotch into her and . . . but, hell, without the Scotch, she wouldn't . . . she just wouldn't, that's all.

ROBERTS (after a pause). Doc, let's make some Scotch!

DOC. Huh?

ROBERTS. As naval officers we're supposed to be resourceful. Frank here's got a great opportunity and I've let him down. Let's fix him up!

DOC. Right! (He goes to desk. Roberts begins removing bottles from medicine chest) Frank, where's the rest of that alcohol we were drinking last night?

PULVER (pulling a large vinegar bottle half filled with colorless liquid from the wastebasket and handing it to Doc). Hell, that ain't even the right color.

DOC (taking the bottle). Quiet! (Thinks deeply) Color . . . (With sudden decision) Coca-Cola! Have you got any?

ROBERTS. I haven't seen a Coke in four months—no, by God, it's five months!

PULVER. Oh, what the hell! *(He rises, crosses to bunk, reaches under mattress of top bunk and produces a bottle of Coca-Cola. The others watch him. Doc snatches the bottle. Pulver says apologetically)* I forgot I had it.

(Doc opens the bottle and is about to pour the Coca-Cola into the vinegar bottle when he suddenly stops.)

DOC. Oh—what shade would you like? Cutty Sark . . . Haig and Haig . . . Vat 69 . . .

PULVER *(interested)*. I told her Johnny Walker.

DOC. Johnny Walker it is! *(He pours some of the Coca-Cola into the bottle)*

ROBERTS *(looking at color of the mixture)*. Johnny Walker Red Label!

DOC. Red Label!

PULVER. It may look like it—but it won't taste like it!

ROBERTS. Doc, what does Scotch taste like?

DOC. Well, it's a little like . . . uh . . . it tastes like . . .

ROBERTS. Do you know what it's always tasted a little like to me? Iodine.

DOC *(shrugs as if to say "Of course" and rises. He takes dropper from small bottle of iodine and flicks a drop in the bottle)*. One drop of iodine—for taste. *(Shakes the bottle and pours some in glass)*

PULVER. Lemme taste her, Doc!

DOC *(stops him with a gesture)*. No. This calls for a medical opinion. *(Takes a ceremonial taste while the others wait for his verdict)*

PULVER. How about it?

DOC. We're on the right track! *(Sets glass down. Rubs hands professionally)* Now we need a little something extra—for age! What've you got there, Doug?

ROBERTS *(reading labels of bottles on desk)*. Bromo-Seltzer . . . Wildroot Wave Set . . . Eno Fruit Salts . . . Kreml Hair Tonic . . .

DOC. Kreml! It has a coal-tar base! And it'll age the hell out of it! *(Pours a bit of Kreml into mixture. Shakes bottle solemnly)* One drop Kreml for age. *(Sets bottle on desk, looks at wrist watch for a fraction of a second)* That's it! *(Pours drink into glass. Pulver reaches for it. Roberts pushes his arm aside and tastes it)*

ROBERTS. By God, it does taste a little like Scotch!

(Pulver again reaches for glass. Doc pushes his arm aside and takes a drink.)

DOC. By God, it does!

(Pulver finally gets glass and takes a quick sip.)

PULVER. It's delicious. That dumb little blonde won't know the difference.

DOC *(hands the bottle to Pulver)*. Here you are, Frank. Doug and I have made the Scotch. The *nurse* is your department. *(Pulver takes the bottle and hides it under the mattress, then replaces the pillows.)*

PULVER *(singing softly)*. Won't know the difference . . . won't know the difference. *(Doc starts to drink from Coca-Cola bottle as Pulver comes over and snatches it from his hand)* Thanks, Doc. *(Puts cap on the bottle and hides it under the mattress. Turns and faces the others)* Thanks, Doug. Jeez, you guys are wonderful to me.

ROBERTS *(putting bottles back in medicine chest)*. Don't mention it, Frank. I think you almost deserve it.

PULVER. You do—really? Or are you just giving me the old needle again? What do you really think of me, Doug—honestly?

ROBERTS *(turning slowly to face Pulver)*. Frank, I like you. No one can get around the fact that you're a hell of a likable guy.

PULVER *(beaming)*. Yeah—yeah . . .

ROBERTS. But . . .

PULVER. But what?

ROBERTS. But I also think you are the most hapless . . . lazy . . . disorganized . . . and, in general, the most lecherous person I've ever known in my life.

PULVER. I am not.

ROBERTS. Not what?

PULVER. I'm not disorganized—for one thing.

ROBERTS. Have you ever in your life finished anything you started out to do? You sleep sixteen hours a day. You pretend you want me to improve your mind and you've never even finished a book I've given you to read!

PULVER. I finished *God's Little Acre*, Doug boy!

ROBERTS. I didn't give you that! *(To Doc)* He's been reading *God's Little Acre* for over a year! *(Takes dog-eared book *from Pulver's bunk)* He's underlined every erotic passage, and added exclamation points—and after a certain pornographic climax, he's inserted the words "well written." *(To Pulver)* You're the Laundry and Morale Officer and I doubt if you've ever seen the laundry.

PULVER. I was down there only last week.

ROBERTS. And you're scared of the Captain.

PULVER. I'm not scared of the Captain.

ROBERTS. Then why do you hide in the passageway every time you see him coming? I doubt if he even knows you're on board. You're scared of him.

PULVER. I am not. I'm scared of myself —I'm scared of what I might do to him.

ROBERTS *(laughing)*. What you might do to him! Doc, he lies in his sack all day long and bores me silly with great moronic plots against the Captain and he's never carried out one.

PULVER. I haven't, huh.

ROBERTS. No, Frank, you haven't. What happened to your idea of plugging up the line of the Captain's sanitary system? "I'll make it overflow," you said. "I'll make a backwash that'll lift him off the throne and knock him clean across the room."

PULVER. I'm workin' on that. I thought about it for half an hour—yesterday.

ROBERTS. Half an hour! There's only one thing you've thought about for half an hour in your life! And what about those marbles that you were going to put in the Captain's overhead—so they'd roll around at night and keep him awake?

PULVER. Now you've gone too far. Now you've asked for it. *(Goes to bunk and produces small tin box from under mattress. Crosses to Roberts and shakes it in his face. Opens it)* What does that look like? Five marbles! I'm collecting marbles all the time. I've got one right here in my pocket! *(Takes marble from pocket, holds it close to Roberts' nose, then drops it in box. Closes box)* Six marbles! *(Puts box back under mattress, turns defiantly to Roberts)* I'm looking for marbles all day long!

ROBERTS. Frank, you asked me what I thought of you. Well, I'll tell you! The day you finish one thing you've started out to do, the day you actually put those marbles in the Captain's overhead, and then have the guts to knock on his door

and say, "Captain, I put those marbles there," that's the day I'll have some respect for you—that's the day I'll look up to you as a man. Okay?

PULVER *(belligerently)*. Okay!

(Roberts goes to the radio and turns it up. While he is listening, Doc and Pulver exchange worried looks.)

RADIO VOICE. . . . intersecting thirty miles north of Hanover. At the same time, General George S. Patton's Third Army continues to roll unchecked into Southern Germany. The abrupt German collapse brought forth the remark from a high London official that the end of the war in Europe is only weeks away—maybe days . . .

(Roberts turns off radio.)

ROBERTS. Where the hell's Dolan with that letter! *(Starts toward the door)* I'm going to find him.

PULVER. Hey, Doug, wait! Listen! *(Roberts pauses at the door)* I wouldn't send in that letter if I were you!

ROBERTS. What do you mean—*that* letter!

PULVER *(hastily)*. I mean any of those letters you been writin'. What are you so nervous about anyway?

ROBERTS. Nervous!

PULVER. I mean about getting off this ship. Hell, this ain't such a bad life. Look, Doug—we're a threesome, aren't we—you and Doc and me? Share and share alike! Now look, I'm not going to keep those nurses all to myself. Soon as I get my little nursie organized today, I'm going to start working on her twin sister—for you.

ROBERTS. All right, Frank.

PULVER. And then I'm going to scare up something for you too, Doc. And in the meantime you've got a lot of work to do, Doug boy—improvin' my mind and watching my grammar. And speaking of grammar, you better watch your grammar. You're going to get in trouble, saying things like "disharmony aboard this ship!" *(Roberts looks at Pulver quickly. Pulver catches himself)* I mean just in case you ever said anything like "disharmony aboard this ship" . . . or . . . uh . . . "harmony aboard this ship" or . . .

ROBERTS. Where's that letter?

PULVER. I don't know, Doug boy . . . *(As Roberts steps toward him, he quickly produces the letter from the blanket)* Here it is, Doug.

ROBERTS (*snatching the letter*). What's the big idea!

(*Roberts goes to desk, reading and preparing to sign the letter. Pulver follows him.*)

PULVER. I just wanted to talk to you before you signed it. You can't send it in that way—it's too strong! Don't sign that letter, Doug, please don't! They'll transfer you and you'll get your ass shot off. You're just running a race with death, isn't he, Doc? It's stupid to keep asking for it like that. The Doc says so too. Tell him what you said to me last night, Doc—about how stupid he is.

ROBERTS (*coldly, to Doc*). Yes, Doc, maybe you'd like to tell me to my face.

DOC (*belligerently*). Yes, I would. Last night I asked you why you wanted to fight this war. And you said: anyone who doesn't fight it is only half-alive. Well, I thought that over and I've decided that's just a crock, Doug—just a crock.

ROBERTS. I take it back, Doc. After seeing my task force last night I don't even feel half-alive.

DOC. You are stupid! And I can prove it! You quit medical school to get into this thing when you could be saving lives today. Why? Do you even know yourself?

ROBERTS. Has it ever occurred to you that the guys who fight this war might also be saving lives . . . yours and mine, for instance! Not just putting men together again, but *keeping* them together! Right now I'd rather practice that kind of medicine—Doctor!

DOC (*rising*). Well, right now, that's exactly what you're doing.

ROBERTS. What, for God's sake!

DOC. Whether you like it or not, this sorry old bucket does a necessary job. And you're the guy who keeps her lumbering along. You keep this crew working cargo, and more than that—you keep them *alive*. It might just be that right here, on this bucket, you're deeper and more truly in this war than you ever would be anywhere else.

ROBERTS. Oh, Jesus, Doc. In a minute, you'll start quoting Emerson.

DOC. *That* is a lousy thing to say!

ROBERTS. We've got nothing to do with the war. Maybe that's why we're on this ship—because we're not good enough to fight. (*Then quietly with emotion*) May-

be there's some omniscient son-of-a-bitch who goes down the line of all the servicemen and picks out the ones to send into combat, the ones whose glands secrete enough adrenalin, or whose great-great-grandfathers weren't afraid of the dark or something. The rest of us are packed off to ships like this where we can't do any harm.

DOC. What is it you want to be—a hero or something?

ROBERTS (*shocked*). Hero! My God, Doc! You haven't heard a word I said! Look, Doc, the war's way out there! I'm here. I don't want to be here—I want to be out there. I'm sick and tired of being a lousy spectator. I just happen to believe in this thing. I've got to feel I'm *good* enough to be in it—to *participate!*

DOC. Good enough! Doug, you're good enough! You just don't have the opportunity. That's mostly what physical heroism is—opportunity. It's a reflex. I think seventy-five out of a hundred young males have that reflex. If you put any one of them—say, even Frank Thurlowe Pulver, here—in a B-29 over Japan, do you know what you'd have?

ROBERTS. No, by God, I don't.

DOC. You'd have Pulver, the Congressional Medal of Honor winner! You'd have Pulver, who, singlehanded, shot down twenty-three attacking Zeroes, then with his bare hands held together the severed wing struts of his plane, and with his bare feet successfully landed the mortally wounded plane on his home field. (*Pulver thinks this over*) Hell, it's a reflex. It's like the knee jerk. Strike the patella tendon of any human being and you produce the knee jerk. Look. (*He illustrates on Pulver. There is no knee jerk. He strikes again—still no reaction*)

PULVER. What's the matter, Doc?

DOC. Nothing. But stay out of B-29's, will you, Frank?

ROBERTS. You've made your point very vividly, Doc. But I still want to get into this thing. I've got to get into it! And I'm going to keep on sending in these letters until I do.

DOC. I know you are, Doug.

ROBERTS (*signs the letter. Then to Doc*). I haven't got much time. I found that out over on the island. That task force I saw last night is on its way to start our last big push in the Pacific. And it went by me, Doc. I've got to catch it. *(He exits)*

PULVER *(after a pause)*. Doc, what are you going to give Doug on his birthday?

DOC. I hadn't thought of giving him anything.

PULVER. You know what? I'm gonna show him he's got old Pulver figured out all wrong. *(Pulls small cardboard roll from under mattress)* Doc, what does that look like?

DOC. Just what it is—the cardboard center of a roll of toilet paper.

PULVER. I suppose it doesn't look like a firecracker.

DOC. Not a bit like a firecracker.

PULVER *(taking a piece of string from the bunk)*. I suppose that doesn't look like a fuse.

DOC *(rising and starting off)*. No, that looks like a piece of string. *(He walks slowly out of the room. Pulver goes on)*

PULVER. Well, you just wait till old Pulver gets through with it! I'm going to get me some of that black powder from the gunner's mate. No, by God, this isn't going to be any peanut firecracker—I'm going to pack this old thing full of that stuff they use to blow up bridges, that fulminate of mercury stuff. And then on the night of Doug's birthday, I'm going to throw it under the Old Man's bunk. Bam—bam—bam! *(Knocks on Roberts' locker, opens it)* Captain, it is I, Ensign Pulver. I just threw that firecracker under your goddamn bunk.

(He salutes as the lights fade out.)

(In the darkness we hear the sound of a winch and shouted orders.)

LCT OFFICER. On the AK—where do you want us?

AK VOICE. Starboard side, up for'd—alongside number two!

LCT OFFICER. Shall we use our fenders or yours?

AK VOICE. No, we'll use ours! Stand off till we finish with the barge!

SCENE THREE

The curtain rises and the lights dim up on the deck. Roberts stands on the hatch cover. Schlemmer, Gerhart and another seaman are sitting on the hatch cover. They are tired and hot. A cargo net, filled with crates, is disappearing off right. Off stage we hear the shouts of men working cargo. Two officers walk across the stage. Everyone's shirt is wet with perspiration.

———

ROBERTS *(calling through megaphone)*. Okay—take it away—that's all for the barge. On the LCT—I'll give you a bow line.

LCT OFFICER *(offstage)*. Okay, Lieutenant.

ROBERTS *(to crew)*. Get a line over!

DOWDY *(offstage)*. Yes, sir.

REBER *(off right)*. Heads up on the LCT!

ROBERTS. That's good. Make it fast. *(Payne, wearing the belt of a messenger, enters from companionway as Dowdy enters from right.)*

PAYNE. Mister Roberts, the Captain says not to give this LCT any fresh fruit. He says he's going to keep what's left for his own mess.

ROBERTS. Okay, okay . . .

PAYNE. Hold your hat, Mister Roberts. I just saw Dolan go in there with your letter. *(He grins and exits as Roberts smiles at Dowdy)*

DOWDY. Here's the list of what the LCT guy wants.

ROBERTS *(reading rapidly)*. One ton dry stores . . . quarter-ton frozen food . . . one gross dungarees . . . twenty cartons toothpaste . . . two gross skivvy shirts . . . Okay, we can give him all that.

DOWDY. Can these guys take their shirts off while we're working?

ROBERTS. Dowdy, you know the Captain has a standing order . . .

DOWDY. Mister Roberts, Corcoran just passed out from the heat.

ROBERTS *(looks at men, who wait for his decision)*. Hell, yes, take 'em off. *(Dowdy exits. Schlemmer, Reber and seaman remove shirts saying, "Thanks, Mister Roberts" and exit right. Roberts calls through megaphone)* LCT, want to swap movies? We've got a new one.

LCT *(offstage)*. What's that?

ROBERTS. *Charlie Chan at the Opera.*

LCT *(offstage)*. No, thanks, we've seen that three times!

ROBERTS. What you got?

LCT *(offstage)*. Hoot Gibson in *Riders of the Range.*

ROBERTS. Sorry I brought the subject up.

DOWDY *(entering from right).* All set, Mister Roberts.

LCT *(offstage).* Lieutenant, one thing I didn't put on my list because I wanted to ask you—you couldn't spare us any fresh fruit, could you?

ROBERTS. You all out?

LCT *(offstage).* We haven't seen any for two months.

ROBERTS *(to Dowdy).* Dowdy, give 'em a couple of crates of oranges.

DOWDY. Yes, sir.

ROBERTS. Compliments of the Captain.

DOWDY. Aye-aye, sir. *(He exits)*

ROBERTS *(to LCT).* Here comes your first sling-load! *(There is the grinding sound of a winch. With hand-signals Roberts directs placing of the sling-load. Then he shouts)* Watch that line!

DOWDY. Slack off, you dumb bastards! Slack off!

(Payne enters. Roberts turns to him sharply.)

ROBERTS. What!

PAYNE. The Captain wants to see you, Mister Roberts.

DOWDY *(offstage).* Goddammit, there it goes! You've parted the line!

ROBERTS. Get a fender over! Quick! *(To Payne)* You go tell the Captain I'm busy! *(Payne exits. Roberts calls offstage)* Get a line over—his bow's coming in!

REBER *(offstage).* Heads up!

GERHART *(offstage).* Where shall we secure?

DOWDY *(offstage).* Secure here!

ROBERTS. No. Take it around the bitt!

DOWDY *(offstage).* Around the bitt!

ROBERTS. That's too much! Give him some slack this time! *(Watches intently)* That's good. Okay, let's give him the rest of his cargo.

GERHART *(entering quickly and pointing toward companionway).* Flash Red! *(He exits. The Captain enters, followed by Payne and Dolan)*

CAPTAIN. All right, Mister! Let's have this out right here and now! What do you mean—telling me you're busy!

ROBERTS. We parted a line, Captain. You didn't want me to leave the deck with this ship coming in on us?

CAPTAIN. You're damn right I want you to leave the deck. When I tell you I want to see you, I mean *now,* Mister! I mean jump! Do you understand?

(At this point a group of men, attracted by the noise, crowd in. They are naked to the waist. They pretend they are working, but actually they are listening to the Captain's fight with Roberts.)

ROBERTS. Yes, Captain. I'll remember that next time.

CAPTAIN. You're damn right you'll remember it! Don't *ever* tell me you're too busy to see me! Ever! *(Roberts doesn't answer. The Captain points to the letter he is carrying)* By God, you think you're pretty cute with this letter, don't you? You're trying to get me in bad with the Admiral, ain't you? Ain't you?

ROBERTS. No, I'm not, Captain.

CAPTAIN. Then what do you mean by writing "disharmony aboard this ship"?

ROBERTS. Because it's true, Captain.

(The men grin at each other.)

CAPTAIN. Any disharmony on this ship is my own doing!

ROBERTS. That's true too, Captain.

CAPTAIN. Damn right it's true. And it ain't gonna be in any letter that leaves this ship. Any criticism of this ship stays on this ship. I got a reputation with the Admiral and I ain't gonna lose it on account of a letter written by some smart-alec college officer. Now you retype that letter and leave out that disharmony crap and I'll send it in. But this is the last one, understand?

ROBERTS. Captain, every man in the Navy has the right to send in a request for transfer . . . and no one can change the wording. That's in Navy regs.

CAPTAIN *(after a pause).* How about that, Dolan?

DOLAN. That's what it says, sir.

CAPTAIN. This goddamn Navy! I never put up with crap like that in the merchant service. All right, I'll send this one in as it is—*dis*approved, like I always do. But there's one thing I don't have to do and that's send in a letter that ain't been written. And, Mister, I'm tellin' you here and now—you ain't gonna write any more. You bring one next week and you'll regret it the rest of your life. You got a job right here and, Mister, you ain't *never* going to leave this ship. Now get on with your work. *(He looks around and notices the men. He shouts)* Where are your shirts?

ROBERTS. Captain, I . . .

CAPTAIN. Shut up! *Answer me, where are your shirts?* *(They stare at him)* Get those shirts on in a goddamn quick hurry.

(The men pick up their shirts, then pause, looking at Roberts.)

ROBERTS. Captain, it was so hot working cargo, I . . .

CAPTAIN *(shouting louder)*. I told you to shut up! *(To the men)* I'm giving you an order: get those shirts on!

(The men do not move.)

ROBERTS *(quietly)*. I'm sorry. Put your shirts on.

(The men put on their shirts. There is a pause while the Captain stares at the men. Then he speaks quietly.)

CAPTAIN. Who's the Captain of this ship? By God, that's the rankest piece of insubordination I've seen. You've been getting pretty smart playing grab-ass with Roberts here . . . but now you've gone too far. I'm givin' you a little promise—I ain't never gonna forget this. And in the meantime, every one of you men who disobeyed my standing order and appeared on deck without a shirt—every one—is on report, do you hear? On report!

ROBERTS. Captain, you're not putting these men on report.

CAPTAIN. What do you mean—I'm not!

ROBERTS. I'm responsible. I gave them permission.

CAPTAIN. You disobeyed my order?

ROBERTS. Yes, sir. It was too hot working cargo in the sun. One man passed out.

CAPTAIN. I don't give a damn if fifty men passed out. I gave an order and you disobeyed it.

LCT *(offstage)*. Thanks a million for the oranges, Lieutenant.

CAPTAIN *(to Roberts)*. Did you give that LCT fresh fruit?

ROBERTS. Yes, sir. We've got plenty, Captain. They've been out for two months.

CAPTAIN. I've taken all the crap from you that I'm going to. You've just got yourself ten days in your room. Ten days, Mister! Ten days!

ROBERTS. Very well, Captain. Do you relieve me here?

CAPTAIN. You're damn right, I relieve you. You can go to your room for ten days! See how you like that!

LCT *(offstage)*. We're waiting on you, Lieutenant. We gotta shove off.

(Roberts gives the megaphone to the Captain and starts off. The Captain looks in direction of the LCT then calls to Roberts.)

CAPTAIN. Where do you think you're going?

ROBERTS *(pretending surprise)*. To my room, Captain!

CAPTAIN. Get back to that cargo! I'll let you know when you have ten days in your room and you'll damn well know it! You're going to stay right here and do your job! *(Roberts crosses to the crew. The Captain slams the megaphone into Roberts' stomach. Pulver enters around the corner of the house, sees the Captain and starts to go back. The Captain sees Pulver and shouts)* Who's that? Who's that officer there?

PULVER *(turning)*. Me, sir?

CAPTAIN. Yes, you. Come here, boy. *(Pulver approaches in great confusion and can think of nothing better to do than salute. This visibly startles the Captain)* Why, you're one of my officers!

PULVER. Yes, sir.

CAPTAIN. What's your name again?

PULVER. Ensign Pulver, sir.

(He salutes again. The Captain, amazed, returns the salute, then says for the benefit of Roberts and the crew:)

CAPTAIN. By God, I'm glad to see one on this ship knows how to salute. *(Then to Pulver)* Pulver . . . oh, yes . . . Pulver. How is it I never see you around?

PULVER *(terrified)*. I've wondered about that myself, sir.

CAPTAIN. What's your job?

PULVER *(trembling)*. Officer in charge of laundry and morale, sir.

CAPTAIN. How long you been aboard?

PULVER. Fourteen months, sir.

CAPTAIN. Fourteen months! You spend most of your time down in the laundry, eh?

PULVER. Most of the time, sir. Yes, sir. *(Roberts turns his face to hide his laughter.)*

CAPTAIN. Well, you do a good job, Pulver, and . . . you know I'd like to see more of you. Why don't you have lunch with me in my cabin today?

PULVER. Oh, I can't today.

CAPTAIN. Can't? Why not?

PULVER. I'm on my way over to the hospital on the island. I've got to go pick up a piece . . . of medical equipment.

ROBERTS *(calling over)*. Why, I'll take care of that. Frank.

CAPTAIN. That's right, Roberts. You finish here and you go over and fetch it.

ROBERTS. Yes, sir. (*He nods and turns away, grinning*)

CAPTAIN (*to Pulver*). Well, how about it?

PULVER. This is something I've got to take care of myself, sir. If you don't mind, sir.

CAPTAIN. Well, some other time then.

PULVER. Yes, sir. Thank you, sir.

CAPTAIN. Okay, Pulver.

(*The Captain baits another salute from Pulver, then exits. Pulver watches him go, then starts to sneak off.*)

ROBERTS (*grinning and mimicking the Captain*). Oh, boy! (*Pulver stops uneasily. Roberts salutes him*) I want to see more of you, Pulver!

PULVER (*furiously*). That son-of-a-bitch! Pretending he doesn't know me! (*He looks at watch and exits. Roberts turns laughing to the crew who are standing rather solemnly*)

DOWDY (*quietly*). Nice going, Mister Roberts.

SCHLEMMER. It was really beautiful the way you read the Old Man off!

GERHART. Are you going to send in that letter next week, Mister Roberts?

ROBERTS. Are we, Dolan?

DOLAN. You're damn right we are! And I'm the baby who's going to deliver it!

SCHLEMMER. He said he'd fix you good. What do you think he'll do?

REBER. You got a promotion coming up, haven't you?

SCHLEMMER. Yeah. Could he stop that or something?

DOLAN. Promotion! This is Mister Roberts. You think he gives a good hoot-in-hell about another lousy stripe?

ALL. Yeah.

GERHART. Hey, Mister Roberts, can I take the letter in next week?

DOLAN (*indignantly*). You can like hell. That's my job—isn't it, Mister Roberts?

GERHART. Can I, Mister Roberts?

ROBERTS. I'm afraid I've promised that job to Dolan.

DOLAN (*pushing Gerhart away*). You heard him. (*To Roberts*) We gotta write a really hot one next week.

ROBERTS. Got any asbestos paper?

(*He starts off, the men follow happily as the lights fade out.*)

SCENE FOUR

The lights come up immediately on the main set. Reber and Gerhart enter from right passageway. As they get around the corner of the house, they break into a run. Reber dashes off through left passageway.

GERHART (*excitedly, descending hatchway*). Hey, Schlemmer! Schlemmer! (*Miss Girard, a young, attractive, blonde Army nurse, and Pulver enter from right passageway.*)

PULVER. Well, here it is.

MISS GIRARD. This is a ship?

PULVER. Unh-hunh.

MISS GIRARD. My sister and I flew over some warships on our way out from the States and they looked so busy—men running around like mad.

PULVER. It's kinda busy sometimes up on deck.

MISS GIRARD. Oh, you mean you've seen a lot of action?

PULVER. Well, I sure as hell haven't had much in the last year . . . Oh, battle action! Yeah . . . Yeah . . .

MISS GIRARD. Then you must have a lot of B.F. on here.

PULVER. Hunh?

MISS GIRARD. You know—battle fatigue?

PULVER. Yeah, we have a lot of that.

MISS GIRARD. Isn't that too bad! But they brief us to expect a lot of that out here. (*Pause*) Say, you haven't felt any yourself, have you?

PULVER. I guess I had a little touch of it . . . just a scratch.

MISS GIRARD. You know what you should do then? You should sleep more.

PULVER. Yeah.

MISS GIRARD. What's your job on the ship?

PULVER. Me? I'm . . . Executive Officer . . .

MISS GIRARD. But I thought that Executive Officers had to be at least a . . .

PULVER. Say, you know what I was thinking? That we should have that little old drink of Scotcharoo right now—

MISS GIRARD. I think so too. You know, I just love Scotch. I've just learned to drink it since I've joined the Army. But I'm already an absolute connoisseur.

PULVER (*dismayed*). Oh, you are?

MISS GIRARD. My twin sister has a nickname for me that's partly because I like a particular brand of Scotch . . . *(Giggles)* and partly because of a little personal thing about me that you wouldn't understand. Do you know what she calls me? "Red Label!" *(They both laugh)* What are you laughing at? You don't know what I'm talking about—and what's more you never will.

PULVER. What I was laughing about is —that's the kind I've got.

MISS GIRARD. Red Label! Oh, you're God's gift to a thirsty nursie! But where can we drink it? This is a Navy ship . . . isn't it?

PULVER. Oh, yeah, yeah, we'll have to be careful . . . We mustn't be seen . . . Lemme see, where shall we go . . . *(Considers)* I have it! We'll go back to my cabin. Nobody'd bother us there.

MISS GIRARD. Oh, you're what our outfit calls an operator. But you look harmless to me.

PULVER. Oh, I don't know about that.

MISS GIRARD. What's your first name— Harmless?

PULVER. Frank.

MISS GIRARD. Hello, Frank. Mine's Ann.

PULVER. Hello, Ann.

MISS GIRARD. All right. We'll have a little sip in your room.

PULVER. Right this way. *(They start off toward left passageway. Insigna, Mannion, Stefanowski, Wiley and Lindstrom enter from right, carrying the spy glass and binoculars. Stefanowski trips on hatch cover. Miss Girard and Pulver turn)* Hello, Mannion . . . Insigna . . . Stefanowski . . .

MANNION *(hoarsely)*. Hello, Mister Pulver . . .

PULVER. This is—Lieutenant Girard. *(The men murmur a greeting.)*

MISS GIRARD. What're you all doing with those glasses?

INSIGNA. We're . . . cleaning them. *(Suddenly pulls out shirt tail and begins lamely polishing spy glass. The others follow his example. More men crowd onto the stage.)*

PULVER. Well, don't work too hard . . . *(They turn to leave, but find themselves hemmed in by the men)* It's getting a little stuffy up here, I guess we better . . . *(Roberts enters, very excited, carrying a piece of paper and a small book)*

ROBERTS *(entering)*. Hey, Insigna . . . Mannion . . . get a load of this . . . Hey, Frank . . . *(He stops short, seeing Miss Girard)*

PULVER. Hiya, Doug boy! This is Ann Girard—Doug Roberts.

ROBERTS. How do you do?

MISS GIRARD *(beaming)*. How do you do? You're Frank's roommate. He's told me all about you.

ROBERTS. Really?

MISS GIRARD. What are you doing on this ship?

ROBERTS. Now there you've got me.

MISS GIRARD. No, I mean what's your job? Like Frank here is Executive Officer.

ROBERTS. Oh, I'm just the Laundry and Morale Officer.

MISS GIRARD. Why, that's wonderful— I've just been made Laundry and Morale Officer in our outfit!

PULVER. Oh, for Christ's sake! *(Mannion and Insigna begin an argument in whispers.)*

MISS GIRARD. Maybe we can get together and compare notes.

ROBERTS. I'd enjoy that very much.

PULVER *(attempting to usher Miss Girard off)*. Look, Doug. Will you excuse us? We're going down to have a little drink.

MISS GIRARD. Frank, I don't think that's very nice. Aren't you going to ask Doug to join us?

PULVER. Hell, no—I mean—he doesn't like Scotch.

ROBERTS. That's right, Miss Girard. I stay true to alcohol and orange juice.

PULVER. Come on, Ann . . .

MISS GIRARD. Wait a minute! A lot of the girls at the hospital swear by alcohol and orange juice. We ought to all get together and have a party in our new dayroom.

INSIGNA *(to Mannion)*. I bet you fifty bucks . . . *(Stefanowski moves Insigna and Mannion away from Miss Girard.)*

MISS GIRARD. Seems to be an argument.

PULVER. Yeah.

MISS GIRARD. Well, anyhow, we're fixing up a new dayroom. *(She looks offstage)* Look, you can see it! The hospital! And there's our new dormitory! That first window . . . *(Pulver takes glasses from Wiley to look at island.)*

INSIGNA *(to Mannion, his voice rising)*. All right, I got a *hundred* bucks says that's the one with the birthmark on her ass. *(There is a terrible silence. Miss Girard, after a moment, takes the glasses from Pulver and looks at the island. After a moment she lowers the glasses and speaks to Pulver.)*

MISS GIRARD. Frank, I won't be able to have lunch with you after all. Would you call the boat, please? *(To Roberts)* Good-bye, Doug. It was nice knowing you. You see, I promised the girls I'd help them hang some curtains and I think we'd better get started right away. Good-bye, everybody. *(To Mannion)* Oh, what's your name again?

INSIGNA. Mine?

MISS GIRARD. No. Yours.

MANNION. Mine? *(Miss Girard nods)* Mannion.

MISS GIRARD. Well, Mannion. I wouldn't take that bet if I were you because you'd lose a hundred bucks. *(To Pulver)* Come on, Harmless. *(She exits, followed by a bewildered Pulver. The men watch her off. Stefanowski throws his cap on the ground in anger)*

MANNION *(to Insigna)*. You loud-mouthed little bastard! Now you've gone and done it!

ROBERTS. Shut up! Insigna, how did you . . .

INSIGNA. We seen her taking a bath.

LINDSTROM. Through these glasses, Mister Roberts! We could see everything!

STEFANOWSKI *(furious)*. You heard what she said—she's going to hang some curtains.

MANNION. Yeah . . .

LINDSTROM. Gee, them nurses was pretty to look at. *(He sighs. There is a little tragic moment)*

ROBERTS. She's got a ten-minute boat ride. You've still got ten minutes.

WILEY. It wouldn't be any fun when you know you're going to be rushed.

LINDSTROM. This was the first real good day this ship has ever had. But it's all over now.

ROBERTS. Well, maybe you've got time then to listen to a little piece of news . . . *(He reads from the paper in his hands)* "When in all respects ready for sea, on or about 1600 today, the *AK 601* will proceed at ten knots via points X-Ray, Yolk and Zebra to Elysium Island, arriving there in seven days and reporting to the Port Director for cargo assignment." *(Emphatically)* "During its stay in Elysium, the ship will make maximum use of the recreational facilities of this port."
(The men look up in slow surprise and disbelief.)

STEFANOWSKI. But that means liberty!

LINDSTROM. That don't mean liberty, Mister Roberts?

ROBERTS. That's exactly what it means!

INSIGNA *(dazed)*. Somebody must've been drunk to send us to a Liberty Port! *(Roberts nods.)*

LINDSTROM. Has the Old Man seen them orders?

ROBERTS. He saw them before I did. *(Now the men are excited.)*

WILEY. Elysium! Where's that?

MANNION. Yeah! Where's that, Mister Roberts?
(The men crowd around Roberts as he sits on the hatch.)

ROBERTS *(reading from guide-book)*. "Elysium is the largest of the Limbo Islands. It is often referred to as the 'Polynesian Paradise.' Vanilla, sugar, cocoa, coffee, copra, mother-of-pearl, phosphates and rum are the chief exports."

INSIGNA. Rum! Did you hear that? *(He gooses Lindstrom.)*

LINDSTROM. Cut that out! *(Dolan gooses Insigna.)*

INSIGNA. Cut that out!

MANNION. Shut up!

ROBERTS. "Elysium City, its capital, is a beautiful metropolis of palm-lined boulevards, handsome public buildings and colorful stucco homes. Since 1900, its population has remained remarkably constant at approximately 30,000."

INSIGNA. I'll fix that! *(The men shout him down.)*

ROBERTS. That's all there is here. If you want the real dope on Elysium, there's one man on this ship who's been there.

STEFANOWSKI. Who's that?

MANNION. Who?

ROBERTS. Dowdy!
(The men run off wildly in every direction, shouting for Dowdy. The call is taken up all over the ship. Roberts listens to them happily, then notices a pair of binoculars. He looks toward the island for a moment, shrugs and is lifting the binoculars to his eyes as the lights fade out.)

SCENE FIVE

During the darkness we can hear the

exciting strains of Polynesian music.

The lights come up slowly through a porthole, casting a strong late-afternoon shaft of light onto motionless white figures. It is the enlisted men's compartment below decks. Except for a few not yet fully dressed, the men are all in white uniforms. The compartment is a crowded place with three-tiered bunks against the bulkheads. Most of the men are crowded around the porthole, downstage left. The men who cannot see are listening to the reports of Insigna, who is standing on a bench, looking out the porthole. The only man who is not galvanized with excitement is Dowdy, who sits calmly on a bench, downstage center, reading a magazine—True Detective.

———

GERHART *(to Insigna).* What do you see now, Sam?

INSIGNA. There's a lot of little boats up forward—up around the bow.

PAYNE. What kind of boats?

INSIGNA. They're little sort of canoes and they're all filled up with flowers and stuff. And there's women in them boats, paddling them . . .

PAYNE. Are they coming down this way?

INSIGNA. Naw. They're sticking around the bow.

STEFANOWSKI. Sam, where's that music coming from?

INSIGNA. There's a great big canoe up there and it's all filled with fat bastards with flowers in their ears playing little old git-tars . . .

SCHLEMMER. Why the hell can't we go up on deck? That's what I'd like to know!

LINDSTROM. When are we going ashore! That's what I'd like to know!

(Insigna suddenly laughs.)

PAYNE. What is it, Sam?

INSIGNA. I wish you could see this . . .

(Chief Johnson enters, looking knowingly at the men, shakes his head and addresses Dowdy.)

JOHNSON. Same story in here, eh? Every porthole this side of the ship!

DOWDY. They're going to wear themselves down to a nub before they ever get over there . . .

LINDSTROM *(takes coin from pocket and thrusts it at Insigna).* Hey, Sam, here's another penny. Make them kids down below dive for it.

INSIGNA *(impatiently).* All right! *(Throws coin out the port)* Heads up, you little bastards!

(The men watch tensely.)

LINDSTROM. Did he get that one too?

INSIGNA. Yeah . . . *(The men relax somewhat)*

LINDSTROM. Them kids don't ever miss!

INSIGNA. Hey, Dowdy—where's that little park again? Where you said all the good-looking women hang out?

DOWDY. For the last time—you see that big hill over there to the right . . .

INSIGNA. Yeah.

DOWDY. You see a big church . . . with a street running off to the left of it.

INSIGNA. Yeah.

DOWDY. Well, you go up that street three blocks . . .

INSIGNA. Yeah, I'm there.

DOWDY. That's the park.

INSIGNA. Well, I'll be damned . . .

LINDSTROM. Hey, show me that park, Sam?

(The other men gather around Insigna, asking to see the park.)

INSIGNA *(the authority now).* All right, you bastards, line up. I'll show you where the women hang out.

(The men form a line and each steps up to the porthole where Insigna points out the park.)

JOHNSON *(to Dowdy).* Smell that shoe polish? These guys have gone nuts!

DOWDY. I went down the ship's store the other day to buy a bar of soap and, do you know, they had been sold out for a week! No soap, no Listerine, no lilac shaving lotion—hell, they even sold eighteen jars of Mum! Now these bastards are bootlegging it! They're gettin' ten bucks for a used jar of Mum!

(Reber, wearing the messenger's belt, enters. The men greet him excitedly.)

STEFANOWSKI. What's the word on liberty, Reber? Is the Old Man still asleep?

MANNION. Yeah, what's the word?

REBER. I just peeked in on him. He's snoring like a baby.

GERHART. Jeez, how any guy can sleep at a time like this!

INSIGNA. I'll get him up! I'm going up there and tap on his door! *(Picks up a heavy lead pipe)*

DOWDY *(grabbing Insigna).* Like hell you are! You're going to stay right here and pray. You're going to pray that he wakes up feeling good and decides he's kept you guys sweating long enough!

MANNION. That's telling the little crud! *(Insigna and Mannion threaten each other.)*

REBER. Hey, Lindstrom. I got good news for you. You can take them whites off.

LINDSTROM. I ain't got the duty *tonight?*

REBER. That's right. You and Mister Roberts got the duty tonight—the twelve to four watch. The Exec just posted the list . . . *(He is interrupted by the sound of static on the squawk box. Instantly all men turn toward it eagerly)*

DOLAN *(on squawk box).* Now hear this! Now hear this!

WILEY. Here we go! Here we go!

STEFANOWSKI *(imitating the squawk box).* Liberty . . . will com-mence . . . immediately!

GERHART. Quiet!

DOLAN *(on squawk box).* Now hear this! The Captain's messenger will report to the Captain's cabin on the double!

REBER. My God! He's awake! *(He runs out)*

PAYNE. Won't be long now!

WILEY. Get going, Mannion! Get into those whites! We're going to be the first ones over the side!

MANNION. Hell, yes! Give me a hand! *(Now there is a general frenzy of preparation—the men put the last-minute touches to shoes, hair, uniforms.)*

GERHART *(singing to the tune of "California, Here I Come").*

Ee-liss-*ee*-um, here I come! . . . Ta-ta-ta-ta-*ta*-da-tah . . .

SCHLEMMER *(to Gerhart).* Watch where you're going! You stepped on my shine!

INSIGNA. Schlemmer . . . Stef . . . Gerhart . . . come here! *(These men gather around him. Lindstrom remains unhappily alone)* Now listen! Stefanowski and me are going to work alone for the first hour and a half! But if you pick up something first . . . *(Produces small map from his pocket)* We'll be working up and down this street here . . . *(They study the map. Now the squawk box is clicked on again. All the men stand rigid, listening.)*

DOLAN *(on squawk box).* Now hear this! Now hear this! The Captain is now going to make a personal announcement. *(Sound of squawk-box switch.)*

CAPTAIN *(on squawk box).* Goddammit, how does this thing work? *(Sound of squawk-box switch again)* This is the Captain speaking. I just woke up from a little nap and I got a surprise. I found out there were men on this ship who were expecting liberty. *(At this point, the lights start dimming until the entire scene is blacked out. The speech continues throughout the darkness. Under the Captain's speech the strains of Polynesian music can be heard)* Now I don't know how such a rumor got around, but I'd like to clear it up right now. You see, it's like this. Because of cargo requirements and security conditions which has just come to my personal attention there will be no liberty as long as we're in this here port. And one other thing—as long as we're here, no man will wear white uniforms. Now I would like to repeat for the benefit of complete understanding and clearness, NO LIBERTY. That is all.

SCENE SIX

The lights come up on the Captain's cabin. Against the left bulkhead is a settee. A chair is placed center. Up center is the only door. The Captain is seated behind his desk, holding a watch in one hand and the microphone in the other, in an attitude of waiting. Just over the desk and against the right bulkhead is a ship's intercommunication board. There is a wall-safe in the right bulkhead. After a moment there is a knock on the door.

———

CAPTAIN. Come in, Mister Roberts. *(As Roberts enters, the Captain puts the microphone on the desk)* Thirty-eight seconds. Pretty good time! You see, I been expectin' you ever since I made my little announcement.

ROBERTS. Well, as long as you're expecting me, what about it—when does this crew get liberty?

CAPTAIN. Well, in the first place, just kinda hold your tongue. And in the second place, sit down.

ROBERTS. There's no time to sit down. When are you going to let this crew go ashore?

CAPTAIN. I'm not. This wasn't my idea—coming to a Liberty Port. One of my officers arranged it with a certain Port Director—gave him a bottle of Scotch whiskey—compliments of the Captain. And the Port Director was kind enough to send me a little thank-you note along with our orders. Sit down, Mister Roberts. *(Roberts sits)* Don't worry about it. I'm not going to make trouble about that wasted bottle of Scotch. I'll admit I was a little pre-voked about not being consulted. Then I got to thinking maybe we oughta come to this port anyway so's you and me could have a little talk.

ROBERTS. You can make all the trouble you want, Captain, but let's quit wasting time. Don't you hear that music? Don't you know it's tearing those guys apart? They're breakable, Captain! I promise you!

CAPTAIN. That's enough! I've had enough of your fancy educated talk. *(Rises, goes to Roberts)* Now you listen to me. I got two things I want to show you. *(He unlocks the wall-safe, opens it and takes out a commander's cap with gold braid "scrambled eggs" on the visor)* You see that? That's the cap of a full commander. I'm gonna wear that cap some day and you're going to help me. *(Replaces cap in safe, goes back to Roberts)* I guess there's no harm in telling you that you helped me get that palm tree by working cargo. Now don't let this go to your head, but when Admiral Finchley gave me that award, he said, "You got a good Cargo Officer, Morton; keep him at it, you're going places." So I went out and bought that hat. There's nothing gonna stand between me and that hat—certainly not you. Now last week you wrote a letter that said "disharmony aboard this ship." I told you there wasn't going to be any more letters. But what do I find on my desk this morning . . . *(Taking letter from desk)* Another one. It says "friction between myself and the Commanding Officer." That ain't gonna go in, Mister.

ROBERTS. How are you going to ˙top it, Captain?

CAPTAIN. I ain't, you are. *(Goes to his chair and sits)* Just how much do you want this crew to have a liberty anyhow? Enough to stop this "disharmony"? To stop this "friction"? *(Leans forward)* Enough to get out of the habit of writing letters ever? Because that's the only way this crew is ever gonna get ashore. *(Leans back)* Well, we've had our little talk. What do you say?

ROBERTS *(after a moment)*. How did you get in the Navy? How did you get on our side? You're what I joined to fight *against*. You ignorant, arrogant, ambitious . . . *(Rises)* jackass! Keeping a hundred and sixty-seven men in prison because you got a palm tree for the work *they* did. I don't know which I hate worse—you or that other malignant growth that stands outside your door!

CAPTAIN. Why, you goddamn . . .

ROBERTS. How did you ever get command of a ship? I realize that in wartime they have to scrape the bottom of the barrel, but where the hell did they ever scrape you up?

CAPTAIN *(shouting)*. There's just one thing left for you, by God—a general court-martial.

ROBERTS. That suits me fine. Court-martial me!

CAPTAIN. By God, you've got it!

ROBERTS. I'm asking for it!

CAPTAIN. You don't have to ask for it, you've got it now!

ROBERTS. If I can't get transferred off here, I'll get court-martialed off! I'm fed up! But you'll need a witness. Send for your messenger. He's down below. I'll say it all again in front of him. *(Pauses)* Go on, call in Reber! *(The Captain doesn't move)* Go on, call him. *(Still the Captain doesn't move)* Do you want me to call him?

CAPTAIN. No. *(He walks upstage, then turns to Roberts)* I think you're a pretty smart boy. I may not talk very good, Mister, but I know how to take care of smart boys. Let me tell you something. Let me tell you a little secret. I hate your guts, you college son-of-a-bitch! You think you're better than I am! You think you're better because you've had everything handed to you! Let me tell you something, Mister—I've worked since I was ten years old, and all my life I've known you superior bastards. I knew you people when I was a kid in Boston and I worked in eating-places and you ordered me around. . . . "Oh, bus-boy! My friend here seems to have thrown up on the table. Clean it up, please." I started going to sea as a steward and I worked for you then . . . "Steward, take my magazine out to the deck chair!" . . . "Steward, I don't like your looks. Please keep out of my way as much as possible!" Well, I took that crap! I took that for years from pimple-faced bastards who weren't good enough to wipe my nose! And now I don't have to take it any more! There's a war on, by God, and I'm the Captain and you can wipe my nose! The worst thing I can do to you is to keep you on this ship! And that's where you're going to stay! Now get out of here! *(He goes to his chair and sits. Roberts moves slowly toward the door. He hears the music, goes to the porthole and listens. Then he turns to the Captain.)*

ROBERTS. Can't you hear that music, Captain?

CAPTAIN. Yeah, I hear it. *(Busies himself at desk, ignoring Roberts)*

ROBERTS. Don't you know those guys below can hear it too? Oh, my God.

CAPTAIN. Get out of here.

(After a moment, Roberts turns from the porthole and slumps against the Captain's locker. His face is strained.)

ROBERTS. What do you want for liberty, Captain?

CAPTAIN. I want plenty. You're through writin' letters—ever.

ROBERTS. Okay.

CAPTAIN. That's not all. You're through givin' me trouble. You're through talkin' back to me in front of the crew. You ain't ever gonna open your mouth—except in civil answer. *(Roberts doesn't answer)* Mister Roberts, you know that if you don't take my terms I'll let you go out that door and that's the end of any hope for liberty.

ROBERTS. Is that all, Captain?

CAPTAIN. No. Anyone know you're in here?

ROBERTS. No one.

CAPTAIN. Then you won't go blabbin' about this to anyone ever. It might not sound so good. And besides I don't want you to take credit for gettin' this crew ashore.

ROBERTS. Do you think I'm doing this for credit? Do you think I'd *let* anyone know about this?

CAPTAIN. I gotta be sure.

ROBERTS. You've got my word, that's all.

CAPTAIN *(after a pause)*. Your word. Yes, you college fellas make a big show about keeping your word.

ROBERTS. How about it, Captain. Is it a deal?

CAPTAIN. Yeah. *(Roberts picks up the microphone, turns on a switch and thrusts the microphone at the Captain)* Now hear

this. This is the Captain speaking. I've got some further word on security conditions in this port and so it gives me great pleasure to tell you that liberty, for the star board section . . .

ROBERTS *(covering the microphone with his hand)*. For the entire crew, goddammit.

CAPTAIN. Correction: Liberty for the entire crew will commence immediately. *(Roberts turns off the microphone. After a moment we hear the shouts of the crew. Roberts goes up to porthole. The Captain leans back on his chair. A song, "Roll Me Over," is started by someone and is soon taken up by the whole crew.)*

ROBERTS *(looking out of the porthole. He is excited and happy)*. Listen to those crazy bastards. Listen to them.

(The crew continues to sing with increasing volume. Now the words can be distinguished:

> Roll me over in the clover,
> Roll me over, lay me down
> And do it again.)

CURTAIN

ACT TWO

SCENE ONE

The curtain rises on the main set. It is now 3:45 A.M. The night is pitch-black, but we can see because of a light over the head of the gangway, where a temporary desk has been rigged; a large ship's logbook lies open on this desk. A small table on which are hospital supplies is at left of the door.

At rise, Roberts, Doc, Lindstrom, Johnson and four seamen are discovered onstage. Lindstrom, in web belt, is writing in the log. Roberts is standing with a pile of yellow slips in his hand; he wears the side-arms of the Officer of the Deck. Johnson and a seaman are standing near the hatchway, holding the inert body of another seaman, who has court plaster on his face. Two more seamen lie on the hatch cover where Doc is kneeling, bandaging one of them. As the curtain rises we hear the sound of a siren off right. Everyone turns and looks—that is, everyone who is conscious.

LINDSTROM. Here's another batch, Mister

ROBERTS—a whole paddy wagon full. And this one's an Army paddy wagon.

ROBERTS. We haven't filed away this batch yet. (*To Doc*) Hurry up, Doc.

JOHNSON (*to Doc, indicating body he is carrying*). Where do we put number twenty-three here, Doc? Sick bay or what?

DOC. Just put him to bed. His condition's only critical.

JOHNSON (*carrying seaman off*). They just roll out of their bunks, Doc. Now I'm stacking 'em on the deck down there—I'm on the third layer already.

VOICE (*offstage*). Okay, Lieutenant! All set down here! You ready?

ROBERTS (*calling offstage—and giving hand signal*). Okay! (*To Doc*) Here they come, Doc! Heads up!

SHORE PATROLMAN'S VOICE (*offstage*). Lieutenant!

ROBERTS. Oh, not you again!

SHORE PATROLMAN'S VOICE (*offstage*). I got a bunch of real beauties for you this time.

ROBERTS (*calling offstage*). Can they walk?

SHORE PATROLMAN'S VOICE (*offstage*). Just barely!

ROBERTS (*calling*). Then send 'em up.

LINDSTROM. Man, oh, man, what a liberty! We got the record now, Mister Roberts! This makes the seventh batch since we went on watch!

(*The sound of a cargo winch and a voice offstage singing the Army Air Corps song are heard. Roberts is looking offstage.*)

ROBERTS (*signaling*). Looks like a real haul this time. Schlemmer, look out!

LINDSTROM. Schlemmer, look out!

ROBERTS. Okay, Doc. (*Doc and Roberts lift the two bodies from the hatch cover and deposit them farther upstage. At this moment, the cargo net appears, loaded with bodies in once-white uniforms and leis. Riding on top of the net is Schlemmer, wearing a lei and singing "Off We Go into the Wild Blue Yonder"*) Let her in easy . . .

LINDSTROM. Let her in easy . . .

(*The net is lowered onto the hatch cover and Lindstrom detaches it from the hook. All start untangling bodies.*)

ROBERTS. Well, they're peaceful anyhow. (*At this point a Shore Patrolman enters from the gangway.*)

SHORE PATROLMAN (*handing Roberts a sheaf of yellow slips*). For your collection.

(*Points down gangway*) Take a look at them.

ROBERTS (*looks offstage*). My God, what did they do?

SHORE PATROLMAN. They done all right, Lieutenant. Six of them busted into a formal dance and took on a hundred and twenty-eight Army bastards. (*Calls off*) All right, let's go!

(*Stefanowski, Reber, Wiley, Payne and Mannion, with his arm around Insigna, straggle on—a frightening sight—followed by a Military Policeman. Insigna's uniform is torn to shreds. Mannion is clad in a little diaper of crepe paper. All have bloody faces and uniforms. A few bear souvenirs —a Japanese lantern, leis, Army caps, a Shore Patrol band, etc. They throw perfunctory salutes to the colors, then murmur a greeting to Roberts.*)

MILITARY POLICEMAN. Duty Officer?

ROBERTS. That's right.

MILITARY POLICEMAN (*salutes*). Colonel Middleton presents his compliments to the Captain and wishes him to know that these men made a shambles out of the Colonel's testimonial dinner-dance.

ROBERTS. Is this true, Insigna?

INSIGNA. That's right, Mister Roberts. A shambles. (*To Mannion*) Ain't that right, Killer?

MANNION. That's right, Mister Roberts.

ROBERTS. You men crashed a dance for Army personnel?

MANNION. Yes, sir! And they made us feel unwelcome! (*To Insigna*) Didn't they, Slugger?

ROBERTS. Oh, they started a fight, eh?

WILEY. No, sir! *We* started it!

STEFANOWSKI. We finished it too! (*To Military Policeman*) Tell Mister Roberts how many of you Army bastards are in the hospital.

MANNION. Go on.

MILITARY POLICEMAN. Thirty-eight soldiers of the United States Army have been hospitalized. And the Colonel himself has a very bad bruise on his left shin!

PAYNE. *I* did that, Mister Roberts.

MILITARY POLICEMAN. And that isn't all, Lieutenant. There were young ladies present—fifty of them. Colonel Middleton had been lining them up for a month, from the finest families of Elysium. And he had personally guaranteed their safety this evening. Well, sir . . .

ROBERTS. Well?

MILITARY POLICEMAN. Two of those young ladies got somewhat mauled, one actually got a black eye, six of them got their clothes torn off and then went screaming off into the night and they haven't been heard from since. What are you going to do about it, Lieutenant?

ROBERTS. Well, I'm due to get relieved here in fifteen minutes—I'll be glad to lead a search party.

MILITARY POLICEMAN. No, sir. The Army's taking care of that end. The Colonel will want to know what punishment you're going to give these men.

ROBERTS. Tell the Colonel that I'm sure our Captain will think of something.

MILITARY POLICEMAN. But . . .

ROBERTS. That's all, Sergeant.

MILITARY POLICEMAN (*salutes*). Thank you, sir. (*He goes off*)

SHORE PATROLMAN. Lieutenant, I been pretty sore at your guys up till now—we had to put on ten extra Shore Patrolmen on account of this ship. But if you knew Colonel "Chicken" Middleton—well, I'd be willing to do this every night. (*To the men*) So long, fellows!

((*The men call "So long." Shore Patrolman exits, saluting Roberts and quarterdeck.*)

ROBERTS. Well, what've you got to say for yourselves?

STEFANOWSKI (*after a moment*). Okay if we go ashore again, Mister Roberts?

ROBERTS (*to Lindstrom*) Is this the first time for these guys?

LINDSTROM (*showing log*). Yes, sir, they got a clean record—they only been brought back once.

ROBERTS (*to Doc*). What do you say, Doc?

(*The men turn eagerly to Doc.*)

DOC. Anybody got a fractured skull?

MEN. No.

DOC. Okay, you pass the physical.

ROBERTS. Go down and take a shower first and get into some clothes.

(*The men rush to the hatchway.*)

STEFANOWSKI. We still got time to get back to that dance!

(*As they descend hatchway, Insigna pulls crepe paper from around Mannion as he is halfway down the hatchway.*)

ROBERTS. How you feeling, Doc?

DOC. These alcohol fumes are giving me a cheap drunk—otherwise pretty routine. When do you get relieved, Doug? (*Takes box from table and gestures for men to remove table. They carry it off*)

ROBERTS. Soon as Carney gets back from the island. Any minute now.

DOC. What are you grinning like a skunk for?

ROBERTS. Nothing. I always grin like a skunk. What have you got in the box?

DOC (*descending hatchway—holding up small packet he has taken from the box*). Little favors from the Doc. I'm going to put one in each man's hand and when he wakes up he'll find pinned to his shirt full instructions for its use. I think it'll save me a lot of work later on. (*His head disappears*)

LINDSTROM. I wish Gerhart would get back here and relieve me. I've got to get over to that island before it runs out of women.

(*Dolan enters from gangway.*)

DOLAN. Howdy, Mister Roberts! I'm drunk as a goat! (*Pulls a goat aboard*) Show him how drunk I am. Mister Roberts, when I first saw her she was eatin', and you know, she just eat her way into my heart. She was eatin' a little old palm tree and I thought to myself, our ship needs a mascot. (*He points out palm tree to goat*) There you are, kid. Chow!

(*Roberts blocks his way.*)

ROBERTS. Wait a minute . . . wait a minute. What's her name?

DOLAN. I don't know, sir.

ROBERTS. She's got a name plate.

DOLAN. Oh, so she has . . . her name is . . . (*Reads from tag on goat's collar*) . . . Property Of.

ROBERTS. What's her last name?

DOLAN. Her last name . . . (*Reads again*) Rear Admiral Wentworth.

(*Approaching siren is heard offstage.*)

ROBERTS. Okay, Dolan, hit the sack. I'll take care of her.

DOLAN. Okay, Mister Roberts. (*Descends hatchway*) See that she gets a good square meal. (*He points to the Captain's palm tree and winks, then disappears. Gerhart enters from gangway*)

LINDSTROM. Gerhart! (*He frantically removes his web belt and shoves it at Gerhart*)

GERHART. Okay, okay—you're relieved.

LINDSTROM (*tosses a fast salute to Roberts and says in one breath*). Requestpermissiontogoashore! (*He hurries down gangway*)

(Shore Patrolman enters from gangway.)

SHORE PATROLMAN. Lieutenant, has one of your men turned up with a . . . *(Sees goat and takes leash)* Oh, thanks. *(To goat)* Come on, come on, your papa over there is worried about you. *(Pulls goat down gangway)*

GERHART. Where's your relief, Mister Roberts?

ROBERTS *(sitting on hatch)*. He'll be along any minute. How was your liberty, Gerhart?

(Gerhart grins. So does Roberts. Doc enters from hatchway.)

DOC. What are you looking so cocky about anyway?

ROBERTS. Am I looking cocky? Maybe it's because for the first time since I've been on this ship, I'm seeing a crew.

DOC. What do you think you've been living with all this time?

ROBERTS. Just a hundred and sixty-seven separate guys. There's a big difference, Doc. Now these guys are bound together. You saw Insigna and Mannion. Doc, I think these guys are strong enough now to take all the miserable, endless days ahead of us. I only hope I'm strong enough.

DOC. Doug, tomorrow you and I are going over there and take advantage of the groundwork that's been laid tonight. You and I are going to have ourselves a liberty. *(Pulver enters slowly from the gangway and walks across the stage. Doc calls Roberts' attention to him.)*

ROBERTS. Hello, Frank. How was your liberty?

(Pulver half turns, shrugs and holds up seven fingers, then exits. A Shore Patrol Officer enters from the gangway and calls offstage. He speaks with a Southern accent.)

SHORE PATROL OFFICER. That's your post and that's your post. You know what to do. *(He salutes the quarter-deck, then Roberts)* Officer of the Deck? *(Roberts nods. The Shore Patrol Officer hesitates a moment)* I hope you don't mind but I've stationed two of my men at the foot of the gangway. I'm sorry but this ship is restricted for the rest of its stay in Elysium. Your Captain is to report to the Island Commander at seven o'clock this morning. I'd recommend that he's there on time. The Admiral's a pretty tough cookie when he's mad, and he's madder now than I've ever seen him.

ROBERTS. What in particular did this?

SHORE PATROL LIEUTENANT. A little while ago six men from your ship broke into the home of the French Consul and started throwing things through the plate-glass living-room window. We found some of the things on the lawn: a large world globe, a small love seat, a lot of books and a bust of Balzac—the French writer. We also found an Army private first class who was unconscious at the time. He claims they threw him too.

ROBERTS. Through the window?

SHORE PATROL LIEUTENANT. That's right! It seems he took them there for a little joke. He didn't tell them it was the Consul's house; he said it was a—what we call in Alabama—a cat-house. *(Roberts and Doc nod)* Be sure that your Captain is there at seven o'clock sharp. If it makes you feel any better, Admiral Wentworth says this is the worst ship he's ever seen in his entire naval career. *(Laughs, then salutes)* Good night, Lieutenant.

ROBERTS *(returning salute)*. Good night. *(The Shore Patrol Lieutenant exits down gangway—saluting the quarter-deck.)*

GERHART. Well, there goes the liberty. That was sure a wham-bam-thank you, ma'am!

DOC. Good night. *(He exits through left passageway)*

GERHART. But, by God, it was worth it. That liberty was worth anything!

ROBERTS. I think you're right, Gerhart.

GERHART. Hunh?

ROBERTS. I think you're right.

GERHART. Yeah.

(He smiles. Roberts looks over the log. Gerhart whistles softly to himself "Roll Me Over" as the lights slowly fade out.)

During the darkness we hear Johnson shouting:

JOHNSON. All right, fall in for muster. Form two ranks. And pipe down.

SCENE TWO

The lights come up, revealing the deck. Morning sunlight. A group of men, right and left, in orderly formation. They are talking.

———

JOHNSON. 'Ten-shun!

(The command is relayed through the ship. The Captain enters from his cabin, followed by Roberts. The Captain steps up on the hatch cover. Roberts starts to fall in with the men.)

CAPTAIN *(calling to Roberts and pointing to a place beside himself on hatch cover)*. Over here, Roberts. *(Roberts takes his place left of Captain)* We're being kicked out of this port. I had a feeling this liberty was a bad idea. That's why we'll never have one again. We're going to erase this blot from my record if we have to work twenty-four hours a day. We're going to move even more cargo than we've moved before. And if there ain't enough cargo work, Mister Roberts here is gonna find some. Isn't that right, Mister Roberts? *(Roberts doesn't answer)* Isn't that right, Mister Roberts?

ROBERTS. Yes, sir.

CAPTAIN. I'm appointing Mister Roberts here and now to see that you men toe the line. And I can't think of a more honorable man for the job. He's a man who keeps his word no matter what. *(Turns to Roberts)* Now, Roberts, if you do a good job—and if the Admiral begins to smile on us again—there might be something in it for you. What would you say if that little silver bar on your collar got a twin brother some day? *(Roberts is startled. The Captain calls offstage)* Officer of the Deck!

OFFSTAGE VOICE. Yes, sir!

CAPTAIN *(to Roberts)*. You wasn't expectin' that, was you? *(Calling offstage)* Get ready to sail!

OFFSTAGE VOICE. Aye-aye, sir!

CAPTAIN. You men are dismissed!

JOHNSON. Fall out!

(The men fall out. Some exit. A little group forms downstage.)

CAPTAIN. Wait a minute! Wait a minute! Roberts, take these men here back aft to handle lines. And see that they work up a sweat. *(Roberts and men look at him)* Did you hear me, Roberts? I gave you an order!

ROBERTS *(carefully)*. Yes, Captain. I heard you.

CAPTAIN. How do you answer when I give an order?

ROBERTS *(after a pause)*. Aye-aye, sir.

CAPTAIN. That's more like it . . . that's more like it! *(He exits into his cabin)*

STEFANOWSKI. What'd he mean, Mister Roberts?

ROBERTS. I don't know. Just what he said, I guess.

GERHART. What'd you let him give you all that guff for?

DOLAN *(stepping up on hatch, carrying a file folder)*. Because he's tired, that's why. He had the mid-watch last night. Your tail'd be dragging too if you had to handle all them customers.

ROBERTS. Come on. Let's get going . . .

DOLAN. Wait a minute, Mister Roberts. Something come for you in the mail this morning—a little love letter from the Bureau. *(Pulls out paper from file folder)* Get a load of this! *(Reads)* "To All Ships and Stations: Heightened war offensive has created urgent need aboard combat ships for experienced officers. *(He clicks his teeth and winks at Roberts)* All commanding officers are hereby directed to forward with their endorsements all applications for transfer from officers with twenty-four months' sea duty." *(Roberts grabs the directive and reads it. Dolan looks at Roberts and smiles)* You got twenty-nine months—you're the only officer aboard that has. Mister Roberts, the Old Man is hanging on the ropes from the working-over the Admiral give him. All he needs to flatten him is one more little jab. And here it is. Your letter. I typed it up. *(He pulls out triplicate letter from file cover—then a fountain pen which he offers to Roberts)* Sign it and I'll take it in—

MANNION. Go on, sign it, Mister Roberts. He'll take off like a bird.

DOLAN. What're you waitin' for, Mister Roberts?

ROBERTS *(handing directive back to Dolan)*. I'll want to look it over first, Dolan. Come on, let's get going.

DOLAN. There's nothing to look over. This is the same letter we wrote yesterday—only quoting this new directive.

ROBERTS. Look, Dolan, I'm tired. And I told you I wanted—

DOLAN. You ain't too tired to sign your name!

ROBERTS *(sharply)*. Take it easy, Dolan. I'm not going to sign it. So take it easy! *(Turns to exit right, finds himself blocked by crew)* Did you hear me? Let's get going! *(Exits)*

STEFANOWSKI. What the hell's come over him?

(*They look at one another.*)

INSIGNA. Aye-aye, sir—for Christ's sake!

MANNION (*after a moment*). Come on. Let's get going.

DOLAN (*bitterly*). "Take it easy . . . take it easy!"

(*The men start to move off slowly as the lights fade out.*)

During the darkness we hear a radio. There is considerable static.

AMERICAN BROADCASTER. Still, of course, we have no official word from the Headquarters of the Supreme Allied Command in Europe. I repeat, there is no official announcement yet. The report that the war in Europe has ended has come from only one correspondent. It has not been confirmed by other correspondents or by SHAEF headquarters. But here is one highly intriguing fact—that report has not been denied either in Washington or in SHAEF headquarters in Europe. IT HAS NOT BEEN DENIED. Right now in those places the newsmen are crowded, waiting to flash to the world the announcement of V-E Day.

SCENE THREE

The lights come up on Roberts' and Pulver's cabin. Doc, at the desk, and Pulver, up in his bunk, are listening to the radio.

———

PULVER. Turn that damn thing off, Doc. Has Doug ever said anything to you about wanting a promotion?

DOC. Of course not. I doubt if he's even conscious of what rank he is.

PULVER. You can say that again!

DOC. I doubt if he's even conscious of what rank he is.

PULVER. That's what I said. He doesn't even think about a promotion. The only thing he thinks about is the war news—up in the radio shack two weeks now—all day long—listening with a headset, reading all the bulletins . . . Anyone who says he's bucking for another stripe is a dirty liar.

DOC. Who says he is, Frank?

PULVER. Insigna, Mannion and some of the other guys. I heard them talking outside the porthole. They were talking loud on purpose so I could hear them—they must've guessed I was lying here on my bunk. What's happened to Doug anyway, Doc?

DOC. How would I know! He's spoken about ten words to me in as many days. But I'm damn well going to find out.

PULVER. He won't talk, Doc. This morning I followed him all around the room while he was shaving. I begged him to talk to me. I says, "You're a fellow who needs a friend and here I am." And I says, "What's all this trouble you're having with the crew? You tell me and I'll fix it up like that." And then I give him some real good advice—I says, "Keep your chin up," and things like that. And then do you know what he did? He walked out of the room just as though I wasn't here.

(*There is a knock on the door.*)

DOC. Come in.

(*Dowdy enters.*)

DOWDY. Doc, Mister Pulver—could we see you officers a minute?

DOC. Sure. (*Gerhart and Lindstrom enter, closing the door*) What is it?

DOWDY. Tell them what happened, Gerhart.

GERHART. Well, sir, I sure don't like to say this but . . . Mister Roberts just put Dolan on report.

LINDSTROM. Me and Gerhart seen him.

PULVER. On report!

GERHART. Yes, sir. Tomorrow morning Dolan has to go up before the Captain—on account of Mister Roberts.

LINDSTROM. On account of Mister Roberts.

GERHART. And we was wondering if you officers could get him to take Dolan off report before . . . well, before—

DOC. Before what, Gerhart?

GERHART. Well, you see, the guys are all down in the compartment, talking about it. And they're saying some pretty rough things about Mister Roberts. Nobody just ever expected to see him put a man on report and . . .

LINDSTROM. He ain't gonna turn out to be like an officer, is he, Doc?

DOWDY. Lindstrom . . .

LINDSTROM. Oh, I didn't mean you, Doc . . . or even you, Mister Pulver!

DOC. That's all right, Lindstrom. What was this trouble with Dolan?

DOWDY. This letter business again!

GERHART. Yes, sir. Dolan was just kiddin' him about not sending in any more letters. And all of a sudden Mister Roberts turned just white and yelled, "Shut up, Dolan. Shut your goddamn mouth. I've had enough." And Dolan naturally got snotty back at him and Mister Roberts put him right on report.

LINDSTROM. Right on report.

(Roberts enters.)

PULVER. Hello, Doug boy. Aren't you listening to the war news?

DOWDY. All right, Doctor. We'll get that medical store room cleaned out tomorrow. *(Dowdy, Gerhart and Lindstrom leave.)*

PULVER. We thought you were up in the radio shack.

ROBERTS *(to Pulver)*. Don't you want to go down to the wardroom and have a cup of coffee?

PULVER *(jumping down from bunk)*. Sure. I'll go with you.

ROBERTS. I don't want any. Why don't you go ahead?

PULVER. Nah. *(He sits back on bunk. There is another little pause)*

ROBERTS. Will you go on out anyway? I want to talk to Doc.

PULVER *(rising and crossing to door)*. All right, I will. I'm going for a cup of coffee. *(Stops, turns and gets cup from top of locker)* No! I'm going up to the radio shack. You aren't the only one interested in the war news. *(He exits)*

ROBERTS *(with emotion)*. Doc, transfer me, will you? *(Doc looks at him)* Transfer me to the hospital on this next island! You can do it. You don't need the Captain's approval! Just put me ashore for examination—say there's something wrong with my eyes or my feet or my head, for Christ's sake! You can trump up something!

DOC. What good would that do?

ROBERTS. Plenty! I could lie around that hospital for a couple of weeks. The ship would have sailed—I'd have missed it! I'd be off this ship. Will you do it, Doc?

DOC. Doug, why did you put Dolan on report just now?

ROBERTS *(angrily)*. I gave him an order and he didn't carry it out fast enough to suit me. *(Glares at Doc, who just studies him. Roberts rises and paces right)* No, that's not true. It was the war. I just heard the news. The war was ending and

I couldn't get to it and there was Dolan giving me guff about something—and all of a sudden I hated him. I hated all of them. I was sick of the sullen bastards staring at me as though I'd sold them down the river or something. If they think I'm bucking for a promotion—if they're stupid enough to think I'd walk ten feet across the room to get anything from that Captain, then I'm through with the whole damn ungrateful mob!

DOC. Does this crew owe you something?

ROBERTS. What the hell do you mean by that?

DOC. You talk as if they did.

(Roberts rises and crosses to bunk.)

ROBERTS *(quietly)*. That's exactly how I'm talking. I didn't realize it but that's exactly the way I've been feeling. Oh, Jesus, that shows you how far gone I am, Doc. I've been taking something out on them. I've been blaming them for something that . . .

DOC. What, Doug? Something what? You've made some sort of an agreement with the Captain, haven't you, Doug!

ROBERTS *(turns)*. Agreement? I don't know what you mean. Will you transfer me, Doc?

DOC. Not a chance, Doug. I could never get away with it—you know that.

ROBERTS. Oh, my God!

PULVER *(offstage)*. Doug! Doc! *(Entering)* Listen to the radio, you uninformed bastards! Turn it up!

(Roberts reaches over and turns up the radio. The excited voice of an announcer can be heard.)

ANNOUNCER. . . . this broadcast to bring you a special news flash! The war is over in Europe! THE WAR IS OVER IN EUROPE! *(Roberts grasps Doc's arm in excitement)* Germany has surrendered unconditionally to the Allied Armies. The surrender was signed in a schoolhouse in the city of Rheims . . .

(Roberts stands staring. Doc turns off the radio. For a moment there is silence, then:)

DOC. I would remind you that there's still a minor skirmish here in the Pacific.

ROBERTS. I'll miss that one too. But to hell with me. This is the greatest day in the world. We're going to celebrate. How about it, Frank?

PULVER. Yeah, Doug. We've got to celebrate!

DOC (*starting to pull alcohol from waste basket*). What'll it be—alcohol and orange juice or orange juice and alcohol?

ROBERTS. No, that's not good enough.

PULVER. Hell, no, Doc! (*He looks expectantly at Roberts*)

ROBERTS. We've got to think of something that'll lift this ship right out of the water and turn it around the other way. (*Pulver suddenly rises to his feet.*)

PULVER (*shouting*). Doug! Oh, my God, why didn't I think of this before. Doug! Doc! You're going to blow your tops when you hear the idea I got! Oh, Jesus, what a wonderful idea! It's the only thing to do. It's the only thing in the whole world to do! That's all! Doug, you said I never had any ideas. You said I never finished anything I started. Well, you're wrong—tonight you're wrong! I thought of something and I finished it. I was going to save it for your birthday, but I'm going to give it to you tonight, because we gotta celebrate . . .

ROBERTS (*waves his hands in Pulver's face for attention*). Wait a minute, Frank! What is it?

PULVER. A firecracker, by God. (*He reaches under his mattress and pulls out a large, wobbly firecracker which has been painted red*) We're gonna throw a firecracker under the Old Man's bunk. Bam-bam-bam! Wake up, you old son-of-a-bitch, IT'S V-E DAY!

ROBERTS (*rising*). Frank!

PULVER. Look at her, Doc. Ain't it a beauty? Ain't that the greatest hand-made, hand-painted, hand-packed firecracker you ever saw?

ROBERTS (*smiling and taking firecracker*). Yes, Frank. That's the most beautiful firecracker I ever saw in my life. But will it work?

PULVER. Sure it'll work. At least, I think so.

ROBERTS. Haven't you tested it? It's got to work, Frank, it's just got to work!

PULVER. I'll tell you what I'll do. I'll take it down to the laundry and test it—that's my laboratory, the laundry. I got all the fixings down there—powder, fuses, everything, all hid behind the soapflakes. And if this one works, I can make another one in two minutes.

ROBERTS. Okay, Frank. Take off. We'll wait for you here. (*Pulver starts off*) Be sure you got enough to make it loud. What'd you use for powder?

PULVER. Loud! This ain't a popgun. This is a firecracker. I used fulminate of mercury. I'll be right back. (*He runs out*)

ROBERTS. Fulminate of mercury! That stuff's murder! Do you think he means it?

DOC (*taking alcohol bottle from waste basket*). Of course not. Where could he get fulminate of mercury?

ROBERTS. I don't know. He's pretty resourceful. Where did he get the clap last year?

DOC. How about a drink, Doug? (*He pours alcohol and orange juice into two glasses*)

ROBERTS. Right! Doc, I been living with a genius. This makes it all worth while—the whole year and a half he spent in his bunk. How else could you celebrate V-E Day? A firecracker under the Old Man's bunk! The silly little son-of-a-bitch!

DOC (*handing Roberts a drink*). Here you are, Doug. (*Doc holds the drink up in a toast*) To better days!

ROBERTS. Okay. And to a great American, Frank Thurlowe Pulver . . . Soldier . . . Statesman . . . Scientist . . .

DOC. Friend of the Working Girl . . . (*Suddenly there is a tremendous explosion. Doc and Roberts clutch at the desk.*)

ROBERTS. Oh, my God!

DOC. He wasn't kidding! That's fulminate of mercury!

CAPTAIN (*offstage*). What was that? (*Roberts and Doc rush to porthole, listening.*)

JOHNSON (*offstage*). I don't know, Captain. I'll find out!

(*We hear the sounds of running feet.*)

ROBERTS. Doc, we've got to go down and get him.

DOC. This may be pretty bad, Doug. (*They turn to start for the door when suddenly a figure hurtles into the room and stops. For a moment it looks like a combination scarecrow and snowman but it is Pulver—his uniform tattered; his knees, arms and face blackened; he is covered with soapsuds and his eyes are shining with excitement. Roberts stares in amazement.*)

PULVER. Jeez, that stuff's terrific!

DOC. Are you all right?

PULVER. I'm great! Gee, you should've been there!

ROBERTS. You aren't burned—or anything?

PULVER. Hell, no. But the laundry's kinda beat up. The mangle's on the other side of the room now. And there's a new porthole on the starboard side where the electric iron went through. And I guess a steam-line must've busted or something—I was up to my ass in lather. And soap-flakes flyin' around—it was absolutely beautiful!

(During these last lines, Doc has been making a brisk, professional examination.)

DOC. It's a miracle. He isn't even scratched!

PULVER. Come on down and see it, Doug. It's a Winter Wonderland!

CAPTAIN *(offstage)*. Johnson!

ROBERTS. Quiet!

JOHNSON *(offstage)*. Yes, sir.

CAPTAIN *(offstage)*. What was it?

JOHNSON *(offstage)*. The laundry, Captain. A steam-line must've blew up.

PULVER *(explaining)*. Steam-line came right out of the bulkhead. *(He demonstrates)* Whish!

CAPTAIN *(offstage)*. How much damage?

JOHNSON *(offstage)*. We can't tell yet, Captain. We can't get in there—the passageway is solid soapsuds.

PULVER. Solid soapsuds. *(He pantomimes walking blindly through soapsuds)*

CAPTAIN *(offstage)*. Tell those men to be more careful.

ROBERTS *(excitedly)*. Frank, our celebration is just getting started. The night is young and our duty's clear.

PULVER. Yeah! What're we gonna do now, Doug?

ROBERTS. Get cleaned up and come with me.

PULVER. Where we goin' now, Doug?

ROBERTS. We're going down and get the rest of your stuff. You proved it'd work—you just hit the wrong target, that's all. We're going to make another firecracker, and put it where it really belongs.

PULVER *(who has slowly wilted during Roberts' speech)*. The rest of my stuff was—in the laundry, Doug. It all went up. There isn't any more. I'm sorry, Doug. I'm awful sorry.

ROBERTS *(sinks into chair)*. That's all right, Frank.

PULVER. Maybe I can scrounge some more tomorrow.

ROBERTS. Sure.

PULVER. You aren't sore at me, are you, Doug?

ROBERTS. What for?

PULVER. For spoilin' our celebration?

ROBERTS. Of course not.

PULVER. It was a good idea though, wasn't it, Doug?

ROBERTS. Frank, it was a great idea. I'm proud of you. It just didn't work, that's all. *(He starts for the door)*

DOC. Where are you going, Doug?

ROBERTS. Out on deck.

PULVER. Wait'll I get cleaned up and I'll come with you.

ROBERTS. No, I'm going to turn in after that. *(To Pulver)* It's okay, Frank. *(He exits)*

(Pulver turns pleadingly to Doc.)

PULVER. He was happy there for a minute though, wasn't he, Doc? Did you see him laughing? He was happy as hell. *(Pause)* We gotta do something for that guy, Doc. He's in bad shape. What's the matter with him anyhow, Doc. Did you find out?

DOC. No, he couldn't tell me. But I know one thing he's feeling tonight and that's panic. Tonight he feels his war is dying before he can get to it. *(He goes to radio and turns up volume)*

PULVER. I let him down. He wanted to celebrate and I let him down. *(He drops his head)*

(Announcer's Voice on radio comes up as the lights fade out.)

During the darkness and under the first part of Scene Four we hear the voice of a British broadcaster:

BRITISH BROADCASTER. . . . we hope that the King and the Queen will come out. The crowds are cheering—listen to them —and at any second now we hope to see Their Majesties. The color here is tremendous—everywhere rosettes, everywhere gay, red-white-and-blue hats. All the girls in their summer frocks on this lovely, mild, historic May evening. And although we celebrate with joyous heart the great victory, perhaps the greatest victory in the history of mankind, the underlying mood is a mood of thanksgiving. And

now, I believe, they're coming. They haven't appeared but the crowd in the center are cheering madly. Handkerchiefs, flags, hands waving—HERE THEY COME! First, Her Majesty, the Queen, has come into view. Then the King in the uniform of an Admiral of the Fleet. The two Princesses standing on the balcony— listen to the crowd—
(Sound of wild cheering.)
(This broadcast continues throughout the blackout and the next scene. Several times the station is changed, from a broadcast of the celebration in San Francisco to the speaker in New York and the band playing "The Stars and Stripes Forever" in Times Square.)

Scene Four

The lights dim up on the main set. It is a few minutes later, and bright moonlight. The ship is under way—this is indicated by the apparent movement of the stars, slowly up and down. A group of men are sitting on the hatch cover in a late bull session. They are Insigna, Mannion, Dolan and Stefanowski. Gerhart stands over them; he has obviously just returned from some mission for the group.

———

GERHART. I'm telling you, that's all it was. A steam pipe busted in the laundry —they're cleaning it up now. It ain't worth going to see.
(The others make way for him and he sits down beside them. Insigna cocks his head toward the sound of the radio.)
INSIGNA. What the hell's all that jabbering on the radio now?
MANNION. I don't know. Something about the King and Queen . . .
(The men listen for a moment without curiosity; then, as the radio fades, they settle back in indolent positions.)
INSIGNA. Well, anyhow, like I was telling you, this big sergeant in Elysium was scared to fight me! Tell 'em how big he was, Killer.
MANNION. Six foot seven or eight . . .
STEFANOWSKI. That sergeant's grown eight inches since we left Elysium . . . Did you see me when I swiped that Shore Patrol band and went around arresting guys? That Shore Patrol Lieutenant said

I was the best man he had. I arrested forty-three guys . . .
MANNION *(smiles at Dolan who is looking depressed)*. Come on, Dolan, don't let him get you down.
INSIGNA. Yeah, come on, Dolan.
(Roberts enters. He looks at the men, who have their backs turned, hesitates, then goes slowly over to them.)
GERHART *(idly)*. What was them croquette things we had for chow tonight? *(Stefanowski looks up and notices Roberts. Instantly he sits upright.)*
STEFANOWSKI. Flash Red!
(The men sit up. There is an embarrassed silence.)
ROBERTS. Good evening. *(The men smile politely. Roberts is very embarrassed)* Did you hear the news? The war's over in Europe.
MANNION *(smiling)*. Yes, sir. We heard.
STEFANOWSKI *(helping out the conversation)*. Sure. Maybe somebody'll get on the ball out here now . . .
(Dolan rises, starts down hatchway.)
ROBERTS. Dolan, I guess I kind of blew my top tonight. I'm sorry. I'm taking you off report.
DOLAN. Whatever you want, sir . . . *(He looks ostentatiously at his watch and yawns)* Well, I guess I'll hit the old sack . . . *(He goes down hatchway)*
MANNION. Yeah, me too . . .
INSIGNA. Yeah . . .
GERHART. It's late as hell.
STEFANOWSKI. I didn't realize how late it was . . .
(All the men get up, then go down the hatchway. Roberts stands looking after them. Now the radio is heard again. Roberts goes to hatchway and sits listening.)
SPEAKER. . . . Our boys have won this victory today. But the rest is up to you. You and you alone must recognize our enemies: the forces of ambition, cruelty, arrogance and stupidity. You must recognize them, you must destroy them, you must tear them out as you would a malignant growth! And cast them from the surface of the earth!
(The end of the speech is followed by a band playing "The Stars and Stripes Forever." Roberts' face lights up and a new determination is in it. He repeats the words "malignant growth." The band music swells. He marches to the palm

tree, salutes it, rubs his hands together and, as the music reaches a climax, he jerks the palm tree, earth and all, from the container and throws it over the side. Then, as the music continues, loud and climactic, he brushes his hands together, shrugs, and walks casually off left singing the tune to himself.)

(For a moment the stage is empty. Then the lights go up in the Captain's cabin. The door to the Captain's cabin opens and the Captain appears. He is in pajamas and bathrobe, and in one hand he carries his watering can. He discovers the empty container. He looks at it, then plunges into his cabin. After a moment, the General Alarm is heard. It is a terrible clanging noise designed to rouse the dead. When the alarm stops, the Captain's voice is heard, almost hysterical, over the squawk box.)

CAPTAIN. General Quarters! General Quarters! Every man to his battle station on the double!

(Johnson, in helmet and life jacket, scurries from hatchway into the Captain's cabin. Wiley enters from right passageway and climbs into the right gun tub. Now men appear from all directions in various degrees of dress. The stage is filled with men frantically running everywhere, all wearing helmets and life preservers.)

INSIGNA *(appearing from hatchway)*. What happened? *(He runs up the ladder and into the left gun tub. Payne enters from left and starts to climb up to left gun tub)* Get the hell out of here, Payne. This ain't your gun—your gun's over there!

DOLAN *(also trying to climb the ladder with Payne)*. Over there . . . over there . . .

(Payne crosses to right gun tub.)

REBER *(entering from hatchway)*. What the hell happened?

SCHLEMMER. Are *we* in an air raid?

PAYNE. Submarine . . . must be a submarine!

GERHART. Hey, Wiley, what happened?

DOWDY *(calling to someone on life raft)*. Hey, get away from that life raft. He didn't say abandon ship!

(During the confusion, Stefanowski, bewildered, emerges from the hatchway and wanders over to right gun tub.)

STEFANOWSKI. Hey, Wiley, Wiley—you sure you're supposed to be up there?

WILEY. Yeah.

STEFANOWSKI *(crossing to left gun tub)*. Hey, Sam. Are you supposed to be up there?

INSIGNA. Yeah, he was here last year!

STEFANOWSKI. Hey, Dowdy. Where the hell's my battle station?

DOWDY. I don't know where your battle station is! Look around!

(Stefanowski wanders aimlessly about. Wiley, in the gun tub right, is receiving reports of battle readiness from various parts of the ship:)

WILEY. Twenty millimeters manned and ready. *(Pause)* Engine room manned and ready. *(Pause)* All battle stations manned and ready.

STEFANOWSKI *(sitting on corner of hatch)*. Yeah, all but mine . . .

JOHNSON'S VOICE *(in Captain's cabin)*. All battle stations manned and ready, Captain.

CAPTAIN'S VOICE. Give me that thing.

JOHNSON'S VOICE *("on mike"—that is, speaking directly into squawk-box microphone. "Off mike" means speaking unintentionally into this live microphone)*. Attention . . . Attention . . . The Captain wishes to . . .

CAPTAIN'S VOICE *(on mike)*. Give me that thing! *(On mike)* All right, who did it? Who did it? You're going to stay here all night until someone confesses. You're going to stay at those battle stations until hell freezes over until I find out who did it. It's an insult to the honor of this ship, by God! The symbol of our cargo record has been destroyed and I'm going to find out who did it if it takes all night! *(Off mike)* Johnson, read me that muster list!

JOHNSON'S *voice (reading muster list off mike)*. Abernathy . . .

MANNION. Symbol of our cargo record? What the hell's that?

(Stefanowski rises, sees empty container, kneels and ceremoniously bows to it.)

DOWDY. For God's sake, Stefanowski, find some battle station!

CAPTAIN'S VOICE. No, not Abernathy . . .

JOHNSON'S VOICE. Baker . . .

CAPTAIN'S VOICE. No . . .

JOHNSON'S VOICE. Bartholomew . . . Becker . . . Billings . . .

Carney . . .
Daniels . . .

(Stefanowski points Dexter . . .
to empty container. Ellison . . .
Dowdy sees it and Everman . . .
spreads the news to Jenkins . . .
the men on left. Kelly . . .
Schlemmer sees it Kevin . . .
and tells the other Martin . . .
men. Now from all Olsen . . .
parts of the ship O'Neill . . .
men enter and ju- CAPTAIN'S VOICE.
bilantly look at the No, not O'Neill . . .
e m p t y container. JOHNSON'S VOICE.
Bits of soil fly into Pulver . . .
the air as the men CAPTAIN'S VOICE.
group around the No, not Pulver. He
empty can.) hasn't the guts . . .
JOHNSON'S VOICE.
Roberts . . .

CAPTAIN'S VOICE *(roaring, off mike).* Roberts! He's the one! Get him up here!

JOHNSON'S VOICE *(on mike).* Mister Roberts will report to the Captain's cabin on the double!

(The men rush back to their battle stations.)

CAPTAIN'S VOICE. Get him up here, I tell you! Get him up here . . .

JOHNSON'S VOICE *(on mike).* Mister Roberts will report to the Captain's cabin on the . . .

CAPTAIN *(on mike).* Give me that thing. *(On mike)* Roberts, you get up here in a goddamn quick hurry. Get up here! Roberts, I'm giving you an order—get the lead out of your pants.

(Roberts appears from left passageway and, walking slowly, enters the Captain's cabin.)

(The men move onstage and Lindstrom gets to a position on the ladder where he can look through the porthole of the Captain's cabin.)

ROBERTS' VOICE. Did you want to see me, Captain?

CAPTAIN'S VOICE. You did it. You did it. Don't lie to me. Don't stand there and lie to me. Confess it!

ROBERTS' VOICE. Confess what, Captain? I don't know what you're talking about.

CAPTAIN'S VOICE. You know damn well what I'm talkin' about because you did it. You've doublecrossed me—you've gone back on your word!

ROBERTS' VOICE. No, I haven't, Captain.

CAPTAIN. Yes, by God, you have. I kept my part of the bargain! I gave this crew liberty—I gave this crew liberty, by God, but you've gone back on *your* word.

(Dowdy takes off his helmet and looks at the men.)

ROBERTS' VOICE. I don't see how you can say that, Captain. I haven't sent in any more letters.

(Dolan, on gun tub ladder, catches Insigna's eye.)

CAPTAIN'S VOICE. I'm not talking about your goddamn sons-a-bitchin' letters. I'm talkin' about what you did tonight.

ROBERTS' VOICE. Tonight? I don't understand you, Captain. What do you think I did?

CAPTAIN. Quit saying that, goddammit, quit saying that. You know damn well what you did. You stabbed me in the back. You stabbed me in the back . . . aaa . . . aa . . .

JOHNSON'S VOICE. Captain! Get over to the washbasin, Captain!

CAPTAIN'S VOICE. Aaaaaaa . . .

INSIGNA. What the hell happened?

DOLAN. Quiet!

JOHNSON *(on mike).* Will the Doctor please report to the Captain's cabin on the double?

(Doc appears from left, pushing his way through the crowd, followed by two Medical Corpsmen wearing Red Cross brassards and carrying first-aid kits and a stretcher. Doc walks slowly; he is idly attaching a brassard and smoking a cigarette. He wears his helmet sloppily.)

DOC. Gangway . . . gangway . . .

DOWDY. Hey, Doc, tell us what's going on.

DOC. Okay. Okay.

(He enters the Captain's cabin followed by the Corpsmen who leave stretcher leaning against the bulkhead. The door closes. There is a tense pause. The men gather around the cabin again. Lindstrom is at the porthole.)

REBER. Hey, Lindstrom, where's the Old Man?

LINDSTROM. He's sittin' in the chair—leaning way forward.

PAYNE. What's the Doc doin'?

LINDSTROM. He's holdin' the waste basket.

REBER. What waste basket?

LINDSTROM. The one the Old Man's got his head in. And he needs it too. *(Pause)*

They're helpin' him over to the couch. *(Pause)* He's lying down there and they're takin' off his shoes. *(Pause)* Look out, here they come.

(The men break quickly and rush back to their battle stations. The door opens and Roberts, Doc and the Corpsmen come out.)

DOC *(to Corpsmen)*. We won't need that stretcher. Sorry. *(Calls)* Dowdy! Come here.

(Dowdy comes down to Doc. He avoids Roberts' eyes.)

ROBERTS. Dowdy, pass the word to the crew to secure from General Quarters.

DOC. And tell the men not to make any noise while they go to their bunks. The Captain's resting quietly now, and I think that's desirable.

ROBERTS. Pass the word, will you, Dowdy?

DOWDY. Yes, Mister Roberts. *(He passes the word to the crew who slowly start to leave their battle stations. They are obviously stalling)*

DOC *(to Roberts)*. Got a cigarette? *(Roberts reaches in his pocket and offers Doc a cigarette. Then he lights Doc's cigarette. Doc notices the men stalling)* Well, guess I'd better get back inside. I'll be down to see you after I get through.

(He enters cabin and stands there watching. The men move offstage, very slowly, saying "Good night, Mister Roberts," "Good night, sir." Suddenly Roberts notices that all the men are saying good night to him.)

DOLAN *(quietly)*. Good night, Mister Roberts. *(Roberts does not hear him)* Good night, Mister Roberts.

ROBERTS. Good night, Dolan.

(Dolan smiles and exits down hatch. Roberts steps toward hatch, removes helmet, looks puzzled as the lights fade out.)

During the darkness, over the squawk box the following announcements are heard:

FIRST VOICE. Now hear this . . . Now hear this . . . C, E and S Divisions and all Pharmacist's Mates will air bedding today —positively!

SECOND VOICE. There is now available at the ship's store a small supply of peanut brittle. Ship's store will be open from 1300 to 1315.

THIRD VOICE. Now, Dolan, Yeoman Sec-

ond Class, report to the radio shack immediately.

SCENE FIVE

The lights come up on the stateroom of Roberts and Pulver. Pulver is lying in the lower bunk. Doc is sitting at the desk with a glass and a bottle of grain alcohol in front of him. Roberts is tying up a sea bag. A small suitcase stands beside it. His locker is open and empty. Wiley picks up the sea bag.

———

WILEY. Okay, Mister Roberts, I'll take these down to the gangway. The boat from the island should be out here any minute for you. I'll let you know.

ROBERTS. Thanks, Wiley.

WILEY *(grinning)*. That's okay, Mister Roberts. Never thought you'd be taking this ride, did you? *(He exits with the bags)*

ROBERTS. I'm going to be off this bucket before I even wake up.

DOC. They flying you all the way to the *Livingston?*

ROBERTS. I don't know. The radio dispatch just said I was transferred and travel by air if possible. I imagine it's all the way through. They're landing planes at Okinawa now and that's where my can is probably running around. *(Laughs a little)* Listen to me, Doc—my can!

PULVER *(studying map by Roberts' bunk)*. Okinawa! Jeez, you be might-y careful, Doug.

ROBERTS. Okay, Frank. This is *too* much to take, Doc. I even got a destroyer! The *Livingston!* That's one of the greatest cans out there.

PULVER. I know a guy on the *Livingston..* He don't think it's so hot.

DOLAN *(entering. He has a file folder under his arm)*. Here you are, Mister Roberts. I typed up three copies of the radio dispatch. I've got to keep a copy and here's two for you. You're now officially detached from this here bucket. Let me be the first.

ROBERTS. Thanks, Dolan. *(They shake hands. Roberts takes papers, and looks at them)* Dolan, how about these orders? I haven't sent in a letter for a month!

DOLAN *(carefully)*. You know how the Navy works, Mister Roberts.

ROBERTS. Yeah, I know, but it doesn't seem . . .

DOLAN. Listen, Mister Roberts, I can tell you exactly what happened. Those guys at the Bureau need men for combat duty awful bad and they started looking through all the old letters and they just come across one of yours.

ROBERTS. Maybe—but still you'd think . . .

DOLAN. Listen, Mister Roberts. We can't stand here beating our gums! You better get cracking! You seen what it said there, "Proceed immediately." And the Old Man says if you ain't off of here in an hour, by God, he's going to throw you off!

ROBERTS. Is that all he said?

DOLAN. That's all he said.

ROBERTS (grinning at Doc). After fighting this for two years you'd think he'd say more than that . . .

CAPTAIN'S VOICE (offstage). Be careful of that one. Put it down easy.

DOC. What's that?

DOLAN. A new enlarged botanical garden. That's why he can't even be bothered about you today, Mister Roberts. Soon as we anchored this morning he sent Olsen over with a special detail—they dug up two palm trees . . . He's busy as a mother skunk now and you know what he's done—he's already set a twenty-four-hour watch on these new babies with orders to shoot to kill. (To Pulver) That reminds me, Mister Pulver. The Captain wants to see you right away.

PULVER. Yeah? What about?

DOLAN. I don't know, sir. (To Roberts) I'll be back to say good-bye, Mister Roberts. Come on, Mister Pulver. (He exits)

PULVER (following Dolan out). What the hell did I do with his laundry this week?

(Roberts smiles as he starts putting on his black tie.)

DOC. You're a happy son-of-a-bitch, aren't you?

ROBERTS. Yep. You're happy about it too, aren't you, Doc?

DOC. I think it's the only thing for you. (Casually) What do you think of the crew now, Doug?

ROBERTS. We're all right now. I think they're nice guys—all of them.

DOC. Uuh-hunh. And how do you think they feel about you?

ROBERTS. I think they like me all right . . . till the next guy comes along.

DOC. You don't think you're necessary to them?

ROBERTS (sitting on bunk). Hell, no. No officer's necessary to the crew, Doc.

DOC. Are you going to leave this ship believing that?

ROBERTS. That's nothing against them. A crew's too busy looking after themselves to care about anyone else.

DOC. Well, take a good, deep breath, Buster. (He drinks some alcohol) What do you think got you your orders? Prayer and fasting? Sending in enough Wheatie box tops?

ROBERTS. My orders? Why, what Dolan said—one of my old letters turned up . . .

DOC. Bat crap! This crew got you transferred. They were so busy looking out for themselves that they took a chance of landing in prison for five years—any one of them. Since you couldn't send in a letter for transfer, they sent one in for you. Since they knew the Captain wouldn't sign it approved, they didn't bother him—they signed it for him.

ROBERTS. What do you mean? They forged the Captain's name?

DOC. That's right.

ROBERTS (rising). Doc! Who did? Which one of them?

DOC. That would be hard to say. You see, they had a mass meeting down in the compartment. They put guards at every door. They called it the Captain's-Name-Signing contest. And every man in this crew—a hundred and sixty-seven of them—signed the Captain's name on a blank sheet of paper. And then there were judges who compared these signatures with the Captain's and selected the one to go in. At the time there was some criticism of the decision on the grounds that the judges were drunk, but apparently, from the results, they chose well.

ROBERTS. How'd you find out about this, Doc?

DOC. Well, it was a great honor. I am the only officer aboard who does know. I was a contestant. I was also a judge. This double honor was accorded me because of my character, charm, good looks and because the medical department contributed four gallons of grain alcohol to the contest. (Pauses) It was quite a thing to see, Doug. A hundred and sixty-seven guys with only one idea in their heads—to do something for Mister Roberts.

ROBERTS (*after a moment*). I wish you hadn't told me, Doc. It makes me look pretty silly after what I just said. But I didn't mean it, Doc. I was afraid to say what I really feel. I love those bastards, Doc. I think they're the greatest guys on this earth. All of a sudden I feel that there's something wrong—something terribly wrong—about leaving them. God, what can I say to them?

DOC. You won't say anything—you don't even know. When you're safely aboard your new ship I'm supposed to write and tell you about it. And at the bottom of the letter, I'm supposed to say, "Thanks for the liberty, Mister Roberts. Thanks for everything."

ROBERTS. Jesus!

(*Pulver enters, downcast.*)

PULVER. I'm the new Cargo Officer. And that's not all—I got to have dinner with him tonight. He *likes* me!

(*There is a polite rap on the door.*)

DOC. Come in. (*Enter Payne, Reber, Gerhart, Schlemmer, Dolan and Insigna, all carrying canteen cups except Insigna whose cup is in his belt. He carries a large, red fire extinguisher*) What's this?

INSIGNA. Fire and rescue squad. Heard you had a fire in here.

(*All are looking at Roberts.*)

ROBERTS. No, but—since you're here—I—

INSIGNA. Hell, we got a false alarm then. Happens all the time. (*Sets extinguisher on desk*) In that case, we might as well drink this stuff. Give me your glass, Mister Roberts, and I'll put a head on it—yours too, Doc. I got one for you, Mister Pulver. (*He fills their glasses from the fire extinguisher*)

ROBERTS. What's in that, a new batch of jungle juice?

INSIGNA. Yeah, in the handy, new, portable container. Everybody loaded?

(*All nod.*)

DOLAN. Go ahead, Sam.

INSIGNA (*to Roberts*). There's a story going around that you're leaving us. That right?

ROBERTS (*carefully*). That's right, Sam. And I . . .

INSIGNA. Well, we didn't want you to get away without having a little drink with us and we thought we ought to give you a little sort of going-away present. The fellows made it down in the machine shop. It ain't much but we hope you like it. (*Reber prompts him*) We all sincerely hope you like it. (*Calls offstage*) All right, you bastards, you can come in now.

(*Enter Lindstrom, Mannion, Dowdy and Stefanowski. Mannion is carrying a candy box. He walks over to Roberts shyly and hands him the box.*)

ROBERTS. What is it?

SCHLEMMER. Open it.

(*Roberts opens the box. There is a deep silence.*)

PULVER. What is it, Doug?

(*Roberts holds up the box. In it is a brass medal shaped like a palm tree attached to a piece of gaudy ribbon.*)

LINDSTROM. It's a palm tree, see.

DOLAN. It was Dowdy's idea.

DOWDY. Mannion here made it. He cut it out of sheet brass down in the machine shop.

INSIGNA. Mannion drilled the words on it too.

MANNION. Stefanowski thought up the words.

STEFANOWSKI (*shoving Lindstrom forward*). Lindstrom gets credit for the ribbon from a box of candy that his sister-in-law sent him. Read the words, Mister Roberts.

ROBERTS (*with difficulty*). "Order . . . order of . . ." (*He hands the medal to Doc*)

DOC (*rises and reads solemnly*). "Order of the palm. To Lieutenant (jg) Douglas Roberts for action against the enemy, above and beyond the call of duty on the night of eight May 1945." (*He passes the medal back to Roberts*)

ROBERTS (*after a moment—smiling*). It's very nice but I'm afraid you've got the wrong guy.

(*The men turn to Dowdy, grinning.*)

DOWDY. We know that, but we'd kinda like for you to have it anyway.

ROBERTS. All right, I'll keep it.

(*The men beam. There is an awkward pause.*)

GERHART. Stefanowski thought up the words.

ROBERTS. They're fine words.

(*Wiley enters.*)

WILEY. The boat's here, Mister Roberts. I put your gear in. They want to shove off right away.

ROBERTS (*rising*). Thanks. We haven't had our drink yet.

REBER. No, we ain't.

(*All get to their feet. Roberts picks up his glass, looks at the crew, and everyone drinks.*)

ROBERTS. Good-bye, Doc.

DOC. Good-bye, Doug.

ROBERTS. And thanks, Doc.

DOC. Okay.

ROBERTS. Good-bye, Frank.

PULVER. Good-bye, Doug.

ROBERTS. Remember, I'm counting on you.

(*Pulver nods. Roberts turns to the crew and looks at them for a moment. Then he takes the medal from the box, pins it on his shirt, shows it to them, then gives a little gestured salute and exits as the lights fade out.*)

During the darkness we hear voices making announcements over the squawk box:

FIRST VOICE. Now hear this . . . now hear this . . . Sweepers, man your brooms. Clean sweep-down fore and aft!

SECOND VOICE. Now hear this! All men put on report today will fall in on the quarter-deck—and form three ranks!

THIRD VOICE. Now hear this! All divisions will draw their mail at 1700—in the mess hall.

SCENE SIX

The lights come up showing the main set at sunset. Doc is sitting on the hatch, reading a letter. Mannion, wearing side-arms, is pacing up and down in front of the Captain's cabin. On each side of the door is a small palm tree in a five-gallon can—on one can is painted in large white letters, "Keep Away"; on the other, "This Means You." After a moment, Pulver enters from the left passageway, carrying a small packet of letters.

———

PULVER. Hello, Mannion. Got your mail yet?

MANNION. No. I've got the palm tree watch.

PULVER. Oh. (*To Doc*) What's your news, Doc?

DOC. My wife got some new wallpaper for the living room.

(*Pulver sits on hatch cover. Dowdy enters wearing work gloves.*)

DOWDY. Mister Pulver, we'll be finished with the cargo in a few minutes.

PULVER. How'd it go?

DOWDY. Not bad. I've got to admit you were right about Number Three hold. It worked easier out of there. Mister Pulver, I just found out what the Captain decided —he ain't going to show a movie again tonight.

PULVER. Why not?

DOWDY. He's still punishing us because he caught Reber without a shirt on two days ago. You've got to go in and see him.

PULVER. I did. I asked him to show a movie yesterday.

DOWDY. Mister Pulver, what the hell good does that do us today? You've got to keep needlin' that guy—I'm tellin' you.

PULVER. Don't worry. I'll take care of it in my own way.

DOWDY (*going off, but speaking loud enough to be heard*). Oh, God, no movie again tonight.

(*Dowdy exits. Pulver starts looking at his packet of mail.*)

PULVER (*looking at first letter*). This is from my mother. All she ever says is stay away from Japan. (*He drops it on the hatch cover*) This is from Alabama. (*Puts it in his pocket and pats it. Looks at third letter*) Doc! This is from Doug!

DOC. Yeah? (*Pulver rips open the envelope*) What does he say?

PULVER (*reading*). "This will be short and sweet, as we're shoving off in about two minutes . . ." (*Pauses and remarks*) This is dated three weeks ago.

DOC. Does he say where he is?

PULVER. Yeah. He says: "My guess about the location of this ship was just exactly right." (*Looks up*) That means he's around Okinawa all right! (*Reads on and chuckles*) He's met Fornell. That's that friend of mine . . . a guy named Fornell I went to college with. Listen to this: "Fornell says that you and he used to load up your car with liquor in Omaha and then sell it at an indecent profit to the fraternity boys at Iowa City. How about that?" We did too. (*Smiles happily*) "This part is for Doc." (*Doc gestures for him to read it*) "I've been aboard this destroyer for two weeks now and we've already been through four air attacks. I'm in the war at last, Doc. I've caught up with that task force that passed me by. I'm glad to be here. I had to be here, I guess. But I'm thinking now of you, Doc, and you, Frank, and Dolan and Dowdy and Insigna and everyone else on that bucket—all the guys everywhere who sail from Tedium to Apathy and back again—with an occasional side trip to Monotony. This is a tough crew on here, and they have a wonderful battle record. But I've discovered, Doc, that the most terrible enemy of this war is the boredom that eventually becomes a faith and, therefore, a sort of suicide—and I know now that the ones who refuse to surrender to it are the strongest of all.

"Right now, I'm looking at something that's hanging over my desk: a preposterous hunk of brass attached to the most bilious piece of ribbon I've ever seen. I'd rather have it than the Congressional Medal of Honor. It tells me what I'll always be proudest of—that at a time in the world when courage counted most, I lived among a hundred and sixty-seven brave men.

"So, Doc, and especially you, Frank, don't let those guys down. Of course, I know that by this time they must be very happy because the Captain's overhead is filled with marbles and . . ." (*He avoids Doc's eyes*) "Oh, hell, here comes the mail orderly. This has to go now. I'll finish it later. Meanwhile you bastards can write too, can't you?

"Doug."

DOC. Can I see that, Frank?
(*Pulver hands him the letter, looks at the front of his next letter and says quietly:*)
PULVER. Well, for God's sake, this is from Fornell!
DOC (*reading Roberts' letter to himself*). ". . . I'd rather have it than the Congressional Medal of Honor." I'm glad he found that out. (*He looks at Pulver, sensing something wrong*) What's the matter? (*Pulver does not answer*) What's the matter, Frank?

(*Pulver looks at him slowly as Dowdy enters.*)
DOWDY. All done, Mister Pulver. We've secured the hatch cover. No word on the movie, I suppose.
DOC (*louder, with terror*). Frank, what is it?
PULVER. Mister Roberts is dead. (*Looks at letter*) This is from Fornell . . . They took a Jap suicide plane. It killed everyone in a twin-forty battery and then it went on through and killed Doug and another officer in the wardroom. (*Pause*) They were drinking coffee when it hit.
DOWDY (*quietly*). Mister Pulver, can I please give that letter to the crew?
DOC. No. (*Holding out Roberts' letter*) Give them this one. It's theirs. (*Dowdy removes gloves and takes the letter from Doc and goes off*) Coffee . . .
(*Pulver gets up restlessly. Doc stares straight ahead. Pulver straightens. He seems to grow. He walks casually over to Mannion.*)
PULVER (*in a friendly voice*). Go on down and get your mail. I'll stand by for you.
MANNION (*surprised*). You will? Okay, thanks, Mister Pulver.
(*Mannion disappears down hatch. As soon as he exits Pulver very calmly jerks the rooted palms, one by one, from their containers and throws them over the side. Doc looks up to see Pulver pull second tree. Doc ducks as tree goes past him. Then Pulver knocks loudly on the Captain's door.*)
CAPTAIN (*offstage. His voice is very truculent*). Yeah. Who is it?
PULVER. Captain, this is Ensign Pulver. I just threw your palm trees overboard. Now what's all this crap about no movie tonight?
(*He throws the door open, banging it against the bulkhead, and is entering the Captain's cabin as the curtain falls.*)

AFTER the production of *Death of a Salesman,* Arthur Miller was celebrated throughout the land as the second new dramatist to have assured the survival of significant play-writing in America. (The first had been Tennessee Williams.) The play won both the Pulitzer Prize and the Drama Critics Circle award, as well as sundry other prizes. Although Miller's earlier play, *All My Sons,* had been well received, there had been reason to doubt its author's originality and dramatic range. Once *Death of a Salesman* opened in Manhattan, only his originality could be questioned, since his materials, including his style of dialogue, were familiar. Except in the opinion of a few fastidious observers, however, the vigor of the new play made an academic matter of the question of how new the subject was. The characters and the background were, indeed, fresh precisely because they were so vividly recognizable, and Miller's compassionate scrutiny of little lives communicated itself spontaneously to his public; or so it seemed to audiences, although the author actually kept a firm hand on his sequence of events and revelations. Miller here employed flexible dramaturgy, moving from a present crisis to eruptive scenes of reminiscence. Consequently, he was able to give his story some of the extensiveness and richness of a novel without losing dramatic power. The play displayed life multi-dimensionally or, so to speak, in depth.

For these and other reasons, Miller was acclaimed as the outstanding new dramatist of the forties or, at the least, Tennessee Williams' equal among the decade's discovered playwrights. Although Miller's language was not regarded as equal to Williams' dialogue, his picture of reality was considered more representative and significant. It was in his favor, too, that he demonstrated to those who were familiar with his earlier work that he was capable of artistic growth, having graduated from the "well-made play" grammar school of modern playwriting. As he himself declared, "the conventional play form forces the writer to siphon everything into a single place at a single time, and squeezes the humanity out of a play. Why shouldn't a play have the depth, the completeness, and the diversity of a novel?"

Death of a Salesman climaxed a slow advance on the Broadway scene and a steady development of skills and powers. Born in 1916 in New York, and reared in suburban Brooklyn, Miller had the usual high school education, enlivened by a modest football career not unusual in the case of a tall raw-boned lad. Going on to the University of Michigan, after two and a half years of clerking in an automobile parts warehouse, he found an understanding teacher in Professor Kenneth E. Rowe, the author of *Write That Play.* Miller turned to playwriting with such devotion that he won the university's Avery Hopwood award for two successive years. In 1937 he also received a substantially larger prize from the Bureau of New Plays, established by the Theatre Guild director Theresa Helburn. Upon leaving college in 1938, he first found employment on the play-writing project of the Federal Theatre. Fortunately, since the W.P.A. project expired four months after he joined it, Miller also revealed a talent for radio writing and was able to settle down to a simple, semi-suburban life in Brooklyn with his wife, a former Michigan classmate. During the war, disqualified for military service by an injury he had sustained while playing football, he worked as a steamfitter in the Brooklyn Navy Yard and wrote patriotic radio scripts and one-acters. He also did some work, in 1942, on the notable Ernie Pyle film *The Story of G.I. Joe,* spending six months with the infantry and going on maneuvers while gathering information for the production. Having kept a diary of his research, Miller published it in 1944 under the title of *Situation Normal.* He published a second book in 1945, a successful novel about race hatred entitled *Focus.* By no means neglecting playwriting, Miller also wrote several full-length plays during his apprenticeship, and one of these, *The Man Who Had All the Luck,* a sprawling chronicle, brought him some recognition in 1944.

In 1947 Miller's nine-year-long wrestling with the dramatic medium reaped its first rewards when *All My Sons* (see page 281) had a good run on Broadway, won the Drama Critics Circle award, and was bought by a motion picture producer. Two years later he had Broadway at his feet and met Willy Loman's prescription for success to the letter; he was not only "liked" but "well liked" for *Death of a Salesman.*

Brooks Atkinson, in *The New York Times,* called *Death of a Salesman* "one of the finest dramas in the whole range of the American theatre," and John Mason Brown referred to the production, brilliantly directed by Elia Kazan, as "one of the modern theatre's most overpowering evenings." John Chapman of the *New York Daily News* concurred, describing it as "one of those unforgettable times in which all is right and nothing is wrong." Even the usually more sceptical Wolcott Gibbs, writing in *The New Yorker,* set it down as "a tremendously affecting work . . . told with a mixture of compassion, imagination, and hard technical competence you don't often find in the theatre today." And the hardly less exacting reviewer of *Time,* Louis Kronenberger, described the play as "so simple, central, and terrible that the run of playwrights would neither care nor dare to attempt it." The play also won considerable success abroad, and was received with particular enthusiasm in Vienna. English reviewers and playgoers took a more reserved view of Willy Loman's story. Ivor Brown, writing in *The New York Times* of August 28, 1949, explained that the salesman is not a national type in England, and that the English have too much contempt for "the life of the party" and "smiles into diamonds" philosophy of success to be stirred by Willy's failure. *Death of a Salesman* won greater commendation from the British as "a skillful piece of stagecraft" than as a waterfall of compassion. Yet for the British, too, the play made substantial claims as a "little man's" tragedy. Ivor Brown noted that "now on both sides of the Atlantic we have stool tragedies, not throne tragedies," and that "it is the clerk, not the king, who inspires the tragedian."

ACT ONE

A melody is heard, played upon a flute. It is small and fine, telling of grass and trees and the horizon. The curtain rises.

Before us is the Salesman's house. We are aware of towering, angular shapes behind it, surrounding it on all sides. Only the blue light of the sky falls upon the house and forestage; the surrounding area shows an angry glow of orange. As more light appears, we see a solid vault of apartment houses around the small, fragile-seeming home. An air of the dream clings to the place, a dream rising out of reality. The kitchen at center seems actual enough, for there is a kitchen table with three chairs, and a refrigerator. But no other fixtures are seen. At the back of the kitchen there is a draped entrance, which leads to the living-room. To the right of the kitchen, on a level raised two feet, is a bedroom furnished only with a brass bedstead and a straight chair. On a shelf over the bed a silver athletic trophy stands. A window opens onto the apartment house at the side.

Behind the kitchen, on a level raised six and a half feet, is the boys' bedroom, at present barely visible. Two beds are dimly seen, and at the back of the room a dormer window. (This bedroom is above the unseen living-room.) At the left a stairway curves up to it from the kitchen.

The entire setting is wholly or, in some places, partially transparent. The roof-line of the house is one-dimensional; under and over it we see the apartment buildings. Before the house lies an apron, curving beyond the forestage into the orchestra. This forward area serves as the back yard as well as the locale of all Willy's imaginings and of his city scenes. Whenever the action is in the present the actors observe the imaginary wall-lines, entering the house only through its door at the left. But in the scenes of the past these boundaries are broken, and characters enter or leave a room by stepping "through" a wall onto the forestage.

From the right, Willy Loman, the Salesman, enters, carrying two large sample cases. The flute plays on. He hears but is not aware of it. He is past sixty years of age, dressed quietly. Even as he crosses the stage to the doorway of the house, his exhaustion is apparent. He unlocks the door,

comes into the kitchen, and thankfully lets his burden down, feeling the soreness of his palms. A word-sigh escapes his lips—it might be "Oh, boy, oh, boy." He closes the door, then carries his cases out into the living-room, through the draped kitchen doorway.

Linda, his wife, has stirred in her bed at the right. She gets out and puts on a robe, listening. Most often jovial, she has developed an iron repression of her exceptions to Willy's behavior—she more than loves him, she admires him, as though his mercurial nature, his temper, his massive dreams and little cruelties, served her only as sharp reminders of the turbulent longings within him, longings which she shares but lacks the temperament to utter and follow to their end.

———

LINDA (*hearing Willy outside the bedroom, calls with some trepidation*). Willy!

WILLY. It's all right. I came back.

LINDA. Why? What happened? (*Slight pause*) Did something happen, Willy?

WILLY. No, nothing happened.

LINDA. You didn't smash the car, did you?

WILLY (*with casual irritation*). I said nothing happened. Didn't you hear me?

LINDA. Don't you feel well?

WILLY. I'm tired to the death. (*The flute has faded away. He sits on the bed beside her, a little numb*) I couldn't make it. I just couldn't make it, Linda.

LINDA (*very carefully, delicately*). Where were you all day? You look terrible.

WILLY. I got as far as a little above Yonkers. I stopped for a cup of coffee. Maybe it was the coffee.

LINDA. What?

WILLY (*after a pause*). I suddenly couldn't drive any more. The car kept going off onto the shoulder, y'know?

LINDA (*helpfully*). Oh. Maybe it was the steering again. I don't think Angelo knows the Studebaker.

WILLY. No, it's me, it's me. Suddenly I realize I'm goin' sixty miles an hour and I don't remember the last five minutes. I'm —I can't seem to—keep my mind to it.

LINDA. Maybe it's your glasses. You never went for your new glasses.

WILLY. No, I see everything. I came back ten miles an hour. It took me nearly four hours from Yonkers.

LINDA (*resigned*). Well, you'll just have

to take a rest, Willy, you can't continue this way.

WILLY. I just got back from Florida.

LINDA. But you didn't rest your mind. Your mind is overactive, and the mind is what counts, dear.

WILLY. I'll start out in the morning. Maybe I'll feel better in the morning. (*She is taking off his shoes*) These goddam arch supports are killing me.

LINDA. Take an aspirin. Should I get you an aspirin? It'll soothe you.

WILLY (*with wonder*). I was driving along, you understand? And I was fine. I was even observing the scenery. You can imagine, me looking at scenery, on the road every week of my life. But it's so beautiful up there, Linda, the trees are so thick, and the sun is warm. I opened the windshield and just let the warm air bathe over me. And then all of a sudden I'm goin' off the road! I'm tellin' ya, I absolutely forgot I was driving. If I'd've gone the other way over the white line I might've killed somebody. So I went on again—and five minutes later I'm dreamin' again, and I nearly— (*He presses two fingers against his eyes*) I have such thoughts, I have such strange thoughts.

LINDA. Willy, dear. Talk to them again. There's no reason why you can't work in New York.

WILLY. They don't need me in New York. I'm the New England man. I'm vital in New England.

LINDA. But you're sixty years old. They can't expect you to keep traveling every week.

WILLY. I'll have to send a wire to Portland. I'm supposed to see Brown and Morrison tomorrow morning at ten o'clock to show the line. Goddammit, I could sell them! (*He starts putting on his jacket*)

LINDA (*taking the jacket from him*). Why don't you go down to the place tomorrow and tell Howard you've simply got to work in New York? You're too accommodating, dear.

WILLY. If old man Wagner was alive I'd a been in charge of New York now! That man was a prince, he was a masterful man. But that boy of his, that Howard, he don't appreciate. When I went north the first time, the Wagner Company didn't know where New England was!

LINDA. Why don't you tell those things to Howard, dear?

WILLY (*encouraged*). I will, I definitely will. Is there any cheese?

LINDA. I'll make you a sandwich.

WILLY. No, go to sleep. I'll take some milk. I'll be up right away. The boys in?

LINDA. They're sleeping. Happy took Biff on a date tonight.

WILLY (*interested*). That so?

LINDA. It was so nice to see them shaving together, one behind the other, in the bathroom. And going out together. You notice? The whole house smells of shaving lotion.

WILLY. Figure it out. Work a lifetime to pay off a house. You finally own it, and there's nobody to live in it.

LINDA. Well, dear, life is a casting off. It's always that way.

WILLY. No, no, some people—some people accomplish something. Did Biff say anything after I went this morning?

LINDA. You shouldn't have criticized him, Willy, especially after he just got off the train. You mustn't lose your temper with him.

WILLY. When the hell did I lose my temper? I simply asked him if he was making any money. Is that a criticism?

LINDA. But, dear, how could he make any money?

WILLY (*worried and angered*). There's such an undercurrent in him. He became a moody man. Did he apologize when I left this morning?

LINDA. He was crestfallen, Willy. You know how he admires you. I think if he finds himself, then you'll both be happier and not fight any more.

WILLY. How can he find himself on a farm? Is that a life? A farmhand? In the beginning, when he was young, I thought, well, a young man, it's good for him to tramp around, take a lot of different jobs. But it's more than ten years now and he has yet to make thirty-five dollars a week!

LINDA. He's finding himself, Willy.

WILLY. Not finding yourself at the age of thirty-four is a disgrace!

LINDA. Shh!

WILLY. The trouble is he's lazy, goddammit!

LINDA. Willy, please!

WILLY. Biff is a lazy bum!

LINDA. They're sleeping. Get something to eat. Go on down.

WILLY. Why did he come home? I

would like to know what brought him home.

LINDA. I don't know. I think he's still lost, Willy. I think he's very lost.

WILLY. Biff Loman is lost. In the greatest country in the world a young man with such—personal attractiveness, gets lost. And such a hard worker. There's one thing about Biff—he's not lazy.

LINDA. Never.

WILLY (*with pity and resolve*). I'll see him in the morning; I'll have a nice talk with him. I'll get him a job selling. He could be big in no time. My God! Remember how they used to follow him around in high school? When he smiled at one of them their faces lit up. When he walked down the street . . . (*He loses himself in reminiscences*)

LINDA (*trying to bring him out of it*). Willy, dear, I got a new kind of American-type cheese today. It's whipped.

WILLY. Why do you get American when I like Swiss?

LINDA. I just thought you'd like a change—

WILLY. I don't want a change! I want Swiss cheese. Why am I always being contradicted?

LINDA (*with a covering laugh*). I thought it would be a surprise.

WILLY. Why don't you open a window in here, for God's sake?

LINDA (*with infinite patience*). They're all open, dear.

WILLY. The way they boxed us in here. Bricks and windows, windows and bricks.

LINDA. We should've bought the land next door.

WILLY. The street is lined with cars. There's not a breath of fresh air in the neighborhood. The grass don't grow any more, you can't raise a carrot in the back yard. They should've had a law against apartment houses. Remember those two beautiful elm trees out there? When I and Biff hung the swing between them?

LINDA. Yeah, like being a million miles from the city.

WILLY. They should've arrested the builder for cutting those down. They massacred the neighborhood. (*Lost*) More and more I think of those days, Linda. This time of year it was lilac and wisteria. And then the peonies would come out, and the daffodils. What fragrance in this room!

LINDA. Well, after all, people had to move somewhere.

WILLY. No, there's more people now.

LINDA. I don't think there's more people. I think—

WILLY. There's more people! That's what's ruining this country! Population is getting out of control. The competition is maddening! Smell the stink from that apartment house! And another one on the other side . . . How can they whip cheese? (*On Willy's last line, Biff and Happy raise themselves up in their beds, listening.*)

LINDA. Go down, try it. And be quiet.

WILLY (*turning to Linda, guiltily*). You're not worried about me, are you, sweetheart?

BIFF. What's the matter?

HAPPY. Listen!

LINDA. You've got too much on the ball to worry about.

WILLY. You're my foundation and my support, Linda.

LINDA. Just try to relax, dear. You make mountains out of molehills.

WILLY. I won't fight with him any more. If he wants to go back to Texas, let him go.

LINDA. He'll find his way.

WILLY. Sure. Certain men just don't get started till later in life. Like Thomas Edison, I think. Or B. F. Goodrich. One of them was deaf. (*He starts for the bedroom doorway*) I'll put my money on Biff.

LINDA. And, Willy—if it's warm Sunday we'll drive in the country. And we'll open the windshield, and take lunch.

WILLY. No, the windshields don't open on the new cars.

LINDA. But you opened it today.

WILLY. Me? I didn't. (*He stops*) Now isn't that peculiar! Isn't that remarkable— (*He breaks off in amazement and fright as the flute is heard distantly*)

LINDA. What, darling?

WILLY. That is the most remarkable thing.

LINDA. What, dear?

WILLY. I was thinking of the Chevvy (*Slight pause*) Nineteen twenty-eight . . . when I had that red Chevvy—(*Breaks off*) That's funny? I coulda sworn I was driving that Chevvy today.

LINDA. Well, that's nothing. Something must've reminded you.

WILLY. Remarkable. Ts. Remember those days? The way Biff used to simonize that car? The dealer refused to believe there was eighty thousand miles on it. (*He shakes his head*) Heh! (*To Linda*) Close your eyes, I'll be right up. (*He walks out of the bedroom*)

HAPPY (*to Biff*). Jesus, maybe he smashed up the car again!

LINDA (*calling after Willy*). Be careful on the stairs, dear! The cheese is on the middle shelf! (*She turns, goes over to the bed, takes his jacket, and goes out of the bedroom*)

(*Light has risen on the boys' room. Unseen, Willy is heard talking to himself, "Eighty thousand miles," and a little laugh. Biff gets out of bed, comes downstage a bit, and stands attentively. Biff is two years older than his brother Happy, well built, but in these days bears a worn air and seems less self-assured. He has succeeded less, and his dreams are stronger and less acceptable than Happy's. Happy is tall, powerfully made. Sexuality is like a visible color on him, or a scent that many women have discovered. He, like his brother, is lost, but in a different way, for he has never allowed himself to turn his face toward defeat and is thus more confused and hard-skinned, although seemingly more content.*)

HAPPY (*getting out of bed*). He's going to get his license taken away if he keeps that up. I'm getting nervous about him, y'know, Biff?

BIFF. His eyes are going.

HAPPY. No, I've driven with him. He sees all right. He just doesn't keep his mind on it. I drove into the city with him last week. He stops at a green light and then it turns red and he goes. (*He laughs*)

BIFF. Maybe he's color-blind.

HAPPY. Pop? Why he's got the finest eye for color in the business. You know that.

BIFF (*sitting down on his bed*). I'm going to sleep.

HAPPY. You're not still sour on Dad, are you, Biff?

BIFF. He's all right, I guess.

WILLY (*underneath them, in the living-room*). Yes, sir, eighty thousand miles—eighty-two thousand!

BIFF. You smoking?

HAPPY (*holding out a pack of cigarettes*). Want one?

BIFF (*taking a cigarette*). I can never sleep when I smell it.

WILLY. What a simonizing job, heh!

HAPPY (*with deep sentiment*). Funny, Biff, y'know? Us sleeping in here again? The old beds. (*He pats his bed affectionately*) All the talk that went across those two beds, huh? Our whole lives.

BIFF. Yeah. Lotta dreams and plans.

HAPPY (*with a deep and masculine laugh*). About five hundred women would like to know what was said in this room. (*They share a short laugh*)

BIFF. Remember that big Betsy something—what the hell was her name—over on Bushwick Avenue?

HAPPY (*combing his hair*). With the collie dog!

BIFF. That's the one. I got you in there, remember?

HAPPY. Yeah, that was my first time—I think. Boy, there was a pig! (*They laugh, almost crudely*) You taught me everything I know about women. Don't forget that.

BIFF. I bet you forgot how bashful you used to be. Especially with girls.

HAPPY. Oh, I still am, Biff.

BIFF. Oh, go on.

HAPPY. I just control it, that's all. I think I got less bashful and you got more so. What happened, Biff? Where's the old humor, the old confidence? (*He shakes Biff's knee. Biff gets up and moves restlessly about the room*) What's the matter?

BIFF. Why does Dad mock me all the time?

HAPPY. He's not mocking you, he—

BIFF. Everything I say there's a twist of mockery on his face. I can't get near him.

HAPPY. He just wants you to make good, that's all. I wanted to talk to you about Dad for a long time, Biff. Something's—happening to him. He—talks to himself.

BIFF. I noticed that this morning. But he always mumbled.

HAPPY. But not so noticeable. It got so embarrassing I sent him to Florida. And you know something? Most of the time he's talking to you.

BIFF. What's he say about me?

HAPPY. I can't make it out.

BIFF. What's he say about me?

HAPPY. I think the fact that you're not settled, that you're still kind of up in the air . . .

BIFF. There's one or two other things depressing him, Happy.

HAPPY. What do you mean?

BIFF. Never mind. Just don't lay it all to me.

HAPPY. But I think if you just got started —I mean—is there any future for you out there?

BIFF. I tell ya, Hap, I don't know what the future is. I don't know—what I'm supposed to want.

HAPPY. What do you mean?

BIFF. Well, I spent six or seven years after high school trying to work myself up. Shipping clerk, salesman, business of one kind or another. And it's a measly manner of existence. To get on that subway on the hot mornings in summer. To devote your whole life to keeping stock, or making phone calls, or selling or buying. To suffer fifty weeks of the year for the sake of a two-week vacation, when all you really desire is to be outdoors, with your shirt off. And always to have to get ahead of the next fella. And still—that's how you build a future.

HAPPY. Well, you really enjoy it on a farm? Are you content out there?

BIFF (with rising agitation). Hap, I've had twenty or thirty different kinds of jobs since I left home before the war, and it always turns out the same. I just realized it lately. In Nebraska where I herded cattle, and the Dakotas, and Arizona, and now in Texas. It's why I came home now, I guess, because I realized it. This farm I work on, it's spring there now, see? And they've got about fifteen new colts. There's nothing more inspiring or—beautiful than the sight of a mare and a new colt. And it's cool there now, see? Texas is cool now, and it's spring. And whenever spring comes to where I am, I suddenly get the feeling, my God, I'm not gettin' anywhere! What the hell am I doing, playing around with horses, twenty-eight dollars a week! I'm thirty-four years old, I oughta be makin' my future. That's when I come running home. And now, I get here, and I don't know what to do with myself. (After a pause) I've always made a point of not wasting my life, and everytime I come back here I know that all I've done is to waste my life.

HAPPY. You're a poet, you know that, Biff? You're a—you're an idealist!

BIFF. No, I'm mixed up very bad. Maybe I oughta get married. Maybe I oughta get stuck into something. Maybe that's my trouble. I'm like a boy. I'm not married, I'm not in business, I just—I'm like a boy.

Are you content, Hap? You're a success, aren't you? Are you content?

HAPPY. Hell, no!

BIFF. Why? You're making money, aren't you?

HAPPY (moving about with energy, expressiveness). All I can do now is wait for the merchandise manager to die. And suppose I get to be merchandise manager? He's a good friend of mine, and he just built a terrific estate on Long Island. And he lived there about two months and sold it, and now he's building another one. He can't enjoy it once it's finished. And I know that's just what I would do. I don't know what the hell I'm workin' for. Sometimes I sit in my apartment—all alone. And I think of the rent I'm paying. And it's crazy. But then, it's what I always wanted. My own apartment, a car, and plenty of women. And still, goddammit, I'm lonely.

BIFF (with enthusiasm). Listen, why don't you come out West with me?

HAPPY. You and I, heh?

BIFF. Sure, maybe we could buy a ranch. Raise cattle, use our muscles. Men built like we are should be working out in the open.

HAPPY (avidly). The Loman Brothers, heh?

BIFF (with vast affection). Sure, we'd be known all over the counties!

HAPPY (enthralled). That's what I dream about, Biff. Sometimes I want to just rip my clothes off in the middle of the store and outbox that goddam merchandise manager. I mean I can outbox, outrun, and outlift anybody in that store, and I have to take orders from those common, petty sons-of-bitches till I can't stand it any more.

BIFF. I'm tellin' you, kid, if you were with me I'd be happy out there.

HAPPY (enthused). See, Biff, everybody around me is so false that I'm constantly lowering my ideals . . .

BIFF. Baby, together we'd stand up for one another, we'd have someone to trust.

HAPPY. If I were around you—

BIFF. Hap, the trouble is we weren't brought up to grub for money. I don't know how to do it.

HAPPY. Neither can I!

BIFF. Then let's go!

HAPPY. The only thing is—what can you make out there?

BIFF. But look at your friend. Builds an estate and then hasn't the peace of mind to live in it.

HAPPY. Yeah, but when he walks into the store the waves part in front of him. That's fifty-two thousand dollars a year coming through the revolving door, and I got more in my pinky finger than he's got in his head.

BIFF. Yeah, but you just said—

HAPPY. I gotta show some of those pompous, self-important executives over there that Hap Loman can make the grade. I want to walk into the store the way he walks in. Then I'll go with you, Biff. We'll be together yet, I swear. But take those two we had tonight. Now weren't they gorgeous creatures?

BIFF. Yeah, yeah, most gorgeous I've had in years.

HAPPY. I get that any time I want, Biff. Whenever I feel disgusted. The only trouble is, it gets like bowling or something. I just keep knockin' them over and it doesn't mean anything. You still run around a lot?

BIFF. Naa. I'd like to find a girl—steady, somebody with substance.

HAPPY. That's what I long for.

BIFF. Go on! You'd never come home.

HAPPY. I would! Somebody with character, with resistance! Like Mom, y'know? You're gonna call me a bastard when I tell you this. That girl Charlotte I was with tonight is engaged to be married in five weeks. (*He tries on his new hat*)

BIFF. No kiddin'!

HAPPY. Sure, the guy's in line for the vice-presidency of the store. I don't know what gets into me, maybe I just have an overdeveloped sense of competition or something, but I went and ruined her, and furthermore I can't get rid of her. And he's the third executive I've done that to. Isn't that a crummy characteristic? And to top it all, I go to their weddings! (*Indignantly, but laughing*) Like I'm not supposed to take bribes. Manufacturers offer me a hundred-dollar bill now and then to throw an order their way. You know how honest I am, but it's like this girl, see. I hate myself for it. Because I don't want the girl, and, still, I take it and—I love it!

BIFF. Let's go to sleep.

HAPPY. I guess we didn't settle anything, heh?

BIFF. I just got one idea that I think I'm going to try.

HAPPY. What's that?

BIFF. Remember Bill Oliver?

HAPPY. Sure, Oliver is very big now. You want to work for him again?

BIFF. No, but when I quit he said something to me. He put his arm on my shoulder and he said, "Biff, if you ever need anything, come to me."

HAPPY. I remember that. That sounds good.

BIFF. I think I'll go to see him. If I could get ten thousand or even seven or eight thousand dollars I could buy a beautiful ranch.

HAPPY. I bet he'd back you. 'Cause he thought highly of you, Biff. I mean, they all do. You're well liked, Biff. That's why I say to come back here, and we both have the apartment. And I'm tellin' you, Biff, any babe you want . . .

BIFF. No, with a ranch I could do the work I like and still be something. I just wonder though. I wonder if Oliver still thinks I stole that carton of basketballs.

HAPPY. Oh, he probably forgot that long ago. It's almost ten years. You're too sensitive. Anyway, he didn't really fire you.

BIFF. Well, I think he was going to. I think that's why I quit. I was never sure whether he knew or not. I know he thought the world of me, though. I was the only one he'd let lock up the place.

WILLY (*below*). You gonna wash the engine, Biff?

HAPPY. Shh! (*Biff looks at Happy, who is gazing down, listening. Willy is mumbling in the parlor*)

HAPPY. You hear that? (*They listen. Willy laughs warmly*)

BIFF (*growing angry*). Doesn't he know Mom can hear that?

WILLY. Don't get your sweater dirty, Biff! (*A look of pain crosses Biff's face*)

HAPPY. Isn't that terrible? Don't leave again, will you? You'll find a job here. You gotta stick around. I don't know what to do about him, it's getting embarrassing.

WILLY. What a simonizing job!

BIFF. Mom's hearing that!

WILLY. No kiddin', Biff, you got a date? Wonderful!

HAPPY. Go on to sleep. But talk to him in the morning, will you?

BIFF (*reluctantly getting into bed*). With her in the house. Brother!

HAPPY (*getting into bed*). I wish you'd have a good talk with him.

(*The light on their room begins to fade.*)

BIFF (*to himself, in bed*). That selfish, stupid . . .

HAPPY. Sh . . . Sleep, Biff.

(*Their light is out. Well before they have finished speaking, Willy's form is dimly seen below in the darkened kitchen. He opens the refrigerator, searches in there and takes out a bottle of milk. The apartment houses are fading out, and the entire house and surroundings become covered with leaves. Music insinuates itself as the leaves appear.*)

WILLY. Just wanna be careful with those girls, Biff, that's all. Don't make any promises. No promises of any kind. Because a girl, y'know, they always believe what you tell 'em, and you're very young, Biff, you're too young to be talking seriously to girls.

(*Light rises on the kitchen. Willy, talking, shuts the refrigerator door and comes downstage to the kitchen table. He pours milk into a glass. He is totally immersed in himself, smiling faintly.*)

WILLY. Too young entirely, Biff. You want to watch your schooling first. Then when you're all set, there'll be plenty of girls for a boy like you. (*He smiles broadly at a kitchen chair*) That so? The girls pay for you? (*He laughs*) Boy, you must really be makin' a hit.

(*Willy is gradually addressing—physically —a point offstage, speaking through the wall of the kitchen, and his voice has been rising in volume to that of a normal conversation.*)

WILLY. I been wondering why you polish the car so careful. Ha! Don't leave the hubcaps, boys. Get the chamois to the hubcaps. Happy, use newspapers on the windows, it's the easiest thing. Show him how to do it, Biff! You see, Happy? Pad it up, use it like a pad. That's it, that's it, good work. You're doin' all right, Hap. (*He pauses, then nods in approbation for a few seconds, then looks upward*) Biff, first thing we gotta do when we get time is clip that big branch over the house. Afraid it's gonna fall in a storm and hit the roof. Tell you what. We get a rope and sling her around, and then we climb up there with a couple of saws and take her down. Soon as you finish the car, boys, I wanna see ya. I got a surprise for you, boys.

BIFF (*offstage*). Whatta ya got, Dad?

WILLY. No, you finish first. Never leave a job till you're finished—remember that. (*Looking toward the "big trees"*) Biff, up in Albany I saw a beautiful hammock. I think I'll buy it next trip, and we'll hang it right between those two elms. Wouldn't that be something? Just swingin' there under those branches. Boy, that would be . . .

(*Young Biff and Young Happy appear from the direction Willy was addressing. Happy carries rags and a pail of water. Biff, wearing a sweater with a block "S," carries a football.*)

BIFF (*pointing in the direction of the car offstage*). How's that, Pop, professional?

WILLY. Terrific. Terrific job, boys. Good work, Biff.

HAPPY. Where's the surprise, Pop?

WILLY. In the back seat of the car.

HAPPY. Boy! (*He runs off*)

BIFF. What is it, Dad? Tell me, what'd you buy?

WILLY (*laughing, cuffs him*). Never mind, something I want you to have.

BIFF (*turns and starts off*). What is it, Hap?

HAPPY (*offstage*). It's a punching bag!

BIFF. Oh, Pop!

WILLY. It's got Gene Tunney's signature on it!

(*Happy runs onstage with a punching bag.*)

BIFF. Gee, how'd you know we wanted a punching bag?

WILLY. Well, it's the finest thing for the timing.

HAPPY (*lies down on his back and pedals with his feet*). I'm losing weight, you notice, Pop?

WILLY (*to Happy*). Jumping rope is good too.

BIFF. Did you see the new football I got?

WILLY (*examining the ball*). Where'd you get a new ball?

BIFF. The coach told me to practice my passing.

WILLY. That so? And he gave you the ball, heh?

BIFF. Well, I borrowed it from the locker room. (*He laughs confidentially*)

WILLY (*laughing with him at the theft*). I want you to return that.

HAPPY. I told you he wouldn't like it!

BIFF (*angrily*). Well, I'm bringing it back!

WILLY (*stopping the incipient argument, to Happy*). Sure, he's gotta practice with a regulation ball, doesn't he? (*To Biff*) Coach'll probably congratulate you on your initiative!

BIFF. Oh, he keeps congratulating my initiative all the time, Pop.

WILLY. That's because he likes you. If somebody else took that ball there'd be an uproar. So what's the report, boys, what's the report?

BIFF. Where'd you go this time, Dad? Gee, we were lonesome for you.

WILLY (*pleased, puts an arm around each boy and they come down to the apron*). Lonesome, heh?

BIFF. Missed you every minute.

WILLY. Don't say? Tell you a secret, boys. Don't breathe it to a soul. Someday I'll have my own business, and I'll never have to leave home any more.

HAPPY. Like Uncle Charley, heh?

WILLY. Bigger than Uncle Charley! Because Charley is not liked. He's liked, but he's not—well liked.

BIFF. Where'd you go this time, Dad?

WILLY. Well, I got on the road, and I went north to Providence. Met the Mayor.

BIFF. The Mayor of Providence!

WILLY. He was sitting in the hotel lobby.

BIFF. What'd he say?

WILLY. He said, "Morning!" And I said, "You got a fine city here, Mayor." And then he had coffee with me. And then I went to Waterbury. Waterbury is a fine city. Big clock city, the famous Waterbury clock. Sold a nice bill there. And then Boston—Boston is the cradle of the Revolution. A fine city. And a couple of other towns in Mass., and on to Portland and Bangor and straight home!

BIFF. Gee, I'd love to go with you some-time, Dad.

WILLY. Soon as summer comes.

HAPPY. Promise?

WILLY. You and Hap and I, and I'll show you all the towns. America is full of beautiful towns and fine, upstanding people. And they know me, boys, they know me up and down New England. The finest people. And when I bring you fellas up, there'll be open sesame for all of us, 'cause one thing, boys: I have friends. I can park my car in any street in New England, and the cops protect it like their own. This summer, heh?

BIFF and HAPPY (*together*). Yeah! You bet!

WILLY. We'll take our bathing suits.

HAPPY. We'll carry your bags, Pop!

WILLY. Oh, won't that be somethin'! Me comin' into the Boston stores with you boys carryin' my bags. What a sensation! (*Biff is prancing around, practicing passing the ball.*)

WILLY. You nervous, Biff, about the game?

BIFF. Not if you're gonna be there.

WILLY. What do they say about you in school, now that they made you captain?

HAPPY. There's a crowd of girls behind him everytime the classes change.

BIFF (*taking Willy's hand*). This Saturday, Pop, this Saturday—just for you, I'm going to break through for a touchdown.

HAPPY. You're supposed to pass.

BIFF. I'm takin' one play for Pop. You watch me, Pop, and when I take off my helmet, that means I'm breakin' out. Then you watch me crash through that line!

WILLY (*kisses Biff*). Oh, wait'll I tell this in Boston!

(*Bernard enters in knickers. He is younger than Biff, earnest and loyal, a worried boy.*)

BERNARD. Biff, where are you? You're supposed to study with me today.

WILLY. Hey, looka Bernard. What're you lookin' so anemic about, Bernard?

BERNARD. He's gotta study, Uncle Willy. He's got Regents next week.

HAPPY (*tauntingly, spinning Bernard around*). Let's box, Bernard!

BERNARD. Biff! (*He gets away from Happy*) Listen, Biff, I heard Mr. Birnbaum say that if you don't start studyin' math he's gonna flunk you, and you won't graduate. I heard him!

WILLY. You better study with him, Biff. Go ahead now.

BERNARD. I heard him!

BIFF. Oh, Pop, you didn't see my sneakers! (*He holds up a foot for Willy to look at*)

WILLY. Hey, that's a beautiful job of printing!

BERNARD (*wiping his glasses*). Just because he printed University of Virginia on his sneakers doesn't mean they've got to graduate him, Uncle Willy!

WILLY (*angrily*). What're you talking about? With scholarships to three universities they're gonna flunk him?

BERNARD. But I heard Mr. Birnbaum say—

WILLY. Don't be a pest, Bernard! (*To his boys*) What an anemic!

BERNARD. Okay, I'm waiting for you in my house, Biff.

(*Bernard goes off. The Lomans laugh.*)

WILLY. Bernard is not well liked, is he?

BIFF. He's liked, but he's not well liked.

HAPPY. That's right, Pop.

WILLY. That's just what I mean. Bernard can get the best marks in school, y'understand, but when he gets out in the business world, y'understand, you are going to be five times ahead of him. That's why I thank Almighty God you're both built like Adonises. Because the man who makes an appearance in the business world, the man who creates personal interest, is the man who gets ahead. Be liked and you will never want. You take me, for instance. I never have to wait in line to see a buyer. "Willy Loman is here!" That's all they have to know, and I go right through.

BIFF. Did you knock them dead, Pop?

WILLY. Knocked 'em cold in Providence, slaughtered 'em in Boston.

HAPPY (*on his back, pedaling again*). I'm losing weight, you notice, Pop?

(*Linda enters, as of old, a ribbon in her hair, carrying a basket of washing.*)

LINDA (*with youthful energy*). Hello, dear!

WILLY. Sweetheart!

LINDA. How'd the Chevvy run?

WILLY. Chevrolet, Linda, is the greatest car ever built. (*To the boys*) Since when do you let your mother carry wash up the stairs?

BIFF. Grab hold there, boy!

HAPPY. Where to, Mom?

LINDA. Hang them up on the line. And you better go down to your friends, Biff. The cellar is full of boys. They don't know what to do with themselves.

BIFF. Ah, when Pop comes home they can wait!

WILLY (*laughs appreciatively*). You better go down and tell them what to do, Biff.

BIFF. I think I'll have them sweep out the furnace room.

WILLY. Good work, Biff.

BIFF (*goes through wall-line of kitchen to doorway at back and calls down*). Fellas! Everybody sweep out the furnace room! I'll be right down!

VOICES. All right! Okay, Biff!

BIFF. George and Sam and Frank, come out back! We're hangin' up the wash! Come on, Hap, on the double! (*He and Happy carry out the basket*)

LINDA. The way they obey him!

WILLY. Well, that's training, the training. I'm tellin' you, I was sellin' thousands and thousands, but I had to come home.

LINDA. Oh, the whole block'll be at that game. Did you sell anything?

WILLY. I did five hundred gross in Providence and seven hundred gross in Boston.

LINDA. No! Wait a minute, I've got a pencil. (*She pulls pencil and paper out of her apron pocket*) That makes your commission . . . Two hundred—my God! Two hundred and twelve dollars!

WILLY. Well, I didn't figure it yet, but . . .

LINDA. How much did you do?

WILLY. Well, I—I did—about a hundred and eighty gross in Providence. Well, no—it came to—roughly two hundred gross on the whole trip.

LINDA (*without hesitation*). Two hundred gross. That's . . . (*She figures*)

WILLY. The trouble was that three of the stores were half closed for inventory in Boston. Otherwise I woulda broke records.

LINDA. Well, it makes seventy dollars and some pennies. That's very good.

WILLY. What do we owe?

LINDA. Well, on the first there's sixteen dollars on the refrigerator—

WILLY. Why sixteen?

LINDA. Well, the fan belt broke, so it was a dollar eighty.

WILLY. But it's brand new.

LINDA. Well, the man said that's the way it is. Till they work themselves in, y'know. (*They move through the wall-line into the kitchen.*)

WILLY. I hope we didn't get stuck on that machine.

LINDA. They got the biggest ads of any of them!

WILLY. I know, it's a fine machine. What else?

LINDA. Well, there's nine-sixty for the washing machine. And for the vacuum cleaner there's three and a half due on the fifteenth. Then the roof, you got twenty-one dollars remaining.

WILLY. It don't leak, does it?

LINDA. No, they did a wonderful job. Then you owe Frank for the carburetor.

WILLY. I'm not going to pay that man! That goddam Chevrolet, they ought to prohibit the manufacture of that car!

LINDA. Well, you owe him three and a half. And odds and ends, comes to around a hundred and twenty dollars by the fifteenth.

WILLY. A hundred and twenty dollars! My God, if business don't pick up I don't know what I'm gonna do!

LINDA. Well, next week you'll do better.

WILLY. Oh, I'll knock 'em dead next week. I'll go to Hartford. I'm very well liked in Hartford. You know, the trouble is, Linda, people don't seem to take to me. (*They move onto the forestage.*)

LINDA. Oh, don't be foolish.

WILLY. I know it when I walk in. They seem to laugh at me.

LINDA. Why? Why would they laugh at you? Don't talk that way, Willy.

(*Willy moves to the edge of the stage. Linda goes into the kitchen and starts to darn stockings.*)

WILLY. I don't know the reason for it, but they just pass me by. I'm not noticed.

LINDA. But you're doing wonderful, dear. You're making seventy to a hundred dollars a week.

WILLY. But I gotta be at it ten, twelve hours a day. Other men—I don't know—they do it easier. I don't know why—I can't stop myself—I talk too much. A man oughta come in with a few words. One thing about Charley. He's a man of few words, and they respect him.

LINDA. You don't talk too much, you're just lively.

WILLY (*smiling*). Well, I figure, what the hell, life is short, a couple of jokes. (*To himself*) I joke too much! (*The smile goes*)

LINDA. Why? You're—

WILLY. I'm fat. I'm very—foolish to look at, Linda. I didn't tell you, but Christmas time I happened to be calling on F. H. Stewarts, and a salesman I know, as I was going in to see the buyer I heard him say something about—walrus. And I—I cracked him right across the face. I won't take that. I simply will not take that. But they do laugh at me. I know that.

LINDA. Darling . . .

WILLY. I gotta overcome it. I know I gotta overcome it. I'm not dressing to advantage, maybe.

LINDA. Willy, darling, you're the handsomest man in the world—

WILLY. Oh, no, Linda.

LINDA. To me you are. (*Slight pause*) The handsomest.

(*From the darkness is heard the laughter of a woman. Willy doesn't turn to it, but it continues through Linda's lines.*)

LINDA. And the boys, Willy. Few men are idolized by their children the way you are.

(*Music is heard as behind a scrim, to the left of the house. The Woman, dimly seen, is dressing.*)

WILLY (*with great feeling*). You're the best there is, Linda, you're a pal, you know that? On the road—on the road I want to grab you sometimes and just kiss the life outa you.

(*The laughter is loud now, and he moves into a brightening area at the left, where The Woman has come from behind the scrim and is standing, putting on her hat, looking into a "mirror" and laughing.*)

WILLY. 'Cause I get so lonely—especially when business is bad and there's nobody to talk to. I get the feeling that I'll never sell anything again, that I won't make a living for you, or a business, a business for the boys. (*He talks through The Woman's subsiding laughter; The Woman primps at the "mirror"*) There's so much I want to make for—

THE WOMAN. Me? You didn't make me, Willy. I picked you.

WILLY (*pleased*). You picked me?

THE WOMAN (*who is quite proper-looking, Willy's age*). I did. I've been sitting at that desk watching all the salesmen go by, day in, day out. But you've got such a sense of humor, and we do have such a good time together, don't we?

WILLY. Sure, sure. (*He takes her in his arms*) Why do you have to go now?

THE WOMAN. It's two o'clock . . .

WILLY. No, come on in! (*He pulls her*)

THE WOMAN. . . . my sisters'll be scandalized. When'll you be back?

WILLY. Oh, two weeks about. Will you come up again?

THE WOMAN. Sure thing. You do make me laugh. It's good for me. (*She squeezes his arm, kisses him*) And I think you're a wonderful man.

WILLY. You picked me, heh?

THE WOMAN. Sure. Because you're so sweet. And such a kidder.

WILLY. Well, I'll see you next time I'm in Boston.

THE WOMAN. I'll put you right through to the buyers.

WILLY (slapping her bottom). Right. Well, bottoms up!

THE WOMAN (slaps him gently and laughs). You just kill me, Willy. (He suddenly grabs her and kisses her roughly) You kill me. And thanks for the stockings. I love a lot of stockings. Well, good night.

WILLY. Good night. And keep your pores open!

THE WOMAN. Oh, Willy!

(The Woman bursts out laughing, and Linda's laughter blends in. The Woman disappears into the dark. Now the area at the kitchen table brightens. Linda is sitting where she was at the kitchen table, but now is mending a pair of her silk stockings.)

LINDA. You are, Willy. The handsomest man. You've got no reason to feel that—

WILLY (coming out of The Woman's dimming area and going over to Linda). I'll make it all up to you. Linda, I'll—

LINDA. There's nothing to make up, dear. You're doing fine, better than—

WILLY (noticing her mending). What's that?

LINDA. Just mending my stockings. They're so expensive—

WILLY (angrily, taking them from her). I won't have you mending stockings in this house! Now throw them out!

(Linda puts the stockings in her pocket.)

BERNARD (entering on the run). Where is he? If he doesn't study!

WILLY (moving to the forestage, with great agitation). You'll give him the answers!

BERNARD. I do, but I can't on a Regents! That's a state exam! They're liable to arrest me!

WILLY. Where is he? I'll whip him, I'll whip him!

LINDA. And he'd better give back that football, Willy, it's not nice.

WILLY. Biff! Where is he? Why is he taking everything?

LINDA. He's too rough with the girls, Willy. All of the mothers are afraid of him!

WILLY. I'll whip him!

BERNARD. He's driving the car without a license!

(The Woman's laugh is heard.)

WILLY. Shut up!

LINDA. All the mothers—

WILLY. Shut up!

BERNARD (backing quietly away and out). Mr. Birnbaum says he's stuck up.

WILLY. Get outa here!

BERNARD. If he doesn't buckle down he'll flunk math! (He goes off)

LINDA. He's right, Willy, you've gotta—

WILLY (exploding at her). There's nothing the matter with him! You want him to be a worm like Bernard? He's got spirit, personality . . .

(As he speaks, Linda, almost in tears, exits into the living-room. Willy is alone in the kitchen, wilting and staring. The leaves are gone. It is night again, and the apartment houses look down from behind.)

WILLY. Loaded with it. Loaded! What is he stealing? He's giving it back, isn't he? Why is he stealing? What did I tell him? I never in my life told him anything but decent things.

(Happy in pajamas has come down the stairs; Willy suddenly becomes aware of Happy's presence.)

HAPPY. Let's go now, come on.

WILLY (sitting down at the kitchen table). Huh! Why did she have to wax the floors herself? Everytime she waxes the floors she keels over. She knows that!

HAPPY. Shh! Take it easy. What brought you back tonight?

WILLY. I got an awful scare. Nearly hit a kid in Yonkers. God! Why didn't I go to Alaska with my brother Ben that time! Ben! That man was a genius, that man was success incarnate! What a mistake! He begged me to go.

HAPPY. Well, there's no use in—

WILLY. You guys! There was a man started with the clothes on his back and ended up with diamond mines!

HAPPY. Boy, some day I'd like to know how he did it.

WILLY. What's the mystery? The man knew what he wanted and went out and got it! Walked into a jungle, and comes out, the age of twenty-one, and he's rich! The world is an oyster, but you don't crack it open on a mattress!

HAPPY. Pop, I told you I'm gonna retire you for life.

WILLY. You'll retire me for life on seventy goddam dollars a week? And your women and your car and your apartment, and you'll retire me for life! Christ's sake, I couldn't get past Yonkers today! Where are you guys, where are you? The woods are burning! I can't drive a car!

(Charley has appeared in the doorway. He is a large man, slow of speech, laconic, immovable. In all he says, despite what he says, there is pity, and, now, trepidation. He has a robe over pajamas, slippers on his feet. He enters the kitchen.)

CHARLEY. Everything all right?

HAPPY. Yeah, Charley, everything's . . .

WILLY. What's the matter?

CHARLEY. I heard some noise. I thought something happened. Can't we do something about the walls? You sneeze in here, and in my house hats blow off.

HAPPY. Let's go to bed, Dad. Come on.

(Charley signals to Happy to go.)

WILLY. You go ahead, I'm not tired at the moment.

HAPPY *(to Willy)*. Take it easy, huh? *(He exits)*

WILLY. What're you doin' up?

CHARLEY *(sitting down at the kitchen table opposite Willy)*. Couldn't sleep good. I had a heartburn.

WILLY. Well, you don't know how to eat.

CHARLEY. I eat with my mouth.

WILLY. No, you're ignorant. You gotta know about vitamins and things like that.

CHARLEY. Come on, let's shoot. Tire you out a little.

WILLY *(hesitantly)*. All right. You got cards?

CHARLEY *(taking a deck from his pocket)*. Yeah, I got them. Someplace. What is it with those vitamins?

WILLY *(dealing)*. They build up your bones. Chemistry.

CHARLEY. Yeah, but there's no bones in a heartburn.

WILLY. What are you talkin' about? Do you know the first thing about it?

CHARLEY. Don't get insulted.

WILLY. Don't talk about something you don't know anything about.

(They are playing. Pause.)

CHARLEY. What're you doin' home?

WILLY. A little trouble with the car.

CHARLEY. Oh. *(Pause)* I'd like to take a trip to California.

WILLY. Don't say.

CHARLEY. You want a job?

WILLY. I got a job, I told you that.

(After a slight pause) What the hell are you offering me a job for?

CHARLEY. Don't get insulted.

WILLY. Don't insult me.

CHARLEY. I don't see no sense in it. You don't have to go on this way.

WILLY. I got a good job. *(Slight pause)* What do you keep comin' in here for?

CHARLEY. You want me to go?

WILLY *(after a pause, withering)*. I can't understand it. He's going back to Texas again. What the hell is that?

CHARLEY. Let him go.

WILLY. I got nothin' to give him, Charley, I'm clean, I'm clean.

CHARLEY. He won't starve. None of them starve. Forget about him.

WILLY. Then what have I got to remember?

CHARLEY. You take it too hard. To hell with it. When a deposit bottle is broken you don't get your nickel back.

WILLY. That's easy enough for you to say.

CHARLEY. That ain't easy for me to say.

WILLY. Did you see the ceiling I put up in the living-room?

CHARLEY. Yeah, that's a piece of work. To put up a ceiling is a mystery to me. How do you do it?

WILLY. What's the difference?

CHARLEY. Well, talk about it.

WILLY. You gonna put up a ceiling?

CHARLEY. How could I put up a ceiling?

WILLY. Then what the hell are you bothering me for?

CHARLEY. You're insulted again.

WILLY. A man who can't handle tools is not a man. You're disgusting.

CHARLEY. Don't call me disgusting, Willy.

(Uncle Ben, carrying a valise and an umbrella, enters the forestage from around the right corner of the house. He is a stolid man, in his sixties, with a mustache and an authoritative air. He is utterly certain of his destiny, and there is an aura of far places about him. He enters exactly as Willy speaks.)

WILLY. I'm getting awfully tired, Ben.

(Ben's music is heard. Ben looks around at everything.)

CHARLEY. Good, keep playing; you'll sleep better. Did you call me Ben?

(Ben looks at his watch.)

WILLY. That's funny. For a second there you reminded me of my brother Ben.

BEN. I only have a few minutes. *(He strolls, inspecting the place. Willy and Charley continue playing)*

CHARLEY. You never heard from him again, heh? Since that time?

WILLY. Didn't Linda tell you? Couple of weeks ago we got a letter from his wife in Africa. He died.

CHARLEY. That so.

BEN *(chuckling)*. So this is Brooklyn, eh?

CHARLEY. Maybe you're in for some of his money.

WILLY. Naa, he had seven sons. There's just one opportunity I had with that man . . .

BEN. I must make a train, William. There are several properties I'm looking at in Alaska.

WILLY. Sure, sure! If I'd gone with him to Alaska that time, everything would've been totally different.

CHARLEY. Go on, you'd froze to death up there.

WILLY. What're you talking about?

BEN. Opportunity is tremendous in Alaska, William. Surprised you're not up there.

WILLY. Sure, tremendous.

CHARLEY. Heh?

WILLY. There was the only man I ever met who knew the answers.

CHARLEY. Who?

BEN. How are you all?

WILLY *(taking a pot, smiling)*. Fine, fine.

CHARLEY. Pretty sharp tonight.

BEN. Is Mother living with you?

WILLY. No, she died a long time ago.

CHARLEY. Who?

BEN. That's too bad. Fine specimen of a lady, Mother.

WILLY *(to Charley)*. Heh?

BEN. I'd hoped to see the old girl.

CHARLEY. Who died?

BEN. Heard anything from Father, have you?

WILLY *(unnerved)*. What do you mean, who died?

CHARLEY *(taking a pot)*. What're you talkin' about?

BEN *(looking at his watch)*. William, it's half-past eight!

WILLY *(as though to dispel his confusion he angrily stops Charley's hand)*. That's my build!

CHARLEY. I put the ace—

WILLY. If you don't know how to play

the game I'm not gonna throw my money away on you!

CHARLEY *(rising)*. It was my ace, for God's sake!

WILLY. I'm through, I'm through!

BEN. When did Mother die?

WILLY. Long ago. Since the beginning you never knew how to play cards.

CHARLEY *(picks up the cards and goes to the door)*. All right! Next time I'll bring a deck with five aces.

WILLY. I don't play that kind of game!

CHARLEY *(turning to him)*. You ought to be ashamed of yourself!

WILLY. Yeah?

CHARLEY. Yeah! *(He goes out)*

WILLY *(slamming the door after him)*. Ignoramus!

BEN *(as Willy comes toward him through the wall-line of the kitchen)*. So you're William.

WILLY *(shaking Ben's hand)*. Ben! I've been waiting for you so long! What's the answer? How did you do it?

BEN. Oh, there's a story in that.

(Linda enters the forestage, as of old, carrying the wash basket.)

LINDA. Is this Ben?

BEN *(gallantly)*. How do you do, my dear.

LINDA. Where've you been all these years? Willy's always wondered why you—

WILLY *(pulling Ben away from her impatiently)*. Where is Dad? Didn't you follow him? How did you get started?

BEN. Well, I don't know how much you remember.

WILLY. Well, I was just a baby, of course, only three or four years old—

BEN. Three years and eleven months.

WILLY. What a memory, Ben!

BEN. I have many enterprises, William, and I have never kept books.

WILLY. I remember I was sitting under the wagon in—was it Nebraska?

BEN. It was South Dakota, and I gave you a bunch of wild flowers.

WILLY. I remember you walking away down some open road.

BEN *(laughing)*. I was going to find Father in Alaska.

WILLY. Where is he?

BEN. At that age I had a very faulty view of geography, William. I discovered after a few days that I was heading due south, so instead of Alaska, I ended up in Africa.

LINDA. Africa!

WILLY. The Gold Coast!

BEN. Principally diamond mines.

LINDA. Diamond mines!

BEN. Yes, my dear. But I've only a few minutes—

WILLY. No! Boys! Boys! *(Young Biff and Happy appear)* Listen to this. This is your Uncle Ben, a great man! Tell my boys, Ben!

BEN. Why, boys, when I was seventeen I walked into the jungle, and when I was twenty-one I walked out. *(He laughs)* And by God I was rich.

WILLY *(to the boys)*. You see what I been talking about? The greatest things can happen!

BEN *(glancing at his watch)*. I have an appointment in Ketchikan Tuesday week.

WILLY. No, Ben! Please tell about Dad. I want my boys to hear. I want them to know the kind of stock they spring from. All I remember is a man with a big beard, and I was in Mamma's lap, sitting around a fire, and some kind of high music.

BEN. His flute. He played the flute.

WILLY. Sure, the flute, that's right! *(New music is heard, a high, rollicking tune.)*

BEN. Father was a very great and a very wild-hearted man. We would start in Boston, and he'd toss the whole family into the wagon, and then he'd drive the team right across the country; through Ohio, and Indiana, Michigan, Illinois, and all the Western states. And we'd stop in the towns and sell the flutes that he'd made on the way. Great inventor, Father. With one gadget he made more in a week than a man like you could make in a lifetime.

WILLY. That's just the way I'm bringing them up, Ben—rugged, well liked, all-around.

BEN. Yeah? *(To Biff)* Hit that, boy—hard as you can. *(He pounds his stomach)*

BIFF. Oh, no, sir!

BEN *(taking boxing stance)*. Come on, get to me! *(He laughs)*

WILLY. Go to it, Biff! Go ahead, show him!

BIFF. Okay! *(He cocks his fists and starts in)*

LINDA *(to Willy)*. Why must he fight, dear?

BEN *(sparring with Biff)*. Good boy! Good boy!

WILLY. How's that, Ben, heh?

HAPPY. Give him the left, Biff!

LINDA. Why are you fighting?

BEN. Good boy! *(Suddenly comes in, trips Biff, and stands over him, the point of his umbrella poised over Biff's eye)*

LINDA. Look out, Biff!

BIFF. Gee!

BEN *(patting Biff's knee)*. Never fight fair with a stranger, boy. You'll never get out of the jungle that way. *(Taking Linda's hand and bowing)* It was an honor and a pleasure to meet you, Linda.

LINDA *(withdrawing her hand coldly, frightened)*. Have a nice—trip.

BEN *(to Willy)*. And good luck with your—what do you do?

WILLY. Selling.

BEN. Yes. Well . . . *(He raises his hand in farewell to all)*

WILLY. No, Ben, I don't want you to think . . . *(He takes Ben's arm to show him)* It's Brooklyn, I know, but we hunt too.

BEN. Really, now.

WILLY. Oh, sure, there's snakes and rabbits and—that's why I moved out here. Why, Biff can fell any one of these trees in no time! Boys! Go right over to where they're building the apartment house and get some sand. We're gonna rebuild the entire front stoop right now! Watch this, Ben!

BIFF. Yes, sir! On the double, Hap!

HAPPY *(as he and Biff run off)*. I lost weight, Pop, you notice? *(Charley enters in knickers, even before the boys are gone.)*

CHARLEY. Listen, if they steal any more from that building the watchman'll put the cops on them!

LINDA *(to Willy)*. Don't let Biff . . . *(Ben laughs lustily.)*

WILLY. You shoulda seen the lumber they brought home last week. At least a dozen six-by-tens worth all kinds a money.

CHARLEY. Listen, if that watchman—

WILLY. I gave them hell, understand. But I got a couple of fearless characters there.

CHARLEY. Willy, the jails are full of fearless characters.

BEN *(clapping Willy on the back, with a laugh at Charley)*. And the stock exchange, friend!

WILLY *(joining in Ben's laughter)*. Where are the rest of your pants?

CHARLEY. My wife bought them.

WILLY. Now all you need is a golf club and you can go upstairs and go to sleep. (*To Ben*) Great athlete! Between him and his son Bernard they can't hammer a nail!

BERNARD (*rushing in*). The watchman's chasing Biff!

WILLY (*angrily*). Shut up! He's not stealing anything!

LINDA (*alarmed, hurrying off left*). Where is he? Biff, dear! (*She exits*)

WILLY (*moving toward the left, away from Ben*). There's nothing wrong. What's the matter with you?

BEN. Nervy boy. Good!

WILLY (*laughing*). Oh, nerves of iron, that Biff!

CHARLEY. Don't know what it is. My New England man comes back and he's bleedin', they murdered him up there.

WILLY. It's contacts, Charley, I got important contacts!

CHARLEY (*sarcastically*). Glad to hear it, Willy. Come in later, we'll shoot a little casino. I'll take some of your Portland money. (*He laughs at Willy and exits*)

WILLY (*turning to Ben*). Business is bad, it's murderous. But not for me, of course.

BEN. I'll stop by on my way back to Africa.

WILLY (*longingly*). Can't you stay a few days? You're just what I need, Ben, because I—I have a fine position here, but I—well, Dad left when I was such a baby and I never had a chance to talk to him and I still feel—kind of temporary about myself.

BEN. I'll be late for my train.

(*They are at opposite ends of the stage.*)

WILLY. Ben, my boys—can't we talk? They'd go into the jaws of hell for me, see, but I—

BEN. William, you're being first-rate with your boys. Outstanding, manly chaps.

WILLY (*hanging on to his words*). Oh, Ben, that's good to hear! Because sometimes I'm afraid that I'm not teaching them the right kind of—Ben, how should I teach them?

BEN (*giving great weight to each word, and with a certain vicious audacity*). William, when I walked into the jungle, I was seventeen. When I walked out I was twenty-one. And, by God, I was rich! (*He goes off into the darkness around the right corner of the house*)

WILLY. . . . was rich! That's just the spirit I want to imbue them with! To walk into a jungle! I was right! I was right! I was right!

(*Ben is gone, but Willy is still speaking to him as Linda, in nightgown and robe, enters the kitchen, glances around for Willy, then goes to the door of the house, looks out and sees him. Comes down to his left. He looks at her.*)

LINDA. Willy, dear? Willy?

WILLY. I was right!

LINDA. Did you have some cheese? (*He can't answer*) It's very late, darling. Come to bed, heh?

WILLY (*looking straight up*). Gotta break your neck to see a star in this yard.

LINDA. You coming in?

WILLY. Whatever happened to that diamond watch fob? Remember? When Ben came from Africa that time? Didn't he give me a watch fob with a diamond in it?

LINDA. You pawned it, dear. Twelve, thirteen years ago. For Biff's radio correspondence course.

WILLY. Gee, that was a beautiful thing. I'll take a walk.

LINDA. But you're in your slippers.

WILLY (*starting to go around the house at the left*). I was right! I was! (*Half to Linda, as he goes, shaking his head*) What a man! There was a man worth talking to. I was right!

LINDA (*calling after Willy*). But in your slippers, Willy!

(*Willy is almost gone when Biff, in his pajamas, comes down the stairs and enters the kitchen.*)

BIFF. What is he doing out there?

LINDA. Sh!

BIFF. God Almighty, Mom, how long has he been doing this?

LINDA. Don't, he'll hear you.

BIFF. What the hell is the matter with him?

LINDA. It'll pass by morning.

BIFF. Shouldn't we do anything?

LINDA. Oh, my dear, you should do a lot of things, but there's nothing to do, so go to sleep.

(*Happy comes down the stairs and sits on the steps.*)

HAPPY. I never heard him so loud, Mom.

LINDA. Well, come around more often; you'll hear him. (*She sits down at the table and mends the lining of Willy's jacket)*

BIFF. Why didn't you ever write me about this, Mom?

LINDA. How would I write to you? For over three months you had no address.

BIFF. I was on the move. But you know I thought of you all the time. You know that, don't you, pal?

LINDA. I know, dear, I know. But he likes to have a letter. Just to know that there's still a possibility for better things.

BIFF. He's not like this all the time, is he?

LINDA. It's when you come home he's always the worst.

BIFF. When I come home?

LINDA. When you write you're coming, he's all smiles, and talks about the future, and—he's just wonderful. And then the closer you seem to come, the more shaky he gets, and then, by the time you get here, he's arguing, and he seems angry at you. I think it's just that maybe he can't bring himself to—open up to you. Why are you so hateful to each other? Why is that?

BIFF *(evasively)*. I'm not hateful, Mom.

LINDA. But you no sooner come in the door than you're fighting!

BIFF. I don't know why, I mean to change. I'm tryin', Mom, you understand?

LINDA. Are you home to stay now?

BIFF. I don't know. I want to look around, see what's doin'.

LINDA. Biff, you can't look around all your life, can you?

BIFF. I just can't take hold, Mom. I can't take hold of some kind of a life.

LINDA. Biff, a man is not a bird, to come and go with the springtime.

BIFF. Your hair . . . *(He touches her hair)* Your hair got so gray.

LINDA. Oh, it's been gray since you were in high school. I just stopped dyeing it, that's all.

BIFF. Dye it again, will ya? I don't want my pal looking old. *(He smiles)*

LINDA. You're such a boy! You think you can go away for a year and . . . You've got to get it into your head now that one day you'll knock on this door and there'll be strange people here—

BIFF. What are you talking about? You're not even sixty, Mom.

LINDA. But what about your father?

BIFF *(lamely)*. Well, I meant him too.

HAPPY. He admires Pop.

LINDA. Biff, dear, if you don't have any feeling for him, then you can't have any feeling for me.

BIFF. Sure I can, Mom.

LINDA. No. You can't just come to see me, because I love him. *(With a threat, but only a threat, of tears)* He's the dearest man in the world to me, and I won't have anyone making him feel unwanted and low and blue. You've got to make up your mind now, darling, there's no leeway any more. Either he's your father and you pay him that respect, or else you're not to come here. I know he's not easy to get along with—nobody knows that better than me—but . . .

WILLY *(from the left, with a laugh)*. Hey, hey, Biffo!

BIFF *(starting to go out after Willy)*. What the hell is the matter with him? *(Happy stops him)*

LINDA. Don't—don't go near him!

BIFF. Stop making excuses for him! He always, always wiped the floor with you! Never had an ounce of respect for you.

HAPPY. He's always had respect for—

BIFF. What the hell do you know about it?

HAPPY *(surlily)*. Just don't call him crazy!

BIFF. He's got no character—Charley wouldn't do this. Not in his own house—spewing out that vomit from his mind.

HAPPY. Charley never had to cope with what he's got to.

BIFF. People are worse off than Willy Loman. Believe me, I've seen them!

LINDA. Then make Charley your father, Biff. You can't do that, can you? I don't say he's a great man. Willy Loman never made a lot of money. His name was never in the paper. He's not the finest character that ever lived. But he's a human being, and a terrible thing is happening to him. So attention must be paid. He's not to be allowed to fall into his grave like an old dog. Attention, attention must be finally paid to such a person. You called him crazy—

BIFF. I didn't mean—

LINDA. No, a lot of people think he's lost his—balance. But you don't have to be very smart to know what his trouble is. The man is exhausted.

HAPPY. Sure!

LINDA. A small man can be just as exhausted as a great man. He works for a company thirty-six years this March, opens up unheard-of territories to their trademark, and now in his old age they take his salary away.

HAPPY (*indignantly*). I didn't know that, Mom.

LINDA. You never asked, my dear! Now that you get your spending money someplace else you don't trouble your mind with him.

HAPPY. But I gave you money last—

LINDA. Christmas time, fifty dollars! To fix the hot water it cost ninety-seven fifty! For five weeks he's been on straight commission, like a beginner, an unknown!

BIFF. Those ungrateful bastards!

LINDA. Are they any worse than his sons? When he brought them business, when he was young, they were glad to see him. But now his old friends, the old buyers that loved him so and always found some order to hand him in a pinch—they're all dead, retired. He used to be able to make six, seven calls a day in Boston. Now he takes his valises out of the car and puts them back and takes them out again and he's exhausted. Instead of walking he talks now. He drives seven hundred miles, and when he gets there no one knows him any more, no one welcomes him. And what goes through a man's mind, driving seven hundred miles home without having earned a cent? Why shouldn't he talk to himself? Why? When he has to go to Charley and borrow fifty dollars a week and pretend to me that it's his pay? How long can that go on? How long? You see what I'm sitting here and waiting for? And you tell me he has no character? The man who never worked a day but for your benefit? When does he get the medal for that? Is this his reward—to turn around at the age of sixty-three and find his sons, who he loved better than his life, one a philandering bum—

HAPPY. Mom!

LINDA. That's all you are, my baby! (*To Biff*) And you! What happened to the love you had for him? You were such pals! How you used to talk to him on the phone every night! How lonely he was till he could come home to you!

BIFF. All right, Mom. I'll live here in my room, and I'll get a job. I'll keep away from him, that's all.

LINDA. No, Biff. You can't stay here and fight all the time.

BIFF. He threw me out of this house, remember that.

LINDA. Why did he do that? I never knew why.

BIFF. Because I know he's a fake and he doesn't like anybody around who knows!

LINDA. Why a fake? In what way? What do you mean?

BIFF. Just don't lay it all at my feet. It's between me and him—that's all I have to say. I'll chip in from now on. He'll settle for half my pay check. He'll be all right. I'm going to bed. (*He starts for the stairs*)

LINDA. He won't be all right.

BIFF (*turning on the stairs, furiously*). I hate this city and I'll stay here. Now what do you want?

LINDA. He's dying, Biff.

(*Happy turns quickly to her, shocked.*)

BIFF (*after a pause*). Why is he dying?

LINDA. He's been trying to kill himself.

BIFF (*with great horror*). How?

LINDA. I live from day to day.

BIFF. What're you talking about?

LINDA. Remember I wrote you that he smashed up the car again? In February?

BIFF. Well?

LINDA. The insurance inspector came. He said that they have evidence. That all these accidents in the last year—weren't—weren't—accidents.

HAPPY. How can they tell that? That's a lie.

LINDA. It seems there's a woman . . . (*She takes a breath as*)

BIFF (*sharply but contained*). What woman?

LINDA (*simultaneously*). . . . and this woman . . .

LINDA. What?

BIFF. Nothing. Go ahead.

LINDA. What did you say?

BIFF. Nothing. I just said what woman?

HAPPY. What about her?

LINDA. Well, it seems she was walking down the road and saw his car. She says that he wasn't driving fast at all, and that he didn't skid. She says he came to that little bridge, and then deliberately smashed into the railing, and it was only the shallowness of the water that saved him.

BIFF. Oh, no, he probably just fell asleep again.

LINDA. I don't think he fell asleep.

BIFF. Why not?

LINDA. Last month ... (*With great difficulty*) Oh, boys, it's so hard to say a thing like this! He's just a big stupid man to you, but I tell you there's more good in him than in many other people. (*She chokes, wipes her eyes*) I was looking for a fuse. The lights blew out, and I went down the cellar. And behind the fuse box —it happened to fall out—was a length of rubber pipe—just short.

HAPPY. No kidding?

LINDA. There's a little attachment on the end of it. I knew right away. And sure enough, on the bottom of the water heater there's a new little nipple on the gas pipe.

HAPPY (*angrily*). That—jerk.

BIFF. Did you have it taken off?

LINDA. I'm—I'm ashamed to. How can I mention it to him? Every day I go down and take away that little rubber pipe. But, when he comes home, I put it back where it was. How can I insult him that way? I don't know what to do. I live from day to day, boys. I tell you, I know every thought in his mind. It sounds so old-fashioned and silly, but I tell you he put his whole life into you and you've turned your backs on him. (*She is bent over in the chair, weeping, her face in her hands*) Biff, I swear to God! Biff, his life is in your hands!

HAPPY (*to Biff*). How do you like that damned fool!

BIFF (*kissing her*). All right, pal, all right. It's all settled now. I've been remiss. I know that, Mom. But now I'll stay, and I swear to you, I'll apply myself. (*Kneeling in front of her, in a fever of self-reproach*) It's just—you see, Mom, I don't fit in business. Not that I won't try. I'll try, and I'll make good.

HAPPY. Sure you will. The trouble with you in business was you never tried to please people.

BIFF. I know, I—

HAPPY. Like when you worked for Harrison's. Bob Harrison said you were tops, and then you go and do some damn fool thing like whistling whole songs in the elevator like a comedian.

BIFF (*against Happy*). So what? I like to whistle sometimes.

HAPPY. You don't raise a guy to a responsible job who whistles in the elevator!

LINDA. Well, don't argue about it now.

HAPPY. Like when you'd go off and swim in the middle of the day instead of taking the line around.

BIFF (*his resentment rising*). Well, don't you run off? You take off sometimes, don't you? On a nice summer day?

HAPPY. Yeah, but I cover myself!

LINDA. Boys!

HAPPY. If I'm going to take a fade the boss can call any number where I'm supposed to be and they'll swear to him that I just left. I'll tell you something that I hate to say, Biff, but in the business world some of them think you're crazy.

BIFF (*angered*). Screw the business world!

HAPPY. All right, screw it! Great, but cover yourself!

LINDA. Hap, Hap!

BIFF. I don't care what they think! They've laughed at Dad for years, and you know why? Because we don't belong in this nuthouse of a city! We should be mixing cement on some open plain, or— or carpenters. A carpenter is allowed to whistle!

(*Willy walks in from the entrance of the house, at left.*)

WILLY. Even your grandfather was better than a carpenter. (*Pause. They watch him*) You never grew up. Bernard does not whistle in the elevator, I assure you.

BIFF (*as though to laugh Willy out of it*). Yeah, but you do, Pop.

WILLY. I never in my life whistled in an elevator! And who in the business world thinks I'm crazy?

BIFF. I didn't mean it like that, Pop. Now don't make a whole thing out of it, will ya?

WILLY. Go back to the West! Be a carpenter, a cowboy, enjoy yourself!

LINDA. Willy, he was just saying—

WILLY. I heard what he said!

HAPPY (*trying to quiet Willy*). Hey, Pop, come on now ...

WILLY (*continuing over Happy's line*). They laugh at me, heh? Go to Filene's, go to the Hub, go to Slattery's, Boston. Call out the name Willy Loman and see what happens! Big shot!

BIFF. All right, Pop.

WILLY. Big!

BIFF. All right!

WILLY. Why do you always insult me?

BIFF. I didn't say a word. (*To Linda*) Did I say a word?

LINDA. He didn't say anything, Willy.

WILLY (*going to the doorway of the living-room*). All right, good night, good night.

LINDA. Willy, dear, he just decided . . .

WILLY (*to Biff*). If you get tired hanging around tomorrow, paint the ceiling I put up in the living-room.

BIFF. I'm leaving early tomorrow.

HAPPY. He's going to see Bill Oliver, Pop.

WILLY (*interestedly*). Oliver? For what?

BIFF (*with reserve, but trying, trying*). He always said he'd stake me. I'd like to go into business, so maybe I can take him up on it.

LINDA. Isn't that wonderful?

WILLY. Don't interrupt. What's wonderful about it? There's fifty men in the City of New York who'd stake him. (*To Biff*) Sporting goods?

BIFF. I guess so. I know something about it and—

WILLY. He knows something about it! You know sporting goods better than Spalding, for God's sake! How much is he giving you?

BIFF. I don't know, I didn't even see him yet, but—

WILLY. Then what're you talkin' about?

BIFF (*getting angry*). Well, all I said was I'm gonna see him, that's all!

WILLY (*turning away*). Ah, you're counting your chickens again.

BIFF (*starting left for the stairs*). Oh, Jesus, I'm going to sleep!

WILLY (*calling after him*). Don't curse in this house!

BIFF (*turning*). Since when did you get so clean?

HAPPY (*trying to stop them*). Wait a . . .

WILLY. Don't use that language to me! I won't have it!

HAPPY (*grabbing Biff, shouts*). Wait a minute! I got an idea. I got a feasible idea. Come here, Biff, let's talk this over now, let's talk some sense here. When I was down in Florida last time, I thought of a great idea to sell sporting goods. It just came back to me. You and I, Biff—we have a line, the Loman Line. We train a couple of weeks, and put on a couple of exhibitions, see?

WILLY. That's an idea!

HAPPY. Wait! We form two basketball teams, see? Two water-polo teams. We play each other. It's a million dollars' worth of publicity. Two brothers, see? The Loman Brothers. Displays in the Royal Palms—all the hotels. And banners over the ring and the basketball court: "Loman Brothers." Baby, we could sell sporting goods!

WILLY. That is a one-million-dollar idea!

LINDA. Marvelous!

BIFF. I'm in great shape as far as that's concerned.

HAPPY. And the beauty of it is, Biff, it wouldn't be like a business. We'd be out playin' ball again . . .

BIFF (*enthused*). Yeah, that's . . .

WILLY. Million-dollar . . .

HAPPY. And you wouldn't get fed up with it, Biff. It'd be the family again. There'd be the old honor, and comradeship, and if you wanted to go off for a swim or somethin'—well, you'd do it! Without some smart cooky gettin' up ahead of you!

WILLY. Lick the world! You guys together could absolutely lick the civilized world.

BIFF. I'll see Oliver tomorrow. Hap, if we could work that out . . .

LINDA. Maybe things are beginning to—

WILLY (*wildly enthused, to Linda*). Stop interrupting! (*To Biff*) But don't wear sport jacket and slacks when you see Oliver.

BIFF. No, I'll—

WILLY. A business suit, and talk as little as possible, and don't crack any jokes.

BIFF. He did like me. Always liked me.

LINDA. He loved you!

WILLY (*to Linda*). Will you stop? (*To Biff*) Walk in very serious. You are not applying for a boy's job. Money is to pass. Be quiet, fine, and serious. Everybody likes a kidder, but nobody lends him money.

HAPPY. I'll try to get some myself, Biff. I'm sure I can.

WILLY. I see great things for you kids. I think your troubles are over. But remember, start big and you'll end big. Ask for fifteen. How much you gonna ask for?

BIFF. Gee, I don't know—

WILLY. And don't say "Gee." "Gee" is a boy's word. A man walking in for fifteen thousand dollars does not say "Gee!"

BIFF. Ten, I think, would be top though.

WILLY. Don't be so modest. You always started too low. Walk in with a big laugh. Don't look worried. Start off with a couple of your good stories to lighten things up.

It's not what you say, it's how you say it—because personality always wins the day.

LINDA. Oliver always thought the highest of him—

WILLY. Will you let me talk?

BIFF. Don't yell at her, Pop, will ya?

WILLY (*angrily*). I was talking, wasn't I?

BIFF. I don't like you yelling at her all the time, and I'm tellin' you, that's all.

WILLY. What're you, takin' over this house?

LINDA. Willy—

WILLY (*turning on her*). Don't take his side all the time, goddammit!

BIFF (*furiously*). Stop yelling at her!

WILLY (*suddenly pulling on his cheek, beaten down, guilt ridden*). Give my best to Bill Oliver—he may remember me. (*He exits through the living-room doorway*)

LINDA (*her voice subdued*). What'd you have to start that for? (*Biff turns away*) You see how sweet he was as soon as you talked hopefully? (*She goes over to Biff*) Come up and say good night to him. Don't let him go to bed that way.

HAPPY. Come on, Biff, let's buck him up.

LINDA. Please, dear. Just say good night. It takes so little to make him happy. Come. (*She goes through the living-room doorway, calling upstairs from within the living-room*) Your pajamas are hanging in the bathroom, Willy!

HAPPY (*looking toward where Linda went out*). What a woman! They broke the mold when they made her. You know that, Biff?

BIFF. He's off salary. My God, working on commission!

HAPPY. Well, let's face it: he's no hot-shot selling man. Except that sometimes, you have to admit, he's a sweet personality.

BIFF (*deciding*). Lend me ten bucks, will ya? I want to buy some new ties.

HAPPY. I'll take you to a place I know. Beautiful stuff. Wear one of my striped shirts tomorrow.

BIFF. She got gray. Mom got awful old. Gee, I'm gonna go in to Oliver tomorrow and knock him for a—

HAPPY. Come on up. Tell that to Dad. Let's give him a whirl. Come on.

BIFF (*steamed up*). You know, with ten thousand bucks, boy!

HAPPY (*as they go into the living-room*). That's the talk, Biff, that's the first time I've heard the old confidence out of you!

(*From within the living-room, fading off*) You're gonna live with me, kid, and any babe you want just say the word . . . (*The last lines are hardly heard. They are mounting the stairs to their parents' bedroom*)

LINDA (*entering her bedroom and addressing Willy, who is in the bathroom. She is straightening the bed for him*). Can you do anything about the shower? It drips.

WILLY (*from the bathroom*). All of a sudden everything falls to pieces! Goddam plumbing, oughta be sued, those people. I hardly finished putting it in and the thing . . . (*His words rumble off*)

LINDA. I'm just wondering if Oliver will remember him. You think he might?

WILLY (*coming out of the bathroom in his pajamas*). Remember him? What's the matter with you, you crazy? If he'd've stayed with Oliver he'd be on top by now! Wait'll Oliver gets a look at him. You don't know the average caliber any more. The average young man today—(*He is getting into bed*)—is got a caliber of zero. Greatest thing in the world for him was to bum around.

(*Biff and Happy enter the bedroom. Slight pause.*)

WILLY (*stops short, looking at Biff*). Glad to hear it, boy.

HAPPY. He wanted to say good night to you, sport.

WILLY (*to Biff*). Yeah. Knock him dead, boy. What'd you want to tell me?

BIFF. Just take it easy, Pop. Good night. (*He turns to go*)

WILLY (*unable to resist*). And if anything falls off the desk while you're talking to him—like a package or something—don't you pick it up. They have office boys for that.

LINDA. I'll make a big breakfast—

WILLY. Will you let me finish? (*To Biff*) Tell him you were in the business in the West. Not farm work.

BIFF. All right, Dad.

LINDA. I think everything—

WILLY (*going right through her speech*). And don't undersell yourself. No less than fifteen thousand dollars.

BIFF (*unable to bear him*). Okay. Good night, Mom. (*He starts moving*)

WILLY. Because you got a greatness in you, Biff, remember that. You got all kinds a greatness . . . (*He lies back, exhausted. Biff walks out*)

LINDA (*calling after Biff*). Sleep well, darling!

HAPPY. I'm gonna get married, Mom. I wanted to tell you.

LINDA. Go to sleep, dear.

HAPPY (*going*). I just wanted to tell you.

WILLY. Keep up the good work. (*Happy exits*) God . . . remember that Ebbets Field game? The championship of the city?

LINDA. Just rest. Should I sing to you?

WILLY. Yeah. Sing to me. (*Linda hums a soft lullaby*) When that team came out—he was the tallest, remember?

LINDA. Oh, yes. And in gold.

(*Biff enters the darkened kitchen, takes a cigarette, and leaves the house. He comes downstage into a golden pool of light. He smokes, staring at the night.*)

WILLY. Like a young god. Hercules—something like that. And the sun, the sun all around him. Remember how he waved to me? Right up from the field, with the representatives of three colleges standing by? And the buyers I brought, and the cheers when he came out—Loman, Loman, Loman! God Almighty, he'll be great yet. A star like that, magnificent, can never really fade away!

(*The light on Willy is fading. The gas heater begins to glow through the kitchen wall, near the stairs, a blue flame beneath red coils.*)

LINDA (*timidly*). Willy dear, what has he got against you?

WILLY. I'm so tired. Don't talk any more.

(*Biff slowly returns to the kitchen. He stops, stares toward the heater.*)

LINDA. Will you ask Howard to let you work in New York?

WILLY. First thing in the morning. Everything'll be all right.

(*Biff reaches behind the heater and draws out a length of rubber tubing. He is horrified and turns his head toward Willy's room, still dimly lit, from which the strains of Linda's desperate but monotonous humming rise.*)

WILLY (*staring through the window into the moonlight*). Gee, look at the moon moving between the buildings!

(*Biff wraps the tubing around his hand and quickly goes up the stairs.*)

CURTAIN

ACT TWO

Music is heard, gay and bright. The curtain rises as the music fades away. Willy, in shirt sleeves, is sitting at the kitchen table, sipping coffee, his hat in his lap. Linda is filling his cup when she can.

WILLY. Wonderful coffee. Meal in itself.

LINDA. Can I make you some eggs?

WILLY. No. Take a breath.

LINDA. You look so rested, dear.

WILLY. I slept like a dead one. First time in months. Imagine, sleeping till ten on a Tuesday morning. Boys left nice and early, heh?

LINDA. They were out of here by eight o'clock.

WILLY. Good work!

LINDA. It was so thrilling to see them leaving together. I can't get over the shaving lotion in this house!

WILLY (*smiling*). Mmm—

LINDA. Biff was very changed this morning. His whole attitude seemed to be hopeful. He couldn't wait to get downtown to see Oliver.

WILLY. He's heading for a change. There's no question, there simply are certain men that take longer to get—solidified. How did he dress?

LINDA. His blue suit. He's so handsome in that suit. He could be a—anything in that suit!

(*Willy gets up from the table. Linda holds his jacket for him.*)

WILLY. There's no question, no question at all. Gee, on the way home tonight I'd like to buy some seeds.

LINDA (*laughing*). That'd be wonderful. But not enough sun gets back there. Nothing'll grow any more.

WILLY. You wait, kid, before it's all over we're gonna get a little place out in the country, and I'll raise some vegetables, a couple of chickens . . .

LINDA. You'll do it yet, dear.

(*Willy walks out of his jacket. Linda follows him.*)

WILLY. And they'll get married, and come for a weekend. I'd build a little guest house. 'Cause I got so many fine tools, all I'd need would be a little lumber and some peace of mind.

LINDA (*joyfully*). I sewed the lining . . .

WILLY. I could build two guest houses,

so they'd both come. Did he decide how much he's going to ask Oliver for?

LINDA (*getting him into the jacket*). He didn't mention it, but I imagine ten or fifteen thousand. You going to talk to Howard today?

WILLY. Yeah, I'll put it to him straight and simple. He'll just have to take me off the road.

LINDA. And Willy, don't forget to ask for a little advance, because we've got the insurance premium. It's the grace period now.

WILLY. That's a hundred . . . ?

LINDA. A hundred and eight, sixty-eight. Because we're a little short again.

WILLY. Why are we short?

LINDA. Well, you had the motor job on the car . . .

WILLY. That goddam Studebaker!

LINDA. And you got one more payment on the refrigerator . . .

WILLY. But it just broke again!

LINDA. Well, it's old, dear.

WILLY. I told you we should've bought a well-advertised machine. Charley bought a General Electric and it's twenty years old and it's still good, that son-of-a-bitch.

LINDA. But, Willy—

WILLY. Whoever heard of a Hastings refrigerator. Once in my life I would like to own something outright before it's broken! I'm always in a race with the junkyard! I just finished paying for the car and it's on its last legs. The refrigerator consumes belts like a goddam maniac. They time those things. They time them so when you finally paid for them, they're used up.

LINDA (*buttoning up his jacket as he unbuttons it*). All told, about two hundred dollars would carry us, dear. But that includes the last payment on the mortgage. After this payment, Willy, the house belongs to us.

WILLY. It's twenty-five years!

LINDA. Biff was nine years old when we bought it.

WILLY. Well, that's a great thing. To weather a twenty-five-year mortgage is—

LINDA. It's an accomplishment.

WILLY. All the cement, the lumber, the reconstruction I put in this house! There ain't a crack to be found in it any more.

LINDA. Well, it served its purpose.

WILLY. What purpose? Some stranger'll come along, move in, and that's that. If only Biff would take this house, and raise a family . . . (*He starts to go*) Good-by, I'm late.

LINDA (*suddenly remembering*). Oh, I forgot! You're supposed to meet them for dinner.

WILLY. Me?

LINDA. At Frank's Chop House on Forty-eighth near Sixth Avenue.

WILLY. Is that so! How about you?

LINDA. No, just the three of you. They're gonna blow you to a big meal!

WILLY. Don't say! Who thought of that?

LINDA. Biff came to me this morning, Willy, and he said, "Tell Dad, we want to blow him to a big meal." Be there six o'clock. You and your two boys are going to have dinner.

WILLY. Gee whiz! That's really somethin'. I'm gonna knock Howard for a loop, kid. I'll get an advance, and I'll come home with a New York job. Goddammit, now I'm gonna do it!

LINDA. Oh, that's the spirit, Willy!

WILLY. I will never get behind a wheel the rest of my life!

LINDA. It's changing, Willy, I can feel it changing!

WILLY. Beyond a question. G'by, I'm late. (*He starts to go again*)

LINDA (*calling after him as she runs to the kitchen table for a handkerchief*). You got your glasses?

WILLY (*feels for them, then comes back in*). Yeah, yeah, got my glasses.

LINDA (*giving him the handkerchief*). And a handkerchief.

WILLY. Yeah, handkerchief.

LINDA. And your saccharine?

WILLY. Yeah, my saccharine.

LINDA. Be careful on the subway stairs. (*She kisses him, and a silk stocking is seen hanging from her hand. Willy notices it.*)

WILLY. Will you stop mending stockings? At least while I'm in the house. It gets me nervous. I can't tell you. Please. (*Linda hides the stocking in her hand as she follows Willy across the forestage in front of the house.*)

LINDA. Remember, Frank's Chop House.

WILLY (*passing the apron*). Maybe beets would grow out there.

LINDA (*laughing*). But you tried so many times.

WILLY. Yeah. Well, don't work hard today. (*He disappears around the right corner of the house*)

LINDA. Be careful!

(*As Willy vanishes, Linda waves to him. Suddenly the phone rings. She runs across the stage and into the kitchen and lifts it.*)

LINDA. Hello? Oh, Biff! I'm so glad you called, I just . . . Yes, sure, I just told him. Yes, he'll be there for dinner at six o'clock, I didn't forget. Listen, I was just dying to tell you. You know that little rubber pipe I told you about? That he connected to the gas heater? I finally decided to go down the cellar this morning and take it away and destroy it. But it's gone! Imagine? He took it away himself, it isn't there! (*She listens*) When? Oh, then you took it. Oh nothing, it's just that I'd hoped he'd taken it away himself. Oh, I'm not worried, darling, because this morning he left in such high spirits, it was like the old days! I'm not afraid any more. Did Mr. Oliver see you? . . . Well, you wait there then. And make a nice impression on him, darling. Just don't perspire too much before you see him. And have a nice time with Dad. He may have big news too! . . . That's right, a New York job. And be sweet to him tonight, dear. Be loving to him. Because he's only a little boat looking for a harbor. (*She is trembling with sorrow and joy*) Oh, that's wonderful, Biff, you'll save his life. Thanks, darling. Just put your arm around him when he comes into the restaurant. Give him a smile. That's the boy . . . Good-by, dear. . . . You got your comb? . . . That's fine. Good-by, Biff dear. (*In the middle of her speech, Howard Wagner, thirty-six, wheels in a small typewriter table on which is a wire-recording machine and proceeds to plug it in. This is on the left forestage. Light slowly fades on Linda as it rises on Howard. Howard is intent on threading the machine and only glances over his shoulder as Willy appears.*)

WILLY. Pst! Pst!

HOWARD. Hello, Willy, come in.

WILLY. Like to have a little talk with you, Howard.

HOWARD. Sorry to keep you waiting. I'll be with you in a minute.

WILLY. What's that, Howard?

HOWARD. Didn't you ever see one of these? Wire recorder.

WILLY. Oh. Can we talk a minute?

HOWARD. Records things. Just got delivery yesterday. Been driving me crazy, the most terrific machine I ever saw in my life. I was up all night with it.

WILLY. What do you do with it?

HOWARD. I bought it for dictation, but you can do anything with it. Listen to this. I had it home last night. Listen to what I picked up. The first one is my daughter. Get this. (*He flicks the switch and "Roll Out the Barrel" is heard being whistled*) Listen to that kid whistle.

WILLY. That is lifelike, isn't it?

HOWARD. Seven years old. Get that tone.

WILLY. Ts, ts. Like to ask a little favor if you . . .

(*The whistling breaks off, and the voice of Howard's daughter is heard.*)

HIS DAUGHTER. "Now you, Daddy."

HOWARD. She's crazy for me! (*Again the same song is whistled*) That's me! Ha! (*He winks*)

WILLY. You're very good!

(*The whistling breaks off again. The machine runs silent for a moment.*)

HOWARD. Sh! Get this now, this is my son.

HIS SON. "The capital of Alabama is Montgomery; the capital of Arizona is Phoenix; the capital of Arkansas is Little Rock; the capital of California is Sacramento . . ." (*And on, and on*)

HOWARD (*holding up five fingers*). Five years old, Willy!

WILLY. He'll make an announcer some day!

HIS SON (*continuing*). "The capital . . ."

HOWARD. Get that—alphabetical order! (*The machine breaks off suddenly*) Wait a minute. The maid kicked the plug out.

WILLY. It certainly is a—

HOWARD. Sh, for God's sake!

HIS SON. "It's nine o'clock, Bulova watch time. So I have to go to sleep."

WILLY. That really is—

HOWARD. Wait a minute! The next is my wife.

(*They wait.*)

HOWARD'S VOICE. "Go on, say something." (*Pause*) "Well, you gonna talk?"

HIS WIFE. "I can't think of anything."

HOWARD'S VOICE. "Well, talk—it's turning."

HIS WIFE (*shyly, beaten*). "Hello." (*Silence*) "Oh, Howard, I can't talk into this . . ."

HOWARD (*snapping the machine off*) That was my wife.

WILLY. That is a wonderful machine. Can we—

HOWARD. I tell you, Willy, I'm gonna

take my camera, and my bandsaw, and all my hobbies, and out they go. This is the most fascinating relaxation I ever found.

WILLY. I think I'll get one myself.

HOWARD. Sure, they're only a hundred and a half. You can't do without it. Supposing you wanna hear Jack Benny, see? But you can't be at home at that hour. So you tell the maid to turn the radio on when Jack Benny comes on, and this automatically goes on with the radio . . .

WILLY. And when you come home you . . .

HOWARD. You can come home twelve o'clock, one o'clock, any time you like, and you get yourself a Coke and sit yourself down, throw the switch, and there's Jack Benny's program in the middle of the night!

WILLY. I'm definitely going to get one. Because lots of time I'm on the road, and I think to myself, what I must be missing on the radio!

HOWARD. Don't you have a radio in the car?

WILLY. Well, yeah, but who ever thinks of turning it on?

HOWARD. Say, aren't you supposed to be in Boston?

WILLY. That's what I want to talk to you about, Howard. You got a minute? (*He draws a chair in from the wing*)

HOWARD. What happened? What're you doing here?

WILLY. Well . . .

HOWARD. You didn't crack up again, did you?

WILLY. Oh, no. No . . .

HOWARD. Geez, you had me worried there for a minute. What's the trouble?

WILLY. Well, tell you the truth, Howard. I've come to the decision that I'd rather not travel any more.

HOWARD. Not travel! Well, what'll you do?

WILLY. Remember, Christmas time, when you had the party here? You said you'd try to think of some spot for me here in town.

HOWARD. With us?

WILLY. Well, sure.

HOWARD. Oh, yeah, yeah. I remember. Well, I couldn't think of anything for you, Willy.

WILLY. I tell ya, Howard. The kids are all grown up, y'know. I don't need much any more. If I could take home—well, sixty-five dollars a week, I could swing it.

HOWARD. Yeah, but Willy, see I—

WILLY. I tell ya why, Howard. Speaking frankly and between the two of us, y'know —I'm just a little tired.

HOWARD. Oh, I could understand that, Willy. But you're a road man, Willy, and we do a road business. We've only got a half-dozen salesmen on the floor here.

WILLY. God knows, Howard, I never asked a favor of any man. But I was with the firm when your father used to carry you in here in his arms.

HOWARD. I know that, Willy, but—

WILLY. Your father came to me the day you were born and asked me what I thought of the name of Howard, may he rest in peace.

HOWARD. I appreciate that, Willy, but there just is no spot here for you. If I had a spot I'd slam you right in, but I just don't have a single solitary spot.

(*He looks for his lighter. Willy has picked it up and gives it to him. Pause.*)

WILLY (*with increasing anger*). Howard, all I need to set my table is fifty dollars a week.

HOWARD. But where am I going to put you, kid?

WILLY. Look, it isn't a question of whether I can sell merchandise, is it?

HOWARD. No, but it's a business, kid, and everybody's gotta pull his own weight.

WILLY (*desperately*). Just let me tell you a story, Howard—

HOWARD. 'Cause you gotta admit, business is business.

WILLY (*angrily*). Business is definitely business, but just listen for a minute. You don't understand this. When I was a boy —eighteen, nineteen—I was already on the road. And there was a question in my mind as to whether selling had a future for me. Because in those days I had a yearning to go to Alaska. See, there were three gold strikes in one month in Alaska, and I felt like going out. Just for the ride, you might say.

HOWARD (*barely interested*). Don't say.

WILLY. Oh, yeah, my father lived many years in Alaska. He was an adventurous man. We've got quite a little streak of self-reliance in our family. I thought I'd go out with my older brother and try to locate him, and maybe settle in the North with the old man. And I was almost decided to go, when I met a salesman in the

Parker House. His name was Dave Single-man. And he was eighty-four years old, and he'd drummed merchandise in thirty-one states. And old Dave, he'd go up to his room, y'understand, put on his green velvet slippers—I'll never forget—and pick up his phone and call the buyers, and without ever leaving his room, at the age of eighty-four, he made his living. And when I saw that, I realized that selling was the greatest career a man could want. 'Cause what could be more satisfying than to be able to go, at the age of eighty-four, into twenty or thirty different cities, and pick up a phone, and be remembered and loved and helped by so many different people? Do you know? when he died—and by the way he died the death of a salesman, in his green velvet slippers in the smoker of the New York, New Haven and Hartford, going into Boston—when he died, hundreds of salesmen and buyers were at his funeral. Things were sad on a lotta trains for months after that. (*He stands up. Howard has not looked at him*) In those days there was personality in it, Howard. There was respect, and comradeship, and gratitude in it. Today, it's all cut and dried, and there's no chance for bringing friendship to bear —or personality. You see what I mean? They don't know me any more.

HOWARD (*moving away, to the right*). That's just the thing, Willy.

WILLY. If I had forty dollars a week— that's all I'd need. Forty dollars, Howard.

HOWARD. Kid, I can't take blood from a stone, I—

WILLY (*desperation is on him now*). Howard, the year Al Smith was nominated, your father came to me and—

HOWARD (*starting to go off*). I've got to see some people, kid.

WILLY (*stopping him*). I'm talking about your father! There were promises made across this desk! You mustn't tell me you've got people to see—I put thirty-four years into this firm, Howard, and now I can't pay my insurance! You can't eat the orange and throw the peel away— a man is not a piece of fruit! (*After a pause*) Now pay attention. Your father— in 1928 I had a big year. I averaged a hundred and seventy dollars a week in commissions.

HOWARD (*impatiently*). Now, Willy, you never averaged—

WILLY (*banging his hand on the desk*).

I averaged a hundred and seventy dollars a week in the year of 1928; and your father came to me—or rather, I was in the office here—it was right over this desk— and he put his hand on my shoulder—

HOWARD (*getting up*). You'll have to excuse me, Willy. I gotta see some people. Pull yourself together. (*Going out*) I'll be back in a little while.

(*On Howard's exit, the light on his chair grows very bright and strange.*)

WILLY. Pull myself together! What the hell did I say to him? My God, I was yelling at him! How could I! (*Willy breaks off, staring at the light, which occupies the chair, animating it. He approaches this chair, standing across the desk from it*) Frank, Frank, don't you remember what you told me that time? How you put your hand on my shoulder, and Frank . . . (*He leans on the desk and as he speaks the dead man's name he accidentally switches on the recorder, and instantly*)

HOWARD'S SON. ". . . of New York is Albany. The capital of Ohio is Cincinnati, the capital of Rhode Island is . . ." (*The recitation continues*)

WILLY (*leaping away with fright, shouting*). Ha! Howard! Howard! Howard!

HOWARD (*rushing in*). What happened?

WILLY (*pointing at the machine, which continues nasally, childishly, with the capital cities*). Shut it off! Shut it off!

HOWARD (*pulling the plug out*). Look, Willy . . .

WILLY (*pressing his hands to his eyes*). I gotta get myself some coffee. I'll get some coffee . . .

(*Willy starts to walk out. Howard stops him.*)

HOWARD (*rolling up the cord*). Willy, look . . .

WILLY. I'll go to Boston.

HOWARD. Willy, you can't go to Boston for us.

WILLY. Why can't I go?

HOWARD. I don't want you to represent us. I've been meaning to tell you for a long time now.

WILLY. Howard, are you firing me?

HOWARD. I think you need a good long rest, Willy.

WILLY. Howard—

HOWARD. And when you feel better, come back, and we'll see if we can work something out.

WILLY. But I gotta earn money, Howard. I'm in no position to—

HOWARD. Where are your sons? Why don't your sons give you a hand?

WILLY. They're working on a very big deal.

HOWARD. This is no time for false pride, Willy. You go to your sons and tell them that you're tired. You've got two great boys, haven't you?

WILLY. Oh, no question, no question, but in the meantime . . .

HOWARD. Then that's that, heh?

WILLY. All right, I'll go to Boston to-morrow.

HOWARD. No, no.

WILLY. I can't throw myself on my sons. I'm not a cripple!

HOWARD. Look, kid, I'm busy this morning.

WILLY (*grasping Howard's arm*). Howard, you've got to let me go to Boston!

HOWARD (*hard, keeping himself under control*). I've got a line of people to see this morning. Sit down, take five minutes, and pull yourself together, and then go home, will ya? I need the office, Willy. (*He starts to go, turns, remembering the recorder, starts to push off the table holding the recorder*) Oh, yeah. Whenever you can this week, stop by and drop off the samples. You'll feel better, Willy, and then come back and we'll talk. Pull yourself together, kid, there's people outside.

(*Howard exits, pushing the table off left. Willy stares into space, exhausted. Now the music is heard—Ben's music—first distantly, then closer, closer. As Willy speaks, Ben enters from the right. He carries valise and umbrella.*)

WILLY. Oh, Ben, how did you do it? What is the answer? Did you wind up the Alaska deal already?

BEN. Doesn't take much time if you know what you're doing. Just a short business trip. Boarding ship in an hour. Wanted to say good-by.

WILLY. Ben, I've got to talk to you.

BEN (*glancing at his watch*). Haven't the time, William.

WILLY (*crossing the apron to Ben*). Ben, nothing's working out. I don't know what to do.

BEN. Now, look here, William. I've bought timberland in Alaska and I need a man to look after things for me.

WILLY. God, timberland! Me and my boys in those grand outdoors!

BEN. You've a new continent at your doorstep, William. Get out of these cities, they're full of talk and time payments and courts of law. Screw on your fists and you can fight for a fortune up there.

WILLY. Yes, yes! Linda, Linda!

(*Linda enters, as of old, with the wash.*)

LINDA. Oh, you're back?

BEN. I haven't much time.

WILLY. No, wait! Linda, he's got a proposition for me in Alaska.

LINDA. But you've got— (*To Ben*) He's got a beautiful job here.

WILLY. But in Alaska, kid, I could—

LINDA. You're doing well enough, Willy!

BEN (*to Linda*). Enough for what, dear?

LINDA (*frightened of Ben and angry at him*). Don't say those things to him! Enough to be happy right here, right now. (*To Willy, while Ben laughs*) Why must everybody conquer the world? You're well liked, and the boys love you, and some-day— (*To Ben*) —why, old man Wagner told him just the other day that if he keeps it up he'll be a member of the firm, didn't he, Willy?

WILLY. Sure, sure. I am building something with this firm, Ben, and if a man is building something he must be on the right track, mustn't he?

BEN. What are you building? Lay your hand on it. Where is it?

WILLY (*hesitantly*). That's true, Linda, there's nothing.

LINDA. Why? (*To Ben*) There's a man eighty-four years old—

WILLY. That's right, Ben, that's right. When I look at that man I say, what is there to worry about?

BEN. Bah!

WILLY. It's true, Ben. All he has to do is go into any city, pick up the phone, and he's making his living—and you know why?

BEN (*picking up his valise*). I've got to go.

WILLY (*holding Ben back*). Look at this boy!

(*Biff, in his high school sweater, enters carrying suitcase. Happy carries Biff's shoulder guards, gold helmet, and football pants.*)

WILLY. Without a penny to his name, three great universities are begging for him, and from there the sky's the limit.

because it's not what you do, Ben. It's who you know and the smile on your face! It's contacts, Ben, contacts! The whole wealth of Alaska passes over the lunch table at the Commodore Hotel, and that's the wonder, the wonder of this country, that a man can end with diamonds here on the basis of being liked! (*He turns to Biff*) And that's why when you get out on that field today it's important. Because thousands of people will be rooting for you and loving you. (*To Ben, who has again begun to leave*) And Ben! when he walks into a business office his name will sound out like a bell and all the doors will open to him! I've seen it, Ben, I've seen it a thousand times! You can't feel it with your hand like timber, but it's there!

BEN. Good-by, William.

WILLY. Ben, am I right? Don't you think I'm right? I value your advice.

BEN. There's a new continent at your doorstep, William. You could walk out rich. Rich! (*He is gone*)

WILLY. We'll do it here, Ben! You hear me? We're gonna do it here!

(*Young Bernard rushes in. The gay music of the Boys is heard.*)

BERNARD. Oh, gee, I was afraid you left already!

WILLY. Why? What time is it?

BERNARD. It's half-past one!

WILLY. Well, come on, everybody! Ebbets Field next stop! Where's the pennants? (*He rushes through the wall-line of the kitchen and out into the living-room*)

LINDA (*to Biff*). Did you pack fresh underwear?

BIFF (*who has been limbering up*). I want to go!

BERNARD. Biff, I'm carrying your helmet, ain't I?

HAPPY. No, I'm carrying the helmet.

BERNARD. Oh, Biff, you promised me.

HAPPY. I'm carrying the helmet.

BERNARD. How am I going to get in the locker room?

LINDA. Let him carry the shoulder guards. (*She puts her coat and hat on in the kitchen*)

BERNARD. Can I, Biff? 'Cause I told everybody I'm going to be in the locker room.

HAPPY. In Ebbets Field it's the club-house.

BERNARD. I meant the clubhouse. Biff!

HAPPY. Biff!

BIFF (*grandly, after a slight pause*). Let him carry the shoulder guards.

HAPPY (*as he gives Bernard the shoulder guards*). Stay close to us now.

(*Willy rushes in with the pennants.*)

WILLY (*handing them out*). Everybody wave when Biff comes out on the field. (*Happy and Bernard run off*) You set now, boy?

(*The music has died away.*)

BIFF. Ready to go, Pop. Every muscle is ready.

WILLY (*at the edge of the apron*). You realize what this means?

BIFF. That's right, Pop.

WILLY (*feeling Biff's muscles*). You're comin' home this afternoon captain of the All-Scholastic Championship Team of the City of New York.

BIFF. I got it, Pop. And remember, pal, when I take off my helmet, that touchdown is for you.

WILLY. Let's go! (*He is starting out, with his arm around Biff, when Charley enters, as of old, in knickers*) I got no room for you, Charley.

CHARLEY. Room? For what?

WILLY. In the car.

CHARLEY. You goin' for a ride? I wanted to shoot some casino.

WILLY (*furiously*). Casino! (*Incredulously*) Don't you realize what today is?

LINDA. Oh, he knows, Willy. He's just kidding you.

WILLY. That's nothing to kid about!

CHARLEY. No, Linda, what's goin' on?

LINDA. He's playing in Ebbets Field.

CHARLEY. Baseball in this weather?

WILLY. Don't talk to him. Come on, come on! (*He is pushing them out*)

CHARLEY. Wait a minute, didn't you hear the news?

WILLY. What?

CHARLEY. Don't you listen to the radio? Ebbets Field just blew up.

WILLY. You go to hell! (*Charley laughs. Pushing them out*) Come on, come on! We're late.

CHARLEY (*as they go*). Knock a homer, Biff, knock a homer!

WILLY (*the last to leave, turning to Charley*). I don't think that was funny, Charley. This is the greatest day of his life.

CHARLEY. Willy, when are you going to grow up?

WILLY. Yeah, heh? When this game is

over, Charley, you'll be laughing out of the other side of your face. They'll be calling him another Red Grange. Twenty-five thousand a year.

CHARLEY (*kidding*). Is that so?

WILLY. Yeah, that's so.

CHARLEY. Well, then, I'm sorry, Willy. But tell me something.

WILLY. What?

CHARLEY. Who is Red Grange?

WILLY. Put up your hands. Goddam you, put up your hands!

(*Charley, chuckling, shakes his head and walks away, around the left corner of the stage. Willy follows him. The music rises to a mocking frenzy.*)

WILLY. Who the hell do you think you are, better than everybody else? You don't know everything, you big, ignorant, stupid . . . Put up your hands!

(*Light rises, on the right side of the forestage, on a small table in the reception room of Charley's office. Traffic sounds are heard. Bernard, now mature, sits whistling to himself. A pair of tennis rackets and an overnight bag are on the floor beside him.*)

WILLY (*offstage*). What are you walking away for? Don't walk away! If you're going to say something say it to my face! I know you laugh at me behind my back. You'll laugh out of the other side of your goddam face after this game. Touchdown! Touchdown! Eighty thousand people! Touchdown! Right between the goal posts. (*Bernard is a quiet, earnest, but self-assured young man. Willy's voice is coming from right upstage now. Bernard lowers his feet off the table and listens. Jenny, his father's secretary, enters.*)

JENNY (*distressed*). Say, Bernard, will you go out in the hall?

BERNARD. What is that noise? Who is it?

JENNY. Mr. Loman. He just got off the elevator.

BERNARD (*getting up*). Who's he arguing with?

JENNY. Nobody. There's nobody with him. I can't deal with him any more, and your father gets all upset everytime he comes. I've got a lot of typing to do, and your father's waiting to sign it. Will you see him?

WILLY (*entering*). Touchdown! Touch— (*He sees Jenny*) Jenny, Jenny, good to see you. How're ya? Workin'? Or still honest?

JENNY. Fine. How've you been feeling?

WILLY. Not much any more, Jenny. Ha, ha! (*He is surprised to see the rackets*)

BERNARD. Hello, Uncle Willy.

WILLY (*almost shocked*). Bernard! Well, look who's here! (*He comes quickly, guiltily, to Bernard and warmly shakes his hand*)

BERNARD. How are you? Good to see you.

WILLY. What are you doing here?

BERNARD. Oh, just stopped by to see Pop. Get off my feet till my train leaves. I'm going to Washington in a few minutes.

WILLY. Is he in?

BERNARD. Yes, he's in his office with the accountant. Sit down.

WILLY (*sitting down*). What're you going to do in Washington?

BERNARD. Oh, just a case I've got there, Willy.

WILLY. That so? (*Indicating the rackets*) You going to play tennis there?

BERNARD. I'm staying with a friend who's got a court.

WILLY. Don't say. His own tennis court. Must be fine people, I bet.

BERNARD. They are, very nice. Dad tells me Biff's in town.

WILLY (*with a big smile*). Yeah, Biff's in. Working on a very big deal, Bernard.

BERNARD. What's Biff doing?

WILLY. Well, he's been doing very big things in the West. But he decided to establish himself here. Very big. We're having dinner. Did I hear your wife had a boy?

BERNARD. That's right. Our second.

WILLY. Two boys! What do you know

BERNARD. What kind of a deal has Bi got?

WILLY. Well, Bill Oliver—very big sporting-goods man—he wants Biff very badly. Called him in from the West. Long distance, carte blanche, special deliveries. Your friends have their own private tennis court?

BERNARD. You still with the old firm, Willy?

WILLY (*after a pause*). I'm—I'm overjoyed to see how you made the grade, Bernard, overjoyed. It's an encouraging thing to see a young man really—really— Looks very good for Biff—very—(*He breaks off, then*) Bernard—(*He is so full of emotion, he breaks off again*)

BERNARD. What is it, Willy?

WILLY (*small and alone*). What—what's the secret?

BERNARD. What secret?

WILLY. How—how did you? Why didn't he ever catch on?

BERNARD. I wouldn't know that, Willy.

WILLY (*confidentially, desperately*). You were his friend, his boyhood friend. There's something I don't understand about it. His life ended after that Ebbets Field game. From the age of seventeen nothing good ever happened to him.

BERNARD. He never trained himself for anything.

WILLY. But he did, he did. After high school he took so many correspondence courses. Radio mechanics; television; God knows what, and never made the slightest mark.

BERNARD (*taking off his glasses*). Willy, do you want to talk candidly?

WILLY (*rising, faces Bernard*). I regard you as a very brilliant man, Bernard. I value your advice.

BERNARD. Oh, the hell with the advice, Willy. I couldn't advise you. There's just one thing I've always wanted to ask you. When he was supposed to graduate, and the math teacher flunked him—

WILLY. Oh, that son-of-a-bitch ruined his life.

BERNARD. Yeah, but, Willy, all he had to do was go to summer school and make up that subject.

WILLY. That's right, that's right.

BERNARD. Did you tell him not to go to summer school?

WILLY. Me? I begged him to go. I ordered him to go!

BERNARD. Then why wouldn't he go?

WILLY. Why? Why! Bernard, that question has been trailing me like a ghost for the last fifteen years. He flunked the subject, and laid down and died like a hammer hit him!

BERNARD. Take it easy, kid.

WILLY. Let me talk to you—I got nobody to talk to. Bernard, Bernard, was it my fault? Y'see? It keeps going around in my mind, maybe I did something to him. I got nothing to give him.

BERNARD. Don't take it so hard.

WILLY. Why did he lay down? What is the story there? You were his friend!

BERNARD. Willy, I remember, it was June, and our grades came out. And he'd flunked math.

WILLY. That son-of-a-bitch!

BERNARD. No, it wasn't right then. Biff just got very angry, I remember, and he was ready to enroll in summer school.

WILLY (*surprised*). He was?

BERNARD. He wasn't beaten by it at all. But then, Willy, he disappeared from the block for almost a month. And I got the idea that he'd gone up to New England to see you. Did he have a talk with you then?

(*Willy stares in silence.*)

BERNARD. Willy?

WILLY (*with a strong edge of resentment in his voice*). Yeah, he came to Boston. What about it?

BERNARD. Well, just that when he came back—I'll never forget this, it always mystifies me. Because I'd thought so well of Biff, even though he'd always taken advantage of me. I loved him, Willy, y'know? And he came back after that month and took his sneakers—remember those sneakers with "University of Virginia" printed on them? He was so proud of those, wore them every day. And he took them down in the cellar, and burned them up in the furnace. We had a fist fight. It lasted at least half an hour. Just the two of us, punching each other down the cellar, and crying right through it. I've often thought of how strange it was that I knew he'd given up his life. What happened in Boston, Willy?

(*Willy looks at him as at an intruder.*)

BERNARD. I just bring it up because you asked me.

WILLY (*angrily*). Nothing. What do you mean, "What happened?" What's that got to do with anything?

BERNARD. Well, don't get sore.

WILLY. What are you trying to do, blame it on me? If a boy lays down is that my fault?

BERNARD. Now, Willy, don't get—

WILLY. Well, don't—don't talk to me that way! What does that mean, "What happened?"

(*Charley enters. He is in his vest, and he carries a bottle of bourbon.*)

CHARLEY. Hey, you're going to miss that train. (*He waves the bottle*)

BERNARD. Yeah, I'm going. (*He takes the bottle*) Thanks, Pop. (*He picks up his rackets and bag*) Good-by, Willy, and don't worry about it. You know, "If at first you don't succeed . . ."

WILLY. Yes, I believe in that.

BERNARD. But sometimes, Willy, it's better for a man just to walk away.

WILLY. Walk away?

BERNARD. That's right.

WILLY. But if you can't walk away?

BERNARD (*after a slight pause*). I guess that's when it's tough. (*Extending his hand*) Good-by, Willy.

WILLY (*shaking Bernard's hand*). Good-by, boy.

CHARLEY (*an arm on Bernard's shoulder*). How do you like this kid? Gonna argue a case in front of the Supreme Court.

BERNARD (*protesting*). Pop!

WILLY (*genuinely shocked, pained and happy*). No! The Supreme Court!

BERNARD. I gotta run. 'By, Dad!

CHARLEY. Knock 'em dead, Bernard! (*Bernard goes off.*)

WILLY (*as Charley takes out his wallet*). The Supreme Court! And he didn't even mention it!

CHARLEY (*counting out money on the desk*). He don't have to—he's gonna do it.

WILLY. And you never told him what to do, did you? You never took any interest in him.

CHARLEY. My salvation is that I never took any interest in anything. There's some money—fifty dollars. I got an accountant inside.

WILLY. Charley, look . . . (*With difficulty*) I got my insurance to pay. If you can manage it—I need a hundred and ten dollars.

(*Charley doesn't reply for a moment; merely stops moving.*)

WILLY. I'd draw it from my bank, but Linda would know, and I . . .

CHARLEY. Sit down, Willy.

WILLY (*moving toward the chair*). I'm keeping an account of everything, remember. I'll pay every penny back. (*He sits*)

CHARLEY. Now listen to me, Willy.

WILLY. I want you to know I appreciate . . .

CHARLEY (*sitting down on the table*). Willy, what're you doin'? What the hell is goin' on in your head?

WILLY. Why? I'm simply . . .

CHARLEY. I offered you a job. You can make fifty dollars a week. And I won't send you on the road.

WILLY. I've got a job.

CHARLEY. Without pay? What kind of a job is a job without pay? (*He rises*) Now, look, kid, enough is enough. I'm no genius but I know when I'm being insulted.

WILLY. Insulted!

CHARLEY. Why don't you want to work for me?

WILLY. What's the matter with you? I've got a job.

CHARLEY. Then what're you walkin' in here every week for?

WILLY (*getting up*). Well, if you don't want me to walk in here—

CHARLEY. I am offering you a job.

WILLY. I don't want your goddam job!

CHARLEY. When the hell are you going to grow up?

WILLY (*furiously*). You big ignoramus, if you say that to me again I'll rap you one! I don't care how big you are! (*He's ready to fight*) (*Pause.*)

CHARLEY (*kindly, going to him*). How much do you need, Willy?

WILLY. Charley, I'm strapped, I'm strapped. I don't know what to do. I was just fired.

CHARLEY. Howard fired you?

WILLY. That snotnose. Imagine that? I named him. I named him Howard.

CHARLEY. Willy, when're you gonna realize that them things don't mean anything? You named him Howard, but you can't sell that. The only thing you got in this world is what you can sell. And the funny thing is that you're a salesman, and you don't know that.

WILLY. I've always tried to think otherwise, I guess. I always felt that if a man was impressive, and well liked, that nothing—

CHARLEY. Why must everybody like you? Who liked J. P. Morgan? Was he impressive? In a Turkish bath he'd look like a butcher. But with his pockets on he was very well liked. Now listen, Willy, I know you don't like me, and nobody can say I'm in love with you, but I'll give you a job because—just for the hell of it, put it that way. Now what do you say?

WILLY. I—I just can't work for you, Charley.

CHARLEY. What're you, jealous of me?

WILLY. I can't work for you, that's all, don't ask me why.

CHARLEY (*angered, takes out more bills*). You been jealous of me all your life, you damned fool! Here, pay your insurance

(*He puts the money in Willy's hand*)

WILLY. I'm keeping strict accounts.

CHARLEY. I've got some work to do. Take care of yourself. And pay your insurance.

WILLY (*moving to the right*). Funny, y'know? After all the highways, and the trains, and the appointments, and the years, you end up worth more dead than alive.

CHARLEY. Willy, nobody's worth nothin' dead. (*After a slight pause*) Did you hear what I said?

(*Willy stands still, dreaming.*)

CHARLEY. Willy!

WILLY. Apologize to Bernard for me when you see him. I didn't mean to argue with him. He's a fine boy. They're all fine boys, and they'll end up big—all of them. Someday they'll all play tennis together. Wish me luck, Charley. He saw Bill Oliver today.

CHARLEY. Good luck.

WILLY (*on the verge of tears*). Charley, you're the only friend I got. Isn't that a remarkable thing? (*He goes out*)

CHARLEY. Jesus!

(*Charley stares after him a moment and follows. All light blacks out. Suddenly raucous music is heard, and a red glow rises behind the screen at right. Stanley, a young waiter, appears, carrying a table, followed by Happy, who is carrying two chairs*)

STANLEY (*putting the table down*). That's all right, Mr. Loman. I can handle it myself. (*He turns and takes the chairs from Happy and places them at the table*)

HAPPY (*glancing around*). Oh, this is better.

STANLEY. Sure, in the front there you're in the middle of all kinds of noise. Whenever you got a party, Mr. Loman, you just tell me and I'll put you back here. Y'know, there's a lotta people they don't like it private, because when they go out they like to see a lotta action around them because they're sick and tired to stay in the house by theirself. But I know you, you ain't from Hackensack. You know what I mean?

HAPPY (*sitting down*). So how's it coming, Stanley?

STANLEY. Ah, it's a dog's life. I only wish during the war they'd a took me in the Army. I coulda been dead by now.

HAPPY. My brother's back, Stanley.

STANLEY. Oh, he come back, heh? From the Far West.

HAPPY. Yeah, big cattle man, my brother, so treat him right. And my father's coming too.

STANLEY. Oh, your father too!

HAPPY. You got a couple of nice lobsters?

STANLEY. Hundred per cent, big.

HAPPY. I want them with the claws.

STANLEY. Don't worry, I don't give you no mice. (*Happy laughs*) How about some wine? It'll put a head on the meal.

HAPPY. No. You remember, Stanley, that recipe I brought you from overseas? With the champagne in it?

STANLEY. Oh, yeah, sure. I still got it tacked up yet in the kitchen. But that'll have to cost a buck apiece anyways.

HAPPY. That's all right.

STANLEY. What'd you, hit a number or somethin'?

HAPPY. No, it's a little celebration. My brother is—I think he pulled off a big deal today. I think we're going into business together.

STANLEY. Great! That's the best for you. Because a family business, you know what I mean?—that's the best.

HAPPY. That's what I think.

STANLEY. 'Cause what's the difference? Somebody steals? It's in the family. Know what I mean? (*Sotto voce*) Like this bartender here. The boss is goin' crazy what kinda leak he's got in the cash register. You put it in but it don't come out.

HAPPY (*raising his head*). Sh!

STANLEY. What?

HAPPY. You notice I wasn't lookin' right or left, was I?

STANLEY. No.

HAPPY. And my eyes are closed.

STANLEY. So what's the—?

HAPPY. Strudel's comin'.

STANLEY (*catching on, looks around*). Ah, no, there's no—

(*He breaks off as a furred, lavishly dressed girl enters and sits at the next table. Both follow her with their eyes.*)

STANLEY. Geez, how'd ya know?

HAPPY. I got radar or something. (*Staring directly at her profile*) Oooooooo . . . Stanley.

STANLEY. I think that's for you, Mr. Loman.

HAPPY. Look at that mouth. Oh, God. And the binoculars.

STANLEY. Geez, you got a life, Mr. Loman.

HAPPY. Wait on her.

STANLEY (*going to the girl's table*). Would you like a menu, ma'am?

GIRL. I'm expecting someone, but I'd like a—

HAPPY. Why don't you bring her—excuse me, miss, do you mind? I sell champagne, and I'd like you to try my brand. Bring her a champagne, Stanley.

GIRL. That's awfully nice of you.

HAPPY. Don't mention it. It's all company money. (*He laughs*)

GIRL. That's a charming product to be selling, isn't it?

HAPPY. Oh, gets to be like everything else. Selling is selling, y'know.

GIRL. I suppose.

HAPPY. You don't happen to sell, do you?

GIRL. No, I don't sell.

HAPPY. Would you object to a compliment from a stranger? You ought to be on a magazine cover.

GIRL (*looking at him a little archly*). I have been.

(*Stanley comes in with a glass of champagne.*)

HAPPY. What'd I say before, Stanley? You see? She's a cover girl.

STANLEY. Oh, I could see, I could see.

HAPPY (*to the Girl*). What magazine?

GIRL. Oh, a lot of them. (*She takes the drink*) Thank you.

HAPPY. You know what they say in France, don't you? "Champagne is the drink of the complexion"—Hya, Biff!

(*Biff has entered and sits with Happy.*)

BIFF. Hello, kid. Sorry I'm late.

HAPPY. I just got here. Uh, Miss—?

GIRL. Forsythe.

HAPPY. Miss Forsythe, this is my brother.

BIFF. Is Dad here?

HAPPY. His name is Biff. You might've heard of him. Great football player.

GIRL. Really? What team?

HAPPY. Are you familiar with football?

GIRL. No, I'm afraid I'm not.

HAPPY. Biff is quarterback with the New York Giants.

GIRL. Well, that is nice, isn't it? (*She drinks*)

HAPPY. Good health.

GIRL. I'm happy to meet you.

HAPPY. That's my name. Hap. It's really Harold, but at West Point they called me Happy.

GIRL (*now really impressed*). Oh, I see. How do you do? (*She turns her profile*)

BIFF. Isn't Dad coming?

HAPPY. You want her?

BIFF. Oh, I could never make that.

HAPPY. I remember the time that idea would never come into your head. Where's the old confidence, Biff?

BIFF. I just saw Oliver—

HAPPY. Wait a minute. I've got to see that old confidence again. Do you want her? She's on call.

BIFF. Oh, no. (*He turns to look at the Girl*)

HAPPY. I'm telling you. Watch this. (*Turning to the Girl*) Honey? (*She turns to him*) Are you busy?

GIRL. Well, I am . . . but I could make a phone call.

HAPPY. Do that, will you, honey? And see if you can get a friend. We'll be here for a while. Biff is one of the greatest football players in the country.

GIRL (*standing up*). Well, I'm certainly happy to meet you.

HAPPY. Come back soon.

GIRL. I'll try.

HAPPY. Don't try, honey, try hard.

(*The Girl exits. Stanley follows, shaking his head in bewildered admiration.*)

HAPPY. Isn't that a shame now? A beautiful girl like that? That's why I can't get married. There's not a good woman in a thousand. New York is loaded with them, kid!

BIFF. Hap, look—

HAPPY. I told you she was on call!

BIFF (*strangely unnerved*). Cut it out, will ya? I want to say something to you.

HAPPY. Did you see Oliver?

BIFF. I saw him all right. Now look, I want to tell Dad a couple of things and I want you to help me.

HAPPY. What? Is he going to back you?

BIFF. Are you crazy? You're out of your goddam head, you know that?

HAPPY. Why? What happened?

BIFF (*breathlessly*). I did a terrible thing today, Hap. It's been the strangest day I ever went through. I'm all numb, I swear.

HAPPY. You mean he wouldn't see you?

BIFF. Well, I waited six hours for him, see? All day. Kept sending my name in.

Even tried to date his secretary so she'd get me to him, but no soap.

HAPPY. Because you're not showin' the old confidence, Biff. He remembered you, didn't he?

BIFF (*stopping Happy with a gesture*). Finally, about five o'clock, he comes out. Didn't remember who I was or anything. I felt like such an idiot, Hap.

HAPPY. Did you tell him my Florida idea?

BIFF. He walked away. I saw him for one minute. I got so mad I could've torn the walls down! How the hell did I ever get the idea I was a salesman there? I even believed myself that I'd been a salesman for him! And then he gave me one look and—I realized what a ridiculous lie my whole life has been! We've been talking in a dream for fifteen years. I was a shipping clerk.

HAPPY. What'd you do?

BIFF (*with great tension and wonder*). Well, he left, see. And the secretary went out. I was all alone in the waiting-room. I don't know what came over me, Hap. The next thing I know I'm in his office—paneled walls, everything. I can't explain it. I—Hap, I took his fountain pen.

HAPPY. Geez, did he catch you?

BIFF. I ran out. I ran down all eleven flights. I ran and ran and ran.

HAPPY. That was an awful dumb—what'd you do that for?

BIFF (*agonized*). I don't know, I just—wanted to take something, I don't know. You gotta help me, Hap, I'm gonna tell Pop.

HAPPY. You crazy? What for?

BIFF. Hap, he's got to understand that m not the man somebody lends that kind of money to. He thinks I've been spiting him all these years and it's eating him up.

HAPPY. That's just it. You tell him something nice.

BIFF. I can't.

HAPPY. Say you got a lunch date with Oliver tomorrow.

BIFF. So what do I do tomorrow?

HAPPY. You leave the house tomorrow and come back at night and say Oliver is thinking it over. And he thinks it over for a couple of weeks, and gradually it fades away and nobody's the worse.

BIFF. But it'll go on forever!

HAPPY. Dad is never so happy as when he's looking forward to something!

(*Willy enters.*)

HAPPY. Hello, scout!

WILLY. Gee, I haven't been here in years! (*Stanley has followed Willy in and sets a chair for him. Stanley starts off but Happy stops him.*)

HAPPY. Stanley!

(*Stanley stands by, waiting for an order.*)

BIFF (*going to Willy with guilt, as to an invalid*). Sit down, Pop. You want a drink?

WILLY. Sure, I don't mind.

BIFF. Let's get a load on.

WILLY. You look worried.

BIFF. N-no. (*To Stanley*) Scotch all around. Make it doubles.

STANLEY. Doubles, right. (*He goes*)

WILLY. You had a couple already, didn't you?

BIFF. Just a couple, yeah.

WILLY. Well, what happened, boy? (*Nodding affirmatively, with a smile*) Everything go all right?

BIFF (*takes a breath, then reaches out and grasps Willy's hand*). Pal . . . (*He is smiling bravely, and Willy is smiling too*) I had an experience today.

HAPPY. Terrific, Pop.

WILLY. That so? What happened?

BIFF (*high, slightly alcoholic, above the earth*). I'm going to tell you everything from first to last. It's been a strange day. (*Silence. He looks around, composes himself as best he can, but his breath keeps breaking the rhythm of his voice*) I had to wait quite a while for him, and—

WILLY. Oliver?

BIFF. Yeah, Oliver. All day, as a matter of cold fact. And a lot of—instances—facts, Pop, facts about my life came back to me. Who was it, Pop? Who ever said I was a salesman with Oliver?

WILLY. Well, you were.

BIFF. No, Dad, I was a shipping clerk.

WILLY. But you were practically—

BIFF (*with determination*). Dad, I don't know who said it first, but I was never a salesman for Bill Oliver.

WILLY. What're you talking about?

BIFF. Let's hold on to the facts tonight, Pop. We're not going to get anywhere bullin' around. I was a shipping clerk.

WILLY (*angrily*). All right, now listen to me—

BIFF. Why don't you let me finish?

WILLY. I'm not interested in stories about the past or any crap of that kind because the woods are burning, boys, you understand? There's a big blaze going on all around. I was fired today.

BIFF (*shocked*). How could you be?

WILLY. I was fired, and I'm looking for a little good news to tell your mother, because the woman has waited and the woman has suffered. The gist of it is that I haven't got a story left in my head, Biff. So don't give me a lecture about facts and aspects. I am not interested. Now what've you got to say to me?

(*Stanley enters with three drinks. They wait until he leaves.*)

WILLY. Did you see Oliver?

BIFF. Jesus, Dad!

WILLY. You mean you didn't go up there?

HAPPY. Sure he went up there.

BIFF. I did. I—saw him. How could they fire you?

WILLY (*on the edge of his chair*). What kind of a welcome did he give you?

BIFF. He won't even let you work on commission?

WILLY. I'm out! (*Driving*) So tell me, he gave you a warm welcome?

HAPPY. Sure, Pop, sure!

BIFF (*driven*). Well, it was kind of—

WILLY. I was wondering if he'd remember you. (*To Happy*) Imagine, man doesn't see him for ten, twelve years and gives him that kind of a welcome!

HAPPY. Damn right!

BIFF (*trying to return to the offensive*). Pop, look—

WILLY. You know why he remembered you, don't you? Because you impressed him in those days.

BIFF. Let's talk quietly and get this down to the facts, huh?

WILLY (*as though Biff had been interrupting*). Well, what happened? It's great news, Biff. Did he take you into his office or'd you talk in the waiting-room?

BIFF. Well, he came in, see, and—

WILLY (*with a big smile*). What'd he say? Betcha he threw his arm around you.

BIFF. Well, he kinda—

WILLY. He's a fine man. (*To Happy*) Very hard man to see, y'know.

HAPPY (*agreeing*). Oh, I know.

WILLY (*to Biff*). Is that where you had the drinks?

BIFF. Yeah, he gave me a couple of—no, no!

HAPPY (*cutting in*). He told him my Florida idea.

WILLY. Don't interrupt. (*To Biff*) How'd he react to the Florida idea?

BIFF. Dad, will you give me a minute to explain?

WILLY. I've been waiting for you to explain since I sat down here! What happened? He took you into his office and what?

BIFF. Well—I talked. And—and he listened, see.

WILLY. Famous for the way he listens, y'know. What was his answer?

BIFF. His answer was—(*He breaks off, suddenly angry*) Dad, you're not letting me tell you what I want to tell you!

WILLY (*accusing, angered*). You didn't see him, did you?

BIFF. I did see him!

WILLY. What'd you insult him or something? You insulted him, didn't you?

BIFF. Listen, will you let me out of it, will you just let me out of it!

HAPPY. What the hell!

WILLY. Tell me what happened!

BIFF (*to Happy*). I can't talk to him!

(*A single trumpet note jars the ear. The light of green leaves stains the house, which holds the air of night and a dream. Young Bernard enters and knocks on the door of the house.*)

YOUNG BERNARD (*frantically*). Mrs. Loman, Mrs. Loman!

HAPPY. Tell him what happened!

BIFF (*to Happy*). Shut up and leave me alone!

WILLY. No, no! You had to go and flunk math!

BIFF. What math? What're you talking about?

YOUNG BERNARD. Mrs. Loman, Mrs. Loman!

(*Linda appears in the house, as of old.*)

WILLY (*wildly*). Math, math, math!

BIFF. Take it easy, Pop!

YOUNG BERNARD. Mrs. Loman!

WILLY (*furiously*). If you hadn't flunked you'd've been set by now!

BIFF. Now, look, I'm gonna tell you what happened, and you're going to listen to me.

YOUNG BERNARD. Mrs. Loman!

BIFF. I waited six hours—

HAPPY. What the hell are you saying?

BIFF. I kept sending in my name but he wouldn't see me. So finally he . . . (*He *continues unheard as light fades low on the restaurant*)

YOUNG BERNARD. Biff flunked math!

LINDA. No!

YOUNG BERNARD. Birnbaum flunked him! They won't graduate him!

LINDA. But they have to. He's gotta go to the university. Where is he? Biff! Biff!

YOUNG BERNARD. No, he left. He went to Grand Central.

LINDA. Grand—You mean he went to Boston!

YOUNG BERNARD. Is Uncle Willy in Boston?

LINDA. Oh, maybe Willy can talk to the teacher. Oh, the poor, poor boy!

(*Light on house area snaps out.*)

BIFF (*at the table, now audible, holding up a gold fountain pen*). . . . so I'm washed up with Oliver, you understand? Are you listening to me?

WILLY (*at a loss*). Yeah, sure. If you hadn't flunked—

BIFF. Flunked what? What're you talking about?

WILLY. Don't blame everything on me! I didn't flunk math—you did! What pen?

HAPPY. That was awful dumb, Biff, a pen like that is worth—

WILLY (*seeing the pen for the first time*). You took Oliver's pen?

BIFF (*weakening*). Dad, I just explained it to you.

WILLY. You stole Bill Oliver's fountain pen!

BIFF. I didn't exactly steal it! That's just what I've been explaining to you!

HAPPY. He had it in his hand and just then Oliver walked in, so he got nervous and stuck it in his pocket!

WILLY. My God, Biff!

BIFF. I never intended to do it, Dad!

OPERATOR'S VOICE. Standish Arms, good evening!

WILLY (*shouting*). I'm not in my room!

BIFF (*frightened*). Dad, what's the matter? (*He and Happy stand up*)

OPERATOR. Ringing Mr. Loman for you!

WILLY. I'm not there, stop it!

BIFF (*horrified, gets down on one knee before Willy*). Dad, I'll make good, I'll make good. (*Willy tries to get to his feet. Biff holds him down*) Sit down now.

WILLY. No, you're no good, you're no good for anything.

BIFF. I am, Dad, I'll find something else, you understand? Now don't worry about anything. (*He holds up Willy's face*) Talk to me, Dad.

OPERATOR. Mr. Loman does not answer. Shall I page him?

WILLY (*attempting to stand, as though to rush and silence the Operator*). No, no, no!

HAPPY. He'll strike something, Pop.

WILLY. No, no . . .

BIFF (*desperately, standing over Willy*). Pop, listen! Listen to me! I'm telling you something good. Oliver talked to his partner about the Florida idea. You listening? He—he talked to his partner, and he came to me . . . I'm going to be all right, you hear? Dad, listen to me, he said it was just a question of the amount!

WILLY. Then you . . . got it?

HAPPY. He's gonna be terrific, Pop!

WILLY (*trying to stand*). Then you got it, haven't you? You got it! You got it!

BIFF (*agonized, holds Willy down*). No, no. Look, Pop, I'm supposed to have lunch with them tomorrow. I'm just telling you this so you'll know that I can still make an impression, Pop. And I'll make good somewhere, but I can't go tomorrow, see?

WILLY. Why not? You simply—

BIFF. But the pen, Pop!

WILLY. You give it to him and tell him it was an oversight!

HAPPY. Sure, have lunch tomorrow!

BIFF. I can't say that—

WILLY. You were doing a crossword puzzle and accidentally used his pen!

BIFF. Listen, kid, I took those balls years ago, now I walk in with his fountain pen? That clinches it, don't you see? I can't face him like that! I'll try elsewhere.

PAGE'S VOICE. Paging Mr. Loman!

WILLY. Don't you want to be anything?

BIFF. Pop, how can I go back?

WILLY. You don't want to be anything, is that what's behind it?

BIFF (*now angry at Willy for not crediting his sympathy*). Don't take it that way! You think it was easy walking into that office after what I'd done to him? A team of horses couldn't have dragged me back to Bill Oliver!

WILLY. Then why'd you go?

BIFF. Why did I go? Why did I go! Look at you! Look at what's become of you!

(*Off left, The Woman laughs.*)

WILLY. Biff, you're going to go to that lunch tomorrow, or—

BIFF. I can't go. I've got no appointment!

HAPPY. Biff, for . . . !

WILLY. Are you spiting me?

BIFF. Don't take it that way! Goddammit!

WILLY (*strikes Biff and falters away from the table*). You rotten little louse! Are you spiting me?

THE WOMAN. Someone's at the door, Willy!

BIFF. I'm no good, can't you see what I am?

HAPPY (*separating them*). Hey, you're in a restaurant! Now cut it out, both of you! (*The girls enter*) Hello, girls, sit down.

(*The Woman laughs, off left.*)

MISS FORSYTHE. I guess we might as well. This is Letta.

THE WOMAN. Willy, are you going to wake up?

BIFF (*ignoring Willy*). How're ya, miss, sit down. What do you drink?

MISS FORSYTHE. Letta might not be able to stay long.

LETTA. I gotta get up very early tomorrow. I got jury duty. I'm so excited! Were you fellows ever on a jury?

BIFF. No, but I been in front of them! (*The girls laugh*) This is my father.

LETTA. Isn't he cute? Sit down with us, Pop.

HAPPY. Sit him down, Biff!

BIFF (*going to him*). Come on, slugger, drink us under the table. To hell with it! Come on, sit down, pal.

(*On Biff's last insistence, Willy is about to sit.*)

THE WOMAN (*now urgently*). Willy, are you going to answer the door!

(*The Woman's call pulls Willy back. He starts right, befuddled.*)

BIFF. Hey, where are you going?

WILLY. Open the door.

BIFF. The door?

WILLY. The washroom . . . the door . . . where's the door?

BIFF (*leading Willy to the left*). Just go straight down.

(*Willy moves left.*)

THE WOMAN. Willy, Willy, are you going to get up, get up, get up, get up?

(*Willy exits left.*)

LETTA. I think it's sweet you bring your daddy along.

MISS FORSYTHE. Oh, he isn't really your father!

BIFF (*at left, turning to her resentfully*). Miss Forsythe, you've just seen a prince walk by. A fine, troubled prince. A hard-working, unappreciated prince. A pal, you understand? A good companion. Always for his boys.

LETTA. That's so sweet.

HAPPY. Well, girls, what's the program? We're wasting time. Come on, Biff. Gather round. Where would you like to go?

BIFF. Why don't you do something for him?

HAPPY. Me!

BIFF. Don't you give a damn for him, Hap?

HAPPY. What're you talking about? I'm the one who—

BIFF. I sense it, you don't give a good goddam about him. (*He takes the rolled-up hose from his pocket and puts it on the table in front of Happy*) Look what I found in the cellar, for Christ's sake. How can you bear to let it go on?

HAPPY. Me? Who goes away? Who runs off and—

BIFF. Yeah, but he doesn't mean anything to you. You could help him—I can't! Don't you understand what I'm talking about? He's going to kill himself, don't you know that?

HAPPY. Don't I know it! Me!

BIFF. Hap, help him! Jesus . . . help him . . . Help me, help me, I can't bear to look at his face! (*Ready to weep, he hurries out, up right*)

HAPPY (*staring after him*). Where are you going?

MISS FORSYTHE. What's he so mad about?

HAPPY. Come on, girls, we'll catch up with him.

MISS FORSYTHE (*as Happy pushes her out*). Say, I don't like that temper of his!

HAPPY. He's just a little overstrung, he'll be all right!

WILLY (*off left, as The Woman laughs*). Don't answer! Don't answer!

LETTA. Don't you want to tell your father—

HAPPY. No, that's not my father. He's just a guy. Come on, we'll catch Biff, and, honey, we're going to paint this town! Stanley, where's the check! Hey, Stanley! (*They exit. Stanley looks toward left.*)

STANLEY (*calling to Happy indignantly*). Mr. Loman! Mr. Loman!

(*Stanley picks up a chair and follows them off. Knocking is heard off left. The Woman enters, laughing. Willy follows her. She is in a black slip; he is buttoning his shirt. Raw, sensuous music accompanies their speech.*)

WILLY. Will you stop laughing? Will you stop?

THE WOMAN. Aren't you going to answer the door? He'll wake the whole hotel.

WILLY. I'm not expecting anybody.

THE WOMAN. Whyn't you have another drink, honey, and stop being so damn self-centered?

WILLY. I'm so lonely.

THE WOMAN. You know you ruined me, Willy? From now on, whenever you come to the office, I'll see that you go right through to the buyers. No waiting at my desk any more, Willy. You ruined me.

WILLY. That's nice of you to say that.

THE WOMAN. Gee, you are self-centered! Why so sad? You are the saddest, self-centeredest soul I ever did see-saw. (*She laughs. He kisses her*) Come on inside, drummer boy. It's silly to be dressing in the middle of the night. (*As knocking is heard*) Aren't you going to answer the door?

WILLY. They're knocking on the wrong door.

THE WOMAN. But I felt the knocking. And he heard us talking in here. Maybe the hotel's on fire!

WILLY (*his terror rising*). It's a mistake.

THE WOMAN. Then tell him to go away!

WILLY. There's nobody there.

THE WOMAN. It's getting on my nerves, Willy. There's somebody standing out there and it's getting on my nerves!

WILLY (*pushing her away from him*). All right, stay in the bathroom here, and don't come out. I think there's a law in Massachusetts about it, so don't come out. It may be that new room clerk. He looked very mean. So don't come out. It's a mistake, there's no fire.

(*The knocking is heard again. He takes a few steps away from her, and she vanishes into the wing. The light follows him, and now he is facing Young Biff, who carries a suitcase. Biff steps toward him. The music is gone.*)

BIFF. Why didn't you answer?

WILLY. Biff! What are you doing in Boston?

BIFF. Why didn't you answer? I've been knocking for five minutes, I called you on the phone—

WILLY. I just heard you. I was in the bathroom and had the door shut. Did anything happen home?

BIFF. Dad—I let you down.

WILLY. What do you mean?

BIFF. Dad . . .

WILLY. Biffo, what's this about? (*Putting his arm around Biff*) Come on, let's go downstairs and get you a malted.

BIFF. Dad, I flunked math.

WILLY. Not for the term?

BIFF. The term. I haven't got enough credits to graduate.

WILLY. You mean to say Bernard wouldn't give you the answers?

BIFF. He did, he tried, but I only got a sixty-one.

WILLY. And they wouldn't give you four points?

BIFF. Birnbaum refused absolutely. I begged him, Pop, but he won't give me those points. You gotta talk to him before they close the school. Because if he saw the kind of man you are, and you just talked to him in your way, I'm sure he'd come through for me. The class came right before practice, see, and I didn't go enough. Would you talk to him? He'd like you, Pop. You know the way you could talk.

WILLY. You're on. We'll drive right back.

BIFF. Oh, Dad, good work! I'm sure he'll change it for you!

WILLY. Go downstairs and tell the clerk I'm checkin' out. Go right down.

BIFF. Yes, sir! See, the reason he hates me, Pop—one day he was late for class so I got up at the blackboard and imitated him. I crossed my eyes and talked with a lithp.

WILLY (*laughing*). You did? The kids like it?

BIFF. They nearly died laughing.

WILLY. Yeah? What'd you do?

BIFF. The thquare root of thixthy twee is . . . (*Willy bursts out laughing; Biff joins him*) And in the middle of it he walked in!

(*Willy laughs and The Woman joins in offstage.*)

WILLY (*without hesitation*). Hurry downstairs and—

BIFF. Somebody in there?

WILLY. No, that was next door.

(*The Woman laughs offstage.*)

BIFF. Somebody got in your bathroom!

WILLY. No, it's the next room, there's a party—

THE WOMAN (*enters, laughing. She lisps this*). Can I come in? There's something in the bathtub, Willy, and it's moving! (*Willy looks at Biff, who is staring open-mouthed and horrified at The Woman.*)

WILLY. Ah—you better go back to your room. They must be finished painting by now. They're painting her room so I let her take a shower here. Go back, go back . . . (*He pushes her*)

THE WOMAN (*resisting*). But I've got to get dressed, Willy, I can't—

WILLY. Get out of here! Go back, go back . . . (*Suddenly striving for the ordinary*) This is Miss Francis, Biff, she's a buyer. They're painting her room. Go back, Miss Francis, go back . . .

THE WOMAN. But my clothes, I can't go out naked in the hall!

WILLY (*pushing her offstage*). Get outa here! Go back, go back!

(*Biff slowly sits down on his suitcase as the argument continues offstage.*)

THE WOMAN. Where's my stockings? You promised me stockings, Willy!

WILLY. I have no stockings here!

THE WOMAN. You had two boxes of size nine sheers for me, and I want them!

WILLY. Here, for God's sake, will you get outa here!

THE WOMAN (*enters holding a box of stockings*). I just hope there's nobody in the hall. That's all I hope. (*To Biff*) Are you football or baseball?

BIFF. Football.

THE WOMAN (*angry, humiliated*). That's me too. G'night. (*She snatches her clothes from Willy, and walks out*)

WILLY (*after a pause*). Well, better get going. I want to get to the school first thing in the morning. Get my suits out of the closet. I'll get my valises. (*Biff doesn't move*) What's the matter? (*Biff remains motionless, tears falling*) She's a buyer. Buys for J. H. Simmons. She lives down the hall—they're painting. You don't imagine—(*He breaks off. After a pause*) Now listen, pal, she's just a buyer. She sees merchandise in her room and they have to keep it looking just so . . . (*Pause. Assuming command*) All right, get my suits. (*Biff doesn't move*) Now stop crying and do as I say. I gave you an order. Biff, I gave you an order! Is

that what you do when I give you an order? How dare you cry! (*Putting his arm around Biff*) Now look, Biff, when you grow up you'll understand about these things. You mustn't—you mustn't over-emphasize a thing like this. I'll see Birnbaum first thing in the morning.

BIFF. Never mind.

WILLY (*getting down beside Biff*). Never mind! He's going to give you those points. I'll see to it.

BIFF. He wouldn't listen to you.

WILLY. He certainly will listen to me. You need those points for the U. of Virginia.

BIFF. I'm not going there.

WILLY. Heh? If I can't get him to change that mark you'll make it up in summer school. You've got all summer to—

BIFF (*his weeping breaking from him*). Dad . . .

WILLY (*infected by it*). Oh, my boy . . .

BIFF. Dad . . .

WILLY. She's nothing to me, Biff. I was lonely, I was terribly lonely.

BIFF. You—you gave her Mama's stockings! (*His tears break through and he rises to go*)

WILLY (*grabbing for Biff*). I gave you an order!

BIFF. Don't touch me, you—liar!

WILLY. Apologize for that!

BIFF. You fake! You phony little fake! You fake! (*Overcome, he turns quickly and weeping fully goes out with his suitcase. Willy is left on the floor on his knees*)

WILLY. I gave you an order! Biff, come back here or I'll beat you! Come back here! I'll whip you!

(*Stanley comes quickly in from the right and stands in front of Willy.*)

WILLY (*shouts at Stanley*). I gave you an order . . .

STANLEY. Hey, let's pick it up, pick it up, Mr. Loman. (*He helps Willy to his feet*) Your boys left with the chippies. They said they'll see you home.

(*A second waiter watches some distance away.*)

WILLY. But we were supposed to have dinner together.

(*Music is heard, Willy's theme.*)

STANLEY. Can you make it?

WILLY. I'll—sure, I can make it. (*Sud-

denly concerned about his clothes) Do I—
I look all right?

STANLEY. Sure, you look all right. (*He
flicks a speck off Willy's lapel*)

WILLY. Here—here's a dollar.

STANLEY. Oh, your son paid me. It's all
right.

WILLY (*putting it in Stanley's hand*).
No, take it. You're a good boy.

STANLEY. Oh, no, you don't have to . . .

WILLY. Here—here's some more, I don't
need it any more. (*After a slight pause*)
Tell me—is there a seed store in the neighborhood?

STANLEY. Seeds? You mean like to plant?
(*As Willy turns, Stanley slips the money
back into his jacket pocket.*)

WILLY. Yes. Carrots, peas . . .

STANLEY. Well, there's hardware stores
on Sixth Avenue, but it may be too late
now.

WILLY (*anxiously*). Oh, I'd better hurry.
I've got to get some seeds. (*He starts off
to the right*) I've got to get some seeds,
right away. Nothing's planted. I don't
have a thing in the ground.

(*Willy hurries out as the light goes down.
Stanley moves over to the right after him,
watches him off. The other waiter has
been staring at Willy.*)

STANLEY (*to the waiter*). Well, whatta
you looking at?

(*The waiter picks up the chairs and moves
off right. Stanley takes the table and follows him. The light fades on this area.
There is a long pause, the sound of the
flute coming over. The light gradually
rises on the kitchen, which is empty.
Happy appears at the door of the house,
followed by Biff. Happy is carrying a large
bunch of long-stemmed roses. He enters
the kitchen, looks around for Linda. Not
seeing her, he turns to Biff, who is just
outside the house door, and makes a gesture with his hands, indicating "Not here,
I guess." He looks into the living-room
and freezes. Inside, Linda, unseen, is
seated, Willy's coat on her lap. She rises
ominously and quietly and moves toward
Happy, who backs up into the kitchen,
afraid.*)

HAPPY. Hey, what're you doing up?
(*Linda says nothing but moves toward
him implacably*) Where's Pop? (*He keeps
backing to the right, and now Linda is in
full view in the doorway to the living-
room*) Is he sleeping?

LINDA. Where were you?

HAPPY (*trying to laugh it off*). We met
two girls, Mom, very fine types. Here, we
brought you some flowers. (*Offering them
to her*) Put them in your room, Ma.
(*She knocks them to the floor at Biff's
feet. He has now come inside and closed
the door behind him. She stares at Biff,
silent.*)

HAPPY. Now what'd you do that for?
Mom, I want you to have some flowers—

LINDA (*cutting Happy off, violently to
Biff*). Don't you care whether he lives or
dies?

HAPPY (*going to the stairs*). Come upstairs, Biff.

BIFF (*with a flare of disgust, to Happy*).
Go away from me! (*To Linda*) What do
you mean, lives or dies? Nobody's dying
around here, pal.

LINDA. Get out of my sight! Get out of
here!

BIFF. I wanna see the boss.

LINDA. You're not going near him!

BIFF. Where is he? (*He moves into the
living-room and Linda follows*)

LINDA (*shouting after Biff*). You invite
him for dinner. He looks forward to it all
day—(*Biff appears in his parents' bedroom, looks around, and exits*)—and then
you desert him there. There's no stranger
you'd do that to!

HAPPY. Why? He had a swell time with
us. Listen, when I—(*Linda comes back
into the kitchen*)—desert him I hope I
don't outlive the day!

LINDA. Get out of here!

HAPPY. Now look, Mom . . .

LINDA. Did you have to go to women tonight? You and your lousy rotten whores!
(*Biff re-enters the kitchen.*)

HAPPY. Mom, all we did was follow Biff
around trying to cheer him up! (*To Biff*)
Boy, what a night you gave me!

LINDA. Get out of here, both of you, and
don't come back! I don't want you tor-
menting him any more. Go on now, get
your things together! (*To Biff*) You can
sleep in his apartment. (*She starts to pick
up the flowers and stops herself*) Pick up
this stuff, I'm not your maid any more.
Pick it up, you bum, you!

(*Happy turns his back to her in refusal.
Biff slowly moves over and gets down on
his knees, picking up the flowers.*)

LINDA. You're a pair of animals! Not
one, not another living soul would have

had the cruelty to walk out on that man in a restaurant!

BIFF (*not looking at her*). Is that what he said?

LINDA. He didn't have to say anything. He was so humiliated he nearly limped when he came in.

HAPPY. But, Mom, he had a great time with us—

BIFF (*cutting him off violently*). Shut up!

(*Without another word, Happy goes upstairs.*)

LINDA. You! You didn't even go in to see if he was all right!

BIFF (*still on the floor in front of Linda, the flowers in his hand; with self-loathing*). No. Didn't. Didn't do a damned thing. How do you like that, heh? Left him babbling in a toilet.

LINDA. You louse. You . . .

BIFF. Now you hit it on the nose! (*He gets up, throws the flowers in the wastebasket*) The scum of the earth, and you're looking at him!

LINDA. Get out of here!

BIFF. I gotta talk to the boss, Mom. Where is he?

LINDA. You're not going near him. Get out of this house!

BIFF (*with absolute assurance, determination*). No. We're gonna have an abrupt conversation, him and me.

LINDA. You're not talking to him!

(*Hammering is heard from outside the house, off right. Biff turns toward the noise.*)

LINDA (*suddenly pleading*). Will you please leave him alone?

BIFF. What's he doing out there?

LINDA. He's planting the garden!

BIFF (*quietly*). Now? Oh, my God!

(*Biff moves outside, Linda following. The light dies down on them and comes up on the center of the apron as Willy walks into it. He is carrying a flashlight, a hoe, and a handful of seed packets. He raps the top of the hoe sharply to fix it firmly, and then moves to the left, measuring off the distance with his foot. He holds the flashlight to look at the seed packets, reading off the instructions. He is in the blue of night.*)

WILLY. Carrots . . . quarter-inch apart. Rows . . . one-foot rows. (*He measures it off*) One foot. (*He puts down a package and measures off*) Beets. (*He puts down another package and measures again*) Let-

tuce. (*He reads the package, puts it down*) One foot—(*He breaks off as Ben appears at the right and moves slowly down to him*) What a proposition, ts, ts. Terrific, terrific. 'Cause she's suffered, Ben, the woman has suffered. You understand me? A man can't go out the way he came in, Ben, a man has got to add up to something. You can't, you can't—(*Ben moves toward him as though to interrupt*) You gotta consider, now. Don't answer so quick. Remember, it's a guaranteed twenty-thousand-dollar proposition. Now look, Ben, I want you to go through the ins and outs of this thing with me. I've got nobody to talk to, Ben, and the woman has suffered, you hear me?

BEN (*standing still, considering*). What's the proposition?

WILLY. It's twenty thousand dollars on the barrelhead. Guaranteed, gilt-edged, you understand?

BEN. You don't want to make a fool of yourself. They might not honor the policy.

WILLY. How can they dare refuse? Didn't I work like a coolie to meet every premium on the nose? And now they don't pay off? Impossible!

BEN. It's called a cowardly thing, William.

WILLY. Why? Does it take more guts to stand here the rest of my life ringing up a zero?

BEN (*yielding*). That's a point, William. (*He moves, thinking, turns*) And twenty thousand—that *is* something one can feel with the hand, it is there.

WILLY (*now assured, with rising power*). Oh, Ben, that's the whole beauty of it! I see it like a diamond, shining in the dark, hard and rough, that I can pick up and touch in my hand. Not like—like an appointment! This would not be another damned-fool appointment, Ben, and it changes all the aspects. Because he thinks I'm nothing, see, and so he spites me. But the funeral—(*Straightening up*) Ben, that funeral will be massive! They'll come from Maine, Massachusetts, Vermont, New Hampshire! All the old-timers with the strange license plates—that boy will be thunder-struck, Ben, because he never realized—I am known! Rhode Island, New York, New Jersey—I am known, Ben, and he'll see it with his eyes once and for all. He'll see what I am, Ben! He's in for a shock, that boy!

BEN (*coming down to the edge of the garden*). He'll call you a coward.

WILLY (*suddenly fearful*). No, that would be terrible.

BEN. Yes. And a damned fool.

WILLY. No, no, he mustn't. I won't have that! (*He is broken and desperate*)

BEN. He'll hate you, William.

(*The gay music of the Boys is heard.*)

WILLY. Oh, Ben, how do we get back to all the great times? Used to be so full of light, and comradeship, the sleigh-riding in winter, and the ruddiness on his cheeks. And always some kind of good news coming up, always something nice coming up ahead. And never even let me carry the valises in the house, and simonizing, simonizing that little red car! Why, why can't I give him something and not have him hate me?

BEN. Let me think about it. (*He glances at his watch*) I still have a little time. Remarkable proposition, but you've got to be sure you're not making a fool of yourself. (*Ben drifts off upstage and goes out of sight. Biff comes down from the left.*)

WILLY (*suddenly conscious of Biff, turns and looks up at him, then begins picking up the packages of seeds in confusion*). Where the hell is that seed? (*Indignantly*) You can't see nothing out here! They boxed in the whole goddam neighborhood!

BIFF. There are, people all around here. Don't you realize that?

WILLY. I'm busy. Don't bother me.

BIFF (*taking the hoe from Willy*). I'm saying good-by to you, Pop. (*Willy looks at him, silent, unable to move*) I'm not coming back any more.

WILLY. You're not going to see Oliver tomorrow?

BIFF. I've got no appointment, Dad.

WILLY. He put his arm around you, and you've got no appointment?

BIFF. Pop, get this now, will you? Everytime I've left it's been a fight that sent me out of here. Today I realized something about myself and I tried to explain it to you and I—I think I'm just not smart enough to make any sense out of it for you. To hell with whose fault it is or anything like that. (*He takes Willy's arm*) Let's just wrap it up, heh? Come on in, we'll tell Mom. (*He gently tries to pull Willy to left*)

WILLY (*frozen, immobile, with guilt in his voice*). No, I didn't want to see her.

BIFF. Come on! (*He pulls again, and Willy tries to pull away*)

WILLY (*highly nervous*). No, no, I don't want to see her.

BIFF (*tries to look into Willy's face, as if to find the answer there*). Why don't you want to see her?

WILLY (*more harshly now*). Don't bother me, will you?

BIFF. What do you mean, you don't want to see her? You don't want them calling you yellow, do you? This isn't your fault; it's me, I'm a bum. Now come inside. (*Willy strains to get away*) Did you hear what I said to you?

(*Willy pulls away and quickly goes by himself into the house. Biff follows.*)

LINDA (*to Willy*). Did you plant, dear?

BIFF (*at the door, to Linda*). All right, we had it out. I'm going and I'm not writing any more.

LINDA (*going to Willy in the kitchen*). I think that's the best way, dear. 'Cause there's no use drawing it out, you'll just never get along.

(*Willy doesn't respond.*)

BIFF. People ask where I am and what I'm doing, you don't know, and you don't care. That way it'll be off your mind and you can start brightening up again. All right? That clears it, doesn't it? (*Willy is silent, and Biff goes to him*) You gonna wish me luck, scout? (*He extends his hand*) What do you say?

LINDA. Shake his hand, Willy.

WILLY (*turning to her, seething with hurt*). There's no necessity to mention the pen at all, y'know.

BIFF (*gently*). I've got no appointment, Dad.

WILLY (*erupting fiercely*). He put his arm around . . . ?

BIFF. Dad, you're never going to see what I am, so what's the use of arguing? If I strike oil I'll send you a check. Meantime, forget I'm alive.

WILLY (*to Linda*). Spite, see?

BIFF. Shake hands, Dad.

WILLY. Not my hand.

BIFF. I was hoping not to go this way.

WILLY. Well, this is the way you're going. Good-by.

(*Biff looks at him a moment, then turns sharply and goes to the stairs.*)

WILLY (*stops him with*). May you rot in hell if you leave this house!

BIFF (*turning*). Exactly what is it that you want from me?

WILLY. I want you to know, on the train, in the mountains, in the valleys, wherever you go, that you cut down your life for spite!

BIFF. No, no.

WILLY. Spite, spite, is the word of your undoing! And when you're down and out, remember what did it. When you're rotting somewhere beside the railroad tracks, remember, and don't you dare blame it on me!

BIFF. I'm not blaming it on you!

WILLY. I won't take the rap for this, you hear?

(*Happy comes down the stairs and stands on the bottom step, watching.*)

BIFF. That's just what I'm telling you!

WILLY (*sinking down into a chair at the table, with full accusation*). You're trying to put a knife in me—don't think I don't know what you're doing!

BIFF. All right, phony! Then let's lay it on the line. (*He whips the rubber tube out of his pocket and puts it on the table*)

HAPPY. You crazy—

LINDA. Biff! (*She moves to grab the hose, but Biff holds it down with his hand*)

BIFF. Leave it there! Don't move it!

WILLY (*not looking at it*). What is that?

BIFF. You know goddam well what that is.

WILLY (*caged, wanting to escape*). I never saw that.

BIFF. You saw it. The mice didn't bring it into the cellar! What is this supposed to do, make a hero out of you? This supposed to make me sorry for you?

WILLY. Never heard of it.

BIFF. There'll be no pity for you, you hear it? No pity!

WILLY (*to Linda*). You hear the spite!

BIFF. No, you're going to hear the truth—what you are and what I am!

LINDA. Stop it!

WILLY. Spite!

HAPPY (*coming down toward Biff*). You cut it now!

BIFF (*to Happy*). The man don't know who we are! The man is gonna know! (*To Willy*) We never told the truth for ten minutes in this house!

HAPPY. We always told the truth!

BIFF (*turning on him*). You big blow, are you the assistant buyer? You're one of the two assistants to the assistant, aren't you?

HAPPY. Well, I'm practically—

BIFF. You're practically full of it! We all are! And I'm through with it! (*To Willy*) Now hear this, Willy, this is me.

WILLY. I know you!

BIFF. You know why I had no address for three months? I stole a suit in Kansas City and I was in jail. (*To Linda, who is sobbing*) Stop crying, I'm through with it. (*Linda turns away from them, her hands covering her face.*)

WILLY. I suppose that's my fault!

BIFF. I stole myself out of every good job since high school!

WILLY. And whose fault is that?

BIFF. And I never got anywhere because you blew me so full of hot air I could never stand taking orders from anybody! That's whose fault it is!

WILLY. I hear that!

LINDA. Don't, Biff!

BIFF. It's goddam time you heard that! I had to be boss big shot in two weeks, and I'm through with it!

WILLY. Then hang yourself! For spite, hang yourself!

BIFF. No! Nobody's hanging himself, Willy! I ran down eleven flights with a pen in my hand today. And suddenly I stopped, you hear me? And in the middle of that office building, do you hear this? I stopped in the middle of that building and I saw—the sky. I saw the things that I love in this world. The work and the food and time to sit and smoke. And I looked at the pen and said to myself, what the hell am I grabbing this for? Why am I trying to become what I don't want to be? What am I doing in an office, making a contemptuous, begging fool of myself, when all I want is out there, waiting for me the minute I say I know who I am! Why can't I say that, Willy? (*He tries to make Willy face him, but Willy pulls away and moves to the left*)

WILLY (*with hatred, threateningly*). The door of your life is wide open!

BIFF. Pop, I'm a dime a dozen, and so are you!

WILLY (*turning on him now in an uncontrolled outburst*). I am not a dime a dozen! I am Willy Loman, and you are Biff Loman!

(*Biff starts for Willy, but is blocked by*

Happy. In his fury, Biff seems on the verge of attacking his father.)

BIFF. I am not a leader of men, Willy, and neither are you. You were never anything but a hard-working drummer who landed in the ash can like all the rest of them! I'm one dollar an hour, Willy! I tried seven states and couldn't raise it. A buck an hour! Do you gather my meaning? I'm not bringing home any prizes any more, and you're going to stop waiting for me to bring them home!

WILLY (*directly to Biff*). You vengeful, spiteful mutt!

(*Biff breaks from Happy. Willy, in fright, starts up the stairs. Biff grabs him.*)

BIFF (*at the peak of his fury*). Pop, I'm nothing! I'm nothing, Pop. Can't you understand that? There's no spite in it any more. I'm just what I am, that's all.

(*Biff's fury has spent itself, and he breaks down, sobbing, holding on to Willy, who dumbly fumbles for Biff's face.*)

WILLY (*astonished*). What're you doing? What're you doing? (*To Linda*) Why is he crying?

BIFF (*crying, broken*). Will you let me go, for Christ's sake? Will you take that phony dream and burn it before something happens? (*Struggling to contain himself, he pulls away and moves to the stairs*) I'll go in the morning. Put him—put him to bed. (*Exhausted, Biff moves up the stairs to his room*)

WILLY (*after a long pause, astonished, elevated*). Isn't that—isn't that remarkable? Biff—he likes me!

LINDA. He loves you, Willy.

HAPPY (*deeply moved*). Always did, Pop.

WILLY. Oh, Biff! (*Staring wildly*) He cried! Cried to me. (*He is choking with his love, and now cries out his promise*) That boy—that boy is going to be magnificent!

(*Ben appears in the light just outside the kitchen.*)

BEN. Yes, outstanding, with twenty thousand behind him.

LINDA (*sensing the racing of his mind, fearfully, carefully*). Now come to bed, Willy. It's all settled now.

WILLY (*finding it difficult not to rush out of the house*). Yes, we'll sleep. Come on. Go to sleep, Hap.

BEN. And it does take a great kind of a man to crack the jungle.

(*In accents of dread, Ben's idyllic music starts up.*)

HAPPY (*his arm around Linda*). I'm getting married, Pop, don't forget it. I'm changing everything. I'm gonna run that department before the year is up. You'll see, Mom. (*He kisses her*)

BEN. The jungle is dark but full of diamonds, Willy.

(*Willy turns, moves, listening to Ben.*)

LINDA. Be good. You're both good boys, just act that way, that's all.

HAPPY. 'Night, Pop. (*He goes upstairs*)

LINDA (*to Willy*). Come, dear.

BEN (*with greater force*). One must go in to fetch a diamond out.

WILLY (*to Linda, as he moves slowly along the edge of the kitchen, toward the door*). I just want to get settled down, Linda. Let me sit alone for a little.

LINDA (*almost uttering her fear*). I want you upstairs.

WILLY (*taking her in his arms*). In a few minutes, Linda. I couldn't sleep right now. Go on, you look awful tired. (*He kisses her*)

BEN. Not like an appointment at all. A diamond is rough and hard to the touch.

WILLY. Go on now. I'll be right up.

LINDA. I think this is the only way, Willy.

WILLY. Sure, it's the best thing.

BEN. Best thing!

WILLY. The only way. Everything is gonna be—go on, kid, get to bed. You look so tired.

LINDA. Come right up.

WILLY. Two minutes.

(*Linda goes into the living-room, then reappears in her bedroom. Willy moves just outside the kitchen door.*)

WILLY. Loves me. (*Wonderingly*) Always loved me. Isn't that a remarkable thing? Ben, he'll worship me for it!

BEN (*with promise*). It's dark there, but full of diamonds.

WILLY. Can you imagine that magnificence with twenty thousand dollars in his pocket?

LINDA (*calling from her room*). Willy! Come up!

WILLY (*calling into the kitchen*). Yes! Yes. Coming! It's very smart, you realize that, don't you, sweetheart? Even Ben sees it. I gotta go, baby. 'By! 'By! (*Going over to Ben, almost dancing*) Imagine? When the mail comes he'll be ahead of Bernard again!

BEN. A perfect proposition all around.

WILLY. Did you see how he cried to me? Oh, if I could kiss him, Ben!

BEN. Time, William, time!

WILLY. Oh, Ben, I always knew one way or another we were gonna make it, Biff and I!

BEN (*looking at his watch*). The boat. We'll be late. (*He moves slowly off into the darkness*)

WILLY (*elegiacally, turning to the house*). Now when you kick off, boy, I want a seventy-yard boot, and get right down the field under the ball, and when you hit, hit low and hit hard, because it's important, boy. (*He swings around and faces the audience*) There's all kinds of important people in the stands, and the first thing you know . . . (*Suddenly realizing he is alone*) Ben, Ben, where do I . . . ? (*He makes a sudden movement of search*) Ben, how do I . . . ?

LINDA (*calling*). Willy, you coming up?

WILLY (*uttering a gasp of fear, whirling about as if to quiet her*). Sh! (*He turns around as if to find his way; sounds, faces, voices seem to be swarming in upon him and he flicks at them, crying*) Sh! Sh! (*Suddenly music, faint and high, stops him. It rises in intensity, almost to an unbearable scream. He goes up and down on his toes, and rushes off around the house*) Shhh!

LINDA. Willy?

(*There is no answer. Linda waits. Biff gets up off his bed. He is still in his clothes. Happy sits up. Biff stands listening.*)

LINDA (*with real fear*). Willy, answer me! Willy!

(*There is the sound of a car starting and moving away at full speed.*)

LINDA. No!

BIFF (*rushing down the stairs*). Pop!

(*As the car speeds off, the music crashes down in a frenzy of sound, which becomes the soft pulsation of a single cello string. Biff slowly returns to his bedroom. He and Happy gravely don their jackets. Linda slowly walks out of her room. The music has developed into a death march. The leaves of day are appearing over everything. Charley and Bernard, somberly dressed, appear and knock on the kitchen door. Biff and Happy slowly descend the stairs to the kitchen as Charley and Ber-nard enter. All stop a moment when Linda, in clothes of mourning, bearing a little bunch of roses, comes through the draped doorway into the kitchen. She goes to Charley and takes his arm. Now all move toward the audience, through the wall-line of the kitchen. At the limit of the apron, Linda lays down the flowers, kneels, and sits back on her heels. All stare down at the grave.*)

REQUIEM

CHARLEY. It's getting dark, Linda.

(*Linda doesn't react. She stares at the grave.*)

BIFF. How about it, Mom? Better get some rest, heh? They'll be closing the gate soon.

(*Linda makes no move. Pause.*)

HAPPY (*deeply angered*). He had no right to do that. There was no necessity for it. We would've helped him.

CHARLEY (*grunting*). Hmmm.

BIFF. Come along, Mom.

LINDA. Why didn't anybody come?

CHARLEY. It was a very nice funeral.

LINDA. But where are all the people he knew? Maybe they blame him.

CHARLEY. Naa. It's a rough world, Linda. They wouldn't blame him.

LINDA. I can't understand it. At this time especially. First time in thirty-five years we were just about free and clear. He only needed a little salary. He was even finished with the dentist.

CHARLEY. No man only needs a little salary.

LINDA. I can't understand it.

BIFF. There were a lot of nice days. When he'd come home from a trip; or on Sundays, making the stoop; finishing the cellar; putting on the new porch; when he built the extra bathroom; and put up the garage. You know something, Charley, there's more of him in that front stoop than in all the sales he ever made.

CHARLEY. Yeah, he was a happy man with a batch of cement.

LINDA. He was so wonderful with his hands.

BIFF. He had the wrong dreams. All, all, wrong.

HAPPY (*almost ready to fight Biff*). Don't say that!

BIFF. He never knew who he was.

CHARLEY (*stopping Happy's movement and reply. To Biff*). Nobody dast blame this man. You don't understand: Willy was a salesman. And for a salesman, there is no rock bottom to the life. He don't put a bolt to a nut, he don't tell you the law or give you medicine. He's the man way out there in the blue riding on a smile and a shoeshine. And when they start not smiling back—that's an earthquake. And then you get yourself a couple of spots on your hat, and you're finished. Nobody dast blame this man. A salesman is got to dream, boy. It comes with the territory.

BIFF. Charley, the man didn't know who he was.

HAPPY (*infuriated*). Don't say that!

BIFF. Why don't you come with me, Happy?

HAPPY. I'm not licked that easily. I'm staying right in this city, and I'm gonna beat this racket! (*He looks at Biff, his chin set*) The Loman Brothers!

BIFF. I know who I am, kid.

HAPPY. All right, boy. I'm gonna show you and everybody else that Willy Loman did not die in vain. He had a good dream. It's the only dream you can have—to come out number-one man. He fought it out here, and this is where I'm gonna win it for him.

BIFF (*with a hopeless glance at Happy, bends toward his mother*). Let's go, Mom.

LINDA. I'll be with you in a minute. Go on, Charley. (*He hesitates*) I want to, just for a minute. I never had a chance to say good-by.

(*Charley moves away, followed by Happy. Biff remains a slight distance up and left of Linda. She sits there, summoning herself. The flute begins, not far away, playing behind her speech.*)

LINDA. Forgive me, dear. I can't cry. I don't know what it is, but I can't cry. I don't understand it. Why did you ever do that? Help me, Willy, I can't cry. It seems to me that you're just on another trip. I keep expecting you. Willy, dear, I can't cry. Why did you do it? I search and search and I search, and I can't understand it, Willy. I made the last payment on the house today. Today, dear. And there'll be nobody home. (*A sob rises in her throat*) We're free and clear. (*Sobbing more fully, released*) We're free. (*Biff comes slowly toward her*) We're free . . . We're free . . .

(*Biff lifts her to her feet and moves up right with her in his arms. Linda sobs quietly. Bernard and Charley come together and follow them, followed by Happy. Only the music of the flute is left on the darkening stage as over the house the hard towers of the apartment buildings rise into sharp focus, and*)

THE CURTAIN FALLS

The Member of the Wedding

BY CARSON McCULLERS

First presented by Robert Whitehead, Oliver Rea and Stanley Martineau at the Empire Theatre in New York on January 5, 1950, with the following cast:

BERENICE SADIE BROWN	Ethel Waters	MRS. WEST	Margaret Barker
FRANKIE ADDAMS	Julie Harris	HELEN FLETCHER	Mitzie Blake
JOHN HENRY WEST	Brandon de Wilde	DORIS	Joan Shepard
JARVIS	James Holden	SIS LAURA	Phyllis Walker
JANICE	Janet de Gore	T. T. WILLIAMS	Harry Bolden
MR. ADDAMS	William Hansen	HONEY CAMDEN BROWN	Henry Scott
	BARNEY MacKEAN	Jimmy Dutton	

ACT ONE

A late afternoon in August.

ACT TWO

Afternoon of the next day.

ACT THREE

Scene One: The wedding day—afternoon of the next day following Act Two.
Scene Two: 4 A.M. the following morning.
Scene Three: Late afternoon, in the following November.

Time: August, 1945
Place: A small Southern town

ALTHOUGH Carson McCullers, who was born in Columbus, Georgia, in 1917, has been writing since the age of sixteen, her first interest was music and the pursuit of a career as a concert pianist. In fact, she came to New York at the age of seventeen in order to study at Columbia University's Juilliard School of Music. This laudable intention died virtually aborning when she lost her tuition money in the subway during her second day in the city. Since she had no other resources, she took on a variety of jobs she was fortunately (in retrospect) unable to retain while settling for an inexpensive writing course at New York University. And fate apparently had her definitely marked for a literary and theatrical career by then, since she found herself living in the same house in Brooklyn as the poet W. H. Auden and the now prominent British opera composer Benjamin Britten.

A year later, Mrs. Carson McCullers (she was married in 1937 to a Southerner, Reeves McCullers) sold two short stories to *Story Magazine* and began a novel, *The Heart Is a Lonely Hunter,* published in 1940, which won her high critical acclaim. In 1941 she published a second book, the short novel *Reflections in a Golden Eye,* which *Time Magazine* compared favorably to *The Turn of the Screw.* Her third and longer novel *The Member of the Wedding,* published in 1946, indicated the addition of a humorous tenderness to her intense talent. In 1951 the last two novels, along with a new novella and six of her stories, were collected in another volume, *The Ballad of the Sad Café.* For these contributions she was awarded two Guggenheim Fellowships and was made a member of the American Academy of Art.

A young Southerner having made a dramatization of *The Member of the Wedding* that did not please her, although it was optioned by the Theatre Guild, Mrs. McCullers decided to dramatize the book herself. In venturing upon this enterprise, she worked without preparation in the field of playwriting, having, in fact, seen only two Broadway productions and a few plays while still at school. All the assistance she had was encouragement from Tennessee Williams, who urged her to make the dramatization. All her novels had stressed the fact of loneliness and human isolation. Her dramatization simply translated this reality into dialogue and dramatic representation. Mrs. McCullers was acutely aware of her intentions and, as she later explained, she was not writing a "conventional" or "literal kind of play." It was, she declared, "an inward play," in which the conflict was inward and the antagonist was not a person, but "a human condition." To give proper realization to her theme, she concerned herself, she declared, with "the weight of time, the hazard of human existence, bolts of chance." As a result the play was inevitably "fragmentary." It could be argued quite reasonably, however, that the "fragmentariness" of the play is an essential expression of the transitory experience Mrs. McCullers was intent upon evoking. A "well-made play," a methodical elaboration of meshing plot elements, would have violated the integrity of the novel's substance.

ACT ONE

A part of a Southern back yard and kitchen. At stage left there is a scuppernong arbor. A sheet, used as a stage curtain, hangs raggedly at one side of the arbor. There is an elm tree in the yard. The kitchen has in the center a table with chairs. The walls are drawn with child drawings. There is a stove to the right and a small coal heating stove with coal scuttle in rear center of kitchen. The kitchen opens on the left into the yard. At the interior right a door leads to a small inner room. A door at the left leads into the front hall. The lights go on dimly, with a dreamlike effect, gradually revealing the family in the yard and Berenice Sadie Brown in the kitchen. Berenice, the cook, is a stout, motherly Negro woman with an air of great capability and devoted protection. She is about forty-five years old. She has a quiet, flat face and one of her eyes is made of blue glass. Sometimes, when her socket bothers her, she dispenses with the false eye and wears a black patch. When we first see her she is wearing the patch and is dressed in a simple print work dress and apron.

Frankie, a gangling girl of twelve with blonde hair cut like a boy's, is wearing shorts and a sombrero and is standing in the arbor gazing adoringly at her brother Jarvis and his fiancée Janice. She is a dreamy, restless girl, and periods of energetic activity alternate with a rapt attention to her inward world of fantasy. She is thin and awkward and very much aware of being too tall. Jarvis, a good-looking boy of twenty-one, wearing an army uniform, stands by Janice. He is awkward when he first appears because this is his betrothal visit. Janice, a young, pretty, fresh-looking girl of eighteen or nineteen, is charming but rather ordinary, with brown hair done up in a small knot. She is dressed in her best clothes and is anxious to be liked by her new family. Mr. Addams, Frankie's father, is a deliberate and absent-minded man of about forty-five. A widower of many years, he has become set in his habits. He is dressed conservatively, and there is about him an old-fashioned look and manner. John Henry, Frankie's small cousin, aged seven, picks and eats any scuppernongs he can reach. He is a delicate, active boy and wears gold-rimmed spectacles which give him an oddly judicious look. He is blond and sunburned and when we first see him he is wearing a sun-suit and is barefooted.

—

(Berenice Sadie Brown is busy in the kitchen.)

JARVIS. Seems to me like this old arbor has shrunk. I remember when I was a child it used to seem absolutely enormous. When I was Frankie's age, I had a vine swing here. Remember, Papa?

FRANKIE. It don't seem so absolutely enormous to me, because I am so tall.

JARVIS. I never saw a human grow so fast in all my life. I think maybe we ought to tie a brick to your head.

FRANKIE *(hunching down in obvious distress)*. Oh, Jarvis! Don't.

JANICE. Don't tease your little sister. I don't think Frankie is too tall. She probably won't grow much more. I had the biggest portion of my growth by the time I was thirteen.

FRANKIE. But I'm just twelve. When I think of all the growing years ahead of me, I get scared.

(Janice goes to Frankie and puts her arms around her comfortingly. Frankie stands rigid, embarrassed and blissful.)

JANICE. I wouldn't worry.

(Berenice comes from the kitchen with a tray of drinks. Frankie rushes eagerly to help her serve them.)

FRANKIE. Let me help.

BERENICE. Them two drinks is lemonade for you and John Henry. The others got liquor in them.

FRANKIE. Janice, come sit down on the arbor seat. Jarvis, you sit down too.

(Jarvis and Janice sit close together on the wicker bench in the arbor. Frankie hands the drinks around, then perches on the ground before Janice and Jarvis and stares adoringly at them.)

FRANKIE. It was such a surprise when Jarvis wrote home you are going to be married.

JANICE. I hope it wasn't a bad surprise.

FRANKIE. Oh, Heavens no! *(With great feeling)* As a matter of fact . . . *(She strokes Janice's shoes tenderly and Jarvis' army boot)* If only you knew how I feel.

MR. ADDAMS. Frankie's been bending my ears ever since your letter came, Jarvis. Going on about weddings, brides, grooms, etc.

JANICE. It's lovely that we can be married at Jarvis' home.

MR. ADDAMS. That's the way to feel, Janice. Marriage is a sacred institution.

FRANKIE. Oh, it will be beautiful.

JARVIS. Pretty soon we'd better be shoving off for Winter Hill. I have to be back in barracks tonight.

FRANKIE. Winter Hill is such a lovely, cold name. It reminds me of ice and snow.

JANICE. You know it's just a hundred miles away, darling.

JARVIS. Ice and snow indeed! Yesterday the temperature on the parade ground reached 102.

(Frankie takes a palmetto fan from the table and fans first Janice, then Jarvis.)

JANICE. That feels so good, darling. Thanks.

FRANKIE. I wrote you so many letters, Jarvis, and you never, never would answer me. When you were stationed in Alaska, I wanted so much to hear about Alaska. I sent you so many boxes of home-made candy, but you never answered me.

JARVIS. Oh, Frankie. You know how it is . . .

FRANKIE (sipping her drink). You know this lemonade tastes funny. Kind of sharp and hot. I believe I got the drinks mixed up.

JARVIS. I was thinking my drink tasted mighty sissy. Just plain lemonade—no liquor at all.

(Frankie and Jarvis exchange their drinks. Jarvis sips his.)

JARVIS. This is better.

FRANKIE. I drank a lot. I wonder if I'm drunk. It makes me feel like I had four legs instead of two. I think I'm drunk. (She gets up and begins to stagger around in imitation of drunkenness) See! I'm drunk! Look, Papa, how drunk I am! (Suddenly she turns a handspring; then there is a blare of music from the club house gramophone off to the right)

JANICE. Where does the music come from? It sounds so close.

FRANKIE. It is. Right over there. They have club meetings and parties with boys on Friday nights. I watch them here from the yard.

JANICE. It must be nice having your club house so near.

FRANKIE. I'm not a member now. But they are holding an election this afternoon, and maybe I'll be elected.

JOHN HENRY. Here comes Mama.

(Mrs. West, John Henry's mother, crosses the yard from the right. She is a vivacious, blonde woman of about thirty-three. She is dressed in sleazy, rather dowdy summer clothes.)

MR. ADDAMS. Hello, Pet. Just in time to meet our new family member.

MRS. WEST. I saw you out here from the window.

JARVIS (rising, with Janice). Hi, Aunt Pet. How is Uncle Eustace?

MRS. WEST. He's at the office.

JANICE (offering her hand with the engagement ring on it). Look, Aunt Pet. May I call you Aunt Pet?

MRS. WEST (hugging her). Of course, Janice. What a gorgeous ring!

JANICE. Jarvis just gave it to me this morning. He wanted to consult his father and get it from his store, naturally.

MRS. WEST. How lovely.

MR. ADDAMS. A quarter carat—not too flashy but a good stone.

MRS. WEST (to Berenice, who is gathering up the empty glasses). Berenice, what have you and Frankie been doing to my John Henry? He sticks over here in your kitchen morning, noon and night.

BERENICE. We enjoys him and Candy seems to like it over here.

MRS. WEST. What on earth do you do to him?

BERENICE. We just talks and passes the time of day. Occasionally plays cards.

MRS. WEST. Well, if he gets in your way just shoo him home.

BERENICE. Candy don't bother nobody.

JOHN HENRY (walking around barefooted in the arbor). These grapes are so squelchy when I step on them.

MRS. WEST. Run home, darling, and wash your feet and put on your sandals.

JOHN HENRY. I like to squelch on the grapes.

(Berenice goes back to the kitchen.)

JANICE. That looks like a stage curtain. Jarvis told me how you used to write plays and act in them out here in the arbor. What kind of shows do you have?

FRANKIE. Oh, crook shows and cowboy shows. This summer I've had some cold shows—about Esquimos and explorers—on account of the hot weather.

JANICE. Do you ever have romances?

FRANKIE. Naw . . . (With bravado) I had crook shows for the most part. You see I never believed in love until now. *(Her look lingers on Janice and Jarvis. She hugs Janice and Jarvis, bending over them from back of the bench)*

MRS. WEST. Frankie and this little friend of hers gave a performance of "The Vagabond King" out here last spring.

(John Henry spreads out his arms and imitates the heroine of the play from memory, singing in his high childish voice.

JOHN HENRY. Never hope to bind me. Never hope to know. *(Speaking)* Frankie was the king-boy. I sold the tickets.

MRS. WEST. Yes, I have always said that Frankie has talent.

FRANKIE. Aw, I'm afraid I don't have much talent.

JOHN HENRY. Frankie can laugh and kill people good. She can die, too.

FRANKIE *(with some pride)*. Yeah, I guess I die all right.

MR. ADDAMS. Frankie rounds up John Henry and those smaller children, but by the time she dresses them in the costumes, they're worn out and won't act in the show.

JARVIS *(looking at his watch)*. Well, it's time we shove off for Winter Hill—Frankie's land of icebergs and snow—where the temperature goes up to 102.

(Jarvis takes Janice's hand. He gets up and gazes fondly around the yard and the arbor. He pulls her up and stands with his arm around her, gazing around him at the arbor and yard.)

JARVIS. It carries me back—this smell of mashed grapes and dust. I remember all the endless summer afternoons of my childhood. It does carry me back.

FRANKIE. Me too. It carries me back, too.

MR. ADDAMS *(putting one arm around Janice and shaking Jarvis' hand)*. Merciful Heavens! It seems I have two Methuselahs in my family! Does it carry you back to your childhood too, John Henry?

JOHN HENRY. Yes, Uncle Royal.

MR. ADDAMS. Son, this visit was a real pleasure. Janice, I'm mighty pleased to see my boy has such lucky judgment in choosing a wife.

FRANKIE. I hate to think you have to go. I'm just now realizing you're here.

JARVIS. We'll be back in two days. The wedding is Sunday.

(The family move around the house toward the street. John Henry enters the kitchen through the back door. There are the sounds of "good-byes" from the front yard.)

JOHN HENRY. Frankie was drunk. She drank a liquor drink.

BERENICE. She just made out like she was drunk—pretended.

JOHN HENRY. She said, "Look, Papa, how drunk I am," and she couldn't walk.

FRANKIE'S VOICE. Good-bye, Jarvis. Good-bye, Janice.

JARVIS' VOICE. See you Sunday.

MR. ADDAMS' VOICE. Drive carefully, son. Good-bye, Janice.

JANICE'S VOICE. Good-bye and thanks, Mr. Addams. Good-bye, Frankie darling.

ALL THE VOICES. Good-bye! Good-bye!

JOHN HENRY. They are going now to Winter Hill.

(There is the sound of the front door opening, then of steps in the hall. Frankie enters through the hall.)

FRANKIE. Oh, I can't understand it! The way it all just suddenly happened.

BERENICE. Happened? Happened?

FRANKIE. I have never been so puzzled.

BERENICE. Puzzled about what?

FRANKIE. The whole thing. They are so beautiful.

BERENICE *(after a pause)*. I believe the sun done fried your brains.

JOHN HENRY *(whispering)* Me too.

BERENICE. Look here at me. You jealous.

FRANKIE. Jealous?

BERENICE. Jealous because your brother's going to be married.

FRANKIE *(slowly)*. No. I just never saw any two people like them. When they walked in the house today it was so queer.

BERENICE. You jealous. Go and behold yourself in the mirror. I can see from the color of your eyes.

(Frankie goes to the mirror and stares. She draws up her left shoulder, shakes her head, and turns away.)

FRANKIE *(with feeling)*. Oh! They were the two prettiest people I ever saw. I just can't understand how it happened.

BERENICE. Whatever ails you?—actin' so queer.

FRANKIE. I don't know. I bet they have a good time every minute of the day.

JOHN HENRY. Less us have a good time.

FRANKIE. Us have a good time? Us?

(She rises and walks around the table)

BERENICE. Come on. Less have a game of three-handed bridge.

(They sit down at the table, shuffle the cards, deal, and play a game.)

FRANKIE. Oregon, Alaska, Winter Hill, the wedding. It's all so queer.

BERENICE. I can't bid, never have a hand these days.

FRANKIE. A spade.

JOHN HENRY. I want to bid spades. That's what I was going to bid.

FRANKIE. Well, that's your tough luck. I bid them first.

JOHN HENRY. Oh, you fool jackass! It's not fair!

BERENICE. Hush quarreling, you two. *(She looks at both their hands)* To tell the truth, I don't think either of you got such a grand hand to fight over the bid about. Where is the cards? I haven't had no kind of a hand all week.

FRANKIE. I don't give a durn about it. It is immaterial with me. *(There is a long pause. She sits with her head propped on her hand, her legs wound around each other)* Let's talk about them—and the wedding.

BERENICE. What you want to talk about?

FRANKIE. My heart feels them going away—going farther and farther away—while I am stuck here by myself.

BERENICE. You ain't here by yourself. By the way, where's your Pa?

FRANKIE. He went to the store. I think about them, but I remembered them more as a feeling than as a picture.

BERENICE. A feeling?

FRANKIE. They were the two prettiest people I ever saw. Yet it was like I couldn't see all of them I wanted to see. My brains couldn't gather together quick enough to take it all in. And then they were gone.

BERENICE. Well, stop commenting about it. You don't have your mind on the game.

FRANKIE *(playing her cards, followed by John Henry)*. Spades are trumps and you got a spade. I have some of my mind on the game.

(John Henry puts his donkey necklace in his mouth and looks away.)

FRANKIE. Go on, cheater.

BERENICE. Make haste.

JOHN HENRY. I can't. It's a king. The only spade I got is a king, and I don't want to play my king under Frankie's ace. And I'm not going to do it either.

FRANKIE *(throwing her cards down on the table)*. See, Berenice, he cheats!

BERENICE. Play your king, John Henry. You have to follow the rules of the game.

JOHN HENRY. My king. It isn't fair.

FRANKIE. Even with this trick, I can't win.

BERENICE. Where is the cards? For three days I haven't had a decent hand. I'm beginning to suspicion something. Come on less us count these old cards.

FRANKIE. We've worn these old cards out. If you would eat these old cards, they would taste like a combination of all the dinners of this summer together with a sweaty-handed, nasty taste. Why, the jacks and the queens are missing.

BERENICE. John Henry, how come you do a thing like that? So that's why you asked for the scissors and stole off quiet behind the arbor. Now, Candy, how come you took our playing cards and cut out the pictures?

JOHN HENRY. Because I wanted them. They're cute.

FRANKIE. See? He's nothing but a child. It's hopeless. Hopeless!

BERENICE. Maybe so.

FRANKIE. We'll just have to put him out of the game. He's entirely too young.

(John Henry whimpers.)

BERENICE. Well, we can't put Candy out of the game. We gotta have a third to play. Besides, by the last count he owes me close to three million dollars.

FRANKIE. Oh, I am sick unto death. *(She sweeps the cards from the table, then gets up and begins walking around the kitchen. John Henry leaves the table and picks up a large blonde doll on the chair in the corner)* I wish they'd taken me with them to Winter Hill this afternoon. I wish tomorrow was Sunday instead of Saturday.

BERENICE. Sunday will come.

FRANKIE. I doubt it. I wish I was going somewhere for good. I wish I had a hundred dollars and could just light out and never see this town again.

BERENICE. It seems like you wish for a lot of things.

FRANKIE. I wish I was somebody else except me.

JOHN HENRY *(holding the doll)*. You serious when you gave me the doll a while ago?

FRANKIE. It gives me a pain just to think about them.

BERENICE. It is a known truth that gray-eyed people are jealous.

(There are sounds of children playing in the neighboring yard.)

JOHN HENRY. Let's go out and play with the children.

FRANKIE. I don't want to.

JOHN HENRY. There's a big crowd, and they sound like they having a mighty good time. Less go.

FRANKIE. You got ears. You heard me.

JOHN HENRY. I think maybe I better go home.

FRANKIE. Why, you said you were going to spend the night. You just can't eat dinner and then go off in the afternoon like that.

JOHN HENRY. I know it.

BERENICE. Candy, Lamb, you can go home if you want to.

JOHN HENRY. But less go out, Frankie. They sound like they having a lot of fun.

FRANKIE. No, they're not. Just a crowd of ugly, silly children. Running and hollering and running and hollering. Nothing to it.

JOHN HENRY. Less go!

FRANKIE. Well, then I'll entertain you. What do you want to do? Would you like for me to read to you out of The Book of Knowledge, or would you rather do something else?

JOHN HENRY. I rather do something else. *(He goes to the back door, and looks into the yard. Several young girls of thirteen or fourteen, dressed in clean print frocks, file slowly across the back yard)* Look. Those big girls.

FRANKIE *(running out into the yard).* Hey, there. I'm mighty glad to see you. Come on in.

HELEN. We can't. We were just passing through to notify our new member.

FRANKIE *(overjoyed).* Am I the new member?

DORIS. No, you're not the one the club elected.

FRANKIE. Not elected?

HELEN. Every ballot was unanimous for Mary Littlejohn.

FRANKIE. Mary Littlejohn! You mean that girl who just moved in next door? That pasty fat girl with those tacky pigtails? The one who plays the piano all day long?

DORIS. Yes. The club unanimously elected Mary.

FRANKIE. Why, she's not even cute.

HELEN. She is too; and, furthermore, she's talented.

FRANKIE. I think it's sissy to sit around the house all day playing classical music.

DORIS. Why, Mary is training for a concert career.

FRANKIE. Well, I wish to Jesus she would train somewhere else.

DORIS. You don't have enough sense to appreciate a talented girl like Mary.

FRANKIE. What are you doing in my yard? You're never to set foot on my Papa's property again. *(Frankie shakes Helen)* Son-of-a-bitches. I could shoot you with my Papa's pistol.

JOHN HENRY *(shaking his fists).* Son-of-a-bitches.

FRANKIE. Why didn't you elect me? *(She goes back into the house)* Why can't I be a member?

JOHN HENRY. Maybe they'll change their mind and invite you.

BERENICE. I wouldn't pay them no mind. All my life I've been wantin' things that I ain't been gettin'. Anyhow those club girls is fully two years older than you.

FRANKIE. I think they have been spreading it all over town that I smell bad. When I had those boils and had to use that black bitter-smelling ointment, old Helen Fletcher asked me what was that funny smell I had. Oh, I could shoot every one of them with a pistol.

(Frankie sits with her head on the table. John Henry approaches and pats the back of Frankie's neck.)

JOHN HENRY. I don't think you smell so bad. You smell sweet, like a hundred flowers.

FRANKIE. The son-of-a-bitches. And there was something else. They were telling nasty lies about married people. When I think of Aunt Pet and Uncle Eustace! And my own father! The nasty lies! I don't know what kind of fool they take me for.

BERENICE. That's what I tell you. They too old for you.

(John Henry raises his head, expands his nostrils and sniffs at himself. Then Frankie goes into the interior bedroom and returns with a bottle of perfume.)

FRANKIE. Boy! I bet I use more perfume than anybody else in town. Want some on you, John Henry? You want some, Berenice? *(She sprinkles perfume)*

JOHN HENRY. Like a thousand flowers.

BERENICE. Frankie, the whole idea of a club is that there are members who are included and the non-members who are not included. Now what you ought to do is to round you up a club of your own. And you could be the president yourself. *(There is a pause)*

FRANKIE. Who would I get?

BERENICE. Why, those little children you hear playing in the neighborhood.

FRANKIE. I don't want to be the president of all those little young left-over people.

BERENICE. Well, then enjoy your misery. That perfume smells so strong it kind of makes me sick.

(John Henry plays with the doll at the kitchen table and Frankie watches.)

FRANKIE. Look here at me, John Henry. Take off those glasses. *(John Henry takes off his glasses)* I bet you don't need those glasses. *(She points to the coal scuttle)* What is this?

JOHN HENRY. The coal scuttle.

FRANKIE *(taking a shell from the kitchen shelf)*. And this?

JOHN HENRY. The shell we got at Saint Peter's Bay last summer.

FRANKIE. What is that little thing crawling around on the floor?

JOHN HENRY. Where?

FRANKIE. That little thing crawling around near your feet.

JOHN HENRY. Oh. *(He squats down)* Why, it's an ant. How did that get in here?

FRANKIE. If I were you I'd just throw those glasses away. You can see good as anybody.

BERENICE. Now quit picking with John Henry.

FRANKIE. They don't look becoming. *(John Henry wipes his glasses and puts them back on)* He can suit himself. I was only telling him for his own good. *(She walks restlessly around the kitchen)* I bet Janice and Jarvis are members of a lot of clubs. In fact, the army is kind of like a club.

(John Henry searches through Berenice's pocketbook.)

BERENICE. Don't root through my pocketbook like that, Candy. Ain't a wise policy to search folks' pocketbooks. They might think you trying to steal their money.

JOHN HENRY. I'm looking for your new glass eye. Here it is. *(He hands Berenice the glass eye)* You got two nickels and a dime.

(Berenice takes off her patch, turns away and inserts the glass eye.)

BERENICE. I ain't used to it yet. The socket bothers me. Maybe it don't fit properly.

JOHN HENRY. The blue glass eye looks very cute.

FRANKIE. I don't see why you had to get that eye. It has a wrong expression—let alone being blue.

BERENICE. Ain't anybody ask your judgment, wise-mouth.

JOHN HENRY. Which one of your eyes do you see out of the best?

BERENICE. The left eye, of course. The glass eye don't do me no seeing good at all.

JOHN HENRY. I like the glass eye better. It is so bright and shiny—a real pretty eye. Frankie, you serious when you gave me this doll a while ago?

FRANKIE. Janice and Jarvis. It gives me this pain just to think about them.

BERENICE. It is a known truth that gray-eyed people are jealous.

FRANKIE. I told you I wasn't jealous. I couldn't be jealous of one of them without being jealous of them both. I 'sociate the two of them together. Somehow they're just so different from us.

BERENICE. Well, I were jealous when my foster-brother, Honey, married Clorina. I sent a warning I could tear the ears off her head. But you see I didn't. Clorina's got ears just like anybody else. And now I love her.

FRANKIE *(stopping her walking suddenly)*. J.A.—Janice and Jarvis. Isn't that the strangest thing?

BERENICE. What?

FRANKIE. J.A.—Both their names begin with "J.A."

BERENICE. And? What about it?

FRANKIE *(walking around the kitchen table)*. If only my name was Jane. Jane or Jasmine.

BERENICE. I don't follow your frame of mind.

FRANKIE. Jarvis and Janice and Jasmine. See?

BERENICE. No. I don't see.

FRANKIE. I wonder if it's against the law to change your name. Or add to it.

BERENICE. Naturally. It's against the law.

FRANKIE *(impetuously)*. Well, I don't care. F. Jasmine Addams.

JOHN HENRY *(approaching with the doll)*. You serious when you give me this? *(He pulls up the doll's dress and pats her)* I will name her Belle.

FRANKIE. I don't know what went on in Jarvis' mind when he brought me that doll. Imagine bringing me a doll! I had counted on Jarvis bringing me something from Alaska.

BERENICE. Your face when you unwrapped that package was a study.

FRANKIE. John Henry, quit pickin' at the doll's eyes. It makes me so nervous. You hear me! *(He sits the doll up)* In fact, take the doll somewhere out of my sight.

JOHN HENRY. Her name is Lily Belle. *(John Henry goes out and props the doll up on the back steps. There is the sound of an unseen Negro singing from the neighboring yard.)*

FRANKIE *(going to the mirror)*. The big mistake I made was to get this close crew cut. For the wedding, I ought to have long brunette hair. Don't you think so?

BERENICE. I don't see how come brunette hair is necessary. But I warned you about getting your head shaved off like that before you did it. But nothing would do but you shave it like that.

FRANKIE *(stepping back from the mirror and slumping her shoulders)*. Oh, I am so worried about being so tall. I'm twelve and five-sixth years old and already five feet five and three-fourths inches tall. If I keep on growing like this until I'm twenty-one, I figure I will be nearly ten feet tall.

JOHN HENRY *(re-entering the kitchen)*. Lily Belle is taking a nap on the back steps. Don't talk so loud, Frankie.

FRANKIE *(after a pause)*. I doubt if they ever get married or go to a wedding. Those freaks.

BERENICE. Freaks. What freaks you talking about?

FRANKIE. At the fair. The ones we saw there last October.

JOHN HENRY. Oh, the freaks at the fair! *(He holds out an imaginary skirt and begins to skip around the room with one finger resting on the top of his head)* Oh, she was the cutest little girl I ever saw. I never saw anything so cute in my whole life. Did you, Frankie?

FRANKIE. No. I don't think she was cute.

BERENICE. Who is that he's talking about?

FRANKIE. That little old pin-head at the fair. A head no bigger than an orange. With the hair shaved off and a big pink bow at the top. Bow was bigger than the head.

JOHN HENRY. Shoo! She was too cute.

BERENICE. That little old squeezed-looking midget in them little trick evening clothes. And that giant with the hang-jaw face and them huge loose hands. And that morphidite! Half man—half woman. With that tiger skin on one side and that spangled skirt on the other.

JOHN HENRY. But that little-headed girl was cute.

FRANKIE. And that wild colored man they said came from a savage island and ate those real live rats. Do you think they make a very big salary?

BERENICE. How would I know? In fact, all them freak folks down at the fair every October just gives me the creeps.

FRANKIE *(after a pause, and slowly)*. Do I give you the creeps?

BERENICE. You?

FRANKIE. Do you think I will grow into a freak?

BERENICE. You? Why certainly not, I trust Jesus!

FRANKIE *(going over to the mirror, and looking at herself)*. Well, do you think I will be pretty?

BERENICE. Maybe. If you file down them horns a inch or two.

FRANKIE *(turning to face Berenice, and shuffling one bare foot on the floor)*. Seriously.

BERENICE. Seriously, I think when you fill out you will do very well. If you behave.

FRANKIE. But by Sunday, I want to do something to improve myself before the wedding.

BERENICE. Get clean for a change. Scrub your elbows and fix yourself nice. You will do very well.

JOHN HENRY. You will be all right if you file down them horns.

FRANKIE *(raising her right shoulder and turning from the mirror)*. I don't know what to do. I just wish I would die.

BERENICE. Well, die then!

JOHN HENRY. Die.

FRANKIE (suddenly exasperated). Go home! (There is a pause) You heard me! (She makes a face at him and threatens him with the fly swatter. They run twice around the table) Go home! I'm sick and tired of you, you little midget.
(John Henry goes out, taking the doll with him.)

BERENICE. Now what makes you act like that? You are too mean to live.

FRANKIE. I know it. (She takes a carving knife from the table drawer) Something about John Henry just gets on my nerves these days. (She puts her left ankle over her right knee and begins to pick with the knife at a splinter in her foot) I've got a splinter in my foot.

BERENICE. That knife ain't the proper thing for a splinter.

FRANKIE. It seems to me that before this summer I used always to have such a good time. Remember this spring when Evelyn Owen and me used to dress up in costumes and go down town and shop at the five-and-dime? And how every Friday night we'd spend the night with each other either at her house or here? And then Evelyn Owen had to go and move away to Florida. And now she won't even write to me.

BERENICE. Honey, you are not crying, is you? Don't that hurt you none?

FRANKIE. It would hurt anybody else except me. And how the wisteria in town was so blue and pretty in April but somehow it was so pretty it made me sad. And how Evelyn and me put on that show the Glee Club did at the High School Auditorium? (She raises her head and beats time with the knife and her fist on the table, singing loudly with sudden energy) Sons of toil and danger! Will you serve a stranger! And bow down to Burgundy! (Berenice joins in on "Burgundy." Frankie pauses, then begins to pick her foot again, humming the tune sadly)

BERENICE. That was a nice show you children copied in the arbor. You will meet another girl friend you like as well as Evelyn Owen. Or maybe Mr. Owen will move back into town. (There is a pause) Frankie, what you need is a needle.

FRANKIE. I don't care anything about my feet. (She stomps her foot on the floor and lays down the knife on the table) It was just so queer the way it happened this afternoon. The minute I laid eyes on the pair of them I had this funny feeling. (She goes over and picks up a saucer of milk near the cat-hole in back of the door and pours the milk in the sink) How old were you, Berenice, when you married your first husband?

BERENICE. I were thirteen years old.

FRANKIE. What made you get married so young for?

BERENICE. Because I wanted to.

FRANKIE. You never loved any of your four husbands but Ludie.

BERENICE. Ludie Maxwell Freeman was my only true husband. The other ones were just scraps.

FRANKIE. Did you marry with a veil every time?

BERENICE. Three times with a veil.

FRANKIE (pouring milk into the saucer and returning the saucer to the cat-hole). If only I just knew where he is gone. Ps, ps, ps . . . Charles, Charles.

BERENICE. Quit worrying yourself about that old alley cat. He's gone off to hunt a friend.

FRANKIE. To hunt a friend?

BERENICE. Why certainly. He roamed off to find himself a lady friend.

FRANKIE. Well, why don't he bring his friend home with him? He ought to know I would be only too glad to have a whole family of cats.

BERENICE. You done seen the last of that old alley cat.

FRANKIE (crossing the room). I ought to notify the police force. They will find Charles.

BERENICE. I wouldn't do that.

FRANKIE (at the telephone). I want the police force, please . . . Police force? . . . I am notifying you about my car . . . Cat! He's lost. He is almost pure Persian.

BERENICE. As Persian as I is.

FRANKIE. But with short hair. A lovely color of gray with a little white spot on his throat. He answers to the name of Charles, but if he don't answer to that, he might come if you call "Charlina." . . . My name is Miss F. Jasmine Addams and the address is 124 Grove Street.

BERENICE (giggling as Frankie re-enters). Gal, they going to send around here and tie you up and drag you off to Milledgeville. Just picture them fat blue police chasing tomcats around alleys and hollering, "Oh Charles! Oh come here, Charlina!" Merciful Heavens.

FRANKIE. Aw, shut up!

(Outside a voice is heard calling in a drawn-out chant, the words almost indistinguishable: "Lot of okra, peas, fresh butter beans . . .")

BERENICE. The trouble with you is that you don't have no sense of humor no more.

FRANKIE *(disconsolately)*. Maybe I'd be better off in jail.

(The chanting voice continues and an ancient Negro woman, dressed in a clean print dress with several petticoats, the ruffle of one of which shows, crosses the yard. She stops and leans on a gnarled stick.)

FRANKIE. Here comes the old vegetable lady.

BERENICE. Sis Laura is getting mighty feeble to peddle this hot weather.

FRANKIE. She is about ninety. Other old folks lose their faculties, but she found some faculty. She reads futures, too.

BERENICE. Hi, Sis Laura. How is your folks getting on?

SIS LAURA. We ain't much, and I feels my age these days. Want any peas today? *(She shuffles across the yard)*

BERENICE. I'm sorry, I still have some left over from yesterday. Good-bye, Sis Laura.

SIS LAURA. Good-bye. *(She goes off behind the house to the right, continuing her chant)*

(When the old woman is gone Frankie begins walking around the kitchen.)

FRANKIE. I expect Janice and Jarvis are almost to Winter Hill by now.

BERENICE. Sit down. You make me nervous.

FRANKIE. Jarvis talked about Granny. He remembers her very good. But when I try to remember Granny, it is like her face is changing—like a face seen under water. Jarvis remembers Mother too, and I don't remember her at all.

BERENICE. Naturally! Your mother died the day that you were born.

FRANKIE *(standing with one foot on the seat of the chair, leaning over the chair back and laughing)*. Did you hear what Jarvis said?

BERENICE. What?

FRANKIE *(after laughing more)*. They were talking about whether to vote for C. P. MacDonald. And Jarvis said, "Why I wouldn't vote for that scoundrel if he was running to be dogcatcher." I never heard anything so witty in my life. *(There is a silence during which Berenice watches Frankie, but does not smile)* And you know what Janice remarked. When Jarvis mentioned about how much I've grown, she said she didn't think I looked so terribly big. She said she got the major portion of her growth before she was thirteen. She said I was the right height and had acting talent and ought to go to Hollywood. She did, Berenice.

BERENICE. O.K. All right! She did!

FRANKIE. She said she thought I was a lovely size and would probably not grow any taller. She said all fashion models and movie stars . . .

BERENICE. She did not. I heard her from the window. She only remarked that you probably had already got your growth. But she didn't go on and on like that or mention Hollywood.

FRANKIE. She said to me . . .

BERENICE. She said to you! This is a serious fault with you, Frankie. Somebody just makes a loose remark and then you cozen it in your mind until nobody would recognize it. Your Aunt Pet happened to mention to Clorina that you had sweet manners and Clorina passed it on to you. For what it was worth. Then next thing I know you are going all around and bragging how Mrs. West thought you had the finest manners in town and ought to go to Hollywood, and I don't know what-all you didn't say. And that is a serious fault.

FRANKIE. Aw, quit preaching at me.

BERENICE. I ain't preaching. It's the solemn truth and you know it.

FRANKIE. I admit it a little. *(She sits down at the table and puts her forehead on the palms of her hands. There is a pause, and then she speaks softly)* What I need to know is this. Do you think I made a good impression?

BERENICE. Impression?

FRANKIE. Yes.

BERENICE. Well, how would I know?

FRANKIE. I mean, how did I act? What did I do?

BERENICE. Why, you didn't do anything to speak of.

FRANKIE. Nothing?

BERENICE. No. You just watched the pair of them like they was ghosts. Then, when they talked about the wedding, them ears of yours stiffened out the size of cabbage leaves . . .

FRANKIE *(raising her hand to her ears)*. They didn't!

BERENICE. They did.

FRANKIE. Some day you going to look down and find that big fat tongue of yours pulled out by the roots and laying there before you on the table.

BERENICE. Quit talking so rude.

FRANKIE *(after a pause)*. I'm so scared I didn't make a good impression.

BERENICE. What of it? I got a date with T. T. and he's supposed to pick me up here. I wish him and Honey would come on. You make me nervous.

(Frankie sits miserably, her shoulders hunched. Then with a sudden gesture she bangs her forehead on the table. Her fists are clenched and she is sobbing.)

BERENICE. Come on. Don't act like that.

FRANKIE *(her voice muffled)*. They were so pretty. They must have such a good time. And they went away and left me.

BERENICE. Sit up. Behave yourself.

FRANKIE. They came and went away, and left me with this feeling.

BERENICE. Hosee! I bet I know something. *(She begins tapping with her heel: one, two, three—bang! After a pause, in which the rhythm is established, she begins singing)* Frankie's got a crush! Frankie's got a crush! Frankie's got a crush on the *wedding!*

FRANKIE. Quit!

BERENICE. Frankie's got a crush! Frankie's got a crush!

FRANKIE. You better quit! *(She rises suddenly and snatches up the carving knife)*

BERENICE. You lay down that knife.

FRANKIE. Make me. *(She bends the blade slowly)*

BERENICE. Lay it down, Devil. *(There is a silence)* Just throw it! You just!

(After a pause Frankie aims the knife carefully at the closed door leading to the bedroom and throws it. The knife does not stick in the wall.)

FRANKIE. I used to be the best knife thrower in this town.

BERENICE. Frances Addams, you goin' to try that stunt once too often.

FRANKIE. I warned you to quit pickin' with me.

BERENICE. You are not fit to live in a house.

FRANKIE. I won't be living in this one much longer; I'm going to run away from home.

BERENICE. And a good riddance to big old bag of rubbage.

FRANKIE. You wait and see. I'm leavin town.

BERENICE. And where do you think you are going?

FRANKIE *(gazing around the walls)*. I don't know.

BERENICE. You're going crazy. That's where you going.

FRANKIE. No. *(Solemnly)* This coming Sunday after the wedding, I'm leaving town. And I swear to Jesus by my two eyes I'm never coming back here any more.

BERENICE *(going to Frankie and pushing her damp bangs back from her forehead)*. Sugar? You serious?

FRANKIE *(exasperated)*. Of course! Do you think I would stand here and say that swear and tell a story? Sometimes, Berenice, I think it takes you longer to realize a fact than it does anybody who ever lived.

BERENICE. But you say you don't know where you going. You going, but you don't know where. That don't make no sense to me.

FRANKIE *(after a long pause in which she again gazes around the walls of the room)*. I feel just exactly like somebody has peeled all the skin off me. I wish I had some good cold peach ice cream. *(Berenice takes her by the shoulders)* *(During the last speech, T. T. Williams and Honey Camden Brown have been approaching through the back yard. T. T. is a large and pompous-looking Negro man of about fifty. He is dressed like a church deacon, in a black suit with a red emblem in the lapel. His manner is timid and over-polite. Honey is a slender, limber Negro boy of about twenty. He is quite light in color and he wears loud-colored, snappy clothes. He is brusque and there is about him an odd mixture of hostility and playfulness. He is very high-strung and volatile. They are trailed by John Henry. John Henry is dressed for afternoon in a clean white linen suit, white shoes and socks. Honey carries a horn. They cross the back yard and knock at the back door. Honey holds his hand to his head.)*

FRANKIE. But every word I told you was the solemn truth. I'm leaving here after the wedding.

BERENICE *(taking her hands from Frankie's shoulders and answering the door).* Hello, Honey and T. T. I didn't hear you coming.

T. T. You and Frankie too busy discussing something. Well, your foster-brother, Honey, got into a ruckus standing on the sidewalk in front of the Blue Moon Café. Police cracked him on the haid.

BERENICE *(turning on the kitchen light).* What! *(She examines Honey's head)* Why, it's a welt the size of a small egg.

HONEY. Times like this I feel like I got to bust loose or die.

BERENICE. What were you doing?

HONEY. Nothing. I was just passing along the street minding my own business when this drunk soldier came out of the Blue Moon Café and ran into me. I looked at him and he gave me a push. I pushed him back and he raised a ruckus. This white M.P. came up and slammed me with his stick.

T. T. It was one of those accidents can happen to any colored person.

JOHN HENRY *(reaching for the horn).* Toot some on your horn, Honey.

FRANKIE. Please blow.

HONEY *(to John Henry, who has taken the horn).* Now, don't bother my horn, Butch.

JOHN HENRY. I want to toot it some. *(John Henry takes the horn, tries to blow it, but only succeeds in slobbering in it. He holds the horn away from his mouth and sings: "Too-ty-toot, too-ty-toot." Honey snatches the horn away from him and puts it on the sewing table.)*

HONEY. I told you not to touch my horn. You got it full of slobber inside and out. It's ruined! *(He loses his temper, grabs John Henry by the shoulders and shakes him hard)*

BERENICE *(slapping Honey).* Satan! Don't you dare touch that little boy! I'm going to stomp out your brains!

HONEY. You ain't mad because John Henry is a little boy. It's because he's a white boy. John Henry knows he needs a good shake. Don't you, Butch?

BERENICE. Ornery—no good!

(Honey lifts John Henry and swings him, then reaches in his pocket and brings out some coins.)

HONEY. John Henry, which would you rather have—the nigger money or the white money?

JOHN HENRY. I rather have the dime. *(He takes it)* Much obliged. *(He goes out and crosses the yard to his house)*

BERENICE. You troubled and beat down and try to take it out on a little boy. You and Frankie just alike. The club girls don't elect her and she turns on John Henry too. When folks are lonesome and left out, they turn so mean. T. T., do you wish a small little quickie before we start?

T. T. *(looking at Frankie and pointing toward her).* Frankie ain't no tattle-tale. Is you? *(Berenice pours a drink for T. T.)*

FRANKIE *(disdaining his question).* That sure is a cute suit you got on, Honey. Today I heard somebody speak of you as Lightfoot Brown. I think that's such a grand nickname. It's on account of your travelling—to Harlem, and all the different places where you have run away, and your dancing. Lightfoot! I wish somebody would call me Lightfoot Addams.

BERENICE. It would suit me better if Honey Camden had brick feets. As it is, he keeps me so anxious-worried. C'mon, Honey and T. T. Let's go! *(Honey and T. T. go out)*

FRANKIE. I'll go out into the yard. *(Frankie, feeling excluded, goes out into the yard. Throughout the act the light in the yard has been darkening steadily. Now the light in the kitchen is throwing a yellow rectangle in the yard.)*

BERENICE. Now Frankie, you forget all that foolishness we were discussing. And if Mr. Addams don't come home by good dark, you go over to the Wests'. Go play with John Henry.

HONEY AND T. T. *(from outside).* So long!

FRANKIE. So long, you all. Since when have I been scared of the dark? I'll invite John Henry to spend the night with me.

BERENICE. I thought you were sick and tired of him.

FRANKIE. I am.

BERENICE (*kissing Frankie*). Good night, Sugar!

FRANKIE. Seems like everybody goes off and leaves me. (*She walks toward the Wests' yard, calling, with cupped hands*) John Henry. John Henry.

JOHN HENRY'S VOICE. What do you want, Frankie?

FRANKIE. Come over and spend the night with me.

JOHN HENRY'S VOICE. I can't.

FRANKIE. Why?

JOHN HENRY. Just because.

FRANKIE. Because why? (*John Henry does not answer*) I thought maybe me and you could put up my Indian tepee and sleep out here in the yard. And have a good time. (*There is still no answer*) Sure enough. Why don't you stay and spend the night?

JOHN HENRY (*quite loudly*). Because, Frankie. I don't want to.

FRANKIE (*angrily*). Fool Jackass! Suit yourself! I only asked you because you looked so ugly and so lonesome.

JOHN HENRY (*skipping toward the arbor*). Why, I'm not a bit lonesome.

FRANKIE (*looking at the house*). I wonder when that Papa of mine is coming home. He always comes home by dark. I don't want to go into that empty, ugly house all by myself.

JOHN HENRY. Me neither.

FRANKIE (*standing with outstretched arms, and looking around her*). I think something is wrong. It is too quiet. I have a peculiar warning in my bones. I bet you a hundred dollars it's going to storm.

JOHN HENRY. I don't want to spend the night with you.

FRANKIE. A terrible, terrible dog-day storm. Or maybe even a cyclone.

JOHN HENRY. Huh.

FRANKIE. I bet Jarvis and Janice are now at Winter Hill. I see them just plain as I see you. Plainer. Something is wrong. It is too quiet.

(*A clear horn begins to play a blues tune in the distance.*)

JOHN HENRY. Frankie?

FRANKIE. Hush! It sounds like Honey. (*The horn music becomes jazzy and pangling, then the first blues tune is repeated. Suddenly, while still unfinished, the music stops. Frankie waits tensely.*)

FRANKIE. He has stopped to bang the spit out of his horn. In a second he will finish. (*After a wait*) Please, Honey, go on finish!

JOHN HENRY (*softly*). He done quit now.

FRANKIE (*moving restlessly*). I told Berenice that I was leavin' town for good and she did not believe me. Sometimes I honestly think she is the biggest fool that ever drew breath. You try to impress something on a big fool like that, and it's just like talking to a block of cement. I kept on telling and telling and telling her. I told her I had to leave this town for good because it is inevitable. Inevitable. (*Mr. Addams enters the kitchen from the house, calling: "Frankie, Frankie."*)

MR. ADDAMS (*calling from the kitchen door*). Frankie, Frankie.

FRANKIE. Yes, Papa.

MR. ADDAMS (*opening the back door*). You had supper?

FRANKIE. I'm not hungry.

MR. ADDAMS. Was a little later than I intended, fixing a timepiece for a railroad man. (*He goes back through the kitchen and into the hall, calling: "Don't leave the yard!"*)

JOHN HENRY. You want me to get the weekend bag?

FRANKIE. Don't bother me, John Henry. I'm thinking.

JOHN HENRY. What you thinking about?

FRANKIE. About the wedding. About my brother and the bride. Everything's been so sudden today. I never believed before about the fact that the earth turns at the rate of about a thousand miles a day. I didn't understand why it was that if you jumped up in the air you wouldn't land in Selma or Fairview or somewhere else instead of the same back yard. But now it seems to me I feel the world going around very fast. (*Frankie begins turning around in circles with arms outstretched. John Henry copies her. They both turn*) I feel it turning and it makes me dizzy.

JOHN HENRY. I'll stay and spend the night with you.

FRANKIE (*suddenly stopping her turning*). No. I just now thought of something.

JOHN HENRY. You just a little while ago was begging me.

FRANKIE. I know where I'm going. (*There are sounds of children playing in the distance.*)

JOHN HENRY. Let's go play with the children, Frankie.

FRANKIE. I tell you I know where I'm going. It's like I've known it all my life. Tomorrow I will tell everybody.

JOHN HENRY. Where?

FRANKIE (*dreamily*). After the wedding I'm going with them to Winter Hill. I'm going off with them after the wedding.

JOHN HENRY. You serious?

FRANKIE. Shush, just now I realized something. The trouble with me is that for a long time I have been just an "I" person. All other people can say "we." When Berenice says "we" she means her lodge and church and colored people. Soldiers can say "we" and mean the army. All people belong to a "we" except me.

JOHN HENRY. What are we going to do?

FRANKIE. Not to belong to a "we" makes you too lonesome. Until this afternoon I didn't have a "we," but now after seeing Janice and Jarvis I suddenly realize something.

JOHN HENRY. What?

FRANKIE. I know that the bride and my brother are the "we" of me. So I'm going with them, and joining with the wedding. This coming Sunday when my brother and the bride leave this town, I'm going with the two of them to Winter Hill. And after that to whatever place that they will ever go. (*There is a pause*) I love the two of them so much and we belong to be together. I love the two of them so much because they are the *we* of me.

THE CURTAIN FALLS.

ACT TWO

The scene is the same: the kitchen of the Addams home. Berenice is cooking. John Henry sits on the stool, blowing soap bubbles with a spool. It is the afternoon of the next day.

———

(*The front door slams and Frankie enters from the hall.*)

BERENICE. I been phoning all over town trying to locate you. Where on earth have you been?

FRANKIE. Everywhere. All over town.

BERENICE. I been so worried I got a good mind to be seriously mad with you. Your Papa came home to dinner today. He was mad when you didn't show up. He's taking a nap now in his room.

FRANKIE. I walked up and down Main Street and stopped in almost every store. Bought my wedding dress and silver shoes. Went around by the mills. Went all over the complete town and talked to nearly everybody in it.

BERENICE. What for, pray tell me?

FRANKIE. I was telling everybody about the wedding and my plans. (*She takes off her dress and remains barefooted in her slip*)

BERENICE. You mean just people on the street? (*She is creaming butter and sugar for cookies*)

FRANKIE. Everybody. Storekeepers. The monkey and monkey-man. A soldier. Everybody. And you know the soldier wanted to join with me and asked me for a date this evening. I wonder what you do on dates.

BERENICE. Frankie, I honestly believe you have turned crazy on us. Walking all over town and telling total strangers this big tale. You know in your soul this mania of yours is pure foolishness.

FRANKIE. Please call me F. Jasmine. I don't wish to have to remind you any more. Everything good of mine has got to be washed and ironed so I can pack them in the suitcase. (*She brings in a suitcase and opens it*) Everybody in town believes that I'm going. All except Papa. He's stubborn as an old mule. No use arguing with people like that.

BERENICE. Me and Mr. Addams has some sense.

FRANKIE. Papa was bent over working on a watch when I went by the store. I asked him could I buy the wedding clothes and he said charge them at Mac-Dougals. But he wouldn't listen to any of my plans. Just sat there with his nose to the grindstone and answered with—kind of grunts. He never listens to what I say. (*There is a pause*) Sometimes I wonder if Papa loves me or not.

BERENICE. Course he loves you. He is just a busy widowman—set in his ways.

FRANKIE. Now I wonder if I can find some tissue paper to line this suitcase.

BERENICE. Truly, Frankie, what makes you think they want you taggin' along with them? Two is company and three is a crowd. And that's the main thing about a wedding. Two is company and three is a crowd.

FRANKIE. You wait and see.

BERENICE. Remember back to the time of the flood. Remember Noah and the Ark.

FRANKIE. And what has that got to do with it?

BERENICE. Remember the way he admitted them creatures.

FRANKIE. Oh, shut up your big old mouth!

BERENICE. Two by two. He admitted them creatures two by two.

FRANKIE (after a pause). That's all right. But you wait and see. They will take me.

BERENICE. And if they don't?

FRANKIE (turning suddenly from washing her hands at the sink). If they don't, I will kill myself.

BERENICE. Kill yourself, how?

FRANKIE. I will shoot myself in the side of the head with the pistol that Papa keeps under his handkerchiefs with Mother's picture in the bureau drawer.

BERENICE. You heard what Mr. Addams said about playing with that pistol. I'll just put this cookie dough in the icebox. Set the table and your dinner is ready. Set John Henry a plate and one for me. (Berenice puts the dough in the icebox. Frankie hurriedly sets the table. Berenice takes dishes from the stove and ties a napkin around John Henry's neck) I have heard of many a peculiar thing. I have knew men to fall in love with girls so ugly that you wonder if their eyes is straight.

JOHN HENRY. Who?

BERENICE. I have knew women to love veritable satans and thank Jesus when they put their split hooves over the threshold. I have knew boys to take it into their heads to fall in love with other boys. You know Lily Mae Jenkins?

FRANKIE. I'm not sure. I know a lot of people.

BERENICE. Well, you either know him or you don't know him. He prisses around in a girl's blouse with one arm akimbo. Now this Lily Mae Jenkins fell in love with a man name Juney Jones. A man, mind you. And Lily Mae turned into a girl. He changed his nature and his sex and turned into a girl.

FRANKIE. What?

BERENICE. He did. To all intents and purposes. (Berenice is sitting in the center chair at the table. She says grace) Lord, make us thankful for what we are about to receive to nourish our bodies. Amen.

FRANKIE. It's funny I can't think who you are talking about. I used to think I knew so many people.

BERENICE. Well, you don't need to know Lily Mae Jenkins. You can live without knowing him.

FRANKIE. Anyway, I don't believe you.

BERENICE. I ain't arguing with you. What was we speaking about?

FRANKIE. About peculiar things.

BERENICE. Oh, yes. As I was just now telling you I have seen many a peculiar thing in my day. But one thing I never knew and never heard tell about. No, siree. I never in all my days heard of anybody falling in love with a wedding. (There is a pause) And thinking it all over I have come to a conclusion.

JOHN HENRY. How? How did that boy change into a girl? Did he kiss his elbow? (He tries to kiss his elbow)

BERENICE. It was just one of them things, Candy Lamb. Yep, I have come to the conclusion that what you ought to be thinking about is a beau. A nice little white boy beau.

FRANKIE. I don't want any beau. What would I do with one? Do you mean something like a soldier who would maybe take me to the Idle Hour?

BERENICE. Who's talking about soldiers? I'm talking about a nice little white boy beau your own age. How 'bout that little old Barney next door?

FRANKIE. Barney MacKean! That nasty Barney!

BERENICE. Certainly! You could make out with him until somebody better comes along. He would do.

FRANKIE. You are the biggest crazy in this town.

BERENICE. The crazy calls the sane the crazy.

(Barney MacKean, a boy of twelve, shirtless and wearing shorts, and Helen Fletcher, a girl of twelve or fourteen, cross the yard from the left, go through the arbor and out on the right. Frankie and John Henry watch them from the window.)

FRANKIE. Yonder's Barney now with Helen Fletcher. They are going to the alley behind the Wests' garage. They do something bad back there. I don't know what it is.

BERENICE. If you don't know what it is, how come you know it is bad?

FRANKIE. I just know it. I think maybe they look at each other and peepee or something. They don't let anybody watch them.

JOHN HENRY. I watched them once.

FRANKIE. What do they do?

JOHN HENRY. I saw. They don't peepee.

FRANKIE. Then what do they do?

JOHN HENRY. I don't know what it was. But I watched them. How many of them did you catch, Berenice? Them beaus?

BERENICE. How many? Candy Lamb, how many hairs is in this plait? You're talking to Miss Berenice Sadie Brown.

FRANKIE. I think you ought to quit worrying about beaus and be content with T. T. I bet you are forty years old.

BERENICE. Wise-mouth. How do you know so much? I got as much right as anybody else to continue to have a good time as long as I can. And as far as that goes, I'm not so old as some peoples would try and make me. I ain't changed life yet.

JOHN HENRY. Did they all treat you to the picture show, them beaus?

BERENICE. To the show, or one thing or another. Wipe off your mouth.

(There is the sound of piano tuning.)

JOHN HENRY. The piano tuning man.

BERENICE. Ye Gods, I seriously believe this will be the last straw.

JOHN HENRY. Me too.

FRANKIE. It makes me sad. And jittery too. *(She walks around the room)* They tell me that when they want to punish the crazy people in Milledgeville, they tie them up and make them listen to piano tuning. *(She puts the empty coal scuttle on her head and walks around the table)*

BERENICE. We could turn on the radio and drown him out.

FRANKIE. I don't want the radio on. *(She goes into the interior room and takes off her dress, speaking from inside)* But I advise you to keep the radio on after I leave. Some day you will very likely hear us speak over the radio.

BERENICE. Speak about what, pray tell me?

FRANKIE. I don't know exactly what about. But probably some eye witness account about something. We will be asked to speak.

BERENICE. I don't follow you. What are we going to eye witness? And who will ask you to speak?

JOHN HENRY *(excitedly)*. What, Frankie? Who is speaking on the radio?

FRANKIE. When I said *we*, you thought I meant you and me and John Henry West. To speak over the world radio. I have never heard of anything so funny since I was born.

JOHN HENRY *(climbing up to kneel on the seat of the chair)*. Who? What?

FRANKIE. Ha! Ha! Ho! Ho! Ho! Ho! *(Frankie goes around punching things with her fist, and shadow boxing. Berenice raises her right hand for peace. Then suddenly they all stop. Frankie goes to the window, and John Henry hurries there also and stands on tiptoe with his hands on the sill. Berenice turns her head to see what has happened. The piano is still. Three young girls in clean dresses are passing before the arbor. Frankie watches them silently at the window.)*

JOHN HENRY *(softly)*. The club of girls.

FRANKIE. What do you son-of-a-bitches mean crossing my yard? How many times must I tell you not to set foot on my Papa's property?

BERENICE. Just ignore them and make like you don't see them pass.

FRANKIE. Don't mention those crooks to me.

(T. T. and Honey approach by way of the back yard. Honey is whistling a blues tune.)

BERENICE. Why don't you show me the new dress? I'm anxious to see what you selected. *(Frankie goes into the interior room. T. T. knocks on the door. He and Honey enter)* Why T. T., what you doing around here this time of day?

T. T. Good afternoon, Miss Berenice. I'm here on a sad mission.

BERENICE *(startled)*. What's wrong?

T. T. It's about Sis Laura Thompson. She suddenly had a stroke and died.

BERENICE. What! Why she was by here just yesterday. We just ate her peas. They in my stomach right now, and her lyin dead on the cooling board this minute. The Lord works in strange ways.

T. T. Passed away at dawn this morning.

FRANKIE (*putting her head in the doorway*). Who is it that's dead?

BERENICE. Sis Laura, Sugar. That old vegetable lady.

FRANKIE (*unseen, from the interior room*). Just to think—she passed by yesterday.

T. T. Miss Berenice, I'm going around to take up a donation for the funeral. The policy people say Sis Laura's claim has lapsed.

BERENICE. Well, here's fifty cents. The poor old soul.

T. T. She was brisk as a chipmunk to the last. The Lord had appointed the time for her. I hope I go that way.

FRANKIE (*from the interior room*). I've got something to show you all. Shut your eyes and don't open them until I tell you. (*She enters the room dressed in an orange satin evening dress with silver shoes and stockings*) These are the wedding clothes. (*Berenice, T. T. and John Henry stare*)

JOHN HENRY. Oh, how pretty!

FRANKIE. Now tell me your honest opinion. (*There is a pause*) What's the matter? Don't you like it, Berenice?

BERENICE. No. It don't do.

FRANKIE. What do you mean? It don't do.

BERENICE. Exactly that. It just don't do. (*She shakes her head while Frankie looks at the dress*)

FRANKIE. But I don't see what you mean. What is wrong?

BERENICE. Well, if you don't see it I can't explain it to you. Look there at your head, to begin with. (*Frankie goes to the mirror*) You had all your hair shaved off like a convict and now you tie this ribbon around this head without any hair. Just looks peculiar.

FRANKIE. But I'm going to wash and try to stretch my hair tonight.

BERENICE. Stretch your hair! How you going to stretch your hair? And look at them elbows. Here you got on a grown woman's evening dress. And that brown crust on your elbows. The two things just don't mix. (*Frankie, embarrassed, covers her elbows with her hands. Berenice is still shaking her head*) Take it back down to the store.

T. T. The dress is too growny looking.

FRANKIE. But I can't take it back. It's bargain basement.

BERENICE. Very well then. Come here. Let me see what I can do.

FRANKIE (*going to Berenice, who works with the dress*). I think you're just not accustomed to seeing anybody dressed up.

BERENICE. I'm not accustomed to seein' a human Christmas tree in August.

JOHN HENRY. Frankie's dress looks like a Christmas tree.

FRANKIE. Two-faced Judas! You just now said it was pretty. Old double-faced Judas! (*The sounds of piano tuning are heard again*) Oh, that piano tuner!

BERENICE. Step back a little now.

FRANKIE (*looking in the mirror*). Don't you honestly think it's pretty? Give me your candy opinion.

BERENICE. I never knew anybody so unreasonable! You ask me my candy opinion, I give you my candy opinion. You ask me again, and I give it to you again. But what you want is not my honest opinion, but my good opinion of something I know is wrong.

FRANKIE. I only want to look pretty.

BERENICE. Pretty is as pretty does. Ain't that right, T. T.? You will look well enough for anybody's wedding. Excepting your own. (*Mr. Addams enters through the hall door.*)

MR. ADDAMS. Hello, everybody. (*To Frankie*) I don't want you roaming around the streets all morning and not coming home at dinner time. Looks like I'll have to tie you up in the back yard.

FRANKIE. I had business to tend to. Papa, look!

MR. ADDAMS. What is it, Miss Picklepriss?

FRANKIE. Sometimes I think you have turned stone blind. You never even noticed my new dress.

MR. ADDAMS. I thought it was a show costume.

FRANKIE. Show costume! Papa, why is it you don't ever notice what I have on or pay any serious mind to me? You just walk around like a mule with blinders on, not seeing or caring.

MR. ADDAMS. Never mind that now. (*To T. T. and Honey*) I need some help down at my store. My porter failed me again. I wonder if you or Honey could help me next week.

T. T. I will if I can, sir, Mr. Addams.

What days would be convenient for you, sir?

MR. ADDAMS. Say Wednesday afternoon.

T. T. Now, Mr. Addams, that's one afternoon I promised to work for Mr. Finny, sir. I can't promise anything, Mr. Addams. But if Mr. Finny changes his mind about needing me, I'll work for you, sir.

MR. ADDAMS. How about you, Honey?

HONEY (shortly). I ain't got the time.

MR. ADDAMS. I'll be so glad when the war is over and you biggety, worthless niggers get back to work. And, furthermore, you sir me! Hear me!

HONEY (reluctantly). Yes—sir.

MR. ADDAMS. I getter go back to the store now and get my nose down to the grindstone. You stay home, Frankie. (He goes out through the hall door)

JOHN HENRY. Uncle Royal called Honey a nigger. Is Honey a nigger?

BERENICE. Be quiet now, John Henry. (To Honey) Honey, I got a good mind to shake you till you spit. Not saying sir to Mr. Addams, and acting so impudent.

HONEY. T. T. said sir enough for a whole crowd of niggers. But for folks that calls me nigger, I got a real good nigger razor. (He takes a razor from his pocket. Frankie and John Henry crowd close to look. When John Henry touches the razor, Honey says) Don't touch it, Butch, it's sharp. Liable to hurt yourself.

BERENICE. Put up that razor, Satan! I worry myself sick over you. You going to die before your appointed span.

JOHN HENRY. Why is Honey a nigger?

BERENICE. Jesus knows.

HONEY. I'm so tensed up. My nerves been scraped with a razor. Berenice, loan me a dollar.

BERENICE. I ain't handing you no dollar, worthless, to get high on them reefer cigarettes.

HONEY. Gimme, Berenice, I'm so tensed up and miserable. The nigger hole. I'm sick of smothering in the nigger hole. I can't stand it no more.

(Relenting, Berenice gets her pocketbook from the shelf, opens it, and takes out some change.)

BERENICE. Here's thirty cents. You can buy two beers.

HONEY. Well, thankful for tiny, infinitesimal favors. I better be dancing off now.

T. T. Same here. I still have to make a good deal of donation visits this afternoon. (Honey and T. T. go to the door)

BERENICE. So long, T. T. I'm counting on you for tomorrow and you too, Honey.

FRANKIE and JOHN HENRY. So long.

T. T. Good-bye, you all. Good-bye. (He goes out, crossing the yard)

BERENICE. Poor ole Sis Laura. I certainly hope that when my time comes I will have kept up my policy. I dread to think the church would ever have to bury me. When I die.

JOHN HENRY. Are you going to die, Berenice?

BERENICE. Why, Candy, everybody has to die.

JOHN HENRY. Everybody? Are you going to die, Frankie?

FRANKIE. I doubt it. I honestly don't think I'll ever die.

JOHN HENRY. What is "die"?

FRANKIE. It must be terrible to be nothing but black, black, black.

BERENICE. Yes, baby.

FRANKIE. How many dead people do you know? I know six dead people in all. I'm not counting my mother. There's William Boyd who was killed in Italy. I knew him by sight and name. An' that man who climbed poles for the telephone company. An' Lou Baker. The porter at Finny's place who was murdered in the alley back of Papa's store. Somebody drew a razor on him and the alley people said that his cut throat shivered like a mouth and spoke ghost words to the sun.

JOHN HENRY. Ludie Maxwell Freeman is dead.

FRANKIE. I didn't count Ludie; it wouldn't be fair. Because he died just before I was born. (To Berenice) Do you think very frequently about Ludie?

BERENICE. You know I do. I think about the five years when me and Ludie was together, and about all the bad times I seen since. Sometimes I almost wish I had never knew Ludie at all. It leaves you too lonesome afterward. When you walk home in the evening on the way from work, it makes a little lonesome quinch come in you. And you take up with too many sorry men to try to get over the feeling.

FRANKIE. But T. T. is not sorry.

BERENICE. I wasn't referring to T. T. He is a fine upstanding colored gentleman, who has walked in a state of grace all his life.

FRANKIE. When are you going to marry with him?

BERENICE. I ain't going to marry with him.

FRANKIE. But you were just now saying . . .

BERENICE. I was saying how sincerely I respect T. T. and sincerely regard T. T. *(There is a pause)* But he don't make me shiver none.

FRANKIE. Listen, Berenice, I have something queer to tell you. It's something that happened when I was walking around town today. Now I don't exactly know how to explain what I mean.

BERENICE. What is it?

FRANKIE *(now and then pulling her bangs or lower lip)*. I was walking along and I passed two stores with a alley in between. The sun was frying hot. And just as I passed this alley, I caught a *glimpse* of something in the corner of my left eye. A dark double shape. And this glimpse brought to my mind—so sudden and clear—my brother and the bride that I just stood there and couldn't hardly bear to look and see what it was. It was like they were there in that alley, although I knew that they are in Winter Hill almost a hundred miles away. *(There is a pause)* Then I turn slowly and look. And you know what was there? *(There is a pause)* It was just two colored boys. That was all. But it gave me such a queer feeling.

(Berenice has been listening attentively. She stares at Frankie, then draws a package of cigarettes from her bosom and lights one.)

BERENICE. Listen at me! Can you see through these bones in my forehead? *(She points to her forehead)* Have you, Frankie Addams, been reading my mind? *(There is a pause)* That's the most remarkable thing I ever heard of.

FRANKIE. What I mean is that . . .

BERENICE. I know what you mean. You mean right here in the corner of your eye. *(She points to her eye)* You suddenly catch something there. And this cold shiver run all the way down you. And you whirl around. And you stand there facing Jesus knows what. But not Ludie, not who you want. And for a minute you feel like you been dropped down a well.

FRANKIE. Yes. That is it. *(Frankie reaches for a cigarette and lights it, coughing a bit)*

BERENICE. Well, that is mighty remarkable. This is a thing been happening to me all my life. Yet just now is the first time I ever heard it put into words. *(There is a pause)* Yes, that is the way it is when you are in love. A thing known and not spoken.

FRANKIE *(patting her foot)*. Yet I always maintained I never believed in love. I didn't admit it and never put any of it in my shows.

JOHN HENRY. I never believed in love.

BERENICE. Now I will tell you something. And it is to be a warning to you. You hear me, John Henry. You hear me, Frankie.

JOHN HENRY. Yes. *(He points his forefinger)* Frankie is smoking.

BERENICE *(squaring her shoulders)*. Now I am here to tell you I was happy. There was no human woman in all the world more happy than I was in them days. And that includes everybody. You listening to me, John Henry? It includes all queens and millionaires and first ladies of the land. And I mean it includes people of all color. You hear me, Frankie? No human woman in all the world was happier than Berenice Sadie Brown.

FRANKIE. The five years you were married to Ludie.

BERENICE. From that autumn morning when I first meet him on the road in front of Campbell's Filling Station until the very night he died, November, the year 1933.

FRANKIE. The very year and the very month I was born.

BERENICE. The coldest November I ever seen. Every morning there was frost and puddles were crusted with ice. The sunshine was pale yellow like it is in winter time. Sounds carried far away, and I remember a hound dog that used to howl toward sundown. And everything I seen come to me as a kind of sign.

FRANKIE. I think it is a kind of sign I was born the same year and the same month he died.

BERENICE. And it was a Thursday towards six o'clock. About this time of day. Only November. I remember I went to the passage and opened the front door. Dark was coming on; the old hound was howling far away. And I go back in the room and lay down on Ludie's bed. I lay myself down over Ludie with my arms spread out and my face on his face. And I pray that the Lord would contage my strength to him. And I ask the Lord to let it be anybody, but not let it be Ludie. And I lay there and pray for a long time. Until night.

JOHN HENRY. How? *(In a higher, wailing voice)* How, Berenice?

BERENICE. That night he died. I tell you he died. Ludie! Ludie Freeman! Ludie Maxwell Freeman died! *(She hums)*

FRANKIE *(after a pause)*. It seems to me I feel sadder about Ludie than any other dead person. Although I never knew him. I know I ought to cry sometimes about my mother, or anyhow Granny. But it looks like I can't. But Ludie—maybe it was because I was born so soon after Ludie died. But you were starting out to tell some kind of a warning.

BERENICE *(looking puzzled for a moment)*. Warning? Oh, yes! I was going to tell you how this thing we was talking about applies to me. *(As Berenice begins to talk Frankie goes to a shelf above the refrigerator and brings back a fig bar to the table)* It was the April of the following year that I went one Sunday to the church where the congregation was strange to me. I had my forehead down on the top of the pew in front of me, and my eyes were open—not peeping around in secret, mind you, but just open. When suddenly this shiver ran all the way through me. I had caught sight of something from the corner of my eye. And I looked slowly to the left. There on the pew, just six inches from my eyes, was this *thumb.*

FRANKIE. What thumb?

BERENICE. Now I have to tell you. There was only one small portion of Ludie Freeman which was not pretty. Every other part about him was handsome and pretty as anyone would wish. All except this right thumb. This one thumb had a mashed, chewed appearance that was not pretty. You understand?

FRANKIE. You mean you suddenly saw Ludie's thumb when you were praying?

BERENICE. I mean I seen *this* thumb. And as I knelt there just staring at this thumb, I begun to pray in earnest. I prayed out loud! Lord, manifest! Lord, manifest!

FRANKIE. And did He—manifest?

BERENICE. Manifest, my foot! *(Spitting)* You know who that thumb belonged to?

FRANKIE. Who?

BERENICE. Why, Jamie Beale. That big old no-good Jamie Beale. It was the first time I ever laid eyes on him.

FRANKIE. Is that why you married him? Because he had a mashed thumb like Ludie's?

BERENICE. Lord only knows. I don't. I guess I felt drawn to him on account of that thumb. And then one thing led to another. First thing I know I had married him.

FRANKIE. Well, I think that was silly. To marry him just because of that thumb.

BERENICE. I'm not trying to dispute with you. I'm just telling you what actually happened. And the very same thing occurred in the case of Henry Johnson.

FRANKIE. You mean to sit there and tell me Henry Johnson had one of those mashed thumbs too?

BERENICE. No. It was not the thumb this time. It was the coat. *(Frankie and John Henry look at each other in amazement. After a pause Berenice continues)* Now when Ludie died, them policy people cheated me out of fifty dollars so I pawned everything I could lay hands on, and I sold my coat and Ludie's coat. Because I couldn't let Ludie be put away cheap.

FRANKIE. Oh! Then you mean Henry Johnson bought Ludie's coat and you married him because of it?

BERENICE. Not exactly. I was walking down the street one evening when I suddenly seen this shape appear before me. Now the shape of this boy ahead of me was so similar to Ludie through the shoulders and the back of the head that I almost dropped dead there on the sidewalk. I followed and run behind him. It was Henry Johnson. Since he lived in the country and didn't come into town, he had chanced to buy Ludie's coat and from the back view it looked like he was Ludie's ghost or Ludie's twin. But how I married him I don't exactly know, for, to begin with, it was clear that he did not have his share of sense. But you let a boy hang around you and you get fond of him. Anyway, that's how I married Henry Johnson.

FRANKIE. He was the one went crazy on you. Had eatin' dreams and swallowed the corner of the sheet. *(There is a pause)* But I don't understand the point of what you was telling. I don't see how that about

Jamie Beale and Henry Johnson applies to me.

BERENICE. Why, it applies to everybody and it is a warning.

FRANKIE. But how?

BERENICE. Why, Frankie, don't you see what I was doing? I loved Ludie and he was the first man I loved. Therefore I had to go and copy myself forever afterward. What I did was to marry off little pieces of Ludie whenever I come across them. It was just my misfortune they all turned out to be the wrong pieces. My intention was to repeat me and Ludie. Now don't you see?

FRANKIE. I see what you're driving at. But I don't see how it is a warning applied to me.

BERENICE. You don't! Then I'll tell you. *(Frankie does not nod or answer. The piano tuner plays an arpeggio)* You and that wedding tomorrow. That is what I am warning about. I can see right through them two gray eyes of yours like they was glass. And what I see is the saddest piece of foolishness I ever knew.

JOHN HENRY *(in a low voice)*. Gray eyes is glass.

(Frankie tenses her brows and looks steadily at Berenice.)

BERENICE. I see what you have in mind. Don't think I don't. You see something unheard of tomorrow, and you right in the center. You think you going to march to the preacher right in between your brother and the bride. You think you going to break into that wedding, and then Jesus knows what else.

FRANKIE. No. I don't see myself walking to the preacher with them.

BERENICE. I see through them eyes. Don't argue with me.

JOHN HENRY *(repeating softly)*. Gray eyes is glass.

BERENICE. But what I'm warning is this. If you start out falling in love with some unheard-of thing like that, what is going to happen to you? If you take a mania like this, it won't be the last time and of that you can be sure. So what will become of you? Will you be trying to break into weddings the rest of your days?

FRANKIE. It makes me sick to listen to people who don't have any sense. *(She sticks her fingers in her ears and hums)*

BERENICE. You just settin' yourself this fancy trap to catch yourself in trouble. And you know it.

FRANKIE. They will take me. You wait and see.

BERENICE. Well, I been trying to reason seriously. But I see it is no use.

FRANKIE. You are just jealous. You are just trying to deprive me of all the pleasure of leaving town.

BERENICE. I am just trying to head this off. But I still see it is no use.

JOHN HENRY. Gray eyes is glass.

(The piano is played to the seventh note of the scale and this is repeated.)

FRANKIE *(singing)*. Do, ray, mee, fa, sol, la, tee, do. Tee. Tee. It could drive you wild. *(She crosses to the screen door and slams it)* You didn't say anything about Willis Rhodes. Did he have a mashed thumb or a coat or something? *(She returns to the table and sits down)*

BERENICE. Lord, now that really was something.

FRANKIE. I only know he stole your furniture and was so terrible you had to call the Law on him.

BERENICE. Well, imagine this! Imagine a cold bitter January night. And me laying all by myself in the big parlor bed. Alone in the house because everybody else had gone for the Saturday night. Me, mind you, who hates to sleep in a big empty bed all by myself at any time. Past twelve o'clock on this cold, bitter January night. Can you remember winter time, John Henry? *(John Henry nods)* Imagine! Suddenly there comes a sloughing sound and a tap, tap, tap. So Miss Me . . . *(She laughs uproariously and stops suddenly, putting her hand over her mouth)*

FRANKIE. What? *(Leaning closer across the table and looking intently at Berenice)* What happened?

(Berenice looks from one to the other, shaking her head slowly. Then she speaks in a changed voice.)

BERENICE. Why, I wish you would look yonder. I wish you would look. *(Frankie glances quickly behind her, then turns back to Berenice)*

FRANKIE. What? What happened?

BERENICE. Look at them two little pitchers and them four big ears. *(Berenice gets up suddenly from the table)* Come on, chillin, less us roll out the dough for the cookies tomorrow. *(Berenice clears the table and begins washing dishes at the sink)*

FRANKIE. If it's anything I mortally despise, it's a person who starts out to tell something and works up people's interest, and then stops.

BERENICE *(still laughing).* I admit it. And I am sorry. But it was just one of them things I suddenly realized I couldn't tell you and John Henry.

(John Henry skips up to the sink.)

JOHN HENRY *(singing).* Cookies! Cookies! Cookies!

FRANKIE. You could have sent him out of the room and told me. But don't think I care a particle about what happened. I just wish Willis Rhodes had come in about that time and slit your throat. *(She goes out into the hall)*

BERENICE *(still chuckling).* That is a ugly way to talk. You ought to be ashamed. Here, John Henry, I'll give you a scrap of dough to make a cookie man. *(Berenice gives John Henry some dough. He climbs up on a chair and begins to work with it. Frankie enters with the evening newspaper. She stands in the doorway, then puts the newspaper on the table.)*

FRANKIE. I see in the paper where we dropped a new bomb—the biggest one dropped yet. They call it a atom bomb. I intend to take two baths tonight. One long soaking bath and scrub with a brush. I'm going to try to scrape this crust off my elbows. Then let out the dirty water and take a second bath.

BERENICE. Hooray, that's a good idea. I will be glad to see you clean.

JOHN HENRY. I will take two baths.

(Berenice has picked up the paper and is sitting in a chair against the pale white light of the window. She holds the newspaper open before her and her head is twisted down to one side as she strains to see what is printed there.)

FRANKIE. Why is it against the law to change your name?

BERENICE. What is that on your neck? I thought it was a head you carried on that neck. Just think. Suppose I would suddenly up and call myself Mrs. Eleanor Roosevelt. And you would begin naming yourself Joe Louis. And John Henry here tried to pawn himself off as Henry Ford.

FRANKIE. Don't talk childish; that is not the kind of changing I mean. I mean from a name that doesn't suit you to a name you prefer. Like I changed from Frankie to F. Jasmine.

BERENICE. But it would be a confusion. Suppose we all suddenly change to entirely different names. Nobody would ever know who anybody was talking about. The whole world would go crazy.

FRANKIE. I don't see what that has to do with it.

BERENICE. Because things accumulate around your name. You have a name and one thing after another happens to you and things have accumulated around the name.

FRANKIE. But what has accumulated around my old name? *(Berenice does not reply)* Nothing! See! My name just didn't mean anything. Nothing ever happened to me.

BERENICE. But it will. Things will happen.

FRANKIE. What?

BERENICE. You pin me down like that and I can't tell you truthfully. If I could, I wouldn't be sitting here in this kitchen right now, but making a fine living on Wall Street as a wizard. All I can say is that things will happen. Just what, I don't know.

FRANKIE. Until yesterday, nothing ever happened to me.

(John Henry crosses to the door and puts on Berenice's hat and shoes, takes her pocketbook and walks around the table twice.)

BERENICE. John Henry, take off my hat and my shoes and put up my pocketbook. Thank you very much. *(John Henry does so)*

FRANKIE. Listen, Berenice. Doesn't it strike you as strange that I am I and you are you? Like when you are walking down a street and you meet somebody. And you are you. And he is him. Yet when you look at each other, the eyes make a connection. Then you go off one way. And he goes off another way. You go off into different parts of town, and maybe you never see each other again. Not in your whole life. Do you see what I mean?

BERENICE. Not exactly.

FRANKIE. That's not what I meant to say anyway. There are all these people here in town I don't even know by sight or name. And we pass alongside each other and don't have any connection. And they don't know me and I don't know them. And now I'm leaving town and there are all these people I will never know.

BERENICE. But who do you want to know?

FRANKIE. Everybody. Everybody in the world.

BERENICE. Why, I wish you would listen to that. How about people like Willis Rhodes? How about them Germans? How about them Japanese?

(Frankie knocks her head against the door jamb and looks up at the ceiling.)

FRANKIE. That's not what I mean. That's not what I'm talking about.

BERENICE. Well, what *is* you talking about?

(A child's voice is heard outside, calling: "Batter up! Batter up!")

JOHN HENRY (in a low voice). Less play out, Frankie.

FRANKIE. No. You go. (After a pause) This is what I mean.

(Berenice waits, and when Frankie does not speak again, says:)

BERENICE. What on earth is wrong with you?

FRANKIE (after a long pause, then suddenly, with hysteria). Boyoman! Manoboy! When we leave Winter Hill we're going to more places than you ever thought about or even knew existed. Just where we will go first I don't know, and it don't matter. Because after we go to that place we're going on to another. Alaska, China, Iceland, South America. Traveling on trains. Letting her rip on motorcycles. Flying around all over the world in airplanes. Here today and gone tomorrow. All over the world. It's the damn truth. Boyoman! (She runs around the table)

BERENICE. Frankie!

FRANKIE. And talking of things happening. Things will happen so fast we won't hardly have time to realize them. Captain Jarvis Addams wins highest medals and is decorated by the President. Miss F. Jasmine Addams breaks all records. Mrs. Janice Addams elected Miss United Nations in beauty contest. One thing after another happening so fast we don't hardly notice them.

BERENICE. Hold still, fool.

FRANKIE (her excitement growing more and more intense). And we will meet them. Everybody. We will just walk up to people and know them right away. We will be walking down a dark road and see a lighted house and knock on the door and strangers will rush to meet us and say: "Come in! Come in!" We will know decorated aviators and New York people and movie stars. We will have thousands and thousands of friends. And we will belong to so many clubs that we can't even keep track of all of them. We will be members of the whole world. Boyoman! Manoboy!

(Frankie has been running round and round the table in wild excitement and when she passes the next time Berenice catches her slip so quickly that she is caught up with a jerk.)

BERENICE. *Is* you gone raving wild? (She pulls Frankie closer and puts her arm around her waist) Sit here in my lap and rest a minute. (Frankie sits in Berenice's lap. John Henry comes close and jealously pinches Frankie) Leave Frankie alone. She ain't bothered you.

JOHN HENRY. I'm sick.

BERENICE. Now no, you ain't. Be quiet and don't grudge your cousin a little bit love.

JOHN HENRY (hitting Frankie). Old mean bossy Frankie.

BERENICE. What she doing so mean right now? She just laying here wore out. (They continue sitting. Frankie is relaxed now)

FRANKIE. Today I went to the Blue Moon—this place that all the soldiers are so fond of and I met a soldier—a redheaded boy.

BERENICE. What is all this talk about the Blue Moon and soldiers?

FRANKIE. Berenice, you treat me like a child. When I see all these soldiers milling around town I always wonder where they came from and where they are going.

BERENICE. They were born and they going to die.

FRANKIE. There are so many things about the world I do not understand.

BERENICE. If you did understand you would be God. Didn't you know that?

FRANKIE. Maybe so. (She stares and stretches herself on Berenice's lap, her long legs sprawled out beneath the kitchen table) Anyway, after the wedding I won't have to worry about things any more.

BERENICE. You don't have to now. No-body requires you to solve the riddles of the world.

FRANKIE *(looking at newspaper)*. The paper says this new atom bomb is worth twenty thousand tons of T.N.T.

BERENICE. Twenty thousand tons? And there ain't but two tons of coal in the coal house—all that coal.

FRANKIE. The paper says the bomb is a very important science discovery.

BERENICE. The figures these days have got too high for me. Read in the paper about ten million peoples killed. I can't crowd that many people in my mind's eye.

JOHN HENRY. Berenice, is the glass eye your mind's eye?

(John Henry has climbed up on the back rungs of Berenice's chair and has been hugging her head. He is now holding her ears.)

BERENICE. Don't yank my head back like that, Candy. Me and Frankie ain't going to float up through the ceiling and leave you.

FRANKIE. I wonder if you have ever thought about this? Here we are—right now. This very minute. Now. But while we're talking right now, this minute is passing. And it will never come again. Never in all the world. When it is gone, it is gone. No power on earth could bring it back again.

JOHN HENRY *(beginning to sing)*.
I sing because I'm happy,
I sing because I'm free,
For His eye is on the sparrow,
And I know He watches me.
BERENICE *(singing)*.
Why should I feel discouraged?
Why should the shadows come?
Why should my heart be lonely,
Away from heaven and home?
For Jesus is my portion,
My constant friend is He,
For His eye is on the sparrow,
And I know He watches me.
So, I sing because I'm happy.
(John Henry and Frankie join on the last three lines.)
I sing because I'm happy,
I sing because I'm free,
For His eye is on the sparrow,
And I know He watches . . .
BERENICE. Frankie, you got the sharpest set of human bones I ever felt.

THE CURTAIN FALLS

ACT THREE

SCENE ONE

The scene is the same: the kitchen. It is the day of the wedding. When the curtain rises Berenice, in her apron, and T. T. Williams in a white coat have just finished preparations for the wedding refreshments. Berenice has been watching the ceremony through the half-open door leading into the hall. There are sounds of congratulations offstage, the wedding ceremony having just finished.

———

BERENICE *(to T. T. Williams)*. Can't see much from this door. But I can see Frankie. And her face is a study. And John Henry's chewing away at the bubble gum that Jarvis bought him. Well, sounds like it's all over. They crowding in now to kiss the bride. We better take this cloth off the sandwiches. Frankie said she would help you serve.

T. T. From the way she's been acting, I don't think we can count much on her.

BERENICE. I wish Honey was here. I'm so worried about him since what you told me. It's going to storm. It's a mercy they didn't decide to have the wedding in the back yard like they first planned.

T.T. I thought I'd better not minch the matter. Honey was in a bad way when I saw him this morning.

BERENICE. Honey Camden don't have too large a share of judgment as it is, but when he gets high on them reefers, he's got on more judgment than a four-year-old child. Remember that time he swung at the police and nearly got his eyes beat out?

T. T. Not to mention six months on the road.

BERENICE. I haven't been so anxious in all my life. I've got two people scouring Sugarville to find him. *(In a fervent voice)* God, you took Ludie but please watch over my Honey Camden. He's all the family I got.

T. T. And Frankie behaving this way about the wedding. Poor little critter.

BERENICE. And the sorry part is that she's perfectly serious about all this fool-ishness. *(Frankie enters the kitchen through the hall door)* Is it all over? *(T. T. crosses to the icebox with sandwiches)*

FRANKIE. Yes. And it was such a pretty wedding I wanted to cry.

BERENICE. You told them yet?

FRANKIE. About my plans—no, I haven't yet told them.

(*John Henry comes in and goes out.*)

BERENICE. Well, you better hurry up and do it, for they going to leave the house right after the refreshments.

FRANKIE. Oh, I know it. But something just seems to happen to my throat; every time I tried to tell them, different words came out.

BERENICE. What words?

FRANKIE. I asked Janice how come she didn't marry with a veil. (*With feeling*) Oh, I'm so embarrassed. Here I am all dressed up in this tacky evening dress. Oh, why didn't I listen to you! I'm so ashamed. (*T. T. goes out with a platter of sandwiches.*)

BERENICE. Don't take everything so strenuous like.

FRANKIE. I'm going in there and tell them now! (*She goes*)

JOHN HENRY (*coming out of the interior bedroom, carrying several costumes*). Frankie sure gave me a lot of presents when she was packing the suitcase. Berenice, she gave me all the beautiful show costumes.

BERENICE. Don't set so much store by all those presents. Come tomorrow morning and she'll be demanding them back again.

JOHN HENRY. And she even gave me the shell from the Bay. (*He puts the shell to his ear and listens*)

BERENICE. I wonder what's going on up there. (*She goes to the door and opens it and looks through*)

T. T. (*returning to the kitchen*). They all complimenting the wedding cake. And drinking the wine punch.

BERENICE. What's Frankie doing? When she left the kitchen a minute ago she was going to tell them. I wonder how they'll take this total surprise. I have a feeling like you get just before a big thunder storm.

(*Frankie enters, holding a punch cup.*)

BERENICE. You told them yet?

FRANKIE. There are all the family around and I can't seem to tell them. I wish I had written it down on the typewriter beforehand. I try to tell them and the words just—die.

BERENICE. The words just die because the very idea is so silly.

FRANKIE. I love the two of them so much. Janice put her arms around me and said she had always wanted a little sister. And she kissed me. She asked me again what grade I was in school. That's the third time she's asked me. In fact, that's the main question I've been asked at the wedding.

(*John Henry comes in, wearing a fairy costume, and goes out. Berenice notices Frankie's punch and takes it from her.*)

FRANKIE. And Jarvis was out in the street seeing about this car he borrowed for the wedding. And I followed him out and tried to tell him. But while I was trying to reach the point, he suddenly grabbed me by the elbows and lifted me up and sort of swung me. He said: "Frankie, the lankie, the alaga fankie, the tee-legged, toe-legged, bow-legged Frankie." And he gave me a dollar bill.

BERENICE. That's nice.

FRANKIE. I just don't know what to do. I have to tell them and yet I don't know how to.

BERENICE. Maybe when they're settled, they will invite you to come and visit with them.

FRANKIE. Oh no! I'm going *with* them. (*Frankie goes back into the house. There are louder sounds of voices from the interior. John Henry comes in again.*)

JOHN HENRY. The bride and the groom are leaving. Uncle Royal is taking their suitcases out to the car.

(*Frankie runs to the interior room and returns with her suitcase. She kisses Berenice.*)

FRANKIE. Good-bye, Berenice. Good-bye, John Henry. (*She stands a moment and looks around the kitchen*) Farewell, old ugly kitchen. (*She runs out*)

(*There are sounds of good-byes as the wedding party and the family guests move out of the house to the sidewalk. The voices get fainter in the distance. Then, from the front sidewalk there is the sound of disturbance. Frankie's voice is heard, diminished by distance, although she is speaking loudly.*)

FRANKIE'S VOICE. That's what I am telling you. (*Indistinct protesting voices are heard*)

MR. ADDAMS' VOICE (*indistinctly*). Now be reasonable, Frankie.

FRANKIE'S VOICE (*screaming*). I have to go. Take me! Take me!

JOHN HENRY (*entering excitedly*). Frankie is in the wedding car and they can't get her out. (*He runs out but soon returns*) Uncle Royal and my Daddy are having to haul and drag old Frankie. She's holding onto the steering wheel.

MR. ADDAMS' VOICE. You march right along here. What in the world has come into you? (*He comes into the kitchen with Frankie who is sobbing*) I never heard of such an exhibition in my life. Berenice, you take charge of her.

(*Frankie flings herself on the kitchen chair and sobs with her head in her arms on the kitchen table.*)

JOHN HENRY. They put old Frankie out of the wedding. They hauled her out of the wedding car.

MR. ADDAMS (*clearing his throat*). That's sufficient, John Henry. Leave Frankie alone. (*He puts a caressing hand on Frankie's head*) What makes you want to leave your old papa like this? You've got Janice and Jarvis all upset on their wedding day.

FRANKIE. I love them so!

BERENICE (*looking down the hall*). Here they come. Now please be reasonable, Sugar.

(*The bride and groom come in. Frankie keeps her face buried in her arms and does not look up. The bride wears a blue suit with a white flower corsage pinned at the shoulder.*)

JARVIS. Frankie, we came to tell you good-bye. I'm sorry you're taking it like this.

JANICE. Darling, when we are settled we want you to come for a nice visit with us. But we don't yet have any place to live. (*She goes to Frankie and caresses her head. Frankie jerks*) Won't you tell us good-bye now?

FRANKIE (*with passion*). We! When you say *we*, you only mean you and Jarvis. And I am not included. (*She buries her head in her arms again and sobs*)

JANICE. Please, darling, don't make us unhappy on our wedding day. You know we love you.

FRANKIE. See! *We*—when you say we, I am not included. It's not fair.

JANICE. When you come visit us you must write beautiful plays, and we'll all act in them. Come, Frankie, don't hide your sweet face from us. Sit up. (*Frankie raises her head slowly and stares with a look of wonder and misery*) Good-bye, Frankie, darling.

JARVIS. So long, now, kiddo.

(*They go out and Frankie still stares at them as they go down the hall. She rises, crosses towards the door and falls on her knees.*)

FRANKIE. Take me! Take me!

(*Berenice puts Frankie back on her chair.*)

JOHN HENRY. They put Frankie out of the wedding. They hauled her out of the wedding car.

BERENICE. Don't tease your cousin, John Henry.

FRANKIE. It was a frame-up all around.

BERENICE. Well, don't bother no more about it. It's over now. Now cheer up.

FRANKIE. I wish the whole world would die.

BERENICE. School will begin now in only three more weeks and you'll find another bosom friend like Evelyn Owens you so wild about.

JOHN HENRY (*seated below the sewing machine*). I'm sick, Berenice. My head hurts.

BERENICE. No you're not. Be quiet, I don't have the patience to fool with you.

FRANKIE (*hugging her hunched shoulders*). Oh, my heart feels so cheap!

BERENICE. Soon as you get started in school and have a chance to make these here friends, I think it would be a good idea to have a party.

FRANKIE. These baby promises rasp on my nerves.

BERENICE. You could call up the society editor of the *Evening Journal* and have the party written up in the paper. And that would make the fourth time your name has been published in the paper.

FRANKIE (*with a trace of interest*). When my bike ran into that automobile, the paper called me Fankie Addams, F-A-N-K-I-E. (*She puts her head down again*)

JOHN HENRY. Frankie, don't cry. This evening we can put up the tepee and have a good time.

FRANKIE. Oh, hush up your mouth.

BERENICE. Listen to me. Tell me what you would like and I will try to do it if it is in my power.

FRANKIE. All I wish in the world, is for no human being ever to speak to me as long as I live.

BERENICE. Bawl, then, misery.

(Mr. Addams enters the kitchen, carrying Frankie's suitcase, which he sets in the middle of the kitchen floor. He cracks his finger joints. Frankie stares at him resentfully, then fastens her gaze on the suitcase.)

MR. ADDAMS. Well, it looks like the show is over and the monkey's dead.

FRANKIE. You think it's over, but it's not.

MR. ADDAMS. You want to come down and help me at the store tomorrow? Or polish some silver with the shammy rag? You can even play with those old watch springs.

FRANKIE *(still looking at her suitcase)*. That's my suitcase I packed. If you think it's all over, that only shows how little you know. *(T. T. comes in)* If I can't go with the bride and my brother as I was meant to leave this town, I'm going anyway. Somehow, anyhow, I'm leaving town. *(Frankie raises up in her chair)* I can't stand this existence—this kitchen—this town—any longer! I will hop a train and go to New York. Or hitch rides to Hollywood, and get a job there. If worse comes to worse, I can act in comedies. *(She rises)* Or I could dress up like a boy and join the Merchant Marines and run away to sea. Somehow, anyhow, I'm running away.

BERENICE. Now, quiet down—

FRANKIE *(grabbing the suitcase and running into the hall)*. Please, Papa, don't try to capture me.

(Outside the wind starts to blow.)

JOHN HENRY *(from the doorway)*. Uncle Royal, Frankie's got your pistol in her suitcase.

(There is the sound of running footsteps and of the screen door slamming.)

BERENICE. Run, catch her.

(T. T. and Mr. Addams rush into the hall, followed by John Henry.)

MR. ADDAMS' VOICE. Frankie! Frankie! Frankie!

(Berenice is left alone in the kitchen. Outside the wind is higher and the hall door is blown shut. There is a rumble of thunder, then a loud clap. Thunder and flashes of lightning continue. Berenice is seated in her chair, when John Henry comes in.)

JOHN HENRY. Uncle Royal is going with my Daddy, and they are chasing her in our car. *(There is a thunder clap)* The thunder scares me, Berenice.

BERENICE *(taking him in her lap)*. Ain't nothing going to hurt you.

JOHN HENRY. You think they're going to catch her?

BERENICE *(putting her hand to her head)*. Certainly. They'll be bringing her home directly. I've got such a headache. Maybe my eye socket and all these troubles.

JOHN HENRY *(with his arms around Berenice)*. I've got a headache, too. I'm sick, Berenice.

BERENICE. No, you ain't. Run along, Candy. I ain't got the patience to fool with you now.

(Suddenly the lights go out in the kitchen, plunging it in gloom. The sound of wind and storm continues and the yard is a dark storm-green.)

JOHN HENRY. Berenice!

BERENICE. Ain't nothing. Just the lights went out.

JOHN HENRY. I'm scared.

BERENICE. Stand still, I'll just light a candle. *(Muttering)* I always keep one around, for such like emergencies. *(She opens a drawer)*

JOHN HENRY. What makes the lights go out so scarey like this?

BERENICE. Just one of them things, Candy.

JOHN HENRY. I'm scared. Where's Honey?

BERENICE. Jesus knows. I'm scared, too. With Honey snow-crazy and loose like this—and Frankie run off with a suitcase and her Papa's pistol. I feel like every nerve had been picked out of me.

JOHN HENRY *(holding out his seashell and stroking Berenice)*. You want to listen to the ocean?

THE CURTAIN FALLS

SCENE TWO

The scene is the same. There are still signs in the kitchen of the wedding: punch glasses and the punch bowl on the drainboard. It is four o'clock in the morning. As the curtain rises, Berenice and Mr. Addams are alone in the kitchen. There is a crepuscular glow in the yard.

———

MR. ADDAMS. I never was a believer in corporal punishment. Never spanked

Frankie in my life, but when I lay my hands on her . . .

BERENICE. She'll show up soon—but I know how you feel. What with worrying about Honey Camden, John Henry's sickness and Frankie, I've never lived through such a anxious night. (*She looks through the window. It is dawning now*)

MR. ADDAMS. I'd better go and find out the last news of John Henry, poor baby. (*He goes through the hall door*)

(*Frankie comes into the yard and crosses to the arbor. She looks exhausted and almost beaten. Berenice has seen her from the window, rushes into the yard and grabs her by the shoulders and shakes her.*)

BERENICE. Frankie Addams, you ought to be skinned alive. I been worried.

FRANKIE. I've been so worried too.

BERENICE. Where have you been this night? Tell me everything.

FRANKIE. I will, but quit shaking me.

BERENICE. Now tell me the A and the Z of this.

FRANKIE. When I was running around the dark scarey streets, I begun to realize that my plans for Hollywood and the Merchant Marines were child plans that would not work. I hid in the alley behind Papa's store, and it was dark and I was scared. I opened the suitcase and took out Papa's pistol. (*She sits down on her suitcase*) I vowed I was going to shoot myself. I said I was going to count three and on three pull the trigger. I counted one—two—but I didn't count three—because at the last minute, I changed my mind.

BERENICE. You march right along with me. You going to bed.

FRANKIE. Oh, Honey Camden!

(*Honey Camden Brown, who has been hiding behind the arbor, has suddenly appeared.*)

BERENICE. Oh, Honey, Honey. (*They embrace*)

HONEY. Shush, don't make any noise; the law is after me.

BERENICE (*in a whisper*). Tell me.

HONEY. Mr. Wilson wouldn't serve me so I drew a razor on him.

BERENICE. You kill him?

HONEY. Didn't have no time to find out. I been runnin' all night.

FRANKIE. Lightfoot, if you drew a razor on a white man, you'd better not let them catch you.

BERENICE. Here's six dolla's. If you can get to Fork Falls and then to Atlanta. But be careful slippin' through the white folks' section. They'll be combing the county looking for you.

HONEY (*with passion*). Don't cry, Berenice.

BERENICE. Already I feel that rope.

HONEY. Don't you dare cry. I know now all my days have been leading up to this minute. No more "boy this—boy that"—no bowing, no scraping. For the first time, I'm free and it makes me happy. (*He begins to laugh hysterically*)

BERENICE. When they catch you, they'll string you up.

HONEY (*beside himself, brutally*). Let them hang me—I don't care. I tell you I'm glad. I tell you I'm happy. (*He goes out behind the arbor*)

FRANKIE (*calling after him*). Honey, remember you are Lightfoot. Nothing can stop you if you want to run away.

(*Mrs. West, John Henry's mother, comes into the yard.*)

MRS. WEST. What was all that racket? John Henry is critically ill. He's got to have perfect quiet.

FRANKIE. John Henry's sick, Aunt Pet?

MRS. WEST. The doctors say he has meningitis. He must have perfect quiet.

BERENICE. I haven't had time to tell you yet. John Henry took sick sudden last night. Yesterday afternoon when I complained of my head, he said he had a headache too and thinking he copies me I said, "Run along, I don't have the patience to fool with you." Looks like a judgment on me. There won't be no more noise, Mrs. West.

MRS. WEST. Make sure of that. (*She goes away*)

FRANKIE (*putting her arm around Berenice*). Oh, Berenice, what can we do?

BERENICE (*stroking Frankie's head*). Ain't nothing we can do but wait.

FRANKIE. The wedding—Honey—John Henry—so much has happened that my brain can't hardly gather it in. Now for the first time I realize that the world is certainly—a sudden place.

BERENICE. Sometimes sudden, but when you are waiting, like this, it seems so slow.

THE CURTAIN FALLS

Scene Three

The scene is the same: the kitchen and arbor. It is months later, a November day, about sunset.

The arbor is brittle and withered. The elm tree is bare except for a few ragged leaves. The yard is tidy and the lemonade stand and sheet stage curtain are now missing. The kitchen is neat and bare and the furniture has been removed. Berenice, wearing a fox fur, is sitting in a chair with an old suitcase and doll at her feet. Frankie enters.

FRANKIE. Oh, I am just mad about these Old Masters.

BERENICE. Humph!

FRANKIE. The house seems so hollow. Now that the furniture is packed. It gives me a creepy feeling in the front. That's why I came back here.

BERENICE. Is that the only reason why you came back here?

FRANKIE. Oh, Berenice, you know. I wish you hadn't given quit notice just because Papa and I are moving into a new house with Uncle Eustace and Aunt Pet out in Limewood.

BERENICE. I respect and admire Mrs. West but I'd never get used to working for her.

FRANKIE. Mary is just beginning this Rachmaninoff Concerto. She may play it for her debut when she is eighteen years old. Mary playing the piano and the whole orchestra playing at one and the same time, mind you. Awfully hard.

BERENICE. Ma-ry Littlejohn.

FRANKIE. I don't know why you always have to speak her name in a tinged voice like that.

BERENICE. Have I ever said anything against her? All I said was that she is too lumpy and marshmallow white and it makes me nervous to see her just setting there sucking them pigtails.

FRANKIE. Braids. Furthermore, it is no use our discussing a certain party. You could never possibly understand it. It's just not in you.

(Berenice looks at her sadly, with faded stillness, then pats and strokes the fox fur.)

BERENICE. Be that as it may. Less us not fuss and quarrel this last afternoon.

FRANKIE. I don't want to fuss either.

Anyway, this is not our last afternoon. I will come and see you often.

BERENICE. No, you won't, baby. You'll have other things to do. Your road is already strange to me.

(Frankie goes to Berenice, pats her on the shoulder, then takes her fox fur and examines it.)

FRANKIE. You still have the fox fur that Ludie gave you. Somehow this little fur looks so sad—so thin and with a sad little fox-wise face.

BERENICE *(taking the fur back and continuing to stroke it).* Got every reason to be sad. With what has happened in these two last months. I just don't know what I have done to deserve it. *(She sits, the fur in her lap, bent over with her forearms on her knees and her hands limply dangling)* Honey gone and John Henry, my little boy gone.

FRANKIE. You did all you could. You got poor Honey's body and gave him a Christian funeral and nursed John Henry.

BERENICE. It's the way Honey died and the fact that John Henry had to suffer so. Little soul!

FRANKIE. It's peculiar—the way it all happened so fast. First Honey caught and hanging himself in the jail. Then later in that same week, John Henry died and then I met Mary. As the irony of fate would have it, we first got to know each other in front of the lipstick and cosmetics counter at Woolworth's. And it was the week of the fair.

BERENICE. The most beautiful September I ever seen. Countless white and yellow butterflies flying around them autumn flowers—Honey dead and John Henry suffering like he did and daisies, golden weather, butterflies—such strange death weather.

FRANKIE. I never believed John Henry would die. *(There is a long pause. She looks out the window)* Don't it seem quiet to you in here? *(There is another, longer pause)* When I was a little child I believed that out under the arbor at night there would come three ghosts and one of the ghosts wore a silver ring. *(Whispering)* Occasionally when it gets so quiet like this I have a strange feeling. It's like John Henry is hovering somewhere in this kitchen—solemn looking and ghost-grey.

A BOY'S VOICE *(from the neighboring yard).* Frankie, Frankie.

FRANKIE *(calling to the boy)*. Yes, Barney. *(To Berenice)* Clock stopped. *(She shakes the clock)*

THE BOY'S VOICE. Is Mary there?

FRANKIE *(to Berenice)*. It's Barney MacKean. *(To the boy, in a sweet voice)* Not yet. I'm meeting her at five. Come on in, Barney, won't you?

BARNEY. Just a minute.

FRANKIE *(to Berenice)*. Barney puts me in mind of a Greek god.

BERENICE. What? Barney puts you in mind of a what?

FRANKIE. Of a Greek god. Mary remarked that Barney reminded her of a Greek god.

BERENICE. It looks like I can't understand a thing you say no more.

FRANKIE. You know, those old-timey Greeks worship those Greek gods.

BERENICE. But what has that got to do with Barney MacKean?

FRANKIE. On account of the figure.

(Barney MacKean, a boy of thirteen, wearing a football suit, bright sweater and cleated shoes, runs up the back steps into the kitchen.)

BERENICE. Hi, Greek god Barney. This afternoon I saw your initials chalked down on the front sidewalk. M.L. loves B.M.

BARNEY. If I could find out who wrote it, I would rub it out with their faces. Did you do it, Frankie?

FRANKIE *(drawing herself up with sudden dignity)*. I wouldn't do a kid thing like that. I even resent you asking me. *(She repeats the phrase to herself in a pleased undertone)* Resent you asking me.

BARNEY. Mary can't stand me anyhow.

FRANKIE. Yes she can stand you. I am her most intimate friend. I ought to know. As a matter of fact she's told me several lovely compliments about you. Mary and I are riding on the moving van to our new house. Would you like to go?

BARNEY. Sure.

FRANKIE. O.K. You will have to ride back with the furniture 'cause Mary and I are riding on the front seat with the driver. We had a letter from Jarvis and Janice this afternoon. Jarvis is with the Occupation Forces in Germany and they took a vacation trip to Luxembourg. *(She repeats in a pleased voice)* Luxembourg. Berenice, don't you think that's a lovely name?

BERENICE. It's kind of a pretty name, but it reminds me of soapy water.

FRANKIE. Mary and I will most likely pass through Luxembourg when we—are going around the world together.

(Frankie goes out followed by Barney and Berenice sits in the kitchen alone and motionless. She picks up the doll, looks at it and hums the first two lines of "I Sing Because I'm Happy." In the next house the piano is heard again, as the curtain falls.)